RIVER OF DEATH

THE CHICKAMAUGA CAMPAIGN

CIVIL WAR AMERICA

Gary Gallagher, Peter S. Carmichael, Caroline E. Janney, and Aaron Sheehan-Dean, editors

This landmark series interprets broadly the history and culture of the Civil War era through the long nineteenth century and beyond. Drawing on diverse approaches and methods, the series publishes historical works that explore all aspects of the war, biographies of leading commanders, and tactical and campaign studies, along with select editions of primary sources. Together, these books shed new light on an era that remains central to our understanding of American and world history.

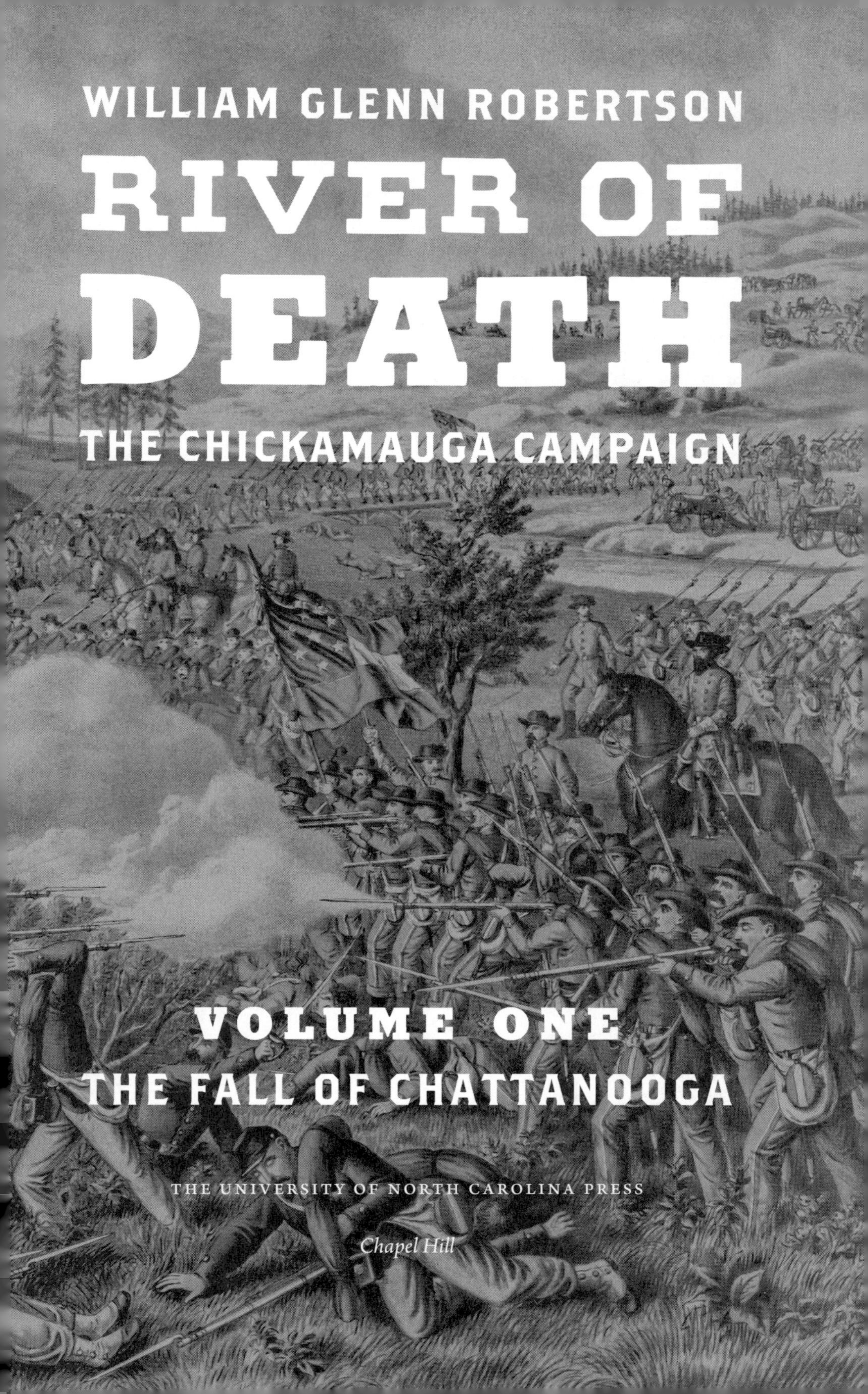

WILLIAM GLENN ROBERTSON

RIVER OF DEATH

THE CHICKAMAUGA CAMPAIGN

VOLUME ONE

THE FALL OF CHATTANOOGA

THE UNIVERSITY OF NORTH CAROLINA PRESS

Chapel Hill

Designed by Jamison Cockerham
Set in Arno, Scala Sans, Cutright, Brothers, and Calt
by Tseng Information Systems, Inc.

Maps created by Hal Jespersen.

Cover illustration: *Battle of Chickamauga*. Created by Kurz & Allison.
Courtesy of the Library of Congress Prints and Photographs Division.

Manufactured in the United States of America

The University of North Carolina Press has been a member
of the Green Press Initiative since 2003.

LIBRARY OF CONGRESS CATALOGING-IN-PUBLICATION DATA
Names: Robertson, William Glenn, 1944– author.
Title: River of death : the Chickamauga Campaign / William Glenn Robertson
Other titles: Civil War America (Series)
Description: Chapel Hill : The University of North Carolina Press, [2018–] |
Series: Civil War America | Includes bibliographical references and index.
Contents: Vol. 1. The Fall of Chattanooga.
Identifiers: LCCN 2018016977 | ISBN 9781469643120 (cloth : alk. paper) |
ISBN 9781469643137 (ebook)
Subjects: LCSH: Chickamauga, Battle of, Ga., 1863. | United States—History—Civil War, 1861–1865—Campaigns. | Tennessee—History—Civil War, 1861–1865—Campaigns.
Classification: LCC E475.81 .R587 2018 | DDC 973.7/35—dc23
LC record available at https://lccn.loc.gov/2018016977

MIX
Paper from
responsible sources
FSC® C013483

For

EMILY POPE WRIGHT

who started me on this path so long ago

» CONTENTS «

» ILLUSTRATIONS «

MAPS

FIGURES

» PREFACE «

I first encountered the Chickamauga battlefield at age ten in June 1954 while on a family trip. When we unexpectedly encountered monuments and cannon while northbound on U.S. Highway 27, I asked to tour the battlefield park. We did so, and my grandmother climbed Wilder Tower with me when no one else would. The memories generated by that trip were reinforced by another visit in the summer of 1966. Thereafter I did not return to Chickamauga for many years, but those two visits remained with me. Sixteen years later, in the spring of 1982, as a military history instructor at the United States Army Command and General Staff College at Fort Leavenworth, Kansas, I had occasion again to think of Chickamauga. The Combat Studies Institute's director asked me to look into the possibility of reconstituting a course from the early days of the Staff College called the Staff Ride. First proposed in 1895 but not implemented until 1906, the Leavenworth Staff Ride was an in-depth study of a historical campaign using as many media as possible in a classroom setting, followed by an extensive visit to sites associated with that campaign. The purpose of the course was not simply historical but to derive timeless lessons in the military art applicable to modern soldiers. The original course lasted only five years, ending in 1911 when the Army mobilized on the Mexican border.

I was unable to revive the Staff Ride at Leavenworth in 1982 and was given additional time to build the course for the following year. As part of the planning process, a fellow instructor and I visited Forts Henry and Donelson, Shiloh, Chickamauga, Chattanooga, and Stones River to assess their suitability for a ten-week course culminating in a multiday site visit. As a result of this survey, I selected Chickamauga as the vehicle through which to return the Staff Ride to the Leavenworth curriculum. Chickamauga was chosen for three reasons: first, it represented a rich and diverse teaching scenario, with a complex campaign culminating in a large multiday battle; second, it was an excellent physical laboratory, preserved as the Chickamauga and Chattanooga National

Military Park with hundreds of monuments and plaques, and an extensive trail network; third, it was logistically supportable, within reach of Leavenworth and capable of sustaining a class of Army officers. My choice was approved and the course operated for the first time in the spring of 1983 with thirteen students and a four-day site visit. Subsequently an additional day was added, permitting study of sites associated with the larger campaign. The course soon became wildly popular, eventually expanding to five iterations per year, and it remained in the Leavenworth curriculum for twenty-five years.

Part of the attraction for the Chickamauga Staff Ride was the opportunity to study a historical campaign in great depth. In order to facilitate the greatest possible degree of student involvement, my colleagues and I gradually provided for student use as many primary sources as we could collect on Chickamauga. All students had to read a common text, initially Glenn Tucker's *Chickamauga: Bloody Battle in the West,* later supplanted by more scholarly works by Peter Cozzens and Steven Woodworth. More important, each student was assigned a historical participant to research as deeply as possible, using the resources gathered by the Staff Ride faculty. As the years passed, and annual faculty research trips assembled ever more primary sources to supplement the *Official Records of the War of the Rebellion,* student analyses became sharper and more knowledgeable. Indeed, many culminated in master's theses, and several resulted in original contributions to knowledge of the campaign and battle. My own insights were also honed by my association with hundreds of professional soldiers, many of them combat veterans, actively studying their profession through the vehicle of the Chickamauga Campaign.

Analysis of the published literature on Chickamauga during the life of the Staff Ride course led me to two conclusions. First the five-week campaign preceding the titanic battle of 18–20 September 1863 was conducted over perhaps the most difficult terrain experienced by two contending Civil War armies. While U. S. Grant's Army of the Tennessee struggled to overcome the swamps and disease of the Mississippi Delta, it always had the support of the U.S. Navy and enjoyed an unbreakable supply line. In contrast, William Rosecrans's Army of the Cumberland had to cross three major mountain ranges and one of America's major rivers just to come to grips with its opponent. Rosecrans was dependent on a single-track railroad stretching back to Louisville, Kentucky, in order to sustain his army in a barren country. Similarly, Braxton Bragg's Army of Tennessee faced the same terrain and was equally dependent on a single rail line to Atlanta. The second conclusion sprang from the first. Although this difficult terrain and the resulting tenuous supply situation was acknowledged in passing by authors writing about Chickamauga throughout the years, the most of their words described the battle and not the campaign. I came to believe that the campaign itself was story worth telling in greater detail. In operational planning, logistical considerations, and engineering, the Chickamauga Campaign had few peers in American Civil War history.

While not a driver in the process through which Chickamauga was selected as a vehicle for the Leavenworth Staff Ride, the campaign itself had great significance in the conduct of the American Civil War. The small city of Chattanooga lay in the midst of a resource-rich region that provided significant quantities of coal, iron, copper, and niter to the Confederate war effort. Chattanooga also stood athwart a primary passage through the multiple ranges of the Appalachian Mountains into the heartland of the Confederacy. As such it represented a door that had to be opened forcibly by the Union and defended by as many military resources as the Confederate government could allocate. Beyond those physical considerations, the mountainous region of East Tennessee and neighboring states was considered by the Lincoln administration to be a hotbed of Unionist sentiment, whose citizens demanded relief from often brutal Confederate domination. For all those reasons—strategic, logistical, and political—the Union sought to seize Chattanooga, and the Confederacy strove to retain possession, setting the stage for a titanic confrontation in the late summer of 1863.

The vast array of primary sources amassed to support the Staff Ride class not only offered the opportunity to study this important campaign in depth but also to illuminate a large number of subordinate issues in a new and more comprehensive way. First, it offered windows into the personalities and thought processes of the contending commanders, Rosecrans and Bragg. Although Rosecrans had been treated relatively well by historians, Bragg had been almost universally vilified over the years, especially by historians like Thomas Connelly and Grady McWhiney. This study attempts to explain the thinking of both senior commanders in terms of what they knew at a given instant and how they responded to that knowledge, a practice not always followed by some earlier writers, who often conflated events and telescoped timelines in order to bolster their preconceived arguments. Wherever possible, this effort to understand factors driving significant decisions extended to the principal subordinates of both commanders. How the personalities of the major figures in the campaign interacted and shaped their decisions proved to be an equally fertile field for analysis.

An often overlooked facet of the campaign was the work performed by the staffs of the principal commanders. Staffs, especially the more senior members, often played a major role in providing advice, filtering opinions, drafting critical orders, and providing eyewitness intelligence to their respective commanders. Thus I have sought to describe the structure of the army staffs and provide capsule biographies of the major figures in terms of age, education, and experience. While space did not permit a similar analysis of lower-level staffs, I have addressed cases where corps, division, and brigade staffs affected events. Often, a poor choice of words or a faulty route taken by a staff officer resulted in significant consequences, and I have examined those consequences fully.

As for intelligence operations, a close reading of Rosecrans's intelligence journal, maintained by Capt. David Swaim, and the diary of Lt. Col. George Brent, Bragg's assistant adjutant general, offers a fairly comprehensive picture of what each commander knew at any given time. When coupled with other sources of information and the extant message traffic, a more detailed analysis of commanders' decisions at every step of the campaign can be made than heretofore. As a result, old canards, such as Bragg's alleged cluelessness about Federal activity beyond the Tennessee River in the early stages of the campaign, can be laid to rest once and for all. Further, several previously unknown espionage operations are revealed. Neither commander was always correct in his understanding of the available intelligence or his response to it, but their performance can be better assessed if the intelligence available to them at a given moment is delineated. This volume offers just such detailed exposition of what Rosecrans and Bragg knew, when they knew it, and how they reacted to it.

Still another facet of the Chickamauga Campaign highlighted in this volume is the role that new technology played in the operations of both armies. Railroads were in their infancy in America at the time of the campaign, barely more than thirty years old. Nevertheless, both armies depended upon single-track railroads to sustain themselves as viable combat organizations. Had the railroads, both North and South, been unable to provide the sinews of war that sustained large field armies in inhospitable terrain, the campaign could not have taken place. Nor could the Army of Tennessee have made a fight of it without the timely arrival by rail of reinforcements from throughout the Confederacy. The railroads, of course, were dispatched by telegraph, another relatively recent invention, and the Army of the Cumberland was able to bring the "singing wire" all the way to the battlefield itself. As for bridge-building, Rosecrans's engineers spanned the wide Tennessee River multiple times with both pontoon and trestle bridges, none of which were less than 1,250 feet in length. The momentary failure of one of those bridges significantly affected the development of the campaign, a fact often unrecognized.

A by-product of the decades-long effort to amass primary sources for students in the Staff Ride course was the collection of vast numbers of letters and diaries from participants in the Chickamauga Campaign. While these highly personal materials seldom shed light on major command decisions or contribute to strategic and operational analysis of the campaign, they offer a wide window into the thoughts, feelings, hopes, and fears of the common soldiers comprising both the Army of the Cumberland and the Army of Tennessee. Caught up in their clinical analyses, military historians often forget that the blue and red blocks and arrows on campaign and battle maps represent thousands of living, breathing, and often suffering individuals, all of whom have a personal story to tell. These individuals lived their lives one day at a time in a rhythm unique to each campaign, without knowing what the future held for them. That rhythm consisted of long periods of mundane activity punctuated by fleeting moments of terror. To tell the story of Chickamauga without acknowledging the varied activities of the men in the ranks is to deny the participants their claim to human dignity. Without their individual experiences, the story of Chickamauga is sterile and incomplete, so I have decided to let them speak for themselves wherever possible.

I address all of these topics, and others of similar significance, comprehensively throughout this volume, which covers the period from 4 July 1863, the end of the Tullahoma Campaign, through 9 September 1863, the date of the occupation of Chattanooga. A second volume will cover the period from 10 September 1863 to mid-October 1863, which includes two major Confederate countermoves, the arrival of large Confederate reinforcements, the Battle of Chickamauga, the withdrawal of the Federal army into Chattanooga, and the relief of William Rosecrans from command of the Army of the Cumberland. Threads initiated in and woven throughout volume 1 will culminate in volume 2.

Though this work is the product of a single author, it owes much to the dedicated efforts of hundreds of others. My grandmother, Emily Wright, financed my initial trip to Chickamauga and nurtured my historical interests. My parents, William and Queenie Robertson, sustained my interest in the American Civil War from my earliest memories and supported my education as a historian. My wife, Janet Vaught Robertson, and our son, William Stewart Robertson, sustained me through my many trips to Chickamauga and expended countless hours in assisting my Chickamauga endeavors. To them I owe more than I can repay.

I also owe thanks to two people I never met, Lt. Col. Arthur Wagner and Maj. Eben Swift, the former for conceiving the Staff Ride as a powerful educational tool and the latter for implementing it. The late Gen. Donn Starry, commander of the Army's Training and Doctrine Command, issued the order to reinstitute the Staff Ride at Leavenworth in 1981, and Col. William Stofft assigned the implementation of that order to me. Some of the officer/historians who have assisted me at Chickamauga over the years include Philip Baker, Gary Bounds, John Boxberger, Randall Briggs, Paul Cal, William Campsey, Thomas Christianson, Steven Clay, Charles Collins, Kelvin Crow, Robert Dalessandro, Michael Derrick, Michael Dunn, Clay Edwards, Karl Farris, Thomas Gleason,

Gary Griffin, Jeffrey "Benny" Gudmens, Curtis King, Kevin Kennedy, Richard Kiper, Gary Linhart, Scott McMeen, Christopher McPadden, Marvin Meek, Andrew Morris, Robert Ramsey, and Edward Shanahan. My thanks also extend to the several thousand United States Army officers who successfully completed the Staff Ride course, many of whom have gone on to general officer rank, and one of whom has become chief of staff of the Army. I have learned much from you all, and your insights have been instrumental in informing mine.

The work of hundreds of librarians and archival assistants has been critical to the richness of detail that supports the judgments in this study. You are far too numerous to mention individually without slighting others who have assisted me in my Chickamauga quest. Thus the list of repositories in the bibliography will have to represent your work over the last thirty-five years of research. Though most of your names escape me, your valiant work does not, and I treasure your efforts on my behalf. Similarly, I am in debt to those individuals who have provided me with primary materials from their personal collections. Your generous assistance is greatly appreciated.

The underpaid and often maligned men and women of the National Park Service, the keepers of the Chickamauga battlefield, also must receive their due. Historian Edward Tinney first taught me about the physical aspects of the park, and Chief Ranger John Cissell taught me how to love it and what it stands for. Most of all, I owe Historian James Ogden III far more than I can articulate. His research assistance, administrative aid, general helpfulness, and true friendship over the past thirty years has gone far to shape this project in more ways than I care to admit. Thanks, Jim!

My thanks also extend to my cartographer, Hal Jesperson, who has turned my rough sketches into professionally drawn maps that simplify yet illuminate the complex troop movements described in the text.

Last, but not least, I wish to pay tribute to the nearly 150,000 soldiers, Americans all, who participated in the Chickamauga Campaign so long ago, 34,000 of whom became casualties. I hope I have rendered to you the honor you all deserve. If not, the fault is mine, not yours.

1

4 July 1863

Maj. Gen. Alexander McCook looked at the sky and was greatly disappointed. Instead of glorious summer sunshine, the leaden clouds promised another day of rain. It had rained virtually every day since 24 June, when the Army of the Cumberland had begun its offensive to drive the Army of Tennessee from its foothold around the towns of Shelbyville and Tullahoma. Although the rain had turned the roads into seemingly bottomless seas of mud, the Federals had successfully driven their opponents from the fertile farmland of Middle Tennessee and beyond the frowning heights of the Cumberland Plateau. McCook's own Twentieth Army Corps, following the line of the Nashville & Chattanooga Railroad, had forded the swollen Elk River with two of its three divisions and was pressing toward the mountain wall visible for miles. Maj. Gen. Philip Sheridan's Third Division occupied the hamlet of Cowan, which lay just short of the long railroad tunnel that took the tracks through the mountain to the Tennessee River valley at Stevenson and Bridgeport, Alabama. Behind Sheridan's troops, Brig. Gen. Jefferson C. Davis's First Division occupied the town of Winchester, near the railroad, where McCook established corps headquarters. West of the raging Elk River, Brig. Gen. Richard Johnson's Second Division settled into the old Confederate fortifications encircling Tullahoma. The momentarily impassable Elk, along with the destruction of the railroad bridge near Estill Springs, ensured that the Army of the Cumberland would soon exhaust its rations, forcing a pause before another advance could begin. To McCook, 4 July seemed a perfect time to have a party. The date was iconic in the history of the nation, the Tullahoma campaign was a resounding success, and the human cost of that success had been minimal. Therefore, McCook reasoned, it was time for a victory celebration. The threatening weather could dampen spirits only so much, so McCook sent invitations to other commands and issued instructions regarding artillery salutes in honor of the day.[1]

McCook's nearest neighbor was Maj. Gen. David Stanley's Cavalry Corps. Although several units were absent, Stanley and his remaining horsemen were camped around the village of Decherd, on the railroad two miles from Winchester. Stanley would have to be invited to McCook's party. Slightly farther away was Maj. Gen. George Thomas's Fourteenth Army Corps. Most of Thomas's command was spread across the fields stretching from the Elk River to the foot of the Cumberland Plateau at the prominent outcropping called Brakefield Point. Maj. Gen. James Negley's Second Division was nearest to the mountain, with Maj. Gen. Lovell Rousseau's First Division camped nearby in support. Several miles northwest of Rousseau and much nearer the Elk River, Brig. Gen. John Brannan's Third Division and Maj. Gen. Joseph Reynolds's Fourth Division established themselves in the sodden fields and woods. Thomas placed his own headquarters near Brannan and Reynolds, six miles north of Decherd. He was probably too far away to respond favorably to McCook's invitation, if indeed one was sent. Certainly not invited was Maj. Gen. Thomas Crittenden, commanding the Twenty-First Army Corps. Crittenden's command was scattered widely west of the Elk River. Brig. Gen. Thomas Wood's First Division rested at Pelham, fifteen miles northeast of Winchester, while Maj. Gen. John Palmer's Second Division guarded the flooded Elk Valley north of Morris's Ford, also fifteen miles distant. Finally, Brig. Gen. Horatio Van Cleve's Third Division garrisoned Murfreesboro, Woodbury, and Manchester. Crittenden himself occupied Hillsboro, seventeen miles from Winchester. Maj. Gen. Gordon Granger's Reserve Corps patrolled the army's rear areas, with its nearest units at Shelbyville and Wartrace. That left only the army commander, Maj. Gen. William Rosecrans, to be invited. Although Rosecrans would soon make Tullahoma his headquarters, he and his staff momentarily rested at Estill Springs, just west of the Elk River. He would definitely receive an invitation to McCook's party.[2]

While McCook planned the day's festivities, the war continued for some soldiers just a few miles from Winchester on the Cumberland Plateau. Although the Federal infantry halted on the plain fronting the mountain wall, Federal cavalrymen probed toward the top of the plateau on two roads. The first, a rough military road, ascended the mountain in the vicinity of Brakefield Point, while the second wound upward from the village of Cowan. Both roads merged at University Place, construction site of an educational institution founded by the Episcopal Church in 1857. Following the laying of the cornerstone on 10 October 1860, little more had been accomplished because of the national crisis. Nevertheless, great plans remained for the University of the South, as it would come to be called. Now Federal horsemen probed toward University Place. On the Brakefield Point road, Col. Edward McCook's Second Brigade of Brig. Gen. Robert Mitchell's First Cavalry Division cautiously led the way. Finding the track seriously obstructed by felled trees and rocks placed by the retreating Confederates, McCook's men abandoned the advance about two miles short of University Place and returned to the plain. On the Cowan Road, one of the primary routes over the Cumberland Plateau, elements of Col.

Louis Watkins's Third Brigade of Mitchell's division initially found the going easier. Watkins began his ascent at 5:30 A.M. with approximately 1,000 men of the Fifth and Sixth Kentucky Cavalry regiments. Three miles from University Place, he paused to deploy three companies of the Fifth Kentucky under Maj. John Owsley as an advance guard, and then resumed the climb. A mile from the junction with the Brakefield Point road, Owsley's men suddenly encountered Confederate pickets. When most of their weapons misfired, the pickets fell back on their reserve company and made a brief stand. Following a confused melee, the Confederates hastily withdrew, Owsley's men gave chase, and the race was on. The time was approximately 8:00 A.M.[3]

The Confederate pickets proved to be three companies of the Eighth Texas Cavalry regiment, part of Col. Thomas Harrison's Brigade of Brig. Gen. John Wharton's Cavalry Division. When the pickets joined their parent unit, Lt. Col. Gustave Cook ordered the Eighth Texas to drive the Federals back. Now it was Major Owsley's turn to retreat, and the Federal advance guard hastened to rejoin Watkins, suffering six wounded in the process. When Owsley reached safety, Watkins decided to escalate the fight. Holding the Fifth Kentucky in reserve, he sent the Sixth Kentucky forward to charge the Eighth Texas. Overmatched, the Texans grudgingly withdrew toward the University Place road junction. Behind them Maj. Gen. Joseph Wheeler assembled more resources to halt the Federal advance. While Harrison reinforced Cook's Eighth Texas with Lt. Col. Paul Anderson's Fourth [Eighth] Tennessee Cavalry regiment, Wheeler called for Col. George Dibrell's Brigade from Brig. Gen. Nathan Bedford Forrest's Cavalry Division to return to University Place. Simultaneously he directed Wharton to form Col. Charles Crews's Brigade a mile in rear of the units fighting at the road junction. Wheeler's moves came just in time, because Watkins's Federals aggressively pushed Harrison's Confederates beyond the junction. Believing that he had gone far enough, Watkins in midmorning decided to end the action and return to Cowan. At a total cost of three killed and fourteen wounded, Watkins had gained more than twenty prisoners and had learned that the Army of Tennessee's rear guard was still atop the Cumberland Plateau. Wheeler's cavalrymen had held their ground at a cost of one killed, six wounded, two missing, and the loss of twenty-five horses. The small fight ended at 9:00 A.M., but Wheeler kept a brigade on the plateau through the afternoon in case the Federals returned. His remaining horsemen descended the mountain, covering the rear of the retreating Confederate infantry.[4]

At Bridgeport, Gen. Braxton Bragg spent the rainy day orchestrating the withdrawal of his army across the Tennessee River. The army consisted of two infantry corps, Wheeler's cavalry, and several thousand troops borrowed from Maj. Gen. Simon Buckner's Department of East Tennessee. The two infantry corps of the army followed separate roads down the mountain, but both roads reached the vicinity of the Tennessee in the valley of Battle Creek. Lt. Gen. Leonidas Polk's Corps arrived first at a pontoon bridge established with some difficulty on the previous day just north of the mouth of the creek. Although Bragg preferred that Buckner cross first, Polk held the bridge for himself, forcing Buckner's men to march downstream to Bridgeport. There they would utilize the massive bridge of the Nashville & Chattanooga Railroad to gain the eastern shore. Behind Polk's command, Lt. Gen. William Hardee's Corps either had to wait for Polk to complete his crossing or march upstream to another pontoon bridge at Kelly's Ferry. Following the infantry, Wheeler's cavalrymen would descend the Cumberland Plateau and cross the river at whatever site was available. Confederate engineers had worked diligently to build the two pontoon bridges and to prepare them for demolition when necessary. In addition, at least one small steamboat plied the river ferrying messages and bringing rations from Bridgeport to the toiling infantry. The railroad from Bridgeport to Chattanooga was also available to facilitate the movement of troops and supplies, and its telegraph line served as a useful communication link to Chattanooga and points beyond. The entire operation was complex, and any delay could be fatal if the Federal Army pushed across the Cumberland Plateau in strength. No commander desired to be caught by a pursuing force with his back to a wide river and his troops in disarray. Braxton Bragg foresaw 4 July 1863 as a day of high anxiety.[5]

Polk began the day at a bivouac six miles east of University Place and moved early toward the river. At 9:30 A.M. he ordered Maj. Gen. Jones Withers, commanding the leading division, to guard the pontoon bridge at Battle Creek. Half an hour later, Polk learned of Wheeler's fight at University Place but was assured that the Confederate cavalrymen were holding their own. He then continued his march to and across the bridge with his remaining division, that of Maj. Gen. Benjamin Cheatham. By midafternoon Polk was satisfied that he would not need the bridge much longer. Although rations had arrived by steamboat, he elected to keep his divisions moving. At 2:30 P.M. Polk told Hardee that the bridge would be free for his use at 4:00 P.M. and that Wheeler would cover his rear. To Wheeler, Polk indicated that he should continue to serve as Hardee's rear guard, that the bridge now belonged to the cavalry, and that Wheeler should dispose of it as he chose. Shortly thereafter, Polk told Capt. Patrick Thomson, one of Bragg's staff officers, that he was leaving the bridge unguarded and undestroyed. A similar message went to Hardee at 4:30 P.M. Thirty minutes later, the last of Polk's command marched from the bridge and headed for Shell Mound Station on the railroad to Chattanooga. Withers's Division camped for the evening at Shell Mound while Cheatham's men bivouacked along the road between Shell Mound and the now unprotected pontoon bridge. Polk himself camped with Withers. At Shell Mound, he found both stocks of provisions and a working railroad. Seizing the former without authority, he ordered them to be distributed to his hungry men. He also told his artillerymen to dismount their guns and ammunition chests for rail transport to Chattanooga while the carriages and teams continued by road. In neither case did Polk concern himself with any other commands or his superior's desires.[6]

Polk's actions left a trail of mischief in their wake. Bragg had expected Polk to leave a brigade west of the Tennessee River to protect the pontoon bridge and only learned otherwise when Captain Thomson returned to army headquarters at Bridgeport. Bragg's chief of staff, Brig. Gen. William Mackall, was miffed that his efforts to provide rations to Polk's men had been disregarded, and he had other uses for the limited railroad equipment than to transport guns seemingly abandoned by Polk at Shell Mound. Hardee decided to find a route across the Tennessee River that would not require him to follow in Polk's wake. At 7:00 P.M. he notified Polk that he was marching upriver toward Kelly's Ferry and would not need the Battle Creek span. The detachment from Buckner's command, having been diverted by Polk to Bridgeport, waited there in hopes of securing space on trains shuttling between that point and Chattanooga. Wheeler's Cavalry Corps remained scattered, with its leading elements at Bridgeport and a brigade just leaving the top of the mountain by nightfall. At the Battle Creek pontoon bridge, engineers waited for someone to decide the fate of the structure left solely in their charge. Hundreds of weary, hungry, and footsore stragglers lined the roads down the mountain, making their way singly or in small groups toward safety beyond the river. At least one of Hardee's men thought of the day in historic terms. As Sgt. Robert Bliss later recounted in a letter to his mother, "We celebrated the 'Glorious Old Fourth' by marching down Cedar Ridge, through Gizzards Cove to the Tennessee. It was a very hot day and hope it may never be my lot again to attend such another celebration." The Army of Tennessee had not been defeated in battle, but it had simply been outmaneuvered by the Federals. Nevertheless, the fact that it had been forced to relinquish Middle Tennessee, the selfish behavior of Polk, and the lack of simple coordination among its senior leaders bode ill for the future.[7]

Entirely unaware of their opponent's disarray, the officers and men of the Army of the Cumberland welcomed the pause in operations. In George Thomas's Fourteenth Corps, 4 July was a day of celebration for two reasons, first, the nation's Independence Day and, second, favorable news from the east, where the Army of the Potomac seemed to be victorious at Gettysburg, Pennsylvania. Thus artillery salutes rolled across the plain until they echoed from the Cumberland Plateau throughout the day. The occasion also called forth extravagant oratory from officers and men alike, and regimental bands played patriotic airs, punctuated by lusty cheers from the men in the ranks. Still, the intermittent rain dampened the festivities somewhat and empty stomachs

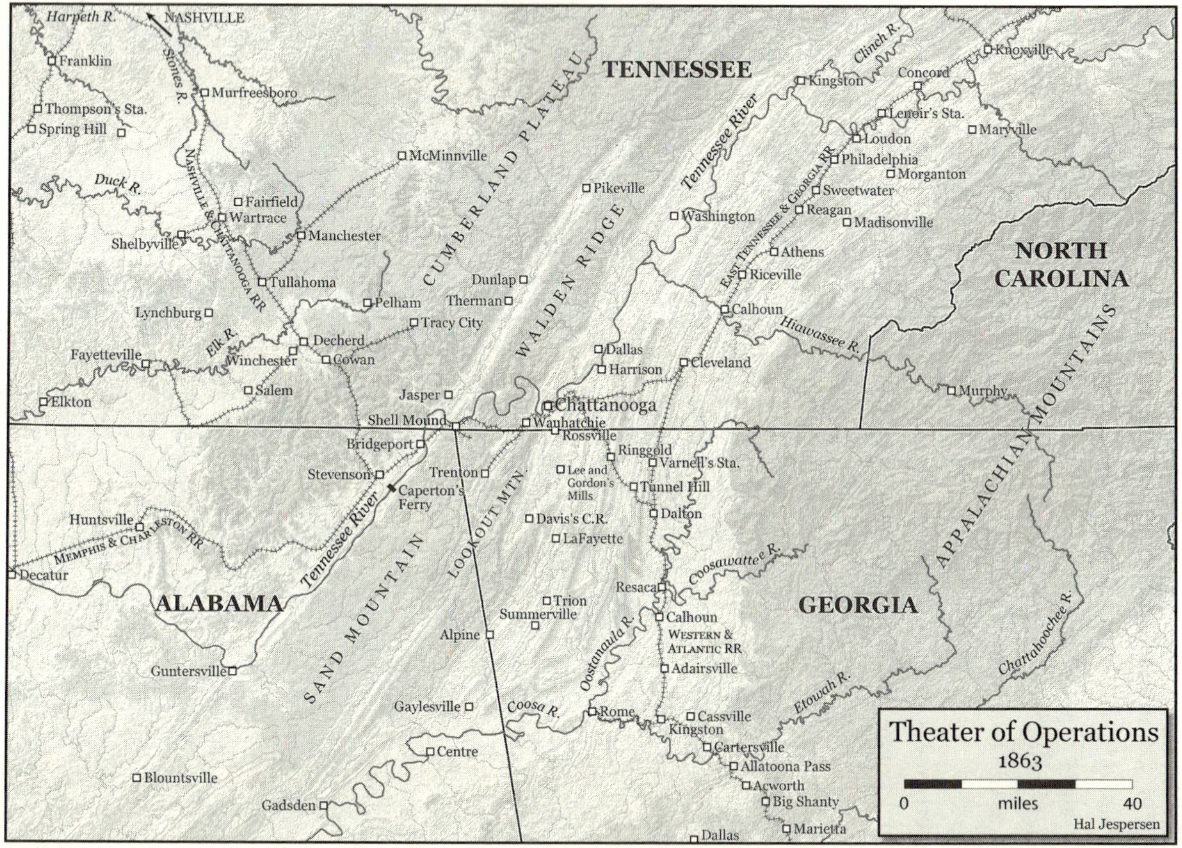
Theater of Operations
1863
0
miles
40
Hal Jespersen
TENNESSEE
NORTH CAROLINA
GEORGIA
ALABAMA
CUMBERLAND PLATEAU
WALDEN RIDGE
LOOKOUT MTN.
SAND MOUNTAIN
APPALACHIAN MOUNTAINS
NASHVILLE
Harpeth R.
Stones R.
Duck R.
Elk R.
Tennessee River
Clinch R.
Hiawassee R.
Coosawattee R.
Oostanaula R.
Coosa R.
Etowah R.
Chattahoochee R.
NASHVILLE & CHATTANOOGA RR
EAST TENNESSEE & GEORGIA RR
WESTERN & ATLANTIC RR
MEMPHIS & CHARLESTON RR
Franklin
Murfreesboro
Thompson's Sta.
Spring Hill
McMinnville
Fairfield
Wartrace
Shelbyville
Manchester
Tullahoma
Lynchburg
Pelham
Tracy City
Dunlap
Therman
Pikeville
Decherd
Winchester
Cowan
Fayetteville
Salem
Elkton
Jasper
Shell Mound
Chattanooga
Wauhatchie
Rossville
Dallas
Harrison
Cleveland
Washington
Kingston
Concord
Knoxville
Lenoir's Sta.
Maryville
Loudon
Philadelphia
Morganton
Sweetwater
Reagan
Madisonville
Athens
Riceville
Calhoun
Murphy
Bridgeport
Stevenson
Caperton's Ferry
Trenton
Ringgold
Varnell's Sta.
Lee and Gordon's Mills
Tunnel Hill
Dalton
Davis's C.R.
LaFayette
Huntsville
Decatur
Resaca
Trion
Summerville
Calhoun
Alpine
Adairsville
Guntersville
Gaylesville
Rome
Cassville
Kingston
Cartersville
Allatoona Pass
Acworth
Big Shanty
Marietta
Dallas
Centre
Blountsville
Gadsden

grumbled at the short rations allocated to the Fourteenth Corps by commissary sergeants. In an effort to rectify the situation, many men left the celebrations early to forage on the local economy. A lucky few found civilian items for sale or confiscation, but most had to content themselves with large quantities of ripe blackberries. In Thomas Crittenden's Twenty-First Corps, which had not yet crossed the Elk, the ration situation was not so dire but the foraging was equally vigorous. Distant from the railroad and telegraph, Crittenden's men did not hear of the Federal success at Gettysburg, so they celebrated only Independence Day with national salutes. In at least one brigade, the men received an unexpected whiskey ration in honor of the day. In other units, the arrival of a supply train brought not only food but also mail and packages from home. In the army's rear, Gordon Granger's Reserve Corps fired the obligatory salutes and searched for ration supplements like their compatriots at the front, but they also spent much of the day holding political gatherings in the occupied areas. In both Shelbyville and Nashville, the troops orchestrated large Unionist meetings among those citizens ready to accept the new political order.[8]

Like his boisterous troops, Rosecrans celebrated the Army of the Cumberland's victory on 4 July. He began the day with the Pioneer Brigade, an engineer unit camped near the destroyed Elk River railroad bridge at Estill Springs. There he received a telegram from Secretary of War Edwin Stanton that forecast success over the Army of Northern Virginia in Pennsylvania. Before leaving to join McCook at Winchester, Rosecrans responded to Stanton with good news of his own. In a brief summary of the campaign just concluded, he described the territory gained, compared his own minimal losses to the much greater damage inflicted on the Army of Tennessee, and promised to resume his advance when the weather and his supply situation improved. Had the incessant rain not intervened, Rosecrans argued, he would have brought Bragg to battle and prevented the Confederate army's escape. Still, the campaign had been a glorious success for Union arms and the army commander could be justly proud of the Army of the Cumberland's efforts. Having put his victory on the record, Rosecrans ordered the telegraph line to be extended from Estill Springs to McCook's advanced units at Cowan, then departed with his staff for Winchester at 10:00 A.M. Unable to use the destroyed rail and road bridges at Estill Springs, Rosecrans's party turned downstream and negotiated a crossing of the turbulent Elk River at Island Ford. From there it was an easy canter to Winchester and McCook's headquarters, which was reached at noon.[9]

When Rosecrans reached Winchester, he found McCook's festivities already under way. Jefferson C. Davis's First Division of the Twentieth Corps occupied the town with the brigades of Col. Sidney Post, Brig. Gen. William Carlin, and Col. Hans Heg. At noon an artillery battery fired a national salute and several regimental bands played patriotic airs. Undeterred by the persistent rain, celebrating soldiers clogged the streets. In the Eighth Kansas Infantry regiment of Heg's Brigade, officers toasted the occasion with whiskey, although the men in the ranks were denied that privilege. At 4:00 P.M. McCook hosted a dinner party for sixty officers. Rosecrans and David Stanley of the Cavalry Corps led the guest list, followed by Brig. Gen. James Garfield, the army's chief of staff, and Brig. Gen. William Carlin. Brigade commanders Post and Heg also attended, as did at least one regimental commander, Col. John Martin of the Eighth Kansas. McCook had hoped to have the dinner in a temporary bower constructed of tree branches, but the rain forced the party indoors. There the dignitaries and their staffs supped, while two regimental bands serenaded the group. A particularly heavy downpour, accompanied by lightning and peals of thunder, washed out the program McCook had planned outside for 6:00 P.M., and the grand party broke up shortly thereafter. While the lesser attendees withdrew to their regimental tents for more whiskey and cigars, Rosecrans, Garfield, and their aides bade farewell to McCook and departed for the rising Elk River on their return to army headquarters at Tullahoma. As they left Winchester, distant echoes of a national salute fired by Philip Sheridan's division five miles away at Cowan reached their ears.[10]

Safely crossing the Elk, Rosecrans and his party reached Tullahoma at 11:30 P.M. Despite the incessant rain, the day had been festive. Still, the trip to Winchester had shown Rosecrans what needed to be done before his army could resume its advance. The divisions beyond the Elk were already beginning to suffer because the delivery of rations had been halted by muddy roads and the broken tracks of the Nashville & Chattanooga Railroad. South of Murfreesboro, the Confederates had removed more than two miles of track near Bell Buckle, had damaged the 350-foot Duck River bridge and a trestle near Normandy, and had destroyed the 540-foot Elk River bridge near Estill Springs. All of this damage would have to be repaired before trains could feed the army beyond the Elk and stockpile supplies for the advance to the Tennessee River valley. The man responsible for maintaining the N&C in working order was John Anderson, military superintendent of railroads. Formerly an official of the Louisville & Nashville Railroad, Anderson had been managing the army's railroad transportation in Kentucky and Tennessee since 1861, serious allegations of inefficiency notwithstanding. Now, with troops reduced to half rations, Anderson needed to rebuild the N&C as quickly as possible. While Rosecrans was at Winchester, Asst. Adj. Gen. Calvin Goddard bombarded Anderson with messages about the necessity for haste. When Rosecrans and Garfield reached army headquarters late that night, they reiterated Goddard's demands. Rosecrans peremptorily ordered Anderson to superintend the repair work in person. Reinforcing the army commander's displeasure, Garfield threatened Anderson with removal if the work was not expedited. McCook's party had been a pleasant interlude, but the problems visible along the railroad quickly brought Rosecrans back to reality. The Tullahoma campaign had been a great success, but the Army of Tennessee waited beyond the Cumberland Plateau. It was time to begin a new campaign.[11]

2

The Army of the Cumberland

» July 1863 «

At the end of the Tullahoma campaign, Maj. Gen. William Starke Rosecrans, commander of the Army of the Cumberland, was just two months short of his forty-fourth birthday. The son of Crandall and Jemima Hopkins Rosecrans of Homer, Ohio, a village in Licking County northeast of Columbus, he was born on 6 September 1819. The first of four boys to survive infancy, he was the acknowledged leader of his siblings and very early gained a reputation for intelligence and a thirst for the knowledge found in books. Homer offered limited opportunities for schooling, so Rosecrans supplemented his formal training with a vigorous personal reading program. Clerking and bookkeeping in the family store further honed his intellect, but family circumstances precluded entry into a private institution of higher education. Thus young Rosecrans set his sights on gaining an appointment to the United States Military Academy. The path to that appointment was not smooth, but he persevered and entered the Academy in 1838. His classmates were James Longstreet, Daniel Harvey Hill, Earl Van Dorn, and John Pope, all of whom he was destined to encounter again during the great conflict besetting the nation a generation later. Among his roommates at one time or another were Longstreet and another Southerner, Alexander Stewart. Upperclassmen he came to know well were George Thomas and William Sherman, while Ulysses Grant was a member of the class that enrolled in 1839. Known to his friends as "Rosy" or "Old Rosy," he graduated fifth out of fifty-six in the class of 1842, a standing that merited a brevet second lieutenant's commission in the Corps of Engineers. The bright but unschooled boy from Homer, Ohio, now had a first-class education and a profession.[1]

Rosecrans's first assignment involved the prevention of shore erosion at Fort Monroe, Virginia, but his ambition pushed him almost immediately to apply for a position at West Point teaching engineering. In 1843 he received both promotion to second lieutenant and the coveted appointment to the engineering faculty under Dennis Hart Mahan. With prospects so favorable, he married Anna Elizabeth Hegeman in August 1843. The teaching assignment was marked by Rosecrans's forsaking his nominal Methodist upbringing to convert to Roman Catholicism in 1844. Following his teaching tour, Rosecrans moved to Newport, Rhode Island, where he spent five years working on coastal fortifications and designing barracks. The work was important, but it kept Rosecrans from participating in the conflict with Mexico that ended in 1848. At the end of the Newport assignment, Rosecrans moved to Bedford, Massachusetts, to work on harbor improvements, but after less than a year he was loaned to the U.S. Navy as "Civil and Constructing Engineer" at the Washington Navy Yard. By this time William and Anna had two children (two others had died in infancy) and life in the nation's capital for a family of four on second lieutenant's pay was becoming difficult. Design and construction work at the Navy Yard kept Rosecrans busy but did not challenge his restless mind. Consequently he searched for other employment, including a failed bid in 1851 to gain an open professorship at the Virginia Military Institute that went to Thomas Jackson. Similarly, Rosecrans unsuccessfully sought the editorship of a Catholic newspaper in Cincinnati in 1853. Even his promotion to first lieutenant in March 1853 did nothing to ameliorate his unhappiness. After his request for a leave of absence during a bout of illness was rejected, Rosecrans decided to leave the army. His resignation became effective in April 1854, just before the birth of his third child.[2]

For the next seven years, Rosecrans strove to make ends meet as a civilian entrepreneur. He began by using his West Point engineering training in several positions involving canal and coal mining ventures in the mountains of Virginia. Ultimately his mining work led him to gravitate into the business of producing kerosene from coal in a refinery located in Cincinnati. Before he perfected his product, one of his experiments went awry, producing an explosion that damaged the refinery and burned his face badly. Although he recovered, Rosecrans thereafter was cursed with a disfigured face that was twisted into a permanent smirk. Undeterred, he continued to improve his manufacturing processes and eventually produced an acceptable kerosene product for home lighting. Additional experimentation led to improvements in the design of both kerosene lamps and the wicks they utilized. Several of these inventions led to European patents. All in all, by the time the secession crisis swept the nation in 1860–61, Rosecrans had finally begun to make economic headway in the world of business. His company was profitable, his family had grown by two additional children, and the life of a military officer seemed far in the past.[3]

The war that began in April 1861 instantly changed life for millions of Americans, including William Rosecrans. The Union's small Regular Army was utterly inadequate to subdue the seceding states, forcing the Lincoln administration to seek a massive influx of volunteers. Those volunteers would need competent officers, placing any sort of officer education at a premium. Rosecrans's West Point training made him a highly marketable commodity, and he quickly returned to the service as a volunteer aide-de-camp and engineer for the state forces of Ohio. At the same time he lobbied friends still in the army for a brigadier general's commission in the volunteer service. He was pleasantly surprised to be commissioned brigadier general in the Regular Army, with date of rank established as 16 May 1861. Ordered to the mountains of western Virginia to command an infantry brigade under Maj. Gen. George McClellan, he played a major role in one of the first small actions of the war, at Rich Mountain on 11 July. Although privately disparaged by McClellan as a "silly fussy goose," Rosecrans persuaded his chief to adopt an aggressive battle plan to outflank Lt. Col. John Pegram's small Confederate force from its strongly fortified mountain position. Rosecrans led the flanking column, took all the risks, received no assistance from McClellan's main body, yet forced the enemy from the field. The fight at Rich Mountain showed Rosecrans to be an excellent operational and tactical thinker who brought a great deal of energy to his movements. Neither Rosecrans nor Pegram could know it, but they would meet again on a much larger field in Tennessee two years later.[4]

The tiny Federal victory at Rich Mountain lifted several careers. To Rosecrans's chagrin, McClellan received most of the credit and was called east to redeem Irvin McDowell's failure at Bull Run. Rosecrans replaced McClellan as commander of the Department of the Ohio, a regional command embracing parts of three states. Department command placed a premium on organizational and administrative skills, which Rosecrans possessed, but he continued to do the work of subalterns whenever their performance did not meet his exacting standards. Rosecrans's Confederate counterpart was Gen. Robert E. Lee, and both men struggled to master the mountainous terrain with inadequate resources as all eyes turned to larger armies both east and west. In September 1861, a Federal departmental reorganization designated Rosecrans's command the Department of Western Virginia, with much smaller geographical responsibilities. As his territory and troop strength declined, Rosecrans appealed to McClellan and the War Department for a larger role. Their response in March 1862 was to create the Mountain Department under Maj. Gen. John Fremont, and absorb Rosecrans's command within it. Rosecrans thus was effectively out of work, forcing him to report to Washington in person for a new assignment. With no suitable command immediately open, Secretary of War Edwin Stanton gave Rosecrans a temporary mission to supervise the movement of a division of troops from one department to another. This seemingly inconsequential assignment, which ultimately had no effect on the conduct of the war, would have a disproportionate effect on Rosecrans's subsequent career.[5]

Although his new assignment was unusual for an officer of Rosecrans's rank and reputation, he readily accepted it. The task involved expediting the movement of Brig. Gen. Louis Blenker's division from east of the Blue Ridge Mountains through the Shenandoah Valley and into the Allegheny Mountains, where it would be assigned to Fremont's command. A secondary task involved coordinating the movement with Maj. Gen. Nathaniel Banks, operating in the Shenandoah Valley. Standing his orders on their head, Rosecrans not only did not join Blenker and push him westward quickly, but after conferring with Banks, forwarded to Washington a rather grandiose plan for a coordinated movement involving three commands larger than Blenker's. Only three months in office, Stanton was under great pressure to establish his dominance at the beginning of what promised to be a critical campaigning season. Imperious and irascible under the best of circumstances, he wanted only results involving Blenker's troops, not gratuitous advice offered without appropriate coordination, and his messages to Rosecrans became increasingly peremptory. Seemingly unaffected by Stanton's strictures, Rosecrans reported that Blenker's men needed basic necessities such as shelter halves, shoes, and back pay, and that he would not resume their westward trek until the War Department supplied them. Again, Rosecrans substituted his judgment for that of the War Department without reference to larger considerations. Ultimately, Rosecrans put Blenker on the road again, but it was far too late to erase Stanton's now fixed opinion of Rosecrans as a potentially troublesome subordinate. For his part, Rosecrans remained supremely confident that his strategic vision was superior to that of most officers, and certainly superior to that of an Ohio lawyer like the secretary of war. Thus, the minor incident involving Blenker's division prefigured future conflicts, when the two strong personalities, Rosecrans and Stanton, met again. Rosecrans had thoughtlessly made an enemy who could hurt him later.[6]

Following an unpleasant final interview with Stanton, Rosecrans was sent west to join the massive group of armies advancing on Corinth, Mississippi, under the command of Maj. Gen. Henry Halleck. Upon Rosecrans's arrival in late May 1862, Halleck assigned him to the Army of the Mississippi, commanded by his West Point classmate Maj. Gen. John Pope. Just as Rosecrans joined Pope as commander of his Right Wing, the Confederates evacuated Corinth. Halleck ordered Pope's army to pursue, with Rosecrans in the lead, but the Confederates escaped. Once again, a superior garnered the credit for actions engineered by Rosecrans, and Pope was ordered to the Eastern Theater in June to assume a larger command. Again, Rosecrans profited from the change, taking command of the Army of the Mississippi and reporting directly to Halleck. When Halleck departed for Washington and command of all the Federal armies in July, his second in command, Ulysses Grant, became Rosecrans's boss. Initially numbering five divisions, Rosecrans's army in September 1862 dwindled to two with the transfer of three divisions to Maj. Gen. Don Carlos Buell's Army of the Ohio. With that diminished force, Rosecrans participated in the battle of Iuka, Mississippi, on 19 September. There an effort by Grant to defeat Confederate forces under Maj. Gen. Sterling Price failed because of an overly complex plan, bad roads, and an alleged acoustic shadow. Following a hard-fought battle in which only Rosecrans's divisions engaged the enemy, Price's forces escaped. Initially positive in his postbattle comments about Rosecrans's performance, Grant adopted a different stance after Northern newspapers praised Rosecrans highly at Grant's expense. When both staffs joined the fray on behalf of their respective chiefs, the rift between the two men widened.[7]

Rosecrans gained further acclaim when he successfully resisted a strong attack on Corinth in early October by the combined Confederate commands of Price and Maj. Gen. Earl Van Dorn, a fellow member of the class of 1842. After a slow start, Rosecrans's pursuit of the retreating Confederates gathered momentum until a cautious Grant ordered its suspension. Fueled by fawning correspondents, Rosecrans's reputation soared. Thereafter, what had begun as a series of substantive disagreements between Rosecrans and Grant on operational matters quickly degenerated into extreme pettiness over slights both perceived and real. In the midst of it all, Rosecrans received notification that he had been promoted to the rank of major general of volunteers, to date from 17 September 1862. That late date angered Rosecrans so much that he complained bitterly to Halleck in an unofficial letter. Halleck responded soothingly, noting his own positive feelings regarding Rosecrans and the efforts made on his behalf against the "objections" of others in Washington. He closed by promising Rosecrans an independent command in the near future and ultimately succeeded in getting the commission backdated to 21 March 1862. On 24 October Halleck made good on his efforts to find more important work for Rosecrans by ordering him to Cincinnati and placing him in command of a new Department of the Cumberland. The troops in the department were primarily Don Carlos Buell's Army of the Ohio, now designated the Fourteenth Army Corps. Buell himself was relieved of command because of his dilatory pursuit of Braxton Bragg's Army of Tennessee after its failed Kentucky campaign. Buell's loss was Rosecrans's gain, and he now had another independent command, in a far more important theater than western Virginia. His departure from Grant's control no doubt pleased both men immensely.[8]

Rosecrans began his new assignment on a sour note when he again ran afoul of Stanton over a small matter. Told that he could select his own staff, Rosecrans appealed directly to President Lincoln when one of his choices was denied promotion. Lincoln referred the matter to Stanton, who forced Halleck to write a scathing note to Rosecrans in which he threatened to withdraw the assignment to command unless Rosecrans behaved more circumspectly. Rosecrans responded with pledges of fealty, but with the national press trumpeting his arrival to save the day in Tennessee, he refused to bend the knee to his superiors in practice. Besides, he had much to do to restore the Fourteenth Corps to fighting trim. His first task was to win the support of his senior subordinate, Maj. Gen. George Thomas. Thomas had outranked Rosecrans until the latter's commission was backdated, and his strong sense of Army proprieties had left him outraged and seeking a transfer to another theater. Rosecrans mollified Thomas by giving him the largest proportion of troops in what Rosecrans had decided to rename the Army of the Cumberland. Whatever its name, Rosecrans's army needed rest, refitting, and reorganization after a grueling campaign before it could resume the offensive. From the moment on 30 October 1862 when he formally assumed command, Rosecrans worked tirelessly to rebuild the Army of the Cumberland's morale and fighting strength. He divided the Fourteenth Corps into three wings: Right, Center, and Left, and placed them under Major Generals Alexander McCook, George Thomas, and Thomas Crittenden respectively. He also gradually concentrated the army around Nashville, facing an equally battle-worn Army of Tennessee. As fall turned into winter, neither army appeared ready to resume campaigning during the cold, wet season that lay ahead.[9]

Halleck's instructions to Rosecrans when he replaced Buell were breathtakingly brief and suitably general for an officer of Rosecrans's intellect and experience: "The great objects to be kept in view in your operations in the field are: First, to drive the enemy from Kentucky and Middle Tennessee; second, to take and hold East Tennessee, cutting the line of railroad at Chattanooga, Cleveland, or Athens, so as to destroy the connection of the valley of Virginia with Georgia and the other Southern States." The manner of accomplishing these tasks was left to Rosecrans's discretion. The Lincoln administration, however, desired speed in execution. Buell had been relieved in part because he had moved too slowly, and Rosecrans would be judged by the same standard. Yet Rosecrans's entire career had been constructed upon his unshakable belief in his own competence and his frequent substitution of his own judgment for that of his superiors. When Washington demanded an immediate forward movement and Halleck threatened him with relief, Rosecrans responded in words echoing the Blenker controversy of April. He would not advance until he deemed his army ready, and to threats of removal he was "insensible." Halleck withdrew the offending words, and Rosecrans continued to gather supplies and drill his men.[10]

At last, on 26 December 1862, the Army of the Cumberland advanced upon Bragg's forces arrayed around Murfreesboro, Tennessee. Rosecrans's movements were uncharacteristically deliberate, and it took four days for his Right, Center, and Left Wings to reach their start lines for an attack scheduled for the last day of the year. Bragg, however, struck first, his men bursting out of the fog on the morning of 31 December and rolling up McCook's right flank. As other Confederate units joined the action, the entire right side of Rosecrans's army reeled backward, bending his command into a U-shape with its supply line to Nashville endangered. Rosecrans himself was in the thick of the fight, so close that his chief of staff, Lt. Col. Julius Garesche, was killed by his side. By nightfall, the Confederate attack was spent, but Rosecrans recognized that a Federal retreat would be disastrous for both his army and his career. He therefore elected to remain on the field and await Bragg's next move. Neither side took any significant action on New Year's Day, but when the Confederates renewed battle on the Federal left on 2 January, Rosecrans crushed the thrust decisively. On the following day, Bragg withdrew to the southeast, establishing defensive positions around Tullahoma and Shelbyville. Rosecrans's victory at Stones River, balancing Federal setbacks in Virginia and northern Mississippi, was welcome news to the beleaguered Lincoln administration. Congratulations flowed to Rosecrans's headquarters in Murfreesboro from the president, from Halleck, from the Ohio and Indiana legislatures, and, most surprising of all, from Edwin Stanton. Congress was so enthused that it passed an official resolution of thanks. From all indications, it appeared that Rosecrans had finally achieved the acclaim that he had long felt was his due.[11]

A grateful nation and grateful leaders demanded further triumphs as soon as possible. Rosecrans, however, saw firsthand the battered condition of the Army of the Cumberland. He also knew that the bulk of his supplies came by rail over a single-track line stretching back to Louisville. That line could be easily interdicted by Confederate cavalry, which still had the edge over Rosecrans's horsemen. Thus Rosecrans importuned the War Department weekly for more supplies, back pay for his soldiers, and, most often, for more and better cavalry. Gradually, these incessant calls for "more" began to drain the reservoir of goodwill he had momentarily stored in Washington after the Stones River victory. This loss of favor accelerated, at least with Stanton, when Rosecrans in one of his responses to the secretary alluded directly to the Blenker episode of the previous year. By declaring himself in the right whenever he asked for something for his troops and denigrating those who denied him the resources, Rosecrans unnecessarily reopened an old wound that this time could not be healed. Nor did he improve his position with his superiors when he responded condescendingly to a clumsy effort by the War Department to induce forward movement by offering a major general's commission in the Regular Army to the first Federal commander to advance. No matter how often Lincoln or Halleck implored him to begin a forward movement, Rosecrans demurred, and arguments that he needed to distract Confederates from Grant's army besieging Vicksburg were counterproductive. Finally, on 23 June, Rosecrans sent the

Army of the Cumberland forward. In a brilliant campaign of maneuver, hindered by incessant rain and deep mud, he forced Bragg not only out of Middle Tennessee but beyond the Tennessee River to Chattanooga. At very low cost in lives, Rosecrans had met the first part of Halleck's charge to him in October 1862. On a personal level, his string of victories that had begun at Rich Mountain two years earlier remained intact.[12]

One of the Union's most successful commanders in the summer of 1863, William Starke Rosecrans was a man of medium build, slightly overweight, with a prominent hooked nose and the disfiguring facial scars from his industrial accident. His rather nondescript physical appearance, however, belied a very strong personality. Highly intelligent, articulate in speech, and vigorous in manner, he never failed to make an impression on those who met him. He was quick to make decisions and firm in defense of them once made. His fervently expressed hatred of the institution of slavery and its supporters was widely known. Similarly, his strong religious convictions were openly displayed through the rosary that he carried, his personal priest who traveled with his headquarters, and his willingness to engage in complex and obscure theological discussions. Rosecrans's personality, in fact, was an open book to those who encountered him, whether private or general officer. After Stones River, no one doubted his physical courage under fire. His administrative skill was also evident in the way he prepared his command for the rigors of campaigning. Superficial observers were thus convinced of Rosecrans's greatness as an army commander. Others, more perceptive, were instead taken by Rosecrans's flaws. Those flaws included an overly boisterous and often profane manner, a volcanic temper expressed in violent outbursts against subordinates, a nervous and excitable demeanor in times of great stress, an extreme simplicity of outlook, and an uncompromising self-righteousness. Even to those who admired him, Rosecrans always seemed to be on the verge of losing control of himself because of his seemingly boundless energy. Worse, he was neither introspective nor a perceptive judge of others. He could relate to other people on a superficial level, but he had no interest in how he appeared to them or understood their motives. He knew how to ingratiate himself with private soldiers, by supporting them against their officers, but he did not understand how that technique displeased midlevel commanders. Supremely self-confident, Rosecrans gave no thought to the possibility that his actions large or small might not win universal approval and acclaim.[13]

To assist him in managing both the Department of the Cumberland and its field army, Rosecrans by July 1863 had gathered a large number of staff officers of varying quality and longevity. The key position, of course, was chief of staff, although the duties of the position varied from army to army. Rosecrans had been much attached to Julius Garesche, who had died by his side at Stones

Rosecrans and his staff, summer 1863. *Front*: Taylor, Barnett, Goddard, Rosecrans, Garfield, Horace Porter, Bond, Thompson, Sheridan. *Rear*: Thoms, Wiles, Ducat, Simmons, Drouillard. (Detail, Collections of Maine Historical Society).

River. In January, Brig. Gen. James A. Garfield had reported to the Army of the Cumberland in hopes of getting a field command, perhaps a division. A volunteer officer from Ohio, Garfield, thirty-one, was an educator, a lawyer, and a state politician. He saw minor action in Kentucky as a colonel, commanded a brigade on the second day at Shiloh, and participated in the advance on Corinth. A strong Republican and abolitionist, he was extremely ambitious, and the slow pace of the war in the West made him restless. Driven from the field by a serious illness, he went to Washington for reassignment and there became a protégé of Secretary of the Treasury Salmon Chase. Nominated for a redrawn congressional district in Ohio in late 1862, he won the seat and expected to remain in the army only until December 1863. Sent to the Army of the Cumberland to fill any vacant command, Garfield was immediately seen by Rosecrans as a compatible personality with whom to while away the evening hours in theological and political discussion. Finally, after a month of intellectual sparring, Rosecrans offered Garfield the chief of staff position. Initially, Garfield had doubts, especially because his religious affiliation, the Disciples of Christ, clashed with the Roman Catholicism of his chief. Ultimately, however, Garfield accepted the position and gradually came to be Rosecrans's confidant as well as the army's primary administrator. When Rosecrans polled the army's senior leaders in early June on the propriety of a general advance, only Garfield strongly favored the movement. He was vindicated by the success of the Tullahoma campaign, but his overt advocacy made him no friends within the army's hierarchy, except its commander.[14]

Garfield's role officially was to organize the paper flow at Army headquarters, receiving all reports, drafting the most important messages, and supervising the junior members of the staff as they handled routine business. Much more important, he served as a sounding board for ideas broached by Rosecrans and frequently offered ideas of his own. His lack of formal military education troubled Rosecrans not at all, although it did cause resentment among some of the army's professional soldiers. Indeed, the month that Garfield spent in Rosecrans's company debating a wide range of topics before his selection as chief of staff solidified the intuitive bond between the two men. Rosecrans came to trust Garfield implicitly in matters large and small. The latter reciprocated to a degree but privately maintained a certain distance from his chief, perceived closeness to whom could become problematic if Rosecrans's star should wane. In fact, their differences over religious questions notwithstanding, the two men were alike in many ways. Both were egotistical, ambitious, intelligent, and extremely self-confident. Neither possessed the capacity to regulate his interactions with others based upon a deep and mature understanding of human nature. No doubt any strong chief of staff would have elicited occasional opposition, but Garfield's lack of a West Point education exacerbated the tendency of the corps and division commanders to denigrate his role and disparage him in private conversations. Garfield spoke for Rosecrans and was obeyed accordingly, but neither man was universally loved by the experienced combat commanders of the Army of the Cumberland.[15]

Assisting Garfield in the management of affairs was a relatively large number of staff officers. The staff was divided into two sections, the army commander's personal staff and the special staff who handled various well-delineated functions. Garfield was part of Rosecrans's personal staff, as were the aides-de-camp. Army regulations called for an officer of Rosecrans's rank to be assisted by only two aides-de-camp, but the army commander enjoyed the services of eight aides in the summer of 1863. Their duties were ill-defined, being essentially whatever Rosecrans desired them to do. Senior in rank among the aides was Col. Joseph McKibbin, forty-one, a former California congressman and War Democrat, who had joined Rosecrans in February from Halleck's staff in Washington. His rank notwithstanding, McKibbin was not the senior aide by title, however. That position was held by Maj. Frank Bond, thirty-three, a Connecticut native and former railroad executive in Ohio and Pennsylvania, who had joined Rosecrans in December 1862. Also serving as aides were Capt. James Drouillard, twenty-three, West Point class of 1861, on the staff since

April; Capt. Charles Thompson, twenty-three, a volunteer engineer officer who had come with Rosecrans from Corinth; Capt. Robert Thoms, twenty-nine, a Cincinnati attorney who had been with Rosecrans at Stones River as a civilian and who had been commissioned in April; Capt. William Farrar, thirty-eight, an attorney and volunteer officer detailed from the Sixty-Fifth Ohio Infantry; and two young first lieutenants, William Porter and James Reynolds, detached from their Ohio regiments as acting aides. Four of the eight (Bond, Thompson, Thoms, and Porter) had passed through the crucible of Stones River with Rosecrans, gaining primacy of place thereby.[16]

Also classed as part of Rosecrans's personal staff were the assistant adjutants general and the assistant inspectors general. The officers in the army's assistant adjutant general's office managed correspondence, orders, and personnel actions. Lt. Col. Calvin Goddard was Rosecrans's principal assistant adjutant general. Goddard, twenty-five, had been with Rosecrans since the latter's western Virginia campaigns and had served variously as aide, assistant adjutant general, and chief of staff since early 1862. He was trusted implicitly and was noted for his exactitude and efficiency in the operation of his office. Goddard's assistants were Maj. William McMichael, twenty-two, assigned since February 1863; Capt. Henry Thrall, twenty-four, another veteran of the western Virginia campaigns, whose assignment also dated to February 1863; Capt. Jonathan Dickson, thirty, a Cincinnati native serving in the office since December 1862; and Capt. David Swaim, twenty-nine, formerly a Garfield aide but assigned to the assistant adjutant's office since April 1863. A close friend of the army's chief of staff, Swaim managed a group of secret agents with the assistance of Capt. William Farrar, one of Rosecrans's aides. Capt. John Young, a Mexican War veteran and Regular Army officer, held the specific title of commissary of musters, maintaining the army's unit records and serving as an assistant adjutant general or aide-de-camp as needed. The assistant inspector general's office surveyed and reported on the army's discipline, training, equipment, and unit administration. Rosecrans's primary assistant inspector general was the highly competent Lt. Col. Arthur Ducat, thirty-three. An Irish immigrant, Ducat had been a civil engineer and insurance underwriter before the war and a volunteer officer in the Twelfth Illinois Infantry. He had been with Rosecrans since Corinth and had held the inspector's position since early April 1863. Capt. Andrew Burt, twenty-three, Eighteenth United States Infantry, and Capt. Gurdon Hubbard Jr., twenty-five, Eighty-Eighth Illinois Infantry, served as Ducat's assistants.[17]

The special staff of the Department and Army of the Cumberland consisted of those agencies that dealt with the technical issues common to the administration of a large and complex organization. Many of these sections were required by army regulations, but some came into being because Rosecrans saw an unfilled need and created a staff position on his own authority. As the army advanced farther from its advanced base of operations at Nashville, many of these sections split into two groups, with officers stationed both in Nashville and the army's field headquarters. Several of the functional areas involved supply of basic necessities: quartermaster, commissary, and ordnance. Others, such as chief of artillery, were purely administrative. Medical support to the troops required both a department medical director and a medical inspector. Engineering functions in the Department of the Cumberland were split between engineers and topographical engineers, even though the two separate corps had been merged by the War Department in March 1863. The recent advances in communication nationwide required both a chief signal officer and a superintendent of the military telegraph. Similarly, the relatively new railroad transportation required specialized managerial skills and thus its own section. Proper discipline within the army required a provost marshal and a judge advocate, while a similar requirement in the Department of the Cumberland caused Rosecrans to establish an army police separate from the provost marshal function. Finally, the army required a paymaster. Many of these staff sections, especially quartermaster, commissary, and railroad, required a large number of officers, clerks, and civilian workers to operate efficiently, making the Federal government a large employer in Middle Tennessee.[18]

The leaders of the staff departments that clothed, equipped, and transported the Army of the Cumberland, that fed it, and that provided weapons and ammunition were arguably the most critical personnel on Rosecrans's special staff. Rosecrans's chief quartermaster was Lt. Col. John Taylor, forty-six, a native of the state of New York and son of a former Speaker of the House of Representatives. A businessman residing in Iowa when the war began, Taylor entered service as a quartermaster captain and soon found himself chief quartermaster of Pope's command in the campaign against Corinth. When Rosecrans replaced Pope, he retained Taylor and arranged for him to be transferred to the Army of the Cumberland when he moved to Tennessee. Taylor's duties involved providing the clothing, camp equipage, transportation, fuel, and incidental needs for all personnel in the department, and the management of the more than 3,000 personnel needed to supply those needs. Taylor's primary assistant was Capt. Henry Hodges, who managed the Nashville quartermaster depot with the assistance of six junior officers. Taylor's counterpart, the chief commissary of subsistence, was Lt. Col. Samuel Simmons, thirty-seven, a native of Pennsylvania and an attorney in Missouri before the war. Beginning his career with Federal volunteers in St. Louis, he later saw service with Grant at Shiloh and Pope around Corinth. Like Taylor, he had served Rosecrans in Mississippi and had accompanied him to Tennessee in the fall of 1862. Also like Taylor, he had been advanced from captain to lieutenant colonel at Rosecrans's request. Simmons's portfolio revolved around one thing: feeding the troops in the Department of the Cumberland. Less fortunate in rank than his compatriots was Rosecrans's chief of ordnance, Capt. Horace Porter, twenty-six. A Pennsylvania native, Porter had graduated from West Point in 1860 as an ordnance officer. After service on the Atlantic coast at Port Royal, the siege of Fort Pulaski, and the battle of Secessionville, where he was slightly wounded, Porter had spent brief tours with the Army of the Potomac and the Department of the Ohio. In February 1863, he joined the Army of the Cumberland as its chief of ordnance. It was his task to keep track of the army's weapons and provide enough quantities of pistol, rifle, carbine, and artillery ammunition to fight multiple battles.[19]

Unlike the quartermaster and commissary departments, some staff positions were manned very lightly. Col. James Barnett, forty-two, was Rosecrans's chief of artillery, a purely administrative position. A native New Yorker but a long-time resident of Cleveland, Barnett raised a battery at the outbreak of the war and served briefly with it in western Virginia before being appointed colonel of the First Ohio Artillery regiment. He then served in various administrative artillery positions in the Army of the Ohio until Rosecrans took command of the Army of the Cumberland and named Barnett his chief of artillery in October 1862. As such, Barnett kept track of the physical condition of the many batteries assigned to the army, advised Rosecrans on general artillery matters, and also served as an advocate at army headquarters for the corps and division chiefs of artillery. Because the army's batteries were apportioned to individual brigades and reported to infantry brigade commanders, Barnett exercised no tactical control of the artillery and thus could not mass fires if the tactical situation demanded it. In contrast to Barnett, Rosecrans's chief of cavalry, Maj. Gen. David Stanley, commanded the Cavalry Corps of the Army of the Cumberland. Stanley, thirty-five, was an 1852 graduate of the United States Military Academy. Long service on the frontier, in Missouri in 1861, and as a division commander under Rosecrans at Iuka and Corinth had seasoned him. A favorite of Rosecrans's, he had been named cavalry chief in November 1862 and promoted to major general not long thereafter. Unlike Barnett, who had no tactical role with the army's artillery, Stanley's field duties as commander of the army's mounted arm occupied him fully, leaving him no time for purely staff functions.[20]

Rosecrans's special staff also included a medical director, Surgeon Glover Perin, thirty-nine. A native of Ohio and a graduate of the Ohio Medical College in Cincinnati in 1846, Perin had been a Regular Army surgeon since 1847. His service record was extensive, commencing with the Mexican War, continuing with frontier duty at various posts, and in the Civil War. He joined the Army of the Cumberland in February 1863 as its medical director, with the rank of major. Finding the army's medical affairs in disarray, Perin worked diligently to improve his department's efficiency. His most notable subordinates were Asst. Surgeon Dallas Bache, assistant medical director; Surgeon Alfred Thurston, who managed the Nashville hospitals in the army's rear; Surgeon Henry Seys, thirty-three, medical inspector; and Surgeon Robert Fletcher, medical purveyor. By mid-1863, the medical department of the Army of the Cumberland consisted of 159 surgeons, 260 assistant surgeons, 84 contract physicians, and 2,500 stewards, clerks, cooks, and nurses scattered throughout the Department of the Cumberland. The primary general hospitals serving the army were in Nashville, where 3,000 beds were available, but other general hospitals deeper in the rear raised the total number of beds to nearly 12,000. At the other end of the system of care, every regiment had an assigned ambulance, with additional ambulances assigned at higher echelons. Finding the ambulance system in place upon his arrival to be utterly unsatisfactory, Perin had worked to bring greater organization to the process of transporting sick and wounded soldiers. By July 1863, he had made some progress, but problems remained, particularly in regard to the maintenance of the ambulances, which was still in the hands of the army's quartermasters. Rosecrans's acknowledged interest in the care of his soldiers' health worked in Perin's favor, as he continued to improve the army's medical services.[21]

Army discipline was another function that required personnel on Rosecrans's special staff. The army's provost marshal was Lt. Col. William Wiles, twenty-six, of Columbus, Indiana. A businessman in the pharmaceutical trade before the war, Wiles was instrumental in the raising of a company in the Twenty-Second Indiana Infantry regiment and served with it until being posted to Rosecrans's staff in May 1862. Appointed provost marshall of the Army of the Mississippi as a lieutenant in July 1862, he followed Rosecrans to the Army of the Cumberland in October of that year and rose steadily in rank thereafter. Wiles's chief subordinates were Capt. Elias Cosper, thirty-nine, prewar banker and member of the Seventy-Fourth Illinois Infantry, first assistant provost marshal, and Capt. Robert Goodwin, twenty-seven, prewar attorney and member of the Thirty-Seventh Indiana Infantry, second assistant provost marshal. Although his office was small, Wiles had many tasks. The provost marshal maintained law and order within the department among soldiers and civilians alike; took charge of prisoners of war captured by the tactical units; was responsible for general rear area security; and controlled the flow of personnel to and from the army, both military and civilian. Manpower came from tactical units detailed as necessary. As part of his duties, Wiles attempted to generate an order of battle for the Confederate Army of Tennessee, relying upon the unit identification and unguarded statements of prisoners. Assisting Wiles in legal matters was Capt. Hunter Brooke, thirty-two, acting judge advocate. Brooke, a long-time resident of Cincinnati and a practicing attorney since 1851, had accompanied Brig. Gen. Robert McCook when that officer was mortally wounded in a notorious incident in August 1862. Taken prisoner, paroled, and exchanged in December, Brooke reported to the Army of the Cumberland as an aide-de-camp to Rosecrans in February 1863 and was assigned as acting judge advocate in April.[22]

Another key staff officer for Rosecrans was Brig. Gen. James St. Clair Morton, his chief engineer. Born in Philadelphia in 1829, Morton was an 1851 graduate of West Point, ranking second in his class. At age thirty-three he possessed an extensive and illustrious record as an army engineer but was considered by some to be quite eccentric. A man of brilliant mind, he wore his hair shoulder length and had a reputation for being too outspoken for his own good. Although he had been Buell's chief engineer in the Army of the Ohio, he endeared himself to his new chief so greatly by his actions at Stones River that Rosecrans obtained his promotion to brigadier general in April 1863. Oddly enough, the promotion was not related to Morton's engineering talents but was a reward for the combat performance of the Pioneer Brigade, which Morton led. The Pioneer Brigade was an ad hoc response to a perceived need in the Army of the Cumberland. Unable to gain engineer assets from Washington, Rosecrans in November 1862 had ordered that two laborers and mechanics be selected from every regiment in the Army of the Cumberland to serve as engineers. Commanded by officers similarly selected, the men were divided into battalions that would serve their respective corps or be amalgamated into a brigade controlled by the army's chief engineer. The brigade thus combined aspects of both engineer and infantry troops, with the emphasis on the former. They had performed well enough as infantry at Stones River, but Rosecrans preferred their engineer skills to be primary, leaving both infantry skills and discipline to suffer. Morton personally commanded the Pioneer Brigade and was thus responsible for its reputation within the army as an undisciplined rabble. A strong rivalry existed between the Pioneers and the army's other engineer force, the First Michigan Engineers and Mechanics regiment, commanded by Col. William Innes.[23]

While Morton was the army's chief engineer, in practice his writ did not extend to the army's topographical engineers, led by Capt. William Merrill, twenty-five. The War Department had combined the two types of engineers into one branch earlier in 1863, but Rosecrans had not implemented the change beyond an informal understanding that Morton would give general directions only and pass any orders to topographical engineers through Merrill. Merrill himself, an 1859 West Point graduate, remained jealous of his prerogatives and conducted the topographical engineer department independently of the army's chief engineer. Merrill's freedom perhaps stemmed from the fact that he had known Rosecrans since 1861 in western Virginia, where he was a staff engineer until his capture. Upon his release, he made a name for himself at the siege of Yorktown, where he was wounded, and with John Pope at Second Manassas. Transferred to Kentucky, he built fortifications until his command joined the Army of the Cumberland in March 1863. Upon arrival, he found the topographical engineer section in disarray. Rosecrans had decreed in December 1862 that every division and brigade in the army detail an officer for topographical duty, but the chief topographical engineer at that time, Capt. Nathaniel Michler, had resisted full implementation of such a decentralized system and had felt Rosecrans's wrath as a result. By the time Michler was forced from the command under the pretense of ill health in May, his office was larger but in Rosecrans's view remained unsatisfactory. Rosecrans then turned to Merrill, a known quantity, and issued minute instructions on the creation of a chain of topographical officers extending from brigade to army. The primary result of Merrill's ascendancy by July was the adoption of an ingenious system of "quick maps," widely reproduced throughout the army using a method initially devised by one of Merrill's assistants, Capt. William Margedant, twenty-seven.[24]

Capt. Jesse Merrill was the Army of the Cumberland's chief signal officer. Merrill, twenty-seven, a volunteer officer from Pennsylvania, was one of the first graduates of the signal camp of instruction in 1861. He was assigned to Buell's army in Kentucky in early 1862 and remained with it as commander of the army's signal detachment. As chief signal officer, Merrill controlled the personnel attached to the normal signal flag detachments and the field telegraph trains. The latter consisted of wagons carrying up to ten miles of gutta-percha-clad copper wire that could be strung across country and connected to Beardslee telegraph instruments, magneto-electric devices that required no galvanic batteries to operate. By the summer of 1863, Captain Merrill commanded a force of thirty-six officers and 125 men. He had detachments at army- and corps-level headquarters and could deploy up to five field telegraph trains within the department. Merrill's chief competitor on Rosecrans's staff was Capt. John Van Duzer, thirty-six, a New Yorker. Initially a printer and newspaper publisher by trade, Van Duzer early saw the potential of the electric telegraph and switched careers to become a railroad telegrapher. In 1861 he was employed by the Federal army in Missouri and soon became a manager of telegraph services. Working first for Halleck, then for Grant, he had been present at Corinth with Rosecrans. The latter connection may have been his undoing. After Rosecrans's departure, Grant arrested him on specious charges and banished him from west Tennessee in December 1862. His superiors in Washington sustained him, however, and in January 1863 he was appointed second assistant superintendent of U.S. military telegraphs and assigned to the Department of the Cumberland. Van Duzer did not yet have military rank but Rosecrans made him an honorary captain to facilitate his work. So titled, Van Duzer managed the army's electric telegraph lines from the front to their interface with the civilian system, using a corps of civilian operators and a construction team.[25]

Another civilian, John B. Anderson, forty-five, managed Rosecrans's railroad lines. A Pennsylvania native, Anderson had begun a career in education but had gravitated into the field of railroad management during the 1850s. In April 1861 he was the superintendent of transportation for the Louisville & Nashville Railroad, a critical link in the transportation network supporting Federal forces in Kentucky and Tennessee. Anderson was appointed military superintendent of railroads in the Department of the Ohio in November 1861, continued in that post under Buell, and was retained in the same capacity in the Department of the Cumberland by Rosecrans in November 1862. Accused by some of inefficiency and mismanagement, he remained in charge of the railroad lines south of Nashville with the honorary rank of colonel.[26]

Two members of Rosecrans's staff illustrate the contradictions in his personality. Converted to Roman Catholicism as an adult, Rosecrans had a strong spiritual bent, manifest in his theological discussions with Garfield and the retention of a personal chaplain, Father Jeremiah Trecy, at army headquarters. A native of Ireland, Trecy, thirty-eight, was ordained in 1851. An advocate of Western colonization, he founded several congregations in the Iowa-Nebraska region before the war but moved to Huntsville, Alabama, for health reasons before the outbreak of hostilities. There he had turned to ministering to Confederate wounded after the battle of Shiloh. Visiting Corinth in the fall of 1862, he met Rosecrans and so impressed the army commander that Rosecrans took Trecy with him when he moved to the Army of the Cumberland. Serving first without pay, Trecy was on the verge of leaving the army until he was offered the chaplaincy of the Fourth United States Cavalry regiment. Thus he remained at headquarters, ministering to the spiritual needs of the Roman Catholics in the army, most notably its commander. Rosecrans's final principal staff officer, William Truesdail, the chief of army police, was a man of quite different mold. A native of New York, Truesdail, forty-eight, was involved in police work, banking, and railroad construction prior to the Civil War. Not long after the war began, he became associated with Pope's command in Missouri as a beef contractor and organizer of police, scouts, and spies. He also developed the distribution of the army's mail. When Pope departed, Truesdail continued his activities under Rosecrans's supervision. Making himself useful to Rosecrans, especially as a spymaster, he accompanied his chief to the Army of the Cumberland. Truesdail was established in Nashville as chief of army police with the purely honorary rank of colonel. He and his detectives not only kept order in the urban areas in the army's rear but also executed counterintelligence missions and acquired military intelligence through a network of scouts and spies. Using methods often more high-handed than legal, Truesdail soon found himself under attack by many parties, including Governor Andrew Johnson. Rosecrans successfully resisted all efforts to discipline Truesdail's operatives, although he did transfer Truesdail from Nashville to the army's field headquarters in June.[27]

Although there were notable exceptions, many of the army's staff officers shared three characteristics. Most were young men in their twenties, many had a strong connection to the state of Ohio, and a significant number had served with Rosecrans in Mississippi. The army commander presided over his retinue with energetic abandon, albeit with an unusual daily schedule. Rosecrans's preferred manner of operation was to rise late, often as late as 10:00 A.M., eat breakfast near noon, go on inspection rides or receive visitors until 4:00 P.M., eat dinner, then throw himself vigorously into paperwork until past midnight. He would then relax with senior staff members until well beyond 2:00 A.M., finally ending his day around 3:00 in the morning. The staff at the field headquarters generally conformed to this pattern, with little business being conducted early. Like Rosecrans himself, the staff was boisterous and electric with energy. The general's supporters found the frenetic pace bracing and indicative of brilliant minds at work, but some line officers privately were appalled at the rowdy spectacle. For example, Col. Emerson Opdycke, commanding the 125th Ohio Infantry regiment, in a letter to his wife, noted that the atmosphere at army headquarters "reminded one of the bar room of a country tavern! This is no exaggeration." Similarly, brigade commander William Hazen disparaged the character flaws and incompetent behavior of many of Rosecrans's primary advisors. As long as the army was in camp, the unusual work schedule and weaknesses of individual officers did not exert a particularly detrimental effect on business, the private complaints of more straitlaced officers notwithstanding. A long and arduous campaign, however, would severely test an organization so constructed and manned. Stones River had been a very short campaign, as had Tullahoma; any advance beyond the Cumberland Plateau and the Tennessee River would necessarily last far longer.[28]

If the army commander and his staff represented the brain of the Army of the Cumberland, its major tactical formations comprised the army's muscular body. Prior to January 1863, the army's infantry and artillery components collectively had been styled the Fourteenth Army Corps, and subdivided into a Right, Center, and Left. On 9 January, Rosecrans reorganized his infantry into three army corps, the Fourteenth (formerly Center), Twentieth (formerly Right), and Twenty-First (formerly Left). In May 1863 he established a Cavalry Corps. As additional infantry and artillery units arrived in the department, many of them from the defunct Army of Kentucky, they were organized into a Reserve Corps on 8 June. Rosecrans's own headquarters was guarded by a regiment and a battalion of infantry, and a regiment of cavalry. Finally, various miscellaneous units, mostly artillerymen in the Nashville defenses, engineer troops like the Pioneer Brigade, and convalescents rounded out the command. In July 1863, the strength of the Army of the Cumberland stood at 4,886 officers and 76,438 men present for duty, a total of 81,324 soldiers present with their commands. The aggregate present, a figure that included detailed men, guardhouse prisoners, and sick soldiers still with the army, numbered 95,682 officers and men. As an indicator of how many soldiers assigned to the Army of the Cumberland were not with it in the field, the aggregate present and absent number stood at 131,636 officers and men. During the same month, the army's artillery contingent manned 22 heavy artillery pieces and 239 light guns.[29]

The largest infantry corps in the Army of the Cumberland was the Fourteenth, consisting of four divisions. The corps reported 22,873 officers and men present for duty and an aggregate present of 27,036 in July 1863, with seventy-two field guns. Its commander was Maj. Gen. George Henry Thomas. Nearly forty-seven years old, Thomas was a native of Southampton County, Virginia. A graduate of the United States Military Academy in 1840, he served in the artillery branch for fifteen years, winning two brevet promotions during the Mexican War. Transferring to the cavalry in 1855, he saw hard service on the Texas frontier until the outbreak of the Civil War. Although he was offered a position in the Confederate Army, Thomas remained steadfast in adherence to the Union. He was rewarded with a commission as brigadier general of volunteers and served briefly in the Valley of Virginia before being transferred to the Kentucky front. There he won the small battle of Mill Springs before becoming part of Buell's Army of the Ohio. Thomas served with Buell at Shiloh, participated in the advance on Corinth, and was Buell's deputy during the Kentucky campaign in the fall of 1862. Along the way he was promoted to major general of volunteers, with date of rank established as 25 April 1862. Offered command of Buell's army before Perryville, Thomas declined, but when Buell was finally removed he briefly contested Rosecrans's right to replace him because of a date of rank issue. Assured that Rosecrans's commission antedated his, Thomas cheerfully acquiesced until he learned that Rosecrans's seniority had been established purely by administrative fiat. Nevertheless, his strong sense of duty kept him in place and Rosecrans rewarded him with command of what became the Fourteenth Corps. At Stones River he had fully justified both Rosecrans's confidence in him and his own strong reputation as a combat leader.[30]

No more than six feet tall, Thomas had a large frame that contributed to the initial impression of an impassive, dull individual hardly fit for his rank. Anyone who remained in his presence for more than a few moments, however, quickly learned otherwise. Thomas was well schooled in his profession, had an extreme sense of honor, and exuded strength of purpose that prevented even his friends from wasting time with small talk. No one who knew him pronounced him brilliant, but all acknowledged his thorough competence in managing thousands of men on campaign and in combat. He had a well-deserved reputation as an officer who could be counted on to keep his head in the most difficult circumstances. The very opposite of Rosecrans, whose excitability in crisis sometimes affected his judgment, Thomas remained firmly in command of his emotions in good times and bad. The troops under his command sensed this steadiness and repaid his leadership with great devotion. To them he was "Old Pap," although he never spoke familiarly to them or curried their favor in any way. To all but his most inner circle, Thomas maintained a reserve of great severity, and even his few confidants knew their place and did not trespass beyond the boundaries Thomas set. Hardly dour, however, he was noted for his lavish and hospitable headquarters establishment. His baggage train was legendary throughout the army, as was the table he set for staff and visitors alike. His general reputation in the Army of the Cumberland was uniformly high with both regular and volunteer officers. Although he was on occasion excessively deliberate in his actions, Thomas was an officer of substance and a leader of men, and all who came in contact with him knew it instantly.[31]

Thomas's First Division numbered 5,066 officers and men present for duty, with an aggregate present of 6,010, in July 1863. The division commander was Maj. Gen. Lovell Harrison Rousseau, forty-four. A native of Kentucky, Rousseau rose from common laborer to attorney and state legislator by 1860, with meritorious service as a Mexican War volunteer. After he raised a regiment, his political connections gained him a brigadier generalship in 1861 and promotion to major general in the fall of 1862. He led a brigade at Shiloh and a division at Perryville and Stones River, always with more impetuosity than skill. Flamboyant in speech and attire but devoid of technical military training, Rousseau was idolized by his men because of his extreme personal courage and his brash demeanor. A more discerning observer, however, disparaged him as "an ass of eminent gifts," and even a friend noted the disparity between Rousseau's words and his deeds. His three brigade commanders were a mixed lot. Col. Benjamin Scribner, thirty-seven, an Indiana native, commanded the First Brigade. A druggist and a veteran of the battle of Buena Vista in the Mexican War, Scribner raised the Thirty-Eighth Indiana Infantry regiment in 1861 and was a brigade commander since November 1862. An earnest, diligent, but colorless leader, he offered basic competence but nothing more. The Second Brigade was commanded by Col. John Starkweather, thirty-three, a native of New York and a Wisconsin attorney. Starkweather was the original colonel of the First Wisconsin Infantry regiment and a brigade commander since September 1862. As such, he fought in the battles of Perryville and Stones River. Known for his strong political connections and stentorian voice, Starkweather awaited his pending promotion to brigadier general. In contrast to his other brigades, Rousseau's Third Brigade was led by a Regular Army officer, Brig. Gen. John King, forty-three. His long career dated from 1838, with service in the Seminole and Mexican Wars and duty on the Texas frontier. King participated in the actions at Shiloh, Corinth, and Stones River, where he received a serious wound in the hand. Promoted to brigadier general in April 1863, he commanded the Regular Brigade of five battalions.[32]

Maj. Gen. James Scott Negley, thirty-six, commanded Thomas's Second Division, which listed 4,699 officers and men present for duty and 5,635 aggregate present in July 1863. Born near Pittsburgh, he served as an enlisted volunteer during the Mexican War, and maintained a strong affiliation with the state militia while pursuing a career in horticulture. Instrumental in raising several Pennsylvania regiments in 1861, he was rewarded with a brigadier general's commission in October. Transferred west, he served on occupation duty in central Tennessee and led Buell's advance on Chattanooga in June 1862. When Buell withdrew to Kentucky, he left Negley to garrison Nashville. At Stones River, Negley satisfactorily led a small division and was promoted to major general in March 1863. Large and rather portly, he was generally affable with all who met him and often regaled his staff with obscure facts on roadside flora. A sensitive man, he did not follow Regular Army rules and conventions. His prior enlisted service made him a strong advocate of the common soldier, and his men responded with equal affection. This openness and democratic style, however, set Negley apart from most of his fellow division commanders, especially those educated at West Point. His First Brigade was led by Brig. Gen. John Beatty, thirty-four, an Ohio banker. An erudite and intelligent personality, Beatty began his military career in western Virginia but quickly moved west, where his success at Perryville brought him a brigadier general's star in November 1862. He gained further accolades at Stones River as a brigade commander. Col. Timothy Stanley commanded Negley's Second Brigade. Descended from an old New England family, Stanley, fifty-three, was an Ohio attorney, industrialist, and politician. The original colonel of the Eighteenth Ohio Infantry regiment, Stanley was promoted to brigade command prior to Stones River. Commander of the Third Brigade was Col. William Sirwell, forty-three. A Pennsylvania businessman and militia officer, Sirwell raised the Seventy-Eighth Pennsylvania Infantry regiment and commanded it through Stones River. He assumed brigade command on 19 June.[33]

The Third Division of the Fourteenth Corps was led by Brig. Gen. John Milton Brannan. Born in Washington, D.C., Brannan, forty-four, was a member of the West Point class of 1841. Commissioned as an artilleryman, he held routine coastal postings until the Mexican War, where he distinguished himself in the battles of Contreras, Churubusco, and Mexico City, gaining one brevet for gallantry and suffering a serious wound. He spent most of the 1850s in Florida, where the outbreak of the Civil War found him. Promoted to brigadier general of volunteers in September 1861, Brannan served in the Department of the South until early 1863. In April he transferred to the Department of the Cumberland as commander of an infantry division. By this time, his private life was a shambles and a subject for soldier gossip. In 1858, Brannan's wife of eight years, Eliza Crane, disappeared, and initially foul play was suspected. She was discovered in Italy, living with Powell Wyman, another artillery officer. By the spring of 1863, Wyman was dead, and the sordid facts revealed in Brannan's divorce proceedings were becoming common knowledge to the troops in the Department of the South. Thus Brannan no doubt was relieved to transfer to the Tennessee front. After a few weeks in the Twenty-First Corps, he received the Third Division of the Fourteenth Corps, a total of 6,343 officers and men present for duty, with an aggregate present of 7,231. The Tullahoma campaign was his first experience as an infantry division commander. Brannan's First Brigade was commanded by Col. Moses Walker, forty-four. An Ohio attorney, Walker raised the Thirty-First Ohio Infantry regiment at the outbreak of the war and led it until gaining brigade command in 1862. His brigade was present at Perryville and Stones River but not heavily engaged. Brig. Gen. James Steedman, forty-six, commanded the Second Brigade. A large, powerful man, Steedman had little formal education but a wealth of practical experience as a printer, forty-niner, editor, and Democratic politician in Ohio before organizing the Fourteenth Ohio Infantry regiment in 1861. His combat résumé began in western Virginia and extended through the battle of Perryville. He had been a brigadier general with a reputation for boldness since July 1862. Brannan's Third Brigade was led by Col. Ferdinand Van Derveer, forty, also from Ohio. An attorney who had distinguished himself as a volunteer in the Mexican War, Van Derveer led the Thirty-Fifth Ohio Infantry regiment at Corinth and Perryville, but missed Stones River. He was promoted to brigade command early in 1863.[34]

Maj. Gen. Joseph Jones Reynolds, forty-one, of Flemingsburg, Kentucky, headed Thomas's Fourth Division. Moving to Indiana as a youth, he graduated from West Point in 1843 as an artilleryman. He served uneventfully in garrison until joining the West Point faculty, where he spent almost nine years. Sent to frontier duty in 1855, he resigned two years later and took an academic position at Washington University. The outbreak of war found him engaged in the grocery business in Indiana with his brother. Appointed brigadier general in the summer of 1861, he served under Rosecrans in western Virginia but resigned early in 1862 because of his brother's death. He assisted in recruiting Indiana units until again commissioned brigadier general in September 1862 and major general two months later. Given a small infantry division, he futilely chased Confederate cavalry in the army's rear until the Tullahoma campaign. His overly cautious decisions at Hoover's Gap, his only fight of consequence, bespoke Reynolds's irresolute view of his own abilities. He was Thomas's least experienced division commander. In July his division numbered 6,465 officers and men present for duty, with an aggregate present of 7,745 soldiers. Reynolds's First Brigade commander, Col. John Wilder, thirty-three, was everything that Reynolds was not. An aggressive and self-assured man, Wilder had early left his New York home and by 1861 was a successful industrialist in Greensburg, Indiana. Joining the Seventeenth Indiana Infantry regiment, he served with it under Reynolds and Rosecrans in western Virginia. Promoted to colonel, he participated in the operations around Corinth, made a gallant but unsuccessful defense of Munfordville, Kentucky, and was given a brigade. By the summer of 1863, he had turned his command into mounted infantry armed with the Spencer rifle, giving his brigade unique capabilities. Less flamboyant was the Second Brigade commander, Col. Milton Robinson, thirty-one. A prewar attorney and colonel of the Seventy-Fifth Indiana Infantry regiment, Robinson gained brigade command in June. Finally, Brig. Gen. George Crook commanded the Third Brigade. Crook, thirty-four, was an 1852 West point graduate with extensive service on the Pacific coast. Appointed colonel of the Thirty-Sixth Ohio Infantry regiment in 1861, he led it in western Virginia. Promoted to brigadier general, he held brigade command at South Mountain and Antietam before transferring west in February 1863. In Reynolds's division since June, Crook was Reynolds's most experienced brigade commander.[35]

Unlike the Fourteenth Corps, Rosecrans's Twentieth Corps consisted of only three infantry divisions. Commanded by Maj. Gen. Alexander McDowell McCook, the corps in July numbered 13,913 officers and men present for duty, with an aggregate present of 16,056 men and 54 artillery pieces. Only thirty-two in the summer of 1863, McCook was an Ohio native and a 1852 West Point graduate. Commissioned into the infantry, McCook spent five years in the American Southwest, participating in various expeditions and skirmishes in New Mexico, Arizona, and Colorado Territories. Posted to West Point in 1858 as an assistant professor of tactics, he was there in April 1861 when the Civil War erupted. He quickly received command of the First Ohio Infantry regiment and led it at First Manassas. Commissioned brigadier general to rank from September 1861, McCook transferred to the western theater, where he led first a brigade then the Second Division of the Army of the Ohio. As a division commander he participated in the capture of Nashville, the second day of the battle of Shiloh, the siege of Corinth, and the advance on Chattanooga. Promoted to major general in July 1862, he received command of a corps in the early stages of the Kentucky campaign and played a major role at Perryville. Upon Buell's relief, Rosecrans retained McCook in corps command as leader of the army's

Right Wing. As such, he participated in the battle of Stones River at the end of 1862. In the reorganization of the army that followed Stones River, McCook's command was designated the Twentieth Corps. When the army resumed its advance in the Tullahoma campaign, the Twentieth Corps served as a fixing force while other elements of the army maneuvered to outflank the Confederates. After a hard-fought but minor action at Liberty Gap, McCook and his men simply followed the other corps as they ushered Bragg's army beyond the Elk River. There they remained in July, staring at the heights of the Cumberland Plateau and garrisoning the towns of Tullahoma, Winchester, Decherd, and Cowan along the Nashville & Chattanooga Railroad.[36]

A heavy-set man approaching 250 pounds (and thereby called "Old Big bellyed McCook" by his men), McCook betrayed his relative youth in his soft facial features. Friendly and boisterous, he participated fully in the drinking and cursing that seemed to pervade the army's officer corps. Nevertheless, many officers harbored grave doubts about McCook's capacity for command at the corps level. His years as a tactics instructor at West Point and his small role in the war's first major battle gained him early promotion and a reputation as a tactician. The list of campaigns and battles in which he participated was also impressive. A closer look at his performance as a corps commander at Perryville and Stones River, however, was troubling. At Perryville, McCook gave ground, lost heavily, barely held his own against a determined attack, and was censured by Buell for not informing him of the deteriorating situation. At Stones River, McCook's corps was surprised, routed, and barely survived, a strikingly similar performance to its actions in Kentucky. Physically courageous and a hero to his staff, Alex McCook was dismissed by many perceptive officers in the Army of the Cumberland. Brigade commanders William Hazen and John Beatty spoke disparagingly of McCook, Hazen deriding his "boastful over-confidence" and Beatty calling him a "chucklehead" and a "blockhead." The caustic reporter William Shanks called McCook "an overgrown school-boy, without dignity." In fact, the genial and well-meaning commander of the Twentieth Corps was grossly immature, unsuited for the high position he occupied. Nevertheless, his membership in the clan of "Fighting McCooks," with its strong Ohio political connections, had raised him to corps command. James Garfield early recognized McCook's incapacity and argued for his replacement, but Rosecrans demurred, even as he agreed with the judgment. Thus Alexander McCook remained commander of the Twentieth Corps in July 1863.[37]

McCook's First Division contained 4,307 officers and men present for duty, with an aggregate present of 4,973. Its commander was probably the most notorious officer in the Army of the Cumberland, Brig. Gen. Jefferson Columbus Davis, thirty-five, of Indiana. A youthful volunteer in the Mexican War, Davis received a direct commission in the Regular Army as an artillery officer at age twenty. A lieutenant at Fort Sumter in 1861, he participated in the action that began the war. A connection to Indiana governor Oliver Morton, gained while serving as a mustering officer, led first to a colonel's appointment and in December 1861 a brigadier general's commission. Davis commanded a division at Pea Ridge in March 1862 and again in the operations around Corinth. While on sick leave, he learned of the Confederate invasion of Kentucky and rushed to offer his services at Louisville. Assigned to organize new units, he quickly came into conflict with the imperious giant Maj. Gen. William "Bull" Nelson, who temporarily banished him beyond the Ohio River. Equally aggressive but small in stature, Davis returned to Louisville and confronted Nelson, then in front of numerous witnesses assassinated the much larger but unarmed officer. Never brought to account for this shocking act, Davis soon returned to duty as a division commander. He fought in that capacity at Stones River and participated in the Tullahoma campaign but remained a marked man. Davis's First Brigade commander was Col. Sidney Post, a New York native. An attorney in Illinois and Kansas Territory before the war, Post in 1861 joined the Fifty-Ninth Illinois Infantry regiment, rising ultimately to command it. Seriously wounded at Pea Ridge, he attained brigade command in September 1862 but illness kept him from seeing action until Stones River. Leading the Second Brigade was Brig. Gen. William Carlin, thirty-three, Davis's most experienced subordinate. An Illinois native and 1850 West Point graduate, Carlin participated in numerous frontier campaigns and rose to captain by 1861. Commissioned colonel of the Thirty-Eighth Illinois Infantry regiment, he quickly gained command of a brigade, leading it at Corinth, Perryville, and Stones River. Col. Hans Heg, thirty-three, commanded Davis's Third Brigade. Born in Norway in 1829, he came to America in 1840 and settled in Wisconsin. A forty-niner, farmer, merchant, and minor Republican officeholder, Heg played a major role in rallying Norwegian Americans to the Union cause in 1861. Appointed colonel of the Fifteenth Wisconsin Infantry regiment, he saw heavy action at Perryville and Stones River and was rewarded with brigade command in May 1863.[38]

McCook's Second Division numbered 5,183 officers and men present for duty in July, with an aggregate present of 6,007. Its commander, Brig. Gen. Richard W. Johnson, thirty-six, had an uneven record. Born in Kentucky to parents of Virginia heritage, he graduated from the United States Military Academy in 1849. He spent the bulk of his prewar career on frontier duty in Texas, first in the infantry, later as a cavalryman. A captain at the outbreak of the war, he began his service in western Virginia but soon transferred to Kentucky, where he gained promotion to brigadier general in late 1861 and command of a brigade in McCook's division. Missing Shiloh because of illness, he participated in the siege of Corinth and Buell's advance on Chattanooga. Sent by Buell with a mixed force to intercept Confederate raider Col. John Morgan in August

1862, Johnson was routed and forced to surrender with part of his command near Gallatin, Tennessee. Exchanged in December, he received command of a division. At Stones River, his division was the first Federal unit to be crushed. The subject of a whispering campaign insinuating treason, he nevertheless retained McCook's and Rosecrans's favor and remained in command. Johnson's First Brigade was led by Brig. Gen. August Willich, fifty-two. Born in Prussia, he was a professional soldier until the revolutionary turmoil of 1846–48. A committed communist, he fled Europe, reaching the United States in 1853. The crisis of 1861 found him editing a German-language newspaper in Cincinnati. As colonel of the all-German Thirty-Second Indiana Infantry regiment, he performed heroically at Shiloh. Promoted to brigadier general in July 1862 and given a brigade, he missed Perryville but was unhorsed and captured at Stones River. Exchanged after four months, "Papa" Willich retained his reputation as a hard-fighting disciplinarian. Less distinguished was Col. Joseph Dodge, thirty-three, commander of the Second Brigade. A teacher, Dodge began his military career as the lieutenant colonel of the Thirtieth Indiana Infantry regiment. Upon the death of the regimental commander at Shiloh, Dodge was promoted to colonel. He missed Perryville and was part of the division's rout at Stones River. The mortal wounding of his brigade commander in that battle raised Dodge to his place. Fellow brigade commander John Beatty called Dodge "a very industrious talker, chewer, spitter, and drinker," implying that he was something of a braggart. Not so Col. Philemon Baldwin, twenty-six, the Third Brigade commander. Beginning the war as a captain in the Sixth Indiana Infantry regiment, Baldwin became colonel of the regiment after participating in the battle of Shiloh. Missing Perryville, he became brigade commander just days before Stones River. A strong performance in that fight brought the young and impetuous Baldwin a recommendation for promotion by Johnson.[39]

Maj. Gen. Philip H. Sheridan, thirty-two, commanded the Third Division of the Twentieth Corps, which numbered 4,414 officers and men present for duty in July 1863 and had an aggregate present of 5,067. The son of Irish immigrants to New York, Sheridan gained appointment to West Point from Ohio and graduated, after a year off for fighting, in 1853. Standing only five inches over five feet and weighing no more than 130 pounds, he had the pugnacity often seen in men of small stature. Other than a slight wound, his prewar career on the frontier was unremarkable. Sheridan began his war service as a quartermaster, first in Missouri and later during the advance on Corinth. Chosen colonel of the Second Michigan Cavalry in May 1862, he won several small actions in Mississippi. By September he was a brigadier general commanding an infantry brigade sent to counter the Confederate invasion of Kentucky. Unexpectedly promoted to lead a division prior to the battle of Perryville, he performed adequately at best in that confused fight. At Stones River, Sheridan's division lost 40 percent of its soldiers but was prominent in the Union victory. Profane and self-assured, by July Sheridan had gained a reputation as a fighter and was a favorite of Rosecrans. His First Brigade commander, Brig. Gen. William Lytle, thirty-six, was one of the best-known figures in the army. A Cincinnati lawyer, politician, and minor poet, Lytle parlayed brief Mexican War service and political connections into the colonelcy of the Tenth Ohio Infantry regiment. Wounded at Carnifex Ferry in western Virginia in 1861, he gained brigade command in early 1862, only to be more seriously wounded and captured at Perryville in October. After exchange and a lengthy convalescence, he was promoted to brigadier general in March 1863. Sheridan's Second Brigade belonged to Col. Bernhard Laibold, thirty-six, a native of the German state of Baden. A resident of St. Louis since childhood, Laibold was prominent in the militia and entered the war as lieutenant colonel of the Second Missouri Infantry regiment. The absence of his colonel gave Laibold regimental command at Pea Ridge and brigade command at Perryville, both of which earned him commendation. He again took brigade command at Stones River when his colonel was killed and retained the brigade as colonel in January 1863. Sheridan's Third Brigade commander was Col. Luther Bradley, forty, a Connecticut native and resident of Illinois. Another prewar militiaman, Bradley began his service as lieutenant colonel of the Fifty-First Illinois Infantry regiment in 1861 and was present at Island No. 10, Corinth, and the defense of Nashville. Promoted to colonel and regimental command in October 1862, he first saw major action at Stones River, where his brigade commander was killed, elevating Bradley to the position. Handling the brigade creditably, Bradley remained in command into 1863.[40]

Like the Twentieth Corps, the Twenty-First Corps contained only three divisions. Led by Maj. Gen. Thomas Leonidas Crittenden, the corps in July 1863 numbered 14,394 officers and men present for duty, with an aggregate present of 17,034 men and fifty-eight cannon. Crittenden, forty-four, was a native of Kentucky and the son of powerful Senator John Crittenden, a prewar voice for compromise between the sections. Educated as an attorney, Thomas Crittenden gravitated into politics until the Mexican War, when he enlisted as an aide to Zachary Taylor. Finishing the war as lieutenant colonel of a Kentucky volunteer regiment, Crittenden parlayed his war service and political connections into a position as U.S. consul in Liverpool, a position he held until 1852. Thereafter he practiced law and engaged in business in Louisville until the crisis of 1861. Although his older brother George joined the Confederacy as a general officer, Thomas held steadfast to the Union, as did his father. Active in the Kentucky State Guard, he became the commander of the loyal faction when Simon Buckner took the remainder into the Confederate Army. In September 1861 Crittenden received an appointment as brigadier general of volunteers, although his formal military education was nonexistent. Later that year the troops under his command were organized into a small division, which he commanded at Shiloh and throughout the operations around Corinth. Promoted to major general in July, he gained corps command in Buell's Army of the Ohio in September. Crittenden led the Second Corps at Perryville in October 1862 and retained corps command when Rosecrans replaced Buell. He commanded the Left Wing of the Army of the Cumberland at Stones River in December 1862. In Rosecrans's January 1863 reorganization of the army, Crittenden's Left Wing became the Twenty-First Corps. As such, it participated in the Tullahoma campaign in June.[41]

A full beard, lank hair falling to his collar, and a penetrating gaze gave Crittenden the physical appearance of a decisive leader, but his actual persona belied such an assessment. In truth, Crittenden was a mild-mannered and inoffensive personality who shrank from controversy and confrontation. Throughout his life he had stood in the long shadow of his father, desperately seeking the older man's approval for his every action. The failure of George Crittenden to rise above his affinity for alcohol placed an even greater burden on his younger brother. Fear of personal failure thus caused Thomas Crittenden to avoid risk wherever possible and remain passive in situations where a more confident individual might have seized an opportunity. His desire to please his father was also reflected in his relationships with other authority figures, especially his military superiors. Despite his obvious personal bravery and exalted rank, Crittenden was a born follower, not a leader. The prominence of his father in national affairs, and the key role of Kentucky early in the war, had much to do with his initial rise in the ranks of general officers. He had neither formal military education nor command experience at regimental or brigade level when he found himself commanding a division in late 1861. After only one day in serious combat at Shiloh, he rose to corps command at Perryville but did not participate seriously in the battle. At Stones River, Rosecrans piecemealed the Left Wing's troops into action, leaving Crittenden few opportunities to lead his command as a unit. A lax administrator between campaigns and a weak disciplinarian, he was nevertheless a favorite with the men in the ranks who saw only his kindliness toward them, not his indecisiveness. James Garfield was not fooled and lumped Crittenden with McCook, but Rosecrans liked Crittenden's accommodating personality and inoffensive demeanor and retained him in command of the Twenty-First Corps.[42]

Crittenden's First Division numbered 4,558 officers and men present for duty, with an aggregate present of 5,245 soldiers. The division's commander, Brig. Gen. Thomas John Wood, thirty-nine, was the antithesis of Crittenden. A Kentuckian like his chief, Wood graduated from West Point in 1845. Initially a member of the Corps of Topographical Engineers, he served with distinction in the Mexican War, winning a brevet for gallantry at Buena Vista. Transferring to the cavalry, he spent the next ten years on the frontier with various cavalry regiments. Upon returning from a two-year leave of absence in Europe, he found the nation in crisis and was sent to Indiana to organize that state's volunteers. Promoted to brigadier general in October 1861, he, like Crittenden, received command of a division in the Army of the Ohio late that year. He arrived at Shiloh too late to affect the outcome, and his division had little to do at Perryville, but at Stones River his command was heavily engaged and he was painfully wounded in the left foot. Small in stature yet feisty in demeanor, Wood was known throughout the army for his experience, erudition, and an especially salty vocabulary. He was considered by at least one observer to be Crittenden's mentor, furnishing all of the corps commander's "military brains." Wood's First Brigade was led by Col. George Buell, twenty-nine, a native of Lawrenceburg, Indiana, and first cousin of Don Carlos Buell. A graduate of Norwich University, Buell worked briefly as a civil engineer before joining the Fifty-Eighth Indiana Infantry regiment in December 1861. Promoted to colonel in June 1862, he led the regiment at Perryville and Stones River. He attained brigade command in January 1863 when his superior transferred to another department. Brig. Gen. George Wagner, thirty-three, commanded Wood's Second Brigade. A native of Ohio but long associated with Indiana, Wagner was a prewar Republican Party stalwart. Appointed colonel of the Fifteenth Indiana Infantry regiment in June 1861, he gained brigade command in February 1862. Present but only lightly involved at Shiloh and Perryville, the brigade participated vigorously in the first day's fight at Stones River. Wagner gained promotion to brigadier general in April 1863. Commander of the division's Third Brigade was Col. Charles Harker, twenty-seven. An orphan from New Jersey, Harker by dint of hard work gained an appointment to West Point, graduating in 1858. After brief frontier service, he organized Ohio troops, receiving command of the Sixty-Fifth Ohio Infantry regiment in November 1861. Arriving too late to fight at Shiloh, Harker ascended to brigade command in July 1862 when his superior, James Garfield, took sick leave. The brigade saw no action at Perryville but was seriously engaged at Stones River. Afterward, Wood recommended him for a brigadier's commission despite his youth and naked ambition.[43]

The Second Division, commanded by Maj. Gen. John McAuley Palmer, forty-five, in July contained 5,165 officers and men, with an aggregate present of 6,233 soldiers. Palmer, a native of Kentucky but resident of Illinois, was an attorney and politician. Initially a Democrat with strong antislavery views, he played a major role in the formation of the Republican Party, unsuccessfully running for Congress on that ticket in 1859. A delegate to the Republican Convention in 1860, he supported the nomination of Abraham Lincoln for president. Such connections brought him the colonelcy of the Fourteenth Illinois Infantry regiment in May 1861 and a brigadier's star in December of the same year. He commanded a brigade and a division in the Army of the Mississippi, performing well at Island No. 10 and the siege of Corinth. His division remained in Nashville during the Kentucky campaign, thus missing Perryville. At Stones River his command played a key role in stabilizing the army's left. As a reward, he was promoted to major general in March 1863. Like George Thomas, Palmer was a steady performer of solid reputation, but his lack of West Point credentials was a source of friction between him and those more classically educated. Leading Palmer's First Brigade was Brig. Gen. Charles Cruft, thirty-seven, from Terre Haute, Indiana. A lawyer and railroad president, Cruft entered the war as colonel of the Thirty-First Indiana Infantry regiment in September 1861. Gaining brigade command soon thereafter, he saw action at Fort Donelson (one wound), Shiloh (three wounds), and the siege of Corinth. Promoted to brigadier general in July 1862, he performed heroically during the rout at Richmond, Kentucky (one wound), but was not engaged at Perryville. At Stones River, Cruft again was in the midst of the heaviest fighting, making him one of the army's most experienced brigade commanders. Equally proficient was the Second Brigade commander, Brig. Gen. William Hazen, thirty-two. A Vermont native raised in Ohio, Hazen graduated from West Point in 1855. After frontier duty in Oregon and Texas (one wound), Hazen was a tactics instructor at West Point when the war broke out. Appointed colonel of the Forty-First Ohio Infantry regiment in September 1861, he soon attained brigade command. Heavily involved on the second day at Shiloh but not engaged at Perryville, Hazen's command was the keystone of the army's defense at Stones River. His performance gained him promotion to brigadier general. Col. William Grose, fifty, led Palmer's Third Brigade. Born in Ohio but a Hoosier since infancy, Grose was an attorney, minor politician, and judge. Joining the Republican Party in 1856, he received the colonelcy of the Thirty-Sixth Indiana Infantry regiment from his patron, Governor Oliver Morton, in October 1861. Grose led the regiment at Shiloh in April 1862 (one wound) and advanced to brigade command when his superior was promoted in August. Not engaged at Perryville, he participated fully at Stones River. An average commander, his record paled in comparison to that of Cruft and Hazen.[44]

The Third Division of the Twenty-First Corps in July numbered 4,506 officers and men present for duty, with an aggregate present of 5,067 soldiers. Its leader was Brig. Gen. Horatio Phillips Van Cleve, fifty-three, a native of New Jersey and West Point graduate in the class of 1831. After uneventful garrison duty in Wisconsin, Van Cleve resigned his second lieutenant's commission in 1836. Thereafter he pursued a variety of occupations—farmer, teacher, civil engineer, surveyor, stockman—in the upper Midwest. The outbreak of war found him in Minnesota, where he became the colonel of the Second Minnesota Infantry regiment in July 1861. He commanded the regiment in the small battle of Mill Springs, Kentucky, in January 1862. Promoted to brigadier general in March, he missed Shiloh but commanded one of Crittenden's brigades in the advance on Corinth. He remained a brigade commander until just before the battle of Perryville, when he succeeded Crittenden in division command. Van Cleve saw no action at Perryville but was heavily engaged at Stones River until wounded in the right leg on the first day of the battle. The oldest division commander in the Army of the Cumberland, his bald head, glasses, and gray beard caused his troops to call him "grand pap." His First Brigade commander was Brig. Gen. Samuel Beatty, forty-two, a Pennsylvanian long associated with Ohio. A farmer with little formal education, Beatty gained military experience as a volunteer officer in the Mexican War. Postwar he served two terms as sheriff of Stark County, Ohio. Forming a company of the Nineteenth Ohio Infantry regiment, he soon was elected colonel. Successful regimental command at Rich Mountain and Shiloh gained him a brigade in May 1862. Unengaged at Perryville, he received a brigadier's star in November. After heavy fighting on the first day at Stones River, he briefly succeeded to division command during Van Cleve's convalescence. Col. George Dick, thirty-four, commanded Van Cleve's Second Brigade. A tobacconist from Ohio, Dick raised a company in the Twentieth Indiana Infantry regiment in July 1861. He shared the fortunes of that regiment on the Atlantic seaboard and in the Army of the Potomac until October 1862, seeing much action and rising to major. In November he was commissioned lieutenant colonel of the Eighty-Sixth Indiana Infantry regiment and rose to command it at Stones River when its colonel was relieved. In January 1863 he gained promotion to colonel and in March attained brigade command. Col. Sidney Barnes, forty-two, led Van Cleve's Third Brigade. A Kentucky attorney, Barnes raised the Eighth Kentucky Infantry regiment and was elected colonel in August 1861. The regiment spent the next year peacefully guarding railroads. Barnes and his unit were present but unengaged at Perryville, after which he took an extended leave of absence to tend to personal affairs in Kentucky, thereby missing Stones River. Without significant combat experience, he nevertheless gained brigade command in April 1863.[45]

Anticipating the need to garrison Middle Tennessee before resuming his advance in the summer of 1863, Rosecrans on 8 June created a Reserve Corps of three divisions. In July it consisted of 17,085 officers and men present for duty, with an aggregate present of 20,359 men and forty guns. It was commanded by Maj. Gen. Gordon Granger, forty, a native of New York and an 1845 West Point graduate. Granger began his career in the Infantry but transferred to the Mounted Rifles just prior to the war with Mexico. During Winfield Scott's advance on Mexico City, he won brevets for gallantry at Contreras/Churubusco and Chapultepec. Postwar, he spent the bulk of his time on frontier duty in Texas and New Mexico. Promoted to captain in May 1861, he was a staff officer at Wilson's Creek, where he received another brevet. Appointed colonel of the Second Michigan Cavalry regiment in September 1861, he joined Pope's force attacking New Madrid, Missouri, and Island No. 10. Promoted to brigadier general in March 1862, he commanded Pope's cavalry in the Army of the Mississippi during its advance on Corinth. When Rosecrans replaced Pope, Granger added an infantry division to his command in August. The following month he and his troops were sent to Kentucky in response to the Confederate invasion of that state. There he was promoted to major general and assumed command of three divisions of mostly new regiments styled the Army of Kentucky. Subsequent reorganizations reduced Granger's command to little more than a division by January 1863. With the threat to Kentucky receding, Granger's command moved to Nashville in February to augment the Department of the Cumberland. From that nucleus Rosecrans created the Reserve Corps. Dour, plain-spoken, and rude to a fault, inflexible of thought, and something of a martinet, Granger was utterly fearless and considered by many of his men to be a strong leader. Others chafed under his draconian disciplinary measures. He also was untried in battle, having seen no combat since Wilson's Creek in the summer of 1861.[46]

Granger's First Division in July 1863 numbered 5,355 officers and men present for duty, with an aggregate present of 6,611 soldiers. It was commanded by Brig. Gen. Absalom Baird, thirty-eight, a Pennsylvanian and a West Point graduate in the class of 1849. An artilleryman by branch, Baird served in Florida, Texas, and at West Point as an instructor prior to 1861. Transferring from line to staff when the war began, he was present at First Bull Run and was an inspector general in the Fourth Corps during the Peninsula campaign. Promoted to brigadier general in April 1862, he commanded a brigade in the Army of the Ohio until October, a district in the Department of the Ohio until November, and a division in Granger's Army of Kentucky until it became part of the Reserve Corps in June 1863. Short in stature but sporting a magnificent mustache and beard, Baird had seen no significant combat action after two years at war. None of his brigade commanders were professional soldiers. Baird's First Brigade commander, Col. Smith Atkins, twenty-seven, of the Ninety-Second Illinois Infantry regiment, was a newspaperman and attorney. He had seen action at Fort Donelson with the Eleventh Illinois Infantry regiment and had been a staff officer at Shiloh. The Second Brigade commander, Col. William Reid, thirty-eight, an attorney, had raised the 121st Ohio Infantry regiment in September 1862, and had witnessed his ill-trained unit's disgrace at Perryville. The regiment's training and discipline had improved little by the time Reid ascended to brigade command in early 1863. The Third Brigade commander, Col. John Coburn, thirty-seven, of the Thirty-Third Indiana Infantry regiment, was an attorney and politician. A brigade commander since October 1862, he and most of his command had been captured in March 1863 at Thompson's Station and only recently exchanged.[47]

Brig. Gen. James Dada Morgan, fifty-two, commanded Granger's Second Division, which in July consisted of 6,638 officers and men present for duty, with an aggregate present of 7,632 soldiers. Originally from Boston, Morgan originally was a merchant seaman but left that profession after a harrowing two weeks in an open boat following a mutiny. He moved to Quincy, Illinois, and began a successful career there as a merchant. Active in militia affairs, he served in an Illinois volunteer regiment during the Mexican War, participating in the battle of Buena Vista. Commissioned colonel of the Tenth Illinois Infantry regiment in the summer of 1861, Morgan in early 1862 gained brigade command in Pope's expedition against New Madrid and Island No. 10, and the operations around Corinth. Promoted to brigadier general in July 1862, he and his brigade transferred to the Army of the Ohio, where they garrisoned Nashville during the Kentucky campaign. Similarly, his brigade guarded the rear of the Army of the Cumberland during the battle of Stones River. For several months during the first half of 1863, Morgan commanded a division in the Fourteenth Corps but by May was only in charge of the post of Nashville. He again attained division command with the formation of the Reserve Corps, but his experience as a combat commander was extremely limited. His First Brigade was commanded by Col. Robert Smith, fifty-six, a farmer who had raised the Sixteenth Illinois Infantry regiment in 1861. Smith's war experience mirrored Morgan's. The Second Brigade was led by Col. Daniel McCook Jr., twenty-nine, younger brother of the Twentieth Corps commander. A law partner of William Sherman, he saw action at Wilson's Creek, served on Alex McCook's staff at Shiloh, then became colonel of the Fifty-Second Ohio Infantry regiment in July 1862. Attaining brigade command two months later, he saw limited action at Perryville and Stones River. Gaunt and in poor health, he nevertheless retained brigade command in July 1863. Col. Charles Doolittle, thirty-one, commanded Morgan's Third Brigade. Born in Vermont, by 1861 he was working in the glass business in Michigan. Joining the Fourth Michigan Infantry regiment as a company officer, he served with the unit during heavy fighting on the Virginia Peninsula (one wound). Appointed colonel of the Eighteenth Michigan Infantry regiment in August 1862, he gained brigade command in November.[48]

The Third Division of the Reserve Corps was led by Brig. Gen. Robert Seaman Granger, forty-seven, a native of Ohio unrelated to Gordon Granger. In July 1863 the command contained 4,694 officers and men present for duty, with an aggregate present of 6,018 soldiers. A West Point graduate in 1838, Granger participated in brief operations against the Seminole Indians, taught at West Point, and served in the occupation of Mexico. He spent the 1850s at several posts in Texas, which did not improve his often precarious health. Captured with most of the regulars in Texas at the outbreak of the Civil War, he was paroled under terms prohibiting service in the field until exchange. He therefore marked time in Ohio and Kentucky until formally exchanged in August 1862. Commissioned brigadier general of volunteers in October, he commanded a brigade in the Army of the Ohio that garrisoned Bowling Green, Kentucky, thereby missing both Perryville and Stones River. Transferring to Nashville in early 1863, Granger filled various interim brigade and divisional commands in the Fourteenth Corps until assigned to command the post of Nashville and a division in the Reserve Corps in June. His combat experience at brigade and division levels was essentially nil. Granger's First Brigade was commanded by Col. Sanders Bruce, thirty-seven, of Kentucky. Brother-in-law and erstwhile business partner of Confederate cavalry commander John Morgan, Bruce formed the Twentieth Kentucky Infantry regiment in late 1861 and gained brigade command shortly thereafter. He led the brigade in the second day's fighting at Shiloh, where he was injured by the fall of his horse. He continued in brigade command during operations around Corinth and until the unit's return to Kentucky in August 1862. Thereafter he commanded several posts in rear areas, most notably at Clarksville, Tennessee. Brig. Gen. William Ward, fifty-four, led Granger's Second Brigade. A native of Virginia long associated with Kentucky, Ward was an attorney and politician. Brief service in the Mexican War and political prominence brought him a brigadier general's commission in September 1861. He became a brigade commander in November and thereafter garrisoned a series of posts in Kentucky and Tennessee, never seeing major combat action.[49]

In addition to the four infantry corps, the Army of the Cumberland also contained a Cavalry Corps, commanded by Maj. Gen. David Sloane Stanley, thirty-five. In July 1863 the Cavalry Corps numbered 10,883 officers and men present for duty, with an aggregate present of 12,636 soldiers and nine cannon. A native of Ohio, Stanley graduated from West Point in 1852 as a cavalryman. He spent the 1850s on frontier duty in Texas, Kansas Territory, and Indian Territory, narrowly escaping death or serious injury several times. He participated in the army's efforts to keep the peace in eastern Kansas in 1856, privately supporting the Free State faction although later in Indian Territory he briefly owned three slaves. Upon the outbreak of war he participated in several small skirmishes in Missouri and guarded the Federal trains at Wilson's Creek in August. Promoted to brigadier general in September 1861, he was out of action for several months with a fractured ankle. In early 1862 he commanded a division in Pope's campaign against New Madrid and Island No. 10. He then moved with Pope to join the siege of Corinth. When Rosecrans replaced Pope, he retained Stanley in division command and relied heavily upon him in the battles of Iuka and Corinth. When he moved to Tennessee, Rosecrans specifically asked that Stanley be transferred to command his mounted units. Reporting in late November 1862, Stanley commanded the Cavalry Corps at Stones River in December, in several minor actions during the first half of 1863, and in the Tullahoma campaign. As a result of his performance, he was promoted to major general. Well-proportioned physically, he wore a full beard and had a serious demeanor that belied his prewar reputation for droll wit. Outspoken and fearless in battle, Stanley was one of the most battle-tested commanders in the Army of the Cumberland.[50]

Stanley's First Division was commanded by Brig. Gen. Robert Byington Mitchell, forty, another Ohio native. In July 1863 the division numbered 5,693 officers and men present for duty, with an aggregate present of 6,763 soldiers. An attorney, Mitchell parlayed service as a junior officer in the Mexican War into a political career in Kansas Territory during the latter half of the 1850s. A delegate to the Democratic Convention in 1860, he organized the Second Kansas Infantry regiment upon the outbreak of war. Seriously wounded at Wilson's Creek in August 1861, he was slow to recover. Appointed brigadier general in April 1862, he commanded a brigade at Ft. Riley, Kansas, in May and took it to Kentucky in June. The following month his brigade became part of the Army of the Mississippi at Corinth. Gaining division command when his superior became ill, Mitchell joined the Army of the Ohio during the Kentucky campaign but was not seriously engaged at Perryville. He next led a division in the Fourteenth Corps, but it remained at Nashville during the battle of Stones River. Thereafter, Mitchell commanded the Nashville garrison until assigned to the First Cavalry Division in May. Known for his mercurial temper and general pomposity, he was disparaged by at least one contemporary. Stanley himself detested Mitchell, claiming he was foisted on the cavalry by Garfield for political reasons. The division's First Brigade was led by Col. Archibald Campbell, thirty-four, a native of Scotland. Campbell entered the war as a captain in the Second Michigan Cavalry regiment and rose to lieutenant colonel by the time of Perryville, where he was wounded. Promoted to colonel in early 1863, he gained brigade command in March, extricating his command from the Thompson's Station debacle that same month. Col. Edward McCook, thirty, commanded Mitchell's Second Brigade. A first cousin of Alex and Daniel McCook, he was an attorney and politician in the Colorado portion of Kansas Territory. Joining the Second Indiana Cavalry regiment in 1861, he was promoted to colonel in April 1862. Gaining brigade command in September, he was present but barely engaged at Perryville. Taking leave in December after suffering a slight head wound, he missed Stones River but returned to brigade command in early 1863. Flamboyant in dress and notorious for rakish behavior, McCook profited from his family's political connections. The Third Brigade was commanded by Col. Louis Watkins, twenty-nine, a Florida native long associated with the District of Columbia. Watkins joined the Regular Army in 1861 as a first lieutenant. While serving in the Fifth U.S. Cavalry, he was severely wounded at the battle of Gaines' Mill in June 1862. Commissioned colonel of the Sixth Kentucky Cavalry regiment in February 1863, he attained brigade command when the Third Brigade was organized early in July.[51]

Brig. Gen. John Basil Turchin, forty-one, commanded the Second Cavalry Division, whose strength in July 1863 stood at 5,187 officers and men present for duty, with an aggregate present of 5,870 soldiers. A native of Russia, Turchin was an 1841 graduate of the Imperial Military School at St. Petersburg. Serving variously as artilleryman, staff officer, and engineer, he participated in the Hungarian War of 1848 and the Crimean War before leaving the Russian Army as a colonel. Immigrating to the United States in 1856, he worked as a civil engineer for the Illinois Central Railroad. Appointed colonel of the Nineteenth Illinois Infantry regiment in June 1861, Turchin perfected his unit's drill, while mounting a vigorous campaign for higher rank. In the spring of 1862 Buell elevated Turchin to brigade command. During an advance into northern Alabama, his troops pillaged the town of Athens. A court-martial convicted Turchin of neglect of duty, conduct unbecoming an officer, and violation of an order to bar females from camp. Accordingly, he was dismissed from the service in August. Powerful friends in Illinois quickly interceded with President Lincoln, who not only reinstated Turchin to command but promoted him to brigadier general. Assigned to the Army of the Cumberland in March 1863, he gained command of the Second Cavalry Division upon its organization in May. No horseman, seriously overweight, and accompanied in the field by his imperious wife, Nadine, Turchin stood even lower in Stanley's estimation than Mitchell. Another foreigner, Col. Robert Horatio George Minty, thirty-one, commanded Turchin's First Brigade. A native of Ireland, Minty initially served in the British Army as an ensign. Immigrating to Michigan in 1853, he was in the railroad business when the war came. By September 1861, he was lieutenant colonel of the Third Michigan Cavalry regiment and served with that unit through the New Madrid, Island No. 10, and Corinth campaigns. Appointed colonel of the Fourth Michigan Cavalry regiment in July 1862, he missed Perryville but participated in the pursuit to Nashville. He gained brigade command in late December and participated fully in the Stones River and Tullahoma campaigns. The Second Brigade was led by Col. Eli Long, twenty-six, a Kentuckian. Educated at the Frankfort Military Institute, Long was appointed a second lieutenant in the First U.S. Cavalry in 1856. He spent most of the next five years on escort duty in Kansas Territory. Transferred to Kentucky as a captain in February 1862, he was part of the escort for both Buell and Rosecrans. Wounded in the left shoulder at Stones River, he was appointed colonel of the Fourth Ohio Cavalry regiment in February 1863. His promotion to brigade command came in June.[52]

Such was the Army of the Cumberland and such were its senior leaders on the eve of their greatest, and last, independent campaign. Led by a seasoned and supremely self-confident commander, supported by a large and generally efficient staff, the army was less well-served by its subordinate leaders at corps-level and below. Thomas had a successful record of achievement as a corps commander, but McCook, Crittenden, Granger, and Stanley either had little experience at that echelon of command or had been tried in the crucible of battle and found wanting. The division commanders were also a mixed bag, with each corps having at least one who was weak, inexperienced, or both. At the brigade level, there were both outstanding combat leaders and political appointees lacking military skill, in more or less equal numbers. Almost to a man, the troops came from the Midwest. Of the 242 individual regiments and batteries in the army in July 1863, Ohio furnished 66, Indiana provided 50, and Illinois rostered 48. Kentucky came next, with 21 units, followed by Michigan with 15 and Wisconsin with 12. The Regular Army provided ten units to the Army of the Cumberland, and Pennsylvania, the only Eastern state represented, sent seven. Loyalist Tennessee units numbered six, Missouri added three, Minnesota sent two, while Kansas and Iowa provided one each. In general, the Fourteenth and Twentieth Corps contained the most combat-tested regiments, while most units of the Twenty-First Corps had seen less fighting, and the Reserve Corps formations mostly lacked serious battle experience. The relatively new Cavalry Corps had yet to prove itself equal to its Confederate opponents. Most of the 172 infantry regiments were armed with either the .58-caliber Springfield rifle musket or the equivalent British Enfield rifle, but a smattering of units carried either 1842-pattern rifled muskets or European imports of varying calibers, and only one brigade was armed with the powerful Spencer repeating rifle. The forty-seven field artillery batteries contained approximately 240 guns, with 118 smoothbore and 122 rifled pieces. Unfortunately, forty-two of the smoothbores were obsolescent six-pounders and twelve-pounder howitzers, while forty-four rifles were the inefficient James pattern. The twenty-four cavalry regiments were equipped with a wide variety of single-shot carbines and revolvers, and they had yet to abandon the saber. All in all, the Army of the Cumberland was a formidable fighting force, especially when compared with its opponent, the Confederate Army of Tennessee.[53]

3

The Army of Tennessee

» July 1863 «

William Rosecrans's Confederate opponent in July 1863 was Gen. Braxton Bragg, the same commander he had faced since November 1862. Two years older than Rosecrans, Bragg was born in Warrenton, North Carolina, on 21 or 22 March 1817, the third son of Thomas Bragg and Margaret Crosland. His father made his living building houses, churches, and public buildings in Warren County. Eventually he became a successful contractor, but he never was able to raise his family's standing in the highly stratified Warrenton society. Believing that education was a proven path to greater community acceptance, he ensured that his sons received the best schooling possible, which meant in young Braxton's case the highly regarded Warrenton Male Academy. Having expended most of his available funds on the education of his older children, in 1827 Thomas Bragg began a campaign to gain his third son a free education at the United States Military Academy. The protracted effort finally bore fruit in 1833 and Braxton Bragg at age sixteen traveled to West Point as a prospective member of the class of 1837. He brought with him a reputation for intelligence and hard work, but also a rather reserved personality. Bragg studied hard enough to graduate fifth in his class of fifty while being convivial enough to be regarded favorably by most of his peers. According to classmate Joseph Hooker, Bragg was "tall, ungainly in his gait, uncouth in manner, but bright and engaging . . . remarked from the beginning for his manliness, independence, and unbending integrity." Hooker also found Bragg to be strongly opinionated, outspoken to a fault, and often brusque with casual acquaintances. Classmates of note were John Sedgwick, John Pemberton, Jubal Early, and two men whose path would intersect with Bragg's in the summer of 1863, William W. Mackall and William H. T. Walker. Bragg's high-class standing gained him an appointment as a second lieutenant in the artillery. Thus at the age of twenty he entered a respectable but hardly lucrative profession, no doubt pleasing his father.[1]

Bragg's initial posting was to the Third Regiment of Artillery, engaged in hostilities with Seminole Indians in Florida. For the next six years he participated unhappily in desultory operations against an elusive foe, punctuated by long periods of boredom, all in a most inhospitable climate. In Florida he demonstrated traits that would mark his entire military career, especially a self-righteousness that tended to characterize opposing views as unworthy. Bragg's intense personality also caused him to overwork himself wherever he perceived duty to be involved, occasionally to the point of harming his health. Brief respites on recruiting duty did little to mollify his displeasure at his Florida posting, so he was great relieved when his unit transferred to Fort Moultrie in South Carolina in 1843. There, as a first lieutenant, he took command of one of the new light artillery companies being formed to make field artillery more relevant to the offensive battlefield. By 1844, Bragg's command, which included Lieutenants George Thomas and John Reynolds, was actively preparing for war. Still, there was time to hector the high command with proposals for improvements to the army's structure, which Bragg offered anonymously in a series of articles in the *Southern Literary Messenger*. Further, he willingly became involved in a controversy between Commanding Gen. Winfield Scott and members of Congress, which led to a gentle but pointed reprimand in April 1844. Bragg's high profile in disputes among the army's senior leaders represented a considerable risk for a young officer. Nevertheless, believing that he was right and his opponents were wrong, he forged ahead. He prevailed in an equally arid controversy over living quarters with his regimental commander in 1845, but by then he had gained a reputation as the most argumentative officer in the army. The episodes illustrated Bragg's intellect, self-confidence, fearlessness, and lack of normal prudence. They also displayed his tendency to see simple policy disagreements in the most personal terms.[2]

Peacetime controversies disappeared in the summer of 1845 because of the growing crisis with Mexico. Bragg's battery was among those units ordered to gather at Corpus Christi, Texas, in preparation for action. There a brevet second lieutenant named Harvey Hill briefly joined the unit. He would transfer to another regiment before the war began, but Bragg and Hill would meet again. When Zachary Taylor's little army advanced to the Rio Grande, Bragg and his battery became part of the garrison of Fort Brown, which soon came under siege. After a successful defense, which brought Bragg promotion to captain, Taylor led his small army to the Mexican city of Monterrey. There, in a series of bloody actions on 21–23 September 1846, Bragg's battery participated fully in the American victory, although its losses were significant. Monterrey brought Bragg a brevet promotion to major and transfer to another battery. Left behind when Winfield Scott took most of the regulars to Veracruz, Bragg was with Taylor's command at Buena Vista on 23 February 1847 when a larger Mexican force attacked. In a heroic performance, Bragg moved his three guns all over the field, always at the critical point, and virtually alone stopped the final Mexican charge. His performance was noted by Col. Jefferson Davis of the First Mississippi Infantry regiment and by Zachary Taylor himself, who noted that Bragg's battery "saved the day." Not long thereafter, an anecdote began to circulate in the United States that Taylor had responded to Bragg's question about ammunition with, "A little more grape, Captain Bragg." While no doubt an incorrect rendering of whatever the profane Taylor may have said, the story gained great currency and became part of the lore surrounding each man. Bragg's performance at Buena Vista gained him yet another brevet, to lieutenant colonel, but there would be no more action for Taylor's little army. Instead, Bragg threw himself into perfecting his battery through iron discipline and incessant drill, causing at least one soldier to attempt his assassination.[3]

Upon returning from Mexico, Bragg endured months of celebratory parties, banquets, and speeches as a bona fide hero. Temporarily assigned to staff duty in New Orleans in 1849, he found the time to court and marry Eliza Brooks Ellis, twenty-three, eldest child of a wealthy Thibodaux, Louisiana, family. Known as Elise to Bragg and her friends, she followed Bragg to his next posting, at Jefferson Barracks, near St. Louis. There Bragg resumed his campaign to improve the army, especially the horse artillery, through letter-writing efforts and the lobbying of his brother John, an Alabama congressman. In an era of reduced military budgets Bragg's efforts bore little fruit, even when Jefferson Davis, his compatriot at Buena Vista, became secretary of war. In 1853, to add insult to injury, Davis assigned Bragg's battery to Fort Gibson in Indian Territory. Elise accompanied her husband to what proved to be a hardship post on the frontier, and moved with him again after eight months to an even more isolated garrison at Fort Washita. After half a year at Fort Washita, Bragg applied for leave, and he and Elise returned to Louisiana in early 1855. While on leave he refused promotion to major and transfer to the First Cavalry regiment because it meant returning to the frontier. Instead he asked for additional leave, which was granted, and permission to travel in Europe, which was not. As 1855 ended, Bragg resumed his efforts to have his battery transferred from the frontier. When his pleas were summarily rejected by Secretary of War Davis, Bragg resigned his commission on the last day of the year. In his view, Davis had forced him to leave the army. Thus, in early 1856, Bragg began a new career. Using his wife's money, he bought a sugar plantation with a labor force of more than 100 slaves. For the next five years he labored with his usual diligence and discipline to make the plantation profitable. He also began to accept minor political offices, including a seat on the Louisiana Military Board, which grew in importance as the Union began to dissolve.[4]

Although Bragg strongly favored a peaceful resolution of the differences between the sections, he was too closely associated with his adopted state's power structure to do anything but follow Louisiana's lead. Thus, when Governor Thomas Moore asked Bragg to negotiate the surrender of the Federal arsenal in Baton Rouge in January 1861, he complied. When Louisiana seceded from the Union, Moore chose Bragg to command the state's military forces, and Bragg threw himself into the task with his customary energy. The appointment lasted only a few weeks because the Confederate government offered Bragg a commission as a brigadier general in early March. Bragg had feared that the animosity he ascribed to Jefferson Davis, stemming from their prewar disagreements over army policy, would retard his rise, but such proved not to be the case. He was immediately ordered to Pensacola, where a standoff had developed between the Federal garrison at Fort Pickens and secessionist units controlling the remainder of the harbor. The situation at Pensacola was remarkably similar to that momentarily prevailing at Charleston, where a Federal garrison at Fort Sumter was threatened by Confederates commanded by P. G. T. Beauregard. At Pensacola, Bragg found a belligerent yet poorly armed rabble facing a small but resolute Federal garrison, with a tenuous truce preventing bloodshed. Using his skills as a trainer of men, Bragg slowly created order and discipline out of the exuberant chaos. In April, the truce was shattered when Federal reinforcements landed, making the task of taking Fort Pickens almost impossible. Bragg developed plans to carry the fort by storm, but he had little confidence in either the plans or his still unready troops. The nation's attention quickly deserted Pensacola when Beauregard forced Fort Sumter's surrender, Abraham Lincoln called for thousands of volunteers, and several other states left the Union. With Fort Pickens too difficult to assault, the Confederate government ordered Bragg to send several of his best units to the new seat of war in Virginia.[5]

Throughout the remainder of 1861 Bragg continued to drill and discipline whatever recruits the new Confederate government could spare for the Pensacola front. He was devoted to establishing standards of training and deportment that few other officers could muster, and he denigrated those who did not meet those standards. To his credit, he did not spare himself, working exceedingly long hours and finding no detail too small for his attention. Given such an attitude and provided with mediocre subordinates, Bragg worked himself beyond his physical capabilities. Seldom free of illness, much of it caused by overwork, he struggled to remain on duty. His physical deterioration was obvious to all, including a foreign visitor who described him as "elderly." He suffered often from migraine headaches, dyspepsia, and boils, and when overcome by those maladies he was decidedly unpleasant to those around him. He quickly gained a reputation for being abrupt and severe in his dealings with others, most of whom were unaware of the cause of his black mood. Every day seemed to bring a new worry, whether in regard to the unpreparedness of his men, the sloth and incapacity of his officers, the lack of support from the Confederate War Department, or his wife's problems managing their plantation in his absence. Hoping to spare Elise the vagaries of travel, he asked her not to visit Pensacola, but she came anyway and briefly had a calming effect on her husband. His foremost concern always was the well-being of his troops, and he visited them often. The Richmond authorities noted his diligence and promoted him to major general in September 1861. In early October the War Department expanded his command to include the entire state of Alabama. Now the port of Mobile was part of Bragg's portfolio, adding new problems to be solved. As the year ended, Jefferson Davis proposed that Bragg take command of the area west of the Mississippi River, but Bragg demurred, realizing that the Trans-Mississippi would be an even more difficult command than the Gulf coast.[6]

The Confederate disaster at Fort Donelson in February 1862 released Bragg from static coastal defense. By all accounts his units were the best-disciplined force available to reinforce Albert Sidney Johnston's crumbling Kentucky-Tennessee front. So reasoning, the War Department ordered Bragg to western Tennessee with 10,000 of his best troops. There Beauregard was in command, and his chief deputy was Maj. Gen. Leonidas Polk, both of whom outranked Bragg. Given command of all forces south of Jackson, Tennessee, Bragg soon moved them to Corinth, Mississippi, to counter a Federal thrust up the Tennessee River. When Johnston reached Corinth, he chose Beauregard to be his second in command and made Bragg the army's chief of staff and a corps commander. Clearly, Johnston recognized the army's great need of system, drill, and discipline, and he was certainly aware of Bragg's reputation as a trainer. By making Bragg his chief of staff, Johnston could bypass the amiable but inefficient Polk. The chief of staff position was ill-defined, and command of a corps was a full-time occupation, but Bragg threw himself into both jobs with his usual vigor. He had little time to improve the army's condition because Johnston in early April 1862 decided to attack the growing Federal concentration at Pittsburg Landing. When the Confederates departed Corinth, Bragg's Second Corps was the army's largest, with more than 13,000 troops. As the march disintegrated into confusion, both Beauregard and Bragg counseled Johnston to abandon the advance, but Johnston resolutely demurred. In the resulting battle of Shiloh, Bragg eventually commanded all troops on the army's right. He had two horses shot from under him as he orchestrated ultimately successful frontal attacks against the Federal enclave known as the Hornet's Nest. When Johnston died on the field, Beauregard made Bragg the army's second in command. As such, he helped the Confederate army withdraw safely to Corinth when it was driven from the field on the battle's second day.[7]

Like all who fought at Shiloh, Bragg had seen nothing like it before. Buena

Vista paled in comparison to the fight near Pittsburg Landing. Indeed, at Shiloh Bragg alone commanded three times the number of troops Zachary Taylor had led in his most famous victory. Bragg fought his portion of the battle just as he had seen Taylor fight, aggressively and frontally, without regard to casualties. After the battle, Bragg ascribed the Confederate failure primarily to the indiscipline of the volunteer soldiers and the incompetence of their officers, two problems he had labored for months to rectify. As Beauregard's troops gathered at Corinth, Bragg used the momentary pause to instill greater discipline within the army. He was especially hard on deserters, inflicting the death penalty on miscreants freely and thereby incurring the everlasting enmity of many common soldiers. The widely reported story of Bragg executing a soldier for shooting a chicken was false, but many men in the ranks believed it. The anti-Bragg feeling was especially strong among the army's Tennessee regiments, whose members had been forced from their state. Beauregard and the War Department, however, were so pleased with Bragg's performance that he was appointed full general in mid-April, the fifth-ranking uniformed officer in the Confederate Army. Never again would he have to worry about being junior to Leonidas Polk and others deemed by him to be similarly deficient in military skills. As before, the time available to Bragg for whipping the army into shape was limited. Just before the Federals closed around the Corinth position, Beauregard evacuated the town, with Bragg conspicuously managing the retreat. By mid-June the Confederates assumed a new defensive posture around Tupelo, Mississippi. There Beauregard deflected an order from Richmond to send Bragg to Louisiana, arguing that he could not be spared. Beauregard then went on sick leave without the War Department's permission. In response, Jefferson Davis relieved Beauregard of command and on 20 June 1862 gave his army to Bragg.[8]

Bragg's Department No. 2 and its Army of the Mississippi represented one of the two major troop concentrations in the entire Confederacy. Encompassing most of Tennessee, parts of Louisiana and Florida, and all of Alabama and Mississippi, Department No. 2 embraced much of the Confederacy's heartland and its field army was second only in importance to the forces defending Richmond. Yet that army had lost Shiloh, evacuated Corinth, and retreated fifty miles southward to avoid destruction. Bragg reorganized the army's leadership, elevating Polk to the meaningless position of second in command, and giving day-to-day direction of the army to Maj. Gen. William Hardee. Desertion remained a problem, and Bragg responded with courts-martial and executions. Many officers were incompetent or lazy, so Bragg instituted examination boards to weed out the misfits. Supplies were short, causing Bragg to argue his needs all the way to Richmond. Gradually the army improved, although the grumbling among those who favored a more relaxed approach grew in volume. When Don Carlos Buell advanced from Corinth across northern Alabama toward Chattanooga, Tennessee, Bragg felt compelled to respond. Chattanooga lay in Maj. Gen. Edmund Kirby Smith's Department of East Tennessee. In an effort to support Smith, Bragg sent a division to Chattanooga by a circuitous rail-water route, proving the feasibility of the concept. In late July he followed with the bulk of the Army of the Mississippi. Bragg's move was bold, unprecedented, and successful, with his army concentrating at Chattanooga before Buell could arrive in strength. At Chattanooga on 31 July Bragg met with Smith in order to plan an offensive movement, either in Tennessee or Kentucky. Bragg hoped that the combined commands could force the Federals to recede from northern Alabama and Mississippi. Those hopes were dashed when Smith elected to move independently. Believing that something yet might be done, Bragg put his army in motion in late August 1862.[9]

When his army left Chattanooga, Bragg's burden of responsibility was enormous. As the commander of Department No. 2, he not only directed his field army but also supervised three subcommands: the Districts of the Gulf, the Mississippi, and the Tennessee. He was beginning an offensive campaign in another officer's department, having reinforced that officer with several of his best units. Kirby Smith's dash for Kentucky aborted Bragg's idea of attacking Buell's army in Tennessee. Thus his only recourse was to head for Kentucky as well, interposing his army between Smith's small command and the Federals. He succeeded in outmaneuvering Buell at Munfordville, but without Smith's command he was unable to prevent the Federal army from entering Louisville. Bragg's every effort to unite with Smith was deflected by the latter, and the campaign devolved into no more than the inauguration of a Confederate governor in Frankfort. The hope of so many Confederates that Kentuckians would rally to their cause was also dashed when residents refused to rise in support. As department commander, Bragg joined Smith in Frankfort for the inaugural ceremony, leaving his army scattered around Bardstown under Polk. In response to vague reports of a Federal advance, Bragg ordered Polk to move toward Frankfort, but Polk refused and withdrew eastward instead. Unable to hold Frankfort with only Smith's troops, Bragg tried to draw Polk nearer, but his efforts failed when Buell's army met Polk's troops outside of Perryville. Reaching the scene before the action commenced, Bragg assumed tactical command and vigorously attacked the lethargic Federals. For a variety of reasons, neither Bragg nor Buell was able to bring all his troops into action, and the result was a bloody stalemate. Withdrawing eastward after the battle, Bragg finally united his own and Smith's commands, but lack of supplies, an absence of support from Kentuckians, and news of a Confederate defeat at Corinth caused him to order a retreat from Kentucky.[10]

Although the Army of the Mississippi successfully extricated itself from Kentucky, the failed invasion left everyone unhappy. The Kentucky campaign represented Bragg's first effort as a department and field army commander in offensive operations. Boldly, he had attempted to coordinate the simultaneous movements of the egotistical Smith, scattered forces in northern Mississippi, and his own army. Distracted by the political side of the campaign, he left the bulk of his army in the hands of Polk, an incompetent and insubordinate officer. Having sent Chief of Staff Thomas Jordan on an errand to Vicksburg before the campaign began, Bragg assumed Jordan's role as well as his own in Kentucky. Constitutionally unwilling to delegate either grand decisions or minutia to others, he worked himself to the point of exhaustion during the campaign. Indeed, on 18 September he confided to his wife that he averaged only four hours of sleep per night. Prodded by the disappointed Kentuckians in the army and the Confederate Congress, politicians and newspaper editors of all stripes began a campaign to have Bragg relieved of command. In his official report, Bragg praised his subordinates, but his magnanimity was not reciprocated. Within the Army of the Mississippi, soldier opinion was divided, but Polk began his own campaign to undermine Bragg, and he was abetted quietly by Hardee. Similarly, Kirby Smith worked assiduously to deflect criticism of his own shortcomings by assailing Bragg in the highest circles. The clamor grew so great that Jefferson Davis called Bragg, Polk, and Smith independently to Richmond for consultation. Afterward, Davis sustained Bragg in command and counseled the subordinates of both Smith and Bragg to leave personalities aside and place the public interest foremost. Meanwhile, the army returned to Chattanooga via Cumberland Gap and Knoxville. By late November 1862 it had advanced to Murfreesboro, where it again confronted Buell's old Army of the Ohio, now based in Nashville as William Rosecrans's Army of the Cumberland.[11]

The failed Kentucky campaign triggered a significant reorganization of the Confederate department system. Convinced that an overall coordinator with plenary powers must be appointed, Jefferson Davis on 24 November 1862 assigned Gen. Joseph Johnston to take command of a new Department of the West. On paper, Johnston supervised Smith's Department of East Tennessee, Bragg's Department No. 2, and the new Department of Mississippi and East Louisiana under Lt. Gen. John Pemberton. Even so, Bragg and the other department commanders retained the right to correspond directly with the War Department. At the same time, Bragg reorganized his field army, on 20 November changing its name from the Army of the Mississippi to the Army of Tennessee. Abolishing the wing organization used in Kentucky, Bragg divided his command into army corps under Polk and Hardee, both recently promoted to lieutenant general. Certainly aware of Polk's dislike and possibly Hardee's as well, Bragg had nevertheless praised them officially and had no choice but to give them critical roles in the army's command structure. When Kirby Smith briefly joined Bragg in early December with the troops he had borrowed during the Kentucky campaign, all three corps commanders were united in opposition to the army's leader. Fortunately for Bragg, Smith soon returned to his old department after President Davis ordered most of his corps to Mississippi. Visiting Tennessee to confer with Bragg and Johnston, Davis ordered Johnston to Mississippi as well. Before they departed, both Davis and Johnston pronounced the Army of Tennessee to be in much better shape than they had expected to find it, testimony to Bragg's disciplinary efforts. Nevertheless, Bragg was left alone among his enemies to contend against the next Federal advance. To add to his woes, in Louisiana his wife and his plantation came under Federal occupation in November when Federal troops entered Thibodaux.[12]

When Rosecrans's army approached Murfreesboro in the waning days of December, Bragg decided to strike first. Early on the last day of the year he sent Hardee's Corps forward from his left with Polk instructed to join the fight as Hardee advanced. When its Right Wing collapsed, the Army of the Cumberland was briefly in danger of being driven from the field, but the Confederate attack stalled in a welter of heavy casualties and disorganized units. Bragg ordered Maj. Gen. John Breckinridge's Division first to reinforce Hardee, then to assist Polk, but the Kentuckian delayed so long that the opportunity was lost. At the end of the day, Rosecrans's line was hammered into a tight semicircle, but it was unbroken. When Bragg tried another attack two days later solely with Breckinridge's troops, it was repulsed easily. Still, Bragg resolved to stand his ground, even in the face of calls by Polk and others to withdraw. Only the rise of Stones River behind him and new information on the strength of the Federal army caused him to change his mind. When Polk and Hardee again called for retreat, Bragg acquiesced. Unpursued, the Army of Tennessee eventually halted thirty miles southeast of Murfreesboro to await another Federal advance. To Bragg's critics it seemed like Perryville all over again: win the field at great cost in blood, then lose heart and withdraw, relinquishing all of the army's hard-won gains. Bragg's critics both in and out of the army redoubled their efforts to get him relieved. Wracked by self-doubt and stung by newspaper gossip that he alone had favored retreat from Murfreesboro, Bragg asked his corps and division commanders if they indeed had counseled a withdrawal. Naively, he couched his request in terms that permitted the disaffected commanders to cast a vote of no confidence. Hardee and two division commanders forthrightly recommended that Bragg relinquish command. Slyly, Polk answered ambiguously, all the while continuing to seek Bragg's removal by writing directly to Jefferson Davis.[13]

Forced once more to resolve a dispute within the Army of Tennessee, Davis sent Johnston to investigate the situation. After interviewing the principals in late January, Johnston declared that Bragg should be sustained in command of the army. He added that should Bragg be removed, he himself was disqualified for the position because of his role in the investigation. Disappointed that Johnston would not take command of the army, Davis momentarily shelved the question. There the matter stood until early March, when new controversies erupted. Bragg preferred charges against Maj. Gen. John McCown, who had performed poorly, and sent his Stones River report to Richmond. The report was highly critical of Breckinridge's performance and caused a political uproar in the capital. His patience exhausted, Davis on 9 March peremptorily summoned Bragg to Richmond for a "conference" and ordered Johnston to assume command of the Army of Tennessee. When Johnston arrived ten days later, he found Bragg tending to his gravely ill wife. Elise Bragg, driven from her Louisiana home by Federal troops, had moved to Winchester to be near her husband and was suffering from a severe case of typhoid fever. Under the circumstances, Johnston refused to send Bragg to Richmond but did assume daily supervision of the army. Freed from administrative minutia, for several weeks Bragg not only ministered to his wife but also continued the war of words with his enemies. First, he bolstered his case against Breckinridge, causing that officer futilely to seek a court of inquiry. Next, he drafted a long review of the Kentucky campaign, discovering in the process that Polk, Hardee, and their subordinates had willfully disobeyed his orders in October 1862. Calling upon all general officers present at Polk's councils of war to state the facts as they knew them, Bragg gained no advantage over his principal opponents, who refused to respond, and succeeded only in placing many junior officers in uncomfortable positions.[14]

As the spring campaigning season neared, the internecine warfare within Bragg's command reached its culmination. By mid-April Elise Bragg was on the mend, but Johnston himself had fallen ill, and he again declined to send Bragg to Richmond. Beset by his own problems, Davis relinquished the idea of summoning Bragg, either temporarily or permanently. Thus Bragg retained command of the Army of Tennessee. By the end of April he was satisfied that Polk, Hardee, and several division commanders had been actively disloyal and were continuing to plot against him. Davis had sustained Bragg in command but had neither rebuked nor removed his primary antagonists, leaving them in place for the next campaign. In May, Johnston departed for Mississippi with more than 11,000 of Bragg's troops. Bragg's sole consolation was that Breckinridge departed as well, going to Mississippi with most of his division. By June, Elise Bragg's condition had improved to the point that she could travel to Cherokee Springs, Georgia, to continue her convalescence. Cheered by the improvement in Elise's health and free of Johnston's direct supervision, Bragg found his own health improved as well. In June, however, the Army of the Cumberland began its long anticipated advance, and all of the old problems resurfaced. Feinting toward the Confederate left, Rosecrans turned Bragg's right at Hoover's Gap.

Braxton Bragg. (Library of Congress)

Bragg initially proposed a counterattack by Polk's Corps, but the Federal advance was too rapid, and the Army of Tennessee was forced to retreat to Tullahoma. There Bragg proposed to make a stand, against the wishes of Polk and Hardee, who once more began to conspire behind their commander's back. Outmaneuvered by a stronger enemy, abandoned by his senior subordinates, and threatened by the rising Elk River in his rear, Bragg nearly broke under the strain. Still, against all odds, he held himself together and extricated his army from almost certain disaster. By 4 July he and the Army of Tennessee had placed the barren Cumberland Plateau between them and the jubilant Federals.[15]

The man who watched his army stream off the Cumberland Plateau in early July 1863 looked much older than his forty-six years. Bragg's health had not been robust since his service in Florida early in his military career. Lt. Col. Arthur Fremantle, a British military observer, in late May described Bragg as "very thin. He stoops, and has a sickly, cadaverous, haggard appearance, rather plain features, bushy black eyebrows which unite in a tuft on the top of his nose, and a stubby iron-gray beard; but his eyes are bright and piercing." The improvement in Bragg's health in June was reversed completely during the Tullahoma operations, causing Hardee to tell Polk on 1 July that "I deeply regret to see General Bragg in his present enfeebled state of health. If we have a fight, he is evidently unable either to examine and determine his line of battle or to take command on the field." Hardee and Polk had contributed greatly to Bragg's poor physical condition, having done much to increase the stress levels on their commander by disobedience, innuendo, and backbiting. Still, Bragg's own personality shared the blame for his condition. Throughout his army career, he had maintained an unwavering devotion to the requirements of duty. Since childhood he had disciplined himself to meet those requirements. He fully expected others to do the same, and when they did not, he was not only disappointed but censorious. He abhorred drunkenness, laziness, and luxurious habits and made every effort to eradicate them from all under his command. Technical incompetence in officers he considered a particular vice. Nor did Bragg suffer pernicious traits in silence, for he was outspoken to a fault. Such a stiff-necked and straitlaced attitude, expressed openly in acerbic tones, won him no friends and cemented his public reputation as a hard, uncaring commander. The fact that Bragg truly grieved over the army's casualties and visited hospitals at every opportunity was lost on those who only heard the volleys executing deserters, even if the number of executions was fewer than rumored.[16]

Elevated to army command in circumstances that some considered illegitimate, Bragg had the misfortune to mount his first campaign tethered to a young egotist, Kirby Smith, and saddled with an incompetent deputy eleven years older than himself, Leonidas Polk. Polk had once outranked Bragg, and he enjoyed a personal relationship with Jefferson Davis that Bragg could never shake. When the Kentucky campaign ended badly, Bragg freely criticized the ungrateful Kentuckians, angering generals like Breckinridge and Buckner. Nor did the seemingly more professional Hardee improve the army's comity, falling under Polk's influence as early as October 1862. Unable to relieve either man, Bragg was forced to maintain a professional relationship with them in the face of their poorly disguised hostility. Polk seems to have been the primary instigator of the discord and Hardee, not much older than Bragg, his acolyte. Unable to call upon his senior subordinates for honest counsel, Bragg had no one to assist him in formulating strategy except his superiors in Richmond and, occasionally, Joseph Johnston. Lacking an adequate chief of staff, he simply redoubled his efforts to handle the army's administrative work himself. The result was a downward spiral in his physical condition. Never a social or convivial person, Bragg became more and more reticent, severe, and abrupt as the stress upon him grew. Upon learning that subordinates had been actively thwarting his directives, he naively believed that simply exposing their behavior would cause them to desist. Having achieved the proof he desired in April, he let the matter drop. Without the power to remove Polk, the original source of friction, he had no other choice, and the army's poisonous command climate continued to fester. Thus it was possible for Hardee to skirt the edge of mutiny on 1 July by calling for Polk, Buckner, and himself to meet privately and act against their commander. The easing of the crisis forestalled the cabal, but the disharmony within the army's high command had by no means run its course.[17]

To the degree that he permitted them to do so, Bragg's staff assisted him. There had been no continuity in the chief of staff position since the beginning of the Kentucky campaign. Bragg had either served as his own chief of staff or used Lt. Col. George William Brent, an assistant adjutant general, until the spring of 1863. On 17 April, Brig. Gen. William Whann Mackall arrived from Mobile to assume the position. Born on 18 January 1817 in Maryland, Mackall was an 1837 West Point graduate, ranking eighth, three numbers below Bragg. Assigned to the First Regiment of Artillery, he served two years in Florida fighting the Seminoles, receiving a severe wound in 1839. In the war with Mexico, Mackall participated in six battles, from Monterrey to Chapultepec, suffering another wound and reaching the brevet rank of major. Transferring from line to staff, for the next fourteen years he was an assistant adjutant general. He resigned his commission in July 1861, accepting the rank of lieutenant colonel in the Confederate Army's adjutant general department. Originally placed on Sidney Johnston's staff, he eventually gained the favor of P. G. T. Beauregard, who obtained Mackall's promotion to brigadier general in late March 1862. Assigned to command Island No. 10, he surrendered that post in early April and was imprisoned in Boston harbor. Exchanged in October, he was ordered to

Mobile, where he served under Buckner for several months. When the War Department assigned him to be Bragg's chief of staff, Mackall seemed to be a good choice, as Bragg considered him a friend. He brought a wealth of combat experience from Mexico, much staff experience in two armies, and firsthand knowledge of Bragg's peculiar personality. He also brought a direct, plainspoken personality of his own, and the baggage of being a Beauregard protégé out of favor with President Davis. During the Tullahoma campaign he assumed a much-needed role as operational advisor to the army commander and coordinator of the staff departments.[18]

Bragg's aides-de-camp were closer to him than his classmate Mackall. In July 1863 his senior aide was Col. Joseph P. Jones, thirty-two, of North Carolina. Dismissed from West Point in 1850, Jones gained a lieutenant's commission in the Second United States Artillery regiment in 1856 before resigning in 1861. Chosen lieutenant colonel of the Fifth North Carolina Infantry regiment in July, he again resigned after court-martial on minor charges in October. Commissioned a lieutenant of artillery, he was posted to Mobile, where he apparently gained Bragg's favor. In August he was announced as captain and assistant inspector general. Thereafter Bragg diligently sought Jones's promotion. The War Department finally acquiesced in a temporary promotion to colonel in April 1863 with service on Bragg's staff. Bragg used Jones most often as an inspector in distant regions of Department No. 2. Closer to Bragg personally was Lt. Col. David Urquhart, thirty-five. A commission merchant in New Orleans, Urquhart began the war as an aide to the Louisiana governor, who loaned him to Bragg just before Shiloh. Urquhart remained with Bragg as a volunteer aide until April 1863, then as a lieutenant colonel in the adjutant and inspector general department. Bragg trusted Urquhart implicitly, using him as a confidential secretary to record contentious meetings with his subordinates. Equally loyal was 1st Lt. Towson Ellis, forty, Bragg's brother-in-law and fellow sugar planter. Cultivated and erudite, Ellis joined Bragg at Pensacola in May 1861 and remained with him as aide. Similarly, 1st Lt. Francis S. Parker Jr., twenty-one, of South Carolina had also been with Bragg since Pensacola. Together, Urquhart, Ellis, and Parker represented a large part of Bragg's most loyal inner circle. Not formally part of the army staff but serving occasionally as a volunteer aide was Isham G. Harris, forty-five, governor of Tennessee.[19]

Lt. Col. George William Brent, forty-two, had served as Bragg's assistant adjutant general for many months, and had on occasion acted as chief of staff. Brent, however, had left the Army of Tennessee shortly after Mackall's arrival and did not return until 26 July. Brent's absence apparently did not involve a personality clash with either Bragg or Mackall. Brent was an 1842 graduate of the University of Virginia and an attorney. A member of the Virginia constitutional convention in 1861, he was a signatory of that state's ordinance of secession. In May 1861 he was appointed major in the Seventeenth Virginia Infantry regiment but in early 1862 transferred to the Adjutant and Inspector General Department. Requested by name by P. G. T. Beauregard, he joined the Army of the Mississippi just prior to Shiloh as an assistant inspector general. Both Beauregard and Bragg sought his promotion to lieutenant colonel, which occurred in July. First assigned to Kirby Smith's command, Brent joined Bragg again in October 1862. Thereafter he served as the army's primary assistant adjutant general. Brent did not see himself as an operational advisor to Bragg but was content with a purely administrative role. By all accounts he was a modest, self-effacing officer who moved serenely through the storms that beset Bragg's command. Loyal to his chief, Brent attempted to moderate Bragg's excesses. Unfortunately, his return clouded the division of labor Mackall had instituted between the chief of staff's and adjutant general's offices. Thereafter, Bragg tended to use Mackall, Brent, and others interchangeably. Brent's primary assistant was Capt. Kinloch Falconer, twenty-four, of Mississippi. An attorney and newspaperman, Falconer began the conflict as a private in the Ninth Mississippi Infantry regiment at Pensacola. Detailed as an enlisted clerk in the adjutant general's office in September 1861, he had quickly gained a commission as a captain in the same office and had served there ever since.[20]

As might be expected of a commander who valued standards and obedience, Bragg had a robust inspector general's office. The senior man was Lt. Col. William K. Beard, thirty-two. A merchant, Beard was commissioned lieutenant colonel of the First Florida Infantry regiment in April 1861 and accompanied that regiment to Pensacola. The regiment moved to Corinth with Bragg but failed to reorganize successfully, leaving Beard without employment until Bragg made him an acting inspector general just before Shiloh. When Bragg took command of the Army of the Mississippi, he appointed Beard as the army's inspector general. Beard immediately created a professional inspector general's office, establishing its chain of command and regularizing its procedures. In garrison, on the march, and on the battlefield the inspector general's personnel monitored unit movements, supervised the quartermaster, commissary, ordnance, and medical functions, maintained the order of battle, and processed prisoners of war. To ensure that his office had its finger on the pulse of the army, Beard placed assistant inspectors at all levels from brigade through corps, each of whom was to forward regular reports on a bimonthly basis. Not only did Beard supervise the field army but his writ also extended to the farthest reaches of Department No. 2, requiring frequent trips to distant sites. In sum, while Mackall and Brent managed Bragg's orders process, Beard and his assistants closely supervised everything else the army did and directed corrective measures if Bragg so desired. Surprisingly, given his propensity to micromanage other departments, Bragg rarely intervened in Beard's affairs, giving that officer and his assistants unusual authority and independence. In July 1863, Beard's office was staffed by Lt. Col. Andrew J. Hays, Maj. William Clare, Maj. Pollok B. Lee, Capt. P. H. Thomson, Capt. James Cooper, and Capt. George W. Carr. Hays, Clare, and Cooper had been with the office for more than half a year, while Lee, Thomson, and Carr were new arrivals.[21]

The staff departments most critical to the army's daily existence were the quartermaster and commissary departments. Maj. Matthew B. McMicken, thirty-one, was Bragg's chief quartermaster. In April 1861 he was appointed captain and assistant quartermaster, and ordered to duty at Pensacola. He initially did not follow Bragg to Corinth, but in July 1862 he was appointed major and assistant to the Army of the Mississippi's chief quartermaster. Dropped from the rolls in August for nonexecution of his bond, he was reinstated in November. McMicken became chief quartermaster in June 1863, charged with providing the clothing, equipment, fuel, and transportation needs for all personnel in the Army of Tennessee and Department No. 2. His sources of supply were the depots at Columbus and Atlanta, Georgia, where he depended upon quartermasters beyond his control to ship the required items. Even though the Tullahoma campaign had not been heavily destructive of equipment, the army was woefully short of transportation, forcing McMicken to husband carefully his approximately 2,200 wagons. He was assisted by Capt. John W. Green, inspector of field transportation, and Maj. Albert J. Smith, chief of the pay department. McMicken's counterpart in the Commissary Department was Maj. Giles M. Hillyer, forty-four, chief commissary of subsistence. A commissary major since September 1861, Hillyer served as post commissary at various places in Mississippi until he joined the Army of Tennessee at Murfreesboro in December 1862. For much of the first half of 1863 he was the depot commissary at Tullahoma, rising to acting chief commissary of the army in late May when his predecessor departed. By July, he was the army's chief commissary, with one assistant, Maj. William H. Ross. Although his primary depot was Atlanta, the bulk of that depot's stock usually was reserved for the Army of Northern Virginia. Hillyer thus was forced to scavenge northern Alabama to provide sufficient food for the army. Both he and McMicken were relatively inexperienced at the field army level.[22]

Bragg's ordnance chief was Lt. Col. Hypolite Oladowski, sixty-four. A native of Poland and former officer in the Russian army, Oladowski immigrated to America following the European upheavals of the 1830s. Enlisting in the U.S. Army, he participated in the Mexican War and by 1861 was an ordnance sergeant at the Baton Rouge Arsenal. Joining the Confederacy, in March he was appointed captain of artillery and posted to Pensacola. By October 1861 he was Bragg's ordnance chief and followed him to Corinth. When Bragg became commander of the Army of the Mississippi, he chose Oladowski to be the army's chief of ordnance, with the rank of lieutenant colonel. The Pole continued in that role throughout Bragg's campaigns with the Army of Tennessee. Widely known for his fractured English, his imaginative profanity, his frugality with ammunition, and his utter loyalty to Bragg, Oladowski provided and maintained the army's weapons while stocking adequate supplies of ammunition for six calibers of infantry weapons and seven artillery types. He was assisted by Capt. Octavius T. Gibbes, Capt. William H. Warren, Capt. William D. Humphries, commander of the Chattanooga Ordnance Depot, and Lt. B. Frank Nichol and his brother Bradford. The Atlanta Arsenal was Oladowski's primary source of supply. Working closely with Oladowski was Lt. Col. James H. Hallonquist, twenty-seven, chief of artillery. Hallonquist stood sixth in the West Point class of 1858, resigning in January 1861 to offer his services to his native South Carolina. Assigned to Pensacola, Hallonquist accompanied Bragg to Corinth, where he was appointed chief of artillery of the Army of the Mississippi, with the rank of major. Promoted to lieutenant colonel in July 1862 as inspector of artillery, he again became chief of artillery in November and remained in that position thereafter. Hallonquist's role was purely administrative, involving simply the organization of batteries and the allocation of guns. Hallonquist's lone assistant was 1st Lt. R. H. Smith Thompson of North Carolina.[23]

Bragg's genuine sympathy for the plight of his wounded and sick soldiers was most obvious in his concern for the army's medical department. In July 1863 that department consisted of two separate organizations, divided between medical care in the field, and medical care in the army's immediate rear. The medical director of the Army of Tennessee was Dr. Edward Archelaus Flewellen, forty-four, of Georgia. Flewellen was an 1851 graduate of Jefferson Medical College in Philadelphia. Upon the outbreak of the war, he joined the Fifth Georgia Infantry regiment as its surgeon, but within a year migrated into hospital administration. In June 1862 he became the Army of the Mississippi's assistant medical director. In late December 1862 Flewellen became the Army of Tennessee's medical director. His charter encompassed all medical activity within the field army, essentially the health of army personnel, casualty collection, organization and operation of field hospitals, and supervision of medical personnel at unit levels. His primary assistant was Surgeon Tobias G. Richardson, thirty-six, medical inspector. Beyond the immediate combat zone, the army's medical affairs were supervised by Surgeon Samuel H. Stout, forty-one, medical director of hospitals. A Tennessean, Stout was an 1848 graduate of the medical school of the University of Pennsylvania. Thereafter, he practiced medicine and farmed in Tennessee until 1861. He began his war service as surgeon of the Third Tennessee Infantry regiment, but his organizational ability soon led him into hospital administration at Nashville in late 1861. When the army retreated from Nashville, Stout was sent to organize hospitals in Chattanooga.

Bragg found him there in July and was profoundly impressed with Stout's work. By the end of 1862 Stout was supervising hospitals in six locations centered on Chattanooga. When Richmond formally separated general and field hospitals in the spring of 1863, Stout became Bragg's medical director of hospitals. Surgeon Lewis T. Pim became Stout's medical inspector in June.[24]

For a commander who considered discipline a cardinal tenet, Bragg's disciplinary staff was remarkably lean. His provost marshal general was Col. Alexander McKinstry, forty-one, of Alabama. An attorney, militia officer, and judge, in April 1862 he was commissioned colonel of the Thirty-Second Alabama Infantry regiment. By July he was absent on detached service, and two months later he took command of the troops left at Chattanooga during the Kentucky campaign. For the remainder of 1862 he served on court-martial duty, and in January 1863 he became Bragg's provost marshal general. As such, it was McKinstry's task to maintain order in the army's rear areas, preventing crime, protecting private property, and processing prisoners. He primarily relied upon Col. James Strawbridge's depleted First Louisiana (Regulars) Infantry regiment, although he occasionally called upon other units as well. Like his Federal counterparts, McKinstry dabbled in espionage, sending agents behind Federal lines to gain information. He also periodically executed disinformation campaigns by planting false stories in local newspapers. Further, he controlled and censored reports of civilian newspaper correspondents traveling with the army. During the summer of 1863, his primary assistants were Captains Charles W. Peden and William A. Reid. Peden had worked in the provost marshal's office since April 1862, at Chattanooga, Murfreesboro, and Tullahoma. Reid had been severely wounded at Shiloh and had been relegated to staff duty ever since. McKinstry worked closely with the army's judge advocate, Lt. Col. Harvey Washington Walter, forty-four. A native of Ohio but resident in Mississippi since 1838, Walter was an attorney, railroad promoter, and member of the Mississippi secession convention of 1861. Initially commissioned as an infantry lieutenant, by October 1861 he was Bragg's judge advocate at Pensacola. He remained with Bragg in that capacity for the next two years, rising to the rank of lieutenant colonel. He was devoted to Bragg personally.[25]

The Army of Tennessee had few technical staff departments to assist its commander. For example, there was no army-level signal corps detachment, no military telegraph superintendent, and no railroad manager. There was, however, a fairly robust engineer department. Bragg's chief engineer was Capt. Stephen Wilson Presstman, thirty-three, a native of Maryland. A civil engineer, Presstman was an infantry captain until seriously wounded in his first fight. In February 1862 he was appointed captain of engineers and three months later transferred to the Army of the Mississippi at Corinth. He served as a corps-level engineer until February 1863, when he became the army's chief engineer.

His primary assistant in early July was Lt. Andrew H. Buchanan, thirty-three, a former professor of mathematics at Cumberland University and a skilled cartographer. Other assistants were Lt. James K. P. McFall, twenty-four, and Lt. Henry C. Force, thirty-one, former enlisted men with railroad construction experience. The office also included Conrad Meister, a German draftsman, assistant engineer J. C. Wrenshall, and clerk George B. Blakemore. Supporting Presstman were other engineer officers at the corps level, as well as the engineers in the District of the Tennessee, based at Chattanooga. That office until June 1863 had been commanded by Maj. James Nocquet, thirty-eight, a native of France. Nocquet had been Bragg's chief engineer until late November 1862, when he had been demoted because of Bragg's dissatisfaction with his performance. Nocquet worked on fortifications and bridges in the Chattanooga area until June 1863, when he was relieved by Capt. John Morris Wampler and sent to the Department of East Tennessee. Wampler, thirty-three, was also a former chief engineer of the Army of Tennessee, but illness in January 1863 had forced him from the position. Wampler's assistant was Lt. James D. Thomas, twenty-eight, a railroad constructor and son of a Tennessee congressman. For heavy construction projects, the engineers could call upon the engineer companies of Capt. George B. Pickett and Capt. G. W. Maxson.[26]

The staff officers who supported Bragg, the Army of Tennessee, and Department No. 2 were diverse in their origin and age, but some patterns are apparent. First, Bragg favored individuals and units from Louisiana or from his early war experiences at Pensacola. Examples of the former are aides Urquhart and Ellis, the battalion-sized First Louisiana Infantry (Regulars) regiment that served as his headquarters and provost guard, as well as Capt. Guy Dreux's two-company cavalry escort. In terms of senior staff, the inspector general, quartermaster, ordnance, artillery, and judge advocate department chiefs had all been with Bragg more or less since his initial appointment on the Gulf coast. Not surprisingly, several of these men remained with Bragg when he moved to Richmond after his tenure with the Army of Tennessee and one, Hypolite Oladowski, was captured with him in Georgia at the end of the war. They, and others like Samuel Stout, remained loyal to Bragg even as newspapers, the public, many generals, and some elements of the government turned against him. Bragg's formal style, his irascible demeanor, his sparing use of praise, and his stern sense of duty, all of which caused casual acquaintances to recoil, seem not to have harmed either these men's working relationship with him or their personal affection for him. A second general characteristic of the staff was their initial lack of military education and experience. Exceptions were Chief of Staff Mackall, Chief of Artillery Hallonquist, and Chief of Ordnance Oladowski, the more common occupations being attorney, editor, and merchant. Still, the staff seems to have performed reasonably well, given the shortages, in numbers and matériel, that beset the Army of Tennessee, and Bragg's penchant for handling much of the administrative load himself. The primary source of that army's dysfunction lay not with the army staff but with its senior tactical commanders and their relationship with the commanding general.[27]

At the conclusion of the Tullahoma campaign in early July 1863, the organization of the Army of Tennessee remained generally the same as it had been in Middle Tennessee. The army's primary combat power was represented by two infantry corps, each consisting of two divisions. A cavalry corps and a separate cavalry division supported the foot soldiers, and artillery batteries were scattered throughout the command at the brigade level. A separate infantry brigade located at Chattanooga, an artillery reserve of five batteries, two companies of engineers, and Bragg's cavalry escort completed the Army of Tennessee. It numbered a total of 3,509 officers and 38,908 men present for duty in early July, with an aggregate present of 49,876 soldiers. The artillery fielded 116 guns. As commander of Department No. 2, Bragg also controlled a brigade of mounted troops in the District of Northern Alabama and a provost battalion in Atlanta. Altogether, Bragg's command numbered 3,628 officers and 40,622 men present for duty, with an aggregate present of 52,122 soldiers. Northeast of Department No. 2 and adjacent to it was Maj. Gen. Simon Buckner's Department of East Tennessee, a much smaller command, although it reached as far as the mountains of Virginia. Ever since Kirby Smith's time, the fate of Buckner's department had been intimately linked with Bragg's, usually as a source of manpower. Indeed, Buckner had brought several thousand reinforcements to participate in the latter stages of the Tullahoma campaign. In July, Buckner controlled five separate infantry brigades and two cavalry brigades. Those formations, augmented by a company of engineers and a small signal detachment, in July numbered 1,026 officers and 14,134 men present for duty, with an aggregate present of 17,814 soldiers. Buckner's artillery consisted of fifty-two guns in thirteen batteries.[28]

Bragg's largest infantry corps belonged to Lt. Gen. Leonidas Polk. Born into a wealthy family in Raleigh, North Carolina, on 10 April 1806, Polk entered West Point in 1823. Embroiled in two minor scandals in his third year, Polk in the spring of 1826 came under the influence of the academy's chaplain, Charles McIlvaine. Baptized by McIlvaine into the Episcopal faith, Polk became the chaplain's chief proselytizer thereafter. Upon graduating eighth in the class of 1827, Polk resigned his commission without spending a single day on active duty. After several years of adolescent wandering, Polk was ordained an Episcopal minister. In 1838 he was selected to be the missionary bishop of the Southwest and three years later became the bishop of Louisiana. The scion of a wealthy family and married into another, Polk thus spent most of the prewar period as an Episcopal bishop and planter, first in Tennessee and later in Louisiana. His record as a planter was mixed, but it permitted him to maintain an establishment of several hundred slaves and a comfortable lifestyle. In 1854, he sold his Louisiana holdings, bought a cotton plantation in Mississippi, and moved his family to New Orleans. Thereafter he attended more closely to his ecclesiastical duties, especially the promotion of an Episcopal institution of higher learning in his native region. That effort came to fruition with a ground-breaking ceremony in October 1860 for the University of the South on the Cumberland Plateau at Sewanee, Tennessee. An ardent defender of the Southern way of life, Polk followed Louisiana's secession by unilaterally severing the Diocese of Louisiana from the national denomination. A friend of Jefferson Davis from their time together at West Point, he offered his services to the Confederacy as a military officer in the spring of 1861. Refusing brigadier general's rank, he accepted a commission as a major general in June, thirty-four years after he had left the U.S. Army as a brevet second lieutenant.[29]

Having never commanded more than his family and his plantation workers or managed anything larger than a state association of clerics, Polk suddenly found himself in charge of Department No. 2, parts of five states centered on the Mississippi River with headquarters at Memphis. In September 1861, in a controversial act, he sent Confederate troops across the Tennessee border to Columbus, Kentucky, technically violating Kentucky's efforts to maintain neutrality. Not long thereafter, Gen. Sidney Johnston appeared with plenary authority in Polk's area and beyond. Polk reverted to district command, and when Johnston in November ordered 5,000 of Polk's troops to be transferred to the Cumberland River front, Polk offered his resignation to Jefferson Davis. While Davis considered his answer, Polk's command fought the minor action at Belmont, Missouri, and shortly thereafter he was seriously injured in an artillery accident, which kept him off duty until December. By that time, Davis had decided to retain Polk, and the bishop continued in Confederate service. In early 1862, he again offered his resignation upon learning that Gen. P. G. T. Beauregard was on his way to assume command in Polk's area. Again he was persuaded to remain in service, but the loss of Forts Henry and Donelson caused Beauregard to order the evacuation of Columbus, a move that Polk opposed. When Beauregard gathered his forces at Corinth, Polk first came into contact with Braxton Bragg, who had brought large reinforcements from Pensacola. Upon the arrival of his forces from Nashville, Johnston reorganized the combined commands into the Army of the Mississippi. As mentioned earlier, Bragg was made not only a corps commander like Polk but also chief of staff, a title that ensured he would have a larger say in the army's councils than the inexperienced bishop. At the battle of Shiloh, Polk finally saw major combat action but was chided by Beauregard for his dilatory approach march. Polk's command also fragmented badly during the battle, but he was not alone in that dereliction.[30]

Beauregard's subsequent removal from command placed Braxton Bragg in charge of the Army of the Mississippi, and Leonidas Polk as well. The relationship between the two men was strained from the beginning. Even before Shiloh, Bragg had complained about indiscipline in Polk's command, especially when compared with his own well-trained units from Pensacola. Bragg favored professional competency in the officer corps, and Polk's thirty-four-year break in service did not elevate him in Bragg's eyes. For his part, Polk found that an officer formerly junior in rank had been promoted above him. Not only that, Bragg now held the command Polk had held at the beginning of the war. Although the evidence is purely circumstantial, Polk may also have held a class bias against Bragg. Polk's mother, Sarah Hawkins, had come from the highest social circles in Warrenton, Bragg's birthplace, and was a near contemporary of Bragg's father, Thomas, who stood far lower in the Warren County hierarchy. Similarly, Polk's wife, Frances, was a member of the wealthy Devereux family, whose property lay in Halifax and Bertie Counties, adjacent to Warren. Although Bragg was eleven years younger than Polk, the Polk women could hardly have been unaware of Braxton Bragg's pedigree and no doubt made it known to the bishop. Thus Bragg's professional biases and Polk's sensibilities and worldview collaborated to make the relationship between the two men adversarial from the moment Bragg assumed command of the army. Just prior to the Kentucky campaign, Bragg attempted to remove Polk from line command by appointing him the army's deputy commander. Unfortunately, during the campaign political necessity separated Bragg from the bulk of the army, leaving Polk in charge. Long prone to substitute his judgment for that of his superiors, Polk on two key occasions violated both Bragg's intent and his direct instructions. After the campaign, Polk privately exploited his friendship with Davis to seek Bragg's removal and worked to turn most of the army's senior officers against him.[31]

The dysfunctional relationship stemming from the Kentucky campaign continued unabated after the Army of Tennessee suffered another setback at Stones River in late December 1862. For the next six months, Polk continued his public defense of his own and his friends' actions at Perryville and Stones River, while also pursuing his relentless private campaign to secure Bragg's departure. In such a poisonous atmosphere, the Army of Tennessee failed to hold Middle Tennessee in July 1863 against a stronger and more united foe. Knowing that he could not relieve Polk, Bragg saw no option but to work with him as best he could. Thus Leonidas Polk in July 1863 remained the Army of Tennessee's senior corps commander. A lieutenant general since 10 October 1862, Polk had changed little since his cadet days. Regal in bearing, physically imposing with graying hair and beard, at fifty-seven he looked the part of a senior officer. Gracious and indulgent to underlings who did not challenge his supremacy, he was beloved by his troops even though he wasted their lives through indecision and incompetence. Physically courageous, he was widely acclaimed for mistakenly riding into Federal lines at Perryville and bluffing his way out. Solicitous of his troops, he was also exceedingly self-indulgent, appropriating for himself and his staff the best of everything that his locality could provide. Hardly an intellectual, military or otherwise, Polk basked in the deference his religious title afforded him. Time was of little concern to him on the battlefield, and superiors' direct orders were often considered little more than suggestions. Polk would have been a difficult subordinate for any commander, and his sybaritic habits alone disqualified him in Bragg's eyes. Still, he commanded the largest corps in the Army of Tennessee. In early July that corps numbered 1,380 officers and 14,895 enlisted men present for duty, with an aggregate present of 18,426 soldiers and thirty-four artillery pieces.[32]

Maj. Gen. Benjamin Franklin Cheatham commanded one of the two divisions in Polk's Corps. Cheatham, forty-two, was born 20 October 1820 near Nashville. During the Mexican War he served with distinction as a company commander at the battle of Monterrey and ended the war as colonel of the Third Tennessee Infantry regiment. Beginning in 1849, he spent four years in the California goldfields, acquiring a reputation as a tough and often violent hotel keeper and minor politician. Upon returning to Tennessee, Cheatham spent the remaining prewar years as a planter, manufacturer's representative, and militia officer. A close friend of Governor Harris, on the outbreak of war he received a brigadier general's commission. He was assigned to Department No. 2 and became Polk's mainstay at Columbus. Promoted to major general in March 1862, he took a small division into the battle of Shiloh, where he displayed both bravery and lack of tactical skill. The indiscipline of his troops, and his penchant for strong drink, soon brought him into Bragg's disfavor. Cheatham's Division bore the brunt of the fighting at Perryville, losing heavily in uncoordinated assaults. At Stones River, he again performed poorly, arriving late and sending his brigades forward piecemeal. Worse, he was reliably reported to be very drunk early in the battle, by one account falling from his horse. Bragg noted Cheatham's behavior and ordered Polk to discipline him, unsuccessfully. Governor Harris claimed he could control Cheatham's behavior, causing Bragg to retain the Tennessean, who nevertheless loathed him. Short and stocky in stature and profane in language, Frank Cheatham was a fearless but exceedingly unskillful division commander. His rough persona, however, endeared "Old Frank" to most of the men in his division. In late summer the infantry component of his command numbered 652 officers and 6,121 enlisted men present for duty, with an aggregate present of 8,104 soldiers. Four artillery batteries added approximately 400 men to the divisional total.[33]

Cheatham's Division contained four brigades. George Maney, almost thirty-seven, was the senior brigadier. Born in Franklin, Tennessee, he was a veteran of the Mexican War and an attorney. In 1861 he led the First Tennessee Infantry regiment in western Virginia, then at Shiloh in April 1862. Promoted to brigadier general, Maney subsequently led a brigade in combat at Perryville and Stones River. Next in seniority was Preston Smith, thirty-nine. Born in Giles County, Tennessee, Smith was also an attorney. When Governor Harris mobilized the Tennessee militia in May 1861, Smith became colonel of the 154th Senior Tennessee Infantry regiment. Initially part of Polk's command at Columbus, he participated in the small action at Belmont in November 1861. He served as both regimental commander and temporary brigade commander at Shiloh, where he was wounded. During the Kentucky campaign he briefly gained division command at the battle of Richmond. Unengaged at Perryville, he was promoted to brigadier general in October 1862 but missed Stones River because of illness. Cheatham's third brigade commander was Brig. Gen. Marcus Wright, thirty-two. Born in Purdy, Tennessee, Wright by 1861 was a clerk of court in Memphis. Commissioned lieutenant colonel of Smith's 154th Senior Tennessee regiment, he fought at Shiloh, where he was wounded in the leg. Upon recovery, he served on Cheatham's staff at Perryville then commanded a conscript camp at McMinnville. Governor Harris campaigned tirelessly for his promotion to brigadier general, which came in December 1862, too late for participation at Stones River. Many brigade members were outraged at his assignment and never reconciled themselves to Wright, who was the weakest of Cheatham's brigadiers. Much more experienced was Col. Otho Strahl, commander of the fourth brigade. A native of Ohio, Strahl, thirty-two, moved to Somerville, Tennessee, in 1855 to study law. Admitted to the bar in 1858, he began practice in Dyersburg. Chosen lieutenant colonel of the Fourth Tennessee Infantry regiment in mid-1861, he saw no action until Shiloh. Elected colonel shortly thereafter, he led his regiment at Perryville, where three horses were shot from under him, and also at Stones River. Strahl's promotion to brigadier general arrived on 23 July 1863.[34]

Maj. Gen. Jones Mitchell Withers of Alabama commanded Polk's second division in early July although his tenure would end before the month closed. Withers, forty-nine, graduated from West Point in 1835, but served only six months before resigning to become a lawyer. Volunteer service in the Creek War and a return to the regular army during the Mexican War gave him considerable experience. Mayor of Mobile in 1861, he left that position to command the Third Alabama Infantry regiment but departed upon being commissioned brigadier general in July. By January 1862 he was back in Mobile, working on the city's defenses as part of Bragg's command. He participated in the move to Corinth and commanded a division in Bragg's corps at Shiloh. Promoted to major general in August, he began to suffer serious bouts of illness that kept him off duty for months at a time. He missed Perryville but led his division with bloody distinction at Stones River. Always favorably disposed toward Bragg, he defended him in the Mobile newspapers in January 1863. Yet the rigors of campaigning were too much for his constitution, and he submitted his resignation on 30 May 1863. Favorably endorsed by Polk, Withers's request reached Bragg in June, and the army commander dutifully forwarded it to Richmond. In the interim he searched for a way to retain Withers's services in some capacity. If Withers were to leave the Army of Tennessee, Bragg would lose one of his strongest and most respected supporters. Withers's Division in late summer consisted of 617 officers and 8,025 enlisted men present for duty, with an aggregate present of 9,921 soldiers in the infantry ranks. Four batteries added approximately 400 additional men and eighteen guns.[35]

Withers's Division also consisted of four brigades. Brig. Gen. Patton Anderson, forty-one, was the senior brigade commander. Born in Winchester, Tennessee, Anderson by 1861 had been a deputy sheriff and attorney in Mississippi, volunteer officer in the Mexican War, Washington Territory official, and Florida planter. Elected colonel of the First Florida Infantry regiment, he led it at Pensacola, where he attracted Bragg's attention. Promotion to brigadier general followed in February 1862. Anderson commanded a brigade at Shiloh and briefly led a division at Perryville, but he reverted to brigade command at Stones River. As senior brigadier, he commanded Withers's Division during its commander's many absences and viewed Bragg as Withers did. Withers's second brigade was commanded by Brig. Gen. Zachariah Deas, forty-three. Born into an aristocratic family in South Carolina and educated in France, Deas became a resident of Mobile in 1835 and amassed a fortune as a cotton broker. A staff officer at First Manassas, he raised the Twenty-Second Alabama Infantry regiment, outfitting it with his own money and becoming its colonel in October 1861. First sent to Mobile, Deas moved to Corinth and fought at Shiloh, sustaining multiple wounds. Upon recovery, he participated in the Kentucky campaign but missed Perryville. He was promoted to brigadier general in December 1862, too late to fight at Stones River. Brig. Gen. Edward Walthall, thirty-two, led Withers's third brigade. Born in Virginia, Walthall moved to Mississippi as a child. An attorney, he joined the Fifteenth Mississippi Infantry regiment in June 1861, rising to lieutenant colonel by the time the regiment fought at Mill Springs. Elected colonel of the Twenty-Ninth Mississippi Infantry regiment just after Shiloh, he participated in the Kentucky campaign but was not at Perryville. In November 1862 he gained brigade command and was promoted to brigadier general in December, but he missed Stones River because of illness. Withers's final brigade commander was Brig. Gen. Arthur Manigault, thirty-eight, of South Carolina. Born into a wealthy Charleston family, he served as a lieutenant during the Mexican War, suffering three wounds. After the war, he was a commission merchant, then a rice planter in Georgetown. Elected colonel of the Tenth South Carolina Infantry regiment, he joined the Army of the Mississippi at Corinth. Manigault saw little action until Stones River, where he gained temporary brigade command. Political intrigue in Richmond held him back until April 1863, when he finally became a brigadier general.[36]

Bragg's second infantry corps commander in early July 1863 was Lt. Gen. William Joseph Hardee, forty-seven. Born in rural Georgia in 1815, Hardee attended West Point, graduating twenty-sixth in the class of 1838, a year behind Bragg. Commissioned in the Second Dragoon regiment, he served in the Seminole War and spent two years at the Cavalry School in Saumur, France. Duty in Louisiana followed, as did promotion to captain. During the Mexican War he served with his regiment from Veracruz to Mexico City, receiving brevet promotions up to lieutenant colonel. Various frontier assignments in Texas followed until 1854, when Hardee was assigned to create a new tactics manual to address coming changes in infantry armament. *Rifle and Light Infantry Tactics* eventually made Hardee famous. After a return to the frontier for two years and promotion to major, Hardee became commandant of cadets at West Point in 1856. Promoted to lieutenant colonel in 1860, he resigned his commission in January 1861 to enter the service of his native state. Because of the manual that bore his name, his service on various boards, and his educational experience, Hardee possessed one of the strongest reputations among American military professionals in 1861. He was certainly well-known to Jefferson Davis. Appointed brigadier general in June 1861, Hardee was sent to train troops, first on the Alabama coast, then in Arkansas. In September he was ordered to Bowling Green, Kentucky, where a Confederate defense line was forming. Promoted to major general in October 1861, he thereafter was among the forces that coalesced at Corinth, first into the Army of the Mississippi and later the Army of Tennessee. Hardee's promotion to lieutenant general came in October 1862. He chose a poor subordinate to lead the attack at Stones River and followed Polk's lead in the disastrous Tullahoma campaign. His corps in early July numbered 1,214 officers and 13,413 enlisted men present for duty, with an aggregate present of 17,332 soldiers and thirty-two guns.[37]

Bragg and Hardee certainly knew each other at West Point in the 1830s. Their careers prior to 1861 were remarkably similar: Seminole War service, southwestern frontier duty, combat distinction in Mexico, tactical innovation. Their only known prewar clash occurred in a contentious court-martial arising from the 1846 Thornton Incident that precipitated the Mexican War. Both men struggled to bring order out of the chaos of Shiloh, with only limited success. Slightly younger than Hardee, Bragg nevertheless outranked him as brigadier and major general, and jumped far beyond him when Bragg was promoted to full general and command of the Army of the Mississippi. Unlike Polk, Hardee was the epitome of a professional army officer, in everything from education to bearing, qualities that mattered greatly to Bragg. Initially Bragg was favorably disposed toward Hardee, giving him the day-to-day control of the army prior to the Kentucky campaign. Yet, during that operation, when Bragg was absent at a critical time, Polk took charge of the army and gradually came to dominate Hardee in ways that went far beyond chain of command issues. By nature an extremely cautious officer, Hardee was happy to serve as a senior advisor without assuming any responsibility. Polk's commanding yet outgoing personality fitted well with the less dominant but equally convivial Hardee. Eventually Hardee came to agree with Polk on almost everything, including the bishop's contempt for Bragg. The army commander noted Hardee's hostile attitude by January 1863 but ascribed it simply to ambition. Although he loved command intrigue and gossip, Hardee was not as skillful as Polk and was occasionally caught expressing anti-Bragg views in writing that Polk avoided. While Polk utilized his private contacts in Richmond to undermine Bragg, Hardee influenced many junior officers in a similar direction, making his corps the more anti-Bragg of the two. By the end of the Tullahoma campaign, Hardee was even trying to assemble a cabal to overthrow Bragg as army commander.[38]

The man most influenced by Hardee was Maj. Gen. Patrick Ronayne Cleburne, thirty-five. Born in Ireland, Cleburne enlisted in the British Army after failing certification as a druggist. Enabled by an inheritance to purchase his discharge, he immigrated to America in 1849. He found work as a druggist's clerk, eventually in Helena, Arkansas. By 1852 he was part owner of a Helena pharmacy and three years later performed heroically during an outbreak of yellow fever. Studying law in his spare time, he became an attorney in 1856 and made political common cause with another Helena resident, Thomas Hindman. Together they won a street fight with political opponents, although Cleburne was so seriously wounded that it affected his health for the remainder of his life. Using his military expertise, Cleburne became a militia captain who participated in the seizure of the Little Rock Arsenal. Elected colonel of the Fifteenth Arkansas Infantry, he moved with Hardee to Bowling Green, where he took command of a brigade. In March 1862 he was promoted to brigadier general and led the brigade with distinction at Shiloh. He participated in the invasion of Kentucky as part of Kirby Smith's command. Leading a two-brigade division, he won the battle of Richmond but was shot in the mouth, losing several teeth. He was wounded in the leg while in action at Perryville but returned to duty quickly. Promoted to major general in December 1862, Cleburne commanded a division at Stones River and was largely responsible for Hardee's success there. Quiet, self-effacing, and courageous, yet eccentric enough to keep a pet raccoon on campaign, Cleburne rose above his precarious health to become one of the better division commanders in Bragg's army. A protégé of Hardee,

Cleburne stood firmly with his mentor and Polk in opposition to Bragg during the first half of 1863. In late summer, Cleburne's Division numbered 606 officers and 6,777 enlisted men present for duty, with an aggregate present of 8,880 infantry soldiers. The infantry was supported by 375 artillerymen organized in four batteries with sixteen guns.[39]

Four brigades comprised Cleburne's Division in July 1863. The senior brigadier was Sterling Wood, forty, of Florence, Alabama, an attorney, politician, and newspaper editor. He organized an infantry company in 1861 and took it to Pensacola, where it merged into the Seventh Alabama Infantry regiment with Wood as its colonel. In late 1861 the regiment moved to Bowling Green, where Wood was promoted to brigadier general and brigade command. Called before a court of inquiry because of questionable behavior at Shiloh, he retained command, was wounded slightly at Perryville and heavily engaged at Stones River. Although Hardee campaigned hard for his promotion, Wood remained a brigadier in July 1863. Next in seniority was Brig. Gen. Thomas Churchill, thirty-nine, of Kentucky. He joined the First Kentucky Mounted Riflemen at the outbreak of the Mexican War but was captured in early 1847. Released at war's end, he moved to Arkansas and became a planter. In 1861 he raised the First Arkansas Mounted Rifles and led it at Wilson's Creek and Pea Ridge. Promoted to brigadier general and given a brigade in March 1862, he fought at Richmond in the Kentucky campaign. Sent to the Trans-Mississippi Theater in December 1862, he surrendered Arkansas Post a month later. Upon release from captivity, he was again assigned to the Army of Tennessee but could not shake the stigma of the surrender. Third in seniority was Brig. Gen. St. John Liddell, forty-seven, of Louisiana. Liddell entered West Point with Hardee but was dismissed after one year. Thereafter, he operated a large plantation in Louisiana, where he became involved in several violent local feuds before 1861. Unable to obtain a command, he joined Hardee as a volunteer aide with colonel's rank. He finally gained brigade command at Corinth in May 1862 and was promoted to brigadier general in June. He led the brigade with distinction at Perryville, Stones River, and Liberty Gap. Although he and Hardee were close friends, Liddell was more open-minded about Bragg. Cleburne's final brigadier was Lucius Polk, thirty, Leonidas Polk's nephew. Born in North Carolina and raised in Tennessee, Polk became an Arkansas planter during the 1850s. Enlisting as a private in Cleburne's company, he advanced to lieutenant before Shiloh, where he was wounded in the face. Elected colonel of the Fifteenth Arkansas Infantry, he led the regiment at Richmond and Perryville, receiving additional wounds each time. Promoted to brigadier general in December 1862, Polk was heavily engaged at Stones River. Modest and utterly fearless, he was a favorite of Cleburne's.[40]

Hardee's other division commander, Maj. Gen. Alexander Peter Stewart, forty-one, was the army's newest major general. Born in Rogersville, Tennessee, Stewart graduated twelfth in the West Point class of 1842, seven numbers behind his roommate William Rosecrans. Assigned to the artillery, he served briefly at Ft. Macon, North Carolina, and then returned to West Point as assistant professor of mathematics. He resigned his commission in May 1845 to become a professor of mathematics at Cumberland University. For the next sixteen years he rotated between positions at Cumberland and Nashville University. In 1855 he served as the city surveyor of Nashville. An opponent of secession, in 1861 he nevertheless accepted a commission as major of artillery. Assigned to Polk's command at Columbus, he built and directed the batteries that blocked the Mississippi River. Promoted to brigadier general in November 1861, he was given a brigade and led it at Shiloh, where it lost heavily. After the retreat from Corinth, Stewart joined Cheatham's Division and participated in the Kentucky campaign. At Perryville, his regiments were committed piecemeal but still captured a battery. At Stones River, he maneuvered his command skillfully, illustrating his growing proficiency as a tactician. Stewart successfully avoided the unseemly backbiting among his superiors in the spring of 1863. When a new division was formed in early June, he took command as a major general. The Tullahoma campaign represented his first experience as a division commander. Scholarly in temperament and modest in demeanor, Stewart was unnaturally calm under fire. He conducted both his personal affairs and his unit's maneuvers with the precision befitting a mathematician. Perceiving these qualities, his men named him "Old Straight." In late summer 1863 his division consisted of 497 officers and 5,756 enlisted men, with an aggregate present of 7,729 infantry soldiers. Approximately 375 artillerymen organized in four batteries with sixteen guns supported the infantry.[41]

Like the army's other infantry divisions, Stewart's command consisted of four brigades. The senior brigadier general was Bushrod Johnson, forty-five. Born in Ohio, Johnson graduated from West Point in 1840. During the Mexican War, he fought in several battles but was ensnared in a commissary scandal of his own making and forced to resign in October 1847. Thereafter he taught at military schools in Kentucky and Tennessee. Long association with the South and inability to return to the U.S. Army caused him to join the Confederacy as a colonel of engineers in 1861. Appointed brigadier general in January 1862, he commanded a brigade at Shiloh, where he was wounded, Perryville, where he had five horses shot from under him, and Stones River, where he lost one-third of his command. Brig. Gen. John Brown, thirty-six, led Stewart's second brigade. A Tennessee lawyer and politician, Brown enlisted as a private in 1861 but was instantly chosen colonel of the Third Tennessee Infantry regiment. He led a brigade at Fort Donelson, where he was captured. Exchanged in August 1862, he was promoted to brigadier general in September and commanded a brigade at Perryville, where he was seriously wounded in the right thigh. He was unable to return to duty until January 1863, thereby missing Stones River. Stewart's third brigade was led by Brig. Gen. William Bate, thirty-seven, also from Tennessee. A steamboat clerk, Bate joined a volunteer regiment during the Mexican War, rising to the rank of lieutenant. After the war, he was a newspaper editor, politician, and attorney. He began the Civil War as a private but soon became the colonel of the Second Tennessee Infantry regiment. At Shiloh, he was seriously wounded in the left leg. He was appointed brigadier general in October 1862 and held rear echelon commands for the remainder of the year. Needing crutches to walk, Bate nevertheless gained brigade command in March 1863. The final brigade commander was Brig. Gen. Henry Clayton, thirty-six, of Georgia. Raised in Alabama and educated in Virginia, Clayton was an attorney, politician, and militia officer. He served for one year as colonel of the First Alabama Infantry regiment at Pensacola and in May 1862 raised the Thirty-Ninth Alabama Infantry regiment. Unengaged at Perryville, he was in the thick of the fight at Stones River, where he was wounded in the right shoulder. Upon recovery in April 1863, he was promoted to brigadier general and received command of a brigade.[42]

Maj. Gen. Joseph Wheeler, twenty-six, commanded the Cavalry Corps. A Georgian, Wheeler was a West Point graduate, standing near the bottom of the class of 1859. He spent a year at the Cavalry School for Practice in Pennsylvania and briefly served in New Mexico Territory, then resigned in April 1861. Commissioned as a Confederate artilleryman, he was sent to Pensacola, where he first impressed Bragg. In September he became colonel of the Nineteenth Alabama Infantry regiment and in early 1862 led it at Shiloh. When Bragg assumed command, he gave Wheeler a cavalry brigade. After a successful raid into western Tennessee, Wheeler joined the invasion of Kentucky, participating in the battle of Perryville. Those activities brought him promotion to brigadier general in late October 1862 and command of the army's mounted force. At Stones River Wheeler's cavalry rampaged in the Federal rear, and two weeks later he mounted a successful raid against river traffic at Harpeth Shoals. Those victories brought him promotion to major general in January 1863, but his attack on the Federal garrison at Dover in February was an abject failure. As a result, another cavalry commander, Nathan Bedford Forrest, refused to serve under Wheeler's command again. At the start of the Tullahoma campaign, Wheeler's lapses of judgment denied Bragg critical information at Hoover's Gap, and he barely escaped capture at Shelbyville. Known as "Little Joe" because of his diminutive stature, or the "War Child" because of his youth, Wheeler by July 1863 had learned how to conduct raids and rearguard actions but not how to maintain discipline or support army objectives. Still, he stood high in Bragg's estimation, an opinion he assiduously cultivated. His Cavalry Corps nominally consisted of three divisions, but John Hunt Morgan's command was absent on a disastrous raid north of the Ohio River. Thus Wheeler reported his strength on 10 July as 438 officers and 4,779 enlisted men present for duty, with an aggregate present of 6,254 soldiers and eight guns.[43]

Wheeler's first division was led by Brig. Gen. John Austin Wharton, thirty-five. A Tennessee native but a Texas resident since childhood, Wharton was an attorney. A member of the Texas secession convention, he was elected captain of a company in the Eighth Texas Cavalry regiment. Commissioned colonel of the regiment just before Shiloh, Wharton led it there with distinction, receiving a serious leg wound. Wounded again in a July 1862 skirmish, he participated in the Kentucky campaign and was promoted to brigadier general in November. He performed well at Stones River and gained division command in January 1863. In the disastrous attack at Dover in February 1863, he was wounded again. Seriously injured in May when his horse drove him into a tree, he recovered by July. Having worked for both Wheeler and Forrest, Wharton much preferred the Tennessean and had an adversarial relationship with "Little Joe." Hot-blooded and impetuous, he was a troublesome subordinate for a young officer accustomed to regular army ways. Col. Charles Crews, thirty-four, commanded Wharton's first brigade. A native Georgian, Crews was a physician. Serving first in the Georgia state forces, he was elected captain in the Second Georgia Cavalry regiment in May 1862. Captured during the Kentucky campaign, he was quickly exchanged and promoted to command the regiment in November. Missing Stones River, he was severely wounded in the hip at Dover in February 1863. He was back in command by the time of the Tullahoma campaign in June. Leading Wharton's second brigade was Col. Thomas Harrison, forty, of Alabama. Harrison was an attorney and Mexican War veteran who dabbled in Texas politics. In 1861 he joined the Eighth Texas Cavalry regiment as its major. In action at Shiloh, Harrison briefly commanded the regiment upon Wharton's wounding. He served with it during the Kentucky campaign and attained regimental command again when Wharton was promoted in November 1862. Slightly wounded at Stones River, he gained brigade command in April 1863. Called "Old Ironsides" by his men because of his charmed life in battle, he was also known for an irascible personality, iron discipline, and an unseemly fondness for alcohol, especially just before battle.[44]

Brig. Gen. William Thompson Martin, forty, commanded Wheeler's second division. A Kentuckian, Martin migrated to Mississippi and became a lawyer and district attorney. In 1861 he raised a cavalry company and took it to Virginia. Promoted to lieutenant colonel, Martin participated in the celebrated ride around the Army of the Potomac during the Peninsula campaign. Elevation to colonel soon followed, and Martin shared the fortunes of the Army of Northern Virginia through the Maryland campaign of September 1862. Selected brigadier general in December, he returned to Mississippi to join Earl Van Dorn as a division commander. When Van Dorn's command moved to Tennessee in early 1863, Martin accompanied it. He retained the division in Wheeler's Cavalry Corps, where it was hoped he would elevate the professionalism of the more rustic western horsemen. His first brigade was led by Col. James Hagan, forty-one, a native of Ireland but a U.S. resident since childhood. Growing up in Pennsylvania, Hagan moved to Alabama in 1837. During the Mexican War he served in a Texas unit at Monterrey and then joined the Third U.S. Dragoons as a captain. Thereafter, he was a planter and Alabama militiaman until 1861. Initially commanding an Alabama cavalry company, he was commissioned major in a Mississippi cavalry regiment and finally was elected colonel of the Third Alabama Cavalry regiment after Shiloh. As such he participated in the Kentucky campaign and small actions near Nashville, in one of which he received a leg wound. Gaining brigade command in early 1863, he was recommended by Wheeler in May for promotion to brigadier general. The promotion was quashed by Bragg because Hagan had become "very dissipated" and "totally unfit for command." Still, he retained his brigade in July 1863. Martin's second brigade was led by Col. Alfred Russell, thirty-six, of Alabama. After service in the Alabama militia during the Mexican War, Russell became a physician in Stevenson, Alabama. In 1861 he joined the Seventh Alabama Infantry regiment as its major and was elected lieutenant colonel of a Tennessee cavalry battalion that became part of the Fourth Alabama Cavalry regiment. Promoted to colonel in November 1862, he served under Nathan Bedford Forrest until the cavalry reorganization in early 1863 placed him in Wheeler's corps. He attained brigade command in May. Russell was considered "temperate" and a "strict disciplinarian" by his division commander.[45]

Bragg's separate cavalry division was led by Brig. Gen. Nathan Bedford Forrest, forty-two. A native Tennessean, Forrest lacked formal education. Nevertheless, he amassed considerable wealth as a Memphis slave trader, property developer, and alderman, then became a Mississippi planter. In 1861 he recruited a battalion of irregular cavalry and outfitted it himself. As a lieutenant colonel he led the battalion in western Kentucky, then to Fort Donelson. Refusing to join the garrison in surrender, he escaped through Federal lines with most of his command. New recruits facilitated creation of the Third Tennessee Cavalry regiment, which Forrest led at Shiloh as its colonel. During the summer of 1862 he gained brigade command, a stunning victory at Murfreesboro, and promotion to brigadier general in July. Injured at Munfordville in the Kentucky campaign, he returned to Tennessee in September. There he recruited a new brigade, leading it with spectacular success in western Tennessee in December 1862. Always best in independent command, Forrest in 1863 chafed under more conventional superiors. At Dover in February he clashed with Wheeler and refused to serve under that officer again. Placed under Earl Van Dorn in March, he soon engaged the Mississippian in an altercation over spoils after a fight at Thompson's Station. Sent by Bragg to apprehend the Federal raider Col. Abel Straight, Forrest again succeeded against all odds. Van Dorn's death in May forced Bragg to retain Forrest's command as a separate entity because of Forrest's antipathy toward Wheeler. A self-made man like Forrest had no patience for the pretensions of a West Pointer little more than half his age. Often wounded, most recently in June, Forrest persevered through every difficulty because of his indomitable will. Though his lack of schooling and mercurial personality hindered his relationship with the army commander, Bragg could hardly argue with Forrest's success.[46]

In early July 1863, Forrest led a two-brigade division consisting of 293 officers and 3,500 enlisted men, with an aggregate present of 4,720 soldiers and twelve artillery pieces. The first brigade commander was Brig. Gen. Francis Armstrong, twenty-seven. Born in the Indian Territory, Armstrong campaigned in the Southwest with his stepfather as a teenager. Commissioned a lieutenant in the Second U.S. Dragoons in 1855, he continued to serve in the Southwest and was promoted to captain in June 1861. He commanded his company at First Manassas and then resigned to join the Confederacy. As a volunteer aide, he assisted Ben McCulloch at Wilson's Creek in 1861 and James McIntosh at Pea Ridge in March 1862. Upon McIntosh's death, he joined Earl Van Dorn, who facilitated his commission as colonel of the Third Louisiana Infantry regiment in May. Two months later, he became an acting brigadier general and Sterling Price's chief of cavalry. As such he participated in the battles of Iuka and Corinth. Given a brigade, he moved to Tennessee in the spring of 1863, where he fought in several actions and was promoted to brigadier general in April. Upon Van Dorn's death, Armstrong's command became part of Forrest's division. Forrest's other brigade commander was Col. George Dibrell, forty-one. Born in Sparta, Tennessee, Dibrell was a farmer, merchant, and delegate to the Tennessee secession convention. When his native state left the Union, Dibrell was elected lieutenant colonel of the Twenty-Fifth Tennessee Infantry regiment. He participated in the fight at Mill Springs and briefly during operations around Corinth. Failing to retain his position when the regiment reorganized, Dibrell recruited a cavalry regiment, the Eighth (Thirteenth) Tennessee, from his home neighborhood. In October 1862 it became part of Forrest's command and saw much action in the West Tennessee Raid of December and in multiple fights in the spring of 1863. Although he had occasionally commanded at the brigade level, Dibrell only gained permanent brigade command in early July, during the Tullahoma campaign.[47]

An additional unit that added firepower to the major combat formations of the Army of Tennessee was the Artillery Reserve. Originally formed in the fall of 1862 but allowed to disintegrate, it was reconstituted in February 1863 in an effort to mass fires more efficiently. Initially placed under Capt. (later Maj.) Felix Robertson, in July it consisted of five batteries and the battalion-sized First Louisiana (Regulars) Infantry regiment. The latter formation not only protected the artillery but also doubled as the muscle for the army's provost marshal. When Col. James Deshler arrived in late June, he replaced the unpopular Robertson. An Alabama native, Deshler, thirty, was an 1854 graduate of West Point, ranking seventh in his class. Commissioned in the Third Artillery regiment, after a year he transferred to the Tenth Infantry regiment and spent the next six years on the frontier, participating in the battle of Blue Water and the Utah Expedition. Rising to first lieutenant in 1858, he abandoned his commission three years later and joined the Confederacy as a captain of artillery. Seriously wounded in western Virginia in October 1861, he was promoted to colonel of artillery and in early 1862 joined the staff of Maj. Gen. Theophilus Holmes. He was Holmes's chief of artillery during the Seven Days battles in Virginia, and was present at the battle of Malvern Hill. Following Holmes to the Trans-Mississippi Department in the fall of 1862, Deshler was given a brigade and sent to Arkansas Post. Surrendered with the garrison in January 1863, he was exchanged in June and assigned to the Army of Tennessee. Needing a Reserve Artillery chief with more rank and tact than Felix Robertson, Bragg gave Deshler the position. In early July his command numbered 40 officers and 655 enlisted men present for duty, with an aggregate present of 783 soldiers and twenty-two guns.[48]

Three other commands augmented Bragg's army in July 1863. First was Brig. Gen. John Jackson's separate infantry brigade. Born in Augusta, Georgia, Jackson, thirty-five, had been an attorney since 1848. Thereafter he practiced law and served in the militia until 1861. Elected colonel of the Fifth Georgia Infantry regiment, he joined Bragg's command at Pensacola. Impressed by the Georgian, Bragg sought Jackson's promotion to brigadier general, which occurred in January 1862. He led a brigade at Shiloh and in the Kentucky campaign. Sent to garrison Bridgeport, Alabama, Jackson's command was summoned in December to join the fight at Stones River, where it suffered heavily. In early January 1863 Jackson was placed in charge of the District of the Tennessee, with headquarters at Chattanooga. His command in early July numbered 111 officers and 1,400 enlisted men present for duty, with an aggregate present of 2,053 soldiers and six guns. The District of Northern Alabama, commanded by Col. Philip Roddey, also reported to Bragg. An Alabamian who was a tailor, sheriff, and steamboat captain before the war, Roddey initially formed a local defense company and scouted along the Tennessee River until October 1862. Promoted to colonel, he raised and commanded the Fourth (Roddey's) Alabama Cavalry regiment. Thereafter, his command was reinforced to brigade strength and moved with Van Dorn's cavalry to Middle Tennessee in the spring of 1863. In late March Roddey returned to northern Alabama, where his brigade guarded the Tennessee River valley from Federal incursions. In early July his command consisted of 110 officers and 1,635 enlisted men, with an aggregate present of 2,042 soldiers and four guns. Finally, because the city of Atlanta had become part of his command, Bragg was responsible for the city's provost battalion. Commanded by Maj. George Lee, thirty-four, the battalion in early July numbered nine officers and seventy-nine enlisted men present for duty, with an aggregate present of 204 soldiers. At Pensacola in 1861 Bragg forced Lee's resignation for theft. Subsequently, Lee became colonel of the Thirty-Eighth Georgia Infantry regiment, but he again resigned after only brief service. Leveraging influential political connections, he became provost marshal and post commandant of Atlanta in July 1862. Bragg attempted to remove Lee, a man "without education or character," in March 1863 but without success.[49]

. . . .

The Army of Tennessee that crossed to the south bank of its namesake river in early July 1863 was a veteran formation. Led by a professional soldier seasoned by experience in three major battles and numerous smaller ones, supported by an adequate staff, sufficiently armed to hold its own against a more powerful foe, and populated by the best young men the region could offer, the army was a remarkably resilient organization. At Shiloh, Perryville, Stones River, and places in between, it had fought with tremendous ardor and some skill, rocking its opponents back on their heels and often winning the field before withdrawing from the contest. In general terms, no fault could be attached to its common soldiers, men who endured greater physical hardships and received less support than perhaps any other major Confederate army. Of Bragg's 135 regiments, battalions, and batteries, Tennessee furnished forty-five, followed by Alabama with thirty-one, Mississippi with nineteen, Georgia with thirteen, and Arkansas with eleven. Five units from Texas, five designated as Confederate, two each from Louisiana and Kentucky, and one each from South Carolina and Missouri completed the total. By branch, the army consisted of eighty infantry units, twenty-seven cavalry formations, and twenty-eight artillery batteries. Virtually all were battle-hardened organizations, and most were led by experienced officers. Similarly, most brigade and division commanders were equal to their responsibilities, although division commander Cheatham and several brigade commanders were shaky. Compared to that of its opponent, the army's armament was decidedly inferior, with 40 percent of the infantry weapons being smoothbores and 60 percent of the artillery consisting of inadequate six-pounder and twelve-pounder howitzer smoothbores.[50]

In truth, the source of the Army of Tennessee's failure lay in neither its numbers nor its obsolescent weaponry. Instead, the army's lack of success could be ascribed primarily to the utter indiscipline of the army's principal subordinate commanders. For good or ill, the Confederate government had placed the Army of Tennessee in the hands of Braxton Bragg, but neither Leonidas Polk nor William Hardee could accept that fact and willingly support the army commander. Beginning with the ill-starred Kentucky campaign, each corps commander in his own way assiduously worked to undermine his chief and his plans. Worse, they turned their junior officers against Bragg at every opportunity. Bragg's personality hindered any effort to conciliate his recalcitrant subordinates, but even a more collegial individual would have been unlikely to have brought Polk and Hardee into line without being able to threaten their removal. Thus Polk could disregard Bragg's direct orders at Perryville, Hardee could select an incompetent officer to lead the assault at Stones River, and both could contemplate mutiny at Elk River. Unless that glaring fault was rectified, the Army of Tennessee would continue to risk a catastrophic failure in the campaign soon to begin.

4

Bragg

» JULY 1863 «

Dawn on 5 July 1863 found the Army of Tennessee in a precarious position astride the wide Tennessee River. Polk's Corps was safely on the east bank, having crossed the river on the pontoon bridge located just upstream from the mouth of Battle Creek. In the lead, Withers's Division lay at Shell Mound Station on the Nashville & Chattanooga Railroad adjacent to the river. Polk himself camped with Withers. Four miles behind Withers, Cheatham's Division rested only a short distance south of the pontoon bridge. The bridge itself was unguarded, except for Capt. George Pickett's engineers who had built it, because Polk considered it of no further value. The army's other infantry corps, Hardee's, was still west of the river, preparing to march upstream into the Grand Canyon of the Tennessee toward another pontoon bridge at Kelly's Ferry. Elements of Cleburne's Division led Hardee's column, followed by Stewart's Division. Covering Hardee's rear was Forrest's Cavalry Division. Wheeler's Cavalry Corps, supporting Polk, was scattered from the valley of Battle Creek downstream to Bridgeport. At Bridgeport itself, Simon Buckner and two brigades from his Department of East Tennessee awaited railroad transportation back to Knoxville. Also at Bridgeport were Braxton Bragg and his staff, attempting with limited success to coordinate the army's retreat.[1]

Bragg's problems began early, with his usual nemesis Polk. On the previous day, Bragg had directed Polk to leave a brigade west of the river to safeguard the pontoon bridge, but Polk had not done so and now at 5:00 A.M. claimed that the order arrived too late. At 7:30 A.M. Polk directed Withers to march eastward to Whiteside Station, on the railroad five miles nearer Chattanooga. He did not tell Bragg what he had done until two hours later, then raised a litany of problems: Withers needed rations; Withers had dismounted his cannon and ammunition chests from their carriages, and had unloaded his ordnance wagons; Withers had 1,200 sick men unable to continue the march into the mountains. To Polk's mind, all of these problems required locomotives and rolling stock from the already overburdened railroad. Exasperated by Polk's attitude, Bragg responded that Chief of Staff William Mackall had sent rations to the pontoon bridge by steamer on the previous day, but Polk had made no use of them. Now Bragg ordered Polk's Corps to march to Chattanooga, reluctantly agreeing to provide rations for Withers's Division and guard the ordnance Withers had abandoned at Shell Mound. Behind Withers, Cheatham's Division advanced only to Shell Mound, thereby protecting Withers's matériel. Cheatham then ordered his own batteries to dismount their guns and ammunition chests for railroad transport as Withers had done. Late in the day, Polk ordered Cheatham not to dismount his guns, but the order came too late for at least one battery, which already had begun the laborious process. In a 5:00 P.M. message to Bragg, Polk calmly apologized for the misunderstanding about the rations, ascribed the dismounting of the artillery to Withers, and blamed Hardee and Wheeler for the unguarded pontoon bridge. When Cheatham indicated that he needed to halt so that his men could cook rations, Polk acquiesced, permitting Cheatham to remain at Shell Mound for the night.[2]

Elsewhere, the retrograde movement proceeded more smoothly. Hardee's Corps made good progress toward Kelly's Ferry. In the lead, Lucius Polk's Brigade found a 300-yard pontoon bridge constructed by Capt. Morris Wampler's engineer detachment. Polk's regiments crossed during the afternoon, following the corps trains, and the remaining seven brigades camped along the road stretching back to the village of Jasper. At Bridgeport, Simon Buckner and the brigades of Archibald Gracie and Robert Trigg boarded trains for Chattanooga and ultimately Knoxville. Wheeler's command also gathered at Bridgeport to cross the two massive bridges that carried the Nashville & Chattanooga Railroad over the Tennessee River. The first bridge, 1,232 feet in length, used nine truss spans and eight stone piers to reach from the west bank of the river to Long Island. Beyond the island, a 428-foot bridge with a swinging draw vaulted the railroad over the main channel of the Tennessee. Planks had been laid on the bridges to facilitate horse and foot travel but there were no guard rails to prevent a forty-foot plunge into the water, requiring the cavalrymen to walk their animals gingerly across the two structures. At dark, when the last elements of Wheeler's command were safely across the river, men from Jackson's Brigade set fire to Bridgeport's public buildings and torched the westernmost two spans of the railroad bridge, dropping them into the river. According to a correspondent of the *Macon Telegraph*, it was "a grand pyrotechnical display," but a costly loss. Alex Morgan, a surgeon with the First Confederate Infantry regiment, was equally appalled: "We crossed just at dark with the town in a blaze + then set fire to the magnificent R. R. Bridge. It reminded me of the night we left Corinth. I did hate to see the fine bridge burnt. . . . It was new + had cost so much labour + money." When the remainder of the army resumed its eastward movement on the next day, Jackson established picket posts on Long Island to await the expected Federal approach.[3]

On 6 July, Withers's Division of Polk's Corps resumed its march toward Chattanooga. Leaving the river, the route followed the railroad through a narrow passage cut by Running Water Creek between Raccoon and Sand Mountains. After a few miles, the Running Water Creek defile opened into the much larger Lookout Valley and faced the massive bulk of Lookout Mountain. Turning north and continuing to follow the railroad, Withers's men passed through Wauhatchie Station and crossed Lookout Creek. Climbing over the lowest elevations of the northern tip of Lookout Mountain, they entered the valley of Chattanooga Creek and halted near the town of Chattanooga. By dark all of Withers's regiments were in camp. Behind them, the soldiers of Cheatham's Division waited at Shell Mound for trains to carry Withers's artillery tubes and ammunition to Chattanooga. Given the necessity of using railroad transportation for Withers's guns, Polk's order to Cheatham forbidding further dismounting of cannon was canceled and Cheatham's artillerymen once more separated their guns, chests, and carriages. When the train arrived, the guns, ammunition, and most of the crews loaded and by 2:00 P.M. were on their way to Chattanooga in style. At one point the weight was too great for the toiling engine, but by dividing the train and moving half the cars up the grade at a time, the trainmen completed the journey before dark. The artillery limbers, carriages, and teams meanwhile made their way to Chattanooga by road. Most of Cheatham's infantrymen advanced no farther than Whiteside Station and camped for the night, but at least one regiment, the Fifty-First Tennessee Infantry, caught a ride on a passing train and rode into Chattanooga well ahead of its less fortunate peers.[4]

Meanwhile, Hardee's Corps still had to negotiate Captain Wampler's pontoon bridge over the Tennessee River at Kelly's Ferry. The rain, which had plagued the army for several weeks, continued to fall, making the planks slippery, but, unit by unit, Hardee's men reached the eastern bank of the river successfully. There had been much straggling on the march, and many soldiers had become separated from their parent commands. Some had simply become exhausted and fallen out of line, while others of a more enterprising nature had separated from the column to forage for better food than the army's commissaries could provide. The pontoon bridge thus represented a choke point where soldiers moving independently could be held until their units crossed, and a provost guard stood at the bridge's western approach to enforce the edict. When Lt. Robert Collins, who had been permitted to travel independently because of illness, approached the bridge, he found himself forbidden to cross until his regiment, the Fifteenth Texas Cavalry (Dismounted), arrived. While waiting, Collins witnessed an altercation between corps commander Hardee and another straggler. When private and general fell struggling into the river, the guards were so distracted that Collins crossed the bridge without notice. Eventually Hardee's two divisions completed their crossing and continued forward five miles to Wauhatchie Station on the railroad, where they bivouacked for the night. Wet, weary, and depressed, Hardee relinquished command to Patrick Cleburne and departed for Chattanooga with his staff.[5]

While the infantry made its way slowly toward Chattanooga, Wheeler's Cavalry Corps set a slightly different course. After crossing the Tennessee River on the Bridgeport railroad bridge, Wheeler's two divisions turned east and toiled up Sand Mountain. The top of the mountain was a wide plateau, stretching more than eight miles before the abrupt descent into Lookout Valley. Wheeler's immediate goal was the town of Trenton, nestled in the narrow Lookout Valley just under twenty miles from Chattanooga. The Tullahoma campaign had been hard on Wheeler's command. He desperately needed to rest his men and horses and, if possible, recruit their strength by an extended period of inaction. Yet there would certainly be a requirement to guard the river line and provide early warning of any further Federal advance. Trenton therefore represented a momentarily quiet location not too far from the Tennessee River where the cavalry could pause and rest while the army commander pondered his next move. Thus Wheeler's Cavalry Corps made its way southeast across the broad Sand Mountain plateau on 6 July and halted for the night several miles from the small village that served as the governmental seat of Dade County, Georgia.[6]

On 7 July the Army of Tennessee began to consolidate around Chattanooga, a city of approximately 2,500 people before the war. Bragg established army headquarters at the commodious house of Reese Bowen Brabson, several blocks east of the city center and a similar distance south of the river. Withers's Division of Polk's Corps, having completed its concentration at Chattanooga, established its camps in Chattanooga Valley just south of the city. Cheatham's Division also entered Chattanooga Valley and bivouacked near the city as well. Polk's artillerymen gathered their guns and ammunition from the railroad depot and united them with their carriages and limbers. Hardee's Corps, temporarily under Cleburne's command, remained in its temporary camps around Wauhatchie Station in Lookout Valley on 7 July but during the next few days gradually moved to more permanent cantonments around Tyner's Station on the Chattanooga branch of the East Tennessee & Georgia Railroad. Most of the regiments moved by rail, a pleasant change from the long, arduous, and rainy marches in Tennessee. Tyner's Station itself lay ten railroad miles east of Chattanooga. Momentarily, Wheeler's two cavalry divisions remained near

Trenton, Georgia, while Forrest's Cavalry Division rested in the Chattanooga area.[7]

The peculiar geography of the territory between Bragg's position at Chattanooga and the Federal positions in Middle Tennessee offered many aspects to be considered as Bragg pondered his next move. By withdrawing to Chattanooga Bragg had placed several obstacles between himself and the Federals. From west to east, the first barrier was the wide Cumberland Plateau, a wild desolate region of mountains, forests, rushing streams, and deep canyons. Sparsely populated, the region was generally known as "the barrens." Oriented from southwest to northeast, the plateau was no less than twenty miles across at its most likely crossing point. Few roads traversed it and they were little more than rocky tracks through the forest, damaging travelers' conveyances at every step. Neither an invading army nor a friendly one could sustain itself in the area from local resources alone. The plateau had been penetrated by the Nashville & Chattanooga Railroad in 1852, when a 2,228-foot tunnel was driven from near Cowan, Tennessee, on the west side to the eastern portal in the valley of Crow Creek. Even with the tunnel, the railroad was plagued by steep grades on the tunnel's approaches, limiting tonnage capacity. Still, the railroad made it possible to surmount the Cumberland Plateau. East of the plateau lay the valley of the Tennessee River. Unbridged at Chattanooga and seldom less than 1,000 feet wide, the Tennessee presented another serious obstacle to the passage of an invading army. The Nashville & Chattanooga Railroad had conquered the river by completing the spans at Bridgeport in 1854. One of those bridges now lay partially in ruins, and Chattanooga would see no more trains from Nashville until the span was rebuilt. These two obstacles, the Cumberland Plateau and the Tennessee River, would assist any defense Bragg might make if the Federals chose to continue their advance toward Chattanooga. They could be surmounted—the railroad had proved that—but the cost would be great in both effort and time.[8]

Several other geographical features had to be factored into Bragg's calculations. The Cumberland Plateau was only the most westerly of a series of mountain ridges, all following generally the same southwest-northeast orientation. Each of these ridges stretched for more than 100 miles on either side of Chattanooga. Complicating any defensive scheme was the Tennessee River, which at Chattanooga cut through all the ridges except the Cumberland Plateau on its generally southwesterly course. The largest of these ridges, but not the tallest, was the ridge next east of the Cumberland Plateau. South of the Tennessee the ridge was called Sand Mountain, with its northern extension known as Raccoon Mountain; north of the river it was called Walden's Ridge. In a series of sinuous curves, the Tennessee River breached the ridge complex, creating a deep and narrow canyon. Studded with rocks in the canyon, the river in seasons of low water represented a challenge to steamboat navigation but not an insurmountable problem. Shortly before entering its canyon, the river curled around the tallest of the mountain ridges, Lookout Mountain, which rose 2,400 feet in elevation above sea level and towered more than 1,000 feet above the valley floor. Both Lookout Mountain and the Sand/Raccoon Mountain ridge separated Chattanooga from the Tennessee River downstream from the city, and few roads crossed the two mountains in an east-west direction. Forces defending the river line southwest of Chattanooga would have difficulty communicating with the city and even greater difficulty being reinforced from it. Northeast of the city, the defensive problem was less difficult to solve. There the defensive barriers were the Cumberland Plateau, Walden's Ridge, and the Tennessee River. Northeast of Chattanooga, the Tennessee's broad valley stretched all the way to Knoxville.[9]

Although shielded by the mountain ranges and the river, an army defending Chattanooga could not sustain itself without secure lines of communication linking it to the remainder of the Confederacy. In 1863 those lines were represented by the three railroads that entered the city. Formerly important, the Nashville & Chattanooga Railroad now was in Confederate hands only to Long Island across from Bridgeport. Much more important was the East Tennessee & Georgia Railroad, which ran from Knoxville, Tennessee, 110 miles to Dalton, Georgia. This line connected to Chattanooga via a thirty-mile branch from the main stem at Cleveland, Tennessee. At Knoxville, the East Tennessee & Georgia met the East Tennessee & Virginia Railroad, which ran 130 miles to Bristol, Virginia, and connected with the railroads of the latter state. Thus the East Tennessee & Georgia Railroad not only permitted communication with the Confederacy's Eastern Theater but also traversed the Department of East Tennessee, a potential source of reinforcements. In addition, it transported 90 percent of the Confederacy's copper ore from mines around Ducktown, Tennessee, ore that was critical in the production of percussion caps and other ordnance. Nevertheless, the East Tennessee & Georgia Railroad was not Bragg's most critical railroad. That honor went to the Western & Atlantic Railroad, which ran from Chattanooga 138 miles south to Atlanta, the army's logistical base. Completed by the state of Georgia in 1850, this railroad carried rations, equipment, and ordnance from Atlanta's warehouses, mills, foundries, and arsenal northward to support Bragg. Although the terrain crossed by the Western & Atlantic was not quite as severe as that facing the Nashville & Chattanooga, the route included many significant bridges and a 1,447-foot tunnel west of Dalton. Bragg found the East Tennessee & Georgia Railroad very useful; he could not remain in Chattanooga if he lost the Western & Atlantic Railroad. All of the railroads shared a common five-foot gauge, facilitating interchange.[10]

Bragg moved quickly to posture his army for defense. On 7 July he issued assignments for protecting the army's flanks. From Kelly's Ferry southward, Wheeler's Cavalry Corps was to guard the river line, while Forrest's Division was given the same task above Chattanooga. Both officers were instructed to arrest any deserters attempting to cross the river. Closer to the city, the responsibility for guarding the river, keeping order in the town, and protecting nearby railroad bridges was assigned to John Jackson, commander of the District of the Tennessee. Now that the parent army had arrived, Jackson's authority was modified on 8 July by General Orders, No. 147, which named Jackson military governor of Chattanooga. Informed that such wording was inappropriate for friendly territory, Bragg changed Jackson's title to "commandant of the post" three days later. Jackson's portfolio not only encompassed the city but also included guarding the river line all the way to Bridgeport, including the railroad bridges over Chattanooga, Lookout, and Running Water Creeks. That sector was soon deemed too large and, on 12 July, Bragg instructed Polk to assign a brigade to replace Jackson's units around Bridgeport and Shell Mound. Polk assigned Anderson's Brigade of Withers's Division to the task. At the same time, Bragg instructed Hardee's Corps to send a brigade to Harrison, twelve miles upstream from Chattanooga, to bolster the army's right. Wood's Brigade from Cleburne's Division received the call. To secure his connection with the Department of East Tennessee, Bragg on 9 July ordered Hardee's Corps to send a brigade to Loudon, on the Tennessee River eighty-five miles from Chattanooga. Acting corps commander Cleburne selected Johnson's Brigade of Stewart's Division and dispatched it by rail the next day. Johnson's specific task was to secure all the railroad bridges between Loudon and Chattanooga from possible Federal incursions.[11]

Sending single infantry brigades to distant flanks was a gesture only. Each brigade was too small to block a serious Federal advance and not mobile enough to cover the vast distances involved. Thus Bragg had to rely primarily on his cavalry to provide useful intelligence on Federal activity beyond the river, and early warning of a Federal advance. Wheeler especially was ordered to place "a small force and many scouts" on the Federal right flank to glean information from beyond the river. Even after this admonition, Wheeler seemed not to take the intelligence mission seriously. Instead, he focused on resting and recruiting his men and horses. On 12 July, Wharton's Division left Trenton for Rome, Georgia, sixty-five miles to the south. It reached Rome two days later after a leisurely march via LaFayette and Trion Factory. Wharton left behind only Col. William Estes's Third Confederate Cavalry regiment from Harrison's Brigade. Estes was told to spread his small regiment along the river from Kelly's Ferry all the way downstream to Gunter's Landing, Alabama, a distance of eighty miles. Momentarily remaining at Trenton was Martin's Division. Martin departed

Trenton for his assigned rest area around Gadsden and Alexandria, Alabama, on 22 July. Gadsden was twenty-five miles from the river and seventy-five miles from Chattanooga. Martin, too, left one regiment, Capt. James Field's Eighth Confederate Cavalry, to picket the river from Gunter's Landing downstream to Decatur, a distance of fifty miles. Numbering only 230 men, Field's command was armed mostly with sabers and pistols. Beyond Decatur, Roddey's Brigade watched the river. Formerly, Roddey had reported directly to army headquarters, but on 22 July his command was brought under Wheeler's authority. The same message ordered Wheeler to make Gadsden his headquarters. While Roddey maintained a small presence north of the Tennessee River to observe Federal activity, Wheeler apparently did not.[12]

North of Chattanooga, Forrest held the intelligence mission in higher esteem than did Wheeler. Geography favored Forrest because the axis of the Federal advance during the Tullahoma campaign had followed the line of the Nashville & Chattanooga Railroad. Extended beyond Middle Tennessee, that line reached the Tennessee River at Bridgeport, Alabama, downstream from Chattanooga. If the Federals followed the axis of the railroad, they would probably approach Chattanooga from the southwest, making Wheeler's sector the critical one. North of the city and beyond the river, Walden's Ridge and the even broader Cumberland Plateau, with their vast stretches of wilderness, gave Forrest a greater buffer of terrain between his command and the nearest Federal forces beyond the mountains. Always aggressive in pursuit of current information on his enemy's location and intentions, Forrest certainly was not content with a passive line of observation posts scattered along the river upstream to the mouth of the Little Tennessee near Loudon. Even though his command had also suffered severely in the previous campaign, Forrest permitted only a minimal rest period before seeking the nearest Federals he could find. On 27 July he ordered one of his brigade commanders, Col. George Dibrell, to take a regiment across the Tennessee River, Walden's Ridge, and the Cumberland Plateau to Sparta, Tennessee. Sparta lay at the western foot of the plateau and was Dibrell's birthplace. It was also the locality where he had raised the Eighth (Thirteenth) Tennessee Cavalry regiment in the fall of 1862. Thus it was no coincidence that Dibrell selected the Eighth (Thirteenth) Tennessee for his expedition to Sparta. If the men needed to recuperate, they could rest and recruit at their own homes. Simultaneously, they could watch the growing Federal presence southwest of Sparta. Certainly their circumstances were different, but Forrest's approach contrasted strongly with Wheeler's.[13]

Having momentarily secured his flanks, Bragg turned to a controversy of long standing in Atlanta. To Bragg's mind, the problem lay with Maj. George Lee, commandant of the post of Atlanta. Bragg and Lee shared a long and unhappy history. At Pensacola in early 1861 Bragg had forced Lee to resign company command in the face of charges that included embezzlement. Lee then was elected lieutenant colonel of the Thirty-Eighth Georgia Infantry regiment. Promoted to colonel in June 1862, he resigned a month later, just as the regiment was becoming heavily involved in the fighting in Virginia. At the same time, he was appointed captain and provost marshal by the War Department and assigned to command the post of Atlanta. Bragg protested Lee's elevation strongly in August, but to no avail. Despite his low social status as a slave overseer and probable illiteracy, Lee developed a web of political connections in the city, and enlisted a private army of citizens exempt from the conscription laws. After the battle of Stones River, several thousand wounded soldiers from the Army of Tennessee crowded facilities in Atlanta. Believing that Lee had neither the managerial skill nor the moral authority to supervise his men, Bragg in February 1863 selected a new commander for the post. A week later, under pressure from Richmond, he suspended the change. Next, Bragg sent John Jackson, commander of the District of the Tennessee, to Atlanta to bring some order to the chaos there. As Jackson began to dismantle Lee's petty empire, Lee responded by threatening resignation. He also directed a letter-writing campaign to the Davis administration that began with the commissary, quartermaster, and ordnance officers stationed in Atlanta, progressed to members of the Confederate Congress, and eventually included Vice President Alexander Stephens. When Davis himself favorably endorsed one of the letters to Secretary of War James Seddon, Bragg was beaten and knew it. Indeed, Lee was promoted to major in the adjutant general corps in late June.[14]

In July this petty squabble assumed greater significance because the Army of Tennessee's retreat to Chattanooga showed that the war was much closer to Atlanta than previously thought. Col. Abel Streight's raid in April indicated that Atlanta was an extremely vulnerable target. The city was Bragg's logistical base, and Bragg wanted someone more competent that Major Lee to organize its defenses. In July, scouts and citizens reported a large Federal cavalry force gathering near Huntsville, Alabama, hardly farther from Atlanta than the Army of Tennessee at Chattanooga. Rebuffed by the War Department in his efforts to replace Lee, Bragg became increasingly anxious about the Federal threat. On 22 July he wrote directly to Davis, complaining that the War Department's arrangements at Atlanta were "totally inadequate and unreliable." At the same time he penned a private letter to Adj. Gen. Samuel Cooper, laying out Lee's inadequacy in detail and hinting that Cooper might want to weigh in on the subject. Apparently unknown to Bragg, several prominent Atlanta residents had already importuned the Richmond authorities to make a change, arguing that Lee's social standing prevented him from succeeding as post commander. The citizens proposed that Maj. Moses Wright, twenty-seven, the efficient commander of the Atlanta Arsenal, be promoted into the position, and the War

Department grudgingly acquiesced on 16 July. Having solved the problem to their satisfaction, Davis and Seddon both responded sharply to Bragg's complaint of 22 July, reminding him that the defense of Atlanta remained his responsibility. Promoted to colonel, Wright quickly opened communication with Bragg's chief of staff and began to calm the bureaucratic waters. He retained Lee as provost marshal but stripped him of his other powers. Bragg, meanwhile, sent Edward Walthall's Brigade from Withers's Division to bolster Wright's 800 "reliable men." He also sent an engineer, Capt. Morris Wampler, to assist in laying out fortifications around the city.[15]

Although the situation in Atlanta was worrisome, other issues also required Bragg's attention. Hardee had become noticeably disaffected and desired a change in his situation. Bragg and Hardee had worked together harmoniously in early 1862, but since the Kentucky campaign Hardee had made common cause with Polk in opposition to Bragg. On 14 July, Hardee suddenly received orders from Richmond transferring him to Mississippi, where he would join Joseph Johnston's command. This surprising order was the result of discussions within the Davis administration about how to resolve the situation in Mississippi, not the situation in Tennessee. By mid-July Johnston's small command was momentarily defending Jackson against the Federal army that had conquered Vicksburg earlier in the month. Certain elements in the Richmond government wanted Johnston removed from command, but Davis was not quite ready for that drastic step. Nevertheless, action was required, so on 13 July Davis nominated Maj. Gen. Daniel Harvey Hill for a third star and ordered him to join Johnston. Just as Hill started, Davis changed his mind and ordered Hill to replace Hardee in Chattanooga, with the latter going to Mississippi instead. This sudden personnel change apparently was triggered by Davis's exasperation with Johnston's performance during the Vicksburg campaign, which generated a verbal war between the two men for the next month. The groundwork, however, had long been laid because of earlier arguments between Davis and Johnston, and through efforts of some of Davis's advisors. Hardee, who longed for a change, departed for Mississippi at once, most likely without knowing he was a pawn in a subtle plan for Johnston's eventual removal. Ironically, within a few days of his arrival, Hardee was writing privately to Polk that he regretted the transfer and wished he was back in the Army of Tennessee. Bragg's views on Hardee's departure are unrecorded, but they could hardly have been negative, given the recent history between the two officers.[16]

Hardee's replacement, Daniel Harvey Hill, arrived in Chattanooga and reported personally to Bragg on Sunday, 19 July. Born into modest circumstances in South Carolina in 1821, Hill turned forty-two a week before his arrival in Tennessee. He graduated from West Point in 1842, along with William Rosecrans and Alexander Stewart. An artilleryman, Hill served in garrison until hostilities neared with Mexico. Joining Zachary Taylor's force on the Mexican border, he spent a brief time in Bragg's battery. Transferred to another unit just as hostilities commenced, he participated with distinction in the battles of Monterrey, Contreras, and Chapultepec. Ending the war as a first lieutenant and brevet major, Hill resigned from the army in 1849 to become professor of mathematics at Washington College in Virginia. Five years later he assumed a similar position at Davidson College in North Carolina. In 1859 he left Davidson to become superintendent of the North Carolina Military Institute in Charlotte. In 1861 Hill offered his services to his adopted state and soon became the colonel of the First North Carolina Infantry regiment. He led the regiment at Big Bethel, one of the first actions of the war, which propelled him to a brigadier's star in July. Similar good fortune around Leesburg, Virginia, a few months later brought Hill promotion to major general in March 1862. Thereafter, he led a division at Yorktown, Williamsburg, Seven Pines, and several battles in the Seven Days campaign. After a brief stint as commander of the Department of North Carolina, Hill returned to his old division in the Army of Northern Virginia. During the Maryland campaign he fought skillfully at South Mountain and heroically defended the Bloody Lane at Antietam. Not seriously engaged at Fredericksburg, Hill proposed to resign from field service because of poor health. Asked to resume command of the Department of North Carolina instead, he accepted the position in February 1863. He was serving in that capacity when Jefferson Davis offered him promotion to lieutenant general and transfer to the West in July.[17]

From his earliest youth, Hill suffered from a variety of maladies, most notably a spinal condition that made sitting for long periods extremely painful. Indeed, he claimed that he had never experienced a day free from pain while in the army. Hill was noted for his extremely acerbic personality, and if his chronic pain was not its only cause, it was certainly a contributing factor. He freely criticized most of his superiors, including Robert E. Lee, and by 1863 had become known army-wide as a "croaker." His reputation as a complainer and disruptive force in command circles had as much to do with his departure from the Army of Northern Virginia in early 1863 as his frail health. So prevalent was this view of Hill as a commander that it prompted Robert Kean, a War Department bureau chief, to comment at the time of his assignment to the West: "Harsh, abrupt, often insulting in the effort to be sarcastic, he will offend many and conciliate none. Nor has he talents to reduce this disadvantage, though brave and loyal." Indeed, none questioned Hill's devotion to the Southern cause, or his personal courage. He was simply not a commander who could work harmoniously with peers and superiors. Hill's association with Bragg as a young lieutenant in 1845 was remembered fondly by the army commander upon Hill's arrival in Chattanooga, Bragg no doubt seeing him as an improvement over the duplicitous Hardee. Yet Hill was instantly unimpressed with his chief, writing years later that Bragg seemed "gloomy and despondent" and "prematurely old." Having just been through a harrowing retreat marked by many disaffected senior commanders, Bragg was clearly showing the strain, but Hill could not empathize with his new chief. From Hill's perspective, the interview ended unsatisfactorily and, though neither officer realized it at the time, the sour note thus struck would prove to be a harbinger of things to come. On 24 July Hill formally assumed command of what was now officially known as Hill's Corps.[18]

The Hardee-Hill exchange was not the only major personnel decision facing Bragg in July. Jones Withers had submitted his resignation from the army in late May because of his failing health. Withers had long been known as an officer favorably disposed to Bragg during the army's recent internecine squabbles, and Bragg was loath to lose his services. He therefore suggested that Withers be offered a position less physically rigorous than division commander in order to recruit his health. The matter was not taken up by the War Department until 9 July, and Secretary of War Seddon did not approve the resignation until six days later. In the interim, Bragg offered Withers's services to Governor John Shorter of Alabama as commander of that state's local defense forces. Shorter was amenable to employing Withers, and Withers accepted the position. Accordingly, his resignation was canceled on 21 July, and Withers departed for his new command. Because the division's senior brigadier, Patton Anderson, was on detached service with his brigade, Polk gave Zachariah Deas the interim command. However practical this decision may have been, it nevertheless angered Anderson, who protested from his headquarters at Taylor's Store, across the river from Bridgeport. A solution was already apparent, however, because the War Department's Special Orders, No. 167, on 15 July assigned Maj. Gen. Thomas Carmichael Hindman to the Army of Tennessee. Hindman was in Richmond serving as president of a court of inquiry on the fall of New Orleans and would not be available for a few weeks. He was a close friend of Patrick Cleburne from prewar days and thus would add that factor to the mix of personalities in the senior leadership of the army. Meanwhile, Deas continued in temporary command of Withers's Division.[19]

Personnel reassignments aside, Bragg during July was involved in an administrative reorganization of the commands on either side of his own Department No. 2. Since November 1862 Bragg's department nominally had been subordinate to Joseph Johnston and his Department of the West. Whatever Jefferson Davis had hoped to achieve with Johnston's super-department had not be realized. When the administration ordered Johnston to Mississippi in May 1863 because of the Vicksburg crisis, the general construed the order as severing his connection to the Army of Tennessee. That construction was not intended by Davis, as evidenced by a long, caustic resume of events he shared with Johnston on 15 July. Sending Hardee, a proven if troublesome commander, to assist or possibly supersede Johnston was Davis's first response. His patience with Johnston fraying, Davis followed on 22 July with a reorganization of departments. In a curt message from Adj. Gen. Samuel Cooper, Johnston's command responsibilities in regard to Bragg's department were abolished. In the same message, Cooper placed Simon Buckner's Department of East Tennessee under Bragg's authority. The latter decision had been under consideration for some time, and indeed had been recommended by Johnston in January and Buckner himself in May. Buckner, of course, was another Bragg opponent, stretching at least as far back as the unhappy Kentucky campaign of 1862. Still, Buckner had brought some of his troops to assist the Army of Tennessee during the Tullahoma campaign, for which Bragg had graciously thanked him. Buckner had often promised cooperation, and now the opportunity to match words with deeds was at hand. Nevertheless, the process of integrating the two departments was just beginning and would not play out for another month.[20]

On 25 July, War Department Special Orders, No. 176, made official the changes summarily outlined by Adjutant General Cooper. Bragg's old Department No. 2 was now named the Department of Tennessee, into which the Department of East Tennessee was merged. The boundaries of the new department were as follows: the territory west of the Blue Ridge Mountains in North Carolina down to the East Tennessee & Georgia Railroad; thence southward along the Western & Atlantic Railroad to Atlanta; west along the Atlanta & West Point Railroad to the Alabama state line; northward to the Tennessee River; thence along that stream to its mouth. In a clarification issued two weeks later, Cooper added several counties stretching along the south bank of the Tennessee River in Alabama, including the Gadsden area. As a result, most of Alabama and a large portion of Georgia were placed outside Bragg's area of responsibility. Operationally, that delineation was momentarily of little concern. Much more important was the official denial of resources, especially food and forage, from the excluded localities to the Army of Tennessee. That army was much larger than either Johnston's small command in Mississippi or Beauregard's coastal defense troops in the Department of South Carolina, Georgia, and Florida. To make matters worse, the reserve food stocks held in warehouses in Atlanta were allocated to the Army of Northern Virginia. Nevertheless, the Army of Tennessee somehow successfully drew upon these stocks in times of need. Thus when the Department of Mississippi begged for 250,000 pounds of bacon from the Atlanta stockpile in late July, there was none to be had. Still, rations remained short in Chattanooga for the Army of Tennessee and would continue to be scarce for some time to come.[21]

The personnel turbulence, bureaucratic turmoil, and logistical shortfalls that plagued Bragg throughout the month of July harmed his already shaky health and left little time to contemplate the largest issue of all—what to do next. Upon reaching Chattanooga Bragg had sought to find a way to regain the initiative. Initially asking Richmond for guidance, he received none. Thus, on 17 July Bragg proposed to Johnston a bold plan for concentrating their respective forces. Bragg believed that the geographical barriers between the Army of the Cumberland and Chattanooga would necessitate a delay of some weeks before Rosecrans resumed his offensive. During that window of opportunity, Bragg proposed to move the bulk of the Army of Tennessee to join Johnston and have the combined force strike hard at the Federals in the Mississippi Valley. In Bragg's formulation, the Army of Tennessee's cavalry and several infantry brigades would remain to guard Chattanooga, while as many as fourteen infantry brigades would make the journey west. If Johnston preferred that Bragg not accompany the troops to Mississippi, Bragg was content to remain at Chattanooga; he left the choice to Johnston. The proposal bore considerable similarity to Bragg's 1862 strategic rail movement from Tupelo, Mississippi, to Chattanooga, prior to the disastrous Kentucky campaign. Its operative principle was the rapid concentration of scarce Confederate resources in order to achieve a momentary numerical superiority over an opposing Federal army. Defeat of the Federal army would in turn permit either further offensive operations or a return to the status quo. Unbeknownst to Bragg, his proposal would reach Johnston just as the latter was evacuating Jackson, Mississippi, in the face of Federal pressure. It also occurred at the moment that the Davis administration abolished Johnston's supervision of the Army of Tennessee.[22]

Beset by so many adverse developments, Johnston never responded to Bragg's proposal. In his postwar memoirs, he acknowledged Bragg's offer but dismissed it as being "too late." Nevertheless, the proposal bespeaks Bragg's aggressive attitude, even after the crushing loss of Middle Tennessee. As the days passed with no word from either Johnston or the Confederate government, Bragg felt keenly that an opportunity was slipping away. On 21 July he expressed those feelings in a private message to fellow department commander Beauregard at Charleston. Beauregard had long advocated the principle of concentration and often offered gratuitous advice on the subject to both the War Department and adjacent commanders. Most recently, in May, he had proposed to Johnston a concentration built around Bragg's army that would destroy the Army of the Cumberland, regain Tennessee and much of Kentucky, block the Mississippi River, and force Grant's army to withdraw from Mississippi or be destroyed. Beauregard had sent a copy of his plan to Bragg, who thanked him and disparaged the timidity of both the government and Johnston. Bragg noted that his army lay within five days' travel from Johnston's command and that he could have nearly been there by the time of his writing. He also argued that holding cities was for detachments only, leaving field armies free to maneuver against an aggressor. This criticism was a clear slap at John Pemberton, whose army had been trapped at Vicksburg and forced to surrender less than three weeks earlier. Bragg closed, "These things are too sad to dwell on." There would be no concentration in Mississippi, and Johnston would soon have no power to direct one, so Bragg's proposal died without a trial. Nevertheless, he still believed in two principles inextricably linked in his mind—concentration followed by aggressive maneuver, and refusal to be tied to particular geographical locations at the expense of freedom of action. Perhaps there would be other opportunities to implement these principles, but not in July 1863.[23]

Bragg received no assistance in the formulation of strategy from his corps commanders. Hardee had departed, and Hill was too new to be of much aid. Polk was not about to offer advice, strategic or otherwise, to a man he scorned. Yet Polk fancied himself a strategist, and he could not refrain from offering solutions to the seemingly intractable problems of the western theater. Characteristically, Polk went straight to the top, penning a long private letter on 26 July to Jefferson Davis. After cunningly linking himself to Bragg's decision to evacuate Middle Tennessee, Polk laid the foundation for the next offensive move by the army. He believed the summer heat would preclude activity in Mississippi by either Johnston or Grant for at least six weeks. When the Federals did stir, Polk believed that Johnston's small command could not check them successfully. If, however, Johnston were to leave a detachment to watch Grant's troops around Vicksburg and bring his remaining forces to Chattanooga, they would represent a formidable reinforcement to the Army of Tennessee. Further, if Buckner's small command from East Tennessee could be added to the mix, the combined Confederate army could destroy the Army of the Cumberland. The victorious Army of Tennessee could then drive to the Mississippi River at Memphis, thereby forcing Grant to withdraw from Mississippi. Admittedly, the Confederates would have to assume considerable risk in Alabama while they implemented their scheme, but Polk believed that risk was worth taking. He reiterated his plan in a letter to Hardee four days later, suggesting that Hardee might share it with Johnston. Polk's plan was the same as that offered by Beauregard in May, and it received the same chilly reception in Richmond. Unbeknownst to Polk, Bragg had already offered to relinquish command to Johnston if their respective forces united. Polk was also apparently unaware that Johnston's superdepartment had just been abolished. No matter; his campaign to have Bragg removed from command of the Army of Tennessee would continue unabated.[24]

As the Army of Tennessee settled into its camps at Chattanooga and Tyner's Station, many men expressed strong opinions on the recent campaign in letters home. There was, however, no common assessment of the performance of the army's leaders. Lt. Joshua Callaway appraised the recent campaign in a letter to his wife, Dulcinea, on 7 July: "My dear, you would doubtless feel disappointed if I were not to give you my opinion of Braggs retreat. A great many are down on him for it, but I confess that, if I understand it & know anything of the comparative strength of the two opposing armies, he has displayed more of the *general* than in all his former career." Similar views were expressed by Capt. Irvine Walker: "Bragg will be again censured by the country for failing to do what was impossible, not only for him, but for the greatest general of the age had he been in his place." Blacksmith Daniel Kelly was more ambivalent. Writing on 10 July, Kelly commented, "The soldiers of this army are now verry much disatisfied with there Gen. . . . as for my self I am no Geneal therefore I find no fault." Pvt. John Magee wrote in his diary on 9 July, "All confidence in Genl Bragg is lost, and I do not believe this army can win a victory under his superintendence." In a letter to his parents on 12 July, Pvt. J. P. Kendall was equally judgmental: "Have lost all confidence in Gen. Bragg—never had much." Within some units, differences of opinion were extreme. Pvt. George Turner of the Eighth Texas Cavalry regiment had a positive view of Bragg's generalship, which he expressed in a letter on 7 July to his father: "Bragg will be censured much for this move but there was no alternative for him. And the manner in which he brought off his army stores, waggons, &c, &c deserves the highest commendation." In contrast, on the same day in the same unit, Chaplain Robert Bunting told a Houston, Texas, newspaper: "I do know that the army has been greatly demoralized by it, and Gen. Bragg has been universally cursed. To say the truth, he was out generaled in every sense of the word."[25]

Soldiers recently assigned to the Army of Tennessee tended to give Bragg the benefit of the doubt when they assessed the campaign just concluded. Surgeon Alex Morgan of Jackson's Brigade wrote, "Every body is abusing Bragg now for falling back without a fight, + very unjustly I think. I am not one of his admirers, but I would like to see him have a fair chance one time." Another unbiased observer of the Army of Tennessee, its commanders, and its morale during this period was Lt. Col. Bolling Hall Jr. in Simon Buckner's command. Having temporarily reinforced the Army of Tennessee during the latter stages of the Tullahoma campaign, Hall and his battalion witnessed the retreat from the perspective of the army's rear guard. Even though his unit had suffered severe hardship, Hall had lost only two men from his command of 360 Alabamians. Back in Knoxville, Hall replied to a letter from his father enclosing newspaper commentary savaging Bragg. On 18 July he responded, "I do not believe the army so badly demoralized as the [Montgomery] Advertizer would have us think. . . . You would be surprised to go into Bragg's army to find really how much his men like him, & the confidence they have in his ability even surpasses their friendship for him. I certainly was surprised after reading the papers." In the same letter, Hall then identified the crux of the Army of Tennessee's command problems: "There is one very remarkable fact which is, that as a general rule the best officers of his army like him while the poorest ones dislike him. Whenever you find an officer who never attends to his duty or who is incompetent he abuses Bragg. I found this a very good rule to judge the qualifications of Braggs officers by."[26]

As the rank and file settled into their camp routines and the unpleasant memories of the retreat from Tullahoma faded, issues other than Bragg's ability as a general rose to greater prominence. For many, the scarcity of rations was a serious and nagging concern. On picket near Bridgeport, Pvt. John Roberts, Seventh Mississippi Infantry regiment, recorded in his diary on 13 July, "We get very little to eat, not half enough." Writing to his wife from Trenton on the same day, Pvt. Nimrod Long of the Fifty-First Alabama Cavalry regiment lamented that his daily beef ration was only one-third of a pound. "We are not having a good time here," he concluded. On 21 July, First Sgt. John Crittenden of the Thirty-Fourth Alabama Infantry regiment was pleased to report to his wife, Bettie, that the daily beef ration had improved to three-fourths of a pound, still inadequate but better than before. Those stationed near Chattanooga and other towns, with money to spend, fared somewhat better. Men like Pvt. Thomas Bigbie of the Thirty-Third Alabama Infantry regiment, who guarded the river at Harrison, Tennessee, found potatoes, cabbage, chickens, and milk available from the locals—but at a steep price because most of the sellers were Unionists. When Wharton's Cavalry Division moved to Rome, Georgia, for rest and recuperation, its men also complained about the locals—not their politics but their price-gouging. Irrepressible Sgt. William Heartsill of the Seventeenth Texas Cavalry (Dismounted) noted both the scarcity of rations and the exorbitant prices charged by citizens, including $2 for single chickens and $10 for a watermelon. In his diary on 22 July, Quartermaster Sgt. John Sparkman of the Forty-Eighth Tennessee Infantry regiment worried that the lack of rations would affect discipline. That discipline was already fraying in some quarters because of the illicit availability of whiskey, according to Lt. Hubert Dent of Dent's (formerly Robertson's) Alabama Battery.[27]

Still, soldiers being soldiers, the most inventive among the lower ranks found ways to supplement what Bragg's commissary issued. Pvt. Nimrod Long at Trenton, who complained about short rations and high prices, also believed that the soldiers he knew lived reasonably well through irregular methods liberally applied. A perfect example of this behavior was described by Pvt. John Roberts on 20 July: "Two of the boys went out and killed a hog. They got an armful of cane and wrapped the cane all around the hog and fetched it up to camp. Going to make a bed of the cane. So said they[,] they brought it in, no one suspicionned a thing. Now this is what I call chicanery. What will soldiers get at next. Hunger makes soldiers do things wrong[,] if they were fed would never be guilty of this." Indeed, Roberts proved quite adept at gathering useful items on the sly, writing on 23 July: "I walked through many a corn field and several young pumpkins stuck to my fingers and when I got to camp I fried them. O how good." Still another dodge was described by Sgt. William Heartsill in his diary entry of 28 July: "Col [Roger] Mills is trying to guard all the corn fields in this County, one hundred from this Regiment on guard to day, I am thinking the remedy will prove more fatal than the disease; for the guards will bring an armful into camp every time they come and will manage to have considerable business on hand that will require their presence quite often." Heartsill also railed against an order prohibiting the men from eating cabbage, a plot, he believed, to save that scarce item for the regiment's officers.[28]

If the inadequacy of rations was a nearly universal complaint, equipment shortages were also a concern. While few men had been lost during the recent campaign, numerous units had been forced to abandon clothing, knapsacks, personal items, and shelter. July was a rainy month in the Tennessee River valley, and units without tents were exposed often to the elements. Until the Quartermaster Department could eradicate the shortfalls in tentage, clothing, and shoes, the men had both their patience and patriotism sorely tried. Pvt. John Roberts, picketing near Bridgeport, rejoiced on 25 July to receive a new pair of shoes, of which only the heel and toe were leather, with the remainder cloth. Nevertheless, such shoes would protect his feet from rocks on the march, if only briefly. First Sgt. John Crittenden wrote to his wife on 9 July: "Bettie I have lost all my cloths. . . . By borrowing I can manage to have my clothes washed." Equally destitute was 2nd Lt. William Cole of the Thirty-Eighth Alabama Infantry regiment. In a plaintive letter to his wife on 18 July, Cole explained the hardships he was enduring: "I have seen more hardships in the last month than I have ever seen in all my previous life. . . . I have lost near all of my clothes. . . . I have not shifting clothes at this time. . . . I have not but one pair of pants. . . . I have one domestic shirt and my striped shirt[,] two pair of old socks and no drawers. . . . So you see that I have lost allmost all that I had. We have no tents and when it rains we have to take it just like the dumb brutes and every thing that we have gets wet and it remains wet for two weeks at the time[,] no clothes to change and it raining all the time." For reasons unknown, Cole focused his anger upon the state of Tennessee, which to his mind was the worst of all Confederate states, Mississippi excluded. Other soldiers complained of a lack of ovens for baking bread.[29]

To keep the men busy, officers instituted regular unit drills and inspections, broken by periodic reviews. The more educated read whatever books and newspapers came to hand, while at least one learned to play chess. The most common occupation was writing letters to loved ones at home. The writers asked for clothing and food, inquired about the health of those at home, and begged their correspondents to write more often. Some offered instructions for maintaining their farms and advice on child raising, but others only shared news of common acquaintances in the army. Indicative of the strong feelings of most married soldiers is a letter Pvt. Benjamin Jackson penned to his wife, Martha, on 8 July: "I will say to you, not to give yourself any trouble about me, for I have gone through with many hardships and am still alive and if it is the will of the Lord we will meet again. Tell the children I want to see them. Tell Missouri to kiss Jimmy Tommy for me. Tell Pa and Ma and all of the family I would like to see them. I remain your husband as ever till death." Unlike Arthur Manigault, who was visited by his wife and son on 25 July, more junior officers were like Lt. Hubert Dent, who sought in vain for lodging for his wife in Chattanooga. Still, some wives who lived in nearby areas of Alabama and Georgia managed to make the arduous trip to the army during July. Other soldiers sought furloughs, which were almost universally denied, with a resultant drop in morale. For example, Lt. Joshua Callaway on 24 July requested a twenty-day furlough to return to his home in Dallas County, Alabama, and had it denied four days later. Momentarily crushed, Callaway rallied and took his case all the way to the army commander, who finally acceded to the lieutenant's request in August. Many supplicants were not so lucky and had to content themselves with corresponding with loved ones whenever paper, ink, and stamps were available. Others availed themselves of army visitors, who agreed to carry their letters home either for free or a nominal fee.[30]

Only a few events broke the monotony of camp life. Regiments with active chaplains were favored with protracted camp meetings. Chaplains in Stewart's Division were especially vigorous. The movement apparently began with the chaplains in Bate's Brigade, spread next to Brown's Brigade, and ultimately led to a coordinated effort by all of the army's chaplains by the end of the month. In addition to holding open meetings for preaching and prayer, the chaplains also ordered Testaments and copies of the *Army and Navy Messenger* for distribution to the faithful. This revival fervor even spread to the cavalry camps, where Chaplain Robert Bunting led a series of meetings that lasted from 21 July to the end of the month. For those not so religiously inclined, other amusements filled the spare hours. Sgt. Maj. James Searcy used some of his free time to walk around Chattanooga, while officers of Wharton's Cavalry Division organized a ball. When news arrived that twenty Whitworth target rifles had been acquired from Great Britain and would be allocated to winners of shooting competitions, many soldiers took a great interest in the events. Ten rifles went to the best marksmen from each corps, and units competed keenly for the honor of having a sharpshooter drawn from their ranks. Even though the number of weapons was miniscule, the competitions occupied the minds of hundreds as the spectators cheered their favorites. Individuals not inclined to collective pursuits spent their spare time exploring their surroundings or simply walking in the woods. One such was Sgt. Talbert Holt, who explained to his sisters on 19 July, "For some time have been all alone in the deep recesses of the woods. I come to such a place for several reasons, as follows. I wanted to be away from the stir of camp, where I hear little else than vulgarity, profanity and foolishness instead of the greatness, goodness, mercy, and majesety [*sic*] of our God." Others visited nearby civilian homes. For example, Pvt. John Roberts found simple delight in repairing broken clocks for citizens near his picket post.[31]

No matter how they filled their time, Bragg's soldiers spent the month of July 1863 in a valiant fight to maintain their morale. Even if the retreat from Tullahoma was necessary, the loss of territory rankled. That loss was especially hard on the army's Tennesseans, who found themselves severed from their homes and families, now behind enemy lines. Events elsewhere also contributed to the army's malaise in early July. As the news of the fall of Vicksburg and Port Hudson shifted from rumor to fact, many soldiers spoke of the detrimental effect on morale. Less concern was felt about the activities of Confederate forces in the Eastern Theater, first because news was less easy to acquire and, second, because almost no units in the army hailed from that locale. As garbled accounts of Morgan's raid into Indiana and Ohio reached the troops, they cheered Morgan's audacity, if not his judgment. Similarly, news of draft riots in New York City prompted rejoicing, as did a persistent rumor that European nations were on the verge of officially recognizing the Confederacy. By the end of the month, the loss of Middle Tennessee and the shock of Vicksburg's fall had diminished somewhat. On 21 July Sgt. Maj. James Searcy told his mother that he tried not to dwell on the recent defeats, and he counseled her to do the same. Five days later he was more emphatic, writing, "We are *not whipped* nor any where near it. The Yankees may overrun the whole country that will not be whipping us—and they will find out so, before they do much more." Writing in similar vein was Maj. Isaac Scherck, commissary of Hill's Corps. Scherck had been away briefly and was pleasantly surprised at the army's state of mind upon his return. In a letter to a friend on 29 July Scherck wrote, "The Army is in fine spirit & defys any of the northern threats & scorns Sewards proposals for peace as read in the late papers by sacrificing our leaders. I felt really refreshed when I returned from home & found the troops who had every reason for being despondent, show their intelligence & determination to resist to the last."[32]

While soldier morale slowly began to rise above the despondency of early July, by the end of the month Bragg's physical and mental condition was deteriorating at an alarming rate. As early as 22 July he had written privately to Samuel Cooper, "For two months my health has been anything but good. Long continued and excessive labor of mind and body have produced its natural result on a frame not robust at best. Were it possible, I should seek some repose, but at present I see no hope." Four days later he reorganized part of his staff, returning Lt. Col. Harvey Walter to his original position of judge advocate and welcoming Lt. Col. George Brent once more as assistant adjutant general. Brent had held the position once before but had been absent from the command for several months. His even-tempered personality had served Bragg and the army well during his earlier tenure, and his return must have relieved at least part of Bragg's administrative concerns. Elise Bragg was still nearby, continuing her convalescence at Cherokee Springs, a spa near Ringgold, less than twenty miles from Chattanooga. On 28 July she suggested to her husband that he come for a visit or, alternatively, she could visit him. With Brent now available to manage the army's paperwork on a daily basis, Bragg elected to join Elise for a few days at Cherokee Springs. Having successfully extricated his army from Middle Tennessee, orchestrated the defense of the Tennessee River line, and weathered major personnel and administrative changes, Bragg clearly needed a few days of relaxation. Even while away from the army, however, he could not leave army business behind. Finding two of Wheeler's units, the Ninth Kentucky Cavalry regiment and Allison's Tennessee Cavalry squadron, in a state of gross indiscipline at Cherokee Springs, "doing some harm and no good," on 30 July he sharply brought the matter to Wheeler's attention. At the end of July Bragg was away from his headquarters, but he was still the commander of the Army of Tennessee.[33]

5

Rosecrans

» JULY 1863 «

With the Army of the Cumberland momentarily halted between the flood-swollen Elk River and the massive Cumberland Plateau, Rosecrans had little time to savor his success in the Tullahoma campaign. Because the seemingly never-ending rain had turned the region's primitive roads into deep rivers of mud, there was no hope that his army could be supplied through animal power alone. Yet the Nashville & Chattanooga Railroad was not immediately able to take up the slack because the Confederates had seriously damaged it in many places. Some of the damage, notably the several miles of missing track around Bell Buckle and Wartrace, could be easily handled by John Anderson's track gangs. Similarly, the damaged Duck River bridge and a long trestle near Normandy could be made serviceable in a short time. The 540-foot Elk River bridge at Estill Springs, however, had been totally destroyed during the Confederate retreat. Until that structure was restored, there could be no forward movement by Rosecrans's army and the troops would suffer serious hunger pangs as rations diminished. The problem could be alleviated by withdrawing to the north side of the Elk River, but that option was not seriously considered by Rosecrans. No ground gained in the Tullahoma campaign would be relinquished, even temporarily. Thus, there was no choice but to repair the Elk River bridge as expeditiously as possible. John Anderson had already been threatened with removal as railroad superintendent on 4 July if he did not become more energetic and he was badgered anew on the next day. Yet his civilian track workers were not bridge builders, so military assets would have to be mobilized for the larger projects. Those assets included William Innes's First Michigan Engineers and Mechanics regiment, consisting primarily of Michigan woodsmen, and the larger Pioneer Brigade of St. Clair Morton.[1]

The location of the army's engineers favored the Pioneer Brigade reconstructing the Elk River railroad bridge. Working in the army's rear, the First Michigan regiment on 5 July moved to Tullahoma, having completed repairs to the Duck River bridge and the Normandy trestle on the previous day. Morton's Pioneer Brigade was already at the Elk River, although its energies were dissipated among several diverse projects. Some soldiers labored to return a grist mill to operation, while others began work on several nearby road bridges. At the site of the railroad bridge, some men began to remove bridge wreckage while others completed a temporary foot bridge across the river. The Elk itself, however, continued to rise in depth and velocity because of the continuing rainfall. On 6 July the rampaging river demolished the Pioneer Brigade's footbridge, stopping all work at the site. Back at Tullahoma, the First Michigan rested and repaired its equipment and tools. Also at Tullahoma, Rosecrans became increasingly impatient to see measurable progress on the railroad reconstruction effort. During the day he dispatched several telegrams to John Anderson, demanding detailed information and berating Anderson for the slowness of his operations. He also forwarded to Anderson a charge by the Nashville commissary of subsistence that a shortage of boxcars was hindering the army's resupply efforts. In like vein, the army commander telegraphed Morton several times, seeking progress reports and demanding a completion date. Exasperated when no answer was forthcoming, Rosecrans telegraphed the McCallum Bridge Company in Cincinnati for an estimate of how long it would take for the company to fabricate a bridge over the Elk. He also rebuked Morton for his men's propensity to steal from divisional wagon trains they helped ford the Elk. At the bridge site, the Pioneer Brigade exhausted its supply of army bread, causing one soldier to confide to his diary: "Began to feel very weak for the want of bread to eat."[2]

The Pioneer Brigade was not alone in lacking rations. That condition prevailed throughout the army's camps, especially those of the Fourteenth and Twentieth Corps around Decherd, Winchester, and Cowan. Not only was the railroad broken north of Tullahoma, but also the road bridges over the Elk were destroyed, and the roads everywhere were quagmires of mud. Writing on 5 July, Capt. Everett Abbott described the situation succinctly: "We have been almost out of provisions several days. . . . Foragers have taken everything eatable from the country. Many people left destitute — some say they are almost starving. Such are calamities of war." Two days later, he reported an even bleaker story: "For miles everything eatable has been taken. A desolate God forsaken country. Soldiers everywhere searching for something to eat. Don't know how citizens will avoid starvation. Soldiers must be fed." In Stanley's brigade, Pvt. William Christian wrote on 6 July, "The boys are almost starved. . . . We all know what it is to be hungry." Christian's sentiments were mirrored on 7 July by Cpl. William Miller: "We have no bread of any kind tonight but one of our boys got some middlings or shorts and we made cakes out of it and a man had to have a stomach like a corn sheller to dijest it." With the daily ration reduced to one piece of hardtack in many Fourteenth and Twentieth Corps regiments, no civilian cows, sheep, hogs, turkeys, chickens, potatoes, or other vegetables were safe from famished soldiers. In Van Cleve's division of the Twenty-First Corps at McMinnville, friendly mountaineers offered produce for sale, but elsewhere the food often was confiscated after bitter confrontation. The situation was eased somewhat by the availability of ripe wild berries of several types. Even the berries, however, were not always enough to remove the general discontent, as Lt. Chesley Mosman reported: "Got so hungry I didn't know what to do. . . . Went a berrying for spite."[3]

The men in the ranks reacted to the lack of rations according to each soldier's temperament. Some, like Lt. Jesse Connelly accepted their fate with equanimity: "Our rations are short, but we can live, and while we have enough to satisfy the cravings of hunger should be content, as I think we are." Others consoled themselves with the knowledge that their Confederate counterparts had much less to eat than did the Federals, yet maintained their fighting spirit, so the temporary dearth of army rations could be easily borne. Such reactions were atypical, with many soldiers instead expressing their frustrations and hunger pangs through cursing, grumbling, and finding fault with the chain of command. In their encounters with civilians, particularly those still loyal to the Confederacy, foragers went about their work of confiscation without much gentility. Even other units were considered fair game for expropriation, as Pvt. John Love demonstrated while accompanying a wagon train struggling through the mud to a depot in the rear. Coming upon a loaded train whose personnel had unloaded a wagon to free it, Love and his compatriots stole three boxes of hardtack and a side of meat for their own use. Cpl. Alanson Ryman proudly wrote his wife about his prowess in keeping himself fed through various subterfuges. An extremely shrewd and frugal soldier, Ryman assured his wife that "you need have no fears of my starving while I stay in the army." With rations so short, few were inclined to share them with civilians. When First Sgt. Axel Reed heard that Confederate civilians and deserters were receiving Federal rations, he resolved to take action. Reed and others wrote a blistering letter to the *Nashville Union* newspaper, exposing the practice and thereby embarrassing John Brannan, his new division commander. Brannan ordered Reed placed under arrest and removed from duty indefinitely. The longer the railroad remained closed, lapses in discipline and complaints such as Reed's would continue to spread across the army.[4]

In the midst of his unsuccessful efforts to restore the Nashville & Chattanooga Railroad to working condition, Rosecrans received a telegram on 7 July from Secretary of War Stanton: "We have just received official information that Vicksburg surrendered to General Grant on the 4th of July. Lee's army overthrown; Grant victorious. You and your noble army now have the chance to give the finishing blow to the rebellion. Will you neglect the chance?" Stung by

Washington's apparent lack of understanding of what the Army of the Cumberland had just accomplished, Rosecrans testily replied: "You do not appear to observe the fact that this noble army has driven the rebels from Middle Tennessee, of which my dispatches advised you. I beg in behalf of this army that the War Department may not overlook so great an event because it is not written in letters of blood." In pointing out that he had won a great victory without suffering the losses incurred by Grant and Meade, Rosecrans spoke no more than the truth. A disinterested observer might also concede the point that casualties were not necessarily the best means by which to judge a commander's success. Nevertheless, prudence dictated that Stanton's implied criticism be noted by silence. Rosecrans, however, continued the habit of plain speaking to his superiors that had already caused him trouble in the past. Passing along Stanton's news of the Vicksburg and Gettysburg victories to Governor Andrew Johnson of Tennessee, Rosecrans made his point in slightly gentler terms: "We may thank God and congratulate ourselves that the ides of July were auspicious for freedom, and for our own army that we have accomplished a great work without bloodshed and were prevented only by the unprecedented rains from giving the coup de grace to Bragg's army." In a brief telegram to his wife, he boasted, "Our losses are but slight not over 600 killed & wounded. Am well. Occupy Bragg's Head Quarters." In honor of all of the Federal victories, Rosecrans ordered a round of artillery salutes to be fired at sunrise on the next day.[5]

Peeved but undistracted by his telegraphic exchange with Stanton, Rosecrans continued to press both John Anderson and St. Clair Morton to accelerate their work on the railroad. On 7 July he bombarded Anderson with orders and complaints: send forward materials to repair the telegraph line, provide handcars for movement on the line, stockpile duplicates for all bridges. Most telling of all, Rosecrans again demanded that more boxcars be found to move rations from Nashville to the army when the railroad was again operating. To Morton, it was more of the same: what are the specifications for the Elk River bridge, when will it be finished, how many cars will it take to bring the pontoon train forward? Although Rosecrans expected that the railroad would be open to the Elk River bridge by 8 July, it was not. Indeed, the telegraph operator at Wartrace reported that two trains had arrived at that point but could go no farther because of weeds clogging the track. For a commander as mercurial as Rosecrans, such excuses were the last straw. Heretofore, Rosecrans had communicated with Anderson solely via aides; now he personally demanded that Anderson produce the railroad's books and accounts for inspection. The army commander closed this chilling telegram with one word: "Push." Anderson responded by once again claiming that he would have one passenger train and four freight trains running soon, certainly by 10 July. That response did not satisfy Rosecrans. With the army on the verge of starvation, many vigorously foraging troops were committing outrages upon the local population. The reports were so numerous that Rosecrans was forced to have Garfield on 8 July admonish his corps commanders to enforce strictly the regulations against unauthorized foraging and severely punish offenders. Clearly, the railroad had to be completed to the Elk River to facilitate wagon hauls to the units on the south side—and it had to be done soon.[6]

Completion of the railroad to the Elk River was only a first step toward sustaining an advance beyond the Cumberland Plateau. The more difficult task was to rebuild the Elk River railroad bridge. Morton's Pioneer Brigade was doing little better than John Anderson's track gangs in completing the structure. Well aware of the rivalry between the Pioneer Brigade and the First Michigan Engineers and Mechanics, Rosecrans resolved to use it to expedite the bridge-building. Coincidentally, Innes's regiment rested at Tullahoma without assignment. Seeing his opportunity, on 8 July Innes sent Lt. Col. Kinsman Hunton to survey the bridge site and Morton's work. The next day, Rosecrans called Innes and Hunton to headquarters to discuss the Elk River bridge. Rosecrans presented Innes with Morton's estimate that he could complete the Elk River bridge in from six to eight weeks but would require assignment of the First Michigan to assist the Pioneer Brigade. In response, Innes and Hunton offered to build the bridge in seven days if the Pioneer Brigade was removed from the project. That sort of confidence was just what Rosecrans was seeking, and he assigned the bridge reconstruction to the First Michigan on the spot. To spur them on, he added an additional incentive. Some months earlier, Rosecrans had created new flags for each of his army corps and had included one for the engineers. Since that time, the flag had been claimed by Morton for the Pioneer Brigade. If Innes and Hunton made good on their promise to complete the bridge in seven days, Rosecrans promised, he would award the engineer flag to Innes's regiment. Innes and Hunton accepted Rosecrans's challenge, and the staff informed Morton that the Pioneer Brigade no longer would work on the bridge. Instead, the Pioneer Brigade was to devote its time to repairing wagon roads and cutting wood for locomotive fuel and railroad ties. Other messages instructed Morton to build platforms at Estill Springs for the imminent arrival of supplies, and formally assigned Innes to take charge of all railroad repairs.[7]

Just after midnight on 9 July, soldiers guarding the Duck River bridge at Normandy witnessed the passing of the first southbound train. At 2:15 A.M. Garfield noted the train's arrival at Tullahoma. After unloading part of its cargo, the train proceeded to Estill Springs to discharge the remainder. A second train passed Normandy at 6:00 A.M. headed to the same destinations. By the end of the day a total of forty-one boxcars loaded with rations had arrived at Tullahoma. There a branch left the main line of the railroad, passed through the town of Manchester, and continued thirty-five miles northeast to McMinnville, at the foot of the Cumberland Plateau. If that line could be restored to working order, it could sustain the Twenty-First Corps with food and forage. Thus Rosecrans on 9 July instructed Anderson to put the branch into operation "at once," with a capacity of sixty to seventy tons per day. This line, officially the McMinnville & Manchester Railroad, had been leased to the Nashville & Chattanooga before the war and had suffered major damage from Federal cavalry raids in the spring. Its numerous trestles and a 225-foot bridge over Hickory Creek had been repaired by the Confederates but its general condition was poor, especially beyond Manchester. It would take the installation of at least 15,000 new railroad ties before the line could be opened as far as McMinnville, where Rosecrans planned to base a division of the Twenty-First Corps. Rosecrans also sought one of the three inspection cars purchased earlier by the government. Having the outward appearance of a passenger coach, these cars were propelled by a small steam engine in one end, and were known as "steam dummies." Built for the Pittsburgh, Fort Wayne, & Chicago Railroad in 1860, the cars were of iron construction and longer than normal coaches. Their carrying capacity of ninety-four passengers and three tons of baggage made them ideal for track inspection duty or general officer transportation. Now Rosecrans wanted one for his personal use.[8]

The completion of the railroad to Estill Springs and the reconstruction of a nearby wagon bridge meant that the units concentrated around Decherd and Winchester now could be resupplied by simply sending their teamsters to Estill Springs. Nevertheless, until a sufficient stockpile of rations was accumulated, Rosecrans's three infantry corps would have to mark time in their camps south of the Elk River. Since they could not, however, all be in one place, they were scattered on the plain facing the forbidding Cumberland Plateau. The bulk of the Army of the Cumberland was clustered around the railroad. The four divisions of Thomas's Fourteenth Corps lay either at the village of Decherd or along roads leading toward Manchester and Hillsboro. All of Thomas's units were concentrated in that area except for Wilder's mounted infantry brigade, camped at Rowesville on the Duck River near Normandy. McCook's Twentieth Corps also lay along the railroad. Davis's First Division occupied the town of Winchester on the Winchester & Alabama Railroad, which joined the N&C two miles to the north at Decherd; Johnson's Second Division garrisoned Tullahoma, site of Rosecrans's headquarters; Sheridan's Third Division was dispersed around Cowan, just short of the railroad tunnel. To the north, Crittenden's Twenty-First Corps held Manchester with Palmer's Second Division; two brigades of Wood's First Division were at Hillsboro, the third being at Pelham; and Van Cleve's Third Division was farthest north, at McMinnville. The reopening of the railroad to McMinnville, which occurred on 11 July, meant that all of Rosecrans's infantry was within reach of a working railroad line. Star-

An Army of the Cumberland steam dummy in 1864. (Library of Congress)

vation no longer threatened the Army of the Cumberland. On 10 July Rosecrans felt secure enough to call forward the remainder of his headquarters staff, with their voluminous files and printing press. On that day, too, six companies of the First Michigan Engineers and Mechanics moved their camp to the Elk River Bridge site.[9]

With his logistical situation improving, Rosecrans turned his attention to expanding his operational area. On 7 July he had ordered Stanley's Cavalry Corps to prepare an expedition to sweep the territory fifty miles southwest of Winchester and beyond the army's right flank. Rosecrans on 10 July clearly established Stanley's objectives. First, Stanley was to examine the territory west of Winchester to Pulaski, Tennessee, then southward to Huntsville and Athens, Alabama, giving special attention to railroads. Second, Stanley was to impress upon the inhabitants that the Federal army intended to maintain control of the area, unlike previous visits. Third, Stanley was to rid the countryside of guerrillas and bushwhackers who were harassing foraging parties. Fourth, Rosecrans wanted Stanley to bring to Winchester as many able-bodied male slaves as he could. Finally, Stanley was to gather all horses and mules he encountered. Rosecrans believed that one division would be sufficient for the mission, but he entrusted the details of the expedition to Stanley. In their camps around Salem, a few miles south of Winchester, Stanley's two divisions commenced their preparations. At the same time, Rosecrans found a role for Wilder's mounted infantry brigade. Nominally subordinate to Reynolds's Fourth Division, Fourteenth Corps, Wilder had already begun to establish his independence. On the same day that he defined Stanley's mission, Rosecrans gave similar orders to Wilder, who was to sweep the territory in Stanley's rear westward to the vicinity of Columbia. Wilder, too, was to confiscate all the able-bodied male slaves, horses, and mules he could find. Aware of the brigade's proclivities, Rosecrans enjoined Wilder "to prevent pillage and marauding." Perhaps coincidentally, on the same day that he received his instructions Wilder presented to the army commander a thoroughbred horse he had captured earlier. The gift prompted a fulsome response from Rosecrans, who later told his wife it was "the finest horse I ever owned."[10]

As Stanley and Wilder would be exploring the territory on the army's right, Rosecrans also desired to know what was happening beyond the Cumberland Plateau. On 7 July Sheridan reported the destruction of the Bridgeport bridge and recommended action to preserve the railroad for Federal use. In response, Rosecrans on 8 July authorized McCook to reconnoiter beyond the plateau as far as Bridgeport. In turn, McCook ordered Sheridan to lead the reconnaissance from Cowan. On 9 July Rosecrans repeated his directive more explicitly. That day Sheridan sent Bradley's Third Brigade to the top of the Cumberland Plateau at University Place and accompanied them himself. On 10 July Sheridan and Bradley probed gingerly forward to a place known locally as Dorn's Burnt Stand, where a rough road led down into Sweeden's Cove and the valley of the Tennessee River. During the afternoon, Sheridan led Col. Daniel Ray's Second Tennessee Cavalry regiment into the cove and nearly to Battle Creek before returning to the top of the mountain. On the next day Sheridan sent Ray's horsemen back into the valley with orders to probe as far as Bridgeport and Stevenson before returning along the railroad to rejoin Bradley's infantry. At the same time, he instructed Col. Bernhard Laibold, commanding his Second Brigade at Cowan, to send two regiments through the tunnel to Tantalon Station and eight miles beyond to Anderson Station. In response, the Second and Fifteenth Missouri Infantry regiments stumbled through the dark tunnel to Tantalon. On 12 July they continued to Anderson Station and discovered that while three small bridges between Tantalon and the tunnel were destroyed, four more between Tantalon and Stevenson remained intact. Sheridan also reported that a Confederate brigade guarded the river across from Bridgeport and that a steamboat was operating on the river. Sheridan returned to Cowan by handcar on 12 July. Laibold's regiments followed two days later, while Bradley's brigade withdrew to University Place and camped there on the same day.[11]

At Tullahoma, the pause in operations allowed Rosecrans to enjoy a brief respite. On 12 July he telegraphed his wife, Anna, in Yellow Springs, Ohio, to join him in Nashville two days later. He then took a train to Estill Springs to inspect the work of the First Michigan Engineers and Mechanics. Innes's regiment had reached the bridge on the previous day, and Rosecrans's arrival found them hard at work shaping the heavy timbers needed to raise the bridge. Using horses provided by Innes, the general and some staff officers toured the site. To the delight of the Michiganders, Rosecrans expressed great pleasure at the speed with which the men worked. On the following day, 13 July, he took the steam dummy up the McMinnville branch line. Stopping first at Manchester, where he was joined by Crittenden and Palmer, the party continued to McMinnville to meet Van Cleve. Writing to his wife after his return to Tullahoma, Rosecrans described McMinnville as a pleasant place: "It has many substantial brick houses and contains quite a large number of union people. As we rode up one of the streets two young ladies stood opposite us and one of them presented me a magnificent boquet." Expecting to hear from Anna upon his return, he was disappointed to find no response. When he finally received Anna's reply the next morning, he discovered that his original message had been delayed a full day. At 11:25 A.M. Rosecrans promptly renewed his invitation: "Come, advise me." Using the full power of his position, he imperiously instructed telegraphers as far north as Louisville to prevent another such delay in service. Before leaving for Nashville on the afternoon of 14 July, Rosecrans immersed himself in administrative trivia and welcoming two new officers to his staff, First Lieutenants Neil Dennison and Henry Cist. At last, Rosecrans boarded the train for Nashville, with Garfield, Goddard, Bond, Drouillard, Thompson, and perhaps others. The junior staff remained at Tullahoma to maintain the headquarters in their commander's absence.[12]

For the next several days, Rosecrans made a series of inspection tours in the Nashville area. Leaving his quarters at the St. Cloud Hotel, on 15 July he traveled south to Franklin to view its fortifications. On the next day, Thursday, he visited the Nashville waterfront and toured the navy gunboats *St. Clair* and *Brilliant*. Both vessels and forts fired salutes in Rosecrans's honor. He inspected hospitals in the city on Friday, 17 July, and took part in a large review of Reserve Corps troops with Granger. In the evenings, Rosecrans followed developments at the front, such as progress on the Elk River bridge, Sheridan's activities around University Place, Stanley's cavalry expedition, and a myriad of administrative matters. Gradually, however, the flow of messages between Nashville and Tullahoma diminished. Although Rosecrans was in no hurry to return to Tullahoma, others in his entourage were more eager to get on with the war. On 17 July, Garfield wrote to his wife, Lucretia: "We have a great work on hands to visit all the hospitals, forts, troops, and quartermaster and commissary departments in this place. We shall also make out the official report of our late campaign before we leave this place which will be probably three days hence." When he was not away from the St. Cloud, Rosecrans spent many hours entertaining visitors. One such visitor on 17 July, Col. John Sanderson, attempted to speak with Rosecrans but was unable to do so: "After Gen Rosecrans' return from the review I called to pay my respects to him at his rooms. I found him surrounded by his staff, & a crowd of visitors, each one of whom had I suppose business of some kind with him. I consequently avoided occupying his time." Sanderson spoke instead to Garfield, who told him to call again later in the evening. Sanderson did so, but just as he was about to be ushered into Rosecrans's suite, Anna Rosecrans and two of the general's children arrived from Louisville. Flustered, Sanderson withdrew, promising to seek an audience with the army commander in the future.[13]

Oy 18 July, upon returning from another round of hospital visits, Rosecrans learned that the Elk River bridge had been completed by the First Michigan Engineers and Mechanics. True to their word, Innes and Hunton had built the 540-foot structure in one week. There had been a brief delay three days earlier when Innes informed the staff at Tullahoma that a request to Morton for two-inch planking had gone unanswered. The staff forwarded the request to Garfield, who responded that the planking would be sent from Nashville. This inquiry elicited the information that Morton was ill and had departed, still smarting from his defeat at the hands of the Michiganders. The bridge itself was completed in midafternoon, 18 July, when the locomotive *Huntsville* pulled the construction train across the structure while a regimental band played "Hail Columbia." Innes then took the train to Decherd and Cowan, through the tunnel, and all the way to Tantalon Station. There, he found that a detachment had repaired the last broken trestle on the railroad, which was now open all the way to Bridgeport. Notifying Rosecrans of the glorious news before he headed for Tantalon, Innes upon his return to Elk River received the army commander's heartfelt thanks through telegrams from Garfield in Nashville and the staff at Tullahoma. Also gratifying to Rosecrans was a report on Wilder's expedition to Columbia. On 12 July Wilder had sent the Seventeenth Indiana and 123rd Illinois Mounted Infantry regiments on the sweep, led by Col. James Monroe.

Although unwell and facing business problems at home, Monroe aggressively led his two regiments on a 160-mile rampage through the towns of Lewisburg, Columbia, Centerville, Mount Pleasant, Mooresville, and Petersburg. Finding only a handful of convalescent and furloughed Confederates, Monroe added them to his haul of slaves and draft animals. The expedition returned to its base at Rowesville near Normandy on 18 July with fifty prisoners, 250 slaves, and 700 horses and mules, having lost only Pvt. Andrew Stewart killed.[14]

Not all the news reaching Rosecrans in Nashville was positive. Most troubling was a report from "scouts" at Tantalon that 3,000 Confederate cavalry had crossed the river on their way to burn the Crow Creek railroad bridges. That news generated a flurry of queries to both McCook and Sheridan. Although the report would prove to be incorrect, it illustrated the difficulty both armies encountered in learning about the other when separated by several mountains and a wide river. Apparently the source of the report was Col. Daniel Ray, who on 17 July informed Sheridan: "It is reported that 300 Rebel cav. crossed the river and went into Sweden's Cove two days ago. . . . P.S. I learn from apparently reliable source that Gunter a guerrilla Capt. is on this side of the river with a squad of men and says he intends to burn all the bridges between Anderson Station and Bridgeport." On the next day Ray reported that a woman named Schwartz claimed that 500 Confederates were near the headwaters of Little Crow Creek, on a mission to burn railroad bridges. As the distance from Tantalon increased, so did the number and aggressiveness of the Confederate raiders. By the time the story reached Nashville the raiders had grown tenfold, precipitating Rosecrans's hasty calls for a response. The problem was compounded by the participation of Mrs. Schwartz. According to Ray, she carried passes permitting both entry and exit through Federal lines, using two names different from her own. Having encountered her before, McCook told Sheridan to "make her go and show where the rebels are and if she is lying hang her." That outcome was forestalled by another telegram from Rosecrans: "Colonel Truesdale says Schwartz is well known to many persons in the Army. She has been in the Secret Service of the Army I am informed two years. I have no doubt about her loyalty and think her safe to trust." In the end, no Confederates were found and Mrs. Schwartz remained at large, although Sheridan threatened to "baptize" her in Crow Creek.[15]

In the absence of any formal system of analyzing the scraps of information that came to hand, people like the elusive Mrs. Schwartz were able to wreak havoc on operations, no matter how benign their intentions. Before crossing the mountains, the Army of the Cumberland received information on Confederate activities from a variety of sources. First were observations by Federal units. Second, current Confederate newspapers occasionally reached the Federals. Third, Confederate deserters often provided information, although their testimony had to be weighed carefully. Fourth, local civilians offered similar bits of news, but again much of it was suspect. The population of East Tennessee was seriously divided over the war, with many citizens opposed to the Confederacy and willing to risk all they had to support the Union cause. Finally, secret agents like Mrs. Schwartz prowled throughout the operational area. Like all the others, they reported what they saw and heard, for what it was worth. All of the various pieces of information were duly recorded by Capt. David Swaim in a ledger titled "Summaries of the News Reaching Headquarters of General W. S. Rosecrans, 1863–64," but without any overt attempt to rank them in order of importance, truthfulness, or precise chronology. William Truesdail ran his personal spy network, while Captains Swaim and Farrar of Rosecrans's staff also dispatched agents. Provost Marshal William Wiles attempted to generate a current order of battle for Bragg's command from prisoner interrogations. Occasionally Rosecrans would receive information from Halleck in Washington, more rarely from Burnside on his left, and almost never from Grant on his right. All of this information was analyzed solely by Rosecrans, and he was supremely confident that he was capable of doing so. Unless he chose to involve Garfield, his estimates of Bragg's location, strength, and intentions were his own. Thus the deficiencies in the system exposed by the phantom Crow Creek bridge burners remained unchanged.[16]

"Summaries of the News" shows a wide variety of sources providing information to Rosecrans in mid-July. At least sixteen Confederate deserters provided statements. While a few provided useful order-of-battle data, most spoke only of the general situation around Chattanooga. Almost universally, they claimed rations were low, Bragg was unpopular, Chattanooga was unfortified, and the city would soon be abandoned. Next in quantity was the information provided by fourteen civilians, many of whom were disaffected East Tennesseans. These civilians moved freely in and out of Chattanooga, crossing the pontoon bridges without challenge. Observing troop movements on the railroads, they ascribed them to a decision to divide Bragg's army between East Tennessee and Mississippi. What they were actually seeing was simply the return of Buckner's command to Knoxville, the movement of Johnson's Brigade to Loudon, and the transfer of Hardee's Corps to Tyner's Station. The most detailed civilian reports came from an Irish foundry worker and two Nashville & Chattanooga brakemen, who provided specific and mostly correct information on affairs in Chattanooga, troop locations, and railroad conditions. Five reports from "scouts" added nothing to the civilian accounts, most describing nonexistent Confederate cavalry movements in the Sequatchie Valley. Three informants characterized as "agents" were associated with William Truesdail. One was the notorious Mrs. Schwartz, who reported on Confederate stragglers around Columbia but earned no entry for her bogus Crow Creek report.

Another agent made it all the way to Atlanta and back via Huntsville with general information on the Atlanta munitions industry and road conditions. The third, who came from Chattanooga, provided good information on Confederate troop dispositions and Bragg's intention to make a stand there. Telegrams from Washington and Louisville and a captured edition of the *Chattanooga Daily Rebel* added nothing useful, nor did most statements forwarded by field commanders.[17]

The one field commander closest to the Confederates, Sheridan, was also the most active. Although Mrs. Schwartz's reports proved to be in error, there was no denying the fact that the Nashville & Chattanooga Railroad remained vulnerable beyond Cowan. It was also equally clear that the railroad was absolutely vital to sustain an advance by the Army of the Cumberland. Maintaining the security of the railroad thus became an instant priority when it was discovered that it was relatively undamaged. Sheridan had pushed Bradley's Third Brigade to the top of the Cumberland Plateau at University Place on 9 July but it had only operated on the plateau, not in the Crow Creek valley where the railroad exited the tunnel. To cover that area, Sheridan sent two-regiment contingents through the tunnel to Tantalon and Anderson Stations on three-day rotations, beginning on 11 July, while the Second Tennessee Cavalry (Union) regiment patrolled to the river. The infantry had to return to Cowan so quickly because the men could only carry rations for three days at a time and the unfinished Elk River bridge prevented the accumulation of supplies at Cowan. Thus Lytle's First and Laibold's Second Brigades shared the onerous duty of protecting the tracks. Because the road over the plateau was virtually impassable, the regiments had to make the disagreeable trip through the long, dark railroad tunnel and return the same way. The Second Brigade's Seventy-Third Illinois Infantry regiment enlivened its passage by having its band play "Yankee Doodle" as the regiment stumbled through the tunnel. The usual practice was for one regiment to be stationed at Tantalon and the other at Anderson. While keeping both the railroad and the working parties of the First Michigan Engineers and Mechanics secure, the forward position at Anderson Station still was eleven miles from Stevenson and twenty-two miles from the Tennessee River bridge at Bridgeport.[18]

Although the threat to the Crow Creek trestles proved to be groundless on 18 July, Sheridan decided, with McCook's approval, to move beyond the Cumberland Plateau in strength. Accordingly, on 19 July he ordered Laibold's entire brigade to march to Stevenson. At the same time, he directed Bradley to make another reconnaissance into the upper end of Sweeden's Cove. Fortuitously, completion of the Elk River bridge on the previous day brought Innes's construction train within Sheridan's orbit. Commandeering the locomotive and flatcar for the day, Sheridan took twenty soldiers down the line, far ahead of Laibold's toiling infantry. The party boldly passed through Stevenson and continued to the Widow's Creek trestle three miles from Bridgeport. Although the trestle was intact, Sheridan prudently directed the party to return to Anderson Station. Unseen by Sheridan, Confederate scouts reported his presence to Patton Anderson at Taylor's Store, a mile east of the river. Having relieved Jackson's Brigade on the evening of 13 July, Anderson had stationed one regiment at Shell Mound and posted the bulk of his command between Taylor's Store and the Bridgeport bridge, with his pickets on Long Island. Keenly interested in the Federal activity in the Crow Creek valley, Anderson regularly sent scouts beyond the river. He also gained control of Capt. Patrick Rice's Company G, Third Confederate Cavalry regiment. Rice had been raised just across the river in Tennessee and knew both the land and its inhabitants well. On the night of 18 July, when the Federals were chasing phantoms along Crow Creek, Rice was across the Tennessee with a small party, burning the highway bridge over the Sequatchie River near Jasper. Anderson's aggressive posture meant that Sheridan's noisy railroad reconnaissance was reported to Chattanooga within forty-eight hours. Learning that the Widow's Creek trestle was still intact, Anderson sent a party across the river on 20 July to destroy it. The next time the Federals appeared, they would find the railroad broken at Widow's Creek.[19]

Sheridan's advance developed slowly in the summer heat. Laibold's four regiments halted only a few miles south of Anderson Station on 19 July. At the same time, Bradley cautiously sent half of his brigade across the plateau once more to Dorn's Burnt Stand, where they could look into the upper reaches of Sweeden's Cove. On the next day, Bradley's regiments returned to University Place, having seen and heard nothing of interest. Wherever they might be, regular Confederate units did not inhabit Sweeden's Cove. Meanwhile, Laibold stationed a regiment at Anderson, posted another at a railroad bridge over Crow Creek, and led his remaining two regiments into Stevenson itself. Named for Vernon Stevenson, president of the Nashville & Chattanooga Railroad and now a Confederate quartermaster major in Atlanta, Stevenson had once been an important railroad junction. In peacetime, it was the place where the Memphis & Charleston Railroad met the Nashville & Chattanooga Railroad, its trains continuing to Chattanooga on trackage rights negotiated in 1858. Originally part of the Confederacy's best east-west route, but severed in multiple places during the campaigns of 1862, the M&C was now little more than two streaks of rust coloring the jungle of weeds obscuring the track. Stevenson itself was only a few dwellings and a one-street business district anchored by two railroad stations and a large frame hotel, grandly titled the Alabama House. Federal troops had occupied Stevenson for several months in 1862 during Buell's dilatory advance on Chattanooga. To protect the junction, Federal soldiers had constructed a small enclosed earthwork named Fort Harker overlooking the stations and a

The Alabama House, Stevenson, Alabama. (Miller, *Photographic History*)

wooden stockade nearer the village. By the time Laibold entered Stevenson, it contained only six families, all Unionist. According to Sgt. William Newlin, the village was "very shabby and unattractive in appearance." The defensive works, however, were in fine shape, and were quickly occupied.[20]

With the railroad now secure as far as Stevenson and supplies only beginning to accumulate, Rosecrans saw no need to hasten back to the front. Thus he remained in Nashville with his family. Two of his corps commanders also took the opportunity to have their wives join them, although in each case that opportunity was marred by family tragedy. Thomas Crittenden was notified by Rosecrans's staff on 16 July that his wife, Catherine, had reached Nashville and would join him at Manchester on the next day. Unfortunately, Crittenden's father, Senator John Crittenden, was near death in Kentucky and on 21 July Crittenden received permission to join the vigil at the patriarch's home. He and his wife departed immediately, leaving Palmer in temporary command of his corps. Fearing he would be too late, Crittenden arrived in Frankfort on 24 July. Senator Crittenden died two days later, with his son at his bedside. Crittenden would remain in Kentucky for several weeks. On 19 July Rosecrans invited Kate McCook, wife of Alexander McCook, to join her husband at Winchester. Married for only six months, McCook was trying to change his image, according to regimental commander Caleb Carlton, who wrote, "It is amusing to see McCook try to be good, he used to be one of the roughest and hardest cases in the army, his wife has made him pious and he has service in his quarters and has stopped drinking, and is doing his best to stop swearing." On the day of Rosecrans's invitation, McCook's father, Maj. Daniel McCook Sr., was participating as an impetuous volunteer during the chase of Morgan's Confederate raiders in Ohio. The elder McCook, sixty-five, was mortally wounded that day at Buffington Island and died two days later. Alex McCook's original plans were to meet Kate at Nashville on 22 July and escort her to Winchester, but news of his father's death caused him to continue northward to Cincinnati for his father's burial on 25 July. In McCook's absence, Sheridan assumed command of the Twentieth Corps and at McCook's suggestion transferred his headquarters from Cowan to Winchester.[21]

In the midst of the Crittenden and McCook tragedies, the headquarters of the Army of the Cumberland moved from Tullahoma to Winchester on 21 July. With the primary staff in Nashville, Maj. William McMichael of the adjutant general's section and Capt. Robert Thoms, a junior aide-de-camp, coordinated the details of the movement. McMichael selected the Mary Sharp College, a female school closed since 1861, as the army's headquarters, and located officers' quarters nearby. Anticipating that Rosecrans would soon arrive with his family, the staff selected a suitable private residence for him as well. McMichael also procured horses for Rosecrans and Garfield. In Rosecrans's absence, much official business that needed his attention had accumulated, but the general made no effort to leave Nashville. As an enticement, Thoms on 22 July wrote to Maj. Frank Bond, Rosecrans's senior aide: "Tell General he will be much more comfortable here than is possible at Nashville." Thoms was most likely correct, as the newest member of the staff, 1st Lt. Henry Cist, informed his mother in a letter on the same day. Describing Winchester as a "truly lovely place," Cist continued, "We found only thirteen pianos in the house. They are fast getting out of tune with the banging that is going on them. But pianos in the South are rarely in tune. We have some two or three members of the staff who are very fine performers and we have been enjoying the music as much as possible. This place is one of the most bitter of all Secessia. There are a number of citizens here and a very large proportion of them are pretty girls at least to us who have not seen any for so long." Cist's opinion of Winchester was echoed by Pvt. Allen Frankenberry, a member of Rosecrans's escort. Frankenberry recorded in his diary that Winchester was "a most beautiful town, full of pretty houses, gardens, trees, flowers, and girls, but all south."[22]

On the day that army headquarters opened for business at Winchester, David Stanley arrived with news of his expedition to Alabama. Before his departure for Nashville, Rosecrans had sent Stanley's Cavalry Corps on a raid that would carry all the way to Huntsville and Athens. On 12 July, Turchin's Second Cavalry Division left its camps around the village of Salem, six miles from Winchester. Clumsy and obese, Turchin cut a poor figure on a horse, an image hardly improved by the presence of his sharp-tongued wife, Nadine. Mitchell's First Cavalry Division followed Turchin's troopers a day later. Stanley left behind Watkins's brigade and the Second Tennessee Cavalry (Union) regiment, scouting for Sheridan. On 15 July, Stanley's divisions united at Huntsville and probed to the Tennessee River. Bragg interpreted Stanley's aggressive actions as the precursor to a raid toward Atlanta, and he reinforced the city. Stanley, however, focused solely on gathering Confederate resources from the Huntsville area. The town was almost devoid of men, as many planters had departed with their male slaves. Those that remained lost their workers to Stanley's cavalrymen, who scoured the surrounding country for male slaves, horses, mules, forage and food of all kinds. Also visited was the town of Athens, the place whose sack the previous year had led to Turchin's court martial. This time the Federals were more circumspect but no less thorough in seizing usable assets. After a few days the Federal cavalrymen left Alabama and returned to the army's right flank. On 22 July Stanley wired Rosecrans that he had subdued the region's inhabitants, had found few Confederates picketing the Tennessee River, and learned most of Wheeler's cavalry was around Kingston, Georgia. He reported capturing 300 slaves, 500 horses, and an equal number of mules. Disgusted with Turchin's dilatory movements and inadequate horsemanship, Stanley renewed his call for Turchin's removal from cavalry command.[23]

The slaves brought within Federal lines by Stanley, like those gathered by Wilder earlier, were not fated to spend the remainder of the campaign as laborers. Federal policy by the summer of 1863 had evolved to the point of raising, equipping, and employing African American combat units, and Rosecrans's Department of the Cumberland was slated to be a major participant. Adjutant General Thomas had been instructed by Secretary of War Stanton in the spring of 1863 to expedite the formation of African American regiments. While he concentrated upon the Mississippi River valley for the bulk of his work, Thomas eventually turned his attention to the Army of the Cumberland. On 12 July, just before he departed Tullahoma for Nashville, Rosecrans wrote Thomas seeking specific instructions on how to implement the process in his department. He also put his staff to work on the administrative details. The point of rendezvous for the slaves was to be the Elk River bridge camp of the First Michigan Engineers, and Innes was placed in overall charge of the process until other officers could be selected for the duty. Commanders of garrisons in the army's rear areas were directed to furnish able-bodied African American men for the project, with another rendezvous site established at Nashville. There was no thought of having any other than white officers for the new commands, and

Rosecrans on 18 July directed that lists of applicants for command positions in the new black regiments should be gathered for selection. As Rosecrans relaxed in Nashville, mustering officers and thousands of blank forms began to arrive at Elk River. When Stanley returned from his expedition on 22 July, he received orders to organize the African Americans he had brought within Federal lines into companies of infantry. Four days later Rosecrans queried Adjutant General Thomas about tables of organization and pay. The creation of African American combat units in Rosecrans's department would be slow and difficult, but he had at least put the process in motion enthusiastically.[24]

By 23 July Rosecrans's delay in leaving Nashville was raising concern both at Winchester and in Washington. Acknowledging the pleas of the staff, Garfield that day expressed his hope that Rosecrans would soon return to the army, but he admitted that he did not know when that would occur. Much more ominous was a curt message from Halleck at 3:00 P.M.: "Telegraph the position of your army, and what is known of Bragg's present position." Before responding, Rosecrans queried Thomas at Decherd for the latest information. Thomas simply repeated the account of an agent that had been forwarded to Nashville two days earlier. In his response to Halleck, Rosecrans summarized the agent's report, which was reasonably accurate, and added a terse summary of his own troop locations. On the following day, Halleck pushed harder, telling Rosecrans that if he waited much longer to resume his advance, Bragg and Johnston might unite against him. Halleck then proceeded to lecture Rosecrans on how to move rapidly by reducing his trains and living off the land. He closed with a clear statement of how Rosecrans's efforts were viewed in Washington: "There is great disappointment felt here at the slowness of your advance. Unless you can move more rapidly, your whole campaign will prove a failure, and you will have both Bragg and Johnston against you." In case Rosecrans did not understand the message conveyed in his official telegram, Halleck sent a second note, marked "private and confidential." Taking umbrage at Rosecrans's tone, Halleck was blunt: "The patience of the authorities here has been completely exhausted, and if I had not repeatedly promised to urge you forward, and begged for delay, you would have been removed from the command. It has been said that you are as inactive as was General Buell, and the pressure for your removal has been almost as strong as it has been in his case." Conceding that Rosecrans's logistical challenges were real, Halleck closed, "The dissatisfaction really exists, and I deem it my duty, as a friend, to represent it to you truly and fairly."[25]

On 25 July, Rosecrans responded directly to Halleck's official message, alluding to his private admonitions as well. He calmly stated that he need not be told to reduce baggage and scavenge the enemy's country because he was already doing those things. He asserted that a dispassionate observer would understand his reasons for not resuming the advance at once. He then suddenly addressed Halleck's private warning about Washington's displeasure: "I confess I should like to avoid such remarks and letters as I am receiving lately from Washington, if I could do so without injury to the public service. You will, I think, find the officers of this army as anxious for success, and as willing to exert themselves to secure it, as any member of the Government can be." Having made his point about Washington interference, Rosecrans returned to the difficulty of sustaining an army in the barren territory between him and Chattanooga. Halleck again responded with two messages. Officially, he patiently reiterated Lincoln's desire to see the citizens of East Tennessee liberated from Confederate control. Privately, he conceded the argument for the moment: "Whatever I have written or telegraphed to you on this subject has been from motives of kindness and friendship. It was my only desire to impress upon you the wishes and expectations of the Government, in order that you might be fully acquainted with those wishes. Having now explained to you frankly that you can have no possible grounds for your tone of displeasure toward me, I shall not again refer to this matter." Halleck had placed Rosecrans on notice that Lincoln's and Stanton's patience was limited. In truth, Rosecrans recognized this, and he responded: "Assure the President that whatever prudence & energy we have shall be put to work to save and hold that region, but these must go together or the last state of those loyal men will be worse than their present condition." He thus acknowledged Lincoln's desire for an immediate advance but failed to understand that Halleck was warning him about Secretary Stanton as well.[26]

In the midst of his discussions with Halleck, another contentious issue between Rosecrans and the War Department remained outstanding. Rosecrans had long contended that he needed a more robust mounted arm to counter the Confederate cavalry facing him. Wilder's mounted infantry brigade had been an expedient response to that need. Now Rosecrans was offered an opportunity to solve the problem more comprehensively through a proposal generated by Lovell Rousseau, commander of the First Division, Fourteenth Corps. Rousseau proposed to raise an independent corps of more than 10,000 recently discharged veterans, mounted and armed with repeating rifles, which would augment Stanley's cavalry. In sum, Rousseau wanted to replicate Wilder's brigade on a much larger scale. The number of horses and weapons required to create such a force was so large that prior War Department approval and support would be required. Needing an assistant to help him advance his scheme, Rousseau selected Col. John Sanderson, commander of the Fifteenth United States Infantry regiment. Only one battalion of Sanderson's unit was presently with the army, leaving Sanderson essentially without a command. Newly arrived, and with little to do, Sanderson readily agreed to join Rousseau. While waiting for Rosecrans to return to the army, Rousseau sent Sanderson and brigade commander John King to explain the scheme to Thomas. Receiving Thomas's assent, Sanderson and Rousseau next journeyed to Nashville to present their plan to Rosecrans. Gaining an audience with the army commander on the evening of 25 July, they obtained his enthusiastic approval. Rosecrans authorized Rousseau to visit the War Department and present the plan to Stanton and Halleck. Sanderson would accompany Rousseau as his prospective chief of staff. Armed with supporting letters misleadingly headed Winchester, Rousseau and Sanderson departed early on 27 July. Rosecrans meanwhile authorized Thomas to appoint a new commander for the First Division.[27]

James Garfield was undoubtedly privy to the tart messages passing between Rosecrans and Halleck, as well as the potential ramifications of Rousseau's mission to Washington. A politician to the core, Garfield could see that Rosecrans was incautiously alienating powerful factions capable of crushing him and all who served him. Already elected to Congress, Garfield could resign at any time, but he preferred to leave after a successful campaign. Too, he was a citizen soldier who did not have the professional's concern for logistics and terrain. Finally, he burned with abolitionist zeal and desperately wanted to advance the cause for which he believed the war was being fought. It is impossible to determine which motives primarily drove Garfield's thinking, but clearly one or more caused him to write privately to his mentor, Salmon Chase, on 27 July. In that letter he bemoaned the fact that Rosecrans whiled away the hours in Nashville. Even as he spoke positively about Rosecrans and his army, Garfield made it plain that he had favored a more aggressive stance well before the Tullahoma campaign. To emphasize the point, he reviewed the controversy in which every general except Garfield had counseled delay in beginning the campaign. To Garfield's mind, the resulting victory offered a great opportunity to continue the campaign as soon as the Elk River bridge was reconstructed. The bridge had been finished for more than a week, yet there was no sign of another advance. Baldly stating that he had urged a different course, Garfield damned Rosecrans's inactivity: "Thus far the General has been singularly disinclined to grasp the situation with a strong hand and make the advantage his own. I write this with more sorrow than I can tell you, for I love every bone in his body. . . . But even the breadth of my love is not sufficient to cover this almost fatal delay. . . . I beg you to know that this delay is against my judgment and my every wish." Garfield thus placed himself on the record as an advocate for a different policy in case events unfolded badly for the Army of the Cumberland.[28]

While Garfield and the War Department fretted over Rosecrans's delays, the infrastructure to support an advance beyond the Cumberland Plateau slowly fell into place. The key to logistical success was the Nashville & Chattanooga Railroad, which would have to carry a much greater volume of traffic than it had before the war. Thus the First Michigan Engineers and Mechanics implemented a detailed program of improving such mundane structures as water tanks. Even with improvements, the line would be overwhelmed if forced to carry all the army's supplies to Stevenson. Because Rosecrans envisioned approaching the Tennessee River on a wide front, he needed other locations to serve as supplementary supply dumps. Just beyond Cowan another railroad left the N&C and climbed the Cumberland Plateau before ending at a small village named Tracy City. Named the Sewanee Railroad when built in the late 1850s to tap rich coal seams on the plateau, the twenty-mile railroad rose 900 feet in eight miles by using grades of nearly 3 percent and curves approaching seventeen degrees. Nevertheless, if the Sewanee Railroad could haul supplies to Tracy City, it could sustain one of Rosecrans's corps in the coming advance. On 22 July, Lieutenant Colonel Hunton led a survey party up the steep track and found it usable. From Decherd, the Winchester & Alabama Railroad ran thirty-two miles to Fayetteville, Tennessee. A company of the First Michigan Engineers labored to put that road in running order to support the Cavalry Corps. Yet most of the activity remained concentrated on the Nashville & Chattanooga main line, which by the end of the month saw up to eight trains per day hauling supplies and passengers to the army. Woe to the commander who interfered with the work of railroad personnel, as Sheridan discovered when he arrested a conductor. A sharp reprimand from Rosecrans restored the conductor to duty, representing an object lesson in the primacy of railroads in the army commander's thinking.[29]

During the final week of July the Federal understanding of Confederate activities became somewhat clearer. First, Van Cleve at McMinnville decided to probe beyond the mountain wall facing him. After infantry expeditions yielded only a few guerrillas, Van Cleve mounted sixty-five artillerymen, placed them under artillery chief Capt. Lucius Drury, and sent them beyond the Cumberland Plateau into the Sequatchie Valley on 22 July. They rode north almost to the head of the long, narrow valley, passing through the villages of Dunlap and Pikeville, before returning to McMinnville via Sparta. Drury's party encountered only a few Confederate commissary personnel buying cattle and a handful of home guards and deserters. After destroying a few weapons and killing a Union sympathizer by mistake, the scouting party reported the Sequatchie Valley essentially free of Confederate forces. While Van Cleve was sweeping the Sequatchie Valley, a Truesdail agent named M. D. Thompson on 25 July reported the result of a daring trip to Atlanta. Under the pretense of visiting his uncle, Thompson gained a pass from the Chattanooga provost marshal's office and boldly took the train southward. At Atlanta he observed an abundance of quartermaster stores but few commissary items. He also noted Moses Wright's efforts to create a local defense force. Returning to Chattanooga by train, Thompson accurately described the Confederate order of battle, Hardee's departure, and the general location of Wheeler's Cavalry Corps. He also noted the brigade at Bridgeport, the small number of railroad bridge guards, and the removal of the Kelly's Ferry pontoon bridge to Chattanooga, then being fortified. Some of his information was corroborated by a deserter from the Fourth Georgia Cavalry regiment. Further confirmation came from Sheridan, who reported on 25 July that a Confederate engineer lieutenant had deserted to the Federals at Stevenson with current information and maps. The "lieutenant" was Conrad Meister, a German-born civilian draftsman who had been working in Stephen Presstman's engineer office.[30]

Unwilling to remain passive in the Crow Creek valley, Sheridan on 25 July informed Garfield that he would reinforce Bernhard Laibold at Stevenson with his remaining regiment, the Forty-Fourth Illinois, and a section of Battery G, First Missouri Artillery. Simultaneously, he sent William Lytle's Twenty-Fourth Wisconsin and Twenty-First Michigan Infantry regiments and a section of the Eleventh Indiana Battery to Anderson Station. While Sheridan was reinforcing Laibold, Confederate commander Patton Anderson was mounting an operation of his own. When the Confederates had evacuated Bridgeport early in the month, they had destroyed everything of value except a steam-powered sawmill. In an effort to recover the machinery, Bragg sent Anderson the small steamboat *Paint Rock* from Chattanooga. When the *Paint Rock* arrived on the morning of 27 July, Anderson loaded a working party and Company A, Ninth Mississippi Sharpshooter battalion, onboard and sent them across the river to Bridgeport. While the laborers were rigging the machinery for movement, they were fired upon by part of the Second Tennessee Cavalry (Union). Capt. William Tucker's sharpshooters repulsed the Federal horsemen at the cost of one man wounded. Nevertheless, Anderson elected to leave the machinery to the Federals and sent the *Paint Rock* back to Chattanooga. When Laibold reported the incident to Sheridan, he noted that the Confederates appeared to be removing more of the railroad bridge as well. Anxious to avoid that outcome, Sheridan told Rosecrans on 28 July that he would visit Bridgeport in force on the next day. This slow but steady growth of the Federal presence at Stevenson and Bridgeport would inevitably become more visible to the Confederates across the river, whether Rosecrans desired it or not.[31]

In his report, Sheridan proposed to occupy Bridgeport in strength by bringing Bradley's Third Brigade forward from University Place. He further suggested that Bradley's position on the mountain be taken by a brigade from another division. Energized by the threat of additional damage to the bridge, Rosecrans agreed to Sheridan's proposal and directed that a brigade from the Fourteenth Corps replace Bradley's troops. The new orders transformed a tentative probe from Stevenson into a much larger operation involving elements from separate corps and requiring supervision by army headquarters.

Until that supervision was in place, Sheridan bore full responsibility for the advance. Recognizing that fact, he issued specific instructions to Laibold: "I want you to be exceedingly careful in your advance on Bridgeport to-morrow morning. Send the cavalry well in your advance and on your right flank. Let your topographical engineer make an accurate sketch of the country and report the result of your reconnaissance. Do not let the enemy draw you into any trap." Laibold began his advance early on 29 July with the Forty-Fourth and Seventy-Third Illinois Infantry regiments, a section of Battery G, First Missouri Light Artillery, and Daniel Ray's Second Tennessee Cavalry (Union) regiment. While he was gone, Sheridan instructed Lytle to repair the road leading from University Place down into the Crow Creek drainage. With the railroad now working to Stevenson, the Cowan tunnel was unsafe for infantry and unsuitable for wagon traffic. The Crow Creek road, merely a rough path, had to be improved for use by wheeled vehicles if Sheridan's movements were to be sustained in the future. With the bulk of the Third Division advancing beyond the Cumberland Plateau, Sheridan planned to bring the division headquarters to Stevenson as soon as the condition of the road would permit. To support Sheridan, the Second Brigade of Reynolds's Fourth Division, Fourteenth Corps, abandoned its camps around Decherd, passed through Cowan, and began its ascent to University Place.[32]

The advance of several brigades beyond the Cumberland Plateau signified to perceptive observers that the Army of the Cumberland's long rest period would soon be ending. Ever since the completion of the railroad to Estill Springs, and especially after the Elk River bridge was restored, life for Rosecrans's soldiers had markedly improved. To keep the men too busy for mischief, commanders instituted a regular schedule of drills, beginning at the company level and proceeding through regimental formations to brigade tactical evolutions. Conducted whenever the weather permitted, the drills were leavened with periodic inspections and culminated in weekly dress parades. Officers with inadequate knowledge of the tactical manual were encouraged to study their drill books diligently. In at least one unit, the Thirty-Sixth Ohio Infantry regiment, they were called upon to recite what they had learned publicly. Beyond the daily drills, long hours were devoted to improving the regimental camps by sweeping the ground, removing trash, and building bowers of foliage to shade the men's shelter tents. In addition, there were large levies for fatigue parties to supplement the work of the Pioneer Brigade. Thus the Eighteenth Ohio Infantry regiment built platforms to keep supplies out of the mud, and the Nineteenth Illinois Infantry regiment unloaded railroad cars and guarded the stacks of boxes and barrels arriving daily. The Seventy-Fifth Indiana Infantry regiment diligently labored to improve the road ascending the Cumberland Plateau to University Place, killing large numbers of rattlesnakes in the process. Regiments throughout the occupied zone scoured the countryside for forage for their animals, stripping the fields bare. While necessary, such foraging caused a few pangs of conscience, as Capt. Thomas Honnell acknowledged to his brother Eli: "We have cleaned out almost everything. We can not get a bit of old corn or hay so we cut grass & oats take wheat & rye out of the shock drive in all the cattle for beef and just sweep everything before us. I don't know how the citizens are going to live."[33]

In several regiments much of the camp improvement work was expended on building houses of worship. At Tullahoma, the Forty-Ninth Ohio Infantry regiment cut and arranged tree branches into a large bower for religious services. Not to be outdone, the Thirty-Sixth Ohio Infantry regiment at Cowan constructed a 500-seat semipermanent structure. The men were so pleased with their handiwork that they engaged the defecting Confederate draftsman, Conrad Meister, to draw pencil sketches of the chapel that would be lithographed in Chicago for souvenirs. Most regiments employed chaplains, who labored diligently but not always successfully in maintaining the spiritual health of their commands. In the Army of the Cumberland, most commands followed the lead of the commanding general, who preferred to rest on Sunday, leaving it for divine services and reflection. Thus many diaries speak of religious services held weekly. Such services often included baptisms, as Pvt. Jackson Webster of the Tenth Wisconsin Infantry regiment recorded on 26 July: "Seen 1 poured and 7 emersed by the Chaplain of the 38th." Before conducting a baptismal service in the afternoon of 19 July at Hillsboro, Chaplain John Hight of the Fifty-Eighth Indiana Infantry regiment attended a fellow chaplain's services. Sadly Hight recalled, "Chaplain Crews preached an able sermon, but the attendance was very poor. . . . I do not think it is on account of any personal dislike on the part of the men, but they simply do not want to hear preaching." Some soldiers attended services for other reasons, as Capt. Daniel Howe of the Seventy-Ninth Indiana Infantry regiment at McMinnville explained, "A good many soldiers went to church in town to-day more I suspect to see the pretty girls than from religious motives." Equally honest was Cpl. William Miller of the Seventy-Fifth Indiana Infantry regiment, who wrote from Decherd on 26 July, "There was preaching in camp but it is very hard to get the majority of the men to meeting."[34]

Spare time in the camps was spent in a variety of ways. The more cerebral soldiers read books and newspapers. Indeed, the railroad brought current Nashville papers, and day-old Louisville and Cincinnati papers. As a supplement, some soldiers in Winchester began publishing their own paper on 12 July. For the nonreaders, swimming was a favorite diversion, while others used smaller streams for bathing and washing their uniforms. Berrying continued to be a favored pastime throughout the area. Some soldiers chose to visit civilian dwellings. When the sound of a piano enticed two men into a Winchester home, they found three pro-Confederate women who cordially conversed with the two young soldiers as if it were peacetime. At Pelham, Musician Hiram Hines and a friend spent all day visiting two families who lived near their camp. At University Place, Pvt. James Riley regularly visited pro-Union families in the valley beyond the mountain, especially if young women were present. Yet not everyone saw the mountain folk in such a positive light. Referring to the residents of Anderson, Pvt. George Cummins was vitriolic: "The most of the inhabitants are ignorant and immoral, abject poverty stricken, God forsaken, hell deserving set of animals in human shape." Conversely, Sgt. John Marshall participated in gathering army rations to feed destitute civilians at Pelham. For those soldiers who preferred to avoid the civilian population, there were many natural wonders to visit. Capt. David Claggett and other officers explored the mountains from their McMinnville camp. Sergeant Marshall marveled at a large cave and spring near his camp at Pelham. Lt. Jesse Connelly and chaplain James Johnston pondered the age of the Old Fort, an ancient fortification near Manchester. Still others remained in camp, whiling away the hours in games like chess and checkers. Soldiers in the First Michigan Engineers and Mechanics organized a circus. At the same time, the junior officers of the command instituted a series of horse races.[35]

For all of the troops, writing and receiving letters was the most common activity beyond the dull routine of the duty day. With the railroad at last operating efficiently, men could correspond with family and friends, hindered only by the occasional lack of paper and stamps. In that way, Lt. Col. William Ward learned on 22 July of the birth of his son. Col. John Parkhurst, a widower, used a letter to justify to his sisters a new child-care arrangement for his minor children. Pvt. Joshua Dewees learned from a letter on 17 July that his brother had been killed at Gettysburg two weeks earlier. Pvt. James Phillips shared some stern advice with his wife on 18 July: "You must learn that baby to get along without so much tending[,] put him in the Cradle and let him lay there and squall if he wants to and not kill your self lugging him around if you have got a cradle[,] if you have not buy one." Often, raw emotions were on display. Surgeon Josiah Cotton told his wife, "I promised you that I would do nothing that would make you or the children blush to meet me, and I have not. I believe that absence has rather increased my love for you. I always loved you more than you would give me credit for." Crushed by his fiancée's seeming rejection of their engagement, Capt. James Love replied, "What have I done? What have I put in those letters that should change you so in one short week?" Other writers simply described their circumstances and asked for items difficult to procure locally. Col. Hiram Strong asked his wife to send him some commercial maps of Virginia, Maryland, and Pennsylvania so that he could follow events in that theater. In a letter to his wife, Cpl. Alanson Ryman was specific in his wants: "You may send me some dried beef and a small cheese and some honey if you can get it. These are about all the articles that I care about except it may be some good whiskey."[36]

Extant soldier letters from the Army of the Cumberland during the month of July 1863 indicate that morale was high, almost without exception. Not only were the men pleased that their own Tullahoma campaign had been so successful, but the Union victories in other areas added to the general feeling that the war would end soon. Through newspapers and letters, Rosecrans's soldiers followed Grant's Vicksburg and Jackson successes, Banks's victory at Port Hudson, and even Meade's incomplete triumph at Gettysburg. They also believed the garbled success stories emanating from the Department of the South, where hard fighting was occurring in Charleston harbor. Only Confederate raider John Morgan's foray north of the Ohio River raised concerns, and then solely in terms of the safety of family and friends. In fact, many soldiers welcomed Morgan's trek through southern Indiana and Ohio, if only to show Northern citizens what war was like. Illustrative is the letter of Pvt. William Forder to his wife, Sarah, on 19 July: "I have no dout but what it is the best thing that ever happened for it will show the Butternuts what the rebs would do if they had a chance." Capt. Henry Richards wrote on 21 July: "The boys out here don't feel much sorry that Morgan has paid some of their friends in Ohio and Indiana this visit." A similar view prevailed regarding the New York City Draft Riots. Lt. Daniel Howe, for example, wrote on 16 July, "I am amazed at the riots in New York. The whole power of the Government should be used to push the draft to the last extremity if it deluges the North with blood." While some expressed strong abolitionist sentiments, others begged to differ. One such was Pvt. Joshua Foster, who told his parents of his anger after reading a Cincinnati newspaper: "Now all that do not belong to the Union Party are Copperheads, and that makes me so mad I don't know how to keep down. I am for The Union and The Constitution as they used to be, yet my party name is Democrat."[37]

During the latter half of the month, army paymasters made their rounds, distributing four months of pay. For a private soldier, the sum amounted to $52 before any deductions were made. An officer's pay was considerably higher. For example, Col. Sidney Post, commanding a brigade in the Twentieth Corps, received $780.80 on 21 July, from which taxes of $17.42 were deducted. The paymaster paid Post $263.38 in cash, and gave him a $500 draft on a government account in Louisville to be mailed to his wife in Galesburg, Illinois. For those men who desired to send money home, several methods were available. In some regiments the regimental chaplain took the money north and distributed it from there. Others utilized officers going home on furlough or recruiting duty. Indiana soldiers could avail themselves of a state-sponsored service whereby stipulated sums could be withheld from their pay, credited to the state, and disbursed by state agents to designated recipients in Indiana. Otherwise, the sole alternative for the soldier attempting to send money home was to place it in a letter and trust to luck. Of course, many men kept their pay and disposed of it in their camps. Pvt. William Christian wrote in his diary on 22 July, "We are living high while the money lasts. Condensed milk, cakes." At least Christian got something for his money. A great many other soldiers immediately engaged in games of chance. In the words of Pvt. John King, "I found that there was a perfect chuck-luck mania passing through the army. Nearly every regiment and company had men, sometimes more or sometimes less, who were daily playing chuck-luck and the only reason I could give for it was that the men all had their pay and there was nowhere the money could be spent." Lt. Jesse Connelly at Manchester noted on 23 July how payday attracted unsavory types: "Gamblers are lurking under the creek bluffs fleecing the unsophisticated of their hard earned pay."[38]

Payday compounded the normal problems of discipline in an army of boisterous young men. Many soldiers used their momentary windfall to purchase liquor, with predictable results. Two days after payday, Pvt. Francis Kiene reported that many men in his unit were drunk. Lt. Chesley Mosman wrote in his diary on 23 July, "Get paid. Universal 4th of July drunk. One man stabbed two of the Company. Fighting drunk." In Granger's Reserve Corps, the situation prompted a response from Rosecrans himself: "A staff officer having reported that there are constantly a great number of intoxicated soldiers at Wartrace, the General Comdg. directs that you make such laws in regard to selling liquors that will insure good order there, and at all places under your command." At University Place, sixteen soldiers partied so openly that they were arrested by the brigade provost guard. At Tullahoma, Chaplain George Phillips recorded, "At night news came of the capture of Morgan and his men, which with the absence of the Col. led some of the officers of the Regt to take a spree and some of them acted like crazy men." In Manchester, Pvt. George Botkin wrote, "Gobbled up a little of Old Bourbon whiskey & get as happy as a coon." Also in Manchester, Col. Charles Rippey "gave an order to some of the boys to get whiskey at the Commissary, and some of them got full and had quite a time." Tolerance for occasional intoxication often extended to other misdeeds. Theft and vandalism were often punished lightly or not at all. When soldiers broke the cornerstone of the University of the South and scattered its contents, Sheridan offered a reward for the "unmitigated raskel" who perpetrated the deed, but nothing came of it. More serious crimes elicited more severe punishment. In one regiment a deserter was drummed out of camp and remanded to prison. A cavalryman was dismissed from the service for burning a cotton mill. And two men from the Pioneer Brigade were sentenced to thirty days' hard labor with ball and chain for attempted rape.[39]

Even while Rosecrans's soldiers rested in their camps, the specter of death walked among them. Analysis of contemporary sources yields a toll of at least twenty soldiers who died or were accidentally killed in the period 5–29 July. The great majority of deaths were caused by typhoid fever and digestive tract disorders. In an age when field sanitation was rudimentary and the army's diet was so uncertain, such losses were to be expected in the field and not infrequent in the civilian population. Some soldiers died in hospitals in Nashville, others in regimental facilities, and still others during movement. While the bodies of some soldiers were shipped home, others were buried in local churchyards or simply in unmarked graves near camp. Even more tragic were accidental deaths stemming from carelessness or errors in judgment. During the month two events stand out. The first case involved soldiers from Wood's First Division, Twenty-First Corps. On the afternoon of 20 July, Pvt. Wilbur Jacquess of the Fifty-Eighth Indiana Infantry regiment joined three friends in an unauthorized foraging expedition near Hillsboro. Originally seeking blackberries, the foragers encountered and killed a sheep. The sheep belonged to a citizen whose property was protected by a provost guard that included Pvt. George Cropp of the Sixty-Fourth Ohio Infantry regiment. The guard twice called for the fleeing foragers to halt, but Jacquess and several others kept running. At a distance of 100 yards, Cropp fired and Jacquess fell dead. Feeling in Jacquess's regiment ran so high against Cropp that a vigilante party unsuccessfully attempted to assassinate him. The second case was equally troubling. On 21 July, at Cowan, a member of the Twenty-First Michigan Infantry regiment was cleaning his gun when it accidentally discharged. The bullet passed into an adjacent tent, instantly killing a sleeping soldier. This incident strongly affected everyone in the brigade, primarily because of the random nature of the death. To be killed in battle was one thing; to be killed while taking a nap was quite another.[40]

Possibly influenced by Confederate activity around Bridgeport, Rosecrans finally determined on 29 July to return to Winchester. Before leaving Nashville, he removed John Turchin from command of the Second Cavalry Division, replacing him with George Crook. Turchin would take command of Crook's old infantry unit, the Third Brigade of Reynolds's Fourth Division, Fourteenth Corps. Rosecrans also initiated an effort to replace the army's chief quartermaster, Lt. Col. John Taylor. He had been unhappy with Taylor's performance for some time, but the final blow to Taylor's standing was a trivial argument over the number of tents left at Tullahoma. Rosecrans requested that Quartermaster General Montgomery Meigs replace Taylor with Capt. Henry Hodges, the chief quartermaster at Nashville. Taylor had been with Rosecrans since their days in Mississippi, but his management style irked both subordinates and superiors alike. The more Rosecrans immersed himself in the details of the quartermaster's department and the nearer he came to resuming active operations, the less he liked Taylor's performance. Taylor responded to the pressure by seeking to resign on the grounds of ill health, and Rosecrans was delighted to make a change. Unfortunately, Captain Hodges was on leave in New York, so Taylor would have to continue in office for a few weeks longer. Still, there was promise of change in a department vital to the army's success in the forthcoming campaign. Thus satisfied, Rosecrans, his family, Garfield, and the remaining senior staff boarded one of the steam dummies and headed to Winchester. On the way, his party stopped at Wartrace, where Pvt. Gifford Robinson saw him: "He is quite common in appearance and actions and talked freely with any and all." Rosecrans reached Decherd around sundown where he found the entire Second Division, Fourteenth Corps, awaiting him. They presented arms and cheered loudly as he passed. At last, after a monthlong interlude, the commander of the Army of the Cumberland was back in the field.[41]

6

Rosecrans Makes a Plan

» 30 July–14 August 1863 «

Refreshed by his fifteen-day sojourn in Nashville and cheered that his wife and three of his children remained with him, Rosecrans quickly resumed his frenetic pace. On the morning of 30 July he inspected the handiwork of the First Michigan Engineers and Mechanics at the Elk River bridge. Braving a violent storm that wrecked camps from Estill Springs to Cowan around noon, he spent the afternoon reconnoitering fifteen miles up the Winchester & Alabama Railroad toward Fayetteville, where much of the army's cavalry was located. During the trip he dictated a flurry of messages to subordinates about projects he deemed to be lagging. Just as they had before Rosecrans left for Nashville, most of these messages involved the Nashville & Chattanooga Railroad in some way. Having found the steam dummy useful as a command vehicle, Rosecrans was incensed when it broke down briefly and demanded that it be repaired at once or a substitute sent from Louisville. Further, he inquired if the dummy could safely transit the Cowan tunnel without modification. Nor was that all. Rosecrans also complained that the locomotive supporting Sheridan's troops beyond the Cumberland Plateau was too weak to pull more than six cars over the mountain, and he wanted it replaced. He also demanded to know the location of the construction train. All these messages fell upon harried railroad superintendent John Anderson in Nashville and assistant superintendent John Beggs at Decherd. Rosecrans's tendency toward micromanagement was exemplified by other messages on the same day: to George Thomas, about pack animal panniers; to Captain O'Connell of the Pioneer Brigade, about the size of woodcuts; to James Morgan at Murfreesboro, about ammunition magazines and tarpaulins. In the midst of all the activity, Rosecrans found the time to authorize a brief leave for Maj. William McMichael, who had kept the headquarters functioning while Rosecrans and his principal staff officers were in Nashville.[1]

On 31 July Rosecrans took the dummy to Cowan, where he met Sheridan, whose division represented the vanguard of the army. Because of the continuing absence of McCook, Sheridan continued in temporary command of the Twentieth Corps, while Lytle commanded Sheridan's division. Sheridan quickly recounted for the army commander what had been done to facilitate the army's advance to the Tennessee River. Laibold's Second Brigade had occupied Stevenson and the Crow Creek valley on 20 July, and in subsequent days Sheridan had tried to push other portions of his division beyond the Cumberland Plateau. His brigade commanders were more cautious than Sheridan, however, and the results were disappointing. Laibold had made only a weak probe to Bridgeport on 29 July, Bradley's Third Brigade had remained atop the mountain because it was short of rations, and only half of Lytle's First Brigade had made it to Anderson Station. Unsatisfied with such slow progress, Sheridan on 30 July urged his subordinates to greater effort. On that day, Lytle sent the remainder of his brigade from Cowan beyond the Cumberland Plateau to Anderson. Lytle himself took a train to Stevenson and was temporarily marooned there when the engine broke down. Sheridan ordered Laibold to return to Bridgeport with the Seventy-Third Illinois and Second Missouri Infantry regiments, making the occupation of that site permanent. At the same time, Bradley's command reached the valley floor at Battle Creek, a few miles north of Bridgeport, and would occupy the works overlooking the railroad bridge on the next day. Thus Sheridan reported to Rosecrans that six regiments were at or near Bridgeport, two at Stevenson, and four on the railroad around Anderson and Tantalon Stations. Sheridan's entire division was now beyond the Cumberland Plateau, the first barrier on the way to Chattanooga.[2]

Pleased by Sheridan's initiative, Rosecrans was less satisfied with the logistical support of the division. The Cumberland Plateau was mostly barren, and the corn crop in Sweeden's Cove, along Crow Creek, and in the Tennessee River valley was not yet ripe. The Nashville & Chattanooga Railroad, therefore, was the lifeline for Sheridan's scattered units. Worst off were Lytle's two regiments at Anderson and Tantalon, which Sheridan complained were out of both rations and forage. Further, Sheridan wanted to take an engine to Bridgeport, but the only one under his control was broken. He knew there were engines at Decherd, but he had been told by the army's quartermaster that John Anderson would have to authorize their use. Knowing how to influence Rosecrans, Sheridan described the situation in dire terms: "Must the men starve on account of culpable negligence?" Rosecrans quickly ordered assistant superintendent Beggs to provide an engine immediately for Sheridan's use. Two companies of the First Michigan Engineers and Mechanics regiment accompanied the train to rebuild the Widows Creek bridge between Stevenson and Bridgeport. Still, the efficient Beggs could not save Anderson from Rosecrans's wrath on another railroad matter. With the Fourth Division of the Fourteenth Corps already spreading across the top of the Cumberland Plateau behind Sheridan, it too would need the rations that only rail transport could provide. The Sewanee Railroad, which climbed the mountain at Cowan before turning northward to the Tracy City coal mines, would be needed to support troops in that vicinity. Steep and crooked, the railroad had not appeared to Anderson to be a viable conduit for supplies, and he had done nothing to facilitate its use, neglecting to procure engines capable of the climb. Now Rosecrans discovered that the engines were unavailable, and he expressed his frustration to Anderson. Declaring that the result would be "millions in delay," Rosecrans pointedly reminded Anderson that he had been warned months before to prepare equipment far in advance of need.[3]

Back at his Winchester headquarters on 1 August, Rosecrans spent a frustrating day. He wanted to take the dummy to Shelbyville in the afternoon, but it was unavailable—another mark of Anderson's inefficient management. When Anderson's reply to Rosecrans's earlier rant arrived, it caused even more dissatisfaction. Unlike the accommodating Beggs, Anderson maddeningly stated that he had been unaware of Rosecrans's desire to use the Sewanee Railroad. Nevertheless, he would endeavor to repair a coal-burning engine to be placed on the road. Thus Anderson offered no apology, pleading simple ignorance instead. Frustrated that the day's plans were thwarted, Rosecrans resumed the contentious dialogue with his superiors in Washington. Writing privately to Halleck, he explained that his Louisville base was 264 miles to the north; his Nashville depot was 83 miles in his rear; and he confronted a 60–70 mile swath of barren country. Thus the railroad must supply the army until it could come to grips with the enemy. That enemy lay beyond a great river and was fortified in a mountainous region offering multiple options for advance or retreat. Rosecrans believed no advance should be attempted unless success was assured. To guarantee that success, he proposed to rebuild the railroad, establish secure supply depots, develop a means to cross the Tennessee River, and prepare to maintain himself beyond it. Only then would he seek the enemy. He would execute that sequence as rapidly as possible, but if the government thought otherwise, it should replace him at once. Rosecrans made the same arguments at greater length in a separate, unofficial letter to Lincoln. After recapitulating his tenure as commander of the Army of the Cumberland, Rosecrans noted how much his army had accomplished, all without water-borne support (like Grant) or short distances and small rivers (like Meade). In his letter to the president, Rosecrans's general tone was respectful, although his arguments occasionally verged on the condescending. Nor did he offer his resignation to Lincoln, as he had to Halleck.[4]

Not everyone in the Army of the Cumberland believed in Rosecrans's methodical plan of campaign. Garfield continued to chafe at the delay, writing to his wife, Lucretia, on 1 August, "I don't feel at all satisfied with the slow progress we are making and I expect to hear complaints and just ones, soon. There are the strongest possible reasons for using every moment now before the rebels can recover from their late disasters." Try as he might, Garfield was unable to accelerate Rosecrans's timetable, a frustration of long standing that may have exacerbated the severe attack of piles then afflicting him. Yet Rosecrans was not to be hurried until the railroad had delivered sufficient supplies to sustain more than a single division beyond the Cumberland Plateau. On 2 August the army commander changed his mind about going to Shelbyville, proposing to visit Bridgeport instead, but when the steam dummy could not be ready in time he reverted to his original destination. Accordingly, assistant superintendent Beggs was bombarded by a flurry of messages from anxious aides until Rosecrans and much of his staff boarded the dummy for Shelbyville. Maj. Frank Bond, Rosecrans's senior aide-de-camp, telegraphed Brig. Gen. Walter Whitaker, temporarily commanding Absalom Baird's Reserve Corps division, that Rosecrans and up to ten guests would be arriving for the evening. Late in the afternoon, Rosecrans's party departed Winchester for the two-mile trip to Decherd, then followed the mail train twenty-eight miles from Decherd to Wartrace. At the latter place the dummy diverged from the main line on the six-mile branch to Shelbyville. Before leaving with his commander, Garfield queried Lieutenant Colonel Hunton of the First Michigan Engineers and Mechanics about progress on the pontoons being constructed at the Elk River camp and the work on the Widows Creek bridge. With the railroad finally delivering tons of supplies, the bridging that would be needed at the Tennessee River was assuming ever-greater importance.[5]

Rosecrans and his party arrived safely at Shelbyville on the evening of 2 August. Shelbyville was the location not only of Whitaker's headquarters but also that of Col. William Reid's Second Brigade. During the morning of 3 August, Reid's troops marched to a field west of town and passed in review before Rosecrans and Garfield. The day was hot and the march disagreeable, but the men took it all in good part. In one of the standard performances so beloved by his troops, Rosecrans addressed each unit individually. To the men of Battery M, First Illinois Light Artillery, he tipped his hat and said, "You are the healthiest, largest and best looking set of men I have yet seen in any battery, and I hope soon to meet you at the front." Refreshed by the general's remarks, the troops returned happily to camp, the heat and dust of the day washed away by their commander's praise. The official party next boarded the dummy and returned to Wartrace, garrisoned by Col. Thomas Champion's First Brigade of Whitaker's division. There the Shelbyville ceremonies were repeated, during an even hotter afternoon. Rosecrans's performance again worked its magical effect on morale. As a member of the 115th Illinois recalled, Rosecrans said "we needed a little more soup, thought we were not quite as fat as the boys in some of the other Regiments" but that "he believed us to be pretty long winded." After telling the brigade it was "one of the finest he had ever seen in the service," and that he "hoped to meet it even nearer the front," Rosecrans and his retinue boarded the dummy and departed for Winchester. During the trip, his aide Capt. James Drouillard forwarded the location of all the army's major elements to Halleck. In a note to John Beggs, he sought to arrange transportation for Rosecrans to Stevenson and Bridgeport on the morrow.[6]

The euphoria Rosecrans may have felt after visiting the troops at Shelbyville and Wartrace did not last long. Upon returning to Winchester, he learned that the dummy had to be modified before it could pass through the Cowan tunnel, delaying his visit to the front for several days. On 4 August two intemperate messages arrived from John Anderson, who railed against a series of complaints about him from several commanders. Sheridan wanted soldiers traveling without orders to be carried without charge, apparently contrary to Rosecrans's policy of half fare. The provost marshal of the Fourteenth Corps condemned the mail and baggage handling on the passenger train, with civilians mingling freely with the mail and baggage agents. Worst of all, Thomas proposed the appointment of an "honest" railroad superintendent. Anderson strongly denied any implication of dishonesty and demanded either proof or disavowal of the charge by Rosecrans. Vexing as these petty quarrels were, they had a ready solution. Far more troubling was a two-sentence telegram from Halleck in Washington: "Your forces must move forward without further delay. You will daily report the movement of each corps till you cross the Tennessee River." If he had thought Washington would accept his timetable after he described the obstacles to an immediate advance, Rosecrans was sorely mistaken. Most galling of all was the requirement to report daily any and all progress, as if he were a child being closely monitored. Gathering an escort from the Fifteenth Pennsylvania Cavalry, he rode to Thomas's headquarters at Decherd, most likely to discuss Halleck's peremptory order. At 5:00 P.M., he responded tartly. Acknowledging receipt of the order, he continued: "As I have been determined to cross the river as soon as practicable, and have been making all preparations, and getting such information as may enable me to do so without being driven back, like Hooker, I wish to know if your order is intended to take away my discretion as to the time and manner of moving my troops?"[7]

Rosecrans was truly miffed that the Lincoln administration seemingly could not understand his military situation. Could Lincoln, Stanton, and Halleck not see that the obstacles facing the Army of the Cumberland were quite different from those encountered by other Federal armies? How could they not be aware of the massive Cumberland Plateau, the wide Tennessee River beyond, and the 2,000-foot mountain ranges guarding Chattanooga? Were they not aware of the fragility of his single-track railroads, vulnerable to Confederate guerrillas throughout their length? Could they not appreciate the risk in relying upon those railroads for food, forage, and ammunition during the army's advance? And what of Rosecrans's opponent, the veteran Army of Tennessee, which had nearly been victorious at Perryville and Stones River? Whenever Rosecrans stepped outside his Winchester headquarters, the Cumberland Plateau dominated his view. Yet Lincoln, Stanton, and Halleck could not see the Cumberland Plateau from Washington, and their worldview was wider than the military geography of southeastern Tennessee. Vicksburg and Gettysburg had been great victories, but the war was by no means won. Worst of all, a precipitous decline in volunteering had forced the government to institute conscription. Less than a month earlier, New York City had exploded in a four-day riot over the draft. That unrest had been quelled at great cost, but a second draft was scheduled to be held in New York on 19 August. In the face of such unrest, the Lincoln administration desperately needed positive news before elections in key venues like Ohio. For Lincoln, Stanton, and Halleck, the Army of the Cumberland had to be part of the solution to what was essentially a political problem. The difficult situation facing Rosecrans therefore was largely irrelevant. Measurable progress simply had to be achieved before the fall elections. Thus the view from Washington did not mesh with the view from Winchester, and a test of wills was about to ensue.[8]

While he awaited an answer from Halleck, Rosecrans on 5 August continued his methodical preparations for an advance on his own timetable. There was some good news around the army. McCook had returned to Winchester on the previous day and resumed command of the Twentieth Corps. His first act was to organize a review of some of his troops for the benefit of his young wife, Kate, who had returned to Winchester with him. Crittenden was still absent from his Twenty-First Corps, but two of his three divisions had organized their supply trains, which were on their way from Murfreesboro to Manchester with twenty days of rations apiece. The army staff ordered railroad managers Anderson and Beggs to modify the dummy so that it could traverse the Cowan tunnel. Elements of the First Michigan Engineers and Mechanics continued to repair track and strengthen bridges. Garfield ordered six companies from the Pioneer Brigade to build platforms at Stevenson for the tons of supplies arriving there. In the rear, train service was interrupted when morning fog caused one train to crash into another, killing three soldiers and injuring many more. The line was blocked for some time, making mail delivery late throughout the army. Rosecrans himself went to the Winchester depot to witness the departure of two of his horses, which were being shipped to Cincinnati. One of the horses, no doubt, was the valuable animal given him by John Wilder the previous month. When the car was late to arrive, Rosecrans's aides expressed the

Army of the Cumberland supply dump, Stevenson, Alabama.
(Behringer-Crawford Museum, Covington, Kentucky)

general's displeasure in another flurry of telegrams to the hapless John Beggs. Toward evening a summer thunderstorm broke over the Winchester-Decherd area. About the same time, Halleck's answer arrived from Washington. It was brief and pointed: "The orders for the advance of your army, and that its movements be reported daily, are peremptory."[9]

Rosecrans spent much of the night thinking about how to respond to Halleck's order, and composed a tentative answer in pencil. On the next morning he called Garfield, Thomas, McCook, and Stanley to a meeting to discuss his response. According to Rosecrans's later statements, he read Halleck's messages to the assembled generals, who were aghast at what they heard. When asked how he planned to respond, Rosecrans read his proposed reply. In the draft, he offered a tentative start date of 10 August for the army's forward movement. He then shed light on the process by which he planned to develop a route across the Tennessee River. Current information indicated that a river crossing between Chattanooga and Bridgeport would be unwise, and he had not yet decided to make the crossing upstream from Chattanooga or downstream from Bridgeport. Most of his troops could not advance until that decision was made and sufficient supplies and bridging equipment accumulated to facilitate the crossing. Rosecrans pointedly concluded, "To obey your order literally would be to push our troops at once into the mountains on narrow and difficult roads, destitute of pasture and forage, and short of water, where they would not be able to maneuver as exigencies may demand, and would certainly cause ultimate delay and probably disaster." Having stated that such a precipitous advance would be foolhardy, Rosecrans again offered his command to Halleck: "If, therefore, the movement which I propose cannot be regarded as obedience to your order, I respectfully request a modification of it, or to be relieved from the command." As Rosecrans remembered it, the corps commanders, led by Thomas, offered their positive support, while Garfield remained silent. Accordingly, Rosecrans finalized his answer and shortly after noon telegraphed it to Washington. Later in the day he directed his corps commanders to maintain ten days' rations and short forage (grain) packed for movement.[10]

Believing that he had answered Washington's challenge successfully, Rosecrans rode to the Elk River bridge to inspect the black regiment forming there. While many in the Army of the Cumberland had reservations about arming blacks, Rosecrans harbored no such doubts. The mounted sweeps during the previous month had brought in hundreds of able-bodied men, most of them now gathered around Estill Springs. There they initially provided a labor pool to support the work of the army's engineers. Under William Innes's supervision, the former slaves were organized into companies temporarily commanded by Innes's officers until a more formal officer selection process could be adopted. Similar activity occurred at Nashville, where other units were being organized under the auspices of Gordon Granger. On the previous day Rosecrans had reported to Adj. Gen. Lorenzo Thomas that 600 men had been enrolled at Estill Springs and 650 at Nashville, with 1,200 more potentially available. "When we get into Georgia, we can raise an army," he enthused. While clerks struggled to complete the voluminous enlistment paperwork, army headquarters issued a call for prospective officers. This call generated much discussion among the army's rank and file. While some vehemently opposed the idea of black soldiers, others saw a chance to escape the enlisted ranks and enthusiastically applied for the positions. Examining boards began to meet at Winchester and Nashville to select candidates from a growing list. John Beatty chaired the Winchester board. Nominally a fair and open procedure, the selection process soon became corrupted by favoritism and command influence. Especially egregious were the promises made, and broken, in regard to the regiment forming at Estill Springs, the Twelfth United States Colored Troops. Certain nearby units, such as the First Michigan Engineers and Mechanics and the Fifteenth Pennsylvania Cavalry, participated actively in the deal-making. Rosecrans himself was not above meddling, leading Kinsman Hunton of the First Michigan Engineers to remark that the army commander's pronouncements on the subject were not to be trusted.[11]

The day of Rosecrans's visit to Estill Springs was also the day established by presidential proclamation as a day of Thanksgiving. Although the occasion was meant to be observed throughout the army, the ceremonies varied according to the whims of division commanders. In the Fourteenth Corps, neither Rousseau's First Division nor Negley's Second Division seem to have taken notice of the proclamation. In contrast, the Third Brigade of Brannan's Third Division held a full schedule of commemorative events. In the Second Minnesota Infantry regiment, the program included sermons delivered by members of the Christian Commission and music from the regimental band. The Eighty-Seventh Indiana Infantry regiment spent the entire day in speeches, sermons, and musical tributes, dampened only by a heavy rain shower just after noon. Similarly, Reynolds's Fourth Division marked the occasion with prayers, sermons, and speeches in at least two of its scattered brigades. Perhaps because it was under Rosecrans's own eye or perhaps because McCook's wife remained in camp, Davis's First Division of the Twentieth Corps threw itself into the spirit of the day in an extravagant fashion at Winchester. The usual round of prayers, sermons, and patriotic songs was supplemented by stirring speeches from McCook and Davis, and musical interludes furnished by three regimental bands. As in Brannan's camp, brief but heavy rain sent people scurrying for cover early in the afternoon. In Tullahoma, miles from corps headquarters, Johnson's Second Division marked the day in much more subdued fashion. The First Brigade's August Willich declared a holiday from work, a practice also followed in Joseph Dodge's Second Brigade. In the Twenty-First Corps, all three brigades of Wood's First Division held services, but all the Second and Third Divisions could muster was a lighter duty day for most soldiers. Reserve Corps units at Wartrace and Shelbyville also followed this pattern. Confronting the enemy beyond the Cumberland Plateau, Sheridan's Third Division of the Twentieth Corps took no part in the day's festivities.[12]

Rosecrans was anxious to visit Sheridan's regiments deployed at Stevenson and Bridgeport. By the morning of 7 August the dummy had been modified to pass through the Cowan tunnel, and Rosecrans and Garfield boarded it for the trip to the front. At least one newspaper reporter accompanied them, "A.L.F." [Alfred Burnett], accredited to the *Cincinnati Commercial*. At Stevenson, the party added Sheridan and continued to Bridgeport. Many soldiers noted Rosecrans's arrival, but Cpl. Edward Crippin was unimpressed: "The old gentleman looks odd in his citizen dress and chip hat." At Bridgeport, Rosecrans found everything much as it had been since Laibold's Second Brigade had occupied the site permanently on 30 July. Now nothing stood but a log shanty and the open shed formerly housing the dismantled sawmill. Everything else, both railroad station and dwellings, lay in ruins. Initially nervous in the face of so many Federal soldiers, the Confederate pickets had gradually become accustomed to their presence and an unofficial truce generally prevailed around the wrecked railroad bridge. Anderson's Brigade guarded the far shore and picketed Long Island. The long bridge from the west bank of the river to Long Island was broken at both ends, but the draw span east of Long Island remained intact. Although they were peaceable, both sides carefully noted the daily arrival of trains on each bank. While their officers worried about security, many men on both sides of the river freely conversed across the wide but shallow western channel. Beginning as good-natured jesting, the conversations occasionally assumed a hard edge. Both Federals and Confederates used the river to swim, bathe, and fish, as did some local females, whose behavior was noted wryly in soldiers' letters and diaries. On the day of Rosecrans's visit, several men from Sheridan's staff enticed Pvt. Daniel Crow of the Third Confederate Cavalry regiment to visit the west bank with the promise of his safe return. Crow paddled across the stream and chatted affably with the Federals before returning to his own lines.[13]

Rosecrans probably never met Private Crow, nor did the Confederate's visit make its way into the army's daily intelligence summary. Nevertheless, the army commander saw much of interest during his first visit to Bridgeport. Clearly, a major construction effort would have to occur before the Nashville & Chattanooga Railroad could be extended beyond the Tennessee River, even without further bridge destruction. Still, the railroad, fragile as it was, could bring supplies all the way to the west bank of the river if need be. As he pondered whether to cross the Tennessee above or below Chattanooga, Rosecrans could see that the Bridgeport crossing site held prominent advantages, especially if the sustainability of the army was a primary driver. Equally significant, Confederate forces in the area were no larger than an infantry brigade in strength, supported by a tiny handful of artillerymen and cavalrymen. Even with a working railroad, Bragg could not quickly reinforce the Bridgeport area and contest a crossing if Rosecrans could keep his preparations secret. The town of Stevenson, eleven miles from Bridgeport and three from the river, was an ideal place for a supply depot and headquarters site. If the Memphis & Charleston Railroad could be returned to operation from Stevenson to Decatur, Alabama (eighty-three miles), where it connected to the Nashville & Decatur Railroad, a second supply line could be opened via that route, easing the pressure on the Nashville & Chattanooga Railroad. Stevenson's primary flaw was that it was visible from the top of Confederate-held Sand Mountain, beyond the Tennessee River and only five miles distant, although heavy vegetation obscured much of that visibility. Even if the Memphis & Charleston could not be reopened, the Stevenson-Bridgeport locality offered much to an army commander seeking a way through the maze of geographical obstacles between him and Chattanooga.[14]

With impressions of Bridgeport fresh in his mind, Rosecrans departed for Winchester. Before leaving Stevenson, he telegraphed Ambrose Burnside, commanding the adjacent Department of the Ohio. Halleck for some time had desired a collaborative advance on East Tennessee by Burnside's and Rosecrans's armies, and the two generals had been exchanging information for several weeks. Now both commanders were under the same peremptory orders to advance, and it was time to coordinate the movements of the two armies. Rosecrans explained to Burnside that he had made the town of McMinnville a supply depot in case Burnside's advance approached Rosecrans's left. He asked Burnside to provide him with concrete information on his plan of campaign so that the Twenty-First Corps could cooperate with Burnside's movements, thereby assuring a united front against Bragg's and Buckner's forces. Burnside was notoriously slow in acting, so Rosecrans urged him to accelerate the process. Resuming his journey to Winchester, the army commander found upon his arrival that Halleck had responded to his churlish note of the previous day. Halleck wrote, "I have communicated to you the wishes of the Government in plain and unequivocal terms. The object has been stated, and you have been directed to lose no time in reaching it. The means you are to employ, and the roads you are to follow, are left to your own discretion." Having successfully forced Halleck to back down, Rosecrans soothingly responded that he was doing everything possible to expedite his advance. He closed, "Will advise you daily." By threatening to resign, Rosecrans had maintained his freedom not only to set the time of his advance but the route as well. Still, he perceived that the hour for commencing his campaign was fast approaching. Thus he informed his mother-in-law, Eliza Hegeman, in Yellow Springs, Ohio, that Anna Rosecrans would be leaving the army on 10 August, one of the potential dates for the campaign to begin.[15]

Rosecrans accelerated the pace of activity on 8 August. For some time Rosecrans's family had been sharing quarters at Yellow Springs with the family of Brig. Gen. Eliakim Scammon, an associate of Rosecrans's from their days in western Virginia. While Anna Rosecrans and three of her children visited the Army of the Cumberland, the youngest children, Carl and Charlotte, remained in Ohio with their grandmother Hegeman. Rosecrans's telegram to Mrs. Hegeman triggered an instant response from Ohio that Charlotte was seriously ill. Rosecrans immediately arranged for his wife and daughters to leave for Yellow Springs that very afternoon. Ominously, he wired Mrs. Hegeman, "Telegraph if Charlotte is worse." Rosecrans's son, Adrian, fourteen, would remain with him a while longer. While an aide arranged his family's travel, Rosecrans turned to army business with his accustomed habit of micromanagement. A flurry of telegrams ensued: to John Anderson, use every available freight car to move supplies forward, and come to headquarters as fast as possible; to Capt. Simon Perkins Jr., assistant quartermaster in Nashville, expedite movement of rail cars, with priority given to forage; to Sheridan, describe the nature of the ground at

Caperton's Ferry on the Tennessee River, and move lumber to Stevenson for shed roofs; to Capt. Ferdinand Winslow, acting chief quartermaster in Nashville, provide 100 horses for the Fifteenth Pennsylvania Cavalry regiment; to John Palmer, move the army's reserve ammunition train from Manchester to Tullahoma at once, and send all extra supplies to McMinnville; to John Van Duzer, run a second telegraph line along the railroad; to Gordon Granger, order the First Battalion Ohio Sharpshooters from Normandy bridge to Winchester; to Calvin Goddard, return at once from leave as several staff members are ill; to Governor Andrew Johnson, please come for a visit tomorrow; and finally, to John Beggs and William Lytle, expedite the transportation of Mrs. Margaret Bybee, Confederate Brig. Gen. Patton Anderson's mother, to Bridgeport.[16]

That same day, Chief Quartermaster John Taylor submitted his estimate of the railroad cars needed daily to supply the army during its campaign. Taylor used planning figures of 45,000 animals and 70,000 men in computing the army's needs, with the capacity of each railroad car placed at eight tons. He expected that fodder or long forage would be procured locally, leaving only the grain or short forage to be transported by rail. Therefore the army's animals would need 450,000 pounds of grain per day, accounting for twenty-eight railroad cars. Standard bacon-based rations for the men equaled 210,000 pounds per day, carried in thirteen cars. Quartermaster stores amounted to 160,000 pounds per day, or ten cars. Medical stores accounted for 32,000 pounds per day, filling only two cars. Finally, "Contingencies" added 112,000 pounds per day, the equivalent of seven freight cars. In total, Taylor estimated that Rosecrans's four corps would require the Nashville & Chattanooga Railroad to deliver at the railhead an average of 964,000 pounds of supplies per day, the equivalent of sixty loaded freight cars. This quantity of supplies had to be delivered every day for the duration of the campaign. Otherwise, the army would have to operate on reduced rations for an extended period while marching over a series of mountain ranges rising at least 1,000 feet above the plain. Taylor's estimate did not account for the army's ammunition needs, which was the province of Capt. Horace Porter's ordnance department, because ammunition moved in regimental wagons or the army's 800-wagon reserve ammunition train. Even without the ammunition, the task facing the 4,000 railroad workers of the Nashville & Chattanooga was enormous. With only thirty locomotives, 350 cars, rapidly deteriorating track, and inadequate sidings, the railroad would be taxed to the utmost. It is likely that Taylor's sixty-car per day estimate on 8 August was the reason that Rosecrans peremptorily summoned John Anderson to Winchester.[17]

On the same day, larger operational and political issues came into clearer focus. Responding to Rosecrans's query, Ambrose Burnside announced that he would probably advance from Stanford, Kentucky, toward Knoxville and

Loudon, Tennessee. Burnside had hoped to await the arrival of the Ninth Corps, which had not yet returned from service on the Mississippi River, but Halleck's order to advance was peremptory. Thus Burnside could send no more than 5,000 cavalry and 7,000 infantry toward Knoxville, beginning on 11 or 12 August. Still, if Rosecrans advanced at the same time, Bragg's and Buckner's forces might be overwhelmed. Cheered by Burnside's message, Rosecrans dispatched his first daily report to Washington in accord with Halleck's directive. In a small act of defiance, he addressed the report to Adj. Gen. Lorenzo Thomas, not Halleck. Thomas, as Rosecrans was probably aware, was fully occupied with the enrollment of black troops, and had not participated in the rancorous discussions between Rosecrans and the War Department. Nevertheless, Rosecrans was following the letter of army protocol, if not the spirit, and informed Thomas, "For the information of the General-in-Chief, I report that our cavalry on the left have moved to Sparta, to attack the rebel advance there. Our forage trains are coming up, but we have not transportation enough to get our supplies up to five days ahead, until the cars lately bought arrive. No other movement of troops to-day." The message offered no indication that an advance was imminent, but it met the requirement for a daily report. Thus, in this passive-aggressive way, Rosecrans continued to operate on a timetable of his own choosing. Coincidentally, in Washington, Lovell Rousseau and John Sanderson finally gained an audience with President Lincoln and presented the proposal to create a new mounted division for service in the theater. Lincoln directed the two officers to Secretary of War Stanton, who simply deferred the matter to Halleck. There the proposal rested, for the time being.[18]

On Sunday, 9 August, Rosecrans maintained his frenetic pace. Responding to Anna's telegram announcing her safe arrival in Nashville, Rosecrans told his wife that he had heard nothing further regarding Charlotte's condition. He then turned to army business. Unexpectedly but pleasantly received was John Anderson's resignation. In response, Rosecrans appointed Col. William Innes as his replacement. Innes, as aggressive as he was efficient, had been lobbying hard for the position for months. He now assumed operational control of railroad activities between Nashville and the front, while at the same time retaining regimental command. Rosecrans lost no time in making new demands on him. With the need for rolling stock so acute, he instructed Innes to purchase twenty cars from the Adams Express Company to augment the barely adequate freight car pool. John Beggs remained as assistant railroad superintendent, and Rosecrans again raised the issue with him of using the Sewanee Railroad to haul supplies to Tracy City. In order to supplement the railroads, Rosecrans looked to the Tennessee River itself. Federal forces controlled the river from its mouth all the way to Muscle Shoals, Alabama, where natural obstructions prevented the passage upstream of all but the most shallow-draft vessels. Therefore Rosecrans directed Capt. Ferdinand Winslow at Nashville to seek two vessels that could pass the shoals and ascend the river to Bridgeport. Such vessels would need naval protection, so Rosecrans telegraphed Capt. Alexander Pennock, commanding the Cairo, Illinois, Naval Station, seeking the location of the Mississippi Marine Brigade. Such last-minute requests bespoke Rosecrans's self-absorption with his problems alone, with no thought to what might be transpiring in other theaters. In like vein, he telegraphed Maj. Gen. Stephen Hurlbut, commanding the District of West Tennessee at Memphis, "Cannot you occupy Florence and so protect our flanks?" This request, sent directly to one of Grant's subordinates, was not only cavalier and tardy but violated army protocol as well.[19]

Writing to Burnside late on 9 August, Rosecrans revealed his thinking. He planned to advance one corps beyond the Cumberland Plateau into the Sequatchie Valley to confront Chattanooga directly. The remainder of his army would close on the Tennessee River around Bridgeport. Still undecided on the army's main crossing point, Rosecrans admitted that Bridgeport looked very promising. If he chose to cross downstream, he promised Burnside that he would demonstrate in front of Chattanooga to distract the Confederates. The advance would begin on the next day but would develop slowly. Rosecrans's remarks show that his campaign plan remained incomplete, with major decisions still pending. First, he calculated that he needed sufficient supplies to subsist his army for twenty days beyond the railhead and enough ammunition to fight two major battles. With a maximum effort, the railroad could sustain the soldiers for twenty days, but the long forage needed by the army's animals had to be procured locally. It was imperative that the local corn crop be ripe enough to provide fodder, and that would not occur until the middle of August. The second consideration was the crossing of the Tennessee River. Rosecrans could not rely upon random small boats or makeshift rafts to make the crossing. Instead, large numbers of pontoons would have to be constructed and brought to the river by rail. The third consideration was how to deceive the Confederates as to the point of crossing. That deception could be provided through a combination of targeted misinformation and ostentatious displays. Fourth, the actual crossing point had to be selected. Finally, a scheme of maneuver would have to be implemented to gain possession of Chattanooga. By 9 August supply accumulation and pontoon construction were nearing completion, and the deception plan was ready for implementation. Rosecrans's note to Burnside indicated that he had not yet reached a final decision on the river crossing sites, and that decision would shape the scheme of maneuver.[20]

As for crossing sites, Rosecrans's most direct course of action was to force a crossing in the vicinity of Chattanooga. A few rough and steep roads led over the Cumberland Plateau and Walden's Ridge to the Tennessee River valley directly opposite Chattanooga, with the nearest railhead at Tracy City. The Sewanee Railroad clearly could not handle the volume of traffic that the Nashville & Chattanooga Railroad provided to Stevenson and Bridgeport. Further, all intelligence sources indicated that Bragg's army was concentrated around Chattanooga, which it was fortifying. The river crossing itself would be difficult enough without opposition and virtually impossible if attempted under the muzzles of Bragg's guns. Burnside's debacle at Fredericksburg graphically illustrated the problem. Logistically tenuous and tactically suicidal, the direct option received only cursory consideration before being rejected. Rosecrans's second option was to cross the river upstream from Chattanooga. While it permitted an unopposed crossing if the deception plan worked, this option was even more difficult to sustain logistically than the direct approach. Again, both the Cumberland Plateau and Walden's Ridge would have to be surmounted, with the nearest railhead being McMinnville, west of the mountain wall. In this option the railroad's task was easier, but the wagon haul was more difficult, and the local forage could not sustain the army's animals. If Rosecrans adopted this option and advanced to the vicinity of Cleveland, he might interpose between Bragg and Buckner, but he would not threaten Bragg's supply line to Atlanta. Without that threat, Bragg could simply maneuver against Rosecrans with Chattanooga secure in his rear. If Burnside moved promptly, there might a chance for a potential merger of his and Rosecrans's armies, with Burnside being the senior officer. If Burnside dallied, Rosecrans might find himself trapped between Bragg and Buckner, with each Confederate force being supported by rail while Rosecrans depended upon an extremely difficult wagon haul from McMinnville.[21]

Rosecrans's third option was to cross at Bridgeport, downstream from Chattanooga. This option placed his railhead directly on the Tennessee River. The Sewanee Railroad could support the army's left, as well as forces involved in the deception plan. Rosecrans's sources indicated that a lone Confederate infantry brigade and some cavalry guarded the river around Bridgeport. A crossing there probably would face little opposition, allowing the engineers to work unimpeded. If Rosecrans could then push large forces beyond Sand and Lookout Mountains, he would seriously threaten Bragg's lifeline to Atlanta. Such a threat would be much more likely to force Bragg to evacuate Chattanooga than an approach from the north. Any battle resulting from adoption of this option would be more likely to develop as a fight for Bragg's supply line than one for Rosecrans's. The initiative would belong to Rosecrans, and Bragg would have to dance to the Federal tune. Logistically, it made the best use of railroad assets and protected the Federal supply line most easily. Operationally, it offered a better chance to force the evacuation of Chattanooga without a fight than either of the other options. It did not tie Rosecrans's movements in any way to Burnside's, a good thing in view of Burnside's record. It also could facilitate Burnside's advance on Knoxville if Buckner moved to join Bragg, as Rosecrans expected him to do. The cooperation between Rosecrans's and Burnside's forces, so earnestly desired by the Lincoln administration, could thus be achieved without literal amalgamation. The more Rosecrans looked at the downstream option, the more promising it appeared. Still, he announced no decision. Instead, he directed all surplus supplies to McMinnville, ordered the occupation of Tracy City, and queried Sheridan about the Tennessee River at Caperton's Ferry, near Stevenson. Even so, the steady stream of trains daily unloading supplies at Stevenson and Bridgeport created the impression that Rosecrans's decision had been made.[22]

An hour before midnight, Rosecrans telegraphed his daily report of activities to Lorenzo Thomas. His only news was that Reynolds's Fourth Division, Fourteenth Corps, had advanced to Tracy City. Rosecrans explained that he was only one day ahead of daily supply requirements, and he needed to be at least five ahead in order to cross the Cumberland Plateau. In fact, the statement that Reynolds had occupied Tracy City was literally untrue. On 9 August, none of Reynolds's three brigades was at Tracy City. Two brigades were atop the Cumberland Plateau around University Place, and one was still in camp at Decherd. All three of the division's units were momentarily in turmoil. Wilder's First Brigade, at Decherd, had long been censured by Reynolds for its lax discipline, aggressive foraging, and disregard of military protocol. While Wilder had been on leave in Indiana, the straitlaced Reynolds made several ineffectual efforts to curb the brigade's excesses. Wilder returned to duty on 9 August and resumed defending his men by cultivating Reynolds's superiors, but the brigade remained at Decherd. The Second Brigade was commanded by Col. Edward King, who had just arrived from convalescent leave. The unit had been at University Place since 29 July. Reynolds's Third Brigade was also experiencing command turmoil. Dissatisfied with Turchin's performance as a cavalryman, Rosecrans had traded him for the brigade's George Crook on 30 July. The switch was strongly favored by many soldiers, who had chafed under Crook's strict policies against foraging, but officers like Col. Caleb Carlton of the Eighty-Ninth Ohio Infantry regiment were dismayed. Nor did they like Nadine Turchin, "not a woman of much delicacy." Turchin and his disgruntled wife moved their new command to University Place on 1 August and encamped a mile beyond King's troops, where they remained. Reynolds himself remained in Decherd. Thus, Rosecrans's report to Thomas notwithstanding, the Fourth Division did not occupy Tracy City on 9 August.[23]

Although Rosecrans's infantry remained quiet on 9 August, some of his horsemen were active on the army's far left flank. At McMinnville, Van Cleve long had wanted a mounted force to patrol the mountains in his front. On 1 Au-

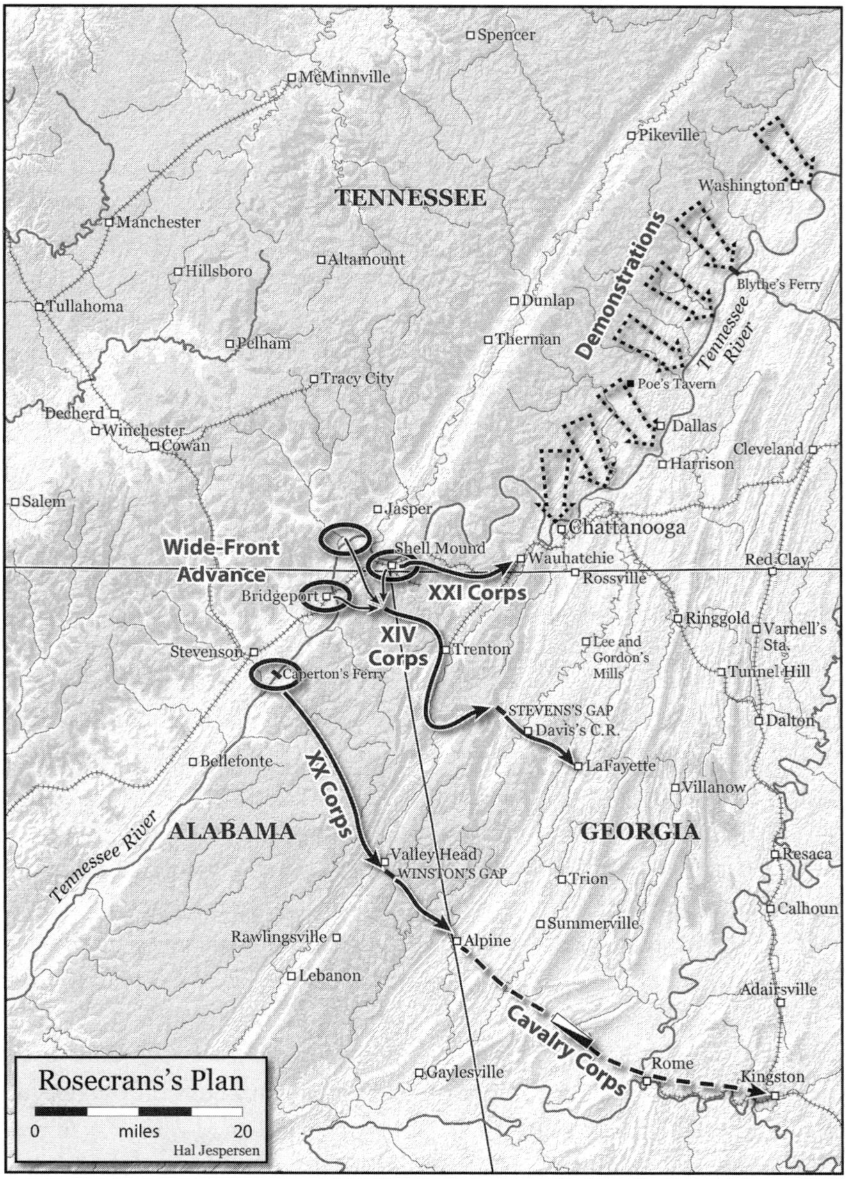

gust Rosecrans had sent him Minty's First Brigade of Crook's Second Cavalry Division. Coincidentally, Forrest had sent Col. George Dibrell with his own Eighth (Thirteenth) Tennessee Cavalry regiment across the Cumberland Plateau to watch the Federals. Dibrell was from Sparta, twenty-five miles northeast of McMinnville. He occupied his own plantation in late July and began to recruit his depleted regiment while watching the Federals at McMinnville. Aware of Dibrell's presence, the aggressive Minty had tried to surprise the Confederates on the night of 4 August by quickly overwhelming their pickets on the Caney

Fork River. Although the Federals captured several pickets, others escaped to alert Dibrell. Having lost the element of surprise, Minty returned to McMinnville. Unhappy with Minty's results, Van Cleve ordered him to try again, using a larger force of 774 troopers. Early on 9 August Minty again crossed the Caney Fork, driving the Confederate pickets through Sparta at a gallop. Warned by the noise, Dibrell delayed the charging Federals with one company and formed his regiment behind Wild Cat Creek. With his right protected by the Calfkiller River and his left covered by a millpond, Dibrell halted Minty's charges. When Minty threatened to outflank the Confederates by sending a regiment across the Calfkiller, Dibrell withdrew his 300 troopers behind Blue Spring Creek and made another stand. Rather than press his luck, Minty elected to return to McMinnville. He admitted losing three killed and two wounded, although Dibrell claimed he killed twelve Federals. Dibrell placed his own loss at four wounded and eight captured, while Minty claimed killing fourteen and capturing ten Confederates. At the end of the day, Dibrell reoccupied Sparta, and Forrest soon reinforced him with 200 men from the Fourth Tennessee Cavalry. The Confederate observation post at Sparta remained viable.[24]

At the other end of the front, the friendly truce at Bridgeport remained in effect on 9 August. Except for unauthorized visits by a few bold soldiers, nothing had been exchanged except occasional newspapers and tobacco carried to midriver. Now there was to be a more formal transfer, as Margaret Bybee, mother of Patton Anderson, was to be repatriated to the Confederacy at Bridgeport in style. Rosecrans instructed assistant superintendent Beggs to place a lounge in her car before her train left Decherd on the afternoon of 8 August. She was escorted from Winchester by Lt. Col. William Ward. The train arrived at Bridgeport too late for her to be sent across the river that day, so Mrs. Bybee was the overnight guest of Ellen Sherman, wife of Col. Francis Sherman of the Eighty-Eighth Illinois Infantry regiment. After the sun banished the morning mist on 9 August, the Federals initiated a formal flag of truce procedure. Lytle assigned two staff officers to accompany the party with a bottle of champagne to commemorate the occasion. At 10:00 A.M., a boat flying a white flag ferried Mrs. Bybee, Mrs. Sherman, Lt. Col. Ward, Lytle's two aides, and several orderlies across the river to Long Island. Awaiting them were several Confederate officers dressed in their most formal attire. While the orderlies unloaded Mrs. Bybee's baggage, the officers of both armies toasted each other's health with the champagne. After the ceremony, the Confederates crossed the drawbridge to the eastern bank of the river while the Federals and Ellen Sherman rowed back to the western shore. That evening at twilight Ward and a delegation from the Tenth Ohio Infantry regiment presented Lytle, their former commander, a token of their esteem. In a touching speech, Lytle accepted the gift, a solid gold Maltese cross encrusted with diamonds and an emerald, suspended from a silver shield. Then, as the shadows lengthened on the river and the music from regimental bands wafted over the valley, for a few moments at least, the war seemed far away.[25]

West of the Cumberland Plateau, the war was also distant, although prescient observers could see signs that the long pause was nearing its end. While Rosecrans fretted about supplies and pontoons and meddling deskbound generals in Washington, his soldiers continued the routine established six weeks earlier. Gone were the starving times of early July; for most, the railroad brought full rations daily, and local apples and peaches were ripening for the harvest. By now, all but the laziest privates had shaded their tents with cedar boughs and crafted rude furniture to make their daily existence more civilized. Capt. James Edmonds expressed the views of many: "Scenery fine, water good and everything calculated to make a soldier's life pleasant." Still, both the scenery and the routine were becoming monotonous, making some commanders nervous. At Tullahoma, August Willich spent early August schooling his four regiments mercilessly in the intricacies of skirmishing and maneuvering solely by the bugle. While not training as hard as Willich's men, all regiments suffered through hours of drill at echelons from company to brigade. Most days also involved standing for long periods in formation for dress parade and inspection. The usual camp diversion of reading newspapers, magazines, books, and religious tracts was supplemented by increased letter writing, now that regular mail service was available. William Carroll advised his sister on 8 August that she did not need his permission to write to a soldier in another regiment: "I suppose you ar [*sic*] of age and ought to have your own way." A letter to William Miller from his wife, Nett, informed him on 7 August that their son Rollie was dangerously ill. That night Miller wrote in his journal, "I hope the next letter will say Rollie is out of danger, if not entirely well." Sadly, the next letter brought the worst of all possible news. Still, Miller resolved to continue doing his duty, even as he consoled his wife by mail.[26]

Many individuals employed more creative diversions than writing letters. Some played marbles and chess, at least one studied the German language, and still more fashioned trinkets from local granite and the cornerstone of the University of the South. One soldier sent home $50 gained from turning buttons into rings. At Winchester and Decherd, soldiers patronized photographic studios. The upwardly mobile stood for examination as prospective officers in the United States Colored Troops. Every Sunday regimental chaplains preached to large congregations, and United States Christian Commission ministers held midweek prayer meetings. Less wholesomely, more and more soldiers found themselves ensnared by the growing availability of illicit alcohol. On 5 August a court-martial convicted a captain in the Ninety-Eighth Illinois Mounted Infantry regiment of drunkenness but recommended mercy.

Two days earlier, five noncommissioned officers in the Seventy-Eighth Pennsylvania Infantry regiment were reduced to the ranks for gross intoxication. In the First Kentucky Infantry regiment, not only were officers arrested but the local "picture galleries" in Manchester were shuttered. A few days later, the sutler of the Thirty-First Indiana was forced to close for selling bottles of "death and destruction." The closure came too late, according to Lt. Jesse Connelly: "Night—the boys are on a general tight. Our company, almost to a man, is tight—some beyond going, others dancing, fiddling, and halloing. Have dispersed them twice and got all quieted down but one or two, and they will quarrel themselves to sleep." Some regiments countered by organizing temperance meetings, but with limited success. The general indiscipline also manifested itself in petty theft and insubordinate behavior, causing some officers to respond with harsh measures. The colonel of the Eighth Kentucky Infantry regiment briefly suspended a man by his thumbs for painting his bare feet black. Believing the punishment barbaric, the man's company commander cut him down, successfully defying the colonel.[27]

Throughout the area, soldiers continued to interact with civilians in their midst. The longer units remained in one place, the more civilians visited their camps, either selling produce or seeking handouts. This familiarity often bred contempt. At Bridgeport, Musician Day Elmore wrote to his parents on 9 August, "The people what few thare is left are very Ignorant." Capt. John McGraw was contemptuous of the women he encountered at Pelham, as he told his wife: "Did I ever tell you about the ladies of this section. Well they are not very intelligent some of them passably good looking but they all of them chew tobacco." In like vein, Cpl. Alanson Ryman wrote his wife from University Place, "Jane you should see some of the women and girls that come to our camp to trade.... They ask for the cash and then go to the sutler for tobacco cigars and all kinds of fancy things. I saw a good looking young woman to day smoking a cigar. It is very amusing to the soldiers." Some interactions went beyond wry commentary, as Pvt. Alva Griest recounted. A civilian selling fruit made remarks the soldiers deemed unpatriotic: "As soon as we heard this our course slightly changed, his oxen were soon loose going over the hill with stones flying after them, his linchpins got out by some means and the wheels rolled down the hill, while his apples were scattered about promiscuously." In contrast, Pvt. James Riley left camp without authorization in order to aid a dying elderly man whose family he had befriended earlier. Assisted by two Confederate soldiers, Riley prepared the body for burial. He then returned to camp to face extra duty, satisfied that his actions were justified.[28]

Although some soldiers tried to assure themselves that the war was winding down, the signs of an impending move grew in intensity as the August days passed. The most obvious indication was the issuing of new clothing by regimental quartermasters to replace missing or ragged items. In the 104th Illinois Infantry regiment, the men were surprised to receive slouch hats instead of the regulation kepis. The knapsacks of several regiments arrived from storage, although some were moldy and others had been robbed. Other signs that the campaign was about to open were the growing stockpiles of rations, the evacuation of sick men to Nashville hospitals, and the arrival of comrades from convalescent camps. Anyone near the tracks could see the increased tempo of railroad operations, especially the heavily loaded trains disappearing southward through the Cowan tunnel. The diary of Lt. Col. William Robinson succinctly expressed the view of many on 6 August: "No news on the front, but soon will be. Army is stirring." The departure of several units of the First Division of the Fourteenth Corps from their Cowan camps also indicated an impending move by the remainder of the army. Scribner's First Brigade marched over the Cumberland Plateau to Anderson Station on 6 August. There Scribner's men relieved the remaining units of Lytle's brigade. When the two regiments joined Lytle at Bridgeport, Sheridan's entire division was concentrated in the Tennessee River valley for the first time. Two days later, the Second Battalion of the Eighteenth United States Infantry regiment from King's Third Brigade departed Cowan for a new camp halfway up the mountain. From that base it initiated heavy repairs to the rough road leading over the Cumberland Plateau. In Rousseau's absence, King normally commanded the division, but he had become ill, and division command devolved temporarily to John Starkweather of the Second Brigade. A volunteer officer, Starkweather was much preferred by some soldiers to King, who strictly enforced the Regular Army's standards of discipline.[29]

Some soldiers would not be making the trip to the Tennessee River, as death continued to claim random individuals in the army's camps. At least six men died from disease in early August, and another was dismembered when he fell under the wheels of a train. A private in the 100th Illinois Infantry regiment almost joined them when he was wounded by the negligent discharge of a weapon in camp. Collectively a small number amid a large host, the soldiers' deaths nevertheless touched their comrades. Cpl. Alanson Ryman wrote poignantly about the death of Pvt. James Meyneke on 3 August: "I made his coffin out of rough pine boards and lined the head end of it and put in a pillow for his head to rest on. Jim was well liked by his comrades and was a good faithful soldier. I was sorry to see him die away from his friends and home but his body will rest as well on these lonely mountains as it would by the side of his father on that knoll by the hillside." Such tragedies were compounded when a single event generated multiple fatalities. A horrendous accident occurred on 8 August in Turchin's brigade at its camp near University Place. On that day, the Twenty-First Indiana Battery spread many of its damp powder bags on canvas tarpaulins to dry them in the sun. Through someone's carelessness, a spark ignited ninety-six cartridges, which exploded in a massive fireball that set nearby trees ablaze. Seven soldiers suffered severe burns, with four of them eventually dying from their injuries. Several of the casualties were infantrymen detailed to the battery earlier from the Eleventh Ohio and Eighteenth Kentucky Infantry regiments. One, Pvt. Samuel Mitchell of the Eighteenth Kentucky, had both ears burned off, suffered facial scarring, and sustained major damage to his right arm and hand. Although he would live for forty-six more years, Private Mitchell's war for the Union ended at University Place on 8 August 1863.[30]

Such tragic accidents did not impede the preparations for an advance. Although Garfield was sick in bed, and ordnance officer Horace Porter was absent on sick leave, the flow of orders from headquarters continued unabated. Corps commanders were admonished to maintain a five-day supply of rations and forage. Capt. Henry Thrall published Special Field Orders, No. 219, which officially appointed William Innes as military superintendent of railroads in place of the ineffectual John Anderson. The order specified Innes's duties to be "repairing, managing, and running the railroads under his charge." He was also empowered to set train schedules, regulate rates, and keep weekly and monthly records to be submitted to the army's chief quartermaster. Innes retained command of the First Michigan Engineers and Mechanics regiment, as well as temporary control of the black regiment forming at Estill Springs. Having thus empowered an aggressive subordinate to improve the efficiency of his railroad operations, Rosecrans spent the remainder of the day attending a grand review of Davis's First Division, Twentieth Corps. As the official party of Rosecrans, McCook, Davis, and Stanley watched, the brigades of Post, Carlin, and Heg passed in review. Seated in a carriage near the parade field was Kate McCook, who some soldiers took to be Mrs. Rosecrans. Afterward, Rosecrans walked among the troops, jocularly admonishing them: "You young men who wish to be corporals and sergeants must stand erect, and then you will be good looking when you get home." According to Lt. Chesley Mosman, "I never saw a more pleasant looking man than the General." Following the review, the official party adjourned to Davis's headquarters for refreshment, although Post appeared to some to have gotten a head start. Upon returning to his own headquarters, Rosecrans entertained Governor Andrew Johnson and Gordon Granger, who had just arrived from Nashville.[31]

Even though the day was extremely hot, several brigades were in motion. With King ill, the "insane" Maj. Samuel Dawson took the remainder of King's brigade of the First Division, Fourteenth Corps, over the mountain to Tantalon Station. There they joined the Second Battalion, Eighteenth United States Infantry, which had preceded them. The heat took its toll. Large numbers staggered behind the long column until they fell by the roadside, where they were left to follow when they could. Nor was the passage of the artillery and baggage trains any easier, as Lt. Augustus Carpenter reported: "Our artillery and transportation had a hard time in getting along. Some places the road wound along the tops of hills, right on the brink of precipices several hundred feet down, and occasionally a wagon would upset, sending its contents helter scelter [*sic*] down the hill." Also marching over the mountain was the division's Second Brigade, temporarily led by Col. Henry Hambright of the Seventy-Ninth Pennsylvania Infantry regiment while Starkweather held divisional command. Hambright's men also suffered under the extreme heat, but their volunteer officers sensibly mitigated their discomfort, unlike the regular officers. The First Division's departure from Cowan freed numerous campsites for other units, notably Stanley's Second Brigade of Negley's Second Division. Stanley's men marched six miles from Decherd to Cowan during the heat of the day, generating even more stragglers. Rosecrans reported all of these movements to Lorenzo Thomas in his nightly summary. He embellished the report by claiming that Negley's entire division had moved to Cowan, and touted the inconclusive fight at Sparta as a significant victory. He also announced that he would be sending a cavalry division to the Tennessee River valley in the near future to protect the Memphis & Charleston Railroad. Beyond that, Rosecrans was still waiting to accumulate sufficient forage to move the remainder of the army over the Cumberland Plateau.[32]

On 11 August, Rosecrans continued to push his staff at a frenetic pace. He bombarded William Innes with peremptory orders: repair the locomotive that assisted trains up the Cowan grade; borrow cars from the Louisville & Nashville Railroad; acquire the Adams Express Company cars. Capt. James Drouillard worked with assistant superintendent Beggs to transport Governor Johnson to Fayetteville. Maj. Frank Bond instructed John Palmer, still commanding the Twenty-First Corps, to evacuate all sick soldiers from his First and Second Divisions to Nashville. Van Cleve's Third Division was to retain its sick at McMinnville until further notice. Capt. Henry Thrall issued Special Field Orders, No. 220, which relieved James Steedman from his brigade in the Third Division, Fourteenth Corps, and assigned him to command the Reserve Corps division formerly led by Absalom Baird. Baird himself was sent to Thomas's Fourteenth Corps for assignment. Both Thrall and Drouillard wired absent staff officers Calvin Goddard and Henry Hodges, recalling them from leave. Capt. Robert Thoms expedited the movement of tools to Stevenson. Finally, Capt. Charles Thompson asked a Louisville Associated Press agent for Burnside's address. Rosecrans himself spent the afternoon reviewing Brannan's Third Division, Fourteenth Corps, at Decherd. He had not reviewed the command before, so his familiar banter played well with most of the men. Pvt. James Thomas later enthused in a letter home, "I think he sertonley is the best man on erth now. . . .

Washington might have bin as good but he was no better than old rosey. . . . I tell you the boys will fight for him to the last." Officers tended to see Rosecrans's performance differently. Lt. Jeremiah Donahower grumbled about the amount of marching on a hot day, while Capt. Everett Abbott was unimpressed: "Rosecrans very pleasant. Not a great man. He seems governed by sense of religious duty more than any officer I know of." Afterward, the official party, which again included McCook, Stanley, and Davis, visited Brannan's headquarters for liquid refreshments.[33]

While Brannan's men sweated on the review field at Decherd, the two brigades of the First Division, Fourteenth Corps, resumed their march along the railroad from Tantalon Station. They crossed the state line into Alabama during the heat of the day, and camped several miles beyond Anderson in the Crow Creek valley. The march was even more difficult than the previous day's had been. At Estill Springs a member of the First Michigan Engineers and Mechanics recorded the temperature as 108 degrees in the shade, and it could hardly have been less around Anderson Station. Again, many of the toiling soldiers fell out of line, some with dangerous cases of sunstroke. Both Hambright's Second Brigade and Dawson's Third Brigade temporarily lost hundreds of men to straggling. Rumors spread that several men in the First Battalion, Sixteenth United States Infantry regiment had died from sunstroke, although regimental returns list no such deaths. The men of Scribner's First Brigade, camped at Anderson Station since 6 August, watched with pity as their fellow soldiers staggered past them. By the end of the day, the First Division was finally united east of the Cumberland Plateau but, to one regular officer, the march was "harder than there was any necessity for." Still, the scenery was beautiful, and hundreds of acres of ripening corn carpeted the valley floor. Also moving on 11 August was Mitchell's First Cavalry Division. Commanded by Col. Edward McCook because Mitchell was absent sick, the division marched from Fayetteville toward Huntsville to secure the line of the Memphis & Charleston Railroad. At McMinnville, several of Van Cleve's regiments began the construction of a protective earthwork. At Bridgeport and Stevenson, Sheridan's brigades issued extra pairs of shoes and rations for ten days. At Decherd, one of Alex McCook's orderlies was killed by the daily passenger train when his horse threw him into the engine's path. In his nightly report to Lorenzo Thomas, Rosecrans noted only the departure of McCook's cavalrymen.[34]

On the next day, 12 August, Rosecrans continued to make demands upon his railroad operators. With the army's forage stocks still insufficient to permit it to cross the Cumberland Plateau, the need for additional freight cars was acute. The immediate requirement was for boxcars, which had prompted the purchase of fifty such cars and an effort to buy twenty cars belonging to the Adams Express Company. In a series of telegrams to the increasingly harassed Innes, staff officers pressed for the acquisition of the Adams equipment. Only when the Adams Company pushed back did army headquarters look elsewhere for cars. Not only boxcars were needed; the pontoons constructed by army engineers would need transportation to Stevenson by flatcar. Rosecrans estimated that thirty-five flatcars would be required, and his staff pressed Innes to provide them. When Innes disregarded multiple queries about the number of cars in inventory, he was pointedly reminded that Rosecrans expected a "full and prompt answer." This was the kind of behavior that had gotten John Anderson in trouble and was an early sign that Innes's relationship with Rosecrans would not be smooth. At Nashville, Capt. Simon Perkins Jr. somehow managed to find enough cars to fill the largest requisition of the summer on 12 August. Sent the previous evening, the order required fifteen carloads to be dispatched to McMinnville, twenty to Tullahoma, ten to Winchester, six to Murfreesboro and Wartrace, and an unspecified number to Decherd. Perkins was admonished, "The Supply for tomorrow must not fail." The efficient Perkins met the requirement, only to be assigned to other duties a few days later. Unfortunately, there was no relief for the equally efficient John Beggs at Decherd. He was directed to make the dummy available at 8:00 A.M. on the following day to take Governor Johnson and Gordon Granger to Fayetteville. He was further called to account for the nonarrival of the daily passenger train from Nashville, delayed because of a problem with the bridge over Stones River at Murfreesboro.[35]

While his staff harassed the railroad managers, Rosecrans himself initiated a telegraphic conversation with Ambrose Burnside. Having discovered that Burnside had reached Camp Nelson in central Kentucky, Rosecrans sought to learn how his plans to attack Knoxville were progressing. Burnside responded that he had been waiting to hear from Rosecrans again before committing his troops to the advance. He offered to accelerate his own timetable, should Rosecrans desire it. Unwilling to commit to a definite time for his own advance and perhaps still unsure of its exact direction, Rosecrans responded vaguely. He did promise that his army would reach (but not cross) the Tennessee River by the time Burnside arrived at Kingston, Tennessee, and closed, "Will keep you advised, and hope to hear from you often." Clearly, Rosecrans expected little from the Department of the Ohio and did not intend to link his own campaign to Burnside's. Halleck and Lincoln had expected Burnside and Rosecrans to collaborate in the liberation of the long-suffering Unionists of East Tennessee. By occasionally offering Burnside vague promises of general support, Rosecrans fulfilled the letter of his orders but hardly the spirit. Rosecrans did not believe he needed Burnside to capture Chattanooga. If Burnside could aid that endeavor, Rosecrans would welcome it, but if not, the Army of the Cumberland would act alone. Rosecrans's most current intelligence reports indicated correctly that Bragg's two infantry corps lay at Chattanooga and just upstream. To

Rosecrans that meant that Bragg expected an attack above the city rather than below. If Burnside's pending advance contributed to that Confederate perception, so much the better for Rosecrans's operations. For his part, Burnside was so overwhelmed by the absence of his Ninth Corps and his own logistical problems that he gave little thought to Rosecrans's movements or how they might affect his own operations.[36]

On Wednesday, 12 August, the thermometer registered only ninety-four degrees at Decherd, and an afternoon thundershower drenched the camps west of the Cumberland Plateau. In the Second Division of the Fourteenth Corps, a portion of the Second Brigade climbed the mountain from its camp at Cowan, driving a herd of 600 cattle to Tantalon Station. At Winchester, Sgt. Peter Keegan encountered Governor Andrew Johnson: "The Gov. invited me to drink with him which I declined, the Gov. 'indulges' himself somewhat freely if his countenance is any indication. For a man of his age, he looks quite fresh & vigorous." Gordon Granger also remained in Winchester and met at length with Alex McCook. Kate McCook was present too, hoping to remain until her husband's corps crossed the mountain. In the First Brigade of Davis's First Division, Lt. Cyrenius Woods died of disease. At Pelham the Ninety-Seventh Ohio Infantry regiment received a new regimental flag from the ladies of Coshocton, Ohio. On the army's far left flank at McMinnville, three regiments from Van Cleve's Third Division grumbled as they continued building a defensive earthwork. At Tullahoma, August Willich scolded the Forty-Ninth Ohio Infantry regiment on its rowdy behavior. In the rear, most of the First Brigade of the First Division, Reserve Corps, left Wartrace and headed for Estill Springs. Two regiments of the Second Brigade moved from Shelbyville to Wartrace to take their place. At Nashville, virtually all of the Second Brigade of the Second Division, Reserve Corps, attended the funeral of Col. David Irons of the Eighty-Sixth Illinois Infantry regiment, another victim of disease. At University Place, soldiers continued crafting souvenirs from local granite, and Nadine Turchin ranted in her diary against West Pointers. At Bridgeport, Sheridan's men reduced their baggage and packed their knapsacks for a movement. Edward McCook's First Cavalry Division reached Huntsville. Hearing nothing from McCook, Rosecrans reported to Lorenzo Thomas that night only the consolidation of Starkweather's division near Stevenson and the familiar complaint about lack of forage.[37]

The next day brought some respite to staff officers and railroad managers alike. William Innes received only one message from headquarters, an order to activate sawmills at Anderson Station to stockpile bridge timbers. Several messages indicated that Rosecrans was seeking alternate pathways over the Cumberland Plateau other than the one leading from Cowan to Anderson. Capt. Robert Thoms queried Thomas about progress in improving the road down the mountain into the valley of Battle Creek. He also instructed Palmer, still commanding the Twenty-First Corps, to open another pathway over the Cumberland Plateau from Pelham. The small amount of headquarters business indicates that Rosecrans was otherwise engaged. Indeed, a special run of the dummy was made on 13 August to carry Governor Johnson, Gordon Granger, and probably Rosecrans to Fayetteville and back to Winchester. Johnson desired to survey Unionist sentiment in the area, but Rosecrans was so unsure of their welcome that he ordered a cavalry regiment to deploy along the railroad. As the cavalrymen patrolled the tracks, they were almost fired upon by the train guard, which had not been informed of their presence. Fortunately, no damage was done, Governor Johnson's party visited Fayetteville as planned, and all returned to Winchester safely. Back at his headquarters, Rosecrans found a message from Burnside and another from Stephen Hurlbut at Memphis. Responding to Rosecrans's request for a demonstration, the Memphis District commander claimed that the addition of Arkansas to his area of responsibility prevented him from assisting the Army of the Cumberland. Instead, Hurlbut brazenly asked Rosecrans to support him with 3,000 cavalry. Nor was there much comfort in Burnside's telegram. He offered 15 August as a tentative date for beginning his own advance, but his units remained widely scattered over central Kentucky. Burnside again promised hearty cooperation with the Army of the Cumberland, but the lack of conviction in his pronouncements was obvious.[38]

The heat that had baked the army's camps continued unabated on 13 August until a strong and widespread afternoon thunderstorm broke the spell. While some units reported only minor showers, the two brigades of Wood's First Division, Twenty-First Corps, at Hillsboro took the full brunt of the storm. Not only did the pouring rain drench everything, but strong winds also tore through the regimental camps, blowing down tents and uprooting trees. Men in the Sixty-Fourth Ohio Infantry regiment had sheltered their tents under large trees, which crashed down upon them, injuring several men severely. Still, the work of preparing the army for its advance had to continue. East of the Cumberland Plateau, near Tantalon, the Eighteenth Ohio Infantry regiment struggled to improve the still rough road over the mountain to Cowan. In the army's rear, Thomas Champion's brigade completed its march from Wartrace to Estill Springs. Farther in the rear, two regiments of William Reid's Second Brigade of what was now James Steedman's First Division, Reserve Corps, settled into the abandoned camps at Wartrace. These small movements represented a further coiling of the spring represented by the army as it readied itself for the grand push across the mountains to the Tennessee River valley. Edward McCook's First Cavalry Division was already in that valley, and on 13 August it advanced eastward beyond Huntsville. Following the line of the Memphis &

Charleston Railroad to Brownsboro through delightful mountain scenery, the division scoured the hills for guerrillas, capturing one and killing him when he tried to escape. In his nightly message to Washington, Rosecrans highlighted McCook's advance, the roadwork being done on the Cumberland Plateau, and his plan to send the Twenty-First Corps to Tracy City on the following day. Again, Rosecrans oversold the day's events. In fact, fewer men were engaged in roadwork than Rosecrans indicated, and Palmer's Twenty-First Corps would not advance to Tracy City on the next day. Nevertheless, a sense of forward movement was communicated, and that was all that seemed to matter in Washington.[39]

On Friday, 14 August, Rosecrans was cheered by the arrival of his assistant adjutant general, Calvin Goddard, who had finally returned from leave. Garfield, bedridden for a week with fever and diarrhea, was too weak to do more than write a brief note to his wife, but Goddard could now direct the flow of official correspondence. His first order of business was to ask the corps commanders and Capt. Patrick O'Connell of the Pioneer Brigade if their commands were ready to begin the campaign. Goddard also wanted to know the amount of rations and forage available, and if provision had been made to care for the sick who could not travel. Thomas reported crisply that the Fourteenth Corps was ready to advance, with eight days of rations and five days of forage, and was gathering its sick soldiers in a convalescent camp at Cowan. McCook replied in a rambling note that the Twentieth Corps had forage for five or six days, while its divisions had rations for periods varying from eleven to seventeen days. He did not address the readiness issue or the disposition of sick solders. Palmer stated that the Twenty-First Corps was ready to advance, with eighteen days of rations and ten days of short forage. Two of his divisions were already evacuating their sick, while Van Cleve held his patients at McMinnville. O'Connell reported that the Pioneer Brigade also was prepared to move, with rations for ten days, forage for three, and his sick accounted for. Stanley did not answer, probably because four of his five brigades were already in the field. Shortly after Palmer reported, Thomas Crittenden arrived at Tullahoma on the way to Manchester. Crittenden did not mention that he was bringing along his nine-year-old son, John, although Rosecrans would hardly have minded, since his own son Adrian remained with the army. Rosecrans himself resumed his bombardment of Innes with detailed questions about rolling stock and train schedules. Major Bond telegraphed John Beggs that henceforth only Rosecrans could use the dummy. Pointedly, Rosecrans made no report to Adjutant General Thomas that night.[40]

Aware that an advance was imminent, the men of the Army of the Cumberland spent the day in various ways. Around Tantalon, the Eighteenth Ohio Infantry regiment continued to improve the road in the Crow Creek valley. West of the mountain, the Ninety-Seventh Ohio Infantry regiment did the same on the road heading uphill from Pelham. Daily drill sessions continued. Sweating details emptied boxcars choking railroad sidings. At Estill Springs the First Michigan Engineers and Mechanics shaped thousands of railroad ties for track improvements. At Stevenson, a detachment from the Pioneer Brigade cleared ground for a field hospital. At McMinnville, several regiments labored for a third day on an earthen fort. Beyond the Cumberland Plateau, Edward McCook's cavalrymen continued their march down the Memphis & Charleston Railroad to Larkinsville. Even with all the work yet to be done, there was time for large numbers of soldiers to enjoy themselves. Many went on foraging expeditions, offering to trade greenbacks, coffee, salt, and soap for fresh produce. The photographic studios remained open, offering opportunities for soldiers to memorialize their service. Mail, new clothing, and convalescent soldiers continued to arrive. In a replay of the previous afternoon, a heavy thunderstorm struck the camps west of the mountain. Without shelter, the Ninety-Seventh Ohio soldiers repairing the mountain road suffered greatly, but the worst of the storm hit Negley's and Brannan's camps at Decherd. There, amid flashes of lightning and peals of thunder, soldiers fought to hold their tents in place, while others were injured by falling trees and flying debris. That evening, the air was cooler and spirits rose in the camps. At Winchester, 700 people attended a minstrel show staged by the Seventy-Fourth Indiana Infantry regiment. At Hillsboro, some officers organized a ball. Finally, at McMinnville, two companies of the Seventy-Ninth Indiana Infantry regiment became so intoxicated that they were forced to stand in formation all night as punishment.[41]

At Bridgeport, 14 August began quietly. A day earlier, Lytle had been concerned about what sounded like chopping noises on Long Island before dawn, but inspection in daylight had shown nothing amiss. Now all remained quiet for a second day, and Lytle's worries had dissipated. Except for those on picket duty, the men of the eight regiments at Bridgeport were free to amuse themselves in the August heat. During the afternoon, the mail was joyfully welcomed. Cpl. William Austin was especially gratified to receive a package of fishing line. In the Twenty-Fourth Wisconsin Infantry regiment, the men formed ranks for inspection and received their second pair of shoes. Soldiers in the Thirty-Sixth Illinois Infantry regiment enjoyed perusing their regimental library, which had arrived a few days earlier. Bought with unit funds, the works by Washington Irving, Lord Macaulay, Walter Scott, Charles Dickens, and other noted authors were by 14 August proving to be popular among men starved of wholesome reading matter. Other soldiers gossiped about the Confederate officer who had just deserted to the Federal side of the river. The afternoon storm that did so much damage at Decherd had deteriorated into a light shower by the time it arrived at Bridgeport. All in all, as Cpl. Edward Crippin put it, unless a soldier was on picket duty, the place made him lazy. Burdened by more responsibilities than Corporal Crippin, Lytle retired early that night, but he had difficulty sleeping. Around midnight he was startled wide awake by someone shouting, "Tell the General the bridge is on fire." Dressing hurriedly, Lytle raced to the fort overlooking the bridge, where he found the night luridly illuminated by the burning drawbridge stretching from Long Island to the far shore. When his two batteries opened, they completed the hellish tableau by exploding shells over the doomed structure. Lytle and his aide, Capt. Alfred Pirtle, could only gape in wonder as the bridge soon collapsed in a shower of sparks.[42]

7

Bragg Bides His Time

» 30 July–14 August 1863 «

Cherokee Springs, Georgia, had long been a place where people sick in body or mind went for recuperation. Located little more than two miles east of Ringgold in a secluded valley, it was watered by Cherokee Branch and several natural springs. In prewar times the springs were known for their alleged medicinal value, but the primary balm may have been the pastoral quality of the small valley. Two miles to the east was a similar establishment, Catoosa Springs. Important enough to have their own small station on the Western & Atlantic Railroad, the two spas were recognized in 1862 as ideal places for sick and wounded Confederate soldiers to recuperate. Thus by the summer of 1863 both Cherokee Springs and Catoosa Springs contained Confederate convalescent camps supervised by Dr. Cary Gamble, surgeon in charge at Ringgold. Campbell rented quarters at a house midway between the two camps, near a stone church erected in 1850 for his wife, Edwarda, and their two young daughters. It was to Cherokee Springs that Elise Bragg came in June to complete her recovery from typhoid fever. Unlike Catoosa Springs, which boasted a three-story main building, Cherokee Springs was primarily a tent hospital. It consisted of three wards, all under canvas, erected in the midst of a grove of large trees. Each ward had a small frame cabin of light construction associated with it to house the sickest patients. Other cabins of similar size served as support facilities, a bakery, and a large kitchen. A covered shelter with open sides was used as the main dining room. There was also a library, and a chapel was under construction. In August 1863, the camp had a capacity of 500 patients but was only half full. Managed by Dr. Samuel Bemiss, who directed three assistant surgeons and numerous orderlies, Cherokee Springs was an effective rehabilitation center. According to Kate Cumming, a nurse who arrived in mid-August, the camp was "one of the most lovely spots I ever beheld." It was to Cherokee Springs that Braxton Bragg had come in late July to recover his own health.[1]

Although Bragg himself was at Cherokee Springs, the bulk of his staff remained in Chattanooga handling the normal administrative tasks of a field army and a department headquarters. Bragg had known for several weeks the general dispositions of the Army of the Cumberland on the far side of the Cumberland Plateau. He also had excellent rail and telegraph communications to Atlanta, and from there to Joseph Johnston's headquarters at Morton, Mississippi, to Simon Buckner's headquarters at Knoxville, and ultimately to Richmond. On 1 August the network delivered a short telegram from Adj. Gen. Samuel Cooper: "If we can spare most of Johnston's army, temporarily, to re-enforce you, can you attack the enemy?" Bragg responded quickly, on the next day telegraphing Cooper with his initial thoughts. If Bragg correctly understood the size of Johnston's force, he thought using most of it to augment his command would offer a reasonable chance for success, everything else being equal. Still, there were difficulties to be considered. It would be hard to cross the Tennessee River and the Cumberland Plateau again, especially in view of the broken Nashville & Chattanooga Railroad. Also, it would take some time for Johnston's troops to arrive at Chattanooga, even before an advance could be considered. If those difficulties could be surmounted, Bragg thought a flank move might be the way to approach the Federals. He promised to consult with Johnston in person and then write Richmond more fully. He wrote to Johnston requesting such a meeting, and Johnston replied on 4 August that he would be willing to meet Bragg in Montgomery, Alabama, to discuss possible cooperation. Within twenty-four hours, however, Bragg telegraphed to both Cooper and Johnston that he was no longer considering an advance. To Cooper, Bragg said the Federals were already across the Cumberland Plateau in strength, but that the deciding factor was an insufficiency of resources. Johnston was told simply that after "full information and reflection" the movement was "inexpedient."[2]

Bragg's sudden change of heart was the result of information he had received from Leonidas Polk. Corresponding privately with William Hardee, Polk had received Hardee's strongly negative assessment of Johnston's force. Not anxious to endure another battle under Bragg's leadership, Polk saw the mountains ringing Chattanooga as a defensive asset, while a hasty advance courted disaster. Thus Polk shared Hardee's dismal view of Johnston's command with Bragg, knowing the effect it would have on the latter's deliberations. Even if not so intended, Polk's input succeeded in quashing Bragg's idea of an offensive. After telegraphing his decision to both Cooper and Johnston, Bragg wrote to each officer at length. As he explained to Cooper, it was mostly a question of numbers. The strength return of 31 July 1863 placed the army's "aggregate present" at 52,429 officers and men. Of that number Bragg considered only his 40,000 infantry and artillerymen to be effective in a fight. He had an additional 10,000 horsemen, but their condition was such that he expected little from them. In contrast, Bragg believed that Rosecrans could deploy at least 60,000 effectives, and Burnside 30,000 more. Therefore, an advance beyond the Tennessee River and Cumberland Plateau against a larger foe would be very risky. When the sorry state of Confederate logistics and the lack of rail support beyond the Tennessee were factored into the equation, an advance would be sheer folly. In contrast, if the Federals incautiously advanced beyond the river and the mountains, Bragg believed the odds favored the Army of Tennessee. Writing to Johnston, he summarized the argument succinctly: "To 'fight the enemy' is a very simple operation when you have the means and can get at him. But with less than half his strength and a large river and fifty to one hundred miles of rugged, sterile mountains, destitute even of vegetation, between you and him, with our limited commissariat, the simple fighting would be a refreshing recreation." Bragg thus rejected an advance as long as the armies' relative positions remained unchanged. When he saw Bragg's answer to Cooper, Jefferson Davis wrote, "However desirable a movement may be, it is never safe to do more than suggest it to a commanding general, and it would be unwise to order its execution by one who foretold failure." Unlike the Lincoln administration's incessant prodding of Rosecrans, Davis would leave matters to his field commander.[3]

Having summarily dismissed any plans for an advance, Bragg resumed his quiet recuperation at Cherokee Springs. Unfortunately, his rest was broken by a swelling cry for furloughs from both officers and men. Bragg had long been loath to authorize furloughs, but during the first weeks of August at least two division commanders, Frank Cheatham and Alexander Stewart, were absent from their commands. Harvey Hill quickly saw that furloughs were necessary to maintain morale. In late July he had proposed a system to distribute furloughs equitably. Bragg had responded favorably, permitting one man out of every twenty to receive a furlough for ten days. Unfortunately, Hill soon reported a serious desertion problem in his corps. Angered, Bragg revoked Hill's authority to manage his own furlough policy. Nor did John Wharton's proposal to permit furloughs in the Eighth Texas Cavalry regiment receive approval. Wharton sought the dispensation for his old regiment, whose men earnestly desired to return to Texas. Knowing that men whose homes were beyond the Mississippi might never return, Bragg denied Wharton's request. The stiff policy on furloughs, as well as the discouraging war news, led to a steady dribble of men from the ranks. To staunch the flow, Bragg sent Capt. Robert Allison's Tennessee cavalry squadron to augment Hill's guards along the Tennessee River. He also ordered Capt. Guy Dreux, commanding his escort, to sweep the riverbank from Chattanooga to the mouth of Chickamauga Creek for deserters. When his inspector general found laxity among the sentinels on the army's left flank, Bragg directed Polk to increase the guards in that sector also. Finally, on 6 August he published General Orders, No. 1, which outlined the War Department policy of amnesty toward those currently absent without permission. Absentees who returned to their commands within twenty days of the proclamation's publication would be welcomed without penalty. Although it was too early for such measures to have much of an effect, the army's trimonthly strength return for 10 August placed the "aggregate present" at 53,418 officers and men, a gain of almost 1,000 soldiers.[4]

Another issue troubling Bragg in early August was the status of Simon Buckner. Special Orders, No. 176, issued in Richmond on 25 July, had renamed Bragg's Department No. 2 as the Department of Tennessee, and Buckner's smaller Department of East Tennessee had been merged into it. Accordingly, Bragg on 6 August issued an order announcing the creation of the Department of Tennessee. It also abolished Buckner's department and designated Buckner's troops as the Third Army Corps. Buckner, however, would continue to administer the district that had formerly been his department. For Bragg, the document resolved the previously problematic relationship between Bragg's army and Buckner's command. Unfortunately, the order displeased Buckner, who on 8 August specified his concerns to Chief of Staff William Mackall. If he had to continue administering his former department, Buckner wanted the full powers of a department commander, especially the authority to convene courts-martial. If that authority was denied, he wished to be relieved of all territorial administration. Although he claimed not to care how the situation was resolved, Buckner would later prove by both word and deed that he cared very deeply about the result. What he really wanted was to retain de facto independence under the distant yet protective wing of the Army of Tennessee. Buckner argued that precedent for such an arrangement was the District (or as Buckner styled it, Department) of the Gulf, which Buckner had commanded before coming to East Tennessee. While within Bragg's command, the District of the Gulf was so geographically isolated that Bragg had essentially left its commander alone. The Department of East Tennessee was inextricably linked to the Department of Tennessee by geography, rail connections, and strategic focus in ways Mobile and its environs never had been, but Buckner refused to recognize the differences between the two commands. He couched his argument in terms of technical issues like court-martial authority, but his pride and status were what was really at stake. His intense dislike of Bragg also inspired his plea for a more independent role.[5]

What initially appeared to be a simple administrative reorganization that would rationalize command relationships in eastern Tennessee and northern Alabama generated controversy at both ends of Bragg's now enlarged domain. When he received no immediate response from Bragg, Buckner wrote on 11 August to Adjutant General Cooper, as earlier correspondence had permitted him to do. In that letter he argued that he should either regain department command, with its concomitant technical authority, under the general umbrella of the Department of Tennessee, or he should become simply a corps commander with no other responsibilities. Again, he claimed that he sought only administrative efficiency and had no personal interest in mind. He took the liberty to append his letter to Mackall to the correspondence with Cooper. For the moment the Davis administration did not answer Buckner's plea. In the meantime, both Bragg and Johnston raised another issue over the boundaries of Bragg's expanded command. Special Orders, No. 176, had defined the western boundary of Bragg's department as a line running north from West Point, Georgia, to the Tennessee River, then along that river all the way to its mouth in Kentucky. This boundary meant that Bragg's territory included only the land on the right bank of the Tennessee. Thus, Patton Anderson's brigade watching the Federals at Bridgeport, Joseph Wheeler's pickets along the river to Gunter's Landing, Wheeler's headquarters and Will Martin's division at Gadsden, and Philip Roddey's command in western Alabama would all be outside of the Department of Tennessee. To correct the problem, the War Department on 4 August issued Special Orders, No. 184, which added nine Alabama counties, all of them either on the left bank of the Tennessee River or around Gadsden, to Bragg's command. This modification permitted Bragg to operate legally in the northernmost counties of Alabama all the way to the Mississippi state line, and Johnston was so notified.[6]

Boundary questions aside, Bragg was most concerned in early August with keeping track of the Army of the Cumberland. On his left flank, Wheeler had assigned only two small regiments of cavalry to watch the river from Bridgeport to Decatur, where Roddey's brigade extended the picket line across northern Alabama. Roddey was told to place scouts north of the river, but no such order to Wheeler is extant. At Bridgeport and Shell Mound, Anderson's Mississippians occasionally crossed the river clandestinely to supplement their observations from the left bank. On Bragg's right flank, Forrest had stationed part of Dibrell's command around Sparta, where it could watch the Federal division at McMinnville. Still, much of the Federal activity in the center of Bragg's front was shielded by the massive Cumberland Plateau and Walden's Ridge. Thus Bragg used various means to penetrate that area. When Col. Benjamin Hill proposed to take part of his Thirty-Fifth Tennessee infantry regiment into the mountains to protect Confederate sympathizers, Bragg saw an opportunity. Both Hill and his regiment were native to the McMinnville area and knowledgeable about the territory from the Sequatchie Valley to the west side of the Cumberland Plateau. For several weeks, beginning in early August, Hill's detachment operated west of the Tennessee River. Similarly, Maj. Charles McDonald's battalion, sometimes styled the Eighteenth Tennessee Cavalry Battalion, also scouted into the mountains west of Chattanooga. Writing to his uncle on 7 August, Pvt. P. B. Clark reported, "We are here on detached service as scouts for Gen Bragg.

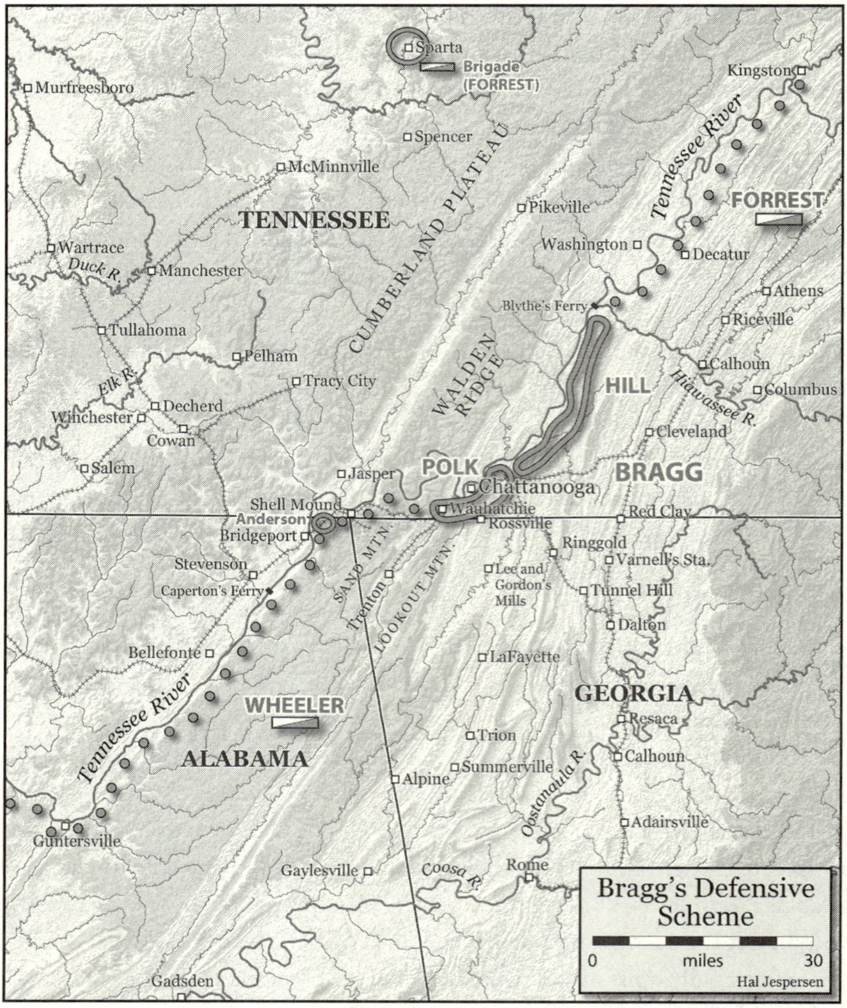

Bragg's Defensive Scheme

We have a pleasant time — the easiest time we have had since I have been out. We send out a scout every fourth or fifth day. Our last scouts report the main body of the enemy at Tulahoma." Finally, Alexander McKinstry, Bragg's provost marshal, managed the activities of a series of agents who passed between the lines of the opposing armies. Like Rosecrans, Bragg had no intelligence staff and had to make his own assessments from these disparate sources.[7]

In addition to intelligence gathering, Bragg was also concerned about intelligence denial. According to Rosecrans's intelligence journal, a steady stream of army deserters and disaffected workers from Chattanooga's industries reached the Federal lines during July and August. Many of them offered information on Confederate unit locations, strength, and morale. Well aware of this leakage, Bragg attempted to reduce the flow of information to the enemy and even occasionally turn it to his advantage. The Tennessee River barred easy escape from Bragg's territory, although it did not stop determined deserters or Federal agents. At least, Bragg reasoned, he could regulate major crossing points like Kelly's Ferry and Brown's Ferry downstream and Blythe's Ferry upstream from the city. The two crossings below Chattanooga seemed to give Bragg the most trouble. They represented the easiest way to reach the Federal lines if a soldier was inclined to desert, but private citizens used those crossings as well. Bragg admonished Inspector General Beard for regulating traffic at Kelly's Ferry too strictly, but in the same letter ordered Beard to secure all boats in the area to discourage deserters. Similar instructions went to Forrest at Kingston. Brown's Ferry was Polk's responsibility, and Bragg ordered him to increase its guard. Still, security remained lax, especially away from the river. When Beard reported passing from the west side of Lookout Mountain into Chattanooga during the night of 8 August without challenge, Bragg demanded better performance from John Jackson, post commander. He also arranged to strengthen the guard at the Western & Atlantic Railroad depot. Every train carried men from McKinstry's provost guard, either detailed men or convalescents from the hospitals. All this vigilance may have deterred casual deserters or spies, but as Rosecrans's intelligence journal shows, it was by no means completely effective. The country was just too wild, the opportunities too great, and the motivations too diverse for Bragg to maintain perfect operational security across such a wide front.[8]

The details of Bragg's headquarters routine during his convalescence at Cherokee Springs are not known. All of the orders emanating from headquarters during the first two weeks of August were headed "Chattanooga," but that may simply have been a bureaucratic convenience. At Cherokee Springs, Bragg did have access to telegraphic services via the Western & Atlantic Railroad, which also provided transportation between Chattanooga and Catoosa Station. Certainly the more often Bragg visited Chattanooga and its vexing distractions, the less a change of scenery and his wife's presence would rejuvenate his health. Much of the army's headquarters business was routine, and most personnel actions could be handled by the staff with minimal guidance from Bragg. The return of George Brent in late July as the army's assistant adjutant general had removed a great deal of pressure from Bragg. Brent's mild, self-effacing personality and his technical proficiency were an almost perfect combination for a staff officer. Unlike the more mercurial Mackall, Brent had no higher ambition than to serve Bragg, and by extension the Army of Tennessee, in the best way possible. Like Rosecrans, Bragg reveled in detail work that should have been beneath his level of attention. Unlike Rosecrans, who dominated his young staff officers with his manic behavior, Bragg was usually willing to listen to a calming influence such as Brent provided. Thus Brent apparently handled much of the army's routine paperwork, leaving Bragg free to clear his head and regain his physical health. Some matters, of course, required Bragg's personal attention, notably his correspondence with both Samuel Cooper and Joseph Johnston. In other cases, Brent signed the documents, serving simply as the army commander's scribe. Acknowledging Brent's contribution, Bragg on 8 August recommended Brent's promotion to colonel in the strongest terms to Adjutant General Cooper. Whether Brent did his work at Chattanooga or Cherokee Springs was immaterial; his obvious value to his commander was not.[9]

While Bragg rested at Cherokee Springs, his soldiers continued to recover from the rigors of the previous campaign. There was still work to be done, but most units maintained some semblance of normal camp life. In Polk's Corps, daily details labored on fortifications rising on Cameron Hill and the bluffs overlooking the landing. On Harvey Hill's front upstream near Harrison, many fords required guards, to keep Federals from approaching and deserters from escaping. Everywhere units drilled and, like their Federal counterparts, participated in onerous inspections and reviews. During a review of Churchill's Brigade, Hill impressed at least one soldier, who stated, "He is a fine looking man and I think is able anuff to sweep the Feds before him as he goes." On 5 August, John Wharton and Col. Thomas Harrison reviewed the Eighth Texas Cavalry regiment. The famed "Terry's Texas Rangers" paraded to the music of the Sixth Arkansas Infantry regiment's brass band, imported from Chattanooga for the occasion. Afterward, the Texans hosted a sumptuous barbecue in honor of Wharton and the ladies of Rome. The men of the regiment presented Wharton with a spirited charger, purchased with their own money. Pvt. Leonidas Giles thought little of the subsequent speeches: "Both speakers pledged the last drop of their blood, etc. Same old story, but a trifle stale by this time." On a more practical note, a number of artillery batteries in Polk's Corps competed in target practice outside of Chattanooga. Some of the shooting was poor, as recorded by a member of Stanford's Mississippi Battery: "Commenced firing at ten oclock with first piece—very unsatisfactory. Each gun has 4 shots allowed it. The second piece followed us. Neither one hit the target a distance of 1400 yards. Will not fire the 3rd and 4th pieces—are unfit." The guns were condemned on the spot and the unit eventually received four new three-inch rifled guns. Other batteries, notably Smith's Mississippi and Fowler's Alabama, performed better. Nevertheless, at least one infantryman was not impressed by what he saw.[10]

Still, all was not seriousness in the camps of the Army of Tennessee. Men wrote letters home, read books and papers, and visited the top of Lookout Mountain to admire the natural curiosity called Rock City. Others visited Chattanooga, among them Lt. James Fraser of the Fiftieth Alabama Infantry regiment, who confided to his diary on 7 August, "Went to Chattanooga had a jolly time. Hope I will not be arrested for going without leave." Surgeon James Brannock of the Fifth Tennessee Infantry regiment attended a musical review in the town in early August. He delighted in the performances of several singers but was disgusted by the audience: "I do not honestly think there was a decent woman present. Prostitutes there were in abundance, & *Confederate Officers* & soldiers lavishing their attentions upon them. Their conduct was in many instances shameful—a disgrace to humanity & an outrage upon common decency." Similar disgust was expressed by Sgt. John Sparkman of the Forty-Eighth Tennessee Infantry regiment, who wrote on 4 August, "I was once in a Mess with an old man who used to curse me for (as he called it) preaching *morality* in camps. Today he is in the Guardhouse for bad conduct while I am still at my post as usual." Sgt. Maj. James Searcy of the Reserve Artillery Battalion also indicted the morals of some soldiers, in a letter to his sister: "The vicinity of an army is the last place in the world I'd like a sister or lady friend of mine to be in. . . . There are several ladies about here—real ladies—who I know are imposed upon by the attentions of perfect rascals." One of those "rascals" may have been Adj. Alexander Moore of the Thirty-Third Alabama Infantry regiment, who boasted to his brother, "I know several women in town & have had a *good time* so far with some of them. Nearly all up here smoke, chew & *curse* some. I have managed to *squeeze* nearly all of my *female acquaintances* in Tenn. so far. There are in fact some very pretty women here & we 'army fellows' play a fast game with them."[11]

Brannock, Sparkman, and Searcy were hardly alone in resisting the urges that possessed many young men with too little to do. Indeed, surviving accounts indicate that large numbers of soldiers took refuge in a renewed wave of religious fervor sweeping through the camps. Harvey Hill set the example for his corps by regularly attending religious services in camp instead of going to church in town. When Rev. S. M. Cherry, the Methodist chaplain of Bate's Brigade, had an audience with the general soon after he took command, Hill encouraged him to begin a brigade-wide revival immediately. Cherry superintended the construction of a large arbor, complete with log seats and a mourner's bench. Thereafter, he and nine other chaplains took turns preaching every night and three times on Sunday. According to the *Chattanooga Daily Rebel,* Hill himself attended the services. In the camp of the Eighth Texas Cavalry near Rome, Rev. Robert Bunting and several associates continued their monthlong revival, breaking the string of nightly meetings only during relocation of the camp. Bunting first used a local church building but eventually utilized soldier labor to construct a new meeting hall from materials remaining from the Wharton barbecue celebration. He thereafter held three services daily. By mid-August at least sixty soldiers had joined Bunting in a "provisional church," and an additional twenty had made professions of faith. Elsewhere, soldiers simply crowded into established churches or attended Sunday services in their regimental areas. Still others, already strong in their faith, expressed themselves privately in letters to loved ones. Sgt. William Honnoll of the Twenty-Fourth Mississippi Infantry regiment was such a man, writing to his sister on 3 August, "I don't want you to think that I am dissatisfied. . . . I am better satisfied then I have been in a long time for I am reconcile to my doom let it be what it may for my sole trust is in god."[12]

Many soldiers in the Army of Tennessee shared Sergeant Honnoll's sense of resignation. Writing to his wife on 13 August, Pvt. Hezekiah Rabb of the Thirty-Third Alabama Infantry regiment believed the Confederacy's future was bleak: "It looks very much to me like the Confederacy is gone up. I sometimes think she will not Quiver but a little longer we are undoubtedly whipped unless there is a Powerful alteration soon though I can't say what will happen." Capt. Irvine Walker, a staff officer in Manigault's Brigade, tried to suppress views like Rabb's. To his fiancée he wrote on 9 August, "The position of affairs generally looks very blue, but I trust in God and the righteousness of our cause." Pvt. Benjamin Burke of the Eighth Texas Cavalry regiment echoed Walker in a letter to his parents: "Some citizens are getting somewhat despondent, though I do not think that kind of a spirit prevails to much extent in the army or among the soldiers." More upbeat was Assistant Surgeon David Godwin of the Fifty-First Tennessee Infantry regiment, who wrote to a friend on 1 August, "Since I wrote you last, the future of this great national drama has undergone a great change; and for a few short days cast a gloom over our entire army, but I am proud to say, that the cloud has almost entirely disappeared; and to day our prospects are more flattering than at any former time." Even those who could not see such a bright future were resolved to fight to the last, as Pvt. Daniel Kelly of Maxson's Company of Sappers and Miners told a cousin on 3 August: "And now Cousin I feel that this unholy war was forsed on me for I was opposed to it at the start but now I am in favor of prosicuting it to the last extremity for if we do not gain our independence I cannot see any thing els but slavery stareing me in the face and reather than submit to this I would reather die and I want to die as my noble brother at Shilo. . . . I want to die battling for my liberty."[13]

As August approached its midpoint, Bragg welcomed a new major general to his army. Ever since the departure of Jones Withers, half of Polk's command had been led temporarily by Brig. Gen. Zachariah Deas. The War Department on 15 July had announced Maj. Gen. Thomas Carmichael Hindman Jr. as Withers's replacement, but Hindman did not arrive until 12 August. A controversial figure, Hindman, thirty-five, was a native of Knoxville, Tennessee, and a graduate of the prestigious Lawrenceville Classical Institute in New Jersey. Moving with his parents to Mississippi, he became first an attorney, then a junior officer in the Mexican War but saw no combat. After a brief foray into Mississippi politics, he moved to the frontier town of Helena, Arkansas, where he soon gained a reputation as a fiery orator, brawler, and duelist. There, too, he developed a lifelong friendship with Helena resident Patrick Cleburne. An Arkansas congressman in 1861, Hindman was an ardent secessionist who worked diligently to remove Arkansas from the Union. He then raised the Second Arkansas Infantry regiment and subsequently was promoted to brigadier general. He commanded a brigade at Shiloh, where he was injured, and shortly thereafter gained promotion to major general. Sent to Arkansas, Hindman commanded the Trans-Mississippi Department until his dictatorial pronouncements led to his demotion to field command. He then led a small army to defeat at Prairie Grove in December 1862. Forced by popular clamor to leave Arkansas, Hindman next chaired the commission investigating the fall of New Orleans. Having completed the commission's work, he now reported to Braxton Bragg for duty. Energetic to a fault, bold in personal demeanor, and quick to take offense, Thomas Hindman packed those qualities into a body little taller than five feet. Dapper in dress and favoring long curls, he wore an elevated shoe and walked with a limp because of a prewar carriage accident. A stronger contrast between him and his friend Cleburne could hardly be imagined.[14]

On the same day that Hindman was announced as a division commander in Polk's Corps, Brig. Gen. James Deshler took command of a brigade in Hill's Corps, the brigade formerly commanded by Thomas Churchill. Deshler had only recently been promoted to brigadier general and placed in charge of the army's Artillery Reserve. Both he and Churchill had been at Arkansas Post in January 1863 when the place had been surrendered, shamefully in the eyes of many. Churchill, however, had commanded the entire garrison, while Deshler had been a brigade commander only. Exchanged in April and sent to the Army of Tennessee in May, the predominately Texas units from the Arkansas Post debacle were organized into a brigade under Churchill but had never reconciled themselves to that fact. Desirous of returning to the Trans-Mississippi Department, where the cavalrymen among them could be remounted, the men of the brigade resented both Churchill and anything to do with Bragg's command. Churchill had struggled to reassert his authority over the brigade, but Deshler was popular with the men, so the change was considered a positive step. The infantry's gain, however, was the Artillery Reserve's loss, because Deshler's departure meant that the hated Maj. Felix Robertson would resume command of the gunners. Even with Deshler in charge, the spirited men of the brigade remained difficult to return to full compliance with army discipline. Col. Roger Mills, commanding the consolidated Sixth and Tenth Texas Infantry and the Fifteenth Texas Cavalry (Dismounted) regiments, was especially disliked. For example, Sgt. William Heartsill recorded in his diary a telling incident that occurred on the night of 14 August: "At night some fellow on the right of the Regiment raised a yell and it spread like 'wild fire' through the command, when what do you think,! orders are immediatly [*sic*] issued by KING ROGER for every man to be quiet or suffer severe punishment, . . . and has it come to this; that the men cannot indulge in a little merriment occasionally without displeasing our RULER, petty tyranny now reigns over this Regiment."[15]

Still another pocket of discontent with the Army of Tennessee's senior leadership appeared within the army's mounted arm. While Joseph Wheeler lacked administrative and disciplinary skills, he remained in favor with Bragg. Such favor did not extend to Nathan Bedford Forrest, although Bragg clearly recognized Forrest's talents. Forrest detested Wheeler and chaffed under Bragg's tight control. Indeed, he seemed to perform best when freed to operate without the constraints of a rigidly hierarchical system. On 9 August Forrest wrote to Samuel Cooper, offering a bargain he felt the War Department might accept. Bowing to military protocol, he sent his letter through Bragg's headquarters, although he did not expect it to be forwarded to Richmond. In the letter, Forrest proposed to leave the Army of Tennessee with a small force and assume command of the territory stretching from Cairo, Illinois, to Vicksburg, Mississippi. There he expected to raise a force of up to 10,000 men, primarily from western Tennessee and northern Mississippi, within sixty days. With that force he intended to so interdict the Mississippi River that only traffic escorted by armored vessels could pass against his will. In other words, Forrest proposed to regain control of a large swath of lost territory and hold that territory until regular Confederate forces could arrive in strength. To support his appeal, Forrest reminded Cooper of his longstanding ties to the area and his intimate knowledge of the region's geography. He asked only for his personal escort (60 men), Maj. Charles McDonald's Eighteenth Tennessee Cavalry Battalion (150 men), and Lt. Col. Thomas Woodward's Second Kentucky Cavalry regiment (250 men). Forrest also requested four rifled artillery pieces, pulled by eight-horse teams, and commanded by Capt. William Carnes. Upon receipt of this remarkable document, Bragg forwarded it to Richmond on 14 August, with the following endorsement: "I know no officer to whom I would sooner assign the duty proposed, than which none is more important, but it would deprive this army of one of its greatest elements of strength to remove General Forrest." There the matter rested, for the time being.[16]

Around Bridgeport, the only troops of Bragg's army that were in daily contact with their Federal opponents spent the first half of August in watchful waiting. When he was sent to the area in July, Patton Anderson had established his base of operations at Taylor's Store, located at a crossing of the railroad approximately a mile from the railroad bridges. From that base, he dispatched daily details to picket the river and occasionally sent raiders across the Tennessee in search of Union guerrillas like the well-known "Bob" White. His line stretched fifteen miles from the mouth of Island Creek, five miles below Bridgeport, to Shell Mound Station on the Nashville & Chattanooga Railroad, ten miles upstream. Four of Anderson's five regiments, his battalion of sharpshooters, and Dent's Alabama Battery camped at Taylor's Store, while the Forty-First Mississippi Infantry regiment bivouacked at Shell Mound. Named for the large quantities of discarded freshwater mussel shells visible there, Shell Mound was another well-established crossing site, opening on the north side of the river into the Sequatchie Valley and the village of Jasper, Tennessee. It was also the site of an extensive saltpeter mining operation in Nickajack Cave, operated by the Confederate Nitre and Mining Bureau. There were other crossing sites within Anderson's sector, notably Alley's Ferry at the mouth of Battle Creek, but Bridgeport and Shell Mound were the most obvious choices for the Federals to use. For much of his front, Anderson's task was straightforward. At the Bridgeport railroad crossing, however, the river was divided into two channels by Long Island. To watch Federal activity around the railroad bridge, Anderson was forced to garrison Long Island with a significant number of pickets, who were quietly rotated every third night. Officers enjoined men on the Long Island detail to be as quiet as possible, situated as they were under the enemy's guns. The pickets also maintained several dugout canoes and skiffs on the east side of the island.[17]

When the Federals had first appeared at Bridgeport, the opposing pickets had fired at each other, but by August an unofficial truce prevailed. The Federals, and some civilians, used the river for bathing, but Anderson's Mississippians rarely joined them. There was some trading of coffee, sugar, tobacco, and newspapers whenever officers were absent. The generally friendly approach was favored by soldiers on both sides, who believed that randomly killing a picket would not affect the war's outcome. The situation at Bridgeport was so relaxed by 1 August that 1st Lt. Hubert Dent endeavored to lodge his wife with a local family. At Shell Mound, which had daily train service from Chattanooga, officers of the Forty-First Mississippi had the same idea. There, Lt. Col. Byrd Williams welcomed his wife, and Lt. J. H. Evans entertained his mother and sister. A major attraction for the civilian guests was Nickajack Cave. At Shell Mound, it was easy to cross the river unopposed, and numerous soldiers foraged liberally on the far bank. When the regiment's cattle escaped their herder, the short rations caused several men to cross the river in search of food. When they illegally killed a hog, they received severe punishment. Lt. John Rand crossed the river to pay for the animal, and took the opportunity to purchase two watermelons at $1.00 each. Rand also noted in his diary on 9 August that the religious fervor sweeping the Chattanooga camps had reached his regiment, with nightly preaching and several baptisms. The men worried about their families in Mississippi that were in the path of the Federals, as Augustus Davis of the Seventh Mississippi Infantry regiment wrote his wife, Julia: "I was glad to hear that the Yanks had fallen back to the river. I feel like I will hear from you occasionally if they will stay on the river, but if they come out to Jackson I know there is no chance to hear—if they come out there you must do the best you can." On 6 August, Pvt. John Roberts of the same regiment recorded in his diary, "I heare the yanks is a coming close to my home. . . . They will soon have my county."[18]

Although Anderson's men could see no immediate end to the tedium of guarding the ruined railroad bridge, watching the languid river, and joking with their Federal counterparts, their leaders were becoming concerned about the situation along the river. The growing number of Federals on the Bridgeport bluff, the increased amount of railroad traffic, and a report that seventy-five Federals had visited Jasper on 8 August all contributed to a growing concern by both Anderson and Bragg. As early as 4 August, Bragg had instructed Anderson to report Federal activity directly to army headquarters. If the Federals crossed the Tennessee above his position, Anderson was to withdraw and rejoin the main army via Trenton. Several days earlier, Anderson had put men to work splitting kindling and stockpiling it near the drawbridge to Long Island. In addition, they kept a barrel of turpentine nearby to accelerate the conflagration if ordered to burn the bridge. Although the flag of truce that returned Anderson's mother to her son on 9 August offered no indication that the Federals were ready to upset the Bridgeport equilibrium, Bragg decided to visit Anderson in person. Ordering chief engineer Stephen Presstman to accompany him, Bragg traveled to Bridgeport on 12 August. There are no accounts of what he learned from Anderson, or any of what he saw during his visit, but Bragg was clearly alarmed. While he pondered what to do, on 13 August he contented himself with ordering John Jackson to increase the guard at the Chattanooga depot significantly. By the following day, 14 August, he had made his decision. In Bragg's estimation, a Federal advance was very likely to begin soon, so it was time to prepare his army to meet it. That meant recalling scattered detachments, like Benjamin Hill's in the Sequatchie Valley and part of the Eighteenth Tennessee Cavalry battalion, also across the river. Most important of all was an order to Patton Anderson: "The General Commanding directs that you abandon the Island at Bridgeport, and burn the Bridge."[19]

That evening, Pvt. John Roberts of the Seventh Mississippi Infantry regiment was part of the detail assigned to replace the pickets on Long Island. He and thirty-five other soldiers quietly crossed the drawbridge and made their way to their picket posts. Eventually Roberts and seventeen other soldiers settled into their positions on the downstream end of the island. While some of his comrades kept watch, Roberts went to sleep. He was soon rudely awakened and informed that the island was to be abandoned. Quietly withdrawing toward the drawbridge, Roberts and several other men were ordered to remove the dugout canoes on the island's shore. Stumbling through the brambles and deadfall to the riverbank in the darkness, they eventually found the canoes and paddled them to safety. Meanwhile the remainder of the detachment crossed the drawbridge. While the pickets of the Seventh Mississippi rallied on the left bank of the river and their officers accounted for everyone, soldiers from the Ninth Mississippi Sharpshooter battalion ignited the piles of turpentine-soaked kindling and fired the drawbridge. As the flames roared high over the doomed structure, Roberts stood in awe of the scene. He recorded: "In a few minutes a canon fired at the brig then a nother sheld the island alover. . . . Some times they wood thra a bawl past us. . . . At last the brig fel in and all quite a gain. . . . Thir was gards plast along the slou before we crost. So we will rest to nite and come on to marrow."[20]

8

To the River

» 15–20 August 1863 «

News of the destruction of the Bridgeport drawbridge reached Winchester, Tennessee, before daylight on the morning of 15 August. If Rosecrans had been waiting to gather a few more days of supplies, he now had reason to initiate the movement at once. Needing more information about what was happening on the Confederate side of the river, he instructed Sheridan and Lytle at Bridgeport to be especially vigilant. During the previous evening, before the bridge fell, Sheridan had brashly suggested that the Confederates might be evacuating Chattanooga. Now Rosecrans wanted to know if there were any other signs that Anderson's men were leaving, such as changes in the appearance of their campfires. No matter what Lytle discovered, Rosecrans informed Sheridan that the entire army would move east of the Cumberland Plateau on the next day. Rosecrans had never liked to conduct operations on Sunday, but the situation had become too unstable to keep the army in its camps, so the advance would begin the next day, Sunday, 16 August. In order for that to happen, the army staff was galvanized into action. With Garfield still ill, Calvin Goddard and his assistants, Maj. William McMichael and Capt. Henry Thrall, initiated drafting, editing, and proofreading two General Orders regarding the treatment of guerrillas and rules for foraging, as well as the all-important movement order for the army's major components. The final draft of the order would not be ready for publication until late in the afternoon, although news of its coming soon began to spread around the army.[1]

While the adjutant general department crafted the movement order, two of Rosecrans's aides-de-camp, Frank Bond and Robert Thoms, scurried to do Rosecrans's bidding on a variety of other subjects. First, Bond telegraphed Sheridan, ordering the manufacture of large numbers of oars for the pontoons building at Estill Springs. He also wrote in Rosecrans's name to James Guthrie, president of the Louisville & Nashville Railroad, seeking the temporary loan of several locomotives and cars. Both Bond and Thoms then wired Innes and Capt. Jonathan Dickson in Nashville on the car issue. Innes had wanted to send two officers north to purchase additional freight cars, a request now denied because 100 had already been ordered. In contrast, Innes was permitted to detail an officer to unload cars arriving by steamboat from other commands, notably Grant's. At Rosecrans's behest, Thoms also dispatched several interrogatories: to the commander of the Pioneer Brigade, can you spare 100 panniers for headquarters use; to George Thomas, how is Reynolds's work on the Doran Cove road down the Cumberland Plateau progressing; to Richard Johnson at Tullahoma, have Reserve Corps units arrived to relieve your division; to Samuel Simmons, the army's chief commissary of subsistence, must the Twentieth Corps go on half rations of sugar; and, to Capt. Edwin Townsend, ordnance officer at Nashville, can you provide arms and equipment for two regiments of black troops. In the midst of this flurry of frenetic activity, Rosecrans himself found the time to upbraid Colonel Innes for usurping the prerogatives of the army's chief telegrapher, John Van Duzer, and to wire Secretary of War Stanton for $10,000 with which to pay secret agents. He also wrote a note to the Democratic State Central Committee of Ohio, stating that although he was a Democrat and favored soldiers' casting ballots, he would not permit "stump orators and canvassers" to visit the army prior to the upcoming elections. He apparently gave no thought to how the note, which found its way to the newspapers, would be received by the Lincoln administration.[2]

Lieutenant Colonel Goddard's handiwork consisted of eight distinct parts. It opened with instructions to George Thomas and the Fourteenth Corps. Thomas was to move his First and Second Divisions to positions just north of Stevenson, while the Third and Fourth Divisions were to cross the Cumberland Plateau into the Sequatchie and Battle Creek valleys, north of Battle Creek itself and near the village of Jasper. The divisions were to carry with them their reserve ammunition, eight days' rations and at least five days' forage. One regiment was to be left at Cowan to guard the depot, the railroad tunnel, and the sick of the corps until they could be evacuated to Nashville. Another regiment was to be left at Tracy City to guard the supply depot to be established there. Thomas's two divisions near Battle Creek were to draw their supplies from Tracy City, while the others were to get their rations from Stevenson. Thomas was to maintain communication between his wings by both courier and signal corps personnel, and his staff officers were authorized to communicate their needs directly to the army's staff department heads. One of Thomas's units, John Wilder's First Brigade of Reynolds's Fourth Division, was assigned a special mission. Wilder, who would receive instructions directly from Rosecrans, was to lead his "Lightning Brigade" of mounted infantry to the Tennessee River at Chattanooga and Harrison and make demonstrations there. The corps was to begin its advance on the next morning. As befitting instructions to the army's senior corps commander, the order was succinct, giving general guidance only and leaving the specific details of route and troop placement entirely to Thomas's discretion.[3]

In contrast to the latitude given Thomas, Section 2 of the operations order gave minute instructions to Thomas Crittenden. Each of Crittenden's divisions was to take a different path across the Cumberland Plateau. Wood's First Division was to cross the mountain beyond Pelham and occupy a road junction called Therman in the Sequatchie Valley, five miles south of Dunlap. The order required Wood to carry ten days' rations and eight days' short forage. On Wood's left, Palmer's Second Division was to move from Manchester beyond the Cumberland Plateau to Dunlap, using the route through Irving College. North of Palmer, Van Cleve was ordered to take two brigades and Minty's cavalry across the plateau and enter the Sequatchie Valley at Pikeville. Minty was to move via Sparta, while the infantry and two cavalry battalions took a more southerly route via Spencer. Van Cleve was to leave an infantry brigade at McMinnville and a cavalry battalion at Sparta to protect the army's left flank. The order required all Twenty-First Corps units to be in the Sequatchie Valley by the night of 18 August. Upon reaching Pikeville, Van Cleve was to send a strong cavalry probe beyond Walden's Ridge into the Tennessee River valley near Blythe's Ferry and Washington. Palmer was to send an infantry brigade into the same valley at Poe's Tavern, where it would support Wilder's demonstrations. Finally, Wood was to send an infantry brigade to the eastern edge of Walden's Ridge, in plain view of Chattanooga. In each case, the advance parties were to act with "a show of modest concealment, indicating strength." If the Confederates moved against them, the brigades should protect themselves; if the Confederates simply reinforced their units east of the river, the brigades should push scouts forward; and if the Confederates disappeared, the brigades should advance to the river and attempt to cross the stream. Finally, the army order specified that each division of the Twenty-First Corps should divide its trains into three sections to bring supplies from the McMinnville and Tracy City depots.[4]

Sections 3 and 4 of the operations order addressed Alexander McCook's Twentieth Corps and David Stanley's Cavalry Corps. With Sheridan's Third Division already deployed at Stevenson and Bridgeport, the order to McCook only addressed his remaining divisions. Johnson's Second Division was ordered to leave Tullahoma and cross the Cumberland Plateau into the Tennessee River valley by a route that would take it near Bellefonte, Alabama. There it would establish itself in a concealed position near the Memphis & Charleston Railroad and open communication with corps headquarters at Stevenson by the night of 19 August. At the same time, Davis's First Division was to march from Winchester over the Cumberland Plateau and also enter the Tennessee River valley, but nearer Stevenson than Johnson's troops. Davis was also to camp on the Memphis & Charleston Railroad, but nearer Stevenson between Mud and Raccoon Creeks. He was to be in position by 20 August. As for the army's cavalry, Stanley's First Division, temporarily under Edward McCook, was already dispersed along the Memphis & Charleston Railroad from Stevenson west to Maysville, guarding major bridges and picketing the Tennessee River. Crook's Second Division, only two brigades strong, was split. Minty's First Brigade was with Van Cleve, on the army's far northern flank, while Long's Second Brigade was to remain in support of army headquarters and move forward with it. Stanley himself was to move with Long and be governed by further instructions from Rosecrans himself.[5]

Sections 5 and 6 delineated the role of Gordon Granger's Reserve Corps. Granger's charter to guard the rear areas of the Army of the Cumberland remained in effect. Specifically, he was to advance to Fayetteville to protect the supply depot vacated by Stanley's cavalry, push a two-brigade force southward to Athens, Alabama, and give the impression that 25,000 men would be advancing on Decatur. These moves, if fully implemented, would protect the far right flank of the Army of the Cumberland. Granger's easternmost unit was a brigade of Unionist Tennessee troops stationed at Carthage, Tennessee, forty-five miles east of Nashville on the Cumberland River. The army operations order required that brigade, minus one regiment, to move seventeen miles south to Alexandria, Tennessee. From there, the command would open communication with the troops Van Cleve had left at McMinnville when his division advanced into the Sequatchie Valley. When circumstances permitted, this force would relieve the McMinnville garrison, permitting Van Cleve's Second Brigade to join its parent unit. To facilitate communications, as the units moved farther from Nashville, a new telegraph line would be built from Gallatin, Tennessee, to Carthage. Elements of Granger's corps therefore would protect the left flank of the Army of the Cumberland as well as its right. Beyond that, Granger was free to deploy the units of his corps as he saw fit. He remained responsible for the safety of the Nashville depot and the army's lines of communication in Tennessee. Those lines included the Cumberland River garrisons at Fort Donelson and Clarksville, Tennessee, as well as the critical Louisville & Nashville and Nashville & Chattanooga Railroads, with garrisons at Murfreesboro and points south. Thus his command was now more widely spread than ever before, and as the main army moved forward the Reserve Corps it would be stretched even farther.[6]

Section 7 of the army operations order addressed logistics. There would be three depots of supplies: Stevenson, Tracy City, and McMinnville, with Stevenson the largest. All three depended upon railroad transportation to provide the requisite amount of food, short forage, equipment, and medical supplies. The easiest location to supply was Stevenson, situated on the main line of the Nashville & Chattanooga Railroad. The primary challenge on that route was the steep grade on both sides of the Cumberland Tunnel. Details from the Pioneer Brigade had been at work for some time on platforms at Stevenson to keep the massive numbers of boxes, barrels, and kegs out of the mud when it rained. The Right Wing of the Fourteenth Corps, the entire Twentieth Corps, all of the Cavalry Corps except Minty's brigade, the Pioneer Brigade, and army headquarters would all be sustained from Stevenson. Much more problematic was the selection of Tracy City as a supply depot. That coal mining settlement lay at the end of the extremely steep and curving track of the Sewanee Railroad. By the time the operations order was issued, Tracy City was unoccupied by troops, and no supplies had been accumulated there. Rosecrans's long-standing concerns about getting the right kind of engines to traverse the line successfully had also not yet borne fruit. The situation was somewhat better at McMinnville, where the McMinnville & Manchester Railroad ran thirty-seven miles to a junction with the main line of the Nashville & Chattanooga Railroad at Tullahoma. Despite poor track and several large trestles, the railroad had been able to support a supply depot at McMinnville for several weeks. No matter how difficult the Tracy City and McMinnville branches were to operate, depots at those villages were expected to sustain the Left Wing of the Fourteenth Corps, the entire Twenty-First Corps, and Minty's cavalry brigade. As for army headquarters, it was scheduled to move to Stevenson on Tuesday, 18 August.[7]

Although it did not articulate a general concept of the army's forthcoming campaign, the operations order of 15 August signaled that Rosecrans had finally decided how to proceed. The detailed instructions to Crittenden's Twenty-First Corps and the more vaguely worded mention of Wilder's expedition clearly showed that the army would implement its deception plan at Chattanooga and upstream, not below the city where troops were instructed to remain completely hidden. Of course, if the deception units discovered that the Confederates were withdrawing, as Sheridan expected them to do, the plan could be adjusted. Nevertheless, the order gave no indication that such was an active possibility. Given the vertical and unforgiving terrain opposite Chattanooga and northward, the location of the Nashville & Chattanooga Railroad, and the difficulty of moving heavy pontoons secretly over multiple mountains in order to reach the river anywhere but near Stevenson, it would appear that Rosecrans had no other rational course of action available to him. Perhaps Rosecrans had known this truth all along and had simply maintained the fiction of multiple avenues of approach with Burnside and others for security reasons when he seemingly left other options open for consideration. It is also possible that he came to his choice through a rational weighing of all of the options before him, as would be expected of a mind of logical and scientific bent. However he reached the final decision, Rosecrans had now produced a detailed operations order for the Army of the Cumberland. Whether he came to adopt the plan rationally or impetuously, his timing in its issuance bore the marks of unseemly haste. The fact that Rosecrans committed the army to a highly unusual Sunday advance, the universal surprise expressed by all echelons, and the resulting chaos at army headquarters all lead to the conclusion that Bragg's unexpected destruction of the Bridgeport drawbridge caused Rosecrans to advance his movement schedule by at least a day, if not more.[8]

As the army staff frantically crafted the operations order, Rosecrans's soldiers blissfully enjoyed a quiet Sunday in camp. Across the army the usual inspections and dress parades took place, as did normal details for picket duty. Those not so engaged received mail from home, wrote letters, washed their clothes, and relaxed. At Manchester, Thomas Prickett of the Ninth Indiana wrote to "Dear Matilda" about the disgusting predilection of Southern women to chew tobacco. At Cowan, artilleryman Eben Sturges Jr. continued his study of the German language. At Tullahoma, August Willich maintained his strict schedule of daily drill. At University Place, the last injured soldier from the 7 August gunpowder explosion finally succumbed. At Decherd, men of the 101st Indiana spent the day cleaning their camp. At Pelham, the Ninety-Seventh Ohio completed work on a road leading up the Cumberland Plateau. At Wartrace, a detail from the 113th Ohio languidly guarded a herd of draft animals. Nor was there greater activity at the front. At Bridgeport, men from the Forty-Second Illinois swam in the Tennessee River, even as smoke continued to rise from the burned drawbridge beyond Long Island. Only a few units were in motion. Having completed their road repair tasks on the plateau, two Fourteenth Corps regiments marched down the mountain to Anderson Station. In the Tennessee River valley, the Ninth Pennsylvania Cavalry moved from Larkinsville to Stevenson, escorting the division commander, Edward McCook. Virtually everyone believed that the campaign would begin soon, but they had no inkling that the operations order even then was being prepared. The day was hot and humid, and around 3:00 P.M. a large thunderstorm developed that both stopped activity and cooled the air. Again, the storm struck most heavily in the camps around Decherd. Dangerous lightning strikes drove the Seventeenth Ohio into an open field for safety, and the tents and bowers of the Tenth Indiana were scattered far and wide. The storm eventually climbed the mountain to University Place, wetting the bivouacs of Edward King's brigade before dissipating.[9]

At the Mary Sharp College in Winchester, a storm of a different kind was brewing. The lengthy operations order not only had to be drafted and proofread, but it also had to be copied multiple times, at least one copy for every major element of the army plus file copies for headquarters. Thomas, McCook, Stanley, and Garfield were nearby and could receive their copies either in person or by courier. Crittenden, however, had only reached Twenty-First Corps headquarters at Manchester on the previous evening. The operations order was too sensitive to be sent by telegraph, and a courier would take too long to arrive by horseback. Rosecrans therefore called for the dummy to carry the operations order to Crittenden's headquarters. When John Beggs was told to send the dummy to Winchester, he replied that Colonel Innes had sent it elsewhere. Wherever the dummy was, it was not available either at Decherd or Winchester. Upon hearing the news, Rosecrans flew into a rage. He dispatched a blistering telegram to Innes: "It seems that one of the 1st acts of your administration has been to take the dummy ordered here for my use away without my consent or knowledge. Now she is wanted to bear dispatches. Such a thing must be amply explained and never again occur while you serve in my command." Beggs also received a telegram from Frank Bond, in which the aide accused Innes of a "very great impropriety," established new rules for the use of the dummy, and demanded that a train be sent to Winchester at once to take the operations order to Crittenden. Even after all the harsh words, Beggs was slow to get the train to Winchester, causing aide Charles Thompson at 9:15 P.M. to demand an explanation for the delay. In order to prevent the Twenty-First Corps from missing the start time completely, Bond and another aide, Robert Thoms, telegraphed guarded messages to Crittenden and Van Cleve that generally outlined the roles they were to play. Having vented his spleen, Rosecrans reported to Adjutant General Thomas that the army would begin its advance in the morning.[10]

The Fourteenth Corps received the operations order at midnight, 15–16 August. Fortunately, the corps was already partially in compliance with the order because the three brigades of Rousseau's First Division had been east of the Cumberland Plateau for several days. Temporarily led by John Starkweather, the division was settled comfortably in camps in the Crow Creek valley stretching east from Anderson Station for several miles. Likewise, half of Stanley's Second Brigade of Negley's Second Division was also at Anderson Station. Thus, fourteen of the twenty-four regiments that constituted the corps' Right Wing were already in the Crow Creek valley. Nevertheless, the remaining ten regiments and three batteries of Negley's command had to abandon their camps at Decherd in great haste to comply with the army and corps directives. First to move was Sirwell's Third Brigade. Sirwell started early, with his rearguard marching at 9:30 A.M. The route led first to Cowan, reached in early afternoon despite a heavy rain that began around noon. From Cowan the rough road led steeply up the mountain. On top of the plateau it passed over the railroad tunnel several hundred feet below. Although the road was difficult, Sirwell's brigade reached the top of the plateau after dark and halted for the night. Behind Sirwell came Beatty's First Brigade, led in Beatty's absence by Col. Absalom Moore of the 104th Illinois Infantry regiment. By the time the First Brigade began its journey, the rain had begun. Traveling behind Sirwell's command on an increasingly deteriorated road, Moore's men periodically halted because teams stalled in front of them. By nightfall, with the brigade still short of the crest, Moore decided to camp on the mountainside until the next day. Behind Moore's tired and wet men, the remaining regiments of Stanley's Second Brigade did not even try to advance. In accord with instructions to leave a unit at Cowan to guard the convalescent camp there, Stanley's Sixty-Ninth Ohio Infantry left the brigade at that point.[11]

Unlike his Right Wing, Thomas's Left Wing was decidedly in trouble. Reynolds's Fourth Division already had its Second and Third Brigades on the mountain at University Place, but Wilder's First Brigade and division headquarters were still at Decherd. Reynolds acknowledged receipt of the order at 4:30 A.M., promising to move promptly, but two factors complicated his efforts. First, Wilder had to visit Thomas's headquarters in Decherd to meet with Rosecrans, Thomas, and Reynolds. There he was given explicit instructions regarding the demonstration he was to make in front of Chattanooga later in the week. His mission made Wilder independent of Reynolds, an arrangement no doubt pleasing to all concerned. Second, Thomas ordered Reynolds to supervise the movements of Brannan's Third Division in addition to his own. Brannan had just gained division command in April, and his only experience in directing its movements had been in the brief Tullahoma campaign. Although Reynolds himself did not have a strong reputation at army headquarters, he had commanded a division since late 1862. Both men had very limited combat experience. Their route was an extremely rough road from the valley floor at Brakefield Point to University Place, thence down into Sweeden's Cove. Wilder's leading regiment, the Seventy-Second Indiana Mounted Infantry, made it up the mountain with ease, but the remainder of the brigade was caught in a heavy downpour as it began the ascent. Lightning flashed around the toiling column, some bolts so near that they drove men to their knees, their skin tingling. The torrent soon began to wash down the hillside, making the rocky road slippery. In the recently mounted Ninety-Second Illinois regiment, soldiers and unsecured gear fell into the muck, paving the road with "frying pans, coffee pots, knives, forks, spoons, bacon, hardtack, and poor riders." Eventually Wilder's troopers reached the crest, where they were above the storm. Unfortunately, the brigade train failed to complete the climb by nightfall, stalling the division train as well. Behind Reynolds's wagons waited Brannan's division.[12]

Brannan apparently was late in getting the order to march. Still, the pickets were recalled and everything packed for movement within a very short time. In Van Derveer's Third Brigade, the Second Minnesota had built an elaborate palisaded camp, with ornamental arches and towers over its gates. When all had departed the three-acre enclosure, a detail burned their handiwork to the ground. The regiment then joined the remainder of the division heading first to Decherd, then north toward Brakefield Point. As it happened, Brannan's men were on the road less than an hour before the violent thunderstorm that would drench so many other units struck them in full fury. The epicenter of the storm seems to have been Decherd, although it was felt over a far wider area. The blinding flashes of lightning and the tremendous peals of thunder brought all movement to a halt. In Connell's First Brigade, Col. Morton Hunter of the Eighty-Second Indiana Infantry regiment ordered his command to fix bayonets, stick their reversed guns into the ground, and move away from their weapons for safety. Several men in the division were struck by lightning and others were injured when a bolt exploded a battery's ammunition chest. Everywhere men donned their rubber ponchos, turned their backs to the storm, and stood the pounding rain and wind as best they could. The heaviest blows lasted thirty minutes, but the rain continued for two hours until the sun reappeared. By that time, the damage had been done. Although the temperature was noticeably cooler, the roads had become muddy streams that made travel extremely disagreeable. Brannan's division resumed its march, but four miles beyond Decherd it halted behind the trains of Reynolds's command. If Brannan was to follow Reynolds up the Cumberland Plateau, he would have to wait until the Brakefield Point road was clear. Thus Brannan's weary division bivouacked in the sodden fields a few miles north of Decherd. The only consolation to the men was that they halted in the midst of unplundered fields of green corn.[13]

Nine miles north of Thomas's stalled Left Wing was Thomas Wood's First Division of the Twenty-First Corps. Wagner's Second Brigade lay at Pelham, four miles from the foot of the Cumberland Plateau. Two infantry brigades and the division headquarters were at Hillsboro, nine miles northwest of Pelham. Wood received his movement orders at dawn, but by the time regimental commanders got the word, it was midmorning. While the troops packed their gear, Wood chose an obscure track called the Park Road for the division's ascent of the plateau. Tramping through the humid countryside, Wagner's regiments reached the foot of the mountain by noon. At that moment the rain sweeping toward them from the northwest arrived in strength. Although the storm in Wood's sector did not have the violence seen at Decherd, the hard rain affected Wood's movements just as it did those of the Fourteenth Corps. The road in the valley quickly turned to mud behind Wagner, while his own brigade could get little traction on the wet rocks of the steep Park Road. In order to prevent his wagons from stalling on the grade, Wagner ordered the teams to be doubled. By sundown only half of Wagner's train had reached the top of the plateau. Knowing that he was delaying the remainder of the division, Wagner ordered fires to be kindled along the road. By that faint and flickering light, regimental details took the doubled teams down the mountain, and dragged the remaining wagons up the slippery road. They did not complete their task until well after midnight. Back in the valley, Buell's First Brigade struggled forward to the foot of the mountain, cursing first the heat, then the rain. Behind Buell, Harker's Third Brigade floundered in the mud only as far as Pelham. At least twelve wagons stuck deeply in the muck could only be freed by unloading them. Col. Emerson Opdycke's 125th Ohio Infantry regiment, the division's rear guard, unloaded wagons, cut downed horses from the traces, and built new paths around mud-holes. At 9:00 P.M., Opdycke halted his men's efforts and sent them into camp.[14]

Fortunately for Crittenden's timetable, John Palmer's Second Division had a much easier time tackling the Cumberland Plateau than did Wood's First Division. Orders to move reached the division around midnight after all had retired for the evening, but Cruft's First Brigade nevertheless got on the road by 8:00 A.M. The division's route led northeast in the general direction of McMinnville before it turned directly east to assault the Cumberland Plateau. In several regiments the men carried their knapsacks in addition to their weapons, ammunition, rations, blankets, ponchos, and shelter halves. The heat and humidity quickly took a toll on the marching soldiers. Their pain increased as the storm sweeping across Middle Tennessee began to pound them. Marching behind Cruft's men, Grose's Third Brigade followed closely on the same track. At least one of Grose's regiments, the Eighty-Fourth Illinois Infantry, left its large tents and knapsacks behind, easing somewhat its burden in the heat and rain and making the march slightly less tedious. Bringing up the rear was Hazen's Second Brigade, escorting the division's train of 300 heavily loaded wagons. Knowing that the march would be difficult for the men on such a hot day, officers in the Forty-First Ohio issued whiskey to those who desired it. Rather than fortify the men for the task ahead, the whiskey only served to sicken some of them as they trudged forward. As a result, a growing body of stragglers trailed the column. At least the men of the Forty-First did not have to carry their knapsacks, as reported by Pvt. George Hodges: "We had no Napsacks to lug, them ware left at Manchester. We may see them again & we may not. I think I rather loose mine than caried it on this march." By the end of the day, the division had reached the hamlet of Viola, thirteen miles from Manchester, and there it halted for the night. The entire movement had been essentially over flat ground, leaving Palmer's ascent of the Cumberland Plateau for another day.[15]

Horatio Van Cleve's Third Division of the Twenty-First Corps received its movement orders from corps headquarters at 11:00 A.M., and Van Cleve had his command on the road ninety minutes later. The orders required Van Cleve to march to Pikeville, a village in the Sequatchie Valley beyond the Cumberland Plateau, with two of his three brigades and Robert Minty's cavalry brigade. Leaving George Dick's Second Brigade to garrison the McMinnville depot, Van Cleve led with Sidney Barnes's Third Brigade, followed by Samuel Beatty's First Brigade and the division train of 150 wagons. The army operations order specified that the infantry column was to travel via the village of Spencer, while Minty was to take most of his horsemen by way of Sparta, brushing aside the Confederate force there. According to Van Cleve's information, however, the Spencer road was impassable, so he followed a lesser road known as the Harrison Trace. This road took a more southerly course than the Spencer road, ultimately climbing to the crest of the Cumberland Plateau and then crossing a virtually uninhabited wilderness until it reached the Sequatchie Valley. Just beyond McMinnville, the infantry column waded the Barren Fork, marched four miles, waded the Collins River, and went into camp at the foot of the mountains. With two river crossings and the rain, which began shortly after the division moved, it was a wet day for everyone concerned, except for Dick's infantrymen and Minty's cavalrymen, who remained snug in their camps at McMinnville. Minty could not move until he received a shipment of forage by rail, due that night, so he planned to go to Sparta on the following day. Van Cleve believed that only a lone Confederate cavalry regiment was at Sparta, so he expected no difficulty for Minty. Similarly, he expected the Cumberland Plateau itself to be his only opposition for the next several days.[16]

The operations order envisioned that the right side of the Army of the Cumberland's advance would consist of the two remaining divisions of the Twentieth Corps. Sheridan's Third Division was already manning the front lines at Bridgeport, so it was not involved. That left Jefferson C. Davis's First Division at Winchester and Richard Johnson's Second Division at Tullahoma to join the remainder of the army beyond the Cumberland Plateau. Kate McCook was still in camp, and her husband seemed to be in no hurry to leave Winchester. Writing from corps headquarters, McCook's aide, Capt. Frank Jones, told his father, "Mrs. McCook, Horace Phillips and young George McCook still remain with us and will go north perhaps tomorrow—certainly if we *move*; which is very probable." Meanwhile, George McCook, eleven, continued to visit and play with Harry Van Derveer, thirteen, son of a brigade commander in the Fourteenth Corps, who was also in camp with the army. George's uncle Alex McCook finally ordered Davis's First Division to begin its advance at 2:00 P.M. on the following day, 17 August, taking a road that would carry the division beyond the Cumberland Plateau into the valley of Raccoon Creek south of Stevenson. Lt. Col. Gates Thruston, the corps chief of staff, enjoined Davis to reduce the division's baggage to a minimum and load his wagons to only half their capacity in order to make the crossing. With another day of grace, soldiers in the division paid no heed to the rain that pelted Winchester in the afternoon and continued their daily routines. For Lt. Chesley Mosman of the Fifty-Ninth Illinois Infantry regiment of Sidney Post's First Brigade, it was an enjoyable day. He recorded in his diary, "Went to church, Anderson and I. Meanwhile inspector came around to inspect the Company and no officer there. He said we had 'the best guns of any company in the Brigade he had seen.' Citizen choir in church. Pretty girls."[17]

Affairs were a bit more hectic in Richard Johnson's Second Division at Tullahoma. Johnson had received a telegram early in the morning from corps headquarters telling him to move on the next day, but a subsequent message advanced his departure time to that very afternoon. Accordingly, Johnson marched at 3:30 P.M., with Philemon Baldwin's Third Brigade leading the column. The brigade had only one hour's notice to break camp, and by the time it departed, rain was widespread in the Tullahoma area. Pvt. David Shideler of the Ninety-Third Ohio Infantry regiment spoke for many when he wrote, "We received marching orders this afternoon. I was lying in my tent at the time and must confess that I was disappointed." Still, Private Shideler was lucky to be among the first to take the road to Elk River, before it was ruined by rain and marching feet. The brigade halted for the night at Estill Springs. Joseph Dodge's Second Brigade followed Baldwin's command, but in Dodge's absence Col. Thomas Rose of the Seventy-Seventh Pennsylvania Infantry regiment led the movement. According to Sgt. Maj. Lyman Widney of the Thirty-Fourth Illinois Infantry regiment, the men were ready to go, after being in camp so long: "The men were never in better spirits since we left camp Butler or Green River; they acted like so many schoolboys just let loose from school." Dodge's brigade also halted at Elk River, but well after dark. In the rear, August Willich's First Brigade escorted the division train. Before departing, Willich formally cashiered an officer of the Forty-Ninth Ohio Infantry regiment for rape, assault and battery, and straggling. By the time they got on the road at 5:30 P.M., following the heavy supply and ammunition wagons, the route had become nearly impassable. Floundering mules and broken wagons blocked the road every few minutes, preventing the brigade from making more than a few miles before halting in the sodden fields at 2:00 A.M. on 17 August.[18]

For those units already beyond the Cumberland Plateau, 16 August was a quiet day. At Bridgeport, William Lytle orchestrated a delicate flag of truce negotiation with Patton Anderson's Confederates. By one account, a Confederate mother desired to pass through the lines to visit her wounded and captured son; by another, a wife sought to cross the river to be with her badly wounded husband. Either way, telegraphic inquiries ascertained that the individual in question was long dead, negating the need for the lady's passage. Elsewhere at Bridgeport the day consisted of routine picket and fatigue duty. In the Thirty-Sixth Illinois Infantry regiment, Pvt. Ebenezer Lamb borrowed a book on the life of Andrew Jackson from the regimental library, while a captain in the Twenty-First Michigan received the news of the death of his son. Lytle informed Sheridan that a deserter had confirmed that the recent Confederate activity was simply Anderson's men cooking rations. At Stevenson, Lytle's aide,

Lt. Alfred Pirtle, joined Sheridan and Edward McCook on a visit to Larkinsville on the Memphis & Charleston Railroad. The officers found the M&C feasible as a supply route, although the track was so choked with weeds that the engine slipped badly. Pirtle commented on the locals, "The people were rebels and ugly looking like they used to be last summer—they are behind the times and don't know the S. C. is 'played out.'" Back at Stevenson, two more of McCook's cavalry regiments arrived from downstream. So did the rain, which appeared with diminished force in late afternoon. In the Crow Creek valley, John Starkweather's three brigades performed road work, suffered through inspection, wrote letters home, and rested in camp. In the Seventy-Ninth Pennsylvania Infantry regiment, which finally received its baggage, Commissary Sgt. William Clark learned that his blanket and shelter half had been stolen. He consoled himself with rumors that Fort Sumter had fallen. At Anderson, the Eighteenth Ohio Infantry regiment of Stanley's brigade spent the day washing clothes, writing letters, and foraging.[19]

While most of the army struggled on 16 August to leave its camps, army headquarters planned its own move. Rosecrans himself continued to pressure President Guthrie of the Louisville & Nashville Railroad to loan the army fifty freight cars. Calvin Goddard instructed the Decherd quartermaster to divert all Winchester-bound supplies to Stevenson. Frank Bond instructed George Thomas to guard the supplies remaining at Decherd with the regiment left at Cowan. Robert Thoms instructed Thomas to clear a site in Stevenson for a large field hospital. Both Goddard and Bond telegraphed Sheridan to select a place in Stevenson for army headquarters to occupy on Tuesday, 18 August. Goddard ordered William Innes to furnish a locomotive, five cars, and the dummy on the same day to move the headquarters. Bond and Charles Thompson reminded John Beggs to be sure to have the dummy available when Rosecrans required it. Thoms ordered Gordon Granger to increase the force guarding the army's reserve ammunition train parked at Tullahoma. Members of the Fifteenth Pennsylvania Cavalry regiment were told to prepare for a move on the next day. Four companies of the Pioneer Brigade reported to the Fourteenth Corps for duty, six companies were assigned to build platforms at Stevenson, 200 men went to Nashville to bring forward the pontoon train, and the remainder of the brigade marched toward Salem for road repair duty. That night, Rosecrans happily informed Lorenzo Thomas, "All three corps are crossing the mountains. It will take till Wednesday night to reach their respective positions. I think we shall deceive the enemy as to our point of crossing. It is a stupendous undertaking." In fact, out of 22 ½ infantry brigades under orders to cross the Cumberland Plateau, only three brigades had reached the crest, and five had not moved at all. The primary cause of the delay was the severe storm, but late distribution of the operations order also contributed to the army's poor performance on 16 August.[20]

On 17 August the struggles of the Fourteenth Corps continued. In Negley's Second Division, Sirwell's Third Brigade descended the mountain six miles to Tantalon Station and camped for the night near some large fields of green corn. The corn provided the only sustenance for the troops as the regiments had exhausted their rations and their wagons remained far behind. Not everyone agreed that the corn was freely available: in the Seventy-Eighth Pennsylvania Infantry regiment, "Col and Lieut Col had a fuss about corn." Three regiments of Beatty's First Brigade also reached Tantalon, while the Forty-Second Indiana Infantry regiment was stuck on the side of the mountain behind the division train. Following the Forty-Second Indiana was the remainder of Stanley's Second Brigade. Several miles to the northeast, Reynolds's and Brannan's commands were still behind schedule. Turchin's Third Brigade left University Place and started down the mountain into the depths of Sweeden's Cove. Little air stirred in the forest as the men made their way down the rough path into the valley. At last they reached level ground and camped at a large pool of water known as Blue Springs. Three regiments of King's Second Brigade joined them there. Searching for wood, men of the Seventy-Fifth Indiana Infantry regiment ran afoul of the brigade commander when they followed their colonel's orders to take nearby fence rails. Confronted by Col. Milton Robinson, King surrendered ungraciously, causing Cpl. William Miller to opine, "Some officers think the private soldier is nothing but a dog and treat them accordingly and if there was no privates we would have no use for officers. About all some officers are real good for is to draw their pay." Left behind was King's 101st Indiana Infantry regiment, which Reynolds retained to assist the division train up the west side of the plateau. After taking all day to boost the wagons up the grade, Reynolds and the 101st Indiana bivouacked just beyond University Place. Because Reynolds took so long to move his train, Brannan advanced his division little more than a mile to the western foot of the Cumberland Plateau.[21]

While Reynolds struggled with his train, other units of the Fourth Division were moving on independent missions. Before taking his brigade into Sweeden's Cove, Turchin detached Col. Caleb Carlton's Eighty-Ninth Ohio Infantry regiment to occupy Tracy City, eleven miles away. The Seventy-Second Indiana Mounted Infantry regiment of Wilder's command was already there. The name of Tracy City was grander than its reality. Founded in the late 1850s as a support center for extensive coal mines owned by the Sewanee Mining Company, the "city" was named for Samuel Tracy, head of the New York consortium that established the mining operation. The company had built the Sewanee Railroad to serve the mines, with its prewar terminus at Tracy City. By the time the Seventy-Second Indiana arrived, Tracy City consisted of only three houses and a depot, although numerous miners' shacks were scattered in the woods. The remainder of Wilder's command left camp near University Place in midmorning after finally getting the brigade train up the mountain. Satisfactory for marching troops, the road was more difficult for wagons, forcing a leisurely pace through the forest. Although the distance was not excessive, it was dark before the brigade reached a ravine holding the headwaters of Big Fiery Gizzard Creek. The bridge over that chasm had been damaged, so the First Brigade halted on the west side of the ravine for the night. Nearby was a large trestle that carried the Sewanee Railroad to Tracy City and the mines. Undeterred by the state of the road, Carlton's Eighty-Ninth Ohio made it all the way to Tracy City. Carlton found neither rations nor a functioning railroad and telegraph station, a poor beginning for a supply depot expected to sustain large numbers of troops. Carlton was not impressed with the hamlet: "It is not a very pretty place a mere hole in the mountains." The surrounding woods were choked with undergrowth, while the clearings were overgrown with brush. Nevertheless, Tracy City finally had been occupied by Federal forces.[22]

Farther north, there was also movement in the Twenty-First Corps sector. Wood's First Division encountered the most difficulty, continuing to struggle on the Park Road. In the lead, Wagner's Second Brigade finally got its regiments and the brigade train on top of the plateau. After marching only a few miles, Wagner's men encountered the damaged bridge on Big Fiery Gizzard Creek, which Wood had instructed Wagner to repair with Wilder's assistance. After pausing for dinner and a brief rest, Wagner's troops passed two miles beyond Tracy City on the road that would eventually lead to Therman in the Sequatchie Valley. There they camped for the night. Behind them, Wood's remaining brigades spent all day battling the mountain grade. In the lead, Buell's First Brigade made every effort to hurry. The wagons were partially unloaded, the teams were doubled, and long ropes were attached to the wagons for men to assist the mules. By using such measures all day and far into the night, Buell's command reached the top of the plateau. There they went into camp, so weary that they were little hindered by the many rattlesnakes infesting their campsite. A brief panic ensued in the 100th Illinois Infantry regiment when a team trod upon a soldier sleeping in the road, but no lasting damage was done, and quiet soon returned. Behind Buell, Harker's Third Brigade also reached the top of the plateau, but so late that once again fires had to be kindled on the roadside for light. Last of all, Emerson Opdycke's 125th Ohio Infantry regiment assisted the 250 half-loaded wagons of the division train until 11:00 P.M. Opdycke joined his men on the ropes used to pull wagons uphill until he became faint and relinquished his place to others. When the teams reached the crest, they unloaded, then returned downhill for their remaining cargo, while the exhausted infantrymen sprawled by the roadside.[23]

Approximately twenty airline miles north of Tracy City, Palmer's Second Division had far less difficulty than Wood because it was not yet at the foot of the plateau. Palmer's men began the day in the hamlet of Viola, located at the foot of an outlying hill mass. Cruft's First Brigade moved at 9:00 A.M., leading the way first north, then east over a 200-foot rise into a narrow valley called Rodger's Hollow. The track eventually entered the wider valley of Scott's Creek, and that valley in turn gave way to the still wider valley forming the watershed of the Collins River. After marching only a few miles in a northerly direction, Cruft halted just beyond a small group of brick buildings known as Irving College. Founded in 1835, the college had suspended operations in 1861. The day was hot, with only a brief shower of rain, straggling was a problem, and several wagons became stuck in the creek bottoms. Nevertheless, by nightfall, Hazen's and Grose's Second and Third Brigades had also reached the vicinity of Irving College. There they found a virtual cornucopia of ripe peaches, apples, and green corn, which greatly supplemented the standard army ration. During the evening, Thomas Crittenden joined them there. All could see the steep escarpment of the Cumberland Plateau looming a mile to the east.

If Palmer only reached the foot of the Cumberland Plateau on 17 August, Van Cleve's Third Division began the day there. Van Cleve had reached Collins River four miles north of Irving College on the previous day. Barnes's Third Brigade easily made it to the top, then marched eight miles into the wilderness before halting on the headwaters of Rocky River. Van Cleve established division headquarters with Barnes. Behind them, Beatty's First Brigade spent the day assisting the 150-wagon train to the crest, then advanced several additional miles before also halting for the night. Both brigades had to contend with rattlesnakes in their bivouacs, and one regiment found the energy to raid a sutler's wagon for bottles of champagne.[24]

Although Rosecrans's order gave the Twentieth Corps no more time to cross the Cumberland Plateau than other units, Alex McCook seemed to be in no hurry to leave the comforts of Winchester. McCook may have been distracted by the departure of his young wife, brother-in-law, and nephew. When Davis's First Division tried to depart Winchester at 2:00 P.M. on 17 August, it found the road blocked by the army headquarters train and its escort. Rosecrans himself cleared the road for Davis. The division's route led initially toward Cowan but turned south well short of that village. Before he left Winchester, Hans Heg, Third Brigade commander, penned a note to his wife: "I am glad to get off for several reasons. We have laid here till it began to be tedious and times go faster when we are stirring around, but the main reason is that as soon as we have made this move, and get through this campaign, I shall get leave of Absence to go home." Some of the men left Winchester with regret, believing that the inhabitants had treated them with respect. Soft from their long stay in camp, many overheated soldiers left the ranks as the afternoon progressed. The goal for the afternoon's march was only the foot of the mountain, five miles from the division's starting point. North of Winchester, the three brigades of Johnson's Second Division left their Elk River bivouacs much earlier than Davis's men. Johnson's leading brigades crossed Boiling Fork Creek and in late morning entered Winchester. In the lead, Baldwin's Third Brigade continued five miles beyond the town, camping on the Salem road. There they were joined by Dodge's Second Brigade, still led by Col. Thomas Rose. In the rear, Willich's First Brigade continued to assist the division train's many mired and broken wagons. By the time Willich rejoined the division, the day was spent. In the Forty-Ninth Ohio Infantry regiment, the men received a whiskey ration, but for Pvt. Francis Kiene it was not helpful: "I stood the day's march very well but this evening while receiving my ration of Whiskey I fainted." For both Davis and Johnson, the Cumberland Plateau still lay ahead.[25]

On the Tennessee River there was little activity on 17 August. At Bridgeport, William Lytle forwarded the news from a Confederate picket who had visited the Federal lines briefly: Bragg intended to hold Chattanooga, reinforcements had arrived from Johnston's army, and 500 men had joined Anderson's brigade along the river. Some soldiers from the Thirty-Sixth Illinois Infantry regiment enjoyed a refreshing swim in the river, while others took advantage of their new regimental library to form a literary society. In Bradley's brigade, regimental bands played in the cool of the evening. Pvt. John McBride of the Fifty-First Illinois Infantry regiment thanked his mother for a box of delicacies: "If you have another chance to dont send any tea or sugar for I have enough to last me a great while now. The cheese, cakes, crackers and candy were very nice. . . . The envelopes and paper could not have come in a better time for our sutler has none worth any thing." Brigade commander Bradley wrote to his wife on the same day: "We are in good heart and temper for work, and if the rebels want to cross bayonets with us again, we shall not deny them. From all indications, they are not in the most confident humor." In Stevenson, Bernhard Laibold's commissary of subsistence noted the arrival of more of McCook's cavalry division. McCook's three brigades were scattered. Watkins's Third Brigade was stationed at Brownsboro to secure the Flint River and Hurricane Creek railroad bridges, McCook's own Second Brigade had one regiment at Paint Rock Bridge and two at Larkinsville, while Campbell's First Brigade took position at Bolivar, near Bridgeport. The Memphis & Charleston Railroad was open to Larkinsville, but McCook wanted service to be extended to Boonsboro. He also desired the return of his Second Tennessee (Union) Cavalry regiment, but it continued to work for Sheridan upstream from Bridgeport.[26]

On the army's far northern flank, Minty's cavalry brigade departed McMinnville for Sparta at 2:00 A.M. with 1,400 troopers. Waiting at Sparta was Dibrell's Eighth (Thirteenth) Tennessee Cavalry regiment, reinforced by 200 men of the Fourth Tennessee Cavalry regiment. On that day half of Dibrell's command was absent gathering supplies from the countryside. By moving so early, Minty hoped to gain the benefit of surprise, but he encountered Dibrell's scouts south of Sparta around 2:00 P.M. Alerted, Dibrell deployed on both sides of the Calfkiller River. Upon reaching Sparta, Minty also divided his command. Around 4:00 P.M. he sent the Fourth Michigan and Seventh Pennsylvania Cavalry regiments east of the Calfkiller, and personally led the Fourth United States Cavalry and the six-company Third Indiana Cavalry west of the stream. As they had on 9 August, Dibrell's men slowly withdrew to a ford across the Calfkiller at Meredith's Mill. Mistakenly believing that he was outnumbered, Minty did not press Dibrell's command and at dark ordered a retreat to Sparta. The Fourth Michigan and Seventh Pennsylvania east of the Calfkiller obeyed quickly, but Minty was slow to follow on his side of the stream. Seeing an opportunity, some of the Fourth Tennessee waited for Minty's column to offer its flank. Carelessly leading the column, Minty was ambushed suddenly by Confederates hidden beyond the Calfkiller. The unexpected blast wounded Lt. Joseph Vale of Minty's staff and an orderly, along with Minty's roan mare and several other horses. In a chaotic counterattack, a trooper of the Fourth United States Cavalry regiment drowned. The handful of Confederates quickly escaped, joining Dibrell's main body on high ground several miles to the north. Minty had gained Sparta again, at a cost of one drowned and fifteen wounded. He claimed to have taken twenty-three prisoners, while Confederate losses were placed at eight killed and thirty-nine wounded. Neither combatant had hurt the other seriously.[27]

On its last day in Winchester, the army staff bombarded railroad superintendent Innes with queries and instructions. With much of the Reserve Corps ordered south, railroad capacity was strained to the utmost. For the moment, the Nashville & Chattanooga Railroad was handling the load, using cars borrowed from the Louisville & Nashville Railroad. Trains carrying supplies for Granger could operate to Stevenson, then head west on the Memphis & Charleston Railroad. A better solution was to open the line through Columbia to Decatur, where it would connect with the reconstructed Memphis & Charleston. A bridge over the Duck River at Columbia needed to be rebuilt, and Innes twice had been informed that materials were available, but he had not expedited the work. Staff officers Frank Bond, William Porter, and James Drouillard relentlessly chided him about the matter. Worse, a serious accident blocked the N&C main line near Wartrace. In the morning, guerrillas derailed a freight train at Lavergne, delaying it for three hours. When the shaken engineer again took fire, he wildly increased speed, wrecking eleven of nineteen cars at Wartrace. At least six guards were injured and the track remained blocked until 2:00 P.M. Another train added the undamaged cars, but it was so underpowered that it nearly stalled in the Cowan tunnel. Behind the wreck, trains waited in sidings for hours, one until 10:00 P.M. Northbound traffic was also affected, causing army headquarters to query Innes three times about the daily passenger train to Nashville. As for good news, Lt. Col. Henry Hodges arrived from leave, replacing John Taylor as the army's chief quartermaster. Also, aide Charles Thompson was announced as the new commander of the Twelfth United States Colored Troops, with the rank of colonel. In his terse daily message to Adjutant General Thomas, Rosecrans candidly admitted that only half of his troops had crested the Cumberland Plateau, blaming the failure on heavy rains and bad roads.[28]

On 18 August, the third day of the Army of the Cumberland's ponderous lurch beyond the Cumberland Plateau, the Right Wing of the Fourteenth Corps finally began to show real progress. Starkweather's First Division remained in place on the railroad just east of Anderson Station. When not repairing the road to Stevenson, Starkweather's men amused themselves fixing up their camps and foraging liberally in the neighborhood. Peaches were both ripe and abundant, and so many soldiers sought them that officers had to curb the absences by instituting roll calls every two hours. Negley's Second Division passed through Starkweather's camps during the day. When Negley himself reached Stanley's Second Brigade, he ordered it to leave Anderson and march down the Crow Creek valley toward Stevenson. Stanley's men were joined on the road by Sirwell's Third Brigade. Before leaving camp, Sirwell's men had to retrace their steps up the mountain to their wagons for rations, then return downhill. The day was hot, with high humidity, causing large numbers of stragglers to dribble from the rear of the marching regiments. Becoming irate, Negley accosted Lt. Col. William Ward, commanding the Thirty-Seventh Indiana Infantry regiment, and capriciously placed him under arrest. Thus encouraged, Stanley's and Sirwell's brigades continued their march far into the evening, finally halting at a large spring three miles short of Stevenson. Far behind them, men of Beatty's First Brigade returned to the crest of the plateau to retrieve the knapsacks dumped from overburdened wagons, then headed south in Negley's wake. They halted just beyond Anderson because Col. Oscar Moore, temporary brigade commander, saw plainly that the exhausted men could go no farther. They had not yet reached their final bivouac sites, but at least the Right Wing's divisions had successfully crossed the Cumberland Plateau. Thomas himself and his headquarters party left Decherd and stopped for the night at the eastern portal of the Cowan tunnel.[29]

Thomas's Left Wing also made progress on 18 August, but not nearly as much as the remainder of the corps. Joseph Reynolds began 18 August with King's and Turchin's brigades camped at the large Blue Spring near the head of Sweeden's Cove. Because Turchin had led the column on the previous day, Reynolds left him at Blue Spring and marched five miles down Sweeden's Cove with King's men to a new bivouac on the lower reaches of Battle Creek, just two

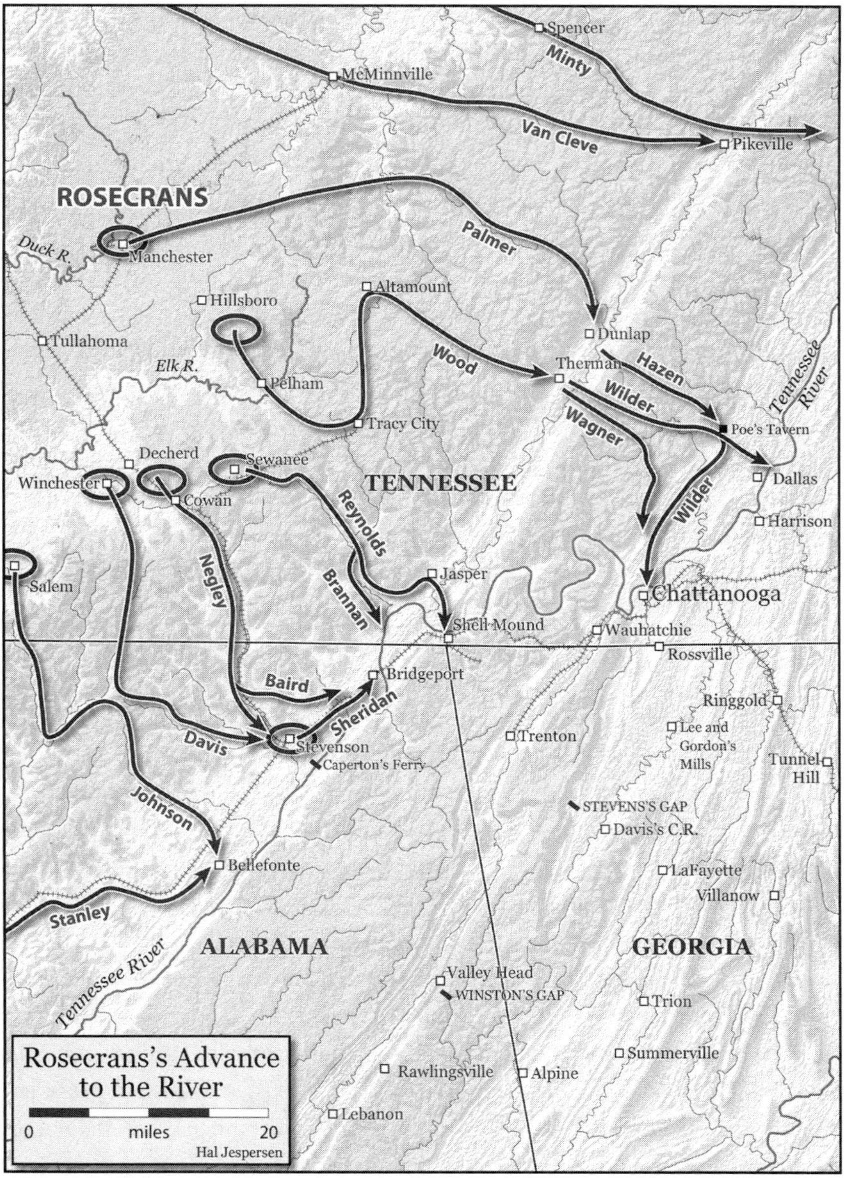

miles from the Tennessee River. A signal detachment with Reynolds ascended the mountain above the camp and reported that it could see trains running on the stub of the Nashville & Chattanooga Railroad between Shell Mound and Anderson's camps near Bridgeport. King's troops, however, were the only elements of Reynolds's command to reach the Tennessee River valley. Turchin's brigade remained at Blue Spring, while Brannan's Third Division spent all day struggling up the western slope of the Cumberland Plateau. Croxton's Second Brigade led the division on the well-worn Brakefield Point pathway to the crest at University Place. Van Derveer followed Croxton with his Third Brigade. Van Derveer was accompanied by his son Harry, thirteen, who delighted in the stirring scenes of the ascent and wrote his chagrinned mother accordingly. Connell's First Brigade was next, followed by the division train. With the road dry, the infantrymen ascended without much difficulty, but the mule teams struggled with the heavy wagons. As teamster Daniel Bruce explained, the day consisted of nothing but "stopping, stalling, and breaking wagons." Still the division was at last atop the plateau. Two brigades settled into camp at University Place, near the desecrated cornerstone of Bishop Polk's college, while the remaining brigade continued to Turchin's old camp two miles nearer the plateau's eastern edge.[30]

Ten miles north of Reynolds's and Brannan's route, John Wilder's Lightning Brigade began the morning of 18 August just short of Tracy City. There a broken bridge over the headwaters of Big Fiery Gizzard Creek delayed the column. Wilder assigned bridge reconstruction to the Ninety-Second Illinois Mounted Infantry regiment, his newest and least-favored unit. While waiting for the road to be opened, he wrote a brief note to his wife explaining his role in the army deception plan. Proudly he told Martha Jane Wilder, "As usual, they have assigned me the most difficult part of the movement." By midmorning the bridge had been improved enough for wagons to cross and the troopers began their march. Passing through the collection of log huts that was Tracy City, they rode in a northerly direction toward the village of Altamont. Several miles short of that settlement the horsemen turned eastward, leaving Altamont to their left. They moved easily, on a generally level road through a sea of trees. Many of those trees were pines, which were unfamiliar to several soldiers from Indiana and Illinois. The men also encountered numerous large rattlesnakes, which seemed to infest the entire Cumberland Plateau. A slight shower of rain cooled the journey briefly, but the march was generally hot and dry. Not long after noon, Wilder's troops encountered the infantrymen of Wagner's Second Brigade of Wood's First Division, Twenty-First Corps. Wagner had preceded Wilder on the road from Tracy City and was halted for lunch when the horsemen arrived. With Wilder having priority of movement, Wagner's men waited several hours for Wilder's brigade and its train to gain the lead. The Lightning Brigade soon passed out of sight, although its wagons delayed Wagner for the remainder of the afternoon. Eventually Wilder's brigade halted for the night at a wilderness road junction known as Bryant's, and Wagner's men bivouacked several miles behind them.[31]

Rosecrans's deception plan called for Wilder to be supported by Crittenden's Twenty-First Corps, which was also struggling to surmount the Cumberland Plateau. Wood's First Division on 18 August remained scattered. Wagner's Second Brigade had already ascended the mountain and made good progress until forced to relinquish the lead to Wilder. Wood's remaining two brigades, however, had yet to complete their climb to the Cumberland Plateau. Both Buell's First Brigade and Harker's Third Brigade spent the morning lifting their last wagons up the grade to the top of the plateau. Along the way, much baggage had to be discarded before the teams could drag the residue forward. Nevertheless, by late morning everything essential was on top of the mountain, and Wood decreed a rest until 1:00 P.M. Harker was so pleased with the performance of Col. Emerson Opdycke's 125th Ohio Infantry regiment that he summoned Opdycke to share a convivial glass of wine. Then, to the accompaniment of regimental bands, Buell's and Harker's men resumed their march toward Tracy City, covering the five miles by dark. There they found Col. Caleb Carlton and his Eighty-Ninth Ohio Infantry regiment. Carlton had been detached from John Turchin's command to protect the supply depot at Tracy City. The wretched settlement loomed large in Rosecrans's mind as a critical supply point not only for Wilder but for most of the Twenty-First Corps as well. Unfortunately, Carlton had nothing to issue because the railroad from Cowan had not yet begun operating. Nor was the telegraph line to Cowan working. Still, Carlton was delighted to see Wood's brigades arrive. Wood and Harker, the latter a West Point classmate of Carlton's, visited the garrison commander and shared recent experiences. Carlton no doubt voiced his pleasure at being detached from Turchin, the Russian's unconventional habits and loose discipline being especially irksome to Regular Army officers. In a letter to his wife describing the reunion, Carlton expressed the hope that his detachment from Turchin would be permanent.[32]

Operating north of Wood's track, Crittenden's other divisions also made progress on 18 August. Twenty-two miles north of Tracy City, Palmer's Second Division left Irving College, forded the Collins River, and followed the narrow valley of Hills Creek until it confronted the steep headwall of the Cumberland Plateau. Leading the ascent, Hazen's Second Brigade fought its way to the summit with three regiments, leaving the Forty-First Ohio Infantry behind to guard the division's train of 300 wagons. Hazen halted eight miles beyond the crest on a relatively level road through the forest. Behind him, most of Cruft's First Brigade reached the summit in midafternoon, then moved two miles farther on Hazen's route. Left behind were Cruft's train and its guards. Finally, Grose's Third Brigade also reached the crest, but only by leaving its wagons at the foot of the mountain as well. By this time the men had exhausted their rations, but occasional peach orchards provided ripe fruit as a substitute. Last of all was the Forty-First Ohio and the division train. Everywhere on the mountain, the soldiers encountered rattlesnakes but were so weary that they lay down in the forest anyway. Five miles north of Palmer, Van Cleve's two brigades similarly were scattered along the rough track known as Harrison's Trace. During the morning Van Cleve and Barnes's Third Brigade waited briefly at the headwaters of Rocky River in order for Beatty's First Brigade to join and then continued through the wilderness for ten more miles. Beatty finally succeeded in raising the division train to the top of the plateau and plodded forward in Barnes's wake. For much of their journey, Van Cleve's troops encountered no sign of human habitation. Exhausted by their labors, both brigades bivouacked in the forest. During the night, a herd of cattle accompanying the column escaped its enclosure and wandered among the sleeping soldiers, knocking over stands of weapons and trampling men. The resulting shouts led to a brief stampede, ruining the night's rest.[33]

Like their compatriots to the north, the men of McCook's Twentieth Corps made progress in their battle with the rugged Cumberland Plateau on 18 August. Davis's First Division began the day at the foot of the mountain a short distance south of Cowan. The route uphill had already been traversed by Rosecrans's headquarters guard units, but the headquarters train was still at the foot of the mountain. Thus the regiments of Post's First Brigade lined the rocky road to assist the heavily loaded wagons. Post's train and the division ordnance train of fifty wagons also required assistance. With great effort, Post's men gradually pushed and pulled the wagons uphill. In midafternoon Carlin's Second Brigade relieved Post's weary soldiers and the process of lifting wagons continued. The regimental historian of the Eighty-First Indiana Infantry regiment wrote, "Just imagine a train of wagons stretched out for miles and a whole brigade of men in their shirt sleeves strung along on each side, tugging at the wheels, pulling at ropes, the drivers using the most emphatic language you ever heard to the mules, then you may form some idea of the scene." All along the road the plateau's ubiquitous rattlesnakes made their appearance but were hardly more than a curiosity to the toiling troops. Eventually, Heg's Third Brigade joined Post and Carlin on top and all moved forward several miles. Fifteen miles southwest of Davis, Johnson's Second Division ascended the foothills of the plateau through White's Gap. East of the gap the three brigades followed a faint road along and through a stream named Larkin's Fork. Willich's First Brigade led the column, followed by Baldwin's Third Brigade, while Dodge's Second Brigade trailed the division train. After a march of fifteen miles, Johnson halted his drenched command. Some traded their wet clothes for army blankets, but others did not, a decision they regretted when the night turned cool. Although surrounded by mountains, Johnson had yet to confront the western escarpment of the Cumberland Plateau.[34]

While his soldiers battled with the mountain on 18 August, Rosecrans's thoughts turned to the next obstacle, the Tennessee River. Thus, Calvin Goddard asked William Innes about the dimensions of the Bridgeport railroad bridge, and Frank Bond queried Capt. Arthur Edwards, a quartermaster officer with Great Lakes maritime experience, about building small steamboats at Bridgeport. Bond charged Innes and Ferdinand Winslow, acting chief quartermaster at Nashville, with preparing lumber to Edwards's specifications at sawmills at Stevenson and Wartrace. Lt. George Burroughs, one of the army's staff engineers, reported that thirty pontoons were at Elk River, ten were at Murfreesboro, and sixty-four were at Nashville. Thirty pontoon wagons were moving forward with part of the Pioneer Brigade. Innes had only seven flatcars at Nashville, and he wanted to use them for other cargo unless Rosecrans decreed otherwise. He also reported that he only had twelve reliable locomotives and many wrecked cars. Nevertheless, Bond ordered him to prepare three hospital cars and ship half a carload of Sanitary Commission supplies each day to Stevenson on the passenger train. Both Innes and John Starkweather at Anderson were told to have idle men cut wood for locomotive fuel. Gordon Granger was ordered to guard the Nashville & Chattanooga Railroad all the way to Tantalon. Informed that no supplies had been stockpiled at Tracy City, and that the Twenty-First Corps would soon exhaust its forage, Rosecrans warned the quartermaster at McMinnville to be prepared to sustain Crittenden's animals. Finally, Rosecrans invited Governor Andrew Johnson to join the army at the front on Thursday. At last, Rosecrans and his staff boarded the dummy and headed for Stevenson. Still seriously ill, Chief of Staff Garfield traveled on a bed carried aboard the car. As their husbands departed for the front, the wives of Alex McCook, David Stanley, Calvin Goddard, Arthur Ducat, and John Taylor left Winchester on the northbound passenger train.[35]

The headquarters party arrived at Stevenson at 1:30 P.M., where they were welcomed by Sheridan and Laibold. David Swaim supervised Garfield's removal from the dummy and transfer to a quiet lodging away from the frenetic activity at the depot. While his staff established headquarters at a small brick house also distant from the depot, Rosecrans took the dummy a short distance down the weed-choked Memphis & Charleston Railroad. He returned to Stevenson at dark on what even then was coming to be called "Rose's buggy." In Rosecrans's absence five freight trains arrived at Stevenson, clogging the junction until their cargo was unloaded. If Stevenson was a hive of activity, Bridgeport exhibited what one diarist called "the dull monotony of camp life." Men in Lytle's brigade spent the day cleaning their camps and listening to preaching by a Christian Commission representative. In Bradley's command some amused themselves by swimming in the river while others watched the continuing trickle of deserters crossing into the Federal lines. One man noted that the river level was dropping, thereby opening more crossing sites. In overall command at Bridgeport, Lytle asked Sheridan about improving the Bridgeport fortifications. If the army was going to advance soon, additional work would be wasted; if not, more effort should be made to secure the Federal position.

Lytle also inquired about the status of the Second Tennessee (Union) Cavalry regiment, which momentarily seemed to be working for no one. Confronting the enemy at Bridgeport, Lytle was only vaguely aware of the massive logistical effort in his rear, and the struggles of the divisions crawling over the Cumberland Plateau. Rosecrans saw it all, and he was pleased, as reflected in his nightly message to Lorenzo Thomas: "My Head Qrs. Moved today to Stevenson Alabama. The commands all moving well, better today than yesterday." Nearly 200 miles to the north, in Crab Orchard, Kentucky, Ambrose Burnside telegraphed Rosecrans that he, too, had begun his advance.[36]

Rosecrans's operations order required that Thomas's Fourteenth Corps reach its final positions by the end of Wednesday, 19 August. In the Right Wing, Starkweather's First Division remained in its designated camps in the Crow Creek valley between Anderson Station and Stevenson. Negley finally consolidated his three brigades around Cave Spring, three and a half miles north of Stevenson. Thomas's Left Wing continued to lag behind. Reynolds's Fourth Division consolidated in camps on Battle Creek, three miles from the Tennessee River. Far behind Reynolds, Brannan's Third Division spent all day descending into the upper reaches of Sweeden's Cove. The day was excessively hot, a temperature of 108 degrees being recorded at Estill Springs. The men had to carry their knapsacks as well as rations, water, guns, and ammunition, causing the usual straggling. Still the brigades of Connell, Croxton, and Van Derveer all successfully negotiated the steep descent and camped near the Blue Spring. Now that the two divisions of the Left Wing were in the valley of Battle Creek, the logistical plan called for them to be sustained from Tracy City. Unaware that there was still no depot at Tracy City, Reynolds opposed sending his wagon trains back up the plateau simply because of the difficulty of the route. He penned a note to Thomas seeking permission to draw rations and forage from Stevenson. The message to Thomas passed through army headquarters, which denied Reynolds's request. When Reynolds's request reached Thomas in the Crow Creek valley, the corps commander supported Reynolds. That evening, Rosecrans relented, permitting Reynolds to draw upon Stevenson for subsistence. At the same time, Rosecrans ordered Reynolds to occupy the village of Jasper, six miles to the east at the mouth of the Sequatchie Valley, on the following day.[37]

The army operations order required Crittenden's Twenty-First Corps to be in position in the Sequatchie Valley by Wednesday night as well. The march of Wood's First Division had been complicated from the beginning by the need to follow Wilder's command. Wilder had an especially long train composed of both wagons and a string of pack mules. On 19 August Wilder's brigade left the top of the plateau and soon began the descent into the Sequatchie Valley. When the leading Ninety-Second Illinois Mounted Infantry regiment encountered

Rosecrans at the N&C Depot, Stevenson, Alabama. (Miller, *Photographic History*)

Confederate pickets near the foot of the mountain, it halted and deployed. Irked by the regiment's caution, which was incompatible with his style of operations, Wilder replaced the Ninety-Second with the Seventy-Second Indiana Mounted Infantry regiment and rushed the handful of defenders. Vastly outnumbered, the small Confederate force hastily retreated through the road junction known as Therman and scattered. The pickets likely belonged to McDonald's Cavalry Battalion, temporarily led by Capt. Philip Allin, which Bragg had sent to picket the Sequatchie Valley. Part of the Seventy-Second drove across the narrow valley to the Sequatchie River, killing and capturing several Confederates, while another company surprised some citizens holding several Union sympathizers in a school. In a report to Reynolds, Wilder claimed that his brigade captured eleven Confederates, although the haul ultimately approached twenty. The brigade then moved six miles north of Therman to the village of Dunlap, which consisted of two log houses, a store, and the one-story Sequatchie County courthouse. Although the village was unimpressive, the surrounding fields of green corn and peach orchards were a different matter. Especially delighted to reach Dunlap were the men of the Eighteenth Indiana Battery, who had slept atop their ammunition chests the previous night because of the rattlesnakes infesting the plateau. Henry Campbell, one of the gunners, found the Sequatchie Valley such a pleasant place that he recorded in his diary, "Wouldn't mind staying here for some time."[38]

Following Wilder to Therman was Wood's First Division. Wagner's Second Brigade reached the valley floor in late afternoon. Wood's remaining brigades were far behind Wagner, but Wood was determined to meet the schedule at all costs. He therefore instructed Buell and Harker to expedite their progress across the relatively flat plateau. Three of Buell's regiments reached the foot of the mountain at Therman soon after dark, but the brigade train and the 100th Illinois Infantry regiment remained on top. Similarly, Harker's brigade raced twenty-eight miles, arriving at Therman around 9:00 P.M. As on the climb uphill, Emerson Opdycke led his 125th Ohio Infantry regiment by personal example. Opdycke walked much of the way, sharing his horse with exhausted soldiers. On reaching the descent, he raised a shout and led his men in a charge down the slope. Like Buell's train, Harker's wagons bivouacked on top of the mountain. Palmer's Second Division also got units into the Sequatchie Valley on 19 August. Cruft's First Brigade arrived first, marching into Dunlap in midafternoon. With Cruft were Crittenden and his young son. Behind Cruft came several regiments from both Hazen's Second Brigade and Grose's Third Brigade, all of which camped around Dunlap. Four regiments remained on the plateau with brigade and division trains. The story was much the same twenty miles northward, where Van Cleve and most of his command descended the mountain to Pikeville. Like Dunlap, Pikeville was unimpressive, Pvt. Marcus Woodcock of the Ninth Kentucky Infantry regiment considering it "neither large, nor populous, nor thriving nor beautiful." In his report to Crittenden Van Cleve noted that most of Minty's cavalry had arrived that evening from Sparta. Minty was scheduled to probe beyond Walden's Ridge on the next day, but his train was far behind him. Van Cleve was also nervous about his tenuous supply route to either McMinnville or Tracy City. Still, Crittenden's Twenty-First Corps had, for the most part, met Rosecrans's schedule.[39]

McCook's Twentieth Corps had mixed success on 19 August. Davis had been given until Thursday, 20 August, to reach a camp southwest of Stevenson, but Johnson was expected to reach the village of Bellefonte, near the Tennessee River, by Wednesday evening. Davis's leading unit, Post's First Brigade, left its camp four miles north of the Alabama state line at 3:00 A.M. Post's regiments marched fourteen miles through sparsely populated woodland until reaching the two-mile descent into the valley of Big Coon Creek. According to Lt. Chesley Mosman, the road down the mountain was the "worst place I ever saw." Nevertheless, the brigade descended successfully and halted at a spring four miles from Stevenson after marching twenty-four miles. Carlin's Second Brigade followed the same path as Post. The only incident occurred when a mail carrier was badly wounded by a bushwhacker. In the rear, Heg's Third Brigade was only able to descend the mountain by nightfall. Meanwhile, army headquarters notified Davis that his wife was at Nashville en route to the army. While Davis was ahead of schedule, Johnson's Second Division was seriously late. Intending to surmount the Cumberland Plateau where the Larkin's Fork met the larger Paint Rock River, Johnson found most of the army's Pioneer Brigade ahead of him. The Pioneers not only were poor marchers, but they were also encumbered by thirty pontoon wagons. Unwilling to follow the Pioneers, Johnson ordered his brigades to turn north up the Paint Rock. After a march of four miles, he turned east up Hurricane Creek for an additional four miles, finally halting at the foot of a rough track ascending the plateau. There his men camped on the farm of a large landowner, whose property they happily stripped of edibles. In the lead, the Thirty-Ninth Indiana Mounted Infantry regiment began to lift its wagons up the mountain, placing only two wagons on top by nightfall. While understandable, Johnson's detour kept him far short of Rosecrans's target for the day.[40]

Elsewhere on 19 August other units continued their preparations. At Bridgeport Sheridan's two brigades packed their knapsacks for storage in the rear. Such orders were definite signs that a forward movement was imminent. Cpl. Edward Crippin of the Twenty-Seventh Illinois Infantry regiment wrote, "Let it come for everyone is tired of this place." At Stevenson, the first scheduled passenger train arrived from Nashville. Also at Stevenson, Capt. John Morledge, Laibold's commissary officer, had an unpleasant encounter with Sheridan at the Alabama Hotel, causing Morledge to record in his diary, "He can hardly bear the weight of two stars on his shoulders." Elsewhere in town, staff officers gained a respite when Rosecrans, Stanley, and Sheridan took the dummy west on the Memphis & Charleston Railroad to visit Edward McCook at Larkinsville. Satisfied that his right flank was protected, Rosecrans returned to Stevenson. In his absence, the First Ohio Sharpshooter battalion and most of the Fifteenth Pennsylvania Cavalry regiment from the army's headquarters guard reached Stevenson via Crow Creek. The headquarters wagon train and the remainder of the Fifteenth Pennsylvania was still on the road. With Rosecrans absent, staff officers generated relatively few directives. Frank Bond ordered William Innes to open sawmills at Wartrace and Stevenson to prepare boat and bridge timbers. Robert Thoms queried Nashville quartermasters about the availability of rope, again for boat-building. James Drouillard wired one of Grant's quartermasters in St. Louis in an effort to secure more railroad cars. That evening, Rosecrans informed Gordon Granger that the Nashville & Decatur Railroad was unworkable as a supply corridor until Granger himself repaired it. In his daily report to Washington, Rosecrans noted his visit to Larkinsville and proclaimed that only the Twentieth Corps was not yet in position. He also wrote to Burnside, concluding, "We want to cross south of Bridgeport, penetrate between Rome and Chattanooga. Let us have full co-operation." Tentative no longer, Rosecrans had at last decided on his next move.[41]

Most of the Fourteenth Corps rested on Thursday, 20 August. Thomas and his elaborate headquarters train left Anderson Station and continued down Crow Creek to Stevenson. The men of Starkweather's and Negley's commands noted his passing, along with the many pontoons on flatcars going south. Unaware of Rosecrans's plans, the soldiers began to improve their camps by clearing the ground and erecting bowers. For the most part, the atmosphere in the camps was festive. In the Nineteenth Illinois Infantry regiment, the band played patriotic airs to the delight of all. Other soldiers played chess, swam in Crow Creek, or fished its waters with limited success. In the Forty-Second Indiana Infantry regiment, Pvt. William Stookey received two letters from his wife, Helen, begging him to come home. Exasperated, Stookey explained that it would take a bribe and six signatures, including Rosecrans's, to get a furlough. He continued facetiously, "As for geting home for twenty or thirty dollars just to sleep with a woman is plaid out. . . . I can get to sleep with them without going two miles from camp and with less than half the money and I never miss an opertunity." In their camps on Battle Creek Reynolds's men resumed the daily routine of inspection and dress parade. Corn and peaches were plentiful in the valley and the fishing was better than at Crow Creek. In Sweeden's Cove, Brannan's soldiers remained in camp around the Blue Spring. Unaware of Rosecrans's permission to draw supplies from Stevenson, Reynolds sent a wagon train up the mountain toward Tracy City. There Caleb Carlton's Eighty-Ninth Ohio Infantry regiment continued to wait for a supply depot to be established. A locomotive had briefly appeared on the previous day, its crew promising to return with two cars of rations, but they had not done so. As Carlton explained to his wife, "Part of two Corps are to draw supplies from here but not a single ration here yet, besides my own rations will be out tonight. How we can live and send back twenty one miles over a difficult mountain road and wagon up supplies is hard to tell."[42]

Supplied or not, both Crittenden and Wilder were determined to continue their operations on 20 August. Even though none of his divisions had completed their descent into the Sequatchie Valley, Crittenden activated the deception plan. At 4:00 A.M. he started Hazen's Second Brigade of Palmer's command up Walden's Ridge from Dunlap. As tall as the Cumberland Plateau but only ten miles across, Walden's Ridge was the final barrier between the Twenty-First Corps and the Tennessee River. Hazen's infantrymen were to support Wilder's brigade, but Wilder got a slow start because he had to mount pack saddles on his mules before ascending the ridge. Wilder left his wagons in the Sequatchie Valley and sent thirty of them to Tracy City for rations. With only two pack mules per company, the horsemen plodded up Walden's Ridge behind Hazen's toiling infantry. Palmer joined the column, leaving Cruft in charge at Dunlap. Arriving at the crest in late morning, Hazen relinquished the lead to Wilder, who soon reached the eastern edge of the escarpment and descended into the Tennessee River valley. His goal was the well-known tavern of Hasten Poe, one of the earliest settlers of the area. At Poe's Tavern the track down Walden's Ridge met a major road running parallel to the Tennessee River. After routing a few Confederate pickets, the Seventy-Second Indiana Mounted Infantry regiment stormed into the road junction. There, four companies rode north, while the remainder of the regiment turned to the south. Suddenly encountering four wagons loaded with wheat, Wilder's men seized them, appropriating the cargo to their own use. As more regiments reached the valley floor, they went into camp around Poe's Tavern. Behind them, Hazen's brigade reached the lip of the escarpment and also halted for the evening. Palmer continued on and spent the night at Poe's. In a message to Reynolds, Wilder reported the capture of six Confederates, a number later raised to eleven. He also informed Reynolds of his tenuous supply situation.[43]

Elsewhere, Crittenden's divisions consolidated their positions. At Dunlap, Cruft's command spent the day repairing vehicles, foraging, and marveling at the mountain scenery and bountiful orchards. An officer in the First Kentucky Infantry regiment noted that Crittenden's young son John remained with him. During the day the last of Palmer's brigades, Grose's, arrived and camped near the village, although the division train was still on the road at nightfall. A few miles south at Therman, Wood's First Division got all its trains down the mountain. Wood also started Wagner's Second Brigade up Walden's Ridge. Wagner's men used the Anderson Road, a former toll road built in the 1840s by Josiah Anderson, a Sequatchie Valley farmer. Leaving his train and part of his battery behind, Wagner reached the top around noon and continued across the tableland. Nightfall found his regiments scattered along the road. At Therman, Wood issued an order thanking his men for their performance on the previous day. Meanwhile, a rumor swept the division's camps that several thousand Confederate cavalrymen were approaching. Everyone grabbed his gun and rushed into line before the rumor was quashed. Far up the valley at Pikeville, Van Cleve's brigades also brought their trains down from the plateau. The men found the citizens of Pikeville willing to sell food for a small sum, although free foraging also improved the men's diet. Van Cleve himself received a watermelon from his staff, no questions asked. Not all welcomed the Federals, and Van Cleve had to admonish a young woman for spitting on a soldier. Even with foraging, Van Cleve continued to worry about supplies. He had a ration train en route from McMinnville, but it could not arrive for two more days. He also planned to send twenty-five of his own wagons and all of Minty's back to McMinnville for rations on the next day. Minty, whose brigade also lay at Pikeville, was especially short of forage. Telling his wife of the day's tribulations, Van Cleve closed, "We are faring very well & I am in excellent health considering."[44]

With the army's Left Wing essentially in place, Rosecrans believed his Right Wing would soon attain its objectives as well. On 20 August the army headquarters train arrived at Stevenson. In the army's rear, Long's Second Brigade of Crook's Second Cavalry Division began to ascend the mountain from Cowan. From Nashville, Daniel McCook's brigade of the Reserve Corps marched southward to Brentwood, evidence of Granger's promise to cover the army's right flank. Only the Twentieth Corps was behind schedule. Davis's First Division covered the last few miles down Big Coon Creek by noon and bivouacked just west of Stevenson, not far from Negley's division. The men immediately turned to improving their new campsite and informing friends and relatives of their new location. One soldier, Pvt. William Ball of the Fifth Wisconsin Battery, proudly told his brother that he had advertised in a Cincinnati newspaper for female correspondents and had gained two. Unlike Private Ball, the men of Johnson's Second Division had no time for such pleasant fantasies. Johnson's detour of the previous day to avoid the undisciplined Pioneer Brigade had placed him hopelessly behind schedule. On 20 August only Dodge's Second Brigade successfully ascended the mountain. The brigade continued its march for eight miles, camping amid a "swarm" of rattlesnakes. In the valley of Hurricane Creek, Willich's First Brigade succeeded only in getting its trains to the top of the mountain, while Baldwin's Third Brigade simply spent the day in camp. With so many soldiers idle, the inhabitants paid the price. As Pvt. Alpheus Bloomfield wrote to his father, "I do not think any of the citizens were personally injured by any of our soldiers, but their crops and property had to suffer. We used rails freely and I do not think any one ever saw peach orchards stripped any quicker." Scheduled to be at Bellefonte on the previous night, Johnson would spend 20 August mired in the mountains. In contrast, the detachment of the Pioneer Brigade reached Bellefonte that day.[45]

At Bridgeport and Stevenson, the pace of operations continued to accelerate. In Lytle's command, the camps bustled with men packing their knapsacks and mess gear for transport to Stevenson by rail. When not packing, numerous soldiers patronized a photographer who had just arrived in camp. Otherwise, men amused themselves by swimming or illicit gambling. At Stevenson, Alex McCook arrived and established corps headquarters nearby. During the afternoon he joined Rosecrans on a reconnaissance to the river. The party's destination was Caperton's Ferry, one of the two crossing points near Stevenson. At Caperton's, the river was little more than 400 yards wide, narrow enough to shout across. Soldiers from both armies used the river for swimming, and there was a tacit agreement not to fire unless a serious crossing was attempted. Taking advantage of the truce and apparently unrecognized, Rosecrans conversed with some of Anderson's Mississippians. According to one of McCook's aides, "One sallow and dirty looking fellow yelled out to us that 'the folks of Mississippi were skeered back into the Union,' also 'he would like to see Old Rosy if he was not *mad*,' also that the Rebels 'were living on whiskey to get in good running condition.'" Another Confederate shouted, "That Dutchman Rosecrans is a pretty good man, but Bragg would turn out all right yet." Clearly the critical problem was no longer the struggle to cross the Cumberland Plateau; it had been replaced by the problem of crossing the wide Tennessee River. Perhaps that concern was reflected in Rosecrans's demeanor when William Carlin saw him that night: "I called to see General Rosecrans, whom I thought to be discouraged or oppressed with anxiety. Garfield looked angry. I was not pleased with the appearance of men and things at headquarters of the Army of the Cumberland, but I knew naught of their cares and causes of worry. Everything outside headquarters seemed to progress smoothly, as if a master mind were directing all."[46]

Had Carlin spoken to Calvin Goddard, he might have understood Rosecrans's anxiety better. Goddard had spent much of the day attempting to accelerate the flow of supplies to Stevenson. When the commander at Clarksville, Tennessee, offered several idle freight cars, Goddard instructed him to send them to Nashville. Goddard informed Innes that eighty new cars were on order, twenty were being purchased from the Adams Express Company, and Grant's quartermaster at St. Louis would be sending some cars to Nashville. He told Innes to give the required sixty-day notice to Adams, authorizing the government to control their cars, and authorized Innes to seek five more locomotives. As for river transportation, Goddard instructed Lytle to detail twenty-five men, six teams, and all necessary tools to Capt. Arthur Edwards's boat-building project. Finally, Goddard wired Capt. Bates Dickson in Nashville to issue a pass to Marietta Davis, wife of Brigadier General Davis, and her escort, Lt. William Davis, the general's brother. When he returned to headquarters, Rosecrans kept the staff at work late into the night. Told that Reynolds could see trains running on the other side of the river, Rosecrans asked Sheridan if placing a battery on Long Island could interdict the movement. Sheridan replied in the negative but stated that a battery emplaced opposite Shell Mound could probably do so. Accordingly, Rosecrans ordered Thomas to have Reynolds strike the railroad with artillery. Reynolds also was told to investigate the mouth of Battle

Creek as another possible crossing point. Later that evening, Rosecrans became agitated about sixteen missing pontoon-laden flatcars and wired Negley and Starkweather to find them, unload them quickly, and rush them back to Nashville. All day trains loaded with pontoons had been coming down the railroad, risking accidents and narrowly avoiding at least one. If Rosecrans wanted the missing pontoons found, other generals would have to spend their evening searching dark sidings in the countryside for them.[47]

Near the end of a very busy day, Rosecrans wired both Henry Halleck and Ambrose Burnside. Earlier, Halleck had queried Rosecrans about a rumor that Bragg had reinforced the Army of Northern Virginia with troops from Chattanooga. At 8:50 P.M. Rosecrans responded: "Reports of deserters and others are against the supposition that any troops have gone to Richmond. Cleburne's and Stewart's divisions are the only ones that could have gone, and they are reported at Atlanta." Substantiating Rosecrans's opinion was deserter William Duncan, Second Tennessee Infantry, whose confusing mixture of fact and fantasy Caleb Carlton forwarded to Garfield during the day. In the main, Rosecrans was correct in asserting that no units of the Army of Tennessee had gone to Virginia. Considering Washington informed, Rosecrans filed no report of operations with Lorenzo Thomas that night. To Burnside, Rosecrans simply telegraphed, "I am very anxious to hear from you." In his response, which may not have reached Rosecrans until after midnight, Burnside indicated that his troops would begin their advance on the next day. Inquiring about the locations of Thomas's and Crittenden's units, Burnside again promised to assist Rosecrans's movements: "I think we will be in time. You may rely on every possible co-operation." Whether Burnside moved or not, Rosecrans had come too far to wait for a man whose reputation for celerity was decidedly mixed. Nine of his ten infantry divisions were now east of the Cumberland Plateau, the Nashville & Chattanooga Railroad was finally working with reasonable efficiency, supplies were rapidly accumulating at Stevenson, and the vital pontoons were finally arriving. Most important of all, the critical effort to mislead Bragg as to the point of crossing the Tennessee River would begin on the next day, Friday, 21 August. As he had always expected to do, Rosecrans would act independently of any timetable other than his own. Secure in his own abilities and confident in his army, Rosecrans would execute his plans without further reference to either Halleck in Washington or Burnside in Kentucky. He was on his own, and was not troubled by that fact in any way as he awaited the dawn.[48]

9

Before the Storm

» 15–21 August 1863 «

As the second half of August began, Braxton Bragg remained at Cherokee Springs, Georgia, with his wife, Elise. Both were attempting to recruit their health, Bragg from the stress of army command and his wife from her life-threatening bout of typhoid fever. On Sunday, 16 August, Bragg and his wife attended public religious services conducted at the Cherokee Springs hospital camp by noted Episcopal priest Charles Quintard. There was, as yet, no chapel at the site, so the congregants worshipped under a large oak tree. Elise Bragg helped lead the singing of hymns, although her husband did not. Civilian nurse Kate Cumming, who had recently joined the hospital's staff, noted in her journal that Bragg still did not look well: "His health is very bad, which is no wonder, as he is so much harassed. He is a member of the church, and, I am told, a sincere Christian. He has done his utmost to have Christianity diffused in the army. Mrs. Bragg has the appearance of being a very modest, lady-like person, as I am told she is. She is also in bad health." Bragg continued in residence at Cherokee Springs throughout the week, all the while pondering the forthcoming movements of Rosecrans's army and the various responses he might make. Meanwhile, the able-bodied patients and the camp attendants resumed their efforts to raise a makeshift chapel from the boughs of trees.[1]

With Federals visible in strength around Bridgeport, the coming campaign must have always been uppermost in Bragg's mind. Until Rosecrans committed himself to an axis of advance, however, Bragg was unwilling to modify his own dispositions. He therefore busied himself with other matters, notably the growing problem of desertion. With rations short, pay hopelessly in arrears, and little to do in the filthy camps, many men sought personal relief by surreptitiously leaving the army. The opportunity was especially enticing for the Mississippi soldiers of Anderson's Brigade, facing the Federals at Shell Mound and Bridgeport. Pvt. John Roberts of the Seventh Mississippi Infantry regiment described the magnitude of the problem in a series of diary entries: 16 August—many deserters, including two from the Seventh Mississippi; 17 August—more desertions, including six from the Ninth Mississippi; 18 August—more deserters. Roberts, who had long firmly supported the Confederate cause, admitted to having second thoughts: "Old Rosey says he will furnish transportation and a suit of clothes to every one who deserts and comes over. He will send them as close home as he can. This is very encouraging if it is true. I want to go home, but I won't do this yet." Pvt. George Lea, another member of the Seventh Mississippi, wrote to his father on 18 August, "Our troops are doing very bad deserting every night almost. There has as many as fifteen left in the last week two from our Regt." The problem was not confined to Anderson's Brigade. On 15 August Bragg authorized an expedition into several counties of Middle Tennessee to capture deserters. Two days later, he instructed Wheeler, Forrest, and Polk to curtail the flow of deserters by patrolling the river more strictly. Whatever good these instructions did, the problem would remain as long as the army was stationary. On 20 August, the total strength of the Army of Tennessee stood at 53,612 officers and men, aggregate present, but if desertion was not checked, that strength would decline precipitously.[2]

Another vexing problem for Bragg involved his new subordinate, Simon Buckner. In July Buckner had proposed to Richmond that some disaffected eastern Tennessee and western North Carolina regiments be removed from his department. He desired to exchange the unhappy regiments for troops from South Carolina or Mississippi. The proposal went nowhere in the War Department bureaucracy and was eventually returned to Buckner with the suggestion that perhaps Bragg or Johnston might arrange such an exchange. By that time Buckner no longer had an independent command, so he placed the matter in Bragg's hands. On 15 August Bragg forwarded Buckner's proposal to Johnston. Buckner had suggested trading the Tennesseans and North Carolinians for Kentuckians in Johnston's army, but Bragg demurred. His experience with Kentuckians during the past year's campaign had soured him forever on residents of that state. Buckner, of course, was a Kentuckian. Each man no doubt knew of the other's biases regarding Kentuckians in Confederate service. Still, the troop exchange issue was a minor irritant in comparison to the controversy regarding Buckner's specific role as an administrator. In Buckner's opinion, subsuming his department into Bragg's larger command made him only a corps commander, yet Bragg expected him to administer his area without sufficient administrative authority. Complaint to the War Department resolved nothing, so on 20 August Bragg attempted to clarify Buckner's status once more. He denied that the new arrangement would cause confusion, arguing that Buckner's concerns about lack of administrative authority were groundless. If any problems arose, Bragg promised to resolve any contentious issues immediately. Finally, Bragg assured Buckner that he was free to organize his corps in his own way. Subsequent events would prove that Buckner remained unsatisfied, and his contentious relationship with Bragg continued to fester.[3]

Random issues of smaller import also distracted Bragg in the last half of the month. On 15 August he had to defuse a minor tempest generated by Edward Walthall in Atlanta. Acting under Bragg's orders, Walthall had gone into the community to impress horses from citizens for use in the army's artillery. Walthall's men apparently were too zealous in their work, seizing horses from people connected with the Georgia State Guard controlled by Governor Joseph Brown. The cries of outrage from his constituents caused Brown to complain to the Confederate government, which ordered Bragg to make amends. Bragg did so, apologizing to Brown for Walthall's excesses and ordering the horses to be returned to their owners. On the following day, Bragg notified Patton Anderson at Bridgeport that a certain Mrs. Webb desired to cross the Tennessee River into the Federal lines and that Anderson should facilitate the crossing. Bragg helpfully suggested that Mrs. Webb should be placed on Long Island and the Federals notified of her presence, but he left the details of the transfer entirely to Anderson. On 17 August Bragg responded to a message from Sterling Wood of Hill's Corps, who asked what troops were on the west bank of the Tennessee River opposite his defenses upstream from Chattanooga. The answer, sent through Hill, informed Wood that any Confederates beyond the Tennessee in Wood's front belonged to Forrest's command, and that Forrest's headquarters was located far to the northeast at Kingston. On the same day that he responded to Wood, Bragg addressed a complaint from Hill himself that the road bridge over Chickamauga Creek near its mouth was becoming impassable. Here the solution was easy, with Bragg simply ordering Capt. Stephen Presstman, the army's chief engineer, to assign men to repair the bridge.[4]

In his message to Hill about the bridge, Bragg also wrote, "Your suggestion in regard to Lieut. Buford has been acted on and the Provost Marshal is looking after her." "Buford" no doubt was the person seen by Sgt. Robert Hodges Jr., of the Twenty-Fourth Texas Cavalry (Dismounted), at Tyner's Station in early August. Writing to his father, Hodges told of being drawn to the station because of a crowd: "Approaching, I enquired what was up. One of the soldiers directed my attention to a youth apparently about seventeen years of age well dressed with a lieutennant's badge on his collar. I remarked that I saw nothing strange. He then told me that the young man was not a man but a female." The female in question was Loreta Janeta Velazquez, already notorious throughout the Confederacy. According to her memoir, *The Woman in Battle*, she was born in Cuba around 1842 and sent to New Orleans to further her education. There she married an army officer, who allegedly died in Confederate service early in the Civil War. To assuage her grief, she claimed to have acquired a uniform and served at the front in the early Virginia battles and at Shiloh. She then married an Arkansas officer named Thomas DeCaulp. Although she claimed he soon died, surviving records indicate he deserted the Confederacy and eventually served in a Wisconsin regiment. At some point, Velazquez adopted the persona of "Lieutenant Harry T. Buford" and traveled widely in uniform, possibly on secret service missions. According to the *Richmond Examiner,* she was released from arrest in Richmond and sent to Atlanta on 15 July 1863. The *Chattanooga Daily Rebel* on 6 August noted her presence in Chattanooga. Again according to the *Richmond Examiner,* she briefly joined the staff of Alexander Stewart but was back in Richmond by the middle of September. Thereafter her adventures continued, but her brief time with Braxton Bragg's command had ended. Whatever Hill suggested to Bragg in her case, as well as whatever the two generals knew about the true identity and mission of "Lieutenant Buford," remains lost to history.[5]

As August passed its midpoint, most of Bragg's units remained in the positions they had occupied in July. On the army's flanks mounted units were charged with monitoring Federal activity beyond the infantry's center of gravity around Chattanooga. Wheeler's Cavalry Corps provided security on the army's left flank, picketing the line of the Tennessee River. Farthest to the west was Philip Roddey's brigade, recently added to Wheeler's command and only nominally under Wheeler's control. Roddey made his headquarters at Tuscumbia, Alabama. From Decatur to Bridgeport, only the Eighth Confederate Cavalry from Hagan's Brigade and the Third Confederate Cavalry from Harrison's Brigade stood watch along the river. Wheeler's two cavalry divisions, Wharton's and Martin's, were far in the rear, camped at Rome, Georgia, and Alexandria, Alabama, respectively. On 20 August, Wheeler's command reported an aggregate present of 8,531 cavalrymen and 302 artillerymen. Of that total, fewer than 500 men from the Third Confederate Cavalry regiment guarded the critical river line stretching from Shell Mound southwest to Gunter's Landing. Wheeler's headquarters remained at Gadsden, Alabama, thirty miles from the river. Most of Wheeler's men enjoyed very pleasant camps, with plenty of ripe fruit and vegetables available at what the men considered extortionate prices. On the army's right flank, there were far fewer horsemen. Nathan Bedford Forrest commanded only a division, which on 20 August numbered only 4,609 cavalrymen and 158 artillerymen, aggregate present. Like Wheeler, Forrest picketed the Tennessee River, but, unlike Wheeler, he maintained an observation post west of the river at Sparta. That force was periodically harassed by Federal cavalry but remained in the area. The Eighteenth Tennessee Cavalry battalion operating in the Sequatchie Valley also nominally belonged to Forrest's command, although it reported directly to Bragg. Forrest made his headquarters west of the Tennessee River, in stark contrast to Wheeler's location east of the stream.[6]

Leonidas Polk spent the third week of August with his wife and two of his daughters, who were visiting him in Chattanooga. The largest formation in the Army of Tennessee, Polk's Corps on 20 August contained 19,124 officers and men, aggregate present, organized into two divisions. The four brigades of Cheatham's Division numbered 8,110 infantrymen. All of the brigades were camped south of Chattanooga in the valley of Chattanooga Creek, between Lookout Mountain on the west and Missionary Ridge on the east. Other than working on the Chattanooga fortifications and improving their camps, Cheatham's men had little to do. A detachment from the Sixteenth Tennessee Infantry regiment was sent into the country south of the city to graze stock near Lafayette, Georgia. Others, like Polk, welcomed their wives for brief visits. Some men were lucky enough to receive delicacies like flour and potatoes from friends and families to supplement their meager rations. The soldiers of Polk's other division welcomed Thomas Hindman on 17 August. The previous commander, Jones Withers, had been a favorite of the troops, so his replacement was viewed with considerable skepticism. In the words of Capt. Irvine Walker, a staff officer in Manigault's Brigade, "We know nothing of Genl. H. as a Division Comdr. Therefore I can't say whether I will like the change. His Arkansas career however does not prepossess us in his favor." On 20 August, Hindman's Division had an aggregate present of 9,992 officers and men. Organized into four brigades, the division was momentarily widely scattered. Anderson's Brigade guarded the Tennessee River around Bridgeport and Shell Mound, Walthall's Brigade remained in Atlanta to counter a possible Federal raid, while Manigault's Brigade and Deas's Brigade lay in camps south of Chattanooga near Cheatham's men. For Hindman's men, too, there was little to do and no prospect of receiving a furlough. Completing the corps were 849 artillerymen with 36 guns, and 173 staff officers and mounted escort.[7]

The other half of Bragg's infantry strength belonged to Harvey Hill. Hill's Corps was just beginning to understand that its new commander was quite different from the more lenient Hardee. Since his arrival, Hill had published a series of orders which made it very clear that old ways would no longer be acceptable and that more strict discipline would be enforced. For example, Special Orders, No. 152, published on 16 August, decreed that anyone caught selling his shoes or uniform clothing would face court-martial. On the following day Hill issued General Orders, No. 43, which set forth his response to President Davis's call for a day of fasting and prayer on Friday, 21 August. In the strongest language, Hill reviewed the events of the previous thirty months and the sacrifices already made, and exhorted his troops to even greater effort: "Is our cause less just? Is the State less precious? Are our hearts less determined? Have we forgotten the battle cry of Manassas, of Shiloh, of Richmond, of Murfreesborough—victory or death!" For that day, Hill suspended all but the most necessary duty so that his men could "humble themselves in prayer and supplication." The corps commander had considerable reason to be concerned about the emotional state of his new command. Writing to his aunt on that very Friday, Pvt. Alfred Peterson, twenty, of the Sixth Arkansas Infantry regiment explained the situation baldly: "The troops at this point are somewhat disheartened from our late misfortunes, and from what I can learn, it is a general thing all over the Southern Army. I believe that there are some men deserting from all parts of the Army though I hope not so many as is represented to be. And those that have deserted, I hope will return as soon as they have visited their people." Yet, even after enumerating the wild rumors of defeat racing through the camps, Peterson was unwilling to abandon the cause: "We are not whipped yet and if we ever are it will be our own fault for I know that we can whip them if we will only all work together."[8]

Slightly smaller than Polk's command, Hill's Corps numbered 17,770 officers and men, aggregate present, on 20 August. The four brigades of Cleburne's Division accounted for 9,105 of the corps total. In mid-August, Cleburne's brigades were widely scattered. One of them, Lucius Polk's, was camped on the East Tennessee & Georgia Railroad at Tyner's Station. A second brigade, Liddell's, lay at Chickamauga Station on the Western & Atlantic Railroad, two miles southwest of Tyner's. The third brigade, Churchill's, lay on the Western & Atlantic Railroad near Graysville, Georgia. Cleburne's fourth brigade, Wood's, was located at Harrison, a village eleven miles upstream from Chattanooga. Wood's men picketed the river all the way to Blythe's Ferry, nineteen miles to the northeast. Wood himself was among those men whose zeal was flagging, as he wrote his wife on 19 August: "The state of the country, and the prospect of a long separation, has made me nearly gloomy." Hill's other division, Stewart's, on 20 August consisted of 7,787 officers and men, aggregate present. Brown's, Clayton's, and Bate's Brigades camped in the vicinity of Tyner's Station. Stewart's fourth brigade, Johnson's, had for some time been guarding critical bridges at Loudon, sixty miles northeast of Tyner's. Life in Stewart's command mirrored that in Cleburne's. Rations were scarce, drill was boring, and the dust and flies were aggravating. As the hot days of August continued, morale plummeted, especially in Clayton's Brigade. Lt. William Cole of the Thirty-Eighth Alabama Infantry regiment plaintively told his wife, Cornelia, on 15 August, "One word in regard to my little children. I hope that they may be spared to live through this war and never be reduced to want and poverty. That one thing causes me to have more trouble than all other things that I have to contend with." More gloomy still was Pvt. Abram Glazener of the Eighteenth Alabama Infantry regiment, who wrote to a friend, "This army is in a bad condition. The men all think we are whipt all out of heart they don't put much confidence in this general, Bragg." A total of 782 artillerymen and 96 staff and escort personnel completed Hill's Corps.[9]

A hundred miles northeast of Chattanooga, Braxton Bragg's newest corps commander was also staring a threat in the face. Simon Buckner's command in mid-August numbered only 17,332 officers and men, aggregate present. Within that total, there were 9,286 infantrymen, 6,702 cavalrymen, 1,261 artillerymen, and 73 engineers and signalmen. Most of Buckner's major units were located on the railroads linking Chattanooga and Knoxville to the Virginia rail system. Most distant was Preston's Brigade at Abingdon, Virginia, on the Virginia & Tennessee Railroad 145 miles northeast of Knoxville. Slightly closer, on the East Tennessee & Virginia Railroad at Zollicoffer, Tennessee (formerly Union, now Bluff City), was Jackson's Brigade, 119 miles from Knoxville. Much nearer Buckner's headquarters at Knoxville was Gracie's Brigade, eighteen miles distant at Strawberry Plains. At Knoxville, Buckner stationed Robert Trigg's Brigade. These units were all available to move along the line of railroads as necessary in order to guard key bridges and repel raiders. Buckner's remaining forces were scattered along the edge of the Cumberland Plateau west and north of Knoxville picketing mountain passes connecting Tennessee and Kentucky. The most important of these gaps was the historic pass through the Appalachian Mountains known as Cumberland Gap. There Buckner placed his final infantry brigade, Frazer's. He covered a series of passes southwest of Cumberland Gap with a mixture of units. Big Creek Gap was held by two infantry regiments, while horsemen of Pegram's Brigade guarded Winters Gap. Buckner's other cavalry brigade, Scott's, lay at Concord, Tennessee, on the railroad fourteen miles southwest of Knoxville, recuperating from its disastrous Kentucky raid. At Winters Gap, Pegram was less than twenty miles from Kingston, headquarters of Forrest's Division. Similarly, Scott at Concord was only fifteen miles from Loudon, the location of Johnson's Brigade. If Buckner was directly threatened from Kentucky, elements of the main army were at least near at hand.[10]

As the August days passed without any apparent Federal movement except around Bridgeport and Stevenson, Bragg continued to ponder what Rosecrans would do next. Bragg was not alone in his concern and the long wait eventually took its toll on men's nerves. Indicative of the tension was a brief panic that struck three companies of the Second Regiment, Georgia State Line guarding several small bridges at Graysville, Georgia. In an effort to test some newly arrived recruits, the Graysville commander mounted a mock night attack upon them, without notifying anyone else of his plan. The recruits scattered in wild panic, but the firing also alarmed Churchill's Brigade, whose camp was nearby. At 10:00 P.M. Col. Roger Mills's Sixth/Tenth/Fifteenth Texas (Consolidated) regiment was rudely awakened and started in great haste toward Graysville.

According to Sgt. William Heartsill, "On we go for the Depot which we at last reach, the night is dark and marching through thickets, over fences, across ditches and pitching, fall, stumbling and splashing about generally characterizes our advent into Graysville." Eventually, a member of Graysville's original garrison appeared and sheepishly explained the cause of the alarm. Most of Mills's command took the excursion in good part, joking with each other about their nocturnal race to the hamlet. Mills's regiment returned to its original encampment by 4:00 A.M. the next morning. That day, 16 August, James Deshler formally assumed command of Churchill's Brigade. On the following day, the men of the brigade were cheered by the receipt of an enormous number of letters from their homes beyond the Mississippi River. Perhaps to prevent another occurrence of problems at Graysville, Patrick Cleburne on 17 August moved Lucius Polk's Brigade from Tyner's Station to a new camp at Graysville. Two days later, Cleburne sent Deshler's Brigade also to the vicinity of Graysville. Liddell's Brigade remained at Chickamauga Station and Wood's Brigade continued to guard the river near Harrison.[11]

On 18 August, Bragg's concern about imminent Federal movement led him to institute extensive precautionary measures. The information driving his decision remains unknown, but clearly he believed that Rosecrans would soon take the offensive. That day he informed Forrest that there were indications of Federal movement on the army's left. On the same day, he told Wheeler that if withdrawal became necessary he should evacuate all able-bodied slaves to serve as teamsters. On 19 August, Bragg ordered Wheeler to withdraw Capt. James Field's Eighth Confederate Cavalry regiment from its posts along the Tennessee River and send it to Chattanooga. No reason was given, but obviously Bragg had decided that Field's men would not encounter the main Federal advance if they remained where they were. At Chattanooga Bragg ordered Hindman to send two brigades beyond Lookout Mountain into the valley of Lookout Creek. On 20 August, when Hindman sought clarification of the order sending Manigault's and Deas's Brigades to Lookout Valley, Bragg explained that they would guard against Federal incursions in that vicinity. Further, Hindman was to leave his artillery and his ordnance train behind until he could repair the rough road over the lower slopes of Lookout Mountain. On the same day, Bragg ordered Polk to expedite construction on the Chattanooga fortifications by working three shifts per day. Rumors soon began to spread that the Army of the Cumberland was "moving about." In Lookout Valley, Manigault's Brigade settled into camp around the Wauhatchie railroad station and sent pickets to the river. Mary Manigault, who happened to be visiting her husband, traveled with the brigade. That night, orders reached Anderson's regiment at Shell Mound to prepare rations for three days and await movement orders. Similar orders were delivered to all units of Polk's Corps, Hill's Corps, and the Reserve

Artillery Battalion near Chattanooga. Clearly, the Army of Tennessee was moving to a higher level of readiness than had been seen for some time.[12]

Just as Bragg had indications of an imminent Federal advance, so too did Simon Buckner in Knoxville. On 19 August one of Buckner's staff officers noted that headquarters had learned that Ambrose Burnside's forces in Kentucky were on the march toward Tennessee. On the next day, Buckner sent a chilling telegram to William Mackall, Bragg's chief of staff. In the telegram he reported that Col. John Palmer, commanding the Fifty-Eighth North Carolina Infantry regiment at Big Creek Gap, believed that a large Federal force was advancing on his position and would arrive in less than forty-eight hours. Buckner warned Mackall that the Cumberland Plateau gaps could not be held without reinforcements, and he wished to know what Bragg wanted him to do. Should he reinforce the gaps with troops from the railroad garrisons, or should he simply wait for orders to withdraw southward toward Chattanooga? Pending an answer from Bragg, Buckner instructed Palmer to call upon the Sixty-Fifth Georgia Infantry regiment at Jacksboro for aid. If that reinforcement proved insufficient, both regiments should move northeast to join Frazer's command at Cumberland Gap. Meanwhile, Pegram was told to move his entire command to Winters Gap. Finally, Buckner ordered Gracie's Brigade to move from Strawberry Plains to Knoxville as rapidly as possible, with arrival no later than the next day, 21 August. Until he received further instructions from the headquarters of the Army of Tennessee, Buckner could only await developments with considerable anxiety.[13]

President Davis had called for 21 August to be a day of fasting and prayer for the Confederate cause. All across the army, officers and men either attended services in their camps or in houses of worship. In Atlanta, Sgt. John Freeman of the Thirty-Fourth Mississippi Infantry regiment of Walthall's Brigade went to church in town. At Tyner's Station, the chaplains of Stewart's Division conducted services in their individual brigades. In Chattanooga, Frank Cheatham and many of his officers attended services at the First Presbyterian Church on Market Street, while others gathered in churches elsewhere in town. At Cherokee Springs, Bragg was in the audience when Chaplain E. M. Green preached in the new brush-arbor chapel. Nurse Kate Cumming, also in the audience, watched Bragg closely and wrote in her daily journal, "As General Bragg was leaving the church, a dispatch was handed to him, seemingly an important one. I hope nothing is the matter." Unfortunately, something was the matter—Federal shells were landing in the streets of Chattanooga.[14]

10

Bombardment

» 21–23 August 1863 «

Well before dawn on 21 August the soldiers of Wilder's brigade stirred in their camps around Poe's Tavern. Their task was to appear ostentatiously at the river crossings upstream of Chattanooga and simulate the advance guard of a mighty host. In order to gain the desired effect, Wilder's command had to be visible but not so overt as to be an obvious deception. Nor was he to provoke a cross-river response by Confederate forces. Wilder was separated from the bulk of Crittenden's Twenty-First Corps in the Sequatchie Valley by the formidable obstacle of Walden's Ridge. Only two brigades, Hazen's above Poe's Tavern and Wagner's overlooking Chattanooga, were within extreme supporting distance. An aggressive response to Wilder's provocations would place his men in considerable danger. Wilder himself was undaunted by either the complexities of the mission or the convoluted command structure controlling it. He nominally belonged to the Fourteenth Corps, yet the entire deception operation belonged to Crittenden's Twenty-First Corps. Crittenden chose to remain at Dunlap in the Sequatchie Valley, leaving John Palmer to supervise the initial deception. Having received his orders directly from Rosecrans, Wilder considered himself to be an independent actor, a role he had enjoyed since the beginning of the Tullahoma campaign. He divided his brigade to cover a wide swath of territory. First, he assigned Col. John Funkhouser of the Ninety-Eighth Illinois Mounted Infantry regiment to lead his own unit and Col. Smith Atkins's Ninety-Second Illinois Mounted Infantry regiment to Harrison's Ferry, supported by two guns from Capt. Eli Lilly's Eighteenth Indiana Battery. Next, Wilder assigned Capt. Jacob Vail and two companies of the Seventeenth Indiana Mounted Infantry regiment to scout along the river near North Chickamauga Creek. Finally, Wilder himself would lead the Seventy-Second Indiana Mounted Infantry regiment, the 123rd Illinois Mounted Infantry regiment, the remainder of the Seventeenth Indiana, and four of Lilly's guns to the river opposite Chattanooga. To Wilder's relief, Palmer decided to accompany Funkhouser's force to Harrison's Ferry.[1]

Southern portion of Chattanooga, with freight station, train shed, and Crutchfield House in view in the distance. (Chattanooga Public Library)

Leading two companies of the 123rd Illinois, Maj. James Connolly around 6:00 A.M. suddenly reached the river opposite the town. The streets of Chattanooga lay 600 yards away, but much closer were twelve Confederate soldiers leading sixty mules from a ferry. The Confederates were utterly surprised by the sudden appearance of the Federals. Connolly's men dashed forward, capturing the drovers. The ferry abruptly backed away, leaving its gangplank behind. Although the Federals inflicted several casualties, including the ferryman, the vessel reached the city safely. For a few moments, no one in Chattanooga reacted, so great was the surprise. Indeed, Connolly had time to water his horses in the river before a few scattered shots from the city caused him to retreat to the shelter of nearby trees. Arriving by midmorning, Wilder surveyed the situation with Lilly. A range of hills known as Stringer's Ridge paralleled the river from Moccasin Bend south of the town to a point well upstream. The ridge stood 350 feet above the plain and was approximately a half mile from the river. Two vessels, the *Paint Rock*, a sternwheeler of 140 tons, and the smaller *Dunbar*, a side-wheeler, lay moored at the foot of Market Street, along with a floating bridge of forty-seven pontoons. Atop Cameron Hill, slightly lower than Stringer's Ridge, was an earthwork with three embrasures. Slightly below it was another work pierced for nine guns, and a water battery below that at river level. Just beyond three large brick warehouses was a small fieldwork commanding the landing. Upstream was another large fortification perched on a sheer rocky bluff, while smaller works crowned hills beyond it. No cannon could be seen. A mile beyond the river stood two railroad stations and the large Crutchfield House hotel. Several church steeples rose above the general clutter of buildings. The streets seemed to be empty of either soldiers or civilians. Taking in everything at a glance from Stringer's Ridge, Wilder ordered Lilly to open fire. By 10:30 A.M., Lilly had gotten his guns into good firing positions on the ridge and sent the first shells screaming toward Chattanooga.[2]

Lilly's first targets were the *Paint Rock* and the *Dunbar*, which he engaged with three guns at a range of 1,600 yards. The right gun bombarded the silent earthwork on Cameron Hill. Firing slowly, Lilly's gunners methodically took the vessels apart. After three shots struck its waterline, the *Paint Rock* sank in shallow water with its upper works badly damaged. The *Dunbar* remained afloat, but its superstructure was wrecked. Lilly next turned his attention to the two large fortifications at either end of the waterfront. Confederate gunners briefly replied until they found they could not reach the Federals. Meanwhile, Lilly's men placed shot after shot through the Confederate embrasures. After an initial flurry of people scrambling in panic from the houses and churches downtown, few citizens were to be seen. As the bombardment continued, only an occasional person dashed from house to house. At one point, a bold civilian drove his carriage back and forth on the riverbank, in apparent defiance of Lilly's gunners, until he was targeted specifically. When a shell burst nearby, he too disappeared out of range. In late afternoon, having expended over 260 rounds, Lilly was firing only an occasional shot toward the ferry moored near the steamboats when suddenly a rifled thirty-two-pounder spoke from the large fort. Unlike the other Confederate rounds, which had fallen laughably short, the heavy shot struck Lilly's position squarely. Bouncing off the ground under gun No. 5, it sliced off the leg of Cpl. Abram McCorkle and killed four horses in the gun team before finally coming to rest against a tree behind the gun limber. The lucky shot ended Lilly's target practice and the Federals departed from Stringer's Ridge at 4:30 P.M. The artillerymen evacuated Corporal McCorkle to Poe's Tavern, but the severe wound caused his death four days later. Wilder's force withdrew several miles to the foot of Walden's Ridge near the beginning of the Anderson Road. Above them camped Wagner's command, distant spectators to the artillery duel.[3]

Fourteen miles upriver, at Harrison's Ferry, John Palmer followed two of Wilder's regiments and a section of Lilly's guns to the riverbank. With Palmer was the Twenty-First Corps chief of staff, Lt. Col. Lyne Starling, and Lt. George Crow, topographical engineer. Col. John Funkhouser first sent four companies of the Ninety-Eighth Illinois under Lt. Col. Edward Kitchell upstream several miles to the village of Dallas. He then led the remainder of his regiment and the eight available companies of Col. Smith Atkins's Ninety-Second Illinois to the vicinity of the ferry landing. A lone Confederate picket saw the Federals approach and escaped to the far shore in a flatboat. Far more cautious than Wilder at Chattanooga, Palmer began a minute investigation of the Confederate fortifications across the river. There seemed to be several distinct works overlooking the ferry, just below the point where Ooltewah Creek entered the river. A handful of Confederates could be seen observing the Federal column. For some time, each side stared at the other. While Palmer and Starling closely observed the Confederate movements, Lieutenant Crow sketched a map of the area. Also observing the scene was Smith Atkins of the Ninety-Second Illinois, who stood near a large frame house close to the river. Suddenly, a Confederate officer approached the river and knelt on one knee. A puff of smoke made it instantly clear that he was firing on the Federals. His bullet missed Atkins but struck Pvt. William Patterson in the arm. The Federals quickly responded with shots of their own. Armed with Enfield rifles, most of the Ninety-Second Illinois could not reach the Confederates. Only three companies of the Ninety-Second had Spencer rifles, so they and the six companies of the Ninety-Eighth Illinois carried the action until Palmer halted the firing. Having learned that the Confederates were alert and that boats would be required to cross the river, Palmer withdrew Funkhouser's command several miles from the river. He then returned to Poe's Tavern and crossed Walden's Ridge to Dunlap.[4]

Farther upstream, Robert Minty also showed his small command to the Confederates. Minty's First Brigade was seriously understrength in view of its role in the deception plan and the need to connect with Burnside's forces. He had been required to leave the battalion of the Third Indiana Cavalry regiment to shield the McMinnville supply depot. He left 200 more troopers at McMinnville because their horses had broken down. By the time he reached Pikeville, Minty could mount only 1,200 men. Nevertheless, he crossed Walden's Ridge early on 21 August with three regiments and two guns of the Chicago Board of Trade Battery. Reaching the hamlet of Morganton at the eastern foot of Walden's Ridge around 9:00 A.M., he pushed forward a mile to Smith's Cross Roads. From there he sent scouts toward the Tennessee River. One group traveled northeast to the village of Washington, while another rode southeast toward Blythe's Ferry. The scouts to Washington encountered a few Confederates, who easily withdrew beyond the Tennessee. Before leaving Washington, the Federals plundered the Rhea County courthouse, scattering county records. At Blythe's Ferry, the Federals found Confederate infantry busily entrenching on the far side of the river. Before Minty's troopers withdrew, the Confederates opened fire, wounding a trooper in the Fourth United States Cavalry. Having shown his command to the Confederates, Minty positioned himself at Smith's Cross Roads. At the moment, there was no sign of Burnside, Van Cleve's supporting infantrymen were beyond Walden's Ridge, and Wilder's nearest units were at Poe's Tavern, fifteen miles to the south. With his rations and forage almost exhausted and his road to the rear unsecured, Minty believed himself to be in a dangerous position. Those fears would grow as the hours passed. Still, as he nervously glanced back at the mountain behind him, Minty and his small band of horsemen were where Rosecrans wanted him to be.[5]

It is unlikely that Braxton Bragg was surprised by the sudden appearance of Federal troops across from Chattanooga on 21 August. Bragg was still at Cherokee Springs, but the army staff was in the city. In Bragg's absence, Leonidas Polk and Frank Cheatham were the senior officers present in the town. Federal activity beyond the Tennessee River had indeed been monitored by the Confederates. The growing Federal presence around Stevenson, Bridgeport, and Jasper had not gone unnoticed by Anderson's Brigade and the Third Confederate Cavalry regiment. Similarly, multiple small detachments roaming beyond the Tennessee River northwest of Chattanooga also were reporting Federal movement into the Sequatchie Valley. Maj. Charles McDonald's Battalion of Forrest's Division, a detachment from Col. Benjamin Hill's Thirty-Fifth Tennessee Infantry regiment from Cleburne's Division, and a detail from several more Tennessee infantry regiments under Lt. James McFerrin of the Thirty-Second Tennessee Infantry from Stewart's Division had all been scouting for some time beyond the river. Unfortunately, only McFerrin's report is extant. In it he noted that his scouts left the west bank of the river only on the night of 20 August under pressure from Wilder's advance. Clearly, Wilder's movements were being reported to the staff of the Army of Tennessee. That information, however, seems not to have been widely disseminated, as Frank Cheatham told a reporter that he was unaware of the Federal approach. As a result, the ferry operator transporting herders across the river at Chattanooga had no inkling that Wilder's Federals were so near on 21 August. In late morning a signal corps detachment atop Raccoon Mountain saw Wilder's men approaching the river, but their warning came too late for an immediate response. Events might have taken a different course had Bragg been in Chattanooga instead of the more lackadaisical Polk, but Bragg was absent and the senior leaders in Chattanooga thought it best to be seen in church that morning.[6]

The citizens of Chattanooga were utterly unprepared for the rain of shells that descended upon their town in midmorning. Although it was Friday, the town's churches were filled with soldiers and civilians attending services in accord with President Davis's proclamation. Polk and his wife were most likely at St. Paul's Episcopal Church at Chestnut and Eighth Streets, where Dr. Charles Quintard was preaching. Cheatham and several subordinates were at the First Presbyterian Church at the corner of Seventh and Market Streets. Henry Watterson, principal reporter for the *Chattanooga Daily Rebel*, was also at the Presbyterian Church, along with correspondents from more distant newspapers. Rev. Benjamin Palmer had just begun a long prayer when Lilly's first shots exploded on the waterfront. As errant shells landed elsewhere in the city, nervous congregants began to depart in haste. Cheatham attempted to quiet the growing unease, but his words had no effect. Throughout the town, men, women, and children rapidly transformed growing concern into abject panic. Lilly's guns were at least 2,500 yards from the Presbyterian Church, but shots that flew over the batteries on Cameron Hill reached well into the town, striking private dwellings, churches, and hospitals indiscriminately. Some people, like reporter John Linebaugh of the *Memphis Daily Appeal,* were restrained by officers as they attempted to reach their quarters near the river. By evening hundreds of citizens had abandoned their homes for rude camps in groves beyond artillery range or found space on departing trains. Not all escaped so easily; according to the *Daily Rebel,* five or six citizens were killed or wounded before the day's bombardment ended. Among the mortally wounded were an unidentified woman and Elizabeth "Lizzie" Roach, twelve, a refugee from Nashville struck in the thigh. Chattanooga had been bombarded before, but the lack of meaningful warning contributed greatly to the shock felt by citizens far beyond the reach of Lilly's guns.[7]

The military reaction to Wilder's appearance was more measured than that of Chattanooga's civilians. In Bragg's absence, Polk orchestrated the army's response. First he sent Lumsden's Alabama Battery from the Artillery Reserve, Scott's Tennessee and Scogin's Georgia Batteries from Cheatham's Division, and Fowler's Alabama Battery from Hindman's Division to occupy the fortifications on the town's waterfront. Armed mostly with smoothbores, the Confederate gunners soon found that their field guns were badly outranged. Only the heavy rifled thirty-two-pounder could reach Lilly's position and it took several hours to mount it and bring it into action. Beyond that direct response, Polk needed information about what might be happening beyond the bulk of Lookout Mountain. By telegraph he queried Anderson about Federal activity in the area of Bridgeport and Shell Mound. Similarly, he telegraphed Hindman, ordering him to keep a strong guard at Kelly's Ferry and maintain contact with Anderson. While waiting to hear from the left of his line, Polk rearranged the defenses of his center and right as well. Cheatham had been guarding several railroad bridges west of Chattanooga for some time, as well as Brown's Ferry downstream. Polk ordered Cheatham to relinquish those posts to Hindman, while extending his pickets upstream to the village of Harrison, the western edge of Hill's sector. Polk instructed Cheatham to utilize his escort, Capt. Thomas Merritt's Company G, Second Georgia Cavalry regiment, for the task. In another message indicating a lack of confidence in Cheatham, Polk directly charged Col. Alfred Vaughan Jr., temporarily commanding Smith's Brigade, to maintain a picket line from Chattanooga downstream to the nose of Lookout Mountain, where it would connect with Hindman's pickets. Finally, Polk ordered Asst. Quartermaster Richard Mason to gather the corps transportation for possible movement. Having taken those actions, Polk waited to hear from Bragg.[8]

Responding quickly to Polk's call for information and action, Hindman rode first through a mile-long gap in Raccoon Mountain to Kelly's Ferry, where he found Capt. Granville Sandusky's Company H, Third Confederate Cavalry, on guard. Sandusky told Hindman that another company of the Third Confederate was at Rankin's Ferry, twelve miles downriver at the mouth of Running Water Creek. Returning to Wauhatchie, Hindman sent a staff officer to investigate Brown's Ferry. Brown's was another well-known crossing site, sixteen miles upstream from Kelly's Ferry by the meandering Tennessee River but only four miles from the Wauhatchie depot. When the staff officer returned, he reported that a small Federal mounted force had appeared across the river that morning and had probably seized a number of wagons belonging to a foraging detail from Hill's Corps. This disturbing news came from two teamsters who swam the river to escape capture. In addition, locals reported a Federal force passing over Walden's Ridge early in the day. Forwarding this information to Polk, Hindman also reported that he was relieving Cheatham's pickets. Deeming Brown's Ferry to be the most critical point, he sent the Fiftieth Alabama Infantry regiment of Deas's Brigade to defend that crossing. He reinforced Captain Sandusky at Kelly's Ferry with sixty infantrymen and ordered another group of similar size to replace Cheatham's men at the railroad bridge over Running Water Creek. Finally, he dispatched thirty men to relieve Cheatham's guards at the Lookout Creek railroad bridge. He asked to be excused from sending anyone to the Chattanooga Creek railroad bridge because the structure was in Cheatham's area. Hindman reminded Polk that he lacked his artillery batteries and ordnance wagons. He also issued an order banishing all dependents visiting the command. Among those affected was brigade commander Arthur Manigault, who reluctantly parted with his wife, Mary, and son, Arthur, twelve, in midafternoon.[9]

When Capt. James Hall's Company K, Twenty-Fourth Alabama Infantry regiment of Manigault's Brigade, arrived at Kelly's Ferry around 6:00 P.M., they discovered approximately 200 Confederate cavalrymen on the far shore of the Tennessee River. The horsemen proved to be McDonald's Tennessee Cavalry Battalion. In Maj. Charles McDonald's absence, Capt. Philip Allin commanded the battalion, which had been monitoring Federal movements west of the Tennessee. Forced from both the Sequatchie Valley and Walden's Ridge by the approach of Wilder's brigade, Allin's men were desperate to cross to the Confederate side of the river. Cut off from Chattanooga, the battalion had reached Kelly's Ferry on the afternoon of 21 August but found no easy means of crossing the stream. Fearing to ride their horses across the river, the cavalrymen spent several hours trying to force their mounts to swim to the Confederate shore.

No horses made the trip willingly, and few made it at all without their riders. By nightfall only a few cavalrymen and their mounts had successfully surmounted the obstacle. Fearing that the Federals would arrive at any time and catch them with their backs to the river, the desperate cavalrymen turned to a final expedient. Finding two small dugout canoes, they began the laborious process of towing single horses across the river. Throughout the night, teams of two men in each dugout worked to rescue Allin's command. On every trip across the river, one man paddled the canoe, while the other held the reins of a horse. The laborious process would not be completed until 2:00 A.M. on 22 August, but surprisingly only one horse drowned during the crossing. With Allin's departure from the west bank of the river, Bragg lost his last major source of information about Federal activity beyond his immediate sight. Over the next several days a handful of stragglers would also make the crossing successfully, but they provided little useful news.[10]

Even before Wilder's bombardment galvanized Polk into action, significant portions of Hill's Corps were in motion. For several weeks, the only infantry guarding the river above the mouth of South Chickamauga Creek had been Wood's Brigade of Cleburne's Division. Wood's four regiments and two battalions were responsible for the thirty miles of riverfront from Sivley's Ford just upstream from Chattanooga to Blythe's Ferry. All told, there were at least twelve possible crossing points to be picketed. Wood guarded Blythe's Ferry with the Thirty-Second/Forty-Fifth Mississippi Infantry regiment and placed the Fifteenth Mississippi Sharpshooter battalion at Doughty's Ferry next downstream. The Forty-Fifth Alabama Infantry regiment monitored Campbell's and Thatcher's Fords, while the Thirty-Third Alabama Infantry regiment covered the crossing sites around Harrison's Ferry. The remaining crossings were left to the Sixteenth Alabama Infantry regiment and the Eighteenth Alabama Infantry battalion. Wood made his headquarters at the village of Harrison. According to "Army of Tennessee," a correspondent of the *Augusta Daily Constitutionalist* and apparently a staff officer at army headquarters, William Mackall received information on 20 August that the river line upstream from Chattanooga was threatened, especially around Blythe's Ferry. The report could have come from one of the detachments forced from the Sequatchie Valley by Wilder's and Minty's advancing troops, or it could have been a reaction to the increasingly nervous dispatches emanating from Buckner in Knoxville. No written orders from army headquarters are extant, but Hill clearly was told to send a brigade to reinforce the Thirty-Second/Forty-Fifth Mississippi at Blythe's Ferry. Although the Blythe's Ferry position belonged to Cleburne's Division, Cleburne momentarily had no troops available to support Wood. Two of his remaining brigades, Polk's and Deshler's, had recently moved from Tyner's Station southward several miles to Graysville and were too distant to be sent quickly. Cleburne's remaining brigade, Liddell's, was being detached to form an army reserve and was unavailable as well.[11]

To support Cleburne, Hill ordered Alexander Stewart, whose division was camped near Tyner's Station, to loan Cleburne a brigade. Stewart selected Clayton's Brigade to reinforce Blythe's Ferry. Clayton was the junior brigadier in the division, and his brigade, though large, was untested in serious action. Nevertheless, shortly after midnight, Clayton put his command on the road toward Blythe's Ferry. Clayton was informed he would be attached temporarily to Cleburne's command. The brigade was well on its way long before Wilder arrived opposite Chattanooga. Clayton's men were unaccustomed to arduous road marches, so he was far short of Blythe's Ferry when a courier reported that Federals had appeared opposite Blythe's Ferry. Clayton accelerated his pace, further discomfiting his men, but soon received another message telling him the emergency had passed. Slackening his speed, he reached the village of Birchwood, four miles from the ferry, around sundown. Leaving his brigade there, Clayton continued forward with a section of guns. Far in his rear, other units from Cleburne's Division were also moving to support the river defenses. Polk's and Deshler's commands moved north at sunrise from their camps around Graysville. In the lead, Polk reached Harrison at noon and halted there. Deshler followed an hour later and advanced a short distance beyond Harrison before stopping for the night. The remainder of Hill's Corps spent the day cooking rations in preparation for instant movement. Later, in both his official report and his postwar writings, Hill took Bragg to task for being surprised on 21 August. The fact that three of his brigades were in motion by dawn of that day, before a single Federal soldier had appeared across the river, renders his charge invalid. Some of Hill's foragers were surprised on the far bank of the Tennessee when Wilder arrived at midmorning, but their predicament reflects more on Hill than Bragg. No one knew where the Federals would appear, but their coming seems to have been at least partially anticipated by the army staff.[12]

Bragg reached Chattanooga from Cherokee Springs at the end of the day. One of his first acts was to order Anderson to leave Bridgeport and Shell Mound and fall back toward Chattanooga. Anderson received the order just as he was completing a report to Polk on his dispositions. Although most of his brigade was camped at Taylor's Store, on the railroad a mile from the ruined bridge, he also guarded Cameron's Ferry, plus Alley's Ferry upstream toward Shell Mound. At Shell Mound itself he had stationed the Forty-First Mississippi Infantry regiment, which also protected Gardenhire's Ferry just beyond Rankin's Ferry. Caperton's Ferry, below Bridgeport, he had left to Capt. John Hoge's Company A, Third Confederate Cavalry regiment. Anticipating movement ever since he had learned of the bombardment of Chattanooga,

Anderson in late afternoon readied his regiments to leave their camps at a moment's notice. While the men packed their meager belongings, several officers struggled to evacuate their visiting wives via the railroad. At least one regiment developed contingency plans to destroy its baggage and cooking utensils if no train was available to carry the impedimenta to Chattanooga. Fortunately, a train arrived in time and the matériel was quickly loaded aboard. Anderson notified Polk that he would move toward Chattanooga via the hamlet of Whiteside, and around 9:00 P.M. the regiments at Taylor's Store took the road toward Shell Mound. After they passed the Shell Mound depot, the Forty-First Mississippi followed, halting often to guard the rear while the remainder of the brigade stumbled forward in the darkness. Anderson's men would march all night, most of them continuing through the canyon of Running Water Creek until they debouched into the much larger valley of Lookout Creek. From there it was only a short distance to Wauhatchie and a reunion with the remainder of the division. Left in place along the river were the now isolated companies of the Third Confederate Cavalry.[13]

Anderson's move was only Bragg's first response to the Federal bombardment. Next, he recalled Walthall's Brigade from Atlanta. Walthall was to report to St. John Liddell at Chickamauga Station for assignment to a new divisional formation. Although Liddell had requested a transfer to Louisiana, Bragg had persuaded him to remain with the Army of Tennessee for one more campaign. As a reward, Liddell received command of a small division consisting of his own brigade and Walthall's. Another circular placed Polk in command of all troops at Chattanooga, including Jackson's Brigade. Next Bragg reviewed the army's troop dispositions with his staff. From Roddey's brigade at Tuscumbia to Forrest's command at Kingston, Bragg's army was draped across a 250-mile front. His infantry, however, was concentrated within the forty-mile stretch from Wauhatchie to Blythe's Ferry, with the sole exception being Johnson's Brigade at Loudon. Johnson served as a tenuous link to Buckner's command, which added another seventy miles of frontage from Loudon to Cumberland Gap. It had long been obvious that Bragg could not hold the river line in strength with his limited forces. Nor, with his inadequate transportation and bridging assets, could he cross the Tennessee River to attack the Army of the Cumberland. Instead, Rosecrans would have to come to him. Therefore, Bragg believed he would have to wait for Rosecrans to commit the Army of the Cumberland to an axis of advance before the Army of Tennessee could respond. The response would be offensive in nature, but it could not be implemented until Rosecrans tipped his hand. Bragg would have to be patient for a while longer. The Federals were beginning to stir, but there might be time for reinforcements to arrive before they acted. Thus he sent a late evening telegram to Joseph Johnston in Mississippi: "Rosecrans and Burnside both moving on us in force. Artillery fired on the town to-day across the river; preparing to cross below. If able to assist us do so promptly."[14]

Unaware of what was transpiring at Chattanooga, Simon Buckner was agitated by problems of his own. Certain that Burnside's army was bearing down upon him, and painfully aware that his strength was inadequate to defend Knoxville and the railroads, he vigorously sought assistance. An earlier request to Mackall for guidance having produced nothing, Buckner asked Adjutant General Cooper if Samuel Jones, commanding in southwestern Virginia, might come to his aid. Knowing that Cooper would not reply immediately, Buckner telegraphed Mackall again. Plaintively, he asked Mackall to tell him which way to withdraw, either northeast toward Abingdon, Virginia, or southwest toward Loudon, Tennessee. With shells falling in the streets of Chattanooga, Mackall was too busy to respond. Verging on insubordination, Buckner again wired Mackall, tartly reminding him that his department had been subsumed into Bragg's for the sole purpose of "concerted action." In return, Buckner had received nothing but silence. Boldly, he threatened to go his own way, knowing that it was an empty threat. He closed by begging, "Please answer." When nothing arrived from Mackall, Buckner resolved to act. Learning from Forrest of the Federal activity in the Sequatchie and Tennessee River valleys below Kingston, Buckner concluded that he had to move closer to Bragg's army. Loudon, not Abingdon, thus would become Buckner's base of operations. To that end, he began to assemble a mobile force of 7,000 troops near Knoxville. Gracie's Brigade arrived during the day from Strawberry Plains. Single regiments were called to Knoxville from Hansonville and Glade Spring in Virginia. Even though he expected Big Creek Gap to be one of Burnside's routes of advance, Buckner replaced its infantry garrison with cavalry. When the concentration was complete, only Frazer's garrison at Cumberland Gap and Jackson's railroad guards would remain in place. Finally, Buckner counseled the presidents of the East Tennessee & Georgia and East Tennessee & Virginia Railroads to remove their rolling stock to places of safety.[15]

Unaware of the turmoil he had created among his enemies, Rosecrans on 21 August maintained his usual routine. Rising late, he planned to handle correspondence until the middle of the day and then travel to Bridgeport to investigate potential crossing points. He wrote first to Thomas Crittenden, thanking him for his prompt movements and expressing the hope that Crittenden's activities would attract Confederate forces posted downstream from Chattanooga. He then sent a brief message to Ambrose Burnside, suggesting that Burnside make contact with Crittenden's troops in the Sequatchie Valley. Finally, he offered a tardy report of the previous day's operations to the adjutant general's office in Washington, predicting, "I think we shall maneuver to cross where they do not expect us." Meanwhile, the army staff prepared for Rosecrans's trip to Bridgeport by calling up the steam dummy for a noon departure from Stevenson and directing William Lytle to provide horses for the general's party. Before departing, Rosecrans ordered George Thomas to investigate the possibility of capturing the Confederate steamer *Paint Rock*, which allegedly was stranded at a shoal below Chattanooga. Col. Caleb Carlton, commanding the Eighty-Ninth Ohio Infantry regiment at Tracy City, had reported during the night that a large number of crewmen from the *Paint Rock* had arrived with news that the vessel was stuck at a shoal known as the "Suck." Vessels attempting to pass upstream usually needed to be warped past the "Suck" by using lines attached to capstans onshore. The crewmen, members of the First Louisiana Infantry regiment, told Carlton that the capstan system was broken, trapping the *Paint Rock*. Carlton's news was out of date because the *Paint Rock* had already reached Chattanooga, only to be sunk later that day by Wilder's artillery. Unaware of those developments, and anxious to gain a vessel to facilitate his crossing, Rosecrans asked Thomas to capture the vessel. He and his son Adrian then boarded the dummy with McCook and Stanley and headed for Bridgeport.[16]

At Bridgeport, six deserters from the Seventh Mississippi Infantry regiment crossed the river into the Federal lines early in the morning. They reported demoralization in their unit and stringent efforts by officers to prevent more desertion. They also stated that Joseph Johnston had arrived in Chattanooga with 10,000 reinforcements for Bragg. Not long thereafter, a flag of truce from Patton Anderson delivered two women to the waiting Federals. The ladies did not impress Lt. Alfred Pirtle, a native of Louisville, Kentucky: "The Mrs. Payne who came over today is some no body from down on Market St bet 9 X 10th. I don't know anything about her. Miss Caruthers is a Rebel I suppose, but wants to get home even if it is in our lines." In early afternoon the dummy arrived with Rosecrans and his party. Soldiers from Bradley's command rushed to greet the generals until their officers, fearing a Confederate reaction, dispersed them. When Lytle and his staff joined the group, the party numbered more than twenty riders. The cavalcade then headed downstream to visit possible crossing sites. Approaching Cameron's Ferry, Lytle and others heard a shot from across the river. They continued their ride until several more bullets whizzed past them, one almost hitting Adrian Rosecrans. Lytle feared the worst: "It occurred to me that the enemy *might* have thrown across the river a small cavalry force and the thought flashed across me that if old Rosey & McCook & Stanley should be *bagged* that I would be censured for not bringing along a stronger escort and catch the d—l generally!" Fortunately, the party soon encountered troopers of the First Tennessee (Union) Cavalry regiment who were picketing the area unbeknownst to Lytle. Rosecrans had seen enough and ordered the party back to Bridgeport. Exhilarated by his brush with danger, he made an impromptu speech to the assembled men, who wildly cheered him. Afterward, Cpl. William Austin of the Twenty-Second Illinois Infantry regiment recorded, "It was the first time I ever heard a cheer for Rosey. The soldiers love him in a different way. They praise him when he is away, and all the time, and there is not a man — a fighting man — in his army who would not rush into the jaws of death and rob it of its terror by their enthusiasm."[17]

Upon returning to Stevenson, Rosecrans forwarded the latest information on Confederate activity to Washington. Some information came from the Mississippi deserters, but the bulk of Rosecrans's news came from one of William Truesdail's "scouts" named M. D. Thompson, who had just reported from Chattanooga. Thompson stated that Joseph Johnston was moving to Knoxville from Mobile with 25,000–50,000 troops. That startling information apparently came from Leonidas Polk, who was present where Thompson dined on the previous night. Polk, he claimed, said that a Confederate invasion of Kentucky would be the best way to counter Rosecrans's advance. Thompson also seemed quite knowledgeable about Anderson's Brigade and reported movement toward Bridgeport by units of Cleburne's Division. Bragg's order of the previous evening to prepare three days' rations was also noted. Other tidbits of information included the caliber of the two heavy guns in Chattanooga, roadwork around Harrison, and the alleged location of Forrest's cavalry at Sparta. Most important of all, Thompson stated that Bragg remained ill at Catoosa Springs. In his report to Washington, Rosecrans emphasized the Johnston and Cleburne movements. In fact, Johnston would only be asked by Bragg for reinforcements that very evening, so the Johnston reference represented only speculation. Similarly, Cleburne's movement was simply the shifting of two brigades from Tyner's Station to Graysville. Cleburne's Division moved on 21 August, the day of Thompson's report, but toward Harrison, not Bridgeport. As for Thompson himself, he probably was Michael D. Thompson, a young Chattanooga merchant who received permission from Federal occupation authorities in 1865 to open a public bathhouse in Chattanooga. Whoever he was, the fact that he reported events only a day old indicates that his transmission method was rapid. Most likely, the information was carried by train to Shell Mound and sent across the river by unknown means. Such a conduit would explain how Thompson knew so much about the troops guarding Bridgeport and far less about the other end of the Confederate line.[18]

While Rosecrans toured the front, his army continued to improve its position. In the Fourteenth Corps sector, Thomas moved his headquarters to the hamlet of Bolivar, between Stevenson and Bridgeport. Division commanders Brannan and Reynolds edged closer to the Tennessee River in accord with orders from army headquarters on the previous day. Brannan ordered Van Derveer's Third Brigade to leave Sweeden's Cove and occupy a new position at the mouth of Battle Creek. There Confederate pickets welcomed them with several rifle shots. There, too, Van Derveer's son Harry saw a live Confederate for the first time. At the same time, Reynolds's command marched five miles northeast to the village of Jasper. Nestled at the foot of the Cumberland Plateau, Jasper lay at the mouth of the Sequatchie Valley. Reynolds's instructions were to find suitable sites from which to interdict the Nashville & Chattanooga Railroad at Shell Mound. At Dunlap, twenty-five miles to the north, Crittenden nervously awaited information about the execution of the army's deception plan. Wagner's Second Brigade of Wood's First Division withdrew from its vantage point overlooking Chattanooga late in the day and Hazen's Second Brigade of Palmer's Second Division descended to Poe's Tavern on the far side of the ridge, but at Dunlap Crittenden knew virtually nothing of their movements. At Pikeville, twenty miles north of Dunlap, Van Cleve struggled with serious logistical issues facing both his own and Minty's commands. At the other end of Rosecrans's line, McCook's Twentieth Corps still had not completed its concentration. Although Richard Johnson and his Second Brigade finally reached the hamlet of Bellefonte, the Second Division's two remaining brigades still struggled to surmount the Cumberland Plateau. So did Long's Second Brigade of Crook's Second Cavalry Division. Deep in the army's rear, the first Reserve Corps brigade to be called forward, Daniel McCook's, left Nashville and halted for the night at Franklin, Tennessee.[19]

Although Patton Anderson attempted to keep his evacuation of Taylor's Store and Shell Mound a secret, his departure was noted almost instantly by Federal units across the Tennessee River. Around midnight, Van Derveer's sentries at the mouth of Battle Creek reported that the opposing infantry pickets had been replaced by cavalrymen. They also reported hearing heavy railroad activity beyond the river. On the morning of 22 August, Van Derveer promptly sent the report to Fourteenth Corps headquarters, but Thomas decided not to forward the information until he could hear from Reynolds, who was supposed to be in the process of interdicting Shell Mound. At Bridgeport, where heavy fog blanketed the river, several deserters from Anderson's Brigade appeared early in the day. They announced that their unit had departed around 9:00 P.M. the previous evening, carrying three days' rations, and was moving to Chattanooga. Lytle, who had been planning to send a flag of truce to protest the previous day's picket firing, instead sent a detachment of sharpshooters from Bradley's brigade across the channel to Long Island. Led by Lt. John Turnbull of Lytle's staff, the Federals exchanged a few shots with members of the Third Confederate Cavalry regiment and later returned to the Federal shore with additional deserting Mississippians. Lytle reported the news of Anderson's departure to Sheridan at Stevenson, who forwarded it to corps and army headquarters. Rosecrans probably would have returned to Bridgeport in response to the news, but the dummy had broken and momentarily was not available. Still, Anderson's departure portended good things for the Federals if Rosecrans decided to cross the river in the vicinity of Bridgeport and Shell Mound. Meanwhile, Cpl. Edward Crippin of the Twenty-Seventh Illinois Infantry regiment summed up the attitude of the common soldier at Bridgeport in his diary: "Rebs left us alone in our glory last night. . . . They never so much as bid us good bye when they started. . . . Well let them go we will visit them shortly."[20]

During Rosecrans's absence from headquarters on the previous day, private letters from Halleck and Lincoln had arrived at Stevenson. With the dummy broken, Rosecrans had time to respond on 22 August. The extraordinary content of the letters must have inflamed his mercurial temper. Halleck's letter, dated 9 August, was a blunt attempt to end the wrangling between Rosecrans and the Lincoln administration. He denied that Stanton was hostile to Rosecrans but said that both Lincoln and Stanton remained unsatisfied with Rosecrans's slow pace. In Halleck's opinion, Rosecrans himself had largely created the problem: "In your official dispatches, as well as in your private notes, you seem to be laboring under the impression that the authorities here were making war on you. There never was a greater mistake. I know of no one here who has not the kindest and most friendly feelings for you. Nevertheless, many of your dispatches have been exceedingly annoying to the War Department. No doubt such was not your intention, but they certainly have been calculated to convey the impression that you were not disposed to carry out the wishes of the Department, at least in the manner and at the time desired." Rosecrans's response was equally blunt. First, he explained that his delays had been caused by the lack of a sufficient mounted force and the difficult terrain in which he was operating. In a passage that must have been especially galling, he compared the terrain Halleck faced during his brief advance on Corinth in 1862 to the far more daunting mountains and rivers encountered by the Army of the Cumberland. Asserting that his actions had the approbation of his senior officers, Rosecrans attacked the War Department for ignoring, with "contemptuous silence," the recent achievements of his army. He believed he was utterly misunderstood by his superiors, Halleck's protestations to the contrary notwithstanding. In a final rhetorical flourish, he gratuitously advised those superiors to try to grasp both his difficulties and his proposed solutions.[21]

Lincoln's letter, dated 10 August, was couched in an entirely different tone from Halleck's. He denied that he had lost confidence in Rosecrans, then explained how his own views had fluctuated over the summer as Grant's campaign against Vicksburg waxed and waned. When Lincoln saw Johnston gathering a force to relieve the Vicksburg garrison, he urged Rosecrans to reduce Grant's risk by attacking Bragg. When Vicksburg capitulated, Lincoln slackened his pressure on Rosecrans to advance. Then, when Rosecrans's continued delays gave Johnston the opportunity to reinforce Bragg, Lincoln again urged Rosecrans forward. Yet when Rosecrans continued to resist, Lincoln admitted his own uncertainty: "The question occurs, Can the thing be done at all?" In effect, Lincoln begged Rosecrans to reassure him that the "thing" could indeed be done. He closed with some gentle yet fatherly words: "Do not misunderstand. I am not casting blame upon you. I rather think by great exertion you can get to East Tennessee; but a very important question is, Can you stay there? I make no order in the case; that I leave to General Halleck and yourself. And now be assured once more that I think of you in all kindness and confidence, and that I am not watching you with an evil eye." In his response, Rosecrans ignored the president's explanation and offered his own opinion of the relationship between Grant's army and his own. He argued that Grant's army now should assist Rosecrans by pinning Johnston's army in place. After repeating the familiar litany of difficulties, Rosecrans once more sought the president's indulgence: "Thanking you for your kindness, may I ask you, when impulsive men suppose me querulous, to believe I am only straightforward and in earnest, and that you may always rely upon my using my utmost efforts to do what is best for our country and the lives and honor of the soldiers of my command." Nowhere in the letter did Rosecrans venture an opinion on Lincoln's specific question; the president would have to be satisfied with his general assertion that he would do his best.[22]

After his unpleasant correspondence with Washington, Rosecrans turned to what he considered more practical concerns. In a note to Burnside, he offered insight into his thinking about his future axis of advance: "Wish to cross below if not hindered. May try it above if enemy move to suit. You will be in good time." The army staff meanwhile labored to improve the logistical infrastructure that would sustain the army's leap across the Tennessee River. In increasingly brusque tones, Calvin Goddard queried Samuel Simmons, the army's chief commissary, about his apparent inability to stockpile rations at Tracy City, where Twenty-First Corps wagon trains impatiently awaited them. Simmons was also pointedly asked when he was going to move his office from Nashville to Stevenson. Calls went out for more laborers to work at the expanding Stevenson logistical base, most notably to Col. Charles Thompson, who continued to organize his Twelfth United States Colored Troops at Estill Springs. William Innes and his deputy Kinsman Hunton received instructions to expedite boat construction by assembling millwrights and sawmill workers at Bridgeport and Stevenson. In one important area, a major personnel change occurred. St. Clair Morton, the army's chief engineer, had been absent on sick leave for a month with "pustular opthalmia" and sought a permanent transfer from the Department of the Cumberland. Rosecrans disliked the eccentric Morton and recommended approval. As Morton's paperwork began its journey to the War Department, Rosecrans appointed Capt. William Merrill of the Topographical Engineers to replace him and assigned Capt. Patrick O'Connell to command the Pioneer Brigade. Merrill immediately ordered O'Connell to detail a battalion to build a platform for quartermaster supplies at Stevenson. With as many as twenty trains per day unloading army supplies at Stevenson, Rosecrans ordered Gordon Granger to transfer two more assistant quartermasters to that post.[23]

Action flared on the Tennessee River during the afternoon and evening of 22 August. Although Wilder's men expected an early return to Stringer's Ridge, he held them back while he visited George Wagner atop Walden's Ridge. In midafternoon he finally sent the Seventeenth and Seventy-Second Indiana Mounted Infantry regiments and a section of Lilly's Eighteenth Indiana Battery to show themselves along the riverfront. Around 5:30 P.M., Lilly again opened fire from Stringer's Ridge, focusing his attention on the "heavy battery" on the terrace below the crest of Cameron Hill. That was the location of the thirty-two-pounder that had mortally wounded one of his men on the previous afternoon. The Confederate gunners replied, again with accuracy, but did no damage. In response, Lilly ordered his gunners to entrench their guns. After firing forty rounds, Lilly withdrew his guns at dusk to their secluded camp behind Stringer's Ridge. Upstream at Harrison's Ferry, more of Wilder's units were also active. Palmer had returned to Dunlap, leaving Hazen in charge of the force at Poe's Tavern. Unlike Palmer, who saw no value in random bombardments, Hazen instructed John Funkhouser to have the attached section of the Eighteenth Indiana Battery open on the Confederates. The gunners sent fifteen shots winging toward the distant earthworks with no discernible effect. Sharpshooters also traded shots with Confederate riflemen, claiming but unable to prove better results. Rather than waste more ammunition, Funkhouser withdrew from the river around 4:00 P.M. and returned to Poe's. Palmer's departure made Hazen the senior officer in the valley, and he acted accordingly. While most of his brigade foraged for beef or operated a small flour mill, he gathered a few volunteers for a daring attempt to cross the river and reach the distant railroad. Unlike Hazen, at Smith's Cross Roads Minty did not again threaten the Confederates holding Blythe's Ferry. In fact, he continued to fantasize about masses of Confederates sweeping down upon him from all directions. Minty dared only to send six scouts toward the river after dark.[24]

Behind the deception units, there was activity as well. On Walden's Ridge, Wagner pushed the remainder of his brigade forward to the rim of the valley. From that vantage point he not only could see Wilder's camps far below but also had a panoramic view of Chattanooga and its environs. Watching the frenetic activity in town, Wagner tried to make sense of what the Confederates were doing. During the day, Wilder ascended the mountain to confer with the infantryman. Unaware that Garfield remained sick, both officers sent him messages agitating for more aggressive action. Wilder focused upon possible signs of the evacuation of Chattanooga, while Wagner proposed a quick strike across the river upstream to develop Confederate intentions. Wilder soon returned to his brigade and prepared to resume the bombardment of Chattanooga. Meanwhile, Wood arrived from his headquarters at Therman. Wood counted six distant plumes of smoke representing what appeared to be brigade camps, stretching from Kelly's Ferry downstream to Harrison upstream. His locations were more or less correct, but his estimate of Confederate strength was too small by half. Still, any sizable Confederate movements in the Chattanooga area could be easily observed from Wagner's perch. Such was not the case in the river canyon downstream, where Wood had sent a detachment to capture the *Paint Rock* allegedly trapped below the "Suck." The *Paint Rock*, of course, was lying within view at the Chattanooga landing, sunk. Wood's men were still on the way when cannon fire and a great light drew attention far downstream toward Shell Mound. There, Reynolds had sent two regiments and a section of guns from King's Second Brigade to interdict the railroad. Just before midnight, four daring soldiers from the Seventy-Fifth Indiana crossed the river to burn a covered railroad bridge near the depot. Encountering Confederates on a similar errand, they succeeded in firing the bridge before escaping. The resulting noise and light were seen as far as Bridgeport, causing much speculation.[25]

On Saturday night Rosecrans finally had some positive news to share with his tormentors in Washington. He described Wilder's bombardment of Chattanooga on the previous day and confirmed that Anderson's Brigade had left his front. He forecast success for Reynolds's expedition to Shell Mound. Finally, he announced the arrival of the Pioneer Brigade at Stevenson with half of the pontoon train. Otherwise, there was no change in the army's posture. In the Fourteenth Corps, the First Division around Anderson Station improved its camps and guarded the pontoons arriving by rail. In Negley's Second Division, camped just outside Stevenson, several regiments spent the day chopping wood to fuel passing trains. John Beatty and his examining board meanwhile continued to examine soldiers seeking commissions in the United States Colored Troops. The First and Second Brigades of Brannan's Third Division joined the Third Brigade at the mouth of Battle Creek. There, they found the pickets from the Third Confederate Cavalry regiment more amiable than Anderson's Mississippians had been. Brannan's men quickly took advantage of the truce to bathe in the river and exchange newspapers with the opposing sentries. In McCook's Twentieth Corps, Davis's First Division relaxed in its camps, writing letters home and swimming in Crow Creek. With the arrival of his First and Third Brigades, Johnson finally consolidated his Second Division at Bellefonte. In decline before the war, Bellefonte had been abandoned by most of its citizens before the Federals' arrival. Absent property owners soon suffered serious depredations, and many of Jackson County's irreplaceable documents were destroyed before the Thirty-Fourth Illinois Infantry regiment restored order as a provost guard. Far to the north, in the Sequatchie Valley, those units of Crittenden's Twenty-First Corps not engaged in the deception operation entertained Unionist visitors at Dunlap and Pikeville or foraged to supplement their dwindling rations. Unable to get supplies from Tracy City, their leaders reluctantly began to send supply trains to McMinnville instead.[26]

In Chattanooga, Wilder's delay in resuming his bombardment permitted Bragg to take stock of his situation. His first thought was to seek reinforcements. Thus he wired Samuel Cooper, "Rosecrans has advanced in heavy force to this side of the mountains. Buckner reports Burnsides moving on him in force. Our line is too long for our present means. Is it possible to send us assistance? The town was raked yesterday by the enemys artillery from commanding heights across the river. This we cannot prevent. Very slight damage." Before Cooper could reply, he received a message from Johnston in Morton, Mississippi, forwarding Bragg's earlier request. Mired in a controversy over the loss of Vicksburg, Johnston was unwilling to assist Bragg without specific authorization from Richmond, asking, "Shall I help him?" A similar message soon followed: "General Bragg telegraphs that he will probably need help, as the enemy is threatening him. Should this be the case, am I authorized in sending it from this department?" Cooper's reply was succinct: "By all means help General Bragg as far as you are able to do so." Believing that Johnston had relinquished command temporarily, Jefferson Davis telegraphed Hardee, asking if he could assist Bragg. Hardee was in Demopolis, Alabama, organizing part of the paroled Vicksburg garrison. He immediately forwarded Davis's query to Johnston for decision. Davis also telegraphed Bragg, "Have you batteries on the commanding heights? Can you attack one of the enemy's columns by a combination of the main body of both yours so as to fight him in detail?" The president's comments offered no solution to Bragg's problems, but better news soon arrived from Johnston, who wired Bragg that he would be sending two divisions by rail. The divisions would move without wagons, which expedited the transfer but would further exacerbate Bragg's transportation difficulties. Nevertheless, the two divisions, which represented half of Johnston's infantry strength, would be a significant addition to Bragg's army, if they could arrive before the Federal army advanced.[27]

The only information reaching Bragg that morning was a report from Blythe's Ferry that Federal cavalry had appeared upstream at Washington and Smith's Cross Roads on the previous day. Thus Rosecrans's forces were widely scattered across his front. In an effort to begin a dialogue with his newest corps commander, Bragg had Chief of Staff Mackall write to Harvey Hill. According to Mackall's note, Bragg proposed "to await developments of the enemy and when his point of attack is ascertained, to neglect all smaller affairs and fall on him with our whole force." Hill must have responded, in a message no longer extant, because later in the day Bragg wrote, "You and Gen. Cleburne both agree with my views and intentions. We must strike with our whole power as soon as the opportunity offers." Without further indication of Federal intentions, Bragg was content to await developments. In the meantime, he acted to preserve the army's assets. Because the hospital complex on Academy Hill had been struck, medical personnel began to evacuate patients to locations farther south on the Western & Atlantic Railroad. Similarly, the removal of military supplies from riverfront warehouses also commenced. After nightfall, engineers began to remove the army's pontoons from the river before Federal gunners could destroy them. The previous day's panic among the citizenry had not dissipated, and a growing procession of refugees left town for safer locales. Some even rented freight cars to haul away their possessions. Among those leaving were Leonidas Polk's wife, Frances, and her two daughters. The remaining citizens rushed to gather extra stocks of food and other necessary items as more and more businesses closed their doors. Chattanooga's own newspaper, the *Daily Rebel*, remained defiantly in place at its Market Street office, although publisher Franc Paul nervously sought a way to evacuate his printing plant from the town. The resumption of the Federal bombardment late in the day accelerated the exodus from Chattanooga by those who had no duty to remain.[28]

An object lesson in the price of disobedience occurred during the afternoon when garrison commander John Jackson conducted a military execution. The condemned man was 1st Lt. William White, twenty-three, of the Fourth (ultimately Twelfth) Georgia Cavalry regiment. During the months of May and June 1863, he had encouraged several soldiers to desert, and on 14 June he deserted his post while on picket. He had then gone to Nashville and met with Federal officers, including Robert Granger of the Reserve Corps. He had then agreed to serve as a recruiting officer for the Federals in the territory just north of the Tennessee River near Jasper. During a sweep of the locality in mid-July by a raiding party from the Forty-First Mississippi Infantry regiment, White was captured. He eventually admitted all to his captors after being identified by local citizens and fully expected to be treated harshly. White was taken to Chattanooga, arraigned, and tried by military court. The charges were advising desertion, persuading soldiers to desert, quitting his guard, disobedience of a lawful order, and holding correspondence with the enemy. White pleaded not guilty, but the court convicted him on all charges and specifications, sentencing him to death by hanging. Bragg approved the sentence, to be applied between 10:00 A.M. and 2:00 P.M. on 22 August. A newspaper correspondent from the *Augusta Chronicle* witnessed the execution and admired White's exceptional composure during the ordeal. Unfortunately, the hangman did not do his work well. As the correspondent reported, "The Rope failed to break his neck, and he died very hard — struggling for three or four minutes. It was a horrid sight." White was not the first Army of Tennessee soldier to be executed in Chattanooga, nor would he be the last.[29]

As Lieutenant White was meeting his end, thousands of soldiers in the Army of Tennessee prepared for action. In Polk's Corps, Cheatham assumed responsibility for guarding the Chattanooga Creek railroad bridge, relieving Hindman's troops. In exchange, detachments from Hindman's Division relieved Cheatham's men guarding railroad bridges west of Lookout Mountain. When the rearguard Forty-First Mississippi Infantry regiment rejoined Anderson's Brigade at Wauhatchie, Hindman's Division was at last complete. At Atlanta, Walthall's Brigade, now assigned to Liddell's new reserve formation, prepared to return to Chattanooga. Unwilling to go, at least fifty men deserted. In the brigade's Twenty-Fourth Mississippi Infantry regiment, men planning a grand military ball in Atlanta saw their hopes dashed as trains arrived to transport them to the front. In Harvey Hill's sector Federal activity was minimal. At Blythe's Ferry, the Thirty-Second/Forty-Fifth Mississippi Infantry regiment saw only a few of Minty's horsemen. Downstream at Harrison's Ferry, the Thirty-Third Alabama Infantry regiment withstood a brief desultory bombardment but nothing more. Weary from their rapid march to Harrison on the previous day, Deshler's and Polk's commands remained in camp. Henry Clayton spent most of the day inspecting the defenses at Blythe's and Doughty's Ferries. He also seized a small steamboat and diverted it into the Hiwassee River. Concerned about what might be lurking upstream from Blythe's Ferry, Clayton attempted to establish contact with Forrest's cavalry by sending an infantry company beyond the unbridged Hiwassee River. Nowhere in his reports to Stewart and Hill did Clayton mention Sterling Wood, whose troops were already manning the river defenses from Blythe's Ferry southward. Wood outranked Clayton by fifteen months, but Hill had placed Clayton in charge along the river, under the general supervision of Cleburne. For some reason, Wood was momentarily not in the chain of command.[30]

As darkness fell in the Tennessee River valley, disturbing information reached the troops at each end of Bragg's attenuated line. On the right, a message addressed to Wood from Col. Samuel Adams at Harrison's Ferry reached Cleburne's headquarters at Harrison. Cleburne was scouting along the river, and Wood was nowhere to be found, so Capt. Irving Buck of Cleburne's staff forwarded the message to Hill. Adams reported that during a flag of truce exchange an officer had learned that the Federals were planning to cross the river in force that night. In response, Hill ordered Stewart to send Brown's Brigade to Sivley's Ford, the site mentioned by Colonel Adams. Stewart at 8:00 P.M.

instructed Brown to move to the river, at the same time warning Bate to prepare to join Brown. While Brown's men stumbled in the darkness toward Sivley's Ford, Bate's soldiers continued their camp meeting, with Rev. Benjamin Palmer as the featured speaker. Hill also wrote to Clayton at Birchwood, implying that Clayton's main focus should be the countryside beyond the Hiwassee, an implication new to Clayton. Clearly, Hill's command of the river line defenses showed some serious deficiencies on 22 August. The absence of Wood and Cleburne forced Hill to feed elements of Stewart's Division into the defensive mix piecemeal. Clayton's role and his authority were especially ambiguous. Fortunately, no Federal crossing materialized. The same could not be said at the other end of Bragg's line. There, at Shell Mound, a very small number of Federal troops had indeed crossed the river and were burning a railroad bridge. Elements of the Third Confederate Cavalry regiment reported the incursion to guards at the Running Water Creek railroad bridge. From there, the telegraph carried the news to Hindman at Wauhatchie, who sent the report to Polk in Chattanooga around midnight. With so few troops immediately available, so many mountains intervening, and no clear picture of the extent of the Federal incursion, there was nothing for Bragg's headquarters to do before dawn.[31]

In Knoxville, Simon Buckner continued the gradual evacuation of his department on 22 August. He had been abandoned by senior officers at Fort Donelson and had no desire to find himself in that position again. Therefore, even though no Federal soldier had yet penetrated the mountains in his front, Buckner was ready to abandon both Knoxville and its vital railroad connections. Having decided to concentrate his mobile forces nearer the Army of Tennessee, he needed only to establish the point of concentration. When Forrest informed him of Federal movements downstream near Washington, Buckner decided that Kingston should be his destination. Notifying Mackall, he explained that he was gathering Preston's command at Knoxville and removing all infantry from Big Creek Gap. Like Bragg's, Buckner's field transportation was inadequate, and he begged Mackall for any spare wagons. During the afternoon, he informed Forrest that he had ordered Pegram's Brigade from Winters Gap to join Forrest at Kingston. He further reported that his infantry was moving to Kingston and would travel at least ten miles in that direction by nightfall. In support of Buckner's decision, Gracie's Brigade changed its destination from Clinton to Kingston while on the march, halting for the night at Campbell's Station. At least one battery of the Ninth Georgia Artillery battalion also joined the exodus from Knoxville. Elsewhere, the Fifty-Eighth North Carolina Infantry regiment withdrew from Big Creek Gap and the Fifth Kentucky Infantry regiment took a train from Abingdon for Knoxville. Buckner told Alfred Jackson, whose small command guarded the railroad link to Virginia, to hold his positions as long as possible, and then either withdraw toward Abingdon,

Virginia, or into the North Carolina mountains. Realizing that Jackson's instructions might sound defeatist, Buckner described them as only temporary expedients: "That you may understand fully, I will say there is no purpose of evacuating East Tennessee, but on the contrary it is proposed to defend it to the last."[32]

....

On Sunday, 23 August, the portion of Wilder's command facing Chattanooga remained out of sight and the Eighteenth Indiana Battery did not return to Stringer's Ridge. Wilder's inaction was purely a function of his growing logistical problems. His brigade had left Cowan with only six days of rations and, even though foraging had been productive, items like sugar and coffee were now in short supply. Further, the expectation that he could draw supplies from Tracy City was proving problematic. Adding to the difficulty was the length of his supply line. Wilder had left his wagons at Therman when he had crossed Walden's Ridge. Beyond Therman he relied on a train of pack mules with limited carrying capacity. Thus his supply line ran, in the best of circumstances, from Tracy City across the Cumberland Plateau on a narrow wagon road that descended steeply into the Sequatchie Valley at Therman. There the supplies had to be transferred to pack mules, taken up the western slope of Walden's Ridge on the old Anderson Road, then brought down the eastern face of the ridge to Wilder's camp at its foot. If there were no supplies at Tracy City, Wilder's quartermaster and commissary officers had to descend the mountain to Cowan and draw their food and forage there. According to Wilder, commissary officers at Cowan previously had been unwilling to provide more than minimal rations for his brigade. The lack of a fully stocked depot at Tracy City was clearly beginning to affect operations. Compounding the problem was the fact that Lilly had expended over 300 rounds in two days of firing, a quarter of his basic load. To acquire rations, Wilder returned his pack train to Therman; to solve the ammunition shortage, he requisitioned 200 rounds of percussion shell, 200 rounds of fuse shell, and 1,000 friction primers for his guns. If the ordnance department could get the ammunition to Tracy City, Wilder stated that his men would move it the remainder of the way to the front. Pending resolution of his supply problems, he postponed further offensive action.[33]

At Smith's Cross Roads, Minty's scouts returned at 3:00 A.M. on 23 August with the disturbing news that Confederates were crossing the river at Blythe's Ferry and downstream at the mouth of Sale Creek. If true, the Sale Creek force would interpose between Minty and Hazen at Poe's Tavern, seventeen miles to the south. If Minty did not act immediately, the Sale Creek force, the Blythe's Ferry force, and Dibrell's men would pin his small command against Walden's Ridge and destroy it. In a brief note to Van Cleve, Minty explained that he was leaving for Poe's Tavern at once. As Minty galloped southward, his courier reached Pikeville a little after 8:00 A.M. Alarmed that Minty was uncovering his front, Van Cleve dispatched Minty's note to Twenty-First Corps headquarters at Dunlap. Crittenden, who had worried about the security of his corps for several days, demanded to know if Van Cleve had authorized Minty's precipitous withdrawal. He stated unequivocally that Minty had acted "imprudently" and that he must either return to his old position or withdraw to Pikeville. Crittenden did not want Van Cleve's two brigades at Pikeville to lack a cavalry screen, and Minty's handful of horsemen represented all the mounted troops available. Denying that he had ordered Minty's retreat, Van Cleve forwarded the corps commander's instructions to the cavalryman. Minty meanwhile was hastening to get his brigade south of Sale Creek. Reaching that point, he found no Confederates at all, and must have realized that he had panicked unnecessarily. Soon he encountered Funkhouser's Ninety-Second and Ninety-Eighth Illinois Mounted Infantry regiments. They had been sent upstream by Hazen, who was responding to deserters' reports of rapid Confederate troop movements beyond the river. After calming the rattled Minty, Funkhouser returned to Poe's Tavern. The entire incident was troubling, especially to Crittenden, who told Rosecrans, "I am much annoyed at this movement of Minty's, as I deem it of the utmost importance that he should be with Van Cleve."[34]

At Stevenson, Rosecrans spent the morning pushing his staff to resolve several issues impeding the army's preparations. Garfield was still too weak to sit up for more than three hours at a time, so the remainder of the staff bore the brunt of Rosecrans's manic style of management. A prime concern was the slow arrival of pontoons. On the previous day Innes had complained that he could ship no more pontoons by rail until cars were unloaded and returned. Unwilling to accept blame, both Goddard and Bond alleged that Innes had not told anyone that the pontoons had reached the front. In addition, Innes was instructed to provide more locomotives for the line to Tracy City. Indeed, the Tracy City supply bottleneck caused others to receive chiding messages from the staff as well. Chief commissary Samuel Simmons was queried about the inadequate stocks at the Tracy City depot. Crittenden's wagons waiting at Tracy City for food and forage found none there, yet Simmons had assured Rosecrans that 20,000 rations had been moved to the village. Thus Bond wanted to know the truth of the matter. The staff also continued to urge Simmons to move his office from Nashville to Stevenson, where he could more closely supervise the commissary officers at the front. In order to soften the peremptory tone of the messages, Drouillard asked Simmons to bring a supply of whiskey because "we are short and dry." Another series of instructions assigned responsibility for defense of the line to McMinnville, which remained a critical supply node because of the Tracy City failure. When the Decherd quartermaster excitedly reported a recent raid on his post that cost him three men, Goddard dismissed the seriousness of the threat. Nevertheless, he instructed Stanley to rush a battalion of the Third Ohio Cavalry regiment from Cowan to Decherd. Upon receipt of Wilder's request for artillery ammunition, Goddard told Thomas that he would send some projectiles to Tracy City as requested but suggested that they could sooner be procured from Reynolds at Jasper.[35]

While his staff worked on logistical issues, Rosecrans concentrated on selecting the army's specific crossing points. He had already visited the sites near Stevenson and had been told by Lt. George Burroughs, one of the army's engineers, that Caperton's Ferry was the best of the lot. He had also surveyed sites downstream from Bridgeport, and had briefly been under fire for his pains. The only site that met his approval in that sector was Bridgeport itself. Seizure of the vicinity would both provide a crossing site and protection for the railroad construction crews. Two infantry brigades of Sheridan's division were at Bridgeport, supported by Daniel Ray's Second Tennessee (Union) Cavalry regiment. The bulk of Rosecrans's cavalry guarded the army's right flank below Stevenson, but the Second Brigade of Crook's Second Cavalry Division had just reached Stevenson and was available for assignment. Rosecrans sent it to guard the river from Bridgeport downstream to Cedar Bluff Ford (Cox's Ferry), near Stevenson. He sent Ray's Tennesseans to assist Reynolds's troops covering the river upriver to Shell Mound. With Caperton's Ferry and Bridgeport tentatively selected as crossing points, Rosecrans needed additional locations to expedite the army's passage over the river. Therefore, he called again for the dummy to take him to Bridgeport. With McCook and Stanley as traveling companions, Rosecrans toured the country northward along the river. He rode as far north as the camp of the Seventy-Fifth Indiana Infantry regiment, which had raided Shell Mound on the previous night. As usual, Rosecrans paused and chatted amiably with the soldiers, who offered to share their evening meal with him. Declining their offer, Rosecrans returned to Bridgeport and the waiting dummy. He had not finished his examination of the area but had begun to form some idea of its suitability for additional crossing sites. Upon his return to Stevenson, Rosecrans instructed Thomas to improve the fords on Battle Creek, build a floating bridge across the same stream, and begin building flatboats at Jasper.[36]

Around the army 23 August was a quiet Sunday. In the Fourteenth Corps, the First Division welcomed Absalom Baird, who replaced acting commander John Starkweather. In the Second Division, many soldiers attended religious services and endured the usual dress parade and inspection in the 90 degree heat. At Battle Creek, Third Division soldiers built arbors for shade or climbed the nearby mountain for a panoramic view of the river valley. At Jasper, Reynolds informed Thomas that he had destroyed the Shell Mound railroad bridge, unaware that even then Thomas was sending him instructions not to do so. His soldiers settled into camp around Jasper, described by Surgeon Josiah Cotton of the Ninety-Second Ohio Infantry regiment as "the most dilapidated town I ever saw." In McCook's Twentieth Corps, First Division soldiers passed the time swatting bugs and trying to keep cool in their sweltering camps along Crow and Mud Creeks. The Second Division continued to dismantle buildings and appropriate unclaimed items at the deserted village of Bellefonte. Meanwhile, Col. Hiram Strong of the Ninety-Third Ohio Infantry regiment successfully tested the unofficial truce that prevailed with the Third Confederate Cavalry's pickets. At Stevenson, some Pioneer Brigade men unloaded pontoons while others stood inspection, attended preaching, or visited the sutler for twenty-five cent pints of beer. In the Twenty-First Corps sector, the *Paint Rock* expedition straggled back to camp without success, while the remainder of the First Division attended religious services or listlessly whiled away the day in its tents. At Dunlap, Second Division soldiers spent their time relaxing in camp and writing letters home. Crittenden attended the service conducted by the chaplain of the Thirty-First Indiana Infantry regiment. At Pikeville, the men of the Third Division, short of rations, were rescued by citizens offering to trade fruit for coffee, sugar, and salt. On the army's right flank, the First Cavalry Division stood guard on the weed-choked Memphis & Charleston Railroad all the way to Huntsville. In the rear, Daniel McCook's Reserve Corps brigade reached Spring Hill on its march to the front.[37]

When Rosecrans returned to Stevenson, he found a message from Crittenden, as well as reports from Wagner and Palmer of their operations on Walden's Ridge. Coupled with messages from Wilder, the reports gave Rosecrans a good understanding of the recent activities of the deception force. Believing that Innes and Simmons had solved the difficulties of getting supplies to Tracy City, he instructed Crittenden to use that depot for his sustenance. Rosecrans agreed that Minty's behavior that morning was puzzling, but he was unwilling to censure Minty and did not worry about a Confederate attack in that quarter. Indeed, Rosecrans believed that Burnside's advance would adequately cover his left flank in just a few days. He projected that Burnside would reach Jamestown, Tennessee, in forty-eight hours, and Jamestown was only sixty-five miles from Pikeville. Crittenden should have Van Cleve try to connect with Burnside, although Minty's small command could hardly do that and simultaneously demonstrate on the river. Having assured Crittenden that all would be well, Rosecrans composed his daily report to the War Department. This time he addressed the report to Henry Halleck himself. In his summary Rosecrans placed great emphasis on the workings of the deception plan. He noted the occupation of Poe's Tavern and again highlighted Wilder's bombardment of Chattanooga. Rosecrans's operations had forced the Confederates to spread their defenses from Washington in the north to Shell Mound in the south. The pontoons for crossing the river were being gathered, assembled, and otherwise prepared for the coming advance. In other words, Rosecrans was making legitimate progress and the next phase of the campaign would soon begin. He closed by repeating Wilder's statement that a large number of locomotives were being towed out of Chattanooga. To Rosecrans, that fact alone bespoke the disarray in the enemy camp: "I think they are a little confused."[38]

In Chattanooga, Bragg did not consider himself confused. The bombardment of the previous two days and the inability of his artillery to respond proved to Bragg that Chattanooga itself was too vulnerable to serve as a base. Responding Davis's telegram suggesting artillery locations, Bragg replied, "We have our batteries in all suitable positions but cannot save this town." Thus, it was time to remove everything valuable, a process that had already begun. In midmorning, Bragg abandoned his offices at the Brabson residence on Fifth Street and moved to the home of Ely Bruce on Montgomery Avenue (now Main Street), a mile from downtown. It was also moving day for the army's four hospitals: the Academy, Gilmer, Foard, and Camp Direction. After consultation with Medical Director Edward Flewellen, and the Chattanooga garrison commander, Surgeon Dudley Saunders, in charge of the Chattanooga hospitals, decided to evacuate them to Marietta, Georgia. Patients at the Foard Hospital left during the morning, but the convalescents at the Academy and Gilmer Hospitals remained a while longer to dismantle the hospital furniture and prepare it for shipment south. Initially, Camp Direction was to be part of the evacuation, but after everything was packed, Bragg ordered Saunders to reestablish it at Chickamauga Station with items from those hospitals leaving town. Camp Direction thus would remain open for a while longer, with a capacity of only 300 patients. The controlled chaos in the hospital department was replicated elsewhere in Chattanooga, as quartermasters and commissaries hastened to move their matériel to safer locations. Likewise, the post office and the telegraph office moved into temporary quarters in the suburbs beyond the range of the Federal guns. Finally, the outflow of private citizens continued as well, leaving the town to its military garrison. The *Chattanooga Daily Rebel* remained in its office on Market Street, although owner Franc Paul continued to seek a way to save his newspaper by removing it from town.[39]

Throughout the day, all attempts to learn more of the Federal intentions were futile. While the disappearance of Lilly's guns measurably facilitated the removal of military items from town, the absence of the enemy did not mean that Bragg's army remained supine. Given the Federal activity around Shell Mound, Bragg decided to destroy the 780-foot covered railroad bridge spanning Running Water Creek near Whiteside. The task fell to Company B, Third Confederate Engineer regiment, covered by part of Anderson's Brigade. The engineers destroyed the bridge, set the wreckage ablaze at 10 A.M., and returned to Wauhatchie. There they found Hindman's Division under orders to return to the east side of Lookout Mountain. The division moved at 5:00 P.M. and continued during the night, leaving the Twenty-Eighth Alabama Infantry regiment of Manigault's Brigade to block the narrow road over the lower slopes of the mountain. In Hill's Corps troops were also active. Lucius Polk's Brigade of Cleburne's Division left its temporary bivouac at Harrison and marched upriver several miles to the vicinity of Thatcher's and Campbell's (Gardenhire's) Ferries, where it occupied a new position on the river. In Stewart's Division, Brown's Brigade reached Sivley's Ford well before daylight. While his men slept, Brown explored his surroundings. Finding no fortifications in place, he requested an engineer to lay out some works but was told that the only available engineer had gone to Blythe's Ferry, at the other end of the corps line. Meanwhile, Bate's Brigade continued its revival services at Tyner's Station, with Reverend Palmer again the featured speaker. Scheduled to last all day, the afternoon services were canceled when orders arrived for the brigade to break camp. In late afternoon Bate's Brigade marched five miles to Boyce Station, on the Western & Atlantic Railroad near a bridge over South Chickamauga Creek. There, Bate would be within supporting distance of Brown's position at Sivley's Ford. Finally, Walthall's Brigade arrived at Chickamauga Station from Atlanta to become part of Liddell's Division.[40]

Bragg's actions materially changed the Army of Tennessee's center of gravity. The destruction of the Running Water Creek bridge signaled that he was conceding the mountainous terrain west of Chattanooga to the Federals. The withdrawal of Hindman's Division east of Lookout Mountain centered Polk's Corps more compactly on Chattanooga. Most of Cheatham's five brigades were either in town or nearby. At least two brigade commanders, Smith and Maney, were absent. Hindman's three brigades were immediately on Cheatham's left, at the eastern foot of Lookout Mountain. Hill's Corps, which had previously occupied camps around Tyner's Station, Chickamauga Station, and Graysville, now had moved to the Tennessee River to increase troop density there. In Cleburne's Division, Wood's and Polk's Brigade manned the river defenses as far north as Blythe's Ferry, while Deshler's Brigade remained in reserve at the village of Harrison. Several of Cleburne's brigade commanders were also absent or indisposed, notably Lucius Polk and Sterling Wood. Stewart's Division had Clayton's Brigade at Birchwood and Brown's Brigade at Sivley's Ford, with Bate's Brigade nearby at Boyce Station. Stewart's fourth brigade, Johnson's, had long been absent at Loudon, guarding the railroad to Knoxville. Forced out of Chattanooga, the army's supply depot was reconstituted at Chickamauga Station on the Western & Atlantic Railroad. There it was guarded by Liddell's newly formed Reserve Division of two brigades. In sum,

Running Water Creek trestle after 1864 reconstruction. (National Archives)

Rosecrans's deception activities had caused Bragg to contract his line downstream of Chattanooga and significantly strengthen it upstream. The Federal gambit also exposed fractures within Hill's Corps, with Hill scrambling command relationships by introducing Clayton's Brigade into Cleburne's sector with an ambiguous charter. Hill's initial response to the crisis clearly indicated that he had not yet mastered the intricacies of corps command in a new and different theater of war.[41]

In Knoxville, Buckner's evacuation of his department continued on 23 August. That day Adjutant General Cooper notified Buckner that there would be no assistance forthcoming from Samuel Jones's adjacent department. Jones, whose primary mission was to safeguard the salt-making facilities at Saltville, Virginia, thought it imprudent to reduce his garrison to assist Buckner, and Cooper chose not to overrule him. Buckner therefore once more telegraphed Mackall in Chattanooga. He reported that Burnside would probably advance via Jamestown, Tennessee, in cooperation with Rosecrans's army. Without revealing the source of his information, Buckner boldly stated that Rosecrans would cross the Tennessee River north of the Hiwassee. Burnside was too strong for Buckner to oppose alone, but if Buckner and Bragg united before Burnside and Rosecrans did, a Confederate victory might be gained over Rosecrans. In fact, if events developed as Buckner expected, his command would represent the right of the Army of Tennessee. He noted in closing that the gathering of his mobile force was almost complete. Indeed, such was the case. On that day, Gracie's Brigade advanced a few more miles on the road to Kingston, while most of Trigg's Brigade marched from Knoxville to occupy Gracie's old camps near Campbell's Station. Scattered regiments, like the Fifty-Eighth North Carolina Infantry at Jacksboro and the Fifty-Fourth Virginia Infantry at Bell's Bridge, also converged on Knoxville to join the units momentarily pausing around Campbell's Station. Additional batteries of the Ninth Georgia Artillery battalion departed Knoxville and took the road to Kingston as well. Behind them, in circumstances that mirrored events at Chattanooga, quartermasters struggled to evacuate military supplies from the city. Still in Knoxville, Buckner met with William Preston and offered him command of the mobile force at Campbell's Station. Preston previously had only led a brigade, but Buckner expected the mobile force to number 8,000 troops, and that would require a division commander.[42]

Buckner had many reasons to nominate Preston to division command. A product of the Kentucky gentry, Preston, forty-six, not only shared Buckner's Kentucky heritage and worldview, but he was extraordinarily well connected. Obtaining a law degree from Harvard College in 1838, he built a prosperous practice in Louisville until the outbreak of the Mexican-American War. Although unexceptional, his war service smoothed Preston's entry into politics. Elected first to the Kentucky legislature, then to the U.S. Congress, in 1858 he was selected by James Buchanan to be the American ambassador to Spain. Like many other Kentuckians of his class, Preston chose to serve the Confederacy in 1861. His eldest sister had been Albert Sidney Johnston's first wife, facilitating his appointment as Johnston's aide with the rank of colonel. Promotion to brigadier general followed, dating from 14 April 1862. A few days later Sidney Johnston's son, William Preston Johnston, a frequent visitor in the Preston home, joined Jefferson Davis's military staff as an aide. Preston commanded a brigade during the Army of Tennessee's retreat from Corinth, and there began his criticism of Bragg. Thereafter, he served briefly in the division of John Breckinridge, a distant cousin. Detached with Kirby Smith during the Kentucky campaign, Preston once more commanded a brigade in Breckinridge's Division at Stones River. He performed gallantly during Breckinridge's disastrous attack on 2 January but thereafter became heavily embroiled in the controversies wracking Bragg's army. Even William Preston Johnston, his nephew in Richmond, noted that "Uncle William" was a ringleader in the opposition to Bragg. His high profile in the anti-Bragg camp contributed to his transfer to southwestern Virginia in late April. Not long afterward, his old brigade departed for Mississippi. Banished to one of the war's backwaters, Preston saw Buckner's offer of division command as the rescue of a declining career.[43]

Not only was Preston rejoining Bragg's army but so was Breckinridge. True to his promise to both Davis and Bragg, Joseph Johnston on 23 August began to transfer two of his four divisions in Mississippi to Chattanooga. Johnston selected Breckinridge's Division, consisting of the brigades of Daniel Adams, Benjamin Helm, and Marcellus Stovall, and three brigades of Walker's Division, commanded by Matthew Ector, States Gist, and Claudius Wilson. For the moment, John Gregg's Brigade of Walker's Division would remain in Mississippi. As of 20 August, Breckinridge's Division had an aggregate present strength of 5,797 officers and men. The aggregate present strength of Walker's four brigades was 8,812 officers and men, so the contingent going to Tennessee could not have been less than 6,000 troops and was probably somewhat larger. Johnston was giving Bragg six of his eleven infantry brigades, although Breckinridge's Division had been part of the Army of Tennessee until loaned to Johnston in May. Given that Bragg's aggregate present infantry and artillery strength on 20 August was only 39,486 officers and men, the nearly 12,000 troops sent by Johnston represented a large reinforcement. The preferred route of travel, however, was long, approximately 700 miles via Mobile. It involved seven railroad companies, two gauge changes, and a ferry trip across Mobile Bay. Johnston had promised that troops would begin to leave Morton, Mississippi, on the afternoon of 23 August, but the first detachment, from Walker's Division, did not depart for Chattanooga until well after dark. He expected the transfer to take at least five days. On the same day, Claudius Wilson, one of Walker's brigadiers, agreed with Johnston's estimate, writing to his wife, Kate, "But I must bring this letter to a close and go to packing up. I did not start with the intention of writing a letter but only a note to inform you of our change of base. I expect to be in Atlanta about the 28th and expect to meet a letter from you there."[44]

Although they had no idea how events would unfold, the soldiers of both armies could clearly see that a major campaign was about to open. On Sunday, 23 August, many men took the opportunity to express their emotions in letters home. Cheered by successes in other theaters, the men of Rosecrans's army were confident of ultimate victory. Thus Lt. Augustus Carpenter of the Nineteenth United States Infantry regiment told his parents, "A month hence if I mistake not will tell a tale. Whether it be for weal or woe time will show. I think by that time no armed force of rebels will prowl around this department and perhaps many of us will fall in fierce engagements which must inevitably follow." Still, the sacrifice would be worth the price. Another junior officer, Lt. Montraville Reeves of the Seventy-Ninth Illinois Infantry regiment, made his resolve clear when he wrote to his brother, "I think I would be willing to serve and if nessesary sacrifise my life on the soil of the Southern States to shield the soil of Illinois from the dreded tramp of an army." Bragg's men wrote in similar vein. From the camp of the Eighth Texas Cavalry in Rome, Georgia, Lt. Frank Batchelor told his wife that his unit did not fear the coming battle: "The Confidence of our Army is still unshaken in Genl Bragg—and with equal chances we are not afraid to see him measure length with Genl Rosecrans or any one else from Yankeedom." Far less sanguine was Cpl. Ezekiah Rorie of the Thirty-Second Mississippi Infantry regiment. Rorie only recently had seen a "wild Yank" for the first time, but he expected to see many more soon and wanted to prepare his family for what might happen: "Dear Mother if it is the Lord's will that I should fall in this battle I beg of you to bear it without misgivings reclicking [recollecting] that many a neighboring mother have borne the same and that your lot is not harder than others. . . . You dear mother will console and sympathize with my wife and little ones and my brothers and sisters will do the same reminding them that they once had a father that loved them dearer than his life."[45]

11

Final Preparations

» 24–27 August 1863 «

On Monday, 24 August, Rosecrans began the final week of campaign preparations with an attempt to resolve a major logistical issue. A shortage of railroad equipment had developed as a result of Rosecrans's expedited accumulation of supplies at the Stevenson railhead. For some time staff officers had been canvassing the army's rear and adjacent commands for additional boxcars, but now the need was for additional locomotives. The obvious source of relief was Grant's Department of the Tennessee, which used river transportation primarily and was not then involved in an active campaign. On 24 August Rosecrans authorized Goddard to query Grant in hopes of securing at least five or six engines. At the same time Goddard wrote to Capt. Charles Parsons, Grant's St. Louis quartermaster, also asking for locomotives. Grant had both locomotives and cars to spare, writing to Parsons on 10 August that he controlled "about one hundred locomotives and fifteen hundred cars of all classes." Grant was willing to share his surplus but circumstances conspired to prevent Rosecrans from profiting from Grant's generosity. Parsons had no spare locomotives at St. Louis, and Rosecrans's message apparently did not reach Grant's Vicksburg headquarters until 2 September. By that time Grant had gone to New Orleans, where his horse fell on him, severely injuring his thigh. In Grant's absence, the request would bounce from desk to desk among staff officers until 10 September, when Grant's railroad superintendent admitted that he could indeed spare six locomotives if ordered to do so. Grant would not return to Vicksburg until 16 September and even then remained in great pain. Rosecrans's request thus received no action for more than three weeks, far too late to bring relief to the hard-pressed William Innes. Relations between Grant and Rosecrans had long been cool at best, but in this instance more mundane factors seem to explain Grant's failure to assist a fellow department commander in a timely manner.[1]

Other problems facing Rosecrans on 24 August were equally vexing but more susceptible to solution. Supply of Twenty-First Corps units in the Sequatchie Valley continued to be difficult, causing Rosecrans to write to chief commissary Samuel Simmons about the issue once more. This time the problem was at McMinnville, where Crittenden had reported only partially filled requisitions, even though Simmons claimed warehouses there contained 200,000 rations. Previously, Tracy City had been the problem, but now Wood was instructed to draw his supplies from that source instead of McMinnville. Only the easy availability of forage and the friendliness of the Sequatchie inhabitants was keeping Twenty-First Corps units adequately supplied. Crittenden's corps also came to Rosecrans's attention in another context. Rosecrans had finally learned of Minty's ignominious flight from Smith's Cross Roads and was displeased not only with Minty but also with Crittenden, Minty's supervisor. To stiffen Crittenden's resolve, Rosecrans instructed Captain Drouillard to reiterate to the corps commander that he alone would be held responsible for Minty's accomplishing his mission. Crittenden should not worry, because Burnside's small army was approaching and would soon make contact with his troops at Pikeville or Smith's Cross Roads. He also authorized Crittenden to draw some supplies from Bridgeport, if McMinnville proved inadequate as a depot. In a separate message, Drouillard instructed Crittenden to open communication with Reynolds, whose two brigades lay at the mouth of the Sequatchie Valley near Jasper. With the construction of a good bridge over Battle Creek, an easy supply route from Bridgeport all the way through Jasper to Pikeville would become a reality. The army's left thus would be tied to its center and its logistical needs met, if necessary, without recourse to either Tracy City or McMinnville.[2]

Rosecrans next looked to his right and rear, where the key commander was Gordon Granger of the Reserve Corps. On 24 August Rosecrans clarified Granger's existing orders and issued new ones. Granger already was charged with securing the Nashville & Chattanooga Railroad, but, lacking cavalry, he had to use foot soldiers for the task. Rosecrans wanted reconstruction of the railroad from Nashville to Decatur, Alabama, to continue, but not at the expense of the protection of the N&C. Granger had placed James Morgan and two of his brigades on the Decatur line, with Tillson's First Brigade stationed at Columbia and Daniel McCook's Second Brigade scattered from Columbia northward rebuilding railroad bridges. Now Rosecrans instructed him to push one of the brigades south to Athens, Alabama, with all possible haste. If a crossing of the Tennessee River was to be effected safely, Granger's Reserve Corps would have to prevent the Confederates from interfering either with the Stevenson supply base or the crossing itself. For the long term, reconstruction of the line from Nashville to Decatur was highly desirable. That route, when linked with the Memphis & Charleston Railroad from Decatur to Stevenson, and the Nashville & Chattanooga Railroad from Stevenson to Nashville, would greatly increase capacity by permitting one-way traffic to the front. Loaded trains could go directly to Stevenson and empty trains could be routed back to Nashville via Decatur. At least, that would be possible when the Decatur line was completed. At the moment, security of the N&C and the army's far right flank was paramount, and Granger's corps was spread widely to accomplish his mission. James Steedman, new commander of Granger's First Division, covered the triangle of territory between Murfreesboro, Shelbyville, and Cowan with his three brigades. Most of Morgan's Second Division was on the railroad to Decatur, while Robert Granger and his Third Division held the remainder of Middle Tennessee, including the army's Nashville base.[3]

Apparently Rosecrans had intended to return to Bridgeport and survey more potential crossing sites that day, but for some reason he did not make the trip. His brief visit to the area earlier had been insufficient to select additional crossing sites upstream from Bridgeport. In preparation for Rosecrans's return, Frank Bond issued warning orders for commanders to prepare for Rosecrans's arrival at Bridgeport. Security had been a problem a few days earlier, when Confederate pickets had fired on the general and his party. Therefore several companies of Rosecrans's escort, the Fifteenth Pennsylvania Cavalry regiment, were sent to Bridgeport. Rosecrans, however, apparently remained at his Stevenson headquarters all day immersed in minutia. He instructed Calvin Goddard to write to the post commander at Cowan: "The General Commanding directs you to assume command of the convalescents at Cowan and see that they are kept under proper discipline. Consult with the surgeon in charge and require the performance of such duty as they are able to perform." Another message from Goddard had large consequences for one soldier. Pvt. Henry McLean, nineteen, of Battery C, Second Illinois Light Artillery regiment, had been convicted of desertion in the spring, and his execution scheduled for the next day at Fort Donelson. In response to a query from Col. Arthur Smith, temporary post commander, Goddard wrote, "In the absence of Col. Lyon, you will of course carry sentence against Private McLean into execution." The appeal to Rosecrans was McLean's last hope, and he was executed by musketry on the following day. Private McLean's impending fate was not mentioned when Rosecrans made his daily report to Halleck. In it, he announced no changes in the position of his units and stated that nothing had been heard from Burnside. He closed by gratuitously asking, "Would like to know if Grant is to do anything to occupy Johnston's attention." Such a brusque query would be bound to elicit a response, whether Rosecrans meant to do so or not.[4]

Along the river 24 August was another day of activity. Wilder's ammunition shortage precluded another shelling of Chattanooga, although companies continued to scout openly along the river. Pvt. Alva Griest of the Seventy-Second Indiana Mounted Infantry regiment worried that the Confederates would discover just how few Federals were in front of the town: "If they know our numbers we would have to vamous I think." Lilly's gunners rejoiced in the arrival of a pack mule laden with sugar, coffee, and whiskey. In a report to army headquarters, Wilder correctly located the Confederate corps facing him, noting the large amount of train traffic, and the presence of many wagons in Chattanooga's streets. Upriver, Hazen sent the Ninety-Second Illinois Mounted Infantry regiment to the river's edge opposite Harrison's Ferry and again bombarded the Confederate positions. After agitating their opponents, the Federals returned to camp, visiting Igou's Ferry, upstream from Harrison's, on the way. Still farther upstream, Minty remained at Sale Creek feeling the heat of official displeasure. During the day he tried to deflect criticism by reporting that he had kept scouts at Washington and Blythe's and Doughty's Ferries since his arrival in the valley. He wrote, "I was under the impression that I was using a good deal of vigilance," and he promised to have 150 troopers at Smith's Cross Roads by nightfall. Far downstream from Chattanooga, men of King's brigade engaged Confederate cavalry pickets and continued to pound the Shell Mound railroad station into rubble. At Bridgeport, several companies of the Thirty-Sixth Illinois Infantry regiment crossed the channel to Long Island for a brief reconnaissance. When the Confederate pickets contested the move, Lytle's artillery opened on them, "causing much scatterment," in the words of Pvt. Edward Tabler of the Fifty-First Illinois Infantry regiment. Finally, from Bridgeport southward as far as the river's great bend beyond Guntersville, Stanley's Cavalry Corps guarded the river, interacting daily with Confederate pickets on the far side.[5]

In the Fourteenth Corps, Thomas reported that he had bridged Battle Creek, the Confederates had probably destroyed the Running Water Creek railroad bridge, and artillery ammunition had been dispatched to Wilder. In the First Division, gathered near Anderson Station, Absalom Baird formally assumed command. Soldiers in Negley's Second Division, camped just outside of Stevenson, noted that 103 pontoons were stockpiled in their area, with others arriving daily. In the Eleventh Michigan Infantry regiment of Stanley's Second Brigade, officers treated their men to a barrel of beer in honor of the regiment's second anniversary. Beer also flowed in Sirwell's Third Brigade, offered by the sutler of the Thirty-Seventh Indiana Infantry regiment. Lt. Robert Dilworth of the Twenty-First Ohio Infantry regiment noted with disgust that his captain, Charles Vantine, was drunk on duty. In Brannan's Third Division at Battle Creek, Medical Director Moody Tolman began to issue quinine to sick men because no whiskey was available. Pvt. Mungo Murray of the Thirty-First Ohio Infantry regiment of Connell's First Brigade wrote his sister expressing great confidence in the "ever-victorious" Rosecrans, and declaring that "this army has yet to learn defeat." Notwithstanding firing heard from both Bridgeport and Shell Mound, Sgt. Axel Reed of the Second Minnesota Infantry regiment of Van Derveer's Third Brigade swam halfway across the Tennessee River and conversed freely with Confederates on the far bank. At Jasper, in Reynolds's Fourth

Division, the men of the 105th Ohio Infantry regiment of King's Second Brigade discarded their battered forage caps for much more practical slouch hats. At Tracy City, where he remained nominally part of Turchin's Third Brigade, Col. Caleb Carlton of the Eighty-Ninth Ohio Infantry regiment unburdened himself in a letter to his wife: "I hope while we are detached to get transferred to some other Brigade and Division for I have but little respect for Reynolds and none for the 'Gallant German Marauder Turchin.'"[6]

In McCook's and Crittenden's commands, there was little for the men to do but make themselves as comfortable as possible in the hot, muggy atmosphere. Davis's First Division of the Twentieth Corps remained in its camps just west of Stevenson, where the temperature reached 94 degrees. Sidney Post, commanding the First Brigade, held a convivial dinner party in honor of the visiting wives of two officers. At Bellefonte, Johnson's Second Division continued to enjoy the excellent foraging and fishing around that abandoned town. The Thirty-Fourth Illinois Infantry regiment of Dodge's Second Brigade guarded the remaining records of Jackson County, salvaged from the wrecked courthouse. Men in the Twenty-Ninth Indiana Infantry regiment memorialized Pvt. John Grover, accidentally killed by a friend while the two wrestled with a musket. At Bridgeport, during the evening some officers of the Fifty-First Illinois Infantry regiment serenaded others with a popular new song, "When This Cruel War Is Over." At Stevenson, the Seventy-Third Illinois Infantry regiment finished storing its knapsacks in preparation for a move. In the Sequatchie Valley, Twenty-First Corps commander Crittenden continued to fret about Minty's retreat and his vexing supply situation. In Wood's First Division, the foraging remained profitable around Therman. In Wagner's Second Brigade, miscreants from the Ninety-Seventh Ohio Infantry regiment absconded with several sheep collected by the brigade's artillerymen. The two brigades of Palmer's Second Division at Dunlap were delighted to receive their first mail since leaving Manchester. Hazen's Second Brigade, meanwhile, lay in its camps around Poe's Tavern, supporting Wilder's and Minty's horsemen. Hazen himself wrote disdainfully to corps headquarters that Minty had run from a Confederate scouting party of only 100 men. At Pikeville, Van Cleve also chided Minty gently: "I trust by this time you have returned to your first position at the crossroads, and that you will be able to watch the movements of the enemy from that point."[7]

At Chattanooga, the fog obscuring the river valley eventually burned away, leaving few Federals visible on the far bank of the river. At Bragg's headquarters no new information arrived indicating what the Army of the Cumberland might do. Federals could be seen in varying numbers from Guntersville, downstream from Chattanooga, to Washington, far upstream. Shelling had occurred at Shell Mound, Chattanooga, and as far north as Harrison's Ferry. Federal soldiers were known to have made at least one brief foray across the river, at Shell Mound. The screen provided by the mountains and river made Rosecrans's intentions momentarily as opaque as the morning fog. The only significant movement seemed to be northeast of Chattanooga, where Buckner was withdrawing from Knoxville. Thus, Bragg and his staff tended to focus on Buckner's movements. As Buckner seemed to be moving south along the East Tennessee & Georgia Railroad toward Loudon, Bragg ordered Bushrod Johnson to leave Loudon when Buckner's troops arrived and move closer to Chattanooga. For Bragg, the major news on 24 August was a telegram from Joseph Johnston in Mississippi. Johnston announced that he was sending an effective force of 9,000 infantry and artillery to Chattanooga. Although Johnston claimed the movement had begun on the previous night, it would take at least four more days to get the last units started from Morton. Johnston was adamant that Bragg not consider the transfer of Breckinridge's and Walker's Divisions permanent: "This is a loan to be promptly returned." Such an attitude seemed churlish on Johnston's part because Breckinridge's command had belonged to the Army of Tennessee until loaned to Johnston several months earlier. Nevertheless, reinforcements were coming, with the Eighth Georgia Battalion of Gist's Brigade and the Thirtieth Georgia Infantry regiment of Wilson's Brigade departing Morton for Tennessee that evening.[8]

One of the division commanders leaving Mississippi was delighted to be departing. Already a controversial character, Maj. Gen. William Henry Talbot Walker, forty-six, would soon inject even more discord into the senior leadership of Bragg's command. Born into a prominent Augusta, Georgia, family in 1816, Walker was an 1837 graduate of West Point, forty-sixth in a class of fifty that included Bragg and Mackall. Slight of build, asthmatic, and academically weak, Walker nevertheless by the time of the Civil War had made a strong reputation as a combat officer. Wounded at least three times in the Second Seminole War and again severely at Molino Del Rey, "Shot Pouch" Walker seemingly lived only to fight. He had chafed during long stints on recruiting duty and other peacetime postings that had included commandant of cadets and tactics instructor at West Point. Married into a prominent Albany, New York, family, he nevertheless offered his services to the South in late 1860. Thereafter, he had floated in and out of the general officer ranks in both Confederate and Georgia state service, but each time he had resigned in a fit of pique over some perceived slight. Reinstated as a Confederate brigadier in March 1863 and posted to the District of Georgia, he and his brigade had participated in the Vicksburg campaign under Johnston. Only lightly engaged in the battle of Jackson, he nevertheless had been promoted to major general and divisional command on Johnston's strong recommendation. Widely known for his bellicosity and exaggerated sense of honor, Walker was a man of the strongest passions. Shortly after his arrival in Chattanooga, he told his eldest child to instruct her siblings, "Tell them I want them to grow up hating the Yankee nation more & more every day & I don't want any cousining or uncling any Northern kin. That is played out. This revolution has d—— the nation for ever in my eyes." Incapable of cloaking his opinions to play army politics, Walker would bring his particular brand of candor to the army at whatever level he was allowed to occupy.[9]

Walker's three brigades had only served together since June. The senior brigadier was States Rights Gist, thirty-two, a native of South Carolina. Born at the height of the Nullification Crisis, Gist was a privileged member of upcountry South Carolina society. A graduate of Harvard Law School, he rose to prominence as an attorney and militia officer by the end of the 1850s. State adjutant general in 1861, he was an aide at First Manassas. Named brigadier general in March 1862, he commanded a brigade on the Atlantic coast until May 1863, when it was called to reinforce Johnston in the Vicksburg campaign. Col. Claudius Charles Wilson, Walker's second brigade commander, was not a professional soldier. Born in Georgia in 1831, Wilson attended Emory College, then read law and quickly became a prominent attorney in Savannah. In September 1861 he was elected colonel of the Twenty-Fifth Georgia Infantry regiment. Thereafter he saw coastal duty until the spring of 1863. Traveling with Walker's Brigade to Mississippi, he rose to brigade command when Walker was promoted. A sensitive man, Wilson, thirty-one, was well liked by his men, even though, like Gist, his combat experience was minimal. In contrast, the third brigade commander, Matthew Duncan Ector, forty-one, had seen a great deal of fighting by September 1863. Born in central Georgia in 1822, Ector was an attorney and legislator in his native state until 1849. After the death of his first wife, he moved to Texas and resumed his legal and political career until 1861. Enlisting as a private in the Third Texas Cavalry regiment, he fought at Wilson's Creek and Pea Ridge. Elected colonel of the Fourteenth Texas Cavalry (Dismounted) in the spring of 1862, he led his unit at the battle of Richmond in the Kentucky campaign. Promotion to brigadier general followed in September 1862, as did brigade command in October. The unit was heavily engaged at Stones River in December. Transferred to Mississippi for the Vicksburg campaign, Ector's Brigade would now be returning to the Army of Tennessee.[10]

If Walker brought increased volatility to the army's officer corps, John Cabell Breckinridge brought malice. Born into a prominent family in Lexington, Kentucky, in 1821, Breckinridge eventually received a law degree from Transylvania University. After a brief sojourn in Iowa, he returned to Lexington and gravitated into Democratic Party politics. Late in volunteering for the Mexican War, he saw no action. Nevertheless, that limited service and a talent for oratory fueled his meteoric rise through the Kentucky state legislature and the U.S. Congress to the vice presidency in the Buchanan administration.

Elected to the Senate, he simultaneously became the presidential nominee of the Southern wing of the fractured Democratic Party. In the fall of 1861 fear of arrest drove him into the Confederacy. Commissioned brigadier general, he took command of the First Kentucky Brigade. His first action came at Shiloh, a week after an unexpected command change elevated him to command the division-sized Reserve Corps. There he led his three brigades ineptly, but his conspicuous personal courage rescued his reputation. Promoted to major general, he joined Van Dorn in Mississippi in the summer of 1862. Sent to capture Baton Rouge, he gained the town but relinquished it when naval support failed to materialize. Learning of a proposed thrust by Bragg into Kentucky, Breckinridge sought to join it. Bragg was amenable, but Breckinridge's unwillingness to go without his troops ensured that he would not arrive before the campaign ended. By now soured on all things Kentuckian, Bragg found Breckinridge's delays unsatisfactory. Thereafter, the execution of a Kentucky deserter, the anti-Bragg activities of a Breckinridge staff officer, and a questionable performance at Stones River made Breckinridge's break with Bragg irremediable. Thereafter he made common cause with Bragg's enemies until his transfer to Mississippi in May 1863 separated the two antagonists. Now Breckinridge, forty-two, would be rejoining his nemesis.[11]

Brig. Gen. Benjamin Hardin Helm, thirty-two, commanded Breckinridge's beloved Kentucky Brigade. The son of a Kentucky governor, Helm was born in Bardstown, Kentucky, in 1831. Graduating from the United States Military Academy in 1852 and commissioned in the dragoons, he resigned after a year because of poor health. Thereafter he became a practicing attorney in his native state. Spurning a commission offered by his brother-in-law, Abraham Lincoln, Helm organized and commanded the First Kentucky Cavalry regiment in 1861. Promoted to brigadier general after Shiloh, he commanded a brigade at Baton Rouge until badly injured when his horse collapsed. After a long recuperation, he took command of the Kentucky Brigade in February 1863. Breckinridge's second brigade commander was Brig. Gen. Daniel Weisiger Adams, forty-two. Born in Frankfort, Kentucky, in 1821, he grew to manhood in Mississippi, where he read law and killed a man who slighted his father. Acquitted of murder, Adams built a legal and political career in New Orleans. Joining the First Louisiana Regular Infantry regiment in early 1861, he commanded it by September. Heavily engaged at Shiloh, he assumed brigade command until a head wound cost him his left eye. Promoted to brigadier general in May 1862, he led a brigade at Perryville and again at Stones River, where he was wounded in the left arm. Upon recovery, "Old Pelican" and his Louisiana brigade followed the division to Mississippi. Breckinridge's third brigade commander was Brig. Gen. Marcellus Augustus Stovall, forty-five. Born at Sparta, Georgia, in 1818, Stovall participated in the Second Seminole War as a militiaman at the age of seventeen. Appointed to West Point in 1836, he withdrew after one year for reasons of health. Thereafter he worked as a merchant in Augusta and Rome, while maintaining strong ties to the Georgia militia. Chosen lieutenant colonel of the Third Georgia Infantry battalion in late 1861, he led that unit for more than a year in East Tennessee. Transferred to Bragg's command, Stovall's strong showing at Stones River gained him promotion to brigadier general in April 1863.[12]

The Federal lethargy, which permitted Johnston to reinforce Bragg, led to much speculation about Rosecrans's plans. Relying upon information received from Chattanooga on 24 August, the *Memphis Daily Appeal* opined that the Federal activity at Bridgeport represented Rosecrans's true intentions, while the upstream movements were only a diversion. Pvt. John Magee of Stanford's Mississippi Battery was certain that either way, Chattanooga would have to be evacuated, a sentiment shared by Bragg. Others disagreed, and indeed there was a lessening of tension in the town on 24 August. Polk ordered Maney's and Smith's Brigades of Cheatham's Division to withdraw from the waterfront to their camps behind the town. Similarly, Cheatham's pickets downstream were also withdrawn, to be replaced by Hindman's men. When Hindman asked for clarification of his duties on the river, Polk refused to act without specific approval from Bragg. Meanwhile, Hindman's three brigades completed their march over the tip of Lookout Mountain, leaving a lone regiment to guard the road into Lookout Valley. In Hill's Corps, one commander took the initiative without waiting for orders. Henry Clayton at Blythe's Ferry had already assumed command in the sector, had stopped the steamboat *Holston* from heading upstream, and was building a bridge over the Hiwassee River at Bunker Hill. Clayton's strong actions displeased the *Holston*'s captain, who escaped and resumed his journey upriver. They also displeased Cleburne, who complained to Hill about Clayton's impertinence. At Chickamauga Station, Liddell absorbed the First Louisiana Infantry regiment into his old brigade, now commanded by Col. Daniel Govan. That night, Franc Paul, publisher of the *Chattanooga Daily Rebel*, bribed a railroad engineer to move his newspaper out of town. Loading his primary press, stocks of newsprint, and most of his staff on two cars spotted behind his office on Market Street, Paul departed for Marietta. Left behind were three employees and a small press to continue reporting the news from the beleaguered town.[13]

Simon Buckner was momentarily still in Knoxville, although many of his mobile units had already begun to depart. In the faint hope that he might still get assistance from Richmond, Buckner plaintively wired Adjutant General Cooper, "Is it not possible to re-enforce me?" Probably not expecting a positive answer, he continued to abandon his former department. Originally he had planned to concentrate at Kingston, but now the village of Loudon, thirty miles southwest of Knoxville, seemed to be a better place, so he directed his troops toward that point. Loudon was the site of a massive railroad bridge on the East Tennessee & Georgia Railroad. Thus Buckner ordered Archibald Gracie, commanding the infantry gathering at Turkey Creek, to march to Loudon. There Gracie was to confer with Bushrod Johnson, whose brigade had been guarding the Loudon bridge since July. In addition to his own brigade, Gracie's force included Trigg's Brigade, which was composed mostly of Floridians. To avoid the heat of the day, Gracie's and Trigg's men began their march at dusk. Also in motion were the Fifty-Eighth North Carolina Infantry regiment and the Sixty-Fifth Georgia Infantry regiment, withdrawing from the mountain passes to the west, and the Sixty-Third Virginia Infantry regiment, coming by rail from Saltville. The Sixty-Third Virginia belonged to Samuel Jones's department, but Buckner had gained its services by promising to give Jones some dismounted cavalry. Writing to Forrest, he again offered to place Pegram's Brigade under Forrest's control. Scott's Brigade was still at Lee's Ferry on the Clinch River, guarding one of the main roads to Knoxville. Buckner instructed Pegram to cooperate with Forrest and maintain contact with Scott. Telling Pegram that Rosecrans was simply waiting at Smith's Cross Roads for Burnside to arrive before advancing on Knoxville, he promised to give Pegram divisional command. As Pegram and Scott were sworn enemies, there could only be trouble with such an arrangement, if adopted.[14]

. . . .

Early on 25 August a cold front swept across the Tennessee River valley, producing rain and falling temperatures. The previous day had been hot and muggy, but now men clutched their blankets closer as they stood around smoky fires. Unpleasant weather did not alter Rosecrans's plans for the day. By late morning, when he took the dummy to Bridgeport, the rain had stopped, but the temperature remained disagreeable. At Bridgeport, Rosecrans met several escort companies and headed upstream to survey potential crossing sites. The cavalcade proceeded first to Brannan's camps, where Rosecrans visited men of the Eighty-Seventh Indiana Infantry regiment. He then crossed Battle Creek and rode to the Shell Mound ferry, where occasional shots were exchanged every day with Confederate pickets. Stopping at the camp of the Seventy-Fifth Indiana Infantry regiment, Rosecrans and his party cautiously advanced to a position where they could view the river. After concluding that the Shell Mound area would suffice, Rosecrans and his retinue rode to Reynolds's headquarters at Jasper. While Rosecrans and Reynolds chatted, a message from Secretary of War Stanton arrived, reporting that Fort Sumter was in ruins and that the Federals were beginning to bombard Charleston itself. Elated, Rosecrans ordered Reynolds to assemble nearby regiments for an impromptu speech. According to a witness, Rosecrans declared, "Charleston! where they first fired on the American flag—where this rebellion began—I want to see it reduced to ashes—I want to see the old flag which waved over it in April '61 and which the Presidt. has carefully preserved, raised again over Fort Sumter by the hands of Gen'l. Anderson." Before leaving Jasper, Rosecrans told Reynolds to spread the glorious news to all of his units. Reynolds complied, awakening many soldiers who had spent a backbreaking day unloading supply wagons. Rosecrans meanwhile returned to Bridgeport and the waiting dummy. It was well past midnight when he arrived at Stevenson.[15]

During Rosecrans's trip to Shell Mound and Jasper, the flow of orders from army headquarters at the "Little Brick" in Stevenson slowed to a trickle. Garfield was still unwell and sent only one routine message on 25 August. Goddard, who had handled Garfield's business during his illness, ordered the Cowan commander to send forward the army's cattle herd escorted by a cavalry company. Otherwise, Goddard sent only two more messages, seeking some mess furniture lost in transit from Nashville. Drouillard wrote to Brannan, offering prefabricated trusses to rebuild the bridge over the Sequatchie River. Thoms denied Crittenden's request to bring Van Cleve's Second Brigade forward from McMinnville because loyal Tennessee units forming in the army's rear were not yet ready. Thoms also instructed Crittenden to gather all the rations he could carry, in preparation for a general advance. On the same day, Chief Quartermaster Henry Hodges answered a query from Quartermaster Gen. Montgomery Meigs. Rousseau's proposal to recruit a new mounted division had been rejected in Washington, but Stanton had agreed to mount Rousseau's existing division if the army's bureau chiefs agreed that it could be done without difficulty. Like Halleck, Meigs opposed the idea, and he had asked on 17 August if the Department of the Cumberland had enough mules to mount Rousseau's command. In office less than a week and consumed with supporting the army's impending advance, Hodges answered Meigs's request only on 25 August. He acknowledged that 5,409 mules were at the Nashville depot but indicated that he had no capacity to provide the number needed to mount a full division. Meigs had quarreled with Rosecrans before, over horses, and was unwilling to support a scheme in which he had no faith. Thus the bureaucratic tug of war continued, even as Rousseau began his return to the army. Horace Porter may have had Meigs in mind when he wrote his mother dismissively about rear echelon officers who were in "the 'not-another-man-or-another-dollar conspiracy.'"[16]

On the long riverfront, the Federals remained quiescent for yet another day. John Wilder continued to await the arrival of artillery ammunition, which finally appeared late in the day. Meanwhile his regiments facing Chattanooga continued to send parties to the river, where they traded shots with the opposing pickets. The Seventy-Second Indiana Mounted Infantry regiment scouted Friar's Island, a potential crossing site north of Chattanooga. Several deserters from the Sixteenth Tennessee Infantry regiment reported that Bragg would soon retreat from Chattanooga and that they expected a Federal crossing at Harrison's Ferry. Upstream, two companies of the Ninety-Second Illinois Mounted Infantry patrolled along the river, and a few scouts from the Ninety-Eighth Illinois Mounted Infantry regiment did the same. They all reported nothing to have changed, although there seemed to be suspicious activity among the troops at Harrison's Ferry. Like the regiments below them, John Funkhouser's Ninety-Second and Ninety-Eighth Illinois contented themselves with moving short distances to better camps or brought forward critical supplies. Hazen's infantrymen remained peacefully in camp at Poe's Tavern but remained ready to support Funkhouser if necessary. Atop Walden's Ridge, Wagner pushed his brigade back to the rim of the valley, where he monitored Confederate railroad activity in Chattanooga. Impatient to begin the advance, Wagner expressed his frustration at the slow pace of the campaign in a report to army headquarters. North of Poe's Tavern, Minty's small brigade sheepishly returned to Smith's Cross Roads from Sale Creek. That evening Minty cautiously pushed the Fourth Michigan Cavalry regiment toward the village of Washington. Even at the downstream sites of Shell Mound and Bridgeport, nothing of note occurred, with only an occasional rifle shot disturbing the peace. Thus the lull established several days earlier continued along the river dividing the two armies.[17]

As Rosecrans surveyed potential crossing sites, his soldiers waited in their camps for the order to advance. Near Stevenson, Pioneer Brigade engineers continued building the quartermaster platform at the depot and drilled on their pontoons. During the day planking was loaded aboard wagons for transport to the river, and additional men were detailed to the pontoon companies. Far in the rear, at Estill Springs, soldiers from the First Michigan Engineers and Mechanics cut and shaped heavy timbers for bridging until a rainstorm temporarily halted their work. In the Fourteenth Corps there was little activity during the day, but signs of an impending move continued to appear. In the First Division, Lt. Howard Burnham assumed command of Battery H, Fifth United States Artillery regiment, while in the Twenty-First Wisconsin Infantry regiment an officer left for home, absconding with his company's morale fund. The 104th Illinois Infantry regiment in the Second Division was detailed to cut wood to fuel the voracious engines endlessly passing their camp. Lt. Eben Sturges Jr. of Battery M, First Ohio Light Artillery regiment, spent the day studying the German language and reading newspapers. In the Twenty-First Ohio Infantry regiment, Capt. Charles Vantine was drunk for a second day, and the regiment received orders to surrender its tents, a sign of imminent movement. Increased daily roll calls in the Seventy-Eighth Pennsylvania Infantry regiment also portended a change in the unit's location. At Battle Creek, the Third Division reduced baggage, issued extra shoes, and loaded rations into wagons. Meanwhile, three men of the Second Minnesota Infantry regiment swam across the river and visited the Confederate pickets. A trickle of Confederate deserters made the crossing in the opposite direction. In the Fourth Division, although much of his day was taken up with unloading wagons, Cpl. Alanson Ryman of the Sixty-Eighth Indiana Infantry regiment still found time to send his wife some apricot seeds and his daughter a handmade ring. Everywhere, the apparent good news from Charleston boosted morale.[18]

Elsewhere in the army, men filled the time in a variety of ways as they awaited the opening of the campaign. In the Twentieth Corps, soldiers in the First Division foraged unsuccessfully for peaches, played cards, and completed paperwork, while regimental bands serenaded division commander Davis and his wife. At Bellefonte, many of the Second Division's regiments drew rations. A disturbing trend, however, was the growing sick list. Sickness was also spreading in the Third Division, especially in the two brigades at Bridgeport. Stanley's cavalrymen did not seem to suffer the same maladies as their infantry counterparts and thus were able to concentrate on preparing themselves for action. Men in the First Wisconsin Cavalry regiment at Larkinsville received a shipment of revolvers, while the Third Ohio Cavalry regiment acquired new supplies of beans, soap, and candles. In the narrow Sequatchie Valley, where nothing but mountains could be seen on all sides, the Twenty-First Corps also impatiently awaited the order to move. Except for Wagner's and Hazen's men, Crittenden's soldiers received no news of what was transpiring elsewhere in the army. Thus, First Division regiments busied themselves with mundane tasks like rigorous drills. In the Second Division, men in the First Kentucky Infantry regiment received a welcome ration of potatoes, while a detail from the Ninetieth Ohio grumbled about being assigned to road repair. With so much time on their hands, grumbling became especially rampant in the Eighty-Fourth Illinois Infantry regiment, where the men strongly disliked their brigade commander, whom they considered a petty tyrant. Division commander Palmer wrote his wife in Illinois about the old-fashioned clothes worn by the local civilians. Even deeper in the mountains, Van Cleve's two brigades had little time to comment on their surroundings, as the men were engaged in either heavy foraging or escorting supply trains crawling over the Cumberland Plateau to McMinnville.[19]

The cold front that made 25 August so disagreeable for the Federals also cast its pall over Chattanooga. Braxton Bragg was up early, summoning Hill to his headquarters for a conference. Hill received the message at 5:30 A.M. and left his own headquarters at the Chickamauga Creek bridge to ride to Bragg's office at the Bruce house on the edge of Chattanooga. While unknown, the subject of their discussion most likely involved the situation on Hill's right flank.

With Buckner sounding the alarm daily about Burnside's approach and the presence of Minty's horsemen around Smith's Cross Roads, a major collaboration between the two Federal forces was certainly possible. If such proved to be the case, Hill's command would represent Bragg's first line of defense. Because Cleburne was absent inspecting the Hiwassee River sector, Hill left Stewart in charge of the corps while he was at Bragg's. There is no indication that Polk attended the Bragg-Hill conference. At any rate, Polk was unworried about recent events. In his first letter to his wife after her departure, Polk downplayed Federal activity, writing, "It is yet doubtful what Rosecrans purposes are. I think he will do nothing hastily. For your satisfaction I may inform you that we are to be reinforced from Johnston's army. These reinforcements are now on the way, and I think will be in time for our operations without doubt. The force promised will aid us greatly and put things easy." If George Brent's diary entry for 25 August is a true indication of Bragg's thinking on that day, the army commander's focus was primarily on Buckner's situation. When a telegram arrived from Buckner describing Burnside's progress toward the gaps in the Cumberland Plateau, Bragg's concern for his right flank grew. Buckner's sources were adamant: "All speak of it as a move concerted with Rosecrans." According to Brent, Bragg surmised that a small group of Federals had already crossed the Tennessee River far upstream from Chattanooga, and he advised Buckner to concentrate his forces and cross the river into the Federal rear.[20]

Another matter of substance crossed Bragg's desk on 25 August. The Army of Tennessee's chief of subsistence, Maj. Giles Hillyer, offered a gloomy report on his department's inventory and a dire prediction for the immediate future. According to Hillyer, he had three depots of his own and could also draw upon depots at Loudon and Atlanta in times of extreme need. His projection for September was startling: "After supplying the army to August 31, inclusive, I shall have on hand in bacon, salt beef, and lard, 900,000 rations; fresh beef none; breadstuffs, 1,100,000 rations; rice and pease, 3,000,000 rations; sugar, 150,000 pounds; vinegar, 1,200,000 rations; soap, 3,000,000 rations, salt, 4,500,000 rations; molasses, 300,000 rations." Hillyer believed he had sufficient quantities of bread, rice, peas, soap, salt, and vinegar to sustain the army indefinitely. Unfortunately, Hillyer's depots had only enough bacon and beef to last until 15 September. Maj. Robert Wilson at Loudon could only provide an additional five days' supply of meat each month, while Maj. James Cummings at Atlanta reported that the needs of the Army of Northern Virginia had first priority on his limited stocks. Hillyer stated that he was trying to procure cattle in northern Alabama but expected to acquire no more than 700 head, only three days' supply. Some bacon could be found in the same area, but the Mobile commissary officer would probably reserve the bacon for the Mobile garrison. Hillyer based his projections on the army's current strength (without the augmentation from Johnston's command) and the allocation of only one-third pound of bacon per daily ration. The latter amount already was causing discontent within the army; to reduce it further would risk massive demoralization. Hillyer concluded, "Upon the whole, general, I can see no reasonable expectation to feed the army with meats beyond the last of September." In response, Bragg authorized Hillyer to seize all beef cattle in the vicinity of the army. He also forwarded Hillyer's report to Commissary Gen. Lucius Northrop, who suggested only that Bragg assume the offensive.[21]

The gloomy weather, troubling supply situation, and virtual evacuation of the town made Chattanooga an unhappy place on 25 August. All connections to the outside world, such as the post and telegraph offices, had moved to the distant suburbs days earlier. The Tennessee state records that had followed Governor Isham Harris to Chattanooga had also been removed. Yet life still flickered in the town's newspaper, the *Daily Rebel*. Although the publisher, the main press, and most of the staff had departed, the remaining employees managed to publish an abbreviated edition on 25 August. Writers Henry Watterson and Albert Roberts and printer Henry Sparks published a one-page *War Bulletin of the Rebel* on that day and remained defiant. Indeed, the *Rebel*, even its truncated form, was essentially the only remaining public institution in what the paper labeled a "war camp." In florid prose, Watterson described how the bustle of commerce had disappeared from the streets, replaced by the dash of cavalry and the rumble of artillery batteries. Still, in Watterson's view, Chattanooga could withstand the worst that Federal guns could inflict upon it: "Rack on and do your worst, Rosecranz and gang, mongrel, puppy; whelp and hound. The mountains are on fire! There are freemen in the crags. There are rifles among the pines." As for news, the *Rebel* reported that three Confederate cavalrymen watering their horses on the riverfront that morning had been killed by Federal sharpshooters. It also described how the body of a Federal officer allegedly killed on the previous day was finally removed, although Wilder's command listed no such casualty. Speculating about the future, the paper cited current rumors that Rosecrans had no intention of crossing in force at Bridgeport but intended to move northward to join Burnside advancing upon Knoxville. Perhaps reflecting the opinion of Confederate headquarters personnel, Watterson stated, "At all events, the impression prevails that if a general engagement takes place at all, it will occur in upper East Tennessee, between this point and Knoxville."[22]

Still, some Confederate units were in motion. Hindman's Division marched across Chattanooga Valley to McFarland's Spring at the western foot of Missionary Ridge. On Hill's front, men in the Thirty-Third Alabama Infantry regiment at Harrison's Ferry improved their works, while Federal sharpshooters harassed them ineffectively. Nearby, soldiers in the Seventeenth Texas Cavalry regiment went fishing after their opponents disappeared upstream. Eighty-five miles to the northeast, Gracie's and Trigg's Brigades entered Loudon after a grueling night march. There they met division commander William Preston, who arrived from Knoxville by train. Buckner remained momentarily at Knoxville, although the bulk of his staff departed for Loudon. With the departure of all other units, only the Sixty-Third Virginia Infantry regiment remained with Buckner. Hoping to coordinate cavalry movements, Forrest rode from Kingston to Loudon but was disappointed to find Buckner still in Knoxville. The arrival of most of Buckner's units at Loudon freed Johnson's Brigade to march six miles down the railroad toward Charleston. Several hundred miles to the southwest, Morton, Mississippi, saw even greater activity as more units of Walker's Division entrained on the first leg of their journey to Chattanooga. Also departing Morton were the first elements of Breckinridge's Division. With Breckinridge absent on leave, Helm supervised the division's departure. Like Walker's men, Breckinridge's Division was forbidden to bring any of its wagons. To conserve scarce railroad cars, the division's artillery horses were to be driven overland via Rome. With even regiments departing Morton piecemeal, the chaotic movement would severely test the capabilities of several railroad companies. The original plan to send everyone via Mobile would soon prove unworkable, to be supplemented by a rail-water route through Selma. The longer the Federals delayed their advance, however, the more of Johnston's men would be able to join Bragg before the great battle occurred that everyone was expecting.[23]

....

Rosecrans returned from his reconnaissance to Shell Mound and Jasper at 2:00 A.M. on Wednesday, 26 August. There he found Halleck's response to his poorly phrased question regarding potential assistance from Grant's Department of the Tennessee. While acknowledging that Burnside had been instructed to cooperate with the Army of the Cumberland, Halleck made it clear that Rosecrans would get no help from the west: "Grant's movements at present have no connection with yours." Although not explicitly acknowledged, the impact of that decision by Halleck was to free Johnston in Mississippi to send troops to reinforce Bragg if the Richmond authorities so desired. When he resumed business much later in the day, Rosecrans made no further reference to Grant's lack of movement. Given the unfriendly relationship between the two department commanders, perhaps Rosecrans had not expected much aid and was hardly disappointed. Supremely confident in his own abilities and those of his army, he had long been prepared to conduct the coming campaign on his own. Rosecrans did request Halleck to provide a replacement for St. Clair Morton, who remained absent on sick leave. With major engineering tasks ahead, Rosecrans believed Capt. William Merrill of the Topographical Engineers was too busy with his mapmaking, Lt. George Burroughs was too junior in rank and experience, and Capt. Patrick O'Connell had his hands full managing the unruly Pioneer Brigade. With the river crossing imminent, there would not be time to get a replacement for Morton to supervise that operation, so Rosecrans would have to assume that responsibility himself. As a commander with strong tendencies toward micromanagement of the smallest details, Rosecrans was certainly comfortable with that situation. Nevertheless, appointment of a chief engineer with appropriate rank and experience would materially assist an army commander engaged in active operations in the enemy's country.[24]

A welcome augmentation to the staff occurred on 26 August with Garfield's return to duty. During the day he ordered the arrest of a citizen named Samuel Love, a mail carrier and ferryman in the Shell Mound neighborhood who had been denounced by his pro-Union neighbors. Removal of Love made a crossing at Shell Mound more secure, if Rosecrans needed it as one of his crossing sites. Garfield also telegraphed the U.S. marshal at Nashville, explaining that the army would be taking possession of the machinery at Brannon's Foundry for railroad purposes and that Colonel Innes would provide the proper receipts. Finally, Garfield queried Lytle at Bridgeport about artillery firing, which proved to be Reynolds at Shell Mound covering the removal of flatboats from the far side of the river. Goddard wrote to Grant's St. Louis quartermaster, seeking all the flatcars, boxcars, and passenger cars he could spare. In an effort to resolve Crittenden's supply difficulties, Goddard decreed that Wood's and Palmer's divisions should draw their rations from Tracy City, while Van Cleve should continue to draw from McMinnville. Goddard directed Thomas to have Brannan detail two regiments to report to Bridgeport with axes for the purpose of cutting bridge timbers. Finally Goddard telegraphed Innes in Nashville regarding three passenger cars Rosecrans had ordered modified for transporting sick and wounded soldiers. Other staff officers were also busy. Bond asked Brannan about improving the Battle Creek bridge. Thoms told Sheridan to have Lytle renovate a derelict sawmill to produce lumber for bridge decking. Thoms also telegraphed Granger to be prepared to move forward to cover the army's rear very soon. Granger was especially instructed to prepare Tennessee cavalry units forming at Carthage for movement to McMinnville, where they would relieve Van Cleve's Second Brigade. Finally, 1st Lt. Henry Cist, a recent addition to the army staff, notified both Steedman and the Murfreesboro quartermaster that Rosecrans desired all wagons, tools, and spare parts to be moved forward to Stevenson.[25]

Along the Tennessee River, the skirmishing continued on 26 August. Wilder had been resupplied with ammunition, but he chose not to resume the bombardment of Chattanooga. Instead, Lilly's gunners spent the day digging pits on Stringer's Ridge to protect them when they did resume firing. In front of the artillerymen, elements of the Seventeenth Indiana pushed forward to the river. North of the Seventeenth, two companies of the Seventy-Second Indiana patrolled from the mouth of Chickamauga Creek to a point opposite the Chattanooga waterfront. They saw no Confederates on their side of the river and few on the far side. The Seventy-Second Indiana sent its pack train over Walden's Ridge for rations, while Wagner's brigade maintained its perch overlooking Wilder's camps. Upstream, Hazen sent a forage train to Thatcher's Ferry and had a section of artillery send a few shells across the river. At Harrison's Ferry, Funkhouser's detachment of Wilder's brigade was also in action. On the previous day several Confederate scouts had briefly crossed the river. Resolved to end the practice, Funkhouser before dawn sent Company E of the Ninety-Second Illinois and Company A of the Ninety-Eighth Illinois to the ferry landing and hid them along the road leading from the river. There they watched at sunrise as a woman in a house signaled to Confederates on the opposite shore. Soon a flatboat crossed the river and unloaded a number of horsemen. As the Confederates advanced inland, the hidden Federals revealed themselves. In the ensuing fight, three Confederates were killed and two captured. The Federals then raced to capture the flatboat and its crew. By crouching and paddling with their hands the Confederates managed to get the boat safely downstream. The firing brought more Federals to the scene and Pvt. John King of the Ninety-Second Illinois recorded the result: "The woman's house at the landing caught fire in less than half an hour afterwards and was burned to the ground with all its contents. We never knew of her being in the 'signal service' afterwards."[26]

Although Wilder's brigade was the most visible, other Federal forces also drew attention to themselves. To the north, Minty pushed the Fourth Michigan Cavalry to Washington and the adjacent Lock's Ferry. After being fired upon ineffectively by Confederates on the opposite bank, they eventually returned to Smith's Cross Roads. At the same time Minty's scouts appeared at Blythe's and Doughty's Ferries downstream. Minty sent Van Cleve a variety of information, some of which was contradictory and most of which was out of date, but his greatest contribution was his presence near Burnside's advancing columns. A plausible case could be made that Burnside's and Rosecrans's forces were about to join hands, a case Buckner made daily to Bragg. Actions at the other end of the long river line were also compelling, however. The activity there was the product of aggressive action by Reynolds, who began another bombardment of the ruined railroad station at Shell Mound. The shelling was intended to cover a daylight raid by a company of the Seventy-Fifth Indiana Infantry regiment to acquire some flatboats. When queried by Thomas, Reynolds proudly announced that he had captured six flatboats, had prospects of gaining two more, and was building still another. Unaware of the purpose of Reynolds's noisy probe, Lytle at Bridgeport sent several companies of the Thirty-Sixth Illinois Infantry regiment again to scout Long Island. Presumably, both Reynolds's and Lytle's forays were seen and reported by men of the Third Confederate Cavalry regiment, but no such report has come to light. That night, however, Federals at widely scattered points in the river valley noticed numerous lights on Sand Mountain, which overlooked the scene. The lights remain unexplained but may have been the work of Confederate signal corps personnel. If reports of the Federal activity at Shell Mound and Bridgeport did reach Bragg's headquarters, they would have exacerbated an already confusing picture of possible Federal intentions.[27]

In the camps of the Army of the Cumberland, the cold, disagreeable weather continued on 26 August. The day was dry, but a brisk wind made it seem like fall. In the Fourteenth Corps, all could plainly see that another movement was rapidly approaching. In the First Division, Capt. William Mitchell of the First Wisconsin Infantry regiment told his father, "Deserters come into our lines daily. They report Bragg's force very much demoralized. My opinion is that the rebels will not make a desperate stand at Chattanooga." Capt. Alfred Hough, a member of Negley's staff, wrote his wife in similar vein: "It does really seem now as if the war was, *beginning* to draw toward the end. The rebellion is certainly growing weaker. I cannot see how we can fail in our movements here." Elsewhere within the division, Captain Vantine of the Twenty-First Ohio Infantry regiment remained intoxicated for a third day, while the Seventy-Eighth Pennsylvania Infantry regiment instituted roll call four times daily to ensure its men would be present for the coming advance. At Battle Creek, soldiers of the Second Minnesota Infantry regiment were disappointed when their newfound Confederate friends shouted across the river that they could no longer accept visitors. Capt. John Beatty, thirty-two, of the same regiment, had another concern, as he told his fiancée, Laura Maxfield, twenty-two: "I am growing old. Libbie I am afraid that you will not like me (love me I mean). I am really. It seems to me that all the freshness of my early youth is gone." In Reynolds's Fourth Division, the Federal successes at Charleston led many soldiers to believe that the war would be over by the end of the year. Lt. Piatt Andrew of the Twenty-First Indiana Battery was not so sure, as he wrote a friend: "It may be that I am mistaken, but I think two years will pass before we are mustered out of the service." First Sgt. Newton Parker of the 105th Ohio Infantry regiment was more focused, recording in his diary, "It is supposed we will have a pretty hot time crossing the river. Guess we will do it if we try, however."[28]

Events elsewhere in the army mirrored the circumstances of the Fourteenth Corps. In their camps near Stevenson, the Pioneer Brigade continued to build platforms to accommodate the hundreds of tons of rations arriving daily at the depot, or drilled with the cumbersome pontoons stockpiled several miles from the river. Except for Sheridan's soldiers at Bridgeport, the unseasonably cold day passed quietly in the Twentieth Corps. Regimental bands continued their nightly serenades for Davis and his wife. At Bellefonte, the Forty-Ninth Ohio Infantry regiment unloaded supplies from railroad cars, while other men improved their camps. In Baldwin's command, the entire brigade drilled as a unit. At Stevenson, Laibold's men heard a rumor that Chattanooga had been occupied by Federal forces. Downstream, the army's horsemen maintained their vigil along the river, fraternizing freely with Confederate pickets and receiving a steady stream of deserters. Sequestered in the Sequatchie Valley, Twenty-First Corps troops also reveled in the good news coming from Charleston. In Wood's First Division, Capt. John Tuttle of the Third Kentucky Infantry regiment was essentially crippled for life when his horse fell on him. At Poe's Tavern, Hazen proudly reported that a mill he had repaired was producing a ton of flour per day. From Pikeville, Van Cleve announced that his supply situation was improving and that he had sent a courier in search of Burnside's troops. In the army's rear, soldiers of the First Michigan Engineers and Mechanics regiment continued to shape logs into large square beams. Unaware of Rosecrans's plans, Pvt. Isaac Roseberry wondered about the utility of their labor: "The co is still getting out timber not knowing wheather it will ever be used or not. This seems to be some thing done to keep the boys out off mischeaf." In Nashville, Granger informed Garfield that he would send additional troops to Athens, Alabama, but that McCook's brigade would not move for three more days. Like Private Roseberry, Granger seemed to understand neither the larger operational picture nor the accelerating tempo at the Tennessee River.[29]

With only minor Federal activity reported from Bridgeport to Blythe's Ferry, Bragg had no more clues about Rosecrans's intentions on 26 August than on the previous day. Knowing he was unable to prevent a Federal crossing, Bragg could only wait for Rosecrans to make his move. He could theorize how he might respond if the Federals crossed downstream of Chattanooga, and could do the same if the Federals crossed above, but such an exercise would amount to idle speculation. Thus Bragg needed reliable news of a major Federal crossing before he could put his own troops into countervailing motion. Unable to place small scouting parties across the river successfully, as proven at Harrison's Ferry, he was totally dependent upon what observers could see from the left bank of the river or from Sand and Raccoon Mountains. In addition, he could draw information from Buckner at Knoxville. Buckner had a robust network of scouts and spies in eastern Kentucky and Tennessee, and they accurately reported the progress of Burnside's columns toward Kingston and Knoxville, information passed to Bragg and Mackall. What the spies could not divine was the exact relationship between Burnside's small army and Rosecrans's much larger one. Even so, Buckner believed that when Burnside was in place, Rosecrans would join him and the united force would cross the Tennessee River between Chattanooga and Knoxville. That analysis remained plausible and, indeed, Buckner was already moving the bulk of his forces to Loudon from Knoxville. By 26 August, Buckner's assessment was becoming ascendant in Bragg's headquarters as well, as recorded in George Brent's diary: "Enemy quiet in our front. He must be waiting until Burnside's movement is unmasked, & then possibly moving by his left effect a junction with Burnside & cross above us here. We can not hold both Knoxville & this place." Bragg's relationship with Brent was strong and of long standing. For Brent to write as he did on 26 August, it is clear that he accurately reflected Bragg's views as well as his own.[30]

Even without new information, the army's senior leaders continued to make prudent small adjustments. Given the general shortage of wagons, and the promise of two more divisions arriving without transportation, Bragg published General Orders, No. 171, which reduced the army's baggage wagons to an absolute minimum. At the same time, he promulgated Special Orders, No. 229, which made several temporary adjustments of significance. One provision ordered the removal of the last hospital in Chattanooga, Camp Direction, to Dalton. Another provision directed the transfer of the army's ordnance stores from Chickamauga Station to Graysville. This measure prudently removed Bragg's reserve ammunition stocks farther from the river. To alleviate the army's shortage of meat, Bragg ordered Wheeler to assist commissary personnel driving cattle from northern Alabama to the vicinity of Chattanooga. Meanwhile, Medical Director Edward Flewellen and the medical director of hospitals, Samuel Stout, disagreed over where to locate the hospitals evacuated from Chattanooga. Flewellen recommended placing them between Kingston and Big Shanty, but Stout believed that course would limit him to Cassville. Flewellen also agreed to place Stout's request to seize church buildings before the army's chief of staff, but he was in no hurry to do so. Oddly, while the army staff was acting with some urgency, Polk seemed to be relaxing the state of readiness of his corps. Division commanders Cheatham and Hindman were told to suspend the requirement to keep three days' cooked rations on hand. They also were instructed to return their artillery batteries to their respective infantry brigades. Otherwise, it was business as usual in Polk's sector, with normal details assigned to load railroad cars and work on the Chattanooga fortifications. The *Daily Rebel* reflected the army's ambivalence as well, reporting conflicting information about events around Bridgeport and devoting much of its diminished space to a whimsical article titled "Shelled Out."[31]

Like their Federal counterparts, Bragg's men had difficulty adjusting to the severe temperature drop that had begun the previous day. In Polk's Corps, the men of the Twelfth Tennessee Infantry regiment did not let the chill dampen their religious fervor, as large crowds attended their nightly revival meeting.

Around McFarland's Spring, Hindman's three brigades settled into their camps in the shadow of Missionary Ridge. They could hear the distant sounds of cannon fire coming from Harrison's Ferry and digested the latest rumors—the enemy was advancing on Knoxville and Harrison's, but Johnston would soon arrive with his entire army. In Hill's Corps, details continued to rotate between their camps and the entrenchments along the river. Hill himself remained at his Chickamauga Bridge headquarters, where a rumor circulated that Knoxville had fallen. Foraging Federals at Thatcher's Ferry threw twenty shells at the pickets of Lucius Polk's Brigade but without doing any damage. Nearby, men of the Seventeenth Texas Cavalry (Dismounted) used the Federal shelling to explain the disturbed earth in a citizen's sweet potato patch they had pillaged. In Stewart's Division, Pvt. Abram Glazener, thirty-eight, of the Eighteenth Alabama Infantry regiment, wrote to his wife, Lavenia, and his seven children: "Always hope for the best whether I get home or not. My ernest prairs is that I may live to see all one time moore." At Chickamauga Station, new brigade commander Daniel Govan drilled his command then released them to attend revival services. In Walthall's Brigade, Capt. Joseph Ward of the Twenty-Fourth Mississippi Infantry regiment continued to regret the cancelation of the ball his unit had been planning in Atlanta. He spoke for many in a letter to his sister: "Our holidays are over and we are once more with the army, cut off from evry source of pleasure and nearly everything to eat. We get nothing but blue beef and musty meal to eat. Yesterday by way of variety they gave us some hard corn for roasting ears."[32]

Away from Chattanooga, reinforcements destined for Bragg's army inched closer. Relieved at Loudon by Buckner's troops, Johnson's Brigade made a rapid march to the southwest, finishing the day just short of Athens. At Loudon, the final elements of Gracie's and Trigg's Brigades arrived, as did McCants's Battery. One artilleryman was not dismayed by the withdrawal, as Lt. Andrew Neal told his mother: "We expect hot work soon and I do not care how soon. I have felt more life the last five days than since we came out of Kentucky." On the same day Buckner arrived at Loudon by train, the Fifty-Eighth North Carolina Infantry regiment reached Lenoir Station, and the Sixty-Third Virginia Infantry regiment departed Knoxville, leaving the town protected only by scattered cavalrymen of Scott's Brigade. At Loudon, Preston formally organized his division, numbering 5,951 officers and men present for duty. Gracie's Brigade with 2,206 soldiers, and Trigg's Brigade, with 1,940, were Preston's largest units, soon to be augmented by a provisional brigade of regiments yet to arrive. In distant Morton, Mississippi, virtually all of Walker's Division had departed for Meridian. Momentarily left behind was Lt. Col. Ellison Capers of the Twenty-Fourth South Carolina Infantry regiment, who had just learned of the death of his infant daughter. Detailed to arrange the burial of Maj. Thomas

Ogier Jr., Walker's division surgeon, Capers caught an eastbound passenger train at 9:30 P.M. By that time, elements of Breckinridge's Division were also beginning to leave Morton. First to go were portions of the Second and Fourth Kentucky Infantry regiments of Helm's Brigade. Helm departed Morton on the same train as Capers, along with fellow brigade commander Marcellus Stovall. As the rickety train lurched through the darkness, the remainder of Helm's and Stovall's Brigades reached the Morton depot and camped for the night.[33]

The four days of relative quiet along the Chattanooga waterfront ended with a thundering crash at 9:30 A.M. on 27 August. A signal station atop Raccoon Mountain provided early warning, but nothing could be done to prevent what was coming. Lilly's four guns entered the pits built on Stringer's Ridge, while the Seventeenth Indiana and 123rd Illinois Mounted Infantry regiments occupied the plain below. When Lilly opened on the town, he elevated his pieces to thirty-five degrees in an effort to reach the railroad depot, train shed, and Crutchfield House, two miles distant. Eventually, the gunners found the range and struck the buildings several times. Still, the effects were so uncertain that Lilly occasionally shifted his aim to the Confederate works downtown, especially the fortification on the lower shoulder of Cameron Hill, location of the only long-range Confederate cannon. That gun fired in response only twice and did no damage. Satisfied that he had disrupted activity at the railroad depot, Lilly around 3:00 P.M. withdrew his guns behind Stringer's Ridge. Upstream, Funkhouser sent four companies to sweep the riverbank southward to the mouth of North Chickamauga Creek, while he took the bulk of the Ninety-Second and Ninety-Eighth Illinois Mounted Infantry regiments to Harrison's Ferry. Using Lilly's First section, he opened fire on the far bank around 9:00 A.M., driving the small number of Confederates to cover. From his vantage point, Funkhouser could see dust clouds moving in the distance and wagons loading or unloading in Harrison itself. After several hours of desultory fire, he moved upstream a short distance to the village of Dallas and fired a few more shots from that position. Tiring of the effort, he then led his two regiments back to camp. The next crossing point upstream was Igou's Ferry. There, Hazen sent the Sixth Kentucky Infantry regiment and two guns of Lt. Giles Cockerill's Battery F, First Ohio Light Artillery regiment, to make additional mischief. Cockerill scattered several Confederates bathing in the river, but again little damage was done. At sunset, Hazen withdrew to Poe's Tavern and relative quiet returned to the Tennessee River valley.[34]

At Stevenson, Rosecrans apparently had reached a decision about crossing sites by 27 August, his personal visits to the river having given him enough information to formulate a plan. The army would cross at four sites, from south to north: Caperton's Ferry, Bridgeport, Battle Creek, and Shell Mound. Caperton's Ferry, most distant from the Confederates, would be the first site to be used. During the day Rosecrans rode with engineer George Burroughs to determine a covered approach to the river. Beginning at the pontoon staging area northwest of Stevenson, Rosecrans and Burroughs traveled to the headquarters of the First Division of the Twentieth Corps. Davis's command occupied a position on the Memphis & Charleston Railroad just west of Stevenson. Satisfied that up to that point the pontoons were safe from prying Confederate eyes, Rosecrans instructed Davis to build a military road to the river. He then returned to his headquarters to resolve issues that he would have little time to address when the campaign got under way. Most pressing was a long-term solution to a vexing problem with his supply lines. Because the Cumberland River was often unusable because of low water and the Louisville & Nashville Railroad lacked capacity, Rosecrans needed a railroad to the deeper Tennessee River. If the Nashville & Northwestern Railroad could be completed, supplies could arrive without interruption. Because Governor Johnson also held military rank, Rosecrans baldly assigned him to direct the project. In turn, Granger's Reserve Corps would protect the road, the army staff would support Johnson's efforts, and the black regiments forming at Estill Springs and Nashville could be used as labor troops. Nowhere did Rosecrans address the political issues raised by such an order, but his supreme self-confidence, expressed in imperious tones, was much on display. He exhibited a similar tone in a message to Quartermaster General Meigs seeking additional funds for his quartermaster account before the army crossed the Tennessee.[35]

The army staff spent 27 August tending to housekeeping details. Garfield supported Rosecrans's orders to Governor Johnson by gathering information on the number of black laborers available. He also instructed Col. Charles Thompson to employ the second black regiment forming to cut locomotive fuel on the Nashville & Chattanooga line to Stevenson. Thompson, a former Rosecrans aide favored with a colonel's commission, was the lead agent to recruit more former slaves and utilize their labor in the army's rear. Goddard gave Sheridan specific instructions on the preparation of bridge timbers at Bridgeport. The message also specified that two of Brannan's regiments wielding axes would report to Sheridan on the next day to shape the timbers. Goddard also established a courier line between Stevenson and Bridgeport. He forwarded to Granger Rosecrans's desires that prisons in the department be inspected and that the inmates work on the fortifications. Edward McCook, commanding the cavalry force at Larkinsville, received permission to employ loyal citizens in the vicinity as auxiliaries. Finally, Goddard informed chief commissary Samuel Simmons that the headquarters mess had exhausted its supply of hams, a situation that should be rectified as soon as possible. Thoms gently chided Granger in Rosecrans's name for not forwarding daily reports of Reserve Corps unit locations. When Granger responded that he had telegraphed an updated accounting daily, Thoms was quick to offer Rosecrans's thanks. The accounting showed that Granger's units were scattered widely over Middle Tennessee, garrisoning Nashville and smaller towns, protecting the Nashville & Chattanooga Railroad, and positioning units to secure Rosecrans's flanks. Finally, Cist, Goddard's most junior assistant, instructed Reynolds to draw supplies from Stevenson, as Bridgeport was not yet a functioning depot. Ironically, Thomas reported on the same day that the supply line to Tracy City was finally working properly, with 60,000 rations accumulated there.[36]

Rosecrans's nightly report to Halleck on 27 August noted simply, "Bridge preparations going forward." Indeed that was the case. Most Pioneer Brigade soldiers spent the day drilling with their cumbersome equipment, then loaded the boats, chesses, and balks on running gear for movement to the river's edge. Other members of the brigade continued work on a long platform near the Stevenson depot to store commissary items. Sheridan that morning offered to build a trestle bridge at Bridgeport very quickly if Rosecrans would give him control of the First Michigan Engineers and Mechanics regiment. In support of that proposal, some members of the Forty-Second Illinois Infantry regiment began building canoes to facilitate the bridge-building. At Battle Creek, Brannan turned to Van Derveer's brigade for the construction skills he needed. The Second Minnesota Infantry regiment contained woodsmen handy with axes and saws who knew how to construct rafts. During the day teams dragged timbers to the bank of Battle Creek, where the process of shaping the timbers into large rafts began. Brannan also assigned soldiers to construct a semipermanent bridge over Battle Creek to facilitate lateral movement within the Fourteenth Corps sector. Upstream at Shell Mound, Reynolds had already secured several flatboats from the far side of the river. Needing more, he assigned soldiers from the 101st Indiana Infantry regiment to gather lumber for additional rafts. Even units on the army's flanks participated in the planning for the river crossing. Capt. James Hawley, Cavalry Corps inspector, tested a ford at Hart's Bar, between Caperton's Ferry and Bridgeport, and found it suitable for both cavalry and infantry. Far to the north, Wagner reported that a crossing at Chattanooga itself did not look promising. Wood apologized for Wagner's gloomy report but promised that "whatever is necessary to be done, if men can do it, shall be done." Even Crittenden, deep in the Sequatchie Valley, sent Garfield a report from Hazen on the possibility of crossing the river north of Chattanooga.[37]

While some elements of Rosecrans's command worked at the river, the remainder of the army marked time. At Bridgeport, Cpl. Edward Crippin of the Twenty-Seventh Illinois Infantry regiment spoke for many when he confided to his diary, "Revalee and roll call at the usual hour. . . . Breakfast over camp to police. . . . Nothing to do time drags heavaly on my hands. . . . No news." After the morning fog burned away, the day proved to be clear and cool, more like

Troops of Timothy Stanley's brigade near Stevenson, Alabama, 27 August 1863. (Behringer-Crawford Museum, Covington, Kentucky)

September than August. Only a few unusual events broke the monotony. In Negley's Second Division, Stanley's Second Brigade was called into formation at 9:00 A.M. for a photographer to record the scene. There had been an attempt to take the photo on the previous afternoon, but by the time the photographer was ready, the light had failed. Thus the Eleventh Michigan, Eighteenth Ohio, and Nineteenth Illinois Infantry regiments, and Battery M, First Ohio Light Artillery regiment, stood for a long hour while their image was recorded for posterity. Nearby, in the Twenty-First Ohio Infantry regiment of Sirwell's Third Brigade, Col. James Neibling departed for Ohio on recruiting duty. He left behind a large but undisciplined regiment, one of whose captains, Charles Vantine, remained intoxicated for a fourth day. At Bridgeport, chilled soldiers of the Forty-Second and Fifty-First Illinois Infantry regiments sent for their blankets that had been stored at Stevenson. Everywhere signs of a move were visible. The 104th Illinois Infantry regiment welcomed several convalescents to its ranks, an indication that hospitals were being purged of those able to fight. In the Twentieth Corps, the Fifty-Ninth Illinois Infantry regiment received orders to put new shoes on its animals, another sign of things to come. In the Sequatchie Valley, Capt. Daniel Howe of the Seventy-Ninth Indiana Infantry regiment was anxious to move: "This is a horribly lonesome place. The valley is not over three miles wide here and the mountain sides look like prison walls." At Therman, Capt. John Tuttle had no time to be lonely, as doctors attempted to stretch his broken leg an inch and a half.[38]

Rosecrans's horsemen were more active than his infantry on 27 August. In Edward McCook's First Division of Stanley's Cavalry Corps, Campbell's First Brigade picketed the river from the village of Bolivar past Cox's and Caperton's Ferries to Bellefonte. It also guarded the railroads in its rear and operated courier lines to connect various headquarters. McCook's Second Brigade, led by Oscar La Grange, continued the picket line southward to Larkinsville. Watkins's Third Brigade protected the Memphis & Charleston Railroad from a base at Maysville, with occasional patrols to Huntsville. Only in Watkins's sector was there much activity, and that involved combatting strong guerrilla activity. Madison County, where Maysville was located, was the home of Capt. Frank Gurley of the Fourth Alabama Cavalry. In August 1862, Brig. Gen. Robert McCook had been passing through the county from Athens, Alabama, to Winchester, Tennessee. Ill with dysentery, McCook was traveling in a makeshift ambulance with only a small escort near the village of New Market when he inadvertently became separated from his brigade. Suddenly encountering Confederate cavalry, the Federals fled but were halted by a fusillade of shots, one of which mortally wounded McCook. Frank Gurley was among the Confederates who captured McCook and was blamed for his death. The prominence of the McCook family and the controversial circumstances had led to reprisals in 1862, and a year later the McCook clan still sought vengeance for what they considered a murder. Thus on 27 August 1863, Edward McCook, Robert's first cousin, informed Rosecrans that Watkins had captured some of Gurley's associates. In a private message to Alex McCook, Robert's brother, he reported, "Watkins last night caught Ragsdale, one of the party with Gurley when Robert was murdered." McCook personally congratulated Watkins and encouraged him to treat such people harshly. Even as McCook wrote, Watkins reported the burning of three bridges on the Memphis & Charleston Railroad. Madison County clearly was not yet pacified.[39]

Like Madison County, Chattanooga felt the hard hand of war on 27 August, as Federal shells pummeled the town for four hours. The fact that Confederate signalmen on Raccoon Mountain reported Wilder's approach before the bombardment had little effect on the outcome. There were still useful supplies remaining in warehouses on the river and commissary wagons were being loaded when the first shells landed around 9:30 A.M. The Federals first targeted the batteries on the river and managed to kill three soldiers and wound three more by the time the bombardment ended at 1:00 P.M. According to a soldier in the Twenty-Fifth Alabama Infantry regiment on picket just downstream, the three were asleep at the time of their deaths and killed by a single shot. The *Chattanooga Daily Rebel* reported that a total of 280 shots were fired into the town during the day's shelling. The *Rebel* reporter also reported much "artful dodging" by the few citizens remaining in Chattanooga and admitted taking refuge in the vault of an abandoned bank next door. Eventually the Federals shifted their attention to the railroad depot, which they hit several times. One of the shells penetrated the army's transportation office near the depot, where Maj. John Bransford and young assistants toiled on paperwork. A clerk named Thomas received a serious wound in the arm, while a second clerk was injured less severely. Another shell struck the kitchen of the Spencer House, one of the few Chattanooga hotels remaining open, and still others lightly damaged the large Crutchfield House hotel across from the depot. Instructed not to reply to the Federal barrage until noon, Confederate gunners fired only two ineffectual shots before Wilder and Lilly decided to end the shooting for the day. In a show of bravado, a young man flew a kite over the waterfront throughout the action, according to Henry Watterson of the *Rebel*.[40]

The bombardment of Chattanooga on 27 August seemed not to affect the growing consensus that the Federal crossing would occur far upstream of the city. At some point during the day, Bragg summoned his officers to a conference. Although no list of attendees has been found, the gathering served as a vehicle for Bragg to explain his vision for the coming campaign. Speaking with more emotion than usual, the army commander stated his opinion that the Federals probably would cross the Tennessee River north of Chattanooga. Rosecrans's particular crossing point, however, was largely irrelevant because Bragg intended to engage the Federals vigorously, either north or south of the city. In forceful terms he instructed the generals to tell their soldiers that the army would fight, not run. Chattanooga would be defended, although not necessarily at the gates of the city itself. He cautioned that hard marching would be involved but that no one should interpret the coming movements as a retreat. Instead, the marches would simply be the means to facilitate a great victory. Referencing the inadequate meat supply, Bragg argued that a victory would alleviate that and other supply difficulties. In sum, by sharing his thinking publicly with his senior generals and instructing them to inform their soldiers, Bragg attempted to forestall the grumbling and defeatism sure to be expressed when the campaign began. For some time Bragg had known that he would have to leave Chattanooga, if only briefly, in order to win a victory—he would not mimic John Pemberton's tactics at Vicksburg. Bragg wanted all to understand what was about to happen and be prepared to do their part to achieve success. The degree to which this message of hope was disseminated throughout the army is unknown, but Bragg's words reached the junior officers of at least two brigades in Hindman's Division. In each case, in letters home, the officers repeated the gist of Bragg's message and expressed confidence that a victory was in the offing.[41]

Two of Bragg's senior commanders echoed his assessment of Federal intentions on 27 August. Polk, who would certainly have attended the meeting, agreed with Bragg that Rosecrans would most likely attack north of Chattanooga. On that day he wrote to his wife, "We think Rosecrans is moving up the river to make his attempt to cross *above* Chattanooga; but his plans are as yet not well developed. He has not crossed at Bridgeport and I think will not, nor at any other place below Chattanooga." In Polk's opinion, Rosecrans would not cross downstream because of the mountain barriers he would confront east of Bridgeport. At Loudon, Buckner also expected Rosecrans to cross north of Chattanooga and merge with Burnside's army. Buckner had several spies in Kentucky, one even traveling with one of Burnside's columns, and their information was definite and timely. The network was managed by Maj. Stoddard Johnston, one of Buckner's staff officers. Johnston sent the latest spy report on 27 August to Mackall, who believed the report credible. Knowing that Buckner's command, essentially Preston's Division and several cavalry brigades, would be little hindrance to Burnside's force, Bragg decided to act. Aware that the two divisions coming from Mississippi would soon arrive, Bragg believed he could spare a division to reinforce Buckner. Stewart's Division of Hill's Corps was less tied to the river than Cleburne's Division, so Bragg selected Stewart to move to Buckner's aid at Loudon. He also directed that Forrest's and Pegram's commands be combined under Forrest, with orders to "develop the designs of the enemy." Given what Bragg knew at the time, the move seemed to be a prudent response to a real threat. Even after Stewart's departure, Bragg's army would grow by one division with the arrival of Walker and Breckinridge. His plan to wait until Rosecrans committed himself remained intact. The decision seemed justified when the leading elements of Walker's Division arrived at Chickamauga Station at 7:00 P.M.[42]

For most of the Army of Tennessee, 27 August passed without incident. In Cheatham's Division, fatigue details continued improving the fortifications and loading supply wagons. In the Twelfth Tennessee Infantry regiment, the men formed for dress parade as usual in the evening, then attended the nightly prayer meeting. Soldiers in Stanford's Mississippi Battery of Strahl's Brigade serenaded Polk. Word spread rapidly about the three men killed while sleeping and the young clerk severely injured in Major Bransford's transportation office. In the Fiftieth Alabama Infantry regiment, 2nd Lt. James Fraser, twenty-two, closed the current volume of his diary: "Many changes have taken place, some for good, some for ill. Life is uncertain and death is sure. How soon it may overtake us, none can tell." Upstream, Fraser's words were prophetic as shells fell in several places, killing a sharpshooter at Harrison's Ferry and wounding several artillerymen in Calvert's Arkansas Battery. In the Thirty-Third Alabama Infantry regiment, Pvt. Hezekiah Rabb, twenty-four, was downcast that his wife had been unable to visit him. Disappointment was evident when he wrote, "My Hopes are almost Thread beare I am badly out of hart of our ever Whiping them. . . . I see nothing in our favor at all they are gaining ground every day on us & believe they will soon carry us up the Spout. . . . Perhaps I may bee too badly disheartened I Quit the subject for the Present." In Stewart's Division, the soldiers of Brown's Brigade strengthened their fortifications at Sivley's Ford. At Chickamauga Station, in Liddell's Division, Pvt. Robert Jarman and his friends in the Twenty-Seventh Mississippi Infantry regiment congratulated themselves on their good fortune in becoming part of the Reserve Division, an indication they would see less action than their peers. As if to prove Jarman's point, Sgt. John Freeman of the Thirty-Fourth Mississippi regiment confided to his diary, "Nothing new having fine time going in washing evry day." On the East Tennessee & Georgia Railroad, the soldiers of Johnson's Brigade completed their tiring march from Loudon to Charleston.[43]

While most of the army remained in place, some mounted units were in motion on 27 August. The weakness of the cavalry screen on the army's left had finally been noted in Chattanooga. Wheeler had long been out of favor at army headquarters because of his laxity in administering his command, with Mackall being especially critical of the young cavalryman. Unfortunately, now that there was a pressing need to improve the army's flank protection, Wheeler's unit nearest that point, Martin's Division, remained in exceedingly poor condition. Since July, Martin's command had been recuperating from the rigors of the previous campaign in camps around Alexandria, Alabama. In order to reinforce the Third Confederate Cavalry regiment scattered along the Tennessee River, the most expedient solution appeared to be the creation of an ad hoc formation. Therefore Lt. Col. Harris Mauldin, commanding the Third Alabama Cavalry regiment of Hagan's Brigade, received orders to form a temporary unit from the best-mounted and equipped men in the brigade and march it north. Mauldin selected 300 troopers and on 27 August led them northward toward Bridgeport, nearly 100 miles away. At the other end of Bragg's line, the departure of Buckner's infantry from the Knoxville area caused the scattered detachments of Scott's Brigade to begin withdrawing from the Knoxville area as they prepared to join the retreat to Loudon. Before they could get away, the men of Col. Charles Goode's Tenth Confederate Cavalry regiment were surprised and routed at Jacksboro, losing nearly fifty troopers to the First East Tennessee Mounted Infantry. At Bell's Bridge, just north of Knoxville, Lt. Winslow Robinson's Louisiana Battery from Scott's command was ordered to remove fifty sacks of corn to safety. Robinson seized a civilian wagon to remove part of the corn, left a small detail to safeguard the remainder, and headed south to Campbell's Station. That night, panic broke out in Knoxville as the railroad east of town was severed by Federal partisans.[44]

On 27 August the first contingent from Johnston's army reached Georgia. Wilson's Brigade of Walker's Division led the movement, which began with a ride on the Southern Railroad of Mississippi from Morton to Meridian, 61 miles. From Meridian, the troops rode the Mobile & Ohio Railroad to Mobile, 134 miles. After a boat trip across Mobile Bay, the soldiers took the Mobile & Great Northern Railroad 50 miles to Pollard. From there, the route ran northeast on the Alabama & Florida Railroad 114 miles to Montgomery. The troops there transferred to the Montgomery & West Point Railroad for an 88-mile journey to West Point, Georgia. The next leg was an 87-mile trip on the Atlanta & West Point Railroad to Atlanta. The Western & Atlantic Railroad's 128-mile line from Atlanta to Chickamauga Station ended the trip. A few of Wilson's men arrived during the evening of 27 August, but most of the brigade was still below Atlanta. Behind them came Ector's and Gist's Brigades, near Montgomery. Following Walker was Breckinridge's command. In the lead was Adams's Brigade, in the vicinity of Mobile. Behind Adams was part of Stovall's Brigade, on trains between Meridian and Mobile. Finally, regiments of Helm's Brigade left Morton for Meridian during the day. Because the Mobile route had reached capacity, two of Stovall's regiments and at least two of Helm's took an alternate path via Selma, Alabama. Their route would be the Southern Railroad of Mississippi from Morton to Meridian, 61 miles; Meridian to McDowell's Bluff, Alabama via the Alabama & Mississippi Rivers Railroad, 53 miles; a short boat ride on the Tombigbee River from McDowell's Bluff to Demopolis; Demopolis to Selma, using more of the Alabama & Mississippi Rivers Railroad, 50 miles; and, finally, a much longer steamboat ride on the Alabama River to Montgomery, 75 miles, where it merged with the Mobile route. While some troops rode in passenger cars, most traveled in or on top of freight cars. Generally unaware of the reason for their movement, Walker's and Breckinridge's soldiers saw the trip simply as a pleasant interlude in an otherwise dull summer.[45]

12

The Crossing Begins

» 28–30 August 1863 «

By long-standing habit, Rosecrans was a late sleeper who usually worked well past midnight when in camp. On Friday, 28 August, he could not follow his normal pattern because he had chosen that day to initiate his army's crossing of the Tennessee River. Rosecrans had decided that the crossing would begin at Caperton's Ferry in McCook's Twentieth Corps sector, where the Pioneer Brigade would erect a 1,250-foot pontoon bridge after the river's east bank was secured. Early in the morning Garfield sent McCook specific instructions placing him in overall charge of the operation. First, he was to supervise the movement of the pontoons to the river via the route selected earlier. Second, McCook was to deploy most of the pontoons on a mile-long stretch of riverfront, reserving some to ferry several infantry regiments across the stream. The entire movement was to be conducted with the greatest secrecy, shielding all activity from any Confederate pickets on the far bank of the river or on Sand Mountain. McCook was to have everything in place by nightfall and safeguard the pontoons until they were launched. Lieutenant Burroughs was assigned to assist McCook for the duration of the operation. Garfield told McCook that Rosecrans wanted the bridge placed just below the point where Crow Creek emptied into the Tennessee River. Because of his recent illness, Garfield had not participated in the earlier surveys made by Rosecrans and Burroughs, and he was unaware of the specific geography of the site or the exact location they had selected. Having given McCook his instructions, Garfield departed with Rosecrans for Bridgeport. Because so many generals and staff officers made the trip, two steam dummies were required. At some point during the visit to Bridgeport, Garfield learned that he had given McCook the incorrect location for the bridge. Without a hint of embarrassment, he ordered Captain Drouillard to send a correction to the corps commander: The Pioneers were to lay the bridge above the mouth of Crow Creek, not below as specified earlier.[1]

Upon arriving at Bridgeport, Rosecrans and his party found a scene of intense activity. Sheridan, who had two brigades at Bridgeport, had promised

Rosecrans on the previous day that he could build a trestle bridge over the river very quickly if he had engineer assistance. Thus Rosecrans found Bradley's Third Brigade already hard at work on various projects related to crossing the river. Three regiments were cutting and shaping timbers, while the fourth was constructing a shipyard for the assembly of small steamboats. Meanwhile, Lytle's Second Brigade manned the old Confederate fortifications overlooking the crossing site. In accord with his customary practice, Rosecrans mingled with the men as they worked, impressing Pvt. Merritt Simonds of the Forty-Second Illinois as "a plain, honest man." Knowing the magnitude of the task ahead, Rosecrans had already directed that Sheridan's soldiers be reinforced by two regiments from Brannan's Third Division of the Fourteenth Corps, but they would not arrive until the evening, and without axes. Indeed, Rosecrans was at Bridgeport before the Eighty-Second Indiana Infantry regiment of Connell's First Brigade and the Fourth Kentucky Infantry regiment of Croxton's Second Brigade left their camps near Battle Creek. While at Bridgeport, Rosecrans also issued two additional orders. Seeing the need for boats to facilitate the construction process, he ordered Burroughs to dispatch four pontoons by rail from Stevenson. He further directed Stanley to send the Second Michigan Cavalry regiment of Campbell's First Brigade to Bridgeport as well. The Michigan horsemen were to drive Confederate pickets from both Long Island and the east bank of the river to prevent them from hindering the work. The bridge builders would be four companies of the First Michigan Engineers and Mechanics, who were already coming by rail from Estill Springs. Finally, before leaving Bridgeport, Rosecrans instructed Maj. William Sinclair of Stanley's staff to have Crook send two regiments of Long's Second Brigade across the river at Hart's Bar, several miles north of Caperton's Ferry.[2]

At Stevenson, McCook and Burroughs began to move the 100-wagon pontoon train to the river at Caperton's Ferry without being seen. The first task was to establish a covert path to the riverbank for the pontoons and their guards. A temporary screen was thrown across the railroad northwest of Stevenson, behind which the pontoons could be moved into the dense woods south of the railroad. When all was ready, Burroughs gave the order to Capt. Patrick O'Connell of the Pioneer Brigade at 10 A.M.: "Commence hauling the pontoon train to the river by the hidden road. Keep it concealed at every step. Stop it in the woods securely hidden & as near Caperton's Ferry as may be." During the afternoon Davis ordered Heg to move his Third Brigade to the river. Heg started his four regiments from their camps at 5:00 P.M., and by midnight had everyone in position near the hidden pontoons. Behind them, soldiers from Post's First Brigade assumed the sentry positions formerly occupied by Heg's men. Hospital Steward David Lathrop of the Fifty-Ninth Illinois Infantry regiment was pleased that the army was finally beginning to move. He explained that the mind-numbing routine of sedentary camp life had a detrimental effect on soldiers, culminating in greater rates of sickness. For the moment, only Davis's division was in motion. In the camps of Johnson's Second Division around Bellefonte, the daily grind of drill, picket duty, camp improvement, and foraging continued unabated. Even among Sheridan's troops at Bridgeport, not everyone was thinking of the pending movement. According to Pvt. James Riley of the Forty-Second Indiana Infantry regiment, "This morning I did not get up very early for there was not much going on in camp." Far different was the experience of Pvt. George Cummins, twenty-three, of the Thirty-Sixth Illinois Infantry regiment, who recorded in his diary: "Last night was up nearly all night with Bro. Stephen. This morning about 6 he died & in an hour we burry him. Last night was a sorrowful time for me. It is hard to see a bro. die, especially away off from home in a strange desolate land."[3]

Although Rosecrans intended multiple crossings of the river, he did not want them to be simultaneous. Only after a secure lodgment was achieved would subsequent crossings be attempted. Yet in two divisions of the Fourteenth Corps aggressive commanders wanted to accelerate the timetable. The First and Second Divisions of the corps remained quietly in their camps on the railroad north of Stevenson on 28 August, but Brannan and Reynolds were anxious to advance. In Brannan's command, only Van Derveer's Third Brigade was posted on the river, at the mouth of Battle Creek. On that day Van Derveer's primary task was to construct a bridge over Battle Creek in order to improve lateral communication within the Federal lines. The bridge required a central pier, so a detail of eighty men from the Thirty-Fifth Ohio Infantry regiment began building a midstream crib of logs and rocks to support the stringers. While they struggled to prevent the crib from breaking apart and floating away, woodsmen from the Second Minnesota Infantry regiment dismantled some abandoned log houses and built a massive raft. The regiment also constructed several smaller flatboats. At 5:00 P.M. Brannan announced that he could place a regiment on the far shore whenever Rosecrans desired it. Surprised, Rosecrans cautioned Brannan not to initiate a crossing without orders. Like Brannan, Reynolds had only part of his division on the river. At Shell Mound, the soldiers of King's Second Brigade for some time had been gathering flatboats and building others. King already had raided twice across the river, and the weak Confederate response had emboldened Reynolds to do more. The constant trickle of deserters provided enough information on Confederate dispositions to offer a high probability of success, so Reynolds authorized King to mount a strong raid after nightfall. King selected six companies of the 101st Indiana Infantry regiment, four companies of the Seventy-Fifth Indiana Infantry regiment, and nine mounted artillerymen from the Nineteenth Indiana Battery, all of whom prepared to cross the river after darkness fell.[4]

Upstream, the units maintaining the fiction that the crossing would occur north of Chattanooga continued their deception at a leisurely pace. Wilder sent the usual pickets to the river facing the town, but most of his troops spent the day foraging. A detail of prisoners built a road up the west side of Stringer's Ridge to Lilly's gun pits, but the gunners did not occupy them on 28 August. Pvt. Alva Griest of the Seventy-Second Indiana joyfully informed his diary about the haul of butter and sweet milk he had obtained from locals and dreamed about the peach cobbler he was going to make. Ominously, he also noted that he could hear a great deal of railroad activity in Chattanooga. To Griest, the sounds meant that the Confederates were either evacuating the town or receiving reinforcements, but he could not choose between the conflicting interpretations. Pvt. William Records of the same regiment also mentioned the way sounds carried across the river from Chattanooga during the cool and windy day. He described two deserters from North Carolina who swam the river, bringing the usual stories of destitution and demoralization in the Army of Tennessee. Far above Wilder, on Walden's Ridge, Wagner chafed at the seemingly lackadaisical Federal movements. Hazen on the previous day had reported deserters' claims that the Confederates were preparing to evacuate the valley, and Wood had forwarded Hazen's message to Wagner. From his vantage point, Wagner saw no evidence of an evacuation, although he did observe a continued shift of Confederate units upriver from Chattanooga. Unwilling to remain a passive spectator, Wagner during the day sent detachments down into the valley to select locations from which to bombard the town. At Poe's Tavern, Hazen himself reported no change in the situation in his sector. During the day he sent only two companies of the Ninety-Second Illinois Mounted Infantry regiment to the river. Minty's brigade was equally quiescent, remaining in its camps around Smith's Cross Roads with only a few men picketing the river.[5]

In the Twenty-First Corps, sequestered in the Sequatchie Valley, the languid pace of operations generated a feeling of unease. At Therman, most of Wood's First Division followed their daily routine, but in the Third Kentucky Infantry regiment the seriously injured Capt. John Tuttle contemplated his dire situation. Wracked with pain, Tuttle wrote, "The Drs. all agree I cannot be removed from here for a considerable length of time and the question is what is to become of me. If left alone or with a small guard the guerrillas are good for me." At Dunlap, the two brigades of Palmer's Second Division spent the day drilling or foraging among the generally pro-Union locals. At Pikeville, Van Cleve continued to seek the return of Dick's Second Brigade, still guarding McMinnville. As he had on the previous day, Capt. Daniel Howe of the Seventy-Ninth Indiana Infantry regiment recorded his displeasure with his surroundings: "I am glad I have something to do, for this is the most lonesome spot I ever was in. It is a beautiful valley, it is true, but it looks too much like a prison. The 'sights' of

Pikeville can be seen in a very few minutes. It is all suburbs and I don't think there is any 'elephant' there." During the evening, a cow stumbled through the camp of the Seventeenth Kentucky Infantry regiment, trampling sleeping soldiers, whose shouts reverberated throughout the valley. Taken up successively by other regiments, the noise took some time to dissipate. Greatly displeased, brigade commander Samuel Beatty called the entire command into line and kept it there all night as punishment. The incident confirmed both the irrepressible nature of the common soldier and the need to relieve tension. Even Crittenden was affected. In response to Van Cleve's invitation to visit his command, Crittenden responded through his adjutant: "The general cannot leave here at present as he is much in the dark, and cannot form any conjectures as to the probable course of events." Wracked by self-doubt, blinded by the frowning mountains, and only tenuously connected to the rest of the army, Crittenden could only hope that orders to begin the campaign would soon arrive.[6]

About the time that Beatty's infantrymen were raising their primal shout at Pikeville, Pioneer Brigade engineers, Fourteenth and Twentieth Corps infantrymen, and Cavalry Corps horsemen were approaching the bank of the Tennessee River in several places. At 7:45 P.M. Captain O'Connell received Rosecrans's final instructions, which were to use no more than fifty-six pontoons at Caperton's Ferry. In the woods near the ferry, O'Connell's engineers continued unloading the cumbersome pontoons, chesses, and balks from wagons, a task that would take until midnight. Near them, Heg's infantrymen stood guard in the darkness or tried to sleep on the rough ground. Approximately six miles upstream at Hart's Bar, cavalrymen from Long's Second Cavalry Brigade completed their own covert path to the river. While commissary officers distributed rations, Long readied a detail of three officers and fifty-two men from the Third Ohio Cavalry to ford the river under cover of darkness. At Bridgeport, Maj. Leonidas Scranton's Second Michigan Cavalry regiment arrived and bivouacked near the river, ready to cross to Long Island. At Battle Creek, Brannan at 9:30 P.M. informed army headquarters that he could cross the river with a regiment to seize the Confederate pickets. Unwilling to have an overeager division commander disrupt his crossing sequence, Rosecrans authorized the raid, but in less than regimental strength. Thomas also approved Brannan's idea, cautioning the division commander not to complicate matters at a site where he believed a pontoon bridge was to be laid. Upstream at Shell Mound, Reynolds prepared to launch his own probe without waiting for permission from higher authority. After dark, King's raiding party gathered at the flatboats moored at the ferry site. Like Brannan, Reynolds had no understanding of Rosecrans's plan, but he was anxious to prove to his superiors that he was an aggressive division commander. King's raid, if successful, would offer an opportunity to burnish his credentials.[7]

By the time Rosecrans composed his nightly summary to Halleck, several thousand troops were massed along the river from Caperton's Ferry to Shell Mound. Rosecrans's message was brief: "Corps in the same position. Pontoons for first bridge at ferry now down and going down to concealed position, with an advanced brigade. The cavalry will begin to cross tonight." Outside army headquarters in the "Little Brick," some distance from the noisy railroad depots, Timothy Stanley assembled a regimental band and many of his brigade officers to serenade for the army commander. Stanley's efforts were apparently not appreciated by the commanding general, as a participant reported: "A dusty ride of four miles and back was what the thing amounted to. Gen. Rosecrans took no notice of the serenade that I could perceive." As Stanley's officers dejectedly returned to their camps, other soldiers of the Army of the Cumberland were already going into action. At Shell Mound, beginning around 10:00 P.M., King's raiding party of 350 Indiana soldiers quietly paddled their flatboats across the Tennessee River to a landing near the shell-damaged railroad depot. Leaving two companies to hold the crossing site, King led eight companies of infantry and the nine mounted men on the road leading up Running Water Creek toward Lookout Valley. Six miles from Shell Mound, King's raiders encountered a few Confederate pickets, forcing them into hasty flight. Posting two companies as a rear guard, King pressed on to the camp of Capt. Thomas Edmondson's Company F, Third Confederate Cavalry regiment. Like the pickets before them, the startled Confederates scattered into the darkness, but King's men managed to capture six prisoners, eleven horses, and assorted weapons. Gathering more plunder as they retraced their steps to Shell Mound, the raiders prepared to return across the river without hindrance. Surprisingly, all along the Tennessee River front from Shell Mound to Caperton's Ferry, the Confederates seemed not to be aware of what was about to happen when dawn broke.[8]

On 28 August Confederate commanders continued to believe that Rosecrans would likely move northward to link with Burnside's force threatening Knoxville. Even when scouts reported that Rosecrans was at Stevenson and that most of his army was concentrated between Stevenson and Jasper, the belief remained strong that the two Federal forces would not remain separated long. Buckner's spy network had been entirely too efficient, providing a clear picture of Burnside's movements, in contrast to the vague reports from downstream. If Brent's diary is any indication of Bragg's thinking, the army commander was actually considering a quick strike against Burnside, even if it meant the temporary abandonment of Chattanooga. Burnside was thought to have fewer than 30,000 troops, and the Confederate rail network could concentrate Bragg's army quickly at Loudon. Stewart's Division was already moving to Buckner's assistance. To replace Stewart, Bragg assigned Walker and Breckinridge to Hill's Corps. When his division reached Chickamauga Station, Breckinridge would support the army's right, while Walker was to prepare to follow Stewart to Buckner's aid. In a note to Hill describing the changes, Mackall enclosed Major Johnston's note detailing the intelligence on Burnside's movements. The chief of staff also noted that an "old citizen from the other side of the river" had just reported Rosecrans's headquarters was at Jasper and that Federal troops were moving up the Sequatchie Valley. In fact, only Reynolds's headquarters was at Jasper, and the Sequatchie Valley movements were only supply trains sustaining the Twenty-First Corps. Not knowing this, Mackall thought the disparate pieces of evidence indicated that Rosecrans was moving north to join Burnside. To Bragg, Mackall, and Brent, it all seemed to make sense because of the lack of visible Federal activity downstream and the desultory bombardment of the town. Both Hill and Polk were already united in the belief that any Federal crossing would occur upstream from Chattanooga.[9]

In the camps of the Army of Tennessee little changed on 28 August. Details from Cheatham's Division continued to load goods from Chattanooga's warehouses on southbound trains. Regiments also continued to hold regular inspections and dress parades, and in the Twelfth Tennessee Infantry regiment nightly prayer meetings drew crowds of the faithful. In Stanford's Mississippi Battery, one man climbed Lookout Mountain as a tourist, while another was delighted to receive a box of clothing from home. Hindman's Division remained quiet in its camps around McFarland's Spring. When an officer in Anderson's Brigade learned that some female visitors had been halted in Dalton because visits to the army were prohibited, he arranged to get a pass to meet them there. In Cleburne's Division, detachments continued to rotate between their camps and the trenches along the river, while rumors about the coming of both Burnside and Johnston spread widely. Cleburne, meanwhile, completed the constitution of a new fraternal order for Confederate officers, the Comrades of the Southern Cross. Stewart's Division was under marching orders, although the news was slow to reach Clayton's Brigade at the far northern end of the river line. At Birchwood, Lt. William Cole, thirty-four, of the Thirty-Eighth Alabama Infantry regiment penned a sorrowful letter to his wife, Cornelia, in Fayette County, Alabama. He wrote, "I commenced last winter at Mobile with two pairs of pants. I lost one of them on our retreat and have been wearing the others evisince. I fear that I will be left entirely naked just about cold weather though I hope the skin will thicken and tough so that I can bear the cold." On a cold and windy day like 28 August, men like Cole saw a bleak future ahead if they could receive no relief: "I am of the impression that we will fall back to Atlanta after we have a fight. . . . It will be too cowardly to fall back. . . . Show the Confederate Spine as well as Judgment. We are to get the worst whipin here that have ever been since we have been engaged."[10]

While most of the army waited, other units were in motion. Brown's and

Bate's Brigades of Stewart's Division marched to Tyner's Station on the East Tennessee & Georgia Railroad and waited patiently for trains that did not arrive until after dark. Many of the units would have to travel all night to cover the seventy-five miles to Loudon. More fortunate was Johnson's Brigade, which had just reached Charleston when it was ordered to return to Loudon. This time Johnson's men boarded trains that rapidly carried them the forty-two miles back to Loudon, where they awaited the remainder of the division. Nor were Stewart's men the only Confederates riding trains on 28 August. Wilson's Brigade of Walker's Division left Atlanta that morning and arrived at Chickamauga Station during the evening. Their numbers were low because many men had taken unauthorized leave to visit their Georgia homes, but most of the absentees would eventually return. Behind them, Ector's Brigade neared Atlanta, while Gist's Brigade was around Montgomery. After Walker's Division came Breckinridge's three brigades. Adams's Brigade was on the rails between Mobile and Montgomery. Stovall's Brigade was split, with the bulk of the brigade awaiting transportation at Mobile, while the remainder took the rail-river route via Selma. The last element to leave Mississippi, Helm's Brigade, was also divided between the two routes, with part of the brigade crossing Mobile Bay to Tensas Landing and the remainder reaching Demopolis on the Selma route. Even Buckner had troops on the move. Still hoping to mount an offensive against Burnside when Stewart arrived, Buckner believed the fight would have to occur south of Clinch River. Accordingly, he continued to draw Pegram's cavalry closer to his infantry at Loudon. Clearly, the decrepit Confederate railroad system could still make a difference in Bragg's strategic and operational calculus. That system, however, momentarily was operating to support a flawed analysis of Federal intentions.[11]

A few minutes after midnight on 29 August, the Third Ohio Cavalry regiment put Rosecrans's plan into motion. Stealthily fifty-five volunteers entered the river near the mouth of Widow's Creek and followed a guide along a winding, invisible underwater ridge stretching across the Tennessee River. All made the crossing safely without being seen by the five Confederate pickets nearby. Surprise was lost when an officer's pistol fired prematurely, causing the Confederates to scatter in the thick foliage. Capturing only one picket, the Federals nevertheless secured the east bank of the stream and signaled for their comrades to begin crossing. Around 2:00 A.M. Long led three regiments into the water. During the crossing the Second Kentucky Cavalry lost two troopers and three horses drowned when they slipped into deep water. At dawn Long led the Second Kentucky southward toward Caperton's Ferry. After a two-mile ride he encountered a Confederate courier carrying a message for Col. William Estes of the Third Confederate Cavalry regiment. Learning that one of Estes's companies guarded Caperton's Ferry, Long accelerated his pace to a gallop. Meanwhile, Crook led the First and Third Ohio Cavalry regiments northward toward Moore's Spring, a well-known landmark two miles east of Bridgeport. Named for the William Moore family, the spring lay in a narrow valley between Hogjaw Ridge and Sand Mountain. From there a road ran over Sand Mountain to Trenton in Lookout Valley. Told by Moore that Capt. P. H. Rice's Company G of the Third Confederate Cavalry regiment was camped on the road leading up the mountain and that Estes's own camp was nearby, Crook sent the First Ohio Cavalry regiment forward. Rice retreated quickly, abandoning his camp to the charging Federals. Col. Estes's camp proved empty as well, although active cooking fires indicated recent occupation. After collecting large quantities of weapons and equipment, capturing six Confederates and killing another, Crook's men continued their pursuit across the top of Sand Mountain on the Trenton Road.[12]

At Caperton's Ferry, the morning mist began to dissipate on the river as the sky brightened. Suddenly, parties of Federal axmen hacked away the foliage hiding more than fifty pontoons from pickets of Capt. John Hoge's Company A, Third Confederate Cavalry regiment. As soon as the brush was removed, hundreds of soldiers from Heg's Third Brigade manhandled the cumbersome pontoons into the stream. Into each pontoon jumped twenty-five men and an officer. Oarsmen took their places on the sides of the ungainly vessels while the remainder of the soldiers crouched low to avoid the shots expected momentarily from the Confederate pickets. Amazingly, the pickets held their fire, having been taken completely by surprise. Heg himself occupied the center of the flotilla, prominently displaying the brigade's colors. He was flanked by men from the Eighth Kansas Infantry regiment and the Fifteenth Wisconsin Infantry regiment, who rowed furiously. At Caperton's the river was approximately 1,250 feet wide, exposing the helpless soldiers in the pontoons for what seemed like hours, although it was little more than ten minutes. Those not rowing lay in the bottom of the pontoons in water that had either leaked or splashed into the boats. Although he did not want to be the first ashore, Capt. James Love of Company K, Eighth Kansas Infantry regiment, found his pontoon in the lead. Love tried to restrain his oarsmen, but he was among the first to land on the east bank. Forming quickly, the Eighth Kansas pushed rapidly beyond a fence and a cornfield to a road paralleling the shore. There they were joined by the Fifteenth Wisconsin. Throwing out skirmishers, the two regiments pursued the Confederate pickets, passing through their abandoned camp without halting. Only a few random shots broke the stillness as the Confederates disappeared in the trees. A mile from the river, the two regiments halted at the foot of Sand Mountain. After a brief pause, Heg sent the Eighth Kansas up the mountain, leaving the Fifteenth Wisconsin to cover the arrival of the remainder of the brigade.[13]

By 10:00 A.M., when the Kansans reached the summit, the panorama spread before them was breathtaking. From their perch 900 feet above the valley, they could see the placid Tennessee River stretched like a silver ribbon across their front. On the river, a swarm of pontoon boats looked like tiny water bugs as the Pioneer Brigade assembled them into a frail bridge. Five miles away, Stevenson was visible, with its frenetic railroad activity and growing supply dumps. Even though the distance was too great to see the thousands of soldiers occupying the valley south of Stevenson, clouds of dust indicated their presence. Soon the Eighth Kansas was joined on the mountain by Long and the Second Kentucky Cavalry regiment, who raced in pursuit of Captain Hoge's fleeing remnants. Catching three Confederate horsemen and an official of the Nitre Bureau, Long and the Second Kentucky turned northward on the mountain, eventually joining Crook and the two Ohio regiments at John Price's farm. On the valley floor, the Pioneer Brigade quickly carried the remainder of Heg's brigade across the river and began to construct the pontoon bridge. As soon as the first boat was anchored in position, another was dropped downstream beside it, anchored, and connected to the first with long timbers called balks. As soon as the balks were secured, flat planks called chesses were laid on the balks as a roadway. The chesses were secured by side rails lashed to the balks by ropes threaded through the chesses. The side rails thus made the roadway somewhat more rigid while still allowing the bridge to flex in response to both the load and wave motion. Although the windy day made the clumsy pontoons difficult to manage, the engineers worked rapidly. Details from Carlin's brigade supplemented their efforts. By 1:00 P.M., McCook announced that the bridge was available for traffic. Among the first units to cross was the First Tennessee (Union) Cavalry regiment. Most of the Tennesseans scouted downriver, while one company climbed the mountain to screen Heg's infantry.[14]

Delighted that the crossing at Caperton's Ferry had been so successful, Rosecrans rode to the bridge with Garfield, McCook, and Negley. Crossing the span, Rosecrans continued to the top of Sand Mountain, where the Eighth Kansas Infantry regiment stood guard over the bridgehead. After bantering with the men, Rosecrans and his party returned to the bridge and continued to Stevenson. On the way, they met a party of officers from Negley's division, which included John Beatty, Timothy Stanley, and Col. Horace Hobart. According to Beatty, Rosecrans "checked up, shook hands, and said: 'How d' ye do?' Garfield gave us a grip which suggested 'vote right, vote early.' Negley smiled affably, and the cavalcade moved on." Beatty and his group then crossed the bridge and explored the lush countryside below the mountain. Returning to the river, they found Pioneer Brigade soldiers frolicking in the river, a practice soon curtailed by brigade order. Meanwhile, Heg ordered the Fifteenth Wisconsin to join the Eighth Kansas on top of Sand Mountain. He wanted to send his remaining two regiments as well, but the road was so bad that he elected to wait until the next day. At dusk, he sent the Eighth Kansas and Fifteenth Wisconsin three miles ahead on top of the plateau, where they established a defensive position. Davis supported Heg by moving Carlin's Second Brigade to the bridge, although he held it on the west shore. At the same time, McCook ordered Davis to bring Post's First Brigade to the bridge early the next morning. He also directed Johnson to move his Second Division from its Bellefonte camps to Crow Creek, near Stevenson, on the next day as well. Pleased with the work of his division, Davis and his wife that evening were Post's guests at a dinner party held at Post's quarters. Stanley and Capt. Joseph Pope, Davis's commissary officer, along with Pope's wife, completed the convivial group. As night settled over Caperton's Ferry, many of Davis's soldiers no doubt expressed relief that the Army of Tennessee had not chosen to contest the crossing.[15]

Eleven miles upstream at Bridgeport, Lytle orchestrated another crossing with a force that had grown to ten regiments of infantry, a regiment of cavalry, two batteries, and a detachment of the First Michigan Engineers and Mechanics. After placing the batteries to cover Long Island, Lytle ordered the Second Michigan Cavalry regiment to begin fording the river shortly after noon. The horsemen entered the water opposite the northern tip of Long Island, a mile and a half north of the railroad bridge. The first troopers experienced difficulty descending the steep fifteen-foot bank, but gradually the movement of men and horses created a safer passage. The river was shallow at the crossing site, causing only a few of the smaller horses to tread water. On the far shore a thick canebrake masked any lurking defenders, but none appeared. Forcing their way through the thicket in single file, the Federal horsemen eventually reached the point where the railroad had crossed the river in happier times. As Lytle watched from the Bridgeport bluff, Maj. Leonidas Scranton arrayed his regiment in battle formation and sent Company M across the narrow river channel toward the far bank. Again, the Federals expected to be met by a thunderous volley; again they were relieved when no shots were fired. With the water only four feet deep, the cavalrymen soon reached the far shore. The remainder of the regiment followed and advanced a mile beyond the river. No Confederates were found, probably because they had withdrawn in the face of Crook's sweep into Hogjaw Valley earlier that morning. Back at Bridgeport, some infantrymen occupied Long Island, while others prepared bridge timbers. Meanwhile, Lytle sent his aide, Capt. Alfred Pirtle, to survey the river with several pontoons that had arrived the previous night. In a letter home, Pirtle noted, "The trip was enjoyed by all of us, being a pleasant break in a monotonous life." For the remainder of Lytle's enlarged command, the day passed quietly. At least one young private, Merritt Simonds, sat for his photograph.[16]

Four miles upriver, Brannan continued to press his superiors for permission to cross the river at the mouth of Battle Creek. At 8:30 A.M. Thomas forwarded to Rosecrans Brannan's assurances that he could seize a bridgehead with a single regiment. Rosecrans had not initially expected to make a crossing in the Battle Creek vicinity and had deployed no bridging assets there. Brannan's insistence that he could accomplish the task without assistance led Rosecrans to let him try. At 9:50 A.M. he authorized Brannan to attempt a limited crossing. Anticipating approval, Brannan at 11:00 A.M. sent a few scouts across the river. When the scouts encountered no Confederates, Brannan renewed his plea to be allowed to cross a regiment. Upon receiving the permission he had so vigorously sought, Brannan assigned the task to Van Derveer's Third Brigade. Van Derveer decided to initiate the crossing cautiously with only two companies. He offered the honor of leading the movement to the Second Minnesota Infantry regiment, builders of the raft and canoes to be used in the crossing. When they demurred, he directed the Thirty-Fifth Ohio Infantry regiment to provide the crossing force. Around 3:00 P.M. Companies A and G of Lt. Col. Henry Boynton's regiment crossed the river by propelling the large raft out of the mouth of Battle Creek. Like the scouts before them, they found no one contesting their advance. Chastened by the ease with which their sister regiment seized the far shore, the Second Minnesota sent four companies across the river after dark. Reporting Van Derveer's success to corps headquarters, Brannan asked to expand the small bridgehead. Thomas responded at 8:45 P.M. with the welcome news that Brannan could cross not only a regiment but also his entire division. Recognizing the raft's inadequacy, Thomas told Brannan to send his trains to the Stevenson depot, fill them with twenty-five days' rations, and direct them to Bridgeport, where a bridge would be constructed within forty-eight hours.[17]

Above Battle Creek, Federal activity on the river was minimal. During the early morning King's raiding party returned from Shell Mound, having driven Confederate pickets deep into Running Water Canyon. The remainder of Reynolds's division spent the day peacefully. Cpl. William Miller of the Seventy-Fifth Indiana Infantry regiment noted the arrival of many Confederate deserters and recorded his impressions: "They say the war is over and I have no doubt they think so, but I can't agree with them for I think there will be a terrible battle in this department within the next thirty days." Opposite Chattanooga, the Seventeenth Indiana Mounted Infantry regiment surveyed a ford at Friar's Island. Otherwise, the aggressive activity was confined to Wagner's Second Brigade. For some time Wagner had pressed for a more active role for his command while watching Wilder's men agitate the Confederates. Unwilling to remain passive and contemptuous of the deception operation's languid pace, Wagner resolved to act. Gathering the Fortieth and Fifty-Seventh Indiana Infantry regiments and a section of the Tenth Indiana Battery, he took them down the mountain to Lilly's gun pits on Stringer's Ridge and proceeded to bombard the town. Wagner's gunners employed two ten-pounder Parrotts, functionally equivalent to Lilly's three-inch ordnance rifles, but neither the quality of their ammunition nor their gunnery skills equaled Lilly's performance. Capt. William Naylor's men fired thirty-eight rounds in a two-hour span ending at 1:00 P.M. with little effect except to amuse Lilly's men. Besides moderating Wagner's thirst for action, the expedition yielded a deserter from the Thirty-Seventh Tennessee Infantry regiment, who stated that Stewart's Division had departed for Cleveland on the previous night. Coupled with some vague information from civilians and Wagner's own observations, the deserter's report indicated that the Confederates were shifting troops upriver. In a note to division headquarters, Wagner duly reported his analysis for consideration by his superiors.[18]

The momentous events taking place in the Tennessee River valley went without notice in the Twenty-First Corps, closeted in the long narrow trench of the Sequatchie Valley. There, the supply lines finally were working satisfactorily, the temperature was comfortable, the foraging was good, and most of the locals remained friendly though they were considered ignorant and poor. Perhaps best of all, the mail was arriving regularly. Letters from home often released powerful emotions, as shown by the response of Pvt. Willis Jones of the Eighty-Fourth Illinois Infantry regiment to a miniature sent by his wife, Rachel: "The more I look at it the better it looks and the better I like it. . . . It looks as tho you was thinking of me. . . . You look as pleasing as you ever did. . . . The baby it looks natural as it did when I left home and there has bin but one day since I got it but what I have looked at them several times. . . . Well I will have to stop this and write about something elce." In the Thirty-First Indiana Infantry regiment, several applicants for commissions in the United States Colored Troops departed for Stevenson to be examined. In many Twenty-First Corps units spirits were high because of rumored successes in South Carolina and the increasing numbers of demoralized deserters offering themselves for capture. The exuberance got out of hand again in Beatty's command, and he held the brigade in line for several hours until near midnight for the offense of "yelling." Van Cleve at Pikeville informed Crittenden that he had finally accumulated sufficient rations for his division and Minty's brigade beyond Walden's Ridge. Like Hazen, whose brigade was also beyond Walden's Ridge, Van Cleve also boasted of operating a local mill for the benefit of his troops. Best of all, Van Cleve stated that a courier from his division had met troops belonging to Burnside's army at Jamestown, Tennessee, sixty miles north of Pikeville, three days earlier. In turn, Crittenden forwarded the good news to Garfield at Stevenson.

While extremely tenuous, the connection between Rosecrans's and Burnside's armies had finally been made.[19]

Soldiers at Stevenson and camped along the railroad were better informed about the progress of the campaign than their compatriots in the Sequatchie Valley. Laibold's Second Brigade of Sheridan's Third Division continued to guard the massive piles of supplies that were rapidly filling the open space around Stevenson. Just outside town, Negley's Second Division remained at rest, its daily routine disturbed only by locomotive whistles. On 29 August, Pvt. William Stookey, twenty-two, of the Forty-Second Indiana Infantry regiment, wrote to his wife, Helen: "I am a very tierd of living away from you my loving Wife. . . . The time is passing away fast and it will not be long till the last year passes by." Capt. Daniel O'Leary of the Fifteenth Kentucky Infantry regiment placed his own hardship in a wider context: "The people of the north know but very little of the trials and privations the poor people have to endure among these mountains. The old men, women and children remain and consequently they were unable to cultivate very much this season and they are deprived of the greater portion of what they did raise, while mothers and daughters of once respectable families sacrifice their honor for a few dollars to enable them to sustain life." In Battery G, First Ohio Light Artillery, two men convicted of stealing $40.00 from a widow were drummed through the camps with their heads partially shaved. At a picket post near Anderson Station, Capt. James Edmonds, twenty-seven, of the Ninety-Fourth Ohio Infantry regiment found his mind wandering back to an earlier time: "I have laid upon my blanket, gazing at the passing clouds, musing most of the day. I am strongly reminded of many such days spent at college when all was 'coleur de rose.'" In the camp of Battery H, Fifth United States Artillery, Lt. Howard Burnham's thoughts also turned to home, as he explained to his mother: "I have been so far in fine health and like this out-door life—everything except waiting three or four days in camp. I suppose Longmeadow [Massachusetts] is looking very pleasant and our place more so, but I shall not probably see it this season."[20]

The units stationed on the army's right and in its rear were not immune to the quickening pace of events on 29 August. At Bellefonte, in Johnson's Second Division rumors began to circulate that their days in camp were nearing an end. Capt. Henry Richards of the Ninety-Third Ohio Infantry regiment wrote to his father disparagingly about the local population: "The inhabitants in the mountains seem very ignorant generally and especially the women, which all chew tobacco and dip snuff." Although Richards chose not to mention it, during the day a soldier in his regiment was drummed out of camp for desertion. In the Twenty-Ninth Indiana Infantry regiment, Pvt. Bergun Brown praised Rosecrans in a letter to his family: "As soon as the occasion requires Old Rose will be on hand. What a blessing to have a commander that the men have confidence in. They work together." That evening the long-awaited orders arrived. In the Reserve Corps, some units were already in motion. During the day, Second Division commander Morgan arrived in Athens, Alabama, with Tillson's First Brigade and part of a cavalry regiment. Sixty miles to the north, Dan McCook's Second Brigade consolidated at Columbia, Tennessee. Morgan's task was to guard the army's right flank by pacifying the restive countryside. Having lost a brother under ambiguous circumstances a year earlier, Dan McCook was in no mood to be gentle with the locals. As he informed Granger, "Some such decided measures as you adopted at Franklin must be adopted here and at Pulaski to break the necks of the rebels." Such bald sentiments could only lead to trouble if McCook's command continued southward. On better terms with civilians around Shelbyville, Fosterville, Wartrace, and Estill Springs, soldiers of Steedman's First Division spent the day foraging for vegetables, apples, and plums. Less pleasant was the work assigned to the 113th Ohio Infantry regiment, stuck with salvaging more than 1,000 sacks of corn from the site of a recent train derailment.[21]

Upon returning from Caperton's Ferry, Rosecrans made several significant decisions. Because the crossing had not faced even token opposition, he decided to bring forward Reserve Corps units on both flanks of the army. On Rosecrans's left, Dick's Second Brigade of Van Cleve's Third Division still garrisoned McMinnville on the far side of the Cumberland Plateau. To leave it there while its parent unit advanced from Pikeville was unacceptable, so Granger was instructed to relieve Dick with several regiments of loyal East Tennesseeans brought from Alexandria, Tennessee. Rosecrans informed Granger that the Alexandria units, soon to be commanded by Brig. Gen. James Spears, would eventually advance to Pikeville. Other Tennessee units were to abandon Carthage, Tennessee, and move to McMinnville as well. On the army's right flank, Rosecrans instructed Granger to cancel Morgan's occupation of Athens, Alabama, and send Morgan to Huntsville instead. Having strengthened his flanks, Rosecrans turned to the inefficiency of the Pioneer Brigade. Although they had built the pontoon bridge in four hours, Rosecrans desired significant changes in the Pioneers' organization. He had not worked well with St. Clair Morton, the army's former chief engineer, but Morton's successors were also unsatisfactory. Capt. William Merrill of the Topographical Engineers was too busy with his own organization, Lt. George Burroughs was too inexperienced, and Capt. Patrick O'Connell lacked the rank to command even the Pioneer Brigade. Earlier, Rosecrans had written to Halleck about the problem; now he asked permission to organize two volunteer engineer regiments from the Pioneer Brigade. The concerns about his engineers notwithstanding, Rosecrans highlighted their performance in his nightly summary for Halleck, reporting simply that the Army of the Cumberland was across the Tennessee River in several places from Caperton's Ferry to Battle Creek, with "no fighting to amount to anything."[22]

If Rosecrans was heartened by the events of 29 August, his opponents in Chattanooga remained in a quandary as to his intentions. The day dawned bright and cool at Bragg's headquarters without any news from the troops guarding the long Tennessee River line. Acting upon his suspicions that the Federal crossing would be upstream from Chattanooga, Bragg resolved early to reinforce Hill's Corps. First he ordered Wharton's Cavalry Division to leave its camps around Rome, Georgia, and move to Hill's sector of the river line, where it would form a screen in front of Hill's Corps. The order went directly to Wharton, bypassing Wheeler, which indicated an elevated level of urgency at army headquarters. Informing Hill of Wharton's instructions, Mackall admitted that Wharton's was the only Cavalry Corps division ready for field service. He also told Hill not to count on the support of Liddell's small two-brigade division, which would remain at Chickamauga Station guarding the army's supply depot. In contrast, the troops arriving from Mississippi would soon be available to reinforce Hill's command, replacing Stewart's Division, which had been sent to assist Buckner. Mackall also shared with Hill several of Bragg's suggestions for the deployment of the new arrivals. According to Mackall, Bragg favored placing one division at Harrison, away from the river, as well as keeping the bulk of Hill's command near the East Tennessee & Georgia Railroad for ease in concentration. He further suggested that Hill strongly protect the village of Charleston, where the railroad crossed the Hiwassee River. Still, Mackall assured Hill, Bragg desired that Hill make his own dispositions as he saw fit. Not yet sure of Hill's abilities as a corps commander, Bragg momentarily was treating the dour and prickly Hill carefully. On the one hand, he wanted to give the North Carolinian free rein within his own sector; on the other, he could not resist making his own wishes known. He thus chose a diplomatic course: offer Hill pointed suggestions but provide them through an intermediary, Mackall.[23]

During the day news of Federal activity arrived from several sources. The ineffectual shelling of Chattanooga initially caused no alarm; the Federal shooting was poor, and nothing significant was hit. At some point during the afternoon, however, Capt. Patrick Rice, commanding Company G, Third Confederate Cavalry regiment, reported that a Federal force had crossed the Tennessee around Shell Mound and Bridgeport, and that his regiment was abandoning Sand Mountain and withdrawing toward Trenton. The captain's message apparently referenced the Federal raid at Shell Mound during the previous night and Crook's drive through Hogjaw Valley and up Sand Mountain beyond Moore's Spring. Surmising that the bombardment and the seemingly limited crossing downstream from Chattanooga represented only a feint, Bragg and his staff believed that a crossing upstream from the city would soon occur. Because the troops from Mississippi were just beginning to arrive, and Stewart's Division had already departed, Hill would need help quickly. Thus army headquarters drafted new orders. Hindman's Division, encamped at McFarland's Spring at the foot of Missionary Ridge, was instructed to march to Chickamauga Bridge, near Hill's headquarters. Subsequently, a second message from Captain Rice ominously reported that a Federal brigade had crossed the Tennessee at and below Bridgeport. That message only served to reinforce Bragg's concern about his army's right flank and the even graver danger to Buckner at Loudon. In fact, Buckner's situation seemed to be of far greater concern than anything happening downstream. Brent's diary characterized the discussion at army headquarters: "Shall we abandon East Tenn? Buckner has not force enough to defend it. To leave him there would endanger his command, & he would be thus rendered useless in the campaign. As we can not go to his assistance it would be better to place him, in such position, as would insure his co-operation with this army, & enable him to fall on Rosecrans with our entire strength."[24]

A final bit of information reaching Bragg on 29 August confirmed his judgment about Federal intentions. At some point during the day, he received a memorandum from Col. Benjamin Hill, commander of the Thirty-Fifth Tennessee Infantry regiment. A native of McMinnville, Hill for some time had been sending scouts west of the Tennessee River. His memorandum placed two divisions of the Twenty-First Corps in the Sequatchie Valley, at Dunlap and Pikeville, and part of the third east of Walden's Ridge. That information was essentially correct. He also correctly identified Wilder's brigade. According to Hill, additional mounted brigades had just come over the ridge with pack mules to join Wilder. Although Hill misidentified the commanders of the divisions and confused Wilder's supply trains with new units, he was more right than wrong about Crittenden's command. Hill then proceeded to go astray by locating Rosecrans at Dunlap and Thomas's Fourteenth Corps moving north in the Sequatchie Valley. According to Hill, McCook's Twentieth Corps was scattered among posts at Murfreesboro, Stevenson, and Bridgeport. He placed Rosecrans's total strength at 45,000 men, organized in three corps of three divisions each, with three brigades in each division. In fact, Hill correctly named seven of Rosecrans's ten infantry division commanders on the river line, but he confused the Reserve Corps with McCook's command. Except for Wilder's and what proved to be Minty's mounted units, Hill also knew nothing of Stanley's Cavalry Corps. He thus provided Bragg with a reasonably accurate order of battle for the units on the river, but he seriously underestimated Rosecrans's strength. Most important of all, he erred badly by reporting the movement of Thomas's command northward in the Sequatchie Valley. Reynolds's occupation of Jasper and the movement of supply trains northward from Stevenson were no doubt the cause of Hill's mistaken analysis. Still, his memorandum aligned nicely with information Bragg had already received from other sources about Federal activity in the Sequatchie Valley.[25]

With hindsight, it is easy to blame Bragg for not perceiving Captain Rice's brief statements to be true indicators of Rosecrans's plans. Indeed, numerous historians have accused Bragg of being a confused, hesitant commander who had lost track of Rosecrans's army. Yet, from Bragg's perspective in the Chattanooga suburbs, a major Federal crossing below Chattanooga did not seem so obvious. Until that moment, the bulk of aggressive Federal activity had been at Chattanooga and above. True, Bragg had reports locating the bulk of the Army of the Cumberland in the Jasper-Stevenson area, but those reports were balanced by the statement of a citizen that the Federal army was shifting northward in the Sequatchie Valley. Now, Colonel Hill offered an even more detailed account, and it too pointed to a northward shift by Rosecrans. Buckner's certainty about his own perilous situation and Hill's description of events in the Sequatchie Valley made it easy for Bragg to see a developing pattern. For him, the movement of large Federal infantry units was the key indicator of Federal intentions. Rice's initial report had focused on cavalry units. His second report, about a brigade crossing below Bridgeport, was unspecific and may have only referred to the Federal cavalry crossing at Hart's Bar. In addition, small Federal probes in the Shell Mound area were common and hardly a cause for alarm. In contrast, Hill had described the movement northward of an entire infantry corps. With Bragg and his generals focused upon Buckner, Hill's information had to be taken seriously. Similarly, Rice's reports could be interpreted as simply a scheme to divert attention from an upstream crossing. Even Col. William Estes, Rice's commander, mentioned only cavalry when he reported a Federal crossing below Bridgeport to Wheeler at 1:00 P.M. Without news of the infantry crossing at Caperton's Ferry, Bragg was not befuddled but was acting rationally in response to what he knew at that moment. Unfortunately, his assessment was incorrect; fortunately, there was still time to get it right.[26]

Bragg's soldiers tended to see the events of 29 August in the same way he did. They regarded the bombardment of Chattanooga as inconsequential. According to Sgt. Robert Bliss of Wood's Brigade, "As I write, the booming of cannon may be heard down the river in the direction of Chattanooga, but we have got so used to this that it is looked upon as nothing." Lt. William Moore of the Twenty-Fifth Alabama disparaged the shelling: "There has been sharp cannonading to-day but we have not heard the result yet. I do suppose however that it will [not] amount to anything only a few men killed on each side, which *does not help at all to make peace,* and ought to be stopped as an inhuman sacrifice of life without any good result." There was desultory skirmishing from Chattanooga to Blythe's Ferry, but that too had become routine. Chattanooga remained "an empty, dismal place," according to Capt. James Hall of the Twenty-Fourth Alabama Infantry regiment. Sergeant Bliss agreed: "Chattanooga has fallen back to Atlanta." Still, some citizens too poor to escape remained camped in the woods just beyond the city limits. The absence of most of the residents tempted some soldiers, who began to plunder locked houses. After the provost guard arrested a dozen miscreants, the *Daily Rebel* vigorously condemned such behavior: "One or two such offenders, swung up by the neck, might serve as an example to other thieves in uniform." Most men in the ranks carried themselves honorably and professionally, filling the day with drill, inspection, dress parade, and in many cases, prayer meetings. Beyond that, all discussed the rumors that reinforcements were coming and that Knoxville and Cumberland Gap had fallen. At least one soldier found time to take a pleasure ride into the countryside near Harrison. Like his counterparts across the river, Sgt. John Sparkman found the local females unappealing: "Nearly all of the women are barefooted and bareheaded. They are not tasty or fashionable and generally homely."[27]

Because of the uncertainty, most large units remained stationary on 29 August. In Polk's Corps, Cheatham's Division continued to occupy camps south of Chattanooga. For the moment, Hindman's Division remained at McFarland's Spring five miles south of town, but Bragg's late-afternoon decision to send it to Chickamauga Bridge would soon set it in motion. Cleburne's Division remained scattered along the river from Harrison to Blythe's Ferry. Liddell's two brigades guarded the army's supply base at Chickamauga Station. Most of Stewart's Division spent the day on trains of the East Tennessee & Georgia Railroad. Three brigades reached Loudon on 29 August, but Clayton's Brigade spent the day trudging from Blythe's Ferry to the railroad at Tyner's Station. At Loudon, Stewart joined Preston's Division. Buckner's cavalry continued to screen the approaches to Knoxville, if only to maintain some contact with Burnside's advancing forces. Similarly, Forrest's Cavalry Division picketed the Tennessee and Clinch Rivers from north of the Hiwassee to a point beyond Kingston. South of Chattanooga, much of Wheeler's Cavalry Corps remained at rest. Wharton's Division at Rome was under orders to join Hill's Corps upstream from Harrison, but it had not yet begun to move. Martin's Division left Alexandria, Alabama, and marched to Gadsden, Wheeler's headquarters. As for Walker's Division, Wilson's Brigade settled into camps around Chickamauga Station, while scattered regiments of Ector's and Gist's Brigades arrived during the day. Breckinridge's leading unit, Adams's Brigade, was north of Montgomery, while Stovall's and Helm's Brigades converged on that city by two routes, part via Mobile and part via Selma. While far better than marching, the rail movement was not without risk, according to Pvt. William Jones of the Forty-First Alabama Infantry regiment: "I will tell you of an awful occurrence that happened as we come a long on the cars. Jaret [Jarrott] Gray was on the top of the cars an fell off when it was running very fast an surposed it killed him. We havant hurd from him yet."[28]

. . . .

By common practice in Rosecrans's army, Sundays normally were days of rest, but 30 August was not a normal Sunday in the Tennessee River valley. The Confederates inexplicably had not opposed the initial crossing, but the advantage could be lost if Rosecrans did not consolidate his tenuous foothold by pushing more troops across the broad stream. Trusting McCook to expedite the flow of men over the Caperton's Ferry bridge, Rosecrans, Garfield, and Sheridan departed for Bridgeport in the dummy in late morning. Behind them, McCook found the frail and narrow bridge to be a limiting factor. Already across the stream, Heg called forward his brigade trains and his two remaining regiments. The steep track up Sand Mountain proved to be another limiting factor, requiring infantrymen to assist the heavily loaded wagons up the mountain. By the end of the day, Heg's command was united on the plateau at a crossroads five miles southeast of Caperton's Ferry. Behind Heg, Carlin's Second Brigade crossed the river during the morning but camped in the lush bottomlands east of the stream. Following Carlin, Post's First Brigade left its camps west of the river and marched to the pontoon bridge. Arriving around 9:00 A.M., Post found a large cattle herd being driven across the bridge, a difficult task that took virtually all day. While waiting, some of Post's men swam or bathed in the river, foraged in the surrounding countryside, or watered their mule teams in the river. Finally, around 4:00 P.M., the brigade took its turn on the swaying structure. Serenaded by the band of the Seventy-Fourth Illinois Infantry regiment, the soldiers managed to avoid being thrown from the undulating bridge. Once across, they too camped at the foot of Sand Mountain. Although Davis would report that his division reached the top of the mountain on 30 August, and McCook would repeat the claim, only Heg's troops occupied the mountaintop at the end of the day. That night McCook ordered Johnson to move his Second Division across the bridge early the next morning, camping in the fields to be vacated by Davis's troops.[29]

While Caperton's Ferry was significant in Rosecrans's plan, the Bridgeport site was far more important to the success of the operation. Not only did Bridgeport offer direct railroad access to the river, it also facilitated the rapid reconstruction of the two massive railroad bridges critical to extending the campaign southward. Arriving at Bridgeport after the morning chill had dissipated, Rosecrans, Garfield, and Sheridan found thousands of men at work. Lytle's and Bradley's brigades, joined by two of Brannan's regiments and a battalion of the First Michigan Engineers and Mechanics, were busily engaged in preparing timbers for a trestle bridge. To complete the trestle span and to bridge the narrower channel beyond Long Island, Rosecrans saw that far more pontoons would be required than the four already on hand. To facilitate the work from both shores simultaneously, Lytle had constructed a shaky footbridge across the narrow channel by utilizing the wreckage of the railroad drawbridge. He also ordered details to improve the bridge approaches and drive a road across Long Island. Intensely interested in the details of the work, Rosecrans crossed the river with Sheridan, who basked in the commanding general's approval. Sheridan had promised a bridge at Bridgeport, but there was still much work to be done at the site. Although the river level was low, it was still "swimming deep" in places, making the arrival of the pontoons critical. Sheridan was also anxious to consolidate his division beyond the stream as rapidly as possible, so he requested the relief of Laibold's Second Brigade from guard duty at Stevenson. Rosecrans agreed, and, before leaving Bridgeport, Garfield directed Thomas to relieve Laibold's men. The army commander and his retinue departed Bridgeport in late afternoon, but Lytle kept most of the troops at their backbreaking labor well into the night. On the far shore, the bulk of the Second Michigan Cavalry regiment guarded the working parties, while Company M made a quick scout to Shell Mound before returning at dark.[30]

Upstream at Battle Creek, Brannan was determined to get his division across the stream. His sole assets were a fifty-foot raft, two canoes, and two flat-bottomed skiffs. Van Derveer began the crossing with the Thirty-Fifth Ohio Infantry regiment, followed by the Eighty-Seventh Indiana Infantry regiment. With so few boats, the process was long and tedious. The large log raft in particular was an unstable platform, but it moved far more personnel than the smaller vessels. At some point Van Derveer and his son Harry crossed in one of the small boats. It was a sight never to be forgotten — the raft on the river, hundreds of men in frenetic activity, the swimming horses, and a regimental band playing onshore. Harry Van Derveer wanted to continue on the campaign, telling his mother, "I believe that school commences Monday. I would like to be there but then I like to be down here with Father." During the afternoon, the Ninth Ohio Infantry regiment attempted to get its horses across the stream by loading the skiffs with twenty-five men, some of whom held long ropes attached to horses. Men onshore then forced the horses to jump into the stream and swim across the river guided by the ropes. One horse tried to jump from the bank directly into a boat, capsizing the skiff and dumping the infantrymen into water twelve feet deep. All were rescued, even the troublesome horse. Finally, in late afternoon the Second Minnesota Infantry regiment crossed without incident, leaving behind the brigade's battery and most of its rations and baggage. Soldiers worked until past midnight to transfer some rations to the far shore, but it would take another day to make Van Derveer's command ready for combat. Fortunately, patrols sent inland to the railroad discovered no Confederates. Brannan had hoped to cross more of the division before the day ended, but Connell's First Brigade placed only two companies on the far shore before operations ceased. Nevertheless, at 7:15 P.M. Brannan reported to corps headquarters that Van Derveer was across and Connell would follow during the evening.[31]

Like Brannan, Reynolds itched to begin crossing the river. At 8:00 A.M. Reynolds informed Fourteenth Corps headquarters that he had ample means for crossing the river at Shell Mound. By capture or construction, Reynolds had collected seven flatboats and an eighth was nearly complete. With that flotilla, Reynolds estimated that he could move 400 men across the stream every hour. The boats could each move a wagon and team, permitting the crossing of a regiment's train in thirty minutes. With no opposition nearby, Reynolds boasted that he could move the Fourth Division across the Tennessee at any time Rosecrans desired. Pending Rosecrans's permission, Reynolds announced that he would send an expedition beyond the river toward Trenton, Georgia, that evening. Before Reynolds's message reached corps headquarters at Bolivar, Thomas at 12:30 P.M. asked Reynolds if it was feasible to take the entire division beyond the stream. If so, Reynolds was to reduce baggage, cross with his troops and a few wagons, and send the remainder of his trains to Stevenson. There they would load enough supplies for twenty-five days and head to Bridgeport, where a bridge was expected to be completed soon. Reynolds responded positively at 2:30 P.M., and redirected his pending reconnaissance toward Chattanooga instead of Trenton. He planned to send most of King's Second Brigade across the river that night to support the reconnaissance. At 4:55 P.M. Thomas authorized Reynolds to cross his entire division at Shell Mound as soon as possible. King immediately began preparations to cross the river in support of the Second Tennessee (Union) Cavalry regiment during the evening. Turchin's Third Brigade was left at Jasper a while longer. There, Surgeon Josiah Cotton of the Ninety-Second Ohio Infantry regiment wrote his wife that the men's morale had never been higher, especially since they were now free from George Crook. Turchin, with his European attitude toward foraging and his lax discipline, was much more to their liking, according to Cotton.[32]

If most of his old brigade was delighted to be rid of him, Crook was equally glad to change commands. An infantryman by education and experience, he had traded places with Turchin at the end of July. According to Crook's biographer, Stanley may have chosen Crook because they were both Ohioans and fellow graduates of the West Point class of 1852. At any rate, Crook on 30 August was participating in his first major operation as a cavalryman. On the previous day he had led the First and Third Ohio Cavalry regiments on a sweep along the shore from Hart's Bar to Bridgeport and beyond to the top of Sand Mountain.

After Long and the Second Kentucky Cavalry regiment arrived from Caperton's Ferry, Crook early in the morning headed for the eastern slope of Sand Mountain. Descending into Lookout Valley, at 8:00 A.M. he burst into Trenton, county seat of Dade County. Trenton was also the terminus of the Wills Valley Railroad, a small company whose dream of connecting Wauhatchie, Tennessee, with Gadsden, Alabama, had been halted by the war. Grading was complete to Gadsden, but track had been laid only between Trenton and Wauhatchie, twenty miles to the north. Finding no opposition at Trenton, Crook scouted some distance along the track toward Wauhatchie. Again no opposition materialized, but prudence dictated caution, so the cavalrymen returned to Trenton. There the Federals procured some "groceries" and tobacco from local stores, then returned to the top of Sand Mountain and camped. Meanwhile, Capt. George Gotwald and a detail of twenty-eight men from Company E, Fourth Ohio Cavalry regiment, fruitlessly searched Sand Mountain for Crook and Long. Dispatched by Stanley with an order for Crook, Gotwald asked everyone he saw along the way from the river to Moore's Spring and beyond for Crook's location, but was rebuffed. He returned across the river, chagrinned to report his failure, but he had at least gained useful information on the roads crossing Sand Mountain into Lookout Valley.[33]

Although the crossings below Chattanooga were at a delicate stage, Rosecrans's deception force made no special effort to distract watching Confederates. In Wilder's command most soldiers relaxed in camp. In keeping with the day, Chaplain Safety Layton of the Seventeenth Indiana Mounted Infantry regiment preached in a local meetinghouse to congregants from several regiments. Pvt. Alva Griest of the Seventy-Second Indiana Mounted Infantry found his peaceful Sunday disturbed by stomach pains caused by too much cobbler and by hordes of mosquitos infesting the river bottom. In the Eighteenth Indiana Battery, Lilly again dispatched a detail over Walden's Ridge to acquire more ammunition from the Tracy City railhead. For Wilder's men, the big news was the presence of William Crutchfield, prominent member of the family that formerly owned Chattanooga's premier hotel. Crutchfield had been a Federal spy since the fall of 1861, and, although no longer associated with the hotel, he and his brother Thomas had continued to observe Confederate activity, which William passed to the Federals from his farm on the river north of town. As Confederate suspicions grew, William Crutchfield crossed the river during the evening of 29–30 August. During the day Wilder made an extensive visual reconnaissance of the Confederate works at Friar's Island, six river miles above Chattanooga. Atop Walden's Ridge, Wagner's command also quietly observed the panorama spread below them. Capt. John McGraw of the Fifty-Seventh Indiana Infantry regiment improved the time by writing his wife, Mary Ann, enclosing three flowers he had picked on the mountaintop. There was a little

The Crutchfield House hotel, Chattanooga, Tennessee. (Chattanooga Public Library)

more activity upstream, where Hazen sent some of Funkhouser's men to the river at Harrison's Ferry. There they exchanged shots with Confederate pickets, losing one man wounded. Most of Hazen's men spent the day participating in a grand review. The event was attended by more than 300 Unionist citizens, some of whom waved crude, homemade national colors.[34]

Away from the river, Sunday, 30 August, was a quiet day, especially for the Twenty-First Corps. Around Therman, Wood's First Division remained at ease, while Palmer's Second Division at Dunlap broke the routine with church services and much letter writing. The religious gatherings drew large numbers of enthusiastic civilians. Mail service into the Sequatchie Valley finally had become regularized, offering the soldiers the opportunity to correspond more frequently with loved ones and friends. In the Eighty-Fourth Illinois Infantry regiment, Pvt. Willis Jones sent his daughter Mellunda Ann some seeds that he had collected. At Pikeville, Van Cleve's Third Division welcomed the battalion of the Third Indiana Cavalry regiment, which arrived during the day from beyond the Cumberland Plateau. Although the unit belonged to Minty's command, Van Cleve planned to use it to establish a better link with Burnside. Having finally amassed enough rations to last sixteen days, he nevertheless dispatched another supply train over the mountains to McMinnville. In contrast to the Twenty-First Corps, McCook's Twentieth Corps was mostly in motion on 30 August. With Davis's First Division consolidating beyond the Tennessee, and Johnson's Second Division marching to Crow Creek from Bellefonte, only Laibold's brigade of Sheridan's Third Division was stationary at Stevenson. Likewise, in Thomas's corps, only Baird's First and Negley's Second Divisions remained in their camps in Crow Creek valley. For them, 30 August was also a day of dress parades, inspections, and preaching by regimental chaplains or representatives of the Christian Commission. Still, on this peaceful Sunday, death continued to stalk the camps. In the Eleventh Michigan Infantry regiment of Stanley's brigade, Pvt. Joseph Shranger of Company E died suddenly and was buried before sunset. In the Seventy-Ninth Pennsylvania Infantry regiment in Baird's division, Pvt. Jacob Ostrander was notified that his wife, Esther, daughter Agnes, and a sister-in-law had drowned in the Monongahela River.[35]

There was more activity on the army's right and rear. While Edward McCook personally reconnoitered a ford near Bellefonte, his staff ordered Watkins's Third Brigade to leave Maysville, Alabama, for Larkinsville, McCook's headquarters. At Larkinsville, McCook's old Second Brigade, commanded by Col. Oscar LaGrange, spent the day idly racing horses in camp or attending church services in town. Those elements of Campbell's First Brigade not already across the river remained stretched along it on both sides of Stevenson. To fill the void left by the eastward movement of Watkins's command, Morgan's Second Division of the Reserve Corps continued its leisurely advance from Middle Tennessee into northern Alabama. Granger ordered Morgan to march from Athens to Huntsville with Tillson's First Brigade. Far behind Tillson was Daniel McCook's Second Brigade, which was just departing Columbia, Tennessee. Leaving a regiment to garrison Columbia, McCook led the remainder of his brigade southward along the line of the damaged Nashville & Decatur Railroad. As he advanced, McCook discovered growing hostility among civilians and an equal propensity for marauding among his men. When he halted for the night at the hamlet of Lynnville, seventeen miles south of Columbia, he ordered another public reading of his standard order against marauding. He also counseled the local citizenry against the random shots from concealment hated by the troops as "bushwhacking." He also established a strong security perimeter around his camp. In more secure areas such as Shelbyville, Wartrace, Tullahoma, Fosterville, and Estill Springs, Steedman's First Division had no need for such drastic precautions. Nevertheless, they remained alert as they guarded the army's Nashville & Chattanooga Railroad lifeline. In the 115th Illinois Infantry regiment at Fosterville, the weekly religious service became a funeral sermon for Musician Amos Wilson, who had died on the previous day. Otherwise, the day was quiet along the lines of communication.[36]

Energized by his visit to Bridgeport, Rosecrans spent the evening dispatching a flurry of orders to maintain the army's forward momentum. Rosecrans first wrote Crittenden a vague note ordering him to "move down secretly and quietly, leaving front as at present," and warning him that detailed instructions would soon arrive in cipher. Drafted by Garfield at 10:00 P.M. but delayed by the encryption process, the instructions left headquarters well after midnight. They directed Crittenden to move down the Sequatchie Valley and cross the river at Shell Mound, Battle Creek, or Bridgeport. Crittenden's wagons were to cross the river via the bridge being constructed at Bridgeport. Crittenden was to leave Hazen, Wagner, Wilder, and Minty in place to maintain the fiction of a pending crossing north of Chattanooga. Garfield explained that Rosecrans expected the Confederates to withdraw from the city and he forecast a battle somewhere between Dalton and Atlanta. Should the Confederates depart, Hazen and Wagner were to cross the river and occupy Chattanooga. At the same time Garfield also wrote to Granger and Morgan. To Granger he indicated that Rosecrans no longer was concerned about the town of Carthage in the army's rear. Instead, he wanted Daniel McCook's brigade to accelerate its movements so as to protect the Nashville & Chattanooga Railroad. Further, Steedman should relieve the regiment garrisoning Cowan so it could rejoin its parent unit. Morgan received specific instructions to advance beyond Huntsville to the Memphis & Charleston Railroad's Flint River bridge and rebuild it. In a note to Samuel Simmons, Garfield gently warned the army's chief commissary that "the General Commanding thinks you ought to be here." Garfield directed Thomas retain King's Third Brigade to guard the railroad until Dan McCook's troops arrived. Finally, Garfield notified Lytle that a train carrying pontoons would arrive at Bridgeport at 11:00 P.M., and a quick return to Stevenson was needed.[37]

Other staff officers were busy Sunday night fleshing out Rosecrans's vision with detailed instructions and queries. Goddard reinforced Garfield's messages to Simmons and Morgan. With the Nashville & Decatur Railroad still severed in several places, Morgan would have to be supplied from Stevenson via the Memphis & Charleston Railroad, and that road, too, was broken at the Flint River bridge. Simmons was to create a supply point for Morgan at the bridge until the span could be reconstructed. Goddard also sought to expedite the advance of the Sixty-Ninth Ohio Infantry regiment from Cowan, where it guarded a camp of several hundred convalescent soldiers. The Sixty-Ninth, which belonged to Stanley's Second Brigade of Negley's division, had been left behind when the Fourteenth Corps crossed the Cumberland Plateau in mid-August. Now it was needed at the front, but McCook's Reserve Corps brigade would be slow to arrive, so Goddard inquired if the convalescent soldiers were armed. Like Garfield, Bond wrote to Simmons counseling him to come to Stevenson. In addition, Bond instructed Stanley to see that the difficult ford at Hart's Bar was properly marked. Crook and Long had lost several men during their original crossing, so proper marking of the passage for their return was important. Similarly, Thoms ordered Lytle to mark the ford at the north end of Long Island and improve its approaches. Thoms also queried Lytle about the amount of flooring being stockpiled at Bridgeport for the bridge. Finally, staff engineer Burroughs instructed O'Connell to move the Pioneer Brigade to Bridgeport to assist in the bridging efforts there. Although signed by staff officers, these messages were essentially generated by Rosecrans in the hours before midnight. As such, they clearly reflected his management style. On the positive side, Rosecrans's grasp of detail was remarkable in breadth of knowledge and span of control. Negatively, that same attention to detail placed on display Rosecrans's worrisome tendency toward what would today be called micromanagement.[38]

The lights burning late in the "Little Brick" on the edge of Stevenson were matched elsewhere on Sunday night. North of Stevenson there was turmoil in Negley's Second Division. Garfield in late morning had ordered Thomas to send a division to Stevenson to relieve Laibold's command, which would then join Sheridan at Bridgeport. Thomas passed the word to Negley, who ordered his three brigades to strike their tents and pack their baggage, a process that continued beyond sunset. Suddenly the order was modified to include only Beatty's First Brigade. Beatty's men began to move at 9:00 P.M., and did not settle into camp at Stevenson until midnight. Negley's remaining brigades spent an uncomfortable night without the tents and camp gear they had so carefully packed for travel. At Bridgeport a detail from the Twenty-Fourth Wisconsin Infantry regiment of Lytle's brigade worked all night unloading pontoons from railroad cars. Lytle himself was vexed by the train conductor, who adamantly refused to return to Stevenson immediately for another load of pontoons. Instead, the conductor held his train at Bridgeport until the next day. At Shell Mound others also worked in the darkness. There King orchestrated the crossing of his Second Brigade and the Second Tennessee (Union) Cavalry regiment to the east side of the river. Reynolds's plan called for Daniel Ray's cavalrymen to probe through Running Water Canyon into Lookout Valley toward Chattanooga. King's infantry would support Ray by advancing to the wrecked railroad bridge over Running Water Creek near the hamlet of Whiteside. If Ray found more Confederates than he could handle, King could cover his withdrawal to Shell Mound. In any case, Reynolds did not want King to return to the Federal side of the river. Crossing first, Ray's 375 horsemen at 10:30 P.M. moved cautiously toward the dark confines of Running Water Canyon. Behind them, King supervised the crossing of his command. By midnight he had gathered a formidable striking force east of the river, and it too took the narrow, rocky road into the mountains.[39]

By midnight on 30 August, Rosecrans believed his campaign was proceeding according to plan. He had placed five infantry brigades and five cavalry regiments east of the Tennessee River without opposition. From the Sequatchie Valley to Caperton's Ferry, friendly civilians and deserting soldiers reported deteriorating Confederate morale and predicted that Bragg would abandon Chattanooga. Recorded in Capt. David Swaim's intelligence log, these reports clearly colored Rosecrans's thinking. In a message to Burnside, he described his plan to outflank Bragg's army on its left. Noting that Bragg might withdraw beyond Dalton, Rosecrans told Burnside, "Our present indications are that he will retreat towards Atlanta." He warned Burnside that the Twenty-First Corps would be moving southward and that Burnside should extend his cavalry in the same direction. Rosecrans's nightly report to the War Department also forecast the future course of the campaign: "The rebs will probably evacuate Chattanooga on hearing we are crossing and take the line of the Georgia R. R. from Ringgold south." In a letter to his wife, he once more predicted Bragg's response: "The indications are that they will retire towards Atlanta." After noting that their son Adrian Louis was still in camp, Rosecrans admitted, "The next three weeks will be an arduous campaign." Had he known that on that very day a spy was ordered to join his entourage, Rosecrans's thoughts would have been quite different. In Washington, Secretary of War Stanton had directed Assistant Secretary Charles Dana to join Rosecrans's command. Stanton's letter of introduction, dated 30 August, stated that Dana "visits your command for the purpose of conferring with you upon any matters which you desire to have brought to the notice of this Department." It would be some time before Dana arrived, and even longer for his true mission to be revealed, but Dana's visit would ultimately play a pivotal role in Rosecrans's career.[40]

The vague reports of Federal activity east of the river notwithstanding, Bragg on 30 August remained focused on Buckner's precarious position at Loudon. If Rosecrans were to throw a heavy force across the river between Chattanooga and Loudon while Burnside drove toward Knoxville, Buckner could be trapped before Bragg could intervene. Therefore the first order of business that Sunday was to order Buckner to abandon Loudon and withdraw nearer to Chattanooga. Accordingly, Mackall drafted an order for Buckner to retreat forty-two miles to Charleston. Located on the East Tennessee & Georgia Railroad just below the Hiwassee River, Charleston offered an easily defended river line and a linkage with the right flank of Hill's defenses around Blythe's Ferry. Mackall instructed Buckner also to withdraw the Cumberland Gap garrison and bring it along, unless Federal movements interposed. If such proved to be the case, Frazer's contingent should retreat eastward. Finally Buckner was to withdraw all bridge guards north of Charleston, as the railroad was useless beyond that point. Buckner was not to destroy the massive railroad bridge at Loudon until absolutely necessary; instead, he was to remove all railroad rolling stock to Charleston. While Mackall wrote to Buckner, Brent wrote to Hill, telling him that Hindman's Division was moving to his support. Further, Brent told Liddell at Chickamauga Station to be prepared to support Hill if called upon. As the day progressed, nothing further arrived from Buckner, but a report from beyond Lookout Mountain indicated that Federal cavalry was operating around Trenton and approaching Wauhatchie. Although Brent believed that the force was "probably not large," the new information caused Bragg to revise his instructions to Wharton's cavalry camped at Rome and Calhoun, Georgia. Earlier, Wharton had been told to move his division to join Hill north of Chattanooga; now he was to halt at LaFayette and picket the routes over Lookout Mountain.[41]

Although army headquarters did not yet consider it significant, Crook's surprise visit to Trenton and his probe toward Wauhatchie caused more activity beyond Lookout Mountain than simply a redirection of Wharton's destination. Around the middle of the day, when news of Crook's approach reached Chattanooga, Brent suggested that Polk withdraw his pickets to the junction of the Nashville & Chattanooga and Wills Valley Railroads. Polk responded baldly, "Any troops which may be beyond Lookout Creek are reporting directly to army headquarters, and are not under my control." Queried further, Polk reiterated that if Bragg wanted the regiment beyond Lookout Mountain, the Twenty-Eighth Alabama Infantry, to be relieved, he would have to authorize it. At the same time, Polk appealed for the relief of the regiment picketing the river (probably the Twenty-Fifth Alabama of Deas's Brigade, another of Hindman's units) and the Thirty-Fourth Alabama Infantry regiment from Manigault's command, serving as the Chattanooga provost guard. With Hindman's Division already in motion to join Hill at Harrison, Polk proposed to replace the three regiments with units from Cheatham's Division, camped just south of Chattanooga. Accepting Polk's logic, Brent approved the change, and Polk immediately instructed Cheatham to use Smith's Brigade. When the orders reached Smith, he sent the consolidated Twelfth/Forty-Seventh Tennessee Infantry regiment beyond the nose of Lookout Mountain into Lookout Valley and edged his remaining regiments closer to the mountain. The relief came too late in the day for the Twenty-Eighth Alabama to join its parent brigade, so it did not race to follow Hindman's Division tramping toward the Tennessee River above Chattanooga. Ultimately, the only effect of the shuffling of units was to transfer the responsibility for guarding the western approach to Chattanooga from Hindman to Cheatham, while Bragg remained focused on bolstering Hill's defenses on the army's right. Meanwhile, word of the Federal probe spread in Cheatham's Division.[42]

Except for the movements of Smith's and Hindman's commands, it was an especially quiet Sunday for the troops in Bragg's army. Although they were occasionally visible, Federals on the far side of the Tennessee River did little to attract attention. The profound lull led a few individuals to predict that any significant Federal crossing would occur below Chattanooga rather than above. After surveying the far shore from a battery in town, Capt. John Harris wrote to his mother, "The river only now separates us. I don't think the force there is a very large one though for I believe that the larger portion intend crossing somewhere below here." In the *Daily Rebel,* Henry Watterson advanced the same idea, quoting a "man from across the river" who said that only a small force of Federals faced the town. Upstream, Cleburne surveyed his thirty-mile front and concluded that if the Federal army attempted a crossing in his sector, he could not concentrate quickly enough to repulse them successfully. Cleburne recommended that Hill shorten the division's frontage and identify concentration points before they were needed. Having already lost Stewart's Division, Hill could do little until Hindman arrived from McFarland's Spring and the divisions coming from Mississippi could reconstitute themselves. Of those reinforcements, several more regiments from Ector's and Gist's Brigades of Walker's Division arrived at Chickamauga Station during the day. Still, in Walker's Division only Claudius Wilson's Brigade was fully formed, and it had suffered large losses during the trip as hundreds of men took unauthorized leave to visit their homes. Scattered on trains and steamboats on both sides of Montgomery, Alabama, most of Breckinridge's Division was far south of Atlanta. At Chickamauga Station, Liddell's Reserve Division continued to guard the army's supply depot. There the men cooked three days' rations in preparation for a move and continued religious meetings of various kinds, including a baptismal ceremony for eleven men in Govan's Brigade.[43]

Bragg's decision to order Buckner to retreat more than forty miles to Charleston was the largest significant action he took on 30 August. Upon receiving the order Buckner was in a quandary: Should he burn the bridges along the way, should he destroy the steamboats in the Tennessee River, and, most important of all, were Bragg's instructions genuine? To authenticate the order, Buckner asked that the answers to his other questions be partially encrypted. While awaiting a response, he arranged for the southward movement of Preston's and Stewart's Divisions, two artillery battalions, Pegram's cavalry, and his supply trains. Clayton's Brigade, just arriving by rail, was sent back to Charleston without debarking. After unloading Clayton's men, the trains were to return to Loudon for Bate's Brigade, and eventually Brown's. Stewart had brought no wagons with him, or any artillery, thereby simplifying the move but precipitating a bureaucratic struggle with Hill over the absent wagons. Stewart's fourth brigade, Johnson's, which had already traveled between Loudon and Charleston several times, was assigned to lead Buckner's main column. A circular from corps headquarters established the order of march: Johnson's Brigade and a battery; a herd of beef cattle; a regiment, battery, and the engineer company; the supply, ammunition, and ambulance trains; Preston's Division with Leyden's and Williams's Artillery Battalions; and finally, McMahon's Brigade of Preston's Division serving as rear guard. Johnson, whose wagons had just reached him, moved promptly on the familiar road to Charleston, but the remainder of Buckner's command was slow to start. As darkness fell, Trigg's Brigade finally departed Loudon in Johnson's wake, but Gracie's Brigade did not leave until the following day. McMahon's rear guard only made four miles, from Lenoir Station north of the river to the south bank at Loudon. The trains returned from Charleston for Bate's Brigade of Stewart's Division, but Brown's Brigade would also have to remain at Loudon overnight.[44]

Buckner next turned to the remnants of his command remaining north of the Tennessee River. Originally placed under Forrest, Pegram was now instructed to concentrate at Lenoir Station to cover Buckner's rear. When Forrest proposed to strike one of Burnside's columns, Buckner dismissed the proposal as being too late. Instead, he wanted Forrest to withdraw from Kingston to the Hiwassee River line, where he would link Buckner's and Hill's troops. As for his last remaining units, Buckner instructed Jackson to withdraw his railroad guards toward Bristol, and Frazer to abandon Cumberland Gap and head for Abingdon. At 9:30 P.M. Buckner informed Mackall that he was preserving the Loudon bridge for the moment and sending his steamboats down to the Hiwassee. Shortly thereafter, he received word from Frazer that he believed he could maintain his position for at least forty days. Intrigued but unwilling to modify Bragg's instructions unilaterally, Buckner at 11:00 P.M. suggested to army headquarters that the Cumberland Gap decision be reconsidered. Pending a response, he wired Frazer to remain in place for another day. For Buckner, abandoning Knoxville and the railroad to Virginia was one thing, but opening the historic passage between Kentucky and Virginia for Federal exploitation was quite another. Once lost, Cumberland Gap might be impossible to regain, and Buckner shrank from taking what might be an irrevocable step. Concern for Buckner's situation already had occupied Bragg's attention for several days, and Buckner's call to revisit the Cumberland Gap issue would ensure that Bragg's focus on his far right flank would continue a while longer. Given what was transpiring below Chattanooga, any concern for Cumberland Gap at such a time ultimately would prove to be misplaced. Bragg, however, could only respond to the information he had, and on 30 August the preponderance of information came from Buckner, not from scattered cavalrymen in Lookout Valley.[45]

13

SURPRISE

» 31 AUGUST–1 SEPTEMBER 1863 «

Monday morning, 31 August 1863, dawned hot and dusty in the Tennessee River valley. Atop Sand Mountain, Hans Heg ordered Lt. Col. James Abernathy of the Eighth Kansas Infantry regiment to lead thirty cavalrymen from the First Tennessee (Union) Cavalry regiment to survey the roads all the way to Trenton, Georgia, in Lookout Valley. Boldly, Abernathy led the Tennesseans forward on the relatively flat top of the mountain. Approaching the descent into Lookout Valley around 9:00 A.M., his small party encountered Confederate pickets, who withdrew hastily down the mountainside. Abernathy followed into the valley and approached Trenton, a village of only a few houses. Several hundred yards from the village his detachment came under fire from Confederates hidden behind fences and buildings. Outnumbered and afraid of being surrounded, Abernathy withdrew up the mountain without loss. He was not pursued and returned the way he had come, reporting to Heg what he had seen. Abernathy saw no sign of Crook's regiments supposed to be on Sand Mountain but did learn that they had visited Trenton on the previous day. He identified his opponents as elements of the Fourth Alabama Cavalry regiment. In fact, Trenton's defenders that morning belonged to Lt. Col. Harris Mauldin, commander of the Third Alabama Cavalry regiment. Mauldin had arrived in Trenton around 5:00 A.M. with approximately 300 of the best-mounted and equipped troopers drawn from Hagan's Brigade of Martin's Division. He had been ordered on 27 August to march from Alexandria, Alabama, northward to Trenton via Big Wills Valley, which became Lookout Valley a short distance before reaching the Georgia border. He had covered forty-five miles since the previous morning and knew little of either the situation or the terrain around Trenton. Fortunately for him, Abernathy's party was small and its mission was limited. Each commander reported the encounter to his respective superior, Mauldin to Wheeler and Abernathy to Heg.[1]

West of Sand Mountain, other elements of the Twentieth Corps slowly lurched into motion. First to move was the remainder of Davis's First Division. Leading the way, Carlin's Second Brigade found it hard to raise its heavily laden wagons over the eroded rock ledges that intersected the path. Detailing soldiers to assist the wagons, Carlin finally reached the top of the mountain. Moving only a short distance beyond the crest, Carlin's men camped near a small stream in early afternoon. Behind Carlin came Post's First Brigade. Again, regiments lined the track to assist laboring mules dragging wagons to the crest. Reaching the top by nightfall and disregarding loud complaints by his men, Post kept the brigade moving until he had passed both Carlin and Heg. It was not until 8:00 P.M. that Davis's division was finally consolidated on the plateau. For Carlin's and Post's commands, the tiring day had been relieved only by the spectacular views from the top of Sand Mountain. Cpl. George Morris of the Eighty-First Indiana Infantry regiment spoke for many when he wrote, "Below was the smiling valley, with its fields of waving grain, while like a silver thread the Tennessee River wound between the high mountains, decked with the brightest foliage, and the bosom of the river was dotted with lovely islands robed in green. In the distance the pontoon bridges could be seen, with a steady stream of blue coats marching over them, their bayonets flashing back the sunlight and the Stars and Stripes waving over them." The troops crossing the bridge belonged to Johnson's Second Division. Moving from their Crow Creek camps, Willich's, Dodge's, and Baldwin's brigades all managed to cross the undulating span successfully during the day and occupied Davis's old campsites in the river bottom. Lt. Col. William Robinson in Dodge's command was not impressed with the scenery. A resident of western Pennsylvania well acquainted with mountains, Robinson confided to his diary, "Hard looking country—air fragrant with miasma—birds look sickly."[2]

With the crossing going well at Caperton's Ferry, Rosecrans saw no need to supervise McCook further and turned his attention to Crittenden's Twenty-First Corps. Having ordered Crittenden to begin moving his scattered divisions to Shell Mound, Rosecrans became concerned that the Confederates might strike the Twenty-First Corps before it could join the remainder of the army. Increasingly there were signs that Bragg was reinforcing his right, above Chattanooga, where the Army of the Cumberland was the weakest. Of course, Rosecrans's deception plan had been crafted with just that outcome in mind. Still, as more and more divisions crossed the river and disappeared into the mountains, Crittenden's vulnerability would increase for a few days. If Bragg chose to cross the river and confront the Twenty-First Corps while the remainder of Rosecrans's army was straddling the Tennessee, the situation could become dangerous. Similarly, if Bragg crossed in strength after Crittenden moved down to Jasper but before Thomas and McCook could threaten Bragg's railroad to Atlanta, the Bridgeport-Stevenson logistical complex would be placed at risk. With those considerations in mind, Rosecrans at 9:00 A.M. had Garfield send Crittenden a list of questions: Were the Confederates moving up the Tennessee River? Was Bragg concentrating on Rosecrans's left flank? Where was Burnside? Where was Forrest's cavalry? Garfield wanted Hazen and Wagner to collect as much information as possible and rush it to army headquarters. Further, Van Cleve's division should hasten to join the remainder of the corps. Like the messages sent to Crittenden on the previous night, this one too would take time to deliver, either via a line of signal stations on mountaintops or by telegraph to Tracy City, thence by courier to Dunlap. Longer messages, especially encrypted ones, were most easily transmitted via Tracy City, but the line of flags and torches seems to have been the preferred method by which Rosecrans communicated with Crittenden.[3]

While Rosecrans pondered Crittenden's situation, his staff dispatched another flurry of detailed instructions to various elements of the army. Goddard ordered the army's reserve ammunition train of 800 heavily loaded wagons from Tullahoma to Cowan, where the Sixty-Ninth Ohio Infantry regiment would shepherd it over the Cumberland Plateau. He also sent a herd of beef cattle to Tracy City for use by the Twenty-First Corps. Finally he instructed the army paymaster not to hurry in paying the troops because of the ongoing operations. Meanwhile, Bond coordinated Reserve Corps movements on the army's flanks. He notified Granger that Rosecrans wanted Morgan to advance to Flint River and Dan McCook to move to Huntsville. He also asked Granger when the loyal Tennessee units would arrive at McMinnville to free Dick's brigade to rejoin Van Cleve. Bond also telegraphed Chief Quartermaster Hodges in search of fifty sledges Rosecrans wanted sent to the front. Thoms enjoined railroad superintendent Innes to maintain the Nashville & Chattanooga Railroad tracks better, so as to avoid wrecks like the one that briefly blocked the track near Murfreesboro that day. He also arranged for a train to travel to Larkinsville to evacuate seriously ill cavalrymen. In early afternoon Rosecrans learned that pontoons were not reaching the Bridgeport construction site as he had directed. A train expected to deliver pontoons to Bridgeport and return to Stevenson for another load had not appeared, wasting valuable time and throwing Rosecrans into a rage. Garfield scorched the telegraph wires to Lytle seeking to know "by whose neglect this criminal delay has occurred," while Thoms asked Lytle for a progress report on the bridge construction. When Lytle blamed a railroad conductor, Thoms directed assistant railroad superintendent Beggs to locate the miscreant. As the staff scrambled to rectify the problem, Rosecrans suddenly decided that he again needed to go to Bridgeport, so the dummy was readied to take him there in late afternoon.[4]

At Bridgeport, the delay in the pontoons' arrival did not affect the thousands of soldiers working on the bridge. During the day most of the Pioneer Brigade joined them. Leaving one company to maintain the Caperton's Ferry

Combination trestle/pontoon bridge under construction at Bridgeport, Alabama, 31 August 1863. (Library of Congress)

bridge, O'Connell sent part if his command by rail with the remaining pontoons, while the remainder marched from Stevenson. Meanwhile many of the infantry laborers and part of the First Michigan continued preparing the timbers for the trestle bridge across the wide channel from Bridgeport to Long Island. During the day they also began to erect the bents that would hold the roadway out of the water, standing them up on the riverbed and connecting them with balks and ropes. While some soldiers struggled in the water with the massive timbers, others improved the bridge approaches. At the same time, telegraphers extended their line across the river, using an insulated cable. To record the scene for posterity, a Cleveland photographer created at least two images of the construction crews at work that day. Lytle described the effort in a letter to his sister: "From my tent on the hill the camp presents a busy appearance. Railroad trains rolling in & out, locomotives whistling, long wagon trains loaded with timbers for the bridges, 'engineers and mechanics' busy as bees, regiments of infantry & cavalry passing and repassing—fatigue parties in every direction." Suddenly a series of telegrams from Stevenson interrupted Lytle. Garfield wanted to know why the train moving pontoons to Bridgeport had not returned for another load, and Thoms wanted to know how the construction gangs were faring. At 3:30 P.M. Lytle placed the blame for the delay on the nameless railroad conductor and reported that the trestle momentarily stretched one-third of the way to Long Island with flooring laid as fast as the bents were secured. When the next telegram from Stevenson disclosed that Rosecrans was on the way to Bridgeport, Lytle hastily closed his letter and prepared to receive the army commander once again.[5]

On both sides of Bridgeport other Federal units were active. Downstream, Crook's cavalrymen recrossed the river at the Hart's Bar ford. Upstream at Battle Creek, the traffic ran in the opposite direction. Brannan was finding it a bit more difficult to get his division across the Tennessee than he had earlier predicted, and he sent no more glowing reports to his superiors. Using its improvised flotilla, Van Derveer's Third Brigade had reached the far shore during the previous day, but its battery and much baggage still remained west of the river. While the Eighty-Seventh Indiana Infantry regiment moved the baggage, the remainder of the brigade bathed, washed their clothes, or foraged across the countryside. When a rumor spread that Bragg had evacuated Chattanooga, Cpl. David Griffin of the Second Minnesota Infantry regiment wrote home: "I do not doubt it much for we were getting them pretty well shut up and they would either have to fight or run away, and as the latter form of warfare was Bragg's favorite mode, they have again taken to the foot race and gone towards 'the last ditch' but where that is I do not know." In Brannan's other brigades, there was no time for speculation about the direction of the campaign; there was a wide river to cross, with inadequate means. The Second Brigade was next to test the makeshift fleet. In brigade command for only two weeks, John Croxton moved four of his five regiments over the river, leaving only the Seventy-Fourth Indiana Infantry regiment and his battery on the Federal shore. Also crossing was Connell's First Brigade. According to Adj. John Inskeep of the Seventeenth Ohio Infantry regiment, the order was, "Get across the river somehow to day." Less skilled than Van Derveer's woodsmen, Connell's soldiers had struggled to build their own watercraft. Nevertheless, they made the crossing without incident, although their battery also remained west of the river. By midnight Brannan's division had mostly made it across the stream, but its baggage, artillery, ammunition wagons, and some officers had yet to reach the eastern shore.[6]

At Shell Mound, Edward King's probe toward Chattanooga began well before dawn. King sent Col. Daniel Ray's cavalrymen through Running Water Canyon into Lookout Valley and toward Chattanooga, while he remained several miles in rear at the village of Whiteside. There a rough road left the valley floor and climbed the mountain wall, providing an alternate route to Trenton. Nearby was the still-smoldering wreckage of the Running Water Creek railroad trestle. Originally a metal-roofed Howe truss 789 feet long and 110 feet high, the bridge had been destroyed by Confederate engineers eight days earlier. Now reduced to an impressive pile of charred timbers and twisted iron surmounted by two large, masonry supports 90 feet high, the bridge impressed King's infantrymen who occupied defensive positions around it. While they waited, some soldiers amused themselves by sending cars from a small coal mine crashing down the mountainside. Ahead of them, Ray's troopers debouched from Running Water Canyon and followed the main road to Wauhatchie in Lookout Valley. Encountering Confederate pickets, Ray pushed them back easily. Suddenly in the early morning light, Ray saw what appeared to be a heavy force of infantry and artillery ahead on the lower slope of Lookout Mountain. Concluding that he was outnumbered, he withdrew to Whiteside. There he proudly displayed a captured Confederate purchasing agent with a wagon load of leather and a saddlebag full of Confederate currency. After the war, Ray claimed to have captured twenty-five Confederates at a cost of two of his own men killed and five wounded, but his written report omitted any such claims. Either way, King at 9:00 A.M. ordered the entire command to withdraw to the river. Reaching Shell Mound Station in early afternoon, King camped with his infantrymen on the east bank of the stream, making the occupation of Shell Mound permanent. Meanwhile, Ray ferried the Second Tennessee back to the west side of the river.[7]

While waiting for their baggage to arrive, a number of King's soldiers explored Nickajack Cave. With an opening 177 feet wide and 48 feet high, the cave extended at least a mile and a half and had been noted in national literature before the war. In 1863, it was a major source of niter, a critical ingredient of gunpowder. Nickajack Cave lay within the territory of District Eight of the Confederate Nitre and Mining Bureau, headquartered in Chattanooga. Originally worked by a private contractor, whose equipment had been wrecked by a brief Federal advance in 1862, the cave had subsequently been operated by the Confederate government. By August 1863 an extensive industrial operation for the production of niter existed inside the cave and just outside its mouth. Miners first dug the niter from the cave floor and placed it in long wooden hoppers or vats. Water was then introduced into the vats, permitting the niter crystals to be leached into kettles. The resulting liquid was boiled outside in furnaces. The concentrated product then was moved to a potash works in Chattanooga, where it was turned into potassium nitrate or saltpeter. The Nickajack Cave apparatus was extensive, and as late as July 1863 at least fifty-three workers toiled there daily. Although the evidence is inconclusive, it appears that the Nickajack Cave works may have been active until late August, when Confederate troops evacuated the Shell Mound vicinity. Federal soldiers exploring the cave could not have known the details of the operation, but they were impressed by its size. Now the works were quiet, but the extensive paths and footbridges throughout the cave proved irresistible to Federal soldiers with time on their hands. One such tourist, Cpl. William Miller of the Seventy-Fifth Indiana Infantry regiment, recorded, "I was back in the cave some distance and it is a rough dismal place and I observed Torches all through it. Some above and some

Abandoned niter works at Nickajack Cave, Tennessee. (Miller, *Photographic History*)

below me. If a man Should Step off of the plank it is no telling where he would land." Miller's musings on 31 August would soon prove prophetic.[8]

Unlike the activity downstream, the riverfront from Chattanooga upstream was quiet on 31 August. In Wilder's command, men spent the day foraging, improving their camps, or writing letters. In the afternoon Lilly ascended Stringer's Ridge to survey recent changes in the Confederate batteries guarding Chattanooga. Wilder sent a report to Rosecrans detailing information he had recently gleaned. Three scouts had penetrated far enough beyond the river to observe the Confederate regiment guarding the entrance to Lookout Valley and believed only cavalry detachments roamed beyond that point. More important, William Crutchfield reported that Buckner had retreated to Loudon, part of Hill's Corps had been sent to support Forrest at Kingston, Wheeler's command was still at Rome and Gadsden, and at least 10,000 troops from Johnston were arriving to reinforce Bragg. Finally, Wilder noted that he had found a good ford at Friar's Island, seven miles upstream from Chattanooga. From his position on Walden's Ridge, Wagner provided additional information. He confirmed the departure of part of Stewart's Division from the river line and forwarded a prisoner captured near Kelly's Ferry. The man described the Third Confederate Cavalry regiment's dispositions and stated that Bragg's greatest fear was a Federal crossing south of the city. Otherwise, Wagner's men spent the day celebrating the arrival of tents, blankets, knapsacks, and mail from the

Sequatchie Valley. A similar shipment reached Hazen's brigade around Poe's Tavern. There the Sixth Kentucky Infantry regiment displayed a large American flag and made itself comfortable for an extended stay. Seeing no indications of a move, officers in the Sixth Ohio Infantry regiment invited the local citizenry to attend a dance Hazen had permitted them to organize. At Smith's Cross Roads, Minty sent most of the Fourth Michigan Cavalry regiment northward in another effort to contact Burnside.[9]

In the Sequatchie Valley, Crittenden was becoming increasingly nervous at his Dunlap headquarters. For some time he had felt isolated in the narrow valley, totally dependent upon signal stations and courier lines for news of the rest of the army. Around 11:45 A.M. he received Rosecrans's brief message of the previous night warning him that movement orders were on their way to him. Without knowledge of the larger picture, Crittenden could make little sense of the message. Expecting that the movement order would arrive via Tracy City, he told Wood to send a courier to the mountain village. While he waited, he worried about Van Cleve's exposed position at Pikeville. At 1:15 P.M. he sent Van Cleve information from Wood forecasting an attack on the Pikeville position and cautioned Van Cleve to "be ready." Fifteen minutes later he dismissed Van Cleve's proposal to establish a secondary supply depot at Pikeville in view of the army's pending advance. With that, Crittenden returned to scanning the road for a courier from Tracy City. At 2:15 P.M., the order finally arrived by signal, and it was encrypted. At last Crittenden had orders he could understand: place the three divisions of the corps in motion toward the Tennessee River at Shell Mound; leave the four-brigade deception force in place; and have Wagner and Hazen occupy Chattanooga if the Confederates evacuated the city. At 4:20 P.M. Crittenden acknowledged the order in a brief note to Garfield, stating that the Twenty-First Corps would begin its march at 6:00 A.M. on the following day. At 7:00 P.M. he informed Garfield that he would locate his headquarters at Jasper five hours after the corps moved. Later still, at 9:30 P.M., he assured Garfield that he would continue beyond Jasper to army headquarters at Stevenson for consultation and further orders. Unsure of himself and uncomfortable in ambiguous situations, Crittenden always performed best when he had specific and precise orders from a superior. Now, he happily prepared to execute just such orders.[10]

Blissfully unaware that their idyll would soon be ending, the men of the Twenty-First Corps continued their daily routine. At Therman, Wood's First Division mustered for pay, as did all other units of the Army of the Cumberland. The periodic mustering determined who was eligible to be paid for the previous two months' service, but did not signify that paymasters would immediately appear. Otherwise, there was little unusual activity in Wood's division. In the Third Kentucky Infantry regiment, officers continued their search for a suitable place to leave the seriously injured Capt. John Tuttle when the division moved south. A few miles north at Dunlap, Palmer's Second Division also mustered for pay. The story was much the same at Pikeville, where Van Cleve's Third Division continued to dispatch heavy guard details with wagon trains shuttling to and from the McMinnville supply depot. There, too, in Samuel Beatty's First Brigade, still another regiment was punished for making noise at night by being forced to stand in line for hours. Of course, everything changed as darkness fell and Crittenden issued orders to each division commander to prepare to leave the Sequatchie Valley. Those orders created a flurry of movement in every regimental camp. What had been a pleasant interlude for most soldiers was now seen to be ending. The foraging had been good, especially the ripe peaches, and the inhabitants had mostly been friendly. Those citizens now would be abandoned to their fate. The rumor mill worked overtime as men speculated on their new destination, which many believed to be Knoxville. Palmer was especially concerned about leaving while his Second Brigade remained beyond Walden's Ridge. Hazen's baggage had to be left under guard at Dunlap until it could be sent to join him. Palmer closed his note to Hazen wistfully: "I leave you very bare of supplies, but [Lt. Charles C.] Peck [chief of transportation] will be here before you will need supplies. I take all from here not now issued. I hope you may get Chattanooga, and that I may speedily see you again."[11]

At Stevenson, stifling clouds of dust covered everything from tents to trees. Thrown up by thousands of marching men, shuffling mules, and churning wagon wheels, the dust was everywhere, choking those who had yet to move to the river. Laibold's Second Brigade of Sheridan's division had been scheduled to march to Bridgeport to join its parent formation, but the movement was postponed for a day, probably because the construction camps took all available room. Beatty's First Brigade of Negley's Second Division, which had relieved Laibold's troops on the previous evening, now assumed responsibility for the town, although an order to store knapsacks indicated that it would not remain in Stevenson for long. A few miles to the north, shielded from the town by a spur of the mountain, Stanley's and Sirwell's brigades grumpily reestablished the camps they had abandoned on the previous evening. North of Negley's troops, in Baird's First Division, King's Third Brigade assumed responsibility for protecting the railroad all the way north to the tunnel. Relieved from guard duty at Tantalon and Anderson Stations, Baird's remaining brigades returned to their camps and mustered for pay. Meanwhile, elements of the Cavalry Corps gradually converged on Stevenson. Nearest at hand was Campbell's First Brigade of McCook's First Division. Campbell's Second Michigan Cavalry regiment had been beyond the river at Bridgeport for several days and remained there. Now Campbell moved the Ninth Pennsylvania Cavalry regiment from Bolivar to Caperton's Ferry and across the river to a temporary camp.

Southwest of Stevenson, LaGrange's Second Brigade left Larkinsville for Bellefonte, arriving after dark. West of Larkinsville, Watkins received orders to move the Third Brigade to Caperton's Ferry, after leaving detachments to guard critical railroad bridges until the Reserve Corps relieved them. Instructed to hurry, Watkins moved quickly, leaving thirty seriously ill troopers at Larkinsville to be rescued by a train early the next day.[12]

As most of Rosecrans's army neared the river crossing sites, a vacuum developed on the army's flanks. On the left, Dick's command could not leave McMinnville until Reserve Corps units arrived to relieve them. Granger selected several loyal Tennessee regiments for the task, placing them under Col. James Shelley. Rosecrans, however, assigned Brig. Gen. James Spears to the command at the same time. A prewar lawyer in Pikeville, Spears had vigorously opposed Lincoln's Emancipation Proclamation and was a divisive force in the East Tennessee Unionist community. Aware of Spears's reputation, Granger had chosen Shelley, but Rosecrans's assignment of Spears delayed the movement briefly. Van Cleve thus would have to wait a bit longer to regain his absent brigade. On the army's right flank, the unit charged with filling the space vacated by the Cavalry Corps was Morgan's Second Division. Morgan had been ordered to move Tillson's First Brigade to Huntsville, but he was in no hurry to leave Athens. Slowly following Tillson was McCook's Second Brigade. On the morning of 31 August, while leaving Lynnville, Tennessee, the Fifty-Second Ohio Infantry regiment had two men slightly wounded by bushwhackers. Enraged, McCook sent Col. Oscar Harmon's 125th Illinois Infantry regiment back to Lynnville with orders to burn five houses. Distressed by the unpleasant task, Harmon selected one home and four businesses: "The people were greatly alarmed. They thought the whole town was going, and the women begged earnestly. Bring such a case home, and their feelings can be easily appreciated." Three hours later, two companies of the Fifty-Second Ohio were fired upon while serving as brigade rear guard. Again the snipers could not be found, and again a nearby property owner paid the price, losing two barns even though the regiment suffered no loss. Maj. James Holmes had no regrets: "How they got on fire I did not know and when I saw them I didn't care much." McCook's troops then resumed their march, halting for the night five miles south of Pulaski, Tennessee.[13]

Upon returning from Bridgeport, Rosecrans prepared his daily report for Halleck. Although the Bridgeport bridge was behind schedule, everywhere else the crossings were going well. By the end of the day, two Twentieth Corps divisions and a cavalry regiment were on the east bank at Caperton's Ferry. At Battle Creek, Brannan had crossed virtually all of his infantry, leaving only some baggage and artillery on the west shore. At Shell Mound, Reynolds had crossed a brigade and was preparing to send another over the river. At Bridgeport, the far shore was secure. Cavalry units had penetrated into Lookout Valley without serious opposition. North of Chattanooga, the deception force continued to attract attention. On the army's flanks, the Twenty-First Corps was preparing to march to the crossing sites, and most of the army's cavalry was nearing Caperton's Ferry. The Reserve Corps was slowly filling the void left by advancing units. Even the railroad was finally delivering the supplies needed to sustain an advance beyond the river. Rosecrans believed Wheeler's cavalry was withdrawing to Rome, leaving him free to enter the mountains south of Chattanooga, and he saw indications that Bragg's army was moving upstream. If true, his campaign plan was unfolding just as he had intended. Completion of the Bridgeport span on the next day would guarantee that the army could sustain itself beyond the river. Coincidentally, Rosecrans's report passed in transit a message from Abraham Lincoln. Unaware of the recent successes, Lincoln nevertheless saw enough progress to end the unpleasant dispute between Rosecrans and the government: "I repeat that my appreciation of you has not abated. I can never forget whilst I remember anything, that about the end of last year and beginning of this, you gave us a hard-earned victory, which, had there been a defeat instead, the nation could scarcely have lived over." For the moment at least, Rosecrans was free to conduct his campaign as he alone saw fit.[14]

The Consolidated Tri-monthly Report of the Department of the Cumberland dated 31 August presents a reasonably accurate picture of the army that Rosecrans would lead across the Tennessee River. At army headquarters, there was an aggregate present of twenty-one officers, with fifteen present for duty. The three units in the headquarters guard counted an aggregate present of 1,214 officers and men, with 1,006 present for duty. The Fourteenth Army Corps showed an aggregate present of 26,608 officers and men with seventy-four cannon, 22,616 being present for duty. The Twentieth Army Corps numbered an aggregate present of 16,734 officers and enlisted men with fifty-four artillery pieces, but only 14,222 soldiers present for duty. The Twenty-First Army Corps had an aggregate present of 17,168 officers and men with fifty-eight cannon, and 14,367 present for duty. The Reserve Corps contained an aggregate present of 20,254 officers and men with fifty-two guns. Its present for duty total was 16,931. The Cavalry Corps contained only two divisions and nine guns, with an aggregate present of 12,701 officers and men. Of that number, only 10,699 were present for duty. Separately recorded was the First Michigan Engineers and Mechanics regiment with an attached battery (885 aggregate present and 808 present for duty) and various unattached artillery units, mostly in the Nashville fortifications (320 aggregate present and 303 present for duty). The army's Pioneer Brigade (605 aggregate present and 425 present for duty), Signal Corps detachment (154 aggregate present and 153 present for duty), and the Convalescent Battalion at Cowan (1,048 aggregate present and 173 present for duty) were subsumed in the totals for their parent units. The grand total for Rosecrans's department thus came to an aggregate present of 95,905 officers and men, with 80,967 present for duty. Because much of the Reserve Corps manned static garrison positions, Rosecrans's primary reliance would be on Thomas's, McCook's, Crittenden's, and Stanley's commands. Together, these corps had an aggregate present of 73,211 officers and men, with 61,904 present for duty.[15]

The last day of the month was also strength reporting day for the Army of Tennessee. The army staff numbered 24 officers aggregate present, with all present for duty. Polk's Corps, which included Cheatham's and Hindman's Divisions, listed an aggregate present of 17,985 officers and men, with 15,559 present for duty, and thirty-four cannon. Hill's Corps, which consisted of Cleburne's, Stewart's, and Walker's Divisions, numbered 20,395 officers and men aggregate present, and 17,445 present for duty, with twenty-eight artillery pieces. Stewart's transfer to Buckner's command came too late to be reflected in the 31 August report. Liddell's Reserve Division claimed an aggregate present of 5,334 officers and men, and 4,506 present for duty, with ten guns. The army's cavalry, comprised of Wheeler's Corps, Forrest's Division, and six escort companies, contained an aggregate present of 14,522 officers and men, and a present for duty strength of 11,672, with twenty cannon. In addition, Bragg's artillery reserve numbered 467 officers and men aggregate present, with a present for duty total of 423, and sixteen guns. He also had three engineer companies, which added 302 officers and men aggregate present and 256 present for duty. Thus, the Army of Tennessee momentarily consisted of 59,027 soldiers aggregate present and 49,885 present for duty, with 108 artillery pieces. Breckinridge's Division, still in the process of arriving, did not appear in the army's totals. According to a report dated 26 August, the division listed 5,775 officers and men aggregate present, and 4,956 present for duty, with 16 artillery pieces. Buckner's command on 10 August numbered an aggregate present of 17,332 officers and men, with 14,733 present for duty. Counting Breckinridge and Buckner as part of the Army of Tennessee gave Bragg 82,134 officers and men aggregate present and 69,574 present for duty. Two small brigades from Buckner's command, at Cumberland Gap and on the railroad to Virginia, were unavailable for immediate service with the main army.[16]

In the Chattanooga suburbs Bragg and his staff continued to believe that the Federals would cross the Tennessee River north of Chattanooga, although Brent acknowledged that "spies & scouts" forecast that the Federals would cross south of the town. Even so, Buckner's situation continued to dominate the thinking of army headquarters. If Frazer believed that he could hold Cumberland Gap for forty days, and if Buckner supported him, then by all means the garrison should remain in place. Thus Mackall tersely responded to Buckner's plea to revisit the issue: "Let Frazier [*sic*] hold the gap." The unspoken belief in Chattanooga was that the coming campaign would be decided in less than forty days, and if the Army of Tennessee was victorious, Frazer could be relieved. If not, Frazer's small command would be inconsequential. Either way, it was essential that Buckner and Forrest manage their withdrawal from East Tennessee safely. With the army's supply situation approaching a crisis, Brent enjoined Buckner to strip the countryside through which he passed of all usable food. Expecting Forrest's cavalry to cover Buckner's withdrawal to Charleston, Brent again ordered Forrest to take position south of the Hiwassee River and connect with Hill's pickets on his left. As for Hill, Bragg still expected the Federal crossing to occur in his sector and worked during the day to funnel reinforcements to him. Liddell received instructions to collect arriving units from Breckinridge's Division and make them available for Hill's use. Unfortunately, Breckinridge's men had serious armament deficiencies, so Lt. Col. Hypolite Oladowski, chief of ordnance, sought better weapons from Atlanta and Richmond. Toward the end of the day, word arrived from Smith's Brigade that the feeble Federal probe of the morning had been repulsed easily and the Federals had disappeared. Thus Bragg, Mackall, and Brent remained convinced that Rosecrans would cross the Tennessee River above Chattanooga rather than below.[17]

For the men in the ranks, the process of waiting for the enemy to reveal his intentions was beginning to wear on their nerves. Soldiers in the Twelfth Tennessee Infantry regiment, on picket beyond Lookout Mountain, were concerned about the skirmishing in their front until at 8:00 A.M. Preston Smith declared that the enemy force had withdrawn. The remainder of the day was quiet, although speculation about Federal intentions was rampant. Rumors spread through Strahl's Brigade of Knoxville's evacuation and Cumberland Gap's fall. In Stanford's Mississippi Battery, Pvt. John Magee, twenty-two, was depressed by the interminable waiting: "Hope brighter times may come. Oh how I wish for a battle, a move or anything to divert my thoughts." In Hindman's Division, lying in temporary camps on Chickamauga Creek, the talk was all about an altercation between Hindman and Polk's staff a week earlier that had prompted several challenges but no duels. Pvt. Thomas Hall of the Twenty-Fourth Alabama Infantry regiment said of the division commander: "Hindman has proven himself to be a regular low-life rowdy. . . . But with all this he may be a good *officer*, and *I* for one will do none the less good fighting on account of him. If he will just lead us into it that is all I want, to encourage me to fight. Or if he keeps out of the way I don't care." On the river line, Cleburne's soldiers occupying the fortifications also worried about the future. In the Tenth Texas Infantry regiment, Pvt. Benjamin Seaton, thirty-two, wrote, "Alas how sad the gloom of hope seams at the present time to look around and see the sad condition we are now placed in is almost anuff to give up all hop of our independence." At Chickamauga Station, Lt. John Bostick of Liddell's staff did not share the downcast mood so prevalent among the enlisted men, advising his sister, "Joe says that Mother has about $200 in Tenn. Bank money and that it can now be sold for near a thousand dollars. Sell it at once before we whip the Yankees and Confederate money goes up."[18]

Unlike Polk's and Hill's troops, Buckner's command was in rapid motion southward from Loudon to Charleston. With prodigious effort, the East Tennessee & Georgia Railroad transported Bate's and Clayton's Brigades forty-two miles to Charleston on 31 August. That evening the trains returned to Loudon for Brown's Brigade. Led by Johnson's Brigade, most of Buckner's Corps moved south by foot. At the end of the day Johnson's weary soldiers finally halted at Athens, twenty-seven miles south of Loudon. Behind Johnson, Preston's Division was scattered along the road for miles, suffering severely from the heat and billowing dust clouds. Preston's men passed through Philadelphia, seven miles south of Loudon, and encamped for the night on both sides of Sweetwater, ten miles beyond Philadelphia. Trigg's and Gracie's Brigades were in front with the two artillery battalions, while McMahon Brigade brought up the rear. Behind the infantry came Pegram's Cavalry Brigade, while Scott's Cavalry Brigade halted at Lenoir Station, seven miles north of Loudon. Forrest's Cavalry Division also crossed to the south bank of the Tennessee. Before leaving Loudon, Buckner notified Samuel Jones, whose Department of Western Virginia adjoined Buckner's now-defunct department, that Jackson's small brigade of railroad guards was withdrawing into his area. Buckner wistfully closed, "Take charge of Southwestern Virginia for me." Ignorant of the larger strategic picture, many of Buckner's men did not understand their seemingly random movements. Lt. William Cole of the Thirty-Eighth Alabama Infantry regiment found the situation utterly inexplicable and decidedly gloomy. As he wrote to his wife after arriving at Charleston, "I think also that we will get badly whiped. . . . I see no chance for any thing else—for the men here in this army are low spirited and a large portion of them think that there is no use of fighting. . . . They think that we are whiped and no chance for anything else—it does appear to me that we are at the end of our row."[19]

South of Chattanooga, other Confederate units were also active on 31 August. Walker's Division spent the day walking from Chickamauga Station four miles to the vicinity of Tyner's Station. That evening, Walker's last brigade commander, Wilson, reached Chickamauga Station. Just beginning to arrive were the leading elements of Breckinridge's Division. In the lead was Adams's Brigade, followed by Stovall's Brigade. Bringing up the rear was Helm's so-called Kentucky "Orphan Brigade." Elements of both the Sixth and Ninth Kentucky Infantry regiments spent the day in transit on the railroad between Montgomery and West Point. After changing cars at the latter, the Kentuckians reached LaGrange around midnight and were fed by the ladies of the town. Breckinridge remained absent on leave, so Helm directed the movement. Moving much more slowly was Wheeler's Cavalry Corps, which headed northward in haphazard fashion to join the main army. Both brigades of Wharton's Division left Calhoun and Rome and slowly marched westward toward the extension of Chattanooga Valley called Broomtown Valley. By evening at least one regiment, the Fourth Tennessee Cavalry regiment of Harrison's Brigade, had arrived at a hamlet known as Dirt Town. The ultimate destination of both brigades was LaFayette, Georgia, approximately twenty-five miles south of Chattanooga. At the same time, Martin's Division was slowly making its way northward from camps near Alexandria, Alabama, toward Broomtown Valley as well. One of Martin's units, the Fifty-First Alabama Cavalry regiment of Hagan's Brigade, made it only to Round Mountain by the end of the day. Approximately forty-five miles to the north, Harris Mauldin's detachment from Hagan's command held Trenton against Federal probes. With Federal cavalry active at Wauhatchie and on Sand Mountain, Mauldin at 11:00 P.M. told Wheeler, "If a large force attacks me I can see no chance to save my train, as there is no gap here where I can go up Lookout Mountain. I shall do the [best I] can under the circumstances, and await your orders."[20]

Unaware of Mauldin's predicament, Confederate officials nevertheless were concerned about Bragg's situation. Tennessee's governor, Isham Harris, on the previous day had appealed to Jefferson Davis for aid for Bragg's command. Harris's message found Davis in the midst of discussions with Gen. Robert E. Lee on a wide range of strategic options. For some time a proposal had existed to send part of Lee's army to assist Bragg temporarily. James Longstreet, the chief military proponent, had congressional allies, but Lee was adamantly opposed to weakening his own command. Believing that he had convinced Davis to keep his army united, Lee on 31 August instructed Longstreet to prepare the command for an offensive movement. Davis, however, had not made a final decision. Until he did, Davis could do little to reinforce Bragg beyond asking Johnston to send aid. Still, Davis could not ignore Governor Harris's candid assessment. Thus, he wrote to Vice President Alexander Stephens in Crawfordville, Georgia, hoping that Stephens could persuade Governor Brown to mobilize the Georgia militia and send it to Chattanooga. He also directed his aide Col. James Chesnut to visit both Brown and Governor John Shorter of Alabama and request assistance from their state forces. Secretary of War Seddon wrote Brown independently: "We are advised that a formidable force of the enemy is advancing on East Tennessee. Cannot the local troops organized by you be thrown to aid?" With the two regiments of the Georgia State Line already deployed along the railroad at critical points from Atlanta to Graysville, the grandly named but woefully inadequate militia known as the Georgia State Guard was all that remained for Brown to provide. In sum, there was little more that could be done by anyone in a timely fashion to assist Bragg and his army.

Therefore, while Harris Mauldin spent an anxious night at Trenton fearing the worst, the discussions about strategy continued at Richmond.[21]

In Chattanooga, George Brent was rudely awakened just before 2:00 A.M. on 1 September by the sudden appearance of a citizen with a disturbing story to tell. The man was Israel Russell, thirty-eight, a prominent farmer from Stevenson. Russell explained that he and his family, along with two Stevenson ministers, had left the town when the Federals arrived. While the Russells continued east beyond Lookout Mountain, the clergymen camped on Sand Mountain. After settling his family safely, Russell decided to return to Stevenson on business. Upon reaching the crest of Sand Mountain, he encountered the two ministers watching the Federal army crossing the Tennessee River at Caperton's Ferry. In an effort to report what he had seen, Russell headed for Chattanooga. According to an account published in 1910 by Rev. Robert Shook, Russell went to LaFayette seeking army headquarters. Russell may indeed have gone to LaFayette, but if so he quickly discovered that Bragg remained in Chattanooga. Upon Russell's arrival in Chattanooga, he first sought friends who could substantiate his character, then went to Polk's headquarters. According to Shook, after hearing Russell's report, Polk sent him to Bragg: "General Bragg listened with great interest, knitting his brows and stroking his knee hard with his fist and said with very great earnestness: 'I am going to strike Rosecrans, and I am going to beat him.'" Shook's account is generally confirmed by an article penned by "Historicus" in the *Richmond Whig* of 30 October 1863, and also by Hill in his undated battle report written after the campaign. Russell's observations at Caperton's Ferry most likely occurred on 30 August, when Post's and Carlin's brigades were crossing the pontoon bridge laid the previous day. If Russell departed Sand Mountain that day and traveled by way of LaFayette, he would not have encountered the Federal units probing Lookout Valley on the last two days of August. No matter how he got to Chattanooga, Russell's arrival created great consternation at Bragg's headquarters.[22]

Bragg's first response to Israel Russell's troubling news was to seek confirmation from other sources. He thought first of Capt. Patrick Rice's Company G, Third Confederate Cavalry, which had covered Bridgeport until driven away by Federal cavalry on 29 August. Brent told Rice that the Federals were reported to be in Lookout (Wills) Valley in strength and ordered him to move down Lookout Mountain until he could observe Trenton. Brent sent the message to Polk for transmission by his signalmen. No one at army headquarters knew that Mauldin's detachment of the Third Alabama Cavalry regiment had held Trenton for nearly a day, because Mauldin's reports had been addressed to Wheeler, who was nowhere near Chattanooga. Bragg next ordered Maj.

Charles McDonald's Eighteenth Tennessee Cavalry battalion, picketing upstream from Chattanooga, to move at once to McLemore's Cove, a V-shaped valley east of Lookout Mountain. If the Federals were already in Lookout Valley, Bragg believed there was nothing to prevent the Federals from continuing their eastward movement toward the railroad. McDonald's small command could move quickly and was better than nothing if Rosecrans's army was indeed on the march. While Brent wrote to McDonald, Mackall requested Polk to provide ten men from his escort, Capt. Leeds Greenleaf's Orleans Light Horse, to protect engineer officers reconnoitering the threatened area. The need to assemble mounted units in the middle of the night to form a screen on and behind Lookout Mountain highlighted the inadequacy of Wheeler's original dispositions. Widely dispersed, the Third Confederate Cavalry regiment had been sufficient while the Federals remained beyond the river, but when Rosecrans advanced, its picket line was quickly shattered. Rice had done his best, but he could neither halt nor delay the Federal advance guard. Still, Bragg and Brent counted on Rice, and they were chagrinned to learn that Polk's signalmen could not contact Rice until daylight because they lacked turpentine to light their signal torches.[23]

Having dispatched horsemen into the night, Bragg next alerted his infantry. Brent informed Hill that the Federal army seemed to have appeared in force in Lookout (Wills) Valley. A second message instructed Hill to cook three days' rations at once so as to be "prepared to move in any direction." With Walker and Breckinridge now part of Hill's Corps, Brent enjoined him to ensure that their ammunition trains were ready for movement. Indicative of the chaos at army headquarters, a third message instantly followed to Hill and Liddell with the same instructions. Later in the day, when no further information was forthcoming, the crisis atmosphere subsided, and Bragg began to adopt a more measured response. Smith's Brigade was nearest the point of concern, but only the Twelfth Tennessee Infantry regiment was posted beyond the tip of Lookout Mountain. Bragg instructed Polk to place an entire brigade west of the mountain and an additional brigade east of it facing the road to Rossville. In addition, he told Polk to return Hindman's Division to its old camps at McFarland's Spring. There it could counter any Federal threat emanating from McLemore's Cove. Finally, Brent told Polk that McDonald had been stripped from the river line because of the emergency. Although he had issued instructions at 3:00 A.M. to cook three days' rations, Polk acted with his usual lack of urgency to reposition his troops. Not until 10:30 A.M. did he order Hindman to return to McFarland's Spring, and the division did not arrive there until twelve hours later. Similarly, Polk ordered Cheatham to send Strahl's Brigade to relieve the Twelfth Tennessee beyond Lookout Mountain and detail Preston Smith's troops to guard the Rossville Road. That move, too, was not completed until late in the day. Exhibiting much more urgency than Polk, inspector general Beard sent an ambulance and wagon to evacuate Mrs. Patton Anderson, her children, and their baggage from Chattanooga. Etta Anderson had been visiting her husband, but Beard knew from the headquarters activity that it was time for her to go.[24]

Unlike his infantry, Bragg's largest cavalry force seemed impervious to army control. The only reports received by Bragg during the previous week seem to have come from Captain Rice at Bridgeport, and possibly from Capt. T. P. Edmondson's Company F, Third Confederate Cavalry regiment, at Shell Mound. Regimental commander William Estes had reported at least once about the Federal incursions across the river to Wheeler, not to Bragg. Similarly, Harris Mauldin also reported only to Wheeler. Mauldin's detachment had moved north on 27 August, but the remainder of Martin's Division did not break camp until two days later. Bypassing Wheeler, Bragg had ordered Wharton's Division to support Hill north of Chattanooga on 29 August but diverted it on the next day to LaFayette. On 31 August, Bragg ordered Wheeler to move his headquarters to Chattanooga, but there was no response. While Brent built a cavalry screen and alerted the army's infantry, Kinloch Falconer attempted to reach Wheeler. At 2:30 A.M., Falconer telegraphed Capt. Thaddeus Foster Jr., quartermaster at Kingston, Georgia, to forward a message to Wheeler: "The Enemy are reported to have crossed into Wills Valley in force at Trenton. The General wishes a report immediately from you, as to the truth of this report, and any facts in regard to the numbers &c of the enemy." Thirty minutes later, Falconer wired "Commanding Officer, Troops Wheeler's Corps, Calhoun, Georgia," that "General Bragg requests that you move rapidly forward to Lafayette and watch the movements of the enemy from Lafayette to McLemore's Cove and *resist* to the last every effort to enter McLemore's Cove. Report frequently to these Head Quarters." Later in the morning Falconer drafted a telegram to Col. Alexander Caldwell, post commander at Rome, introducing his clerk Alfred Carothers, who was bearing "important dispatches to Generals Wheeler and Wharton." For some reason, the telegram was not sent; whether or not Carothers took the train to Rome is unknown.[25]

During the day Bragg learned more about the location of Wheeler's divisions, although nothing was heard from Wheeler himself. In some fashion, army headquarters learned that Wharton was approaching LaFayette and that Martin had reached Trenton, although most of Martin's command remained far to the south. By that time Falconer had stopped trying to reach Wheeler, and Brent assumed the task of coordinating the movements of Wheeler's Corps. First, Brent ordered Martin to locate the Federals and report immediately to Chattanooga. Next, he wrote to Wharton, assumed to be near LaFayette. Explaining Martin's instructions, he ordered Wharton to support Martin's efforts: "You must closely watch the passes of the mountains, and guard vigilantly against any raids upon our connections. They must be repelled." Finally, Brent enclosed a dispatch for Philip Roddey, commanding a small brigade in northern Alabama. The message ordered Roddey to leave one regiment in Alabama and join Wheeler with his command as rapidly as possible. Under the best of circumstances it would be some time before Roddey could join the main army. Wharton's and Martin's commands, however, were at last becoming available to investigate Federal movements south of Chattanooga. Still, there was no word from Wheeler himself, and Bragg urgently needed better control of the cavalry on the army's left flank. Thus he sent Maj. Pollok Lee, an assistant inspector general, to join Wharton's Division and report periodically. Lee's instructions were apparently verbal, but clearly he could serve as a trusted liaison between army headquarters and Wheeler's Cavalry Corps. Bragg told Wharton to assist Lee and facilitate his communications with army headquarters. Normally such a liaison officer would have been sent to Wheeler, but in Wheeler's absence, Wharton was the senior officer in the command. Wharton's response to the presence of a "headquarters spy" is unrecorded but can hardly have been positive.[26]

The crisis on the army's left flank sent ripples throughout Bragg's command. For all his differences with Forrest, Bragg recognized the Tennessean's skills in the aggressive collection of intelligence. Thus Brent sent two messages to Forrest on 1 September via Buckner's headquarters, still believed to be at Loudon. In no uncertain terms Brent ordered Forrest to cross the Hiwassee River and bring his entire command to Chattanooga as soon as possible. Forgetting that Forrest earlier had been given control of Buckner's cavalry, Brent told Forrest that Buckner's horsemen would serve as his rear guard and protect the massive Loudon bridge. As for Buckner himself, Brent ordered him to continue his withdrawal to the line of the Hiwassee River. Buckner was to be sure to salvage all the railroad rolling stock he could move within Confederate lines. Formally ratifying a tentative decision made earlier, Brent issued Special Orders, No. 14, which assigned Stewart's Division to Buckner's Corps as of 1 September. Aware that Stewart's command had left its wagons behind when it moved to Loudon by rail, Brent wrote to Hill about the matter. Aware of the developing tension between army headquarters and Hill, Brent was polite in the extreme: "The General desires that you will as far as the public service will admit, let Genl. Stewart have his transportation." Until Hill relinquished the wagons, their absence remained a sore subject in Stewart's command. Brent next looked to the army's rear. Fearing another raid toward Atlanta, he warned Col. Moses Wright, commanding the Atlanta Arsenal, of a potential Federal approach from either Rome or the Western & Atlantic Railroad. Finally, Brent informed Carter Stevenson in Demopolis, Alabama, that the Vicksburg parolees would be gathered near Atlanta under strict control until they could be reactivated in the Army of Tennessee. With the larger issues momentarily addressed, both Brent and Falconer turned to more mundane matters, such as locating 2,000 pairs of shoes for Walker's and Breckinridge's men.[27]

South of Chattanooga, the news of a potential Federal incursion into the army's rear created concern in several quarters. Security for the railroad to Atlanta had been vested in the Georgia State Line since July. Controlled by Governor Brown and his adjutant general, Maj. Gen. Henry Wayne, Col. Edward Galt's First Regiment and Col. James Wilson's Second Regiment were scattered along the railroad. Headquartered at Resaca, Galt covered the sector south to Atlanta, with detachments at Chattahoochee Bridge, Etowah Bridge, Pettis Creek Bridge, and Resaca. Wilson's regiment guarded the railroad from Resaca to just north of Graysville, which included Dalton, Tunnel Hill, and several bridges around Catoosa Platform and Graysville. At least six cannon supported the infantry, and fortifications covered the major river crossings. Wayne established his own headquarters at Cartersville. During the crisis of 1 September, Bragg notified Wayne to "look out for trouble along the line of the road." Wayne's command was not under Bragg's control, but Brown did not prevent cooperation between the State Line and the Army of Tennessee. Such was not the case with Confederate medical personnel, attempting to relocate hospitals evacuated from Chattanooga. On 1 September Surgeon Dudley Saunders was in the midst of securing equivalent space on the railroad south of Dalton. He found several suitable buildings in Marietta but was blocked at every turn by Brown's representatives. Saunders estimated that a battle would create at least 6,000 seriously wounded, and he already was accommodating 4,000 sick. Brown's refusal to permit use of the Georgia Military Institute buildings at Marietta for hospital purposes was especially galling to Saunders. He begged Stout to intervene with Brown, saying, "*Privately* I do not like the spirit shown by Gov Brown, there is too much of the demagogue." With battle increasingly imminent and only 6,000 available beds, Saunders feared an impending medical disaster.[28]

Throughout the army perceptive soldiers saw that something was stirring on 1 September. Rumors of the Federal probe toward Lookout Mountain gradually spread through the camps. On the river, fraternization with the enemy now was sternly prohibited. Orders to cook three days' rations also meant possible movement. Many units were already in motion. Hindman's Division spent the day returning to its old camps at McFarland's Spring. More units from Breckinridge's Division arrived at Chickamauga Station. Martin's Cavalry Division continued to straggle northward from Alabama, while Wharton's troopers reached LaFayette in late afternoon. At Charleston, Stewart's soldiers reveled in their transfer to Buckner's Corps. According to Maj. Harry Thornton, "All the men and officers are delighted with the new arrangement—

and the transfer to Buckner. He has a kind of popularity, rather based upon his showy military deportment than upon any solid services—while D. H. Hill after his career in Virginia in command of Alabamians is not cordially respected by them." In the Thirty-Eighth Alabama Infantry regiment, Sgt. Talbert Holt commemorated his fourth wedding anniversary in a letter to his wife, Carrie, and stated, "Big battle to be fought soon, hope I wont be in it." During the day, Johnson's Brigade reached Charleston. Yet to arrive was Preston's Division, which stopped for the night at Riceville. With Forrest's Cavalry Division and Pegram's Brigade heading for the Hiwassee also, the only unit remaining at Loudon was Scott's Cavalry Brigade. Scott's troopers manned the entrenchments north of the river with two mountain howitzers, sending their horses and the remainder of Robinson's Battery to the south bank. In Chattanooga, Pvt. William Whitehead of Company H, Second Kentucky Infantry regiment, was executed by musketry for desertion. Cpl. John James of the Thirty-Ninth Alabama Infantry regiment told his wife of his role: "I had to unlock the handcuffs from a captive to be shot. He was shot in a few moments after I took the handcuffs off of him."[29]

Unaware that the Confederates had discovered the Caperton's Ferry crossing, Rosecrans believed that Bragg remained focused upstream. In fact, there was concern that the Confederates might cross the river and strike the Twenty-First Corps. At 10:00 A.M. Garfield telegraphed Thomas: "Have you any news touching the reported movement of the enemy into East Tennessee?" Thomas replied that he had none. When no other sources indicated such a movement, Garfield relaxed. Writing to his wife, Lucretia, he calmly announced, "We must delay our movement till we can ascertain the truth of this rumor. If it be true we will turn back and fight him on this side. If not we will try to find him beyond the mountains." His health having returned, Garfield boasted, "No man in this army can fill my place during this moment. It would take him several months to learn the character and condition of affairs as I know them and to hold that influence with the commanding General that I do." Garfield's placid demeanor seemingly had an effect. At 2:00 P.M. Rosecrans asked Sheridan for a progress report on the Bridgeport bridge. When told that the work would not be completed until the next day, he seemed content to let the matter rest. Thus the staff spent the day resolving smaller issues. Garfield ordered Thomas to improve the roads between the Battle Creek and Bridgeport enclaves and rebuked Steedman at Murfreesboro for delaying telegraphic communication from the rear. Goddard ordered Steedman to relieve the Sixty-Ninth Ohio Infantry regiment at Cowan. Bond instructed Morgan to bring his infantry to the Flint River bridge, leaving his cavalry at Huntsville. Thoms also tried to secure the relief of the Sixty-Ninth Ohio, as well as the Eighty-Ninth Ohio Infantry regiment at Tracy City. Thoms offered the 60,000 rations and 700 sacks of grain at Tracy

City to any Twenty-First Corps units that might want them. Finally, Thoms instructed Chief Quartermaster Hodges to negotiate with civilian bridge companies for the reconstruction of the Tennessee River and Running Water Creek railroad bridges.[30]

In the Twentieth Corps sector, there was no movement on 1 September. On Sand Mountain, Davis's men spent the day winnowing their baggage in accord with General Orders, No. 28, which limited regiments, batteries, and brigade headquarters to only three wagons apiece. The three regimental wagons could carry a wall tent, regimental and company desks, cooking utensils, 500 pounds of medical supplies, camp tools, officers' baggage (limited to 80 pounds each), and three days' forage for the regimental animals. Division headquarters were limited to ten wagons each: four for camp equipage, baggage, desks, and three days' forage; four for shoes (800 pairs), some clothing, and blacksmith tools; and two for officers' commissary supplies. Division ammunition trains were to carry 110 rounds of small arms ammunition per man and 250 artillery rounds per gun. A few wagons in the ammunition train were loaded with axes, spades, and picks for road repair and entrenching. All other wagons were to be grouped into a divisional supply train, divided into four sections carrying six days' rations each. Every wagon was required to carry three days' short forage for its team. McCook on 1 September permitted an additional wagon per division to carry medical supplies. As Sheridan had already reduced his wagons below the number required by corps headquarters, he was allowed to go his own way. The order reduced the transportation of the Twentieth Corps to approximately 750 wagons and more than 100 ambulances, pulled by 4,500 mules and just over 200 horses. In order to meet the requirement, hard choices had to be made. Regiments accustomed to nine wagons had to be content with three. Most tents were forbidden, leaving the men only their shelter halves. Officers had to reduce their personal baggage to subsistence levels, which some took in stride, while others grumbled. Everything not taken had to be sent to Stevenson and stored, possibly never to be seen again.[31]

Everywhere in the corps area, the winnowing process continued all day. On Sand Mountain, Hans Heg had no difficulty, as he told his wife, Gunild: "I can take along all I have got." In Johnson's division, Col. Hiram Strong of the Ninety-Third Ohio Infantry regiment found the reduction more painful: "I took an old valise of Col. Martin's put in it such articles of indispensable necessity as the journey required and sent my trunk back." Sgt. Maj. Lyman Widney of the Thirty-Fourth Illinois Infantry regiment was philosophical: "So anxious are we to lighten our loads that very few have retained any clothing but what they are wearing and one blanket preferring a scanty wardrobe to carrying a heavy pack over the mountains and at the same time filling the position of 'assistant mule' by helping to drag baggage wagons and artillery over steep and rocky mountain roads." Less accepting was Surgeon Luther Waterman of the First Division. Given the reduction of medical supplies to only 500 pounds per regiment, Waterman foresaw a situation in which those supplies would probably be unavailable just when most needed. Had he known that Marietta Davis, twenty-five, the division commander's wife, was traveling with two large trunks, he would have been even more peeved. Still, General Orders, No. 28, was generally obeyed in the two Twentieth Corps divisions beyond the river. For those men who finished their sorting and packing early, the remainder of the day was theirs. In Davis's division, the soldiers lazed about their camps or surveyed their surroundings. Johnson's men washed clothes, bathed, swam, and frolicked in the river. Late in the day, corps chief of staff Gates Thruston issued orders for the next move. Davis was to advance to the far side of Sand Mountain, descend into Wills Valley, and halt at William Winston's plantation. At the same time, Johnson was to ascend Sand Mountain and occupy Davis's old camps. Both men were told that McCook and his staff would join Johnson on the mountain during the day. That night Davis and his wife dined again with Colonel Post at his headquarters on the mountain.[32]

At Bridgeport, the frenzy of activity continued on 1 September. With more than 1,000 men on the job, work on the trestle bridge continued from both the western bank of the river and Long Island. In the middle of the channel the water was at least eleven feet deep, requiring pontoons to span the gap. While some men extended the trestle, others constructed a bridge of twenty-six pontoons from Long Island to the east bank. Meanwhile, a handful of Confederate prisoners toiled on the approaches and the road across the island. Around 3:30 P.M., Lt. George Burroughs declared the pontoon bridge ready for use. That left only the combination trestle-pontoon structure to be completed, a much more complex task. During the day, Laibold's Third Brigade of Sheridan's division moved from Stevenson to Bridgeport. With his command now united, Sheridan moved his headquarters to Bridgeport as well, relieving Lytle at the construction site. Freed of larger responsibilities, Lytle attempted to have a group photograph made of himself and his staff, but the effort was unsuccessful. During the afternoon, wagons from Brannan's division began to accumulate near the bridge. While waiting to cross, teamsters and guards washed away the ubiquitous dust by bathing in the river. Two such soldiers, privates Harvey Cotterman, twenty, and David C. Moler, twenty-one, both of Company G, Thirty-First Indiana Infantry regiment, unfortunately got into deeper water than they could handle. When one struggled, the other went to his aid, and both drowned in full view of hundreds of men working on the bridge. As darkness fell, Lt. Col. Kinsman Hunton of the First Michigan Engineers and Mechanics estimated that the bridge would be available for use before noon on the next day. At 9:30 P.M., Sheridan promised Rosecrans that the bridge would be completed even earlier, by 9:00 A.M. Anxious to leave the river behind, Sheridan asked permission to cross his division as soon as the bridge was ready, permission readily granted by Rosecrans.[33]

Upstream, Brannan and Reynolds expanded their toeholds east of the river. At Battle Creek, Brannan ordered his three brigades to move inland, even though their artillery batteries and wagons had not yet crossed. First to advance was Van Derveer's Third Brigade. During the morning Van Derveer and his staff rode east three miles on the Shell Mound road to Graham's Station, where the brigade joined him during the afternoon. Meanwhile, Connell's First Brigade took the road past Taylor's Store and halted at Moore's Spring. Croxton's Second Brigade followed Connell only as far as Taylor's Store. From there Croxton furnished working parties that spent the day ferrying artillery pieces, rations, and baggage across the river. While so engaged, Pvt. Henry Winkler of the Tenth Indiana Infantry regiment was kicked in the head by a fractious mule on one of the makeshift rafts. Knocked unconscious, he fell into the river and drowned, his body disappearing in the current. Still the work went on as the men continued to manhandle artillery pieces across the stream. Similar craft were in use at Shell Mound, where Reynolds supervised the transfer of his two brigades east of the river. First to move were the detachments of King's Second Brigade left behind with the brigade trains when most of the command crossed the river two days earlier. After bringing over the brigade's baggage, the new arrivals joined their parent units near the ruined railroad depot. Those not so occupied splashed and swam in the river. Again, tragedy struck, as Pvt. Robert Commons of Company I, Seventy-Fifth Indiana Infantry regiment, drowned in full view of 500 horrified onlookers. The drowning did not stop the ferrying process, as Turchin's Third Brigade crossed the river during the afternoon. Like Van Derveer, Turchin had a regimental band play patriotic airs while the rafts, flatboats, and skiffs plied the wide river. Across the stream at last, Turchin's men also camped near the depot. Reynolds now had his division securely on the eastern shore, although he and his staff remained west of the stream.[34]

For the units executing Rosecrans's deception plan, news of downstream events came only through rumors brought by supply trains crossing Walden's Ridge. The regiments under Wilder's direct command spent the day quietly, with no bombardment of the city. Pickets at several crossings showed themselves to their opponents but initiated no contact. Similarly, Wagner's infantrymen remained quiescent on Walden's Ridge. In the Fifty-Seventh Indiana Infantry regiment, the men were delighted to receive a shipment of mail. During the day, Wagner's regiments welcomed their rear detachments, which had remained in the Sequatchie Valley until the Twenty-First Corps began moving southward. Farther up the river valley, Hazen continued his efforts to distract any watching Confederates. During the morning he dispatched elements of the Ninety-Second Illinois Mounted Infantry regiment, supported by part of the Forty-First Ohio Infantry regiment, to demonstrate at Igou's Ford, not far above Harrison's Ferry. Later, he sent portions of the Ninety-Eighth Illinois Mounted Infantry regiment and four cannon, supported by the Ninth Indiana and 124th Ohio Infantry regiments, to Thatcher's Ferry. Hazen had heard that the Confederates were planning to raid across the river to a grist mill his troops were operating, and he wanted to forestall that possibility. The guns fired a few rounds across the river without response, but Hazen's point had been made. Meanwhile, he attempted to exchange Col. Isaac Suman's Ninth Indiana for the Sixth Ohio Infantry regiment. The latter had been attached to Hazen's command for some time but was under orders to return to Grose's brigade. Suman and Hazen were both strong personalities who mutually desired to sever their relationship. Nevertheless, Palmer, the division commander and a citizen soldier like Suman, denied Hazen's request for a divorce. North of Hazen's command, Minty's brigade remained quietly at Smith's Cross Roads, foraging and hoping not to be noticed in its exposed position.[35]

With specific orders finally in hand, Crittenden executed them with a will. Buell's First Brigade of Wood's First Division led the way from Therman at 6:30 A.M. As the temperature rose and the dust clouds billowed, the march became exceedingly unpleasant. Still, Pvt. William Carroll was ready to go: "I want to get out of this valley and get away from the mountains. . . . I like to be in a level country whair you don't have to clime a mountain every time you move." Following Buell was Harker's Third Brigade. Unwilling to leave the injured Captain Tuttle to an uncertain fate, Wood had ordered him to be transported with the column, though he had to endure "the most excruciating pain it was every my fortune to suffer." Wood halted near Jasper in midafternoon after a grueling march of twenty miles. Close behind him was Palmer's Second Division. His troops also were plagued by the heat and the "shoe mouth deep" dust. Palmer's troops rested more often than Wood's had done and thus halted five miles short of Jasper at the end of the day. Even though the regimental bands played lively music and tributaries of the Sequatchie River provided relief from the dust, some men still complained that the day's march had been too long. Such a charge could hardly be lodged against Van Cleve, who halted several miles short of Dunlap in early afternoon. He too was glad to be leaving the Sequatchie Valley, where "the people are happy in their ignorance, as they rarely see the outside of the valley, and consequently cannot know that others can live, or do live, better than they." Traveling with the column on horseback was Mrs. Alexander Stout, wife of the colonel of the Seventeenth Kentucky Infantry regiment. At least one officer saw her presence as unseemly, writing, "If she were my wife I would send her home." Far ahead of his toiling infantry, Crittenden reached Jasper in early afternoon. There he learned that Reynolds would not relinquish his rafts until he had ferried a supply train across the Tennessee, so the Twenty-First Corps would have to wait around Jasper for at least a day.[36]

With the Bridgeport bridge still unfinished and the rafts at Battle Creek and Shell Mound slow, the Caperton's Ferry span represented the best hope for expanding the Federal presence beyond the river on 1 September. During the day drovers pushed a herd of cattle across the stream, and the First Tennessee (Union) Cavalry regiment crossed as well. Campbell's First Brigade of McCook's division thus became the first complete cavalry brigade beyond the river. Rosecrans needed to concentrate his Cavalry Corps so that it could lead the Twentieth Corps into the mountains, but the Federal cavalrymen remained scattered. McCook's Second Brigade reached Caperton's during the day but was not ready to begin an expedition. His Third Brigade, marching from Larkinsville, was also unready to cross. Long's Second Brigade of Crook's command was nearby, but his men spent the day issuing equipment, shoeing horses, and washing their mounts in the river. Thus the Cavalry Corps would not be ready to use the pontoon bridge for at least another day. Impatient, Rosecrans suggested to Negley that his division use the bridge while the cavalry was still coming forward. Thomas agreed, ordering Negley to advance along the river's eastern shore to Taylor's Store after crossing at Caperton's. Negley himself planned to cross at the Hart's Bar ford, and elements of Rosecrans's escort guided him to that difficult crossing point. After learning that at least one cavalryman had drowned there, Negley elected to use the pontoon bridge after all. Already at Stevenson, Beatty's First Brigade was the first of Negley's units to move. Handing eighty-six Confederate prisoners to other units, Beatty's men left the town in midafternoon and crossed the bridge just before dark. Their road led toward Sand Mountain for a little over a mile, then turned northward to parallel the river. Beatty himself remained in Stevenson for several hours, adjourning the examining board he chaired. By the time he crossed it was dark, and he spent several anxious hours until he found his command six miles beyond the bridge.[37]

The late decision to send Negley's division across the river meant that two brigades would have to negotiate the shaky pontoon bridge at night. Stanley's Second Brigade left Cave Spring near sunset and traversed the dusty road to the river. Along the way, Pvt. William Christian of the Nineteenth Illinois Infantry regiment met his father, who offered his son an extra pair of shoes. The chance meeting filled Christian with foreboding: "I feel as though I would not see father again," he wrote. By the time Stanley reached the bridge, darkness had fallen. The waning three-quarter moon had not yet risen, yet the crossing point was illuminated. Large bonfires blazed at both ends of the bridge and hundreds of campfires twinkled on the far bank where Johnson's division lay, but clouds of dust diffused the light. Sgt. Joseph Johnston vividly recalled that the fires "threw a faint glare over the smooth current revealing the long low bridge with the hobgoblin forms of the troops bobbing up and down." Crouched in each pontoon was a soldier ready to bail any water that splashed into it. The scene filled Lt. Eben Sturges Jr. with pride: "As I crossed the bridge that night feeling it beneath my feet almost as steady and, for our purposes, as stable as a turnpike, I felt proud of the yankee enterprise that had constructed it." After crossing, Stanley's men stumbled through the camps of sleeping Twentieth Corps soldiers and took the river road northward. Sirwell's Third Brigade followed in Stanley's footsteps. The moon had now risen in a cloudless sky, adding its pale illumination to the lurid scene. In the Seventy-Fourth Ohio Infantry regiment the men boisterously shouted and sang, while Capt. Robert Findley and Lt. Edward Ballard clutched tightly the six quarts of commissary whiskey they had just purchased in Stevenson for $1.00. The rowdy men of the Twenty-First Ohio Infantry gleefully whistled the "Rogue's March" as they made their way over the span. It was midnight before Sirwell completed his crossing, and his command marched only two miles beyond the bridge before halting to rest fitfully beside the road.[38]

When Rosecrans dispatched his nightly summary to Washington at 10:30 P.M., Negley's troops were still crossing the river. Thus he stated that only four divisions were across the stream. He also reported, erroneously, that one of Stanley's cavalry divisions was beyond the Tennessee. Rosecrans expected the Bridgeport bridge to be completed before dawn and that Sheridan's division would then cross to the east bank. Two Reserve Corps brigades were also on the march, with their advance at Huntsville. All was going according to design and the Army of the Cumberland was well on its way to completing the most difficult and dangerous part of the campaign plan. Although he did not say so, Rosecrans had safely placed nearly half of his available infantry beyond the stream. With the arrival of Negley's division on the far shore, fourteen of the thirty infantry brigades in the Fourteenth, Twentieth, and Twenty-First Corps were across the river with only negligible losses. Only one cavalry brigade had crossed, but four others were gathered at Caperton's Ferry ready to move on the next day. As soon as the Bridgeport bridge was completed, Sheridan's division would cross the river, as would two brigades of Baird's division of the Fourteenth Corps. Two of Crittenden's divisions were near Jasper, within striking distance of the Shell Mound rafting site, and the third was only a day's march behind them. The only point of concern was the worrisome bottleneck growing at Bridgeport, where hundreds of wagons and ambulances from several divisions had gathered to await the completion of the bridge. Even at Bridgeport, the engineers had promised imminent success. If the Army of Tennessee remained quiescent just a little longer, Rosecrans would able to consolidate his hold on the east bank of the river without fear of being thrown back across the stream. All in all, at the end of Tuesday, 1 September 1863, prospects never looked brighter for Rosecrans and the Army of the Cumberland.[39]

14

Sand Mountain

» 2–4 September 1863 «

At 6:00 A.M. on Wednesday, 2 September, Lieutenant Colonel Hunton reported to Sheridan that the Bridgeport bridge was available for infantry to cross the stream and that wagons could use the structure by noon. The first troops to use the bridge were pickets from the Thirty-Sixth Illinois Infantry regiment, who had been on duty on Long Island, and who crossed to Bridgeport to rejoin their fellows in Lytle's First Brigade. Lytle's troops led the division across the rickety structure at noon, followed by Bradley's Third Brigade. Laibold's Second Brigade brought up the rear, crossing in midafternoon. Thereafter, Sheridan's command followed the railroad to Taylor's Store and turned up a narrow track over Hogjaw Ridge. Surmounting the ridge, the Federals descended into Hogjaw Valley and sprawled around Moore's Spring to await their wagons carrying rations and camp equipage. Already at Moore's Spring was Beatty's First Brigade, the vanguard of Negley's Second Division. Even though Negley had already selected campsites for the brigades of Stanley and Sirwell, still toiling up the dusty road from Caperton's, Sheridan's men paid no heed and seized the best remaining camping grounds for themselves. Outraged by their behavior, Negley complained to Thomas, but Sheridan's soldiers remained in place. Clearly Sheridan's aggressive spirit had been transmitted to his troops, and the fact that the divisions belonged to two different corps only exacerbated the situation. Even though all the units of the Army of the Cumberland were laboring toward a common goal, that fact did not preclude friction between commands. Indeed, much of the friction sprang from the personalities of senior leaders who had taken the measure of their peers during the previous year's campaigning. Small in stature but bold and pugnacious to a fault, West Pointer Sheridan, thirty-two, was contemptuous of the portly and affable Negley, thirty-seven, a citizen soldier whose date of rank preceded Sheridan's by a month. On 2 September the dispute was minor, with only campsites being at issue, but more significant differences lay ahead.[1]

The Bridgeport bridge figured large in Rosecrans's plans, as both Sheridan's command and Baird's division were slated to use it. Even more important, hundreds of baggage wagons, supply wagons, ammunition wagons, and ambulances waited to make their way gingerly across the river. Already in position were Sheridan's and Brannan's trains, and the trains of Long's Second Brigade, Second Cavalry Division. Coming from the Sequatchie Valley were the trains of Crittenden's Twenty-First Corps, all of which were to cross at Bridgeport in lieu of being slowly ferried across the stream at Shell Mound. Baird's division trains and the wagons of miscellaneous organizations completed the mob of teamsters, mules, and wagons fighting for a place in the single line of wheeled vehicles forming below the Bridgeport fortifications. Somehow, the baggage wagons of Connell's First Brigade of Brannan's division were first in line when Sheridan's infantry exited the bridge. In midafternoon Connell's teamsters began negotiating the spindly trestles and bobbing pontoons to Long Island. The wagons of Connell's infantry regiments went first, and the wagons of his artillery battery brought up the rear of the column. For a brief time, all went well, but suddenly around 3:30 P.M. the trestle section from the midchannel pontoons to Long Island suffered a catastrophic collapse. The baggage wagons of Battery D, First Michigan Light Artillery, had almost reached the safety of the island when the falling trestle bents dumped five heavily loaded wagons, their drivers, and their mule teams into the river. According to a newspaper correspondent who was present, "One moment the bridge, with its creeping monstrous burden, was quietly spanning the olive waters of the Tennessee; the next there was a corresponding line of partly submerged wagons, a maelstrom of struggling mules, a confused clambering among the pale and frantic drivers, and a tangled, loose raft of timbers, bubbling up end-wise from the wreck, and sweeping about with lessening swiftness into the tumbled current."[2]

For a moment, onlookers gaped in shock as approximately 700 feet of trestlework dropped into the stream. At the site of the collapse the water was little more than four feet deep, but the mules were so tangled in harness and bridge debris that they could not escape the wreck. Rescuers manning spare pontoons eventually freed all but one of the mules, which drowned before it could be saved. Similarly, the pontoons facilitated the salvage of most of the cargo. Emptied of their loads, the now buoyant wagons were eventually poled to shore. The rescue complete, the men of the First Michigan Engineers and Mechanics began the painful task of reconstructing their handiwork. They were assisted by Pioneer Brigade engineers, who had laid the pontoon bridge on the other side of Long Island. There had long been a rivalry between the two units, with the Michiganders casting aspersions on the capabilities of the Pioneers. Now Pioneer Brigade soldiers had the satisfaction of seeing random pieces of their tormenters' work floating lazily down the river, while their own bridge stood "solid as a rock." Examination of the wreckage and eyewitness accounts

Pontoon bridge built by Pioneer Brigade over ship channel of Tennessee River at Bridgeport, Alabama. (Michigan Organizations at Chickamauga)

revealed that the bridge had failed initially where it joined the free-floating pontoons in the deepest part of the channel. In their haste to construct the trestle, Hunton's men had not braced the bents but simply stood them in the stream, relying on the balks to keep the trestle upright and rigid. The flowing water had eroded the streambed around the bents, making them unstable. As each heavily laden wagon crossed the structure, it caused the bents to oscillate, and the vibration eventually caused the connection between the pontoons and the trestle to break. With no anchor on one end and no support in the riverbed holding them vertical, the bents folded toward the island like a house of cards under the weight of the wagons. This explanation for the disaster became obvious after the bridge's collapse, but the pressure to finish the bridge quickly had been intense. Haste had made waste.[3]

With no inkling of the looming disaster, Rosecrans and his staff spent the morning coordinating the movements of the army's most distant units. At 10:00 A.M., Garfield instructed Crittenden to send one brigade to Shell Mound and a second to Battle Creek. Either Crittenden or Palmer was to cross the river and deploy the Twenty-First Corps troops to the left or rear of Reynolds's division. Crittenden was also enjoined to gather his trains behind his right and improve the road net around Shell Mound. At 11:00 A.M. Garfield telegraphed Granger, Innes, and Col. Charles Thompson, forbidding the dispersal of Thompson's regiment of United States Colored Troops in anything smaller than battalion size. For the moment, Thompson's newly formed command would be allowed to continue training at Elk River Bridge as a unit. Finally,

Garfield instructed Morgan of the Reserve Corps to use Tillson's First Brigade to relieve the Fourteenth Corps garrisons along the Nashville & Chattanooga Railroad, in lieu of Dan McCook's Second Brigade, which would now continue toward Stevenson. Goddard wrote to Granger about command relationships at McMinnville, now that the Reserve Corps was assuming responsibility for that post. In addition, he wired Morgan at Flint River to protect a sawmill at Larkinsville, as the army would need its lumber. He firmly admonished McCook for delaying Negley's trains at the Caperton's Ferry bridge on the previous night. Bond suggested to Sheridan that he follow Negley up Sand Mountain via Moore's Spring. Bond, too, wired Granger, suggesting ways to protect the large amount of supplies at Carthage. Thoms's task for the day was to arrange the transportation of one of Rosecrans's horses to Cincinnati. Finally, at 2:00 P.M. Garfield invited Crittenden to join Rosecrans, Thomas, and McCook at Bridgeport at 6:00 P.M. if possible, while Drouillard warned Sheridan that he would soon have important visitors. By the time the meeting convened, the crisis at the bridge would drastically change its agenda.[4]

McCook's orders for the day required him to cross Sand Mountain into Wills Valley and advance to a point known as Valley Head, where it would seize the crossing of Lookout Mountain known as Winston's Gap. McCook himself remained at Stevenson, but Davis's First Division had been on Sand Mountain for two days. According to the plan, Davis would advance to Winston's Gap, Johnson would follow Davis in support, and Sheridan would rejoin the corps at Winston's after crossing Sand Mountain behind the Fourteenth Corps. The sooner McCook's troops topped Lookout Mountain, Rosecrans reasoned, the greater pressure there would be on the Army of Tennessee to evacuate Chattanooga. Therefore, the Twentieth Corps needed to resume its advance quickly. Preceded by two companies of the First Tennessee (Union) Cavalry regiment, Post's First Brigade marched from the present crossroads of Flat Rock at 6:00 A.M. and headed southeasterly into the forest. Although elevated far above the valleys on its flanks, Sand Mountain was relatively flat on top. Covered with pines and hardwoods, the mountain was virtually unpopulated. Only occasionally did the men of the Twentieth Corps encounter residents, mostly women and children living in extreme poverty. They were friendly enough, with several expressing pleasure at seeing the U.S. flag again. According to Lt. Chesley Mosman, there were "some very pretty women to be seen." Less impressed was Sgt. Lewis Day, who opined, "The few people—citizens—that we saw, did not look as though they knew enough to last them through the week, nor did their actions belie their looks." Other than a few Confederate cavalry scouts flushed by Davis's advance guard, the march proved to be tiring but uneventful. In late afternoon Post's men descended the eastern slope of Sand Mountain and camped at its foot, several miles short of William Winston's plantation.

Behind them, Carlin's and Heg's brigades followed Post's track. By the time Heg's men halted for the day, night had fallen, but they too were at the foot of the mountain.[5]

Because of their rapid march, Davis's three brigades found themselves alone in the narrow four-mile wide trough between Sand and Lookout Mountains. The terrain where they halted for the night, however, was more complex than anyone had anticipated. In fact, there was not one valley separating Sand and Lookout Mountains, but four, depicted on modern maps as Sand Valley, Dugout Valley, Big Wills Valley, and Railroad Valley. Behind the Federals, Sand Mountain rose more than 450 feet above them at Troxel's Gap. In their front were three small, parallel ridges. No more than 200 feet tall, the ridges stood athwart the direct route to Winston's plantation and the road up Lookout Mountain. They also divided the terrain into discrete compartments. Post stopped in the first compartment, Sand Valley, but Carlin and Heg continued forward into Dugout Valley, camping on the small farm of Philip Young. Lt. Chesley Mosman of the Fifty-Ninth Illinois Infantry regiment dismissed any concerns about the division's precarious situation: "It seems queer for Rosecrans to move his men down in rear of the Rebel Army and thus invite an attack . . . but I'll let old Rosey boss the job." In both valleys, Davis's men wreaked havoc on the chickens, hogs, and potatoes their pleasant surroundings offered. Their nearest support was Johnson's Second Division, which spent the day heaving its wagon train up the west face of Sand Mountain. Pvt. Francis Kiene of the Forty-Ninth Ohio Infantry regiment found the road only dusty, but Pvt. Oliver Protsman of the First Ohio Infantry regiment claimed the track up the mountain was "the Worst road wee have Ever encountered." Ill with fever, Lt. Col. William Robinson of the Seventy-Seventh Pennsylvania Infantry regiment took quinine, but his only relief came in reaching the crest: "Sick and weary of a soldier's life, but the air feels purer, and by morning I hope to be better. More quinine." Johnson's division halted for the night only two miles beyond the crest, nearly twenty miles behind Davis.[6]

Although the Twentieth Corps momentarily was in front, Stanley's Cavalry Corps was expected to lead the Army of the Cumberland's flanking movement. Stanley's command, however, was not yet in position to play its assigned role. Campbell's First Brigade of the First Cavalry Division was scattered from the Bridgeport crossing site to the river valley below Caperton's Ferry. During the morning, LaGrange's Second Brigade and Watkins's Third Brigade, received orders to march at 12:30 P.M. to the pontoon bridge. Moving the skittish horses and mule-drawn wagons over the bridge took all afternoon but was completed without incident. With the difficult track up Sand Mountain clogged by Johnson's infantrymen, the two brigades turned south a short distance and camped at the mouth of Raccoon Creek. Meanwhile, the Second Michigan

Cavalry regiment from the First Brigade left its camp across from Bridgeport and scouted twelve miles up Sand Mountain on the road eventually to be taken by Negley and Sheridan. Finding no enemy on the road to Trenton, they returned to Moore's Spring with the news that the way was clear. Meanwhile, Crook's Second Cavalry Division also crossed the river. With Minty's First Brigade absent, Crook's command momentarily consisted only of Long's Second Brigade. Most of Long's troopers had used the difficult ford at Hart's Bar during the initial seizure of the east bank of the river, so the cavalry commanders considered it safe for continued use. The Chicago Board of Trade Battery and the division trains would cross via the Bridgeport bridges, but Long's four regiments would use the ford. In a dramatic scene, Long's troopers safely threaded their way through the twists of the ford to the east bank, although some men had to swim for their lives in the process. Long then led the Second Kentucky toward the Bridgeport bridges to meet the train, while Crook marched the remaining regiments toward Caperton's Ferry. Meanwhile, the battery made it across the Bridgeport bridge before it fell in midafternoon, but the division train had not yet crossed when the bridge collapsed.[7]

Thomas's Fourteenth Corps mostly lay still on 2 September, with only Baird's First Division in motion toward the Bridgeport crossing site. Starkweather's Second Brigade traveled to Stevenson from the Crow Creek valley, then took the dusty road to Bridgeport via Bolivar. As they passed Stevenson, they were joined by the First Wisconsin Infantry regiment, which had been clearing ground for a hospital. Capt. John Otto of the Twenty-First Wisconsin Infantry regiment was not impressed with Stevenson, "a conglomerate of several dozen miserable looking shanties erected in a barren sandy plain." In an effort to avoid eating Starkweather's dust, the First Brigade's Benjamin Scribner received permission to use a shortcut from Anderson Station over the mountain behind Stevenson, a poor choice because the unimproved track was almost impossibly difficult. Eventually Scribner's exhausted men reached Widow's Creek and followed it to the Bridgeport road, where they joined Starkweather's troops. By the time they neared Bridgeport, the bridge had fallen, so Baird's two brigades camped a few miles short of the crossing site. Beyond the stream, Negley's Second Division concentrated around Moore's Spring in Hogjaw Valley, intermixed with Sheridan's division. At Battle Creek, Brannan crossed the river, but his wagons did not. In the Tenth Indiana Infantry regiment, men searched for the previous day's drowning victim by firing a cannon over the water. While his compatriots foraged aggressively, Musician Billings Sibley wrote his mother that, except for the ignorant inhabitants, "this is a most beautiful country and should like to live here if it was not so far out of the world." At Shell Mound, Reynolds also moved across the river but experienced delay in getting his trains to the east bank. His men meanwhile swam, foraged, visited Nickajack Cave, and viewed the boundary stone marking the junction of Tennessee, Alabama, and Georgia. On a sadder note, soldiers in the Seventy-Fifth Indiana Infantry regiment sorrowfully recovered the body of drowning victim Robert Commons and buried him nearby.[8]

At Jasper, Crittenden was again without specific orders. At 8:45 A.M. he wrote to Garfield, "General Reynolds informs me that he will be through crossing at Shellmound at 2 P.M. Shall I then commence crossing?" In a tone that never would have been used with Thomas or even McCook, Garfield at 10:00 A.M. gave Crittenden detailed instructions on how to locate his troops on the far shore. At 3:00 P.M. Crittenden ordered Wood to send a brigade to the Shell Mound crossing site. At the same time he instructed Palmer to dispatch a brigade to Battle Creek. Realizing that the lateness of the hour meant that any crossing necessarily would occur at night, both Wood and Palmer questioned the need for haste. At 4:40 P.M. Crittenden's assistant adjutant general responded peremptorily, "The general cannot change the order as to crossing, as he is directed to effect it as rapidly as possible, and General Reynolds has informed him that the crossing would be clear this (4) p.m." Reluctantly, Wood selected Buell's First Brigade to march to Shell Mound during the evening to see if Reynolds would be true to his word. Palmer chose Grose's Third Brigade for the trip to Battle Creek but almost immediately postponed Grose's departure until the following morning. Crittenden meanwhile received the invitation from Garfield to meet with Rosecrans, Thomas, and McCook at Bridgeport at 6:00 P.M., a time Crittenden could not meet. All the while, Van Cleve pushed his Third Division southward through the heat and dust toward Jasper. Van Cleve's arrival meant that the long sojourn of the Twenty-First Corps in the isolated Sequatchie Valley was finally finished. The soldiers in the ranks speculated endlessly about their destination, but at least one officer harbored doubts about how it all would end. In a letter to his wife from Jasper on 2 September, Palmer exclaimed, "I am well satisfied that Rosecrans though a good soldier in the face of the enemy is not the man to conduct a complicated campaign. He lacks steadiness and breadth of thought."[9]

With Rosecrans's army precariously straddling the Tennessee River, the role of the deception force had never been more important. At the same time, with the Twenty-First Corps leaving the Sequatchie Valley, the deception force had never been more alone. Still, the four brigades assigned to mislead the Confederates stuck to their task. In Wilder's command, the day passed peacefully, broken only by the capture of two Confederate scouts. Interrogation of the scouts yielded only that Forrest's command was nearby. Wilder's artillerymen spent the day unpacking 400 rounds of ammunition that had arrived on the previous evening. Wilder himself studied dust plumes rising from the direction of Tyner's Station and Ringgold and concluded that a large body of troops had moved to that vicinity. He also received a report from John Funkhouser, who reported a great deal of "chopping or pounding" within the Confederate lines and concluded that they were either repairing wagons or building boats. Wilder sent the information to Rosecrans and, in a separate note, told Reynolds that he could cross the river at Williams Island whenever he wished. From Poe's Tavern, Hazen also reported increased Confederate activity. In response he moved units ostentatiously toward the river and played band music at several widely separated locations. On Walden's Ridge, Wagner's brigade welcomed the arrival of regimental baggage from the Sequatchie Valley. In the Ninety-Seventh Ohio Infantry regiment, a detail of carpenters and boatmen worked on boats to ferry the command across the river. North of Hazen, Minty continued to worry about his exposed position. A flurry of deserters from the Twenty-Sixth Tennessee Infantry regiment brought news of Buckner's withdrawal and the concentration of Forrest's cavalry. Minty feared an attack by Forrest and urgently voiced his concerns to Hazen, Crittenden, and Rosecrans. Still, he continued to display his command at the river, especially at Blythe's Ferry. Minty also reported making contact with Burnside's forces near Kingston.[10]

Behind the front the Reserve Corps was stirring to life. At McMinnville, Col. James Shelley arrived with three loyal Tennessee regiments to relieve Dick's Second Brigade. Shelley's own regiment had remained at Carthage, where the unpopular James Spears had just taken command. Both Shelley and Spears complained to Rosecrans about the confused command situation. Meanwhile, Dick prepared his brigade to move to the front. At the other end of the department, Second Division commander Morgan arrived at Flint River with Tillson's First Brigade. There he received orders to bring Tillson's troops to Stevenson and relieve King's Third Brigade of Baird's division along the railroad. Not knowing the location of McCook's Second Brigade, which was somewhere behind him, Morgan held Tillson's command at rest for another day. As for McCook, the three regiments with him spent a long day marching through what Pvt. Thomas Burns called the "largest woods I ever saw." Their throats parched from the suffocating dust and lack of water, McCook's men staggered into Athens by the end of the day. McCook's last unit, the Eighty-Sixth Illinois Infantry regiment, remained far behind at Columbia, waiting to be relieved by troops from Clarksville and Fort Donelson. In Morgan's Third Brigade, Col. Heber Le Favour's Twenty-Second Michigan Infantry regiment prepared to leave Nashville for Stevenson. In the midst of their preparations, friends of deceased Pvt. Lewis Yerkes, twenty-one, borrowed enough money to have their comrade's body embalmed and shipped to his Michigan home. Along the line of the railroad, Champion's First Brigade of Steedman's Second Division remained in its camps at Estill Springs, Fosterville, and Tullahoma. Reid's Second Brigade quietly garrisoned Shelbyville and Wartrace, while the 121st Ohio

Infantry regiment marched to Cowan to relieve another Fourteenth Corps unit, the Sixty-Ninth Ohio Infantry regiment. Coburn's Third Brigade held Murfreesboro, while elements of Robert Granger's Third Division patrolled Nashville, Clarksville, and Carthage.[11]

At Bridgeport the fall of the trestle threatened to derail all of Rosecrans's plans. Not only was Baird's division prevented from crossing the river, but the failure to move the trains of several units created supply problems. Sheridan's division had made it across the stream but, without the division's wagons, the troops lacked blankets and rations. Sheridan's men shamelessly begged such items from Negley's division, even after rudely appropriating the best camping places around Moore's Spring. Some of Brannan's troops were in similar circumstances. Thus Lieutenant Colonel Hunton quickly sent hundreds of men into the waist-deep water to wrestle the heavy timbers back into an upright position. This time, Hunton ordered the bents to be braced, in the manner of carpenter's sawhorses. In the midst of the rebuilding effort, Rosecrans arrived on the dummy with Thomas and McCook. Originally scheduled as a review of the campaign plan, the meeting now became an effort to craft a new and very tentative movement schedule. Worse, the Twenty-First Corps was unrepresented because Crittenden did not appear. Rosecrans asked Hunton to explain the problem and his proposed solution, chiding him about the original lack of bracing. Still, there was no point in blaming Hunton and his engineers; whatever their guilt in the original failure, they were now the only people who could rectify the problem. Thus Hunton remained in charge of the reconstruction effort. With nothing further to be seen or done by the generals, Rosecrans and his party returned to Stevenson. After thinking about the problem on the brief train trip, Rosecrans asked Hunton if troops could use the bridge while the engineers were working. Hunton replied affirmatively, but before any significant movement occurred, the bridge crashed into the stream again shortly after 9:00 P.M. Apprised of the collapse, Rosecrans at 10:30 P.M. ordered Hunton to remove his men from the water until daylight.[12]

The collapse of the trestle bridge was not the only bad news Rosecrans received on 2 September. Grant's quartermaster at St. Louis informed him of bureaucratic delays in shipping forty spare freight cars to Louisville. Another message, from Halleck, provided minimal information on Burnside's progress toward Knoxville. Undaunted, Rosecrans continued to conduct business far into the night. He asked the president of the Louisville & Nashville Railroad to expedite the movement of material to rebuild the Bridgeport railroad bridges. He importuned Secretary of War Stanton to replenish his contingency fund, saying, "I am going now where it will be much needed." News also arrived from Crittenden, who had finally reached Bridgeport. In response, the staff quickly arranged for the dummy to bring Crittenden to Stevenson. At

10:30 P.M., Crittenden and his staff reached army headquarters. Thirty minutes later, Rosecrans sent Halleck his daily summary of significant events. His chief focus was the bridge disaster, although Rosecrans minimized its severity and its effect on the timing of the army's advance. Instead, Rosecrans heralded the fact that Sheridan's division had gotten across the stream, Crittenden's corps was beginning to cross in boats, and one of McCook's divisions was probably at Valley Head. He also projected that Stanley's cavalry would push southward to Rawlingsville in Wills Valley on the next day. Rosecrans noted that Confederate rumors placed Burnside in Knoxville already. Indeed, Rosecrans could have been even more positive about developments than he actually was in his report to Halleck. Sheridan's and Stanley's crossings meant that by the end of the day he had placed seventeen of his thirty infantry brigades and four of his five cavalry brigades on the east bank of the river. At Shell Mound, Buell was even then ferrying a Twenty-First Corps brigade across the stream. Slowly but surely, the Army of the Cumberland was surmounting its first major obstacle, a process that the Bridgeport disaster would only delay, not halt.[13]

Rosecrans's troubles on 2 September were entirely invisible to Bragg, who still had no accurate picture of what the Federals were doing. Dispatches from both Mauldin and Wharton, no longer extant, apparently indicated that a very large force of Federals had crossed the river below Bridgeport and was somewhere on Sand Mountain. Trenton seemed to be threatened by a slightly smaller party. Still, the ubiquitous Captain Rice reported at 10:00 A.M. from a signal station on Lookout Mountain that no enemy was visible on the valley floor. For the moment, major elements of Rosecrans's army had disappeared. At noon, Bragg convened a conference at his headquarters in the Chattanooga suburbs. Present were Polk, Hill, Cheatham, Hindman, Cleburne, Walker, Wheeler, Liddell, and Mackall. According to Liddell, Bragg opened the session by stating that Rosecrans had crossed the river below Chattanooga with two corps while threatening the city directly with two more. He then called for comment, beginning with Liddell, the junior man present. Taken aback, Liddell suggested that the Federals were apparently seeking to cross Lookout Mountain and threaten the railroad to Atlanta, forcing the army to evacuate Chattanooga in order to protect its supply line. In Liddell's opinion, such a move offered a splendid opportunity for Bragg to counterattack the Federal flanking column after it had advanced beyond the support of the remaining Federal units. When Polk mildly objected that surely Rosecrans would not be so incautious, Liddell responded that his easy victory in the Tullahoma campaign had made Rosecrans overconfident. The reference to Tullahoma brought a smile to Polk's face but not to Bragg's, and Liddell realized that inadvertently he had raised a controversial issue. Hill quickly defused the situation by proposing a rapid crossing of the Tennessee River and the Cumberland Plateau, followed by an invasion of Middle Tennessee. Liddell countered that neither the army's transportation nor the food available in "the barrens" could sustain such a course of action.[14]

Bragg suddenly stood and dismissed Hill's proposal out of hand. Satisfied with what he had heard about Rosecrans's probable course of action, he posed a new question: Should the army make an immediate attack on that portion of Rosecrans's army that was across the river below Bridgeport? Again, Bragg looked directly at Liddell. Making the most of his opportunity, Liddell launched into his opinion. To Liddell, the question was simply one of timing. If the Federals operating below Bridgeport were struck too soon, they would simply recoil quickly across the river. Chattanooga having been evacuated, the Federals opposite the city would capture it before the Army of Tennessee could return. The difficulty in crossing Lookout Mountain also caused Liddell to counsel delay. He argued that it would be wiser to let the Federals struggle across the mountains, far from their base, before striking them a mortal blow. Liddell therefore expected that the decisive battle would be fought somewhere south of Chattanooga near the town of LaFayette. Upon hearing Liddell, Bragg queried the others for their opinions. According to Liddell, all except Wheeler reluctantly agreed with him. Noting Wheeler's silence and harboring animosity toward him dating to Stones River, Liddell pointedly asked Bragg to seek Wheeler's opinion. Bragg refused to do so, in Liddell's opinion a transparent attempt to disguise Wheeler's inadequacies. The council then adjourned, leaving Liddell smugly confident of victory if his proposal was adopted. Following the council, Bragg telegraphed Secretary of War Seddon: "Rosecrans' main force has crossed the Tennessee below Bridgeport opposite Stevenson. He is sixty miles from us with two ranges of barren mountains interposed. Unable to hold so long a line without sacrificing my force in detail. Buckner has been drawn this way so as to secure a junction at any time. Burnsides was sixty miles from Knoxville at last accounts. We shall assail either party or both whenever practicable." For the moment, St. John Liddell had carried the day.[15]

As the generals dispersed, the army staff went into action. First, George Brent issued a series of instructions to the frontline cavalry commanders. Mauldin at Trenton was told to scout the enemy's positions on Sand Mountain and determine their intentions. In order to report what he learned quickly, Mauldin was to establish a courier line directly to Chattanooga. A similar order was sent to Wharton at LaFayette. Wheeler's other division commander, Martin, was simply told to "report promptly and frequently" to army headquarters. Brent next turned to the question of arms for those men without them, especially the new arrivals from Mississippi. First, he polled both Polk and Hill for the number of unarmed men. Next, he telegraphed Josiah Gorgas at Richmond to see if any arms were in transit. At the same time, chief of ordnance Oladowski specified to Moses Wright, Atlanta Arsenal commander, the number of rounds he required for each of the army's 104 artillery pieces. He pointedly told Wright, "Send only few canister for each gun." In personnel matters, Brent notified Buckner that Col. John Kelly would be sent to replace Col. James McMahon as a brigade commander in Preston's Division. A native of Alabama and a West Point attendee before resigning in 1860, Kelly, twenty-three, was the colonel of the Eighth Arkansas Infantry regiment in Liddell's command. Distinguished in action at Shiloh and Perryville, and wounded at Stones River, Kelly had long been recognized as a rising star. Brent duly notified Liddell of his loss and Buckner's gain, while Kelly headed to join his new command at Charleston. With a major battle looming in the near future, Chief Quartermaster McMicken dispatched Capt. Robert Gribble to Dalton and Marietta to accelerate the establishment of hospitals for the expected influx of casualties. Gribble was assigned to work with the efficient if abrasive Samuel Stout, medical director of hospitals. In order to resolve the continuing impasse over the use of the Georgia Military Institute for hospital purposes, Bragg himself appealed to Governor Brown for their use.[16]

Two critical issues remained unresolved at the end of the day. First, Chief Commissary of Subsistence Giles Hillyer calculated the army's supply of meat and bread would be exhausted in three weeks. Either food had to be released from Atlanta stocks earmarked for the Army of Northern Virginia, or the shrinking territory controlled by the Army of Tennessee had to be scoured anew, or Federal stocks had to be captured. If nothing was done, the army would have to retreat or begin to starve. The second issue was linked with the first. In order to act decisively, Bragg needed more timely information on Federal movements. To date, that kind of information had not been furnished by Wheeler's Cavalry Corps. Since July only two small regiments had picketed the army's left flank and there apparently had been no system to notify Bragg in a timely fashion if that line was penetrated. Any reports generated went up the chain eventually to Wheeler's headquarters at Gadsden. Wheeler apparently had made nothing of any reports he received and seems to have been out of communication with Bragg until he reached Chattanooga on 2 September. When Bragg learned that the picket line had been penetrated and Sand Mountain overrun by large Federal forces, he had to communicate directly with individual units, bypassing Wheeler entirely. Significant Federal forces spilling over Sand Mountain into Wills/Lookout Valley was bad enough; if they crossed Lookout Mountain the army's lifeline to Atlanta would be in peril. With food running low, loss of the railroad would be disastrous and Chattanooga would most certainly be lost. Liddell's proposed counterstrike could only succeed if Bragg received timely information on Federal activity beyond his flank, and Wheeler had not provided it. Wheeler finally appeared at army headquarters on 2 September, but according to Liddell he contributed nothing to the discussion. If Bragg was indeed shielding Wheeler from overt criticism, as Liddell believed, continuing to do so would place at grave risk his army's chances for success.[17]

On 2 September Chief of Staff Mackall wrote privately to Wheeler chastising him for his failures: "I am uneasy about the state of affairs. It is so vitally important that the general should have full and correct information. One misstep in the movement of this army would possibly be fatal." He explained what should have been obvious to Wheeler, that the loss of Sand Mountain left Lookout Mountain as the army's final picket line on its left flank. Mackall was blunt: "The passage at Caperton's Ferry broke the line, and a week has passed and we don't know whether or not an army has passed. If this happens on Lookout, say to-night, and the enemy obtain that as a screen to their movements, I must confess I do not see myself what move we can make to answer it." When Wheeler received Mackall's rebuke is unknown, but he generated a flurry of orders before the day was over. Special Orders, No. 68, issued while Wheeler was still at Chattanooga, ordered Wharton to picket the routes over Lookout Mountain from Wills Valley and patrol the crest of the mountain from Chattanooga to Gadsden. Information gained should be reported to Bragg, Wheeler, and to the bridge guards at Resaca and Etowah. Another message ordered Wharton to place one brigade at Alpine, Georgia, on the road from Valley Head, and the other at LaFayette. Wheeler also directed Martin to concentrate most of his command between LaFayette and Dalton. The only portion of Martin's Division not to move toward LaFayette was Mauldin's detachment holding Trenton. Wheeler now wanted Mauldin to form a line from Kelly's Ford on the Tennessee to Lookout Mountain in the vicinity of Wauhatchie. Wheeler's orders thus relinquished control of approximately ten miles of Lookout Valley to any Federals who might appear. From Wauhatchie south, Wharton's La Fayette brigade was responsible for blocking any Federal incursions. Until Martin's command could get itself together, Wharton's division was all that stood between the Army of the Cumberland and the rear of the Army of Tennessee.[18]

In the ranks, word of the Federal crossing had spread widely, and discussions turned to the great battle that all expected to occur soon. Capt. James Hall was confident, writing to his father, "There is no doubt in my mind that a general engagement is imminent and there is just as little doubt about our success." Artificer D. L. Kelly was not so sanguine of victory, opining, "Cousin Jane you would like to hear some glorious ware news from this part of the Confederacy I no but I have no good newes to tell you but of a sertainty we are on the eave of a grate Battle and perhaps the greatest one that has bin faught during the war. All seem to be in good spirits . . . but the thing looks very dark to me." With the return of Hindman's Division to McFarland's Spring, Polk's Corps was reunited in Chattanooga Valley. Most of Hindman's men spent the day resting after their grueling night march, although several hundred were detailed to work on fortifications. In Cheatham's Division, Brig. Gen. Otho Strahl's Brigade guarding Lookout Valley was on high alert, but even there not everyone was actively watching for the enemy's approach. In the Fifth Tennessee Infantry regiment, those soldiers not on picket duty found that they could make marbles from the malleable stone surrounding them and whiled away the dull hours shaping the playthings. In Hill's Corps, Cleburne's Division spent the day gradually withdrawing from the upper Tennessee River crossings and concentrating near Harrison. Elements of Breckinridge's Division were still arriving at Chickamauga Station, but Stovall and Breckinridge remained absent. As the last units arrived, they marched to Tyner's Station, where the division was concentrating. Walker's Division was already at Tyner's, organizing its trains and preparing for either movement or action. In Liddell's Division, guarding the army's dwindling supplies at Chickamauga Station, many soldiers attended religious gatherings, a phenomenon widely observed in Bragg's army on 2 September.[19]

Cleburne's gradual withdrawal from the river fords to Harrison meant that the bulk of Bragg's infantry would soon be concentrated for rapid movement in any direction. This concentration would uncover at least seven crossings between Harrison and Blythe's Ferry unless other troops occupied the now thinly held defenses. Cleburne's departing men were to be replaced by Forrest's cavalry, which was to connect with Buckner's command holding the line of the Hiwassee River. During the day James Wheeler's and Dibrell's Brigades from Forrest's Division continued their march toward the Tennessee River from Charleston. Also moving in that direction was part of Pegram's command. Behind the horsemen, Preston's Division occupied positions five miles west of Charleston, where it guarded the Hiwassee line from Candies Creek to Charleston itself. Stewart's Division momentarily remained at Charleston, around Buckner's headquarters. Forty-two miles north of the Hiwassee, a portion of Scott's Brigade still held a bridgehead beyond the Tennessee River at Loudon, where a 1,700-foot rail and road bridge spanned the stream. Somewhere between Loudon and Charleston, Scott's remaining troopers covered Buckner's train, toiling toward safety south of the Hiwassee. At 4:00 P.M., Buckner exercised his right to contact Secretary of War Seddon directly, informing him that Cumberland Gap was still guarded by Frazer's Brigade, Jackson's railroad guards and a few cavalry units had withdrawn to Virginia, and that he held the line of the Hiwassee River as Bragg's Right Wing. Buckner admitted that he knew nothing of Rosecrans's movements, but that Burnside appeared to be moving toward a junction with the Army of the Cumberland under cover of the mountains beyond the Tennessee. Still, Buckner was upbeat: "The present concentration gives up temporarily the country between this place and Bristol. The best hopes are entertained of this concentration. Troops in fine spirits."[20]

What seemed so hopeful at Charleston did not look quite so positive to

Pvt. William Sloan of the Fifth Tennessee Cavalry regiment of Scott's Brigade. The most advanced vidette north of the Loudon bridge, Sloan suddenly saw a Federal cavalry column round a bend in front of him. The Federals proved to be part of Burnside's Twenty-Third Army Corps. Firing a shot that downed one horse and rider, Sloan dashed a half-mile south to the picket reserve, chased all the while by shots from the pursuing Federals. After briefly checking the Federal horsemen, Sloan's comrades raced across the bridge on decking that had been laid between the rails to facilitate the passage of troops. While other members of the regiment manned the entrenchments on the north side of the river, Sloan and his companions fired piles of turpentine-soaked wood on the bridge's lower deck. A masterpiece of prewar bridge design, the massive two-story, tin roofed structure soon became fully involved in flames. As the fire consumed the span, the Tennesseans continued to keep the Federals from the bridge. When the fire had mostly done its work, they left their trenches and crossed the river on a large flatboat. Their retreat was covered by fire from two three-inch rifles of Robinson's Louisiana Battery. Unable to fire on the flatboat, Federal gunners shelled Loudon itself, setting a house ablaze and causing some casualties. Confederate efforts to destroy the flatboat were unsuccessful, but the destruction of the bridge was complete. With no reason to remain at Loudon longer, the Fifth Tennessee headed south, halting late at night at Athens, twenty-five miles to the south. Behind them, the Federals quickly occupied the south bank of the river, but their hopes of using the railroad were dashed. Learning of the fight at Loudon, Buckner at 8:30 P.M. informed Bragg that the bridge was probably gone. More significant, Buckner stated that Federal cavalry had entered Knoxville, severing the direct connection to Virginia. Plaintively, he asked Brent, "Shall I move my infantry in vicinity of Georgetown to sustain cavalry?"[21]

. . . .

If not quickly reversed, the loss of the railroad between Knoxville and Loudon would have far-reaching effects on Confederate planning. The East Tennessee & Georgia Railroad represented part of a direct 540-mile route from central Virginia to Chattanooga. Any reinforcements sent from Virginia to Bragg's army would most readily be dispatched along that route. Now, that direct link had been severed. Meanwhile, Davis's discussions with Lee about Confederate strategy continued in Richmond. Lee argued vigorously to keep the Army of Northern Virginia intact and on the offensive in its home territory. Yet Davis for some time had been aware of Bragg's precarious situation. A recent note from Senator Landon Haynes of Tennessee had prematurely announced the fall of Knoxville, while a telegram from Governor Isham Harris had bluntly called for reinforcements to be sent to the Army of Tennessee. Davis had already tapped Johnston's command for aid and was cajoling Governor Brown of Georgia for militia assistance. Lee's arguments notwithstanding, his army was another potential source of aid for Bragg's beleaguered command. While Lee was in Richmond, James Longstreet commanded the Army of Northern Virginia. For six months Longstreet had advocated shifting troops from Lee to Bragg, usually with himself as the detachment's leader. In August, he again had approached Secretary of War Seddon and Senator Louis Wigfall of Texas with the scheme, but those efforts had seemingly failed on 31 August. Longstreet now saw the Tennessee crisis as another opportunity to advance his proposal. On 2 September he acknowledged Lee's orders to prepare the army for offensive action but again pressed for the adoption of his own plan: "I know but little of the condition of our affairs in the west, but am inclined to the opinion that our best opportunity for great results is in Tennessee. If we could hold the defensive here with two corps and send the other to operate in Tenn. with that army I think that we could accomplish more than by an advance from here."[22]

Expecting the collapsed trestle to be repaired quickly, Rosecrans early on 3 September issued the instructions that would drive his campaign for several days. The document reflected his plan to threaten both Bragg's supply line and Chattanooga in order to force him to withdraw southward without a fight. Crafted by Garfield, the order established the objectives for each corps and often specified how to attain them. First, the Cavalry Corps was to advance via Rawlingsville across Lookout Mountain to the vicinity of Rome. Stanley was to "push forward with audacity, feel the enemy strongly, and make a strong diversion in that direction." The order specified that Stanley's First Division was to take the direct road over Sand Mountain from Caperton's Ferry to Valley Head, while the Second Division was to cross Sand Mountain to Trenton, then follow Wills Valley to Valley Head. Next, McCook was to gather the Twentieth Corps at Valley Head and seize Winston's Gap on Lookout Mountain. Thomas was to consolidate the Fourteenth Corps at Trenton and send a division to seize two gaps on Lookout Mountain. Specifically, Thomas was to occupy Frick's Gap northeast of Trenton with one brigade, while sending the remainder of the division via a cul-de-sac valley named Johnson's Crook to capture Stephens's Gap southeast of Trenton. The Twenty-First Corps was to advance from Shell Mound up the canyon of Running Water Creek as far as the village of Whiteside. From there Crittenden was to probe toward Chattanooga via Lookout Valley with one division and ascend Sand Mountain via Murphy's Hollow with his remaining units. The order formally gave Hazen command of the deception forces, but detached a regiment each from Minty's and Wilder's commands to join Thomas and Crittenden. Hazen was to continue the deception indefinitely and, if the opportunity arose, cross the river and seize Chattanooga. Finally,

King's brigade of Baird's division was to remain in place on the railroad until relieved by Morgan's Reserve Corps division. All movements were to be completed by the close of the next day, 4 September.[23]

While Confederate leaders pondered their next moves, Pioneer Brigade soldiers worked all night in the murky Tennessee River to restore the trestle bridge. Rosecrans had ordered work halted until daylight, but that order did not reach the Pioneers. At dawn the men from the First Michigan Engineers and Mechanics resumed work, and together the two units struggled in the shallow water to erect the fallen bents and connect the trestle to the pontoons. The work was exceedingly difficult, slow, and tedious, but this time Hunton assured Garfield that the bridge would be much stronger than before. Meanwhile, more than 1,000 wagons and ambulances awaited a chance to cross the stream. Baird moved his two available brigades to Bridgeport and assumed command of the reconstruction effort. Upon reaching the river, some of Baird's men seized the opportunity to wash away the choking dust that covered everything. Unwilling to remain in Stevenson all day while the work continued at Bridgeport, Rosecrans joined Baird during the afternoon and established the priority of movement across the span. First to cross would be Sheridan's trains, followed by the trains of Crook's Second Cavalry Division. After Crook's wagons would come Brannan's division trains, followed by Baird's division and its trains. Bringing up the rear would be the large trains of the Twenty-First Corps. The entire process would take several days, the pace being driven first by the engineers and then by the skill of teamsters coaxing their mule teams across the shaky trestles and swaying pontoons. Drouillard, one of Rosecrans's aides, recorded completion of the bridge at 1:00 P.M., but diaries of Pioneer Brigade members indicate that the bridge was not reopened for several more hours. Even then, Pvt. Isaac Roseberry wrote, "After much hard work and waiding in water waist deep we got it ready so teams could cross by diner but the general opinion is that it will go down again." Should it do so, the already worrisome delay in executing Rosecrans's campaign plan would be extended.[24]

For the two divisions camped around Moore's Spring, only Sheridan's command had to wait for its wagons. Negley's division was under no such restraint, having crossed its trains at Caperton's Ferry two days earlier. Therefore Negley ordered his three brigades to begin their ascent of Sand Mountain. Sirwell's Third Brigade led the way, distributing men along the track to assist the wagons and battery. Soon the temperature began to climb, making the hard pull up the mountain even more disagreeable. Unwilling to remain spectators, both Negley and Sirwell stripped off their uniform coats and put their shoulders to the wheels of several wagons. To encourage the men even more, the Twenty-First Ohio Infantry regiment's band played a spritely version of "Dixie" as the heavily laden wagons crawled up the grade. Traveling with the column was a regimental sutler whose wagon overturned, spilling its contents to the delight of the nearby soldiers. Sirwell's command finally reached the top of the mountain and marched three miles across the plateau to a deep ravine. Providentially, Negley's men found an abandoned sawmill in the ravine whose lower story could serve as a bridge foundation. Two companies soon began to transform mill into bridge. As Sirwell's brigade camped around what they called Warren's Mill, Stanley's Second Brigade was toiling up the mountain. Stanley's battery had difficulty making the climb. Only by hitching twelve horses on each gun was it able to reach the crest, and three horses died in the process. On top at last, Stanley's men moved only a slight distance before halting for the night. Beatty's First Brigade brought up the rear. Escorting the division ammunition train, part of Beatty's command reached the top, but the remainder remained at the foot of the mountain with the division supply train. Weary as he was, Cpl. George Harris of the Forty-Second Indiana Infantry regiment was impressed: "We have a fair view of the river, Bridgeport, the rail road, battle creek and the mountains all around, as nice a view as I ever saw."[25]

At Shell Mound, Reynolds's Fourth Division began its ascent of Sand Mountain during the afternoon. Reynolds's route lay southward in Nickajack Cove to the headwaters of Cole City Creek. The cove's walls abounded with exposed coal seams that had been exploited by small mining operations like the Castle Rock Coal Company. The tracks of the Nicojack Railroad & Mining Company extended eight miles up the cove on a gradually ascending grade. Thus Reynolds's leading unit, Turchin's Third Brigade, had an easy pathway up Sand Mountain. On top, the road crossed relatively flat terrain until it reached the eastern edge of the mountain. After an easy descent, Turchin's men entered Slygo Valley, drained by Squirrel Town Creek, where they found the extensive plantation of William Cole. Concerned about his surroundings, Turchin sent scouts to the nearby Trenton-Chattanooga road. Ominously, lights could be seen atop Lookout Mountain in the distance. Behind Turchin, King's Second Brigade halted on the mountain. Brannan's train had been caught by the collapse of the Bridgeport trestle, so his Third Division only moved to Turchin's old camps at Shell Mound. While waiting, many of his men visited Nickajack Cave, as hundreds had done earlier. Unfortunately, the cave remained a dangerous place, literally full of pitfalls. As forecast by another soldier earlier, the cave claimed a life when Cpl. Samuel McIlvaine of the Tenth Indiana Infantry regiment slipped and was mortally injured in a fall. Slightly less unlucky was a man in McIlvaine's brigade who was shot in the leg by a soldier aiming at a pig. During the day corps commander Thomas moved his headquarters from Bolivar to Moore's Spring via Stevenson and Caperton's Ferry. While a regimental band played "The Star-Spangled Banner" at Moore's Spring, Thomas issued orders for the next day: Baird was to follow Negley as soon as he could cross the river; Reynolds was to seize Frick's Gap on Lookout Mountain; and Negley was to move toward Stephens's Gap via Brown's Spring, where Thomas planned to join him.[26]

Shell Mound was a popular place on 3 September. Not only was Reynolds's division leaving and Brannan's division arriving, but units of the Twenty-First Corps were beginning to appear as well. Reynolds did not complete the transfer of his train across the river until 2:00 P.M., thereby delaying the passage of Wood's First Division across the stream. By seizing boats and rafts idled by Reynolds during the previous night, Buell had been able to transport his First Brigade over the river by 6:00 A.M. His baggage train, however, remained snarled in the traffic jam at Bridgeport. While they waited, Buell's men visited Shell Mound's tourist sites, Nickajack Cave, and the surveyor's marker delineating where three states met. By midafternoon, Reynolds's train was finally over the river, and Wood hurried Harker's Third Brigade to the crossing site. For the next seven hours, Harker pushed his regiments across the river, using Reynolds's motley collection of rafts and boats. Next in line was a herd of cattle. After efforts to force the animals to swim across the stream failed, they were finally transported by raft in small groups, a tedious and time-consuming process. Behind the cattle came Cruft's First Brigade of Palmer's Second Division. Ordered initially to Battle Creek, Cruft received new orders diverting his brigade to Shell Mound and his wagons to Bridgeport. Before leaving Jasper, the band of the Ninetieth Ohio Infantry regiment serenaded the locals with "Yankee Doodle," while other men looted the few civilian stores. It was nearly midnight when Cruft's men began to cross the river with the aid of the rising moon. Earlier, Palmer and Grose's Third Brigade reached Battle Creek around noon. Finding insufficient rafts and boats, Grose had to construct more before beginning his crossing. It would take all night for Grose to place three regiments on the far bank, sending one regiment with his trains to Bridgeport. Behind Palmer's command, two brigades of Van Cleve's Third Division reached Jasper and went into camp. At the same time, Dick's Second Brigade departed McMinnville on its long journey over the Cumberland Plateau.[27]

The collapse of the Bridgeport bridge significantly affected the movements of McCook's Twentieth Corps. Dawn of 3 September found Davis's First Division camped in the tangled terrain several miles short of Winston's Gap. Instead of continuing his advance, Davis had been told during the night to go no farther than absolutely necessary to get water. With Sheridan delayed on the far side of Sand Mountain and his request for cavalry denied, Davis had no choice but to remain where he was. During the morning Carlin sent scouting detachments all the way to Winston's, but in the afternoon he withdrew nearer Sand Mountain and formed line of battle with the remainder of the division. Meanwhile, Johnson's Second Division marched slowly across the top of Sand

Mountain but halted before descending into Wills Valley. During the hot and dusty march some men of the Fifteenth Ohio Infantry regiment discovered an abandoned distillery. Their attempt to make peach brandy failed, but soldiers of the Thirty-Ninth Indiana Mounted Infantry succeeded well enough to become gloriously drunk. Speeding past both foot soldiers and wagons, McCook and his staff joined Johnson in early afternoon. The headquarters train was far in the rear, so McCook decided not to descend the mountain that day. Also on the mountain road was Stanley's Cavalry Corps. Although Rosecrans had expected the cavalry to reach Rawlinsville, several miles south of Winston's, to protect Davis's southern flank, Stanley decided that Rawlinsville was beyond reach on 3 September. He halted Edward McCook's First Division at Davis's position and sent Long's Second Brigade of Crook's Second Division to occupy Winston's. Stanley did not descend into the valley, camping instead with Alex McCook and Johnson a mile short of the brow of Sand Mountain. His trains were scattered from there all the way back to Caperton's Ferry. Until the news from Bridgeport was better, both McCook and Stanley would pause for at least a day before tackling Lookout Mountain.[28]

Unaware that their mission was increasingly irrelevant, the deception force remained highly visible on 3 September. For Wilder's regiments facing Chattanooga, most of the day was consumed in foraging for vegetables, meat, and fodder. Men in the Seventy-Second Indiana Mounted Infantry regiment were overjoyed to receive the first mail in two weeks, as well as their regimental baggage. Atop Walden's Ridge, soldiers in Wagner's brigade also engaged in routine tasks, except for those men building small boats to cross the river flowing placidly below them. Upstream at Poe's Tavern, Hazen received orders to assume command of the entire deception force. Necessitated by Crittenden's departure from the Sequatchie Valley, the order placed almost 7,000 troops under Hazen's control. He wasted no time in making his wishes known, especially to Col. John Funkhouser of the Ninety-Eighth Illinois Mounted Infantry regiment of Wilder's brigade. Funkhouser had cooperated with Hazen but had not been under his command. Now Hazen made clear who was in charge, ordering Funkhouser to provide him an escort company and changing the position of his units. Styling himself Commander, U.S. Forces, Left Flank of the Army, Hazen elevated Col. Oliver Payne of the 124th Ohio Infantry regiment to temporary command of his old brigade. He then began an inspection tour of his new domain, which he believed stretched seventy-five miles from Williams Island to Kingston and included at least twenty crossing points. He also ordered boats to be gathered in North Chickamauga Creek for crossing the river. Fearing that Minty's brigade was at risk if the Confederates pushed across the river, Hazen sought Minty's assessment of the situation. Meanwhile, Minty sent the band of the Fourth Michigan Cavalry regiment to the riverbank to serenade his opponents with the "Bonnie Blue Flag," "Yankee Doodle," and other familiar tunes. The concert prompted a brief but cordial visit to the Federal side of the stream by several men under cover of a flag of truce.[29]

In Nashville, Granger encountered difficulty in accomplishing his two most critical tasks. First, he had to maintain control of the growing territory in the army's rear. The departure of Dick's brigade added McMinnville to the list of places needing protection. Rosecrans had wanted the Fifth Iowa Cavalry regiment to move from Murfreesboro to McMinnville, but Granger protested that such a move would leave the railroad without mounted protection. In response, Rosecrans lectured his Reserve Corps commander as if he were a green lieutenant, specifying exactly how the Fifth Iowa could be divided to handle both tasks. As for McMinnville, Rosecrans was clear: "You must take care of McMinnville. It is too important for us to lose; see to that." Such a message from Rosecrans spoke volumes about both men and their relationship. If Granger was passive and unimaginative in managing the army's sprawling rear area, Rosecrans was overly immersed in micromanaging that same area. Compounding the problem was James Spears, the controversial officer Rosecrans had foisted upon Granger for command of the McMinnville garrison. Spears was so hated by the loyal Tennessee units at McMinnville that twenty-seven officers petitioned Rosecrans for his transfer. To their chagrin, Rosecrans adamantly retained Spears in command. As for Granger's other principal task, the protection of the Stevenson base, Granger had momentarily left that to Morgan's Second Division. Morgan and Tillson's First Brigade were at the broken Flint River bridge, between Huntsville and Stevenson, while Daniel McCook's Second Brigade was mostly gathered at Athens, Alabama. Rosecrans wanted Tillson's command to relieve King's brigade at Stevenson, but Morgan demurred until McCook's troops could reach Huntsville. On 3 September neither Tillson nor McCook moved at all, and one of McCook's regiments was still at Columbia. The urgency much in evidence at Bridgeport and Shell Mound was nowhere to be seen in Granger's Reserve Corps.[30]

Around midnight Rosecrans reported to Halleck that the Bridgeport trestle had been repaired, most of the army was across the river, and that Valley Head, Winston's Gap, and Rawlingsville had probably been seized. In fact, only cavalry had reached Valley Head because of the pause ordered when the Bridgeport trestle fell. Nor had Rawlingsville or Winston's Gap been gained by that time. As for the bulk of the army being across the river, at the time Rosecrans wrote only nineteen of the army's thirty infantry brigades were on the east bank with two more in the midst of crossing. In contrast, four of the army's five cavalry brigades were finally beyond the river. There was a small note of concern in the message: "Have you any news from Burnside, any reason to think forces will be sent from Virginia to East Tenn, any that Johnston has sent any force up this way?" Still, according to Rosecrans, the plan was being executed essentially on schedule. Garfield was equally sanguine, writing a friend, "If I live through this campaign I now think I shall go to Congress. I am inclined to believe there will be work of great importance before that body, and if our campaign and that of the other armies are successful, the work of fighting will be substantially ended." Less sure of success was Pvt. Baldwin Colton of the Fifteenth Pennsylvania Cavalry regiment, who told his father, "A man was telling me yesterday that Rosecrans told his regiment he hoped they would all be home Christmas. I am sure it will not be before spring and likely not then." Rosecrans was indeed optimistic about the campaign just beginning. In preparation for leaving Stevenson, he arranged to have one of his horses, an accompanying servant, and a favorite saddle transported to Cincinnati. At the same time, Goddard ordered the Alabama House Hotel to be emptied so that a contractor could fill it with railroad workers. Even after the Army of the Cumberland moved on, the railroad lifeline would have to continue to function without fail.[31]

Much of Rosecrans's optimism can be ascribed to intelligence reports collected by Capt. David Swaim. On 3 September Swaim recorded the testimony of one John Sherlock. Sherlock had been dispatched from Winchester on 7 August with orders to penetrate Confederate lines. Establishing himself at his grandmother's house fifteen miles south of Chattanooga, he dispatched a disabled former Confederate soldier into town to gather information. All went well until 21 August, when a patrol led by Sherlock's brother-in-law surrounded the house where Sherlock and a deserter were eating dinner. The deserter was shot and killed, but Sherlock escaped to Lookout Mountain. Sustained by another Union family, he continued to receive information from his informant until 30 August, when he began his return to Federal lines. Crossing the river at Shell Mound, Sherlock reported directly to army headquarters. First, he described a conversation with Confederate artillerymen grazing horses in McLemore's Cove. "They all said the South was whipped and that the soldiers wouldn't fight to do any good any more." Next, his informant "learned that it is Braggs intention to fight if the Federals crossover at Chattanooga but if they cross at Shellmount & advance by way of Chattanooga Valley over Lookout Mountain through Stevens Gap aiming to cut him off from Dalton & Rome that he will fall back to Dalton & fight there." Sherlock correctly located the positions of Bragg's two corps but placed Confederate effective infantry strength at only 16,000 men. He mistakenly reported that Bragg had received no aid from either Johnston or anyone else but correctly identified the movement of Stewart's Division to Loudon. Another statement was equally intriguing: "The secesh soldiers I heard talk said there would not be a fight at Chattanooga because the d——d Yankees would not come out and fight them fair, but try to surround & cut them off as they always did." Sherlock's report dovetailed with those of recent deserters, reinforcing Rosecrans's natural optimism.[32]

Just as Rosecrans relied upon agents like John Sherlock, Bragg also used "scouts and spies" to determine Federal movements and intentions. By the morning of 3 September Bragg's headquarters in Chattanooga had received new reports from the cavalrymen he had dispatched in haste on the previous day. Both Wharton and McDonald sent reports to Chattanooga. The messages, no longer extant, apparently contained no information useful enough to be recorded in Brent's headquarters diary. More informative was a report from Maj. Pollok Lee, sent by Bragg to provide an independent source of news from Wheeler's cavalry. According to Lee, three Federal cavalry regiments and an infantry brigade were at Cash's Store on Sand Mountain, equidistant from Caperton's Ferry and Winston's. Another report, from an unknown source, placed three Federal infantry brigades moving toward Trenton from Caperton's. No word came from Trenton itself, because Mauldin's detachment had been ordered by Wheeler to withdraw northward toward Wauhatchie. The lack of definite information on Rosecrans's movements troubled Brent: "Altho' a week has elapsed, we have little or no information concerning him. The passes of Sand Mountain are not guarded, & the enemy may get into Will's Valley & occupy Lookout before we are informed of his movement." Unaware that the Federal advance had been delayed at least twenty-four hours because of the failure of the Bridgeport trestle, Brent feared that a rapid Federal advance would soon wash over Lookout Mountain into the Confederate rear. He continued, "It is easy to see that if Rosecrans crossed the River on Friday, Saturday & Sunday last in force, that he may by a rapid move place himself on our rear before we know it. Is the movement on our left a feint or not? No one as yet has been able to answer." Bragg's thoughts on this day are unrecorded. He might have been just as concerned as Brent, but without a clearer view of the situation, he did not dare order the Army of Tennessee into motion.[33]

While they awaited more information, Bragg prepared the army for either movement or action. First, he requested a report from all corps commanders on the strength and location of their outposts. As for the Western & Atlantic Railroad, Bragg ordered Inspector General Beard to closely inspect the railroad guards stationed along the line. McDonald's Eighteenth Tennessee Cavalry battalion was released from its temporary duty in Lookout Valley and ordered to rejoin Forrest's command. Similarly, Rice's company of the Third Confederate Cavalry received orders to rejoin its parent command. As for Forrest himself, his stock was momentarily ascendant at army headquarters, especially when compared to Wheeler's lackluster performance. Bragg now officially placed Buckner's cavalry directly under Forrest's command. Forrest thus became a corps commander, leading his old division, now under Frank Armstrong, and John Pegram's Division from Buckner's command. Along with the new command came an order to picket the Tennessee River in front of both Hill's and Buckner's Corps. Knowing that his army was too small to meet Rosecrans's force on equal terms, Bragg also cast about for men to bolster his ranks. He called upon Gideon Pillow, the regional conscription officer, to "send us all the men you can, we need them." At the same time, he recalled the Ninth Tennessee Cavalry regiment, which had been assisting Pillow in scouring the backcountry for deserters. In anticipation of using the thousands of Confederates paroled at Vicksburg in July, he sent Col. Joseph Jones, his senior aide, to select a camp outside Atlanta where they could be assembled. Those men could not be returned to action until formally exchanged, but Bragg anticipated that they would be available soon. For those troops already on hand but without arms, Ordnance Chief Oladowski directed the issuance of 760 guns to Polk's Corps and 500 to Hill's.[34]

Neither Polk nor Hill assisted Bragg in divining Federal intentions on 3 September. While formally cordial, Polk despised the army commander and ventured no advice unless required to provide it. He did, however, respond to Bragg's query about the location of his outposts. Hindman's Division near Rossville guarded the main road through Missionary Ridge to points south, Smith's Brigade covered Chattanooga Valley, and Strahl's Brigade on the northern toe of Lookout Mountain blocked the roads to both Trenton and Shell Mound. Late in the day Strahl forwarded to Polk news from scouts that a Federal column estimated at 40,000 men was crossing Sand Mountain and heading southwest in Wills Valley. Strahl reported, "None coming in this direction." This information eventually reached army headquarters but apparently was forwarded by Polk without comment. The army's senior corps commander thus remained a passive observer only. In contrast, Hill at least shared his thoughts with Bragg. In Hill's opinion, the Federal goal was to secure East Tennessee by gaining control of the region's railroads. He anticipated that Rosecrans would advance northward in Wills/Lookout Valley until he controlled the railroad into Chattanooga from the west, while Burnside held the line from Knoxville. Hill thought that Chattanooga was being spared destruction because the Federals wanted to seize it intact. He expected a concerted movement by Rosecrans, Burnside, and Grant in order to achieve their objective. He concluded, "I know the country too imperfectly & have too little confidence in my own judgment to counsel any particular course of action but I have felt so uneasy about the delay that I cannot refrain from expressing my anxiety." At least Hill favored seizing the initiative to disrupt the Federal timetable. Bragg, of course, had already reached the same conclusion. The only question remaining was the all-important one of correctly timing the Confederate riposte.[35]

For the men in the ranks, 3 September was a day of increasing tension. In Polk's Corps soldiers spread rumors that only one of Rosecrans's divisions had crossed the Tennessee River. Prayer meetings continued in the Eighteenth Tennessee Infantry regiment of Smith's Brigade, as they did in other units across the army. In Hindman's Division, heavy details went to Chattanooga to work on a magazine. Hindman himself toured the camps to gauge the division's morale. Apparently there was considerable work for Hindman to do, as Pvt. Marion Brindley explained to his sister: "There is much despondency in the army, many deserters and many others feeling whipped and ready to desert." Yet Brindley was not one of them: "I do not despair of final success. When I do I shall be willing to die the death of a martyr upon any battle field on Southern soil, subjugated, I have little desire to live, at best, and when I die I have nothing to leave Mary and Luta better than the ashes of a fallen patriot on some blood-stained battle field." In Hill's Corps, resolve seems to have been equally strong among the troops, although a few took refuge in whiskey. Ordnance Sgt. Robert Bliss defended Bragg, who "has been the Atlas whose shoulders had to bear mountain loads of ridicule, contempt and criticism from the press, stay at home generals and dispirited soldiers . . . and when Mr. Rosecranz crosses the Tennessee let him learn that he does not 'catch a tartar.' These are the general opinions current." Equally confident of victory was Capt. Bryan Marsh, though his reasoning was somewhat different. To his wife, "Mit," he wrote, "We are confident that we will teach Rosey a lesson should he cross the river. Gen Brag will be compelled to fight this time no chance to run." Like Private Brindley, Captain Marsh was willing to sacrifice his life for the cause: "When I think of the treatment of the wimen and children in Middle Tenn by the cowardly curs I am willing to undergo any deprivation on my part and rather than to submit let me dy and near see the only ones on earth that I love again."[36]

Confederate activity on 3 September centered on consolidation of units. Cleburne's Division continued to withdraw from positions along the river and trudge through the choking dust toward Harrison. Quartermaster Sergeant John Sparkman wondered what it meant: "I do not understand the movements but things look to me like we will retreat soon. I yet have hopes that we will come out of this thing well." At Tyner's Station, Breckinridge's stragglers continued to reach camp, as did Marcellus Stovall. The new arrivals were in poor shape according to a Florida officer: "Our men are in a sad condition so many ragged & barefoot and it is very hard to walk over these rocky roads without good shoes." In Walker's Division, also at Tyner's, Claudius Wilson warned his wife: "Should the fight commence before I get time to write you again I will telegraph you & if I am wounded, will try to get to Atlanta where you must meet me." At Charleston, thirty-three miles from Tyner's Station, Buckner also consolidated his command. That day he formally merged Stewart's and

Preston's Divisions into a corps and exhorted the soldiers to "discharge the duties of patriots and of men." During the afternoon Buckner sent Gracie's and Kelly's Brigades westward several miles to Georgetown and planned to follow them with Trigg's Brigade as soon as Stewart organized his transportation. He also notified Pegram that his cavalry division had been assigned to Forrest's command. Having recently passed through territory untouched by foraging soldiers, Buckner's men were eating well and in high spirits. According to Lt. Quintus Adams, "The Army of Tennessee so far as I have seen is in excellent condition and capable of rendering the most efficient service, and if we should have a passage at arms during the fall I can not but anticipate the most splendid results to our arms." Ominously, both Buckner's and Forrest's recent movements were reported openly in the *Memphis Daily Appeal* on the same day, under the byline "Ashantee," a pseudonym for reporter John Linebaugh.[37]

Bragg's cavalry remained in disarray on 3 September. On the army's right, Forrest's newly minted corps was beginning to establish a screen for Hill's and Buckner's infantry. Armstrong's Division slowly replaced Cleburne's pickets from the village of Harrison northward toward Blythe's Ferry. James Wheeler's Brigade (formerly Armstrong's) occupied the river frontage around Harrison, with Dibrell's Brigade extending the line to Wheeler's right. Meanwhile, Pegram's Division remained scattered. In addition to the division, Pegram retained command of his old brigade pending the arrival of a new brigadier. He stretched his brigade along the Hiwassee River toward Blythe's Ferry, shielding Preston's infantry at Georgetown. Col. George Hodge's command, four small Kentucky and Virginia battalions now added to the division, protected Charleston. A Confederate congressman from Kentucky and a prominent supporter of President Davis, Hodge had recently arrived from Richmond. Scott's Brigade was still making its way to Charleston after burning the Loudon Bridge. With Hodge a novice and Scott unalterably opposed to Pegram, the division lacked cohesion. In Wheeler's corps, the main problem was not cohesion but lack of urgency in executing Bragg's orders. Wheeler had instructed Wharton on 2 September to send only one brigade by "easy marches" to Alpine, Georgia, a tiny settlement in Broomtown Valley at the eastern foot of Lookout Mountain. Alpine lay on the road from Winston's to Summerville and, ultimately, to Rome. Wharton apparently chose Crews's Brigade, because Harrison's Brigade remained at LaFayette all day on 3 September. Meanwhile, most of Martin's Division was still straggling forward in small groups to a concentration point northeast of LaFayette. At the same time, under Wheeler's orders, Mauldin's detachment evacuated Trenton and formed a new picket line in the northern end of Lookout Valley. Satisfied with his deployments, which left Lookout Mountain mostly uncovered, Wheeler apparently remained in Chattanooga, for unknown reasons.[38]

Rosecrans's faith in his engineers was not misplaced, because at 6:27 A.M. on 4 September Hunton telegraphed from Bridgeport that "the bridge stands well," even though one of the trestles had broken during the night. It had been quickly replaced and slight improvements had been made to several others. Sheridan's entire train was now beyond the river, as were 130 wagons of the Cavalry Corps. Hunton indicated that he would resume sending wagons across the stream at 7:00 A.M. Anticipating Hunton's success, Rosecrans confirmed his decision to move army headquarters across the river. About the same time that Hunton was directing traffic across the Bridgeport trestle, the infantry portion of Rosecrans's guard departed Stevenson for Caperton's Ferry with the headquarters wagon train. One company of the Fifteenth Pennsylvania Cavalry regiment accompanied the column, while most of the regiment headed for the tortuous Hart's Bar ford. Several companies waited outside the "Little Brick" for the army staff to dispatch a final flurry of messages. Garfield wrote first to Morgan at Flint River, telling him not to worry about garrisoning Huntsville but to "close up this way with your force as soon as possible." He next instructed King, soon to be the senior officer at Stevenson, to deploy a new company of Alabama volunteer cavalry to patrol the Memphis & Charleston Railroad around Larkinsville. He also told King that all dispatches addressed to Rosecrans now should be forwarded to Bridgeport and beyond. At the same time Goddard wired Innes in Nashville, again reminding him not to divide Thompson's regiment of United States Colored Troops until it was fully organized. Thereafter, Rosecrans and his staff departed the "Little Brick" for the last time and headed for Bridgeport. By Rosecrans's order, the cavalcade rode at a gallop, often abandoning the road in favor of a more direct route through fields and woods. According to one of the escorts, the trip was "the most disagreeable ride I ever was on, the dust was so thick I could not see ten feet from me."[39]

Upon reaching Bridgeport in midmorning, Rosecrans found hundreds of heavily laden wagons slowly trundling across Hunton's handiwork, while hundreds more awaited their turn. The bridge was working so well that some of the Michigan engineers were ordered to return to the Elk River bridge. Rosecrans spent several hours at Bridgeport before crossing the river, taking full advantage of the last opportunity to use the telegraph line to Stevenson, Nashville, and Washington. During his stay at Bridgeport, he received a flurry of reports from Wilder, Minty, and Burnside, which explained that Minty's and Burnside's men had met near Kingston, that Confederates were leaving East Tennessee, and that there was much activity around Chattanooga. All of the information was at least forty-eight hours old, and in some cases even older. Nevertheless, Rosecrans took the opportunity to share it with Halleck. The only sour note was his nagging concern about Bragg's being reinforced from Virginia: "Is it not possible that Lee's movements are intended to cover the temporary detaching of troops to Bragg?" In a congratulatory message to Burnside, Rosecrans declared that his own objective was the Western & Atlantic Railroad and appealed for cooperation: "I hope you will close down upon our left as soon as possible, and at once throw cavalry in that direction to cover our flank. I have much evidence to show that Johnston is re-enforcing Bragg with a considerable force." His growing concern about Confederate reinforcements was also obvious in two telegrams to Granger. In the first, Garfield instructed Granger to "leave minimum garrisons in all your posts and come forward with all the force you can possibly spare. We want you with us and will I think be able to feed you and ourselves." The second telegram assured Granger that Innes would expedite the movement of any units Granger could send. Finally, Rosecrans instructed both Wagner and Hazen to be prepared to cross the river.[40]

At Bridgeport there was little for Rosecrans to do except survey the ongoing efforts to heave his army and all its impedimenta across the broad Tennessee River. He watched as members of the Pioneer Brigade closed small gaps in the bridge planking with freshly cut brush, and no doubt smiled at the antics of Twenty-First Corps soldiers attempting to force a herd of cattle into the river. Instantly perceiving the need for a second bridge, he ordered King at Stevenson to send two companies of Pioneers at that place to Bridgeport. The men of the First Michigan Engineers already on the way back to Elk River also were halted at Stevenson and put to work building more pontoons. Finally, in midafternoon, Rosecrans and his retinue crossed the bridge and headed for Sand Mountain. With a large staff, headquarters train, and escort the size of a small brigade, Rosecrans needed a route over the mountain that would not hinder his infantry corps. He thus selected a track that led downstream four miles from Bridgeport, thence up the mountain by way of Long Island Creek. The site selected for the night's camp was at the foot of the mountain near what was then called Cave Spring (now Gross Spring), approximately eight miles from Bridgeport. Elements of the Fifteenth Pennsylvania Cavalry regiment arrived first and established a courier line to the telegraph office at Bridgeport. By the time Rosecrans, Garfield, and the staff arrived around 6:00 P.M., the headquarters train and its escort had already reached Cave Spring via the road from Caperton's Ferry. Well aware that Thomas's command was lagging behind its schedule, Garfield informed McCook that the Fourteenth Corps would not reach its designated position in Lookout Valley until forty-eight hours later. Garfield admitted that Rosecrans and the staff had miscalculated the condition of the roads and the difficulty of ascending the mountain. McCook therefore would have to wait a little longer before Sheridan could join him.[41]

Thomas's command was indeed behind schedule. Leading Thomas's right column, Negley's Second Division continued its struggle to surmount the deep ravine atop Sand Mountain. Around 7:00 A.M. Negley sent Sirwell's Third Brigade across the makeshift bridge, followed by some of the division's trains. When the bridge showed signs of failure, he halted any further advance until the span could be strengthened. After two companies of the Twenty-First Ohio Infantry regiment made repairs, the long column resumed its advance. Behind Sirwell came Stanley's Second Brigade, while Beatty's First Brigade followed with the division's wagons. After marching eight miles across the plateau, Sirwell's leading regiments reached the eastern edge of the mountain. Making their way down the steep track, they halted around Brown's Spring, a well-known water source. At Brown's Spring the Federals found themselves in Back Valley, little more than three miles southwest of Trenton. By evening Stanley's men and half of Beatty's joined Sirwell there. Although Negley reported that his entire train was down the mountain by 8:00 P.M., Beatty's account and soldier diaries indicate that many wagons halted for the night atop Sand Mountain. Following Negley's command was Sheridan's division. Anxious to rejoin the Twentieth Corps, Sheridan complained all day to Garfield about the slow pace of Negley's train. At last, at 12:15 P.M., his division began to ascend, with Bradley's Third Brigade leading the way. The cloudless sky magnified the sun's heat, and the dust billowed as the troops toiled up the grade. Wreckage from the passage of Negley's train was evident, and several of Bradley's wagons joined the tally of destroyed vehicles. Artillery batteries required ten horses to a gun to complete the ascent. Still, the view from the summit was magnificent, as thousands of men, animals, and wagons could be seen carpeting the valley. Bradley halted for the night just beyond Negley's mill/bridge. Behind him, Lytle's First Brigade also made the climb, but Laibold's Second Brigade remained at the foot of Sand Mountain.[42]

Commanding the left column of Thomas's advance, Reynolds began the day on top of Sand Mountain several miles from its eastern edge. Turchin's Third Brigade had descended the mountain during the previous night and lay on Cole's plantation at the headwaters of Squirrel Town Creek. A mile in front of the brigade, the Eleventh Ohio Infantry regiment and a section of guns blocked the Wauhatchie-Trenton Road. Reynolds joined Turchin by midmorning and reported his situation to Thomas. Acknowledging his mission to seize Frick's Gap on Lookout Mountain, he explained that he could not yet do so. He had heard nothing from Baird, sorely missed Wilder's mounted regiments, and again requested the return of the Eighty-Ninth Ohio Infantry regiment from Tracy City. Meanwhile, Reynolds's Second Brigade spent the day crawling across the plateau and descending the eastern slope to join Turchin. With only two-thirds of his division present, Reynolds no doubt felt secure in his decision not to press farther toward Trenton or Frick's Gap. His decision was especially pertinent because neither Brannan's Third Division nor Baird's First Division was nearby. Camped between Shell Mound and Bridgeport, Brannan's troops could not move until their supply train arrived during the afternoon. He later reported placing one brigade and its train atop Sand Mountain, but only one regiment indicated any movement on that day. In fact, most of Brannan's soldiers spent the day bathing, foraging, and gaping at Nickajack Cave and the tristate cornerstone. Their mood was festive, with officers making social calls on the locals and regimental bands gaily playing patriotic airs. As for the First Division, two of Baird's brigades were at last able to take their place in the long line of wagons and men awaiting their turn to use the Bridgeport bridge. During the afternoon both Scribner's First Brigade and Starkweather's Second Brigade crossed the river and camped on the east bank. Baird's instructions were to follow Negley, but with Sheridan's trains clogging the road, he would be some time in negotiating Sand Mountain.[43]

Unlike Thomas, who remained at Moore's Spring, McCook wanted to get closer to the front. Early in the morning he rode down Sand Mountain and followed Long's cavalry brigade to the extensive plantation of William Winston, fifty-nine. Carrying the honorary title of "Colonel," Winston was a prominent attorney, planter, and president of the Wills Valley Railroad, whose uncompleted right of way ran in front of his imposing home. The small settlement was known as Valley Head, but "Colonel Winston's" and Winston's Gap were alternate names for the locality. Behind Winston's house, a steep track ascended Lookout Mountain. It was Winston's Gap, but McCook was disappointed. Arriving around 10:30 A.M., he wrote to Garfield, "There is no such place as Winston's Gap. Winston lives at the foot of Lookout Mountain." McCook reported that he was exploring the road up Lookout Mountain and ordering forward Davis and Johnson. Meanwhile, Stanley sent Edward McCook's First Cavalry Division down Wills Valley toward Rawlingsville. To Thomas, McCook wrote, "All my information leads me to believe that the grand concentration is taking place at Chattanooga. Joe Johnston is reported to be there; also Longstreet from Virginia." During the afternoon Davis's division advanced to Winston's and sprawled across the planter's extensive fields. Marietta Davis and her traveling companion, Mrs. Joseph Pope, were highly visible as Davis's men settled into camp. Behind them, Johnson's troops in late afternoon marched down Sand Mountain and occupied Davis's old camps at the farm of William Lee. By now, many perceptive men understood they were the lever to pry Bragg out of Chattanooga. In early evening both McCook and Stanley reported that Valley Head and Winston's Gap had been secured. Only a minuscule number of Confederates had been seen. After sending an infantry regiment to guard the top of Winston's Gap and dispatching the Thirty-Ninth Indiana Mounted Infantry regiment northward with a message for Thomas, Alex McCook retired for the night.[44]

At Shell Mound, Crittenden's Twenty-First Corps continued its consolidation. Each of Crittenden's three divisions lacked a brigade. Buell's and Harker's brigades of Wood's First Division had been across the river since the previous evening, but their supply wagons remained mired in the traffic jam at Bridgeport. Thus Wood's men had time to bathe in the river and tour Nickajack Cave. Even Col. Emerson Opdycke of the 125th Ohio Infantry regiment explored the cavern, nearly tumbling to his death when his torch failed. Cruft's brigade of Palmer's command also remained camped at Shell Mound, having completed its crossing before dawn. Cruft's men, too, seized the opportunity to visit Nickajack Cave, while others inspected the ruins of the brick railroad station. His wagons also waited patiently in line at Bridgeport. Downstream at Battle Creek, Palmer watched Grose's brigade complete its crossing, which had begun the previous night. Grose used log rafts to ferry both men and artillery pieces across the Tennessee, but his trains remained stuck in the crush at Bridgeport. The remainder of the brigade reached Shell Mound during the afternoon, giving the men time to swim in the river, visit Nickajack Cave, and vandalize the tristate boundary stone. With Palmer and Wood across, only Van Cleve's division remained west of the river. Beatty's brigade crossed during the morning, followed by Barnes. Van Cleve described the scene to his wife: "Sketch a river 600 yds wide, six flat boats, some filled with men, some with men and horses, some with artillery, some with wagons, coming over, the landing place on each side covered with men, horses, wagons, artillery, all life & action." One boat carrying seventy men foundered in midstream, but an empty boat rescued everyone. Van Cleve himself crossed at 3:30 P.M. on a raft, holding the bridle of his horse, Bessie. His trains and their extensive escorts meanwhile joined the throng at Bridgeport. Crittenden and his staff rode to Bridgeport, crossed the river, and followed the stream back to Shell Mound, arriving shortly after 8:30 P.M.[45]

Even though most of the Army of the Cumberland was safely across the Tennessee River, the deception force continued its charade. Early in the morning Hazen formally notified Minty of his new authority and instructed Minty to begin contracting his lines southward. At 10:00 A.M. he ordered the Sixth Kentucky Infantry regiment to make a noisy demonstration at the mouth of North Chickamauga Creek. Augmented with a battery and a full complement of musicians, the Kentuckians spent the day building fires, making loud music, and shelling the far shore, all without noticeable effect. At the same time, he detached the Ninety-Second Illinois Mounted Infantry regiment and sent it back over Walden's Ridge to Shell Mound via the Sequatchie Valley. Nominally part of Wilder's command, the Ninety-Second had been serving under Hazen's supervision for some time; now it was slated to become the mounted vanguard of the Fourteenth Corps. During the evening Hazen forwarded the testimony of a deserter from the Forty-Fifth Tennessee Infantry regiment, who truthfully reported the gradual Confederate infantry withdrawal from the river. From their vantage point on Walden's Ridge, soldiers in Wagner's brigade also noted increased activity around Chattanooga and in the valley behind it. Wagner, however, momentarily had other concerns. He believed that he outranked Hazen and by right should command the deception force. In a polite but firm note to Garfield, forwarded through proper channels, he made his case, but agreed to abide by Rosecrans's decision. Meanwhile, he recognized Hazen's authority. According to his usual custom, Wilder appeared to take no notice of the new chain of command, and his men continued to patrol and forage aggressively in the bottomlands under their control. As for Minty, he acknowledged Hazen's authority and offered him part of the large stocks of provisions still held at Pikeville. He also reported that a new Confederate regiment had appeared at Blythe's Ferry but did not mention that one of his troopers had crossed the river and found no Confederates.[46]

In the army's rear, Reserve Corps units continued to shift positions. In response to Rosecrans's appeal for reinforcements, Granger reported that he had issued movement orders to Walter Whitaker's First Brigade of Steedman's First Division. Divided among Estill Springs, Fosterville, and Tullahoma, Whitaker's men spent the day unaware that their pleasant interlude was coming to an end. Whitaker's departure would leave the division's Second Brigade holding the towns of Shelbyville, Wartrace, and Cowan, while the Third Brigade garrisoned Murfreesboro. In Nashville, Col. Heber Le Favour's Twenty-Second Michigan Infantry regiment received an order to move to the front on the next day as well. As for the Second Division, scattered throughout northern Alabama, Morgan notified Garfield that he would move at noon to Stevenson via Larkinsville with Tillson's First Brigade. He expected that Daniel McCook's Second Brigade probably would reach Huntsville that same day. Detachments of the Tenth Ohio Cavalry regiment would patrol the railroad back to Huntsville, but the departure of the infantry ended construction work on the Flint River bridge. Morgan was indeed correct about McCook's brigade. It left Athens early that day and marched all the way to Huntsville. Somewhere along the road, Pvt. George Mathers of Battery I, Second Illinois Light Artillery, was bitten by either an insect or a venomous reptile. Carried along with the marching column, Mathers received only whiskey as a treatment. He died before reaching Huntsville and was buried beside the road. After McCook threatened vengeance upon anyone molesting Mathers's grave, the column continued to Huntsville. Far behind, the Eighty-Sixth Illinois Infantry regiment was relieved from duty at Columbia and followed in McCook's wake, camping for the night near the burned village of Lynnville, a place that had already experienced McCook's wrath firsthand.[47]

As night fell in Long Island Cove, Rosecrans found himself in a different world. Within a short time he had moved from the capacious Mary Sharp College in Winchester, to the much smaller but still comfortable "Little Brick" in Stevenson, and finally to a rude cabin below Sand Mountain. Previously, steam dummies had carried him quickly and comfortably throughout his department; now he was reduced to riding a horse over barely passable tracks. Before leaving Bridgeport, he could telegraph Washington and expect a reasonably rapid response; now he stood at the end of a courier line that lengthened every step he took into the mountains. Rosecrans could hardly have been unaware of the significance of the moment. After watching him cross the trestle bridge at Bridgeport, Pvt. Reuben Jones wrote, "'Rosecrans is on the War Path.' Saw him on the bank of the river—as I looked upon him and watched his continence as he descended to cross, I thought I saw a hesitancy in his step and a look of melancholy abstraction rested on his face—no doubt he was contemplating the *unseen future* as he Crossed this Rubicon." That night, even the immediate future was unclear. Although Rosecrans had placed twenty-five of his thirty infantry brigades, most of his cavalry, and thousands of wagons across the river by the end of the day, he really knew little of their locations. Eleven infantry brigades and four cavalry brigades had successfully crossed Sand Mountain and were somewhere in Lookout/Wills Valley, but Rosecrans could not be sure of any of it. His 11:00 P.M. message to Halleck was telling: "The troops are probably nearly in position this side of the river. Thomas near Trenton; Crittenden near Whiteside's; two divisions of McCook's at Valley Head; Sheridan en route for that point. No reports have reached me this evening from the front." The bridge fiasco and a serious miscalculation of the difficulty in crossing Sand Mountain had cost the army at least one precious day, and perhaps two. Nevertheless, after the weeks and months of preparation, the die was cast at last.[48]

On 4 September Bragg remained at the Montgomery Avenue home of Ely Bruce on the outskirts of Chattanooga. Although the news reaching him was maddeningly vague, a clearer picture of Federal activity was slowly emerging. According to Brent, "A large force of the enemy has unquestionably crossed below Trenton & is moving down Wills Valley. Also a large force is in the valley near Trenton. The conclusion would seem, from all reports that McCook's and Thomas' Corps have crossed below, & that Crittenden's Corps is still on the north bank of the River." Except for the Twenty-First Corps, which was crossing at Shell Mound that day, Brent's statement generally reflected reality. Recognizing the imminent threat to his supply line, Bragg resolved to counter it with a unit large enough to be a blocking force but small enough to avoid weak-

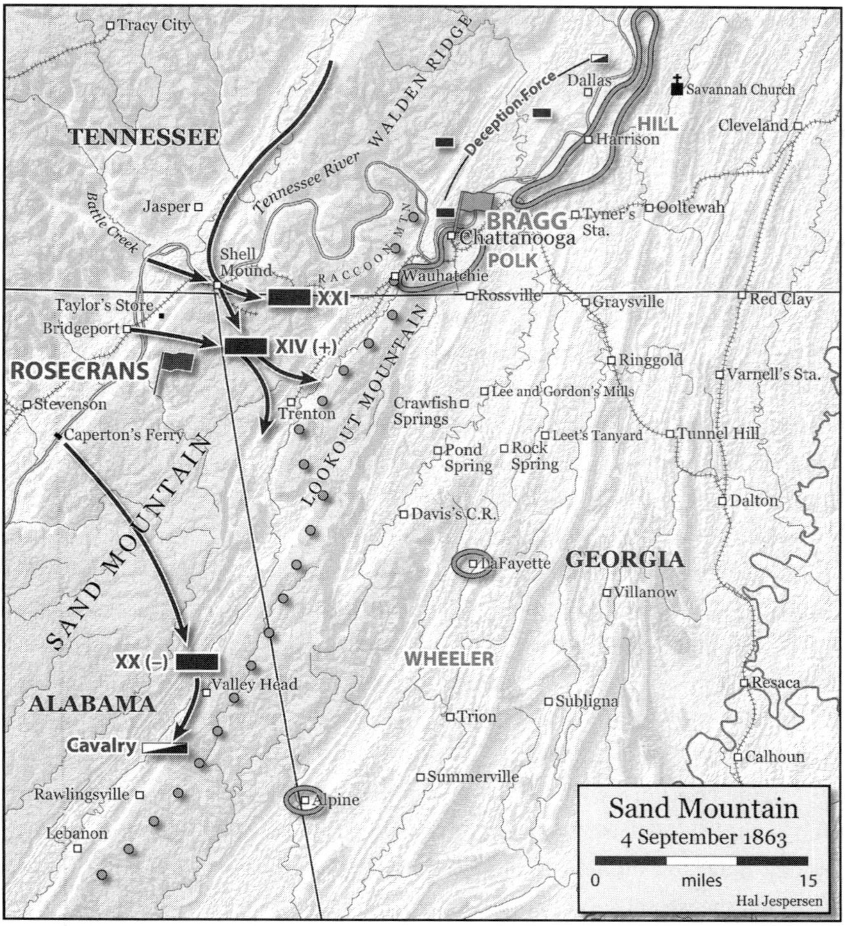

Sand Mountain
4 September 1863

ening his positions around Chattanooga. He selected Walker's Division, just completing its concentration around Tyner's Station. Brent promptly ordered Hill to send Walker's Division to Rome to counter any Federal thrust from Wills Valley. The reason for the move was clear: "Our present information is that a force of three arms having crossed Sand Mountain, is in march towards Rome or Atlanta." Brent told Walker that Roddey's Brigade should soon join him from Alabama to serve as a screen for the infantry. If any more cavalrymen proved to be in the area, Walker was to appeal to them for additional assistance. Because Walker's artillery batteries were still in transit, the orders authorized him to reunite his guns and teams in Atlanta before sending them to Rome by rail via Kingston. Further, Walker should remain in touch with Chattanooga by telegraph. Under no circumstances was he to permit the Federals to reach the all-important Western & Atlantic Railroad. A copy of Walker's instructions was sent to Wheeler, who had just departed Chattanooga. In a letter to Samuel Cooper, Bragg mentioned the threat to his supply line, and promised,

"No effort will be spared to bring him to an engagement whenever the chances shall favor us."[49]

Not long after dispatching Walker, Bragg reassessed his decision to wait for the Federal advance to develop further. If the Fourteenth and Twentieth Corps were in Wills Valley, the Twenty-First Corps was probably isolated west of the river. Perhaps a crossing north of Chattanooga might catch the Federals off guard. It was a tempting proposition, and a bold one. At 10:00 A.M. Bragg wrote a personal note to Hill: "If you can cross the river, now is our time to crush the corps opposite. What say you: Or if we could draw the enemy over. We must do something and that soon. We have a pontoon bridge here, but it is not portable, and the crossing here would be under fire. By selecting fords Forrest promises to cross infantry on his horses." Bragg suggested that Hill consult Cleburne, "Then give me your views or call with C. & see what our resources are." In a postscript, he noted that several steamboats in the Hiwassee River could be used either as a diversion or in a real crossing. On the previous day, Hill had expressed a desire to act offensively, so Bragg may have thought he would find a kindred spirit. The only potentially false note in Bragg's message was his suggestion to consult Cleburne. Such consultation made perfect sense to Bragg, who thought highly of Cleburne's judgment, but it may have rankled Hill, so new to both the area and the Army of Tennessee. There was no immediate answer from Hill, nor would there be. Bragg did not expect an immediate response, but he remained optimistic while he waited for Hill to ponder the matter. A report from scout S. G. Ballard, who had returned from across the river on the previous day, may have influenced Bragg's thinking. Ballard more or less accurately described the various units of the Federal deception force and noted the general movement of the Twenty-First Corps southward. While he waited for Hill to comment, Bragg telegraphed Hill to send only one of Walker's three brigades to Rome. He also ordered his engineers to return his pontoon train to the river, a move noted with alarm by some of Wilder's men.[50]

Extant soldier accounts indicate that 4 September was a quiet Friday in the Army of Tennessee. In Polk's command, dress parades and religious services were held as usual, while the corps commander issued a circular prescribing hard labor for miscreants. Two deserters from the Forty-First Mississippi Infantry regiment who returned voluntarily to the ranks forfeited their sergeant's stripes and were confined. A sterner punishment was meted out to Capt. Jabez Rhodes, thirty-eight, of Company C, First Confederate Infantry regiment, whose execution took place as scheduled. Rhodes had been court-martialed on charges of drunkenness, making false returns, embezzlement of substitute funds, and advising men in his own company to desert the cause. In an effort to avoid the charges, he had offered his resignation, and his friends had appealed to President Davis for clemency. Given the crisis facing the army, Bragg strongly opposed leniency, and Rhodes was convicted. Sentenced to be executed by musketry, he stood before a firing squad shortly after noon and freely admitted his guilt. After Asst. Provost Marshal William Reid read the findings of the court, a minister offered the condemned man a few words of solace. Both then withdrew to safety, and the firing party from the Second Georgia Sharpshooter battalion ended Rhodes's life with a thunderous volley. Meanwhile, in those units of Hill's Corps still near the river, sentries observed minimal Federal activity, although occasional shots still winged their way across the stream. The noisy demonstration at Chickamauga Landing received little attention and elicited no concern. Near Chickamauga Station, the morning passenger train for Atlanta experienced a minor derailment, which blocked local movement for several hours. By the time Gist's Brigade of Walker's Division was ready to depart for Rome in late afternoon the track had been repaired successfully. The first contingent, consisting of the Twenty-Fourth South Carolina Infantry regiment, two companies of the Forty-Sixth Georgia Infantry regiment, and Gist's staff, departed Chickamauga Station at sunset.[51]

There was movement on both of Bragg's flanks on 4 September. On the army's left, Wheeler continued his dilatory approach to the passes over Lookout Mountain. By the end of the day, Wharton had reached Alpine on the road from Winston's to Rome. There he learned from a scout that a few Federal troops had appeared atop the mountain at Winston's Gap. Ominously, local civilians reported many more Federals filling Wills Valley. With only Crews's Brigade at Alpine and Harrison's Brigade at Brownstown, midway between LaFayette and Alpine, Wharton could do no nothing but notify Wheeler of the Federal presence. Martin's Division remained scattered, with Martin at LaFayette, Mauldin's command in Lookout Valley around Wauhatchie, and many men still marching up from Alabama with remounts. At least one of Martin's regiments, the Fifty-First Alabama Cavalry, made a futile march over Taylor's Ridge toward Dalton before returning to the vicinity of LaFayette. Wheeler himself was somewhere between Chattanooga and Alpine, out of communication with anyone. On the army's right, Buckner spent most of the day perfecting his Hiwassee River defense line. Concerned about his eastern flank, he ordered Hodge to guard four fords upstream from Charleston. Meanwhile, Preston and Pegram surveyed the situation at Blythe's Ferry. At the same time, Stewart's Division linked with Preston's two brigades on the Hiwassee west of Charleston. Part of Scott's cavalry still shielded Charleston north of the Hiwassee, and Trigg's Brigade garrisoned the town. It was all for naught at 10:00 P.M., when a telegram arrived from Brent: "Leave a Brigade at your present position and fall back with your entire command without delay to some suitable point midway between this place and the Hiawassee. Be prepared to move promptly in any direction." The message reflected Bragg's desire to strike across the river with his right, requiring Buckner's Corps to be close at hand. Unaware of Bragg's reasoning, Buckner must have wondered what could have prompted such a drastic move.[52]

15

Lookout Valley

» 5–6 September 1863 «

The operations order approved by Rosecrans early on 3 September envisioned that by the end of the next day the Twenty-First Corps would be threatening Chattanooga, the Fourteenth and Twentieth Corps would control several gaps on Lookout Mountain, and the Cavalry Corps would be threatening Rome. Because of the collapse of the Bridgeport span and gross misjudgment in the difficulty of crossing Sand Mountain, Rosecrans's army had fallen well short of that aggressive timeline. Still, the Confederate response had been minimal, so perhaps nothing had been lost. Tucked into Long Island Cove at the western foot of Sand Mountain, Rosecrans remained optimistic that his campaign was proceeding according to plan. He intended to cross Sand Mountain and descend into Lookout Valley at Trenton during the day, joining the Fourteenth Corps. Prior to his departure, he had Garfield prepare instructions for several of the most distant units. At 8:30 A.M. Garfield explained to Stanley the reasons for the delays besetting the main army and expressed the hope that Stanley could still threaten Bragg's supply line. The timing of the thrust was left to Stanley's discretion, but Garfield implied that Rosecrans expected him to move soon. Thirty minutes later, Garfield instructed Granger to forego garrisoning Huntsville, Alabama, but to protect the Larkinsville sawmill and the Paint Rock Creek railroad bridge. Morgan was to guard the Nashville & Chattanooga Railroad east of the Cumberland Plateau with one brigade and prepare to send Daniel McCook's brigade to join the main army. Similarly, Granger was to bring forward most of Steedman's First Division from Middle Tennessee. Garfield asked Granger to forecast both the number of troops coming forward and the timing of Granger's own arrival at Bridgeport, so that army headquarters could release the deception force. Finally, Garfield sent a brief note to Crittenden, granting him permission to modify slightly the route of the Twenty-First Corps into Lookout Valley.[1]

In his note to Crittenden, Garfield indicated that while Rosecrans expected to go to Trenton that afternoon, the headquarters would not move until the next day because the road across Sand Mountain was hopelessly clogged with the trains of several divisions. Unable to get to Trenton expeditiously, Rosecrans decided to while away the long afternoon by exploring a large cave located near the head of Long Island Cove. Known to the Federals as Hill's Cave, the cavern had been used by contractors Daniel Hill and King Newby to mine niter for the Confederate government. The diggings were far smaller than those at Nickajack Cave, as was the cavern's mouth, but the cave's passages extended for several miles. The allure of the cave proved irresistible to a man of Rosecrans's curiosity, and he decided to spend the afternoon exploring its mysteries to a depth of at least 800 feet. He was accompanied by Goddard, engineer officers Merrill and Burroughs, and numerous officers and men from the Tenth Ohio Infantry and Fifteenth Pennsylvania Cavalry regiments. The party gradually traversed a series of expansive rooms and narrow passageways, one of the latter involving a crawl of more than fifty feet, until they reached a space known to modern cavers as the Registry Room. There Rosecrans and Goddard inscribed their names, and the two engineers scratched their initials, far up a vertical shaft. Below that point, less exalted visitors left their own names as well. In exiting the cave Rosecrans apparently stuck in one of the narrow passageways and was extricated with some difficulty. According to Pvt. Baldwin Colton, who met Rosecrans coming out, "The General was much excited and perspiring at every pore, and oh, tell it not in Gath, he was much frightened." Chastened by the experience, Rosecrans soon returned to the task of orchestrating the campaign. His inscription on the cave wall in Long Island Cove, however, stands as mute testimony to his momentary escape from the cascading delays afflicting his carefully crafted plan.[2]

The trains clogging the road across Sand Mountain belonged to Negley's division, and behind them toiled Sheridan's three brigades and several hundred more wagons. As he awaited the arrival of his train, Negley sought to expand his control of the territory beyond Brown's Spring. The division's camps lay directly at the foot of Sand Mountain in Back Valley and were separated from the main Lookout Valley by a range of low hills. Leaving the remainder of his division at Brown's, Negley ordered Sirwell to scout into Lookout Valley with two regiments and a section of guns. Their route took them first to Trenton, where they found themselves in a region of nascent industrialization. Little more than two miles from Brown's Spring the reconnaissance party came to the Macon Iron Works, which had been under construction since the previous year. Created to take advantage of small local deposits of iron ore and coal from the extensive Sand Mountain mines, the Macon Iron Works represented a minor attempt to add to the Confederacy's meager stock of iron products. In its unfinished state, the establishment posed no threat to Negley's men, who stripped it of everything usable and moved on. In another mile they came to Payne's (or Sitton's, as the locals styled it) Mill, a water-powered gristmill on Lookout Creek. Stocked with 400 bushels of wheat ready for grinding, the mill had far greater utility for the invading Federals than an incomplete ironworks, so the Seventy-Eighth Pennsylvania Infantry regiment became both guards and millers. Leaving the Pennsylvanians to their work, Sirwell pushed forward down Lookout Valley with the Twenty-First Ohio and the artillery section. Several miles southward, they found the Empire State Iron Works, also still under construction. Only the first of a planned series of furnaces was operational, but it too was abandoned. Leaving the second ironworks behind, Sirwell finally halted for the night at the gristmill of James Cureton, where another small quantity of wheat was confiscated. No Confederates appeared to molest the Federals in their march.[3]

While Sirwell searched for potential threats, other Fourteenth Corps units consolidated their hold on the Trenton area. In Negley's command, Beatty's and Stanley's brigades made themselves comfortable in Back Valley. During the day, two of Beatty's regiments assisted the division train down Sand Mountain, while other soldiers foraged liberally in the relatively untouched region. Many heard the booming of artillery in the direction of Chattanooga, while others noted the passage of two of Sheridan's brigades toward Trenton. In Lytle's First Brigade, Pvt. John Ely was concerned: "It is now very evident to me that our corps has been sent off here to the Right for the purpose of flanking Chattanooga. But I am almost afraid for the result, if Bragg retreats it will be all right, but if he shows fight I cannot see how our corps is to be saved from destruction." During the afternoon Reynolds's two brigades appeared, marching from their camps at Cole's Spring. Turchin's Third Brigade entered Trenton itself, with King's Second Brigade following close behind. Capt. Augustus Ward of the Thirty-Sixth Ohio disparaged the village: "Small place, court house and church and the public buildings. . . . This is a hard poor country so far. I don't like it." Division commander Reynolds, however, was satisfied, establishing his headquarters near the courthouse and appropriating a church for divine services. Reynolds's arrival, coupled with the appearance of most of Sheridan's division, placed seven Federal brigades in the Trenton area by the end of the day. Two Fourteenth Corps divisions, however, still lagged behind. Brannan's Third Division remained scattered along the rough mountain track from Nickajack Cave to Warren's Mill. Several wagons and at least one artillery caisson fell into the abyss during the climb, killing several horses. Similarly, Baird's two brigades only began to ascend the mountain from Moore's Spring. As for corps commander Thomas, he and his extensive retinue camped at Warren's Mill with Connell's brigade of Brannan's command.[4]

According to Rosecrans's plan, Crittenden's Twenty-First Corps was to threaten Chattanooga from the northern end of Lookout Valley, while Thomas's Fourteenth Corps served as the connection with McCook's and Stanley's forces at Valley Head. Crittenden's pathway through the mountains was to be the canyon cut by Running Water Creek, a relatively easy passage into Lookout Valley. Although rough, that road was far less difficult than the routes farther to the south. Nevertheless, Crittenden was slow to move, primarily because most of his trains had been caught by the collapse of the Bridgeport trestle. Thus, the Twenty-First Corps spent much of the day resting at Shell Mound, permitting Van Cleve to visit the tristate monument and Pvt. Henry Bowlby to drown in the river while bathing. The longer he delayed, the more Crittenden risked exposing Thomas's units around Trenton to attack. By the afternoon of 5 September, Crittenden put his three divisions in motion for Running Water Canyon, following the railroad. Wood's division began its march toward the canyon at 2:30 P.M., followed in order by Palmer's division and Van Cleve's men. Only the divisions' ammunition trains accompanied the long column. Some of the corps supply trains were still crossing the Bridgeport spans at that time and would not reach Shell Mound until dark. Crittenden maintained corps headquarters at Shell Mound until 4:00 A.M. the next morning, although his escort from the Fourth Michigan Cavalry regiment departed during the afternoon after a visit to Nickajack Cave. During the morning Crittenden had asked permission to send Palmer's command over the mountain via the route passing Gordon's Coal Mines. While waiting for an answer, he discovered that Brannan's division clogged that route, so he explained to Garfield that he had been unaware that the route belonged to Brannan. His apologetic tone contrasted sharply with communications from the other corps commanders and spoke volumes about the Crittenden-Rosecrans relationship.[5]

Crittenden's orders to his division commanders were specific. Wood was to march along the railroad through Running Water Canyon until he had passed the small settlement of Whiteside, where he was to halt for the night. On the following day, he was to enter Lookout Valley and probe the Confederate defenses at the tip of Lookout Mountain. Palmer was to follow Wood to Whiteside, then take a narrow track up Sand Mountain through a defile known as Murphy's Hollow. Palmer was to halt upon reaching the road from Shell Mound via Gordon's Coal Mines. Van Cleve was to follow Palmer while maintaining a connection with Wood's units in Running Water Canyon. Few wagons beyond ammunition carriers were to be taken. Harker's Third Brigade of Wood's command began the movement in midafternoon. In a futile effort at stealth, Wood forbade the use of bugles and drums. For four miles the road paralleled the river, but eventually it entered the mouth of Running Water Canyon, where it was constricted by Raccoon and Sand Mountains. Inadvertently leading the advance on a railroad handcar was a five-man wire party intent on advancing the telegraph line from Shell Mound. Reaching the ruins of the Running Water Creek railroad trestle, they halted while telegrapher George

Peirce climbed a bridge pier. He was immediately accosted by Confederate cavalrymen, who ordered him to "come down from there." While Peirce and his comrades headed for Chattanooga under guard, Harker's Federals arrived. Finding the road blocked by the massive pile of wreckage, they cleared a path and continued to Whiteside, halting around 8:00 P.M. Behind Wood, Palmer's division turned up the Murphy's Hollow road and stumbled through the darkness for several hours until Palmer finally called a halt. Last in the column, Van Cleve's two brigades followed Palmer's men on the "indescribably rough road." Around midnight, Van Cleve's men halted short of Murphy's Hollow for a few hours of fitful rest.[6]

The lunge across the river by the bulk of the Army of the Cumberland left Hazen's deception force increasingly isolated. Ominously, the reappearance of Confederate pontoons in the river seemingly foretold a more aggressive Confederate posture. Momentarily unaware of the pontoon activity, Hazen spent the morning orchestrating his demonstration at Harrison and attempting to draw Minty's brigade nearer his infantry. At 8:00 A.M. he reported that visible Confederate movements were concentrated around Tyner's Station. Hazen's firing at Harrison momentarily created a flurry of anxiety in Wilder's command. At 10:00 A.M. Wilder reported that the Confederate pontoon bridge appeared to be operational and that there was much activity in the Confederate camps he could see. The message was transmitted by flag signal from a new station linking Wilder with the Sequatchie Valley signal line and ultimately to the telegraph line at Shell Mound and Bridgeport. From there it would have to be carried by courier into the depths of Long Island Cove to reach Rosecrans. Given the lengthy transmission time for the message, and Rosecrans's absence from headquarters, Wilder would not receive a reply for many hours. Unwilling to wait, in late morning he sent the Seventy-Second Indiana Mounted Infantry and 123rd Illinois Mounted Infantry regiments to the river and ordered the first section of the Eighteenth Indiana Battery to fire on the pontoons from Stringer's Ridge. Lilly's men expended at least twenty rounds, striking the pontoons five times and sinking two of them. Confederate gunners responded with a few shots of their own but did no damage. Using his new signal capability, Wilder throughout the afternoon reported his "indifferent success," noting that several spare pontoons were available to replace those he had destroyed.[7]

Although Hazen remained untroubled, others in the deception force became exceedingly nervous as the day progressed. Atop Walden's Ridge, the noise of Hazen's morning demonstration at Harrison caused Wagner to start two regiments down the mountain to assist in repelling an apparent assault. Upon learning that no attack was occurring, Wagner's men retraced their steps. Their feelings of dread were exacerbated anew by Lilly's afternoon bombardment of the Chattanooga waterfront. As evening neared, Wilder became so concerned that he began to think seriously about retreat. At nightfall he ordered all of his baggage trains and caissons to ascend Walden's Ridge. At the same time he moved his three regiments nearer the river. In a series of notes to Hazen, Wilder explained that a downstream crossing would sever his 1,200 men from the main army. He detailed several troubling observations: flatboats formerly moored at the city waterfront had disappeared and had probably gone downstream to the mouth of Chattanooga Creek, where a great deal of noise had been heard; infantry pickets upstream from Chattanooga had apparently been replaced by cavalrymen; and, finally, ambulance traffic from Chattanooga toward Tyner's Station had increased. Deserters from the Thirty-Fourth Alabama Infantry regiment stated that Longstreet's Corps from Virginia was arriving and that a cavalry force massed upstream was ready to cross at Friar's Island. Confusingly, deserters from the Nineteenth Tennessee Infantry regiment reported that only Breckinridge's Division had arrived from Johnston's army, Jackson's Brigade was preparing to cross the river, but that Bragg was only feigning a crossing to cover his retreat. The mix of direct observations and deserter statements led Wilder to consider a Confederate assault likely, and he notified Wagner accordingly. At 11:00 P.M. Wagner again sent two regiments down the ridge, accompanied by a section of guns. While Wilder and Wagner fretted, only Minty at Smith's Cross Roads seemed unconcerned about Confederate activity.[8]

At Valley Head, McCook's First and Second Divisions remained at ease in William Winston's plantation fields. Without Sheridan's Third Division, still entangled with Fourteenth Corps elements around Trenton, McCook did not feel strong enough to advance on Lookout Mountain in force, a mission already assigned to Stanley's Cavalry Corps. In many units the mail arrived, but rumors soon spread that it would be the last until Chattanooga fell. For soldiers like Pvt. Chauncy Brooks, such rumors were cruel. In a letter to his fiancée, Brooks explained the value of getting mail regularly: "I get so lonsom somtimes that I dont know what to do with my self, but when I get so I eather get your letters and read them over or sit down and write to you. It is comfort to me to eather. I love your kind letters dearly so pleas write often for it cheers me to here from my intended bride." Other writers, like Capt. Philip Welshimer, had divined Rosecrans's campaign plan: "It seems that we are flanking the Rebles in order to force them back from Chattanooga. If we fail in this the impression is we will move on Chattanooga from their rear." He cautioned his wife not to be unduly alarmed, because nothing could be as bad as the Stones River fight had been. Col. John Martin warned his sister not to be surprised if no letters reached her for some time. Noting that it was his fortieth birthday, Capt. Henry Richards waxed philosophical: "I have seen enough confusion during the past year, and I feel like ending the balance of my life in quiet." Richards worried about how their war experiences might affect men in the ranks: "It seems now that nothing but the strictest military regulations can control them." Other writers were more positive, noting the large numbers of citizens either joining the Union army or migrating to the North. One teamster even bragged about conquering Sand Mountain with "the best pulling teem in the train." As for McCook himself, he penned a brief note to Garfield at 6:30 P.M. stating that he had nothing new to report and was simply awaiting further developments.[9]

Rosecrans's order of 3 September required Stanley to drive beyond Lookout Mountain toward Rome. The force sent to Rome "should push forward with audacity, feel the enemy strongly, and make a strong diversion in that direction." Stanley, however, hesitated to commence such an aggressive movement. With Minty absent, he had only four cavalry brigades available, and they were not yet complete. During the day several supply trains arrived, along with the regiments guarding them, but others were still toiling across Sand Mountain. Thus Stanley decided to wait until his force was larger and his supplies more secure before beginning his raid. In the meantime, his division commanders reconnoitered the area aggressively. Edward McCook sent Archibald Campbell and two regiments fifteen miles down Wills Valley to the hamlet of Lebanon. Campbell chased a handful of Confederate scouts all the way to Lebanon but captured only a few winded horses and a small stock of whiskey. McCook also sent part of the Fourth Kentucky Cavalry regiment up Lookout Mountain toward Davis's Gap. The Kentuckians surprised pickets from Crews's Brigade, capturing eleven and driving the remainder down the mountain. Meanwhile, Crook led most of Long's Second Brigade up Lookout Mountain on the direct road to Rome. Encountering Confederates on the far edge of the plateau busily obstructing the road, the Federals gave chase. Reaching the descent into Broomtown Valley, Crook led two dismounted companies down to the valley floor. When the fleeing Confederates escaped, he ordered a gradual withdrawal to Valley Head after dark. While awaiting Crook's return, Stanley wrote to Garfield that he did not wish to begin his movement without Minty's brigade, "unless the general desires me to go sooner." Fearing he would be overruled, he initiated a frantic search for tools and explosives suitable for wrecking railroads. Like its compatriots elsewhere in the valley, Stanley's command was not yet ready to implement the next stage of Rosecrans's campaign plan.[10]

The pause by most of the Army of the Cumberland on 5 September did not extend to Granger's Reserve Corps. Early in the day Granger reported that he would be sending two regiments from the Third Brigade of Morgan's Second Division to Stevenson within the next two days. The Twenty-Second Michigan Infantry would leave Nashville by train that very day, and the 108th Ohio Infantry would follow soon thereafter. Whitaker's First Brigade of Steedman's First Division would march for Stevenson on 7 September, the same day that Granger himself planned to depart for the front. He planned to garrison Mc-

Minnville with the Fifth Iowa Cavalry regiment and a battery. Unmentioned was Reid's Second Brigade of Steedman's command, but it too was preparing to move south from Wartrace. At 6:15 P.M., Granger reported that Morgan would bring approximately 4,000 men forward, Steedman would furnish 3,500 more, and the two regiments from the Nashville garrison would add another 1,000, for a grand total of 8,500 reinforcements. Approximately 6,000 of the troops would reach the Tennessee River in four days, while Granger would arrive two days earlier. In Steedman's command the day was spent concentrating scattered detachments, packing gear, and preparing the regiments for movement. Already moving, Morgan's two brigades continued their leisurely advance toward Stevenson. On 5 September Tillson's First Brigade neared Larkinsville. Meanwhile, Dan McCook's Second Brigade passed through Huntsville to Hurricane Creek with the band of the Fifty-Second Ohio Infantry regiment jauntily playing "Dixie" and "Hail, Columbia" on the way. Far behind, the Eighty-Sixth Illinois Infantry regiment made it only to Pulaski. In a movement unrelated to that of the Reserve Corps, the Ninety-Second Illinois Mounted Infantry regiment departed Wilder's command by way of Walden's Ridge and the Sequatchie Valley to join the Twenty-First Corps as its scouting force.[11]

By the time he wrote to Halleck on the evening of 5 September, Rosecrans had placed twenty-five of the thirty infantry brigades in the Fourteenth, Twentieth, and Twenty-First Corps east of the river. Only John King's brigade guarding Stevenson and Bridgeport, Dick's brigade marching to Jasper, and the three infantry brigades of the deception force remained west of the stream. Four of Rosecrans's cavalry brigades were also east of the Tennessee, with only Minty's brigade absent with the deception force. Although Thomas, McCook, and Crittenden were all behind schedule, they had gained relatively secure positions on Sand Mountain or in Lookout/Wills Valley. On the army's right, Stanley's cavalry was preparing for a strike beyond Lookout Mountain toward Bragg's supply line, with the Twentieth Corps in support. On the army's left, the Twenty-First Corps soon would threaten Chattanooga from the north end of Lookout Valley, while the Fourteenth Corps in the center was poised to seize passes over Lookout Mountain. If Bragg continued to remain passive, Rosecrans would eventually sever his supply line to Atlanta and force him to stand a siege at Chattanooga. If Bragg withdrew southward to preserve his connection to Atlanta, Chattanooga would fall without a fight. Believing it unwise to detail his plans, Rosecrans said only that he was across the Tennessee in force. He expressed some concern about Confederate pontoon activity, but with Granger coming forward with all available reserves, he implied that he could handle the situation. He did not mention his afternoon foray into the cave. Nor did he tell his wife of his underground adventures. In a brief telegram to Anna, Rosecrans instead outlined his expectations for the future: "We will be in Georgia tomorrow. A great battle will probably ensue should the Rebels think they can stand, this side of Atlanta." He asked for the prayers of the Roman Catholic community, and closed with the comforting news that their son Louis, still with the army, was safe.[12]

For several days, Rosecrans had queried Halleck about persistent rumors that troops from Virginia would soon be reinforcing Bragg. On 3 September he wrote, "Have you any news from Burnside? any reason to think forces will be sent from Virginia to East Tennessee?" On 4 September he telegraphed Halleck, "Is it not possible that Lee's movements are intended to cover the temporary detaching of troops to Bragg?" Halleck's response was dispatched at 12:30 P.M. on 5 September: "There is no reason here to suppose that any of Lee's troops have been detached, except, perhaps, a small force to Charleston, S.C." That statement would soon prove to be incorrect. Davis and Lee had finally agreed that a significant number of troops from the Army of Northern Virginia should indeed move to reinforce the Army of Tennessee. As a result, Lee on 4 September asked Longstreet for an estimate of the time such a movement would require. On 5 September, the day of Halleck's reassurance to Rosecrans, Longstreet replied that he was unable to provide the answer. Maj. Frederick Sims of the Confederate Railroad Bureau was not so ignorant of such matters. Instructed to initiate the coordination process, Sims began at once to contact the affected railroad companies. For planning purposes he estimated the number of troops at 20,000 men and fifty cannon, with transit time estimated at five days. The direct route from central Virginia to Chattanooga involved only four railroads and was approximately 540 miles in length. The troops would travel via the Orange & Alexandria Railroad to Lynchburg, where they would take the Virginia & Tennessee Railroad to Bristol, thence southward on the East Tennessee & Virginia Railroad to Knoxville, and finally the East Tennessee & Georgia Railroad to Chattanooga. After giving him the requirement, Sims asked Thomas Dodamead, superintendent of the Virginia & Tennessee Railroad, if his road needed assistance with locomotives and cars, and Sims promised, "You shall be advised in time to prepare."[13]

As Sims began to coordinate the troop movement in earnest, disturbing news arrived from southwestern Virginia. When Buckner withdrew from Knoxville in late August, only Alfred Jackson's small command south of Bristol and Frazer's garrison at Cumberland Gap had remained to hold the area. The withdrawal had been designed to prevent Buckner from being overwhelmed, but it had left Knoxville and the railroad corridor vulnerable to a Federal thrust. Now Jackson reported that Federal forces of unknown size were operating on the railroad near Jonesborough, Tennessee. The presumption that Burnside was moving to join Rosecrans had led the Richmond authorities to believe that only transient raids threatened the railroad to Virginia. In an effort to clarify the confused situation, Davis late on 5 September queried Bragg sharply about Federal movements. In the interim, the adjustment of departmental boundaries seemed momentarily sufficient as a response. Accordingly, Samuel Cooper assigned the southwestern Virginia portion of Buckner's old department and the units east of Knoxville to Maj. Gen. Samuel Jones, commanding the Department of Western Virginia. Jones immediately left his Dublin, Virginia, headquarters for Bristol, hoping to meet Jackson and learn what was happening on the East Tennessee & Virginia Railroad. Privately, Davis was told that Jackson was "a very nervous person under responsibility, although undoubtedly brave and energetic." Bristol was 100 miles southwest of Dublin, and Knoxville was 130 miles beyond Bristol. In light of such distances and his limited assets, Jones could hardly have had a more difficult task than to maintain the security of the railroad. Given the fact that Burnside's advance guard had occupied Knoxville three days earlier, a fact unknown to Jones, the War Department, or the Railroad Bureau, it was already impossible.[14]

In Chattanooga, Bragg on 5 September continued to prepare his mobile forces for a possible strike across the river upstream from the town. He reiterated his order that Walker send only one brigade to Rome as a counterweight to a Federal thrust from Wills Valley. With his remaining brigades Walker was to form a new command, the Reserve Corps, by joining his division with that of Liddell. Liddell's small two-brigade division had previously been designated the army's reserve, an arrangement Liddell had brokered with Bragg earlier. Walker would thus command both the Reserve Corps and his old division, while Liddell retained command of his division only. Brent notified Hill that Walker's troops no longer were part of his corps. Walker himself was pleased at the promotion, as he explained to his eldest daughter, Mary: "I have met all the Genls of any note here Polk D. H. Hill, Forrest, Buckner Breckinridge Cheatham, Cleburne &c &c. They all speak very confidently. Genl Bragg's health is quite delicate but he is improving. He has responsibilities and cares enough to break down a hearty man. He has been very kind & friendly to me. He and Genl Mackall & Col Rutlege whom I have met here are old classmates. I have a separate command, Genl Liddell's (another classmate) Division and mine united & called the Reserve." Liddell, himself a man of extreme passions, was unhappy about the new arrangement: "General Walker was well-known to be a crack-brained fire-eater, always captious or caviling about something whimsical and changeable and hardly reliable. I was very much annoyed by such a man in business relations, though otherwise I regarded him as honorable and high-strung in all engagements. We were very friendly but constantly differed in our views." When Liddell asked Mackall how the appointment had come about, the chief of staff responded, "It was done contrary to my wishes." If nothing else, Bragg in his elevation of Walker had at least found an officer anxious to fight without any reservations whatsoever.[15]

While he pondered his options, Bragg during the day received several new items of information. Hazen's morning bombardment and Wilder's languid afternoon shelling made it clear that Federal units remained just across the river. More important was a scout's report about Federal activity on the previous day in Wills Valley and on Sand Mountain. Neither the scout's identity nor the time his report reached Bragg is extant. Nevertheless, his information was stunning in its accuracy. The scout correctly placed Davis's and Johnson's divisions of the Twentieth Corps in Wills Valley and noted the crossing of Sheridan's and Baird's divisions at Bridgeport. Most chilling of all, the scout accurately described the progress of 10,000 Federal infantrymen across Sand Mountain, including their bridge-building at Gunter's Mill. According to the scout, the head of the Federal column had reached Lookout Valley southwest of Trenton by the end of the previous day. At one point he had encountered a Federal regiment on Sand Mountain whose commander inquired about the route to Johnson's Crook and boasted that the railroad to Atlanta was within his grasp. The scout's report was duly entered into Brent's diary: "Reports thicken & confirm the belief that the enemy has passed to our left in force." Therefore it was all the more imperative that Wheeler's horsemen be more active. In a message to Wheeler, Brent laid out the requirement plainly: "We are still without definite information as to the positions & designs of the enemy. It is absolutely necessary we should have it. Use every possible effort to obtain it, and forward at once." Shortly thereafter, Brent was even more direct: "The General Commanding directs that you will without delay move with your command into the [Wills/Lookout] valley, drive in the enemy's pickets and assail him, so as to develop his designs, strength and position." In case Wheeler was hesitant, Brent closed, "This must be done even at the sacrifice of troops."[16]

As the day progressed, Bragg continued to assess his situation. Somehow, army headquarters had come into possession of a 26 August 1863 issue of the *New York Times*, which contained several articles of interest. One piece, copied from the *Chicago Evening Journal* of an earlier date, clearly explained most of the Federal movements that had already occurred. According to the reporter, writing from Winchester on 18 August, Crittenden's Twenty-First Corps would face Chattanooga and cross the Tennessee River just above the city so as to interpose between Buckner's and Bragg's forces. Meanwhile, Thomas's Fourteenth Corps and McCook's Twentieth Corps would cross below Chattanooga and drive on Rome. Bragg would be forced to withdraw southward in haste, probably not halting until reaching Atlanta. Johnston was believed to be at Atlanta already, so the Army of the Cumberland would try to strike Bragg before he and Johnston could unite. A separate article, in the same *New York Times*, explained Burnside's role: "It was absolutely necessary, however, that the exposed left flank of Rosecrans' army should be covered while he makes a right swinging move on Chattanooga. This is the whole purpose of the co-operation of Burnside's column." During the day Bragg forwarded the relevant snippets from the *Times* to Richmond. He explained that the Federal plan described in the newspapers mirrored in most respects what he was actually seeing develop on the ground. Only Crittenden's movements had not yet fully materialized; otherwise, the newspapers spoke the truth. The scout's statement placing McCook and Thomas in Wills/Lookout Valley corroborated the paper's account. Bragg argued that his decision to bring Buckner's command nearer to Chattanooga had thwarted the Federal designs. Although he gave no details about his next move, he confidently predicted, "The movements of Buckner have frustrated one part of the plan. We shall strive now to turn it to our advantage." Yet, pending a response from Hill, Bragg remained undecided on a specific offensive response.[17]

While he waited to hear from Hill, Bragg busied himself with lesser matters. The one piece of information lacking was the exact location of Crittenden's Twenty-First Corps. He could see the Federals demonstrating across the river in small numbers, but the towering heights of Walden's Ridge screened many dangerous possibilities. Troubled by some vague statements in the scout's report that appeared to refer to the area north of Trenton, he enjoined Mauldin to have his scouts be more specific in naming locations and roads in the future. He raised other concerns with Polk. Polk's signalmen had for some time operated a station atop the west brow of Lookout Mountain that transmitted to Chattanooga via a relay station on Raccoon Mountain. As that station was growing in importance, he ordered Polk to detail an infantry company to protect it. He also instructed Polk to establish a closer connection between Hindman's camps at McFarland's Spring and Smith's Brigade near the foot of Lookout Mountain. Finally, he ordered Polk to maintain a two-man guard over the army's pontoons still lying in the river. After issuing so many minute instructions to his senior corps commander, Bragg also promised to act on charges Polk recently had leveled against Hindman for insubordination. Essentially a foolish argument between Hindman and Polk's staff over a camping site, the dispute hardly merited official notice in view of the situation facing the Army of Tennessee. Nevertheless, Bragg promised that action would be taken as "soon as the exigencies of the service will permit." He ended the day by ordering Buckner to move his corps southward on the following day to the village of Ooltewah on the railroad between Cleveland and Tyner's Station. In an effort to hold as much territory as possible, he instructed Buckner to leave one brigade on the Hiwassee River at Charleston to watch for Burnside.[18]

In beleaguered Chattanooga and its environs, everyone continued to wait for something to happen. According to *Mobile Tribune* correspondent Samuel Reid, Chattanooga itself was a virtual ghost town, with only a few commercial establishments open for business. The much reduced *Chattanooga Daily Rebel,* however, still struggled to publish a one-page edition. Soldiers still manned the forts on the river, but otherwise the city streets were deserted. In Polk's Corps, several hundred detailed men returned to their regiments. The sounds of the various Federal bombardments echoed throughout Polk's encampments but were no longer seen as indicators of coming events. Only in Strahl's Brigade, occupying the mouth of Lookout Valley, was there any sign of concern, and that was simply a requirement for soldiers to remain close at hand in camp. Still, most men were of similar belief as Pvt. Henry Wulff, who wrote to a friend, "We are expecting a very hard fought battle to take place shortly up in this vicinity." Farther upstream, all remained quiet in Hill's Corps as well, but veteran soldiers saw ominous signs that the calm would soon be shattered. Although he may have been in the area, Breckinridge apparently had not resumed formal command of his division, leaving Helm in charge at Tyner's Station. In Cleburne's Division, coordination problems arose with Forrest's cavalrymen, as the latter slowly relieved the infantry regiments holding the defensive positions along the river. The Seventeenth Texas Cavalry (Dismounted) regiment spent the day moving its camp to a new location, described by one diarist as "a pleasant camping place; rather too much so to stay long." In Walker's new Reserve Corps, elements of Gist's Brigade continued to depart for Rome. Across the army, from Tyner's Station to Chattanooga Valley, many soldiers continued to attend religious services and impromptu camp meetings. In at least two commands, visitors from home brought much-needed stocks of new clothing and delicacies far removed from army rations.[19]

Troops on Bragg's flanks continued to change position on 5 September. The Twenty-Fourth South Carolina Infantry regiment of Gist's Brigade reached Rome around sunrise. Several mountain ranges west of Rome, Wheeler finally joined Wharton at the hamlet of Alpine. Harrison's Brigade of Wharton's Division also reached Alpine, joining Crews's Brigade already picketing Lookout Mountain. Not yet in receipt of Bragg's orders to push beyond Lookout Mountain, Wheeler contented himself with blocking the roads at Henderson's, Neal's, Tap's, Standifer's, Leavell's, and Davis's Gaps with trees and large rocks. Such barriers would do little to halt a large Federal force and would hinder any offensive movement by Wheeler's men. Clearly, Wheeler saw no prospect of any movement beyond Lookout Mountain, aggressive or otherwise. He would send scouts forward, but would not probe the Federal positions in a serious way. Wheeler's other division, Martin's, remained all day at LaFayette, still gathering its limited strength. East of Alpine, a detachment from Hagan's Brigade bringing horses to Martin's command reached Summerville. There rumors of Federals nearby caused the detachment to depart hastily after dark toward LaFayette. Far to the southwest, the Eighth Confederate Cavalry regiment, also of Hagan's Brigade, finally left its lonely picket posts on the Tennessee River and headed northeast in search of the Army of Tennessee. In the north, on Bragg's other flank, Buckner's Corps was also in motion. Although Buckner himself during the day moved only along the railroad from Charleston to Cleveland, his troops continued to sidle westward toward the Tennessee River. Two brigades of Preston's Division pushed close to Harrison. Ten miles to the north, Stewart's Division halted around Savannah Church. Left increasingly isolated was Trigg's Brigade, still gamely holding the line of the Hiwassee River at Charleston. There Trigg's men were so bereft of support that they were forced to forage locally in order to have any rations at all.[20]

During the evening, new information caused Bragg to alter his assessment. First, a courier arrived around 11:00 P.M., carrying Hill's response to Bragg's suggestion of an offensive movement. Although Hill's note is not extant, its content can be inferred from the accompanying response of Cleburne, which has survived. Late to receive Hill's query, Cleburne generally favored a strike across the river, but with serious reservations. Most notably, the near impossibility of crossing his artillery would prevent him from overcoming Federal defensive positions. Pending new orders, Cleburne would continue to withdraw his division from the river to campsites around Ooltewah. He noted further that two of his regiments had not yet been relieved from their picket posts on the river. Clearly Cleburne was skeptical of any river crossing, and Hill no doubt added skepticism of his own. At any rate, Mackall quickly acknowledged receipt of the messages and on Bragg's behalf approved Cleburne's continued movement toward Ooltewah. Mackall's telegram was brief, probably because army headquarters now was wrestling with more troubling information. Three Federal prisoners, including telegrapher George Peirce, had just arrived in Chattanooga. During the night they were brought to army headquarters, where Bragg himself led the interrogation. Peirce would later claim that he feigned ignorance and around midnight was dispatched to the guardhouse. Perhaps he succeeded in his subterfuge, but at least two privates were captured with him, and they may have been more talkative. Certainly the Federals knew of the movements of Crittenden's three divisions, which they had inadvertently led toward Lookout Valley. No matter who gave up the secret, Bragg now knew more about the location of the Twenty-First Corps than he had had earlier in the day. On Bragg's direction, Brent telegraphed both Hill and Buckner to come to army headquarters as soon as possible.[21]

Bragg's information that a significant Federal force was on the verge of debouching into the northern reaches of Lookout Valley was correct. Early on the morning of Sunday, 6 September, Wood's First Division, Twenty-First Corps, resumed its march eastward from Whiteside. Although only Buell's and Harker's brigades were present, Wood's orders required him to push into Lookout Valley and probe toward Chattanooga. In the lead, Harker placed the Third Kentucky Infantry regiment in skirmish order at the head of his column and began to advance not long after sunrise. Almost instantly the Kentuckians encountered opposing skirmishers, most likely some of Mauldin's cavalrymen. With a large numerical advantage, Harker made slow but steady progress. Gradually Running Water Canyon widened to reveal the imposing Lookout Mountain, rising far above some intermediate hills. Approximately five miles from Whiteside, Harker reached Lookout Valley itself. The Confederate skirmishers continued their fighting withdrawal but changed their direction to the northeast. Harker slowly followed them, and Buell followed Harker. As the division entered the main valley, Wood and others noticed a signal station high on Lookout Mountain furiously transmitting messages over their heads to another station on Raccoon Mountain. Still, Harker pushed on for two more miles. Crossing the Tennessee state line, in early afternoon he reached Wauhatchie, junction of the Nashville & Chattanooga and Wills Valley Railroads. There, on the bank of Black Creek, the Federals stopped and assumed a defensive posture. Confederate skirmishers remained visible, and Wood believed many more Confederates were concealed on the lower slope of Lookout Mountain. The more he assessed the ground around the railroad station, the more he believed it to be utterly indefensible with the force he then commanded. Nor was there any source of reinforcement nearby—Wood and his small command were completely alone.[22]

Had he been free to select his own route into Lookout Valley, Crittenden would probably have chosen a different path for the Twenty-First Corps than Running Water Canyon. On the previous day, he had sought permission to follow Reynolds's route from Shell Mound on a rough track called the Nickajack Road. Told that Brannan's troops had been assigned to follow Reynolds, Crittenden was forced to use Running Water Canyon at least as far as Whiteside. At that hamlet the Murphy's Hollow Road climbed out of the canyon for three miles to a junction with the Nickajack Road on top of Sand Mountain. Preferring to remain near the Fourteenth Corps in such forbidding terrain, Crittenden had sent Palmer's and Van Cleve's divisions up the Murphy's Hollow Road from Whiteside, while Wood met the requirement for a reconnaissance toward Chattanooga. Like Wood, Palmer and Van Cleve each lacked a brigade, making it even more important to remain within supporting distance of Fourteenth Corps units. While Wood began his advance in Running Water

Canyon, Palmer sent Cruft's and Grose's brigades up Murphy's Hollow. The road was clogged with fallen trees, slowing the advance. Behind Palmer's men, Van Cleve's brigades entered Murphy's Hollow as well. Crittenden, who had spent the night at Shell Mound, soon appeared with his staff and quickly made his way to the head of the column. Shortly after 9:00 A.M., he reached the junction of the Murphy's Hollow and Nickajack Roads on top of Sand Mountain. There Crittenden found the Nickajack Road filled with regiments of Brannan's division. Momentarily unable to move farther, Crittenden at 9:35 A.M. wrote a long note to Garfield. In it, he described his location, passed along some information from Wood about Confederate cavalry detachments at Kelly's Ferry, and stated that he was forwarding a message to Burnside that had inadvertently been sent to him. Other than the fact that the cavalry regiment he had requested had not reported, Crittenden gave no indication he saw any difficulties ahead.[23]

Finding Brannan's men filling the Nickajack Road, Crittenden halted Palmer and Van Cleve, whose soldiers sprawled on the roadside in Murphy's Hollow and filled their canteens at Murphy's Spring. Brannan, meanwhile, was in no hurry. With Van Derveer's Third Brigade still struggling up the western side of Sand Mountain with the division's trains, he remained at Gordon's Coal Mines to await their arrival. At the road junction where Crittenden and Palmer waited, Connell's First Brigade was very near the eastern brow of the mountain where the Nickajack Road dropped precipitously into Slygo Valley. Separated from the much larger Lookout Valley by an intervening ridge, Slygo Valley was the location of William Cole's extensive plantation and Cole's Academy. Reynolds's division had passed through the Slygo Valley two days previously, on its way to Trenton, so Cole was hardly surprised when Connell's Federals appeared. Behind Connell, Croxton's Second Brigade slowly began its descent to the same area. Eventually, Croxton's men also established campsites on Cole's property. Glad to have the dry and dusty Sand Mountain behind them, they found themselves in an idyllic setting, with good water and no Confederates to disturb them. Brannan remained atop Sand Mountain to greet Van Derveer's men and the struggling trains. Exhausted by the climb, Van Derveer's troops halted soon after reaching the summit. The attenuation of Brannan's division furnished an opening for Crittenden to descend the mountain as well. Palmer led Cruft's First Brigade into the Nickajack Road and thence down the track into the Slygo Valley. Grose's Third Brigade followed Cruft. Because Brannan's men had already appropriated the best campsites near Cole's Spring, Palmer's two brigades were forced to continue to Cole's Academy. Crittenden himself remained at the junction of Murphy's Hollow and Nickajack Roads, where he established Twenty-First Corps headquarters. Van Cleve's division did not climb out of Murphy's Hollow but remained dispersed along the road on both sides of Murphy's Spring.[24]

As Crittenden worked to untangle Palmer and Van Cleve from Brannan's command on top of Sand Mountain, Wood at Wauhatchie was becoming increasingly nervous. Resistance had noticeably stiffened, the road beyond Wauhatchie climbed through heavily wooded terrain, and the signalmen far above him continued their inscrutable conversations over his head. To Wood, all signs pointed toward a strong Confederate force ready to pounce on his small command. After considering his predicament for an hour, at 2:00 P.M. he offered corps headquarters some advice: "As my position here, if the enemy is in force in Chattanooga, is hazardous, all the routes leading here should be promptly explored, and some part of the force with General Crittenden should be advanced at once, at least in supporting distance." Told that Crittenden probably was in Lookout Valley eight miles south of Wauhatchie, Wood sent his note in that direction. His only means of communication were courier lines manned by a company of the Thirty-Ninth Indiana Mounted Infantry regiment that stretched back to Whiteside and southward down Lookout Valley. Unknown to Wood, Twenty-First Corps headquarters was at neither place, but on Sand Mountain at the junction of Murphy's Hollow and Nickajack Roads. Growing more alarmed when no reply from Crittenden arrived, Wood wrote again at 4:00 P.M. By that time he had learned that Crittenden's headquarters was still on Sand Mountain, so he repeated his earlier information in a dispatch sent via Whiteside. Noting that he had been skirmishing with the Confederates all day, he again asked that Twenty-First Corps units be moved within supporting distance. He also suggested that the direct road from Trenton to Wauhatchie might be a better route by which to bring that assistance. Staring at the Confederate signal flags waving above him on Lookout Mountain, Wood remarked, "*You* don't know what *I* am going to *do*, for I'll be damned if I know myself."[25]

Just before 5:00 P.M., Capt. John Leavell of Company G, Thirty-Ninth Indiana Mounted Infantry regiment, arrived at Crittenden's headquarters with Wood's first message. Crittenden responded quickly, acknowledging that Rosecrans's order to reconnoiter toward Chattanooga had been accomplished, but he gave no orders to withdraw from Wauhatchie. If Wood needed to withdraw, he should retreat via Lookout Valley toward Trenton. Any decision to fall back would be Wood's alone; no one would be moving toward him. Although Captain Leavell reported that Wood had been skirmishing with the Confederates all day, Crittenden was skeptical because Wood had not mentioned it in his 2:00 P.M. note. Dismissing Leavell to return to Wood, Crittenden next wrote to Garfield explaining what he had done. He admitted that Wood's position was "quite hazardous," but deserters' statements indicated that only Strahl's Brigade was in front. Crittenden closed by stating that if Wood withdrew, the decision would be his alone. Having absolved himself of any consequences that might develop, Crittenden sent the dispatch by courier to Reynolds at Trenton for forwarding to Rosecrans. He remained at the Nickajack/Murphy's Hollow Road junction on top of Sand Mountain. At 7:00 P.M., Wood's second dispatch arrived. Capt. Percival Oldershaw responded for Crittenden: "The general commanding appreciates your position as hazardous, and urges the greatest vigilance, as he is in no position to bring on an engagement in the absence of all advices from department headquarters, where I have sent all information promptly." In an effort to reassure Wood, Oldershaw repeated the deserters' statements that only Strahl's Brigade confronted Wood. He noted that one of Van Cleve's regiments was at Whiteside, that both Palmer's and Brannan's divisions were at the Cole plantation, and that Reynolds's division was at Trenton. Wood therefore knew where all the friendly units were, but still there were no orders for him to withdraw or for anyone else to move to his aid.[26]

As night fell at Wauhatchie, Wood's troops prepared to spend the evening in close proximity to whatever Confederate forces were concealed in the woods beyond Black Creek. Wood himself, however, was not prepared to accept passively the disaster he fully expected to occur the next day. During the afternoon he had interrogated citizens and a prisoner taken by his skirmishers. Collectively, their statements indicated that Cheatham's Division lay just beyond the jutting point of Lookout Mountain, and Hindman's Division was only a few miles beyond Cheatham. The frenetic activity of the Confederate signalmen on the heights, which continued after dark with lights replacing flags, clearly indicated that Wood's position and strength had been well known in Chattanooga for several hours. In the gathering darkness, sounds coming from beyond the Federal picket line were interpreted by several officers as Confederate attack preparations. Unlike Crittenden, who seemed unwilling to move without positive orders from Rosecrans, Wood believed he needed to act decisively to save his command from potential annihilation. Accordingly, he decided to withdraw his two brigades under cover of darkness to a more defensible position. At 10:00 P.M., Buell's and Harker's troops stealthily moved to the road, formed column, and departed, leaving their pickets in place along the creek for two more hours. The division trains did not encumber the column, having been left with the corps trains near Whiteside. No Confederates molested the marching Federals, who halted on a range of small hills approximately two miles south of Wauhatchie. There Wood's troops covered both the road to Whiteside through Running Water Canyon and the main road through Lookout Valley toward Trenton. If he were to be attacked there, Wood could make a fighting withdrawal in either direction. With their minds now more at ease, Wood and his men lay down to rest for the remainder of the night in their new position.[27]

Wood's reconnaissance toward Chattanooga was not the only offensive movement made by the Federals on 6 September. Negley's division was under orders to probe south from its camps at Brown's Spring toward a crossing of

Lookout Mountain known as Stephens's Gap. Unaware that the division would soon depart Brown's Spring, Stanley early in the morning sent the Eighteenth Ohio Infantry regiment beyond Trenton to climb Lookout Mountain above Payne's [Sitton's] Mill. The regiment scaled the mountain, drove off a handful of Confederate pickets, and scouted briefly on the plateau before returning to camp. They found the camps of their brigade and division empty. Just before noon Negley led the division southward with Beatty's First Brigade at the head of the column. Reaching Cureton's Mill a little after 1:00 P.M., Negley continued his march to the large plantation of Benjamin Easley. Easley, sixty-three, was the largest slave owner in Dade County, and his property included a store, blacksmith shop, and private racetrack. Although Negley initially planned to leave one of his brigades at Easley's, pressure from Sheridan's division on his heels caused him to continue his march southward. A little more than a mile beyond Easley's, the road to Stephens's Gap diverged eastward toward the great horseshoe bend of Lookout Mountain called Johnson's Crook. Near the intersection, at the junction of Lookout and Hurricane Creeks a few miles short of the mountain, Negley posted Stanley's and Sirwell's brigades and established division headquarters. Still in the lead, Beatty's brigade turned into the narrow side valley and headed for the steep mountain wall two miles to the east. Arriving at Hugh McKaig's house at the foot of the mountain at 5:00 P.M., Beatty sent the Forty-Second Indiana Infantry regiment cautiously up the rough track toward the crest. Halfway up they were fired upon by Confederate skirmishers, who wounded one of the Federals in the leg. With night approaching, Beatty withdrew to the foot of the mountain.[28]

Behind Negley, other units were also on the move. Forced to follow Negley's troops all the way from the river, Sheridan cursed the delays preventing him from joining his own Twentieth Corps. Disputes over campsites and slow wagon trains showcased the widely divergent personalities of the impetuous Sheridan and the affable Negley. Now, with Negley's troops once more moving forward, Sheridan quickly put his division on the road. Riding ahead, he told Negley that he wanted Easley's plantation for his own use, so Negley continued southward. The end of the day found Sheridan's division encamped along the road stretching from James Cureton's property on Lookout Creek south to Easley's. Still on Sand Mountain, Baird's division was just beginning to follow the route blazed by Negley and Sheridan several days earlier. With their trains finally out of the way, Baird spent the day lifting his own artillery and wagons up the western side of Sand Mountain. The passage of thousands of troops had not improved the road, forcing Baird to deploy infantrymen to assist the struggling teams. Amid clouds of swirling dust and sulphurous oaths from drivers, the guns, wagons, and a herd of cattle slowly crawled up the mountainside. In some cases battery commanders used ten horses per gun to reach the crest. Nevertheless, Baird's men gained the summit before dark. They then continued along the road to Warren's [Gunter's] Mill, where they halted and camped at the improvised bridge constructed earlier by Negley. Ahead of Baird, Thomas and his entourage crossed to the eastern side of Sand Mountain and established corps headquarters at Brown's Spring. Of all of the Fourteenth Corps divisions, only Reynolds's did not move on 6 September. While King's and Turchin's brigades foraged vigorously in the tiny courthouse hamlet of Trenton, Reynolds himself attended preaching in a local church. During the day, the distant booming of cannon could be heard in the direction of Chattanooga.[29]

Twenty-three miles south of Reynolds at Trenton and fifteen miles south of Negley at Johnson's Crook, the Twentieth Corps spent a quiet Sunday at Valley Head. During the morning McCook forwarded to Garfield a statement from Crook recounting the testimony of an elderly civilian named Crow. Encountered during Crook's earlier foray into Broomtown Valley, the old man offered secondhand information that the Army of Tennessee was under orders to withdraw toward Atlanta. Otherwise, McCook spent a remarkably relaxed day. No orders forecast departure from William Winston's increasingly ravaged plantation, so the men of Davis's and Johnson's divisions spent the day in various pleasurable pursuits. In Post's First Brigade of Davis's command, there was preaching in the regiments during the morning and more preaching at division headquarters in the afternoon. According to Lt. Chesley Mosman, the surge of religious fervor was probably generated by the presence of Marietta Davis. Another junior officer, Leroy Mayfield, recorded in his diary, "Day passes drearily away, as always does the Sabbath in the army." In a letter to his wife in Wisconsin, Heg also noted the presence of Marietta Davis: "She is a young, fine intelligent Woman but not handsome." In Johnson's Second Division, letter writing, preaching, dress parade, and a band concert helped many pass the time on a very hot day. Col. Thomas Harrison had no illusions about the loyal mountain people who lived in the vicinity: "I have seldom found so degraded a population as lives in this country." Pvt. Alpheus Bloomfield explained to his sister that the army's morale was high: "You may look for stirring news from this portion of the army, before the coming forty days." The news was already bad for Lt. Philander Miller, who had his shoulder straps cut off publicly and received a dishonorable discharge for refusing to take his company on picket.[30]

Alex McCook was in no hurry to leave his pleasant camp at Winston's. He needed Sheridan's division to join the corps, but, even more important, the Cavalry Corps was slated to lead the advance, not the Twentieth Corps. McCook's role was to serve as a strong support to Stanley's horsemen as they pushed beyond Lookout Mountain to threaten Bragg's supply line to Atlanta and force the evacuation of Chattanooga. Although the failure of the Bridgeport bridge and the difficulty in crossing Sand Mountain had put everything behind schedule, Rosecrans still expected Stanley to initiate his part of the plan quickly. Stanley, however, was reluctant to begin his expedition, especially after learning of the army's delays. He lacked Minty's brigade, and his trains with their escorts were still toiling across Sand Mountain. In addition, he lacked tools for railroad wrecking and was unsure what support the Twentieth Corps might provide. Thus his cavalrymen remained relatively inactive on 6 September. In Edward McCook's First Division, most of the day was spent in search of forage. Although some wagons had arrived on the previous night, most of the division's trains and the Fourth Indiana Cavalry regiment were still on Sand Mountain. According to a man in the Second Michigan Cavalry regiment, food was scarce and the sick list lengthening, although the unit's mail did arrive. Other than dispatching a few scouts to the top of Lookout Mountain, McCook did little more than send a few prisoners to corps headquarters. In Crook's Second Division, the day's work consisted solely of moving Long's camps several miles southward to escape Davis's marauding infantrymen. Meanwhile, the Second Kentucky Cavalry regiment continued to plod forward on Sand Mountain with Crook's train and the Chicago Board of Trade Battery. At 10:00 P.M., Stanley summarized his situation for Garfield. Like Alex McCook, he offered the testimony of a "reliable" citizen that Bragg's army had been ordered to retreat. As for his own inertia, Stanley blamed the delay on the slow movement of his supply trains.[31]

With seven Federal divisions in Lookout Valley visible to Confederate pickets from Wauhatchie to Valley Head, the deception force's mission was complete. In fact, the deception force was now itself being deceived. During the previous night some of Wilder's men stationed opposite Chattanooga had heard considerable hammering inside the town. Coupled with the pontoons still lashed to the riverbank and the appearance of cavalry at the upstream fords, a credible case for a Confederate crossing could be made. In response, Wilder's command had spent a sleepless night under arms and Wagner sent half his brigade to the valley floor. By 6:00 A.M., Hazen began to doubt that a crossing was imminent, but prudence required covering all contingencies. Having already ordered all trains up Walden's Ridge, he instructed Wilder and Wagner to block all routes into the Sequatchie Valley and told Minty to be prepared to return to Walden's Ridge if threatened. By 10:00 A.M., Hazen was certain that there would be no Confederate attack, so he turned to the question of whether he or Wagner should be the true commander of the "U.S. Forces, Left Flank." In long letters to both Garfield and Goddard he argued that he outranked Wagner by as many as twenty numbers but would return to a subordinate position if necessary. While Hazen defended his seniority, Wilder and Wagner began to notice significant new activity in front of them. It appeared that a Confederate division-sized unit with its trains was moving from the vicinity of Tyner's Station toward Chattanooga. Recent deserters from Breckinridge's Division reported that their command was the only reinforcement Bragg had received. Also, Wagner somehow discovered in early afternoon that Wood's division had reached the vicinity of Wauhatchie. Wagner had been preparing to return his two regiments to the top of Walden's Ridge, but in light of Wood's advance, he bombarded Chattanooga with sections of the Tenth and Eighteenth Indiana Batteries. Confederate response was minimal, but Wagner could do no more.[32]

In the army's rear, reinforcing units continued to move forward. Detached from Wilder's command, the men of the Ninety-Second Illinois Mounted Infantry regiment walked their horses across the wildly swaying spans at Bridgeport and marched to Shell Mound. There, they explored Nickajack Cave, taking their band inside to bounce patriotic airs off the cavern's walls. In the Sequatchie Valley, Dick's Second Brigade of Van Cleve's division resumed its march toward the Bridgeport crossing. During the day, the Twenty-Second Michigan Infantry regiment, coming by train from Nashville, reached Bridgeport and camped on Long Island. At the same time both Whitaker's First Brigade and Reid's Second Brigade of Steedman's First Division concentrated at Tullahoma and Estill Springs before heading over the Cumberland Plateau to Stevenson. Meanwhile, the 108th Ohio Infantry regiment left the Nashville garrison and took a train for Bridgeport. At Larkinsville, Morgan reported that most of his Second Division was also heading for Stevenson. Tillson's First Brigade reached Bellefonte by nightfall. A day's march behind Tillson, Daniel McCook left his bivouac at Hurricane Creek and headed for Larkinsville. He soon became distracted when his column passed the ancestral home of Frank Gurley, the alleged killer of his older brother Robert in 1862. Throughout their march, McCook's men had been seeking an opportunity to gain revenge and had treated a number of civilians badly along the way. Now, McCook had another opportunity for vengeance, and he sent Maj. James Holmes and a detail from the Fifty-Second Ohio Infantry regiment to destroy all Gurley property within reach. By the time Holmes was finished, the orgy of destruction had consumed, by one soldier's account, twenty-five structures, an orchard, and all of the fences within sight. Holmes then rejoined the brigade, which halted for the night west of Larkinsville. Meanwhile, the Eighty-Sixth Illinois Infantry regiment of McCook's command finally crossed the Alabama state line on its way to Huntsville.[33]

With more than half of his divisions beyond Sand Mountain, it was time for Rosecrans to join them. Slow to leave Long Island Cove, headquarters consumed the remainder of the day crossing Sand Mountain and descending to Brown's Spring. From there, Rosecrans rode ahead to Trenton, arriving around sunset. First Sgt. Newton Parker, who saw the party pass, noted in his diary that the army commander "looks well." Although it would be some time before the remainder of the staff arrived, and the First Ohio Battalion Sharpshooters would not straggle in until the next day, Rosecrans began work immediately. Stanley reported that Wharton's Division held the Lookout Mountain passes, and that a citizen had heard that Bragg had been ordered to retreat. Contradictory information came from Crittenden, who provided deserters' testimony that Johnston was in Chattanooga with heavy reinforcements and that Buckner was at Cleveland. The deserters placed Bragg's strength at 50,000 men, as did a scout who arrived during the evening. All reports except Stanley's indicated that Bragg would probably make a stand at Chattanooga. In response to the news, Rosecrans issued a flurry of orders. At 9:30 P.M., Garfield told Sheridan to remain in Lookout Valley to support the Fourteenth Corps at Stephens's Gap. Thirty minutes later, he instructed Stanley to proceed with his push toward the Western & Atlantic Railroad: "The enemy appear [*sic*] to be preparing for making a stand at Chattanooga, and it is of the utmost importance that his line of communication be broken." At 11:30 P.M., Garfield approved Crittenden's dispositions and ordered him to send Wood "to feel the enemy at the point of Lookout Mountain, and find out certainly what he is doing." In contrast to what he told Stanley, Garfield informed Crittenden that "there is considerable evidence today that the enemy is preparing to fall back on Dalton, and has already moved part of his force." Rosecrans's nightly report to Halleck indicated still another possibility: "Enemy still in force in Chattanooga, threatening to cross the river."[34]

If Lookout Mountain was a formidable barrier to the Army of the Cumberland, it was a powerful defensive shield for the Army of Tennessee. By the early morning hours of 6 September, Bragg saw clearly that the shield was in grave danger of being breached, placing his supply line at risk. Scout reports and interrogation of the captured telegraph party had finally clarified the location of Rosecrans's three primary army corps. There were large concentrations of Federal troops at Valley Head, Trenton, and Running Water Canyon, all poised to push across Lookout Mountain. With major Federal elements as near to Atlanta as the Army of Tennessee, the city itself was potentially in peril. While he awaited the arrival of his senior commanders, Bragg at 3:00 A.M. sought additional reinforcements from Johnston. Unaware that Johnston was absent in Montgomery, he wrote, "Hasten a Division of Infantry to Atlanta if you can spare it only for a few days. It will save that depot and give me time to defeat the enemy's plans." Simultaneously, Bragg informed Davis of his request. Hardee, commanding at Morton during Johnston's absence, forwarded the request but opposed the transfer. Johnston agreed in principle with Hardee, but in light of the recent Vicksburg fiasco he was unwilling to risk being blamed for another city's loss. Consequently, he telegraphed Bragg, "I can spare no troops without risking Mobile; but if it is to save Atlanta I will send two small brigades for a few

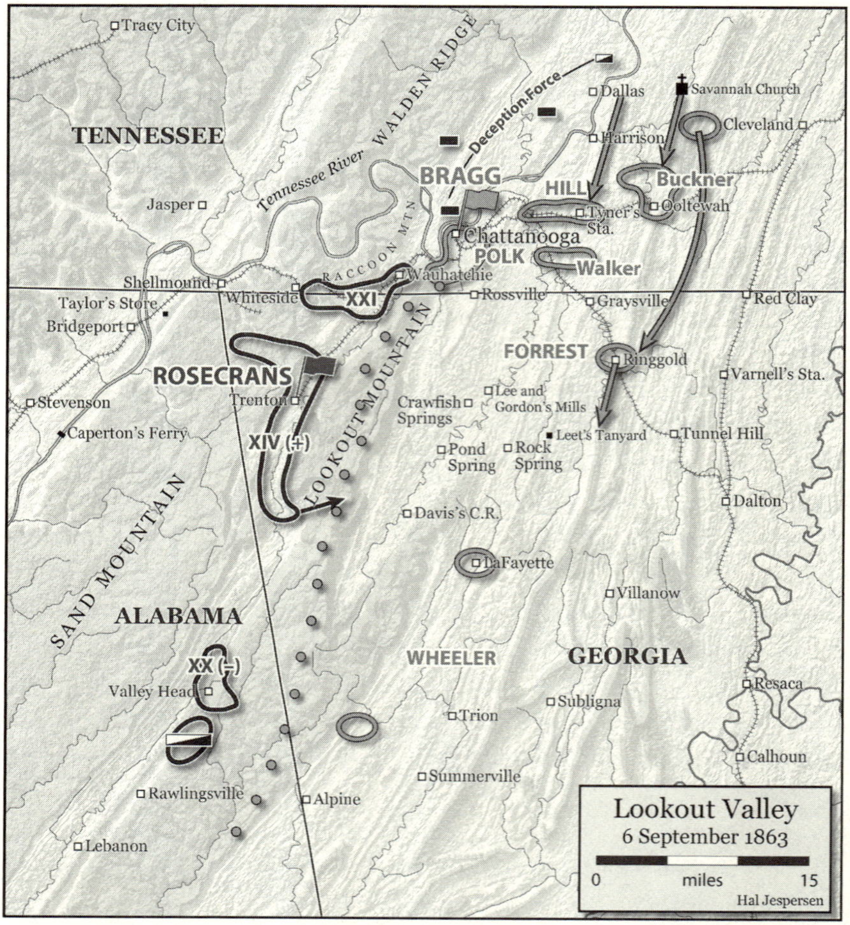

days. Reply and tell me the plan to be defeated." At the same time, he sought Richmond's permission to make the loan. Before receiving an answer, Johnston told Hardee to send the brigades of Brig. Gen. John Gregg and Brig. Gen. Evander McNair to the Army of Tennessee. Hardee dutifully notified Bragg that the two brigades, approximately 2,500 men, would soon be on their way. The orders sending Gregg and McNair to Atlanta specified that no field transportation was to go with them. Johnston was willing to loan soldiers to Bragg in an emergency, but not wagons.[35]

At some point between 3:00 A.M. and 9:00 A.M. on 6 September Bragg apparently met with his senior commanders. No record of this meeting has come to light, but the previous night's call for Hill and Buckner to rush to headquarters, Buckner's presence later that day in Chattanooga, Hill's apparent absence from his headquarters during the day, Forrest's early morning movements toward Rome, and Brent's early rising all point to such a meeting. At the conference Bragg offered his assessment of the available intelligence. It was obvious that the Federal force at Valley Head was nearer to Rome than the Army of Tennessee was. If the railroad was to be saved, the army would have to move southward from Chattanooga. Bragg had long anticipated making the Federals commit themselves before he moved against them, and that Chattanooga would have to be evacuated in the process. Now the wire party's disclosure of the location of the Twenty-First Corps brought the entire Federal array into focus; it was time to act, and act rapidly. Beginning at 9:00 A.M. urgent telegrams flowed from army headquarters. In the belief that Rome was in the most immediate danger, Brent sent three telegrams to States Gist, whose brigade was near the threatened spot. Brent's instructions were peremptory: "Destroy all bridges but one, and defend that; if unable to hold it, destroy it, and retire towards Atlanta." Bragg himself wired Davis: "Rosecrans' army has certainly crossed Tennessee River. Reported now as moving toward Rome. We shall move on him promptly." Bragg admitted that he did not know Burnside's location but stated that he could only deal with one Federal army at a time. Knowing that Davis would not favor the loss of Chattanooga, he explained, "We are obliged to make great sacrifices and abandon territory; in striking at one we must open the country to the other. Atlanta should be strengthened as far as possible." In another telegram, Bragg promised assistance to Governor Brown: "Will do all I can to equip your troops, every available man should be ready to defend Atlanta."[36]

Bragg's admission that he had lost track of Burnside's command highlighted the need to dispose of the last remnants of Buckner's old department. Most of Buckner's troops were resting near Savannah Church, northeast of Chattanooga, but he remained in charge of three brigades around Charleston, Alfred Jackson's scattered units on the railroad south of Bristol, and John Frazer's lonely garrison at Cumberland Gap. First, Buckner's two mobile divisions needed to be put on the road southward to Ooltewah. At 9:00 A.M., with Buckner in Chattanooga, Mackall ordered Stewart, the senior officer present, to begin the movement. Bragg also wanted Trigg's Brigade, which Buckner had left at Charleston, to be moved to Ooltewah as well. No mention was made of Hodge's cavalry command, which guarded Hiwassee fords eastward into the mountains. Momentarily, Scott's Brigade beyond the Hiwassee was the only unit in contact with any of Burnside's units. That day Jackson's remnants were formally incorporated into Samuel Jones's Department of Western Virginia, as was Frazer's command at Cumberland Gap, although Buckner was unaware of it. Under instructions received from Bragg at the morning conference, Buckner telegraphed Jones to have Frazer evacuate the gap and withdraw toward Abingdon. Before receiving Buckner's telegram, which traveled by a roundabout route, Jones ordered Frazer to remain where he was. Later, when Buckner's message arrived at Abingdon, Jones refused to act, eventually telegraphing

Secretary of War Seddon for instructions. Believing that the reinforcements moving from Virginia to Tennessee would pass through his department, Jones strongly preferred that Frazer hold the gap. There the matter stood at the end of the day. Until the authorities at Richmond decreed otherwise, Bragg's decision to withdraw Frazer from danger was nullified. Thus Frazer continued to stand his ground in the mountain fortress with his small command.[37]

While Buckner fretted over the fate of Cumberland Gap, Brent drafted the circular that would result in the evacuation of Chattanooga. It envisioned the army moving southward in two parallel columns toward Rome. Polk was to lead the westernmost column, taking a route through Rossville Gap to a crossing of Chickamauga Creek just north of Snow Hill, past the town of LaFayette, and ultimately to Summerville. Hill's Corps was to follow Polk's route, with Polk leaving two regiments in Chattanooga and at the point of Lookout Mountain as a rear guard. Several miles to the east, Walker's Corps would move southward via Graysville and Ringgold to Maddox Gap, where it would cross to the east side of Taylor's Ridge, then continue via Subligna to Mount Hickory. Buckner's Corps was to follow Walker. The Reserve Artillery was divided between Polk and Hill, while the army's supply train moved with Walker. Forrest was to cover Polk's front with Dibrell's Brigade, while his remaining regiments guarded the army's rear as it moved south. Mauldin's Third Alabama Cavalry regiment, still guarding the north end of Lookout Valley, was to join Forrest's rear guard even though it nominally belonged to Wheeler. Wheeler's orders to probe the Federal positions at Valley Head remained unchanged. The circular specified that the troops were to carry six days' rations. Finally, all hospital patients were to be sent south of Resaca. Although the circular specified no time for execution beyond "immediately," it described an orderly movement that would ultimately place the army's major elements at Summerville and Mount Hickory, on one of the main roads to Rome. After finishing the circular, Brent joined other staff officers in dispatching more telegrams. At 10:00 A.M. he wrote to Col. Moses Wright, commanding at Atlanta: "Should the enemy advance defend Atlanta at every hazard and to the last extremity." At the same time his assistant Kinloch Falconer instructed the quartermaster at Marietta to send the army's papers to Atlanta for safekeeping.[38]

Sunday, 6 September, was a beautiful day, although the dry conditions had placed a heavy coating of dust on everything. Throughout Polk's and Walker's camps men began their morning with religious services. In Cheatham's Division, Sgt. Edwin Rennolds heard a "good" sermon by one of the company officers, while Capt. Alfred Fielder rejoiced in the baptism of three young soldiers. Similar scenes occurred in Liddell's Division, with sixteen men being baptized in Chickamauga Creek. Before the morning was far advanced, however, orders arrived for all regiments to cook three days' rations, strike their tents, and pack their baggage for a movement. Camp rumors soon began to circulate, with some men arguing that the army was headed for Rome, while others speculated about the pontoon bridge floating just above the city wharf. Claudius Wilson waxed philosophical in a letter to his wife, Kate: "We are in the midst of stirring times, making history and it becomes us only to see to it that the page which records our share in it, shall record nothing dishonorable to ourselves or disastrous to our cause." Suddenly, in late morning the work was interrupted in two brigades by an alarm. Strahl, whose brigade guarded the north end of Lookout Valley, reported, "Enemy just in front of my pickets. Send battery, if you can, immediately." What Strahl saw was the arrival of Wood's division in his front at Wauhatchie. Strahl's artillery, Stanford's Mississippi Battery, had gone to Chattanooga to receive new guns in exchange for their condemned pieces. Cheatham responded to Strahl's plea by reinforcing him with the Thirteenth Tennessee Infantry regiment of Smith's Brigade. He also sent the battery back toward the toe of Lookout Mountain, but halted it before it came into action. When the Federals at Wauhatchie remained quiescent, Cheatham concluded they were not a serious threat and returned to preparing for his division's departure from Chattanooga. Strahl, meanwhile, deployed the Thirteenth Tennessee as skirmishers in front of his position.[39]

Hill's Corps was on the road even before receipt of the movement order. Already under orders to move to new camps between Tyner's Station and Ooltewah, Cleburne's Division marched as planned during the morning and reached Tyner's by noon. There they received the order to cook three days' rations. Breckinridge's Division meanwhile left its Tyner's Station camps and marched westward toward Chattanooga. Breckinridge himself had just returned from leave and seemed not to understand the situation. Having left their wagons in Mississippi, Helm's Brigade was forced to leave its baggage at Tyner's under guard and Stovall's Brigade marched with rations for only one day. Breckinridge was told only to go to Chattanooga, but because he had not yet regained control, his three brigades moved under a welter of confusing orders from corps and army staff officers. By the end of the day, Helm's and Adams's Brigades had reached Chattanooga and camped a mile south of the town. Stovall's Brigade had followed what seemingly was Hill's intent and had continued southward to Rossville, where it halted for the night. At 6:45 P.M. Breckinridge admitted to Hill that he had no idea where his brigades were and apologized for their disarray. Circumstances were no better in Cleburne's Division, which had occupied Breckinridge's old camps at Tyner's Station for only three hours when the army's movement orders reached them. Cleburne apparently wanted to concentrate at Chickamauga Bridge then head south from there without going to Chattanooga. His intentions were thwarted when someone ordered the brigades to follow Breckinridge. By the time Cleburne discovered the error, even his artillery batteries were west of Chickamauga Creek. He halted the guns and sent them southward by his preferred route. The infantry brigades made a long, exhausting march through the town and southward beyond Breckinridge's camps. It was near midnight when the last of Cleburne's men staggered into temporary bivouacs in the shadow of Lookout Mountain.[40]

The mistakes of the day revealed serious deficiencies in both Bragg's and Hill's headquarters. Left with little to do by Bragg's reliance upon the efficient and self-effacing Brent, Chief of Staff Mackall apparently inserted himself into the minutia of divisional movements without reference to Hill. In Mackall's defense, he may have acted because of the disarray within Hill's Corps. Hill himself was new to corps command, and his troop list had recently been in great flux. Breckinridge had been absent on leave for some time, leaving Helm to manage the division's transfer to the Army of Tennessee and its recent operations. An efficient corps staff would have published a detailed movement order for the divisions, specifying order of march, time of movement, and bivouac sites. According to Hill's inspector general, Maj. Alphonso Avery, no such order was issued on 6 September. To Archer Anderson, Avery wrote, "It is absolutely essential, if the corps is expected to prove any thing else than a mob on the march, to publish an order with regard to the manner of conducting marches." To Hill himself, Avery observed, "While the divisions receive orders from Corps Hd Qrs & at the same time from Hd Qrs of the army, we will have nothing but confusion." Hill's location and activities during the day are unknown. Col. Taylor Beatty, judge of Hill's military court, left corps headquarters at 2:30 P.M., passed through Chattanooga, and ended the day near Rossville, but he made no mention of Hill. Hill clearly did not manage the day's activities or prepare for the next day's work. Exasperated by the amateurish performance, Cleburne himself complained to Hill that his infantry lacked artillery support. As for the next day's movements, "You have not prescribed the order of march. Must I or Breckinridge move first? Please inform me on this point and should our trains proceed or follow the troops." With an active campaign looming, clearly Hill's Corps had much work to do before it could be considered an efficient part of the Army of Tennessee.[41]

Buckner's Corps fared little better than Hill's on 6 September. The corps was even more of an ad hoc formation than Hill's, having been created only on 3 September. Stewart's Division was a solid, veteran formation, with strong leadership at the brigade and division levels, but Preston's Division had been formed only on 26 August, and its troops were inexperienced. William Preston, forty-six, was a Kentucky lawyer and politician who had strong political connections in Richmond but whose only significant battle experience had been at the brigade level at Stones River. Like his friend Breckinridge, Preston was an extreme opponent of Bragg who had been banished from the army in the spring of 1863. When the day began, the corps was under orders to march to the railroad at Ooltewah. Stewart's Division departed Savannah Church at 3:00 P.M. and covered the thirteen miles to Ooltewah with relative ease. In at least one Tennessee unit, many men deserted rather than leave their native state. Preston's Division, meanwhile, did not leave its camps north of Harrison until sundown. In Gracie's Brigade, Pvt. John Hall wrote to his father, "Our men are in fine spirits and eager for a fight. Don't like the idea of leaving E. Tenn. Will probably discourage them very much. There is no telling where we will stop. I am not discouraged. Feel confident of our success." In Kelly's Brigade, Pvt. Joseph Espey was less sanguine, telling his sister, "The darkning cloud that seem to be ore us loseing may be raised and a thousand rays of light may burst forth or it may continue still to lose. But let us allway hope for the better." Kelly's men had only reached Tyner's Station when they stopped at midnight. Trigg's Brigade spent the day still guarding the Hiwassee River crossings, twenty-four miles north of Ooltewah. When Buckner's order to rejoin the corps reached Trigg, the First Florida Cavalry (Dismounted) regiment was able to take a train to Ooltewah at midnight, but other regiments remained behind, destroying items useful to the enemy. Like Hill, Buckner thus found his command unready to begin a general withdrawal.[42]

Bragg's cavalry loomed large in his plan to leave Chattanooga. At 1:00 P.M. Wheeler received orders to probe aggressively into Wills Valley to learn more about the Federals massing at Winston's plantation. Convinced that Neal's Gap, eight miles north of Alpine, was the most likely Federal approach route, he immediately ordered Wharton to concentrate there and remove the obstructions blocking the road to Winston's. Almost instantly he reversed himself and halted the movement. After consulting with Wharton, Maj. Pollok Lee, and Capt. Salvanus Steele, his engineer, Wheeler elected to do nothing. In a long letter to Brent, he detailed his reasons for disobeying Bragg's explicit orders: It would take a long time to remove the obstructions, and Neal's Gap should remain blocked; he could learn nothing new by entering Wills Valley; the march would exhaust his horses; the enemy could cross the mountain on either side of him and race unimpeded to Rome; and the Federals were in sufficient strength to prevent his movement. Thus he would await further orders from army headquarters. Martin's Division also remained inactive at LaFayette. Unlike Wheeler, Forrest saw no reason to remain passive on 6 September. Brent's circular called for Forrest to lead the way southward with one division, while his second division guarded the army's rear. Forrest construed that order to mean rushing quickly to Wheeler's support. If the Federals were making another raid toward Rome, Forrest planned to be there to stop them. Believing there was no time to lose, he immediately dispatched Dibrell's Brigade southward from Ringgold. He also informed Wheeler that Armstrong's other brigade, under

James Wheeler, would follow at 2:00 P.M. The rearguard duties would be left to Pegram's lone brigade, Scott's and Hodge's Brigades being still on the Hiwassee around Charleston. Forrest himself gathered his escort at Ringgold for an early departure southward on the next morning.[43]

Ripples from Bragg's decision to retreat spread far beyond Chattanooga Valley. At Rome, Gist anxiously awaited the arrival of his remaining regiments from Kingston. At Cartersville, ninety miles south of Chattanooga, Lt. George Gordon saw a train of multiple engines and cars being removed from the scene of potential conflict. Southbound passenger trains were crowded with civilians also fleeing the area. Gordon was contemptuous: "Whole families, often consisting of the father at a desk, the mother on a sofa and a collection of children with furniture fill a box (or freight) car, and so with a little variety, for the whole train. And I think them fools. Fleeing like craven cowards." Nearby, Henry Wayne received official notice of the Federal threat and began an inspection of his two regiments defending the Western & Atlantic Railroad. In Chattanooga, Medical Director Edward Flewellen ordered Samuel Stout to evacuate all hospitals north of Resaca. Stout had already surveyed suitable locations, but Marietta's Georgia Military Institute continued to be withheld by Governor Brown. Originally, Flewellen had hoped to retain the hospitals within the limits of Bragg's command, but that proved impossible because no one knew where the armies would move next. Hospitals located at Ringgold, Catoosa Springs, Cherokee Springs, Tunnel Hill, Dalton, Calhoun, and Adairsville were affected. Their new locations were projected to be in towns south and west of Atlanta, but it would be some time before they could operate efficiently. Momentarily, hospital administrators struggled to reassign medical personnel, weed out malingerers, place all the truly ill on trains, and pack the hospital baggage for shipment. At the Cherokee Springs hospital, nurse Kate Cumming was anxious: "I suppose the cooks will be up all night, preparing rations. We will have to spread comforts on the floor to rest on for the night, as our bedding has been carried off. We do not expect to leave before morning. If the enemy do not capture us I shall be thankful."[44]

As night fell, thousands of soldiers cooked their travel rations, loaded wagons and freight cars, or stumbled along dusty roads in Chattanooga Valley. In widely separate parts of the Confederacy, other soldiers began preparations to join the Army of Tennessee. In Mississippi, Gregg's and McNair's units received orders to prepare for their trip to Atlanta. At Meridian Frank Hayley hurriedly wrote to his wife, Laura: "We have just received orders to cook three days rations and get ready to move immediately. I expect we will go to Chattanooga Tennessee, and I expect it will be a long time before we draw again." In Richmond, Lee spent the day conferring with Quartermaster General Alexander Lawton on the transfer of several of his divisions to assist Bragg. As the infeasibility of the Knoxville route became evident, the Railroad Bureau's Major Sims began to plot an alternate pathway through the Carolinas. Unfortunately, the new route would be longer and more complex, delaying the arrival of the reinforcements. Nor was the question of the contingent's commander fully settled. Davis strongly preferred Lee, but Lee demurred, satisfied that officers already in Tennessee could handle the task. Of course, Longstreet for some time had been lobbying Senator Wigfall and Secretary of War Seddon to be given the position. With Lee unwilling to go, Davis unwilling to force him, and Seddon pressing Longstreet's case, at some point on 6 September Longstreet by default became the commander of the troops traveling to Tennessee from Virginia. The warning order for the men of Longstreet's First Corps was telegraphed to their central Virginia camps that afternoon. That order reached the Fifteenth Alabama Infantry regiment on Sunday night, just as a protracted camp meeting closed with a half dozen candidates anxious for baptism. Rather than wait for an uncertain future to offer a better opportunity, the unit's chaplain found a suitable place in a swamp to conduct the ceremony at midnight. All then turned to the task of cooking travel rations for the journey to Tennessee.[45]

Not long before nightfall, Bragg learned that Johnston had responded positively to his plea for troops to save Atlanta. At 5:00 P.M. he acknowledged Johnston's offer without elaboration: "Please send the Brigades for such time as you can spare them." According to reports from Strahl in Lookout Valley and signalmen on Lookout Mountain, the Federal force at Wauhatchie had become passive. Polk's Corps was ready to move by nightfall, and Walker's Corps at Chickamauga Station was also ready for departure. Hill's Corps, however, was scattered on the roads from Harrison through Chattanooga to Lookout Mountain. Cleburne's Division had been separated from its artillery, and Breckinridge had no idea where his brigades were. Likewise, Buckner's Corps was still clogging the roads from Ooltewah to Tyner's Station, with most of a brigade still at Charleston. At nightfall, half of the army was exhausted from a frustrating march through heat and choking dust but was still short of its assembly areas. Meeting with Bragg, Polk and Hill vigorously urged a suspension of the movement, although Mackall strongly disagreed. Clearly, Hill's and Buckner's men were in no condition to continue their march all night. The Federal inaction at Wauhatchie perhaps indicated that Rosecrans was not yet ready to leap over the Lookout Mountain barrier, giving the Army of Tennessee more time to gather itself. Thus, at 8:00 P.M., Bragg instructed Brent to issue new instructions: "Suspend all further movements until further orders." The delay also would permit more orderly evacuation of the army's depot at Chickamauga Station. Across the army, except for those units still marching, time stood still.

The travel rations had been cooked, the tents had been struck, and the wagons had been loaded, but there would be no departure from Chattanooga that night. According to Lt. William Richmond of Polk's staff, "The feeling is one of great doubt as to the movements of the enemy, all want to fight him but the question is can we make him fight us?"[46]

16

Bragg Leaves Town

» 7–8 September 1863 «

Monday, 7 September, found most of the Army of the Cumberland scattered for more than thirty miles along the narrow trench of Lookout/Wills Valley. Behind the Federals frowned the massive bulk of Sand Mountain, separating the army from its base at Stevenson. In front, stretching north and south as far as the eye could see, Lookout Mountain completely cloaked Bragg's army from prying eyes. At Trenton, Rosecrans needed to assess the situation quickly and energize his widely separated corps. On the left, Crittenden's Twenty-First Corps was to threaten Chattanooga directly from the north end of Lookout Valley. On the right, Stanley's Cavalry Corps, backed by McCook's Twentieth Corps, was to drive eastward beyond Lookout Mountain toward Rome and ultimately the Western & Atlantic Railroad. In the center, Thomas's Fourteenth Corps was to seize a passage over Lookout Mountain while maintaining contact with Crittenden's and McCook's units. If the plan succeeded, Bragg would evacuate Chattanooga without a fight and withdraw toward Atlanta. In some respects, Rosecrans's scheme resembled his successful Tullahoma campaign. At Tullahoma, Rosecrans had turned Bragg's right; now, with any luck, he would turn Bragg's left and pry the Confederates out of their mountain stronghold. The key to success would be synchronized action. First, Crittenden would have to maintain his threatening posture toward Chattanooga to fix Confederate attention in the north and provide intelligence on the Army of Tennessee's location. Second, Thomas would have to surmount Lookout Mountain in at least one place where a road led downward into the valley beyond. Finally, Stanley would have to cross Lookout Mountain quickly in order to mount a credible thrust toward Bragg's supply line. Backed by the power of McCook's infantry, Stanley's cavalrymen would thus play the key role in forcing a Confederate retreat from Chattanooga. Even though not all of his army had yet completed its painful journey over Sand Mountain, it was time for the next phase of Rosecrans's campaign to begin.[1]

Following his normal routine, Rosecrans kept his staff working into the early morning hours of 7 September, even though their trip over Sand Mountain had been exhausting. Around 3:00 A.M., a message arrived at Trenton from the Twenty-First Corps. Dispatched by Capt. John McCook of Crittenden's staff at 12:15 A.M., the message included copies of Wood's messages of 2:00 and 4:00 P.M. the previous day. In both messages Wood had considered his position at Wauhatchie "hazardous." McCook stated in Crittenden's name that he would "await further advice from you before ordering him [Wood] to advance." Perhaps it was simply the lateness of the hour or the rigors of a long day, but McCook's seemingly innocent message caused Rosecrans to fly into a rage. Displeased that the Twenty-First Corps was apparently not going to move without more prodding, Rosecrans instructed senior aide Frank Bond to write Crittenden at 3:15 A.M.: "The general commanding directs that you order General Wood to make a reconnaissance in force, as was intended by the order sent through General Garfield." Also irked that McCook, not Crittenden, had signed the note, even though McCook indicated he was acting under Crittenden's instructions, Rosecrans specifically rebuked Crittenden for not placing his own name on the messages. Again speaking for Rosecrans, Bond wrote, "He also directs me to say that all communications for him from your headquarters must be signed by the general commanding the corps." Probably aware that Captain McCook was the younger brother of Alexander McCook, Rosecrans chose to have Bond sign the rebuke. Clearly, Crittenden must follow army protocol to the letter, but Rosecrans believed himself unfettered by the same rules. Taken by itself, this seemingly insignificant episode would have mattered little in a long campaign, but it was indicative of larger issues that would resonate in the future: Rosecrans's increasing irascibility and his growing mistrust of Crittenden's competence.[2]

Rosecrans's rebuke reached Crittenden on Sand Mountain a little before 5:00 A.M. and triggered immediate action. Mortified that he had displeased the army commander, Crittenden attempted to get Wood moving. His staff dutifully forwarded to Wood Garfield's original message of 11:30 P.M., 6 September, calling for Wood "to feel the enemy at the point of Lookout Mountain, and find out certainly what he is doing." Further, Wood was to waste no time in making the reconnaissance. At 9:15 A.M., Crittenden told Garfield that he had ordered Wood forward upon receipt of Bond's message. He also abjectly apologized for the lapse in staff protocol: "I acknowledge the correctness of the reproof, and it shall not occur again, be I well or ill, sleepy or wide awake, in or out of bed." Believing that he had satisfied Rosecrans, Crittenden now waited to hear from Wood. At approximately 8:00 A.M., Wood received Crittenden's order, as well as the copy of Garfield's original instructions. The packet did not include Rosecrans's explicit order of 3:15 A.M., probably because that order was incorporated within Rosecrans's embarrassing rebuke to Crittenden. Thus Wood did not know of Rosecrans's displeasure or his peremptory directive to "make a reconnaissance in force," far stronger language than Garfield's more benign phrase "to feel the enemy." Crittenden's instructions placed Wood in a quandary. In his opinion, he already had felt the enemy on the previous day, risking his two brigades in a dangerous position at Wauhatchie for many hours without the possibility of support. Now Crittenden had ordered him to return to that "hazardous" position and beyond it in order to learn what he already knew and had already reported. Without knowledge of the language in Rosecrans's 3:15 A.M. message, which gave Crittenden no option, Wood saw Crittenden's order as an extreme interpretation of Rosecrans's wishes. The more he thought about it, the more Wood believed his superiors did not understand what he faced. Otherwise they would not have sent him such an order.[3]

Before advancing, Wood spent several hours selecting defensive positions for his two brigades. While doing so, he decided to remonstrate with Crittenden once more about the reconnaissance. For Wood, the key point was the lack of support for any advance he might make. Crittenden had earlier suggested that Van Cleve's division could assist Wood, but Van Cleve's men were scattered along the Murphy's Hollow Road on their way up Sand Mountain from Whiteside. If the Confederates attacked him, Wood believed the fight would be resolved long before Van Cleve could intervene. Thus, Wood argued that Palmer's division should move north in Lookout Valley to within two miles of Wood's rear and support his advance. Crittenden had already rejected Wood's request because it did not conform to the original orders from army headquarters. Having served with Crittenden for more than a year, Wood was well acquainted with his indecisiveness, inflexibility of mind, and literal interpretation of orders. He saw no need for Crittenden to be bound by specific locations identified in the operations order that was by now four days old. As a professional soldier, Wood was confident that a small deviation from the original order fell within Crittenden's discretion. Thus he vigorously pressed for his proposal in a long and strongly worded message to Crittenden at 11:30 A.M. One sentence leaped out: "I cannot believe General Rosecrans desires such a blind adherence to the mere letter of his order for the general disposition of his forces as naturally jeopardizes the safety of the most salient portions of it, and certainly cripples the force and vigor and accuracy of its reconnaissances." Wood gratuitously suggested that if Crittenden did not feel comfortable making the decision on Palmer alone, he should appeal to Rosecrans personally for permission to act. Finally, Wood stated that although he had already made a reconnaissance on the previous day, he would send a brigade northward in accord with Crittenden's instructions.[4]

Wood selected Harker's Third Brigade to make the reconnaissance. Harker led the brigade forward around 1:00 P.M. and soon reached the Wauhatchie railroad junction. Wood had ordered Harker to advance to Lookout Creek, directly under the tip of Lookout Mountain, if possible, but to go no farther. Not far beyond Wauhatchie, he encountered cavalry pickets, who retired precipitately. Covered by a heavy skirmish line, Harker continued forward until he met infantry pickets, which also fell back. A few hundred yards farther, the brigade reached the substantial home of Elisha Parker, seventy-three. There the road forked, the right-hand fork following the Nashville & Chattanooga Railroad northeast to a crossing of Lookout Creek, while the left-hand road continued northward before turning east to another crossing. Choosing the right fork, Harker pushed his skirmish line to the bank of the creek but held the remaining troops just in front of Parker's house. Suddenly, several Confederate cannon opened with a crash on Harker's troops. For at least fifteen minutes the Confederate gunners rained uncomfortably accurate fire on Harker's men from the lower slope of Lookout Mountain. Hindered by many shells that did not explode, the Confederates drew little blood. Still, Cpl. Herman Beitel of Company F, Sixty-Fifth Ohio Infantry regiment, was killed instantly when a shell fragment took off the top of his head. Shortly thereafter, Harker decided to rejoin Buell's First Brigade in the rear at the mouth of Running Water Canyon. Before leaving, he interviewed Elisha Parker, who claimed to hold Unionist sympathies. Parker indicated that only Strahl's Brigade was in Harker's immediate front but that many more Confederates were nearby. A prisoner also indicated that Bragg had received heavy reinforcements from Mississippi and South Carolina. Having added only marginally to their store of knowledge, Harker's soldiers slowly withdrew from Lookout Creek and Wauhatchie, carrying Corporal Beitel's body with them.[5]

During the day, Crittenden remained at his headquarters atop Sand Mountain. There he overheard someone mention in exaggerated terms Wood's slight withdrawal from Wauhatchie during the previous night. Crittenden claimed that the news came from one of Wood's staff officers who had arrived at corps headquarters early that morning, but Wood would later deny that any of his staff had been there that day. The incorrect information probably came from a member of the Thirty-Ninth Indiana Mounted Infantry regiment who had accompanied Wood's division. Already embarrassed by Rosecrans's rebuke, Crittenden became angry at the fact that Wood had not told him of the slight withdrawal, again placing him in Rosecrans's bad graces. In late morning Crittenden sent Lt. Col. Lyne Starling, chief of staff, and Maj. John Mendenhall, chief of artillery, to survey the Trenton Road all the way to Wood's position. During their absence, Wood's 11:30 A.M. message arrived. Not only did it confirm Wood's withdrawal from Wauhatchie and his delay in initiating the second reconnaissance, it also contained the inflammatory wording about "blind adherence to the mere letter" of orders. His earlier anger instantly rekindled, Crittenden heatedly composed an emotional message to Garfield. In it he charged that Wood had "neglected his duty" by delaying Harker's reconnaissance, had endangered his command by withdrawing on the Trenton Road instead of the Whiteside Road, and had been slow to report the skirmishing on the previous day. He told Garfield that he could send Palmer to Wood's support but would not do so unless Rosecrans ordered it. No doubt pleased that he had exposed Wood's malfeasance in high places, Crittenden directed that a copy of his message be sent to Wood. He seemed utterly unaware of how his whining message might be perceived at Rosecrans's headquarters.[6]

During the afternoon the controversy continued to boil. At some point Starling and Mendenhall returned from their excursion to Wood's position. What they reported is unknown, but before the day was over, Crittenden ordered Palmer to move to Wood's support at 3:00 A.M. on the next day. About the same time that Crittenden's order seemingly vindicated Wood's analysis of the situation, Wood received his copy of Crittenden's heated 2:00 P.M. message to Rosecrans accusing Wood of serial errors of judgment and dereliction of duty. Outraged, at 6:00 P.M. Wood began drafting a scathing response to Crittenden's charges. When Harker returned, Wood paused long enough to report the results of the reconnaissance but soon returned to his writing. Completing the 3,500-word missive shortly before midnight, Wood addressed it to Garfield and forwarded it, as protocol required, through corps headquarters. In the message Wood first explained that his "blind obedience" reference applied only to the army operations order, not the order for a reconnaissance. Second, he denied that he had delayed Harker's reconnaissance unnecessarily, explaining that he had been forced to protect his remaining troops before sending Harker forward. Third, he expended many words in explaining why he had withdrawn from Wauhatchie during the previous night. He took full responsibility, arguing passionately that the security of his command was enhanced by the move. Last, Wood admitted that Crittenden's charge of imprecise messages on 6 September was correct but was simply an "unintentional oversight." He then attacked Crittenden's apparent reliance upon staff officers of limited experience instead of a professional soldier like Wood. Believing that his honor and professionalism had been called into question, Wood closed by apologizing for the length of his missive and appealed to army headquarters for justice. Given the cascade of words he sent at 11:50 P.M. to Twenty-First Corps headquarters, he must have known the episode would not end there.[7]

While Wood and Crittenden traded charges and countercharges, the remainder of the Twenty-First Corps idled in its camps. In Palmer's Second Division, Cruft's and Grose's men continued to occupy the pleasant camping grounds around Cole's Academy. Similarly, Van Cleve's Third Division sprawled beside the Murphy's Hollow Road on both sides of Murphy's Spring.

While some men foraged for corn, others took the opportunity to write letters home. In late morning Cruft sent the thirty-five men of Company K, Thirty-First Indiana Infantry regiment, to scale Lookout Mountain and establish a signal station. The Hoosiers found a track that led up the mountain to what the locals called Nickajack Gap. As they ascended, they found Confederate pickets in large numbers and a sharp skirmish erupted. After losing one man wounded, signal officer Julian Fitch called for assistance while Company K withdrew. In response Cruft sent two regiments to the base of the mountain but soon recalled them to their original camps. Little had been gained except the knowledge that a rough track existed over Lookout Mountain at Nickajack Gap. Even less occurred to break the monotony in Van Cleve's command, tucked away in Murphy's Hollow. Foraging opportunities were fewer there, so the men amused themselves by writing letters and rolling rocks down the mountain. A few thought they could hear artillery fire, but they were uncertain of its location. With Wood no longer covering the Running Water Canyon road, Van Cleve assigned the Twenty-First Kentucky Infantry regiment of Barnes's brigade to garrison Whiteside. Far behind them, Dick's Second Brigade finally reached Bridgeport, crossed the river, and camped just beyond the stream. Late in the day, Palmer's division had a distinguished visitor—the army commander. Riding up from Trenton with part of his staff, Rosecrans visited with the men around Cole's Academy. Although he made it as far as Cole's Spring, where he talked with Brannan around 7:00 P.M., Rosecrans apparently did not ascend Sand Mountain to speak with Crittenden before returning to Trenton.[8]

South of Trenton, on 7 September Thomas's Fourteenth Corps consolidated its position in Lookout Valley and began its assault on Lookout Mountain. Leading the way was Negley's Second Division, whose probe of the previous day had met resistance. Now Negley advanced in strength, with Beatty's First Brigade leading the division up the mountain. At 9:00 A.M. Beatty began the ascent with two regiments. The two units met no Confederates, their only opposition being the steepness of the grade. At noon Beatty started his remaining regiments up the mountain, along with two guns. Negley followed Beatty with part of Stanley's Second Brigade. Any Confederate pickets who might have been watching the Federals sweating their way up the mountain chose not to reveal themselves. Around 11:00 A.M. Beatty's Fifteenth Kentucky Infantry regiment reached the crest unopposed and found Lookout to be, like Sand Mountain, mostly flat on top. Negley himself arrived around noon and remained for several hours. He sent patrols several miles to the east and expedited the arrival of the remainder of Beatty's and Stanley's men. At a crossroads two miles beyond the crest a few Confederate cavalrymen appeared, but they made no effort to interfere with the Federal occupation of the road junction. Far below, in Johnson's Crook, Stanley's Eighteenth Ohio Infantry regiment began the arduous task of assisting the division's wagons up the mountain. The day was warm, broken only by the briefest of afternoon showers that did virtually nothing to tamp down the dust. Behind the Eighteenth Ohio, Sirwell's Third Brigade advanced only to the foot of the mountain. Returning to the valley at 5:00 P.M., Negley reported his success to corps headquarters at Brown's Spring. He also requested a cavalry detachment to serve as couriers and funds to purchase information from the locals. Lacking those resources, he had been forced to use infantrymen to carry messages and had used his own money to reward informants. During the day, Thomas received the Ninety-Second Illinois Mounted Infantry regiment of Wilder's command, but he assigned it to Reynolds, not Negley.[9]

Negley's thrust up Lookout Mountain was only the tip of the spear represented by the Fourteenth Corps. Behind Negley's infantry were hundreds of wagons ready to begin the backbreaking pull up the grade. While awaiting his turn, teamster William Christian found time for a little sightseeing: "I went down to the iron works just off the main road. I went into a deserted house there and found a black man who said he had the small pox. I left mighty sudden." By the end of the day, the road behind Negley's trains was clogged with more troops. Baird's First Division had been ordered to follow Negley's command, but he was delayed all day by wagons in front. Baird began the day still on Sand Mountain, but he hastened Scribner's First Brigade down to the valley floor at Brown's Spring, then after only a brief rest, hurried it on in Negley's wake. Scribner closed on Negley's rear well after dark. Behind him, Starkweather's Second Brigade was only able to negotiate the descent of Sand Mountain to Brown's Spring. Its progress was hindered by many broken wagons and the requirement to guard a large herd of beef cattle moving with Baird's division. Behind Baird, Reynolds's Fourth Division continued to occupy Trenton, a settlement of "two churches, three stores, court-house, mill, and blacksmith shop." Ordered to relieve one of Negley's units left to grind corn at Payne's (Sitton's) Mill, Reynolds dispatched King's Second Brigade to do that and guard the Empire Iron Works several miles south of Trenton as well. In addition, Reynolds was told to send a brigade up Lookout Mountain to secure Frick's Gap. With only Turchin's Third Brigade remaining in Trenton, Reynolds promised to send Van Derveer's Third Brigade of Brannan's Third Division to seize the gap early the next day. Van Derveer's troops were just then descending Sand Mountain to join the remainder of Brannan's division at Cole's Spring several miles north of Trenton. Van Derveer began to prepare for what he considered a most dangerous mission, but when Rosecrans arrived around dark, he canceled the brigade's participation on the spot.[10]

South of the Fourteenth Corps, in what was arguably the most critical sector of Rosecrans's campaign plan, there was little activity on 7 September. David

Stanley had been told repeatedly that his thrust over Lookout Mountain toward Rome and Bragg's supply line was critical to the success of the campaign. He had procrastinated, never refusing to move but offering a series of excuses that amounted to the same thing. On the previous night, Garfield had sent Stanley the clearest order yet to begin the operation, yet Stanley continued to sit. At 10:30 A.M. he responded with a curious message that reflected his inner turmoil. In it, Stanley announced that he would begin the raid on the following day but stated baldly that he had little hope for success. He had asked for Minty's brigade to join him, but that had been denied, leaving him with only thirteen regiments. Stanley thought his corps was utterly inadequate for the task: "My force is so small that I cannot make proper detachments for striking the road and at the same time fight the force of the enemy." In Stanley's opinion, he faced two full Confederate cavalry divisions, who would probably deny him the half day he needed on the railroad to wreck it effectively. Success could only be assured if Minty joined him and Wilder mounted a diversion toward Chattanooga at the same time. Knowing that those two conditions were not likely to be met, Stanley feared the outcome. Still, he offered, "I will do the best I can." Dispatching the message to Trenton by courier, he ordered McCook and Crook to put their regiments in fighting trim for an early start on the next day. In Long's brigade, the Second Kentucky Cavalry regiment arrived with the brigade train, giving Stanley a fourteenth regiment. A detachment of the Fourth Ohio Cavalry regiment, sent up Lookout Mountain to chase bushwhackers, was recalled from its fruitless errand. Suddenly, another order came from Stanley's headquarters: the movement ordered for the next day was canceled![11]

Until Stanley departed on his raid, Alex McCook's Twentieth Corps could do nothing but wait. As he had for several days, McCook continued to enjoy the grudging hospitality of William Winston, even as Winston's plantation was stripped of all food and fence rails. McCook's headquarters was surrounded by the camps of Davis's First Division. On top of the mountain, elements of Carlin's Second Brigade protected the rough, winding route back to the valley. Carlin's perimeter extended a short distance to the east, where a branch of the Little River passed over the spectacular DeSoto Falls into a rock-lined basin. Beyond the falls, foragers seeking ripe fruit trees found not only an orchard but also a larger force of Confederates. Before they could disengage, Pvt. Elisha Stroud was killed and several of his compatriots captured. Clearly, danger lurked in the thickets atop Lookout Mountain. For the bulk of the Twentieth Corps, however, 7 September was spent pleasantly in Wills Valley. Bored men amused themselves by continuing the despoliation of Winston's property. One soldier sent home an arrowhead he had acquired at his campsite, to be kept "among the curiosities." Several miles north of Winston's, Johnson's Second Division was equally bored. As forage for their animals disappeared, and the stench from poorly constructed latrines grew, Johnson's men moved their camps a short distance to escape the filth. The day was hot and dusty until a small but fierce thunderstorm cooled the air in midafternoon. The storm was barely felt by Sheridan's Third Division as it toiled southward past the mouth of Johnson's Crook. Sheridan began the march early, before the sun rose above Lookout Mountain. In the Eighty-Eighth Illinois Infantry regiment, Pvt. John Ely was transfixed as the light fell on Fox Mountain to the west, writing, "Oh I would like to stay here a day and drink in this beauty." Sheridan halted early, with his division stretched from Stevens's Mill northward to the plantation of Confederate officer James Nisbet.[12]

While his strike force at Valley Head dallied, Rosecrans's deception force opposite Chattanooga grew increasingly nervous. Until the command of "U.S. Forces, Left Flank" was settled, Hazen dutifully relinquished that role to Wagner. Still, at 6:00 A.M., he addressed a note directly to army headquarters reporting large dust clouds on the far side of the river on the previous day and an unusual quiet along the river. Unlike Hazen, Wagner was unwilling to remain passive. Apprised of Wood's operations in Lookout Valley on the previous day, Wagner had already sent two of his regiments down to the river. Now he sought to do more in support of Wood's dangerous position. At 6:00 A.M. he informed Wood that he was increasing his force opposite Chattanooga to three regiments and a section of guns. Together, Wagner and Wilder controlled the area across from the large Williams Island, just downstream from Chattanooga. Wagner offered to join Wood at Williams Island, but Wood's troops were unable to take advantage of the offer. At 10:00 A.M., Wagner informed army headquarters that Confederate cavalry had replaced the infantry pickets above Chattanooga and that the pontoon bridge on the Chattanooga waterfront had been broken up. In late morning he decided to distract Confederate attention by bombarding Chattanooga. Heavier than many of the previous bombardments, the shelling elicited no response. Upstream, Wilder sent the Seventeenth Indiana Mounted Infantry regiment to observe the ford at Friar's Island, where he hoped to cross the next morning. Still farther upstream, as signs multiplied that the Confederates were leaving the line of the river, Hazen told Minty to attempt a crossing at Sale Creek on the next day. If successful, Minty should ride southward to meet Hazen's troops in the vicinity of Harrison's Ferry. Minty resisted, pleading his brigade's weakness, and Hazen acquiesced. Although none of the Federals could yet be sure of what was happening, a consensus began to develop slowly that Bragg's army might be leaving town.[13]

The quickening sense of urgency that gripped Rosecrans's deception force also affected Granger's Reserve Corps. During the day, Tillson's First Brigade of Morgan's Second Division finally entered Stevenson. Most of Daniel McCook's Second Brigade passed through Larkinsville on the way to Bellefonte. Reaching the latter place, the band of the Fifty-Second Ohio Infantry regiment broke into patriotic airs to discomfit the citizens but was chagrinned to learn there was no audience in the abandoned settlement. A day's march behind McCook, the Eighty-Sixth Illinois Infantry regiment finally crossed into Alabama and continued for another twelve miles. Beyond the Cumberland Plateau, Steedman put two of his three brigades into motion. Three regiments of Whitaker's First Brigade left Estill Springs early for Decherd, where the fourth regiment joined. The united brigade then continued to Winchester, "a dreadfully stinken place," and finally halted at Cowan for the night. Like Whitaker's men, several regiments of Reid's Second Brigade also headed for Cowan from Tullahoma and Shelbyville. Three of Reid's regiments made it to Decherd for the night, while the fourth awaited them at Cowan. While his troops marched, Steedman himself took the train, where he encountered a detail from the Eighteenth United States Infantry regiment, returning from Nashville. The regulars had been drinking heavily and were very boisterous, but the general simply cautioned the detail's commander to see that his soldiers did not injure themselves and returned to his own car without another word. Such empathy for those in the ranks endeared Steedman to his men. Elsewhere, several unattached regiments were also moving to the front. At Cowan, the Sixty-Ninth Ohio Infantry regiment received orders to head for Stevenson and report to the Reserve Corps. At Bridgeport, the Twenty-Second Michigan Infantry regiment, already under Reserve Corps control, awaited its new brigade assignment. Finally, on the Cumberland Plateau, the Eighty-Ninth Ohio Infantry regiment prepared to leave Tracy City and march to Bridgeport.[14]

At the end of the day, Rosecrans returned to Trenton after visiting Palmer's and Brannan's divisions. Uppermost in his mind was the necessity to get Stanley's raid started. Having received Stanley's tepid promise to move on the next day, Rosecrans instructed Garfield at 8:30 P.M. to encourage his reluctant cavalry commander with strong words of support. Claiming that most of the Confederate cavalry was not yet in Stanley's front, Garfield expressed Rosecrans's confidence that Stanley could succeed in his mission. He assured Stanley that McCook's Twentieth Corps would advance several brigades beyond Lookout Mountain to hold the way open for his return. As he had done before, Garfield reiterated the importance of Stanley's raid to the success of the overall campaign plan: "Even should you fail in thoroughly breaking the railroad, you would at least make a strong diversion in that direction." At 8:45 P.M., Garfield wrote to McCook about his role in Stanley's thrust. As was customary in communications with McCook, the instructions were detailed and specific. McCook was told to guard the route over Lookout Mountain with one brigade, while at the same time he was to push forward two additional brigades to occupy the hamlet of Alpine at the eastern foot of the mountain. Expecting Stanley's raid to be of brief duration, Garfield instructed McCook to carry rations for only three days, with the mission probably lasting no longer than four. To prevent McCook from becoming nervous about his own isolated situation, Garfield shared the belief prevailing at army headquarters that Bragg's army, estimated at 50,000 men, remained at Chattanooga. Although Garfield ascribed the information about the Confederates to Wood, the numbers actually came from deserters and scouts. The inference in both of Garfield's messages was that there was still time to implement the bold dash toward Bragg's supply line with little risk of failure.[15]

Although Stanley's raid was on Rosecrans's mind on the night of 7 September, he had other concerns as well. Part of the problem was the general lack of information reaching headquarters. When Crittenden forwarded Wood's account of Harker's reconnaissance, he drew a sharply worded retort that the report lacked specific details. A more friendly inquiry went to Thomas, asking if he had any "news," particularly of Negley's operations at Stephens's Gap. The unsuccessful efforts during the day to extend the telegraph line from Whiteside to Trenton via Wood's position were also troubling. A report from Granger that the Louisville & Nashville Railroad was not moving sufficient commissary supplies drew a strongly worded plea to President James Guthrie for better service. Increasingly agitated, Rosecrans flogged his staff, addressing minute items such as the state of repairs to a magazine in Nashville and the purchase of supplies for a Nashville hospital for "public women." John King at Stevenson was told to accommodate Archbishop John Purcell of Cincinnati, who would soon arrive to visit the army. Finally, at midnight, Rosecrans crafted his daily report to Halleck. Perhaps it was the accumulated aggravations of the day, but he was in a foul mood by that time. Halleck's most recent telegram had declared, "You give me no information of the position of Bragg and Buckner. If they have united, it is important that you and Burnside unite as quickly as possible, so that the enemy may not attack you separately." For a weary army commander at a critical juncture in his campaign, Halleck's gratuitous advice was unwelcome, and Rosecrans responded heatedly: "Your dispatch of yesterday received with surprise. You have been often and fully advised that the nature of the country makes it impossible for this army to prevent Johnston from combining with Bragg." Because Burnside's campaign had been mounted independently, by Halleck's design, any problems that might have developed were Halleck's fault: "Your apprehensions are just, and the legitimate consequences of your orders."[16]

Just as Burnside's activities in East Tennessee were a source of friction between Rosecrans and Halleck, so too were they problematic for Bragg and the Confederate government. On the previous day, Bragg had instructed Buckner to order the evacuation of Cumberland Gap, the order to be passed through

Samuel Jones. Very reluctantly, Buckner had obeyed, but Jones had stayed the order until he received guidance from Richmond. Fundamentally misunderstanding what had happened during Burnside's advance to Knoxville, Davis and Secretary of War Seddon ordered Jones on 7 September to use his own discretion in the matter. Seddon postulated that "Generals Bragg and Buckner probably acted on misinformation as to force threatening. You have better information and must exercise fully your own judgment." Seddon also notified Bragg of Davis's decision but softened the assessment from "misinformation" to "erroneous impression." Indeed, Davis and Seddon believed that aggressive action by Jones could save both Cumberland Gap and the railroad to Chattanooga. Jones himself was equally ignorant about the status of Burnside's invasion of East Tennessee. Before he heard from Richmond, Jones telegraphed Buckner that he was expecting to receive reinforcements. Thus augmented, he believed he could restore the status quo: "May be able to open communication to Knoxville. Perhaps you did not know condition of things when you telegraphed order in regard to Cumberland Gap." That very morning, at his headquarters in Knoxville, Burnside wrote to Rosecrans's aide Robert Thoms: "We have full possession of East Tennessee except Cumberland gap, which is still held by the enemy. I have a force moving against it from the Kentucky side, and I move from here at once in person with a force to attack it from this side. Will telegraph you from the gap, I hope." Far more realistic in their appreciation of the actual situation, Confederate Railroad Bureau personnel completed their plans to send 18,000 troops from Virginia to Tennessee by way of the Carolinas.[17]

Upon the entreaties of Polk and Hill on the previous day, Bragg had suspended the evacuation of Chattanooga Valley. Now it was time to decide what to do next, and for that he needed more information. At 7:00 A.M. Brent instructed Inspector General Beard to send two officers into Lookout Valley to learn the position and strength of the Federal force lately at Wauhatchie. Bragg had already sent senior aide Joseph Jones to a signal station atop Lookout Mountain on the same mission but without result. Thirty minutes later, Brent notified Forrest that although the infantry movement was held in abeyance, Forrest should continue to assist Wheeler in developing information on the Federals in Wills Valley. At 9:00 A.M., Brent telegraphed Buckner at Ooltewah to have Hodge's makeshift cavalry brigade probe the Federal column reportedly advancing on Charleston. Bragg continued to hope that Wheeler would soon report the results of the reconnaissance he had ordered two days earlier. Those hopes were dashed when a long message from Wheeler arrived from Alpine. In it, Wheeler complained that his force was too small to probe beyond Lookout Mountain to discover the strength and intentions of the Federals concentrated at Winston's plantation. Although Wheeler claimed that the Federals were too strong for him to act, a contrary view was offered in a note from Pollok

Lee, one of Bragg's inspector generals. Earlier, Lee had been sent to provide an independent appraisal of Wheeler's situation, and now he and Wheeler were at odds in their assessment. Thus Bragg learned nothing about what was happening in the southern reaches of the Lookout/Wills Valley corridor. Shortly after 11:00 A.M. shells began falling on Chattanooga. The noisy bombardment could do little damage because virtually everything of military value had long been moved out of range, but it was disconcerting nonetheless. In early afternoon, as the Federal shelling continued, Bragg resolved once more to evacuate Chattanooga, and he instructed Brent to prepare a new movement order.[18]

As before, the army would depart in two massive columns, with one significant change in the order of march. Originally, Polk's Corps headed the westernmost column; now Hill's Corps would lead the way. With Federals still active in northern Lookout Valley, Polk would have to block the road over the toe of Lookout Mountain while Hill departed Chattanooga Valley. Everything else was the same, with Walker leading the eastern column, followed by Buckner. The movement was slated to begin after nightfall. Because some units had arrived at Chattanooga without wagons and ambulances, Brent's circular authorized Chief Quartermaster McMicken to seize wagons from any corps in order to ensure that all divisions shared the limited assets equally. After publishing the circular, Bragg and Brent turned their attention to the smaller units that would be at risk and to the cavalry screen that would cover the army's retreat. Brent reminded Polk to withdraw the signalmen from Lookout Mountain, as well as the cavalry detachment protecting it. Col. Edmund Rucker, twenty-eight, commander of Rucker's First Tennessee Legion from Pegram's Division, was assigned to be Polk's and Hill's rear guard. As such, Rucker was given Mauldin's detachment, as well as Allison's Cavalry Squadron, and Company D of McDonald's Battalion. Polk was to use this odd collection of mounted units to replace the infantry pickets from Smith's Brigade when they withdrew after dark from their positions guarding Lookout Creek. With Forrest heading to assist Wheeler around Alpine, only Pegram's command remained to serve as Buckner's and Walker's rear guard. Unfortunately, two of Pegram's brigades were still fending off Burnside's probes along the Hiwassee River, leaving only Pegram's old brigade available. Except for Rucker's command, most of Pegram's men were still scattered along the Tennessee River upstream from Chattanooga around Harrison. Now they were to relieve Allison's Squadron below Friar's Island and hold their positions as long as possible before following Buckner's infantry.[19]

Although sunset would not occur until 7:00 P.M., most of Hill's Corps spent the afternoon pushing forward to the base of Missionary Ridge. First, Hill sternly admonished his officers: "The success of arms depends more upon celerity than any one thing else. To insure this quality in the corps, commanders of every grade will remain habitually with their commands and will give their personal attention to every movement." The order mentioned no names, but certainly Breckinridge had been among those guilty of slack behavior the previous evening. Hill decreed that his corps would travel with six days' rations, while sick soldiers and all baggage should be sent to the rear at once. Later, Hill issued another circular establishing the order of march. Cleburne's Division would lead the column, followed by the corps trains, with Breckinridge's Division bringing up the rear. An artillery battery was to follow Cleburne's lead brigade and another to precede Breckinridge's last brigade. Breckinridge was to notify Polk when his last unit was in motion. The requirement for officers to accompany their troops was reiterated: "The utmost efforts must be made to prevent the disgraceful practice of straggling. This can only be done by the greatest vigilance on the part of all officers and their habitual presence with the troops." Thus chastised, Cleburne's Division left Chattanooga and marched across the floor of Chattanooga Valley to the Rossville Gap in Missionary Ridge. In Breckinridge's Division, Stovall's Brigade was already in its assembly area, but Adams's and Helm's Brigades had some marching to do despite the day's heat and dust. A detail from Helm's Brigade was ordered to move the division's baggage to Chickamauga Station. Lacking even a single wagon, the men went into the countryside to "press" civilian vehicles. Finding only one oxcart, the Kentuckians spent the remaining daylight hours shuttling back and forth over the two-mile route from their camp. Night found the detail at the depot with "mountains of baggage" but no train to move it farther.[20]

While Hill's troops readied for an evening departure, Polk's Corps waited patiently with folded tents and loaded wagons. In order to assist Breckinridge, Polk ordered his divisions to relinquish five six-horse wagons apiece. In addition, he detailed 150 men to load ammunition on railroad cars that evening. Polk's staff drafted the corps movement order and distributed it to division commanders at 3:00 P.M. Cheatham's Division would be the first to leave its camps in Chattanooga Valley, followed by Hindman's Division, which was already near the Rossville Gap. The artillery and trains of the brigades would be distributed throughout the long column with their respective units. Brigade ambulances were to be gathered into division ambulance trains following each division. Provost guards were to police the column, arresting stragglers and keeping unit intervals tightly closed. Surgeons were to examine all stragglers "and see that none loiter or fall out except those with proper certificates or permits." With Chattanooga and the upstream fords now picketed by Pegram's cavalry, the only infantry units in contact with the Federals during the afternoon were Polk's. At the toe of Lookout Mountain, Smith's Brigade completed its relief of Strahl's command. Around 3:00 P.M. some Federal officers appeared across the river and proposed to trade newspapers. Some men from the Thirteenth Tennessee Infantry regiment made a brief visit, but Confederate officers prohibited reciprocity. Shortly thereafter, Harker's skirmishers appeared at Wauhatchie and pushed toward the mouth of Lookout Creek. Two guns from Carnes's Tennessee Battery, stationed a few hundred feet up the mountain, opened with solid shot and shell on the Federals clustered near the Elisha Parker House. According to a Confederate diarist, "A general stampede occurred among the enemy. They are now out of sight. All quiet at dark." At corps headquarters, Polk's aide William Richmond visited some young ladies to say goodbye and found them in tears. By nightfall, he too was ready to leave Chattanooga.[21]

Throughout the day, army headquarters continued to function at the Ely Bruce home. Bragg wrote to Samuel Cooper, explaining that Burnside was in Knoxville with 25,000 men, far too many for him to confront while simultaneously contending with Rosecrans's army. "Rosecrans is yet beyond the mountains on this side of Tennessee, moving with great caution, and threatening our communications." Unsure of how far he would have to retreat, Bragg instructed Brent to telegraph Henry Wayne of the Georgia State Guard to plank the railroad bridge at Resaca. Wayne was already on his way to Resaca to inspect its defenses. Brent also informed Col. Robert Garland, commanding at Kingston, that the army had no weapons to arm any militia activated by Governor Brown. As the hours passed, the staff's focus shifted to the tons of ammunition and rations remaining at Chickamauga Station. Falconer, Brent's assistant, telegraphed Capt. James Horbach, quartermaster at Chickamauga Station: "Are there any troops at Chickamauga? If so, put as many as necessary to work loading the cars with stores." Later, Brent telegraphed, "Put every man to work to load stores on the cars." Fearing that still more laborers would be needed, Brent telegraphed Buckner at Ooltewah to send a brigade to Chickamauga Station until everything was removed to safety. Brent also telegraphed Maj. J. W. Davis, commanding at Cleveland, to gather all government property there and take it to Dalton. At Chickamauga Station, Captain Horbach wired Medical Director Flewellen that seventy-four sick soldiers were at the depot awaiting transportation. The problem did not just exist at Chattanooga. During the day the hospital personnel at Cherokee Springs also headed south, first in two overloaded wagons to Ringgold, then in a filthy boxcar to Dalton. Traveling with nurse Kate Cumming and others were the wife and children of brigade commander Patton Anderson.[22]

As the sun dipped behind the massive bulk of Lookout Mountain, the western column of the Army of Tennessee began to move. Hill's Corps led the way with Cleburne's Division in front. As the shadows lengthened and the smell of cooked meat hung in the air, the troops left McFarland's Spring and entered the Rossville Gap. The moon would not rise until after midnight, so only the stars guided the soldiers as they passed through the defile. Thereafter the road to LaFayette was relatively flat, and the march marred only by billowing clouds of dust raised by thousands of tramping feet. Although the men saw little in the darkness, they headed southward through heavy woods broken only by small fields cleared by subsistence farmers with names like McDonald, Kelly, Brotherton, and Viniard. Around midnight, after a march of eight miles, Cleburne's van halted on Chickamauga Creek near a grist mill owned by the Lee and Gordon families. At the rear of the column, Sgt. William Heartsill wrote, "This may not be a retreat but it looks very much like one." Heartsill consoled himself with the hope that Johnston, not Bragg, led the army. Not all of Cleburne's Division was present. Two regiments of Polk's Brigade inadvertently had been left behind on the river when the division concentrated in Chattanooga Valley. Rushing to join the column, the men of the Forty-Eighth Tennessee made it only as far as Tyner's Station after a march of more than twenty miles. Finding the army gone, the Tennesseans spent the remainder of the night cooking rations in the abandoned camp. Breckinridge's Division followed Cleburne. Except for the detail securing the division's baggage at Chickamauga Station, Breckinridge's men encountered few difficulties except for the choking dust. In the Third Florida Infantry regiment of Stovall's command, the men sang as they marched, even though many were barefoot. It was well beyond midnight when the division halted in the dust short of Lee and Gordon's Mill.[23]

According to the movement order, Polk's Corps was to follow Hill out of the Chattanooga Valley on 7 September, but with Hill's units not beginning to move until dark and clogging the narrow road through the Rossville Gap, Polk's troops could not begin their own journey southward. Thus Hindman's and Cheatham's Divisions did not march that night. Hindman's command remained in its camps near McFarland's Spring, watching Hill's troops pass for much of the night. Their rations were cooked, their tents were struck, and their wagons were loaded, but they received no orders to march. Hindman himself visited Deas's Brigade, where he "made a beautiful little speech to the Brigade on the duties of the soldier, 'On the march and in the battle.'" One of Deas's units, the Thirty-Ninth Alabama Infantry regiment, remained in Chattanooga, serving as the police force of Col. Alexander McKinstry, the provost marshall. Cpl. John James, thirty-three, a member of the Thirty-Ninth, wrote to his wife from the nearly abandoned town: "My dear, I want you to write as often as you can. I hope that you will soon get well and I want you to pray for me. O that I could be with you and talk with each other. My dear, if we never meet any more on earth, I hope that we will meet in Heaven." Like Hindman's troops, most of Cheatham's Division remained stationary as well. In Strahl's Brigade, one soldier slept without his blanket, expecting any moment to be called into line, but neither he nor his companions were disturbed all evening. Stanford's Mississippi Battery did move forward to McFarland's Spring, but it remained there all night with horses harnessed as the road continued to be filled with Hill's men. On the far side of Lookout Mountain, Smith's Brigade checked Harker's reconnaissance not long before dark. Apparently forgotten in the rush to close Polk's headquarters, Smith's command was unaware that the army was beginning its retreat. At 9:00 P.M. Polk finally remembered Smith, instructing signal officer Mercer Otey to send a message to Smith through the signal station atop Lookout Mountain, a task which occupied the entire night.[24]

If Bragg's western column was slow off the mark on the evening of 7 September, his eastern column fared only slightly better. Leading that column was Walker's Reserve Corps. At sunset Liddell's Division took the road that led southeast toward Graysville, just south of the Georgia state line. Continuing past Graysville without a pause, Govan's Brigade pushed on toward Ringgold, reaching it at dawn on the next day. Following Govan was Walthall's Brigade, which stopped well short of Ringgold around midnight. Behind Liddell came Walker's Division. From Tyner's Station, Walker's troops marched to Chickamauga Station and plodded through the billowing dust after Liddell. With Gist's Brigade absent at Rome, only Ector's and Wilson's brigades made the trip. Even then, one of Wilson's regiments was held at Chickamauga Station to load supplies on railroad cars. Buckner's Corps was slated to follow Walker southward. By the evening, most of Buckner's command had reached Ooltewah, six miles east of Tyner's. There Buckner issued orders organizing divisional ambulance trains and forcing a draconian reduction in the amount of officers' baggage: "Where transportation for ammunition & subsistence for the men is so limited, it scarcely becomes an officer to include trunks, bedsteads, tables (except for desks) chairs and other luxuries as part of his campaigning equipage." During the evening Stewart's and Preston's Divisions left Ooltewah behind. Rather than take the direct road to Ringgold, they first marched westward to Tyner's Station, then to Chickamauga Station, and finally southward toward Graysville, which they would not reach until the next day. Momentarily left at Ooltewah was Johnson's Brigade, slated to assist in the evacuation of the army's Chickamauga Station base. Also left behind was the Seventh Florida Infantry regiment, guarding several steamboats trapped on the Hiwassee River near Charleston. On receiving positive orders to burn the boats, the Floridians complied at midnight and headed southward toward Cleveland.[25]

Even as the Army of Tennessee was withdrawing from Chattanooga and the line of the Tennessee River, reinforcements were coming from other parts of the Confederacy. At Enterprise, Mississippi, Gregg's Brigade boarded trains that would take it to Atlanta via a roundabout route through Mobile. McNair's Brigade, which had departed Enterprise a day earlier, was already well on its way to Montgomery. Johnston had loaned the two brigades in response to

Bragg's statement that Atlanta was in grave danger. Every request from Johnston for more information on the nature of the threat, however, had gone unanswered by Bragg. On 7 September, Johnston tried again: "I have put the brigades in motion, but they are also necessary in Mississippi; so let me know why they are wanted that I may judge between Atlanta and Mississippi." This message, too, would be ignored. Neither brigade brought its wagons, further complicating the already desperate shortage of wagons in the Army of Tennessee. In Virginia, Quartermaster General Lawton assured Lee that all preparations had been made for moving Longstreet's Corps to Tennessee, and that the troops nearest Fredericksburg would be the first to go. Major Sims of the Railroad Bureau announced that the maximum flow rate would be 3,000 men per day and that he had ordered trains carrying that number to arrive at stations just south of Fredericksburg on the following day. Sims also telegraphed Maj. John Whitford at Goldsboro, North Carolina, that the troop movement would entail 18,000 men in five days, with the first units arriving at Weldon, North Carolina, on 9 September. While the railroad men hammered out the details of their trip, Longstreet's troops began to gather outlying detachments and cook travel rations. Elements of Hood's Division at dark headed for several railroad stations below Fredericksburg, while McLaws's Division prepared to leave Waller's Tavern near the North Anna River for Hanover Junction on the next day.[26]

Although Rosecrans's headquarters apparently did not begin functioning early on 8 September, major elements of the Twenty-First Corps were active well before dawn. At 3:00 A.M., Palmer drafted a quick note to his wife in Illinois. Explaining that his division would soon move nearer Chattanooga, Palmer wrote, "I am not quite well but think I will be just as soon as I can sleep one night soundly. Hard marching gives every one inordinate appetites for food and that produces its usual consequences." Around 4:00 A.M. Grose's Third Brigade and Cruft's First Brigade departed from their pleasant camps around Cole's Spring and headed for the Trenton-Wauhatchie Road, a mile distant. Reaching that thoroughfare, they turned north. After a march of another three miles they halted on the floor of Lookout Valley at 7:00 A.M., approximately a mile and a half behind the defensive position occupied since the previous day by Wood. Given their location in the shadow of imposing Lookout Mountain, Palmer kept the two brigades under arms all day. Still, he was not intimidated by his situation, and planned to reconnoiter all the way to the top of Lookout Mountain near the seasonal settlement of Summertown. At 10:00 A.M. he announced his intentions to corps headquarters, but after sending the message reconsidered and decided to launch only small probes on the valley floor to the foot of the mountain. In the meantime, Van Cleve marched Beatty's First Brigade and Barnes's Third Brigade out of Murphy's Hollow, down Sand Mountain, and halted them in Palmer's old camps on the Cole plantation. Like Palmer, Van Cleve lacked a brigade, because Dick's Second Brigade had not yet joined from McMinnville. Dick's men, however, were closer than Van Cleve knew. Having marched from Bridgeport early that morning, they would reach Whiteside in late afternoon. Coincidentally, Van Cleve also wrote to his wife on 8 September: "I have been troubled with dysentery for a few days, and consequently cannot boast of feeling very well."[27]

In front of both Palmer and Van Cleve, Wood rested his command all day while watching for signs of Confederate intentions. Meanwhile, he continued his war of words with Crittenden. During the morning, Crittenden's pejorative endorsement on Wood's long missive to Garfield came to hand. Dismissing Wood's arguments, Crittenden denied that he had charged Wood with anything but unconscionably delaying the reconnaissance on the previous day and he repeated the charge. Crittenden's strictures prompted Wood to write again to Garfield. This time Wood expended more than 1,500 words, reprising the charges that Crittenden had dropped and arguing that his actions were prudent: "With imperfect knowledge of the facts by which my action was necessarily controlled; with imperfect knowledge of the dangers which environed my command, and which I had to guard against, and without first affording me an opportunity to make an explanation in regard to the matter, General Crittenden sits in judgment on my conduct and makes a grave and hurtful charge against me to the commanding general of the army." Wood need not have bothered, because Garfield, acting under Rosecrans's instructions, at 2:00 P.M. dispatched a rebuke to Wood that validated Crittenden's position. As the charges and rebuttals bounced back and forth from division to corps to army, Crittenden refused to end the controversy, although he changed his mode of attack. During the afternoon, Rosecrans had received a report that Wagner's brigade was short of ammunition, causing Garfield to question Crittenden on the subject at 2:00 P.M. Seizing an opportunity to berate Wood and simultaneously raise his standing at army headquarters, Crittenden wrote to Wood at 5:40 P.M. peremptorily asking what Wood knew about the situation. Sensing the potential danger in such a seemingly innocuous question, Wood placidly replied that Wagner could hardly be low on ammunition because he had done little firing and in three messages that day had not raised such an issue.[28]

Even as they continued to bicker, the senior officers of the Twenty-First Corps worried about their precarious situation. Potentially Bragg's entire army could debouch from behind Lookout Mountain and overwhelm Wood's and Palmer's divisions before anyone else could intervene. Palmer was initially the most anxious to discover what mischief lay concealed on the mountain's precipitous slopes. Deciding that his initial plan to send troops to the top of the mountain was too aggressive without Crittenden's prior approval, he contented himself with dispatching a regiment from each of his brigades to the base of Lookout. Cruft's Second Kentucky Infantry regiment discovered a rough track leading upward on what was known locally as Powell's Trace. Meanwhile, Grose detailed the Thirty-Sixth Indiana Infantry regiment to a similar task. While awaiting the results, Palmer visited Wood. For some time cannonading had been heard in the direction of Chattanooga, but its meaning was unclear. Upon returning to his command, Palmer found a note from Crittenden approving his plans for an aggressive reconnaissance but proposing a delay until the following day, when Van Cleve could participate. As night fell, Wood received indications that Chattanooga was being evacuated, and he rode to Palmer's headquarters to propose a reconnaissance of his own, if Palmer could support him. With Crittenden's instructions in hand, Palmer declined. Wood at 10:00 P.M. sent his own proposal for a reconnaissance to corps headquarters, now located near Van Cleve's position. Crittenden had just returned from a visit to army headquarters at Trenton when Wood's message arrived. Having learned that the entire army probably would be in motion on the next day, he rejected Wood's proposal but agreed to submit it to Rosecrans for final decision. Clearly, Crittenden was turning to his other two division commanders for action, thereby denying Wood any of the glory that might be achieved on the next day.[29]

South of the fractious Twenty-First Corps, Thomas's Fourteenth Corps was also active early on 8 September. At 4:00 A.M., Negley began to consolidate his position atop Lookout Mountain at Johnson's Crook. First to move was Beatty, who was told to secure the track down the mountain at Cooper's Gap with two regiments from his First Brigade. Beatty marched before dawn with the Fifteenth Kentucky and 104th Illinois Infantry regiments. Encountering cavalry pickets, Beatty's men pressed forward, driving the handful of Confederates down the mountain. While the Fifteenth Kentucky continued to the base of the slope, the 104th Illinois halted halfway down and assumed a defensive posture. There it remained all day, with nothing to do but watch a large dust cloud rise in the valley east of Lookout far to the north. Four hours after Beatty moved, Stanley's Second Brigade sent the Eleventh Michigan Infantry regiment to clear Stephens's Gap of any obstructions. It also encountered cavalry videttes and easily pushed them to the base of the mountain. Clearing the road into the valley proved more difficult, because the Confederates had clogged the passage with fallen trees and rocks. Stanley's weary men would not return to the top of Lookout Mountain until after midnight. Back in Lookout Valley, Sirwell's Third Brigade helped the division's supply train climb the west side of the mountain. Sirwell distributed his regiments along the grade to assist the struggling teams painfully pulling the heavily laden wagons up the steep incline.

After a hard day's effort, much of the train had reached the crest by nightfall, so Sirwell took three of his regiments up as well. The Seventy-Eighth Pennsylvania Infantry regiment remained at the western base of the mountain in Johnson's Crook. In a 7:20 P.M. report to corps headquarters, Negley described the day's efforts and, in passing, mentioned the ominous dust cloud rising in the valley an estimated nine miles to the north toward Chattanooga. He surmised that the rising dust signified the possibility that reinforcements were arriving to join Bragg's army.[30]

Negley's route via Johnson's Crook and Stephens's Gap was the designated pathway for the entire Fourteenth Corps, but until he completed the journey no other divisions could follow. Rosecrans's campaign plan did not anticipate that Thomas would be the first to push east of Lookout Mountain, a task assigned to Stanley and McCook. If the Army of Tennessee was to be pried out of Chattanooga without a fight, Rosecrans needed to put pressure on Bragg's supply line far enough south of the city to ensure that the Confederate retreat would not halt until well toward Atlanta. Thus Negley's cautious probing beyond the mountain was fully in accord with the original plan. His difficulty in getting his trains up Lookout, however, meant that the remaining Fourteenth Corps divisions would not move at all on 8 September. Baird's First Division spent the entire day idling in camp at the mouth of Johnson's Crook. Baird chafed at the delay, knowing that it would permit the men of his two brigades to commit depredations during their liberal foraging in the neighborhood. John King's Third Brigade meanwhile began to concentrate around Stevenson in preparation for joining the division. At Trenton, Reynolds's Fourth Division also remained stationary. Turchin's Third Brigade garrisoned Trenton itself, while Edward King's Second Brigade guarded both Payne's (Sitton's) Mill and the Empire State Iron Works. Like Baird's men, Reynolds's troops had little to do, giving them opportunity for mischief. After dark some of King's soldiers set fire to a large number of worker's huts and stacks of wood ready for the iron furnaces, creating a conflagration difficult to extinguish. North of Trenton, the soldiers of Brannan's Third Division remained in their pleasant camps at the Cole plantation, where they welcomed the arrival of Van Cleve's division. Corps headquarters remained at Brown's Spring, but Thomas planned to move to Easley's plantation on the next day. That evening Thomas ordered Negley to advance his entire division to the eastern foot of Lookout Mountain in the morning.[31]

Crittenden and Thomas moved slowly because Rosecrans expected greater effort from Stanley and McCook. In the camps of the Cavalry Corps, however, the only movement on the morning of 8 September was thousands of disgruntled men unsaddling their horses and unpacking their gear. Although he had promised to cross Lookout Mountain that morning, Stanley decided not to do so. His specific reasons remain unclear, but some things are known.

First, Stanley was a cautious commander who in the past had been philosophically opposed to deep strikes. Abel Streight's disastrous raid in the spring no doubt remained much on his mind. Second, although he had soundly defeated Wheeler at Shelbyville in June, Stanley truly may have believed that without Minty's brigade he would be seriously overmatched in a fight. Third, innate character flaws may have been at play. According to a modern author, Stanley "suffered bouts of depression and uncontrollable drinking, the latter after periods of intense pressure." Certainly the pressure on Stanley was great, with Rosecrans and Garfield demanding that he leap into the unknown world beyond Lookout Mountain. In October, Assistant Secretary of War Charles Dana would claim that "a few months ago General Stanley defeated an important operation by being drunk at the critical moment." Finally, Stanley may simply have been a victim of poor health, so poor that he would relinquish command a week later. The diagnosis, severe dysentery, required evacuation from the front and an extended convalescence. In his memoirs Stanley gave no explanation for his unusual behavior on 8 September, although in a later letter to Rosecrans he promised to explain himself fully when the two met. He simply wrote to Garfield at 7:00 P.M. that he had not moved as promised because of a lack of horseshoes. Given the time he had been at Valley Head, this excuse was risible. Clearly, more was at play than horseshoes, but whether it was stress, alcoholism, dysentery, or a combination of these factors is impossible to discern.[32]

Stanley's decision meant that McCook's Twentieth Corps would not be crossing Lookout Mountain on 8 September. Davis's First Division, slated to support Stanley, remained mostly inactive around the Winston plantation. While Post's First Brigade spent the day improving the tortuous road up Lookout, Lt. Chesley Mosman of the Fifty-Ninth Illinois Infantry regiment strolled to the top to survey the scene. There he found the men of Carlin's Second Brigade amusing themselves by rolling large rocks down the steep slopes. In the evening Post held a brigade dress parade attended by Davis and his wife. Several miles to the north, the three brigades of Johnson's Second Division moved to new camps at Long's Spring, a march of approximately three miles. There they had an excellent source of freshwater, and were on the direct road between Trenton and Valley Head. So good was the location that McCook relocated corps headquarters to Long's Spring as well. With Sheridan's Third Division seven miles north of Long's Spring at Stevens's Mill, McCook's headquarters was now centrally located for the first time since crossing the river. Sheridan's soldiers themselves remained in camp all day. Some men improved the time by washing their dusty uniforms in Lookout Creek, while others spent the day reading or writing letters. Still others, bent on improving their army rations, foraged in the neighborhood, which had not yet been stripped of edibles. Some inhabitants tried to secure their provisions by burying them, but to no avail.

Sheridan's men were in a relaxed mood, lying in a pleasant valley surrounded by forest-clad mountains untouched by war. That night Lytle was serenaded by the band of the Twenty-Fourth Wisconsin Infantry regiment, and Bradley wrote his wife, "I think the rebels will collect their forces at or near Atlanta, and try to defend that point, and very likely a severe battle will come off there, but I do not believe it will be fought very soon." Pvt. Henry Williams was even more optimistic, writing to his mother that "faith in General Rosecrans is unbounded."[33]

Stanley's four brigades took advantage of the extra day of preparation. Several detachments arrived with new horses to replace those too debilitated to make the climb. Even so, a number of men remained dismounted. They were sent back to Stevenson and eventually to the remount depot at Nashville, missing the campaign entirely. Having expended their first day's travel rations in camp, Stanley's men received an additional issue to reconstitute their three days of supply. Still others took the opportunity to winnow their baggage to the absolute minimum needed for the trip. During the morning, each division sent a battalion up the mountain to scout the route and drive away any prying Confederate eyes. In Edward McCook's First Division a battalion of the Second Michigan Cavalry regiment climbed the mountain and scouted southward, finding nothing. Crook's Second Division had better luck, with a battalion of the Fourth Ohio Cavalry regiment seizing a lone Confederate. With Minty's First Brigade still absent, Crook had only the services of Long's Second Brigade and a portion of the Chicago Board of Trade Battery at his disposal. Nevertheless, Stanley decided that Crook and Long would lead the expedition, and he ordered Crook to send Long's ambulances and a section of guns to the crest before dark. Notified at 3:00 P.M., the guns moved an hour later and, accompanied by Long's ambulances, slowly ascended the mountain. Although Stanley had specified that only a battalion of cavalry accompany the wheeled vehicles, Crook decided to have Long's entire brigade follow them up the mountain. At 5:00 P.M. Long's troopers began the climb, which continued until they camped on the plateau five hours later. Both Stanley and Crook accompanied Long. Meanwhile, Edward McCook ordered his First Division to begin its own journey up the mountain at 4:00 A.M. the next day. Most of Stanley's trains would remain parked in Winston's dusty fields. The hour was late, far too late in William Rosecrans's estimation, but at last the Cavalry Corps was lurching into motion.[34]

If Stanley was reluctant to move, Rosecrans's deception force was not. Looking down on Chattanooga, Wagner became increasingly convinced that the Confederates were leaving the town. At 8:00 A.M. he informed Hazen that he would soon open with artillery in support of Wood. Two hours later he reported to army headquarters that only cavalry garrisoned the town. At noon he forwarded the report of a deserter that Bragg's army had gone "toward Rome."

When shots fired toward the lower slopes of Lookout Mountain elicited no response, Wagner informed Rosecrans that only Cheatham's Division was present and the Confederate pontoon bridge had been broken up. During the afternoon, he used Wilder's battery and his own to shell the town from progressively shorter distances. By the end of the day the guns were firing at the Confederate fortifications from little more than 500 yards away, receiving only scattered shots from a handful of sharpshooters. While Wagner satisfied himself that Chattanooga was virtually empty, Wilder concentrated two regiments and parts of two batteries opposite Friar's Island. Planted in corn, the fifty-acre island shielded Federal movements somewhat, and when Federal artillery fire elicited no significant response, Wilder decided to ford the shallow channel separating the island from the west bank. During the afternoon the Seventeenth Indiana waded to the island, losing only one man, Joseph Wilson, drowned. The Confederate response now strengthened and for the first time included artillery fire. Wilder therefore postponed further action until the next day, although he still favored Friar's Island as a crossing point. The only sour note was provided by Minty, who reported that a crossing by Pegram's Division was imminent. In light of that, he preferred to wait for the arrival of his last battalion from McMinnville before moving in any direction. Thus Minty remained inert at Sale Creek, anxiously awaiting an imaginary Confederate onslaught.[35]

The army's lack of movement on 8 September permitted the units of the Reserve Corps to close the gap that separated them from the front. Granger himself remained ill in Nashville, so he instructed Morgan to expedite the movement. Morgan was to send Daniel McCook's brigade and Steedman's command to Bridgeport, while holding Stevenson with Tillson's brigade. Granger promised Morgan that he would arrive at Stevenson on the next day. As Tillson's soldiers assumed responsibility for guarding the massive Stevenson supply dump and nearby railroad bridges, the other brigades made slow but steady progress toward the river. Three of Daniel McCook's regiments entered Stevenson during the day, and the Eighty-Sixth Illinois Infantry reached Huntsville. Steedman's two brigades encountered more difficulty than McCook as they crossed the Cumberland Plateau from Cowan to the Crow Creek valley. Whitaker's First Brigade left Cowan early and marched over the mountain to Anderson Station. While the exhausted infantrymen bathed in Crow Creek, the brigade's teamsters struggled with many broken wagons and remained far behind. Left at Cowan were two doctors and 200 convalescent soldiers who had hoped to take the train to Stevenson but whose paperwork was not in order. Following Whitaker was the Second Brigade, now led by newly arrived Col. John Mitchell, who by seniority replaced Col. William Reid. Mitchell's men also encountered difficulty on the mountain road. Numerous wagons broke down and the 113th Ohio Infantry regiment was forced to abandon its portable bakery. Mitchell's artillerymen broke two caissons and, perhaps in frustration, amused themselves by mindlessly throwing rocks down the railroad tunnel's air shafts. Nevertheless, Mitchell's brigade also entered the upper reaches of Crow Creek valley by the end of the day. Some miles to the north, the Eighty-Ninth Ohio Infantry regiment prepared to leave Tracy City for Bridgeport. Ominously, the few citizens remaining at the Tracy City coal mines elected to leave with them.[36]

With most of his army motionless, Rosecrans was well aware that the momentum he had gained was in danger of dissipating if he did not initiate further action. The Tennessee River and Sand Mountain had been overcome; now only the great wall of Lookout Mountain prevented him from completing the movement that would pry the Army of Tennessee out of its Chattanooga stronghold. For his plan to succeed, Rosecrans needed two things: first, Stanley and McCook must mount a credible threat to Bragg's supply line, and, second, accurate information about Bragg's response to that threat must be obtained. Given those two conditions, Rosecrans could retain the initiative. He had Stanley's promise that he would begin his advance that morning, late but perhaps not too late. As for information on Confederate movements, Lookout Mountain prevented Rosecrans from seeing what Bragg's army was doing, and the long-range observations of the deception force were a poor substitute for direct knowledge. Wood's two visits to the Wauhatchie area had provided little information, and Rosecrans's frustration was evident in the rebuke he had Garfield send Wood. Virtually all of Rosecrans's mounted units were absent on the army's flanks, but he deployed what little remained to penetrate the Lookout Mountain wall near Trenton. He dispatched Col. William Palmer's Fifteenth Pennsylvania Cavalry regiment to find routes up the mountain, no matter how tortuous. In addition, Col. Smith Atkins's Ninety-Second Illinois Mounted Infantry regiment had just reported for duty at Trenton. Originally slated to join Crittenden's command, it was now assigned by Reynolds also to seek routes up Lookout's forbidding flanks. The searches generated two alternative routes up the mountain, the Nickajack Trace approximately two miles north of Trenton and a similar path slightly farther south known as the McKaig Trace. Neither of these two discoveries, however, yielded any information on Confederate activities or intentions.[37]

As the day ended, critical information arrived at Rosecrans's Trenton headquarters. First, McCook forwarded a report from a deserter from Company D, Fourth [Eighth] Tennessee Cavalry regiment. Pvt. Richard Owen correctly placed Wharton's Division around Alpine and Summerville, and Martin's Division around LaFayette. Owen also correctly identified eight of the nine regiments in Wharton's Division. If he credited Owen's story, Rosecrans thus knew the size and dispositions of the Confederate units facing Stanley. Next, a scout known as "D. M. W." reported in great detail on what he had learned during a month's stay in Chattanooga Valley. Quoting a Union sympathizer whose railroad travel had been disrupted by troop movements, "D. M. W." stated that Breckinridge's Division had joined Bragg with from 12,000 to 20,000 soldiers. The scout explained that Johnston was not with the new arrivals, he having been confused with Brig. Gen. Bushrod Johnson. "D. M. W." also reported that Buckner's troops had been at Loudon and were expected to continue moving southward. Most important of all, he stated that the Confederate pickets on Lookout Mountain had been withdrawn that morning and that most of Bragg's army was concentrated at the foot of Missionary Ridge. According to a talkative cavalryman, the scout said, Bragg had been flanked out of Chattanooga and was withdrawing to a better position in order to defeat the Federals in detail. This statement correctly reflected Bragg's intentions, but it seems to have been overlooked in the general euphoria that swept through the headquarters. On the strength of the scout's report, corroborated by Wagner's observations, Rosecrans approved Crittenden's reconnaissance to the top of Lookout Mountain on the next day. He ordered Thomas to support Crittenden with the Ninety-Second Illinois and also with Brannan's division if necessary. Anticipating that Crittenden's move would show the Confederates gone from Chattanooga, Rosecrans at 10:00 P.M. ordered Wagner to cross the Tennessee and join what was expected to be a pursuit.[38]

Suddenly the festive mood at army headquarters was broken. A courier arriving from Crook mentioned in passing that the Cavalry Corps had not begun its advance that day. Rosecrans instantly flew into a rage and dictated a scathing response to Stanley: "I learn from him that your command lies at the foot of the mountain on this side, intending to move in the morning. I am sorry to say you will be too late." In biting language, Rosecrans castigated Stanley for not following his instructions: "So far your command has been a mere picket guard for our advance. Orders accompany this, which I hope to see effectually executed." At 11:00 P.M., Garfield revoked Stanley's orders to strike for Bragg's railroad, replacing them with a much more modest task. Stanley now was to send one brigade from Alpine northward toward the southern end of Missionary Ridge while at the same time advancing another brigade eastward toward Summerville. "The enemy is believed to be in full retreat, and it is most important to know where he is going and by what routes. You have not a moment to lose in starting these expeditions." Garfield promised Stanley that McCook would support each of the cavalry's thrusts with an infantry brigade. To ensure that McCook understood his role, Garfield addressed a detailed message to him: "From all the evidence before us it appears that the enemy is evacuating Chattanooga and moving south; a part of his force has already reached the northern spur of Missionary Ridge. We must know as speedily as possible what route he is taking." McCook's brigades were not to go beyond the eastern foot of Lookout Mountain. In both messages, Garfield's grasp of the complex geography between Alpine and Chattanooga was weak, especially in regard to the brigade slated to advance northward toward Missionary Ridge. Nevertheless, the new orders were dispatched to Valley Head. Shortly thereafter, Rosecrans drafted his nightly report to Washington: "Information to-night leads to the belief that the enemy have decided not to fight us at Chattanooga."[39]

At 6:00 A.M. on 8 September, Bragg rode out of Chattanooga for the last time. The headquarters party was accompanied for a time by Polk and his staff. Polk's official family was in disarray that morning, his assistant adjutant general, Lt. Col. Thomas Jack, being too inebriated to perform duty. Henry Watterson, editor of the *Chattanooga Daily Rebel* and a severe critic of Bragg, had planned to accompany Polk but, perhaps unwilling to share the road with his nemesis, he did not. Nevertheless, Watterson and the *Daily Rebel* ceased publication in the paper's namesake city forever. Also departing was the correspondent of the *Mobile Tribune*, Samuel Reid, who left for Dalton around midday. Left to occupy the waterfront fortifications were troopers from Rucker's First Tennessee Legion. Having buried its heavy guns, the Reserve Artillery battalion departed with Breckinridge's Division. Even as most of the Army of Tennessee left Chattanooga Valley, organized detachments remained beyond Missionary Ridge at Chickamauga Station. At the depot described by one soldier as "a city in the woods," hundreds of men loaded the baggage of various units and large quantities of army rations on freight cars. Few trains arrived to remove the precious cargo because local railroad managers were rapidly removing all of their engines and rolling stock to Dalton and beyond. Thus John Jackman and his detail from Helm's Brigade waited all day for an engine to carry the division's baggage to safety. As for the stores, which by one estimate amounted to at least 90,000 rations, Bragg on the previous evening had ordered Buckner to send a brigade to guard and remove the stores. In midafternoon, Johnson's Brigade arrived from Ooltewah. Witnessing the chaos beginning to overwhelm the "city in the woods," they became increasingly restive. Aware that the army was abandoning Tennessee, some soldiers decided not to accompany it into Georgia. Still, most of Johnson's men loaded boxcars in the hope that more locomotives would arrive before the Federals did.[40]

The desperation so evident at Chickamauga Station was also visible far beyond Chattanooga Valley. At 2:00 A.M., Scott's Brigade burned the railroad bridge at Charleston and headed south. Reaching Cleveland at 7:00 A.M., Scott found quartermaster and commissary officers hastily trying to remove all government property. Tempers flared as the magnitude of the task overwhelmed military courtesy. To escape the chaos, Scott's troopers quickly resumed their march southward. When a detachment of the Seventh Florida Infantry regiment of Trigg's Brigade reached Cleveland around 10:30 A.M., it found discipline rapidly breaking down. The weary Floridians had just marched all night from the Hiwassee River, where they had burned several small steamboats. Their rations had long since been exhausted, and their foraging had proved futile. Suddenly coming upon large unsecured quantities of government rations, as well as a train preparing to head south to Dalton, the Floridians "conscripted" a bag of flour and some bacon and boarded the train without permission. The train left Cleveland just before noon and deposited the now well-fed men in Dalton at 4:00 P.M. At Dalton there was less desperation but much disorganization. Reporting from the town, correspondent John Linebaugh of the *Memphis Daily Appeal* (published in Atlanta) told his readers that Chattanooga was probably lost and Dalton might soon share its fate. Dalton was the junction of the East Tennessee & Georgia and Western & Atlantic Railroads. Nurse Kate Cumming had just spent an uncomfortable night there in a car packed with doctors, nurses, patients, and the wife and three small children of Patton Anderson. Cumming's train finally resumed its journey to Atlanta in midmorning. Sixteen miles south of Dalton, it passed Confederate engineers at Resaca flooring the Oostanaula River railroad bridge for the passage of troops. Just east of the bridge, Henry Wayne added six cannon Bragg had sent from Atlanta to the fortifications defending the structure.[41]

Unaware of the chaos behind them, the soldiers of Bragg's right column spent the day marching toward LaFayette. In the lead was Cleburne's Division of Hill's Corps. Having marched well into the previous night, Cleburne's men spent the morning cooking rations around Lee and Gordon's Mill until orders arrived to move. Around 11:00 A.M. they crossed Chickamauga Creek and continued toward LaFayette, thirteen miles away. Along the way, they passed the imposing home of widow Clarissa Hunt, "Snow Hill," then the even larger plantation of John Henderson. As Cleburne's men marched, the heat began to build and billowing clouds of dust rose far into the sky. It would be well after dark when Cleburne's brigades halted just north of LaFayette. Following Cleburne's weary men was Breckinridge's Division, which did not leave its camps until the middle of the afternoon. Night found them sprawled along the road several miles north of LaFayette. Polk's Corps followed Hill. Hindman's Division led the way, leaving its camps around McFarland's Spring well after sunrise. Marching in a leisurely fashion, the three brigades covered the eight miles to Lee and Gordon's Mill by late afternoon. At 5:00 P.M. they were in camp east of Chickamauga Creek in the vicinity of Snow Hill. The Thirty-Ninth Alabama Infantry regiment was far behind, not having been relieved of its provost guard duties in Chattanooga until late morning. Behind Hindman came four brigades of Cheatham's Division. Cheatham's march was also leisurely, with at least one regiment not departing its camp until noon. Momentarily left behind was Smith's Brigade, still holding the toe of Lookout Mountain. Smith with-

Lee and Gordon's Mill on Chickamauga Creek. (National Archives)

drew to McFarland's Spring only at 11:00 A.M. and did not leave there to join his division until 7:00 P.M. The remainder of Cheatham's men had finished their refreshing baths in Chickamauga Creek when Smith's soldiers finally arrived. Polk and his staff, now separated from Bragg, took up residence at the house of Joseph and Matilda Scott and their nine children, three-fourths of a mile north of Lee and Gordon's Mill.[42]

Like Polk's Corps, Walker's and Buckner's troops were also slow to move as they made their way south. Walker led the long column, with Liddell's Division at its head. Having marched all night to reach Ringgold, Liddell's soldiers rested at the village for most of the day. Around 3:00 P.M. Walthall's Brigade took the dusty road leading southward. The road lay in the valley of East Chickamauga Creek, with Taylor's Ridge rising to the east and the much lower Chickamauga Hills (now Peavine Ridge) paralleling it to the west. Govan's Brigade departed Ringgold two hours later and followed Walthall's tracks in the dust. Liddell's leading element made only six miles before stopping for the night beside the road. Behind Liddell's two brigades came Walker's own division. Although no sources indicate where Walker's men ended the day, the Thirtieth Georgia Infantry regiment only reached Ringgold because it had spent the previous night loading freight cars at Chickamauga Station. Following Walker was Buckner's Corps. In the lead, Preston reached Graysville at dawn after marching all night. He rested his command until noon, and then directed it to Ringgold, which was reached by nightfall. Trailing Preston's men was Williams's artillery battalion, which used the Graysville pause to feed its horses. Behind the artillery was Stewart's Division. Sources are lacking, but at least one regiment, the Eighteenth Tennessee Infantry, halted at Graysville for the night. With Preston's troops clogging the road and camping just north of Ringgold, Stewart's Division could hardly have advanced much beyond Graysville by the end of the day. While at Graysville, Buckner used the railroad telegraph line to wire Samuel Cooper about Cumberland Gap. He shed all responsibility for the order to abandon the post, placing it solely on Bragg's shoulders: "My own judgment has been to hold it, and I had so instructed." Unaware that Bragg's order had already been countermanded by Samuel Jones with Richmond's approval, Buckner wanted Cooper to be aware of his difference with Bragg on the question.[43]

Now that the Army of Tennessee was marching south from Chattanooga, it was moving behind the screen of cavalry pickets finally put in place by Wheeler. For several days, Wheeler had had scouts from Wharton's Division atop Lookout Mountain covering the passes into Broomtown Valley around the hamlet of Alpine. Wheeler himself had established his headquarters at Summerville, eight miles to the east. There, in a manner reminiscent of Stanley's timidity, he had resisted all orders by Bragg to probe aggressively toward the Federal concentration at Winston's plantation. Wheeler's maddening inaction had forced Bragg to send Forrest all the way from the army's right to its left in order to gain information on Federal activity beyond Lookout Mountain. Not long before 8:00 A.M., Forrest arrived at a place variously known as Gore's or Mount Hickory, five miles east of Summerville. At that time he courteously announced his presence in Wheeler's area of operations and stated that his orders from Bragg were to impede any Federal advance toward Rome. Armstrong's Brigade was with him and Dibrell's Brigade was four hours behind Armstrong. If Wheeler had no news, Forrest proposed to cross Lookout Mountain and see for himself. His aggressive spirit contrasted strongly with Wheeler's passivity. Forrest was unwilling to let the Federals beyond the mountain determine the course of events: "If the enemy does not advance we must move on them." Forrest then rode to Summerville and, apparently with Wheeler's agreement, developed a plan to send a small reconnaissance party to discover Federal intentions. He began by selecting 100 well-mounted and well-armed men for the mission. Roused to action by Forrest's determination to act, Wheeler instructed Wharton to pick 300 men of his own to join Forrest's party. The expedition was to depart from Alpine at 9:00 A.M. on the following day.[44]

North of Alpine and west of LaFayette, Martin's Division also guarded Lookout Mountain. Martin had been at LaFayette for some days, resting his much-depleted division. His situation was unenviable. The commander of his largest brigade, James Hagan, had not long before been denied promotion to brigadier general because of dissipation. Of Hagan's four regiments, the Eighth Confederate Cavalry had not yet arrived from its distant posting on the river line. Another regiment, Mauldin's Third Alabama, was temporarily attached to Pegram's rear guard trailing the army out of Chattanooga. Martin's other brigade, Russell's, consisted of only two regiments. At 4:45 A.M. on 8 September, Martin explained his situation to Wheeler in near apocalyptic terms. First he reported that his pickets had been driven from the western face of the mountain on the previous evening by a large Federal force. He expected to lose the eastern face at any moment, giving the Federals free access to McLemore's Cove, the V-shaped valley formed by Lookout Mountain and its spur, Pigeon Mountain. There were four gaps in Pigeon Mountain: Blue Bird, Dug, Catlett's, and Worthen's. "I have obstructed them and will defend them, but I cannot, if the enemy come on in force, hold them, as infantry can get up in hundreds of places." Similarly, the Federals could outflank Martin by skirting Pigeon Mountain's northern end. Martin bitterly complained that Wheeler had given him no instructions for such an eventuality, and indeed had not even communicated with him recently. Therefore, when the Federals pressed him, as he expected them to do soon, he planned to withdraw through LaFayette all the way to Taylor's Ridge and form a new defense line there. He had already sent his trains to Taylor's Ridge. Frustrated that his superior had seemingly abandoned him, and unaware that the entire Army of Tennessee was approaching his rear, Martin dispatched a copy of his message to army headquarters, wherever that might be, and awaited the day's events with trepidation.[45]

Even though written at LaFayette, Martin's message took all day to reach Bragg. By dark, army headquarters had been established adjacent to Lee and Gordon's Mill, where the road to LaFayette crossed West Chickamauga Creek. During the day, Bragg had sent only one message, an order to Buckner to leave a brigade at Ringgold to protect supplies. The message forecast that headquarters would be near LaFayette on the following evening. After his tent was erected, Bragg wrote to Polk, seeking news from the rear guard. None was immediately forthcoming, perhaps because at least eight members of Polk's staff were cavorting in Chickamauga Creek, while Thomas Jack and ordnance officer Arthur Rutledge were still inebriated. During the evening, Martin's message forecasting the imminent loss of Lookout and Pigeon Mountains reached headquarters. Bragg had planned to continue toward Summerville, but Martin's report caused him to change his mind. If the Federals were so near, it was time to concentrate and prepare for battle. At 11:30 P.M., Brent drafted new orders. First, he instructed Hill to cover the roads leading to LaFayette from Pigeon Mountain, as well as a road running west into McLemore's Cove from Rock Spring.

Brent predicted that Walker would reach LaFayette and Buckner would reach Rock Spring by the next evening. Second, Brent ordered Walker to continue his march southward until he reached Shipp's (now Maddox) Gap in Taylor's Ridge. Walker was then to send the army's trains beyond Taylor's Ridge and march westward to LaFayette. The message forecast a possible battle on the next day somewhere between LaFayette and Rock Spring. Finally, Brent ordered Forrest and Wheeler to move to LaFayette, leaving pickets at the Lookout Mountain passes. No written message to Polk is extant, but somehow he got instructions, because a junior staff officer ordered Hindman to march at 6:00 A.M., followed by Cheatham two hours later. Further moves would have to await the arrival of more information.[46]

Bragg intended to make his fight with the troops at hand, unaware that large reinforcements were beginning to move to his aid. He knew that Johnston was sending two brigades from Mississippi to Atlanta but knew nothing of the decision to send several divisions from Virginia to northern Georgia. That day in Richmond, Frederick Sims telegraphed quartermasters and railroad superintendents in four states, warning them to prepare for the massive troop movement. First, Sims told Thomas Dodamead, superintendent of the Virginia & Tennessee Railroad, that the troops would not be using his company because of the Federal occupation of Knoxville. Sims's new and longer route not only required the services of far more railroads but would greatly strain the capacity of some companies. He was especially concerned about the ability of the Wilmington & Manchester Railroad to handle the traffic expeditiously, so he established two separate routes through North Carolina. The two streams of troops would reunite at Kingville, South Carolina. Sims projected that approximately 3,000 troops could be shipped each day for seven days, in increments of 1,500 men every twelve hours, beginning at 8:00 P.M. that night. All would take the Richmond & Petersburg Railroad to Petersburg, then the Petersburg Railroad to Weldon. At Weldon, the flow would be divided, with half going via the Wilmington & Weldon Railroad to Wilmington and the remainder taking the Raleigh & Gaston Railroad to Raleigh. The routing of individual trains at Weldon was to be handled by Maj. John Whitford, one of Sims's primary assistants, from his office at Goldsboro. Sims asked Whitford to pass the word to railroad managers in North Carolina, while he notified superintendents in South Carolina and Georgia. Thus telegrams flashed to Thomas Sharp of the Charlotte & South Carolina Railroad, Henry Peake of the South Carolina Railroad, Henry Drane of the Wilmington & Manchester Railroad, George Yonge of the Georgia Railroad, and quartermaster Maj. Thomas Peters, regional transportation coordinator in Atlanta.[47]

Of the troops moving to join Bragg, Gregg's Brigade negotiated the tedious crossing of Mobile Bay before boarding trains for Montgomery. Hospital Stew-

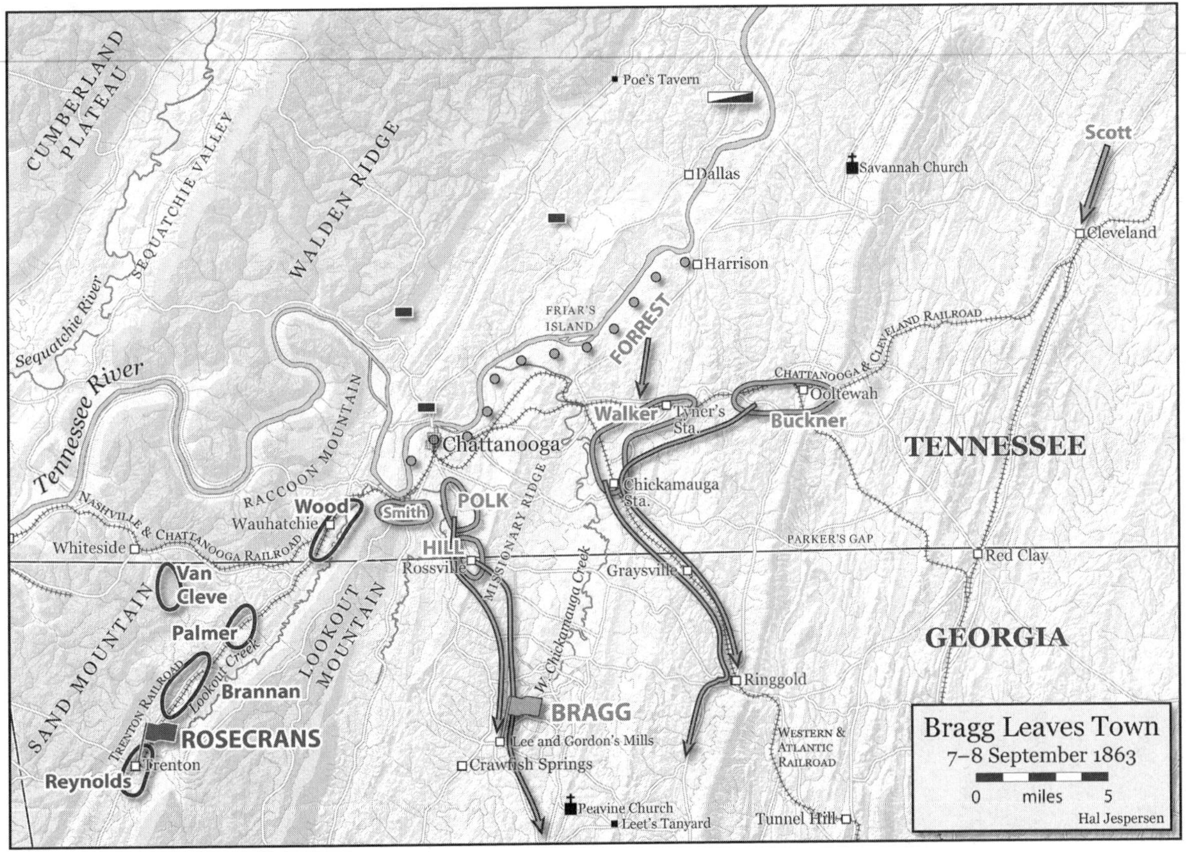

Bragg Leaves Town
7–8 September 1863
0 miles 5
Hal Jespersen
CUMBERLAND PLATEAU
SEQUATCHIE VALLEY
Sequatchie River
WALDEN RIDGE
Tennessee River
Poe's Tavern
Dallas
Savannah Church
Scott
Cleveland
Harrison
FRIAR'S ISLAND
FORREST
CHATTANOOGA & CLEVELAND RAILROAD
Ooltewah
Walker
Tyner's Sta.
Buckner
TENNESSEE
Chattanooga
RACCOON MOUNTAIN
Chickamauga Sta.
NASHVILLE & CHATTANOOGA RAILROAD
Wood
Wauhatchie
Smith
POLK
MISSIONARY RIDGE
PARKER'S GAP
Whiteside
HILL
Rossville
Graysville
Red Clay
Van Cleve
SAND MOUNTAIN
LOOKOUT MOUNTAIN
W. Chickamauga Creek
Palmer
Lookout Creek
GEORGIA
TRENTON RAILROAD
Brannan
Ringgold
BRAGG
ROSECRANS
Lee and Gordon's Mills
WESTERN & ATLANTIC RAILROAD
Trenton
Crawfish Springs
Reynolds
Peavine Church
Leet's Tanyard
Tunnel Hill

ard John Farris, twenty-six, of the Forty-First Tennessee Infantry regiment marveled at the experience of crossing the bay: "It was the first time in my life I had even been where . . . my eyes could see no land." Advance elements of McNair's Brigade meanwhile reached Montgomery via the rail-river route through Selma. In central Virginia, Longstreet put his corps into motion. First to go was Maj. Gen. John Hood's Division, which moved toward railheads on the Richmond, Fredericksburg & Potomac Railroad from its camps around Fredericksburg. Hood himself was already in Richmond, recuperating from his Gettysburg wound, leaving Brig. Gen. Evander Law to manage the loading process. First to board trains was Henry Benning's Brigade, which loaded at Guinea Station, twelve miles south of Fredericksburg. Next was Jerome Robertson's Brigade, which marched to Milford, nine miles south of Guinea, and departed southward that evening. Finally, Law's Brigade, commanded by James Sheffield, marched southward on the Telegraph Road toward Hanover Junction. Southwest of Fredericksburg, Maj. Gen. Lafayette McLaws's division left Waller's Tavern and marched toward the Virginia Central Railroad at Beaver Dam Station. There the brigades of William Wofford, Goode Bryan, Benjamin Humphreys, and Joseph Kershaw found no trains, so they continued eastward on the railroad toward Hanover Junction. By the end of the day, Wofford and Bryan had reached the junction, but Humphreys and Kershaw halted several miles west of that point. Last of all, Maj. Gen. George Pickett's Division departed Orange Court House and marched for Richmond by way of Gordonsville and Louisa Court House. Although Longstreet's move was supposed to be secret, that same day the *New York Herald* reported that a large force of infantry belonging to Longstreet's Corps had gone south, destination unknown.[48]

17

THE FALL OF CHATTANOOGA

» 9 SEPTEMBER 1863 «

As watches ticked past midnight, announcing the beginning of Wednesday, 9 September, lights burned brightly in army headquarters at Trenton. Rosecrans's normal routine kept staff officers active beyond midnight every night, though business often ended with the daily message to Washington. Thereafter, it was time for conviviality lasting several hours. As a result, little business was transacted early in the morning because everyone slept late. Easy to follow in garrison, this pattern wore less well when active campaigning required the headquarters to function both early in the morning and late at night. Gradually the sleep deficit grew, and without noticing it, men became ever more physically weary and mentally dull. On this night, however, there was something new to keep the officers' adrenalin flowing. All new information seemed to indicate that the Army of Tennessee was leaving Chattanooga or had already gone. During the previous afternoon Crittenden had accepted Palmer's proposal to send troops up Lookout Mountain at first light and had ordered Van Cleve to do the same. At the same time, he had rebuffed Wood's proposal to make a reconnaissance of his own. At 1:00 A.M., not long after dispatching his daily report to Washington, Rosecrans gave final approval to Crittenden's probe, which now included the Ninety-Second Illinois Mounted Infantry regiment from Thomas's Fourteenth Corps as a support. At 2:30 A.M., Frank Bond confirmed disapproval of Wood's proposal. At the same time, Bond exuberantly forecast the imminent fall of Chattanooga. Five minutes later, he instructed Capt. Jesse Merrill, the army's chief signal officer, to be present when the probes began, in order to transmit any information they might generate. In response to these instructions, eight miles north of Trenton, William Grose began to move toward the mountain with three regiments. His goal was a steep and narrow pathway up the shoulder of the mountain called Powell's Trace. Three miles north of

Trenton, Samuel Beatty led his brigade across Lookout Valley to the foot of the mountain preparatory to ascending the faint Nickajack Trace.[1]

At the very time that Grose and Beatty were stumbling through the darkness on the floor of Lookout Valley, a message reached Trenton from George Wagner: "The enemy has evacuated Chattanooga. They left to-day. Will occupy the place to-morrow." The message, which arrived around 3:00 A.M., had been more than six hours in transit, first by signal torch from Walden's Ridge to Shell Mound, then by telegraph to Whiteside and up Murphy's Hollow, where a courier carried it to army headquarters. Instantly, all thoughts of levity or sleep vanished, and Rosecrans quickly dictated a series of orders to Crittenden, Wagner, and Thomas. At 3:30 A.M. Garfield ordered Crittenden to "throw your whole command forward (with five days' rations) without delay, and make a vigorous pursuit." In a final sentence, which spoke volumes about Rosecrans's view of Crittenden's competence, Garfield counseled Crittenden to take only wagons enough for a five-day pursuit but to carry an ample supply of ammunition. At the same time that Garfield wrote to Crittenden, Goddard directed Wagner to push across the Tennessee River as rapidly as possible and join Crittenden's column in pursuit. Like Crittenden, Wagner was to take with him only enough wagons to keep the troops supplied for five days with both food and ammunition. Finally, Garfield wrote to Thomas, also at 3:30 A.M. In a very brief note, he shared the contents of Wagner's dispatch, canceled the movement of the Ninety-Second Illinois Mounted Infantry to support Crittenden's probes, and ordered Thomas to prepare the Fourteenth Corps for instant movement. Most important, he informed Thomas that "the general commanding desires you to call on him at once to consult in regard to arrangements for the pursuit." These 3:30 A.M. messages indicate that Rosecrans, with the possible advice of Garfield, had already decided upon the army's new course of action before consulting Thomas. Pursuit it would be. Thus the die was cast: Chattanooga, so long the objective, now would be replaced by a chase after the elusive Army of Tennessee.[2]

Thomas's original plan for the day was to move corps headquarters from Brown's Spring to Easley's Plantation, seven miles south of Trenton, so as to follow his divisions in their trek across Lookout Mountain. Now he rode to army headquarters, probably arriving not long after sunrise, which occurred shortly after 6:00 A.M. Neither Rosecrans, Thomas, nor any other participant recorded the ensuing discussion, and the only account of the meeting comes from Thomas's chaplain, Thomas Van Horne, who was himself not present. After the war and at Thomas's request, Van Horne wrote a history of the Army of the Cumberland, published in 1875 after Thomas's death. Subsequently, he published a biography of Thomas in 1882. In it he asserted for the first time that during the meeting with Rosecrans, Thomas vigorously opposed an immediate pursuit of Bragg's army. At the time, Rosecrans's major elements were widely scattered along the length of Lookout/Wills Valley. The army's supply lines were tenuous, dependent upon single-track railroads, rickety pontoon bridges, and long wagon-hauls over two mountains. Instead of a hasty pursuit on widely divergent routes, the army's scattered corps, Thomas believed, would be better served by marching directly to Chattanooga using Lookout Mountain as a shield. There the army could consolidate its position and amass sufficient supplies to sustain any subsequent advance. If this was indeed Thomas's view, it was certainly in keeping with his cautious and methodical nature. Rosecrans rejected all of Thomas's proposals and entreaties. In a private letter in 1884, Van Horne wrote that Thomas "told me that on the morning of the 9th of September he had presented one military reason after another against the pursuit of Bragg's army and for the occupation of Chattanooga and the establishment of reliable communications. He said Rosecrans assented in every instance and Thomas then said 'Why don't you do this then?' The reply was 'they expect more of me.'" Clearly, Halleck's threats and Lincoln's gentle chiding had had their effect on Rosecrans's thinking.[3]

If Thomas was cautious, Wagner was aggressive. Chaffing under the cautious Hazen, he had questioned Hazen's seniority and had gained command of the deception force. As soon as he gained control, he had ordered increased activity opposite Chattanooga and upstream at Friar's Island. On the previous afternoon a call for volunteers to swim the river and secure boats for a crossing brought forth several soldiers willing to attempt the passage, but darkness prevented their effort. Now, as the sun burned away the mist on the river, the same men readied themselves to try again. Confederate pickets from Rucker's Legion withdrew from the river around 8:00 A.M., giving the men of the Ninety-Seventh Ohio Infantry regiment their opportunity. More than twenty years later, Capt. William Naylor of the Tenth Indiana Battery claimed that he crossed alone with the help of a civilian in a canoe and was fired upon by the withdrawing Confederates, but no one else mentions his exploit. Somewhat more substantial is the claim that three men from Company C, Ninety-Seventh Ohio—Sgt. Andrew Hossum, twenty-three, Cpl. William Jackson, nineteen, and Pvt. Jacob Kraps, twenty-three—were the first Federal soldiers to cross the river. They used a small boat paddled by a black man. Having made the crossing, the three, with the possible assistance of friendly civilians, untied a mule-powered ferry and propelled it back to the Federal shore. By now it was well after daylight, and hundreds of Federals witnessed the bold crossing. Seizing the moment, Lt. Col. Milton Barnes of the Ninety-Seventh Ohio quickly loaded Companies C and I and the regimental colors on the ferry and sent it back across the stream. There Barnes deployed the companies as skirmishers and sent some of the men to the fortifications at Cameron Hill, where they raised the colors. Visible to Wagner's brigade and part of Wilder's command, the flag elicited universal cheers. The time could hardly have been later than 10:00 A.M. and probably was somewhat earlier.[4]

At 5:45 A.M., about the time Sergeant Hossum's party was negotiating for a boat to take them across the river, Crittenden received Rosecrans's 3:30 A.M. order to advance on Chattanooga and quickly passed it to his division commanders. Nearest Chattanooga was Wood's First Division. Buell's First Brigade was already preparing for a possible reconnaissance, so it became the first unit to take the road. Harker's Third Brigade followed at 8:00 A.M., much to his annoyance. A mile south of Harker's position, Palmer's Second Division also received Crittenden's order to advance in haste. The order came too late to recall Grose and his three regiments clawing their way up Powell's Trace, so Grose's two remaining regiments were attached to Cruft's First Brigade. Cruft and his expanded command took the road at 8:00 A.M., moving with the division's artillery and baggage train. They quickly found themselves slowed by Wood's wagons. Several miles south of Palmer, Van Cleve also received the order to march on Chattanooga. Beatty's First Brigade was also beyond recall and was well on its way up Lookout Mountain on the Nickajack Trace. Thus Van Cleve marched from Cole's Spring with only Barnes's Third Brigade and the division's artillery and trains. Dick's Second Brigade had finally reached Whiteside on the previous afternoon and continued toward Lookout Valley, eventually joining Van Cleve's column during the day. Also in motion was Smith Atkins's Ninety-Second Illinois Mounted Infantry regiment. When their orders to sweep the top of Lookout Mountain were canceled, Atkins reported to army headquarters and was told to lead the Twenty-First Corps into Chattanooga. Pleased to operate independently without interference from Wilder or Reynolds, Atkins headed northward to overtake Crittenden's column. Driving his men forward relentlessly, Atkins passed Palmer and Van Cleve before they got on the road and soon reached Wood's leading brigade.[5]

Upon finding Wood's troops filling the road as they approached the steep grade up the slope of Lookout Mountain, Atkins confronted Wood and demanded the right of way. Sensing that Chattanooga was about to fall to his command, Wood at first demurred but ultimately made way for the horsemen. When Atkins's advance met Confederate skirmishers, he dismounted Company F and sent it up the mountain. The Confederates, part of the Third Alabama Cavalry regiment, stubbornly resisted and overlapped the Federal line. Wood soon appeared with the Twenty-Sixth Ohio Infantry regiment of Buell's brigade, and Atkins reluctantly asked for assistance. In response, the infantrymen deployed on the hillside to the right of the Ninety-Second Illinois and forced the Confederates to retreat. Just as Atkins was about to resume his advance, shells began to land uncomfortably near his command. The artillery fire came from a section of Lilly's Eighteenth Indiana Battery. Positioned on Stringer's Ridge, Lilly's gunners could not distinguish friend from foe and fired indiscriminately into the trees along the road. Irked by the unhelpful shelling, Atkins briefly considered having a man swim the river, but changed his mind when a soldier claimed he could stop the gunners with a makeshift signal flag. Using a handkerchief and a stick, the soldier soon attracted the attention of Lilly's gun crews and the firing ceased. Just as Atkins prepared to resume his advance, Wood called him to a conference. Ordering two companies to chase Mauldin's Alabamians toward Rossville while the remainder of the regiment prepared to dash into Chattanooga, Atkins sourly rode back to Wood's position. If Wood was attempting to delay the Ninety-Second Illinois until more of his infantrymen could catch up, he failed because Atkins refused to hold his men back. Breaking free from Wood, he sent his command down the mountain with the regimental colors leading the way. By the time Wood rode to the front with Harker and Harker's flag, Atkins and the Ninety-Second Illinois were already in Chattanooga Valley racing for the city.[6]

Thundering over the Chattanooga Creek bridge, Atkins and seven companies of his regiment entered Chattanooga on Chestnut Street. Just beyond the railroad depot they halted at the Crutchfield House, a large brick three-story building formerly owned by the Unionist Crutchfield brothers. On top, Atkins's men unfurled the regimental colors and proclaimed the capture of the city. According to Atkins, the time was 10:00 A.M. An hour later, in a dispatch to both army headquarters and division commander Reynolds, he announced the capture of Chattanooga and reported the Confederate army heading south. Detailing a company to secure the city, Atkins prepared to head upriver in search of scattered Confederate defenders. His independence ended around noon with the arrival of Crittenden, who sent him to Friar's Island to facilitate Wilder's crossing. Atkins was satisfied that his were the first troops to enter Chattanooga, but it is probable that the handful of men from the Ninety-Seventh Ohio of Wagner's brigade had beaten him to the prize by a few minutes. Eventually men from the two regiments met in the nearly deserted downtown and the capture of Chattanooga was complete. While the Ninety-Second Illinois paused, Wagner kept the mule-powered ferry in full operation, transferring his four regiments to the foot of Market Street. The ferry was small, holding only part of a regiment or two full wagon teams at a time, so the process continued throughout the afternoon and into the night. Meanwhile, Wood's other brigades entered the city. Buell's First Brigade arrived at noon, followed by Harker's Third Brigade an hour later. Col. Emerson Opdycke of the 125th Ohio Infantry regiment led Harker's troops because Harker had raced ahead with Wood. By 2:00 P.M. Wood had complete control of Chattanooga. The race to be first to enter the city appeared unseemly to Chaplain John Hight of the

Fifty-Eighth Indiana Infantry regiment: "There is a great rush now to get to the front. There was not so much of a desire to rush that way awhile ago. Now that the dog is dead, everybody wants to get in at the burial."[7]

The city that Federal troops had fantasized about for so long was a disappointment to many. There had always been something of a raw, frontier style to the town, which had not yet removed the rocks from its streets when the war came. Now, after weeks of bombardment, Chattanooga had a dilapidated and badly worn appearance. There were holes in numerous buildings, with most damage near the river and around the railroad depot. Even more obvious was the silence. Most inhabitants had left the city shortly after the shelling had commenced, leaving their property abandoned. The unfortunate few who either could not leave or chose to remain now found their city under new ownership. Not all were displeased at the result, and some readily offered information about the city's former masters and the routes taken by the departing Army of Tennessee. Most notable was a merchant named Jesse Thompson, forty-six, who told the Federals that Bragg's army had retreated on the previous day in two columns, one via the LaFayette Road and the other via Ringgold. In both cases, the army's destination was Rome, Georgia: "If we pursue vigorously they will not stop short of Atlanta." Most intriguing was Thompson's assessment of Bragg's army: "Troops badly demoralized; all feel that they are whipped; one-seventh of the troops mostly naked; the rations for three days would make one good meal." Thompson established his credentials by claiming that he had a son in Rosecrans's secret service. Indeed he did, as Michael Thompson, twenty-five, also a Chattanooga merchant, had been reporting to William Truesdail's organization since at least July. The sympathies of the Crutchfield brothers were well known, but the Thompsons apparently operated clandestinely. Unlike the Crutchfields, the Thompsons, and a few others, Chattanooga's remaining citizens waited quietly to see what would happen next. Rev. Thomas McCallie feared the worst, but he was happily surprised: "Here was a peaceable occupation of a city without any violence or outrage of any kind."[8]

Having occupied Chattanooga, Crittenden turned his attention to the remainder of the Twenty-First Corps. Originally following in Wood's wake, Palmer's and Van Cleve's divisions were redirected by Crittenden in early afternoon toward Rossville. Three of Palmer's regiments and four of Van Cleve's were still engaged in sweeping the crest of Lookout Mountain to disperse any lingering Confederates. Crittenden was aware that Grose had gained Summertown by noon, but he had not yet learned of Beatty's progress farther south. He had now reached the limit of the instructions received eight hours earlier and did not know how to proceed without further guidance. At 2:00 P.M. he wrote to Garfield, plaintively seeking that guidance: "Shall I order the train of my corps to follow my command? I have received no further orders from you,

Market Street in Chattanooga, Tennessee, with Stringer's Ridge in background. (Chattanooga Public Library)

as you stated I would in your dispatch reporting the evacuation." Crittenden added, "There are various rumors of Bragg having stated that he just wanted to get us in here, that he is not far off, &c., but I am not a bit scared." If Crittenden did not fear the Confederates, he also had no idea of what to do next. With Hazen still west of the river, Grose and Beatty on Lookout Mountain, and Wagner dependent on a tiny ferry, Crittenden's command was scattered. Just as he was about to send his message to Trenton, he received a dispatch from Rosecrans. Six hours in transit, the dispatch nevertheless furnished the guidance that Crittenden sought. Rosecrans wanted Crittenden to leave one brigade to garrison Chattanooga and lead the balance of the corps in a pursuit conducted with the "utmost vigor." He anticipated that the pursuit would lead Crittenden toward Ringgold and Dalton, while at the same time Thomas was moving on LaFayette and McCook was marching on Alpine. Crittenden was to retain Wilder's brigade until he was near the Fourteenth Corps, when it would revert to Thomas's control. If Crittenden encountered a Confederate force too large for him to handle, he was to assume a defensive posture and notify army headquarters promptly.[9]

Far above Crittenden, two of his brigades were sweeping the heights of Lookout Mountain for random Confederates. At first light Grose had led three of his regiments up the horse trail known as Powell's Trace. Near the top, pickets from Mauldin's Third Alabama Cavalry regiment briefly barred the way, but Grose's men quickly dispersed the Confederates, gained the crest, and turned north toward Summertown, three miles away. Also scaling the mountain was topographical engineer William Margedant, accompanied only by a corporal. Margedant's goal was the tip of Lookout Mountain, with its magnificent view and a flagpole hosting a Confederate flag. Arriving at the point of the mountain, Margedant suddenly found himself in the presence of Confederate cavalrymen. Equally surprised, the two groups acknowledged each other and peacefully went their separate ways. Finding the flag gone, Margedant unsuccessfully attempted to remove its rock foundation as a souvenir. The Confederates meanwhile left the crest via a good road that descended the mountain's eastern side. Soon Grose's men arrived from Summertown. They spent some time marveling at the stupendous view and ransacking nearby houses. Some found a large cache of sweet potatoes, while others discovered a barrel of whiskey in an abandoned building. Gathering their booty, Grose's command then began descending into Chattanooga Valley, where their parent division could be seen toiling toward Rossville. Several hours behind Grose was Beatty. At the top of the narrow Nickajack Trace, Beatty's men found themselves eight miles from Summertown and nine from the tip of the mountain. After resting several hours they marched northward, meeting no resistance except an angry young woman at Summertown who denounced them roundly. Reaching Lookout House, they found everything valuable already in the pockets of Grose's troops and could only gape at the view for a few moments in late afternoon before they also descended the mountain.[10]

Except for Wagner, the Federal deception force found itself unable to exploit the Confederate departure. Although he had built some boats and believed the Confederates facing him were weak, Hazen also could not disregard Minty's reports about a Confederate crossing in force. At 6:00 A.M. he wrote to Rosecrans expressing Minty's concern and promising to survey the area in person. An hour later he told Wilder that he would be visiting Minty and that Wilder should use extreme caution until the situation was clarified. The normally aggressive Wilder took Hazen's cautionary note to heart. He had pushed the Seventeenth Indiana Mounted Infantry regiment across a shallow channel to Friar's Island during the previous night but now doubted the wisdom of that action. With the far shore still guarded by artillery, Wilder withdrew the Seventeenth Indiana and opened a bombardment with a section of his Eighteenth Indiana Battery. By the time the men of the Seventeenth Indiana returned to camp, news of the fall of Chattanooga reached them. Also, the Confederate pickets at Friar's Island had disappeared. In response, Wilder in late afternoon managed to get portions of the Seventy-Second Indiana and Ninety-Eighth Illinois Mounted Infantry regiments across the river at Friar's Island, where they found the Ninety-Second Illinois awaiting them. With his baggage still atop Walden's Ridge, Wilder at 10:00 P.M. informed the Twenty-First Corps that he would not finish crossing the river until the following afternoon. Delayed by his jaunt to Sale Creek to see Minty, Hazen was even less ready to push his brigade over the Tennessee. With one regiment on Walden's Ridge guarding baggage and the others scattered around the valley, Hazen did not concentrate his command on the bank of the river until well past midnight. North of Hazen's position, Minty spent the entire day looking for the imaginary Confederates that continued to occupy his mind. With two battalions absent, Minty's command was quite small, but his inordinate fear of a thrust by Forrest's cavalry kept him from either providing useful information or preparing for a forward movement on 9 September.[11]

If Crittenden was unsure what to do, there was absolutely no doubt at Rosecrans's headquarters. Given the timing of messages emanating from Trenton since before midnight, Rosecrans and his principal staff officers had not slept when dawn came. An hour after providing guidance to Crittenden, Rosecrans had Garfield write to McCook. Explaining that Wagner had declared Chattanooga evacuated, that Crittenden was in the process of occupying the city, and that Thomas was driving on LaFayette, Garfield gave McCook explicit instructions: "The general commanding directs you to move as rapidly as possible on Alpine and Summerville, for the purpose of intercepting the enemy in his retreat; move on so as to strike him in flank, if possible." He explained that the Twentieth Corps could inflict great damage on Bragg if all went as Rosecrans planned. Garfield admonished McCook not to wait for his trains but to leave both his and Stanley's wagons to follow under a strong guard. At 9:30 A.M., Garfield wrote to Stanley, sharing Wagner's news and announcing that "a vigorous pursuit has been ordered by the whole army." Further, Garfield described Rosecrans's plans for his three infantry corps. Because uncertainty remained about Bragg's route and because Stanley had been a disappointment so far, Rosecrans and Garfield were unsure about the role to be played by the army's cavalry. Garfield therefore wrote, "The general commanding leaves your operations to your own discretion, with the general direction to cover our extreme right flank and move upon Rome or such other point as shall do the enemy most serious harm." The vague set of instructions contrasted strongly with the explicit directions provided to Stanley earlier, an indication that Rosecrans no longer considered his Cavalry Corps a major factor in the rapidly changing situation. Finally, Garfield told Stanley that McCook would protect his trains and that Minty's brigade would remain under Crittenden's control for several more days.[12]

McCook's headquarters on 9 September was at Long's Spring, twenty-one miles south of Trenton and two miles north of Winston's plantation at Valley Head. At 6:45 A.M. he received Garfield's instructions written at 11:00 P.M. on the previous night. The drive toward Rome and the Western & Atlantic Railroad was canceled; Stanley simply was to make two brigade-sized probes east of Lookout Mountain. McCook was to support those probes with two infantry brigades as far as the eastern foot of the mountain. The remainder of the Twentieth Corps was to prepare for rapid movement because Rosecrans anticipated the Confederate evacuation of Chattanooga. Finally, the message enjoined McCook to hold Winston's Gap and be alert to any Confederate activity south of his position. In addition to the message to McCook, the courier also brought dispatches for Stanley. The dispatches included Rosecrans's excoriation of Stanley for his failure to move against Bragg's supply line, and Garfield's instructions for the two-brigade probe. It is possible but unlikely that McCook read the embarrassing message to Stanley, given the personal nature of the communication. At any rate, McCook told Garfield at 8:30 A.M. that he had forwarded the dispatches to Stanley, although they would probably not reach him before the cavalry descended the mountain. Perhaps reflecting Stanley's views, McCook ventured the opinion that all of Wheeler's cavalry was in their front, making Stanley's task all the more difficult. He doubted that the small probes could accomplish much, but he was hopeful that some information might be gained. Even if Stanley was unsuccessful, McCook expected to gather intelligence on his own and would send it to army headquarters that night. He attached statements from several recent deserters describing the Confederate cavalry concentration opposite Stanley's route. However Stanley fared, McCook promised that the Twentieth Corps would act promptly, writing, "I will now mount my horse and go to the gap in person, so as to be better able to superintend things there."[13]

Thirty minutes before McCook replied to Garfield, his chief of staff, Gates Thruston, sent messages to all three division commanders. The messages to Sheridan and Johnson simply ordered them to be prepared to move in any direction. A much longer message to Davis closely paraphrased Garfield's 11:00 P.M. dispatch calling for two infantry brigades to support the cavalry probes into Broomtown Valley. Drafted in haste, Thruston's dispatch was virtually incoherent. Somewhat later, he crafted a much clearer set of instructions for Davis, ordering him to move with two brigades up Lookout Mountain in support of Stanley's probes. Thruston was emphatic that Davis's infantry must not go beyond the eastern foot of the mountain or explore Broomtown Valley. Davis's remaining brigade was to advance to the top of Lookout Mountain, leaving one regiment at Winston's plantation to guard the division's remaining artillery, its trains, and its sick soldiers. Stanley's trains and convalescents would be protected by Willich's First Brigade of Johnson's command, which could support Davis's guard if needed. Davis was permitted to accompany whichever brigade he preferred. The specific details of cooperation Thruston left to Davis and Stanley. The mission was expected to last only four days, so the troops would carry only three days' rations. Already prepared to ascend Lookout Mountain,

Carlin's and Heg's men started early but were forced to wait for the rear of Stanley's cavalry to clear the road. Through some mistake, both brigades took their trains up the mountain and had to pause while the wagons were sent back to the vast wagon park around Winston's. They then continued across the top of Lookout Mountain but on divergent paths. Heg and his men headed for a descent of the mountain called Neal's Gap, while Carlin and his command took the road toward Alpine that descended through Henderson's Gap. Heg eventually found his road blocked by fallen trees and rocks, ensuring that only Carlin's troops would make it down the eastern slope before night halted the infantry's progress.[14]

Stanley began the day on top of Lookout Mountain near its western edge. Unable to delay any longer, he planned to move with the advance guard, Long's Second Brigade of Crook's Second Cavalry Division. At daylight Long's troopers took the road that eventually led down the mountain at Henderson's Gap to Alpine. Far behind them, Edward McCook's First Cavalry Division left Wills Valley around 6:00 A.M. and commenced to ascend the mountain. Long led the way with his Second Kentucky Cavalry regiment, closely followed by his remaining regiments and a section of the Chicago Board of Trade Battery. By standard practice, whenever a road junction or house was passed, scouts left the column to investigate them. During one such investigation, Pvt. John Smith encountered a Confederate soldier at a residence near the road. Commanding the Confederate to surrender, Smith somehow lost his advantage and was killed, his riderless horse returning to the column while the Confederate escaped. Reaching Henderson's Gap, the Federals suddenly found more Confederate pickets and an obstructed passage. Quickly driving the Confederates back, the column halted while a detail of men spent an hour opening the road. During this pause, a courier arrived with the dispatches from army headquarters that Alex McCook had forwarded from Long's Spring. Stanley, Crook, Long, and other officers were together waiting for the road to be cleared when the messages, including Rosecrans's blistering rebuke of Stanley, were read. According to Crook, Stanley was visibly shaken: "Gen. Stanley was taken sick. In fact, he was sick then." In addition to Rosecrans's personal attack on Stanley, the messages reduced Stanley's mission to a simple two-brigade reconnaissance in Broomtown Valley. Already ill, whether from stress, alcohol, or some other malady, Stanley had no choice but to continue the advance down the mountain. As he did so, rumors of Rosecrans's harsh words began to spread in Crook's division. With the road now clear, Long's brigade resumed its march down the mountain.[15]

Around noon, while a hundred dismounted men completed improvements to the road, 1st Lt. George Hosmer led Company A, Second Kentucky Cavalry regiment, toward the three or four houses comprising the village of Alpine. Behind them the regiment watered its horses at a spring. Hosmer's company soon passed beyond a slight rise known as Shinbone Ridge. Soon it encountered several Confederate cavalry units, which charged and forced Hosmer to give ground. Hosmer's call for assistance brought Col. Thomas Nicholas and the dismounted men to his aid. The First, Third, and Fourth Ohio Cavalry regiments also rode to the front, along with staff officers, servants, and orderlies from brigade headquarters. Passing beyond Shinbone Ridge, the noncombatants found themselves in the midst of a sharp firefight and hastily fled to the rear. The panic almost broke the remainder of the Second Kentucky, but Lt. Col. Elijah Watts steadied his command and took it forward. East of Shinbone Ridge, Watts found broad open fields gradually rising toward a wooded area where the Confederates were standing firm. In the midst of the field, Hosmer's company held a slight knoll forward of the Federal line. Crook now took charge of the action, and sent the Ohio regiments to the right while the Second Kentucky formed on the left of the road. The Confederates contested the ground briefly before the threat to their flank became too difficult to ignore. With a section of the Chicago Board of Trade Battery and Watkins's Third Brigade arriving, the Confederates withdrew on two different roads. As darkness neared, Crook scouted on one road with some of Long's men, while Watkins investigated the other. Finding significant numbers of Confederates blocking their way, the Federals withdrew to Alpine, where Carlin's brigade joined them. At a cost of four killed and eleven wounded, Stanley had gained the Alpine crossroads, twelve prisoners, and several captured dispatches, but little else.[16]

During the time that the Cavalry Corps was working its way down Henderson's Gap and securing Alpine, Alex McCook endeavored to support Stanley's efforts. As he had promised, in midmorning he ascended Lookout Mountain and found Davis's two brigades at a road junction just beyond the crest. Garfield had told Stanley to send a cavalry brigade on each road, but Stanley was well beyond the junction when the orders arrived, so all of the cavalry had gone toward Henderson's. Thus Heg's command continued toward Neal's Gap alone, although Stanley promised to send a brigade toward Neal's Gap from Alpine via the floor of Broomtown Valley. Believing he had done all he could to support the cavalry, McCook started back down the mountain, intending to return to his headquarters at Long's Spring. On his way, he stopped at Winston's plantation and visited Sidney Post, commanding Davis's First Brigade. After conferring with McCook, Post sent the Twenty-Second Indiana, Fifty-Ninth Illinois, and Seventy-Fifth Illinois Infantry regiments up the now well-worn road up to Winston's Gap. The Seventy-Fourth Illinois Infantry regiment remained at the foot of the mountain to guard the division's artillery and trains. Having thus arranged for Stanley to be supported, for Davis's southern flank to be guarded, and for the trains to be protected, McCook returned to his headquarters at Long's Spring. From there he wrote to Garfield at 4:00 P.M. According to McCook, Stanley believed that his modification regarding Neal's Gap would still meet Rosecrans's instructions. Further, McCook thought that Stanley's force of 5,800 troopers was sufficient to "whip all before him." Although McCook admitted that he did not know Stanley's specific orders, he ventured the opinion that Stanley's objective was Summerville or possibly LaFayette. McCook had no knowledge of the fight at Alpine or of Stanley's rapidly deteriorating physical condition. Nor did he know that Heg's command had been stopped by major obstructions in the Neal's Gap road. To McCook, it appeared that all was going well, and he so reported to Garfield.[17]

Around 6:00 P.M. McCook received Garfield's 9:30 A.M. dispatch reporting the fall of Chattanooga and Rosecrans's orders for a vigorous pursuit. The Twentieth Corps was to move as rapidly as possible over Lookout Mountain toward Alpine and Summerville without waiting for its trains. Responding at 6:35 P.M., McCook promised to march at 3:00 A.M. the next morning: "I will do my best, and will have Johnson's division and two brigades of Davis' at Alpine to-morrow night, and Sheridan will be on top of the mountain." McCook complained about having to protect Stanley's trains but promised to get them moving as well. In passing, he noted that Garfield's dispatch had been nine hours in transit, which accounted for his late start. McCook also offered the testimony of a civilian named Taylor, who had been informed by a man named Robertson that Bragg's army was moving by both road and rail to a concentration point at Rome. In closing, he promised to communicate with Thomas as soon as he was east of Lookout Mountain and report to Rosecrans via Winston's as often as possible. At 7:40 P.M. McCook ordered Johnson, whose camps lay near Long's Spring, to move at daybreak with his entire command to Winston's. There he was to leave his baggage and supply wagons with Post and ascend the mountain with only his ammunition train. McCook expected Johnson to reach the eastern side of the mountain by the end of the following day. He wrote in similar vein to Sheridan at 8:15 P.M. Sheridan was to move at daybreak to Winston's and ascend Lookout Mountain, halting two miles beyond the crest. Finally, Post received instructions to get Davis's guns and wagons on the road at 3:00 A.M. so as not to delay Johnson and Sheridan. Post then was to begin moving all the Twentieth Corps transportation and that of the Cavalry Corps up the mountain. Contrary to what Rosecrans would later claim, McCook's orders clearly required him to take his entire corps to the eastern side of Lookout Mountain, and he intended to do so promptly.[18]

At 10:00 A.M., in a dispatch to Thomas, Garfield confirmed that "a general pursuit of the enemy by the whole army" was what Rosecrans desired. Summarizing the orders to Crittenden, Wagner, and McCook, Garfield instructed Thomas "to move your command as rapidly as possible to La Fayette and make every exertion to strike the enemy in flank, and, if possible, to cut off his escape." He promised that Wilder would return to Fourteenth Corps control when the Federals reached LaFayette. With Crittenden entering Chattanooga Valley and McCook struggling across Lookout Mountain into Broomtown Valley more than forty miles apart, Thomas would have to cross Lookout Mountain quickly to connect the army's widely separated flanks. Thomas, however, was not a man to hurry. With a steep pull facing any unit ascending Lookout Mountain at Johnson's Crook, he saw no reason to rush the entire corps to the foot of the mountain, only to have the divisions wait interminably for their turn to ascend the rough road. Negley's Second Division was ready to descend the eastern slope of Lookout, but his trains would take all day to reach the valley floor. Baird's First Division was just starting to ascend the western slope, while King's brigade had not yet crossed the river far in the rear. Reynolds's Fourth Division remained camped at Trenton and the Empire Iron Works. Brannan's Third Division was camped around Cole's Spring, five miles north of Trenton. With two divisions already struggling on the mountain, Thomas saw no need to hurry Reynolds and Brannan southward to Johnson's Crook. Thus the Third and Fourth Divisions of the Fourteenth Corps did not leave their camps on 9 September, Rosecrans's "vigorous pursuit" order notwithstanding. They did receive warning orders to move on the next day, and Reynolds moved his headquarters a short distance southward to Cureton's Mill, but nothing more was done. Thomas himself left Trenton and rode southward toward Easley's plantation, to which his headquarters train was already moving.[19]

From the top of Stephens's Gap, Negley surveyed McLemore's Cove, a checkerboard of small fields, pastures, and woodland. Formed by Lookout Mountain on the west and a spur of Lookout named Pigeon Mountain on the east, the V-shaped valley was essentially an eighteen-mile cul-de-sac with its open end to the north. Entry into the valley was by Dougherty's Gap in the south, Stephens's and Cooper's Gaps in the west, a series of four gaps in Pigeon Mountain (Blue Bird, Dug, Catlett's, and Worthen's) to the east, and the open northern end only a few miles south of Lee and Gordon's Mill. Both West Chickamauga Creek and Missionary Ridge had their origins in McLemore's Cove. From Negley's position, the road from Stephens's Gap to LaFayette led straight across the floor of the cove to Dug Gap. At that point McLemore's Cove was six miles wide, and LaFayette was approximately five miles east of Dug Gap. On the morning of 9 September, Negley knew nothing of events at Chattanooga, or of Rosecrans's decision to begin a headlong pursuit of Bragg's army. Instead, that morning he was governed by his orders of the previous night, which specified that he was to secure the top of the mountain while moving his division to its eastern foot. Told to move at 8:00 A.M., Negley did so promptly, sending Stanley's Second Brigade down the rough track that had been reconnoitered on the previous day. Stanley moved cautiously and took several hours to reach the valley floor, near homesteads owned by Jesse Stephens, Amanuel Rogers, and Wiley Bailey. At the same time, Beatty's First Brigade completed its descent of Cooper's Gap, three and a half miles north of Stanley's route. Beatty then marched southward along the foot of Lookout Mountain until he joined Stanley on the Stephens and Rogers farms. By 4:00 P.M., when most of Sirwell's Third Brigade arrived, Negley's division was essentially complete. Only one regiment was absent, assisting the division's trains on the mountain. An hour later, even the trains arrived in the valley.[20]

The view from Negley's new position was both breathtaking and frightening. To his rear was the frowning wall of Lookout Mountain, looming 1,200 feet above him. The mountain was a serious obstacle to the arrival of reinforcements and a possible trap for his division if he had to retreat in haste. To the east, bands of forest clothed several small ridges approximately 150 feet in height blocking his path, the most prominent being Missionary Ridge. Although they held a few slaves, the cove's inhabitants were Unionist in sympathy, offering essentially correct information about Confederate strength and movements in the immediate area. At 1:30 P.M., before his concentration was complete, Negley informed Thomas that the citizens reported a large Confederate force of all arms gathered just beyond Pigeon Mountain around Dug Gap. Negley's own scouts had traded shots with Confederate cavalrymen as the Federals slowly pushed eastward beyond the first small ridge. There, at a crossroads named for Wiley Bailey, another slaveholding Unionist, a large body of Confederate cavalry stood in formation. Clearly, Negley's presence was known to the Confederates. In order to learn more, Negley decided to push his defensive perimeter forward. Lacking cavalry of his own, he gathered twelve mounted men from his headquarters under Lt. Charles Cooke, an aide, and sent them forward. He ordered Stanley to take the three regiments of his brigade forward as well. The Confederate cavalrymen, a portion of the Fifty-First Alabama Cavalry regiment, gave ground easily in the face of Stanley's advance. Stanley's infantrymen and Cooke's detachment chased the Confederates a mile beyond Missionary Ridge until they rallied at West Chickamauga Creek. With night approaching and Stanley's position seriously exposed, Negley elected to return Stanley to the division's defensive perimeter near the foot of Lookout Mountain. He left some pickets to occupy the crest of Missionary Ridge east of Bailey's Cross Roads.[21]

Upon returning to his headquarters at Jesse Stephens's spring, Negley pondered his situation. Earlier he had been told of a large concentration of Confederates just east of Pigeon Mountain. Now, Wiley Bailey offered a different assessment. Bailey claimed that he had just returned from Ringgold and along the way had seen large numbers of soldiers and wagons, all allegedly heading for Dalton. According to Bailey, "The general impression among the citizens was that Bragg was falling back to Rome and Atlanta, and that Breckinridge's command was left to bring up the rear." Bailey saw only a handful of regiments at LaFayette and only the Fifty-First Alabama Cavalry regiment west of the town. If true, such an assessment represented good news, because Negley received new instructions shortly after 8:00 P.M. His new orders required him to march on LaFayette on the next morning with or without his trains. He was told that all of the other divisions of the corps were under movement orders as well. Negley acknowledged receipt of the order at 8:30 P.M. and promised to move promptly toward LaFayette at 8:00 A.M. He concluded, "All the information I have received this evening from my scouts and others induces the belief that there is no considerable rebel force this side of Dalton." That being the case, Negley was unconcerned that Baird's two brigades remained on the opposite side of Lookout Mountain, at least twelve hours of difficult marching behind him. Nor was he concerned that Reynolds's two brigades around Trenton, fourteen miles and a mountain from him, and Brannan's three brigades, nineteen miles away and also beyond Lookout Mountain, had not yet begun to move. Even though Negley was not told about Bragg's departure from Chattanooga, both Reynolds's and Brannan's men received the joyous news during the night. Some soldiers wondered why their commands were not already in motion toward the fleeing enemy.[22]

In contrast to the Fourteenth Corps, on 9 September Granger's Reserve Corps was far more active. Daniel McCook's Second Brigade of Morgan's Second Division marched from Stevenson to Bridgeport during the afternoon, although one regiment remained far behind near Huntsville. Their place at Stevenson was taken by Whitaker's and Mitchell's brigades of Steedman's First Division. Although scenic, their march from Anderson Station was tiresome because of the extreme heat and ubiquitous dust. Some soldiers were entranced by the high mountains surrounding them, but most were disappointed when they reached Stevenson. The small village consisted of twenty nondescript buildings clustered along a single street dominated by the two railroad stations and the hotel. Far more imposing were the massive piles of supplies being deposited in dumps along the railroad for the army's future use. Even though the main army had departed, the town was still full of soldiers. Tillson's First Brigade of Morgan's command served as garrison, a company of Charles Thompson's African American regiment worked around the depot, empty wagon trains and their escorts were constantly arriving from across the river, and King's brigade of the Fourteenth Corps was nearby at Bolivar. Gordon Granger himself was on his way from Nashville, in company with Assistant Secretary of War Charles Dana. When Granger arrived that evening, he found a new message from Rosecrans. It announced Chattanooga's fall and gave Granger detailed instructions for his subsequent operations. Rosecrans told Granger to send King's brigade forward, build fortifications to protect the Bridgeport bridges, provide forage for the trains shuttling between the army and the river, and organize the army's rear so that Granger himself could join the main army with part of his corps. Perhaps aware of Granger's occasionally dilatory tendencies, Rosecrans admonished him, "Bend every energy to the prompt execution of these things."[23]

Having put virtually his entire army into motion by 10:00 A.M. on 9 September, Rosecrans and his senior staff rested for much of the day. They had been up all night, first because of Rosecrans's nocturnal habits, then because of Wagner's glorious news, and finally because of the need to send orders directing a "vigorous pursuit" to the army's far-flung parts. Rosecrans, Garfield, and several others then must have caught a few hours of fitful sleep after seeing Thomas off toward Johnson's Crook in midmorning. Calvin Goddard found time to telegraph his wife about the evacuation of Chattanooga but did not sign another message until after nightfall. Young 1st Lt. Henry Cist shared the good news in a letter to his mother: "You can well imagine our feelings at this gratifying result and our General feels the best of all." During much of the day, the limited business conducted at headquarters fell to aides Frank Bond, Henry Thrall, and James Drouillard. The latter attempted to have John Purcell, archbishop of Cincinnati, travel to Chattanooga via Shell Mound, but the archbishop's party was already on the way to Trenton in three ambulances with the army's returning chief engineer, St. Clair Morton. That evening, the headquarters was once again fully staffed. At 7:40 P.M., Goddard arranged transportation for Charles Dana to Chattanooga on the next day. Less than an hour later, Rosecrans sent his daily report to Halleck. After all the harsh words exchanged between the two men over the pace of the campaign, it must have been gratifying for Rosecrans to write, "Chattanooga is ours, without a struggle and East Tennessee is free. Our movements on the enemy's flank and rear progress while the tail of his retreating column will not escape unmolested." This simple statement belied what a glorious day it had been for Rosecrans. Chattanooga was his, the enemy appeared to be in disorderly flight, the army's supply line was secure, and the cost was minuscule. The army's staff had already begun to plan Rosecrans's triumphal entry into Chattanooga on the morrow.[24]

Like Rosecrans, Bragg spent a restless night as 9 September opened for the Army of Tennessee. Just before midnight he had issued orders for his infantry to continue marching toward a concentration near LaFayette in the morning. Throughout the night Col. Edmund Rucker forwarded a series of reports that showed the Federals slow to capitalize on the Confederate departure from the river. That slowness gave Bragg time to consider his next move. Martin's frantic report, which forecast a Federal tide washing across McLemore's Cove and lapping at the crest of Pigeon Mountain, told Bragg that such a Federal threat

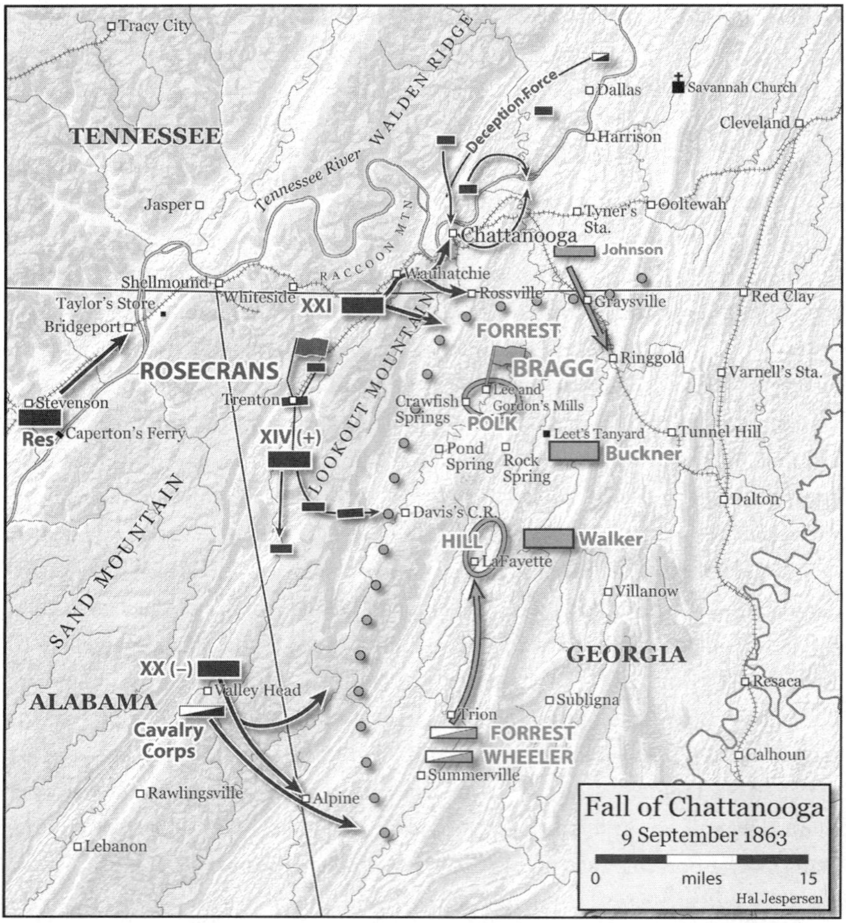

presented both a risk and an opportunity. If the Federals were in McLemore's Cove in strength, they could seize LaFayette or exit the cove at its northern mouth and approach Bragg's position at Lee and Gordon's Mill. Either way, the Federals potentially threatened Bragg's hope to wrest the initiative from the Army of the Cumberland. If the Federals in McLemore's Cove were relatively few and remained quiescent, however, they offered an opportunity to defeat Rosecrans's army in detail. Bragg urgently needed more information on the widely scattered parts of Rosecrans's army. At 5:30 A.M., he decided to modify the movement orders he had issued before midnight. Kinloch Falconer, one of Brent's assistants, at that hour canceled the movement of Polk's Corps. Scheduled to move within the hour, Hindman's Division was halted just in time. Cheatham's Division, ordered to march at 8:00 A.M., had more time to react to the new directive. Cryptically, Falconer told Polk that further instructions would soon arrive. The orders for the remainder of the army remained unchanged. Hill was to continue his march to LaFayette from Rock Spring,

Walker was to secure the army's trains behind Taylor's Ridge and continue to LaFayette as well, while Buckner took Hill's old position at Rock Spring. With Polk's Corps remaining at Lee and Gordon's Mill, by the end of the day the Army of Tennessee would be arrayed on a north-south line thirteen miles in length.[25]

While he awaited new information, Bragg assigned Brent and Falconer to build a cordon around the northern and eastern sides of McLemore's Cove while at the same time completing the army's concentration. The first order, at 7:00 A.M., went to Harris Mauldin, whose Third Alabama Cavalry regiment was to head southward east of Lookout Mountain and throw a screen across the mouth of McLemore's Cove. Mauldin would no longer be subordinate to Rucker but would report directly to army headquarters. Thirty minutes later, Falconer ordered Polk to establish a line of infantry pickets from Snow Hill westward to James Gordon's property at Crawfish Spring. From there Polk's men would eventually connect with Mauldin's troopers. Also at 7:30 A.M., Brent wrote to Hill. Still reliant on Martin's overwrought message of the previous day, Bragg feared that the Federals in McLemore's Cove had already seized Pigeon Mountain. Thus he wanted Hill to picket the road leading from LaFayette to Dug Gap and another road diverging from the main Gordon's Mill–LaFayette road at the house of Dr. Peter Anderson. The latter road entered McLemore's Cove through a low pass in Pigeon Mountain known as Worthen's Gap. At 8:00 A.M. Brent instructed Wheeler to use Martin's Division to establish a picket line in McLemore's Cove from Lookout Mountain to Anderson's house as soon as Wheeler or Forrest arrived at LaFayette. In peremptory language, he forbade Wheeler from beginning a raid, as Wheeler had proposed earlier. At 8:30 A.M., Brent told Walker to bring the army's trains with him to LaFayette instead of sending them east of Taylor's Ridge. Similarly, Brent several times modified the role of the brigade guarding the army's reserve supply and ammunition trains moving toward Dalton. Eventually, as Bragg's plans evolved, Brent ordered Buckner to move his corps to Anderson's house as rapidly as possible, bringing the detached brigade with him.[26]

As Bragg pondered a possible counteroffensive, the army's rear guard was pressed severely by the advance of the Twenty-First Corps. With Forrest and Armstrong's Division absent, the cavalry units following the army out of Chattanooga mostly belonged to Pegram's Cavalry Division. Along the river north of Chattanooga, Pegram's Brigade still guarded the crossing at Friar's Island. It was this command that delayed Wilder's thrust across the river for much of the day. In Chattanooga itself, Rucker held off Wagner's Federals with his First Tennessee Legion. The bulk of Mauldin's Third Alabama Cavalry regiment meanwhile guarded the northern end of Lookout Mountain, both on top and on the Wauhatchie-Chattanooga road. Rucker withdrew his pickets around

8:00 A.M., slowly moving back through the town as Federals converged on it from two directions. Some, in fact, waited near the partially completed Fort Cheatham, coolly watching the Ninety-Second Illinois race past them into town. They then withdrew toward Rossville. Simultaneously, Mauldin's Alabamians were pushed off Lookout Mountain's lower slope by Buell's infantry and forced from the top of the mountain by Grose's brigade. They also headed for Rossville. Pegram's men remained a little longer at Friar's Island but departed around noon when threatened by the Ninety-Second Illinois approaching their flank. Around the same time, Rucker informed Bragg that he had been forced from Chattanooga. Rucker reported in person at 2:00 P.M. At that time his command held a position a mile beyond McFarland's Spring west of the Rossville Gap, and his headquarters was a similar distance east of the gap. An hour later, Mauldin appeared. He reported being driven from Lookout Mountain, losing three men killed and ten wounded. Mauldin complained bitterly that Rucker had given him no assistance. With the army's rear guard clearly in disarray, Bragg at 3:00 P.M. summoned Forrest to his headquarters for new instructions.[27]

During the day, with the exception of Polk's Corps, Bragg's army gradually concentrated. Hill began the day at LaFayette under the assumption that Polk was following him southward. When Bragg ordered him to guard the road from Anderson's house into McLemore's Cove, Hill understood neither its purpose nor its location. Hill's lack of geographical knowledge was surpassed only by his unwillingness to consult Bragg directly. Instead, he ordered Breckinridge at Rock Spring to contact Bragg personally if the message was equally unclear to him. Also unwilling to seek guidance from a man he despised, Breckinridge apparently understood the requirement and deployed Helm's Brigade at Anderson's for much of the day. With Hill's approval, Breckinridge also permitted his command to cook several days' rations before continuing the march to LaFayette. In the midst of the process, he ordered the march resumed, and most of the division reached LaFayette in midafternoon. From there, Sgt. Washington Ives, nineteen, of the Fourth Florida Infantry wrote to his father: "We are a dirty tired and naked set for 3/4 of the men have not a single pair of shoes and no drawers, only one shirt, hat and pair of pants a piece. . . . The whole army is in good spirits but it is bad to see barefoot men marching on such roads. . . . I tell you it is enough to make you shed tears to see what some of the boys are enduring." Cleburne's Division spent most of the day at LaFayette cooking rations. In the afternoon, some regiments moved toward the Pigeon Mountain gaps west of town, where they found no Federals. Behind them, Walker's Reserve Corps continued its dusty march toward LaFayette, arriving in late afternoon. Similarly, Buckner's command marched westward from the vicinity of Ringgold. Stewart's Division took the lead, followed by Preston's Division. Stewart halted in the evening at Rock Spring Church, not far from Dr. Anderson's, with Preston nearby at Pea Vine Church. Thus by the end of the day, Bragg's major elements were within supporting distance of each other.[28]

Although the army was reasonably well concentrated, scattered units remained separated from their commands. Johnson's Brigade of Stewart's Division departed the nearly deserted Chickamauga Station at 8:00 A.M. They ended the day four miles beyond Graysville, not far from Ringgold. Also leaving Chickamauga Station was John Jackman's detail from Helm's Brigade, charged with removing the brigade's baggage by train before the Federals arrived. After waiting all night for a train, the men finally departed Chickamauga Station early on 9 September. At Graysville, five miles down the line, the cars carrying the Kentuckians' baggage were placed on a siding, leaving the detail to fend for itself. Somehow, Jackman prevailed upon the last train passing through to attach his cars. The train made it to Ringgold safely but was forced to wait there to follow a passenger train filled with refugees. Eventually, Jackman and Helm's baggage made it safely to Dalton that night. At Dalton, they found everything in confusion. Dalton was a chokepoint where everything evacuated from Knoxville, Loudon, and Cleveland met everything evacuated from Chattanooga. The Seventh Florida Infantry regiment happened to be at Dalton during the day on its way to rejoin its command, Trigg's Brigade. Forced to commandeer rations without permission on their way from the Hiwassee River, the regiment continued its irregular habits at Dalton, where the men got rations of flour and salt, but no meat. When several men were drafted to load rail cars, they took the opportunity to appropriate a large side of bacon and a box of tobacco for their own use. Seeing their commander's wife in a standing passenger train, the men serenaded her with "Let Me Kiss Him for His Mother" and "The Homespun Dress." Much satisfied with their day's work, the Floridians "went back to camp, took a smoke and turned in." Not as lucky as the Floridians, the Forty-Eighth Tennessee and Third/Fifth Confederate Infantry regiments, late to be relieved from the river, spent the day following the dusty road through Ringgold toward LaFayette.[29]

On 9 September Bragg's cavalry forces remained in disarray. At Summerville, nine miles east of Alpine, Wheeler intended to support Forrest in a reconnaissance up Lookout Mountain. That plan was canceled when orders arrived for Wheeler to concentrate his command at LaFayette, sixteen miles north of Summerville. Wheeler was also instructed to tell Forrest that he should move to LaFayette as well. In response, both Forrest and Wheeler in midmorning headed north, leaving the Lookout Mountain passes picketed by only a handful of men. Thus when Stanley's advance finally pushed down Henderson's Gap to Alpine it encountered only detachments from Crews's and Harrison's Brigades. Easily routed by Stanley's overwhelming numbers, the pickets lost few men, mostly to capture. At some point in the afternoon Stanley's men intercepted three messages from Wheeler, one of them indicating that Wheeler's headquarters had moved to LaFayette. Upon his arrival at that place, Wheeler received Bragg's orders to have Martin's Division picket the northern reaches of McLemore's Cove. Martin already had detachments in the Cove, especially Col. John Morgan's Fifty-First Alabama Cavalry regiment. Portions of that unit faced James Negley's tentative advance beyond Bailey's Cross Roads late in the day. Although Negley claimed the capture of two soldiers, Pvt. William Dodson later stated that he was the only man taken. As for Forrest, when he received Bragg's summons in late afternoon to come to army headquarters, he did so immediately. According to one of Buckner's staff officers who happened to share the road with him, Forrest was angry at Bragg initially but soon claimed he was "all right with the old man." Bragg instructed Forrest to go to Dalton and resume control of the cavalry on the army's right flank and rear. With Armstrong's Division by his side, Forrest would need to bring some order to Pegram's Division, elements of which were scattered from Rossville to Ringgold to the East Tennessee & Georgia Railroad north of Dalton.[30]

Throughout the day, Bragg remained at his headquarters adjacent to Lee and Gordon's Mill, in the midst of Polk's Corps. The staff issued General Orders, Number 178, which required the baggage of officers below the rank of division commander to be discarded, in favor of carrying more rations for the troops. Bragg wrote to Secretary of War Seddon, agreeing with the government's decision to hold Cumberland Gap and explaining why he left Chattanooga: "Rosecrans' main force had obtained my left and rear. I followed and endeavored to bring him to action and secure my connections. This may compel the loss of Chattanooga, but is unavoidable." (Neither Bragg nor the authorities in Richmond were aware that, at that very moment, John Frazer was surrendering the Cumberland Gap garrison unconditionally to Burnside's forces.) At some point during the afternoon, Bragg and Polk had lunch together. Polk's two divisions, meanwhile, idled in camp. Cheatham's Division was treated to a patriotic speech of considerable duration by Governor Isham Harris of Tennessee, who was traveling with the army. With time on their hands, Polk's soldiers cooked rations for the next two days but also became rowdy, causing Polk to forbid the unauthorized firing of guns in camp. When Rucker appeared and acknowledged being driven from Chattanooga, Polk assigned an infantry regiment to assist in picketing the army's rear. Around 5:00 P.M. a fusillade of shots from the direction of Crawfish Spring caused momentary alarm at corps headquarters. An order placing Smith's Brigade under arms was soon canceled when the cause was found to be soldiers shooting hogs. In the process, Smith himself was found to be in a drunken rage, requiring the intervention of Lt. William Richmond of Polk's staff, Capt. John Harris of Smith's staff, and Col. Alfred

Vaughan Jr., the senior regimental commander. Clearly, Polk's command was not well in hand on the evening of 9 September. Polk himself was debilitated that day by a bout of rheumatism.[31]

Had he known that large reinforcements were finally moving toward him, Bragg might have felt more sanguine about the coming battle he expected near LaFayette. Nearest at hand were the two brigades sent by Johnston from Mississippi. During the day major elements of both Gregg's and McNair's Brigades reached Montgomery. There the all-rail route from Mobile and the water/rail route through Selma converged, creating a significant traffic bottleneck. The shortage of locomotives and cars caused most of the units to remain in Montgomery for the night, giving many men an opportunity to attend the theater. In Virginia a much larger group of soldiers also was beginning to ride the rails. Because Hood's Division had reached the railheads first, Quartermaster General Lawton notified McLaws that his division would have to wait at Hanover Junction until at least three of Hood's brigades were dispatched southward. Thus, while Hood's troops rolled south, McLaws's four brigades did no more on 9 September than establish camps near the junction and relinquish their wagons and teams. Although the Army of Tennessee was already grossly deficient in field transportation, Longstreet's First Corps would be bringing none to northern Georgia. Meanwhile, the Railroad Bureau scrambled to gather additional locomotives and rolling stock. The limited capacity of the railroads involved had caused Sims to divide the route southward at Weldon, North Carolina, where Capt. Hiram Troutman was in charge. Initially, Troutman was not told of either the magnitude of the movement or the destination of the troops. After frantically querying his counterparts at Richmond and Petersburg, he received the necessary information and began to assign the arriving troops to different routes. Some were to travel on the Raleigh & Gaston Railroad to Raleigh, thence onward to Charlotte, and finally into South Carolina. Others were to take the Wilmington & Weldon Railroad to Wilmington before also entering South Carolina.[32]

Benning's Brigade was the first of Longstreet's units to arrive at Weldon. The command had departed Richmond before dawn on 9 September and reached Weldon in late morning. Finding no trains immediately available for the Wilmington line, Troutman decided to send the bulk of Benning's men via Raleigh. The two available trains of the Raleigh & Gaston Railroad could only accommodate three of Benning's four regiments, some 1,200 men, so the 350 men of the Fifteenth Georgia Infantry regiment remained at Weldon. That unit was shifted to the Wilmington corridor at 4:00 P.M. when the Wilmington & Weldon Railroad's trains began to appear. Troutman also informed his counterparts at Raleigh and Wilmington that 1,500 troops would leave Weldon daily, half in the morning and half in the evening. That estimate halved the number of 3,000 per day shipped from Richmond that Major Sims had been using. Troutman had hardly accommodated the last of Benning's command when Robertson's Brigade began to arrive at Weldon. With Wilmington & Weldon equipment now available, Troutman informed the Wilmington quartermaster that Robertson's 1,800 soldiers would leave Weldon at 11:00 P.M. Robertson's men had not spent much time in Richmond but were there long enough for some to become intoxicated and disorderly before their departure. More mischief occurred in Raleigh, where soldiers of Benning's command destroyed the office and equipment of the *Raleigh Standard*, an anti-Davis administration newspaper. While editor W. W. Holden cowered in the executive mansion, Governor Zebulon Vance and Lt. Col. William Shepherd, commander of the Second Georgia Infantry regiment, quickly restored order. The chastened rioters returned to the railroad station, some carrying printer's type in their pockets. Benning's men departed Raleigh for Charlotte shortly after midnight, but repercussions from their actions continued to spread in Raleigh for several days.[33]

Around the same time that the false alarm occurred in Polk's Corps, George Brent wrote in his diary, "Up to 5 PM no intelligible information from the other side of Lookout Mt." Polk's aide William Richmond wrote in similar vein: "We are in utter darkness so far as the enemy's whereabouts in force and his movements are concerned." Rucker had kept Bragg apprised of the large Federal force that had occupied Chattanooga and pushed his cavalrymen east of Missionary Ridge. Wheeler, however, had done little to provide clarity on the Federal threat at Alpine. Indeed, the most recent information from Wheeler's scouts was contradictory and outdated. Bragg had long been concerned about Wheeler's inability or unwillingness to probe the Federal positions aggressively, even sending Forrest to gain what Wheeler apparently could not. Now, with a clear threat developing in McLemore's Cove, Bragg had called Wheeler to LaFayette, removing him from the developing situation at Alpine. Still, the tentative Federal probe east of Lookout Mountain, and the slowness with which it developed, gave Bragg time to look elsewhere for an opportunity to strike part of Rosecrans's army. At some point after nightfall, Bragg finally received actionable information from Martin's cavalrymen in McLemore's Cove. A courier, apparently Maj. Augustus Johnson of the First Alabama Cavalry regiment, brought word from Martin that a force of approximately 5,000 Federals had reached the foot of Lookout Mountain via Stephens's and Cooper's Gaps and had halted there. Unlike his message of the previous day, which had forecast the loss of both McLemore's Cove and Pigeon Mountain, Martin's new report brimmed with optimism. A sizable Federal force had incautiously entered the cul-de-sac of McLemore's Cove and now stood with its back to Lookout

Mountain, which would delay any possibility of rapid reinforcement if it were to be assailed. Martin thus saw an opportunity for a Confederate counterstroke and suggested it to Bragg in what he later described as "a somewhat lengthy communication."[34]

The fortuitous arrival of accurate information from McLemore's Cove galvanized Bragg into action. He saw at once that his army was positioned to strike a possibly decisive blow against an isolated segment of Rosecrans's army, while simultaneously protecting his own flanks. The primary instrument for such a blow was Polk's Corps, although Polk himself was not the man for the task. Cheatham's Division, supported by Forrest's cavalrymen, seemed ample to hold the army's right and rear, leaving Hindman's Division free to enter the cove. If Hindman passed through Worthen's Gap and moved southward, he could assail the left flank of the unsuspecting Federal force. Hill's Corps already had Cleburne's Division guarding Blue Bird, Dug, and Catlett's Gaps in Pigeon Mountain. Cleburne could fix the Federals in front while Hindman struck them in flank. Faced with overwhelming numbers and trapped against the forbidding wall of Lookout Mountain, the Federals could be destroyed or dispersed into the southern reaches of the Cove. Either way, a significant portion of Rosecrans's army would be removed from the campaign. Although his son many years later claimed that Polk had suggested the plan, there is no other evidence of that. Indeed, a subsequent message indicates that Polk was only informed of the movement as it was being executed. At any rate, at 10:00 P.M. Mackall instructed Hindman to place his command under arms and called him to army headquarters. Hurriedly alerting his brigade commanders to be ready to march in an hour's time, Hindman hastened to Lee and Gordon's Mill from the vicinity of Snow Hill. There he learned that some 4,000 or 5,000 Federals were camped at the foot of Stephens's Gap, while another unknown number was at Cooper's Gap. Bragg ordered Hindman to enter McLemore's Cove and engage the Federal forces there in cooperation with part of Hill's Corps. The junction of the two Confederate forces was expected to occur in the vicinity of Davis's Cross Roads, midway between Missionary Ridge and Pigeon Mountain.[35]

At 11:45 P.M. Kinloch Falconer issued Hindman's and Hill's written instructions. Hindman's orders required him to meet Hill's contingent at Davis's Cross Roads and, if he proved to be the senior officer present, to lead the united force toward Stephens's Gap. Hill's orders varied slightly. If Hill chose to lead his contingent personally, he would command the expedition as ranking officer; if Hill did not lead Cleburne's Division forward from Pigeon Mountain, Cleburne would be subordinate to Hindman. Because the decision to attack was conceived so hastily, Bragg had no time to consult Hill. Therefore, he deferred to Hill's rank, and Falconer drafted the instructions accordingly. In case Hill was unable to provide troops for the expedition, he was to notify Hindman. Hill was also to provide a cavalry force to screen his advance because Hindman had no cavalry of his own. Finally, Hill's orders made no mention of a Federal force at the foot of Cooper's Gap. Both messages were dispatched just before midnight. Hindman received his orders directly, but a courier had to carry Hill's orders through the night thirteen miles to LaFayette. Prior to the arrival of his orders, Hill would have no inkling that Bragg was planning an attack and that his troops were to participate. As his men prepared to move, Patton Anderson rode in search of Hindman. He finally found the division commander studying maps with Mackall. Told of the Federal dispositions, Anderson openly expressed concern about the force of unknown size at Cooper's Gap, which would be on Hindman's right when he advanced into the Cove. Mackall responded, "*That* was an important question," but said nothing more. Clearly Mackall had doubts, but Bragg had made his decision, and Hindman's orders stood. Not long thereafter, Falconer wrote to Buckner explaining the movement, and to Polk, simply detaching Hindman from Polk's command. At Snow Hill, more than 7,500 soldiers of Hindman's Division prepared to go on the offensive. The Army of Tennessee was about to retaliate for the loss of Chattanooga.[36]

. . . .

The hot dusty day of 9 September 1863 ultimately would prove to be a turning point in the campaign. Beginning in late June Rosecrans's Army of the Cumberland had inexorably pushed Bragg's Army of Tennessee southward. First in the Tullahoma campaign, then in a series of leaps over challenging geographical barriers, and finally through its entry into Chattanooga, Rosecrans had reconquered southeastern Tennessee for the Union. At minimal cost, he had achieved the objectives established by the War Department when he took command in the fall of 1862. Throughout it all, he had maintained the initiative, forcing Bragg to react at a disadvantage. Now, rather than pausing to gather his scattered units, Rosecrans cast aside cautionary advice and elected to throw his army into headlong pursuit of the seemingly demoralized Confederates. That decision, made essentially alone and with little rest early on 9 September, would prove to be a fateful one, because Bragg was not yet ready to concede defeat. Outmaneuvered at Tullahoma, Bragg had safely extricated his army from potential destruction. Withdrawing behind the Tennessee River, he knew that his army could not defend the long river line. His only hope was to wait for Rosecrans to commit himself, then maneuver aggressively in the tangled terrain south of Chattanooga and strike a blow when opportunity offered. Now, on the evening of 9 September, the opportunity to regain the initiative had appeared in McLemore's Cove. A young staff officer who saw Bragg that day was impressed enough to temper his unfavorable opinion of the army commander.

To Lt. Henry Foote Jr., Bragg was "a tall, muscular man, with iron-gray beard, clipped close, a stern mouth, and an iron-looking jaw." Such a man was not likely to acquiesce in his army's destruction without at least one more throw of the dice. Chattanooga might have been lost momentarily, but Bragg resolved on the evening of 9 September that it would not be lost without a fight.[37]

» APPENDIX «

ORDER OF BATTLE

ARMY OF THE CUMBERLAND
31 AUGUST 1863
MAJ. GEN. WILLIAM S. ROSECRANS

General Headquarters

First Battalion Ohio Sharpshooters: Capt. Watson C. Squire
Tenth Ohio Infantry: Lt. Col. William M. Ward
Fifteenth Pennsylvania Cavalry: Col. William J. Palmer

Fourteenth Army Corps: Maj. Gen. George H. Thomas

Escort
First Ohio Cavalry, Company L: Capt. John D. Barker

Provost Guard
Ninth Michigan Infantry: Col. John G. Parkhurst

FIRST DIVISION: BRIG. GEN. ABSALOM BAIRD

First Brigade: Col. Benjamin F. Scribner
Thirty-Eighth Indiana: Lt. Col. Daniel F. Griffin
Second Ohio: Lt. Col. Obadiah C. Maxwell
Thirty-Third Ohio: Col. Oscar F. Moore
Ninety-Fourth Ohio: Maj. Rue P. Hutchins
Tenth Wisconsin: Lt. Col. John H. Ely

Second Brigade: Brig. Gen. John C. Starkweather
Twenty-Fourth Illinois: Col. Geza Mihalotzy
Seventy-Ninth Pennsylvania: Col. Henry A. Hambright
First Wisconsin: Lt. Col. George B. Bingham
Twenty-First Wisconsin: Capt. Henry Turner

Third Brigade: Brig. Gen. John H. King

Fifteenth United States, First Battalion: Capt. Albert H. Dod
Sixteenth United States, First Battalion: Maj. Sidney Coolidge
Eighteenth United States, First Battalion: Capt. George W. Smith
Eighteenth United States, Second Battalion: Capt. Henry Haymond
Nineteenth United States, First Battalion: Maj. Samuel K. Dawson

Artillery

Indiana Light, Fourth Battery (Second Brigade): Lt. David Flansburg
First Michigan Light, Battery A (First Brigade): Lt. George W. Van Pelt
Fifth United States, Battery H (Third Brigade): Lt. Howard M. Burnham

SECOND DIVISION: MAJ. GEN. JAMES S. NEGLEY

First Brigade: Brig. Gen. John Beatty

104th Illinois: Lt. Col. Douglas Hapeman
Forty-Second Indiana: Lt. Col. William T. B. McIntire
Eighty-Eighth Indiana: Col. George Humphrey
Fifteenth Kentucky: Col. Marion C. Taylor
Third Ohio: Capt. Leroy S. Bell (detached at Nashville)

Second Brigade: Col. Timothy R. Stanley

Nineteenth Illinois: Lt. Col. Alexander W. Raffen
Eleventh Michigan: Col. William L. Stoughton
Eighteenth Ohio: Capt. John Jumper
Sixty-Ninth Ohio: Maj. James J. Hanna (detached at Cowan, Tennessee)

Third Brigade: Col. William Sirwell

Thirty-Seventh Indiana: Lt. Col. William D. Ward
Twenty-First Ohio: Lt. Col. Dwella M. Stoughton
Seventy-Fourth Ohio: Capt. Joseph Fisher
Seventy-Eighth Pennsylvania: Lt. Col. Archibald Blakeley

Artillery: Capt. Frederick Schultz

Illinois Light, Bridges's Battery (First Brigade): Capt. Lyman Bridges
First Ohio Light, Battery G (Third Brigade): Capt. Alexander Marshall
First Ohio Light, Battery M (Second Brigade): Capt. Frederick Schultz

THIRD DIVISION: BRIG. GEN. JOHN M. BRANNAN

First Brigade: Col. John M. Connell

Eighty-Second Indiana: Col. Morton C. Hunter
Seventeenth Ohio: Lt. Col. Durbin Ward
Thirty-First Ohio: Lt. Col. Frederick W. Lister
Thirty-Eighth Ohio: Col. Edward H. Phelps

Second Brigade: Col. John T. Croxton
Tenth Indiana: Col. William B. Carroll
Seventy-Fourth Indiana: Col. Charles W. Chapman
Fourth Kentucky: Lt. Col. P. Burgess Hunt
Tenth Kentucky: Col. William H. Hays
Fourteenth Ohio: Lt. Col. Henry D. Kingsbury

Third Brigade: Col. Ferdinand Van Derveer
Eighty-Seventh Indiana: Col. Newell Gleason
Second Minnesota: Lt. Col. Judson W. Bishop
Ninth Ohio: Col. Gustave Kammerling
Thirty-Fifth Ohio: Lt. Col. Henry V. N. Boynton

Artillery
First Michigan, Light, Battery D (First Brigade): Capt. Josiah W. Church
First Ohio Light, Battery C (Second Brigade): Lt. Marco B. Gary
Fourth United States, Battery I (Third Brigade): Lt. Frank G. Smith

FOURTH DIVISION: MAJ. GEN. JOSEPH J. REYNOLDS

First Brigade: Col. John T. Wilder
Ninety-Second Illinois: Col. Smith D. Atkins
Ninety-Eighth Illinois: Col. John J. Funkhouser
123rd Illinois: Col. James Monroe
Seventeenth Indiana: Lt. Col. Henry Jordan
Seventy-Second Indiana: Col. Abram O. Miller

Second Brigade: Col. Edward A. King
Sixty-Eighth Indiana: Capt. Harvey J. Espy
Seventy-Fifth Indiana: Lt. Col. William O'Brien
101st Indiana: Lt. Col. Thomas Doan
105th Ohio: Maj. George T. Perkins

Third Brigade: Brig. Gen. John B. Turchin
Eighteenth Kentucky: Lt. Col. Hubbard K. Milward
Eleventh Ohio: Col. Philander P. Lane
Thirty-Sixth Ohio: Col. William G. Jones
Eighty-Ninth Ohio: Col. Caleb H. Carlton (detached at Tracy City, Tennessee)
Ninety-Second Ohio: Col. Benjamin D. Fearing

Artillery
Indiana Light, Eighteenth Battery (First Brigade): Capt. Eli Lilly
Indiana Light, Nineteenth Battery (Second Brigade): Capt. Samuel J. Harris
Indiana Light, Twenty-First Battery (Third Brigade): Capt. William W. Andrew

Twentieth Corps: Maj. Gen. Alexander M. McCook

Escort

Second Kentucky Cavalry, Company I: Lt. George W. L. Batman

Provost Guard

Eighty-First Indiana Infantry, Company H: Capt. William J. Richards

FIRST DIVISION: BRIG. GEN. JEFFERSON C. DAVIS

First Brigade: Col. P. Sidney Post

Fifty-Ninth Illinois: Lt. Col. Joshua C. Winters
Seventy-Fourth Illinois: Col. Jason Marsh
Seventy-Fifth Illinois: Col. John E. Bennett
Twenty-Second Indiana: Col. Michael Gooding

Second Brigade: Brig. Gen. William P. Carlin

Twenty-First Illinois: Col. John W. S. Alexander
Thirty-Eighth Illinois: Lt. Col. Daniel H. Gilmer
Eighty-First Indiana: Capt. Nevil B. Boone
101st Ohio: Lt. Col. John Messer

Third Brigade: Col. Hans C. Heg

Twenty-Fifth Illinois: Lt. Col. James S. McClelland
Thirty-Fifth Illinois: Lt. Col. William P. Chandler
Eighth Kansas: Col. John A. Martin
Fifteenth Wisconsin: Lt. Col. Ole C. Johnson

Artillery

Minnesota Light, Second Battery: Lt. Albert Woodbury
Wisconsin Light, Fifth Battery: Capt. George Q. Gardner
Wisconsin Light, Eighth Battery: Lt. John D. McLean

SECOND DIVISION: BRIG. GEN. RICHARD W. JOHNSON

First Brigade: Brig. Gen. August Willich

Eighty-Ninth Illinois: Lt. Col. Duncan J. Hall
Thirty-Second Indiana: Lt. Col. Frank Erdelmeyer
Thirty-Ninth Indiana: Col. Thomas J. Harrison
Fifteenth Ohio: Lt. Col. Frank Askew
Forty-Ninth Ohio: Maj. Samuel F. Gray

Second Brigade: Col. Joseph B. Dodge

Thirty-Fourth Illinois: Lt. Col. Oscar Van Tassell
Seventy-Ninth Illinois: Col. Allen Buckner
Twenty-Ninth Indiana: Lt. Col. David M. Dunn
Thirtieth Indiana: Lt. Col. Orrin D. Hurd
Seventy-Seventh Pennsylvania: Col. Thomas E. Rose

Third Brigade: Col. Philemon P. Baldwin
Sixth Indiana: Lt. Col. Hagerman Tripp
Fifth Kentucky: Col. William W. Berry
First Ohio: Lt. Col. Bassett Langdon
Ninety-Third Ohio: Col. Hiram Strong

Artillery: Capt. Peter Simonson
Indiana Light, Fifth Battery: Lt. Alfred Morrison
First Ohio Light, Battery A: Capt. Wilbur F. Goodspeed
Ohio Light, Twentieth Battery: Capt. Edward Grosskopff

THIRD DIVISION: MAJ. GEN. PHILIP H. SHERIDAN

First Brigade: Brig. Gen. William H. Lytle
Thirty-Sixth Illinois: Col. Silas Miller
Eighty-Eighth Illinois: Col. Francis T. Sherman
Twenty-First Michigan: Col. William B. McCreery
Twenty-Fourth Wisconsin: Lt. Col. Theodore S. West

Second Brigade: Col. Bernhard Laibold
Forty-Fourth Illinois: Col. Wallace W. Barrett
Seventy-Third Illinois: Maj. James I. Davidson
Second Missouri: Maj. Arnold Beck
Fifteenth Missouri: Col. Joseph Conrad

Third Brigade: Col. Luther P. Bradley
Twenty-Second Illinois: Lt. Col. Francis Swanwick
Twenty-Seventh Illinois: Col. Jonathan R. Miles
Forty-Second Illinois: Col. Nathan Walworth
Fifty-First Illinois: Lt. Col. Samuel B. Raymond

Artillery: Capt. Henry Hescock
First Illinois Light, Battery C: Capt. Mark H. Prescott
Indiana Light, Eleventh Battery: Capt. Arnold Sutermeister
First Missouri Light, Battery G: Lt. Gustavus Schueler

Twenty-First Army Corps: Maj. Gen. Thomas L. Crittenden

Escort
Fifteenth Illinois Cavalry, Company K: Capt. Samuel B. Sherer

FIRST DIVISION: BRIG. GEN. THOMAS J. WOOD

First Brigade: Col. George P. Buell
100th Illinois: Col. Frederick A. Bartleson
Fifty-Eighth Indiana: Lt. Col. James T. Embree
Thirteenth Michigan: Col. Joshua B. Culver
Twenty-Sixth Ohio: Lt. Col. William H. Young

Second Brigade: Brig. Gen. George D. Wagner
Fifteenth Indiana: Col. Gustavus A. Wood
Fortieth Indiana: Col. John W. Blake
Fifty-Seventh Indiana: Lt. Col. George W. Lennard
Ninety-Seventh Ohio: Lt. Col. Milton Barnes

Third Brigade: Col. Charles G. Harker
Third Kentucky: Col. Henry C. Dunlap
Sixty-Fourth Ohio: Col. Alexander McIlvain
Sixty-Fifth Ohio: Lt. Col. Horatio N. Whitbeck
125th Ohio: Col. Emerson Opdycke

Artillery: Capt. Cullen Bradley
Indiana Light, Eighth Battery: Capt. George Estep
Indiana Light, Tenth Battery: Capt. William A. Naylor
Ohio Light, Sixth Battery: Capt. Cullen Bradley

SECOND DIVISION: MAJ. GEN. JOHN M. PALMER

First Brigade: Brig. Gen. Charles Cruft
Thirty-First Indiana: Col. John T. Smith
First Kentucky: Lt. Col. Alva R. Haddock
Second Kentucky: Col. Thomas D. Sedgewick
Ninetieth Ohio: Col. Charles H. Rippey

Second Brigade: Brig. Gen. William B. Hazen
Ninth Indiana: Col. Isaac C. B. Suman
Sixth Kentucky: Lt. Col. George T. Shackelford
Forty-First Ohio: Col. Aquila Wiley
124th Ohio: Col. Oliver H. Payne

Third Brigade: Col. William Grose
Eighty-Fourth Illinois: Col. Louis H. Waters
Thirty-Sixth Indiana: Lt. Col. Oliver H. P. Carey
Twenty-Third Kentucky: Lt. Col. James C. Foy
Sixth Ohio: Col. Nicholas L. Anderson
Twenty-Fourth Ohio: Col. David J. Higgins

Artillery: Capt. William E. Standart
First Ohio Light, Battery B: Lt. Norman A. Baldwin
First Ohio Light, Battery F: Lt. Giles J. Cockerill
Fourth United States, Battery H: Lt. Harry C. Cushing
Fourth United States, Battery M: Lt. Francis L. D. Russell

Unattached
110th Illinois (battalion): Capt. E. Hibbard Topping

THIRD DIVISION: BRIG. GEN. HORATIO P. VAN CLEVE

First Brigade: Brig. Gen. Samuel Beatty
Seventy-Ninth Indiana: Col. Frederick Knefler
Ninth Kentucky: Col. George H. Cram
Seventeenth Kentucky: Col. Alexander M. Stout
Nineteenth Ohio: Lt. Col. Henry G. Stratton

Second Brigade: Col. George F. Dick
Forty-Fourth Indiana: Lt. Col. Simeon C. Aldrich
Eighty-Sixth Indiana: Maj. Jacob C. Dick
Thirteenth Ohio: Lt. Col. Elhannon M. Mast
Fifty-Ninth Ohio: Lt. Col. Granville A. Frambes

Third Brigade: Col. Sidney M. Barnes
Thirty-Fifth Indiana: Maj. John P. Dufficy
Eighth Kentucky: Lt. Col. James D. Mayhew
Twenty-First Kentucky: Col. S. Woodson Price
Fifty-First Ohio: Col. Richard W. McClain
Ninety-Ninth Ohio: Col. Peter T. Swaine

Artillery: Capt. Lucius H. Drury
Indiana Light, Seventh Battery (Second Brigade): Capt. George R. Swallow
Pennsylvania Light, Twenty-Sixth Battery (First Brigade): Capt. Alanson J. Stevens
Wisconsin Light, Third Battery (Third Brigade): Lt. Cortland Livingston

Reserve Corps: Maj. Gen. Gordon Granger

FIRST DIVISION: BRIG. GEN. JAMES B. STEEDMAN

First Brigade: Col. Thomas R. Champion
Ninety-Sixth Illinois: Lt. Col. Isaac L. Clarke
115th Illinois: Col. Jesse H. Moore
Eighty-Fourth Indiana: Lt. Col. Samuel Orr
Fortieth Ohio: Lt. Col. William Jones

Second Brigade: Col. William P. Reid
Seventy-Eighth Illinois: Col. William H. Benneson
Ninety-Eighth Ohio: Lt. Col. John S. Pearce
113th Ohio: Lt. Col. Darius B. Warner
121st Ohio: Lt. Col. Henry B. Banning

Third Brigade: Col. John Coburn
Thirty-Third Indiana: Maj. Levin T. Miller
Eighty-Fifth Indiana: Col. John P. Baird
Nineteenth Michigan: Lt. Col. William R. Shafter
Twenty-Second Wisconsin: Col. William L. Utley

Artillery
First Illinois Light, Battery M (Second Brigade): Lt. Thomas Burton
Ohio Light, Ninth Battery (Third Brigade): Capt. Harrison B. York
Ohio Light, Eighteenth Battery (First Brigade): Capt. Charles C. Aleshire

SECOND DIVISION: BRIG. GEN. JAMES D. MORGAN

First Brigade: Col. John Tillson

Tenth Illinois: Lt. Col. McLain F. Wood
Sixteenth Illinois: Lt. Col. James B. Cahill
Sixtieth Illinois: Col. William B. Anderson
Tenth Michigan: Lt. Col. Christopher J. Dickerson
Fourteenth Michigan: Lt. Col. Henry R. Mizner

Second Brigade: Col. Daniel McCook Jr.

Eighty-Fifth Illinois: Col. Caleb J. Dilworth
Eighty-Sixth Illinois: Lt. Col. David W. Magee
125th Illinois: Col. Oscar F. Harmon
Fifty-Second Ohio: Maj. James T. Holmes

Third Brigade: Col. Heber Le Favour

Eighteenth Michigan: Lt. Col. George Spalding
Twenty-Second Michigan: Lt. Col. William Sanborn
106th Ohio: Lt. Col. Gustavus Tafel
108th Ohio: Lt. Col. Carlo Piepho

Artillery

Second Illinois Light, Battery I (Second Brigade): Capt. Charles M. Barnett
First Ohio Light, Battery E (Third Brigade): Capt. Warren P. Edgarton
Wisconsin Light, Tenth Battery (First Brigade): Capt. Yates V. Beebe

THIRD DIVISION: BRIG. GEN. ROBERT S. GRANGER

First Brigade: Col. Sanders D. Bruce

Eighty-Third Illinois: Lt. Col. Elijah C. Brott
Twenty-Eighth Kentucky: Col. William P. Boone
102nd Ohio: Col. William Given
Thirteenth Wisconsin: Col. William P. Lyon

Second Brigade: Col. Benjamin Harrison

102nd Illinois: Col. Franklin C. Smith
105th Illinois: Col. Daniel Dustin
129th Illinois: Col. Henry Case
Seventieth Indiana: Lt. Col. James Burgess
Seventy-Ninth Ohio: Lt. Col. Azariah W. Doan
Eightieth Illinois: Capt. James Cunningham

Third Brigade: Brig. Gen. James G. Spears

Third Tennessee: Col. William Cross
Fifth Tennessee: Col. James T. Shelley
Sixth Tennessee: Col. Joseph A. Cooper

Artillery

Second Illinois Light, Battery C (First Brigade): Capt. James P. Flood
Second Illinois Light, Battery H (First Brigade): Capt. Henry C. Whittemore
First Michigan Light, Battery E (Second Brigade): Capt. John J. Ely
Tennessee Light, First Battery (Third Brigade): Capt. Ephraim P. Abbott

Pioneer Battalion: Capt. Milton Kemper

Cavalry Corps: Maj. Gen. David S. Stanley

Escort

Fourth Ohio Cavalry, Company D: Capt. Philip H. Warner

FIRST DIVISION: COL. EDWARD M. MCCOOK

First Brigade: Col. Archibald P. Campbell

Second Michigan: Maj. John C. Godley
Ninth Pennsylvania: Lt. Col. Roswell M. Russell
First Tennessee: Lt. Col. James P. Brownlow

Second Brigade: Col. Oscar H. La Grange

Second Indiana: Maj. Joseph B. Presdee
Fourth Indiana: Col. John A. Platter
Second Tennessee: Col. Daniel M. Ray
First Wisconsin: Lt. Col. Henry Pomeroy

Third Brigade: Col. Louis D. Watkins

Fourth Kentucky: Col. Wickliffe Cooper
Fifth Kentucky: Lt. Col. William T. Hoblitzell
Sixth Kentucky: Maj. Louis A. Gratz
Seventh Kentucky: Lt. Col. Thomas T. Vimont

Artillery

First Ohio Light, section Battery D (Second Brigade): Lt. Nathaniel M. Newell

SECOND DIVISION: BRIG. GEN. GEORGE CROOK

First Brigade: Col. Robert H. G. Minty

Third Indiana (battalion): Lt. Col. Robert Klein
Fourth Michigan: Maj. Horace Gray
Seventh Pennsylvania: Maj. James J. Seibert
Fourth United States: Capt. James B. McIntyre

Second Brigade: Col. Eli Long

Second Kentucky: Col. Thomas P. Nicholas
First Ohio: Lt. Col. Valentine Cupp
Third Ohio: Lt. Col. Charles B. Seidel
Fourth Ohio: Lt. Col. Oliver P. Robie

Third Brigade: Col. William W. Lowe

Fifth Iowa: Maj. Alfred B. Brackett
Tenth Ohio (detached): Lt. Col. William E. Haynes
Fifth Tennessee (detached): Col. William B. Stokes

Artillery

Chicago Board of Trade Battery: Capt. James H. Stokes

Unattached Commands

Pioneer Brigade: Capt. Patrick O'Connell

First Battalion: Capt. Charles J. Stewart
Second Battalion: Capt. Correll Smith
Third Battalion: Capt. Robert Clements

Artillery Reserve (Nashville)

Indiana Light, Twelfth Battery: Capt. James E. White
Indiana Light, Twentieth Battery: Lt. George F. Armstrong

Camp Spears (Nashville): Brig. Gen. Alvan C. Gillem

Fourth Tennessee Infantry (seven companies): Col. Daniel Stover
Tenth Tennessee Infantry: Lt. Col. James W. Scully
Third Tennessee Cavalry (seven companies): Col. William C. Pickens
First Alabama Cavalry (two companies): Col. William C. Pickens

Gallatin, Tennessee: Col. Henry K. McConnell

Thirteenth Indiana Battery: Capt. Benjamin S. Nicklin
Seventy-First Ohio: Capt. Solomon J. Houck

Elk River Bridge, Tennessee

First Michigan Engineers and Mechanics: Lt. Col. Kinsman A. Hunton
Second Kentucky Battery: Capt. John M. Hewett

ARMY OF TENNESSEE
9 SEPTEMBER 1863
GEN. BRAXTON BRAGG

Escort: Capt. Guy Dreux

Dreux's Company Louisiana Cavalry: Lt. O. De Buis
Holloway's Company Alabama Cavalry: Capt. E. M. Holloway

Engineer Battalion: Capt. Stephen W. Presstman

GEORGIA STATE LINE (TEMPORARILY ATTACHED):
ADJ. GEN. HENRY C. WAYNE

First Regiment: Col. Edward M. Galt
Second Regiment: Col. James Wilson

Polk's Corps: Lt. Gen. Leonidas Polk

Escort

Greenleaf's Company Louisiana Cavalry: Capt. Leeds Greenleaf

CHEATHAM'S DIVISION: MAJ. GEN. BENJAMIN F. CHEATHAM

Escort

Company G, Second Georgia Cavalry: Capt. Thomas M. Merritt

Jackson's Brigade: Brig. Gen. John K. Jackson

First Georgia (Confederate), Second Battalion: Maj. James Clarke Gordon
Fifth Georgia: Col. Charles P. Daniel
Second Georgia Battalion Sharpshooters: Maj. Richard H. Whiteley
Fifth Mississippi: Lt. Col. W. L. Sykes
Eighth Mississippi: Col. John C. Wilkinson

Smith's Brigade: Brig. Gen. Preston Smith

Eleventh Tennessee: Col. George W. Gordon
Twelfth/Forty-Seventh Tennessee: Col. William M. Watkins
Thirteenth/154th Tennessee: Col. Alfred J. Vaughan Jr.
Twenty-Ninth Tennessee: Col. Horace Rice
Dawson's Battalion Sharpshooters: Maj. J. W. Dawson

Maney's Brigade: Brig. Gen. George Maney

First/Twenty-Seventh Tennessee: Col. Hume R. Field
Fourth Tennessee (Provisional Army): Col. James A. McMurry
Sixth/Ninth Tennessee: Col. George C. Porter
Twenty-Fourth Tennessee Battalion Sharpshooters: Maj. Frank Maney

Wright's Brigade: Brig. Gen. Marcus J. Wright

Eighth Tennessee: Col. John H. Anderson
Sixteenth Tennessee: Col. David M. Donnell
Twenty-Eighth Tennessee: Col. Sidney S. Stanton
Thirty-Eighth Tennessee/Murray's Tennessee Battalion: Col. John C. Carter
Fifty-First/Fifty-Second Tennessee: Lt. Col. John G. Hall

Strahl's Brigade: Brig. Gen. Otho F. Strahl

Fourth/Fifth Tennessee: Col. Jonathan J. Lamb
Nineteenth Tennessee: Col. Francis M. Walker
Twenty-Fourth Tennessee: Col. John A. Wilson
Thirty-First Tennessee: Col. Egbert E. Tansil
Thirty-Third Tennessee: Col. Warner P. Jones

Artillery: Maj. Melancthon Smith

Carnes's Tennessee Battery: Capt. William W. Carnes
Scogin's Georgia Battery: Capt. John Scogin
Scott's Tennessee Battery: Lt. John H. Marsh
Smith's Mississippi Battery: Lt. William B. Turner
Stanford's Mississippi Battery: Capt. Thomas J. Stanford

HINDMAN'S DIVISION: MAJ. GEN. THOMAS C. HINDMAN

Escort

Lenoir's Company Alabama Cavalry: Capt. T. M. Lenoir

Anderson's Brigade: Brig. Gen. Patton Anderson
Seventh Mississippi: Col. William H. Bishop
Ninth Mississippi: Maj. T. H. Lynam
Tenth Mississippi: Lt. Col. James Barr
Forty-First Mississippi: Col. William F. Tucker
Forty-Fourth Mississippi: Col. Jacob H. Sharp
Ninth Mississippi Battalion Sharpshooters: Maj. W. C. Richards

Deas's Brigade: Brig. Gen. Zachariah C. Deas
Nineteenth Alabama: Col. Samuel K. McSpadden
Twenty-Second Alabama: Lt. Col. John Weedon
Twenty-Fifth Alabama: Col. George D. Johnston
Thirty-Ninth Alabama: Col. Whitfield Clark
Fiftieth Alabama: Col. John G. Coltart
Seventeenth Alabama Battalion Sharpshooters: Capt. James F. Nabers

Manigault's Brigade: Brig. Gen. Arthur M. Manigault
Twenty-Fourth Alabama: Col. Newton N. Davis
Twenty-Eighth Alabama: Col. John C. Reid
Thirty-Fourth Alabama: Maj. John N. Slaughter
Tenth/Nineteenth South Carolina: Col. James F. Pressley

Artillery
Garrity's Alabama Battery: Capt. James Garrity
Dent's Alabama Battery: Capt. S. H. Dent
Waters's Alabama Battery: Lt. Charles W. Watkins

Hill's Corps: Lt. Gen. Daniel H. Hill

CLEBURNE'S DIVISION: MAJ. GEN. PATRICK R. CLEBURNE

Escort
Sanders's Company Tennessee Cavalry: Capt. C. F. Sanders

Wood's Brigade: Brig. Gen. Sterling A. M. Wood
Sixteenth Alabama: Maj. John H. McGaughy
Thirty-Third Alabama: Col. Samuel Adams
Forty-Fifth Alabama: Col. Ephriam B. Breedlove
Eighteenth Alabama Battalion: Maj. John H. Gibson
Thirty-Second/Forty-Fifth Mississippi: Col. Mark P. Lowrey
Fifteenth Mississippi Battalion Sharpshooters: Maj. A. T. Hawkins

Polk's Brigade: Brig. Gen. Lucius E. Polk
First Arkansas: Col. John W. Colquitt
Third/Fifth Confederate: Col. James A. Smith
Second Tennessee: Col. William D. Robison
Thirty-Fifth Tennessee: Col. Benjamin J. Hill
Forty-Eighth Tennessee: Col. George H. Nixon

Deshler's Brigade: Brig. Gen. James Deshler
Nineteenth/Twenty-Fourth Arkansas: Lt. Col. A. S. Hutchison
Sixth Texas Infantry/Tenth Texas Infantry/Fifteenth Texas Cavalry (dismounted), Col. Roger Q. Mills
Seventeenth/Eighteenth/Twenty-Fourth/Twenty-Fifth Texas Cavalry (dismounted): Col. F. C. Wilkes

Artillery: Maj. T. R. Hotchkiss
Calvert's Arkansas Battery: Lt. Thomas J. Key
Douglas's Texas Battery: Capt. James P. Douglas
Semple's Alabama Battery: Capt. Henry C. Semple

BRECKINRIDGE'S DIVISION: MAJ. GEN. JOHN C. BRECKINRIDGE

Escort
Foules's Company Mississippi Cavalry: Capt. H. L. Foules

Helm's Brigade: Brig. Gen. Benjamin H. Helm
Forty-First Alabama: Col. Martin L. Stansel
Second Kentucky: Lt. Col. James W. Hewitt
Fourth Kentucky: Col. Joseph P. Nuckols
Sixth Kentucky: Col. Joseph H. Lewis
Ninth Kentucky: Col. John W. Caldwell

Adams's Brigade: Brig. Gen. Daniel W. Adams
Thirty-Second Alabama: Maj. John C. Kimbell
Thirteenth/Twentieth Louisiana: Col. Randall L. Gibson
Sixteenth/Twenty-Fifth Louisiana: Col. Daniel Gober
Nineteenth Louisiana: Lt. Col. Richard W. Turner
Fourteenth Louisiana Battalion: Maj. J. E. Austin

Stovall's Brigade: Brig. Gen. Marcellus A. Stovall
First/Third Florida: Col. William S. Dilworth
Fourth Florida: Col. Wylde L. L. Bowen
Forty-Seventh Georgia: Capt. William S. Phillips
Sixtieth North Carolina: Lt. Col. James M. Ray

Artillery: Maj. Rice E. Graves
Cobb's Kentucky Battery: Capt. Robert Cobb
Graves's Kentucky Battery: Lt. S. M. Spencer
Mebane's Tennessee Battery: Capt. John W. Mebane
Slocomb's Louisiana Battery: Capt. C. H. Slocomb

Reserve Corps: Maj. Gen. William H. T. Walker

WALKER'S DIVISION: MAJ. GEN. WILLIAM H. T. WALKER

Gist's Brigade: Brig. Gen. States R. Gist
Forty-Sixth Georgia: Col. Peyton H. Colquitt
Eighth Georgia Battalion: Lt. Col. Leroy Napier
Sixteenth South Carolina: Col. James McCullough
Twenty-Fourth South Carolina: Col. Clement H. Stevens

Ector's Brigade: Brig. Gen. Matthew D. Ector
Stone's Alabama Battalion Sharpshooters: Maj. T. O. Stone
Pound's Mississippi Battalion Sharpshooters: Capt. M. Pound
Twenty-Ninth North Carolina: Col. William B. Creasman
Ninth Texas: Col. William H. Young
Tenth Texas Cavalry (dismounted): Lt. Col. C. R. Earp
Fourteenth Texas Cavalry (dismounted): Col. John L. Camp
Thirty-Second Texas Cavalry (dismounted): Col. Julius A. Andrews

Wilson's Brigade: Col. Claudius C. Wilson
Twenty-Fifth Georgia: Lt. Col. A. J. Williams
Twenty-Ninth Georgia: Col. William J. Young
Thirtieth Georgia: Lt. Col. James S. Boynton
First Georgia Battalion Sharpshooters: Maj. Arthur Shaaff
Fourth Louisiana Battalion: Lt. Col. John McEnery

Artillery
Ferguson's South Carolina Battery: Lt. R. T. Beauregard
Howell's Georgia Battery: Capt. Evan P. Howell

LIDDELL'S DIVISION: BRIG. GEN. ST. JOHN R. LIDDELL

Liddell's Brigade: Col. Daniel C. Govan
Second/Fifteenth Arkansas: Lt. Col. Reuben F. Harvey
Fifth/Thirteenth Arkansas: Col. Lucius Featherston
Sixth/Seventh Arkansas: Col. David A. Gillespie
Eighth Arkansas/First Louisiana (Regulars): Lt. Col. George F. Baucum

Walthall's Brigade: Brig. Gen. Edward C. Walthall
Twenty-Fourth Mississippi: Lt. Col. R. P. McKelvaine
Twenty-Seventh Mississippi: Col. James A. Campbell
Twenty-Ninth Mississippi: Col. William F. Brantly
Thirtieth Mississippi: Col. Junius I. Scales
Thirty-Fourth Mississippi: Maj. William G. Pegram

Artillery: Capt. Charles Swett
Fowler's Alabama Battery: Capt. William H. Fowler
Warren Light Artillery (Mississippi) Battery: Lt. H. Shannon

Buckner's Corps: Maj. Gen. Simon B. Buckner

Escort

Clark's Company Tennessee Cavalry: Capt. J. W. Clark

STEWART'S DIVISION: MAJ. GEN. ALEXANDER P. STEWART

Johnson's Brigade: Brig. Gen. Bushrod R. Johnson

Seventeenth Tennessee: Lt. Col. Watt W. Floyd

Twenty-Third Tennessee: Col. Richard H. Keeble

Twenty-Fifth Tennessee: Lt. Col. R. B. Snowden

Forty-Fourth Tennessee: Lt. Col. John L. McEwen Jr.

Bate's Brigade: Brig. Gen. William B. Bate

Fifty-Eighth Alabama: Col. Bushrod Jones

Thirty-Seventh Georgia: Col. Anthony F. Rudler

Fourth Georgia Battalion Sharpshooters: Maj. T. D. Caswell

Fifteenth/Thirty-Seventh Tennessee: Col. Robert C. Tyler

Twentieth Tennessee: Col. Thomas B. Smith

Brown's Brigade: Brig. Gen. John C. Brown

Eighteenth Tennessee: Col. Joseph B. Palmer

Twenty-Sixth Tennessee: Col. John M. Lillard

Thirty-Second Tennessee: Col. Edmund C. Cook

Forty-Fifth Tennessee: Col. Anderson Searcy

Twenty-Third Tennessee Battalion: Maj. Tazewell W. Newman

Clayton's Brigade: Brig. Gen. Henry D. Clayton

Eighteenth Alabama: Col. James T. Holtzclaw

Thirty-Sixth Alabama: Col. Lewis T. Woodruff

Thirty-Eighth Alabama: Lt. Col. Augustus R. Lankford

Artillery

First Arkansas Battery: Capt. John T. Humphreys

Dawson's Georgia Battery: Lt. R. W. Anderson

Eufaula Artillery (Alabama) Battery: Capt. McDonald Oliver

Company E, Ninth Georgia Artillery Battalion: Lt. William S. Everett

PRESTON'S DIVISION: BRIG. GEN. WILLIAM PRESTON

Gracie's Brigade: Brig. Gen. Archibald Gracie Jr.

Forty-Third Alabama: Col. Young M. Moody

First Alabama Battalion (Hilliard's Legion): Lt. Col. John H. Holt

Second Alabama Battalion (Hilliard's Legion): Lt. Col. Bolling Hall Jr.

Third Alabama Battalion (Hilliard's Legion): Lt. Col. John W. A. Sanford

Fourth Alabama Battalion (Hilliard's Legion): Maj. John D. McLennan

Sixty-Third Tennessee: Lt. Col. Abraham Fulkerson

Trigg's Brigade: Col. Robert C. Trigg

First Florida Cavalry (dismounted): Col. George T. Maxwell
Sixth Florida: Col. Jesse J. Finley
Seventh Florida: Col. Robert Bullock
Fifty-Fourth Virginia: Lt. Col. John J. Wade

Kelly's Brigade: Col. John H. Kelly

Sixty-Fifth Georgia: Col. Robert H. Moore
Fifth Kentucky: Col. Hiram Hawkins
Fifty-Eighth North Carolina: Col. John B. Palmer
Sixty-Third Virginia: Maj. James M. French

Artillery Battalion: Maj. Austin Leyden

Jeffress's Virginia Battery: Capt. William C. Jeffress
Peeples's Georgia Battery: Capt. Tyler M. Peeples
Wolihin's Georgia Battery: Capt. Andrew M. Wolihin

Corps Reserve Artillery: Maj. Samuel C. Williams

Baxter's Tennessee Battery: Capt. Edmund D. Baxter
Darden's Mississippi Battery: Capt. Putnam Darden
Kolb's Alabama Battery: Capt. R. F. Kolb
McCants's Florida Battery: Capt. Robert P. McCants

Army Reserve Artillery: Maj. Felix H. Robertson

Barret's Missouri Battery: Capt. Overton W. Barret
Havis's Georgia Battery: Capt. M. W. Havis
Lumsden's Alabama Battery: Capt. Charles L. Lumsden
Massenburg's Georgia Battery: Capt. T. L. Massenburg

Wheeler's Cavalry Corps: Maj. Gen. Joseph Wheeler

WHARTON'S DIVISION: BRIG. GEN. JOHN A. WHARTON

First Brigade: Col. Charles C. Crews

Seventh Alabama: Col. James C. Malone Jr.
Second Georgia: Lt. Col. R. M. Ison
Third Georgia: Col. Robert Thompson
Fourth Georgia: Col. Isaac W. Avery

Second Brigade: Col. Thomas Harrison

Third Confederate: Col. William N. Estes
Third Kentucky: Lt. Col. J. W. Griffith
Fourth [Eighth] Tennessee: Lt. Col. Paul F. Anderson
Eighth Texas: Lt. Col. Gustave Cook
Eleventh Texas: Col. George R. Reeves
White's Tennessee Battery: Capt. B. F. White Jr.

MARTIN'S DIVISION: BRIG. GEN. WILLIAM T. MARTIN

First Brigade: Col. James Hagan
First Alabama: Lt. Col. D. T. Blakey
Third Alabama: Lt. Col. T. H. Mauldin
Fifty-First Alabama: Col. John T. Morgan
Eighth Confederate: Lt. Col. John S. Prather

Second Brigade: Col. Alfred A. Russell
Fourth Alabama (Russell's): Lt. Col. J. M. Hambrick
First Confederate: Capt. C. H. Conner
Wiggins's Arkansas Battery: Lt. J. P. Bryant

Roddey's Brigade (Northern Alabama): Brig. Gen. Philip D. Roddey
Fifth Alabama: Col. Josiah Patterson
Fifty-Third Alabama: Col. Moses W. Hannon
Unorganized Alabama Battalion: Capt. W. R. Julian
Fourth Alabama (Roddey's): Lt. Col. W. A. Johnson
Ferrell's Georgia Battery: Capt. C. B. Ferrell

Forrest's Cavalry Corps: Brig. Gen. Nathan B. Forrest

Escort
Jackson's Company Tennessee Cavalry: Capt. J. C. Jackson

ARMSTRONG'S DIVISION: BRIG. GEN. FRANK C. ARMSTRONG

Armstrong's Brigade: Col. James T. Wheeler
Third Arkansas: Col. Anson W. Hobson
Second Kentucky: Lt. Col. Thomas G. Woodward
Sixth Tennessee: Lt. Col. James H. Lewis
Eighteenth Tennessee Battalion: Maj. Charles McDonald

Dibrell's Brigade: Col. George G. Dibrell
Fourth Tennessee: Col. William S. McLemore
Eighth [Thirteenth] Tennessee: Capt. Hamilton McGinnis
Ninth Tennessee: Col. Jacob B. Biffle
Tenth Tennessee: Col. Nicholas N. Cox
Eleventh Tennessee: Col. Daniel W. Holman
Shaw's Battalion/Hamilton's Battalion/Allison's Squadron: Maj. Joseph Shaw
Huggins's Tennessee Battery: Capt. A. L. Huggins
Morton's Tennessee Battery: Capt. John W. Morton Jr.

PEGRAM'S DIVISION: BRIG. GEN. JOHN PEGRAM

Pegram's Brigade: Brig. Gen. John Pegram
First Georgia: Col. James J. Morrison
Sixth Georgia: Col. John R. Hart
Sixth North Carolina: Col. George N. Folk
Rucker's First Tennessee Legion: Col. Edmund W. Rucker
Huwald's Tennessee Battery: Capt. Gustave A. Huwald

Scott's Brigade: Col. John S. Scott

Tenth Confederate: Col. Charles T. Goode

First Louisiana: Lt. Col. James O. Nixon

Second Tennessee: Col. Henry M. Ashby

Fifth Tennessee: Col. George W. McKenzie

Robinson's Louisiana Battery: Lt. Winslow Robinson

Hodge's Brigade: Col. George B. Hodge

Second Kentucky Battalion, Mounted Rifles: Lt. Col. Thomas Johnson

Third Kentucky Battalion, Mounted Rifles: Lt. Col. Ezekiel F. Clay

Jessee's Kentucky Battalion, Mounted Rifles: Maj. George M. Jessee

Twenty-Seventh Virginia Battalion: Maj. Sylvester P. McConnell

» NOTES «

ABBREVIATIONS

ADAH	Alabama Department of Archives and History, Montgomery, Ala.
AHS	Atlanta Historical Society, Atlanta, Ga.
ALPL	Abraham Lincoln Presidential Library, Springfield, Ill.
AU	Auburn University, Auburn, Ala.
BGSU	Bowling Green State University, Bowling Green, Ohio
BPL	Birmingham Public Library, Birmingham, Ala.
BU	Baylor University, Waco, Tex.
CCNMP	Chickamauga and Chattanooga National Military Park, Ft. Oglethorpe, Ga.
CHS	Chicago Historical Society, Chicago, Ill.
CI	The Citadel, Charleston, S.C.
CIHS	Cincinnati Historical Society, Cincinnati, Ohio
CPL	Chattanooga Public Library, Chattanooga, Tenn.
CU	Carroll University, Waukesha, Wisc.
DP	DePauw University, Greencastle, Ind.
DPL	Danville Public Library, Danville, Ill.
DU	Duke University, Durham, N.C.
EU	Emory University, Atlanta, Ga.
FHS	Filson Historical Society, Louisville, Ky.
GDAH	Georgia Department of Archives and History, Morrow, Ga.
GHS	Georgia Historical Society, Savannah, Ga.
HC	Hill College, Hillsboro, Tex.
HL	Huntington Library, San Marino, Calif.
HPL	Rutherford B. Hayes Presidential Library, Fremont, Ohio
HSP	Historical Society of Pennsylvania, Philadelphia, Penn.
IHS	Indiana Historical Society, Indianapolis, Ind.
ISHL	State Historical Society of Iowa, Des Moines, Iowa
ISL	Indiana State Library, Indianapolis, Ind.
IU	Indiana University, Bloomington, Ind.
KC	Knox College, Galesburg, Ill.
KMNMP	Kennesaw Mountain National Military Park, Kennesaw, Ga.

KSHS Kansas State Historical Society, Topeka, Kans.
KYHS Kentucky Historical Society, Frankfort, Ky.
LC Library of Congress, Washington, D.C.
LCA Eli Lilly & Company Archives, Indianapolis, Ind.
LSU Louisiana State University, Baton Rouge, La.
LV Library of Virginia, Richmond, Va.
MAC Marietta College, Marietta, Ohio
MC Museum of the Confederacy, Richmond, Va.
MDAH Mississippi Department of Archives and History, Jackson, Miss.
MDHS Maryland Historical Society, Baltimore, Md.
MHM Missouri History Museum, St. Louis, Mo.
MHS Minnesota Historical Society, St. Paul, Minn.
MU Miami University, Miami, Ohio
NAHA Norwegian-American Historical Association, Northfield, Minn.
NARA National Archives and Records Administration, Washington, D.C.
NC Navarro College, Corsicana, Tex.
NCDAH North Carolina Department of Archives and History, Raleigh, N.C.
NCWM National Civil War Museum, Harrisburg, Penn.
NIU Northern Illinois University, DeKalb, Ill.
NL Newberry Library, Chicago, Ill.
NLM National Library of Medicine, Bethesda, Md.
NSHS Nebraska State Historical Society, Lincoln, NE
NYPL New York Public Library, New York, N.Y.
OHS Ohio Historical Society, Columbus, Ohio
OR *War of the Rebellion: A Compilation of the Official Records of the Union and Confederate Armies*. 70 vols. in 128. Washington, D.C.: Government Printing Office, 1880–1901. Unless otherwise cited, all references to *OR* are to series 1. *OR* citations take the following form: volume number (part number, where applicable):page number.
SCHS South Carolina Historical Society, Charleston, S.C.
SLRH Smith Library of Regional History, Oxford, Ohio
SOR *Supplement to the Official Records of the Union and Confederate Armies*. 100 vols. Wilmington, N.C.: Broadfoot, 1994–2001.
SRNB Stones River National Battlefield, Murfreesboro, Tenn.
TCU Texas Christian University, Ft. Worth, Tex.
TSLA Tennessee State Library and Archives, Nashville, Tenn.
TU Tulane University, New Orleans, La.
UAK University of Akron, Akron, Ohio
UCB University of California, Berkeley, Berkeley, Calif.
UCLA University of California, Los Angeles, Los Angeles, Calif.
UDC United Daughters of the Confederacy
UF University of Florida, Gainesville, Fla.
UFL Urbana Free Library, Urbana, Ill.
UGA University of Georgia, Athens, Ga.
UI University of Illinois, Urbana-Champaign, Ill.
UK University of Kentucky, Lexington, Ky.
UM-B University of Michigan Bentley Library, Ann Arbor, Mich.
UM-C University of Michigan Clements Library, Ann Arbor, Mich.

UNC	University of North Carolina, Chapel Hill, N.C.
UND	University of Notre Dame, South Bend, Ind.
US	University of the South, Sewanee, Tenn.
USAHEC	United States Army Heritage and Education Center, Carlisle, Penn.
UT	University of Tennessee, Knoxville, Tenn.
UTC	University of Tennessee at Chattanooga, Chattanooga, Tenn.
UTX	University of Texas, Austin, Tex.
VCPL	Vigo County Public Library, Terre Haute, Ind.
VHS	Virginia Historical Society, Richmond, Va.
VM	Valentine Museum, Richmond, Va.
VMI	Virginia Military Institute, Lexington, Va.
VT	Virginia Polytechnic Institute and State University, Blacksburg, Va.
WC	Wabash College, Crawfordsville, Ind.
WHS	Wisconsin Historical Society, Madison, Wisc.
WIU	Western Illinois University, Macomb, Ill.
WMU	Western Michigan University, Kalamazoo, Mich.
WRHS	Western Reserve Historical Society, Cleveland, Ohio
WSU	Wright State University, Fairborn, Ohio
WU	Winthrop University, Rock Hill, S.C.
WVM	Wisconsin Veterans Museum, Madison, Wisc.
WVU	West Virginia University, Morgantown, W.Va.
YU	Yale University, New Haven, Conn.

CHAPTER 1

1. *OR* 52(1):392; Heg, *Letters*, 226–28; Fisher, *Staff Officer's Story*, 71; Post Diary, 4 July 1863, KC; Himoe Diary, 4 July 1863, NAHA; Dodge, *Old Second Division*, 507.

2. Hempstead Diary, 4 July 1863, UM-B; *OR* 23(1):444, 549, 572, 575–77; Kendall Diary, 4 July 1863, HL; Robert Burns to Davidson, 4 July 1863, MHS; *OR* 23(2):513, 531; XIV Corps Journal, Thomas Papers, NARA; Hapeman Diary, 4 July 1863, ISHL; Shotts Diary, 4 July 1863, and Benedict Diary, 4 July 1863, both in SRNB; Small Diary, 4 July 1863, Hollingsworth Diary, 4 July 1863, and Howe Diary, 4 July 1863, all in IHS; *OR* 52(1):393; Walker Diary, 4 July 1863, USAHEC; Van Cleve to Starling, 6 July 1863, Van Cleve Papers, MHS; J. M. Branum, *National Tribune*, 13 December 1900; Partridge, *Ninety-Sixth Illinois*, 143; "Summaries of the News," 4 July 1863, NARA.

3. Sewanee: The University of the South, "About Sewanee, University History," http://www.sewanee.edu/about/university-history (9 January 2010); Kendall Diary, 4 July 1863, HL; Leeper Diary, 4 July 1863, SRNB; *OR* 23(1):549–50; Corbitt Diary, 4 July 1863, EU.

4. *OR* 23(1):550–52, 616–17; Corbitt Diary, 4 July 1863, EU; Bunting, *Letters*, 171–72; Batchelor and Turner, *Batchelor-Turner Letters*, 59, 62–63; Rabb, "Rabb Letters," 211–12; Macmurphy Diary, 4 July 1863, http://www.terrystexasrangers.org/diaries/macmurphy_gl/index.html (21 June 2009); C. W. Love to his parents, 8 August 1863, http://www.terrystexasrangers.org/letters/love_cw/1863_08_20.htm (19 December 2009).

5. U.S. Congress, House of Representatives, *Atlas of Chickamauga*, "Military Map Showing the Theater of Operations"; "Special Orders, No. 176," 3 July 1863, Bragg Papers, WRHS; *OR* 23(1):626; *OR* 23(2):897–900.

6. *OR* 23(1):625–27; *OR* 23(2):897–99; Moorman, "Moorman Memorandum," 75.

7. *OR* 23(1):617, 626–27; *OR* 23(2):899–900; *SOR* 13:909; *SOR* 17:323; Wyeth, *Sabre*,

232; Heartsill, *Fourteen Hundred,* 137; Collins, *Chapters,* 137; Coleman Diary, 4 July 1863, UNC; Robert L. Bliss to his mother, 14 July 1863, Bliss Letters, ADAH.

8. Fitch, *Echoes,* 125–26; Frank M. Phelps to his friends, 17 July 1863, Phelps Letters, Lewis Leigh Collection, USAHEC; Hinkley Diary, 4 July 1863, WHS; Webster Diary, 4 July 1863, Civil War Miscellaneous Collection, USAHEC; Johnston, *Soldier Boy,* 44; Otto, *Mudsill,* 149–50; Hough, *Soldier,* 105–6; Hapeman Diary, 4 July 1863, ALPL; Shotts Diary, 4 July 1863, SRNB; Christian Diary, 4 July 1863, CCNMP; Inskeep Diary, 4 July 1863, OHS; Small Diary, 4 July 1863, IHS; Price Diary, 4 July 1863, Civil War Miscellaneous Collection, USAHEC; Reed Diary, 4 July 1863, CCNMP; Kitchell Diary, 4 July 1863, ALPL; Miller Journal, 4 July 1863, IHS; Taylor Diary, 4 July 1863, SRNB; Ward Diary, 4 July 1863, Booth Papers, OHS; Josiah D. Cotton to his wife, 4 July 1863, Cotton Papers, LC; Hight, *Fifty-Eighth Indiana,* 150; Woodruff, *Fifteen Years,* 269; Kerwood, *Fifty-Seventh Indiana,* 193; Marshall Diary, 4 July 1863, OHS; Hinman, *Sherman Brigade,* 394–95; George Sowers to his brother, 5 July 1863, Sowers Letter, Earl Hess Collection, USAHEC; Clark, *Tigers,* 71; Busbey Diary, 4 July 1863, SRNB; Everett Letter Excerpts, 5 July 1863, WIU; Simmons, *Eighty-Fourth Illinois,* 61–62; Woodcock, *Southern Boy,* 174; Partridge, *Ninety-Sixth Illinois,* 143; J. M. Branum, *National Tribune,* 13 December 1900; Members, *Battery M, First Illinois,* 71; Winans Diary, 4 July 1863, CCNMP.

9. "Summaries of the News," 4 July 1863, NARA; *OR* 23(2):511–12; Rosecrans to Stanton, 4 July 1863, DC, Telegrams Sent, NARA; *OR* 52(1):392.

10. Heg, *Letters,* 226–27; Post Diary, 4 July 1863, KC; Mosman, *Rough Side,* 62–63; John Russell to his sister, 10 July 1863, Russell Letters, *Civil War Times Illustrated* Collection, USAHEC; Colyer Diary, 4 July 1863, ALPL; Himoe Diary, 4 July 1863, NAHA; Love Diary, 4 July 1863, and James E. Love to Molly, 5 July 1863, Love Papers, MHM; James G. Watson to [addressee unknown], 6 July 1863, Watson Letters, UI; Smith, *Private Smith's Journal,* 80–81.

11. "Summaries of the News," 4 July 1863, NARA; *OR* 23(1):583; James M. Sligh to his mother, 14 July 1863, Sligh Family Papers, UM-B; *SOR* 42:387; *OR* 20(2):5–6; Hoffman, *"Brave Mechanics,"* 56; *OR* 23(2):503; Taylor, *"Supply,"* 72–73; Goddard to Anderson, 4 July 1863 (two messages), Rosecrans to Anderson, 4 July 1863, and Garfield to Anderson, 4 July 1863, all in DC, Telegrams Sent, NARA.

CHAPTER 2

1. Lamers, *Edge of Glory,* 8–15; Wert, *Longstreet,* 31; Elliott, *Soldier of Tennessee,* 9; Reid, *Ohio in the War,* 1:311–12; Heitman, *Historical Register,* 1:846.

2. Lamers, *Edge of Glory,* 15–17; Reid, *Ohio in the War,* 1:312–13; Mulhane, *Memorial of Rosecrans,* 50; Heitman, *Historical Register,* 1:846; "History of Major General William Starke Rosecrans," http://rosecransheadquarters.org/History/RosecransBio (3 October 2010).

3. Lamers, *Edge of Glory,* 17–19; Reid, *Ohio in the War,* 1:313–14.

4. Lamers, *Edge of Glory,* 20–36; Reid, *Ohio in the War,* 1:314–16; Heitman, *Historical Register,* 1:846; McClellan, *McClellan Papers,* 44; Newell, *Lee vs. McClellan,* 116–17, 124–33; *OR* 2:214–18.

5. *OR* 2:762; Welcher, *Union Army,* 1:33, 212, 2:126–27; Newell, *Lee vs. McClellan,* 256, 262–71; Lamers, *Edge of Glory,* 39–72; *OR* 12(3):67.

6. *OR* 12(3):71, 74, 77, 81–82, 86–87, 89, 92, 96, 99–100, 105, 132, 168, 186–87; Thomas and Hyman, *Stanton,* 182–85; Lamers, *Edge of Glory,* 73–80.

7. Lamers, *Edge of Glory*, 81–130; Welcher, *Union Army*, 2:187–91, 620–23; Cozzens, *Darkest Days*, 68–134.

8. Lamers, *Edge of Glory*, 131–82; Reid, *Ohio in the War*, 1:326–27; Cozzens, *Darkest Days*, 301–4; "Rosecrans's Campaigns," in U.S. Congress, *Report of the Joint Committee*, 3:23; *OR* 16(2):652, 653; *OR* 17(2):239, 251, 283, 286–87; Welcher, *Union Army*, 2:20, 159, 268. For a detailed analysis of the Grant/Rosecrans feud, see Varney, *General Grant*, 31–121; and Rose, *Grant under Fire*, 151–63.

9. Lamers, *Edge of Glory*, 177–92; *OR* 52(1):295, 297; *OR* 17(2):291; *OR* 16(2):654–55, 657, 663; *OR* 20(2):11; Welcher, *Union Army*, 2:159–60.

10. *OR* 16(2):640–41; *OR* 20(2):117–18, 123–24.

11. Lamers, *Edge of Glory*, 181–247; *OR* 20(1):186–88; *OR* 20(2):300, 306.

12. Lamers, *Edge of Glory*, 248–91; Reid, *Ohio in the War*, 1:335–37; *OR* 23(2):34, 37–38, 60, 66, 72, 95, 111, 138, 146, 154–55, 171, 191, 207, 232, 255–56, 270–71, 320–21, 369, 383; Welcher, *Union Army*, 1:832–39.

13. Olmsted, *Defending the Union*, 538–42, 583; Cooney, "War Letters," 163–65; Carlin, *Memoirs*, 90–91; William S. Rosecrans to George B. Pearson, 1 November 1863, Rosecrans Papers, UCLA; Garfield, *Wild Life*, 224–28; Beatty, *Citizen Soldier*, 229–30, 235–36, 249, 256–64, 308; Shanks, *Recollections*, 258, 261–62; Villard, *Memoirs*, 212; Palmer, *Turncoat*, 120–21; Cox, "Chickamauga Crisis," 329; Kimberly and Holloway, *Forty-First Ohio*, 43. For an admiring summary of Rosecrans's life and career up to July 1863, see Moore, *Rosecrans*, 5–90.

14. Fitch, *Annals*, 41–47; Reid, *Ohio in the War*, 1:739–51; Smith, *Garfield*, 1:269–70, 273–78, 307–8; Garfield, *Wild Life*, 229–36, 240; Sanderson Journal, 15 October 1863, OHS; *OR* 23(2):394–97, 403–11, 413–15, 417–18, 420–24, 433–34; Peskin, *Garfield*, 169–75.

15. Reid, *Ohio in the War*, 1:751–53; Smith, *Garfield*, 1:279–80, 287, 307–9, 358–59; Sanderson Journal, 15 October 1863, OHS; Beatty, *Citizen Soldier*, 224–26; Stanley, *Memoirs*, 131–32; Peskin, *Garfield*, 173–81, 217.

16. *Washington (D.C.) Evening Times*, 2 July 1896; Heitman, *Historical Register*, 1:229, 384, 673, 800, 956, 958; Powell, *Officers (Volunteer)*, 52; *Society of the Army of the Cumberland: Twenty-Fourth Reunion*, 228–29; Hunt and Brown, *Brevet Brigadier Generals*, 611; *OR* 20(1):199, 219; Fitch, *Annals*, 51–55; *OR* 23(2):82, 153, 208–9; Howe, *Historical Collections*, 1:200; *Official Roster, Ohio*, 5:479, 505; *OR* 30(1):63.

17. Heitman, *Historical Register*, 1:267, 373, 385, 461, 938, 959, 1067; *Society of the Army of the Cumberland: Twenty-Third Reunion*, 171–74; *Society of the Army of the Cumberland: Twenty-Fourth Reunion*, 240–46; *OR* 23(2):36, 101–2, 208–9, 225, 504–5; *Official Roster, Ohio*, 1:23; *OR* 20(2):215; *OR* 30(1):63; *New York Times*, 18 August 1897; Garfield, *Wild Life*, 145, 180, 252; *Memoir of Ducat*, 5–44; Mattes, *Indians*, 10–13; Hubbard, *Autobiography*, xxvi.

18. Jones, *Right Hand*, viii–ix. For a slightly different way of characterizing the staff of the Army of the Cumberland during Rosecrans's tenure, see Richardson, "Rosecrans' Staff," 21–24.

19. Heitman, *Historical Register*, 1:799, 887, 947; Fitch, *Annals*, 265–81, 301–2; Taylor, *"Supply,"* 106–7; *OR* 20(2):215; *OR* 23(2):36.

20. Heitman, *Historical Register*, 1:192, 915; Hunt and Brown, *Brevet Brigadier Generals*, 31; Fitch, *Annals*, 199–205, 298–300; *OR* 30(1):233–36; *OR* 20(2):94; Mammay, "Union Artillery," 28–29; Warner, *Generals in Blue*, 470; Stanley, *Memoirs*, 118–21.

21. Heitman, *Historical Register*, 1:178, 425, 705, 960; Fitch, *Annals*, 49–50, 289–92; *OR* 30(1):222, 227; *OR* 23(2):116; Lyman, "Some Aspects," 211–12; Rubenstein, "Medical Support," 21–25; Duncan, *Medical Department*, 279.

22. Heitman, *Historical Register*, 1:248, 329, 464; Fitch, *Annals*, 282–88; *OR* 23(2):225; Richardson, "Rosecrans' Staff," 36–37; *OR* 30(1):228–30.

23. Heitman, *Historical Register*, 1:731; Warner, *Generals in Blue*, 336–37; Fitch, *Annals*, 180–91; *OR* 20(1):186; *OR* 20(2):6–7, 306; Bickham, *Rosecrans' Campaign*, 81–82; Hazen, *Narrative*, 405–8; Shiman, "Engineering and Command," 88–93, 103–4.

24. Heitman, *Historical Register*, 1:705; *OR* 30(3):912–13; *OR* 23(2):376–77; Shiman, "Engineering and Command," 96–99; William C. Margedant to William S. Rosecrans, 21 September 1887, Rosecrans Papers, UCLA; Cone, *Concise History*, 2:347.

25. Heitman, *Historical Register*, 1:705, 982; Brown, *Signal Corps*, 56–57, 176–77, 457–59, 486; *OR*, Series 3, 3:958–59; Furey, *Past and Present*, 197; Fitch, *Annals*, 303–8; Plum, *Military Telegraph*, 1:173, 175, 256, 264–68, 303–5.

26. Weber, *Northern Railroads*, 136, 187; *OR* 20(2):5–6; Taylor, *"Supply,"* 72–73; http://www.kshs.org/p/anderson-family-papers/13973 (4 December 2010).

27. Fitch, *Annals*, 326–30, 346–56; Conyngham, "Soldiers of the Cross," 19–41, UND; Miller, *Both Prayed*, 115; Durham, *Nashville*, 200–204, 228–29, 240–46; Durham, *Reluctant Partners*, 33–37; *OR* 30(1):183; *OR* 23(2):380; *Cincinnati Daily Commercial*, 31 October and 3 November 1863; Johnson, *Johnson Papers*, 6:xxxiii–iv, 205–6; Feis, "Truesdail's Army Police," 34–45.

28. Fitch, *Annals*, 257–64; Olmsted, *Defending the Union*, 538–42; Sanderson Journal, 27 September 1863, OHS; Emerson Opdycke to his wife, 16 November 1863, Opdycke Papers, OHS; William B. Hazen to Benson H. Lossing, 23 August 1866, Hazen Letter, Palmer Collection, WRHS.

29. Welcher, *Union Army*, 2:269, 322, 331, 348, 369; *OR* 23(2):574. The Aggregate Present category "shows the total number with the army in every capacity. It includes all arms of the service, wagon trains, medical department, special details, men under arrest, and the sick in camp,—in fact, all for whom rations must be provided." The Present for Duty category "includes all who were present with their commands and ready for duty, whatever their duties might be. It embraced musicians, company cooks, quartermasters and commissaries, hospital corps, and other noncombatants." Fox, *New York at Gettysburg*, 1:101–2.

30. *OR* 23(2):572; Warner, *Generals in Blue*, 500–501; Van Horne, *Life of Thomas*, 84–89; *OR* 16(2):657, 663; Fitch, *Annals*, 56–66; William S. Rosecrans to *Evening Bulletin*, 7 October 1882, Rosecrans Papers, UCLA. Biographies of Thomas abound. The most recent are Einolf, *Thomas*; Bobrick, *Master of War*; and Wills, *Thomas*.

31. Villard, *Memoirs*, 213–14; Shanks, *Recollections*, 75–80; Jones, "Recollections," 12–13; Beatty, *Citizen Soldier*, 304; Palmer, *Turncoat*, 121–22; Scribner, *Soldiers*, 116–18; Johnson, *Reminiscences*, 308–9.

32. *OR* 23(2) 572, 574–75; Lee, *Kentuckian*, 5–116; Warner, *Generals in Blue*, 268–69, 412–13, 472–73; Welsh, *Medical Histories, Union*, 284; *OR* 30(1):211; Scribner, *Soldiers*, 11–19, 276–79; Shanks, *Recollections*, 195–241; Fitch, *Annals*, 79–87; Hough, *Soldier*, 63; Historical Sketch, Benjamin Scribner, http://www.indianahistory.org/library/manuscripts/collection_guides/sc1322.html (21 February 2011); Perry, *Thirty-Eighth Indiana*, 14–15; Hunt and Brown, *Brevet Brigadier Generals*, 542; Beatty, *Citizen Soldier*, 270, 280, 303–4; Starkweather, *Military Services*, 5; Johnson, *Brave Men*, 333; Johnson, *Reminiscences*, 240–41.

33. *OR* 23(2):572, 575; Fitch, *Annals*, 91–111; Shanks, *Recollections*, 293–94; Warner, *Generals in Blue*, 27–28, 341–42; Beatty, *Citizen Soldier*, 268; James, "Negley," 69–78; Barclay, "Negley," 11–26; Hunt and Brown, *Brevet Brigadier Generals*, 581; Warren, *Stanley Families*, 161–62; Gancas, *Gallant Seventy-Eighth*, 1–15, 196.

34. *OR* 23(2):572, 575; Warner, *Generals in Blue*, 42–43, 473, 522; *New York Times*, 16 February 1859; *New York Tribune*, 24 April 1860; Davis, *Incredible Civil War*, 163; *OR*, Series 3, 1:854–58; Hunt and Brown, *Brevet Brigadier Generals*, 645; *Portrait, Marion and Hardin Counties*, 434; Brennan, *Biographical Cyclopaedia*, 1:201–2; Shanks, *Recollections*, 276–79, 281, 288; Reid, *Ohio in the War*, 1:784–86, 890; Hafendorfer, *Perryville*, 449–50; *OR* 20(1):178, 211.

35. Warner, *Generals in Blue*, 102–3, 397–98; Eicher and Eicher, *High Commands*, 451; Kapaun, "Reynolds," 8–15; Williams, *Wilder*, 1–14; Beatty, *Citizen Soldier*, 295; Hunt and Brown, *Brevet Brigadier Generals*, 513; *OR* 23(1):454; Boatner, *Civil War Dictionary*, 209; Crook, *Autobiography*, 95–101; *OR* 23(2):398.

36. *OR* 23(2):573; Warner, *Generals in Blue*, 294; Fitch, *Annals*, 73–78; Reid, *Ohio in the War*, 1:806–9; Powell and Shippen, *Officers (Regular)*, 258; Welcher, *Union Army*, 2:322, Whalen and Whalen, *Fighting McCooks*, 69–77, 127–31, 167, 178–88. For an extensive summary of McCook's life and career prior to July 1863, see Fanebust, *McCook*, 29–168.

37. Isaac N. Schnorf to his brother and sister, 7 July 1863, Schnorf Letter, OHS; Jones, "Recollections," 9–10; Beatty, *Citizen Soldier*, 211–12, 235–36, 295; *OR* 16(1):1031; Reid, *Ohio in the War*, 1:751–52, 806–9; Hazen, *Narrative*, 151–52; Shanks, *Recollections*, 249; Whalen and Whalen, *Fighting McCooks*, 170; Stanley, *Memoirs*, 120; Boatner, *Civil War Dictionary*, 526; Fanebust, *McCook*, 168–69.

38. *OR* 23(2):573; Warner, *Generals in Blue*, 69–70, 115–16; Hughes and Whitney, *Davis in Blue*, 100–126; Sones, "Davis," 1–79; Cozzens, "Forgotten Hero," 75–85; Carlin, *Memoirs*, 10–93; Johnson, *Reminiscences*, 241–42; Heg, *Letters*, 2–37.

39. *OR* 23(2):573; Warner, *Generals in Blue*, 253–54, 365–66; Dodge, *Old Second Division*, 461–73; *OR* 16(1):871–76; Fitch, *Annals*, 152–54; Reinhart, *Gallant Dutchmen*, 10–11, 16–18; Stewart, "Bachelor General," 131–39; Dodge Family Association, "Col Joseph B Dodge," http://www.dodgefamily.org/Biographies/J/ColJosephDodge.shtml (10 April 2011); Beatty, *Citizen Soldier*, 252–53; *Indiana at Chickamauga*, 130; Briant, *Sixth Indiana*, 70, 126, 171; *OR* 20(1):336–38; Baldwin, *Baldwin Genealogy*, 468.

40. *OR* 23(2):573; Morris, *Sheridan*, 1–40, 78–112; Greiner, *General Phil Sheridan*, 230–31; W. S. Rosecrans, *National Tribune*, 28 June 1883; Warner, *Generals in Blue*, 40–41, 287–88, 437–38; Lytle, *For Honor*, 2–27; Scharf, *History of Saint Louis*, 1–448; Smith, *Stones River (Union)*, 218–19, 231. The Second Brigade commander signed his name Bernhard Laibold on an official document in 1865. Bernhard Laibold, Loyalty Oath, 18 March 1865, Dexter P. Tiffany Collection, MHM.

41. *OR* 23(2):573; Eubank, *Shadow of the Patriarch*, 2–27, 37–38, 44–56, 71–121; Warner, *Generals in Blue*, 100; Welcher, *Union Army*, 2:161, 164, 193–94, 198, 205.

42. Lyman, *Meade's Headquarters*, 116–17; Beatty, *Citizen Soldier*, 235–36; Eubank, *Shadow of the Patriarch*, 7–8, 19–20, 78, 93, 116, 127; Shanks, *Recollections*, 249; Hazen, *Narrative*, 152.

43. *OR* 23(2):573; Welcher, *Union Army*, 2:194, 799–800; Welsh, *Medical Histories, Union*, 377; Beatty, *Citizen Soldier*, 235–37; Warner, *Generals in Blue*, 207, 533–34, 569; Smith, *Stones River (Union)*, 318, 332–56; Tuttle, *Kentucky Captain*, 91, 113; Shanks, *Recollections*, 295; Manville, "Wood," 9–13; Hunt and Brown, *Brevet Brigadier Generals*, 88; Eicher and Eicher, *High Commands*, 152, 280, 546. For a detailed, and not altogether laudatory, summary of Wood's career prior to the Chickamauga Campaign, see Lee, *Wood*, 5–114.

44. *OR* 23(2):573; Palmer, *Recollections*, 23–24, 71–74, 80–81; Warner, *Generals in Blue*, 104–5, 192–93, 225–26, 358–59; Fitch, *Annals*, 119–32; Smith, *Stones River (Union)*, 357–409;

Welcher, *Union Army*, 2:185–90, 192–94; Eicher and Eicher, *High Commands*, 193, 291, 415; Welsh, *Medical Histories, Union*, 85–86, 144, 165; Reid, *Ohio in the War*, 1:765–67; Hazzard, *Henry County*, 1:137–41; Hazen, *Narrative*, v–x.

45. *OR* 23(2):573; Warner, *Generals in Blue*, 28–29, 521–22; Eicher and Eicher, *High Commands*, 128, 209, 541; Welsh, *Medical Histories, Union*, 25, 349–50; Fitch, *Annals*, 174–75; Lott, "Van Cleve," 14–26, 42–44, 49–52, 58–60; Smith, *Stones River (Union)*, 295–96, 313; Barnes, Carnahan, and McCain, *Eighty-Sixth Indiana*, 546–53; "Sidney M. Barnes," http://www.rootsweb.ancestry.com/arsebast/Bios/barnessid.html (22 August 2011); "Col. Sidney Barnes," http://www.kentuckyregiments.org/8thky/staff/barnesfam.htm (22 August 2011); Dyer, *Compendium*, 1:450.

46. *OR* 23(2):398–99, 573; Warner, *Generals in Blue*, 181; Cullum, *Register*, 2:237–39; Eicher and Eicher, *High Commands*, 262–63; Welcher, *Union Army*, 2:181–83, 185–90; Shanks, *Recollections*, 268, 271, 273–75; *Ninety-Second Illinois*, 85–87. For a summary of Granger's career, including statements regarding his personality by contemporaries, see Conner, *Granger*, 9–76.

47. *OR* 23(2):573; Warner, *Generals in Blue*, 15; Eicher and Eicher, *High Commands*, 112, 178; Baird, *Profile*, 11, 32–37, 60–66, 73–75, 84–86, 94–98; "Stephenson County Illinois Biographies — Smith D. Atkins," https://www.accessgenealogy.com/illinois/biography-of-gen-smith-d-atkins.htm (24 August 2011); Welcher, *Union Army*, 2:831–32; "A Brief History of the 121st Ohio Volunteer Infantry," http://121stovi.com/history.html (24 August 2011); *Commemorative Biographical Record*, 88–89; Hunt, *Colonels in Blue*, 108–9.

48. *OR* 23(2):28, 156, 196, 297, 378; Warner, *Generals in Blue*, 128–29, 295, 334–35; Eicher and Eicher, *High Commands*, 212, 374, 397; Welcher, *Union Army*, 2:130, 161, 163, 181, 185, 187, 189–90, 204; Hunt and Brown, *Brevet Brigadier Generals*, 570; *Portrait, Hancock, McDonough and Henderson Counties*, 219–20; Reid, *Ohio in the War*, 1:904–5; Smith, *Stones River (Union)*, 570–71; Welsh, *Medical Histories, Union*, 211; Whalen and Whalen, *Fighting McCooks*, 129–30, 159–60.

49. *OR* 23(2):573; Warner, *Generals in Blue*, 182, 538–39; Eicher and Eicher, *High Commands*, 263, 553; Cullum, *Register*, 1:719–20; Welsh, *Medical Histories, Union*, 136–37; Welcher, *Union Army*, 2:158, 162, 193–94, 198, 200, 205, 794–96, 805; Ramage, *Rebel Raider*, 30, 41–43; "Lexington Rifles," http://www.lexingtonrifles.com/1857-651.htm (August 2011); "Sanders Dewees Bruce," http://www.findgrave.com/cgi-bin/fg.cgi?page=gr&GRid=10581242 (28 August 2011); *New York Times*, 1 February 1902.

50. *OR* 23(2):573; Warner, *Generals in Blue*, 470; Eicher and Eicher, *High Commands*, 504–5; Reid, *Ohio in the War*, 1:796–98; Cullum, *Register*, 2:478–79; Stanley, *Memoirs*, 40–42, 54, 78–79; Belcher, *Stanley*, 1–141.

51. *OR* 23(2):29, 93, 197, 298, 573; Warner, *Generals in Blue*, 296, 328–29, 543–44; Eicher and Eicher, *High Commands*, 374, 392, 556; Welsh, *Medical Histories, Union*, 212, 233, 360–61; Welcher, *Union Army*, 2:84, 159, 161, 164, 190, 349, 819; "Mitchell, Robert Byington," http://www.newmexicohistory.org/filedetails.php?fileID=23530 (29 August 2011); Beatty, *Citizen Soldier*, 307; Stanley, *Memoirs*, 135; Noe, *Perryville*, 284, 291–92, 380; "Col Archibald P Campbell," http://www.findagrave.com/cgi-bin/fg.cgi?page=gr&GRid=32460450 (30 August 2011); "Archibald Campbell GAR Post #161," http://www.macombmicw.com/campbell.html (30 August 2011); Thatcher, *Hundred Battles*, 115–18; Fitch, *Annals*, 207; Whalen and Whalen, *Fighting McCooks*, 290–99.

52. *OR* 23(2):183, 246, 573; Warner, *Generals in Blue*, 283, 511; Eicher and Eicher, *High Commands*, 352, 391, 537; Welcher, *Union Army*, 2:349; East, "Lincoln's Russian General,"

106–18; Turchin, *Chickamauga*, 5; Stanley, *Memoirs*, 135–37; Fitch, *Annals*, 205–13; Powell, *Officers (Volunteer)*, 313; Reid, *Ohio in the War*, 1:861; Welsh, *Medical Histories, Union*, 205; Vale, *Minty*, 366–70.

53. *OR* 23(2):572–80, 967–68; Davis, "Ordnance Logistics," 100–115.

CHAPTER 3

1. McWhiney, *Bragg*, 1–25; Seitz, *Bragg*, 1–3; Martin, *Bragg*, 3–13; Hess, *Bragg*, 1–2; Wellman, *County of Warren*, 62–63, 80, 83, 90, 118. McWhiney places Bragg's birthdate at 21 March, and Hess cites him, but all other sources indicate 22 March.

2. McWhiney, *Bragg*, 26–51; Seitz, *Bragg*, 3–4; Martin, *Bragg*, 14–29; Hess, *Bragg*, 2–4; Cullum, *Register*, 1:663; McKinney, *Education*, 29–39.

3. McWhiney, *Bragg*, 52–100; Seitz, *Bragg*, 5–11; Martin, *Bragg*, 30–64; Hess, *Bragg*, 4–5; Bridges, *Maverick General*, 19. For a mixed view of Bragg as a battery commander, see French, *Two Wars*, 62–64.

4. McWhiney, *Bragg*, 101–150; Seitz, *Bragg*, 11–19; Martin, *Bragg*, 64–89; Hess, *Bragg*, 5–12. For a positive view of Bragg as a battery commander during the 1850s, see John M. Geissler, *National Tribune*, 12 March 1891.

5. McWhiney, *Bragg*, 151–77; Seitz, *Bragg*, 20–51; Martin, *Bragg*, 90–101; Hess, *Bragg*, 15–18; Hay, "Bragg," 268–70.

6. McWhiney, *Bragg*, 175–98; Seitz, *Bragg*, 52–84; Martin, *Bragg*, 100–111; Hess, *Bragg*, 18–27; Taylor, *Destruction*, 100; Russell, *Diary*, 207; Welsh, *Medical Histories, Confederate*, 23; *OR* 6:788–89, 797–98.

7. McWhiney, *Bragg*, 202–52; Seitz, *Bragg*, 85–122; Martin, *Bragg*, 112–47; Hay, "Bragg," 271, 276–77; Hess, *Bragg*, 28–42; *OR* 10(1):463–70. Modern accounts of the Battle of Shiloh that cover Bragg's role fully include Sword, *Bloody April*; Daniel, *Shiloh*; and Cunningham, *Shiloh*.

8. McWhiney, *Bragg*, 253–60; Seitz, *Bragg*, 123–32; Martin, *Bragg*, 148–53; Hess, *Bragg*, 43–47; Hay, "Bragg," 277–79; McDonough, *Shiloh*, 150; Haughton, *Training*, 78–84; Daniel, *Soldiering*, 107–10; Urquhart, "Bragg's Advance," in *Battles and Leaders*, 3:609; S. H. Stout, "Reminiscences of General Braxton Bragg," Bragg Papers, WRHS; Watson, *Life*, 368–69; *OR* 17(2):606, 612, 614.

9. *OR* 10(1):780–86; *OR* 17(2):627–28, 636, 644–45, 647–48, 649, 651–52, 655–56, 658, 667–68, 677; McWhiney, *Bragg*, 261–81; Seitz, *Bragg*, 133–67; Martin, *Bragg*, 154–67; Hess, *Bragg*, 47–57; Hay, "Bragg," 280–82; Haughton, *Training*, 86–88; Daniel, *Soldiering*, 109–11. For analysis of Bragg's options and his relationship to Kirby Smith, see Connelly, *Heartland*, 187–224; McDonough, *War in Kentucky*, 71–85; and Noe, *Perryville*, 25–41.

10. McWhiney, *Bragg*, 281–321; Seitz, *Bragg*, 168–97; Martin, *Bragg*, 167–203; Hess, *Bragg*, 59–73; Hay, "Bragg," 282–90; *OR* 16(1):1087–97. Although occasionally overdrawn in its criticisms of Bragg, Connelly, *Heartland*, 224–70, is the best analysis of the events of the Kentucky Campaign from the Confederate perspective. For a more positive view of Bragg's performance in Kentucky, see Hewitt, "Braxton Bragg."

11. McWhiney, *Bragg*, 321–36; Seitz, *Bragg*, 197–207; Martin, *Bragg*, 203–15; Hess, *Bragg*, 74–92; Hay, "Bragg," 290–91, 294; Braxton Bragg to Elise Bragg, 18 September 1862, Bragg Papers, MHM; *OR* 16(1):1088; *OR* 17(2):680; Hughes, *Hardee*, 133–35; Parks, *Smith*, 242–45; Parks, *Polk*, 279–80; Polk, *Polk*, 2:158; Liddell, *Record*, 97–98; Davis, *Davis*, 473–74.

12. McWhiney, *Bragg*, 337–46; Seitz, *Bragg*, 207–38; Martin, *Bragg*, 215–19; Hess, *Bragg*,

78; Hay, "Bragg," 291–92; Woodworth, *Davis and His Generals*, 184–87; Parks, *Smith*, 247–50; Symonds, *Johnston*, 182–93; *OR* 20(2):384–85, 411–12; Davis, *Davis*, 475, 481–84; Connelly, *Autumn*, 3–43; *OR* 15:166, 171–72.

13. McWhiney, *Bragg*, 347–79; Seitz, *Bragg*, 239–76; Martin, *Bragg*, 220–50; Hess, *Bragg*, 93–112; Hay, "Bragg," 293–97; *OR* 20(1):663–72, 682–84, 698–702; *OR* 52:407; Parks, *Polk*, 293–95; Hughes, *Hardee*, 147–49; Davis, *Breckinridge*, 331–49; Symonds, *Stonewall of the West*, 116–18; Woodworth, *Davis and His Generals*, 186–96; Connelly, *Autumn*, 44–77. For modern accounts of the Battle of Stones River, see McDonough, *Stones River*; Cozzens, *No Better Place*; and both volumes of Smith, *Stones River*.

14. McWhiney, *Bragg*, 380–88; Seitz, *Bragg*, 276–302; Martin, *Bragg*, 250–58; Hess, *Bragg*, 113–33; Hay, "Bragg," 297–303; *OR* 16(1):1097–107; *OR* 23(2):613–14, 624, 626–27, 632–33, 640–41, 652–54, 658–59, 674, 684, 698, 708, 745, 757–61; Kean, *Confederate Government*, 42; Woodworth, *Davis and His Generals*, 196–99; Davis, *Davis*, 491–98; Connelly, *Autumn*, 77–92; Johnston, *Narrative*, 161–64; Symonds, *Johnston*, 196–201; Hughes, *Hardee*, 150; Parks, *Polk*, 300–302. For a spirited but not altogether convincing defense of Breckinridge, see Davis, *Breckinridge*, 349–62. Davis admits that one of Breckinridge's staff officers, Theodore O'Hara, had played a role in instigating the controversy by feeding false information to a Chattanooga newspaper.

15. McWhiney, *Bragg*, 388; Hallock, *Bragg*, 7–22; Seitz, *Bragg*, 303–12; Martin, *Bragg*, 257–67; Hess, *Bragg*, 133–52; Davis, *Davis*, 495–99; *OR* 23(1):618–27; *OR* 23(2):745, 826, 830, 841, 849; Beers, *Memories*, 88–89; Woodworth, *Davis and His Generals*, 198–99, 222–28; Connelly, *Autumn*, 93–134; Parks, *Polk*, 302–16; Hughes, *Hardee*, 150–57; Woodworth, "Tullahoma Campaign," 157–82. For detailed analysis of operations in the Tullahoma Campaign, see Bradley, *Tullahoma*; Brewer, "Tullahoma Campaign"; and Morris, "Forgotten Decisiveness."

16. Fremantle, *Diary*, 115; Welsh, *Medical Histories, Confederate*, 23; Hallock, *Bragg*, 3–6; *OR* 23(1):623; *OR* 52(2):499; Johnston, *Life of Johnston*, 544–48; *OR* 23(2):652, 656–57; S. H. Stout, "Reminiscences of General Braxton Bragg," Bragg Papers, WRHS; Taylor, *Destruction*, 100; Bunch, *Military Justice*, 89, 101–2. Just before the Battle of Stones River, Bragg told St. John Liddell, "General, I have no children. Hence, I look upon the soldiers of my army as my own—as *my* children." Liddell, *Record*, 106.

17. McWhiney, *Bragg*, 216–18, 254–55, 334, 342; Seitz, *Bragg*, 206–7; Connelly, *Autumn*, 21, 70–73; Woodworth, *Davis and His Generals*, 5–6, 94, 106–7, 162–66; Davis, *Breckinridge*, 328; Johnston, *Life of Johnston*, 544–48; S. H. Stout, "Reminiscences of General Braxton Bragg," Bragg Papers, WRHS; *OR* 23(1):623. While he often differed with Bragg, St. John Liddell, in speaking of the discord within the general officer corps of the Army of Tennessee, commented, "He was not popular with his generals; hence, I feared that zealous cooperation on their part was wanting. If he had caused one or two of us to be shot, I firmly believe the balance would have done better." Liddell, *Record*, 113–14.

18. Warner, *Generals in Gray*, 203–4; Davis and Hoffman, *Confederate General*, 4:126–27; Eicher and Eicher, *High Commands*, 359; Cullum, *Register*, 1:667–68; Daniel and Bock, *Island No. 10*, 114–41, 147; *OR* 8:807–9; *OR* 52(2):499; Johnson, "Confederate Staff Work," 61–63; Gow, "Chiefs of Staff," 347–57; Gow, "Military Administration" (dissertation), 52–55.

19. Heitman, *Historical Register*, 1:581; Jordan, *NC Troops*, 4:127; Joseph P. Jones CSR, NARA; David Urquhart CSR, NARA; *OR* 23(1):621; *OR* 52(2):745–46; Urquhart, "Bragg's Advance," in *Battles and Leaders*, 3:608n; Statement of Urquhart, 29 June 1863, Bragg

Papers, WRHS; Towson Ellis CSR, NARA; Hughes, *Yale's Confederates*, 68; McWhiney, *Bragg*, 183; Francis S. Parker Jr., CSR, NARA; J. Stoddard Johnston CSR, NARA; Davis, *Breckinridge*, 361–62; Elliott, *Harris*, 147–48; *OR* 20(1):671; Hughes, *Pride*, 14n.

20. *OR* 23(2):824–25, 933; Gow, "Military Administration" (dissertation), 53–54, 56–57, 160; Goode, *Virginia Cousins*, 239; George William Brent CSR, NARA; Kinloch Falconer CSR, NARA; Nelson, *Nation's Agony*, 200; "Maj Kinloch Falconer," http://www.findagrave.com/cgi-bin/fg.cgi?page=gr&GRid=11526454 (22 October 2011).

21. William K. Beard CSR, Andrew J. Hays CSR, William Clare CSR, Pollok B. Lee CSR, P. H. Thomson CSR, James Cooper CSR, and George W. Carr CSR, all in NARA; Gow, "Military Administration" (dissertation), 169–80. Major Lee's given name is generally listed as "Pollock," but he signed documents as "Pollok B. Lee." Maj. Gustavus A. Henry Jr. and Capt. William A. Reid are listed by June Gow as working in Beard's office during this period, but they did not join until after the Battle of Chickamauga, by which time Thomson had departed. Gustavus A. Henry Jr., CSR, William A. Reid CSR, P. H. Thomson CSR, all in NARA.

22. Lawrence W. O'Bannon CSR, Matthew B. McMicken CSR, John W. Green CSR, Albert J. Smith CSR, Giles M. Hillyer CSR, William H. Ross CSR, all in NARA; *OR* 23(1):584; *OR* 23(2):680, 688–89, 700, 764–65, 769–73, 854, 858; *OR* 51(2):738; Goff, *Confederate Supply*, 151–52.

23. "Death of a Polish Refugee," *New York Times*, 25 August 1878; Buck, *Cleburne*, 204–5; Dawson, *Reminiscences*, 104–5; Hypolite Oladowski CSR, Octavius T. Gibbes CSR, William D. Humphries CSR, William H. Warren CSR, B. Frank Nichol CSR, Bradford Nichol CSR, all in NARA; *OR* 23(2):762–63; *OR* 30(4):495; Cullum, *Register*, 2:701; James H. Hallonquist CSR, and R. H. Smith Thompson CSR, both in NARA; Daniel, *Cannoneers*, 78–79.

24. Edward A. Flewellen CSR, Samuel H. Stout CSR, Tobias G. Richardson CSR, and Lewis T. Pim CSR, all in NARA; *OR* 20(2):461; *OR* 23(2):933; Schroeder-Lein, *Confederate Hospitals*, 25–68, 189–90, 193; Cunningham, *Doctors in Gray*, 55–57; Rubenstein, "Medical Support," 27–29.

25. Alexander McKinstry CSR, James Strawbridge CSR, Charles W. Peden CSR, William A. Reid CSR, Harvey W. Walter CSR, John B. Sale CSR, all in NARA; Owen, *History of Alabama*, 4:1125–26; Rowland, *Encyclopedia of Mississippi*, 2:894–95; Salling, *Louisianians*, 81–83, 158; Bragg, "Postwar Letter," 75–79; "Mem. a/c Amount paid by Col. McKinstry, 8–15 September 1863," "Recd. of Capt. Reid Asst Pro Mar Genl Twenty dollars a/c Secret service, Samuel Gilliam, 4 October 1863," H. W. Walter to Braxton Bragg, 7 October 1863, all in Bragg Papers, WRHS; Andrews, *South Reports*, 339, 348; *OR* 23(2):824–25, 885, 860, 933; Radley, *Watchdog*, 6, 200–217.

26. Stephen W. Presstman CSR, Andrew H. Buchanan CSR, James K. P. McFall CSR, Henry C. Force CSR, James Nocquet CSR, John M. Wampler, CSR, James D. Thomas CSR, George B. Pickett CSR, G. W. Maxson CSR, all in NARA; Kundahl, *Confederate Engineer*, 185–87, 190–200, 218–20, 263–66.

27. Salling, *Louisianians*, 158; *OR* 23(2):958; Bergeron, *Louisiana Confederate Military Units*, 69–71, 176; William W. Mackall CSR, William K. Beard CSR, Matthew B. McMicken CSR, Hypolite Oladowski CSR, James H. Hallonquist CSR, Harvey W. Walter CSR, all in NARA; Martin, *Bragg*, 465; S. H. Stout, "Reminiscences of General Braxton Bragg," Bragg Papers, WRHS; Johnson, "Confederate Staff Work," 131–36; Gow, "Military Administration" (article), 191–94.

28. *OR* 23(1):586; *OR* 23(2):945–46; Daniel, *Cannoneers*, 92–93.

29. Robins, *Bishop*, 10–145; Parks, *Polk*, 21–170; Polk, *Polk*, 1:320–22; Davis, *Davis*, 28, 343, 346; Cullum, *Register*, 1:391; *OR* 52(2):115.

30. *OR* 52(2):115; Robins, *Bishop*, 151–68; Parks, *Polk*, 171–240; Polk, *Polk*, 2:67; *OR* 4:513–14, 522, 539; *OR* 7:746–47.

31. Braxton Bragg to Elise Bragg, 23 March 1862, Bragg Papers, MHM; *OR* 10(2):338–41; *OR* 17(2):336, 628; Martin, *Bragg*, 117–18; Parks, *Polk*, 14, 54, 279–81; "Finding Aid for the John Devereux Papers, 1712–1892," http://www.archives.ncdcr.gov/ead/eadxml/pc_deve reux_john.xml (9 November 2011); McWhiney, *Bragg*, 328–29; Connelly, *Autumn*, 19–23; Woodworth, *Davis and His Generals*, 156–58, 162. Bragg, apparently referring to Polk just before the Kentucky Campaign, spoke of a senior officer as "an old woman, utterly worthless." Taylor, *Destruction*, 100.

32. *OR* 16(1):1097–107; *OR* 20(1):698–704; *OR* 23(2):632, 729–30; Parks, *Polk*, 299–302; Robins, *Bishop*, 174–79; Connelly, *Autumn*, 21, 87–91; Woodworth, *Davis and His Generals*, 29–30, 222; Taylor, *Destruction*, 100; Braxton Bragg to Elise Bragg, 23 March 1862, Bragg Papers, MHM; Fremantle, *Diary*, 111–16; Liddell, *Record*, 100–101; *OR* 23(1):585. According to St. John Liddell, Polk "possessed all the requisites of a great soldier, except strategy and tactical combination."

33. Losson, *Forgotten Warriors*, 5–97; Johnson, "Benjamin Franklin Cheatham"; *OR* 17(2):628, 673; *OR* 23(2):624, 957; Liddell, *Record*, 119; Braxton Bragg to Maj. E. T. Sykes, 8 February 1873, J. F. H. Claiborne Papers, UNC; Elliott, *Harris*, 133–34; McWhiney, *Bragg*, 353–54n, 374; Connelly, *Autumn*, 84–85; Woodworth, *Davis and His Generals*, 189–91; Davis and Hoffman, *Confederate General*, 1:174–81.

34. *OR* 23(2):941, 957–58; Davis and Hoffman, *Confederate General*, 4:150–51, 5:182–83, 6:14–17, 164–65; Warner, *Generals in Gray*, 210, 283–84, 295–96, 346–47; Eicher and Eicher, *High Commands*, 362, 498, 515, 583–84; Welsh, *Medical Histories, Confederate*, 201, 240; Elliott, *Harris*, 134–35; Wright, *Diary*, 1–8; Warner, "George Earl Maney," 130–32; Cummings, "Otho French Strahl," 341–50.

35. Jones M. Withers, CSR, NARA; *OR* 23(2):720, 925, 957; Davis and Hoffman, *Confederate General*, 6:154–55; Warner, *Generals in Gray*, 342–43; Eicher and Eicher, *High Commands*, 577–78; Welsh, *Medical Histories, Confederate*, 238–39; McWhiney, *Bragg*, 381; Manigault, *Carolinian*, 78.

36. "Sketch of General Anderson's Life," James Patton Anderson Papers, UNC; Raab, *Anderson*, 5–81; Owen, *History of Alabama*, 3:475; Manigault, *Carolinian*, 3–76; Davis and Hoffman, *Confederate General*, 1:22–25, 2:60–63, 4:152–53, 6:104–7; Warner, *Generals in Gray*, 7–8, 70–71, 210–11, 325–26; Eicher and Eicher, *High Commands*, 104, 205, 362–63, 552; Welsh, *Medical Histories, Confederate*, 7–8, 53, 153, 228; "Gen. E. C. Walthall," 305.

37. Cullum, *Register*, 1:717–18; Hughes, *Hardee*, 3–98; Davis and Hoffman, *Confederate General*, 3:58–61; Warner, *Generals in Gray*, 124–25; Eicher and Eicher, *High Commands*, 278–79; Welsh, *Medical Histories, Confederate*, 93; Woodworth, *Davis and His Generals*, 162–65; *OR* 23(1):586.

38. Hughes, *Hardee*, 25–30; Martin, *Bragg*, 41; McWhiney, *Bragg*, 328–29, 375; *OR* 16(1):1097–98, 1101–3; *OR* 17(2):627–28; *OR* 20(1):623; *OR* 52(2):407; Connelly, *Autumn*, 21–22, 90–91; Woodworth, *Davis and His Generals*, 156–58, 165–66, 195, 199, 222. According to Bragg in January, "There is no man here to command an army. The one who aspires to it is a good drill-master, but no more, except that he is gallant. He has no ability to organize and supply an army, and no confidence in himself when approached by an enemy."

39. Davis and Hoffman, *Confederate General*, 1:198–201; Warner, *Generals in Gray*, 53–54;

Eicher and Eicher, *High Commands,* 176; Welsh, *Medical Histories, Confederate,* 40–41; Liddell, *Record,* 103, 122–23; Nash, *Biographical Sketches,* 7–73; Buck, *Cleburne,* 78–79; Purdue and Purdue, *Cleburne,* 1–119; Symonds, *Stonewall of the West,* 9–133; Joslyn, *Meteor,* 53–64; *OR* 23(2):957. Further evidence of Cleburne's eccentric nature can be found in Drake, *Annals,* 241–49.

40. Davis and Hoffman, *Confederate General,* 1:186–87, 4:74–75, 5:48–49, 6:158–59; Warner, *Generals in Gray,* 49–50, 187–88, 243–44, 344–45; Eicher and Eicher, *High Commands,* 172–73, 348, 433, 579; Welsh, *Medical Histories, Confederate,* 37–38, 140, 175, 239–40; *OR* 6:820; *OR* 10(2):606–7; S. A. M. Wood, CSR, NARA; Owen, *History of Alabama,* 4:1799–1800; Liddell, *Record,* 11–125; Robert D. Meade to Frank L. Polk, 4 March 1931, Leonidas Polk Papers (microfilm ed.), UNC.

41. Cullum, *Register,* 2:124; Davis and Hoffman, *Confederate General,* 6:10–11; Warner, *Generals in Gray,* 293–94; Eicher and Eicher, *High Commands,* 511; Elliott, *Soldier of Tennessee,* 1–98; Wingfield, *Stewart,* 9–41; *OR* 16(1):1104–5; *OR* 23(2):957.

42. Davis and Hoffman, *Confederate General,* 1:70–73, 130–33, 196–97, 3:180–85; Warner, *Generals in Gray,* 19–20, 35–36, 52–53, 157–58; Eicher and Eicher, *High Commands,* 121, 146–47, 196–97, 320; Welsh, *Medical Histories, Confederate,* 15–16, 29, 40; Cullum, *Register,* 2:47–48; Cummings, *Yankee Quaker,* 15–248; Morris, "Eastern Ohio Quaker," 52–55; Jordan, "Military Career of Henry D. Clayton," 127–30; "Gen. William B. Bate," 336–37; Kelly, "Back in the Saddle," 27–29.

43. Cullum, *Register,* 2:730–31; Davis and Hoffman, *Confederate General,* 6:124–29; Warner, *Generals in Gray,* 332–33; Eicher and Eicher, *High Commands,* 563; Welsh, *Medical Histories, Confederate,* 232; Longacre, *Soldier,* 1–108; Dyer, *Wheeler,* 1–107; Powell, *Failure,* xx–xxiii, 2–7; *OR* 23(1):586.

44. Davis and Hoffman, *Confederate General,* 3:70–71, 6:122–23; Warner, *Generals in Gray,* 127, 331–32; Eicher and Eicher, *High Commands,* 190, 283, 562–63; Welsh, *Medical Histories, Confederate,* 95, 231–32; Allardice, *More Generals,* 66–67; Charles C. Crews, CSR, NARA; Powell, *Failure,* xxx–xxxi; Longacre, *Soldier,* 53, 92, 128; "Thomas Harrison," http://www.tshaonline.org/handbook/online/articles/fhaaf (23 November 2011).

45. Davis and Hoffman, *Confederate General,* 4:162–63; Warner, *Generals in Gray,* 214–15; Eicher and Eicher, *High Commands,* 366, 599, 609; Allardice, *More Generals,* 111–13, 204–5; James Hagan, CSR, and Alfred A. Russell, CSR, NARA; Heitman, *Historical Register,* 1:485–86; Powell, *Failure,* xxvii–xxviii, xxxii–xxxiii.

46. Davis and Hoffman, *Confederate General,* 2:138–45; Warner, *Generals in Gray,* 92–93; Eicher and Eicher, *High Commands,* 240; Welsh, *Medical Histories, Confederate,* 70–72; Steiner, *Medical-Military Portraits,* 297–337; Morton, *Artillery,* 11–17; Weller, "Nathan Bedford Forrest"; Powell, *Failure,* xviii–xx; *OR* 23(1):586; Daniel, *Cannoneers,* 92. Biographies of Forrest are numerous. Useful older studies are Wyeth, *Forrest;* and Jordan and Pryor, *Campaigns of Forrest.* The best modern biographies are Hurst, *Forrest;* and Wills, *Battle from the Start.*

47. Davis and Hoffman, *Confederate General,* 1:42–45, 2:68–69; Warner, *Generals in Gray,* 12–13, 72–73; Eicher and Eicher, *High Commands,* 107–8, 209; Heitman, *Historical Register,* 1:169; Powell, *Failure,* xxiii–xxiv, xxxiii–xxxiv; Daniel, *Cannoneers,* 92.

48. Davis and Hoffman, *Confederate General,* 2:66–67, 5:100–101; Warner, *Generals in Gray,* 71–72, 260–61; Eicher and Eicher, *High Commands,* 594, 609; Cullum, *Register,* 2:579–80; Daniel, *Cannoneers,* 79–80, 88–92; *OR* 23(1):586; *OR* 23(2):944.

49. Davis and Hoffman, *Confederate General,* 3:148–49, 5:104–5; Warner, *Generals in Gray,* 150–51, 262; Eicher and Eicher, *High Commands,* 315–16, 458; Brown, "Unlucky in

Command," 5–18; Smith, *Stones River (Army of Tennessee)*, 332–37; George W. Lee, CSR, NARA; *OR* 20(2):489; *OR* 23(1):586; *OR* 23(2):615, 620, 656–57, 728.

50. *OR* 23(2):941–45; Hypolite Oladowski to Moses H. Wright, 13 August 1863, Letters Sent, Ordnance Office, Army of Tennessee, NARA.

CHAPTER 4

1. *OR* 23(1):626–27; *OR* 23(2):899–900; Manigault, *Carolinian*, 76; Fraser Diary, 5 July 1863, CCNMP; *SOR* 45:81, 92, 153; *SOR* 78:609; *SOR*, 79:394, 426, 559, 562, 565; Smith Diary, 5 July 1863, CCNMP; Sparkman Diary, 5 July 1863, BPL; Daniel Diary, 5 July 1863, SRNB; Talbert Holt Letter, undated, Partin Papers, AU; Moore Diary, 5 July 1863, UDC Collection, and Dowda Diary, 5 July 1863, GDAH; Corbitt Diary, 5 July 1863, EU; Jordan and Pryor, *Campaigns of Forrest*, 293; *SOR* 17:307, 323; *SOR* 13:909, 912–14, 916.

2. *OR* 23(1):626–27; *OR* 23(2):899–901; *SOR* 78:609; *SOR* 79:394, 471; Brown Notebook, CCNMP; Magee Diary, 5 July 1863, DU; Moorman, "Moorman Memorandum," 75.

3. Kundahl, *Confederate Engineer*, 228; Sparkman Diary, 5 July 1863, BPL; *SOR* 79:426; Coleman Diary, 5 July 1863, UNC; Armstrong Diary, 5 July 1863, ADAH; Dillon Diary, 5 July 1863, TSLA; Talbert Holt Letter, undated, Partin Papers, AU; Moore Diary, 5 July 1863, UDC Collection, GDAH; Johnson Diary, 5 July 1863, NARA; *SOR* 17:307, 323; *SOR* 13:909, 911–14, 916; *SOR* 79:559, 562, 565, 570, 576, 579; Dowda Diary, 5 July 1863, GDAH; Bunting, *Letters*, 172; Macmurphy Diary, 5 July 1863, http://www.terrystexasrangers.org/diaries/macmurphy gl/index.html; Cowles, *OR Atlas*, Plate 112.1; Prince, *N., C.& St. L.*, 6; *Macon (Ga.) Telegraph*, 10 July 1863; Alex Morgan to his wife, 20 July 1863, Morgan Letters, BU; *OR* 23(2):907. Modern engineering studies indicate that the longer of the two Bridgeport bridges was 1,470 feet in length, not the 1,232 feet described in the *OR Atlas*. See Rick Garro and Hal Lewis, "CSX Bridge 122.6 over Tennessee River Slough near Bridgeport, Alabama," http://www.arema.org/files/library/1999_Conference_Proceedings/00012.pdf.

4. *OR* 23(1):627; *SOR* 45:77, 133, 164, 183, 714; *SOR* 46:95, 179, 289; *SOR* 13:164; Fraser Diary, 6 July 1863, CCNMP; Manigault, *Carolinian*, 76; C. Irvine Walker to Ada Sinclair, 8 July 1863, Regimental Papers, WRHS; Moorman, "Moorman Memorandum," 75–76; *SOR* 77:144; Freeman Diary, 6 July 1863, TSLA; *SOR* 78:609; *SOR* 79:405, 471; *OR* 23(2):901–2; Magee Diary, 6 July 1863, DU.

5. Coleman Diary, 6 July 1863, UNC; Smith Diary, 6 July 1863, CCNMP; Armstrong Diary, 6 July 1863, ADAH; Williamson, *Forty-Fifth Mississippi*, 119; *SOR* 46:68–69; *SOR* 80:81; Daniel Diary, 6 July 1863, SRNB; *SOR* 14:543; Dillon Diary, 6 July 1863, TSLA; Talbert Holt letter, undated, Partin Papers, AU; Moore Diary, 6 July 1863, UDC Collection, GDAH; Johnson Diary, 6 July 1863, NARA; *SOR* 78:714, 787; *SOR* 79:34, 67; Collins, *Chapters*, 139–42; Heartsill, *Fourteen Hundred*, 137–38; *OR* 23(2):901–2.

6. Dowda Diary, 6 July 1863, GDAH; Bunting, *Letters*, 172–73; Dodd, *Diary*, 20–21; Macmurphy Diary, 6 July 1863, http://www.terrystexasrangers.org/diaries/macmurphy_gl/index.html; Corbitt Diary, 6 July 1863, EU.

7. Hoobler, *Cities under the Gun*, 115; Armstrong, *Hamilton County*, 2:17; Clifton, *Chattanooga*, 132; McAdory Memorandum, ADAH; *SOR* 76:804, 814; *SOR* 77:142, 147; Freeman Diary, 7 July 1863, TSLA; Moorman, "Moorman Memorandum," 76; *OR* 23(1):627; *SOR* 78:550, 609, 701; *SOR* 79:9, 195, 265, 394, 402, 426; Worsham, *Old Nineteenth*, 82; Magee Diary, 7 July 1863, DU; Coleman Diary, 7 July 1863, UNC; Daniel

Diary, 7–9 July 1863, SRNB; Moore Diary, 7 July 1863, UDC Collection, GDAH; Estes Diary, 9 July 1863, MC; Heartsill, *Fourteen Hundred*, 138; Armstrong Diary, 7–9 July 1863, ADAH; Smith Diary, 7 July 1863, CCNMP; Seaton, *Bugle*, 36; Corbitt Diary, 7 July 1863, EU; Audley Anderson to Margaret Anderson, 8 July 1863, NC; Macmurphy Diary, 7 July 1863, http://www.terrystexasrangers.org/diaries/macmurphy_gl/index.html; Lindsley, *Annals*, 2:692.

8. For a comprehensive description of the terrain around Chattanooga, see Connelly, *Autumn*, 139–46. For the Cowan tunnel, see Prince, *N., C. & St. L.*, 6; and Arbuckle, *Cowan Pusher*, 22, 74–75.

9. Connelly, *Autumn*, 142–44.

10. Govan and Livingood, *Chattanooga Country*, 133–36, 149–53; Prince, *N., C. & St. L.*, 6–8, 32–33; Schult, *N., C. & St. L.*, 4–13; Robertson, "Rails to the River of Death," 50–52; Goff, *Confederate Supply*, 32; Vandiver, *Ploughshares*, 201; *OR*, Series IV, 3:990.

11. *OR* 23(2):902, 904–5, 907; Alex Morgan to his wife, 9 July 1863, Morgan Letters, BU; Purdue and Purdue, *Cleburne*, 203–4; Williamson, *Forty-Fifth Mississippi*, 119; *SOR* 13:639; Armstrong Diary, 12 July 1863, ADAH; Johnson Diary, 9 July 1863, Johnson Papers, NARA; Order and Letter Book, Hardee's Corps, MC.

12. *OR* 23(2):904, 914, 923, 925–26; Longacre, *Soldier*, 108–9; Macmurphy Diary, 12–14 July 1863, http://www.terrystexasrangers.org/diaries/macmurphy_gl/index.html; Corbitt Diary, 12–14 July 1863, EU; Dodd, *Diary*, 21; Patton Anderson to Thomas Jack, 16 July 1863, in P. H. Rice (Third Confederate Cavalry), CSR, NARA; Miller, "History of the Eighth Confederate Cavalry, 1861–1865," ADAH; William T. Presley to "Dearest Henrie," 28 July 1863, Presley Letters, UND; Dodson, *Campaigns*, 99; "Tri-monthly Return of Cavalry Corps of the Army of Tennessee, Trenton, Ga., 10 July 1863," private collection.

13. Jordan and Pryor, *Campaigns of Forrest*, 293–94; Dyer, *Diary*, 16; *OR* 23(1):847; Lindsley, *Annals*, 2:651, 657.

14. *OR* 1:451; *OR* 23(2):656, 910, 924. Voluminous correspondence regarding this case can be found in George W. Lee, CSR, NARA. The U.S. Federal Census of 1860 for Twiggs County, Georgia, lists George W. Lee, thirty-one, as an overseer.

15. *OR* 23(2):909–10, 918–19, 924–25, 930–31; *OR* 52(2):511–12; Moses H. Wright, CSR, and George W. Lee, CSR, both in NARA; Norman, *Colonel Burton's*, 40, 97; Sykes, *Walthall's Brigade*, 525; Freeman Diary, 26 July 1863, TSLA; *SOR* 45:714, 784, 811, 829; *SOR* 46:95, 97; Kundahl, *Confederate Engineer*, 231–32.

16. *OR* 23(2):902, 904–5, 908–9; Kean, *Confederate Government*, 81, 83; Manuscript Notes (undated), Hill Papers, NCDAH; *OR* 24(1):201–13; Davis, *Davis*, 509–10; Polk, *Polk*, 2:228–29; Hughes, *Hardee*, 158.

17. Davis and Hoffman, *Confederate General*, 3:102–5; Warner, *Generals in Gray*, 136–37; Eicher and Eicher, *High Commands*, 296–97; Welsh, *Medical Histories, Confederate*, 100–101; Cullum, *Register*, 2:135; Bridges, *Maverick General*, 16–194.

18. Welsh, *Medical Histories, Confederate*, 100–101; Davis and Hoffman, *Confederate General*, 3:104; Kean, *Confederate Government*, 81; Hill, "Chickamauga," in *Battles and Leaders*, 3:639.

19. Jones M. Withers, CSR, NARA; Bragg to Shorter, 18 July 1863, Bragg, Letters and Telegrams Sent, NARA; *OR* 23(2):912, 938; Neal and Kremm, *Lion of the South*, 33, 161–64; Symonds, *Stonewall of the West*, 36–41.

20. *OR* 24(1):202–7, 232; *OR* 23(2):843, 924; *OR* 20(2):495; Bragg to Buckner, 7 July 1863, Buckner Papers, HL.

21. *OR* 23(2):931, 934–35, 964; Connelly, *Autumn*, 157.

22. *OR* 52(2):508.

23. Johnston, *Narrative*, 211; *OR* 23(2):836–38, 920.

24. *OR* 23(2):932–33, 937–38.

25. Joshua K. Callaway to Dulcinea Callaway, 7 July 1863, Callaway Papers, UT; C. Irvine Walker to Ada Sinclair, 8 July 1863, Walker Letters, Regimental Papers, WRHS; D. L. Kelly to Miss S. J. Honnoll, 10 July 1863, Honnoll Family Papers, EU; Magee Diary, 9 July 1863, DU; J. P. Kendall to his parents, 12 July 1863, William D. Kendall Papers, HL; Joseph Branch O'Bryan to his sister, 9 [8] July 1863, O'Bryan Letters, TSLA; Batchelor and Turner, *Batchelor-Turner Letters*, 59; Bunting, *Letters*, 173. See also John R. Hurley to his sisters, 11 July 1863, Hurley Letters, VMI: "So I am afraid we will be whiped but the yankies cant whip us for they cant catch us. If they come down here I think we will run to Atlanta and then to Montgomery. I believe I had rather fight a little than run so mutch."

26. Alex Morgan to his wife, 20 July 1863, Morgan Letters, BU; Bolling Hall Jr. to Bolling Hall Sr., 18 July 1863, Bolling Hall Family Papers, ADAH.

27. Roberts Diary, 7 July 1863, private collection; Nimrod W. E. Long to his wife, 13 July 1863, Long Papers, EU; John Crittenden to "Dear Bettie," 21 July 1863, Crittenden Letters, UT; Thomas T. Bigbie to his parents, 16 July 1863, Bigbie Letters, AU; Bunting, *Letters*, 177; Heartsill, *Fourteen Hundred*, 139; John W. Sparkman Diary, 22 July 1863, BPL; Oldham Diary, 30 July 1863, CCNMP; Hubert Dent to his wife, 11 July 1863, Dent Collection, AU. See also Alex Morgan to his wife, 20 July 1863, Morgan Letters, BU.

28. Thomas Warrick to his wife, 26 July 1863, Warrick Papers, ADAH; Nimrod W. E. Long to his wife, 13 July 1863, Long Papers, EU; Roberts Diary, 20 and 23 July 1863, private collection; Heartsill, *Fourteen Hundred*, 140.

29. Jackson, *So Mourns*, 55–56; Thomas T. Bigbie to his parents, 16 July 1863, Bigbie Letters, AU; Heartsill, *Fourteen Hundred*, 139, 140; Turner, "Co. G, 6th Texas," 162; John R. Hurley to his sisters, 7 July 1863, Hurley Letters, VMI; Roberts Diary, 25 July 1863, private collection; John Crittenden to "Dear Bettie," 9 July 1863, Crittenden Letters, UT; William D. Cole to his wife, 17–18 July 1863, Cole Letters, Civil War Miscellaneous Collection, USAHEC; Oldham Diary, 16 July 1863, CCNMP.

30. Armstrong Diary, 18 July 1863, ADAH; Freeman Diary, 12 July 1863, TSLA; Heartsill, *Fourteen Hundred*, 140; Daniel Diary, 31 July 1863, Civil War Miscellaneous Collection, USAHEC; Sparkman Diary, 26 July 1863, BPL; James T. Searcy to "Dear Stella," 28 July 1863, Searcy Letters, ADAH; J. P. Kendall to his parents, 12 July 1863, W. D. Kendall Papers, HL; J. W. Ward to his mother, 19 July 1863, CSA Records, UT; J. L. Bostick to his sister, 19 July 1863, Bostick Family Collection, TSLA; Jackson, *So Mourns*, 56; Manigault, *Carolinian*, 78; Hubert Dent to his wife, 11 July 1863, Dent Collection, AU; John Crittenden to "Dear Bettie," 21 July 1863, Crittenden Letters, UT; William B. Honnoll to his sister, 16 July 1863, Honnoll Family Papers, EU; Callaway, *Callaway Letters*, xii, 116–21; James A. Hall to Bolling Hall Sr., 28 July 1863, Bolling Hall Family Papers, ADAH; Robert Lewis Bliss to his mother, 14 July 1863, Bliss Letters, ADAH; Thomas T. Bigbie to his wife, 15 July 1863, Bigbie Letters, AU; William G. Young to "N. D.," 24 July 1863, Young Letters, HC; Simeon C. Wilkerson to his wife, 18 July 1863, Wilkerson Letters, NC; William T. Presley to "Dearest Henrie," 30 July 1863, Presley Letters, UND.

31. S. M. Cherry, "Church Leader," *Chattanooga (Tenn.) Free Press*, 21 September 1938, clipping in CPL; Daniel Diary, 16 July 1863, SRNB; James T. Searcy to "Dear Georgia," 12 July 1863, and to "Dear Stella," 17 July 1863, Searcy Letters, ADAH; Bunting, *Letters*, 178–82; Dodd, *Diary*, 21; John Crittenden to "Dear Bettie," 21 July 1863, Crittenden Letters, UT; Joshua K. Callaway to Dulcinea Callaway, 19 July 1863, Callaway Papers, UT;

Daniel C. Govan to James S. Fullerton, 22 May 1894, CCNMP; Fraser Diary, 24 July 1863, CCNMP; Talbert Holt to his sisters, 19 July 1863, Holt Letters, AU; Roberts Diary, 28 July 1863, private collection.

32. John Crittenden to "Dear Bettie," 9 July 1863, Crittenden Letters, UT; Magee Diary, 9, 16, and 27 July 1863, DU; Archie McLaurin to his sister, 9 July 1863, McLaurin Letters, WHS; Davis Diary, 8 July 1863, TSLA; Freeman Diary, 21 July 1863, TSLA; James T. Searcy to his mother, 21 July 1863, and to "Dear Stella," 26 July 1863, Searcy Letters, ADAH; Isaac Scherck to Oscar Stuart, 29 July 1863, Stuart and Family Papers, MDAH. For other indications of morale in the Army of Tennessee at this time, see Sparkman Diary, 9 July 1863, BPL; Dillon Diary, 10 July 1863, TSLA; Joshua K. Callaway to Dulcinea Callaway, 11 and 23 July 1863, Callaway Papers, UT; Pleasant B. Clark to Henry H. Wells, 11 July 1863, Wells Papers, UNC; Robert Lewis Bliss to his mother, 14 July 1863, Bliss Letters, ADAH; Roberts Diary, 19 July 1863, private collection; Jamison and McTigue, *Letters and Recollections*, 68–69.

33. *OR* 23(2):925, 933, 938; Gow, "Military Administration" (article), 191; Beers, *Memories*, 88; Hallock, *Bragg*, 34; Bragg to Cooper, 8 May 1863, in George W. Brent, CSR, NARA.

CHAPTER 5

1. Garfield to Anderson, 4 July 1863, Thoms to Holdridge, 5 July 1863, Drouillard to Anderson, 5 July 1863, Garfield to Anderson, 5 July 1863, and Thompson to Anderson, 5 July 1863, all in DC, Telegrams Sent, NARA; Hoffman, *"Brave Mechanics,"* 149–51.

2. *OR* 23(1):582–83; McCullough Diary, 5–6 July 1863, ISL; Meredith Diary, 5–6 July 1863, Harrisburg Civil War Roundtable Collection, USAHEC; James M. Sligh to his mother, 7 July 1863, Sligh Family Papers, UM-B; Drouillard to Anderson, 6 July 1863, Thompson to Anderson, 6 July 1863, Goddard to Anderson, 6 July 1863, Garfield to Anderson, 6 July 1863, Drouillard to Morton, 6 July 1863 (two messages), Goddard to Morton, 6 July 1863, and Rosecrans to McCallum Bridge Co., 6 July 1863, all in DC, Telegrams Sent, NARA.

3. Jones Diary, 5–6 July 1863, SRNB; Everett F. Abbott to his mother, 5–7 July 1863, Chamberlain Papers, IHS; Christian Diary, 7 July 1863, CCNMP; Miller Journal, 7 July 1863, IHS; Barnes, Carnahan, and McCain, *Eighty-Sixth Indiana*, 144; Kempfer, *Salem Light Guard*, 119; Hinman, *Sherman Brigade*, 395; John M. Barnard to Margaret Barnard, 7 July 1863, Barnard Letters, IHS; Mosman, *Rough Side*, 63; Frank M. Phelps to his friends, 5 July 1863, Lewis Leigh Collection, Phelps Letters, USAHEC; Newlin, *Seventy-Third Illinois*, 187–88. For other accounts of a similar nature, see Johnston Diary, 6 July 1863, Johnston Collection, CHS; Ward Diary, 5 July 1863, Ward Papers, DP; Albertson, *Letters Home*, Letter 90; Marshall Diary, 5–6 July 1863, OHS; Price Diary, 6–7 July 1863, Civil War Miscellaneous Collection, USAHEC; Lyman S. Widney, *National Tribune*, 31 October 1901; Woodcock, *Southern Boy*, 174; Heg, *Letters*, 228; Kiene, *Journal*, 160; Kerwood, *Fifty-Seventh Indiana*, 194.

4. Connelly Diary, 6 July 1863, IHS; John M. Barnard to Margaret Barnard, 7 July 1863 (two letters) and 11 July 1863, Barnard Letters, IHS; Inskeep Diary, 6 July 1863, OHS; Newlin, *Seventy-Third Illinois*, 187; Caleb H. Carlton to his wife, 15 July 1863, Carlton Papers, LC; Busbey Diary, 17 July 1863, SRNB; Wright, *Eighth Kentucky*, 166; John C. Love to his parents, 13 July 1863, Love Letters, UM-B; Alanson R. Ryman to Jane Ryman, 7 July 1863, Ryman Letters, IHS; Reed Diary, 7–10 July 1863, CCNMP.

5. *OR* 23(2):518; Rosecrans to Stanton, 7 July 1863, Rosecrans to A. Johnson, 7 July 1863, and Goddard to Thomas, McCook, Stanley, G. Granger, Morton, and R. S. Granger, 7 July 1863, all in DC, Telegrams Sent, NARA; Rosecrans to Anna Rosecrans, 7 July 1863, Rosecrans Papers, UCLA.

6. Drouillard to Anderson, 7 July 1863 (two messages), Goddard to Anderson, 7 July 1863, Bond to Morton, 7 July 1863, Drouillard to Morton, 7 July 1863, Garfield to Stanley, 7 July 1863, Bond to Anderson, 8 July 1863, and Rosecrans to Anderson, 8 July 1863, all in DC, Telegrams Sent, NARA; Anderson to Garfield, 8 July 1863, DC, Telegrams Received, NARA; *OR* 23(2):522.

7. Travis Account, UM-C; James W. Sligh to his wife, 20 July 1863, Sligh Family Papers, UM-B; Goddard to Morton, 9 July 1863 (two messages), and McMichael to Morton, 9 July 1863, all in DC, Telegrams Sent, NARA. The timeline presented above differs from that offered in Hoffman, *"Brave Mechanics,"* 155, and is based upon the headquarters telegrams cited.

8. Smith Diary, 8–9 July 1863, CCNMP; Jones Diary, 9 July 1863, SRNB; Welk Diary, 9 July 1863, BGSU; Protsman Diary, 9 July 1863, WSU; Talbot Diary, 8–9 July 1863, SRNB; Moon Diary, 9 July 1863, KSHS; Beck Diary, 9 July 1863, KSHS; Garfield to Anderson, 2:30 P.M., 8 July 1863, Garfield to Stanley, 2:15 A.M., 9 July 1863, Garfield to McCook, 9 July 1863, Bond to Anderson, 2:30 P.M., 9 July 1863, Drouillard to Anderson, 9 July 1863, Garfield to Anderson, 9 July 1863, and Garfield to Crittenden, 2:30 P.M., 10 July 1863, all in DC, Telegrams Sent, NARA; Drouillard Diary, 9 July 1863, Rosecrans Papers, UCLA; Prince, *N., C. & St. L.*, 26; Kundahl, *Confederate Engineer*, 208–11; White, *Passenger Car*, 581; Quartermaster's Stores Transferred by Capt. W. F. Harris, Assistant Quartermaster U.S.A., Louisville, Ky., to J. B. Anderson, Genl. Manager of Military Railways, 1863, Anderson Family Papers, KSHS. For photographs of these cars, see Abdill, *Civil War Railroads*, 139, 162. Theories on the origin of the name "steam dummy" can be found in Bianculli, *Trains and Technology*, 1:169–71.

9. *OR* 23(1):582; XIV Corps Journal, Thomas Papers, NARA; Wilder to Rosecrans, 10 July 1863, Rosecrans Papers, UCLA; Mosman, *Rough Side*, 62; Pickering Diary, 9 July 1863, HL; Lytle, *For Honor*, 181; Morledge Diary, 10 July 1863, KMNMP; Crippin, "Diary," 275; Connelly Diary, 9–10 July 1863, IHS; Smith, *Samuel Thomas Smith*, 76; Hinman, *Sherman Brigade*, 398; Woodcock, *Southern Boy*, 175; Moses F. Yoder to his brother, 10 July 1863, Yoder Papers, LC; Drouillard Diary, 11 July 1863, Rosecrans Papers, UCLA; Goddard to Atwater, 10 July 1863 (two messages), DC, Telegrams Sent, NARA; Stearns Diary, 10 July 1863, UM-B.

10. Garfield to Stanley, 7 July 1863, DC, Telegrams Sent, NARA; *OR* 23(2):526–28; Wilder to Rosecrans, 10 July 1863, and Rosecrans to Anna Rosecrans, 11 July 1863, both in Rosecrans Papers, UCLA; Wilder, General Orders, No. 15, 10 July 1863, Lilly Papers, LCA.

11. *OR* 23(2):519, 521–22, 524; Sheridan to Thruston, 4:30 P.M., 7 July 1863, Sheridan to McCook, 11 July 1863, and Sheridan to McCook, undated but 11 July 1863, all in DC, Letters Received, NARA; Garfield to McCook, 8 July 1863, DC, Telegrams Sent, NARA; Thruston to Sheridan, 8 July 1863, Moore to Lee, 9 July 1863, Thruston to Sheridan, 10 July 1863 (two messages), Moore to Lee, 11 July 1863, Conrad to Lee, 14 July 1863, and Bradley to Lee, 14 July 1863, all in Sheridan Papers, LC; Austin Diary, 9–14 July 1863, ALPL; Riley, *Diary*, 48–49; Tabler Diary, 9–14 July 1863, private collection; Crippin, "Diary," 275; Burns Diary, 9–14 July 1863, CCNMP; Colburn/Gray Diary, 9–14 July 1863, private collection; *SOR* 22:168; *SOR* 24:35; *OR* 52(1):398; Newlin, *Seventy-Third Illinois*, 190–91; *OR* 23(1):824; Morledge Diary, 12 July 1863, KMNMP. Possibly named originally for a local

family named Sweeten, the valley known as Sweeden's Cove during the Civil War is now called Sweden Cove on modern maps.

12. Rosecrans to Anna Rosecrans, 12 and 14 July 1863, Bond to Innes, 12 July 1863, Rosecrans to Busch, 11:30 A.M., 14 July 1863, Rosecrans to Anderson, 11:30 P.M. [A.M.], 14 July 1863, Rosecrans to Granger, 14 July 1863, and Goddard to Smith, 14 July 1863, all in DC, Telegrams Sent, NARA; Decker Diary, 13 July 1863, WHS; James W. Sligh to his wife, 13 July 1863, James M. Sligh to his mother, 20 July 1863, and Sligh Diary, 12 July 1863, all in Sligh Family Papers, UM-B; Stearns Diary, 12 July 1863, UM-B; Rosecrans to Anna Rosecrans, 11 July 1863, and Drouillard Diary, 12–14 July 1863, both in Rosecrans Papers, UCLA; *OR* 23(2):531; W. A. Smith to his parents and sister, 15 July 1863, Smith Papers, UM-C; Brown Diary, 14 July 1863, ALPL; Williams, *Extracts*, 77.

13. Drouillard Diary, 14–17 July 1863, Rosecrans Papers, UCLA; Silverstone, *Warships*, 169, 178; Winans Diary, 16–17 July 1863, CCNMP; Hewes, *Tenth Michigan*, 43; Thrall to Goddard, 15 July 1863, and Thoms to Garfield, 16 July 1863, both in DC, Telegrams Sent, NARA; *OR* 52(1):413–14; Garfield, *Wild Life*, 288; Sanderson Journal, 17 July 1863, OHS.

14. Drouillard Diary, 18 July 1863, Rosecrans Papers, UCLA; Garfield to Innes, 5:30 P.M., 18 July 1863, Thompson to Innes, 8:30 P.M. and 8:45 P.M., 18 July 1863, Thrall to Goddard, 15 July 1863, Thoms to Garfield, 8:15 P.M., 15 July 1863, Garfield to Innes, 10:00 P.M., 15 July 1863, Thompson to Morton, 12 July 1863, and Thrall to Rosecrans, 18 July 1863, all in DC, Telegrams Sent, NARA; *OR* 23(1):826; James W. Sligh to his wife, 20 July 1863, and Sligh Diary, 13 and 18 July 1863, both in Sligh Family Papers, UM-B; Stearns Diary, 18 July 1863, UM-B; Meredith Diary, 18 July 1863, Harrisburg Civil War Roundtable Collection, USAHEC; Roseberry Diary, 18 July 1863, EU; Connolly, *Three Years*, 105, 108–11; Banta Diary, 13–18 July 1863, CCNMP; Kemper Diary, 13–18 July 1863, OHS; *SOR* 28:371; Baumgartner, *Blue Lightning*, 100.

15. Rosecrans to Sheridan, 9:45 P.M., 18 July 1863, and Rosecrans to McCook, 9:45 P.M., 18 July 1863, both in DC, Telegrams Sent, NARA; *OR* 23(2):542, 543; Rosecrans to Sheridan, 18 July 1863, Ray to Sheridan, 17 July 1863 and 18 July 1863, McCook to Sheridan, 18 July 1863, Rosecrans to McCook, 18 July 1863, and Thruston to Sheridan, 11:15 P.M., 18 July 1863, all in Sheridan Papers, LC. For an earlier interaction between Mrs. Schwartz and Twentieth Corps personnel, see Thruston to Sheridan, 13 July 1863, in Sheridan Papers, LC.

16. *Tennesseans in the Civil War*, 321; *OR* 30(1):228–33; Frank Shearer to his sister, 8 July 1863, Shearer Papers, OHS; "Summaries of the News," NARA; *OR* 23(2):528. For a discussion of the various sources of information available to commanders, see Fishel, "Methodology of Intelligence," 99–106.

17. "Summaries of the News," 256–87, NARA.

18. Austin Diary, 9–12 July 1863, ALPL; Burns Diary, 9–12 July 1863, CCNMP; Tabler Diary, 9–12 July 1863, private collection; Riley, *Diary*, 48–49; Moore to Lee, 11 July 1863, and Ray to Sheridan, 11 July 1863, both in Sheridan Papers, LC; Sheridan to McCook (two messages), 11 July 1863, and Sheridan to Thruston, 11 July 1863, all in DC, Letters Received, NARA; *OR* 52(1):413–15; *OR* 23(1):824; Marcoot, *Five Years*, 31; Cooley Diary, 13 and 18–20 July 1863, WHS; Eugene Comstock to his parents, 21 July 1863, Comstock Papers, WHS; Henry Drake to his brother, 21 July 1863, Drake Letters, WHS; Pecoy Diary, 13–16 July 1863, CCNMP; Lamb Diary, 13–16 July 1863, CCNMP; Cummins Diary, 14–16 July 1863, Cummins Papers, ALPL; Newlin, *Seventy-Third Illinois*, 192–96; Thomas J. Frazee to his parents, 18 July 1863, Frazee Papers, ALPL; *SOR* 25:358; *OR* 23(2):543–44.

19. *OR* 52(1):415; Sheridan to Thruston, 5:30 P.M., 19 July 1863, DC, Letters Received,

NARA; Bradley to Lee, 19 July 1863, Sheridan Papers, LC; Newlin, *Seventy-Third Illinois*, 195–96; *OR* 23(2):911, 914–16, 918, 923; Higdon Account, CCNMP; Anderson to Jack, 16 July 1863, in P. H. Rice, CSR, NARA; U.S. Federal Census, 1850 and 1860, Marion County, Tennessee.

20. Riley, *Diary*, 49; *SOR* 23:232, 248, 267, 371, 386; Burns Diary, 19–20 July 1863, CCNMP; Tabler Diary, 19–20 July 1863, private collection; Bradley to Sheridan, 20 July 1863, and Laibold to Lee, 21 July 1863, both in Sheridan Papers, LC; John Holden McBride to his mother, 20 July 1863, McBride Correspondence, NSHS; Newlin, *Seventy-Third Illinois*, 195–96; Thomas J. Frazee to his sister, 26 July 1863, Frazee Papers, ALPL; Prince, *N., C. & St. L.*, 6; Woodall, *Stevenson Story*, 81, 99–116; Sheridan to Thruston, 5:30 P.M., 19 July 1863, DC, Letters Received, NARA.

21. Thompson to Crittenden, 16 July 1863, Garfield to Crittenden, 21 July 1863, and Garfield to McCook, 10:00 P.M., 19 July 1863, all in DC, Telegrams Sent, NARA; Eubank, *Shadow of the Patriarch*, 42; Kirwan, *Crittenden*, 472–73; Whalen and Whalen, *Fighting McCooks*, 212–14; Caleb Carlton to his wife, 17 July 1863, Carlton Papers, LC; Frank J. Jones to his father, 21 July 1863, Jones Papers, CIHS; *OR* 52(1):417; Thruston to Sheridan, 22 July 1863, Sheridan Papers, LC.

22. McMichael to Thomas and Crittenden, 8:30 P.M., 20 July 1863, McMichael to McCook, 10:50 P.M., 20 July 1863, Reynolds and Porter to Jones, 20 July 1863, McMichael to Garfield, 22 July 1863, Thoms to Bond, 22 July 1863, and Thoms to Garfield, 22 July 1863, all in DC, Telegrams Sent, NARA; "Mary Sharp College," in Tennessee Historical Commission, *Tennessee Historical Markers*, 228; Henry M. Cist to his mother, 22 July 1863, Cist Family Papers, CIHS; Frankenberry Diary, 21 July 1863, WVU.

23. *OR* 23(1):542, 825; Thoms to Garfield, 9:30 P.M., 16 July 1863, DC, Telegrams Sent, NARA; Hempstead Diary, 13–21 July 1863, UM-B; Thomas Diary, 14–21 July 1863, Thomas Collection, UT; Kendall Diary, 13–21 July 1863, HL; Mendenhall Diary, 14–21 July 1863, IHS; Harris Diary, 13–15 July 1863, IHS; *SOR* 86:698, 712; Turchin, "Diary," 49–51; Merrill, *Diary*, 39–41; Read Diary, 13–21 July 1863, KSHS; Persons Diary, 13–21 July 1863, WHS; Haines, "Fourth Michigan Cavalry," UM-B; Curry, *Four Years*, 106; Prickitt, *Company H*, 94–95; Crane Diary, 20–21 July 1863, and Smith to Ruger, 27 April 1867, both in Ruger Correspondence, Thomas Papers, NARA; Crofts, *Third Ohio Cavalry*, 104–5; Lester Diary, 13–21 July 1863, ALPL; George Shuman to Fannie Shuman, 15 July 1863, Shuman Letters, Harrisburg Civil War Roundtable Collection, USAHEC; Carter, *First Tennessee Cavalry*, 79; Greenwood Diary, 13–21 July 1863, Knight Family Papers, UAK; Robert Burns to his brother, 16 July 1863, Burns Letters, MHS; George Kryder to his wife, 18 July 1863, Kryder Papers, BGSU; Pape-Findley, *Fourth Ohio Cavalry*, 152; *OR* 23(2):548–49; Stanley, *Memoirs*, 137, 151–52.

24. *OR* Series 3, 3:100–101; Cornish, *Sable Arm*, 111–19, 214; Rosecrans to Thomas, 12 July 1863, Goddard to Dickson, 12 July 1863, Goddard to Innes, 14 July 1863, Porter to Bakhaus, 15 July 1863, Thompson to Lyon, 18 July 1863, Thompson to Thrall, 10:00 P.M., 18 July 1863, Garfield to Young, 20 July 1863, Bond to Stanley, 22 July 1863, and Rosecrans to Thomas, 26 July 1863, all in DC, Telegrams Sent, NARA.

25. Garfield to Thoms, 8:15 P.M., 23 July 1863, and Rosecrans to Thomas, 23 July 1863, both in DC, Telegrams Sent, NARA; *OR* 23(2):550–52.

26. *OR* 23(2):552, 554–56; Rosecrans to Halleck, 25 July 1863, DC, Telegrams Sent, NARA. The copy of Rosecrans to Halleck arguing for delay is dated 24 July 1863 in DC, Telegrams Sent, NARA, but apparently was not sent until the following morning, as reported in *OR* 23(2):555.

27. Sanderson Journal, 21–30 July 1863, OHS; Bond to Thrall, 25 July 1863, and Rosecrans to Thomas, 26 July 1863, both in DC, Telegrams Sent, NARA; *OR* 23(2):559–60, 599–600. Lee, *Kentuckian*, 117, argues that the plan was Rosecrans's idea, but John Sanderson's account makes it clear that Rousseau was the originator of the scheme. Others in addition to Sanderson were also promised a place in Rousseau's prospective new command. Hough, *Soldier*, 116–18.

28. Garfield, *Wild Life*, 220–21, 290–91; Smith, *Garfield*, 1:309–12. For a digest of comments in reaction to the publication of Garfield's letter, see *Indianapolis Journal*, 10 March 1882; and *National Tribune*, 18 March 1882.

29. Sligh Diary, 22 and 24 July 1863, and James M. Sligh to his mother, 22 July 1863, both in Sligh Family Papers, UM-B; Stearns Diary, 22 July 1863, UM-B; Roseberry Diary, 22–27 July 1863, EU; Prince, *N., C. & St. L.*, 31; Arbuckle and Shook, *Mountain Goat*, 2–10; *OR* 23(2):560, 564, 565; *OR* 52(1):419; Garfield to Thomas 28 July 1863, and Bond to Sheridan, 27 July 1863, both in DC, Telegrams Sent, NARA; John C. Love to his parents, 26 July 1863, Love Letters, UM-B. For a detailed description of the railroad between Cowan and Stevenson during this period, see *Cincinnati Daily Commercial*, 4 August 1863.

30. *OR* 23(1):827; *Wisconsin State Journal*, 15 August 1863; *SOR* 63:275; Decker Diary, 23–26 July 1863, WHS; Morgan and Murphy, *Seventh Indiana Battery*, 20–21; David Clark to his sister, 26 July 1863, Clark-Williams Family Letters, OHS; Van Cleve to Ruger, 24 May 1867, Thomas Papers, NARA; "Summaries of the News," 294–96, NARA; *OR* 23(2):556–57, 564; Drouillard to Sheridan, 28 July 1863, DC, Telegrams Sent, NARA; Kundahl, *Confederate Engineer*, 265; Conrad Meister CSR, NARA. The possibility exists that "M. D. Thompson" was Michael D. Thompson, age twenty-five in 1863, a merchant living in Chattanooga in 1860, and who received permission from Federal occupation authorities to open a public bathhouse there in May 1865. U.S. Federal Census, 1860 and 1870, Hamilton County, Tennessee; Union Provost Marshals' Files, NARA.

31. *OR* 23(2):556, 564, 933–34; *OR* 52(1):418; *SOR* 23:354, 371, 382, 387; Otto, *Eleventh Indiana Battery*, 32–33; Cooley Diary, 26–27 July 1863, WHS; Roberts Diary, 27 July 1863, private collection; *SOR* 45:168.

32. *OR* 23(2):564, 567; *OR* 52(1):420; Garfield to Sheridan, 28 July 1863, DC, Telegrams Sent, NARA; Fuller to Lee, 29 July 1863, Sheridan to Lytle, 29 July 1863, and Thruston to Lytle, 29 July 1863, all in Sheridan Papers, LC; Newlin, *Seventy-Third Illinois*, 198; Mauzy, *Sixty-Eighth Indiana*, 10; Floyd, *Seventy-Fifth Indiana*, 113; Miller Journal, 29 July 1863, IHS; "Second Years History," Essington Papers, IHS; Tourgee, "Diary," 116; *SOR* 67:121, 125, 130, 136, 152, 162; Morse, *Diaries*, 30; *SOR* 30:512, 528, 553; Hollingsworth Diary, 29 July 1863, IHS; Parker Diary, 29 July 1863, HL.

33. Christian Diary, 11 and 26 July 1863, CCNMP; Ward Diary, 11 and 13 July 1863, Ward Papers, DP; Millen Diary, 23 July 1863, SRNB; Hollingsworth Diary, 15 and 26 July 1863, IHS; Ward Diary, 18 and 27 July 1863, Booth Papers, OHS; John M. Barnard to Margaret Barnard, 25 July 1863, Barnard Letters, OHS; Lyon Diary, 12 and 28 July 1863, OHS; Howe Diary, 23 July 1863, IHS; Pickering Diary, 11–12 and 29 July 1863, HL; Carpenter Diary, 19 July 1863, SRNB; Mosman, *Rough Side*, 64; Inskeep Diary, 13 and 19 July 1863, OHS; Hinchberger Diary, 21–22 July 1863, CCNMP; Lucius Brown to his sister, 26 July 1863, Brown Letters, EU; Harden, *Ninetieth Ohio*, 85–86; Benedict Diary, 13 July 1863, SRNB; Shotts Diary, 25 July 1863, SRNB; Kiene, *Journal*, 162; Miller Journal, 23 July 1863, IHS; Bruce Diary, 10 and 29 July 1863, ISL; Johnston, *Soldier Boy*, 47–48; Taylor Diary, 26 July 1863, SRNB; Lamb Diary, 20 July 1863, CCNMP; Thomas C. Honnell to Eli Honnell, 26 July 1863, Honnell Letters, OHS.

34. Kiene, *Journal*, 162; Pecoy Diary, 23–24 and 26 July 1863, CCNMP; Lamb Diary, 26 July 1863, CCNMP; Bennett and Haigh, *Thirty-Sixth Illinois*, 442–43; Mulhane, *Memorial of Rosecrans*, 54; Ward Diary, 19 July 1863, Ward Papers, DP; Small Diary, 19 July 1863, IHS; Webster Diary, 26 July 1863, USAHEC; Morris, *Eighty-First Indiana*, 52; Hollingsworth Diary, 19 July 1863, IHS; Andrew, *Letters*, 62–63; Mosman, *Rough Side*, 65; Hines Diary, 12 July 1863, Hiram Hines Manuscript Collection, ISL; Connelly Diary, 12 and 26 July 1863, IHS; Walker Diary, 19 July 1863, Harrisburg Civil War Roundtable Collection, USAHEC; Hight, *Fifty-Eighth Indiana*, 153, 158; Howe Diary, 19 July 1863, IHS; Miller Journal, 26 July 1863, IHS.

35. Bruce Diary, 19 July 1863, ISL; Hough, *Soldier*, 118; Hollingsworth Diary, 13 July 1863, IHS; Galpin Diary, 25, 28–29 July 1863, Galpin Family Papers, WHS; Heg, *Letters*, 231; Busbey Diary, 13, 20–21, and 25 July 1863, SRNB; Opdycke Diary, 22 July 1863, Opdycke Papers, OHS; Patton Diary, 17 July 1863, CCNMP; Webster Diary, 21 and 28 July 1863, USAHEC; Wheeler Diary, 20–21 July 1863, OHS; Mosman, *Rough Side*, 64–65; Alfred Pirtle to his sister, 12 July 1863, Pirtle Letters, FHS; Butler, *Letters Home*, 76–79; Love Diary, 19 July 1863, Love Papers, MHM; Christian Diary, 28 July 1863, CCNMP; Taylor Diary, 17 July 1863, SRNB; Morse, *Diaries*, 30; Hines Diary, 18–19 July 1863, Hiram Hines Manuscript Collection, ISL; Marshall Diary, 17–18 July 1863, OHS; Walker Diary, 9 July 1863, Harrisburg Civil War Roundtable Collection, USAHEC; Benedict Diary, 27 July 1863, SRNB; Kiene, *Journal*, 161; Dean Diary, 15 July 1863, private collection; Harden, *90th Ohio*, 85; Riley, *Diary*, 49–50; Cummins Diary, 16 July 1863, Cummins Papers, ALPL; Claggett Diary, 26 July 1863, CCNMP; Connelly Diary, 19 July 1863, IHS; Sligh Diary, 28 July 1863, Sligh Family Papers, UM-B.

36. Lytle, *For Honor*, 183; Cooley Diary, 14 July 1863, WHS; Billings D. Sibley to his father, 14 July 1863, Sibley Papers, MHS; Colyer Diary, 14 July 1863, ALPL; Smith, *Samuel Thomas Smith*, 77–78; Ward Diary, 22 July 1863, Ward Papers, DP; John Parkhurst to his sisters, 12 July 1863, Parkhurst Papers, UM-B; Dewees Diary, 17 July 1863, CCNMP; Phillips, *Diary*, 152–53; Josiah D. Cotton to his wife, 26 July 1863, Cotton Papers, LC; James E. Love to "Dearest Molly," 25 July 1863, Love Papers, MHM; Hiram Strong to his wife, 15 July 1863, Strong Letters, CCNMP; Alanson R. Ryman to Jane Ryman, 15 July and 23 July 1863, Ryman Letters, IHS.

37. James S. Thomas to his sister, 10 July 1863, Thomas Letters, IHS; Ben Mabrey to Lou Mabrey, 11 July 1863, Mabrey Letters, IHS; James E. Love to "Dearest Molly," 18 July 1863, Love Papers, MHM; John W. Switzer to his sister, 28 July 1863, Switzer Letter, IHS; George W. Dodd to his brother, 10 July 1863, Dodd Papers, ALPL; Hiram Strong to his wife, 15 July 1863, Strong Letters, CCNMP; Franklin B. Howard to his sister, 23 July 1863, Howard Letters, WHS; Connolly, *Three Years*, 107–8; Butler, *Letters Home*, 80–82; Clark Diary, 17 July 1863, Clark Papers, USAHEC; Bircher, *Drummer-Boy*, 67; Hough, *Soldier*, 111, 114–15; Undated newspaper clipping, Marsh Family Papers, ALPL; L. Dwight Hinkley to his father, 21 July 1863, Hinkley Papers, WHS; Ward Diary, 23 July 1863, Ward Papers, DP; Small Diary, 27 July 1863, IHS; Cooley Diary, 15 July 1863, WHS; Lyman S. Widney, *National Tribune*, 31 October 1901; Benedict Diary, 18 July 1863, SRNB; Opdycke Diary, 15 July 1863, Opdycke Papers, OHS; John W. Nesbitt to his parents and sisters, 21 July 1863, Nesbitt Letters, CCNMP; Thomas Prickett to "Dearest Matilda," 12 July 1863, Prickett Letters, IHS; James M. Sligh to his mother, 14 July 1863, Sligh Family Papers, UM-B; John S. McGraw to his wife, 19 July 1863, McGraw Papers, ISL; William Forder to Sarah Forder, 19 July 1863, Forder Letters, IHS; Richards, *Letters*, 34–35; Howe Diary, 15–16 July 1863, IHS; Joshua D. Foster to his parents, 18 July 1863, Foster Letters, CCNMP.

38. Webster Diary, 17 July 1863, Civil War Miscellaneous Collection, USAHEC; Bircher, *Drummer-Boy*, 67; Albertson, *Letters Home*, Letters 93 and 95; Reed Diary, 17 July 1863, MHS; Dilworth Journal, 23 July 1863, HC; Hollingsworth Diary, 18 July 1863, IHS; Miller Journal, 18 July 1863, IHS; Lamb Diary, 27 July 1863, CCNMP; Heg, *Letters*, 232; Opdycke Diary, 21 and 24 July 1863, Opdycke Papers, OHS; Post Diary, 21–22 July 1863, Post Papers, KC; Himoe Diary, 22 July 1863, NAHA; John S. McGraw to his wife, 24 July 1863, McGraw letters, ISL; Bennett and Haigh, *Thirty-Sixth Illinois*, 443; Hight, *Fifty-Eighth Indiana*, 158; Marshall Diary, 27 July 1863, OHS; Dewees Diary, 26 July 1863, CCNMP; William Forder to his parents, 23 July 1863, Forder Letters, IHS; Robert J. Bates to his parents, 8 August 1863, Bates Letters, WHS; William W. Blair to his daughter, 18 July 1863, Blair Papers, IHS; Christian Diary, 22–23 July 1863, CCNMP; King, *Three Years*, 101–2; Connelly Diary, 23 July 1863, IHS. For a general account of morale in the Army of the Cumberland during this period, see Dalessandro, "Morale in the Army of the Cumberland."

39. Kiene, *Journal*, 163; Mosman, *Rough Side*, 65–66; Thompson to Whitaker, 23 July 1863, DC, Telegrams Sent, NARA; Crippin, "Diary," 276; Phillips Diary, 26 July 1863, Phillips Collection, HL; Botkin Diary, 28 July 1863, Baker Correspondence, OHS; Harden, *90th Ohio*, 86; Morledge Diary, 26 July 1863, KMNMP; Austin Diary, 15 July 1863, ALPL; Tabler Diary, 15, 17, 20, and 23 July 1863, private collection; Burns Diary, 16–17, 20, and 23 July 1863, CCNMP; John L. McBride to his mother, 20 July 1863, McBride Correspondence, NSHS; Calkins, *One Hundred and Fourth Illinois*, 104; Kendall Diary, 12 July 1863, HL; Meredith Diary, 19 July 1863, Harrisburg Civil War Roundtable Collection, USAHEC.

40. Wheeler Diary, 6 July 1863, OHS; Barringer Diary, 14 July 1863, private collection; Tourgee, "Diary," 113; Miller Journal, 22 July 1863, IHS; Pecoy Diary, 17 July 1863, CCNMP; Clark Diary, 16 July 1863, Clark Papers, USAHEC; Simmons, *84th Illinois*, 63; Hight, *Fifty-Eighth Indiana*, 151, 154–56; Floyd, *Seventy-Fifth Indiana*, 113; Gates Diary, 20 and 25 July 1863, IHS; Hollingsworth Diary, 23 July 1863, IHS; Alanson R. Ryman to Jane Ryman, 27 July 1863, Ryman letters, IHS; Bruce Diary, 20 July 1863, ISL; Members, *Battery M, First Illinois*, 72; Partridge, *Ninety-Sixth Illinois*, 147; *Wisconsin State Journal*, 5 August 1863; Cummins Diary, 21 July 1863, Cummins Papers, ALPL; Lytle, *For Honor*, 187.

41. Tourgee, "Diary," 114–15; Andrew, *Letters*, 63–64; Connelly Diary, 22 July 1863, IHS; Garfield to McMichael, 28 July 1863, Bond to Taylor, 26 July and 27 July 1863, and Rosecrans to Meigs, 27 July 1863, all in DC, Telegrams Sent, NARA; Taylor, *"Supply,"* 95, 122, 128–30; Drouillard Diary, 29 July 1863, Rosecrans Papers, UCLA; Robinson Diary, 29 July 1863, Robinson Papers, ALPL; Hinchberger Diary, 29 July 1863, CCNMP; Millen Diary, 29 July 1863, SRNB; Ward Diary, 29 July 1863, Ward papers, DP; Christian Diary, 30 July 1863, CCNMP; Shotts Diary, 29 July 1863, SRNB.

CHAPTER 6

1. Drouillard Diary, 30 July 1863, Rosecrans Papers, UCLA; McCullough Diary, 30 July 1863, ISL; Sligh Diary, 30 July 1863, Sligh Family Papers, UM-B; Stearns Diary, 30 July 1863, UM-B; Clark Diary, 30 July 1863, Clark Papers, USAHEC; Bond to Anderson, 30 July 1863 (two messages), Thompson to Beggs, 30 July 1863 (two messages), Thompson to Custer, 30 July 1863 (two messages), Bond to Thomas, 30 July 1863, Bond to O'Connell, 30 July 1863, Bond to Morgan, 30 July 1863, and Garfield to Dickson, 30 July 1863, all in DC, Telegrams Sent, NARA.

2. Newlin, *Seventy-Third Illinois*, 195–200; David F. Lawler to his parents, 4 August 1863,

Lawler Letter, private collection; *SOR* 48:351; *SOR* 23:354, 371, 382, 386–87; Cooley Diary, 26 July 1863, IHS; Otto, *11th Indiana Battery*, 32–33; Fuller to Lee, 29 July 1863, Thruston to Lytle, 29 July 1863, Thruston to Bradley, 29 July 1863, Sheridan to Lytle, 29 July 1863, Bradley to Lee, 29 July 1863, and Lytle to Lee, 30 July 1863, all in Sheridan Papers, LC; *OR* 23(2):568; Miller Journal, 29 July 1863, IHS; XIV Corps Journal, Thomas Papers, NARA; *OR* 52(1):421, 424–25; *SOR* 22:659; *SOR* 25:371; Burns Diary, 30–31 July 1863, CCNMP; Tabler Diary, 30–31 July 1863, private collection; Riley, *Diary*, 50; Crippin, "Diary," 277; Colburn/Gray Diary, 30–31 July 1863, private collection.

3. Thompson to Anderson, 6 P.M., 31 July 1863, and Rosecrans to Anderson, 31 July 1863, both in DC, Telegrams Sent, NARA; Stearns Diary, 31 July 1863, UM-B.

4. Drouillard to Beggs, 1 August 1863, DC, Telegrams Sent, NARA; Anderson to Rosecrans, 1 August 1863, QMG, USMRR, Letters Sent, NARA; *OR* 23(2):585–86; *OR* 52(1):427–28.

5. Garfield, *Wild Life*, 291; Drouillard to Beggs, 2 August 1863 (three messages), Thompson to Beggs, 2 August 1863 (two messages), Drouillard to O'Connell, 2 August 1863, Drouillard to Commanding Officer, Stevenson, 2 August 1863, Bond to Whitaker, 2 August 1863, and Garfield to Hunton, 2 August 1863, all in DC, Telegrams Sent, NARA.

6. Drouillard Diary, 3 August 1863, Rosecrans Papers, UCLA; Members, *Battery M, First Illinois*, 73; Robinson Diary, 3 August 1863, ALPL; Van Vleck, *Leader*, 145; Patton Diary, 2–3 August 1863, CCNMP; Imboden, *Army of the Cumberland*, 7; Royse, *115th Illinois*, 80; Partridge, *Ninety-Sixth Illinois*, 147–48; Drouillard to Halleck, 3 August 1863, and Drouillard to Beggs, 3 August 1863, both in DC, Telegrams Sent, NARA; *OR* 23(2):590.

7. Drouillard to Beggs, 3 August 1863, DC, Telegrams Sent, NARA; Anderson to Rosecrans, 4 August 1863 (two messages), QMG, USMRR, Letters Sent (Anderson), NARA; *OR* 23(2):592; Frankenberry Diary, 4 August 1863, WVU.

8. For Rosecrans's perspective, see Boynton, *Chattanooga Letters*, 9–10; and Boynton, "Chickamauga Campaign," 327–29. For Stanton's perspective, see Thomas and Hyman, *Stanton*, 276–83. For the New York Draft Riot crisis of July–August 1863, see Murdock, *Patriotism Limited*, 63–80; and Geary, *We Need Men*, 105–6.

9. Drouillard Diary, 4–5 August 1863, Rosecrans Papers, UCLA; Frank J. Jones to his father, 5 August 1863, Jones Papers, CIHS; Thompson to Beggs, 5 August 1863 (three messages), Thompson to Anderson, 5 August 1863, Thoms to Anderson, undated [5 August 1863], Garfield to Simmons, 5 August 1863, Drouillard to Beggs, 5 August 1863, all in DC, Telegrams Sent, NARA; Clark Diary, 5 August 1863, Clark Papers, USAHEC; Sligh Diary, 5 August 1863, Sligh Family Papers, UM-B; Stewart, *52nd O.V.I.*, 50–51; Mosman, *Rough Side*, 67; Shotts Diary, 5 August 1863, SRNB; Frankenberry Diary, 5 August 1863, WVU; *OR* 23(2):592. The passage of Tom (Rosecrans's servant) and Rosecrans's horses northward generated message traffic among quartermasters at Nashville, Louisville, and Cincinnati until their safe arrival on 7 August. Taylor, *"Supply,"* 116–17.

10. William S. Rosecrans, *National Tribune*, 25 March 1882; Rosecrans to McCook, 9 November 1879, Rosecrans Papers, UCLA; *OR* 23(2):594; Bond to Palmer, 6 August 1863, DC, Telegrams Sent, NARA. It is possible but unlikely that Maj. Gen. John Palmer, temporarily commanding the Twenty-First Corps, was present at the Winchester conference. Palmer's headquarters was at Manchester, Tennessee, thirty miles from Winchester, while Thomas's headquarters was at Decherd, two miles from Winchester, and McCook's headquarters was in Winchester itself.

11. Frankenberry Diary, 6 August 1863, WVU; Stearns Diary, 1 August 1863, UM-B; Bond to Willett, 1 August 1863, Rosecrans to Lorenzo Thomas, 5 August 1863, Thrall to Gordon Granger, 5 August 1863, all in DC, Telegrams Sent, NARA; Charles F. Weller to "Kate," 6 August 1863, Charles Weller Letters, *Civil War Times Illustrated* Collection, USAHEC; Kiene, *Journal*, 164; Puntenny, *Thirty-Seventh Indiana*, 43–44; Beatty, *Citizen Soldier*, 309, 312; James Thomas to his sister, 14 August 1863, James S. Thomas Letters, IHS; Sligh Diary, 3 and 5 August 1863, Sligh Family Papers, UM-B; Samuel S. Boyd, newspaper clipping, 10 September 1863, Boyd Family Papers, UCB; Cox, "Gone for a Soldier," 64; Dyer, *Compendium*, 3:1726.

12. Albertson, *Letters Home*, Letter 97; Keegan, *Diaries*, 18–19; Phillips, *Diary*, 22; Brown Diary, 6 August 1863, ALPL; Josiah Dexter Cotton to his wife, 10 August 1863, Cotton Papers, LC; George B. Turner to his mother, 9 August 1863, Turner Papers, OHS; Mosman, *Rough Side*, 67; Society, Seventy-Fourth Illinois, *Reunion Proceedings*, 20; Patterson Diary, 6 August 1863, ALPL; Isaac P. Rule to his brother, 7 August 1863, Rule Letters, HPL; James G. Watson to [addressee unknown], 6 August 1863, Watson Letters, UI; Kiene, *Journal*, 164; Widney Diary, 6 August 1863, KMNMP; Hight, *Fifty-Eighth Indiana*, 164–65; Hines Diary, 6 August 1863, Hiram Hines Manuscript Collection, ISL; Kerwood, *Fifty-Seventh Indiana*, 196; Marshall Diary, 6 August 1863, OHS; Gillis Diary, 6 August 1863, OHS; Opdycke Diary, 6 August 1863, Opdycke Papers, OHS; Connelly Diary, 6 August 1863, IHS; *History, Seventy-Ninth Indiana*, 81; Howe Diary, 6 August 1863, IHS; Partridge, *Ninety-Sixth Illinois*, 148; Royse, *115th Illinois*, 80–81; Robinson Diary, 6 August 1863, Robinson Papers, ALPL; Schwartz, *Diary*, 9; McAdams, *Soldier Life*, 35; Patton Diary, 6 August 1863, CCNMP.

13. Drouillard Diary, 7 August 1863, Rosecrans Papers, UCLA; "A. L. F. Letter from Stevenson, Ala.," *Cincinnati Commercial*, 12 August 1863; Riley, *Diary*, 51; Tabler Diary, 1–7 August 1863, private collection; Edward Curtis to his aunt, 10 August 1863, Curtis Letters, NL; Burns Diary, 1–7 August 1863, CCNMP; Austin Diary, 1–7 August 1863, ALPL; Lamb Diary, 1–7 August 1863, CCNMP; Sherman, *Quest*, 57–58; Crippin, "Diary," 277; Hugh A. McLaurin to his father, 7 August 1863, McLaurin Letters, WHS; Eugene Comstock to his parents, 3–10 August 1863, Comstock Papers, WHS; Augustus Davis to Julia Davis, 1 August 1863, Davis Letters, SRNB; Roberts Diary, 1–7 August 1863, private collection; Smith, *Private Smith's Journal*, 84–85; Smith, *Memoirs*, 55. Private Crow's allegiance to the Confederacy may have been weakened by his visit to the Federals at Bridgeport, because he deserted his unit on 25 September 1863. Daniel Crow, CSR, NARA.

14. Droullard to Innes, 7 August 1863, DC, Telegrams Sent, NARA; *OR* 30(1):51.

15. *OR* 23(2):597, 598; Drouillard to Burnside, 7 August 1863, Rosecrans to Halleck, 7 August 1863, and Thompson to Mr. Hagerman [Eliza Hegeman], 7 August 1863, all in DC, Telegrams Sent, NARA. Mrs. Hegeman had been a part of the Rosecrans household since at least 1850. U.S. Federal Census, 1850 (Newport, Rhode Island) and 1860 (Hamilton County, Ohio).

16. Rosecrans to Mr. E. Hagerman [Eliza Hegeman], 8 August 1863, Thompson to Dr. Fletcher, 8 August 1863, Thompson to Beggs, 8 August 1863, Rosecrans to Anderson, 8 August 1863, Thompson to Anderson, 8 August 1863, Rosecrans to Perkins, 8 August 1863, Garfield to Sheridan, 8 August 1863, Thoms to Sheridan, 8 August 1863, Rosecrans to Winslow, 8 August 1863, Thompson to Palmer, 8 August 1863, Bond to Palmer, 8 August 1863 (two messages), Drouillard to Van Duzer, 8 August 1863, Porter to Granger, 8 August 1863, Thompson to Goddard, 8 August 1863, Rosecrans to Johnson, 8 August 1863, Bond

to Johnson, 8 August 1863, Thompson to Beggs, 8 August 1863 (two messages), Thompson to Lytle, 8 August 1863, all in DC, Telegrams Sent, NARA; *OR* 52(1):433; Lamers, *Edge of Glory*, 45.

17. *OR* 23(2):601; *OR* 30(1):184; *OR*, Series III, 4:883; Taylor, *"Supply,"* 121–22.

18. *OR* 23(2):600, 601; Sanderson Journal, 9 August 1863, OHS. For an analysis of Burnside's situation, see Marvel, *Burnside*, 264–67.

19. Anderson to Rosecrans, 8 August 1863, QMG, USMRR, Letters Sent (Anderson), NARA; Drouillard Diary, 9 August 1863, Rosecrans Papers, UCLA; Hoffman, *"Brave Mechanics,"* 160; Rosecrans to Anna Rosecrans, 9 August 1863, Bond to Innes, 9 August 1863, Drouillard to Beggs, 9 August 1863, Bond to Winslow, 9 August 1863, Drouillard to Pennock, 9 August 1863, Bond to Hurlbut, 9 August 1863, all in DC, Telegrams Sent, NARA.

20. Rosecrans to Burnside, 9 August 1863, DC, Telegrams Sent, NARA; *OR* 23(2) 602; Rosecrans to Alexander McCook, 9 November 1879, and Rosecrans to Robert Hunter, 25 August 1881, both in Rosecrans Papers, UCLA; William S. Rosecrans, *National Tribune*, 25 March 1882; *OR* 30(1):47; Rosecrans to Ezra Carman, 10 December 1888, Carman Papers, NYPL.

21. Wells, "Campaign of Chickamauga," 208–9; *OR* 30(1):49. For Rosecrans's view of cooperation with Burnside, see his testimony in U.S. Congress, *Report of the Joint Committee* 3:29, 34.

22. Wells, "Campaign of Chickamauga," 208–9; Rosecrans, quoted in Gilbert C. Kniffin to Daniel H. Hill, 26 August 1884, D. H. Hill Papers, LV; Rosecrans to Robert Hunter, 25 August 1881, Rosecrans Papers, UCLA; Thompson to Palmer, 8 August 1863, Drouillard to Thomas, 7 August 1863, and Drouillard to Sheridan, 9 August 1863, all in DC, Telegrams Sent, NARA.

23. Rosecrans to Lorenzo Thomas, 9 August 1863, DC, Telegrams Sent, NARA; *OR* 30(3):3; Henry Jordan to John T. Wilder, 1 August 1863, Wilder Papers, ISL; W. H. H. Terrell to John T. Wilder, 8 August 1863, and John T. Wilder to his wife, 18 August 1863, Wilder Papers, UTC; Baumgartner, *Blue Lightning*, 107–18; Griest Diary, 9 August 1863, CCNMP; Kitchell Diary, 9 August 1863, ALPL; Brown Diary, 9 August 1863, ALPL; Campbell Diary, 9 August 1863, CCNMP; King, *King Family*, 266; Heitman, *Historical Register*, 1:599; Alanson R. Ryman to Jane Ryman, 4 August 1863, Ryman Letters, IHS; High, *Sixty-Eighth Indiana*, 279–81; Mauzy, *Sixty-Eighth Indiana*, 10; Floyd, *Seventy-Fifth Indiana*, 113; Morse, *Diaries*, 30–31; Hollingsworth Diary, 29 July and 9 August 1863, IHS; Miller Journal, 9 August 1863, IHS; Ward Diary, 30 July–2 August 1863, Booth Papers, OHS; Kempfer, *Salem Light Guard*, 120–21; Josiah D. Cotton to his wife, 30 July and 1 August 1863, Cotton Papers, LC; George B. Turner to his father, 4 and 7 August 1863, and to his mother, 13 August 1863, Turner Papers, OHS; Owen Diary, 31 July 1863, AU; Caleb Carlton to his wife, 31 July 1863, Carlton Papers, LC; Turchin, "Diary," 55–56; Horton, *Eleventh Ohio*, 262–63; Scott, *Lane*, 187–88; Andrew, *Letters*, 66–67; Williams, *Extracts*, 83–84. Although the printed version of Rosecrans's telegram to Lorenzo Thomas in *OR* 30(3):3 is dated 12:30 A.M., 11 August 1863, the version in DC, Telegrams Sent, NARA is dated 11:00 P.M., 9 August 1863, which makes more sense. The fact that there is a Rosecrans report to Thomas shortly after midnight on 11 August covering the events of the previous day is a clear indication that the date reported in *OR* 30(3):3 is a copying error. As to why Rosecrans reported a spurious Reynolds move to Tracy City on 9 August, the record is silent. Perhaps Rosecrans believed the report himself, because the headquarters diary kept by Capt. James Drouillard for 9 August also reports the movement. Drouillard Diary,

9 August 1863, Rosecrans Papers, UCLA. If not, Rosecrans was knowingly perpetrating a fraud upon the War Department, a charge difficult to lodge without documentary proof of intent.

24. *OR* 23(2):556, 595; Robert H. G. Minty, *National Tribune*, 25 February 1892; Haines, "Fourth Michigan Cavalry," UM-B; Vale, *Minty*, 197, 200–201; *OR* 23(1):845–48; Robertson, *Michigan in the War*, 653–54; McLain Diary, 4–5 and 8–11 August 1863, ISHS; Decker Diary, 3 August 1863, WHS; Tilford Diary, 4–5 August 1863, FHS; Jordan and Pryor, *Campaigns of Forrest*, 294–96; Lindsley, *Annals*, 2:657–58; Wyeth, *Forrest*, 213–14.

25. Raab, *Anderson*, 5; Thompson to Beggs (two messages), and Thompson to Lytle, 8 August 1863, DC, Telegrams Sent, NARA; Alfred Pirtle to his mother, 10 August 1863, and Alfred Pirtle to "Dear Jane," 13 August 1863, both in Pirtle Papers, FHS; "Letter from Alabama," *Cincinnati Daily Commercial*, 18 August 1863; Sherman, *Quest*, 59–60; Day Elmore to his parents, 9 August 1863, Elmore Letters, CHS; Austin Diary, 9 August 1863, ISLH; Tabler Diary, 9 August 1863, private collection; Cooley Diary, 9 August 1863, WHS; Pecoy Diary, 9 August 1863, CCNMP.

26. Harold J. Bartlett to his family, 1 August 1863, Bartlett Letters, UM-B; Edmonds Diary, 1 August 1863, USAHEC; Stearns Diary, 4 August 1863, UM-B; Kiene, *Journal*, 164; Pickering Diary, 4–5, 8 August 1863, HL; Johnston, *Soldier Boy*, 49–50; Dilworth Journal, 5 and 7 August 1863, HC; Joseph Bruff to Anna Bruff, 1 August 1863, private collection; Hight, *Fifty-Eighth Indiana*, 163–64; Gsell Diary, 1 August 1863, CCNMP; Ward Diary, 8 August 1863, Ward Papers, DP; Sturges, Diary, 1–8 August 1863, Sturges Papers, *Civil War Times Illustrated* Collection, USAHEC; Bruce Diary, 2 August 1863, ISL; Gates, *Rough Side*, 67; Busbey Diary, 1–2 August 1863, SRNB; Opdycke Diary, 1–2 August 1863, Opdycke Papers, OHS; Christian Diary, 7–8 August 1863, CCNMP; Walker Diary 6 August 1863, Harrisburg Civil War Roundtable Collection, USAHEC; George Marsh Jr. to his brother, 2 August 1863, Marsh Family Papers, ALPL; William J. Carroll to his sister, 8 August 1863, Carroll Papers, UM-B; Miller Journal, 7 and 9 August 1863, IHS.

27. Webster Diary, 1 August 1863, Civil War Miscellaneous Collection, USAHEC; Christian Diary, 9 August 1863, CCNMP; Sturges Diary, 4–8 August 1863, Sturges Papers, *Civil War Times Illustrated* Collection, USAHEC; Miller Journal, 2–3 August 1863, IHS; Alanson R. Ryman to Jane Ryman, 4 August 1863, Ryman Letters, IHS; John H. Hoffman to his wife, 31 July 1863, Hoffman Letters, Civil War Miscellaneous Collection, USAHEC; Gsell Diary, 2 August 1863, CCNMP; Hinchberger Diary, 3–4 August 1863, CCNMP; Kitchell Diary, 1 and 5 August 1863, ALPL; Brunsted, "Canadian Recruit," 165–66; Sligh Diary, 31 July 1863, Sligh Family Papers, UM-B; "Civil War Diary 1863 of Robert Thomas McKee," 12 August 1863, http://mckee-burns.pasttracker.com/mckee/cw_mckee/mckee_robert_t_cw_diary_1 (15 June 2013); Meredith Diary, 31 July 1863, Civil War Miscellaneous Collection, USAHEC; Colyer Diary, 5–6 August 1863, ALPL; Kiene, *Journal*, 164; Marshall Diary, 7 August 1863, OHS; Alpheus S. Bloomfield to his sister, 8 August 1863, Bloomfield Letters, OHS; Elbert Squire to his mother, 8 August 1863, Squire Letters, SRNB; Hight, *Fifty-Eighth Indiana*, 163–64; Dilworth Journal, 2 and 5 August 1863, HC; Opdycke Diary, 2 August 1863, Opdycke Papers, OHS; Donahower Account, 9 August 1863, Donahower Papers, MHS; Griest Diary, 9 August 1863, CCNMP; Keegan, *Diaries*, 18; Blackburn, *Letters*, 133; Busbey Diary, 31 July 1863, SRNB; Botkin Diary, 31 July 1863, Baker Correspondence, OHS; Connelly Diary, 4–5 August 1863, IHS; Phillips Diary, 4 August 1863, Phillips Collection, HL; Ward Diary, 31 July 1863, DP; Gates, *Rough Side*, 66; Shotts Diary, 5 August 1863, SRNB; Wright, *Eighth Kentucky*, 166–69.

28. DeWayne K. Calkins to his family, 5 August 1863, Calkins Letters, CCNMP; Day

Elmore to his parents, 9 August 1863, Elmore Letters, CHS; John S. McGraw to his wife and children, 9 August 1863, McGraw Letters, ISL; Alanson R. Ryman to Jane Ryman, 4 August 1863, Ryman Letters, IHS; Riley, *Diary*, 51. Similar opinions can be found in Fradenburgh, *In Memoriam*, 66–67; Samuel Shepardson to his sister, 8 August 1863, Shepardson Letters, ISL; James M. Forbes to his sister, 3 August 1863, Forbes Collection, HL; James P Mitchell Reminiscences, Mitchell Papers, OHS, and Thomas J. Frazee to his sister, 3 August 1863, Frazee Papers, ALPL.

29. Charles Bailer to his sister, 7 and 14 August 1863, Bailer Letters, WRHS; Brown, "Soldier of the 92nd," 119; Webster Diary, 3 and 5–6 August 1863, Civil War Miscellaneous Collection, USAHEC; Knapp Diary, 5–6 August 1863, WHS; Christian Diary, 5–6 August 1863, CCNMP; Morse, *Diaries*, 31; Phillips, *Diary*, 22; "War Reminiscences," Marsh Family Papers, ALPL; Shotts Diary, 1 August 1863, SRNB; Miller Journal, 7 August 1863, IHS; Hapeman Diary, 8 August 1863, ALPL; Calkins, *One Hundred and Fourth Illinois*, 106; Kirkpatrick, *Experiences*, 45; Dilworth Journal, 6 August 1863, HC; Otto, *Mudsill*, 151–52; Marshall Diary, 8 August 1863, OHS; Ward Diary, 8 August 1863, Booth Papers, OHS; Robinson Diary, 6 August 1863, WRHS; Hight, *Fifty-Eighth Indiana*, 164–65; Genco, *Sound*, 105; Hinkley Diary, 5–6 August 1863, Hinkley Papers, WHS; *SOR* 41:107, 128, 147, 162, 174; Frank M. Phelps to his friends, 1 and 10 August 1863, Phelps Letters, Lewis Leigh Collection, USAHEC; Robert J. Bates to his parents, 8 August 1863, Bates Letters, WHS; Angus Waddle to his sister, 8 August 1863, McCoy Papers, MHM; Cooley Diary, 6–8 August 1863, WHS; Wilcox Diary, 8 August 1863, Wiley Sword Collection, USAHEC; Lucius Brown to "Dear Charles," 18 August 1863, Brown Letters, EU; Unit Return, Eighteenth US Infantry, August 1863, NARA; XIV Corps Journal, 10 August 1863, Thomas Papers, NARA.

30. Alanson R. Ryman to Jane Ryman, 4 August 1863, Ryman Letters, IHS; Gates Diary, 7 August 1863, IHS; Howe Diary, 31 July 1863, IHS; Sligh Diary, 31 July 1863, Sligh Family Papers, UM-B; Marshall Diary, 2 August 1863, OHS; Shotts Diary, 4 August 1863, SRNB; Hinchberger Diary, 4 August 1863, CCNMP; John Wilcox to his wife, 5 August 1863, Wilcox Letters, CCNMP; Woodruff, *Fifteen Years*, 270; Andrew, *Letters*, 68–71; John T. Booth, *National Tribune*, 25 September 1890; Josiah D. Cotton to his wife, 10 August 1863, Cotton Papers, LC; George B. Turner to his mother, 9 August 1863, Turner Papers, OHS; Turchin, "Diary," 57, 59; Horton, *Eleventh Ohio*, 96–97; William Tyson CSR, and Samuel Mitchell CSR, NARA; "Surviving Sewanee: The Samuel Mitchell Story," http://survivingsewanee.com/Sept_%2014_samuel_mitchell.html (4 April 2012). The four men killed by the explosion were Corp. Ezra Hess and Corp. Nathan Rector (Twenty-First Indiana Battery), Corp. Joseph Wyrick (Eleventh Ohio Infantry), and Musician William Tyson (Eighteenth Kentucky Infantry).

31. Beatty, *Citizen Soldier*, 312; Garfield, *Wild Life*, 292; Caleb Carlton to his wife, 10 August 1863, Carlton Papers, LC; Drouillard Diary, 10 August 1863, Rosecrans Papers, UCLA; Special Field Orders, No. 219, Extract, 10 August 1863, Anderson Family Papers, KSHS; *OR* 52(1):435; Frankenberry Diary, 10 August 1863, WVU; Frank J. Jones to his mother, 11 August 1863, Jones Papers, CIHS; Mosman, *Rough Side*, 67; William H. Ball to his brother, 10 August 1863, Ball Letters, USAHEC; Colyer Diary, 10 August 1863, ALPL; Post Diary, 10 August 1863, Post Papers, KC; Society, Seventy-Fourth Illinois, *Reunion Proceedings*, 21; Isaac P. Rule to his brother, 13 August 1863, Rule Letters, HPL; Dodd Diary, 10 August 1863, Dodd Papers, ALPL.

32. Hough, *Soldier*, 84; Johnson, *Brave Men*, 369–71; Lucius Brown to his sister, 15 August 1863, and to "Charley," 18 August 1863, Brown Letters, EU; Barringer Diary, 10

August 1863, private collection; Unit Returns, First and Second Battalions, Eighteenth US Infantry, NARA; Charles Bailer to his sister, 14 August 1863, Bailer Letters, WRHS; Jones Diary, 10 August 1863, SRNB; Augustus B. Carpenter to his parents, 16 August 1863, Carpenter Letters, YU; Tarbell Diary, 10 August 1863, Harrisburg Civil War Roundtable Collection, USAHEC; Henry Drake to his brother, 12 August 1863, Drake Letters, WHS; Clark Diary, 10 August 1863, Clark Papers, USAHEC; Johnston, *Soldier Boy*, 51–52; Henry C. Taylor to his parents, 9 August 1863, and to his brother, 16 August 1863, Taylor Papers, WHS; Otto, *Mudsill*, 153; Kelsey M. Adams to his brother, 12 August 1863, Adams Letters, WHS; Galpin Diary, 10 August 1863, Galpin Family Papers, WHS; *SOR* 21:622, 635; *SOR* 27:573; *SOR* 72:502, 515; *SOR* 87:115, 121; *SOR* 88:248, 256–57; Shotts Diary, 10 August 1863, SRNB; Johnston Diary, 10 August 1863, Johnston Collection, CHS; Christian Diary, 10 August 1863, CCNMP; *SOR* 65:544, 556; Lewis Tripp to his parents and sister, 16 August 1863, Tripp Letters, Civil War Miscellaneous Collection, USAHEC; Sturges Diary, 10 August 1863, Sturges Papers, *Civil War Times Illustrated* Collection, USAHEC; Rosecrans to Lorenzo Thomas, 10 August 1863, DC, Telegrams Sent, NARA; *OR* 30(3):4.

33. *OR* 30(3):4–5; Bond to Innes, 11 August 1863, Drouillard to Beggs, 11 August 1863, Bond to Palmer, 11 August 1863, Drouillard to Goddard, 11 August 1863, Thrall to Dickson, 11 August 1863, and Thompson to Tyler, 11 August 1863, all in DC, Telegrams Sent, NARA; Drouillard Diary, 11 August 1863, Rosecrans Papers, UCLA; Inskeep Diary, 11 August 1863, OHS; Harold J. Bartlett to his family, 12 August 1863, Bartlett Letters, UM-B; Price Diary, 11 August 1863, Civil War Miscellaneous Collection, USAHEC; Small Diary, 11 August 1863, IHS; John R. Dow to his sister, 15 August 1863, Dow Letters, FHS; James Thomas to his sister, 14 August 1863, Thomas Letters, IHS; Wheeler Diary, 11 August 1863, OHS; Albertson, *Letters Home*, Letter 98; Keegan, *Diaries*, 19–20; Davidson Diary, 11 August 1863, NCWM; Donahower Account, 11 August 1863, Donahower Papers, MHS; Everett F. Abbott to his mother, 12 August 1863, Chamberlain Papers, IHS; Harry Van Derveer to his mother, 15 August 1863, Van Derveer Letters, SLRH; Frankenberry Diary, 11 August 1863, WVU.

34. Webster Diary, 11 August 1863, Civil War Miscellaneous Collection, USAHEC; Knapp Diary, 11 August 1863, WHS; Robert Newell Elder to his sister, 12 August 1863, Elder Letters, OHS; Lucius Brown to his sister, 15 August 1863, and to "Charley," 18 August 1863, Brown Letters, EU; Barringer Diary, 11 August 1863, private collection; Charles K. Bailer to his sister, 14 August 1863, Bailer Letters, WRHS; *Memorial of Burnham*, 20; Augustus B. Carpenter to his parents, 16 August 1863, Carpenter Letters, YU; Jones Diary, 11 August 1863, SRNB; Unit Returns: Fifteenth, Sixteenth, Eighteenth, and Nineteenth United States Infantry, NARA; Clark Diary, 11 August 1863, Clark Papers, USAHEC; Johnston, *Soldier Boy*, 52; Otto, *Mudsill*, 153–54; Kelsey M. Adams to his brother, 12 August 1863, Adams Letters, WHS; Galpin Diary, 11 August 1863, Galpin Family Papers, WHS; Roseberry Diary, 11 August 1863, EU; Beatty, *Citizen Soldier*, 308–9; *OR* 52(1):435; James M. Chatfield to his wife, 10 August 1863, Chatfield Letters, WVM; L. S. Scranton to Edward Ruger, 8 June 1867, Ruger Correspondence, Thomas Papers, NARA; Hempstead Diary, 11 August 1863, UM-B; Thomas Diary, 11 August 1863, UT; Merrill, *Diary*, 46; Read Diary, 11 August 1863, KSHS; Persons Diary, 11 August 1863, WHS; Kendall Diary, 11 August 1863, HL; Mendenhall Diary, 12 [11] August 1863, IHS; Leeper Diary, 11 August 1863, SRNB; Kiene, *Journal*, 165; Hollingsworth Diary, 11 August 1863, IHS; T. S. McCawley to R. R. Reeves, 11 August 1863, Montraville Reeves Papers, UI; Johnston Diary, 11 August 1863, Johnston Collection, CHS; Christian Diary, 11 August

1863, CCNMP; Woodcock, *Southern Boy*, 179; Lamb Diary, 11 August 1863, CCNMP; Newlin, *Seventy-Third Illinois*, 203; Austin Diary, 11 August 1863, ALPL; Simonds Diary, 11 August 1863, Simonds Papers, NIU; Tabler Diary, 11 August 1863, private collection; Prickitt, *Company H*, 99; John C. Love to his parents, 14 August 1863, Love Letters, UM-B; *OR* 30(3):4.

35. Bond to Innes, 12 August 1863 (four messages), Drouillard to Innes, 12 August 1863, Thoms to Innes, 12 August 1863, Thoms to O'Neill, 12 August 1863, Thompson to Beggs, 12 August 1863, Drouillard to Beggs, 12 August 1863, Thrall to Dickson, 12 August 1863; Thompson to Winslow, 12 August 1863, and Bond to Winslow, 12 August 1863, all in DC, Telegrams Sent, NARA; Taylor, *"Supply,"* 123–24; Dilworth Journal, 12 August 1863, HC; Miller Journal, 12 August 1863, IHS; Kiene, *Journal*, 165; Busbey Diary, 12 August 1863, SRNB.

36. *OR* 30(3):14, 16–18; Rosecrans to Burnside, 12 August 1863, and Bond to Burnside, 12 August 1863, both in DC, Telegrams Sent, NARA; E. Vicar to M. P. Bestow, 10 August 1863, DC, Letters Received, NARA; "Summaries of the News," 12 August 1863, NARA; Marvel, *Burnside*, 267–69.

37. Dilworth Journal, 12 August 1863, HC; Shotts Diary, 12 August 1863, SRNB; Lewis Tripp to his parents and sister, 16 August 1863, Tripp Letters, Civil War Miscellaneous Collection, USAHEC; Christian Diary, 12 August 1863, CCNMP; Keegan, *Diaries*, 20; Frank J. Jones to his father, 12 August 1863, Jones Papers, CIHS; Rogers, "Diary," 10; Marshall Diary, 12 August 1863, OHS; Woodcock, *Southern Boy*, 179; Kiene, *Journal*, 165; Partridge, *Ninety-Sixth Illinois*, 152; Nelson G. Huson to his parents, 15 August 1863, Huson Letters, HL; Hoch Journal, 12 August 1863, UI; Smith, *Write*, 146; Robinson Diary, 12 August 1863, Robinson Papers, ALPL; Royse, *115th Illinois*, 82; Sowers Diary, 12 August 1863, CCNMP; McAdams, *Soldier Life*, 36; Patton Diary, 12 August 1863, CCNMP; Holmes, *Then and Now*, 116; Porter Diary, 12 August 1863, OHS; Boon, *Letters*, 66; Armstrong Diary, 12 August 1863, CCNMP; Miller Journal, 12 August 1863, IHS; Turchin, "Diary," 58–59; Cummins Diary, 12 August 1863, Cummins Papers, ALPL; Burns Diary, 12 August 1863, CCNMP; Austin Diary, 12 August 1863, ALPL; *OR* 30(3):11, 15; R. M. Russell to Edward Ruger, 12 June 1867, Ruger Correspondence, Thomas Papers, NARA; Hempstead Diary, 12 August 1863, UM-B; Thomas Diary, 12 August 1863, UT; Merrill, *Diary*, 46; Read Diary, 12 August 1863, KSHS; Persons Diary, 12 August 1863, WHS; Kendall Diary, 12 August 1863, HL; Leeper Diary, 12 August 1863, SRNB; Thoms to Lorenzo Thomas, 12 August 1863, DC, Telegrams Sent, NARA.

38. *OR* 30(3):14–15, 19–22; Thompson to Beggs, 12 August 1863, Bond to Innes, 13 August 1863, and Thoms to Palmer, 13 August 1863, all in DC, Telegrams Sent, NARA; Drouillard Diary, 13 August 1863, Rosecrans Papers, UCLA; Prickitt, *Company H*, 99; Crofts, *Third Ohio Cavalry*, 110; Crane Diary, 13 August 1863, Thomas Papers, NARA.

39. Willis Jones to his wife, 13 August 1863, Jones Papers, NC; *History, Seventy-Ninth Indiana*, 81; Howe Diary, 13 August 1863, IHS; Marshall Diary, 13 August 1863, OHS; Dewees Diary, 13 August 1863, CCNMP; Dilworth Journal, 13 August 1863, HC; Hinchberger Diary, 13 August 1863, CCNMP; Mosman, *Rough Side*, 67–68; Colyer Diary, 13 August 1863, ALPL; Hollingsworth Diary, 13 August 1863, IHS; Morse, *Diaries*, 31; Pecoy Diary, 13 August 1863, CCNMP; Lamb Diary, 13 August 1863, CCNMP; Austin Diary, 13 August 1863, ALPL; Riley, *Diary*, 51; Crippin, "Diary," 278; Burns Diary, 13 August 1863, CCNMP; Tabler Diary, 13 August 1863, private collection; Williams Diary, 13 August 1863, CCNMP; Hight, *Fifty-Eighth Indiana*, 166; Hinman, *Sherman Brigade*, 400; Opdycke Diary, 13 August 1863, Opdycke Papers, OHS; Clark, *Tigers*, 76; Shotts Diary, 13 August

1863, SRNB; Christian Diary, 13 August 1863, CCNMP; Johnston Diary, 13 August 1863, Johnston Collection, CHS; Partridge, *Ninety-Sixth Illinois*, 152; Hoch Journal, 13 August 1863, UI; *SOR* 25:693; Schwartz, *Diary*, 9; Imboden, *Army of the Cumberland*, 8; Sowers Diary, 13 August 1863, CCNMP; J. W. Branum, *National Tribune*, 20 December 1900; McAdams, *Soldier Life*, 36; Widney Diary, 13 August 1863, KMNMP; *OR* 30(3):19, 106; R. M. Russell to Edward Ruger, 12 June 1867, Ruger Correspondence, Thomas Papers, NARA; Hempstead Diary, 13 August 1863, UM-B; Thomas Diary, 13 August 1863, UT; Merrill, *Diary*, 46; Read Diary, 13 August 1863, KSHS; Persons Diary, 13 August 1863, WHS; Kendall Diary, 13 August 1863, HL; Leeper Diary, 13 August 1863, SRNB; Rosecrans to Lorenzo Thomas, 13 August 1863, DC, Telegrams Sent, NARA.

40. Garfield, *Wild Life*, 292; *OR* 30(3):27–29; Busbey Diary, 20 August 1863, SRNB; Goddard to Palmer, 14 August 1863, Goddard to O'Connell, 14 August 1863, Rosecrans to Innes, 14 August 1863, Bond to Beggs, 14 August 1863 (two messages), Thoms to Crittenden, 14 August 1863, and Rosecrans to Ripley, 14 August 1863, all in DC, Telegrams Sent, NARA.

41. Shotts Diary, 14 August 1863, SRNB; Dewees Diary, 14 August 1863, CCNMP; Marshall Diary, 14 August 1863, OHS; Price Diary, 14 August 1863, Civil War Miscellaneous Collection, USAHEC; Hollingsworth Diary, 14 August 1863, IHS; Taylor Diary, 14 August 1863, SRNB; Tuttle, *Kentucky Captain*, 140; Shideler Diary, 14 August 1863, CCNMP; Lyon Diary, 14 August 1863, OHS; Mosman, *Rough Side*, 68; Millen Diary, 14 August 1863, SRNB; Morledge Diary, 14 August 1863, KMNMP; Roseberry Diary, 14 August, EU; Larew Diary, 13–14 August 1863, IHS; Woodcock, *Southern Boy*, 179; *OR* 30(3):106; Daniel V. Culver to "Friend Anna," 29 August 1863, Clinton Family Papers, CU; Hempstead Diary, 14 August 1863, UM-B; Thomas Diary, 14 August 1863, UT; Merrill, *Diary*, 47; Read Diary, 14 August 1863, KSHS; Persons Diary, 14 August 1863, WHS; Kendall Diary, 14 August 1863, HL; Leeper Diary, 14 August 1863, SRNB; McAdams, *Soldier Life*, 36; Christian Diary, 14 August 1863, CCNMP; Pickering Diary, 14 August 1863, HL; Baumgartner, *Yankee Tigers II*, 84; Inskeep Diary, 14 August 1863, OHS; Sturges Diary, 14 August 1863, Sturges Papers, *Civil War Times Illustrated* Collection, USAHEC; Cutter, *Our Battery*, 128; Burns Diary, 14 August 1863, CCNMP; Hapeman Diary, 14 August 1863, ALPL; Dilworth Journal, 14 August 1863, HC; Ward Diary, 14 August 1863, Ward Papers, DP; Keegan, *Diaries*, 20; Stearns Diary, 14 August 1863, UM-B; Meredith Diary, 14 August 1863, USAHEC; Society, Seventy-Fourth Illinois, *Reunion Proceedings*, 20–21; *History, Seventy-Ninth Indiana*, 81; Huntzinger Diary, 14 August 1863, http://www.lafavre.us/huntzinger/hunt_3.htm (23 May 2016).

42. Lytle to Lee, 13 August 1863, Sheridan Papers, LC; *OR* 30(3):20; Burns Diary, 14–15 August 1863, CCNMP; Pecoy Diary, 14 August 1863, CCNMP; Austin Diary, 14–15 August 1863, ALPL; Cooley Diary, 13–14 August 1863, WHS; Eugene E. Comstock to his parents, 15 August 1863, Comstock Papers, WHS; Bennett and Haigh, *Thirty-Sixth Illinois*, 444–45; Tabler Diary, 14–15 August 1863, private collection; Crippin, "Diary," 278; Lytle, *For Honor*, 195–96; Sherman, *Quest*, 60–61; Alfred Pirtle to his sister, 15 August 1863, Pirtle Papers, FHS; Cummins Diary, 15 August 1863, Cummins Papers, ALPL; Chauncy H. Peck to his brother, 16 August 1863, Peck Letters, CCNMP; Lamb Diary, 15 August 1863, CCNMP; Otto, *11th Indiana Battery*, 33–34; Simonds Diary, 15 August 1863, Simonds Papers, NIU; Colburn/Gray Diary, 15 August 1863, private collection; Riley, *Diary*, 52; Amandus Silsby to his father, 20 August 1863, Silsby Letters, CCNMP; Edward W. Curtis to his cousin, 17 August 1863, Curtis Letters, NL; Eugene Comstock to his parents, 15 August 1863, Comstock Papers, WHS.

CHAPTER 7

1. Beers, *Memories*, 88–89; Cumming, *Kate*, 126–29; *Chattanooga Area Civil War Sites Assessment*, 105–8; Boyd, *Historical Markers*, 36, 38.

2. *OR* 23(2):948, 950, 952; Bragg to Cooper, 5 August 1863, and Bragg to Johnston, 5 August 1863, both in Bragg Letters and Telegrams, NARA.

3. Bragg to Cooper, 5 August 1863, and Bragg to Johnston, 5 August 1863, both in Bragg Letters and Telegrams, NARA; *OR* 23(2):952–53; *OR* 52(2):514; Leonidas Polk to Kenneth Rayner, 14 August 1863, Polk Papers, US.

4. Circular, 5 August 1863, Letters Sent, Polk's Command, NARA; *OR* 23(2):954–55, 957; Brent to D. H. Hill, 30 July 1863, 1 August 1863, and 4 August 1863, Brent to Wharton, 3 August 1863, Brent to Beard, 8 August 1863, Brent to Dreux, 10 August 1863, and Brent to Polk, 10 August 1863, all in Bragg Papers, WRHS; Alex E. Spence to his parents, 5 August 1863, Spence Letter, CCNMP.

5. *OR* 23(2):931, 954, 962–63. For an excellent discussion of the place of the District of the Gulf in the Confederate command structure, see Bergeron, *Confederate Mobile*, 26–30. In the author's opinion, Arndt Stickles, in *Buckner*, 224–25, gives far too much credit to Buckner's ostensible reasons for his protest.

6. Bragg to Cooper, 6 August 1863, Bragg Papers, WRHS; *OR* 23(2):931, 952–53, 962–64. The Alabama counties added to Bragg's territory in the amended order were Franklin, Lawrence, Morgan, Blount, Saint Clair, Calhoun, Cherokee, De Kalb, and Marshall.

7. *OR* 23(2):914, 916, 923, 925–26; Anderson to Jack, 16 July 1863, in Paul H. Rice, CSR, NARA; Jordan and Pryor, *Campaigns of Forrest*, 294–96; Brent to D. H. Hill, 29 July 1863 and 31 July 1863, Brent to B. J. Hill, 14 August 1863, all in Bragg Papers, WRHS; *Tennesseans in the Civil War*, 55–58, 248–50; Davis and Hoffman, *Confederate General*, 3:100–101; "About General Benjamin Jefferson Hill," http://www.angelfire.com/in/scvcamp1615/bjhill.html (17 August 2012); P. B. Clark to "Uncle Henry," 7 August 1863, Wells Papers, UNC; Mackall to Wheeler, 12 July 1863, and "Mem. a/c Amount paid by Col. McKinstry," 8–15 September 1863, both in Bragg Papers, WRHS.

8. "Summaries of the News," 258–308, NARA; *OR* 30(3):29; Brent to D. H. Hill, 29 July 1863, Brent to Forrest, 6 August 1863, Brent to Beard, 8 August 1863, Brent to Jackson, 10 August 1863, Brent to Polk, 10 August 1863, Brent to McKinstry, 11 August 1863, Brent to Flewellen, 13 August 1863, and Brent to Jackson, 13 August 1863, all in Bragg Papers, WRHS.

9. Brent to Wheeler, 6 August 1863, Brent to Walthall, 11 August 1863, and Bragg to Cooper, 8 August 1863, all in Bragg Papers, WRHS; Gow, "Military Administration" (dissertation), 56–57.

10. Polk to Deas and Maney, 6 August 1863, Polk to Deas, 11 August 1863, Polk to Cheatham, 12 August 1863, all in Letters Sent, Polk's Command, NARA; Willie H. Moore to Jennie Parsons, 12 August 1863, Parsons Letters, ADAH; Thomas B. Hall to his sister, 8 August 1863, Hall Family Papers, ADAH; Coleman Diary, 5 August 1863, UNC; Fraser Diary, 1 and 3 August 1863, CCNMP; Freeman Diary, 3–5 August 1863, TSLA; Corbitt Diary, 6–10 August 1863, EU; Seaton, *Bugle*, 37; Bunting, *Letters*, 182–88; Dodd, *Diary*, 21; W. Nicholson to his sister, 11 August 1863, http://www.terrystexasrangers.org/letters/nicholson_w/1863_08_11.htm (19 December 2009); B. F. Burke to his parents, 6 August 1863, http://www.terrystexasrangers.org/letters/burke_bf/1863_08_06.htm (19 December 2009); Gilbert L. Macmurphy Diary, 5 August 1863, http://www.terrystexasrangers.org/diaries/macmurphy_gl/index.html (21 June 2009); Giles, in Blackburn,

Giles, and Dodd, *Trilogy*, 43; Magee Diary, 6–8 August 1863, DU; Brown Notebook, 6 August 1863, CCNMP; Swett, "Warren Light Artillery," http://www.perryvillebattlefield.org/html/ms-swett-charles-cs.html (24 July 2012); Sparkman Diary, 6 August 1863, BPL.

11. Fraser Diary, 1 and 7 August 1863, CCNMP; David G. Godwin to "Miss B.," 1 August 1863, Godwin Letters, TSLA; James M. Brannock to "My Darling," 3 August 1863, Brannock Letters, VHS; Sparkman Diary, 4 August 1863, BPL; James Searcy to his sister, 9 August 1863, Searcy Letters, ADAH; Alexander M. Moore to his brother, 2 August 1863, Sydenham Moore Family Papers, ADAH.

12. S. M. Cherry, "Church Leader," *Chattanooga (Tenn.) Free Press*, 21 September 1938, CPL; *Chattanooga (Tenn.) Daily Rebel*, 4 August 1863; Bunting, *Letters*, 188–89; Sparkman Diary, 2 August 1863, BPL; Daniel Diary, 9 August 1863, Civil War Miscellaneous Collection, USAHEC; James Searcy to his sister, 9 August 1863, Searcy Letters, ADAH; William B. Honnoll to his sister, 3 August 1863, Honnoll Family Papers, EU.

13. Hezekiah Rabb to his wife, 3 August 1863, Rabb Letters, USAHEC; C. Irvine Walker to Ada Sinclair, Walker Letters, WRHS; Benjamin F. Burke to his parents, 6 August 1863, http://www.terrystexasrangers.org/letters/burke_bf/1863_08_06.htm (21 June 2009); David G. Godwin to "Miss B.," 1 August 1863, Godwin Letters, TSLA; Daniel L. Kelly to "Miss S. J. Honnoll," Honnoll Family Papers, EU.

14. *OR* 30(4):495; Cumming, *Kate*, 34, 125; Neal and Kremm, *Lion of the South*, 1–162; Warner, *Generals in Gray*, 137–38; Eicher and Eicher, *High Commands*, 297–98; Davis and Hoffman, *Confederate General*, 3:106–9; Nash, *Biographical Sketches*, 52–79; Welsh, *Medical Histories, Confederate*, 102.

15. *OR* 30(4):495; Davis and Hoffman, *Confederate General*, 1:186–87, 2:66–67; Eicher and Eicher, *High Commands*, 172–73, 594; Warner, *Generals in Gray*, 49–50, 71–72; Heartsill, *Fourteen Hundred*, 122, 127–42; Roger Q. Mills to his wife, 16 August 1863, Mills Papers, UTX; McCaffrey, "Only a Private," 63; Oliphant, *Only a Private*, 43; Daniel, *Cannoneers*, 79–80, 88–89.

16. *OR* 23(2):955–56; *OR* 30(4):507–9; Wyeth, *Forrest*, 245–47; Wills, *Battle from the Start*, 130–31; Hurst, *Forrest*, 131–32.

17. *OR* 23(2):911, 926; Cowles, *OR Atlas*, Plate 80.12; Rand Diary, 1–14 August 1863, MDAH; Roberts Diary, 1–14 August 1863, private collection; Cullens, "Adventures"; William Gabbett to Colonel [Lt. Col. I. M. St. John], 14 August 1863, Cumming Papers, GHS; Smith, *Civil War Tour for Cavers*, 81–82; S. Hubert Dent to his wife, 1 August 1863, Dent Collection, AU; Skellie, *Lest We Forget*, 541–51.

18. Augustus F. Davis to Julia Davis, 1 August 1863, Davis Letters, SRNB; S. Hubert Dent to his wife, 1 August 1863, Dent Collection, AU; Rand Diary, 5–10 August 1863, MDAH; Roberts Diary, 6 August 1863, private collection; Hugh A. McLaurin to his father, 7 August 1863, McLaurin Letters, WHS; Richard B. Pittman to his wife, 13 August 1863, Pittman Letters, CCNMP; Cullens, "Adventures"; Skellie, *Lest We Forget*, 541–51.

19. Brent to Anderson, 4 August 1863, Brent to Presstman, 11 August 1863, Brent to Jackson, 13 August 1863, Brent to B. J. Hill, 14 August 1863, Brent to Allin, 14 August 1863, and Brent to Anderson, 14 August 1863, all in Bragg Papers, WRHS; Roberts Diary, 1 and 3 August 1863, private collection; Skellie, *Lest We Forget*, 542, 546.

20. Roberts Diary, 14 August 1863, private collection; Skellie, *Lest We Forget*, 549.

CHAPTER 8

1. Rosecrans to Sheridan, 15 August 1863, DC, Telegrams Sent, NARA; *OR* 30(3):29, 33–39, 115.

2. Bond to Sheridan, 15 August 1863, Bond to Guthrie, 15 August 1863, Bond to Dickson, 15 August 1863, Thoms to Innes, 15 August 1863, Bond to Innes, 15 August 1863, Thoms to Commanding Officer Pioneers, 15 August 1863, Thoms to Thomas, 15 August 1863, Thoms to Johnson, 15 August 1863, Thoms to Simmons, 15 August 1863, Thoms to Townsend, 15 August 1863, Rosecrans to Innes, 15 August 1863, and Goddard to Stanton, 15 August 1863, all in DC, Telegrams Sent, NARA; *OR* 30(3):33, 38–39; *Wisconsin State Journal*, 5 September 1863.

3. *OR* 30(3):35–36.

4. *OR* 30(3):36–37.

5. *OR* 30(3):37.

6. *OR* 30(3):37.

7. *OR* 30(3):37–38; Larew Diary, 15–17 August 1863, IHS; Kundahl, *Confederate Engineer*, 208–11.

8. *OR* 30(3):36–37, 52; Hight, *Fifty-Eighth Indiana*, 167; Everett F. Abbott to his mother, 17 August 1863, Chamberlain Papers, IHS; Bickham, *Rosecrans' Campaign*, 172.

9. Hinchberger Diary, 15 August 1863, CCNMP; Ward Diary, 15 August 1863, Ward Papers, DP; Lyon Diary, 15 August 1863, OHS; *History, Seventy-Ninth Indiana*, 81–82; Shideler Diary, 15 August 1863, CCNMP; Busbey Diary, 15 August 1863, SRNB; Mosman, *Rough Side*, 68; Colyer Diary, 15 August 1863, ALPL; Morse, *Diaries*, 31; Hines Diary, 15 August 1863, Hines Manuscript Collection, ISL; George H. Alverson to his father, 15 August 1863, Alverson Letters, Civil War Miscellaneous Collection, USAHEC; Frank M. Phelps to "Dear Friends," 15 August 1863, Phelps Letters, Lewis Leigh Collection, USAHEC; John S. Glenn to his sister, 15 August 1863, Glenn Papers, ALPL; Thomas Prickett to "Dearest Matilda," 15 August 1863, Prickett Letters, IHS; Sturges Diary, 15 August 1863, Sturges Papers, *Civil War Times Illustrated* Collection, USAHEC; Pickering Diary, 15 August 1863, HL; Turchin, "Diary," 59; Bruce Diary, 15 August 1863, ISL; Marshall Diary, 15 August 1863, OHS; McAdams, *One Hundred and Thirteenth Ohio*, 36; Riley, *Diary*, 52; Shotts Diary, 15 August 1863, SRNB; Christian Diary, 15 August 1863, CCNMP; *SOR* 21:358; *SOR* 63:460; *OR* 30(3):43; Frank J. Jones to his mother, 15 August 1863, Jones Papers, CIHS; Inskeep Diary, 15 August 1863, OHS; DeVelling, *Seventeenth Ohio*, 73; Price Diary, 15 August 1863, Civil War Miscellaneous Collection, USAHEC; Keegan, *Diaries*, 20; Kitchell Diary, 15 August 1863, ALPL; Miller Journal, 15 August 1863, IHS.

10. Thoms to Beggs, 15 August 1863, Rosecrans to Innes, 15 August 1863, Bond to Innes, 15 August 1863, Bond to Beggs, 15 August 1863, Thompson to Beggs, 15 August 1863, Thoms to Crittenden, 15 August 1863, Bond to Van Cleve, 15 August 1863, Bond to Crittenden, 15 August 1863, and Thoms to Lorenzo Thomas, 15 August 1863, all in DC, Telegrams Sent, NARA; *OR* 30(3):32–33, 40, 42.

11. *OR* 30(3):47–49, 289; Millen Diary, 16 August 1863, SRNB; Hinchberger Diary, 16 August 1863, CCNMP; Gibson, *Seventy-Eighth Pennsylvania*, 83; Nupp Diary, 16 August 1863, CCNMP; Weaver Diary, 16 August 1863, SRNB; Blackburn, *Letters*, 136; John W. Baldwin to his wife, 19 August 1863, Baldwin Papers, OHS; Dilworth Journal, 16 August 1863, HC; Shanks Diary, 16 August 1863, BGSU; Canfield, *21st Ohio*, 104; Ward Diary, 16 August 1863, Ward Papers, DP; *SOR* 62:349; Beatty, *Citizen Soldier*, 319; Harris Diary, 16 August 1863, CCNMP; Hapeman Diary, 16 August 1863, ALPL; Calkins, *One Hundred and*

Fourth Illinois, 106; Belknap, *Michigan*, 109; Sturges Diary, 16 August 1863, Sturges Papers, *Civil War Times Illustrated* Collection, USAHEC.

12. Wilder, "Preliminary Movements," 1; *OR* 30(1):445; *OR* 30(3):49–51; Caleb Carlton to his wife, 10 August 1863, Carlton Papers, LC; Griest Diary, 16 August 1863, CCNMP; Records Diary, 16 August 1863, and Reminiscences, Records Manuscript Collection, ISL; McGee, *72nd Indiana*, 144; Kemper Diary, 16 August 1863, OHS; Kitchell Diary, 16 August 1863, ALPL; *SOR* 28:37; Cort, *Letters*, 100–101; *Ninety-Second Illinois*, 94–95; Colehour Account, 16 August 1863, SRNB; Brown Diary, 16 August 1863, *Civil War Times Illustrated* Collection, USAHEC; King, *Three Years*, 102–4; Campbell Journal, 16 August 1863, CCNMP; Phillips, *Diary*, 23; Runion Diary, 16 August 1863, http://civilwar.illinoisgenweb.org/scrapbk/runiondiary2.html (23 March 2013).

13. Judson Bishop to his brother, 22 August 1863, Bishop Papers, MHS; Donahower Account, 16 August 1863, Donahower Papers, MHS; Inskeep Diary, 16 August 1863, OHS; Wheeler Diary, 16 August 1863, OHS; Hunter, *Eighty-Second Indiana*, 53; Price Diary, 16 August 1863, Civil War Miscellaneous Collection, USAHEC; Bishop, *Story*, 91; Keegan, *Diaries*, 20–21; Reed Diary, 16 August 1863, Reed Papers, MHS; Davidson Diary, 16 August 1863, NCWM; Albertson, *Letters Home*, Letter 99; *OR* 30(1):397–98; DeVelling, *Seventeenth Ohio*, 73; Frederick Marion to his sister, 21 August 1863, Marion Letters, ALPL; Small Diary, 16 August 1863, IHS; Shaw, *Tenth Indiana*, 211; Everett F. Abbott to his mother, 17 August 1863, Chamberlain Papers, IHS; Martling Diary, 16 August 1863, Martling Manuscript Collection; ISL; Bruce Diary, 16 August 1863, ISL.

14. *OR* 30(1):625, 678–79; Hight, *Fifty-Eighth Indiana*, 167; Hines Diary, 16 August 1863, Hines Manuscript Collection, ISL; Kerwood, *Fifty-Seventh Indiana*, 198–99; Marshall Diary, 16 August 1863, OHS; Dewees Diary, 16 August 1863, CCNMP; Woodruff, *Fifteen Years*, 273–74; Hinman, *Sherman Brigade*, 405–6; Mallory Diary, 16 August 1863, HP; Gillis Diary, 18 August 1863, OHS; Clark, *Tigers*, 81; Emerson Opdycke to his wife, 17 and 20 August 1863, and Opdycke Diary, 16 August 1863, Opdycke Papers, OHS; Joseph Bruff to his wife, 20 August 1863, private collection; Rice, *Yankee Tigers*, 61–62; Baumgartner, *Yankee Tigers II*, 85–86, 88.

15. Busbey Diary, 16 August 1863, SRNB; Hyde Diary, 16 August 1863, KYHS; Botkin Diary, 16 August 1863, and George W. Botkin to his friends, 23 August 1863, Baker Correspondence, OHS; *SOR* 34:56, 58, 106, 112; Mason Diary, 16 August 1863, SRNB; Dillman Diary, 16 August 1863, IU; Connelly Diary, 16 August 1863, IHS; McKee Diary, 16 August 1863, http://mckee-burns.pasttracker.com/mckee/cw_mckee/mckee_robert_t_cw_diary_1 (15 June 2013); *SOR* 66:372, 376; Harden, *90th Ohio*, 90; Cutter, *Our Battery*, 128; Simmons, *84th Illinois*, 66; Suiter Diary, 16 August 1863, ALPL; Hannaford, *Sixth Ohio*, 441; *SOR* 62:769, 780; Glisan Diary, 16 August 1863, CCNMP; Williams Diary, 16 August 1863, CCNMP; Palmer Journal, 16 August 1863, CCNMP; Kimberly and Holloway, *Forty-First Ohio*, 46–47; Albert G. Hart to his wife, 20 August 1863, Hart Papers, WRHS; George W. Hodges to his wife, 31 August 1863, Hodges Papers, WRHS; *SOR* 67:573; Johnston Diary, 16 August 1863, FHS.

16. *OR* 30(3):36, 53, 60–61, 960–61; Van Cleve to Ruger, 24 May 1867, Thomas Papers, NARA; Woodcock, *Southern Boy*, 179–80; Benedict Diary, 16 August 1863, SRNB; *History, Seventy-Ninth Indiana*, 82; Tilford Diary, 16 August 1863, FHS; Huntzinger Diary, 16 August 1863, http://www.lafavre.us/huntzinger/hunt_3.htm (23 May 2016); Wright, *Eighth Kentucky*, 171; Barnes, Carnahan, and McCain, *Eighty-Sixth Indiana*, 153; McCain, *Song*, 84–85; Gasherie Decker to his sister, 22 August 1863, Decker Letters, WHS; Hurd Diary, 16 August 1863, private collection; Claggett Diary, 16 August 1863, CCNMP; Howe

Diary, 16 August 1863, IHS; A. L. Gibson to "Dear Friend," J. C. Jessup Letters, IHS; Morgan and Murphy, *Seventh Indiana Battery,* 21.

17. *OR* 30(3):37, 51, 115–16, 959–60; Frank J. Jones to his father, 16 August 1863, Jones Papers, CIHS; Ferdinand Van Derveer to Emily Van Derveer, 12 August 1863, and Harry Van Derveer to Emily Van Derveer, 15 August 1863, both in Van Derveer letters, SLRH; Colyer Diary, 16 August 1863, ALPL; Mosman, *Rough Side,* 68. Horace Phillips, sixteen, was Kate McCook's brother, and George McCook, eleven, was the son of George W. McCook, Alexander McCook's brother.

18. *OR* 30(3):115, 960; Moon Diary, 16 August 1863, KSHS; Beck Diary, 16 August 1863, KSHS; Shideler Diary, 16 August 1863, CCNMP; William McKean to his sister, 24 August 1863, McKean Letters, OHS; Ashmun Diary, August 1863, CCNMP; Wagner Reminiscences, *Civil War Times Illustrated* Collection, USAHEC; Richards, *Letters,* 17–18; Lyon Diary, 16 August 1863, OHS; Doll, *Sixth Indiana,* 66; Lyman S. Widney to his parents, 23 August 1863, Widney Letters, CCNMP; Talbot Diary, 16 August 1863, SRNB; Bergun H. Brown to his parents, 24 August 1863, Brown Papers, IHS; Robinson Diary, 16 August 1863, Regimental Papers, WRHS; J. Grosskopf to Edward Ruger, 23 June 1867, Ruger Correspondence, Thomas Papers, NARA; Kiene, *Journal,* 166; Stahl Diary, 16 August 1863, BGSU; Cope, *Fifteenth Ohio,* 298; Pickering Diary, 16 August 1863, HL; Welk Diary, 16 August 1863, BGSU; Davidson, *Battery A,* 80. The cashiered officer was 2nd Lt. Harvey H. John, Forty-Ninth Ohio Infantry regiment.

19. Lytle, *For Honor,* 194; Austin Diary, 16 August 1863, ALPL; Simonds Diary, 16 August 1863, Simonds Papers, NIU; Burns Diary, 16 August 1863, CCNMP; Crippin, "Diary," 278; Lamb Diary, 16 August 1863, CCNMP; Pecoy Diary, 16 August 1863, CCNMP; Chauncy H. Peck to his brother, 16 August 1863, Peck Letters, CCNMP; Otto, *11th Indiana Battery,* 34; Riley, *Diary,* 52; Tabler Diary, 16 August 1863, private collection; William D. Hynes to his father, 16 August 1863, Hynes Letters, ISL; *OR* 30(3):52; Alfred Pirtle to "Dear Jim," 19 August 1863, Pirtle Papers, FHS; Newton Jones to his father, 15 August 1863, Jones Papers, WHS; Morledge Diary, 16 August 1863, KMNMP; Newlin, *Seventy-Third Illinois,* 203; Webster Diary, 16 August 1863, Civil War Miscellaneous Collection, USAHEC; Clark Diary, 16 August 1863, Clark Papers, USAHEC; Henry C. Taylor to his brother, 16 August 1863, Taylor Papers, WHS; Schotts Diary, 16 August 1863, SRNB.

20. Thoms to Guthrie, 16 August 1863, Goddard to Johnson, 16 August 1863, Bond to Thomas, 16 August 1863 (two messages), Thoms to Thomas, 16 August 1863, Goddard to Sheridan, 16 August 1863, Bond to Sheridan, 16 August 1863, Goddard to Innes, 16 August 1863 (two messages), Bond to Beggs, 16 August 1863, Thompson to Beggs, 16 August 1863, Thoms to Granger, 16 August 1863, Rosecrans to Lorenzo Thomas, 16 August 1863, all in DC, Telegrams Sent, NARA; *SOR* 87:118, 121; Johnston, *Soldier Boy,* 52; *OR* 30(3):46–47, 52; Kirk, *Fifteenth Pennsylvania Cavalry,* 226; Frankenberry Diary, 16 August 1863, WVU; Roseberry Diary, 16 August 1863, EU; *OR* 30(1):929; Meredith Diary, 16 August 1863, Harrisburg Civil War Roundtable Collection, USAHEC.

21. Hinchberger Diary, 17 August 1863, CCNMP; Millen Diary, 17 August 1863, SRNB; Gibson, *Seventy-Eighth Pennsylvania,* 83; Nupp Diary, 17 August 1863, CCNMP; Weaver Diary, 17 August 1863, SRNB; Dilworth Journal, 17 August 1863, HC; Shanks Diary, 17 August 1863, BGSU; Ward Diary, 17 August 1863, IHS and DP; Hapeman Diary, 17 August 1863, ALPL; Calkins, *One Hundred and Fourth Illinois,* 106–7; Harris Diary, 17 August 1863, CCNMP; Thornton, *Gallantry,* 156; Sturges Diary, 17 August 1863, Sturges Papers, *Civil War Times Illustrated* Collection, USAHEC; Turchin, "Diary," 60; Williams, *Extracts,* 87; *SOR* 63:165, 177, 186; Horton, *Eleventh Ohio,* 97; Josiah D. Cotton to his wife, 18 August

1863, Cotton Papers, LC; Owen Diary, 17 August 1863, AU; George B. Turner to his father, 18 August 1863, Turner Papers, OHS; *SOR* 34:477; Ward Diary, 17 August 1863, Booth Papers, OHS; Phillips, *Turchin*, 99–100; John T. Booth, *National Tribune*, 25 September 1890; *SOR* 27:643, 648; *OR* 30(1):469; Mauzy, *Sixty-Eighth Indiana*, 10; High, *Sixty-Eighth Indiana*, 52; Gates Diary, 17 August 1863, IHS; Taylor Diary, 17 August 1863, SRNB; Alanson R. Ryman to Jane Ryman, 25 August 1863, Ryman Letters, IHS; Morse, *Diaries*, 31; Parker Diary, 17 August 1863, HL; Tourgee, "Diary," 116; Essington, "Second Years History," Essington Papers, IHS; Shera Diary, 17 August 1863, FHS; Floyd, *Seventy-Fifth Indiana*, 116–17; Miller Journal, 17 August 1863, IHS; Hollingsworth Diary, 17 August 1863, IHS; *OR* 30(3):58; Inskeep Diary, 17 August 1863, OHS; Wheeler Diary, 17 August 1863, OHS; DeVelling, *Seventeenth Ohio*, 73; Hunter, *Eighty-Second Indiana*, 53–54; Small Diary, 17 August 1863, IHS; Price Diary, 17 August 1863, Civil War Miscellaneous Collection, USAHEC; Everett F. Abbott to his mother, 17 August 1863, Chamberlain Papers, IHS; Keegan, *Diaries*, 21; Martling Diary, 17 August 1863, ISL; Donahower Account, 17 August 1863, Donahower Papers, MHS; Reed Diary, 17 August 1863, MHS; Bishop, *Story*, 91; Davidson Diary, 17 August 1863, NCWM; Albertson, *Letters Home*, Letter 99.

22. Arbuckle and Shook, *Mountain Goat*, 2–6; Griest Diary, 16–17 August 1863, CCNMP; Benefiel, *Souvenir, Seventeenth Indiana*, unpaginated; *OR* 30(1):445; Banta Diary, 17 August 1863, CCNMP; Kemper Diary, 17 August 1863, OHS; Records Diary, 17 August 1863, Records Manuscript Collection, ISL; Kitchell Diary, 17 August 1863, ALPL; Campbell Journal, 17 August 1863, CCNMP; Phillips, *Diary*, 23; Runion Diary, 17 August 1863, http://civilwar.illinoisgenweb.org/scrapbk/runiondiary2.html (23 March 2013); Brown Diary, 17 August 1863, ALPL; *SOR* 25:498, 552; Cort, *Letters*, 101; Caleb Carlton to his wife, 20 August 1863, Carlton Papers, LC; *SOR* 66:313, 321.

23. *OR* 30(1):625; Marshall Diary, 17 August 1863, OHS: Dewees Diary, 17 August 1863, CCNMP; Hines Diary, 17 August 1863, ISL; Hight, *Fifty-Eighth Indiana*, 167–68; Woodruff, *Fifteen Years*, 274; Hinman, *Sherman Brigade*, 406; Mallory Diary, 17 August 1863, HPL; Gillis Diary, 18 August 1863, OHS; Joseph Bruff to his wife, 20 August 1863, Bruff Letters, private collection; Emerson Opdycke to his wife, 20 August 1863, and Opdycke Diary, 17 August 1863, Opdycke Papers, OHS.

24. Busbey Diary, 17 August 1863, SRNB; Hyde Diary, 17 August 1863, KYHS; Botkin Diary, 17 August 1863, and George W. Botkin to his friends, 23 August 1863, Baker Correspondence, OHS; Mason Diary, 17 August 1863, SRNB; Connelly Diary, 17 August 1863, IHS; McKee Diary, 17 August 1863, http://mckee-burns.pasttracker.com/mckee/cw_mckee/mckee_robert_t_cw_diary_1 (15 June 2013); Harden, *90th Ohio*, 90; Cutter, *Our Battery*, 129–30; 46:218; Johnston Diary, 17 August 1863, FHS; Suiter Diary, 17 August 1863, ALPL; Simmons, *84th Illinois*, 70–71; Hannaford, *Sixth Ohio*, 441–42; Glisan Diary, 17 August 1863, CCNMP; Williams Diary, 17 August 1863, CCNMP; *OR* 30(3):61; Wright, *Eighth Kentucky*, 171–72; Woodcock, *Southern Boy*, 180; Benedict Diary, 17 August 1863, SRNB; Hurd Diary, 17 August 1863, private collection; Claggett Diary, 17 August 1863, CCNMP; Howe Diary, 17 August 1863, IHS; *History, Seventy-Ninth Indiana*, 82; Tilford Diary, 17 August 1863, FHS; Huntzinger Diary, 17 August 1863, http://www.lafavre.us/huntzinger/hunt_3.htm (23 May 2016).

25. *OR* 30(3):59, 961; Post Diary, 17 August 1863, KC; Mosman, *Rough Side*, 68; Lathrop, *Fifty-Ninth Illinois*, 212; *SOR* 25:37; Mayfield Diary, 17 August 1863, IU; *SOR* 87:40, 47, 67; William H. Ball to his brother, 25 August 1863, Farlin Q. Ball Letters, WHS; *SOR* 21:432; Colyer Diary, 17 August 1863, ALPL; Patterson Diary, 17 August 1863, MHM; *SOR* 23:19; Day, *One Hundred and First Ohio*, 142; Morris, *Eighty-First Indiana*, 52–53; *SOR* 43:663;

SOR 22:49, 566; Himoe Diary, 17 August 1863, NAHA; "Scandinavian," *Wisconsin State Journal*, 31 August 1863; *SOR* 88:5; *SOR* 33:549; Heg, *Letters*, 236; Stahl Diary, 17 August 1863, BGSU; Kiene, *Journal*, 166; Pickering Diary, 17 August 1863, HL; Welk Diary, 17 August 1863, BGSU; Thomas J. Harrison to his wife, 17 August 1863, Harrison Letters, IHS; Dean Diary, 17 August 1863, private collection; Widney Diary, 17 August 1863, KMNMP; Talbot Diary, 17 August 1863, SRNB; Bergun H. Brown to "Dear Folks at Home," Brown Papers, IHS; Robinson Diary, 17 August 1863, Regimental Papers, WRHS; Doll, *Sixth Indiana*, 66; Lyon Diary, 17 August 1863, OHS; Moon Diary, 17 August 1863, KSHS; Beck Diary, 17 August 1863, KSHS; Shideler Diary, 17 August 1863, CCNMP; William McKean to his sister, 24 August 1863, McKean Letters, OHS; Ashmun Diary, August 1863, CCNMP.

26. *OR* 30(3):43, 54, 59, 61–62, 106; Mann Diary, 17 August 1863, in *Chattanooga (Tenn.) Times*, 25 April 1937; Pecoy Diary, 17 August 1863, CCNMP; Austin Diary, 17 August 1863, ALPL; John L. McBride to his mother, 17 August 1863, McBride Correspondence, NSHS; Luther Bradley to his wife, 17 August 1863, Bradley Papers, USAHEC; Morledge Diary, 17 August 1863, KMNMP; Hempstead Diary, 17 August 1863, UM-B; Thomas Diary, 16–17 August 1863, UT; Carter, *First Tennessee Cavalry*, 83; Merrill, *Diary*, 47; Persons Diary, 17 August 1863, WHS; Kendall Diary, 17 August 1863, HL; Harris Diary, 17 August 1863, IHS.

27. *OR* 30(1):920–21; Robert H. G. Minty, *National Tribune*, 25 February 1892; Vale, *Minty*, 205–10; Sipes, *Seventh Pennsylvania Cavalry*, 74–75; Haines, "Record," UM-B; Robert Burns to "My Dear Davidson," 25 August 1863, Burns Letter, MHS; Robertson, *Michigan*, 654; McLain Diary, 17 August 1863, ISHS; Pickerill, *Third Indiana Cavalry*, 57; *OR* 30(2):527; Lindsley, *Annals*, 2:658–59; Jordan and Pryor, *Campaigns of Forrest*, 296–98.

28. Weller Journal, 17 August 1863, *Civil War Times Illustrated* Collection, USAHEC; Kirk, *Fifteenth Pennsylvania Cavalry*, 226; Wilson, *Column South*, 82–83; Frankenberry Diary, 17 August 1863, WVU; Smith Diary, 17 August 1863, CCNMP; Drouillard to Innes, 17 August 1863 (two messages), Porter to Innes, 17 August 1863, Bond to Innes, 17 August 1863 (two messages), Bond to Burroughs, 17 August 1863 (two messages), Porter to Granger, 17 August 1863, Drouillard to Hodges, 17 August 1863, Thompson to Beggs, 17 August 1863, Thompson to Hunton, 17 August 1863, and Rosecrans to Lorenzo Thomas, 17 August 1863, all in DC, Telegrams Sent, NARA; *OR* 30(3):55–57; Roseberry Diary, 17 August 1863, EU; Porter Diary, 17 August 1863, OHS; Stewart, *52nd O.V.I.*, 52; Boon, *Letters*, 67; Charles R. Thompson CSR, NARA.

29. *OR* 30(3):68; Webster Diary, 18 August 1863, Civil War Miscellaneous Collection, USAHEC; Robert Newell Elder to his sister, 18 August 1863, Elder Letters, OHS; Kelsey M. Adams to his brother, 18 August 1863, Adams Letters, WHS; Hinkley Diary, 18 August 1863, Hinkley Papers, WHS; *SOR* 29:147; Clark Diary, 18 August 1863, Clark Papers, USAHEC; Johnston, *Soldier Boy*, 53; Shotts Diary, 18 August 1863, SRNB; Eben P. Sturges to his mother, 19 August 1863, and Sturges Diary, 18 August 1863, both in Sturges Papers, *Civil War Times Illustrated* Collection, USAHEC; Christian Diary, 18 August 1863, CCNMP; Johnston Diary, 18 August 1863, Johnston Collection, CHS; *SOR* 21:358; Gibson, *Seventy-Eighth Pennsylvania*, 83; Millen Diary, 18 August 1863, SRNB; Hinchberger Diary, 18 August 1863, CCNMP; Nupp Diary, 18 August 1863, CCNMP; Weaver Diary, 18 August 1863, SRNB; Dilworth Journal, 18 August 1863, HC; Shanks Diary, 18 August 1863, BGSU; Ward Diary, 18 August 1863, Ward Papers, DP; Blackburn, *Letters*, 136; John W. Baldwin to his wife, 19 August 1863, Baldwin Papers, OHS; Hapeman Diary, 18 August 1863, ALPL; Calkins, *One Hundred and Fourth Illinois*, 107–8; undated newspaper clipping,

Marsh Family Papers, ALPL; Harris Diary, 18 August 1863, CCNMP; Carpenter Diary, 18 August 1863, SRNB.

30. *OR* 30(1):398, 469; *OR* 30(3):69; Floyd, *Seventy-Fifth Indiana*, 117; Miller Journal, 18 August 1863, IHS; Essington, "Second Years History," Essington Papers, IHS; High, *Sixty-Eighth Indiana*, 52; Shera Diary, 18 August 1863, FHS; Tourgee, "Diary," 116–17; Morse, *Diaries*, 31; Parker Diary, 18 August 1863, HL; Taylor Diary, 18 August 1863, SRNB; *SOR* 27:643; Andrew, *Letters*, 71; Josiah D. Cotton to his wife, 18 August 1863, Cotton Papers, LC; Ward Diary, 18 August 1863, Booth Papers, OHS; Owen Diary, 18 August 1863, AU; Price Diary, 18 August 1863, Civil War Miscellaneous Collection, USAHEC; Small Diary, 18 August 1863, IHS; Orville T. Chamberlain to his brother, 21 August 1863, Chamberlain Papers, IHS; Harry Van Derveer to his mother, 18 August 1863, and Ferdinand Van Derveer to his wife, 19 August 1863, both in Van Derveer Letters, SLRH; Keegan, *Diaries*, 21; Donahower Account, Donahower Papers, MHS; Albertson, *Letters Home*, Letter 99; Bishop, *Story*, 91; Reed Diary, 18 August 1863, MHS; Martling Diary, 18 August 1863, Martling Manuscript Collection, ISL; Bircher, *Drummer-Boy*, 69; Bruce Diary, 18 August 1863, ISL; Davidson Diary, 18 August 1863, NCWM; Inskeep Diary, 18 August 1863, OHS; Wheeler Diary, 18 August 1863, OHS; Frederick Marion to his sister, 21 August 1863, Marion Letters, ALPL; Hunter, *Eighty-Second Indiana*, 54.

31. Brown Diary, 18 August 1863, *Civil War Times Illustrated* Collection, USAHEC; Phillips, *Diary*, 23; *SOR* 25:498; John T. Wilder to his wife, 18 August 1863, Wilder Papers, UTC; Records Diary, 18 August 1863, and Reminiscences, Records Manuscript Collection, ISL; Kitchell Diary, 18 August 1863, ALPL; Connolly, *Three Years*, 114; Banta Diary, 18 August 1863, CCNMP; Kemper Diary, 18 August 1863, OHS; Campbell Journal, 18 August 1863, CCNMP; *OR* 30(3):69–70; Marshall Diary, 18 August 1863, OHS; Dewees Diary, 18 August 1863, CCNMP; Hines Diary, 18 August 1863, Hines Manuscript Collection, ISL.

32. *OR* 30(1) 625; Hight, *Fifty-Eighth Indiana*, 168; Woodruff, *Fifteen Years*, 274–75; Hinman, *Sherman Brigade*, 406; Mallory Diary, 18 August 1863, HPL; Gillis Diary, 18 August 1863, OHS; Emerson Opdycke to his wife, 20 August 1863, and Opdycke Diary, 18 August 1863, both in Opdycke Papers, OHS; Joseph Bruff to his wife, 20 August 1863, Bruff Letters, private collection; *SOR* 67:608; Clark, *Tigers*, 81; Caleb Carlton to his wife, 20 August 1863, Carlton Papers, LC.

33. Johnston Diary, 18 August 1863, FHS; *SOR* 34:218–19; Albert G. Hart to his wife, 20 August 1863, Hart Papers, WRHS; Busbey Diary, 18 August 1863, SRNB; Hyde Diary, 18 August 1863, KYHS; Botkin Diary, 18 August 1863, and George W. Botkin to his friends, 23 August 1863, Baker Correspondence, OHS; Connelly Diary, 18 August 1863, IHS; McKee Diary, 18 August 1863, http://mckee-burns.pasttracker.com/mckee/cw_mckee/mckee_robert_t_cw_diary_1 (15 June 2013); Mason Diary, 18 August 1863, SRNB; Dillman Diary, 18 August 1863, IU; Harden, *90th Ohio*, 90; *SOR* 34:112; Glisan Diary, 18 August 1863, CCNMP; Hannaford, *Sixth Ohio*, 442; Williams Diary, 18 August 1863, CCNMP; Suiter Diary, 18 August 1863, ALPL; Walker Diary, 18 August 1863, Harrisburg Civil War Roundtable Collection, USAHEC; *OR* 30(3):70; Horatio Van Cleve to his wife, 18 August 1863, Van Cleve Papers, MHS; Benedict Diary, 18 August 1863, SRNB; Hurd Diary, 18 August 1863, private collection; *History, Seventy-Ninth Indiana*, 82; Tilford Diary, 18 August 1863, FHS; Huntzinger Diary, 18 August 1863, http://www.lafavre.us/huntzinger/hunt_3.htm (23 May 2016); Howe Diary, 18 August 1863, IHS; Andrew L. Gibson to John C. Jessup, 20 August 1863, Jessup Letters, IHS; Woodcock, *Southern Boy*, 180; Claggett Diary, 18 August 1863, CCNMP; Wright, *Eighth Kentucky*, 172.

34. Post Diary, 18 August 1863, KC; Charles F. Weller to "My Dear Kate," 22 August 1863, Weller Letters, *Civil War Times Illustrated* Collection, USAHEC; James Harvey Houston to his mother and sister, 18 August 1863, Houston Letters, CCNMP; Mayfield Diary, 18 August 1863, IU; Herr, *Nine Campaigns*, 356; Mosman, *Rough Side*, 68; *SOR* 24:432; Society, Seventy-Fourth Illinois, *Reunion Proceedings*, 93, 103–4; Lathrop, *Fifty-Ninth Illinois*, 213; *SOR* 87:40; Dodd Diary, 18 August 1863, ALPL; *SOR* 21:515; Patterson Diary, 18 August 1863, ALPL; *SOR* 23:19; Colyer Diary, 18 August 1863, ALPL; Morris, *Eighty-First Indiana*, 53; Isaac P. Rule to his brother, 20 August 1863, Rule Letters, HPL; Day, *One hundred and First Ohio*, 142–43; Himoe Diary, 18 August 1863, NAHA; James K. Weir to his mother, 23 August 1863, CCNMP; *Wisconsin State Journal*, 31 August 1863; *OR* 30(3):115; Kiene, *Journal*, 166–67; Stahl Diary, 18 August 1863, BGSU; Cope, *Fifteenth Ohio*, 298–99; Pickering Diary, 18 August 1863, HL; Welk Diary, 18 August 1863, BGSU; Davidson, *Battery A*, 81; Dean Diary, 18 August 1863, private collection; Willoughby Diary, 18 August 1863, ISL; Widney Diary, 18 August 1863, KMNMP; Lyman S. Widney to his parents, 23 August 1863, CCNMP; Lyman S. Widney, *National Tribune*, 31 October 1901; Talbot Diary, 18 August 1863, SRNB; Bergun H. Brown to his family, 24 August 1863, Brown Papers, IHS; Robinson Diary, 18 August 1863, Regimental Papers, WRHS; *SOR* 62:498; Moon Diary, 18 August 1863, KSHS; Beck Diary, 18 August 1863, KSHS; Shideler Diary, 18 August 1863, CCNMP; Richards, *Letters*, 18; Lyon Diary, 18 August 1863, OHS; Protsman Diary, 18 August 1863, WSU.

35. Goddard to Innes, 18 August 1863, Bond to Innes, 18 August 1863 (four messages), Bond to Winslow, 18 August 1863 (two messages, Goddard to Starkweather, 18 August 1863, Bond to Granger, 18 August 1863, Bond to Chief Quartermaster, McMinnville, 18 August 1863, and Bond to Andrew Johnson, 18 August 1863, all in DC, Telegrams Sent, NARA; *OR* 30(3):67–68, 70; Le Duc, *Recollections*, 101; Innes to Rosecrans, 18 August 1863, DC, Letters Received, NARA; Drouillard Diary, 18 August 1863, Rosecrans Papers, UCLA; Garfield, *Wild Life*, 293; Smith, *Garfield*, 1:315–16; Henry H. Seys to his wife, 20 August 1863, Seys Letters, UM-C.

36. Drouillard Diary, 18 August 1863, Rosecrans Papers, UCLA; Garfield, *Wild Life*, 293; Morledge Diary, 18 August 1863, KMNMP; Newlin, *Seventy-Third Illinois*, 203; Woodall, *Stevenson Story*, 118; Larew Diary, 19 August 1863, IHS; Simonds Diary, 18 August 1863, Simonds Papers, NIU; Lamb Diary, 18 August 1863, CCNMP; Pecoy Diary, 18 August 1863, CCNMP; Cooley Diary, 18 August 1863, WHS; Austin Diary, 18 August 1863, ALPL; Burns Diary, 18 August 1863, CCNMP; Tabler Diary, 18 August 1863, private collection; Riley, *Diary*, 52; Lytle to Sheridan, 18 August 1863, Sheridan Papers, LC; *OR* 30(3):67, 69, 72; Bond to Lorenzo Thomas, 18 August 1863, DC, Telegrams Sent, NARA.

37. Clark Diary, 19 August 1863, Clark Papers, USAHEC; Johnston, *Soldier Boy*, 53; Hapeman Diary, 19 August 1863, ALPL; Calkins, *One Hundred and Fourth Illinois*, 108–9; *SOR* 29:206, 209; Harris Diary, 19 August 1863, CCNMP; Shotts Diary, 19 August 1863, SRNB; Christian Diary, 19 August 1863, CCNMP; Johnston Diary, 19 August 1863, Johnston Collection, CHS; Sturges Diary, 19 August 1863, Sturges Papers, *Civil War Times Illustrated* Collection, USAHEC; Gibson, *Seventy-Eighth Pennsylvania*, 83; Nupp Diary, 19 August 1863, CCNMP; Millen Diary, 19 August 1863, SRNB; Hinchberger Diary, 19 August 1863, CCNMP; Weaver Diary, 19 August 1863, SRNB; Dilworth Journal, 19 August 1863, HC; Shanks Diary, 19 August 1863, BGSU; *SOR* 65:690; Ward Diary, 19 August 1863, Ward Papers, DP; Miller Journal, 19 August 1863, IHS; Uriah J. Loop to his sister, 20 August 1863, Loop Letters, IHS; Hollingsworth Diary, 19 August 1863, IHS; Tourgee, "Diary," 117; Morse, *Diaries*, 32; Parker Diary, 19 August 1863, HL; Ward Diary, 19 August 1863, Booth

Papers, OHS; Owen Diary, 19 August 1863, AU; George B. Turner to his mother, 23 August 1863, Turner Papers, OHS; Phillips, *Turchin*, 100; *SOR* 34:477; *SOR* 63:162; *OR* 30(1):398; Inskeep Diary, 19 August 1863, OHS; Wheeling Diary, 19 August 1863, OHS; DeVelling, *Seventeenth Ohio*, 73; Frederick Marion to his sister, 21 August 1863, Marion Letters, ALPL; Hunter, *Eighty-Second Indiana*, 54; Price Diary, 19 August 1863, Civil War Miscellaneous Collection; USAHEC; Small Diary, 19 August 1863, IHS; Orville T. Chamberlain to his brother, 21 August 1863, Chamberlain Papers, IHS; Bruce Diary, 19 August 1863, ISL; Keegan, *Diaries*, 21; Martling Diary, 19 August 1863, Martling Manuscript Collection, ISL; Donahower Account, 19 August 1863, Donahower Papers, MHS; Judson Bishop to his brother, 22 August 1863, Bishop Papers, MHS; Albertson, *Letters Home*, Letter 100; Reed Diary, 19 August 1863, MHS; Davidson Diary, 19 August 1863, NCWM; Bircher, *Drummer-Boy*, 69; Roseberry Diary, 19 August 1863, EU; Bond to Reynolds, 19 August 1863, Goddard to Thomas, 19 August 1863, and Goddard to Simmons, 19 August 1863, all in DC, Telegrams Sent, NARA; *OR* 30(3):75–78.

38. *OR* 30(1):445; *OR* 30(3):78, 87; Wilder, "Preliminary Movements," 1–2; McGee, *72nd Indiana*, 144–45; Records Diary, 19 August 1863, and Reminiscences, Records Manuscript Collection, ISL; Phillips, *Diary*, 23; Brown Diary, 19 August 1863, ALPL; *SOR* 25:498; King, *Three Years*, 105–6; Cort, *Letters*, 101; Kitchell Diary, 19 August 1863, ALPL; Connolly, *Three Years*, 114–15; Banta Diary, 19 August 1863, CCNMP; Kemper Diary, 19 August 1863, OHS; Campbell Journal, 19 August 1863, CCNMP; Brent to Allin, 11 August 1863, Bragg Papers, WRHS.

39. *OR* 30(1):617, 625–26; Marshall Diary, 19 August 1863, OHS; Dewees Diary, 19 August 1863, CCNMP; Hines Diary, 19 August 1863, Hines Manuscript Collection, ISL; Kerwood, *Fifty-Seventh Indiana*, 199–200; Hight, *Fifty-Eighth Indiana*, 168; Woodruff, *Fifteen Years*, 275; *SOR* 67:608; Emerson Opdycke to his wife, 20 August 1863, and Opdycke Diary, 19 August 1863, Opdycke Papers, OHS; Mallory Diary, 19 August 1863, HPL; Gillis Diary, 21 August 1863, OHS; Busbey Diary, 19–20 August 1863, SRNB; Hyde Diary, 19 August 1863, KYHS; Botkin Diary, 19 August 1863, and George W. Botkin to his friends, 23 August 1863, Baker Correspondence, OHS; *SOR* 34:66, 112–13, 219, 288, 439; Connelly Diary, 19 August 1863, IHS; McKee Diary, 19 August 1863, http://mckee-burns.pasttracker.com/mckee/cw_mckee/mckee_robert_t_cw_diary_1 (15 June 2013); Mason Diary, 19 August 1863, SRNB; Harden, *90th Ohio*, 90; *SOR* 66:372; Cutter, *Our Battery*, 130; *OR* 30(3):78–79; Chapin, "Diary," 231; Johnston Diary, 19 August 1863, FHS; G. W. Hodges to "Marana," 31 August 1863, Hodges Papers, WRHS; Albert G. Hart to his friends, 23 August 1863, Hart Papers, WRHS; Glisan Diary, 19 August 1863, CCNMP; *SOR* 62:786; Hannaford, *Sixth Ohio*, 442; Williams Diary, 19 August 1863, CCNMP; Suiter Diary, 19 August 1863, ALPL; Simmons, *84th Illinois*, 71–72; Walker Diary, 19 August 1863, Harrisburg Civil War Roundtable Collection, USAHEC; Palmer Journal, 19 August 1863, CCNMP; Benedict Diary, 19 August 1863, SRNB; *History, Seventy-Ninth Indiana*, 82–83; Tilford Diary, 19 August 1863, FHS; Huntzinger Diary, 19 August 1863, http://www.lafavre.us/huntzinger/hunt_3.htm (23 May 2016); Howe Diary, 19 August 1863, IHS; Woodcock, *Southern Boy*, 180–81; Brasher Diary, 19 August 1863, CCNMP; Claggett Diary, 19 August 1863, CCNMP; Morgan and Murphy, *7th Independent Battery*, 21; Wright, *Eighth Kentucky*, 172; Moses F. Yoder to unknown correspondent, 25 August 1863, Yoder Papers, LC.

40. *OR* 30(3):37, 115; Post Diary, 19 August 1863, Post Papers, KC; Mayfield Diary, 19 August 1863, IU; *SOR* 24:432; Mosman, *Rough Side*, 68–69; Society, Seventy-Fourth Illinois, *Reunion Proceedings*, 93–94; Lathrop, *Fifty-Ninth Illinois*, 213; *SOR* 25:37; *SOR* 87:40; Dodd Diary, 19 August 1863, Dodd Papers, ALPL; *SOR* 21:515; Colyer Diary, 19

August 1863, ALPL; William P. Carlin, *National Tribune*, 2 April 1885; Patterson Diary, 19 August 1863, MHM; *SOR* 23:19; Morris, *Eighty-First Indiana*, 53–54; Day, *One Hundred and First Ohio*, 143; Isaac P. Rule to his brother, 20 August 1863, Rule Letters, HPL; Himoe Diary, 19 August 1863, NAHA; *Wisconsin State Journal*, 31 August 1863; Burt to Assistant Quartermaster, 19 August 1863, Davis Papers, IHS; Kiene, *Journal*, 167; Stahl Diary, 19 August 1863, BGSU; Cope, *Fifteenth Ohio*, 299; Pickering Diary, 19 August 1863, HL; Welk Diary, 19 August 1863, BGSU; Davidson, *Battery A*, 81; Willoughby Diary, 19 August 1863, Willoughby Collection, ISL; Dean Diary, 19 August 1863, private collection; Widney Diary, 19 August 1863, KMNMP; Lyman S. Widney to his parents, 23 August 1863, Widney Letters, CCNMP; Lyman S. Widney, *National Tribune*, 31 October 1901; Talbot Diary, 19 August 1863, SRNB; Bergun H. Brown to his family, 24 August 1863, Brown Papers, IHS; Robinson Diary, 19 August 1863, Regimental Papers, WRHS; *SOR* 62:498; Shideler Diary, 19 August 1863, CCNMP; Richards, *Letters*, 18; Demoret, *Ninety-Third Ohio*, 19–20; Lyon Diary, 19 August 1863, OHS; Moon Diary, 19 August 1863, KSHS; Beck Diary, 19–20 August 1863, KSHS; Protsman Diary, 19 August 1863, WSU; Wagner Reminiscences, 19 August 1863, *Civil War Times Illustrated* Collection, USAHEC; Meredith Diary, 19 August 1863, Harrisburg Civil War Roundtable Collection, USAHEC; McCullough Diary, 19 August 1863, ISL; Schwartz, *Diary*, 28; William M. Parkinson to his brother, 22 August 1863, Parkinson Papers, OHS; *OR* 30(1):929.

41. Cooley Diary, 19 August 1863, WHS; Lamb Diary, 19 August 1863, CCNMP; Pecoy Diary, 19 August 1863, CCNMP; Sherman, *Quest*, 60; Burns Diary, 19 August 1863, CCNMP; Tabler Diary, 19 August 1863, private collection; John Wilcox to his wife, 19 August 1863, Wilcox Letters, CCNMP; Crippin, "Diary," 278; Newlin, *Seventy-Third Illinois*, 204; Morledge Diary, 19 August 1863, KMNMP; Persons Diary, 19 August 1863, WHS; Newton Jones to his father, 21 August 1863, Jones Papers, WHS; *OR* 30(3):74–75, 77–78, 80–81, 106; Charles A. Smith Diary, 19 August 1863, CCNMP; Frankenberry Diary, 19 August 1863, WVU; Kirk, *Fifteenth Pennsylvania Cavalry*, 226–27; Weller Journal, 19 August 1863, *Civil War Times Illustrated* Collection, USAHEC; Wilson, *Column South*, 83; Bond to Reynolds, 19 August Drouillard to Parsons, 19 August 1863, Rosecrans to Granger, 19 August 1863, and Thoms to Lorenzo Thomas, 19 August 1863, all in DC, Telegrams Sent, NARA.

42. *OR* 30(3):77, 86–87; Carpenter Diary, 20 August 1863, SRNB; Clark Diary, 20 August 1863, Clark Papers, USAHEC; Johnston, *Soldier Boy*, 53; Henry C. Taylor to his brother, 20 August 1863, Taylor Letters, WHS; Galpin Diary, 20 August 1863, Galpin Family Papers, WHS; Wilcox Diary, 20 August 1863, Wiley Sword Collection, USAHEC; Hough, *Soldier*, 127; Hapeman Diary, 20 August 1863, ALPL; Harris Diary, 20 August 1863, CCNMP; Shotts Diary, 20 August 1863, SRNB; Christian Diary, 20 August 1863, CCNMP; Johnston Diary, 20 August 1863, Johnston Collection, CHS; Sturges Diary, 20 August 1863, Sturges Papers, *Civil War Times Illustrated* Collection, USAHEC; Millen Diary, 20 August 1863, SRNB; Hinchberger Diary, 20 August 1863, CCNMP; Weaver Diary, 20 August 1863, SRNB; Ward Diary, 20 August 1863, Ward Papers, DP; William R. Stookey to "Dear and Loving Wife," 20 August 1863, Stookey Letters, IHS; Owen Diary, 20 August 1863, AU; Miller Journal, 20 August 1863, IHS; Uriah J. Loop to his sister, 20 August 1863, Loop Letters, IHS; Hollingsworth Diary, 20 August 1863, IHS; Tourgee, "Diary," 117; Morse, *Diaries*, 32; George B. Turner to his mother, 23 August 1863, Turner Papers, OHS; Parker Diary, 20 August 1863, HL; Inskeep Diary, 20 August 1863, OHS; Wheeler Diary, 20 August 1863, OHS; Price Diary, 20 August 1863, Civil War Miscellaneous Collection, USAHEC; Small Diary, 20 August 1863, IHS; Whit Isreal to his wife, 20 August 1863,

Isreal Letters, CCNMP; Martling Diary, 20 August 1863, Martling Manuscript Collection, ISL; Keegan, *Diaries*, 21; Bircher, *Drummer-Boy*, 70; Bishop, *Story*, 91; Reed Diary, 20 August 1863, MHS; Davidson Diary, 20 August 1863, NCWM; McClave Diary, http://www.89thohio.com/Mcclave/mcclave02.htm (5 May 2012); Caleb Carlton to his wife, 20 August 1863, Carlton Papers, LC.

43. *OR* 30(3):87, 90–91; *SOR* 34:219, 241; Johnston Diary, 20 August 1863, FHS; *SOR* 28:12; Hannaford, *Sixth Ohio*, 442; *SOR* 62:769; Glisan Diary, 20 August 1863, CCNMP; *OR* 30(1):445; Griest Diary, 19–20 August 1863, CCNMP; McGee, *72nd Indiana*, 145–47; Records Diary, 20 August 1863, and Reminiscences, Records Manuscript Collection, ISL; King, *Three Years*, 106–7; Cort, *Letters*, 101; *SOR* 25:498; Brown Diary, 20 August 1863, *Civil War Times Illustrated* Collection, USAHEC; *Ninety-Second Illinois*, 96; Kitchell Diary, 20 August 1863, ALPL; Banta Diary, 20 August 1863, CCNMP; Kemper Diary, 20 August 1863, OHS; Campbell Journal, 20 August 1863, CCNMP.

44. Palmer Journal, 19 August 1863, CCNMP; *OR* 30(3):91–92; Busbey Diary, 20 August 1863, SRNB; Hyde Diary, 20 August 1863, KYHS; Botkin Diary, 20 August 1863, Baker Correspondence, OHS; Mason Diary, 20 August 1863, SRNB; Connelly Diary, 20 August 1863, IHS; Harden, *90th Ohio*, 90; Williams Diary, 20 August 1863, CCNMP; Walker Diary, 20 August 1863, Harrisburg Civil War Roundtable Collection, USAHEC; Suiter Diary, 20 August 1863, ALPL; Willis Jones to his wife, 20 August 1863, Jones Papers, NC; *OR* 30(1):626, 679; Woodruff, *Fifteen Years*, 275–76; *SOR* 27:587; Joseph Bruff to his wife, 20 August 1863, Bruff Letters, private collection; Marshall Diary, 20 August 1863, OHS; Dewees Diary, 20 August 1863, CCNMP; Hines Diary, 20 August 1863, Hines Manuscript Collection, ISL; Kerwood, *Fifty-Seventh Indiana*, 200; Hudson, "Anderson Road," 165; Baumgartner, *Yankee Tigers II*, 86; Hight, *Fifty-Eighth Indiana*, 168–69; Hinman, *Sherman Brigade*, 407–8; Benedict Diary, 20 August 1863, SRNB; Hurd Diary, 20 August 1863, private collection; Howe Diary, 20 August 1863, IHS; *History, Seventy-Ninth Indiana*, 83; Claggett Diary, 20 August 1863, CCNMP; Tilford Diary, 20 August 1863, FHS; Huntzinger Diary, 20 August 1863, http://www.lafavre.us/huntzinger/hunt_3.htm (23 May 2016); Wright, *Eighth Kentucky*, 173–74; Horatio Van Cleve to his wife, 20 August 1863, Van Cleve Papers, MHS.

45. Kirk, *Fifteenth Pennsylvania Cavalry*, 227; Weller Journal, 20 August 1863, *Civil War Times Illustrated* Collection, USAHEC; Crofts, *Third Ohio Cavalry*, 111; Prickitt, *Company H*, 100; Feagles Diary, 20 August 1863, CCNMP; Crane Diary, 20 August 1863, Thomas Papers, NARA; Crane Diary, 20 August 1863, CIHS; Pape-Findley, *Fourth Ohio Cavalry*, 153; Curry, *Four Years*, 107; O. O. Smith to Edward Ruger, 27 April 1867, Ruger Correspondence, Thomas Papers, NARA; John C. Fleming to his sister, 28 August 1863, Fleming Letters, NL; Porter Diary, 20 August 1863, OHS; Stewart, *52nd O.V.I.*, 52; Holmes, *Then and Now*, 4, 117, 119; Thomas M. Burns to his father, 9 September 1863, Burns Letters, VT; Aten, *Eighty-Fifth Illinois*, 97–98; Kinnear, *Eighty-Sixth Illinois*, 19; Putney Diary, 20 August 1863, KMNMP; Post Diary, 20 August 1863, Post Papers, KC; Mayfield Diary, 20 August 1863, IU; Mosman, *Rough Side*, 69; Lathrop, *Fifty-Ninth Illinois*, 213; Society, Seventy-Fourth Illinois, *Reunion Proceedings*, 94; *SOR* 87:40; Dodd Diary, 20 August 1863, Dodd Papers, ALPL; Colyer Diary, 20 August 1863, ALPL; Patterson Diary, 20 August 1863, MHM; Isaac P. Rule to his brother, 20 August 1863, Rule Letters, HPL; Morris, *Eighty-First Indiana*, 54; *SOR* 66:685; *SOR* 43:671; Heg, *Letters*, 237; Himoe Diary, 20 August 1863, NAHA; *Wisconsin State Journal*, 31 August 1863; *SOR* 22:574; *SOR* 33:550; *SOR* 87:67; William H. Ball to his brother, 20 August 1863, Ball Letters, USAHEC; Widney Diary, 20 August 1863, KMNMP; Lyman S. Widney to his parents, 23 August 1863, Widney

Letters, CCNMP; Lyman S. Widney, *National Tribune*, 31 October 1901; Talbot Diary, 20 August 1863, SRNB; Bergun H. Brown to his family, 24 August 1863, Brown Papers, IHS; Robinson Diary, 20 August 1863, Regimental Papers, WRHS; *SOR* 62:498; Cope, *Fifteenth Ohio*, 299; Kiene, *Journal*, 167; Stahl Diary, 20 August 1863, BGSU; Pickering Diary, 20 August 1863, HL; Welk Diary, 20 August 1863, BGSU; Davidson, *Battery A*, 82; Shideler Diary, 20 August 1863, CCNMP; Lyon Diary, 20 August 1863, OHS; Moon Diary, 20 August 1863, KSHS; Beck Diary, 20 August 1863, KSHS; Protsman, Diary, 20 August 1863, WSU; Doll, *Sixth Indiana*, 66–67; Briant, *Sixth Indiana*, 220–22; Holm, *Fifth Indiana Battery*, 27; Richards, *Letters*, 18; Henry Richards to his father, 29 August 1863, Gilbert-Richards Papers, MU; Alpheus S. Bloomfield to his father, 23 August 1863, Bloomfield Letters, OHS; Meredith Diary, 20 August 1863, Harrisburg Civil War Roundtable Collection, USAHEC; McCullough Diary, 20 August 1863, ISL; Schwartz, *Diary*, 28.

46. Cooley Diary, 20 August 1863, WHS; Pecoy Diary, 20 August 1863, CCNMP; Eugene E. Comstock to his parents, 15 August 1863, Comstock Papers, WHS; Austin Diary, 20 August 1863, ALPL; Burns Diary, 20 August 1863, CCNMP; Tabler Diary, 20 August 1863, private collection; Crippin, "Diary," 279; Simonds Diary, 20 August 1863, Simonds Papers, NIU; Riley, *Diary*, 52; Frank J. Jones to his parents, 21 August 1863, Jones Papers, CIHS; Kirk, *Fifteenth Pennsylvania Cavalry*, 227; Wilson, *Column South*, 84; Frankenberry Diary, 20 August 1863, WVU; William P. Carlin, *National Tribune*, 2 April 1885.

47. Goddard to Bruce, 20 August 1863, Goddard to Lytle, 20 August 1863, Goddard to Dickson, 20 August 1863, Thoms to Sheridan, 20 August 1863, and Goddard to Negley, 20 August 1863, all in DC, Telegrams Sent, NARA; *OR* 30(3):84–85, 89; Boon, *Letters*, 65–67. An additional contributor to the tension at Stevenson may have been the forced removal of certain females from the area. According to Charles Johnston of the Seventy-Ninth Indiana Infantry regiment, a visitor waiting to join his command, "Bragg left all the old strumpets behind when he crossed the River. The boys says the mountains was full of them when they came here first. They gathered up a car load or two and sent them off." Charles W. Johnston to his wife, 23 August 1863, Johnston/Rhoades Family Correspondence, UND. See also J. W. M., *Cincinnati Commercial*, 9 September 1863.

48. *OR* 30(3):83, 88, 92; Thoms to Halleck, 20 August 1863, and Thoms to Burnside, 20 August 1863, both in DC, Telegrams Sent, NARA.

CHAPTER 9

1. Cumming, *Kate*, 129–30.

2. Roberts Diary, 16–18 August 1863, private collection; George Lea to his father, 18 August 1863, Lea Family Papers, USAHEC; Brent to Hughes, 15 August 1863, Brent to Forrest, 17 August 1863, and Falconer to Polk, 17 August 1863, all in Bragg Papers, WRHS; *OR* 30(4):502, 519.

3. *OR* 23(2):964–65; Brent to Buckner, 20 August 1863, Bragg Papers, WRHS; Brent to Buckner, 20 August 1863, Buckner Papers, HL.

4. Freeman Diary, 13 August 1863, TSLA; Sykes, *Walthall's Brigade*, 525–26; Bragg to Joseph E. Brown, 15 August 1863, and Bragg to Seddon (telegram), 15 August 1863, both in Bragg Letters, NARA; Brent to Anderson, 16 August 1863, A. A. G. to S. A. M. Wood, 17 August 1863, Brent to Presstman, 17 August 1863, and A. A. G. to General [D. H. Hill], 17 August 1863, all in Bragg Papers, WRHS.

5. A. A. G. to General [D. H. Hill], 17 August 1863, Bragg Papers, WRHS; Darst, "Robert Hodges, Jr.," 37–38; Oldham Diary, 5 August 1863, CCNMP; Blanton and Cook, *They*

Fought Like Demons, 9–19, 68–70, 153–54, 176–83, 197; Leonard, *All the Daring*, 252–62; *Richmond Examiner*, 16 July 1863 and 16 September 1863; *Chattanooga (Tenn.) Daily Rebel*, 4 and 6 August 1863; Ridley, *Battles and Sketches*, 495. Velazquez tells her own story in *The Woman in Battle: A Narrative of the Exploits, Adventures and Travels of Madame Loreta Janeta Velazquez, Otherwise Known as Lieutenant Harry T. Buford, Confederate States Army*. According to Velazquez, she was released from Castle Thunder in Richmond and sent south by Provost Marshal Charles Winder with fake dispatches for Maj. Gen. Earl Van Dorn in order to test her. The Richmond papers indicate her release came in July 1863, but Van Dorn had been dead since March of that year. Therefore her claim to have delivered the fake dispatches to Van Dorn personally after a delay at Charlotte, North Carolina, was clearly false. She was witnessed at Chattanooga and Tyner's Station in early August in both newspaper and soldier accounts. She speaks glowingly of Brig. Gen. Frank Armstrong of Forrest's Cavalry Division, and indeed her alleged fiancé, Thomas DeCaulp, was a member of the Third Arkansas Cavalry, one of Armstrong's units. Again, according to newspaper accounts, she was back in Richmond by mid-September, although her own testimony indicates that she accompanied Longstreet's Corps from Charlotte to Atlanta during the same time period. From there she once more sought to find Thomas DeCaulp. According to his CSR, Thomas DeCaulp deserted to the Federals on 14 September and was quickly sent north. Thomas DeCaulp CSR, NARA. The story told by Velazquez, however, is that she married DeCaulp in Atlanta but that he soon died in a Federal hospital in Chattanooga. In truth, he was serving in the Federal army in Minnesota. With so much of her story false, it is impossible to surmise what her actual purpose was in coming to Chattanooga in August 1863, but she clearly was there for several weeks. Velazquez's amazing life has been painstakingly reconstructed by William C. Davis in *Inventing Loreta Velasquez: Confederate Soldier Impersonator, Media Celebrity, and Con Artist*. Surprisingly, Davis does not credit her visit to Chattanooga and Tyner's Station as factual, although the Bragg Papers, Hodges letter, Oldham Diary, and *Daily Rebel* of 6 August 1863 all confirm it.

6. *OR* 30(4):500–501, 505, 507, 518, 574; *OR* 23(2):915, 923, 953; George Knox Miller to "My dear Cellie," 15 September 1863, Miller Letters, UNC; Compiled Service Records of Confederate Soldiers Who Served in Military Organizations Raised Directly by the Confederate Government, Third Confederate Cavalry, Muster Roll, 30 April–31 December 1863, Companies A, B, C, G, I, NARA; C. W. Love to his parents, 15 August 1863 and 20 August 1863, Love Family Letters, TCU; John W. Hill to his sister, 15 August 1863, Hill Papers, UTX; *OR* 23(1):847; *OR* 30(2):527; Jordan and Pryor, *Campaigns of Forrest*, 296; P. B. Clark to his uncle, 7 August 1863, Wells Papers, UNC.

7. Leonidas Polk to Susan Rayner, 15 August 1863, Polk Papers, US; *OR* 30(4):518; Etter Diary, 15–16 August 1863, SRNB; Magee Diary, 15 and 17 August 1863, DU; Brown Notebook, 16 August 1863, CCNMP; Owen, "Confederate Surgeon," 148; Newton N. Davis to his wife, 23 July 1863, Davis Letters, ADAH; C. Irving Walker to Ada Sinclair, 16 August 1863, Walker Letters, Regimental Papers, WRHS; Manigault, *Carolinian*, 78; Daniel Diary, 16 August 1863, Civil War Miscellaneous Collection, USAHEC; Freeman Diary, 20 August 1863, TSLA; Fraser Diary, 15 August 1863, CCNMP; Rand Diary, 15–17 August 1863, MDAH; John Crittenden to his wife, 16 August 1863, Crittenden Letters, UTX.

8. Special Orders, No. 152, Hardee's Corps, Special Orders, Circulars, and General Orders, NARA; *OR* 30(4):503; Alfred M. Peterson to his aunt, 21 August 1863, Peterson Letter, CCNMP.

9. *OR* 30(4):503, 523; *SOR* 26:276; *SOR* 91:208, 424; Sparkman Diary, 17 August 1863, BPL; Seaton, *Bugle*, 37–38; Heartsill, *Fourteen Hundred*, 141; *SOR* 58:62; Coleman Diary, 11

August 1863, UNC; Sterling A. M. Wood to his wife, 19 August 1863, Wood Papers, ADAH; Talbert Holt to his wife, 15 August 1863, Holt Letters, Partin Papers, AU; Bodenhamer Memoirs, 20 August 1863, TSLA; Moore Diary, 12 August 1863, UDC Collection, GDAH; Lindsley, *Annals*, 1:355; *SOR* 91:34; William D. Cole to his wife, 15 August 1863, Cole Letters, Civil War Miscellaneous Collection, USAHEC; Abram M. Glazener to his wife, 17 August 1863, Glazener Letters, *Civil War Times Illustrated* Collection, USAHEC.

10. *OR* 23(2):945–46, 948–49, 962; *OR* 30(4):521, 537; *OR* 23(1):839–42; Francis L. Wadsworth to his mother, 9 August 1863, CCNMP.

11. Seaton, *Bugle*, 38; Heartsill, *Fourteen Hundred*, 141–42; Bragg, *Joe Brown's Army*, 68; Special Orders, No. 152, Hardee's Corps, Special Orders, Circulars, and General Orders, NARA; *SOR* 26:276; *SOR* 91:208, 424; Alexander M. Moore to his brother, 19 August 1863, Sydenham Moore Family Papers, ADAH.

12. Brent to Forrest, 18 August 1863, Brent to Wheeler, 18 August 1863 (two messages), Brent to Polk, 19 August 1863, Brent to Hindman, 20 August 1863, and Brent to Polk, 20 August 1863, all in Bragg Papers, WRHS; *OR* 30(4):510; Brown Notebook, 19–20 August 1863, CCNMP; Magee Diary, 20 August 1863, DU; C. Irving Walker to Ada Sinclair, 22 August 1863, Walker Letters, Regimental Papers, WRHS; Thomas B. Hall to Bolling Hall Sr., 21 August 1863, Bolling Hall Family Papers, ADAH; Manigault, *Carolinian*, 91; *SOR* 88:804; *SOR* 89:145; Rand Diary, 20 August 1863, MDAH; Assistant Adjutant General to Cheatham and Hindman, 20 August 1863, Letters Sent, Polk's Command, NARA; Daniel Diary, 21 August 1863, SRNB; Bodenhamer Memoirs, 20 August 1863, TSLA; James Searcy to his mother, 22 August 1863, Searcy Letters, ADAH.

13. Johnston Diary, 19 August 1863, J. Stoddard Johnston Military Papers, FHS; *OR* 30(4):520–21.

14. *OR* 30(4):503; Freeman Diary, 21 August 1863, TSLA; S. M. Cherry, "Church Leader," *Chattanooga (Tenn.) Free Press*, 21 September 1938, CPL; S. J. A. Frazier, "Chickamauga," *Chattanooga (Tenn.) Lookout*, 20 May 1909, clipping in CPL; S. J. A. Frazier, "Soldier," *Chattanooga (Tenn.) Times*, 23 October 1921, clipping in CPL; Quintard, *Doctor Quintard*, 77; Cumming, *Kate*, 130.

CHAPTER 10

1. *OR* 30(1):445; *OR* 30(3):120–22, 124; Benefiel, *Souvenir, Seventeenth Indiana*, unpaginated; Kemper Diary, 21 August 1863, OHS; *SOR* 25:498; Campbell Journal, 21 August 1863, CCNMP; McGee, *72nd Indiana*, 147.

2. Connolly, *Three Years*, 115–17; Jerome B. Quinn, *National Tribune*, 4 October 1900; *Chattanooga (Tenn.) Daily Rebel*, 30 August 1863; *OR* 30(1):445; *OR* 30(3):123–24; Wilder, "Preliminary Movements," 2; Gibson and Gibson, *Dictionary of Transports*, 89, 249; Map, Lilly Papers, LCA; Campbell Journal, 21 August 1863, CCNMP; Map, Campbell Journal, WC.

3. *OR* 30(1):445; *OR* 30(3):122–24; Wilder, "Preliminary Movements," 2; Lilly Report, 1 September 1863, Lilly Papers, LCA; Campbell Journal, 21 August 1863, CCNMP. Wilder on 24 August 1863 identified the larger vessel as the *Tennessee*, and that designation was followed by Baumgartner (*Blue Lightning*, 129), but the vast majority of evidence, including Wilder's subsequent statements, indicates that the vessel sunk at the Chattanooga wharf on 21 August 1863 was the *Paint Rock*. Raised by the Federals, the *Paint Rock* subsequently served the Army of the Cumberland after its withdrawal into Chattanooga following the Battle of Chickamauga. *OR* 30(3):890.

4. *OR* 30(3):120–21 and map; *Ninety-Second Illinois,* 96–97; Cort, *Letters,* 101–2; King, *Three Years,* 107; *SOR* 25:498–99; Kitchell Diary, 21 August 1863, ALPL.

5. *OR* 30(1):921; *OR* 30(3):90, 124–25; Vale, *Minty,* 211–14; Potter Diary, 21 August 1863, Potter Papers, UM-B; McLain Diary, 21 August 1863, ISHS.

6. Cumming, *Kate,* 130; *Augusta (Ga.) Daily Constitutionalist,* 5 September 1863; Rand Diary, 16 August 1863, MDAH; Brent to Allin, 11 August 1863 and 14 August 1863, and Brent to B. J. Hill, 14 August 1863, Bragg Papers, WRHS; *OR* 30(4):535–36; *Memphis Daily Appeal,* 10 September 1863 and 5 November 1863; *Charleston (S.C) Mercury,* 24 August 1863; *Chattanooga (Tenn.) Daily Rebel,* 30 August 1863; Otey, "Signal Corps," 130. Some men from an Alabama infantry regiment, which served as the army's provost guard in Chattanooga, may have been captured on the far bank of the river. Thomas Warrick to his wife, 9 August 1863, Warrick Papers, ADAH; Thomas B. Hall to Bolling Hall Sr., 22 August 1863, Bolling Hall Family Papers, ADAH.

7. *Memphis Daily Appeal,* 22 August 1863, reprinted in *Augusta (Ga.) Daily Constitutionalist,* 25 August 1863; Leonidas Polk to Frances Polk, 25 August 1863, Polk Papers, US; Quintard, *Doctor Quintard,* 77; S. J. A. Frazier, "Chickamauga," *Chattanooga (Tenn.) Lookout,* 20 May 1909, clipping in CPL; S. J. A. Frazier, "Soldier," *Chattanooga (Tenn.) Times,* 23 October 1921, clipping in CPL; Queenie Lee Rowles, "Stories," *Chattanooga (Tenn.) Times,* 23 December 1906, clipping in CPL; Watterson, *Autobiography,* 2:308–9; Wall, *Watterson,* 42–43; Andrews, *South Reports,* 346n; Thomas H. McCallie, "Bragg Headquarters," *Chattanooga (Tenn.) Free Press,* 21 September 1938, clipping in CPL; Zella Armstrong, "Mrs. Davenport," *Chattanooga (Tenn.) Times,* 12 July 1937, clipping in CPL; Louisa Emma Corbin, "War Experience," CPL; J. N. Heiskel to Glenn Tucker, 29 January 1962, and Glenn Tucker to J. N. Heiskel, 17 February 1962, Tucker Correspondence, CCNMP; Armstrong, *Hamilton County,* 2:21, 24–25; Newton N. Davis to Bettie Davis, 22 August 1863, Davis Letters, ADAH; Daniel L. Kelly to "Miss Lou Honnoll," 28 August 1863, Honnoll Family Papers, EU; *Chattanooga (Tenn.) Daily Rebel,* 22 August 1863, reprinted in *Atlanta Daily Intelligencer,* 28 August 1863; *Augusta (Ga.) Chronicle,* 25 August 1863; *Chattanooga (Tenn.) Daily Rebel,* 22 August 1863, reprinted in *Augusta (Ga.) Chronicle,* 25 August 1863; *Charleston (S.C) Mercury,* 24 August 1863; *Augusta (Ga.) Daily Constitutionalist,* 25 August 1863; *Macon (Ga.) Telegraph,* 24 August 1863; U.S. Federal Census of 1860, Davidson County, Tennessee. Although two brief articles in *Confederate Veteran* claim that the mortally wounded child was named Higginbotham, contemporary newspaper accounts agree that she was a daughter of Francis G. Roach (or Roche) of Nashville, and the description of the Roach family in the 1860 census matches statements in other accounts of the tragedy. Smith, untitled, 164; Lewis, "Reminiscences," 243.

8. James T. Searcy to George Searcy, 25 August 1863, Searcy Letters, ADAH; Lumsden Diary, 21 August 1863, ADAH; Moore Memoirs, CCNMP; Magee Diary, 21 August 1863, DU; *OR* 30(4):524–25; Polk to Hindman, 21 August 1863, Polk to Cheatham, 21 August 1863, Polk to Vaughan, 21 August 1863, and Polk to Mason, 21 August 1863, all in Letters Sent, Polk's Command, NARA. According to records at CCNMP for September 1863, of the thirteen guns in the three batteries Polk sent into the Chattanooga works, only one was a rifled piece, a ten-pounder Parrott in Lumsden's Battery. That gun alone had sufficient range to reach Lilly's position, thereby accounting for the small number of return shots. Monument Inscriptions, CCNMP.

9. *OR* 30(4):523–24; *SOR* 79:407; Fraser Diary, 21 August 1863, CCNMP; Manigault, *Carolinian,* 91–92. Manigault claimed that as many as 100 wagons were lost on 21 August,

although Wilder announced the capture of only four. *OR* 30(3):123. Col. Taylor Beatty, Hill's judge advocate, acknowledged the loss of "several" wagons. Beatty Diary, 22 August 1863, UNC. At least some of the mules were saved by men from the Thirty-Ninth Alabama Infantry regiment. John R. Hurley to his sisters, 26 August 1863, Hurley Letters, VMI.

10. Thomas B. Hall to Bolling Hall Sr., 22 August 1863, and James A. Hall to Bolling Hall Sr., 26 August 1863, both in Bolling Hall Family Papers, ADAH.

11. *OR* 30(2):136; E. B. Rorie to his mother, 23 August 1863, Rorie Letter, CCNMP; Williamson, *45th Mississippi*, 119–20; Coleman Diary, 11 August 1863, UNC; *OR* 30(4):534; Smith Diary, 21 August 1863, CCNMP; Armstrong Diary, 21 August 1863, ADAH; Sterling A. M. Wood to his wife, 19 August 1863, Wood Papers, ADAH; *Augusta (Ga.) Daily Constitutionalist*, 5 September 1863; Heartsill, *Fourteen Hundred*, 142; Sparkman Diary, 17 August 1863, BPL; Liddell, *Record*, 131, 133. According to a list prepared for Bragg in October, nine of the potential crossing points were above Harrison. J. C. Wrenshall, "Report of Reconnaissance, Fords and Ferries on Tennessee River between Harrison & Hiwassee River," Bragg Papers, WRHS.

12. *OR* 30(4):532–34; Abram M. Glazener to his wife, 26 August 1863, Glazener Letters, USAHEC; Sparkman Diary, 21 August 1863, BPL; Estes Diary, 21 August 1863, MC; Bevens, *Reminiscences*, 40; *SOR* 14:276, 280; *SOR* 79:208, 221; Heartsill, *Fourteen Hundred*, 143; Seaton, *Bugle*, 38; Daniel Diary, 21 August 1863, SRNB; Dillon Diary, 21 August 1863, TSLA; *OR* 30(2):136–37; Hill, "Chickamauga," in *Battles and Leaders*, 3:639–40.

13. Brent Diary, 21 August 1863, Bragg Papers, WRHS; *OR* 30(4):525; Rand Diary, 21–22 August 1863, MDAH; *SOR* 45:82, 84, 92, 156, 211; Record of Events, Third Confederate Cavalry regiment, NARA. Several of Anderson's men took the movement order as an opportunity to desert. Richard B. Pittman to his wife, 7 [27] August 1863, Pittman Letters, CCNMP.

14. *OR* 30(4):523, 529, 531; Liddell, *Record*, 131, 133; Brent Diary, 21 August 1863, Bragg Papers, WRHS; Mackall to Hill, 22 August 1863, Hill Papers, LV; Aquila Wiley, draft article on strategy, Wiley Papers, WRHS.

15. *OR* 30(4):526–27; *SOR* 17:330; *SOR* 35:306, 310, 313, 315; Dugger Diary, *Watauga (N.C.) Democrat*, 14 May 1891.

16. *OR* 30(3):98–102; Rosecrans to Crittenden, 21 August 1863, Rosecrans to Kelton, 21 August 1863, Rosecrans to Burnside, 21 August 1863, Bond to Mr. Carter, 21 August 1863, Thoms to Lytle, 21 August 1863, and Thoms to Thomas, 21 August 1863, all in DC, Telegrams Sent, NARA.

17. *OR* 30(3):102; Alfred Pirtle to Hattie Pirtle, 21 August 1863, Pirtle Letters, FHS; Drouillard Diary, 21 August 1863, Rosecrans Papers, UCLA; Lytle, *For Honor*, 198–99; Cooley Diary, 21 August 1863, WHS; Simonds Diary, 21 August 1863, Simonds Papers, NIU; Burns Diary, 21 August 1863, CCNMP; Colburn/Gray Diary, 23 August 1863, private collection; Robert S. Walker, "Union Soldier's Diary," *Chattanooga (Tenn.) Times*, 25 April 1937, clipping in CPL; Beatty, *Citizen*, 321; Austin Diary, 21 August 1863, ALPL.

18. Rosecrans to Kelton, 21 August 1863, DC, Telegrams Sent, NARA; *OR* 30(3):109–10 [misdated 22 August]; "Summaries of the News," 309, NARA; U.S. Federal Census, 1860 and 1870, Hamilton County, Tennessee; Union Provost Marshals' Files, NARA.

19. *OR* 30(1):258, 398; Edward P. Burlingame, "History of L Co.," Putnam Collection, MAC; Grebner, *Ninth Ohio*, 139; Martling Diary, 21 August 1863, Martling Manuscript Collection, ISL; Keegan, *Diaries*, 21–22; Robert Tribbett to his brother, 21 August 1863, Tribbett Letters, IHS; Albertson, *Letters Home*, Letter 100; Bishop, *Story*, 92; Reed Diary, 21 August 1863, MHS; Bircher, *Drummer-Boy*, 70; Judson Bishop to his brother, 22 August

1863, Bishop Papers, MHS; Donahower Account, 21 August 1863, Donahower Papers, MHS; Davidson Diary, 21 August 1863, NCWM; Ferdinand Van Derveer to his wife, 22 August 1863, Van Derveer Letters, SLRH; Shera Diary, 21 August 1863, FHS; High, *Sixty-Eighth Indiana*, 52; Gates Diary, 21 August 1863, IHS; *SOR* 29:796; Mauzy, *Sixty-Eighth Indiana*, 110; Miller Journal, 21 August 1863, IHS; Floyd, *Seventy-Fifth Indiana*, 118; Essington, "Second Years History," Essington Papers, IHS; Tourgee, "Diary," 117; Morse, *Diaries*, 32; *SOR* 67:125; Taylor Diary, 21 August 1863, SRNB; Hollingsworth Diary, 21 August 1863, IHS; *SOR* 30:521; *SOR* 27:643; Turchin, "Diary," 60; George B. Turner to his mother, 23 August 1863, Turner Papers, OHS; Owen Diary, 21 August 1863, AU; Williams, *Extracts*, 87; *SOR* 63:166; *SOR* 34:477; Andrew, *Letters*, 71; *SOR* 648; *OR* 30(3):102, 104, 107, 114–16, 964–65; Kerwood, *Fifty-Seventh Indiana*, 201; Marshall Diary, 21 August 1863, OHS; *SOR* 28:12, 27; *SOR* 67:593; *SOR* 62:802; Glisan Diary, 21 August 1863, CCNMP; Robinson Diary, 21 August 1863, Regimental Papers, WRHS; Isaiah Decker to his parents, 27 August 1863, Decker Letters, SRNB; Obreiter, *Seventy-Seventh Pennsylvania*, 125; Bergun H. Brown to "Dear Friends at home," 24 August 1863, Brown Papers, IHS; Lyman S. Widney, *National Tribune*, 31 October 1901; Widney Diary, 21 August 1863, KMNMP; Lyman S. Widney to his parents, 23 August 1863, Widney Letters, CCNMP; Talbot Diary, 21 August 1863, SRNB; Edward Grosskopff to Edward Ruger, 23 June 1867, Ruger Correspondence, Thomas Papers, NARA; Kiene, *Journal*, 167–68; Stahl Diary, 21 August 1863, BGSU; Cope, *Fifteenth Ohio*, 299; Pickering Diary, 21 August 1863, HL; Welk Diary, 21 August 1863, BGSU; Davidson, *Battery A*, 82; Chapin, "Diary," 231; Willoughby Diary, 21 August 1863, Willoughby Manuscript Collection, ISL; Dean Diary, 21 August 1863, private collection; Lyon Diary, 21 August 1863, OHS; Moon Diary, 21 August 1863, KSHS; Beck Diary, 21 August 1863, KSHS; Protsman Diary, 21 August 1863, WSU; Shideler Diary, 21 August 1863, CCNMP; Ashmun Diary, August 1863, CCNMP; Doll, *Sixth Indiana*, 67; Crane Diary, 21 August 1863, CIHS; Prickitt, *Company H*, 100–101; Curry, *Four Years*, 107; Porter Diary, 21 August 1863, OHS; Holmes, *Then and Now*, 4, 117, 119–20; Stewart, *52nd O.V.I.*, 52; Thomas M. Burns to his father, 9 September 1863, Burns Letters, VT; Aten, *Eighty-Fifth Illlinois*, 98; Boon, *Letters*, 67; Kinnear, *Eighty-Sixth Illinois*, 19; Alexander M. Ayers to his wife, 21 August 1863, Ayers Papers, EU.

20. Judson Bishop to his brother, 22 August 1863, Bishop Papers, MHS; *OR* 30(3):113, 116–17; Simonds Diary, 22 August 1863, Simonds Papers, NIU; Tabler Diary, 22 August 1863, private collection; Bond to Innes, 22 August 1863, DC, Telegrams Sent, NARA; Crippin, "Diary," 279.

21. *OR* 23(2):601–2; *OR* 30(3):110.

22. *OR* 52(1):433–34, 439. For a slightly different view of Lincoln's 10 August 1863 letter, see Williams, *Lincoln and His Generals*, 275–77.

23. Rosecrans to Burnside, 22 August 1863, Rosecrans to Andrew Johnson, 22 August 1863 (two messages), Goddard to Simmons, 22 August 1863 (two messages), Thoms to Simmons, 22 August 1863, Goddard to Sweet, 22 August 1863, Thoms to Thompson, 22 August 1863, Goddard to Innes, 22 August 1863, 22 August 1863, Thoms to Hunton, 22 August 1863, and Goddard to Granger, 22 August 1863, all in DC, Telegrams Sent, NARA; Morton to Townsend, 14 August 1863, with Rosecrans endorsement, 21 August 1863, Letters Received, AGO, 1861–1870, NARA; *OR* 30(3):111–12, 126–27; Kelsey M. Adams to his brother, 24 August 1863, Adams Letters, WHS; Merrill to O'Connell, 22 August 1863, Burroughs Papers, NARA.

24. *OR* 30(3):120, 122, 135–36, 139; Records Diary and Reminiscences, 22 August 1863, Records Manuscript Collection, ISL; Campbell Journal, 22 August 1863, CCNMP; Lilly

Report, 1 September 1863, Lilly Papers, LCA; Kemper Diary, 22 August 1863, OHS; Hazen, *Narrative*, 163; Kitchell Diary, 22 August 1863, ALPL.

25. John S. McGraw to his family, 23 August 1863, McGraw Letters, ISL; Hines Diary, 22 August 1863, Hines Manuscript Collection, ISL; Kerwood, *Fifty-Seventh Indiana*, 200–201; Marshall Diary, 22 August 1863, OHS; Dewees Diary, 22 August 1863, CCNMP; *OR* 30(3):101, 114–16, 118–20, 137; *OR* 30(1):439, 469, 652; Hight, *Fifty-Eighth Indiana*, 169; Woodruff, *Fifteen Years*, 278; Gates Diary, 22 August 1863, IHS; Miller Journal, 22 August 1863, IHS; Floyd, *Seventy-Fifth Indiana*, 118; Essington, "Second Years History," Essington Papers, IHS; Parker Diary, 22 August 1863, HL; Hollingsworth Diary, 22 August 1863, IHS; *SOR* 27:643; Burns Diary, 22 August 1863, CCNMP.

26. Rosecrans to Kelton, 22 August 1863, DC, Telegrams Sent, NARA; *OR* 30(3):111, 113–14, 116, 118, 125, 966; Clark Diary, 22 August 1863, Clark Papers, USAHEC; Johnston, *Soldier Boy*, 53; Shotts Diary, 22 August 1863, SRNB; Hinchberger Diary, 22 August 1863, CCNMP; Dilworth Journal, 22 August 1863, HC; Harris Diary, 22 August 1863, CCNMP; Hapeman Diary, 22 August 1863, ALPL; Beatty, *Citizen Soldier*, 320–21; Ward Diary, 22 August 1863, Ward Papers, DP; Inskeep Diary, 22 August 1863, OHS; Wheeler Diary, 22 August 1863, OHS; Hunter, *Eighty-Second Indiana*, 54; Small Diary, 22 August 1863, IHS; Price Diary, 22 August 1863, Civil War Miscellaneous Collection, USAHEC; Shaw, *Tenth Indiana*, 211; Everett F. Abbott to his mother, 22 August 1863, Chamberlain Papers, IHS; John R. Dow to his brother, 22 August 1863, Dow Letters, FHS; Grebner, *Ninth Ohio*, 139; Davidson Diary, 22 August 1863, NCWM; Martling Diary, 22 August 1863, Martling Manuscript Collection, ISL; Reed Diary, 22 August 1863, CCNMP; Mosman, *Rough Side*, 69; Colyer Diary, 22 August 1863, ALPL; Kiene, *Journal*, 168; Stahl Diary, 22 August 1863, BGSU; Pickering Diary, 22 August 1863, HL; Welk Diary, 22 August 1863, BGSU; Cope, *Fifteenth Ohio*, 300; Davidson, *Battery A*, 82; Lyon Diary, 22 August 1863, OHS; Moon Diary, 22 August 1863, KSHS; Beck Diary, 22 August 1863, KSHS; Protsman Diary, 22 August 1863, WSU; Shideler Diary, 22 August 1863, CCNMP; William McKean to his sister, 24 August 1863, McKean Letters, OHS; Ashmun Diary, August 1863, CCNMP; Richards, *Letters*, 18–19; Doll, *Sixth Indiana*, 67; Robinson Diary, 22 August 1863, Regimental Papers, WRHS; Widney Diary, 22 August 1863, KMNMP; Lyman S. Widney to his parents, 23 August 1863, Widney Letters, CCNMP; Talbot Diary, 22 August 1863, SRNB; Busbey Diary, 22 August 1863, SRNB; Botkin Diary, 22 August 1863, Baker Correspondence, OHS; Connelly Diary, 22 August 1863, IHS; Williams Diary, 22 August 1863, CCNMP; Claggett Diary, 22 August 1863, CCNMP; Benedict Diary, 22 August 1863, SRNB; Nance and Bastian, "Old Bellefonte," 17–21.

27. Bragg to Cooper, 22 August 1863, Letters and Telegrams Sent, Bragg, NARA; *OR* 30(4) 518, 529–31; *OR* 52(2):517; *OR* 24(3):1058; Hughes, *Hardee*, 159–60.

28. Brent Diary, 22 August 1863, Bragg Papers, WRHS; *OR* 30(4):531; Mackall to Hill, 22 August 1863, Hill Papers, LV; Bragg to Hill, 22 August 1863, Letters and Telegrams Sent, Bragg, NARA; Schroeder-Lein, *Confederate Hospitals*, 122; Moore Memoirs, CCNMP; Daniel L. Kelly to "Miss Lou Honnoll," 28 August 1863, Honnoll Family Papers, EU; Andrews, *South Reports*, 347n; Armstrong, "Mrs. Davenport," *Chattanooga (Tenn.) Times*, 12 July 1937, clipping in CPL; McCallie, "Bragg Headquarters," *Chattanooga (Tenn.) Free Press*, 21 September 1938, clipping in CPL; Lumsden Diary, 22 August 1863, ADAH; Leonidas Polk to Frances Polk, 25 August 1863, Polk Papers, US; Paul, "Chattanooga Rebel," 276.

29. William H. White, CSR, NARA; Rand Diary, 28 July and 23 August 1863, MDAH; *Augusta (Ga.) Daily Constitutionalist*, 29 August 1863.

30. Polk to Cheatham, 22 August 1863, and Polk to Hindman, 22 August 1863, both in Letters Sent, Polk's Command, NARA; Rand Diary, 22 August 1863, MDAH; Freeman Diary, 22 August 1863, TSLA; Joseph W. Ward to his sister, 22 August 1863, Ward Letters, CSA Records, UTX; James R. Riggs to his sisters, 26 August 1863, Riggs Civil War Letters, ADAH; *OR* 30(4):532–34; E. B. Rorie to his mother, 23 August 1863, Rorie Letter, CCNMP; Armstrong Diary, 22 August 1863, ADAH; Heartsill, *Fourteen Hundred*, 143; Sparkman Diary, 22 August 1863, BPL; Warner, *Generals in Gray*, 53, 344.

31. *OR* 30(4):531–32, 534–35, 539; Bodenhamer Memoirs, 22–23 August 1863, TSLA; S. M. Cherry, "Church Leader," *Chattanooga (Tenn.) Free Press*, 21 September 1938, clipping in CPL; Record of Events, Third Confederate Cavalry regiment, NARA.

32. *OR* 30(4):536–37; *SOR* 13:905, 909, 929; *SOR* 17:694; Samuel R. Miller to "Dear Cath," 25 August 1863, Miller Family Papers, VHS; Bishop, "58th North Carolina," 4; J. W. Dugger Diary, *Watauga (N.C.) Democrat*, 14 May 1891; *SOR* 35:306.

33. *OR* 30(3):123, 135–36; Records Diary and Reminiscences, 23 August 1863, Records Manuscript Collection, ISL; Kemper Diary, 23 August 1863, OHS; Campbell Journal, 23 August 1863, CCNMP; Brown Diary, 22–24 August 1863, ALPL; Brown Diary, 23 August 1863, *Civil War Times Illustrated* Collection, USAHEC; Phillips, *Diary*, 156.

34. *OR* 30(3):137–40; *SOR* 25:499, 529; Kitchell Diary, 23 August 1863, ALPL; McLain Diary, 22–23 August 1863, ISHS.

35. Garfield, *Wild Life*, 293; *OR* 30(3):111–12, 132, 142; Goddard to Innes, 23 August 1863 (two messages), Bond to Innes, 23 August 1863, Thoms to Simmons, 22 August 1863, Bond to Simmons, 23 August 1863, Drouillard to Simmons, 23 August 1863, Goddard to Granger, 23 August 1863, Goddard to Dick, 23 August 1863, Thoms to Granger, 23 August 1863, and Goddard to Johnson, 23 August 1863, all in DC, Telegrams Sent, NARA; Crofts, *Third Ohio Cavalry*, 110.

36. *OR* 30(3):99, 134–35, 141–43; Prickitt, *Company H*, 101; Crofts, *Third Ohio Cavalry*, 111; Curry, *Four Years*, 107; Pape-Findley, *Fourth Ohio Cavalry*, 153; Crane Diary, 23 August 1863, Thomas Papers, NARA; Crane Diary, 23 August 1863, CIHS; Thoms to Beggs, 23 August 1863, DC, Telegrams Sent, NARA; Alfred Pirtle to his parents, 25 August 1863, Pirtle Papers, FHS; Colburn/Gray Diary, 23 August 1863, private collection; Miller Journal, 23 August 1863, IHS.

37. *OR* 30(3):106, 132–33; Shotts Diary, 23 August 1863, SRNB; Christian Diary, 23 August 1863, CCNMP; Thornton, *Gallantry*, 159; Millen Diary, 23 August 1863, SRNB; Hinchberger Diary, 23 August 1863, CCNMP; Ward Diary, 23 August 1863, Ward Papers, DP; Ward Diary, 23 August 1863, IHS; Owen Diary, 23 August 1863, AU; Dilworth Journal, 23 August 1863, HC; Loyal B. Wort to his wife, 23 August 1863, Wort Letters, BGSU; Price Diary, 23 August 1863, Civil War Miscellaneous Collection, USAHEC; Bruce Diary, 23 August 1863, ISL; Reed Diary, 23 August 1863, MHS; Moody C. Tolman to F. H. Gross, 23 August 1863, Tolman Papers, MHS; Tourgee, "Diary," 117; Parker Diary, 23 August 1863, HL; Hollingsworth Diary, 23 August 1863, IHS; Josiah D. Cotton to his wife, 23 August 1863, Cotton Papers, LC; Mosman, *Rough Side*, 69–70; Mayfield Diary, 23 August 1863, IU; Colyer Diary, 23 August 1863, ALPL; Kiene, *Journal*, 168; Pickering Diary, 23 August 1863, HL; Welk Diary, 23 August 1863, BGSU; Alpheus S. Bloomfield to his father, 23 August 1863, Bloomfield Letters, OHS; Robinson Diary, 22–23 August 1863, Regimental Papers, WRHS; Montraville Reeves to his brother, 23 August 1863, Reeves Papers, UI; Talbot Diary, 23 August 1863, SRNB; Moon Diary, 23 August 1863, KSHS; Beck Diary, 23 August 1863, KSHS; Hiram Strong to his wife, 23 August 1863, Strong Letters, CCNMP; Newlin, *Seventy-Third Illinois*, 205; Schwartz, *Diary*, 28–29; Larew Diary, 23 August 1863,

IHS; Meredith Diary, 23 August 1863, Harrisburg Civil War Roundtable Collection, USAHEC; Woodruff, *Fifteen Years*, 278–79; Hight, *Fifty-Eighth Indiana*, 169–70; Hines Diary, 23 August 1863, Hines Manuscript Collection, ISL; Opdycke Diary, 23 August 1863, OHS; Joseph Bruff to Anna Bruff, 23 August 1863, Bruff Letters, private collection; Busbey Diary, 23 August 1863, SRNB; Botkin Diary, 23 August 1863, Baker Correspondence, OHS; Walker Diary, 23 August 1863, Harrisburg Civil War Roundtable Collection, USAHEC; Connelly Diary, 23 August 1863, IHS; Claggett Diary, 23 August 1863, CCNMP; Benedict Diary, 23 August 1863, SRNB; Tilford Diary, 23 August 1863, FHS; Hempstead Diary, 23 August 1863, UM-B; Harris Diary, 23 August 1863, IHS; Kendall Diary, 23 August 1863, HL; Porter Diary, 23 August 1863, OHS; Holmes, *Then and Now*, 4, 117, 120; Boon, *Letters*, 65.

38. Thoms to Crittenden, 23 August 1863, and Thoms to Halleck, 23 August 1863, both in DC, Telegrams Sent, NARA; *OR* 30(3):131, 138.

39. Bragg to Davis, 23 August 1863, Letters and Telegrams Sent, Bragg, NARA; *OR* 52(2):517; Brent Diary, 23 August 1863, Bragg Papers, WRHS; Armstrong, *Hamilton County*, 2:17; Cumming, *Kate*, 95–96, 116; Schroeder-Lein, *Confederate Hospitals*, 122–23; *OR* 30(4):538; *Chattanooga (Tenn.) Daily Rebel*, 25 August 1863, quoted in *Macon (Ga.) Telegraph*, 27 August 1863; *Memphis Daily Appeal*, 24 August 1863; Oldham Diary, 23 August 1863, CCNMP; Newton N. Davis to his wife, 26 August 1863, Davis Letters, ADAH; Paul, "Chattanooga Rebel," 276.

40. *OR* 30(4):538–40; AAG to Cheatham, 23 August 1863, Letters Sent, Polk's Command, NARA; Brent Diary, 23 August 1863, Bragg Papers, WRHS; *SOR* 45:95, 149, 153, 714, 836; *SOR* 46:99, 184, 311; *SOR* 76:804; *SOR* 77:145; Record of Events, B/Third Confederate Engineer regiment, NARA; "Summaries of the News," NARA; Joshua K. Callaway to his wife, 27 August 1863, Callaway Papers, UTX; *SOR* 79:208, 213, 221, 426; *SOR* 14:2766, 280; Sparkman Diary, 23 August 1863, BPL; Estes Diary, 23 August 1863, MC; Bodenhamer Memoirs, 23 August 1863, TSLA; S. M. Cherry, "Church Leader," *Chattanooga (Tenn.) Free Press*, 21 September 1938, clipping in CPL; *SOR* 18:195–97; *SOR* 78:765; Freeman Diary, 23 August 1863, TSLA.

41. AAGenl to Comdg Officers, Smith's and Maney's Brigades, 24 August 1863, Letters Sent, Polk's Command, NARA; *OR* 30(4):539, 544–45; John W. Harris to his mother, 30 August 1863, Harris Letters, TSLA; Armstrong Diary, 23 August 1863, ADAH; Williamson, *45th Mississippi*, 119–20; Heartsill, *Fourteen Hundred*, 143; Daniel Diary, 23 August 1863, SRNB.

42. *OR* 30(4):540; Brown Diary, 23 August 1863, CCNMP; Samuel R. Miller to "Dear Cath," 25 August 1863, Miller Family Papers, VHS; Holmes, *Diary*, 17; *SOR* 17:323, 328, 330, 693–94; Watson Journal, 23 August 1863, CCNMP; Bishop, "58th North Carolina," 5; J. W. Dugger Diary, *Watauga (N.C.) Democrat*, 14 May 1891; *SOR* 61:441; James M. Wysor to his father, 24 August 1863, Wysor Letters, VHS; Owen, *Camp and Battle*, 265–66.

43. Warner, *Generals in Gray*, 246; Eicher and Eicher, *High Commands*, 439; Schlinger, *Last Cavalier*, 1–146; Connelly and Jones, *Politics of Command*, 55–57, 65–67; Davis, *Breckinridge*, 4–10. Five years younger than Preston, Breckinridge was Preston's second cousin, once removed.

44. *OR* 30(4):515–16, 518, 538, 540–41; Black, *Railroads*, 182–83; Claudius C. Wilson to Kate Wilson, 23 August 1863, Wilson Papers, GHS. Except for the addition of a sixty-one-mile segment of the Southern Railroad of Mississippi from Morton to Meridian, the route was the same as that taken by Bragg's entire army in the summer of 1862.

45. Augustus B. Carpenter to his parents, 23 August 1863, Carpenter Letters, YU;

Montraville Reeves to his brother, 23 August 1863, Reeves Papers, UI; Batchelor and Turner, *Batchelor-Turner Letters*, 68; Ezekiah B. Rorie to his mother, 23 August 1863, Rorie Letter, CCNMP.

CHAPTER 11

1. Goddard to Grant, 24 August 1863, and Goddard to Parsons, 24 August 1863, both in DC, Telegrams Sent, NARA; *OR* 30(3):144–45, 171; Grant, *Papers*, 9:164–65, 219, 221–23.

2. Drouillard to Simmons, 24 August 1863, Bond to Wood, 24 August 1863, and Drouillard to Crittenden, 24 August 1863 (two messages), all in DC, Telegrams Sent, NARA; *OR* 30(3):147, 153, 154; Glisan Diary, 24 August 1863, CCNMP.

3. Goddard to Granger, 24 August 1863, DC, Telegrams Sent, NARA; *OR* 30(3):155–56; *OR* 52(1):440; Winans Diary, 24 August 1863, CCNMP; Hewes, *Tenth Michigan*, 46–47; Porter Diary, 24 August 1863, OHS; Boon, *Letters*, 67; Holmes, *Then and Now*, 4, 117, 120; Royse, *115th Illinois*, 83; Van Vleck, *Leader*, 160.

4. Bond to Capt. Cramer, 24 August 1863, Goddard to Commanding Officer, Cowan, 24 August 1863, Goddard to Col. A. A. Smith, 24 August 1863, and Thoms to Halleck, 11:50 P.M., 24 August 1863, all in DC, Telegrams Sent, NARA; *SOR* 81:311–12, 320; Wilson, *Column South*, 84; Kirk, *Fifteenth Pennsylvania Cavalry*, 227; Alotta, *Civil War Justice*, 76; *OR* 30(3):147.

5. Smith Diary, 24 August 1863, CCNMP; Dilworth Journal, 24 August 1863, HC; *SOR* 40:371; Griest Diary, 24 August 1863, CCNMP; Kemper Diary, 24 August 1863, OHS; Campbell Journal, 24 August 1863, CCNMP; *OR* 30(3):151–52, 154, 166–67; *Ninety-Second Illinois*, 97–98; Atkins, *Chickamauga*, 5–6; King, *Three Years*, 108–9; *SOR* 37:525, 529; Miller Journal, 24 August 1863, IHS; Pecoy Diary, 24 August 1863, CCNMP; Burns Diary, 24 August 1863, CCNMP; Anonymous letter to "Friend Lib," 30 August 1861 [1863], Civil War Voices http://www.soldierstudies.org/blog/2011/03/camp-roberts-alabama-1861-august-30th/ (24 January 2012); Tabler Diary, 24 August 1863, private collection; Curry, *Four Years*, 107–8; Nourse Diary, 24 August 1863, DU; *OR* 30(1):910–11.

6. *OR* 30(3):149–50; Clark Diary, 24 August 1863, Clark Papers, USAHEC; Jones Diary, 24 August 1863, SRNB; Shotts Diary, 24 August 1863, SRNB; Eben P. Sturges to his mother, 24 August 1863, Sturges Papers, *Civil War Times Illustrated* Collection, USAHEC; Thornton, *Gallantry*, 159; Bloom Diary, 124 August 1863, CCNMP; Ward Diary, 24 August 1863, Ward Papers, DP; Ferdinand H. Gross to Moody C. Tolman, 24 August 1863, Tolman Papers, MHS; Mungo P. Murray to "Dear Sister Annie," 24 August 1863, Murray Letters, USAHEC; Reed Diary, 24 August 1863, Reed Papers, MHS; Tourgee, "Diary," 117; Calleb H. Carlton to his wife, 24 August 1863, Carlton Papers, LC.

7. Dilworth Journal, 24 August 1863, HC; Rogers, "Diary," 11; Mosman, *Rough Side*, 70; Post Diary, 24 August 1863, Post Papers, KC; Bergun H. Brown to "Dear Folks at home," 24 August 1863, Brown Papers, IHS; Protsman Diary, 24 August 1863, WSU; Lyman S. Widney to his parents, 23 August 1863, Widney Letters, CCNMP; Widney Diary, 24–29 August 1863, KMNMP; Kiene, *Journal*, 168; Cooley Diary, 24 August 1863, WHS; Thomas J. Frazee to his sister, 24 August 1863, Frazee Papers, ALPL; *OR* 30(3):153–54, 157; Emerson Opdycke to his wife, 24 August 1863, Opdycke Papers, OHS; *OR* 30(1):652; Marshall Diary, 24 August 1863, OHS; Busbey Diary, 24 August 1863, SRNB; Botkin Diary, 24 August 1863, Baker Correspondence, OHS; Connelly Diary, 24 August 1863, IHS; Harden, *90th Ohio*, 90.

8. *Chattanooga (Tenn.) Daily Rebel*, 25 August 1863; Brent Diary, 24 August 1863, Bragg Papers, WRHS; Johnston, *Narrative*, 253–54; *OR* 30(4):540–41; *SOR* 18:285–88; Adamson, *Thirtieth Georgia*, 32; UDC Collection, vol. 1, GDAH.

9. *Natchez (Miss.) Weekly Courier*, 20 May 1863; Brown, *Life of Walker*, 1–163; Davis, "Georgia Firebrand," 1–8; Warner, *Generals in Gray*, 323–24; Davis and Hoffman, *Confederate General*, 6:98–99; Eicher and Eicher, *High Commands*, 551; Boatner, *Civil War Dictionary*, 886; Welsh, *Medical Histories, Confederate*, 226–27; Walker to [Mary Cresswell Walker], undated fragment, Walker Papers, DU.

10. Cisco, *States Rights Gist*, 1–96; Davis and Hoffman, *Confederate General*, 2:94–95, 194–97, 6:144–45; Stroud, *Ector's Texas Brigade*, 1–125; Warner, *Generals in Gray*, 80–81, 106–7, 339; Boatner, *Civil War Dictionary*, 260, 344, 930; Eicher and Eicher, *High Commands*, 222, 256, 573; Welsh, *Medical Histories, Confederate*, 60, 80–81, 236.

11. Davis, *Breckinridge*, 3–368; Davis and Hoffman, *Confederate General*, 1:126–27; Warner, *Generals in Gray*, 34; Boatner, *Civil War Dictionary*, 82–83; Eicher and Eicher, *High Commands*, 143–44; Welsh, *Medical Histories, Confederate*, 27. For a recent study, from Bragg's perspective, see Martin, *Bragg*, 168–69, 205, 218, 232–33, 236–40, 247, 252–54. A minutely detailed account of the participation of Breckinridge and his division at Stones River can be found in Smith, *Stones River (Army of Tennessee)*, 326–75, 519–78. Smith generally validates Bragg's charges against Breckinridge. The staff officer was Theodore O'Hara, a college classmate of Breckinridge's who had been fired by Bragg at Pensacola.

12. McMurtry, *Helm*, 1–41; Johansson, "Adams," 87–103; Davis and Hoffman, *Confederate General*, 1:2–3, 3:86–87, 6:12–13; Warner, *Generals in Gray*, 1, 132, 294–95; Boatner, *Civil War Dictionary*, 3, 393, 810; Eicher and Eicher, *High Commands*, 99, 293, 515; Welsh, *Medical Histories, Confederate*, 1–2, 97–98, 207; Bragg, *Distinction*, 1–73. Helm's wife, Emilie Todd Helm, was the half-sister of Mary Todd Lincoln.

13. *Memphis Daily Appeal* 25 August 1863; Magee Diary, 24 August 1863, DU; Jack to Commanding Officers, Smith's and Maney's Brigades, 24 August 1863, Jack to Cheatham, 24 August 1863 (two messages), and Jack to Hindman, 24 August 1863 (four messages), all in Letters Sent, Polk's Command, NARA; Moorman, "Moorman Memorandum," 77; *OR* 30(4):544–45; *SOR* 45:84, 133; *SOR* 46:184, 305; Rand Diary, 24 August 1863, MDAH; Fraser Diary, 24 August 1863, CCNMP; Newton N. Davis to his wife, 26 August 1863, Davis Letters, ADAH; Thomas B. Hall to his father, 26 August 1863, Hall Family Papers, ADAH; Manigault, *Carolinian*, 92; Henry D. Clayton to Archer Anderson, 24 August 1863, Hill Papers, LV; Special Orders, No. 276, 24 August 1863, Bragg Papers, WRHS; Paul, "Chattanooga Rebel," 276–77; Livingood, "*Chattanooga Rebel*," 50; Armstrong, *Hamilton County*, 1:157.

14. *OR* 30(4):546–47, 605, 644; *SOR* 13:905, 909, 919, 929; Brown Diary, 24 August 1863, CCNMP; Watson Journal, 24 August 1863, CCNMP; *SOR* 17:323; Holmes, *Diary*, 17; J. W. Dugger Diary, *Watauga (N.C.) Democrat*, 14 May 1891; *SOR* 84:817, 821–24; Powell, *Failure*, 22–23.

15. Webster Diary, 25 August 1863, Civil War Miscellaneous Collection, USAHEC; Ward Diary, 25 August 1863, Ward Papers, DP; Sturges Diary, 25 August 1863, Sturges Papers, *Civil War Times Illustrated* Collection, USAHEC; Weaver Diary, 25 August 1863, SRNB; Keegan, *Diaries*, 22; Colyer Diary, 25 August 1863, ALPL; Kiene, *Journal*, 168; Mayfield Diary, 25 August 1863, IU; Simonds Diary, 25 August 1863, Simonds Papers, NIU; Opdycke Diary, 25 August 1863, Opdycke Papers, OHS; Alfred Pirtle to his parents, 25–26 August

1863, Pirtle Papers, FHS; Burns Diary, 25 August 1863, CCNMP; Tabler Diary, 25 August 1863, private collection; Drouillard Diary, 25 August 1863, Rosecrans Papers, UCLA; Wilson, *Column South*, 84; Kirk, *Fifteenth Pennsylvania Cavalry*, 227; *SOR* 69:341, 363, 398, 412; Palmer, *Letters*, 79–80; Albertson, *Letters Home*, Letter 100; Miller Journal, 25 August 1863, IHS; Morse, *Diaries*, 32; Ward Diary, 25 August 1863, Booth Papers, OHS; Josiah D. Cotton to his wife, 26 August 1863, Cotton Papers, LC; Andrew, *Letters*, 72; *OR* 30(3):159; Alanson R. Ryman to Jane Ryman, 25–26 August 1863, Ryman Letters, IHS; Gates Diary, 25 August 1863, IHS.

16. Garfield to Dickson, 25 August 1863, Goddard to J. H. Bingham [Brigham], 3 P.M., 25 August 1863, Goddard to Dickson, 25 August 1863, Goddard to Mrs. Goddard, 25 August 1863, Drouillard to Brannan, 25 August 1863, and Thoms to Crittenden, 25 August 1863, all in DC, Telegrams Sent, NARA; *OR* 30(3):62–63, 162–63, 165; Sanderson Journal, 16 and 24 August 1863, Sanderson Papers, OHS; Taylor, *"Supply,"* 122; Horace Porter to his mother, 25 August 1863, Porter Papers, LC. For an able summary of Rosecrans's prior argument with Meigs over horses, see Weigley, *Quartermaster General*, 261–66.

17. *OR* 30(3):164–66, 178, 190; Records Diary, 25 August 1863, Records Manuscript Collection, ISL; Griest Diary, 25 August 1863, CCNMP; McGee, *72nd Indiana*, 148; Kemper Diary, 25 August 1863, OHS; Campbell Journal, 25 August 1863, CCNMP; *SOR* 25:537; James Dawson to unknown recipient, 25 August 1863, Dawson Letters, AHS; Phillips, *Diary*, 23; Brown Diary, 25 August 1863, ALPL; Kitchell Diary, 25 August 1863, ALPL; Johnston Diary, 25 August 1863, FHS; McLain Diary, 25 August 1863, ISHS; Marshall Diary, 25 August 1863, OHS; Hines Diary, 25 August 1863, Hines Manuscript Collection, ISL; Miller Journal, 25 August 1863, IHS.

18. Shultz, *Diary*, 29; Larew Diary, 25 August 1863, IHS; McCullough Diary, 25 August 1863, ISL; Rolison Diary, 25 August 1863, *Civil War Times Illustrated* Collection, USAHEC; Roseberry Diary, 25 August 1863, EU; Stearns Diary, 25 August 1863, UM-B; *Memorial of Burnham*, 21–22; Henry C. Taylor to his parents, 25 August 1863, Taylor Papers, WHS; Hapeman Diary, 25 August 1863, ALPL; Sturges Diary, 25 August 1863, Sturges Papers, *Civil War Times Illustrated* Collection, USAHEC; Dilworth Journal, 25 August 1863, HC; Hinchberger Diary, 25 August 1863, CCNMP; Thomas Stephenson to his grandparents, 25 August 1863, Stephenson Letter, CCNMP; Reed Diary, 25 August 1863, MHS; Harold J. Bartlett to "Dear ones at home," 25 August 1863, Barlett Letters, UM-B; Everett F. Abbott to his mother, letter extract, Chamberlain Papers, IHS; Grebner, *Ninth Ohio*, 139; Morse, *Diaries*, 32; Parker Diary, 25 August 1863, HL; Miller Journal, 25 August 1863, IHS; Alanson R. Ryman to Jane Ryman, 25–26 August 1863, Ryman Letters, IHS; Gates Diary, 25 August 1863, IHS; Josiah D. Cotton to his wife, 26 August 1863, Cotton Papers, LC; Andrew, *Letters*, 72.

19. Mayfield Diary, 25 August 1863, IU; Colyer Diary, 25 August 1863, ALPL; James E. Love to "Dearest Molly," 30 August 1863, Love Papers, MHM; Mosman, *Rough Side*, 70; William H. Ball to his brother, 25 August 1863, F. Q. Ball Letters, WHS; Kiene, *Journal*, 168; Willoughby Diary, 25 August 1863, Willoughby Manuscript Collection, ISL; Robinson Diary, 25 August 1863, Regimental Papers, WRHS; George A. Cummins to M. L. Todd, 25 August 1863, Cummins Papers, ALPL; Bradley to Lee, 25 August 1863, Sheridan Papers, LC; Merrill, *Diary*, 49; Prickitt, *Company H*, 101; Connelly Diary, 25 August 1863, IHS; Opdycke Diary, 25 August 1863, Opdycke Papers, OHS; Busbey Diary, 25 August 1863, SRNB; Harden, *90th Ohio*, 90; Simmons, *84th Illinois*, 73–74; John M. Palmer to his wife, 25 August 1863, Palmer Papers II, ALPL; Benedict Diary, 25 August

1863, SRNB; Woodcock, *Southern Boy*, 182; Claggett Diary, 25 August 1863, CCNMP; Moses F. Yoder to his brother, 25 August 1863, Yoder Papers, LC; *OR* 30(3):91 [misdated 20 August].

20. *OR* 30(4):553, 554; Leonidas Polk to Frances Polk, 25 August 1863, Polk Papers, US; Brent Diary, 25 August 1863, Bragg Papers, WRHS.

21. *OR* 30(4):547–53; Special Orders, No. 228, Bragg Papers, WRHS. For a detailed description of how the food shortages affected individual soldiers, see Lt. Hannibal Paine (Twenty-Sixth Tennessee Infantry regiment) to Mary L. Paine, 5 August 1863, Paine Letters, CCNMP.

22. James A. Hall to his father, 26 August 1863, and Thomas B. Hall to his father, both in Hall Family Papers, ADAH; Magee Diary, 25 August 1863, DU; Newton N. Davis to his wife, 26 August 1863, Davis Letters, ADAH; *Augusta (Ga.) Daily Constitutionalist*, 26 August 1863; Armstrong, *Hamilton County*, 1:157; Livingood, "*Chattanooga Rebel*," 51; *Chattanooga (Tenn.) Daily Rebel*, 25 August 1863; *Memphis Daily Appeal*, 25 and 28 August 1863; *Macon (Ga.) Telegraph*, 27 August 1863. In Moorman, "Moorman Memorandum," 77, the number of cavalrymen shot is placed at two.

23. Rand Diary, 25 August 1863, MDAH; *SOR* 45:84, 154, 171, 183; *SOR* 46:289; Fraser Diary, 25 August 1863, CCNMP; Newton N. Davis to his wife, 26 August 1863, Davis Letters, ADAH; Fielder Diary, 25 August 1863, TSLA; Armstrong Diary, 25 August 1863, ADAH; Heartsill, *Fourteen Hundred*, 143–44; *SOR* 13:624, 911, 919, 925; *SOR* 79:352, 562; Brown Diary, 25 August 1863, CCNMP; *SOR* 17:304; Watson Journal, 25 August 1863, CCNMP; Holmes, *Diary*, 17; Johnston Diary, 25 August 1863, Johnston Military Papers, FHS; Owen, *Camp and Battle*, 266; Andrew J. Neal to his mother, 26 August 1863, Neal Letters, UDC Collection, vol. 4, GDAH; *SOR* 44:577; *SOR* 35:307, 310; J. W. Dugger Diary, *Watauga (N.C.) Democrat*, 14 May 1891; *SOR* 84:817, 821; Dyer, *Diary*, 19; Johnson Diary, 25 August 1863, Johnson Papers, NARA; *SOR* 78:714; Steinmeyer Memoir, UNC; Capers Diary, 25 August 1863, CI; *SOR* 77:217, 230; *SOR* 36:287, 420, 446; Pasco Diary, 25 August 1863, CCNMP; *OR* 30(4):541, 547; John C. Breckinridge to B. S. Ewell, 23 August 1863, John C. Breckinridge CSR, NARA.

24. *OR* 30(3):162, 170; Rosecrans to Halleck, 26 August 1863, DC, Telegrams Sent, NARA.

25. *OR* 30(3):171–74, 178; Garfield to Reynolds, 26 August 1863 (two messages), Garfield to E. H. Glascock, 26 August 1863, Garfield to Lytle, 26 August 1863, Goddard to Parsons, 26 August 1863, Goddard to Perkins, 26 August 1863, Goddard to Simmons, 26 August 1863, Bond to Brannan, 26 August 1863, Thoms to Sheridan, 26 August 1863 (two messages), Thoms to Granger, 26 August 1863, Cist to Steedman, 26 August 1863, and Cist to Warren, all in DC, Telegrams Sent, NARA.

26. *OR* 30(3):176–77; Campbell Journal, 26 August 1863, CCNMP; *SOR* 28:371; Records Diary and Reminiscences, 26 August 1863, Records Manuscript Collection, ISL; McGee, *72nd Indiana*, 148; Marshall Diary, 26 August 1863, OHS; Hines Diary, 26 August 1863, Hines Manuscript Collection, ISL; *SOR* 25:499, 529, 537; James Dawson to his wife, 26 August 1863, Dawson Letters, AHS; Phillips, *Diary*, 23; *Ninety-Second Illinois*, 98–99; King, *Three Years*, 109; Belser L. Wyman to his mother, 28 August 1863, Wyman Letters, ADAH.

27. *OR* 30(3):172–75, 190–91; McLain Diary, 26 August 1863, ISHS; *SOR* 41:807; *OR* 30(1):469; Miller Journal, 26 August 1863, IHS; Mayfield Diary, 26 August 1863, IU; Mosman, *Rough Side*, 70; Bennett and Haigh, *Thirty-Sixth Illinois*, 445; Record of Events,

Third Confederate Cavalry regiment (Companies A, F, G., K), NARA; Goddard to Lytle, 26 August 1863, DC, Telegrams Sent, NARA.

28. Webster Diary, 26 August 1863, Civil War Miscellaneous Collection, USAHEC; Ward Diary, 26 August 1863, Ward Papers, DP; Smith Diary, 26 August 1863, CCNMP; Carpenter Diary, 26 August 1863, SRNB; Johnston, *Soldier Boy*, 53; William S. Mitchell to his father, 26 August 1863, Mitchell Letters, CCNMP; Hough, *Soldier*, 130–32; Dilworth Journal, 26 August 1863, HC; Hinchberger Diary, 26 August 1863, CCNMP; Reed Diary, 26 August 1863, MHS; John Reed Beatty to Laura Maxfield, 26 August 1863, Beatty Papers, MHS; Andrew, *Letters*, 72; Parker Diary, 26 August 1863, HL; Rosecrans to Halleck, 26 August 1863, DC, Telegrams Sent, NARA; *OR* 30(3):171.

29. Larew Diary, 26 August 1863, IHS; Shultz, *Diary*, 29; Mayfield Diary, 26 August 1863, IU; Willoughby Diary, 26 August 1863, Willoughby Manuscript Collection, ISL; Robinson Diary, 26 August 1863, Regimental Papers, WRHS; Isaiah Decker to his parents, 27 August 1863, Decker Letters, SRNB; Mosman, *Rough Side*, 70; Kiene, *Journal*, 168–69; Shideler Diary, 26 August 1863, CCNMP; Lyon Diary, 26 August 1863, OHS; Protsman Diary, 26 August 1863, WSU; Jonas Jones and Samuel Heath to "Friend Lodge," 26 August 1863, Lodge Collection, UI; *OR* 30(3):176–79; Nourse Diary, 26 August 1863, DU; Peletiah Bond to Cornelia Bond, 26 August 1863, "Bond & Edwards Civil War Letters," http://www.genealogy105.com/1863p2.html (2 April 2012); Marshall Diary, 26 August 1863, OHS; Connelly Diary, 26 August 1863, IHS; Tuttle, *Kentucky Captain*, 140–41; Walker Diary, 26 August 1863, Harrisburg Civil War Roundtable Collection, USAHEC; Williams Diary 26 August 1863, CCNMP; Stearns Diary, 26 August 1863, UM-B; Roseberry Diary, 26 August 1863, EU; Partridge, *Ninety-Sixth Illinois*, 153.

30. Brent Diary, 26 August 1863, Bragg Papers, WRHS. For glimpses of Buckner's spy network, see *OR* 30(4):540, 554; and Johnston Diary, 19, 23, and 27 August 1863, Johnston Military Papers, FHS.

31. *OR* 30(4):556–57; Special Orders, No. 229, Bragg Papers, WRHS; E. A. Flewellen to S. H. Stout, 26 August 1863, and Stout endorsement, Stout Papers, MC; Jack to Cheatham and Hindman, 26 August 1863 (two messages), Jack to Cheatham, 26 August 1863, and Jack to J. K. Jackson, 26 August 1863, all in Letters Sent, Polk's Command, NARA; *Chattanooga (Tenn.) Daily Rebel*, 26 August 1863, as reprinted in *Memphis Daily Appeal*, 28 August 1863, *Augusta (Ga.) Daily Constitutionalist*, 30 August 1863, and *Macon (Ga.) Telegraph*, 27 August 1863; Armstrong, *Hamilton County*, 1:156; Livingood, "*Chattanooga Rebel*," 46.

32. Brown Notebook, 26 August 1863, CCNMP; Fielder Diary, 26 August 1863, TSLA; *SOR* 46:184; Rand Diary, 26 August 1863, MDAH; Fraser Diary, 26 August 1863, CCNMP; James A. Hall to Bolling Hall Sr., 26 August 1863, Bolling Hall Family Papers, ADAH; Newton N. Davis to his wife, 26 August 1863, Davis Letters, ADAH; Armstrong Diary, 26 August 1863, ADAH; Beatty Diary, 26 August 1863, UNC; Sparkman Diary, 26 August 1863, BPL; Estes Diary, 26 August 1863, MC; *SOR* 14:276; *SOR* 79:424; Heartsill, *Fourteen Hundred*, 144; Abram M. Glazener to his wife, 26 August 1863, Glazener Letters, USAHEC; Daniel Diary, 26 August 1863, Civil War Miscellaneous Collection, USAHEC; Joseph W. Ward to his sister, 26 August 1863, Ward Letters, CSA Records, UTX.

33. Johnson Diary, 26 August 1863, NARA; Black, *Letters*, 58; *SOR* 79:566, 579; Andrew J. Neal to his mother, 26 August 1863, Neal Letters, UDC Collection, vol. 4, GDAH; Johnston Diary, 26 August 1863, Johnston Military Papers, FHS; J. W. Dugger Diary, *Watauga (N.C.) Democrat*, 14 May 1891; *SOR* 84:817; Davis Diary, 26 August 1863,

TSLA; Leverich Diary, 26 August 1863, LSU; Owen, *Camp and Battle*, 266–67; Allardice, *Confederate Colonels*, 248; Capers Diary, 24–26 August 1863, CI; Jones, *Enlisted*, 108–9; *SOR* 35:206, 208, 210, 282, 340, 346; Green, *Johnny Green*, 85; Jackman Journal, 26 August 1863, LC; Pasco Diary, 26 August 1863, CCNMP.

34. *OR* 30(3):217; *SOR* 28:371; Kemper Diary, 27 August 1863, OHS; Eli Lilly Report, 1 September 1863, Lilly Papers, LCA; Henry Campbell Journal, 27 August 1863, CCNMP; *SOR* 25:499, 525, 529; Phillips, *Diary*, 24; James A. Dawson to his wife, 28 August 1863, Dawson Letters, AHS; Kitchell Diary, 27 August 1863, ALPL; *SOR* 34:207, 219, 236, 241; Johnston Diary, 27 August 1863, FHS.

35. *OR* 30(3):184–85, 202; Frankenberry Diary, 27 August 1863, WVU; Rosecrans to Meigs, 27 August 1863, DC, Telegrams Sent, NARA. Construction of the Nashville & Northwestern Railroad had commenced before the outbreak of the war, but it had made little progress westward by August 1863. Governor Johnson's involvement, and also that of Colonel Innes, would become problematic by early 1864, but by then Rosecrans no longer commanded the Department of the Cumberland. *OR*, Series III, 5:943–44.

36. Garfield to Gillem, 27 August 1863, Garfield to Thompson, 27 August 1863 (two messages), Goddard to Lytle, 27 August 1863, Goddard to Granger, 27 August 1863, Goddard to Lt. Sanderson, 27 August 1863, Goddard to Simmons, 27 August 1863, Thoms to Granger, 27 August 1863 (two messages), and Cist to Reynolds, 27 August 1863, all in DC, Telegrams Sent, NARA; Goddard to Sheridan, 27 August 1863, DC, Letters Sent, NARA; *OR* 30(3):184–86, 192–93.

37. Thoms to Halleck, 27 August 1863, DC, Telegrams Sent, NARA; Shultz, *Diary*, 29; Meredith Diary, 27 August 1863, Harrisburg Civil War Roundtable Collection, USAHEC; Larew Diary, 27 August 1863, IHS; *OR* 30(3):185–89, 193–94; Simonds Diary, 27 August 1863, Simonds Papers, NIU; Colburn/Gray Diary, 27 August 1863, private collection; Bircher, *Drummer-Boy*, 70–71; Reed Diary, 27 August 1863, MHS; Hollingsworth Diary, 27 August 1863, IHS.

38. Webster Diary, 27 August 1863, Civil War Miscellaneous Collection, USAHEC; Harris Diary, 27 August 1863, CCNMP; Millen Diary, 27 August 1863, SRNB; Hinchberger Diary, 27 August 1863, CCNMP; Hollingsworth Diary, 27 August 1863, IHS; Colyer Diary, 27 August 18963, ALPL; Connelly Diary, 27 August 1863, IHS; Williams Diary, 27 August 1863, CCNMP; Schwartz, *Diary*, 10; Crippin, "Diary," 279; McCullough Diary, 27 August 1863, ISL; Christian Diary, 26–27 August 1863, CCNMP; Shotts Diary, 26–27 August 1863, SRNB; Sturges Diary, 27 August 1863, Sturges Papers, *Civil War Times Illustrated* Collection, USAHEC; Dilworth Journal, 27 August 1863, HC; McMahan, "Battle," Twenty-First Ohio Infantry Regiment Collection, BGSU; Quinlin and Haugh, *Duty*, 46; Simonds Diary, 27 August 1863, Simonds Papers, NIU; Burns Diary, 27 August 1863, CCNMP; Hapeman Diary, 27 August 1863, ALPL; Mosman, *Rough Side*, 70; James Prosser to Sarah A. Prosser, 27 August 1863, Neeley Manuscripts, IU; Howe Diary, 27 August 1863, IHS; Tuttle, *Kentucky Captain*, 141.

39. *OR* 30(3):106, 186, 194; McCahan Diary, 27 August 1863, HSP; Kendall Diary, 27 August 1863, HL; Merrill, *Diary*, 50; Persons Diary, 27 August 1863, WHS; Harris Diary, 27 August 1863, IHS; *OR* 16(1):838–41, (2):289–90. For modern accounts of the McCook-Gurley episode, see Whalen and Whalen, *Fighting McCooks*, 134–40, and Steenburn, *Man Called Gurley*, 106–30. Gurley himself was captured in October 1863, tried by a military court for McCook's "murder" in early 1864, convicted and sentenced to death, but never executed. Frank B. Gurley, CSR, NARA.

40. Brent Diary, 27 August 1863, Bragg Papers, WRHS; *Chattanooga (Tenn.) Daily Rebel*,

28 and 29 August 1863, reprinted in *Memphis Daily Appeal*, 31 August 1863; Joseph Branch O'Bryan to his sister, 30 August 1863, O'Bryan Letters, TSLA; Moorman, "Moorman Memorandum," 77; William W. Mackall to Daniel H. Hill, 28 August 1863, Hill Papers, LV; Willie Moore to "Miss Jennie," 29 August 1863, Parsons Letters, ADAH; Richard B. Pittman to his wife, 7 [27] August 1863, Pittman Letters, CCNMP; Armstrong, *Hamilton County*, 1:157; Campbell Journal, 27 August 1863, CCNMP.

41. Brent Diary, 27 August 1863, Bragg Papers, WRHS; Willie Moore to "Miss Jennie," 29 August 1863, Parsons Letters, ADAH; James A. Hall to Bolling Hall Sr., 29 August 1863, Hall Family Papers, ADAH.

42. Leonidas Polk to Frances Polk, 27 August 1863, Polk Papers, US; J. Stoddard Johnston to William W. Mackall, 27 August 1863, and William W. Mackall to Daniel H. Hill, 28 August 1863, both in Hill Papers, LV; Johnston Diary, 27 August 1863, Johnston Military Papers, FHS.

43. Polk to Cheatham, 27 August 1863, and Polk to Jackson, 27 August 1863, both in Letters Sent, Polk's Command, NARA; Fielder Diary, 27 August 1863, TSLA; Brown Notebook, 27 August 1863, CCNMP; Willie Moore to "Miss Jennie," 29 August 1863, Parsons Letters, ADAH; Rand Diary, 27 August 1863, MDAH; Fraser Diary, 27 August 1863, CCNMP; *Chattanooga (Tenn.) Daily Rebel*, 30 August 1863; Sparkman Diary, 27 August 1863, BPL; Hezekiah Rabb to his wife, 27 August 1863, Rabb Letters, Michael Musick Collection, USAHEC; Bodenhamer Memoirs, 27 August 1863, TSLA; Robert A. Jarman Account, CCNMP; Freeman Diary, 27 August 1863, TSLA; Johnson Diary, 27 August 1863, Johnson Papers, NARA; *SOR* 78:714; *SOR* 79:39, 352.

44. William W. Mackall to Daniel H. Hill, 28 August 1863, Hill Papers, LV; *OR* 30(2):520, 577; Stevenson, "Smith," 42; *SOR* 13:61; Sloan Diary, 27–28 August 1863, TSLA; Leverich Diary, 27 August 1863, LSU; Johnston Diary, 28 August 1863, Johnston Military Papers, FHS.

45. A. P. Adamson to N. C. Adamson, 28 August 1863, UDC Collection, vol. 1, GDAH; Adamson, *Thirtieth Georgia*, 32–33; George A. Gordon to "Dear Krilla," 30 August 1863, Gordon Letters, UTX; Reynolds, *Worthy*, 102; Capers Diary, 27–29 August 1863, Capers Papers, CI; Jones, *Enlisted*, 109; Ellis Diary, 27 August 1863, LSU; Pasco Diary, 27 August 1863, CCNMP; Ives, *Journal and Letters*, 40–41; *SOR* 61:455; *SOR* 35:213, 266, 326, 404; Bush Diary, 27 August 1863, CCNMP; Jackman Journal, 27 August 1863, LC; Green, *Johnny Green*, 85; *SOR* 13:698. The location of some units is estimated, but is in accord with the fragmentary evidence listed above. Distances are taken from station lists in David L. Bright, "Confederate Railroads," http://www.csa-railroads.com (5 May 2013).

CHAPTER 12

1. *OR* 30(3):202–3; Drouillard to McCook, 28 August 1863, and Bond to Beggs, 28 August 1863, both in DC, Telegrams Sent, NARA; Tabler Diary, 28 August 1863, private collection.

2. *OR* 30(3):187, 200, 203–5; Tabler Diary, 28 August 1863, private collection; Burns Diary, 28 August 1863, CCNMP; Austin Diary, 28 August 1863, ALPL; Crippin, "Diary," 279; James S. McCarty to his brother, 29 August 1863, McCarty Letters, SRNB; Simonds Diary, 28 August 1863, Simonds Papers, NIU; Colburn/Gray Diary, 28 August 1863, private collection; Pecoy Diary, 28 August 1863, CCNMP; Cooley Diary, 28 August 1863, WHS; Hunter, *Eighty-Second Indiana*, 54; *SOR* 34:162, 171, 174; Drouillard to Burroughs, 28 August 1863, and Drouillard to Stanley, 28 August 1863, both in DC, Telegrams Sent,

NARA; James W. Sligh to his wife, 28 August 1863, and Sligh Diary, 28 August 1863, both in Sligh Family Papers, UM-B; Roseberry Diary, 28 August 1863, EU.

3. Newlin, *Seventy-Third Illinois*, 206; Burroughs to O'Connell, 28 August 1863, Burroughs Papers, NARA; William M. Parkinson to his brother, 7 September 1863, Parkinson Papers, OHS; Heg, *Letters*, 238; *OR* 30(1):496–97, 528, 929; Meredith Diary, 28 August 1863, Harrisburg Civil War Roundtable Collection, USAHEC; Shultz, *Diary*, 29; McCullough Diary, 28 August 1863, ISL; *SOR* 22:25, 61, 555; *SOR* 33:550; *SOR* 88:5; Himoe Diary, 28 August 1863, NAHA; John A. Martin to his sister, 30 August 1863, Martin Letters, KSHS; Mayfield Diary, 28 August 1863, IU; Lathrop, *Fifty-Ninth Illinois*, 213–14; Mosman, *Rough Side*, 70; Kiene, *Journal*, 169; Phillips Diary, 28 August 1863, HL; Pickering Diary, 28 August 1863, HL; Willoughby Diary, 28 August 1863, ISL; Lyon Diary, 28 August 1863, OHS; Shideler Diary, 28 August 1863, CCNMP; Riley, *Diary*, 52; Cummins Diary, 28 August 1863, Cummins Papers, ALPL. In a letter home, George Cummins was bitter: "For a year past Steve had not been able for the service. I had tried several times to get a discharge for him but in vain, but now he is done soldiering, they can't drive him any more, the demon's gun no more will point toward his breast. He will no more stand on the picket post while the assassin lurks in the bushes waiting a chance to send the deadly missle into his breast." George A. Cummins to "My Cher Fille," 30 August 1863, Cummins Papers, ALPL.

4. Webster Diary, 28 August 1863, Civil War Miscellaneous Collection, USAHEC; Edmonds Diary, 28 August 1863, USAHEC; Johnston, *Soldier Boy*, 54; Charles Bailer to his sister, 28 August 1863, Bailer Letters, Regimental Papers, WRHS; Harris Diary, 28 August 1863, CCNMP; Bloom Diary, 28 August 1863, CCNMP; Shotts Diary, 28 August 1863, SRNB; Dilworth Journal, 28 August 1863, HC; Hinchberger Diary, 28 August 1863, CCNMP; Keegan, *Diaries*, 23; Keil, *Thirty-Fifth Ohio*, 120; Martling Diary, 28 August 1863, Martling Manuscript Collection, ISL; Bircher, *Drummer-Boy*, 71; Donahower Account, 28 August 1863, Donahower Papers, MHS; Albertson, *Letters Home*, Letter 101; Turchin, "Diary," 60; *OR* 30(3):200; *OR* 30(1):468–69; Parker Diary, 28 August 1863, HL; Miller Journal, 28 August 1863, IHS.

5. Griest Diary, 28 August 1863, CCNMP; Records Diary, 28 August 1863, and Records Reminiscences, both in Records Manuscript Collection, ISL; Kemper Diary, 28 August 1863, OHS; Campbell Journal, 28 August 1863, CCNMP; *OR* 30(3):203–4; Marshall Diary, 28 August 1863, OHS; Dewees Diary, 28 August 1863, CCNMP; *SOR* 25:537; Phillips, *Diary*, 24; Johnston Diary, 28 August 1863, FHS; Brown Diary, 28 August 1863, ALPL; *SOR* 41:807; McLain Diary, 28 August 1863, ISHS. For an example of cross-river repartee by opposing pickets, see Kirkland N. Cowing to his brother, 30 August 1863, Cowing Letter, private collection.

6. Tuttle, *Kentucky Captain*, 141; Busbey Diary, 28 August 1863, SRNB; Botkin Diary, 28 August 1863, Baker Correspondence, OHS; Connelly Diary, 28 August 1863, IHS; Glisan Diary, 28 August 1863, CCNMP; Palmer Journal, 28 August 1863, CCNMP; Williams Diary, 28 August 1863, CCNMP; Walker Diary, 28 August 1863, Harrisburg Civil War Roundtable Collection, USAHEC; Howe Diary, 28 August 1863, IHS; Claggett Diary, 28 August 1863, CCNMP; Woodcock, *Southern Boy*, 182–83; *OR* 30(3):970.

7. Merrill to O'Connell, 7:45 P.M., 28 August 1863, Burroughs Papers, NARA; Meredith Diary, 28 August 1863, Harrisburg Civil War Roundtable Collection, USAHEC; Shultz, *Diary*, 29; Himoe Diary, 28 August 1863, NAHA; Nourse Diary, 28 August 1863, DU; Crofts, *Third Ohio Cavalry*, 111; Prickitt, *Company H*, 102; Crane Diary, 28 August 1863, Thomas Papers, NARA; Crane Diary, 28 August 1863, CIHS; Hempstead Diary, 28 August

1863, UM-B; *SOR* 41:752; *OR* 30(3):201–2; Goddard to Brannan, 28 August 1863, DC, Telegrams Sent, NARA; *OR* 30(1):468–69; Miller Journal, 28 August 1863, IHS.

8. Rosecrans to Halleck, 28 August 1863, DC, Telegrams Sent, NARA; *OR* 30(3):199; Frankenberry Diary, 28 August 1863, WVU; Sturges Diary, 28 August 1863, Sturges Papers, *Civil War Times Illustrated* Collection, USAHEC; *OR* 30(1):468–69; Floyd, *Seventy-Fifth Indiana*, 119; Miller Journal, 28 August 1863, IHS; J. Newt Conklin to Gen. H. V. Boynton, 30 January 1902, Unit Files, CCNMP.

9. Brent Diary, 28 and 29 August 1863, Bragg Papers, WRHS; *OR* 30(4):561; Mackall to Hill, 28 August 1863, and J. Stoddard Johnston to "My Dear Sir," 27 August 1863, both in Hill Papers, LV; Polk to Frances Polk, 27 August 1863, Polk Papers, US; Brent to Beard, 28 August 1863, Brent Papers, TU.

10. Cheatham to Jackson, 28 August 1863, Letters Sent, Polk's Command, NARA; Fielder Diary, 28 August 1863, TSLA; Magee Diary, 28 August 1863, DU; Brown Notebook, 28 August 1863, CCNMP; Beatty Diary, 28 August 1863, UNC; Heartsill, *Fourteen Hundred*, 144–45; Seaton, *Bugle*, 38; Sparkman Diary, 28 August 1863, BPL; Perdue and Perdue, *Cleburne*, 205; Quintard, *Doctor Quintard*, 81–82; *SOR* 3:255–56; William D. Cole to his wife, 28 August 1863, Cole Letters, Civil War Miscellaneous Collection, USAHEC.

11. *SOR* 3:255–56; Dillon Diary, 28 August 1863, TSLA; *SOR* 18:195, 199; *SOR* 78, 714, 765; *SOR* 79:39, 246, 352; Johnson Diary, 25–28 August 1863, Johnson Papers, NARA; A. P. Adamson to N. C. Adamson, 28 August 1863, UDC Collection, vol. 1, GDAH; Adamson, *Thirtieth Georgia*, 33; George A. Gordon to "Dear Krilla," 30 August 1863, Gordon Letters, UTX; Reynolds, *Worthy*, 102; Capers Diary, 28 August 1863, CI; Pasco Diary, 27–28 August 1863, CCNMP; Bush Diary, 28 August 1863, CCNMP; Jackman Journal, 28 August 1863, LC; Green, *Johnny Green*, 85; *SOR* 35:408, 425; *OR* 30(4):562; Sloan Diary, 28 August 1863, TSLA; Leverich Diary, 28 August 1863, LSU.

12. *OR* 30(1):926–28; Curry, *Four Years*, 108; *SOR* 61:546, 556; George Kryder to Elisabeth Kryder, 30 August 1863, Kryder Papers, BGSU; Marshall, *Niver*, 21; Crofts, *Third Ohio Cavalry*, 111; Feagles Diary, 29 August 1863, CCNMP; Prickitt, *Company H*, 102; Elijah S. Watts to Edward Ruger, 17 June 1867, O. O. Smith to Edward Ruger, 27 April 1867, Ruger Correspondence, and Crane Diary, 29 August 1863, all in Thomas Papers, NARA; Crane Diary, 29 August 1863, CIHS; Pape-Findley, *Fourth Ohio Cavalry*, 153; Record of Events, Company G, Third Confederate Cavalry regiment, NARA.

13. *OR* 30(1):485, 528–29; *OR* 30(3):219, 970–72; Heg, *Letters*, 238–39, 246–48; *SOR* 33:571, 577, 587; John A. Martin to his sister, 30 August 1863, Martin Letters, KSHS; James E. Love to "Dearest Molly," 30 August 1863, Love Papers, MHM; *Report of the Adjutant General of the State of Kansas*, 120–21; Fisher, *Staff Officer's Story*, 78; *SOR* 22:49, 61, 67, 73, 555, 564, 567, 572, 574, 576; James G. Watson to [addressee unknown], 30 August 1863, Watson Letters, UI; Himoe Diary, 29 August 1863, NAHA; *SOR* 88:6, 25, 29, 33, 38, 48, 54.

14. *OR* 30(1):485, 529, 926–28; Meredith Diary, 29 August 1863, Harrisburg Civil War Roundtable Collection, USAHEC; Shultz, *Diary*, 30; McCullough Diary, 29 August 1863, ISL; Larew Diary, 29 August 1863, IHS; Isaac P. Rule to his brother, 31 August 1863, Rule Letters, HPL; William M. Parkinson to his brother, 7 September 1863, Parkinson Papers, OHS; Newlin, *Seventy-Third Illinois*, 207; Thomas Diary, 29 August 1863, UT. The distance to be spanned was 1,254 feet. Although Lieutenant Burroughs was instructed to use no more than fifty-six pontoon boats, the number counted by the Pioneer Brigade personnel varied from fifty-nine to seventy-six. If the pontoons were spaced at twenty-foot intervals, the lower number is most likely nearer the actual number used. For an excellent

generic account of a pontoon bridge, in both word and diagram, see Coggins, *Arms and Equipment*, 104–5.

15. Drouillard Diary, 29 August 1863, Rosecrans Papers, UCLA; *Cincinnati Daily Commercial*, 4 September 1863; Frankenberry Diary, 29 August 1863, WVU; Kirk, *Fifteenth Pennsylvania Cavalry*, 228; *SOR* 69:341; Heg, *Letters*, 248; John A. Martin to his sister, 30 August 1863, Martin Letters, KSHS; Beatty, *Citizen Soldier*, 323–24; Hiram Russell to his wife and children, 30 August 1863, Russell Letters, SRNB; McCullough Diary, 29 August 1863, ISL; *OR* 30(1):497, 529; *OR* 30(3):971–72; *SOR* 23:19, 48–49; Patterson Diary, 29 August 1863, MHM; Colyer Diary, 29 August 1863, ALPL; *SOR* 66:685, 691, 702, 712, 726; Post Diary, 29 August 1863, KC.

16. Hempstead Diary, 29 August 1863, UM-B; John Wasson to his uncle, 18 October 1863, Wasson Letters, DeYoung Collection, WMU; Pirtle, "Leaves," CIHS; Alfred Pirtle to "Dear Jim," 30 August 1863, Pirtle Letters, FHS; Eugene E. Comstock to his parents, 30 August 1863, Comstock Papers, WHS; *OR* 30(3):220; Pecoy Diary, 29 August 1863, CCNMP; Cummins Diary, 29 August 1863, Cummins Papers, ALPL; Cooley Diary, 29 August 1863, WHS; Burns Diary, 29 August 1863, CCNMP; Tabler Diary, 29 August 1863, private collection; Colburn/Gray Diary, 29 August 1863, private collection; Austin Diary, 29 August 1863, ALPL; Crippin, "Diary," 279; James S. McCarty to his sister, 29 August 1863, McCarty Letters, SRNB; Riley, *Diary*, 52; Simonds Diary, 29 August 1863, Simonds Papers, NIU.

17. *OR* 30(3):215–16; Goddard to Thomas, 9:50 A.M., 29 August 1863, DC, Letters Sent, NARA; Davidson Diary, 29 August 1863, NCWM; Keil, *Thirty-Fifth Ohio*, 121; Albertson, *Letters Home*, Letter 101; Bishop, *Story*, 93; Martling Diary, 29 August 1863, Martling Manuscript Collection, ISL; Harry Van Derveer to "Dear Mother," 30 August 1863, Van Derveer Letters, SLRH.

18. *OR* 30(1):220–21, 468–69; Hollingsworth Diary, 29 August 1863, IHS; Morse, *Diaries*, 32; Taylor Diary, 29 August 1863, SRNB; Williams, *Extracts*, 88; Ward Diary, 29 August 1863, Booth Papers, OHS; Owen Diary, 29 August 1863, AU; Miller Journal, 29 August 1863, IHS; *SOR* 28:371; Banta Diary, 29 August 1863, CCNMP; Kemper Diary, 29 August 1863, OHS; Records Diary and Reminiscences, 29 August 1863, Records Manuscript Collection, ISL; Griest Diary, 29 August 1863, CCNMP; Phillips, *Diary*, 24; Kitchell Diary, 29 August 1863, ALPL; Hines Diary, 29 August 1863, Hines Manuscript Collection, ISL; John S. McGraw to "Dear Wife and Children," 30 August 1863, McGraw Letters, ISL; Kerwood, *Fifty-Seventh Indiana*, 201; Marshall Diary, 29 August 1863, OHS; Campbell Journal, 29 August 1863, CCNMP; *Chattanooga (Tenn.) Daily Rebel*, 30 August 1863; *OR* 23(2):968; Brent Diary, 29 August 1863, Bragg Papers, WRHS.

19. Joseph Bruff to Anna Bruff, 29 August 1863, Bruff Letters, private collection; David W. Norton to "DearMollie," 24–29 August 1863, Norton Letters, ALPL; Thomas Prickett to "Dearest Matilda," 29 August 1863, Prickett Letters, IHS; Busbey Diary, 29 August 1863, SRNB; Botkin Diary, 29 August 1863, Baker Correspondence, OHS; Glisan Diary, 29 August 1863, CCNMP; Benedict Diary, 29 August 1863, SRNB; Willis Jones to Rachel Jones, 29 August 1863, Jones Papers, NC; McKee Diary, 29 August 1863, http://mckee-burns.pasttracker.com/mckee/cw_mckee/mckee_robert_t_cw_diary_1 (15 June 2013); John E. Cummins to "Dear Hattie," 29 August 1863, McCray Research Archive, BGSU; Howe Diary, 29 August 1863, IHS; Huntzinger Diary, 29 August 1863, http://www.lafavre.us/huntzinger/hunt_3.htm (23 May 2016); *OR* 30(3):220, 222.

20. Newlin, *Seventy-Third Illinois*, 206–7; Morledge Diary, 29 August 1863, KMNMP; Christian Diary, 29 August 1863, CCNMP; Shotts Diary, 29 August 1863, SRNB; Millen

Diary, 29 August 1863, SRNB; William R. Stookey to Helen Stookey, 29 August 1863, Stookey Letters, IHS; Daniel O'Leary to "My dear Wife," 29 August 1863, O'Leary Letters, KMNMP; Shanks Diary, 29 August 1863, BGSU; Dilworth Journal, 29 August 1863, HC; Hinchberger Diary, 29 August 1863, CCNMP; Ward Diary, 29 August 1863, Ward Papers, DP; Nupp Diary, 29 August 1863, CCNMP; Weaver Diary, 29 August 1863, SRNB; John W. Baldwin to his wife, 29 August 1863, Baldwin Papers, OHS; Edmonds Diary, 29 August 1863, USAHEC; *Memorial of Burnham*, 22–23.

21. Kiene, *Journal*, 169; Pickering Diary, 29 August 1863, HL; Willoughby Diary, 29 August 1863, Willoughby Manuscript Collection, ISL; Dean Diary, 29 August 1863, private collection; Henry Richards to his father, 29 August 1863, Gilbert-Richards Papers, MU; Wilson, *Memoirs*, 194–95; Shideler Diary, 29 August 1863, CCNMP; Bergun H. Brown to his parents and sisters, 29 August 1863, Brown Papers, IHS; Robinson Diary, 29 August 1863, Regimental Papers, WRHS; Oliver P. Hunt to "Jennie," 29 August 1863, Hunt letters, UFL; *OR* 30(3):223, 239; Winans Diary, 29 August 1863, CCNMP; Hewes, *Tenth Michigan*, 48; Holmes, *Then and Now*, 4, 120; Porter Diary, 29 August 1863, OHS; Armstrong Diary, 29 August 1863, CCNMP; Schwartz, *Diary*, 10; Robinson Diary, 29 August 1863, ALPL; Patton Diary, 29 August 1863, CCNMP; McAdams, *One Hundred and Thirteenth Ohio*, 37.

22. *OR* 30(3):170, 199, 213, 222–23; Goddard to Granger, 29 August 1863 (two messages), Goddard to Commanding Officer, McMinnville, 11:45 P.M., 29 August 1863, Goddard to Simmons, 29 August 1863, Rosecrans to Totten, 29 August 1863, Garfield to Bassford, 29 August 1863, and Thoms to Halleck, 29 August 1863, all in DC, Telegrams Sent, NARA; Hunt, *Colonels in Blue*, 25.

23. Brent Diary, 29 August 1863, Bragg Papers, WRHS; *OR* 30(4):565; Mackall to Hill, 29 August 1863, Hill Papers, LV.

24. Brent Diary, 29 August 1863, Bragg Papers, WRHS; Moorman, "Moorman Memorandum," 78; Record of Events, Company G, Third Confederate Cavalry regiment, NARA.

25. "Memorandum furnished by Col. B. J. Hill, 35th Tenn. Regt Aug 29, 1863," Bragg Papers, WRHS.

26. *OR* 30(4):564. For negative assessments of Bragg during this period, see especially Connelly, *Autumn of Glory*, 168–70; and Hallock, *Bragg*, 46–48. Only slightly less judgmental is Cozzens, *This Terrible Sound*, 47–49. Also critical, though by no means objective, is Hill, "Chickamauga," in *Battles and Leaders*, 3:640. It is not difficult to make Bragg appear confused and irresolute during the period 21–29 August 1863 if no direct connection is made between actions taken on a given day and the specific information available at that moment, particularly if the writer disregards any pretense of a detailed timeline. Performed in strict chronological order, however, a careful analysis linking Bragg's knowledge at a particular instant to his subsequent decisions yields a considerably more sympathetic picture, that of a commander responding rationally to developing events as he perceived them, however misguided hindsight eventually would show the response to be.

27. Fielder Diary, 29 August 1863, TSLA; Brown Notebook, 29 August 1863, CCNMP; Magee Diary, 29 August 1863, DU; Robert L. Bliss to his mother, 29 August 1863, Bliss Letters, ADAH; James A. Hall to Bolling Hall Sr., 29 August 1863, Bolling Hall Family Papers, ADAH; William H. Moore to "Miss Jennie," 29 August 1863, Parsons Letters, ADAH; *Chattanooga (Tenn.) Daily Rebel*, 30 August 1863; J. N. Honnoll to C. C. Honnoll, 29 August 1863, Honnoll Family Papers, EU; *SOR* 14:278; *Memphis Daily Appeal*, 31 August 1863, quoting *Chattanooga (Tenn.) Daily Rebel*, 29 August 1863; *Augusta (Ga.) Chronicle*,

4 September 1863, quoting *Chattanooga (Tenn.) Daily Rebel*, 1 September 1863; Sparkman Diary, 29 August 1863, BPL.

28. Brent Diary, 29 August 1863, Bragg Papers, WRHS; *OR* 30(4):564; Fielder Diary, 29 August 1863, TSLA; Armstrong Diary, 29 August 1863, ADAH; Estes Diary, 29 August 1863, MC; Freeman Diary, 29 August 1863, TSLA; Dillon Diary, 29 August 1863, TSLA; William D. Cole to his wife, 28–31 August 1863, Civil War Miscellaneous Collection, USAHEC; *SOR* 18:195, 198, 285; *SOR* 78:765–66, 793, 801; *SOR* 79:246; Johnson Diary, 29 August 1863, Johnson Papers, NARA; Moore Diary, 29 August 1863, UDC Collection, GDAH; Bolling Hall, Jr. to Bolling Hall Sr., 29 August 1863, Bolling Hall Family Papers, ADAH; Sloan Diary, 29 August 1863, TSLA; Leverich Diary, 29 August 1863, LSU; Dyer, *Diary*, 19; Corbitt Diary, 29 August 1863, EU; Stevenson, "Smith," 42; Shields Diary, 29 August 1863, http://freepages.genealogy.rootsweb.ancestry.com/~sassytazzy/family/surnames/shields (1 February 2009); George A. Gordon to "Dear Krilla," 30 August 1863, Gordon Letters, UTX; Capers Diary, 28 August 1863, Capers Papers, CI; Jackman Journal, 29 August 1863, LC; Pasco Diary, 27–29 August 1863, CCNMP; Bush Diary, 28 August 1863, CCNMP; William R. Jones to Mary F. Jones, 29 August 1863, Jones Letters, ADAH. Private Gray must have survived his fall, because his Compiled Service Record shows him present in October, and absent without leave in November 1863. Jarrott Gray CSR, NARA.

29. Alfred Pirtle to "Dear Jim," 30 August 1863, Pirtle Letters, FHS; [unknown] to "Friend Lib," 30 August 1861 [1863], Civil War Voices http://www.soldierstudies.org/blog/2011/03/camp-roberts-alabama-1861-august-30th/ (24 January 2012); John A. Martin to his sister, 30 August 1863, Martin Letters, KSHS; James E. Love to Eliza Mary Wilson, 30 August 1863, Love Papers, MHM; *OR* 30(1):485, 497, 505, 511, 513, 529; *SOR* 22:61, 555, 572, 574, 577; James G. Watson to [addressee unknown], 30 August 1863, Watson Letters, UI; *OR* 30(3):972–73; Patterson Diary, 30 August 1863, ALPL; Isaac P. Rule to his brother, 31 August 1863, Rule Letters, HPL; Colyer Diary, 30 August 1863, ALPL; *SOR* 21:515; *SOR* 23:19, 49; *SOR* 43:663, 671; *SOR* 66:679, 685, 691; Post Diary, 30 August 1863, Post Papers, KC; Mosman, *Rough Side*, 70–71; Lathrop, *Fifty-Ninth Illinois*, 214–15; Herr, *Nine Campaigns*, 140; *SOR* 24:393, 412; Mayfield Diary, 30 August 1863, IU; *SOR* 25:37–38; Society, Seventy-Fourth Illinois, *Reunion Proceedings*, 21; *SOR* 87:40, 67.

30.[Unknown] to "Friend Lib," 30 August 1861 [1863], Civil War Voices http://www.soldierstudies.org/blog/2011/03/camp-roberts-alabama-1861-august-30th/ (24 January 2012); *OR* 30(3):231, 235–36; Lytle, *For Honor*, 198; Pecoy Diary, 30 August 1863, CCNMP; Cooley Diary, 30 August 1863, WHS; Simonds Diary, 30 August 1863, Simonds Papers, NIU; Riley, *Diary*, 52; Burns Diary, 30 August 1863, CCNMP; Tabler Diary, 30 August 1863, private collection; Crippin, "Diary," 279; Hempstead Diary, 30 August 1863, UM-B.

31. Keegan, *Diaries*, 23; Martling Diary, 30 August 1863, Martling Manuscript Collection, ISL; Grebner, *Ninth Ohio*, 139; Albertson, *Letters Home*, Letter 101; John Reed Beatty to "Dearest Laura," 30 August 1863, Beatty Papers, MHS; Reed Diary, 30 August 1863, MHS; Donahower Account, 30 August 1863, Donahower Papers, MHS; Bircher, *Drummer-Boy*, 71; Bishop, *Story*, 92–93; Davidson Diary, 30 August 1863, NCWM; Harry Van Derveer to his mother, 30 August 1863, Van Derveer Letters, SLRH; *OR* 30(3):232; Inskeep Diary, 30 August 1863, OHS; Wheeler Diary, 30–31 August 1863, OHS; DeVelling, *Seventeenth Ohio*, 73; Moses B. Walker, "History of the 1st Brigade," Thomas Papers, NARA; Albert J. Baldwin to his parents, 6 September 1863, Baldwin Letters, UND.

32. *OR* 30(1):439, 468; *OR* 30(3):233–34; Ward Diary, 30 August 1863, Booth Papers, OHS; Josiah D. Cotton to his wife, 30 August 1863, Cotton Papers, LC.

33. Magid, *Crook*, 157; *OR* 30(1):926; *OR* 30(4):574; Crofts, *Third Ohio Cavalry*, 111;

SOR 61:546; Feagles Diary, 30 August 1863, CCNMP; Elijah S. Watts to Edward Ruger, 17 June 1867, Ruger Correspondence, Thomas Papers, NARA; George A. Gotwald to A. O. Smith, 31 August 1863, DC, Letters Received, NARA; Confederate Railroads, Wills Valley Railroad, http://www.csa-railroads.com/Wills_Valley.htm (11 January 2014).

34. Records Diary and Reminiscences, 30 August 1863, Records Manuscript Collection, ISL; Kemper Diary, 30 August 1863, OHS; Griest Diary, 30 August 1863, CCNMP; Campbell Journal, 30 August 1863, CCNMP; *OR* 30(3):251; Invoice, William Crutchfield, 27 September 1867, Accounts of Secret Service Agents, NARA; Thomas Crutchfield Jr. to James R. Hood, 27 December 1863, Crutchfield Family Papers, TSLA; Marshall Diary, 30 August 1863, OHS; W. E. Doyle, *National Tribune*, 22 June 1899; Smith, *Samuel Thomas Smith*, 80–81; Hines Diary, 30 August 1863, Hines Manuscript Collection, ISL; John S. McGraw to Mary Ann McGraw, 30 August 1863, McGraw Letters, ISL; Kitchell Diary, 30 August 1863, ALPL; *SOR* 25:508, 529, 537; Glisan Diary, 30 August 1863, CCNMP; Jonathan B. Holmes to "Anna My Friend," 30 August 1863, private collection; Johnston Diary, 30 August 1863, FHS. Paid at the rate of $50 per month for his service to the Union from 1 November 1861 to 1 November 1864, William Crutchfield received $1,800 from the government in September 1867.

35. Busbey Diary, 30 August 1863, SRNB; Botkin Diary, 30 August 1863, Baker Correspondence, OHS; Connelly Diary, 30 August 1863, IHS; Smith, *Thirty-First Indiana*, 58; McKee Diary, 30 August 1863, http://mckee-burns.pasttracker.com/mckee/cw_mekee/mckee_robert_t_cw_diary_1 (15 June 2013); Harden, *90th Ohio*, 91; Williams Diary, 30 August 1863, CCNMP; Walker Diary, 30 August 1863, Harrisburg Civil War Roundtable Collection, USAHEC; Christopher Wetsel to "Dear Brother Granville," 28–30 August 1863, Wetsel Letters, WIU; Willis Jones to Mellunda Ann Jones, 30 August 1863, Jones Papers, NC; Howe Diary, 30 August 1863, IHS; *OR* 30(3):237–38; Woodcock, *Southern Boy*, 183; Tilford Diary, 30 August 1863, FHS; *History, Seventy-Ninth Indiana*, 83; Cope, *Fifteenth Ohio*, 302; Welk Diary, 30 August 1863, BGSU; Pickering Diary, 30 August 1863, HL; Dean Diary, 30 August 1863, private collection; Kiene, *Journal*, 169; Phillips Diary, 30 August 1863, HL; Stahl Diary, 30 August 1863, BGSU; Davidson, *Battery A*, 82; Widney Diary, 30 August 1863, KMNMP; Talbot Diary, 30 August 1863, SRNB; Robinson Diary, 30 August 1863, Regimental Papers, WRHS; Lyon Diary, 30 August 1863, OHS; Moon Diary, 30 August 1863, KSHS; Beck Diary, 30 August 1863, KSHS; Protsman Diary, 30 August 1863, WSU; Doll, *Sixth Indiana*, 67; Shideler Diary, 30 August 1863, CCNMP; Ashmun Diary, 30 August 1863, CCNMP; Morledge Diary, 30 August 1863, KMNMP; Newlin, *Seventy-Third Illinois*, 207; Webster Diary, 30 August 1863, Civil War Miscellaneous Collection, USAHEC; Clark Diary, 30 August 1863, Clark Papers, USAHEC; Lucius Brown to "Dear Sister Gennie," 30 August 1863, Brown Letters, EU; Robert J. Bates to his parents, 30 August 1863, Bates Letters, WHS; Christian Diary, 30 August 1863, CCNMP; Johnston Diary, 30 August 1863, Johnston Collection, CHS; Shotts Diary, 30 August 1863, SRNB; Ward Diary, 30 August 1863, Ward Papers, DP; Dilworth Journal, 30 August 1863, HC; Hinchberger Diary, 30 August 1863, CCNMP; Johnston, *Soldier Boy*, 54; Bloom Diary, 30 August 1863, CCNMP.

36. *OR* 30(3):239–41; Charles H. Sowle to his mother, 30 August 1863, Sowle Papers, DU; Kendall Diary, 30 August 1863, HL; Merrill, *Diary*, 50; Read Diary, 30 August 1863, KSHS; Harris Diary, 30 August 1863, IHS; Hastings Clinton to "Rette," 30 August 1863, and Daniel V. Culver to "Friend Anna," 30 August 1863, both in Clinton Family Papers, CU; Roswell M. Russell to Edward Ruger, 12 June 1867, Ruger Correspondence, Thomas Papers, NARA; Carter, *First Tennessee Cavalry*, 83; Kinnear, *Eighty-Sixth Illinois*, 20–21;

Stewart, *52nd O.V.I.*, 53; Holmes, *Then and Now*, 4, 120–21; Hewes, *Tenth Michigan*, 48; Porter Diary, 30 August 1863, OHS; Armstrong Diary, 30 August 1863, CCNMP; Partridge, *Ninety-Sixth Illinois*, 153–54; Robinson Diary, 30 August 1863, ALPL; Patton Diary, 30 August 1863, CCNMP; McAdams, *One Hundred and Thirteenth Ohio*, 37; Schwartz, *Diary*, 10; Van Vleck, *Leader*, 162–64.

37. *OR* 30(1):601; *OR* 30(3):230–31, 235–36, 238, 974; Rosecrans to Crittenden, 30 August 1863, Garfield to Crittenden, 10:00 P.M., 30 August 1863, Garfield to Granger, 30 August 1863, Garfield to Morgan, 30 August 1863, Garfield to Simmons, 30 August 1863, Garfield to Thomas, 10:00 P.M., 30 August 1863, and Farfield to Lytle, 9:30 P.M., 30 August 1863, all in DC, Telegrams Sent, NARA.

38. Goddard to Simmons, 30 August 1863, Goddard to Morgan, 30 August 1863, Goddard to Commanding Officer, Cowan, 30 August 1863, Bond to Simmons, 30 August 1863, and Thoms to Lytle, 30 August 1863 (two messages), all in DC, Telegrams Sent, NARA; *OR* 30(3):230, 234–35, 239–40; Burroughs to O'Connell, 9:00 P.M., 30 August 1863, Burroughs Papers, NARA.

39. Beatty, *Citizen Soldier*, 324; Hapeman Diary, 30 August 1863, ALPL; Calkins, *One Hundred and Fourth Illinois*, 110; Harris Diary, 30 August 1863, CCNMP; Johnston Diary, 30 August 1863, Johnston Collection, CHS; Christian Diary, 30 August 1863, CCNMP; Shotts Diary, 30 August 1863, SRNB; Sturges Diary, 30 August 1863, Sturges Papers, *Civil War Times Illustrated* Collection, USAHEC; Ward Diary, 30 August 1863, Ward Papers, DP; Weaver Diary, 30 August 1863, SRNB; John W. Baldwin to his wife, 31 August 1863, Baldwin Papers, OHS; Dilworth Journal, 30 August 1863, HC; John C. Leonard to E. F. Kleckner, 31 August 1863, Leonard/Kleckner Letters, CCNMP; Hinchberger Diary, 30 August 1863, CCNMP; Cooley Diary, 30 August 1863, WHS; *OR* 30(1):439, 468, 911; *OR* 30(3):233, 256; Gates Diary, 30 August 1863, IHS; Shera Diary, 31 August 1863, FHS; Mauzy, *68th Indiana*, 11; High, *68th Indiana*, 175; Miller Journal, 30 August 1863, IHS; Hollingsworth Diary, 30 August 1863, IHS; Parker Diary, 30 August 1863, HL; Morse, *Diaries*, 32; Taylor Diary, 30 August 1863, SRNB; *SOR* 67:130.

40. Entries for 30 August 1863, "Summaries of the News," 314–322, NARA; Rosecrans to Burnside, 30 August 1863, and Rosecrans to Colonel Kelton, 30 August 1863, both in DC, Telegrams Sent, NARA; *OR* 30(3):229–30, 242, 244; William Rosecrans to Anna Rosecrans, 10:30 P.M., 30 August 1863, Rosecrans Papers, UCLA; Dana, *Recollections*, 104–5. Rosecrans's message to Colonel Kelton at the War Department was apparently delayed in transit, and is also misdated 31 August in the *Official Records*. The copy in DC, Telegrams Sent, NARA is correctly dated 30 August 1863 and there is a subsequent report for 31 August. According to James H. Wilson, Dana was supposed to visit Burnside first but found that to be impossible. Wilson, *Dana*, 254.

41. Mackall to Buckner, 30 August 1863 (two messages), Brent to Hill, 30 August 1863 (two messages), Brent to Liddell, 30 August 1863 (two messages), and Brent Diary, 29–30 August 1863, all in Bragg Papers, WRHS.

42. *OR* 30(4):566–67; Polk to Brent, 30 August 1863, Polk to Cheatham, 30 August 1863, and Polk to Hindman, 30 August 1863, all in Letters Sent, Polk's Command, NARA; Manigault, *Carolinian*, 92; William H. Moore to "Miss Jennie," 29 August 1863, Parsons Papers, ADAH; Thomas Warrick to Martha Warrick, 9 August 1863, Warrick Papers, ADAH; Fielder Diary, 30 August 1863, TSLA; Moorman, "Moorman Memorandum," 78; Joshua K. Callaway to Mrs. D. Callaway, 2 September 1863, Callaway Papers, UTX; *SOR* 45:95, 149, 171, 190; Scrapbook, Rietti Papers, MDAH; *SOR* 46:184, 314; Rand Diary, 30 August 1863, MDAH; Fraser Diary, 1 September 1863, CCNMP; *SOR* 76:805; *SOR* 77:142;

Newton N. Davis to his wife, 31 August 1863, Davis Letters, ADAH; Thomas B. Hall to Bolling Hall Sr., 31 August 1863, Hall Family Papers, ADAH; Magee Diary, 30 August 1863, DU.

43. Lumsden Diary, 30 August 1863, ADAH; John W. Harris to his mother, 30 August 1863, Harris Letters, TSLA; *Chattanooga (Tenn.) Daily Rebel*, 30 August 1863; Cleburne to Hill, 30 August 1863, D. H. Hill Papers, LV; "Gist's Brigade," and Capers Diary, 30 August 1863, both in Capers Papers, CI; *SOR* 77:233; *SOR* 61:46; Claudius C. Wilson to "Dear Kate," 3 September 1863, Wilson Papers, GHS; Jackman Journal, 30 August 1863, LC; Green, *Johnny Green*, 85; Bush Diary, 30 August 1863, CCNMP; Pasco Diary, 30 August 1863, CCNMP; Daniel Diary, 30 August 1863, SRNB; Joseph W. Ward to his mother, 30 August 1863, Ward Letters, CSA Records, UTX; Freeman Diary, 30 August 1863, TSLA.

44. *OR* 30(4):567, 570–71; William D. Cole to his wife, 28–31 August 1863, Cole Letters, Civil War Miscellaneous Collection, USAHEC; Dillon Diary, 30–31 August 1863, TSLA; Moore Diary, 30 August 1863, UDC Collection, GDAH; *SOR* 78:766; *SOR* 79:246; *SOR* 17:304, 757; *SOR* 14:258; Harry I. Thornton to William Mackall, 1 September 1863, Mackall Papers, UNC; Brent to Stewart, 1 September 1863, and Brent to Hill, 1 September 1863, both in Bragg Papers, WRHS; Johnson Diary, 30 August 1863, Johnson Papers, NARA; Holmes, *Diary*, 17; Watson Journal, 30 August 1863, CCNMP; *SOR* 13:905; Sexton Diary, 31 August 1863, CCNMP; Joseph S. Espey to his sister, 3 September 1863, Espey Family Papers, UNC.

45. *OR* 30(4):567–72; Lindsley, *Annals*, 2:692–93; Powell, *Failure*, 22–23; *OR* 30(2): 608, 616.

CHAPTER 13

1. Hapeman Diary, 31 August 1863, ALPL; McCullough Diary, 31 August 1863, ISL; *OR* 30(3):254–55; *OR* 30(4):574. Because Mauldin's command was a composite one, it is possible that a few personnel from the Fourth Alabama Cavalry regiment were with Mauldin, but it is more likely that Lieutenant Colonel Abernathy erred in his identification. While both the Third and Fourth Alabama Cavalry regiments were in Martin's Division, the Fourth was in Russell's Brigade, not Hagan's.

2. *OR* 30(3):254; Patterson Diary, 31 August 1863, MHM; *SOR* 23:19; Colyer Diary, 31 August 1863, ALPL; Morris, *Eighty-First Indiana*, 55; *SOR* 21:473, 507; Dodd Diary, 31 August 1863, Dodd Papers; ALPL; Muster roll, Company F, Twenty-First Illinois Infantry regiment, 31 August 1863, Blackburn Papers, ALPL; Day, *One Hundred and First Ohio*, 143–44; Isaac P. Rule to his brother, 31 August 1863, Rule Letters, HPL; *SOR* 66:685; *SOR* 43:663; Post Diary, 31 August 1863, Post Papers, KC; Mosman, *Rough Side*, 71; *OR* 30(1):510–11, 542; Lathrop, *Fifty-Ninth Illinois*, 215–16; *SOR* 24:393; Mayfield Diary, 31 August 1863, IU; *SOR* 25:38; Cope, *Fifteenth Ohio*, 302; Welk Diary, 31 August 1863, BGSU; Pickering Diary, 31 August 1863, HL; Dean Diary, 31 August 1863, private collection; Thomas J. Harrison to his wife, 31 August 1863, Harrison Letters, IHS; J. W. Bartmess to his wife, 31 August 1863, Bartmess Letters, IHS; Phillips Diary, 31 August 1863, and George S. Phillips to his wife, 15 September 1863, both in Phillips Collection, HL; Stahl Diary, 31 August 1863, BGSU; Kiene, *Journal*, 169; *SOR* 28:843; Davidson, *Battery A*, 82–83; Alpheus S. Bloomfield to his sister, 6 September 1863, Bloomfield Letters, OHS; Widney Diary, 31 August 1863, KMNMP; Talbot Diary, 31 August 1863, SRNB; Edward Payne to "ama mia," 1 September 1863, Payne Papers, ALPL; J. Grosskoff to Edward Ruger, 23 June 1867, Ruger Correspondence, Thomas Papers, NARA; Lyon Diary, 31 August 1863, OHS;

Moon Diary, 31 August 1863, KSHS; Beck Diary, 31 August 1863, KSHS; Protsman Diary, 31 August 1863, WSU; Wagner Reminiscences, *Civil War Times Illustrated* Collection, USAHEC; Doll, *Sixth Indiana*, 67; Richards, *Letters*, 19; Hiram Strong to his wife, 4 September 1863, Strong Letters, CCNMP; Shideler Diary, 31 August 1863, CCNMP; Ashmun Diary, 31 August 1863, CCNMP; Holm, *Fifth Indiana Battery*, 28; Robinson Diary, 31 August 1863, Regimental Papers, WRHS.

3. *OR* 30(3):256, 974; *OR* 30(1):240; Brown, *Signal Corps*, 472.

4. "Summaries of the News," 323–25, NARA; Goddard to Pelham, 31 August 1863 (two messages), Goddard to Commanding Officer, Tullahoma, 31 August 1863, Goddard to Commanding Officer, Decherd, 31 August 1863, Goddard to Allen, Louisville, 31 August 1863, Bond to Granger, 31 August 1863, Bond to Hodges, 31 August 1863, Thoms to Innes, 31 August 1863, Thoms to Beggs, 31 August 1863 (five messages), Thoms to Watkins, 31 August 1863, Garfield to Lytle, 1:30 P.M., 31 August 1863, and Thoms to Lytle, 31 August 1863, all in DC, Telegrams Sent, NARA; *OR* 30(3):248–50, 255–56, 259–60; Drouillard Diary, 31 August 1863, Rosecrans Papers, UCLA; Runion Diary, 31 August 1863, http://civilwar.illinoisgenweb.org/scrapbk/runiondiary2.html (23 March 2013).

5. McCullough Diary, 31 August 1863, IHS; Shultz, *Diary*, 30; Meredith Diary, 31 August 1863, Harrisburg Civil War Roundtable Collection, USAHEC; George Burroughs to Patrick O'Connell, 7:30 P.M., 31 August 1863, Burroughs Papers, NARA; *OR* 30(1):929; Roseberry Diary, 31 August 1863, EU; Pecoy Diary, 31 August 1863, CCNMP; Simonds Diary, 31 August 1863, Simonds Papers, NIU; Riley, *Diary*, 53; Burns Diary, 31 August 1863, CCNMP; Tabler Diary, 31 August 1863, private collection; Austin Diary, 31 August 1863, ALPL; Crippin, "Diary," 279; Lytle, *For Honor*, 198; *OR* 30(3):255–56; Pirtle, "Leaves," CHS. The bridge photographer was probably Thomas T. Sweeny (1833–91), already known in Cleveland, Ohio, for landscape panoramas. One of the Bridgeport photographs is attributed to Sweeny by the Minnesota Historical Society. For a capsule biography of Sweeny, see Haverstock, Vance, and Meggitt, *Artists in Ohio*, 845.

6. Crofts, *Third Ohio Cavalry*, 111; Feagles Diary, 31 August 1863, CCNMP; Prickitt, *Company H*, 102; O. O. Smith to Edward Ruger, 27 April 1867, and Elijah Watts to Edward Ruger, 17 June 1867, both in Ruger Correspondence, Thomas Papers, NARA; Crane Diary, 31 August 1863, CIHS; Bircher, *Drummer-Boy*, 71; Reed Diary, 31 August 1863, MHS; Davidson Diary, 31 August 1863, NCWM; Martling Diary, 31 August 1863, Martling Manuscript Collection, ISL; Keegan, *Diaries*, 23; Albertson, *Letters Home*, Letter 101; Price Diary, 31 August 1863, Civil War Miscellaneous Collection, USAHEC; Small Diary, 31 August 1863, IHS; Shaw, *Tenth Indiana*, 211; Chase, *Fourteenth Ohio*, 45; Letter excerpt, Everett F. Abbott to his mother, Chamberlain Papers, IHS; Moses B. Walker, "History of the 1st Brigade," Ruger Correspondence, Thomas Papers, NARA; DeVelling, *Seventeenth Ohio*, 74; McNeil, *Recollections*, 4–5; Inskeep Diary, 31 August 1863, OHS; Wheeler Diary, 31 August 1863, OHS; Gierhart Reminiscences, Gierhart Papers, OHS.

7. *OR* 30(1):469–70, 911; Mauzy, *Sixty-Eighth Indiana*, 11; Shera Diary, 31 August 1863, FHS; Miller Journal, 30–31 August 1863, IHS; Essington, "Second Years' History," Essington Papers, IHS; *SOR* 30:512, 528, 537; Hollingsworth Diary, 31 August 1863, IHS; Parker Diary, 31 August 1863, HL; Taylor Diary, 31 August 1863, SRNB; D. M. Ray to Edward Ruger, 6 October 1867, Ruger Correspondence, Thomas Papers, NARA; J. M. Nash to William Rosecrans, 30 August 1863, DC, Letters Received, NARA; Muster Roll, Company B, Third Engineer Regiment, Record of Events, NARA; *OR*, Series 3, 5:953.

8. Smith, *Civil War Tour for Cavers*, 81–90; Smith, *Niter District Eight*, 13–18; Miller Journal, 31 August 1863, IHS. A handful of soldiers from the Second Michigan Cavalry

regiment had already visited Nickajack Cave briefly on the previous day, during a reconnaissance from their bridgehead at Bridgeport. Hempstead Diary, 30 August 1863, UM-B.

9. Griest Diary, 31 August 1863, CCNMP; Records Diary, 31 August 1863, and Reminiscences, Records Manuscript Collection, ISL; Kitchell Diary, 31 August 1863, ALPL; McManus, *Morning*, 103–4; Brown Diary, 31 August 1863, ALPL; Phillips, *Diary*, 24; John H. Rippetoe to Mary Rippetoe, 31 August 1863, Rippetoe Letters, VCPL; Campbell Journal, 31 August 1863, CCNMP; *OR* 30(3):251–52, 257–58; Kerwood, *Fifty-Seventh Indiana*, 202; Hines Diary, 31 August 1863, Hines Manuscript Collection, ISL; Dewees Diary, 31 August 1863, CCNMP; Marshall Diary, 31 August 1863, OHS; Albert G. Hart to his wife, 31 August 1863, Hart Papers, WRHS; Johnston Diary, 31 August 1863, FHS; Glisan Diary, 31 August 1863, CCNMP; Vale, *Minty*, 214; George W. Chase to his brother and sister, 31 August 1863, Chase Letters, UM-B.

10. *OR* 30(1):601, 617; *OR* 30(3):257, 259, 974–75.

11. *SOR* 65:419, 438, 441; Tuttle, *Kentucky Captain*, 142; Goddard to Allen, Louisville, 31 August 1863, DC, Telegrams Sent, NARA; Busbey Diary, 31 August 1863, SRNB; Hyde Diary, 31 August 1863, KYHS; Botkin Diary, 31 August 1863, Baker Correspondence, OHS; Williams Diary, 31 August 1863, CCNMP; *SOR* 62:803, 830; Walker Diary, 31 August 1863, Harrisburg Civil War Roundtable Collection, USAHEC; Harden, *90th Ohio*, 91; *SOR* 66:635; Woodcock, *Southern Boy*, 183–84; Tilford Diary, 31 August 1863, FHS; Howe Diary, 31 August 1863, IHS; Huntzinger Diary, 31 August 1863, http://www.lafavre.us/hunt zinger/hunt_3.htm (23 May 2016); *History, Seventy-Ninth Indiana*, 84; Benedict Diary, 31 August 1863, SRNB; Claggett Diary, 31 August 1863, CCNMP; *OR* 30(3):258.

12. Frankenberry Diary, 31 August 1863, WVU; Morledge Diary, 31 August 1863, KMNMP; Newlin, *Seventy-Third Illinois*, 207; Hapeman Diary, 31 August 1863, ALPL; Harris Diary, 31 August 1863, CCNMP; Bloom Diary, 31 August 1863, CCNMP; Johnston Diary, 31 August 1863, Johnston Collection, CHS; Christian Diary, 31 August 1863, CCNMP; Shotts Diary, 31 August 1863, SRNB; Lewis Tripp to his parents and sister, 1 September 1863, Tripp Letters, Civil War Miscellaneous Collection, USAHEC; Sturges Diary, 31 August 1863, Sturges Papers, *Civil War Times Illustrated* Collection, USAHEC; Ward Diary, 31 August 1863, Ward Papers, DP; Weaver Diary, 31 August 1863, SRNB; John C. Leonard and Tilden Kleckner to E. F. Kleckner, 31 August 1863, Leonard/Kleckner Letters, CCNMP; Hinchberger Diary, 31 August 1863, CCNMP; Millen Diary, 31 August 1863, SRNB; Hinkley Diary, 31 August 1863, Hinkley Papers, WHS; Frank M. Phelps to "Dear Friends," 31 August 1863, Phelps Letters, Lewis Leigh Collection, USAHEC; Webster Diary, 31 August 1863, Civil War Miscellaneous Collection, USAHEC; *SOR* 29:147; Johnston, *Soldier Boy*, 54; Clark Diary, 31 August 1863, Clark Papers, USAHEC; Barringer Diary, 31 August 1863, private collection; Augustus B. Carpenter to his parents, 2 September 1863, Carpenter Letters, YU; Hempstead Diary, 31 August 1863, UM-B; Roswell M. Russell to Edward Ruger, 12 June 1867, Ruger Correspondence, Thomas Papers, NARA; George Shuman to "My own dear Fannie," 3 September 1863, Shuman Letters, Harrisburg Civil War Roundtable Collection, USAHEC; Dan T. Wooten to "Dear Friend Mell," 31 August 1863, Green Letters, IHS; Mendenhall Diary, 31 August 1863, IHS; Kendall Diary, 31 August 1863, HL; Harris Diary, 31 August 1863, IHS; Merrill, *Diary*, 50; Orson Clinton to "Dear friend Anna," 2 September 1863, Clinton Family Papers, CU; Read Diary, 31 August 1863, KSHS; Persons Diary, 31 August 1863, WHS; *SOR* 86:698; *OR* 30(3):260–61; Thoms to Beggs, 31 August 1863 (three messages), and Thoms to Watkins, 31 August 1863, all in DC, Telegrams Sent, NARA.

13. *OR* 30(3):260; Warner, *Generals in Blue*, 466–67; Winans Diary, 31 August 1863, CCNMP; Porter Diary, 31 August 1863, OHS; Thomas M. Burns to his father, 9 September 1863, Burns Letters, VPI; Armstrong Diary, 31 August 1863, CCNMP; Stewart, *52nd O.V.I.*, 53–54; Harmon, *Life and Letters*, 99–100; Holmes, *Then and Now*, 121–23; George Dillon to his wife, 9 September 1863, Dillon Letters, DPL. Some of McCook's soldiers believed Lynnville to be near the site of the mortal wounding of Brig. Gen. Robert L. McCook in August 1862, and also the home of McCook's alleged killer, Capt. Frank Gurley. In fact, McCook died approximately forty miles to the southeast, near Hazel Green, Alabama, and Gurley's home was twenty miles farther still near Gurley, Alabama. See also Steenburn, *Man Called Gurley*, 18, 106–30.

14. *OR* 30(3):244–45; *OR* 52(1):439, 442; Thoms to Halleck, 31 August 1863, and Drouillard to Beggs, 31 August 1863, both in DC, Telegrams Sent, NARA.

15. *OR* 30(3):267–76; Consolidated Tri-monthly Report, Department of the Cumberland, 31 August 1863, Polk Papers, US. According to definitions of the time, Aggregate Present "shows the total number with the army in every capacity. It includes all arms of the service, wagon trains, medical department, special details, men under arrest, and the sick in camp,—in fact, all for whom rations must be provided." Present for Duty "includes all who were present with their commands and ready for duty, whatever their duties might be. It embraced musicians, company cooks, quartermasters and commissaries, hospital corps, and other noncombatants." An additional category, Present for Duty Equipped, "included only those who were actually available for line of battle at the date of the regimental reports." Fox, *New York at Gettysburg*, 1:101–2. On 31 August 1863, the Department of the Cumberland's Present for Duty Equipped total was 80,425 officers and men. The Present for Duty Equipped total for the Fourteenth, Twentieth, Twenty-First, and Cavalry Corps was 61,114 soldiers of all ranks.

16. *OR* 23(2):940–46; *OR* 30(4):557; *OR* 52(2):520; Abstract from Return of the Army of Tennessee, for August 31, 1863, Polk Papers, US.

17. Brent Diary, 31 August 1863, Bragg Papers, WRHS; Mackall to Buckner, 31 August 1863, Brent to Buckner, 31 August 1863 (two messages), Brent to Forrest, care of Buckner, 31 August 1863, and Brent to Liddell, 31 August 1863, all in Bragg Papers, WRHS; Oladowski to Wright, 31 August 1863 (two messages), and Oladowski to Gorgas, 31 August 1863, all in Ordnance Office, Army of Tennessee, Letters Sent, NARA; *Chattanooga (Tenn.) Daily Rebel*, 1 September 1863, as reprinted by the *Augusta (Ga.) Chronicle*, 4 September 1863.

18. Rennolds Diary, 31 August 1863, CCNMP; Fielder Diary, 31 August 1863, TSLA; Moorman, "Moorman Memorandum," 78; Magee Diary, 31 August 1863, DU; Joshua K. Callaway to Dulcinea Callaway, 2 September 1863, Callaway Papers, UTX; Thomas B. Hall to Bolling Hall Sr., 31 August 1863, Hall Family Papers, ADAH; *SOR* 45:183; Scrapbook, Rietti, Papers, MDAH; *SOR* 46:193, 289; Heartsill, *Fourteen Hundred*, 146; Sparkman Diary, 31 August 1863, BPL; *SOR* 14:278, 286; *SOR* 79:227; Seaton, *Bugle*, 38–39; J. L. Bostick to his sister, 31 August 1863, Bostick Family Collection, TSLA. A tantalizing glimpse of the controversy between Hindman and Polk's staff can be found in the summary of William B. Richmond to Alexander H. Polk, 29 August 1863, as offered for sale by Raynors' Historical Collectible Auctions, 22 September 2011.

19. *OR* 30(4):575; *OR* 52(2):520–21; Dillon Diary, 31 August 1863, TSLA; Moore Diary, 31 August 1863, UDC Collection, GDAH; *SOR* 79:35, 246, 352, 559; *SOR* 18:196, 199; Johnson Diary, 31 August 1863, Johnson Papers, NARA; *SOR* 78:714, 793; Owen, *Camp and Battle*, 269; Holmes, *Diary*, 17; Watson Journal, 31 August 1863, CCNMP; Joseph S.

Espey to his sister, 3 September 1863, Espey Family Papers, UNC; Sexton Diary, 31 August 1863, CCNMP; *SOR* 13:905, 909, 919, 925; Brown Diary, 31 August 1863, CCNMP; Huwald Account, Nutt Papers, UNC; Sloan Diary, 31 August 1863, TSLA; Leverich Diary, 31 August 1863, LSU; Dyer, *Diary*, 19; Jordan and Pryor, *Campaigns of Forrest*, 298–99; William D. Cole to his wife, 28–31 August 1863, Cole Letters, Civil War Miscellaneous Collection, USAHEC.

20. Capers Diary, 31 August 1863, and "Gist's Brigade," both in Capers Papers, CI; Ellison Capers to his wife, 1 September 1863, Capers Papers, DU; *SOR* 77:221; Gentry Diary, 31 August 1863, CCNMP; *SOR* 80:726; Claudius C. Wilson to his wife, 3 September 1863, Wilson Papers, GHS; *SOR* 36:431; Pasco Diary, 31 August 1863, CCNMP; Jackman Journal, 31 August 1863, LC; Green, *Johnny Green*, 85; Bush Diary, 31 August 1863, CCNMP; Corbitt Diary, 31 August 1863, EU; Poole, *Cracker Cavaliers*, 86; Shields Diary, 31 August 1863, http://freepages.genealogy.rootsweb.ancestry.com/~sassytazzy/family.surnames/shields (1 February 2009); *SOR* 13:61; *OR* 30(4):574; Stevenson, "Smith," 42.

21. *OR* 52(2):519–20; Freeman, *Lee's Lieutenants*, 3:163–65; Wert, *Longstreet*, 300–301; Piston, *Tarnished Lieutenant*, 65–67; Robertson, "Bull of the Woods," 117–19; *OR* 51(2):761; *OR* 30(4):575; Bragg, *Joe Brown's Army*, 67–72.

22. Brent Diary, 1 September 1863, Bragg Papers, WRHS; Shook, "Timely Information"; U.S. Federal Census, 1860, Jackson County, Alabama; *Richmond Whig*, 30 October 1863; *OR* 30(2):137. The identity of "Historicus" has not been determined with certainty, although some inferences can be drawn. The writer was intimately familiar with Polk's Corps and was critical of Braxton Bragg. Further, large portions of the "Historicus" text were repeated verbatim in William Polk's article on Chickamauga published in 1882 and his subsequent two-volume biography of his father, both without attribution to any outside source. Polk, "Chickamauga," 2–3; Polk, *Polk*, 2:219–23. A member of his father's staff during the campaign and a fierce defender of Leonidas Polk's record, William Polk had firsthand knowledge of events, the literary skill to craft a coherent narrative, and a motive for making that narrative detrimental to the reputation of the army commander. Finally, both Leonidas Polk and his personal staff were in Atlanta on 23 October 1863, mounting a campaign to have the general restored to duty. "Historicus" wrote from "North Georgia" on that date, and the *Richmond Whig* clearly offered a better platform for influencing the government than the various papers published in Atlanta. Circumstantial evidence thus points to William Polk as "Historicus," at least until a better candidate surfaces.

23. Brent Diary, 1 September 1863, Bragg Papers, WRHS; Brent to Rice, 2:00 A.M., 1 September 1863 (two messages), Brent to McDonald, 2:00 A.M. 1 September 1863 (two messages), and Brent to Lieutenant [W. N. Mercer] Otey, 1 September 1863, all in Bragg Papers, WRHS; *OR* 30(4):579.

24. Brent Diary, 1 September 1863, Bragg Papers, WRHS; Brent to Hill, 2:00 A.M., 1 September 1863 (two messages), Brent to Hill and Liddell, 2:00 A.M., 1 September 1863, and Brent to Polk, 1 September 1863, all in Bragg Papers, WRHS; *OR* 30(4):579; Jack to Cheatham and Hindman, 3:00 A.M., 1 September 1863, and Jack to Hindman, 10:30 A.M., 1 September 1863, both in Letters Sent, Polk's Command, NARA; *SOR* 45:84, 146, 164, 201; *SOR* 46:187, 314; Rand Diary, 1–2 September 1863, MDAH; Fraser Diary, 2 September 1863, CCNMP; McAdory Memo, Twenty-Fifth Alabama File, ADAH; James A. Hall to Bolling Hall Sr., 2 September 1863, Hall Family Papers, ADAH; Joshua K. Callaway to Dulcinea Callaway, 2 September 1863, Callaway Papers, UTX; Fielder Diary, 1 September 1863, TSLA; Moorman, "Moorman Memorandum," 78; Rennolds Diary, 1 September

1863, CCNMP; W. K. Beard to Henrietta Adair Anderson, 1 September 1863, Anderson Papers, UF.

25. Brent Diary, 27–31 August 1863, Bragg Papers, WRHS; *OR* 30(4):564–65, 574, 580; Stevenson, "Smith," 42; *SOR* 13:61; *OR* 30(2):520; Falconer to Foster, 2:30 A.M., 1 September 1863, Falconer to Commanding Officer, Troops Wheeler's Corps, Calhoun, Georgia, and Falconer to Caldwell, 1 September 1863, all in Bragg Papers, WRHS. Carothers, a young merchant clerk from Bardstown, Kentucky, had joined the Army of Tennessee in October 1862, during Bragg's invasion of the state. Nominally a private in Company F, First Kentucky Cavalry regiment, he was posted immediately to Bragg's staff as a clerk and remained so in September 1863. Alfred R. Carothers CSR, NARA; U.S. Federal Census, 1860, Bullitt County, Kentucky.

26. Brent Diary, 1 September 1863, Bragg Papers, WRHS; Brent to Martin, 1 September 1863, Brent to Wharton, 1 September 1863 (three messages), Brent to Roddey, 1 September 1863, Brent to Wharton and Martin, 1 September 1863, and Brent to Lee, 1 September 1863, all in Bragg Papers, WRHS. Wheeler's biographers cast little light on Wheeler's location during this period. Dyer, *Wheeler*, 110–11, claims he was at Gadsden, Alabama, until 1 September, but offers no source. Longacre, *Soldier*, 109–10, does not attempt a guess. Powell, *Failure*, 45, asserts that Wheeler entered LaFayette with Wharton on 1 September but provides no documentation. Certainly Bragg and his staff did not believe that Wheeler was with Wharton on 1 September.

27. Brent to Forrest, 1 September 1863 (two messages), Brent to Buckner, 1 September 1863 (two messages), Brent to Stewart, 1 September 1863, Brent to Hill, 1 September 1863, Brent to Wright, 1 September 1863, Brent to Stevenson, 1 September 1863, Brent to McMicken, 1 September 1863, Brent to Hill and Polk, 1 September 1863, and Brent to Polk, 1 September 1863, all in Bragg Papers, WRHS.

28. Bragg, *Joe Brown's Army*, 66–73; *OR* 3 (4):580; Brodnax Memoirs, FHS; Dudley D. Saunders to Samuel H. Stout, 1 September 1863, Stout Papers, MC; Schroeder-Lein, *Confederate Hospitals*, 123–24. Brown did not relinquish the Georgia Military Institute to Saunders, even after Stout's personal intervention.

29. Neal Diary, 1 September 1863, NC; Moorman, "Moorman Memorandum," 78; Rennolds Diary, 1 September 1863, CCNMP; Fielder Diary, 1 September 1863, TSLA; Brown Notebook, 1 September 1863, CCNMP; Heartsill, *Fourteen Hundred*, 146; Sparkman Diary, 1 September 1863, BPL; Estes Diary, 1 September 1863, MC; Daniel Diary, 1 September 1863, SRNB; *OR* 30(4):580; Orders Received, First Kentucky Brigade, NARA; *SOR* 45:84, 146, 164, 201; *SOR* 46:187, 314; Fraser Diary, 2 September 1863, CCNMP; McAdory Memorandum, 1 September 1863, ADAH; James A. Hall to Bolling Hall Sr., 2 September 1863, Hall Family Papers, ADAH; Joshua K. Callaway to Dulcinea Callaway, 2 September 1863, Callaway Papers, UTX; Jackman Journal, 1 September 1863, LC; *SOR* 35:203, 273, 332, 408; *SOR* 13:698; *SOR* 36:288, 420, 452; Pasco Diary, 1 September 1863, CCNMP; *SOR* 17, 260; Shields Diary, 1 September 1863, http://freepages.genealoby.rootsweb.ancestry.com/~sasswytazzy/family.surnames/shields (1 February 2009); Wyeth, *Sabre*, 238; Corbitt Diary, 1 September 1863, EU; Poole, *Cracker Cavaliers*, 86; *SOR* 79:39, 352, 550, 797; Harry I. Thornton to "My Dear General" [William W. Mackall], 1 September 1863, Mackall Papers, UNC; Hiram Talbert Holt to "Dear Carrie," 1 September 1863, Holt Letters, AU; Johnson Diary, 1 September 1863, Johnson Papers, NARA; Harder Reminiscences, 1 September 1863, TSLA; Owen, *Camp and Battle*, 269; *SOR* 84:824; Holmes, *Diary*, 17; Watson Journal, 1 September 1863, CCNMP; Joseph S. Espey to his sister, 3 September 1863, Espey Family Papers, UNC;

Massey, *Reminiscences*, 180; *SOR* 13:913, 925; Brown Diary, 1 September 1863, CCNMP; Dyer, *Diary*, 20; *SOR* 35:41; Lindsley, *Annals*, 2:693; Huwald Account, Nutt Papers, UNC; Sloan Diary, 1 September 1863, TSLA; Leverich Diary, 1 September 1863, LSU; John A. James to "Dear Companion," 7 September 1863, UDC Collection, vol. 8, GDAH; William Jasper Whitehead CSR, NARA. Whitehead had enlisted in October 1862, deserted in November or December 1862, and had been held in confinement since at least March 1863.

30. *OR* 30(3):279–82, 285–86, 289–91; Garfield, *Wild Life*, 293–94; Rosecrans to Sheridan, 2:00 P.M., 1 September 1863, Garfield to Steedman, 1 September 1863; Goddard to Granger, 1 September 1863, Goddard to Pelham, 1 September 1863, Bond to Morgan, 1 September 1863, Thoms to Granger, 1 September 1863, Thoms to Carlton, 1 September 1863, Thoms to Crittenden, 1 September 1863, Thoms to Minty, 1 September 1863, and Thoms to Hodges, 1 September 1863 (two messages), all in DC, Telegrams Sent, NARA.

31. *OR* 30(1):510; *SOR* 24:441; Mayfield Diary, 1 September 1863, IU; Isaac P. Rule to his brother, 3 September 1863, Rule Letters, HPL; Colyer Diary, 1 September 1863, ALPL; Cope, *Fifteenth Ohio*, 302; Kiene, *Journal*, 169–70; *SOR* 62:541; Doll, *Sixth Indiana*, 67; Shideler Diary, 1 September 1863, CCNMP; Moon Diary, 1 September 1863, KSHS; Beck Diary, 1 September 1863, KSHS; *OR* 30(3):252–53, 976; Thruston to Johnson and Davis, 1 September 1863, and Thruston to Sheridan, 1 September 1863, both in Twentieth Corps, Letters Sent, NARA.

32. Heg, *Letters*, 240; Hiram Strong to his wife, 4 September 1863, Strong Letters, CCNMP; Widney Diary, 1 September 1863, KMNMP; Talbot Diary, 1 September 1863, SRNB; U.S. Surgeon-General's Office, *Medical and Surgical History*, 1:appendix, 275; Dennis Memoir, HPL; Mosman, *Rough Side*, 71; Dean Diary, 1 September 1863, private collection; Kiene, *Journal*, 169; *OR* 30(3):285, 975; Thruston to Johnson, 1 September 1863, Twentieth Corps, Letters Sent, NARA; Post Diary, 1 September 1863, Post Papers, KC.

33. Simonds Diary, 1 September 1863, Simonds Papers, NIU; Riley, *Diary*, 53; Tabler Diary, 1 September 1863, private collection; Burns Diary, 1 September 1863, CCNMP; Austin Diary, 1 September 1863, ALPL; Crippin, "Diary," 279; James S. McCarty to his mother, 1 September 1863, McCarty Letters, SRNB; Pecoy Diary, 1 September 1863, CCNMP; Cooley Diary, 1 September 1863, WHS; Harold J. Bartlett to "Dear Ma and Eugene," 9 September 1863, Bartlett Letters, UM-B; Meredith Diary, 1 September 1863, Harrisburg Civil War Roundtable Collection, USAHEC; Shultz, *Diary*, 30; McCullough Diary, 1 September 1863, ISL; Larew Diary, 1 September 1863, IHS; Roseberry Diary, 1 September 1863, EU; *OR* 30(3):280, 285–86; Newlin, *Seventy-Third Illinois*, 207–8; *SOR* 23:340; *SOR* 25:4; *SOR* 48:284; Thomas J. Frazee to his sister, 4 September 1863, Frazee Papers, ALPL; Smith, *Private Smith's Journal*, 85; Pirtle, "Leaves," CIHS; Bradley to Lee, 1 September 1863, Sheridan Papers, LC; Thoms to Sheridan, 1 September 1863, DC, Telegrams Sent, NARA.

34. *OR* 30(3):284; Inskeep Diary, 1 September 1863, OHS; Wheeler Diary, 1 September 1863, OHS; Benjamin B. Mabrey to his wife, 29 [2] September 1863, Mabrey Letters, IHS; Harold J. Bartlett to "Dear Ma and Eugene," 9 September 1863, Bartlett Letters, UM-B; Price Diary, 1 September 1863, Civil War Miscellaneous Collection, USAHEC; Small Diary, 1 September 1863, IHS; Shaw, *Tenth Indiana*, 211; *SOR* 34:162, 172; Everett F. Abbott to his mother, 2 [1] September 1863, Chamberlain Papers, IHS; J. D. Myers, *National Tribune*, 29 March 1900; Reed Diary, 1 September 1863, MHS; Bishop, *Story*, 93; Davidson Diary, 1 September 1863, NCWM; Bircher, *Drummer-Boy*, 71; Martling Diary, 1 September 1863, Martling Manuscript Collection, ISL; Alanson R. Ryman to Jane Ryman, 9 September 1863, Ryman Letters, IHS; Miller Journal, 1 September 1863, IHS;

Floyd, *Seventy-Fifth Indiana*, 121; Essington, "Second Years History," Essington Papers, IHS; Hollinsworth Diary, 1 September 1863, IHS; Morse, *Diaries*, 32; Tourgee, "Diary," 118; Taylor Diary, 1 September 1863, SRNB; Hartzell, *Ohio Volunteer*, 121; Parker Diary, 1 September 1863, HL; *SOR* 67:136, 152; Williams, *Extracts*, 88; *OR* 30(1):476; Turchin, "Diary," 61; Steward Diary, 1 September 1863, *Chattanooga (Tenn.) Free Press*, 21 September 1938, clipping in CPL; *SOR* 63:162; Ward Diary, 1 September 1863, Booth Papers, OHS; *SOR* 34:466; *SOR* 27:648.

35. Records Diary and Reminiscences, 1 September 1863, Records Manuscript Collection, ISL; Griest Diary, 1 September 1863, CCNMP; Campbell Journal, 1 September 1863, CCNMP; Hines Diary, 1 September 1863, Hines Manuscript Collection, ISL; Dewees Diary, 1 September 1863, CCNMP; Marshall Diary, 1 September 1863, OHS; Phillips, *Diary*, 25; *OR* 30(3):287–88; Andrew C. Parker to his wife, 1 September 1863, Parker Letters, HPC; Johnston Diary, 1 September 1863, FHS; Hannaford, *Sixth Ohio*, 443; Glisan Diary, 1 September 1863, CCNMP; *OR* 30(1):925; McLain Diary, 1 September 1863, ISHS; *SOR* 41:807.

36. Woodruff, *Fifteen Years*, 279; Hight, *Fifty-Eighth Indiana*, 170; William J. Carroll to his sister, 1 September 1863, Carroll Papers, UM-B; Hinman, *Sherman Brigade*, 408; *SOR* 65:389, 419; Mallory Diary, 1 September 1863, HPL; Gillis Diary, 5 September 1863, OHS; Tuttle, *Kentucky Captain*, 142; Opdycke Diary, 1 September 1863, and Emerson Opdycke to his wife, 2 September 1863, both in Opdycke Papers, OHS; Joseph Bruff to Anna Bruff, 2 September 1863, Bruff Family Letters, private collection; Clark, *Tigers*, 83; *SOR* 67:603; *SOR* 62:413; *OR* 30(1):601,624–25, 651, 709–10, 721; Busbey Diary, 1 September 1863, SRNB; Hyde Diary, 1 September 1863, KYHS; George W. Botkin to Liddie C. Baker, 5 September 1863, Baker Correspondence, OHS; *SOR* 34:56, 106, 281, 429, 568; McKee Diary, 1 September 1863, http://mckee-burns.pasttracker.com/mckee/cw_mckee/mckee_robert_t_cw_diary (15 June 2013); Mason Diary, 1 September 1863, SRNB; Smith, *Thirty-First Indiana*, 58; Connelly Diary, 1 September 1863, IHS; Dillman Diary, 1 September 1863, IU; *SOR* 28:788; Marshall Diary, 1 September 1863, OHS; Harden, *90th Ohio*, 91; *SOR* 66:376; Palmer Journal, 1 September 1863, CCNMP; *SOR* 63:666; Walker Diary, 1 September 1863, Harrisburg Civil War Roundtable Collection, USAHEC; Christopher Wetsel to his wife, parents and family, 4 September 1863, Wetsel Letters, WIU; Suiter Diary, 1 September 1863, ALPL; Simmons, *84th Illinois*, 75; Williams Diary, 1 September 1863, CCNMP; Grose, *36th Indiana*, 172; *OR* 30(3):286–87, 289; Horatio Van Cleve to his wife, 1 September 1863, Van Cleve Papers, MHS; Woodcock, *Southern Boy*, 184; Tilford Diary, 1 September 1863, FHS; Huntzinger Diary, 1 September 1863, http://www.lafavre.us/huntzinger/hunt_3.htm (23 May 2016); *History, Seventy-Ninth Indiana*, 84; Howe Diary, 1 September 1863, IHS; Benedict Diary, 1 September 1863, SRNB; Hurd Diary, 1 September 1863, private collection; Claggett Diary, 1 September 1863, CCNMP; Wright, *Eighth Kentucky*, 176; J. E. Cummins to "Dear Hattie," 1 September 1863, Cummins Letters, McCray Archive, BGSU; Claiborne J. Walton to "My Dear Nannie," 3–4 September 1863, Walton Letter, Hess Collection, USAHEC; Moses F. Yoder to Samuel Yoder, 7 September 1863, Yoder Papers, LC.

37. Kiene, *Journal*, 169–70; *OR* 30(1):324–25, 905, 912; Carter, *First Tennessee Cavalry*, 85; Hempstead Diary, 1 September 1863, UM-B; *SOR* 41:721, 761; *SOR* 33:746; Kendall Diary, 1 September 1863, HL; Mendenhall Diary, 1 September 1863, IHS; Baum Diary, 1 September 1863, IHS; Harris Diary, 1 September 1863, IHS; Leeper Diary, 1 September 1863, SRNB; Merrill, *Diary*, 50–51; Read Diary, 1 September 1863, KSHS; Persons Diary, 1 September 1863, WHS; *SOR* 86:654; *Wisconsin State Journal*, 17 October 1863; *OR*

30(3):261, 283; Nourse Diary, 1 September 1863, DU; Lester Diary, 1 September 1863, ALPL; Crofts, *Third Ohio Cavalry*, 112; Feagles Diary, 1 September 1863, CCNMP; Prickitt, *Company H*, 102; Crane Diary, 1 September 1863, CIHS; Hough, *Soldier*, 133; Wilson, *Column South*, 85; Beatty, *Citizen Soldier*, 327; *SOR* 29:219; Harris Diary, 1 September 1863, CCNMP; Kirkpatrick, *Experiences*, 46; *SOR* 26:118; George Marsh Jr. to his brother, 1 September 1863, Marsh Family Papers, ALPL; Hapeman Diary, 1 September 1863, ALPL; *SOR* 20:439.

38. Bloom Diary, 1 September 1863, CCNMP; Sheffield Diary, 1 September 1863, CCNMP; Thornton, *Gallantry*, 160; Christian Diary, 1 September 1863, CCNMP; Joseph S. Johnston to his mother, 5 September 1863, and Johnston Diary, 1 September 1863, Johnston Collection, CHS; Fenton Reminiscence, ALPL; Haynie, *Nineteenth Illinois*, 215; *SOR* 21:358; Shotts Diary, 1 September 1863, SRNB; Launcelot L. Scott, *National Tribune*, 27 October 1910; Eben P. Sturges to "Dear Folks," 5 September 1863, Sturges Papers, *Civil War Times Illustrated* Collection, USAHEC; *OR* 30(1):378, 383, 386, 393, 396, 1063; *SOR* 65:673; Millen Diary, 1 September 1863, SRNB; Andrew G. Wickham to his parents, September 1863, UT; Blackburn, *Letters*, 145; Weaver Diary, 1 September 1863, SRNB; John W. Baldwin to his wife, 1 September 1863, Baldwin Papers, OHS; Hinchberger Diary, 1 September 1863, CCNMP; Gibson, *Seventy-Eighth Pennsylvania*, 83; Nupp Diary, 1 September 1863, CCNMP; Ward Diary, 1 September 1863, Ward Papers, DP; Puntenny, *Thirty-Seventh Indiana*, 47–48; Adams, "Diary," 648; Dilworth Journal, 1 September 1863, HC; Shanks Diary, 1 September 1863, BGSU; Vance, *God's War*, 269–70; Canfield, *Twenty-First Ohio*, 104. Sun and moon data can be found at http://aa.usno.navy.mil/cgi-bin/aa_pap.pl (4 April 2014). William H. Christian and his father, David W. Christian of the Fifty-First Illinois Infantry regiment, both survived the war. U.S. Federal Census, 1860 and 1870, Cook County, Illinois.

39. Thoms to Halleck, 1 September 1863, and Thoms to Sheridan, 1 September 1863, both in DC, Telegrams Sent, NARA; *OR* 30(3):279, 280, 283; Webster Diary, 1 September 1863, Civil War Miscellaneous Collection, USAHEC; Perry, *Thirty-Eighth Indiana*, 79–80; Clark Diary, 1 September 1863, Clark Papers, USAHEC; George Desforges to his sister, 5 September 1863, Desforges Letters, Civil War Miscellaneous Collection, USAHEC; Henry Clay Taylor to his parents, 1 September 1863, Taylor Papers, WHS; Thomas M. Burns to his father, 9 September 1863, Burns Letters, VT; Holmes, *Then and Now*, 5, 119, 123; Porter Diary, 1 September 1863, OHS; Armstrong Diary, 1 September 1863, CCNMP; Winans Diary, 1 September 1863, CCNMP.

CHAPTER 14

1. *OR* 30(3):300, 303; *OR* 30(1):325, 578–79, 582, 589; Pirtle, "Leaves," CIHS; Alfred Pirtle to his mother, 2 September 1863, and Alfred Pirtle to Jane Pirtle, 3 September 1863, both in Pirtle Letters, FHS; Cummins Diary, 2 September 1863, Cummins Papers, ALPL; Bennett and Haigh, *Thirty-Sixth Illinois*, 448–49; Walker, "Union Soldier's Diary," *Chattanooga (Tenn.) Times*, 25 April 1937, CPL; *SOR* 22:161, 164, 585, 601; Pecoy Diary, 2 September 1863, CCNMP; Ely Diary, 2 September 1863, CCNMP; Daniel E. Barnard to his sister, 9 September 1863, Howe Barnard Family Papers, NL; *SOR* 25:4, 13, 350, 354; A. E. Stebbins, *National Tribune*, 19 October 1899; Goodale Account, http://www.21stmichigan.us/goodalestory.htm (18 March 2012); Quiner, *Military History*, 724; Cooley Diary, 2 September 1863, WHS; Merrill, *Soldier*, 2:436; *SOR* 27:603; Otto, *11th Battery*, 35; Newlin, *Seventy-Third Illinois*, 208–9; Thomas J. Frazee to his sister, 4 September 1863,

Frazee Papers, ALPL; *SOR* 23:201, 208, 340, 371; *SOR* 48:304, 339; Luther P. Bradley to his mother, 3 September 1863, and Luther P. Bradley to "Buel," 8 September 1863, both in Bradley Papers, USAHEC; *SOR* 21:527, 531; Austin Diary, 2 September 1863, ALPL; Crippin, "Diary," 279; Simonds Diary, 2 September 1863, Simonds Papers, NIU; Lyman H. Needham to his brother and sister, 12 September 1863, Needham Papers, ALPL; Riley, *Diary*, 53; Burns Diary, 2 September 1863, CCNMP; *SOR* 24:28, 43; Tabler Diary, 2 September 1863, private collection; Smith, "Recollections," Smith Papers, ALPL; Moody Diary, 2 September 1863, SRNB; Colburn/Gray Diary, 2 September 1863, private collection; Hapeman Diary, 2 September 1863, ALPL; Harris Diary, 2 September 1863, CCNMP; Christian Diary, 2 September 1863, CCNMP; Dilworth Journal, 3 September 1863, HC; Eicher and Eicher, *High Commands*, 404, 483.

2. *OR* 30(1):269; *OR* 30(3):307, 978; Prickitt, *Company H*, 102–3; Feagles Diary, 2 September 1863, CCNMP; Inskeep Diary, 2 September 1863, OHS; Bruce Diary, 2 September 1863, ISL; Harold J. Bartlett to "Dearest Ma and Eugene," 9 September 1863, Bartlett Letters, UM-B; Benjamin B. Mabrey to his wife, 2 September 1863, Mabrey Letters, IHS; Joseph W. Miller, in *Cincinnati Daily Commercial*, 3 September 1863 and 9 September 1863.

3. Goodale Account, http://www.21stmichigan.us/goodalestory.htm (18 March 2012); Rosecrans to Halleck, 2 September 1863, DC, Telegrams Sent, NARA; *OR* 30(3):296, 326–27; John W. Miller, *Cincinnati Daily Commercial*, 9 September 1863; Roseberry Diary, 2 September 1863, EU; McCullough Diary, 2 September 1863, ISL; Meredith Diary, 2 September 1863, Harrisburg Civil War Roundtable Collection, USAHEC; George Burroughs to Patrick O'Connell, 7:30 P.M., 31 August 1863, Burroughs Papers, NARA; Hoffman, *"Brave Mechanics,"* 162–63.

4. Garfield to Crittenden, 10:00 A.M., 2 September 1863, Garfield to Granger, 11:00 A.M., 2 September 1863, Garfield to Innes, 11:00 A.M., 2 September 1863, Garfield to Thompson, 2 September 1863, Garfield to Morgan, 2 September 1863, Goddard to Granger, 2 September 1863, Goddard to Morgan, 2 September 1863, Bond to Sheridan, 2 September 1863, Bond to Granger, 2 September 1863, Thoms to Irvin, 2 September 1863, Thoms to Beggs, 2 September 1863, Garfield to Crittenden, 2:00 P.M., 2 September 1863, and Drouillard to Sheridan, 2 September 1863, all in DC, Telegrams Sent, NARA; *OR* 30(3):298, 302, 303, 305, 309, 310, 314.

5. *OR* 30(3):303, 976–77; *OR* 30(4):127; James P. Brownlow to Sir, 30 May 1867, Ruger Correspondence, Thomas Papers, NARA; Post Diary, 2 September 1863, Post Papers, KC; Mayfield Diary, 2 September 1863, IU; *SOR* 28:537; *OR* 30(1):510–11, 529; Mosman, *Rough Side*, 71–72; Herr, *Nine Campaigns*, 356; *SOR* 25:38; William P. Carlin, *National Tribune*, 2 April 1885; *SOR* 21:449, 456; Patterson Diary, 2 September 1863, MHM; Isaac P. Rule to his brother, 3 September 1863, Rule Letters, HPL; *SOR* 23:19; Colyer Diary, 2 September 1863, ALPL; *SOR* 66:679, 702; Day, *One Hundred and First Ohio*, 143–44; *SOR* 43:664, 671; John A. Martin to his sister, 5 September 1863, Martin Letters, KSHS; James E. Love to "Molly," Love Papers, MHM; *SOR* 33:541, 587; Himoe Diary, 2 September 1863, NAHA; *SOR* 22:61, 73, 561, 567; *SOR* 87:67.

6. U.S. Geological Survey, 1:24,000 Series, Alabama Quadrangles: Ider, Sulphur Springs, Dugout Valley, and Valley Head; "Survey from Winson's to Lebanon by L. H. Case, Sept. 5th 1863," Adjutant General's Office, Union Battle Reports, NARA; William P. Carlin, *National Tribune*, 2 April 1885; Mosman, *Rough Side*, 72; Cope, *Fifteenth Ohio*, 303; Pickering Diary, 2 September 1863, HL; Welk Diary, 2 September 1863, BGSU; Kiene, *Journal*, 170; Phillips Diary, 2 September 1863, and George Phillips to his wife, 2 September

1863, Phillips Collection, HL; Willoughby Diary, 2 September 1863, Willoughby Manuscript Collection; ISL; Dean Diary, 2 September 1863, private collection; *SOR* 27:405, 689; Chapin, "Diary," 232; *SOR* 28:774, 837; Davidson, *Battery A*, 83; *SOR* 25:156; Bergun H. Brown to his friends, 2–4 September 1863, Brown Papers, IHS; Lyon Diary, 2 September 1863, OHS; Moon Diary, 2 September 1863, KSHS; Beck Diary, 2 September 1863, KSHS; Protsman Diary, 2 September 1863, WSU; E. T. Hooker to "My Dear Jessie," 7 September 1863, private collection; *SOR* 62:541; Ashmun Diary, 2 September 1863, CCNMP; Shideler Diary, 2 September 1863, CCNMP; Hiram Strong to his wife, 4 September 1863, Strong Letters, CCNMP; Henry Richards to his father, 4–5 September 1863, Gilbert-Richards Papers, MU; Briant, *Sixth Indiana*, 223; Doll, *Sixth Indiana*, 67; *SOR* 34:198; Robinson Diary, 2 September 1863, Regimental Papers, WRHS; Widney Diary, 2 September 1863, KMNMP.

7. *OR* 30(3):315; *OR* 30(1):907–9, 918, 927; Thomas Diary, 2 September 1863, UT; D. M. Ray to Edward Ruger, 6 October 1867, Ruger Correspondence, Thomas Papers, NARA; Kendall Diary, 2 September 1863, HL; Mendenhall Diary, 2 September 1863, IHS; Baum Diary, 2 September 1863, IHS; *SOR* 86:654, 690; Merrill, *Diary*, 51; Orson Clinton to "Dear Friend Anna," 2 September 1863, Clinton Family Papers, CU; Read Diary, 2 September 1863, KSHS; *Wisconsin State Journal*, 17 October 1863; Persons Diary, 2 September 1863, WHS; Leeper Diary, 2 September 1863, SRNB; Harris Diary, 2 September 1863, IHS; Greenwood Diary, 2 September 1863, Knight Family Papers, UAK; Eli Long to Edward Ruger, 15 June 1867, Ruger Correspondence, Thomas Papers, NARA; Curry, *Four Years*, 108; George Kryder to his wife, 7 September 1863, Kryder Papers, BGSU; *SOR* 61:687; Crofts, *Third Ohio Cavalry*, 112; Crane Diary, 2 September 1863, CIHS; Pape-Findley, *Fourth Ohio Cavalry*, 157; O. O. Smith to Edward Ruger, 27 April 1867, Ruger Correspondence, Thomas Papers, NARA; Crane Diary, 2 September 1863, Thomas Papers, NARA; Thomson Diary, 2 September 1863, CCNMP; Elijah Watts to Edward Ruger, 17 June 1867, Ruger Correspondence, Thomas Papers, NARA; *Historical Sketch, CBOT Battery*, 24; Nourse Diary, 2 September 1863, DU; *SOR* 20:456; Lester Diary, 2 September 1863, ALPL; Prickitt, *Company H*, 102–3.

8. *OR* 30(1):269, 325, 386, 393, 398; Johnston, *Soldier Boy*, 54–55; Clark Diary, 2 September 1863, Clark Papers, USAHEC; *SOR* 72:502, 515; Henry A. Hambright Report, 1889, Union Battle Reports, NARA; *SOR* 87:106, 129; *SOR* 88:253, 257, 267; Otto, *Mudsill*, 158; Galpin Diary, 2 September 1863, Galpin Family Papers, WHS; *SOR* 21:358, 376, 622, 641, 652; Hinkley Diary, 2 September 1863, and Lucius D. Hinkley to his mother, 8 September 1863, both in Hinkley Papers, WHS; Robert J. Bates to his parents, 5 September 1863, and Bates Memorandum, Bates Papers, WHS; Wallace W. Darrah to his father, 8 [2] September 1863, Darrah Papers, NC; Webster Diary, 2 September 1863, Civil War Miscellaneous Collection, USAHEC; Knapp Diary, 2 September 1863, WHS; Robert Newell Elder to his sister, 4 September 1863, OHS; Frank M. Phelps to his friends, 9 September 1863, Phelps Letters, Lewis Leigh Collection, USAHEC; Edmonds Diary, 2 September 1863, USAHEC; *Record, Ninety-Fourth Ohio*, 36; Bloom Diary, 2 September 1863, CCNMP; Sheffield Diary, 2 September 1863, CCNMP; Johnston Diary, 2 September 1863, and Joseph S. Johnston to his mother, 5 September 1863, both in Johnston Collection, CHS; Haynie, *Nineteenth Illinois*, 215; Christian Diary, 2 September 1863, CCNMP; Sturges Diary, 2 September 1863, Sturges Papers, *Civil War Times Illustrated* Collection, USAHEC; Blackburn, *Letters*, 145–46; *SOR* 65:678; Andrew G. Wickham to his parents, September 1863, Wickham Letter, UT; Weaver Diary, 2 September 1863, SRNB; John W. Baldwin to his wife, 5 September 1863, Baldwin Papers,

OHS; Dilworth Journal, 3 September 1863, HC; Adams, "Diary," 648; Canfield, *Twenty-First Ohio*, 104; Shanks Diary, 2 September 1863, BGSU; Ward Diary, 2 September 1863, Ward Papers, DP; *SOR* 62:350; Nupp Diary, 2 September 1863, CCNMP; Millen Diary, 2 September 1863, SRNB; Hinchberger Diary, 2 September 1863, CCNMP; Gibson, *Seventy-Eighth Pennsylvania*, 83; Keegan, *Diaries*, 23–24; Inskeep Diary, 2 September 1863, OHS; Wheeler Diary, 2 September 1863, OHS; Price Diary, 2 September 1863, Civil War Miscellaneous Collection, USAHEC; Small Diary, 2 September 1863, IHS; Ferdinand Van Derveer to his wife, 2 September 1863, Van Derveer Letters, SLRH; Billings D. Sibley to his mother, 2 September 1863, Sibley Papers, MHS; Donahower Account, 2 September 1863, Donahower Papers, MHS; Reed Diary, 2 September 1863, MHS; Martling Diary, 2 September 1863, Martling Manuscript Collection; Williams, *Extracts*, 88–89; Alanson R. Ryman to Jane Ryman, 9 September 1863, Ryman Letters, IHS; Miller Journal, 2 September 1863, IHS; Essington, "Second Years' History," Essington Papers, IHS; Hollingsworth Diary, 2 September 1863, IHS; Parker Diary, 2 September 1863, HL; Morse, *Diaries*, 32; Tourgee, "Diary," 118; John T. Booth, *National Tribune*, 25 September 1890; Ward Diary, 2 September 1863, Booth Papers, OHS; Phillips, *Turchin*, 101; Josiah D. Cotton to his wife, 2 September 1863, Cotton Papers, LC; George B. Turner to his father, 4 September 1863, Turner Papers, OHS; Owen Diary, 2 September 1863, AU.

9. *OR* 30(3):304–5, 307–9, 978–79; *OR* 30(1):602; Garfield to Crittenden, 10:00 A.M., 2 September 1863, and Garfield to Crittenden, 2:00 P.M., 2 September 1863, both in DC, Telegrams Sent, NARA; Mallory Diary, 2 September 1863, HPL; Hight, *Fifty-Eighth Indiana*, 170; Caleb Carlton to his wife, 2 September 1863, Carlton Papers, LC; Tilford Diary, 1–2 September 1863, FHS; *History, Seventy-Ninth Indiana*, 84; Howe Diary, 2 September 1863, IHS; Huntzinger Diary, 2 September 1863, http://www.lafavre.us/huntzinger/hunt_3.htm (23 May 2016); Benedict Diary, 2 September 1863, SRNB; Hurd Diary, 2 September 1863, private collection; Claggett Diary, 2 September 1863, CCNMP; Woodcock, *Southern Boy*, 183–84; Brasher Diary, 1–3 September 1863, CCNMP; John M. Palmer to his wife, 2 September 1863, Palmer Papers II, ALPL.

10. *OR* 30(3):301, 306–7, 316–17, 327; Griest Diary, 2 September 1863, CCNMP; Records Diary, 2 September 1863, Records Manuscript Collection, ISL; Campbell Journal, 2 September 1863, CCNMP; *OR* 30(1):760; Johnston Diary, 2 September 1863, FHS; *SOR* 28:27; William B. Hazen to Benson H. Lossing, 23 August 1866, Palmer Collection, WRHS; Dewees Diary, 2 September 1863, CCNMP; Marshall Diary, 2 September 1863, OHS; Vale, *Minty*, 214–15; McLain Diary, 2 September 1863, ISHS.

11. *OR* 30(3):192, 274, 309, 311–314, 329; John H. Hoffman to his wife, 2 September 1863, Hoffman Letters, Civil War Miscellaneous Collection, USAHEC; Ferree Diary, 2 September 1863, SRNB; Decker Diary, 2 September 1863, WHS; *OR* 30(1):872; Hewes, *Tenth Michigan*, 48–49; Porter Diary, 2 September 1863, OHS; Holmes, *Then and Now*, 5; Thomas M. Burns to his father, 9 September 1863, Burns Letters, VT; Armstrong Diary, 2 September 1863, CCNMP; Fahnestock Diary, 2 September 1863, ALPL; Keeler Diary, 2 September 1863, Keeler Papers, UM-B; Robinson Diary, 2 September 1863, ALPL; Schwartz, *Diary*, 11; Patton Diary, 2 September 1863, CCNMP.

12. Pirtle, "Leaves," CIHS; Alfred Pirtle to his sister, 3 September 1863, Pirtle Letters, FHS; Ely Diary, 2 September 1863, CCNMP; Smith, *Private Smith's Journal*, 85; Simonds Diary, 2 September 1863, Simonds Papers, NIU; Smith, "Recollections," Smith Papers, ALPL; Moody Diary, 2 September 1863, SRNB; Inskeep Diary, 2 September 1863, OHS; Keegan, *Diaries*, 24; Martling Diary, 2 September 1863, Martling Manuscript Collection, ISL; Davidson Diary, 2 September 1863, NCWM; *OR* 30(3):304, 326–2 7; McCullough

Diary, 2 September 1863, ISL; Meredith Diary, 2 September 1863, Harrisburg Civil War Roundtable Collection, USAHEC; Roseberry Diary, 2 September 1863, EU; Garfield to Hunton, 8:30 P.M., 2 September 1863, Garfield to Sheridan, 9:30 P.M., 2 September 1863, and Garfield to Hunton, 10:30 P.M., 2 September 1863, all in DC, Telegrams Sent, NARA.

13. *OR* 30(3):296–98; Rosecrans to James Guthrie, 9:35 P.M., 2 September 1863, Rosecrans to Stanton, 2 September 1863, Thoms to Beggs, 2 September 1863, Thoms to Crittenden, 2 September 1863, Drouillard to Beggs, 2 September 1863, and Rosecrans to Halleck, 2 September 1863, all in DC, Telegrams Sent, NARA; Drouillard Diary, 2 September 1863, Rosecrans Papers, UCLA; *OR* 30(1):653; Woodruff, *Fifteen Years,* 279–80; Hight, *Fifty-Eighth Indiana,* 170.

14. Brent to Mauldin, 2 September 1863, Brent to Wharton, 2 September 1863, Brent to Polk, 2 September 1863, Brent to Hill, 2 September 1863, and Brent to Liddell, 2 September 1863, all in Bragg Papers, WRHS; *OR* 30(4):584; Brent Diary, 2 September 1863, Bragg Papers, WRHS; Liddell, *Record,* 134–36.

15. Liddell, *Record,* 136; Bragg to Seddon, 2 September 1863, Bragg Papers, WRHS; *OR* 30(4):583–84.

16. Brent to Mauldin, 2 September 1863, Brent to Wharton, 2 September 1863, Brent to Martin, 2 September 1863, Brent to Liddell, 2 September 1863 (two messages), Brent to Polk, 2 September 1863, Brent to Hill, 2 September 1863, Brent to Gorgas, 2 September 1863, and Brent to Buckner, 2 September 1863, all in Bragg Papers, WRHS; Oladowski to Wright, 2 September 1863, Letters Sent, Ordnance Office, AT, NARA; Brent Diary, 2 September 1863, Bragg Papers, WRHS; Eicher and Eicher, *High Commands,* 329; Davis and Hoffman, *Confederate General,* 4:2; John H. Kelly CSR, NARA; Allardice, *Confederate Colonels,* 248; McMicken to Gribble, 2 September 1863, Army of Tennessee Files, KMNMP; Bragg to Brown, 2 September 1863, Bragg Papers, WRHS.

17. Brent Diary, 2 September 1863, Bragg Papers, WRHS; Liddell, *Record,* 136.

18. *OR* 30(4):584–86.

19. James A. Hall to Bolling Hall Sr., 2 September 1863, Hall Family Papers, ADAH; D. L. Kelly to S. J. Honnoll, 2 September 1863, Honnoll Family Papers, EU; *SOR* 45:87, 151, 211; *SOR* 46:65, 72, 74, 289; Rand Diary, 2 September 1863, MDAH; *SOR* 13:679; Fraser Diary, 2 September 1863, CCNMP; Manigault, *Carolinian,* 92; Polk to Hindman, 2 September 1863, Letters Sent, Polk's Command, NARA; Moorman, "Moorman Memorandum," 78; Fielder Diary, 2 September 1863, TSLA; Rennolds Diary, 2 September 1863, CCNMP; Magee Diary, 2 September 1863, DU; Brown Notebook, 2 September 1863, CCNMP; Etter Diary, 2 September 1863, SRNB; Coleman Diary, 2 September 1863, UNC; Smith Diary, 2 September 1863, CCNMP; Heartsill, *Fourteen Hundred,* 146; *SOR* 80:160, 181; *SOR* 14:280; *SOR* 79:221; Sparkman Diary, 2 September 1863, BPL; *SOR* 35:408; Jackman Journal, 2 September 1863, LC; Pasco Diary, 2–4 September 1863, CCNMP; *SOR* 61:455; Claudius C. Wilson to his wife, 3 September 1863, Wilson Papers, GHS; Capers Diary, 2 September 1863, CI; Grammer Diary, 2 September 1863, CCNMP; Freeman Diary, 2 September 1863, TSLA; Brief Narrative, http://www.perryvillebattlefield.org/html/ms-swett-charles-cs.html (24 July 2012).

20. Coleman Diary, 2 September 1863, UNC; *SOR* 46:64–65, 72, 74; Heartsill, *Fourteen Hundred,* 146; *SOR* 14:215, 220, 280–81; *SOR* 79:156, 221, 246, 550; Sparkman Diary, 2 September 1863, BPL; Dyer, *Diary,* 20; *SOR* 78:125; Davis Diary, 2 September 1863, TSLA; *OR* 30(4):586–87; Owen, *Camp and Battle,* 269; *SOR* 13:912, 917; Brown Diary, 2 September 1863, CCNMP; Holmes, *Diary,* 17; Ulmer, *Stockton Correspondence,* 220; Watson Journal, 2 September 1863, CCNMP; Dugger/White Diary, *Watauga (N.C.)*

Democrat, 14 May 1891; Joseph S. Espey to his sister, 3 September 1863, Espey Family Letters, UNC. Although Hess (*Knoxville Campaign*, 14) gave the Loudon railroad bridge's length at 900 feet, and a Federal soldier estimated it to be 370 yards (Rudy Diary, 4 September 1863, UK), the Federal railroad constructor who rebuilt it claimed in an official report that it was 1,700 feet in length (*OR*, Series 3, 5:942).

21. Sloan Diary, 2 September 1863, TSLA; *OR* 30(3):333–34; Allen Memoirs, TSLA; Allen, "Loudon Bridge," 44; Allen, *Reminiscences*, 31–32; Leverich Diary, 2 September 1863, LSU; Rudy Diary, 4–5 September 1863, UK; *OR* 30(4):587.

22. *OR* 51(2):761; *OR* 52(2):519–20; *OR* 30(4):565–66, 575; Freeman, *Lee's Lieutenants*, 3:163–65; Wert, *Longstreet*, 300–301; Piston, *Tarnished Lieutenant*, 65–67; Robertson, "Bull of the Woods," 117–19; Longstreet, *Manassas to Appomattox*, 434–35; James Longstreet to "General" [Robert E. Lee], 2 September 1863, Longstreet Papers, GDAH.

23. *OR* 30(3):322–23.

24. Larew Diary, 2–3 September 1863, IHS; McCullough Diary, 3 September 1863, ISL; Meredith Diary, 3 September 1863, Harrisburg Civil War Roundtable Collection, USAHEC; Shultz, *Diary*, 31; *OR* 30(3):326–27, 341–42; Memorandum, Robert J. Bates Letters, WHS; Wallace W. Darrah to his father, 8 [3] September 1863, Darrah Papers, NC; Frank M. Phelps to his friends, 9 September 1863, Phelps Letters, Lewis Leigh Collection, USAHEC; Webster Diary, 3 September 1863, Civil War Miscellaneous Collection, USAHEC; Robert Newell Elder to his sister, 4 September 1863, Elder Letters, OHS; Clark Diary, 3 September 1863, Clark Papers, USAHEC; *Record, Ninety-Fourth Ohio*, 36; Drouillard Diary, 3 September 1863, Rosecrans Papers, UCLA; Roseberry Diary, 3 September 1863, EU.

25. *OR* 30(1):325, 383–84, 386, 393, 396, 1063; James S. Negley to George E. Flynt, 3 September 1863, DC, Letters Received, NARA; Hough, *Soldier*, 133–34n; Blackburn, *Letters*, 146; Andrew G. Wickham to his parents, September 1863, UT; Nupp Diary, 3 September 1863, CCNMP; Weaver Diary, 3 September 1863, SRNB; John W. Baldwin to his wife, 5 September 1863, Baldwin Papers, OHS; Shanks Diary, 3 September 1863, BGSU; Dilworth Journal, 3 September 1863, HC; Adams, "Diary," 648–49; Canfield, *Twenty-First Ohio*, 104; Ward Diary, 3 September 1863, Ward Papers, DP; Puntenny, *Thirty-Seventh Indiana*, 48; Archibald Blakely, in Skinner, *Pennsylvania at Chickamauga*, 217; Hinchberger Diary, 3 September 1863, CCNMP; Gibson, *Seventy-Eighth Pennsylvania*, 84; Millen Diary, 3 September 1863, SRNB; Bloom Diary, 3 September 1863, CCNMP; Sheffield Diary, 3 September 1863, CCNMP; Joseph S. Johnston to his mother, 5 September 1863, and Johnston Diary, 3 September 1863, both in Johnston Collection, CHS; Christian Diary, 3 September 1863, CCNMP; Haynie, *Nineteenth Illinois*, 215; *SOR* 21:358, 376; Eben P. Sturges to "Dear Folks," 5 September 1863 and 2 October 1863, and Sturges Diary, 3 September 1863, all in Sturges Papers, *Civil War Times Illustrated* Collection, USAHEC; Beatty, *Citizen Soldier*, 327; Hapeman Diary, 3 September 1863, ALPL; Calkins, *One Hundred and Fourth Illinois*, 110–11; Kirkpatrick, *Experiences*, 46; Harris Diary, 3 September 1863, CCNMP.

26. Williams, *Extracts*, 89; John T. Booth, *National Tribune*, 25 September 1890; Ward Diary, 3 September 1863, Booth Papers, OHS; Owen Diary, 3 September 1863, AU; George B. Turner to his father, 4 September 1863, Turner Papers, OHS; *SOR* 34:477; Lyle, *Lights*, 278–79; Steward Diary, 3 September 1863, *Chattanooga (Tenn.) Free Press*, 21 September 1938, CPL; *SOR* 63:162, 166; Andrew, *Letters*, 74; *SOR* 27:652; *OR* 30(1):246, 264, 398, 470; Mauzy, *Sixty-Eighth Indiana*, 11; Shera Diary, 3 September 1863, FHS; Alanson R. Ryman to Jane Ryman, 9 September 1863, Ryman Letters, IHS; Gates Diary,

3 September 1863, IHS; High, *Sixty-Eighth Indiana*, 54; Floyd, *Seventy-Fifth Indiana*, 121; Miller Journal, 3 September 1863, IHS; Hollingsworth Diary, 3 September 1863, IHS; Parker Diary, 3 September 1863, HL; Morse, *Diaries*, 32–33; Tourgee, "Diary," 118; Taylor Diary, 3 September 1863, SRNB; *SOR* 27:637; Inskeep Diary, 3 September 1863, OHS; Wheeler Diary, 3 September 1863, OHS; DeVelling, *Seventeenth Ohio*, 74; Albert J. Baldwin to his parents, 6 September 1863, Baldwin Letters, UND; Hunter, *Eighty-Second Indiana*, 54; Price Diary, 3 September 1863, Civil War Miscellaneous Collection, USAHEC; Small Diary, 3 September 1863, IHS; Letter excerpt, Everett F. Abbott to his mother, 4 September 1863, Chamberlain Papers, IHS; Chase, *Fourteenth Ohio*, 45; Bishop, *Story*, 93–94; Bircher, *Drummer-Boy*, 71–72; Reed Diary, 3 September 1863, MHS; Keegan, *Diaries*, 24; Martling Diary, 3 September 1863, Martling Manuscript Collection, ISL; Davidson Diary, 3 September 1863, NCWM; *OR* 30(3):323–25; Bennett, *Ninth Michigan*, 33; Carpenter Diary, 3 September 1863, SRNB.

27. John Levering Account, CCNMP; *OR* 30(3):344, 980–82; *OR* 30(1):626, 653, 687, 701, 726, 740, 751, 754, 780, 788; Hight, *Fifty-Eighth Indiana*, 170–71; Woodruff, *Fifteen Years*, 280; Charles G. Harker to N. T. Stratton, 1 October 1863, Harker Letters, private collection; Hinman, *Sherman Brigade*, 408; Mallory Diary, 3 September 1863, HPL; Gillis Diary, 5 September 1863, OHS; Joseph Bruff to his wife, 9 September 1863, Bruff Family Collection, private collection; Emerson Opdycke to his wife, 4 September 1863, and Opdycke Diary, 3 September 1863, both in Opdycke Papers, OHS; Duncan Thompson to his parents, 8 September 1863, Thompson Letters, Brookes Collection, USAHEC; *SOR* 62:413; *SOR* 65:389, 419; *SOR* 67:603; McKee Diary, 3 September 1863, http://mckee-burns.pasttracker.com/mckee/cw_mckee/mckee_robert_t_cw_diary_1 (June 2013); Mason Diary, 3 September 1863, SRNB; Smith, *Thirty-First Indiana*, 58; Connelly Diary, 3 September 1863, IHS; Dillman Diary, 3 September 1863, IU; Harden, *90th Ohio*, 91, 96–97; Marshall Diary, 3 September 1863, OHS; Busbey Diary, 3 September 1863, SRNB; Hyde Diary, 3 September 1863, KYHS; George W. Botkin to Liddie C. Baker, 5 September 1863, Baker Correspondence, OHS; *SOR* 34:58, 106; Cutter, *Our Battery*, 130–31; Glisan Diary, 3 September 1863, CCNMP; Hannaford, *Sixth Ohio*, 443; *SOR* 62:780; Williams Diary, 3 September 1863, CCNMP; Grose, *Thirty-Sixth Indiana*, 172–73; Suiter Diary, 3 September 1863, ALPL; Simmons, *84th Illinois*, 76; Walker Diary, 3 September 1863, Harrisburg Civil War Roundtable Collection, USAHEC; Christopher Wetsel to his wife, 4 September 1863, Wetsel Letters, WIU; Palmer Journal, 3 September 1863, CCNMP; Benedict Diary, 3 September 1863, SRNB; Hurd Diary, 3 September 1863, private collection; Woodcock, *Southern Boy*, 184; Claggett Diary, 3 September 1863, CCNMP; Tilford Diary, 3 September 1863, FHS; *History, Seventy-Ninth Indiana*, 84; Howe Diary, 3 September 1863, IHS; Huntzinger Diary, 3 September 1863, http://www.lafavre.us/huntzinger/hunt_3.htm (23 May 2016); Claiborne J. Walton to "My Dear Nannie," Walton Letter, Hess Collection, USAHEC; *SOR* 30:279; Barnes, Carnahan, and McCain, *Eighty-Sixth Indiana*, 145; Moore Diary, 3 September 1863, CCNMP; McCain, *Song*, 87; *SOR* 63:267; Rerick, *Forty-Fourth Indiana*, 91; Morgan and Murphy, *7th Indiana Battery*, 22; Decker Diary, 3 September 1863, WHS.

28. *OR* 30(1):485, 510–11, 894, 898–99, 901, 903, 909, 912; *OR* 30(3):325–26, 331, 333, 977; Post Diary, 3 September 1863, Post Papers, KC; Mayfield Diary, 3 September 1863, IU; Mosman, *Rough Side*, 72–73; Patterson Diary, 3 September 1863, ALPL; *SOR* 23:19; Colyer Diary, 3 September 1863, ALPL; *SOR* 43:664; *SOR* 28:837; Cope, *Fifteenth Ohio*, 303; Pickering Diary, 3 September 1863, HL; Welk Diary, 3 September 1863, BGSU; Phillips Diary, 3 September 1863, Phillips Collection, HL; Kiene, *Journal*, 170; Willoughby Diary,

3 September 1863, Willoughby Manuscript Collection, ISL; Dean Diary, 3 September 1863, private collection; Davidson, *Battery A*, 83; *SOR* 25:156; Bergun H. Brown to his friends, 2–4 September 1863, Brown Papers, IHS; Robinson Diary, 3 September 1863, Regimental Papers, WRHS; Lyon Diary, 3 September 1863, OHS; Moon Diary, 3 September 1863, KSHS; Beck Diary, 3 September 1863, KSHS; Protsman Diary, 3 September 1863, WSU; *SOR* 62:541; Ashmun Diary, 3 September 1863, CCNMP; Shideler Diary, 3 September 1863, CCNMP; Demoret, *Ninety-Third Ohio*, 21; Hiram Strong to his wife, 4 September 1863, Strong Letters, CCNMP; Briant, *Sixth Indiana*, 223; Doll, *Sixth Indiana*, 67; Roswell M. Russell to Edward Ruger, 12 January 1867, and Leonidas S. Scranton to Edward Ruger, 8 June 1867, both in Ruger Correspondence, Thomas Papers, NARA; *SOR* 41:722; Hempstead Diary, 3 September 1863, UM-B; Thomas Diary, 3 September 1863, UT; Carter, *First Tennessee Cavalry*, 85–86; Kendall Diary, 3 September 1863, HL; Baum Diary, 3 September 1863, IHS; Leeper Diary, 3 September 1863, SRNB; Merrill, *Diary*, 51; Orson Clinton to his sister, 5 September 1863, Clinton Family Papers, CU; Read Diary, 3 September 1863, KSHS; Persons Diary, 3 September 1863, WHS; *Wisconsin State Journal*, 17 October 1863; Harris Diary, 3 September 1863, IHS; *SOR* 33:746; Greenwood Diary, 3 September 1863, Knight Family Papers, UAK; Nourse Diary, 3 September 1863, DU; Lester Diary, 3 September 1863, ALPL; Curry, *Four Years*, 108; George Kryder to his wife, 7 September 1863, Kryder Papers, BGSU; Crofts, *Third Ohio Cavalry*, 112; Feagles Diary, 3 September 1863, CCNMP; Crane Diary, 3 September 1863, Thomas Papers, NARA; Crane Diary, 3 September 1863, CIHS; Pape-Findley, *Fourth Ohio Cavalry*, 157; Prickitt, *Company H*, 103; Thomson Diary, 3 September 1863, CCNMP.

29. Griest Diary, 3 September 1863, CCNMP; Records Diary and Reminiscences, 3 September 1863, Records Manuscript Collection, ISL; Campbell Journal, 3 September 1863, CCNMP; Marshall Diary, 3 September 1863, OHS; Hines Diary, 3 September 1863, Hines Manuscript Collection, ISL; *OR* 30(1):759–60; *OR* 30(3):327–28, 356; McLain Diary, 3 September 1863, ISHS; Haines, "Fourth Michigan Cavalry," UM-B; Robertson, *Michigan in the War*, 654.

30. *OR* 30(3):328–31; Winans Diary, 3 September 1863, CCNMP; Porter Diary, 3 September 1863, OHS; Holmes, *Then and Now*, 5; Thomas M. Burns to his father, 9 September 1863, Burns Letters, VT; Fahnestock Diary, 3 September 1863, ALPL; Armstrong Diary, 3 September 1863, CCNMP; Putney Diary, 3 September 1863, KMNMP.

31. *OR* 30(3):321; Rosecrans to Halleck, 3 September 1863, Thoms to Captain Perkins, A. Q. M. Nashville, 3 September 1863, Thoms to Captain Irwin, A. Q. M. Nashville, 3 September 1863, Thoms to Colonel Smith, Murfreesboro, 3 September 1863, and Goddard to King, 3 September 1863, all in DC, Telegrams Sent, NARA; Smith, *Garfield*, 1:318; Colton, *Journal and Correspondence*, 153.

32. "Summaries of the News," 325–27, NARA. Sherlock's base was probably in McLemore's Cove, known to be populated by many Union sympathizers. The name Sherlock was probably a pseudonym, as no Sherlocks were listed in northwestern Georgia in the Federal Censuses of 1850, 1860, or 1870.

33. Brent Diary, 3 September 1863, Bragg Papers, WRHS.

34. Brent to Polk, Hill, Buckner, Wheeler, and Forrest, 3 September 1863, Brent to Beard, 3 September 1863, Brent to McDonald, 3 September 1863, Brent to Rice, 3 September 1863, Brent to Buckner, 3 September 1863, Brent to Hill, 3 September 1863, Brent to Pillow, 3 September 1863 (two messages), Brent to Wright, 3 September 1863, Brent to Commanding Officer, Paroled Prisoners, 3 September 1863, and Brent to Jones, 3 September 1863, all in Bragg Papers, WRHS; Special Orders, No. 237, Bragg

Papers, WRHS; Oladowski to Wright, 3 September 1863, and Oladowski to Humphries, 3 September 1863, both in Letters Sent, Ordnance Office, Army of Tennessee, NARA. George Brent recorded the favorable view of Forrest in his headquarters diary: "Forrest is the best of our cavalry commanders. He has been uniformly successful: Kept his men in good order, & in an improving condition. He is brave & active, & a man of excellent judgment. Had he been educated & cultivated he would have made a higher reputation. He is honest zealous, & his heart is in the work in which he is engaged." Brent Diary, 3 September 1863, Bragg Papers, WRHS. For Gideon Pillow's activities as conscription officer during this period, see Hughes and Stonesifer, *Pillow*, 267–72.

35. *OR* 30(4):588; Brent Diary, 4 September 1863, Bragg Papers, WRHS; Hill to Bragg, 3 September 1863, Hill Papers, LV.

36. Moorman, "Moorman Memorandum," 78; Rennolds Diary, 3 September 1863, CCNMP; Fielder Diary, 3 September 1863, TSLA; Freeman Diary, 3 September 1863, TSLA; Rand Diary, 3 September 1863, MDAH; Fraser Diary, 3 September 1863, CCNMP; Thaddeus Marion Brindley to his sister, 3 September 1863, Brindley Letters, CCNMP; Freeman Diary, 3 September 1863, BPL; Robert L. Bliss to his father, 3 September 1863, Bliss Letters, ADAH; Marsh, "Confederate Letters," 27–28.

37. Coleman Diary, 3 September 1863, UNC; Heartsill, *Fourteen Hundred*, 146; *SOR* 14:291; Sparkman Diary, 3 September 1863, BPL; Pasco Diary, 3 September 1863, CCNMP; *SOR* 35:206, 208, 210; Claudius C. Wilson to his wife, 3 September 1863, Wilson Papers, GHS; *OR* 30(4):590–92; Abram H. Glazener to his wife, 3 September 1863, Glazener Letters, *Civil War Times Illustrated* Collection, USAHEC; Ulmer, *Stockton Correspondence*, 220; Quintus S. Adams to his mother, 3 September 1863, Adams Letters, *Civil War Times Illustrated* Collection, USAHEC; *Memphis Daily Appeal*, 3 September 1863. Linebaugh wrote from Dalton, Georgia.

38. Dyer, *Diary*, 20; Davis Diary, 3 September 1863, TSLA; *OR* 30(4):585–86, 589, 590–91; Sloan Diary, 3 September 1863, TSLA; Leverich Diary, 3 September 1863, LSU; Davis and Hoffman, *Confederate General*, 3:110; Corbitt Diary, 3 September 1863, EU; Dodd, *Diary*, 22; Stevenson, "Smith," 43–44; Shields Diary, 3 September 1863, http://freepages.genealogy.rootsweb.ancestry.com/~sassytazzy/family/surnames/shields (1 February 2009). For John Pegram's command difficulties, see Griggs, *Pegram*, 74–75. For the composition of Hodge's Brigade, see *OR* 23(2):945, and *OR* 31(3):582, 747, 771.

39. *OR* 30(3):342–43, 346, 353; Smith Diary, 4 September 1863, CCNMP; Kirk, *Fifteenth Pennsylvania Cavalry*, 222, 228, 280; Wilson, *Column South*, 85; *SOR* 69:312, 320, 322, 341, 347, 354, 363, 370, 379, 386, 391, 398, 405, 412; Frankenberry Diary, 4 September 1863, WVU; Garfield to Morgan, 4 September 1863, and Goddard to Innes, 4 September 1863, both in DC, Telegrams Sent, NARA.

40. Roseberry Diary, 4 September 1863, EU; Larew Diary, 4 September 1863, IHS; Meredith Diary, 4 September 1863, Harrisburg Civil War Roundtable Collection, USAHEC; Shultz, *Diary*, 31; McCullough Diary, 4 September 1863, ISL; *OR* 30(3):297, 301, 316, 339, 348–49, 351, 357–58; Rosecrans to Halleck, 4 September 1863, and Garfield to Granger, 4 September 1863 (two messages), all in DC, Telegrams Sent, NARA. The copy of Rosecrans's message to Halleck printed in the *Official Records* indicates it was sent from Stevenson, but the copy in the Department of the Cumberland telegraph log places its origin at Bridgeport, a more likely location given Rosecrans's early departure from the Stevenson headquarters and subsequent messages by both Rosecrans and Garfield from Bridgeport.

41. Shultz, *Diary*, 31; McCullough Diary, 4 September 1863, ISL; *OR* 30(3):339–44, 352;

Bond to Morgan, 1 P.M., 4 September 1863, Drouillard to King, 4 September 1863, and Rosecrans to Halleck, 4 September 1863, all in DC, Telegrams Sent, NARA; Burroughs to O'Connell, 5 September 1863, Burroughs Papers, NARA; Hiram Russell to his wife and children, 5 September 1863, Russell Letters, SRNB; Roseberry Diary, 4 September 1863, EU; Kirk, *Fifteenth Pennsylvania Cavalry*, 222, 228; Frankenberry Diary, 4 September 1863, WVU; Smith, *Civil War Tour for Cavers*, 43.

42. *OR* 30(1):325, 384, 386, 393, 396, 1063; Hough, *Soldier*, 134; Blackburn, *Letters*, 146–47; Weaver Diary, 4 September 1863, SRNB; John W. Baldwin to his wife, 5 September 1863, Baldwin Papers, OHS; Adams, "Diary," 649; Dilworth Journal, 4 September 1863, HC; Shanks Diary, 4 September 1863, BGSU; Ward Diary, 4 September 1863, Ward Papers, DP; Archibald Blakely, in Skinner, *Pennsylvania at Chickamauga*, 217; Gibson, *Seventy-Eighth Pennsylvania*, 83–84; Nupp Diary, 4 September 1863, CCNMP; Millen Diary, 4 September 1863, SRNB; Hinchberger Diary, 4 September 1863, CCNMP; Bloom Diary, 4 September 1863, CCNMP; Sheffield Diary, 4 September 1863, CCNMP; Johnston Diary, 4 September 1863, Johnston Collection, CHS; Christian Diary, 4 September 1863, CCNMP; Fenton Reminiscences, ALPL; Haynie, *Nineteenth Illinois*, 215; *SOR* 21:358, 376; Shotts Diary, 4 September 1863, SRNB; Sturges Diary, 4 September 1863, Sturges Papers, *Civil War Times Illustrated* Collection, USAHEC; Beatty, *Citizen Soldier*, 327–28; Calkins, *One Hundred and Fourth Illinois*, 111; Hapeman Diary, 4 September 1863, ALPL; Harris Diary, 4 September 1863, CCNMP; Kirkpatrick, *Experiences*, 46; *SOR* 20:439; *OR* 30(3):347; Sheridan, *Memoirs*, 1:273–74; Smith, *Private Smith's Journal*, 86–87; Luther Bradley to his wife, 8 September 1863, Bradley Papers, USAHEC; Austin Diary, 4 September 1863, ALPL; Crippin, "Diary," 280; Lyman H. Needham to his brother and sister, 12 September 1863, Needham Papers, ALPL; *SOR* 23:208, 248; Riley, *Diary*, 53; Simonds Diary, 4 September 1863, Simonds Papers, NIU; Tabler Diary, 4 September 1863, private collection; Burns Diary, 4 September 1863, CCNMP; Moody Diary, 4 September 1863, SRNB; Colburn/Gray Diary, 4 September 1863, private collection; Pirtle, "Leaves," CIHS; Mann Diary, 4 September 1863, Robert W. Walker, "Union Soldier's Diary," *Chattanooga (Tenn.) Times*, 25 April 1937, clipping in CPL; Pecoy Diary, 4 September 1863, CCNMP; Cummins Diary, 4 September 1863, Cummins Papers, ALPL; Bennett and Haigh, *Thirty-Sixth Illinois*, 449; Cooley Diary, 4 September 1863, WHS; Ely Diary, 4 September 1863, CCNMP; E. E. Stebbins, *National Tribune*, 19 October 1899; Merrill, *Soldier*, 2:436; Newlin, *Seventy-Third Illinois*, 209–10.

43. *OR* 30(3):341–42, 344; Levering Account, CCNMP; O. Q. Herrick, Report of Chickamauga Campaign, 19 February 1864, Union Battle Reports, NARA; Williams, *Extracts*, 89; Turchin, "Diary," 61–62 [date incorrect]; *OR* 30(1):398, 470, 476; Ward Diary, 4 September 1863, Booth Papers, OHS; Owen Diary, 4 September 1863, AU; George B. Turner to his father, 4 September 1863, Turner Papers, OHS; Steward, "Bodies Found," *Chattanooga (Tenn.) Free Press*, 21 September 1938, clipping in CPL; Mauzy, *Sixty-Eighth Indiana*, 11; Shera Diary, 4 September 1863, FHS; Alanson R. Ryman to Jane Ryman, 9 September 1863, Ryman Letters, IHS; Gates Diary, 4 September 1863, IHS; Miller Journal, 4 September 1863, IHS; Essington, "Second Years' History," Essington Papers, IHS; Hollingsworth Diary, 4 September 1863, IHS; Parker Diary, 4 September 1863, HL; *SOR* 67:140; Tourgee, *Thousand*, 207; Morse, *Diaries*, 33; Taylor Diary, 4 September 1863, SRNB; *SOR* 27:570, 637, 643; Inskeep Diary, 4 September 1863, OHS; Wheeler Diary, 4 September 1863, OHS; Walker, "History," Thomas Papers, NARA; DeVelling, *Seventeenth Ohio*, 74; Hunter, *Eighty-Second Indiana*, 54; Albert J. Baldwin to his parents, 6 September 1863, Baldwin Letters, UND; Price Diary, 4 September 1863, Civil War

Miscellaneous Collection, USAHEC; Small Diary, 4 September 1863, IHS; Abbott Extract, 4 September 1863, Chamberlain Papers, IHS; Chase, *Fourteenth Ohio*, 45; *SOR* 34:162; John R. Beatty to "Libbie Dear," 4 September 1863, Beatty Papers, MHS; Albertson, *Letters Home*, Letter 102; Reed Diary, 4 September 1863, MHS; Bruce Diary, 4 September 1863, ISL; Keegan, *Diaries*, 24; Martling Diary, 4 September 1863, Martling Manuscript Collection, ISL; Davidson Diary, 4 September 1863, NCWM; Memorandum, Bates Letters, WHS; Frank M. Phelps to his friends, 9 September 1863, Phelps Letters, Lewis Leigh Collection, USAHEC; *Record, Ninety-Fourth Ohio*, 36; Wallace W. Darrah to his brother, 9 September 1863, Darrah Papers, NC; Lucius W. Hinkley to his mother, 8 September 1863, Hinkley Papers, WHS; Webster Diary, 4 September 1863, Civil War Miscellaneous Collection, USAHEC; *SOR* 29:107, 142; Edmonds Diary, 4 September 1863, USAHEC; Clark Diary, 4 September 1863, Clark Papers, USAHEC; Johnston, *Soldier Boy*, 55; *SOR* 72:532; *SOR* 87:124; H. C. Hobart Report, Union Battle Reports, NARA; Galpin Diary, 4 September 1863, Galpin Family Papers, WHS; Haddock, "Sketch," Haddock Papers, IHS; U.S. Surgeon-General's Office, *Medical and Surgical History*, 1:appendix, 270; *Memorial of Burnham*, 24.

44. *OR* 30(3):344–46, 353–55, 982–83; *OR* 30(1):485, 497, 510–11, 513, 529, 890, 899, 901, 903, 905, 909, 912; *OR* 30(4):127; Thruston to Davis (two messages), 11 A.M. and 6 P.M., 4 September 1863, both in Twentieth AC, Letters Sent, NARA; Brewer, *Alabama*, 235; Post Diary, 4 September 1863, Post Papers, KC; Nathaniel P. Charlot to "My Dear Harriet," undated, Charlot Papers, AU; Mayfield Diary, 4 September 1863, IU; Mosman, *Rough Side*, 73–74; Herr, *Nine Campaigns*, 356; *SOR* 25:38, 65; Society, Seventy-Fourth Illinois, *Reunion Proceedings*, 40; Dodge, *Seventy-Fifth Illinois*, 90; *SOR* 87:41, 48, 67; *SOR* 23:20; Isaac P. Rule to his brother, 6 September 1863, Rule Letters, HPL; Colyer Diary, 4 September 1863, ALPL; Patterson Diary, 4 September 1863, ALPL; *SOR* 43:664, 671; Heg, *Letters*, 240–41; John A. Martin to his sister, 4 September 1863, Martin Letters, KSHS; James E. Love to "Molly," 6 September 1863, and Love Autobiography, Love Papers, MSM; *SOR* 33:541; Himoe Diary, 4 September 1863, NAHA; *SOR* 88:6; *SOR* 22:61; Cope, *Fifteenth Ohio*, 303; Pickering Diary, 4 September 1863, HL; Welk Diary, 4 September 1863, BGSU; George Phillips to his wife, 2–4 September 1863, and Phillips Diary, 4 September 1863, Phillips Collection, HL; Kiene, *Journal*, 170; Stahl Diary, 4 September 1863, BGSU; *SOR* 27:405; Dean Diary, 4 September 1863, private collection; Willoughby Diary, 4 September 1863, Willoughby Manuscript Collection, ISL; Davidson, *Battery A*, 83; Widney Diary, 4 September 1863, KMNMP; Bergun H. Brown to his friends, 2–4 September 1863, Brown Papers, IHS; Robinson Diary, 4 September 1863, Regimental Papers, WRHS; Lyon Diary, 4 September 1863, OHS; Protsman Diary, 4 September 1863, WSU; *SOR* 62:541; Moon Diary, 4 September 1863, KSHS; Beck Diary, 4 September 1863, KSHS; Ashmun Diary, 4 September 1863, CCNMP; Shideler Diary, 4 September 1863, CCNMP; Henry Richards to his father, 4–5 September 1863, Gilbert-Richards Papers, MU; Doll, *Sixth Indiana*, 68; Briant, *Sixth Indiana*, 223; Roswell M. Russell to Edward Ruger, 12 June 1867, and Leonidas S. Scranton to Edward Ruger, 8 June 1867, both in Ruger Correspondence, Thomas Papers, NARA; *SOR* 41:752; Thatcher, *Hundred Battles*, 140; Hempstead Diary, 4 September 1863, UM-B; *SOR* 41:722; Thomas Diary, 4 September 1863, UT; Carter, *First Tennessee Cavalry*, 86; Kendall Diary, 4 September 1863, HL; Baum Diary, 4 September 1863, IHS; *SOR* 86:654; Leeper Diary, 4 September 1863, SRNB; Orson Clinton to his sister, 5 September 1863, Clinton Family Papers, CU; Merrill, *Diary*, 51–52; *Wisconsin State Journal*, 17 October 1863; Read Diary, 4 September 1863, KSHS; Persons Diary, 4 September 1863, WHS; Harris Diary, 4 September 1863, IHS; *SOR* 33:746; Curry, *Four*

Years, 108; Crofts, *Third Ohio Cavalry*, 112; Crane Diary, 4 September 1863, Thomas Papers, NARA; Thomson Diary, 4 September 1863, CCNMP; Crane Diary, 4 September 1863, CIHS.

45. *OR* 30(1):602, 687, 701, 710, 721, 726, 740, 751, 754, 788–90, 798, 802, 807, 837, 842–44, 846, 848; Decker Diary, 4 September 1863, WHS; McCain, *Song*, 87; Hinman, *Sherman Brigade*, 408; Clark, *Tigers*, 83–84; *SOR* 34:90, 150, 429, 568; Joseph Bruff to his wife, 9 September 1863, Bruff Family Collection, private collection; Emerson Opdycke to his wife, 4 September 1863, and Opdycke Diary, 4 September 1863, both in Opdycke Papers, OHS; McKee Diary, 4 September 1863, http://mckee-burns.pasttracker.com/mckee/mckee_robert_t_cw_diary_1 (15 June 2013); Mason Diary, 4 September 1863, SRNB; Connelly Diary, 4 September 1863, IHS; Smith, *Thirty-First Indiana*, 58; Busbey Diary, 4 September 1863, SRNB; Hyde Diary, 4 September 1863, KYHS; George W. Botkin to Liddie C. Baker, 5 September 1863, Baker Correspondence, OHS; Cutter, *Our Battery*, 131–32; John M. Palmer to his wife, 2–4 September 1863, Palmer Papers II, ALPL; Jonathan B. Holmes to "Anna," 7 September 1863, private collection; Glisan Diary, 4 September 1863, CCNMP; *SOR* 62:781–86; Williams Diary, 4 September 1863, CCNMP; Grose, *36th Indiana*, 173; Christopher Wetsel to his wife, 4 September 1863, Wetsel Letters, WIU; Walker Diary, 4 September 1863, Harrisburg Civil War Roundtable Collection, USAHEC; Suiter Diary, 4 September 1863, ALPL; Simmons, *84th Illinois*, 77–78; Palmer Journal, 4 September 1863, CCNMP; Van Cleve to Edward Ruger, 24 May 1867, Ruger Correspondence, Thomas Papers, NARA; *OR* 30(3):347–48, 350; Horatio Van Cleve to his wife, 4 September 1863, Van Cleve Papers, MHS; Tilford Diary, 4 September 1863, FHS; *History, Seventy-Ninth Indiana*, 84; Howe Diary, 4 September 1863, IHS; Huntzinger Diary, 4 September 1863, http://www.lafavre.us/huntzinger/hunt_3.htm (23 May 2016); Benedict Diary, 4 September 1863, SRNB; Hurd Diary, 4 September 1863, private collection; Woodcock, *Southern Boy*, 184–85; Claggett Diary, 4 September 1863, CCNMP; Morgan and Murphy, *Seventh Indiana Battery*, 22; Claiborne J. Walton to his wife, 3–4 September 1863, Walton Letter, Earl Hess Collection, USAHEC; Wright, *Eighth Kentucky*, 176–77; Moses F. Yoder to his brother, 7 September 1863, Yoder Papers, LC; *SOR* 66:635; Potter Diary, 4 September 1863, Potter Papers, UM-B.

46. *OR* 30(3):349–50, 355–56; *SOR* 34:207, 219, 227; Johnston Diary, 4 September 1863, FHS; Runion Diary, 4 September 1863, http://civilwar.illinoisgenweb.org/scrapbk/runiondiary2.html (23 March 2013); Brown Diary, 4 September 1863, *Civil War Times Illustrated* Collection, USAHEC; Albert Woodcock to his wife, 7 September 1863, Woodcock Papers, NC; *SOR* 25:499, 518; King, *Three Years*, 110; Phillips, *Diary*, 25, 157; *Ninety-Second Illinois*, 99; Dewees Diary, 4 September 1863, CCNMP; Marshall Diary, 4 September 1863, OHS; Hines Diary, 4 September 1863, Hines Manuscript Collection, ISL; Griest Diary, 4 September 1863, CCNMP; Joshua D. Foster to his parents, 9 September 1863, Foster Letters, CCNMP; Records Diary, 4 September 1863, and Records Reminiscences, Records Manuscript Collection, ISL; McLain Diary, 4 September 1863, ISHS.

47. *OR* 30(3):329, 351–52; Schwartz, *Diary*, 11; Keeler Diary, 4 September 1863, UM-B; Winans Diary, 4 September 1863, CCNMP; Hewes, *Tenth Michigan*, 49; Patton Diary, 4 September 1863, CCNMP; McAdams, *One Hundred and Thirteenth Ohio*, 38; Porter Diary, 4 September 1863, OHS; Armstrong Diary, 4 September 1863, CCNMP; Holmes, *Then and Now*, 5, 123; Thomas M. Burns to his father, 9 September 1863, Burns Letters, VT; Putney Diary, 4 September 1863, KMNMP; Brown, Murphy, and Putney, *Behind the Guns*, 52; Kinnear, *Eighty-Sixth Illinois*, 21; Fahnestock Diary, 4 September 1863, ALPL.

48. Jones Diary, 4 September 1863, SRNB; Rosecrans to Halleck, 4 September 1863, DC, Telegrams Sent, NARA; *OR* 30(3):339. At least three members of the First Battalion, Ohio Sharpshooters, part of Rosecrans's escort, spent the night in a private dwelling in the cove, so it is unlikely that Rosecrans did otherwise. Smith Diary, 4 September 1863, CCNMP.

49. Brent Diary, 4 September 1863, Brent to Hill, 4 September 1863, and Brent to Walker, 4 September 1863, all in Bragg Papers, WRHS; *OR* 30(4):594–95; Bragg to Cooper, 4 September 1863, Bragg Letters and Telegrams, NARA; *OR* 30(2):21.

50. Bragg to Hill, 10 A.M., 4 September 1863, Hill Papers, LV; *OR* 30(4):594; Scout Book, Army of Tennessee, 4 September 1863, MC; Brent to Hill, 4 September 1863, Bragg Papers, WRHS; Lumsden Diary, 4 September 1863, ADAH; Connolly, *Three Years*, 118.

51. Moorman, "Moorman Memorandum," 78; Fielder Diary, 4 September 1863, TSLA; Grammer Diary, 4 September 1863, CCNMP; Freeman Diary, 4 September 1863, TSLA; Magee Diary, 4 September 1863, DU; Etter Diary, 4 September 1863, SRNB; Circular, Polk's Corps, 4 September 1863, Letters Sent, Polk's Command, NARA; Rand Diary, 4 September 1863, MDAH; *Augusta (Ga.) Chronicle*, 6 and 9 September 1863; *Richmond Daily Dispatch*, 7 September 1863; *Macon (Ga.) Telegraph*, 21 September 1863, clipping in Civil War Miscellany, GDAH; *Richmond Examiner*, 22 September 1863; Davis, *Papers*, 9:343; Jabez R. Rhodes CSR, NARA; U.S. Federal Census, 1850, Newton County, and 1860, Fulton County, Georgia; Dyer, *Diary*, 20; Sparkman Diary, 4 September 1863, BPL; Coleman Diary, 4 September 1863, UNC; Fraser Diary, 4 September 1863, CCNMP; Isaac Madden [Miller] to his mother, 4 September 1863, Madden Letters, TSLA; *Charleston (S.C) Mercury*, 7 September 1863; Capers Diary, 4 September 1863, Capers Papers, CI. Two days before Rhodes's execution, his commander, Lt. Col. Jacob W. Aderhold, was cashiered from the service for also misappropriating substitute fees. Jacob W. Aderhold CSR, NARA.

52. *OR* 30(4):589, 595–98; Corbitt Diary, 4 September 1863, EU; Dodd, *Diary*, 22; Stevenson, "Smith," 43–44; Shields Diary, 4 September 1863, http://freepages.genealogy.rootsweb.ancestry.com/~sassytazzy/family/surnames/shields/ (1 February 2009); Owen, *Camp and Battle*, 269; *SOR* 13:917; *SOR* 79:550; Holmes, *Diary*, 17; Watson Journal, 4 September 1863, CCNMP; Jackson, *So Mourns*, 61–62; Dugger/White Diary, 4 September 1863, *Watauga (N.C.) Democrat*, 21 May 1897; Dillon Diary, 4 September 1863, TSLA; *SOR* 18:196; *SOR* 78:685, 756; Johnson Diary, 4 September 1863, Johnson Papers, NARA; Sloan Diary, 4 September 1863, TSLA; Leverich Diary, 4 September 1863, LSU; Brent to Buckner, 10:00 P.M., 4 September 1863, Bragg Papers, WRHS.

CHAPTER 15

1. *OR* 30(3):322–23, 369, 373–74; Garfield to Granger, 9:00 A.M., 5 September 1863, and Garfield to Crittenden, 5 September 1863, both in DC, Telegrams Sent, NARA.

2. *OR* 30(3):369; Kirk, *Fifteenth Pennsylvania Cavalry*, 228; Weller Journal, 5 September 1863, *Civil War Times Illustrated* Collection, USAHEC; Drouillard Diary, 5 September 1863, Rosecrans Papers, UCLA; Smith, "Rosecrans' Visit," 37, 40–45; Smith, *Civil War Tour for Cavers*, 43–46; Colton, *Journal and Correspondence*, 154; Wilson, *Column South*, 85–86; Knight Account, VMI.

3. *OR* 30(1):325, 384, 393; *OR* 30(3):363–64; Hough, *Soldier*, 134, 136; Dilworth Journal, 5 September 1863, HC; Shanks Diary, 5 September 1863, BGSU; Adams, "Diary," 649; Canfield, *21st Ohio*, 104–5; Gibson, *Seventy-Eighth Pennsylvania*, 83; Archibald Blakely, in Skinner, *Pennsylvania at Chickamauga*, 217–18; Nupp Diary, 5 September 1863, CCNMP;

Millen Diary, 5 September 1863, SRNB; Hinchberger Diary, 5 September 1863, CCNMP. The Empire State Iron Works is described in McCallie, *Iron Ores of Georgia*, 72.

4. Beatty, *Citizen Soldier*, 328–29; William R. Stookey to his wife, 5 September 1863, Stookey Letters, IHS; *SOR* 29:206; Harris Diary, 5 September 1863, CCNMP; Kirkpatrick, *Experiences*, 46; Hapeman Diary, 5 September 1863, ALPL; Calkins, *One Hundred and Fourth Illinois*, 111; Oliver Shelly to his brother, 5 September 1863, Shelly Letters, IHS; Christian Diary, 5 September 1863, CCNMP; Johnston Diary, 5 September 1863, and Joseph S. Johnston to his mother, 5 September 1863, Johnston Collection, CHS; Sheffield Diary, 5 September 1863, CCNMP; Bloom Diary, 5 September 1863, CCNMP; Shotts Diary, 5 September 1863, SRNB; Sturges Diary, 5 September 1863, and Eben Sturges to the "folks," 5 September 1863, both in Sturges Papers, *Civil War Times Illustrated* Collection, USAHEC; Blackburn, *Letters*, 147; Weaver Diary, 5 September 1863, SRNB; John W. Baldwin to his wife, 5 September 1863, Baldwin Papers, OHS; Ward Diary, 5 September 1863, Ward Papers, DP; Pirtle, "Leaves," CIHS; *OR* 30(1):246, 269–70, 398, 470, 476, 582; Pecoy Diary, 5 September 1863, CCNMP; Mann Diary, 5 September 1863, *Chattanooga (Tenn.) Times*, 25 April 1937, clipping in CPL; *SOR* 22:585, 610; Cooley Diary, 5 September 1863, WHS; John Wilcox to his wife, 5 September 1863, CCNMP; Daniel E. Barnard to his sister, 9 September 1863, Howe Barnard Family Papers, NL; Merrill, *Soldier*, 2:436; Riley, *Diary*, 53; Simonds Diary, 5 September 1863, Simonds Papers, NIU; Lyman H. Needham to his siblings, 12 September 1863, Needham Papers, ALPL; *SOR* 23:208, 248; Burns Diary, 5 September 1863, CCNMP; Moody Diary, 5 September 1863, SRNB; Colburn/Gray Diary, 5 September 1863, private collection; Tabler Diary, 5 September 1863, private collection; *SOR* 24:47; Crippin, "Diary," 280; *SOR* 22:181; Austin Diary, 5 September 1863, ALPL; Miller Journal, 5 September 1863, IHS; Parker Diary, 5 September 1863, HL; Morse, *Diaries*, 33; Tourgee, "Diary," 118; Tourgee, *Thousand*, 400; Taylor Diary, 5 September 1863, SRNB; *SOR* 67:121; Alanson R. Ryman to Jane Ryman, 9 September 1863, Ryman Letters, IHS; *SOR* 29:820; Gates Diary, 5 September 1863, IHS; Hollingsworth Diary, 5 September 1863, IHS; *SOR* 30:512, 518; *SOR* 27:570, 644; A. T. Ward Diary, 5 September 1863, Booth Papers, OHS; John T. Booth, *National Tribune*, 25 September 1890; Owen Diary, 5 September 1863, AU; George B. Turner to his mother, 9 September 1863, Turner Papers, OHS; Steward Diary, 5 September 1863, *Chattanooga (Tenn.) Free Press*, 21 September 1938, clipping in CPL; *SOR* 63:162, 172; *SOR* 34:477; Levering Account, CCNMP; John R. Dow to "My Dear Ann," 6 September 1863, Dow Letters, FHS; Inskeep Diary, 5 September 1863, OHS; DeVelling, *Seventeenth Ohio*, 74–75; Wheeler Diary, 5 September 1863, OHS; Frederick Marion to his sister, 7 September 1863, Marion Letters, ALPL; Harold J. Bartlett to his sister, 9 September 1863, Bartlett Letters, UM-B; Albert J. Baldwin to his parents, 6 September 1863, Baldwin Letters, UND; Shaw, *Tenth Indiana*, 212; Small Diary, 5 September 1863, IHS; Price Diary, 5 September 1863, Civil War Miscellaneous Collection, USAHEC; Chase, *Fourteenth Ohio*, 45; Bircher, *Drummer-Boy*, 72; Bishop, *Story*, 94; Reed Diary, 5 September 1863, MHS; Albertson, *Letters Home*, Letter 103; Donahower Account, Donahower Papers, MHS; Bruce Diary, 5 September 1863, ISL; Martling Diary, 5 September 1863, Martling Manuscript Collection, ISL; Davidson Diary, 5 September 1863, NCWM; Keegan, *Diaries*, 24; Hinkley Diary, 5 September 1863, and Lucius D. Hinkley to his mother, 8 September 1863, Hinkley Papers, WHS; Memorandum, and Robert T. Bates to his parents, 5 September 1863, both in Bates Letters, WHS; Webster Diary, 5 September 1863, Civil War Miscellaneous Collection, USAHEC; F. W. Perry, *National Tribune*, 21 September 1893; Frank M. Phelps to his friends, 9 September 1863, Phelps Letters, Lewis Leigh Collection, USAHEC; Perry, *Thirty-Eighth Indiana*,

81; *SOR* 29:155; Edmonds Diary, 5–6 September 1863, USAHEC; *SOR* 88:282; Clark Diary, 5 September 1863, Clark Papers, USAHEC; Johnston, *Soldier Boy*, 55–56; Henry A. Hambright Report, 1889, Union Battle Reports, NARA; Galpin Diary, 5 September 1863, Galpin Family Papers, WHS; *SOR* 72:502, 516; William S. Mitchell to his father, 6 September 1863, Mitchell Letters, CCNMP; George Desforges to his sister, 5 September 1863, Desforges Letters, Civil War Miscellaneous Collection, USAHEC; *SOR* 87:106, 112; *SOR* 21:646, 652; *OR* 30(3):363; Bennett, *Ninth Michigan*, 33; Carpenter Diary, 5 September 1863, SRNB.

5. *OR* 30(3):322–23, 369–70; *OR* 30(1):602; Potter Diary, 5 September 1863, UM-B; John J. McCook to Garfield, 3:30 P.M., 5 September 1863, DC, Letters Received, NARA; Horatio Van Cleve to his wife, 4–5 September 1863, Van Cleve Papers, MHS; Suiter Diary, 5 September 1863, ALPL; Harden, *Ninetieth Ohio*, 91; McCain, *Song*, 87; Decker Diary, 5 September 1863, WHS.

6. *OR* 30(3):370, 983–84; Plum, *Military Telegraph*, 2:65–66; *Augusta (Ga.) Daily Constitutionalist*, 8 September 1863; *Richmond Whig*, 8 September 1863; *OR* (1):626, 651, 653, 687–88, 699, 703, 706, 710, 721, 726, 740, 751, 754, 790, 802, 807, 837, 843, 845, 848; Woodruff, *Fifteen Years*, 280; Hight, *Fifty-Eighth Indiana*, 58; *SOR* 44:153; Diary, 5 September 1863, HPL; Gillis Diary, 8 September 1863, OHS; Opdycke Diary, 5 September 1863, and Emerson Opdycke to his wife, 6 September 1863, Opdycke Papers, OHS; *SOR* 67:603, 627; Joseph Bruff to his wife, 9 September 1863, Bruff Family Collection, private collection; *SOR* 65:389; Duncan Thompson to his parents, 8 September 1863, Timothy Brookes Collection, USAHEC; *SOR* 62:413; John M. Palmer to his wife, 2–7 September 1863, Palmer Papers II, ALPL; McKee Diary, 5 September 1863, http://mckee-burns.pasttracker.com/mckee/cw_mckee/mckee_robert_t_cw_diary_1 (15 June 2013); Mason Diary, 5 September 1863, SRNB; Connelly Diary, 5 September 1863, IHS; Dilman, *Dillman*, 8; Dillman Diary, 5 September 1863, IU; Hyde Diary, 5 September 1863, KYHS; Busbey Diary, 5 September 1863, SRNB; *SOR* 34:74, 90, 106, 113, 429, 440, 568; Marshall Diary, 5 September 1863, OHS; Suiter Diary, 5 September 1863, ALPL; Harden, *90th Ohio*, 91; Cutter, *Our Battery*, 131–33; *SOR* 62:781, 786; Glisan Diary, 5 September 1863, CCNMP; Hannaford, *Sixth Ohio*, 443; Willis Jones to his wife, 5 September 1863, Jones Papers, NC; Simmons, *84th Illinois*, 76–77; Walker Diary, 5 September 1863, Harrisburg Civil War Roundtable Collection, USAHEC; Williams Diary, 5 September 1863, CCNMP; Palmer Journal, 5 September 1863, CCNMP; Horatio Van Cleve to his wife, 4–5 September 1863, Van Cleve Papers, MHS; Van Cleve to Edward Ruger, 24 May 1867, Ruger Correspondence, Thomas Papers, NARA; Benedict Diary, 5 September 1863, SRNB; Reep Manuscript, private collection; Hurd Diary, 5 September 1863, private collection; Woodcock, *Southern Boy*, 185–86; Patton Diary, 5 September 1863, TSLA; Tilford Diary, 5 September 1863, FHS; *History, Seventy-Ninth Indiana*, 84–85; Howe Diary, 5 September 1863, IHS; Huntzinger Diary, 5 September 1863, http://www.lafavre.us/huntzinger/hunt_3.htm (23 May 2016); Claggett Diary, 5 September 1863, CCNMP; Wright, *Eighth Kentucky*, 177; Moses F. Yoder to his brother, 7 September 1863, Yoder Papers, LC.

7. *OR* 30(3):365–66, 371, 377; Johnston Diary, 5 September 1863, FHS; *SOR* 34:207, 227; Joshua D. Foster to his parents, 5 September 1863, Foster Letters, CCNMP; Records Diary and Reminiscences, 5 September 1863, Records Manuscript Collection, ISL; Campbell Journal, 5 September 1863, CCNMP.

8. Marshall Diary, 5 September 1863, OHS; Dewees Diary, 5 September 1863, CCNMP; Hines Diary, 5 September 1863, Hines Manuscript Collection, ISL; Griest Diary,

5 September 1863, CCNMP; Kemper Diary, 5 September 1863, OHS; McGee, *72nd Indiana*, 151–52; *OR* 30(3):366–67, 371–72, 393.

9. Mayfield Diary, 5 September 1863, IU; Mosman, *Rough Side*, 74; Pickering Diary, 5 September 1863, HL; Kiene, *Journal*, 170; Chauncy Brooks to his fiancée, 5 September 1863, Brooks Papers, ISL; Philip Welshimer to his wife, 5 September 1863, Welshimer Letters, CCNMP; Rollin Olson to his wife and children, 5–7 September 1863, Olson Letters, WHS; John A. Martin to his sister, 5 September 1863, Martin Letters, KSHS; Henry Richards to his father, 4–5 September 1863, Gilbert-Richards Papers, MU; "Cam," 5 September 1863, in *Dayton (Ohio) Weekly Journal*, 15 September 1863; Eli Clampitt to his brother, 5 September 1863, Clampitt Letters, ISL; Widney Diary, 5 September 1863, KMNMP; *OR* 30(3):367–68.

10. *OR* 30(3):322, 374–76; Frankenberry Diary, 5 September 1863, WVU; Thomas Diary, 5 September 1863, Thomas Collection, UT; Read Diary, 5 September 1863, KSHS; Merrill, *Diary*, 52; Persons Diary, 5 September 1863, WHS; Leeper Diary, 5 September 1863, SRNB; Harris Diary, 5 September 1863, IHS; Prickitt, *Diary*, 103; Elijah S. Watts to Edward Ruger, 17 June 1867, Roswell M. Russell to Edward Ruger, 12 June 1867, and James P. Brownlow to Edward Ruger, 30 May 1867, all in Ruger Correspondence, Thomas Papers, NARA; *OR* 30(1):895, 899, 903, 905, 909, 917–18; Carter, *First Tennessee Cavalry*, 86; George Shuman to his wife, 7 September 1863, Shuman Letters, Harrisburg Civil War Roundtable Collection, USAHEC; Curry, *Four Years*, 108–9; Crofts, *Third Ohio Cavalry*, 112; George Kryder to his wife, 7 September 1863, Kryder Papers, BGSU; Feagles Diary, 5 September 1863, CCNMP; Crane Diary, 5 September 1863, Thomas Papers, NARA; Crane Diary, 5 September 1863, CIHS. According to Crook's report, only the First and Third Ohio Cavalry regiments participated in his scout, but Fourth Ohio Cavalry sources indicate that regiment took part as well.

11. *OR* 30(3):372–73; *OR* 52(1):442; Partridge, *Ninety-Sixth Illinois*, 154; *SOR* 25:499, 686; Sowers Diary, 5 September 1863, CCNMP; Royse, *115th Illinois*, 93; Robinson Diary, 6 September 1863, ALPL; Imboden, *Army of the Cumberland*, 9; *SOR* 26:413, 425; Schwartz, *Diary*, 11; Keeler Diary, 5 September 1863, UM-B; *SOR* 43:400, 406; Patton Diary, 5 September 1863, CCNMP; McAdams, *One Hundred and Thirteenth Ohio*, 38; Winans Diary, 5 September 1863, CCNMP; Hewes, *Tenth Michigan*, 49; Porter Diary, 5 September 1863, OHS; Holmes, *Then and Now*, 5, 123; Thomas M. Burns to his father, 9 September 1863, Burns Letters, VT; Fahnestock Diary, 5 September 1863, ALPL; Kinnear, *Eighty-Sixth Illinois*, 22; Armstrong Diary, 5 September 1863, CCNMP; Brown, Murphy, and Putney, *Behind the Guns*, 53; Putney Diary, 5 September 1863, KMNMP; Brown Diary, 5 September 1863, ALPL; Cort, *Letters*, 103; *Ninety-Second Illinois*, 99; Phillips, *Diary*, 25, 157; King, *Three Years*, 110; Albert Woodcock to his wife, 7 September 1863, Woodcock Papers, NC; Runion Diary, 5 September 1863, http://civilwar.illinoisgenweb.org/scrapbk/runiondiary2.html (23 March 2013).

12. Moore Diary, 5 September 1863, CCNMP; Rosecrans to Halleck, 5 September 1863, DC, Telegrams Sent, NARA; *OR* 30(3):361–62; Rosecrans to Anna Rosecrans, 5 September 1863, Rosecrans Papers, UCLA.

13. *OR* 30(3):321, 339, 361; *OR* 29(2):699; Frederick W. Sims to Thomas Dodamead, 5 September 1863 (two messages), Sims Letter Book, HL.

14. Kean, *Confederate Government*, 102–3; Jones, *War Clerk's Diary*, 2:32–33; *OR* 30(4):602–4, 606–7, 616, 623; *OR* 52(2):521.

15. Brent Diary, 5 September 1863, Bragg Papers, WRHS; Brent to Walker, 5 September 1863 (two messages), Brent to Hill, 5 September 1863, Falconer to Walker, 5 September

1863, and Falconer to Williams, 5 September 1863, all in Bragg Papers, WRHS; Walker to [Mary Cresswell Walker], undated fragment, Walker Papers, DU; Liddell, *Record*, 131, 136–37.

16. Brent Diary, 5 September 1863, Bragg Papers, WRHS; Scout Book, Army of Tennessee, 5 September 1863, MC; Brent to Wheeler, 5 September 1863 (two messages), Bragg Papers, WRHS; *OR* 30(4):602.

17. *New York Times*, 26 August 1863; *OR* 30(4):599–600.

18. Brent to Mauldin, 5 September 1863, Brent to Polk, 5 September 1863 (four messages), Brent to Buckner, 5 September 1863, and Mackall to Hill, 5 September 1863, all in Bragg Papers, WRHS; *OR* 30(4):600; Brent Diary, 5 September 1863, Bragg Papers, WRHS. The signal station on Lookout Mountain may be the one described in Evans, *Inventory and Assessment, Dade County*, 181–86. The charges and specifications preferred against Hindman can be found in Thomas C. Hindman CSR, NARA. Pvt. Thomas B. Hall of the Twenty-Fourth Alabama Infantry regiment described the incident, which occurred on the night of 23–24 August, in a letter to his father: "When we halted Gen Hindman found Polks staff camped on the spot where he had picked out his Head quarters and he went up and roused them calling them 'a set of d——d unprincipled curs' and other such epithets as that. Next day Poks [*sic*] Inspec. Gen'l challenged him but Hindman would not accept. Cheatham's Inspector Genl who bore the challenge considered himself insulted by the refusal in some way and he challenged him. Hindman would not accept. Two more of Polk's staff then challenged him but he as many times refused. I understand that he wrote Polk a note but the note was returned unread. These little facts I learn are so." Thomas B. Hall to Bolling Hall Sr., 31 August 1863, Hall Family Papers, ADAH. According to Lt. William B. Richmond, Polk's aide-de-camp, "It will now be seen if Bragg is the man he has assumed to be to make men 'feel the sting of discipline.'" William B. Richmond to Alexander H. Polk, 29 August 1863, quoted in Raynor's Historical Collectible Auctions, Lot no. 212, September 2011, http://hcaauctions.com/LotDetail.aspx?inventoryid=27261 (14 January 2014).

19. Reid Diary, 5 September 1863, Reid Family Papers, LC; Andrews, *South Reports*, 347; Polk to Hindman, 5 September 1863, and Polk to Cheatham, 5 September 1863, both in Letters Sent, Polk's Command, NARA; Brent Diary, 5 September 1863, Bragg Papers, WRHS; Fielder Diary, 5 September 1863, TSLA; Oldham Diary, 5 September 1863, CCNMP; Moorman, "Moorman Memorandum," 79; Rennolds Diary, 5 September 1863, CCNMP; Brown Notebook, 5 September 1863, CCNMP; Lumsden Diary, 5 September 1863, ADAH; Daniel Diary, 6 September 1863, SRNB; Henry T. Wulff to "Friend Clay," 5 September 1863, Wulff Collection, CHS; Coleman Diary, 5 September 1863, UNC; Sparkman Diary, 5 September 1863, BPL; Anderson to Helm, 5 September 1863, Letters, First Kentucky Brigade, NARA; Cleburne to Anderson, 5 September 1863, Hill Papers, LV; Heartsill, *Fourteen Hundred*, 146; Claudius C. Wilson to his wife, 5 September 1863, Wilson Papers, GHS; Grammer Diary, 5 September 1863, CCNMP; Bush Diary, 5 September 1863, CCNMP; Joshua K. Callaway to his wife, 5 September 1863, Callaway Papers, UTX; Rand Diary, 5 September 1863, MDAH; Pasco Diary, 5 September 1863, CCNMP.

20. Capers Diary, 5 September 1863, Capers Papers, CI; *OR* 30(4):601; Dodd, *Diary*, 23; Corbitt Diary, 5 September 1863, EU; Stevenson, "Smith," 43–44; Shields Diary, 5 September 1863, http://freepages.genealogy.rootsweb.ancestry.com/~sassytazzy/family/surnames/shields (1 February 2009); George Knox Miller to "My Dear Cellie," 15 September 1863, Miller Letters, UNC; Van Sheliha to Stewart, General Orders no. 12, 5 September 1863, Orders and Circulars, Army of Tennessee, NARA; Owen, *Camp and*

Battle, 269; *SOR* 13:917, 925; Dugger Diary, 5 September 1863, *Watauga (N.C.) Democrat*, 21 May 1891; Joseph S. Espey to his sister, 3–6 September 1863, Espey Family Papers, UNC; *SOR* 19:194; Dillon Diary, 5 September 1863, TSLA; *SOR* 78:685; Johnson Diary, 5 September 1863, Johnson Papers, NARA; Watson Journal, 5 September 1863, CCNMP.

21. Cleburne to Hill, 10:00 P.M., 5 September 1863, Hill Papers, LV; *OR* 30(4):601; Mackall to Hill, 5 September 1863, Brent to Hill, 5 September 1863, and Brent to Buckner, 5 September 1863, all in Bragg Papers, WRHS; Plum, *Military Telegraph*, 2:65–66; *Augusta (Ga.) Daily Constitutionalist*, 8 September 1863; *Richmond Whig*, 8 September 1863.

22. *OR* 30(1):626, 653, 682, 688, 699, 701, 703, 706; Hinman, *Sherman Brigade*, 409; Mallory Diary, 6 September 1863, HPL; Emerson Opdycke to his wife, 9 September 1863, and Opdycke Diary, 6 September 1863, both in Opdycke Papers, OHS; Joseph Bruff to his wife, 9 September 1863, Bruff Family Collection, private collection; *SOR* 34:146, 150; *SOR* 65:390; *SOR* 67:603, 611; Duncan Thompson to his parents, 8 September 1863, Thompson Letters, Timothy Brookes Collection, USAHEC; Gillis Diary, 8 September 1863, OHS; Woodruff, *Fifteen Years*, 280; Hight, *Fifty-Eighth Indiana*, 171–72.

23. *OR* 30(3):369, 390–91; *OR* 30(1):710, 721, 726–27, 740, 751, 790; McKee Diary, 6 September 1863, http://mckee-burns.pasttracker.com/mckee/cw_mckee/mckee_robert_t_cw_diary_1 (15 June 1863); Mason Diary, 6 September 1863, SRNB; Connelly Diary, 6 September 1863, IHS; Hyde Diary, 6 September 1863, KYHS; Busbey Diary, 6 September 1863, SRNB; *SOR* 34:74, 90, 568; Marshall Diary, 6 September 1863, OHS; Harden, *90th Ohio*, 91, 97; Cutter, *Our Battery*, 133–34; *SOR* 62:781, 786; Glisan Diary, 6 September 1863, CCNMP; Hannaford, *Sixth Ohio*, 443; Simmons, *84th Illinois*, 78; Suiter Diary, 6 September 1863, ALPL; Walker Diary, 6 September 1863, Harrisburg Civil War Roundtable Collection, USAHEC; Williams Diary, 6 September 1863, CCNMP; Grose, *36th Indiana*, 173; Van Cleve to Edward Ruger, 24 May 1867, Ruger Correspondence, Thomas Papers, NARA.

24. *OR* 30(3):385–86, 987; John R. Dow to "My Dear Ann," 6 September 1863, Dow Letters, FHS; Bishop, *Story*, 94; Billings D. Sibley to "Anna," 6 September 1863, Sibley Papers, MHS; Albertson, *Letters Home*, Letter 103; Reed Diary, 6 September 1863, MHS; Bircher, *Drummer-Boy*, 72; Bruce Diary, 6 September 1863, ISL; Martling Diary, 6 September 1863, Martling Manuscript Collection, ISL; Davidson Diary, 6 September 1863, NCWM; Keegan, *Diaries*, 24; Inskeep Diary, 6 September 1863, OHS; DeVelling, *Seventeenth Ohio*, 75; Wheeler Diary, 6 September 1863, OHS; Frederick Marion to his sister, 7 September 1863, Marion Letters, ALPL; *SOR* 34:186; Albert J. Baldwin to his parents, 6 September 1863, Baldwin Letters, UND; Price Diary, 6 September 1863, Civil War Miscellaneous Collection, USAHEC; Small Diary, 6 September 1863, IHS; S. Hendricks, *National Tribune*, 5 November 1891; *OR* 30(1):726–27, 740, 751, 790, 837, 843, 845, 848; Mason Diary, 6 September 1863, SRNB; Connelly Diary, 6 September 1863, IHS; Busbey Diary, 6 September 1863, SRNB; Marshall Diary, 6 September 1863, OHS; Simmons, *84th Illinois*, 78; Suiter Diary, 6 September 1863, ALPL; Van Cleve to Edward Ruger, 24 May 1867, Ruger Correspondence, Thomas Papers, NARA; Benedict Diary, 6 September 1863, SRNB; Patton Diary, 6 September 1863, TSLA; Claggett Diary, 6 September 1863, CCNMP; *History, Seventy-Ninth Indiana*, 85; Howe Diary, 6 September 1863, IHS; Huntzinger Diary, 6 September 1863, http://www.lafavre.us/huntzinger/hunt_3.htm (23 May 2016); Tilford Diary, 6 September 1863, FHS; Evans, *Inventory and Assessment, Dade County*, 33–48.

25. *OR* 30(3):986–87; Chapin, "Diary," 233; Potter Diary, 6 September 1863, Potter

Papers, UM-B; Joseph Bruff to Anna Bruff, 12 November 1863, Bruff Family Collection, private collection.

26. *OR* 30(3):985, 987–88. In his 7:00 P.M. message to Wood, Oldershaw stated that he (and presumably corps headquarters) was a mile and a half from "Naylor's" on the Trenton/Wauhatchie Road. The location identified as "Naylor's" on Federal maps probably referenced Taylor's Spring, which was just east of the Trenton/Wauhatchie road near its junction with the Nickajack Road down Sand Mountain. A mile and a half from Taylor's Spring would place the Twenty-First Corps headquarters in the midst of the camps occupied by Palmer's and Brannan's divisions on the Cole property.

27. *OR* 30(1):627, 653, 688, 699, 703, 706; *OR* 30(3):420–22, 681–84, 852–53; Woodruff, *Fifteen Years*, 280; Hight, *Fifty-Eighth Indiana*, 171–72; Hinman, *Sherman Brigade*, 409–10; Joseph Bruff to Anna Bruff, 9 September 1863, Bruff Family Collection, private collection; Opdycke Diary, 6 September 1863, and Emerson Opdycke to his wife, 6 and 7 September 1863, all in Opdycke Papers, OHS; Duncan Thompson to his parents, 8 September 1863, Thompson Letters, Timothy Brookes Collection, USAHEC; Mallory Diary, 6 September 1863, HPL; Gillis Diary, 8 September 1863, OHS; *SOR* 62:413.

28. *OR* 30(1):325–26, 384, 386, 393, 1063; *OR* 30(3):383–85; Shanks Diary, 6 September 1863, BGSU; Adams, "Diary," 649; Dilworth Journal, 6 September 1863, HC; Ward Diary, 6 September 1863, Ward Papers, DP; Ward Diary, 6 September 1863, IHS; Nupp Diary, 6 September 1863, CCNMP; Millen Diary, 6 September 1863, SRNB; Hinchberger Diary, 6 September 1863, CCNMP; Weaver Diary, 6 September 1863, SRNB; John W. Baldwin to his wife, 5–12 September 1863, Baldwin Papers, OHS; Blackburn, *Letters*, 147; Shotts Diary, 6 September 1863, SRNB; Johnston Diary, 6 September 1863, Johnston Collection, CHS; Christian Diary, 6 September 1863, CCNMP; Haynie, *Nineteenth Illinois*, 215; *SOR* 21:358, 376; Sheffield Diary, 6 September 1863, CCNMP; Bloom Diary, 6 September 1863, CCNMP; Sturges Diary, 6 September 1863, Sturges Papers, *Civil War Times Illustrated* Collection, USAHEC; Beatty, *Citizen Soldier*, 329; *SOR* 28:206; Harris Diary, 6 September 1863, CCNMP; Hapeman Diary, 6 September 1863, ALPL; Calkins, *One Hundred and Fourth Illinois*, 112; George Marsh Jr. to his brother, 7 September 1863, Marsh Family Papers, ALPL; Evans, *Inventory and Assessment, Dade County*, 131–38. The Seventy-Eighth Pennsylvania Infantry regiment of Sirwell's Third Brigade was left behind at Payne's [Sitton's] Mill near Trenton, where it continued to operate the mill.

29. *OR* 30(1):246, 270, 579, 582, 589; *OR* 30(3):383, 388–89; Eugene Comstock to his father, 6 September 1863, Comstock Papers, WHS; Pirtle, "Leaves," CIHS; Alfred Pirtle to his mother, 6 September 1863, Pirtle Letters, FHS; Pecoy Diary, 6 September 1863, CCNMP; Bennett and Haigh, *Thirty-Sixth Illinois*, 449–50; *SOR* 22:181, 187, 610, 667; Cooley Diary, 6 September 1863, WHS; Eugene E. Comstock to his father, 6 September 1863, Comstock Papers, WHS; Ely Diary, 6 September 1863, CCNMP; Daniel E. Barnard to his sister, 9 September 1863, Howe Barnard Family Papers, NL; Merrill, *Soldier*, 2:436; Newlin, *Seventy-Third Illinois*, 210–12; *SOR* 23:208, 341; *SOR* 48:284, 292; Riley, *Diary*, 53; Simonds Diary, 6 September 1863, Simonds Papers, NIU; Lyman H. Needham to his brother and sister, 12 September 1863, Needham Papers, ALPL; Melville Cox Follett Diary, 6 September 1863, http://ehistory.osu.edu/exhibitions/letters/follett_melville/default (17 January 2009); Colburn/Gray Diary, 6 September 1863, private collection; Moody Diary, 6 September 1863; Burns Diary, 6 September 1863, CCNMP; Tabler Diary, 6 September 1863, private collection; *SOR* 24:47; Crippin, "Diary," 280; Austin Diary, 6 September 1863, ALPL; Jones Diary, 6 September 1863, SRNB; Hinkley Diary,

6 September 1863, and Lucius D. Hinkley to his mother, 8 September 1863, Hinkley Papers, WHS; Memorandum, and Robert J. Bates to his parents, 9 September 1863, both in Bates Letters, WHS; Wallace W. Darrah to his brother, 9 September 1863, Darrah Papers, NC; Webster Diary, 6 September 1863, Civil War Miscellaneous Collection, USAHEC; Frank M. Phelps to his friends, 9 September 1863, Lewis Leigh Collection, USAHEC; *SOR* 29:155; Nelson Purdum, "Thirty-Third Ohio," Purdum Papers, OHS; Edmonds Diary, 6–7 September 1863, USAHEC; *Record, Ninety-Fourth Ohio*, 36; *SOR* 27:570; *SOR* 87:106, 112, 253, 282; Otto, *Mudsill*, 159–61; Clark Diary, 6 September 1863, Clark Papers, USAHEC; Johnston, *Soldier Boy*, 56–57; Galpin Diary, 6 September 1863, Galpin Family Papers, WHS; Hambright Report, Union Battle Reports, NARA; *SOR* 72:502, 521; *SOR* 21:646, 653; Bennett, *Ninth Michigan*, 33; Miller Journal, 6 September 1863, IHS; Parker Diary, 6 September 1863, HL; Morse, *Diaries*, 33; Tourgee, "Diary," 118; Luman G. Grist to his parents, 6 September 1863, Grist Letter, CCNMP; Taylor Diary, 6 September 1863, SRNB; Shera Diary, 6 September 1863, FHS; Alanson R. Ryman to Jane Ryman, 9 September 1863, Ryman Letters, IHS; Hollingsworth Diary, 6 September 1863, IHS; Turchin, "Diary," 62; Williams, *Extracts*, 90; Ward Diary, 6 September 1863, Booth Papers, OHS; Owen Diary, 6 September 1863, AU; Phillips, *Turchin*, 101–2; Josiah D. Cotton to his wife, 6 September 1863, Cotton Papers, LC.

30. *OR* 30(3):388–90, 984; Thruston to Sheridan, 12:30 P.M., 6 September 1863, Sheridan Papers, LC; Thruston to Davis, 6 September 1863, Twentieth Army Corps, Letters Sent, NARA; Mosman, *Rough Side*, 74–75; Mayfield Diary, 6 September 1863, IU; *SOR* 24:393; Colyer Diary, 6 September 1863, ALPL; *SOR* 23:20; Heg, *Letters*, 243; James E. Love to "Molly," 6 August [September] 1863, Love Papers, MHM; Phillips Diary, 6 September 1863, Phillips Collection; HL; Kiene, *Journal*, 170–72; Pickering Diary, 6 September 1863, HL; Cope, *Fifteenth Ohio*, 303; Thomas J. Harrison to his wife, 6 September 1863, Harrison Letters, IHS; Willoughby Diary, 6 September 1863, ISL; Alpheus S. Bloomfield to his sister, 6 September 1863, Bloomfield Letters, OHS; Robinson Diary, 6 September 1863, Regimental Papers, WRHS; Moon Diary, 6 September 1863, KSHS; Protsman Diary, 6 September 1863, WSU; W. L. Patterson to his parents, 6 September 1863, Patterson Family Papers, WSU; Beck Diary, 6 September 1863, KSHS; Shideler Diary, 6 September 1863, CCNMP.

31. *OR* 30(3):374–75, 397–98; *OR* 30(1):895, 901, 909; Frankenberry Diary, 6 September 1863, WVU; Kirk, *Fifteenth Pennsylvania Cavalry*, 223–24; Leonidas S. Scranton to Edward Ruger, 8 June 1867, William G. Brownlow to Edward Ruger, 30 May 1867, and Elijah S. Watts to Edward Ruger, 17 June 1867, all in Ruger Correspondence, Thomas Papers, NARA; Hempstead Diary, 6 September 1863, UM-B; *SOR* 41:722; Thomas Diary, 6 September 1863, Thomas Collection, UT; *SOR* 86:713; Merrill, *Diary*, 52; Persons Diary, 6 September 1863, WHS; Kendall Diary, 6 September 1863, HL; Baum Diary, 5–6 September 1863, IHS; Harris Diary, 6 September 1863, IHS; Curry, *Four Years*, 109; *Proceedings, Thirtieth Reunion*, 16; Crofts, *Third Ohio Cavalry*, 112; Prickitt, *Company H*, 103; Feagles Diary, 6 September 1863, CCNMP; Crane Diary, 6 September 1863, Thomas Papers, NARA; Crane Diary, 6 September 1863, CIHS; George Kryder to his wife, 7 September 1863, Kryder Papers, BGSU; Thomson Diary, 6 September 1863, CCNMP; Nourse Diary, 6 September 1863, DU; Lester Diary, 6 September 1863, ALPL.

32. Campbell Journal, 6–7 September 1863, CCNMP; Records Diary, 6 September 1863 and Records Reminiscences, Records Manuscript Collection, ISL; Kemper Diary, 5–6 September 1863, OHS; Griest Diary, 6 September 1863, CCNMP; Unidentified Diary, Seventy-Second Indiana Infantry, 6 September 1863, Meisner Collection, ISL; Joshua D.

Foster to his parents, 9 September 1863, Foster Letters, CCNMP; *OR* 30(3):385–87, 392–94, 396–99; Hines Diary, 6 September 1863, Hines Manuscript Collection, ISL; Marshall Diary, 6 September 1863, OHS; Dewees Diary, 6 September 1863, CCNMP; Smith, *Samuel Thomas Smith*, 81; Elias D. Work to his sister, 6 September 1863, Work Letters, IHS; Albert G. Hart to his wife, 7 September 1863, Hart Papers, WRHS; *SOR* 25:518, 525, 552.

33. Brown Diary, 6 September 1863, ALPL; *SOR* 25:499, 508; Runion Diary, 6 September 1863, http://civilwar.illinoisgenweb.org/scrapbk/runiondiary2.html (23 March 2013); Brown Diary, 6 September 1863, *Civil War Times Illustrated* Collection, USAHEC; *Ninety-Second Illinois*, 99; King, *Three Years*, 111–12; Phillips, *Diary*, 25, 157; Albert Woodcock to his wife, 7 September 1863, Woodcock Papers, NC; Barnes, Carnahan, and McCain, *Eighty-Sixth Indiana*, 158; Moore Diary, 6 September 1863, CCNMP; McCain, *Song*, 87; Decker Diary, 6 September 1863, WHS; Keeler Diary, 6 September 1863, UM-B; *SOR* 43:391, 404; *OR* 30(1):852; *OR* 30(3):397; Partridge, *Ninety-Sixth Illinois*, 154; Nelson G. Huson to his parents, 6 September 1863, Huson Letters, HL; Sowers Diary, 6 September 1863, CCNMP; Royse, *115th Illinois*, 93; Robinson Diary, 6 September 1863, Robinson Papers, ALPL; Royse Diary, 6 September 1863, Royse Manuscript Collection, ISL; *SOR* 26:407, 413; Schwartz, *Diary*, 11; Patton Diary, 6 September 1863, CCNMP; J. M. Brannum, *National Tribune*, 20 December 1900; McAdams, *One Hundred and Thirteenth Ohio*, 38; William L. Broaddus to his wife, 9 September 1863, Broaddus Papers, DU; Van Vleck, *Leader*, 166; Members, *Battery M, 1st Illinois*, 76; Winans Diary, 6 September 1863, CCNMP; Hewes, *Tenth Michigan*, 49; Porter Diary, 6 September 1863, OHS; Holmes, *Then and Now*, 5, 123–24; Thomas M. Burns to his father, 9 September 1863, Burns Letters, VT; Putney Diary, 6 September 1863, KMNMP; Armstrong Diary, 6 September 1863, CCNMP; Fahnestock Diary, 6 September 1863, ALPL; Kinnear, *Eighty-Sixth Illinois*, 22.

34. Garfield, *Wild Life*, 294–95; Drouillard Diary, 6 September 1863, Rosecrans Papers, UCLA; Kirk, *Fifteenth Pennsylvania Cavalry*, 228–29; Wilson, *Column South*, 86; Knight Account, 6 September 1863, VMI; *SOR* 68:412; Miller Journal, 6 September 1863, IHS; Morse, *Diaries*, 33; Parker Diary, 6 September 1863, HL; Williams, *Extracts*, 90; C. A. Smith Diary, 6–7 September 1863, CCNMP; "Summaries of the News," 333–36, NARA; Garfield to Sheridan, 9:30 P.M., 6 September 1863, Sheridan Papers, LC; *OR* 30(3):381, 390–91, 397–98; Rosecrans to Halleck, 6 September 1863, DC, Telegrams Sent, NARA.

35. Bragg to Johnston, 3:00 A.M., 6 September 1863, and Bragg to Davis, 3:00 A.M., 6 September 1863, both in Bragg Papers, WRHS; *OR* 30(4):607–8.

36. Brent Diary, 6 September 1863, Brent to Hill, 5 September 1863, Brent to Buckner, 5 September 1863, Brent to Commanding Officer, Rome, Georgia, 6 September 1863, Brent to Gist, Rome, 9:00 A.M., 6 September 1863, Brent to Gist, via Kingston, 9:00 A.M., 6 September 1863, Bragg to Brown, 9:00 A.M., 6 September 1863, all in Bragg Papers, WRHS; Beatty Diary, 6 September 1863, UNC; *OR* 30(4):615, 618; Bragg to Davis, 6 September 1863, Bragg Letters and Telegrams Sent, NARA; *OR* 52(2):522.

37. Mackall to Stewart, 9:00 A.M., 6 September 1863, and Brent Diary, 6 September 1863, both in Bragg Papers, WRHS; Sloan Diary, 6 September 1863, TSLA; Leverich Diary, 6 September 1863, LSU; *OR* 30(4):616–18.

38. Circular, 6 September 1863, Bragg Papers, WRHS; Circular, 6 September 1863, Hill Papers, LV; Circular, 6 September 1863, Buckner Papers, HL; *OR* 30(4):610–11; Brent to Wright, 10:00 A.M., 6 September 1863, Mackall to Wright, 10:00 A.M., 6 September 1863, Falconer to Quartermaster, Marietta, Georgia, 10:00 A.M., 6 September 1863, and Falconer to McMicken, 6 September 1863, all in Bragg Papers, WRHS.

39. Lumsden Diary, 6 September 1863, ADAH; Daniel Diary, 6 September 1863,

SRNB; Fielder Diary, 6 September 1863, TSLA; Moorman, "Moorman Memorandum," 79; Rennolds Diary, 6 September 1863, CCNMP; *OR* 30(4):614; Brown Notebook, 6 September 1863, CCNMP; Magee Diary, 6 September 1863, DU; Etter Diary, 6 September 1863, SRNB; Neal Diary, 6 September 1863, NC; Rand Diary, 6 September 1863, MDAH; Fraser Diary, 6 September 1863, CCNMP; Thomas B. Hall to Bolling Hall Sr., 6 September 1863, Hall Family Papers, ADAH; Joshua K. Callaway to his wife, 6 September 1863, Callaway Papers, UTX; Claudius C. Wilson to his wife, 6 September 1863, Wilson Papers, GHS; Grammer Diary, 6 September 1863, CCNMP; Swett, "Warren Light Artillery," http://www.perryvillebattlefield.org/html/ms-swett-charles-cs.html (24 July 2012); James R. Riggs to his sister, 6 September 1863, Riggs Letters, ADAH; Freeman Diary, 6 September 1863, TSLA.

40. Cleburne to Hill, 10:00 P.M., 5 September 1863, and Cleburne to Anderson, 5 September 1863, both in Hill Papers, LV; *OR* 30(4):601, 613; Milner Diary, 6 September 1863, ADAH; J. H. Smith Diary, 6 September 1863, CCNMP; *SOR* 13:641–42, 698; Armstrong Diary, 6 September 1863, ADAH; Williamson, *45th Mississippi*, 120; *SOR* 46:72; Coleman Diary, 6 September 1863, UNC; Seaton, *Bugle*, 39; *SOR* 80:74, 160, 181; Heartsill, *Fourteen Hundred*, 146; Sparkman Diary, 6 September 1863, BPL; *SOR* 79:221; Breckinridge to Anderson, 6:45 P.M., 6 September 1863, Avery to Hill, 6 September 1863, and Buck to Cleburne, 6 September 1863, all in Hill Papers, LV; Cleburne to Hill, 6 September 1863, Hill Papers, NCDAH; *SOR* 35:199, 203, 254, 273, 404, 408; Jackman Journal, 6 September 1863, LC; Bush Diary, 6 September 1863, CCNMP; John McGrath to "Friend Danl," 24 September 1863, McGrath Papers, LSU; *SOR* 36:297, 434, 456; Pasco Diary, 6 September 1863, CCNMP; Ives, *Journal and Letters*, 41–42.

41. Avery to Anderson, 6 September 1863, and Avery to Hill, 6 September 1863, both in Hill Papers, LV; Beatty Diary, 6 September 1863, UNC; Cleburne to Hill, 6 September 1863, Hill Papers, NCDAH.

42. *OR* 30(4):592; Elliott, *Soldier of Tennessee*, 86; Owen, *Camp and Battle*, 266–67, 269; Schlinger, *Last Cavalier*, 1–148; Warner, *Generals in Gray*, 246; Boatner, *Civil War Dictionary*, 668; Davis and Hoffman, *Confederate General*, 5:54–57; Eicher and Eicher, *High Commands*, 439; Brent Diary, 5 September 1863, Bragg Papers, WRHS; Dillon Diary, 6 September 1863, TSLA; *SOR* 78:685; Johnson Diary, 6 September 1863, Johnson Papers, NARA; Harder Reminiscences, TSLA; *SOR* 13:925, 929; *SOR* 79:559; John E. Hall to Bolling Hall Sr., 6 August [September] 1863, Hall Family Papers, ADAH; *SOR* 19:194; Joseph S. Espey to his sister, 3–6 September 1863, Espey Family Papers, UNC; Dugger Diary, 6 September 1863, *Watauga (N.C.) Democrat*, 21 May 1891; Watson Journal, 6 September 1863, CCNMP; Holmes, *Diary*, 17.

43. *OR* 30(4):614–15; Isaac B. Ulmer to his mother, 6 September 1863, Ulmer Papers, UNC; Stevenson, "Smith," 44–45; Shields Diary, 6 September 1863, http://freepages.genealogy.rootsweb.ancestry.com/~sassytazzy/family/surnames/shields (1 February 2009); Jordan and Pryor, *Campaigns of Forrest*, 305–6; Davis Diary, 6 September 1863, TSLA; Huwald Account, Nutt Papers, UNC; Sloan Diary, 6 September 1863, TSLA; Leverich Diary, 6 September 1863, LSU; Dyer, *Diary*, 20.

44. Capers Diary, 6 September 1863, Capers Papers, CI; Ellison Capers to his wife, 6 September 1863 (two letters), Capers Papers, DU; George A. Gordon to "Dear Krilla," 6 September 1863, Gordon Letters, UTX; Wayne to Brown, 13 September 1863, Cuyler Collection, UGA; Flewellen to Stout, 6 September 1863, Flewellen to Ussery, 6 September 1863, Flewellen to McFadden, 6 September 1863, Flewellen to Tucker, 6 September 1863, and Flewellen to Ryan, all in Letters Sent, Medical Director, Army of Tennessee, NARA;

Currey to Stout, 5 September 1863, Stout Papers, MC; Stout, "Outline," 70–71; Schroeder-Lein, *Confederate Hospitals*, 123–24; Cumming, *Kate*, 137.

45. Frank M. Hayley to his wife, 6 September 1863, Hayley Letter, CCNMP; *OR* 30(4):608; *OR* 29(2):700–701; James Longstreet to Louis T. Wigfall, 18 August 1863, Wigfall Papers, LC; Jordan Account, ADAH; Jordan, *Events*, 49–50; Giles, *Rags and Hope*, 195–96.

46. Bragg to Johnston, 5:00 P.M., 6 September 1863, Brent to Walker, 8:00 P.M., 6 September 1863 (two messages), Brent to Buckner, 8:00 P.M., 6 September 1863, Brent to Buckner, 6 September 1863, Brent to Polk, 6 September 1863, Brent to Mauldin, 6 September 1863, and Brent Diary, 6–7 September 1863, all in Bragg Papers, WRHS; Oladowski to Humphries, 6 September 1863, and Oladowski to Rains, 6 September 1863, both in Letters Sent, Ordnance Office, Army of Tennessee, NARA; Fielder Diary, 6 September 1863, TSLA; Neal Diary, 6 September 1863, NC; Rand Diary, 6 September 1863, MDAH; Fraser Diary, 6 September 1863, CCNMP; Thomas B. Hall to Bolling Hall Sr., 6 September 1863, Hall Family Papers, ADAH; Daniel Diary, 6 September 1863, SRNB; Cleburne to Hill, 6 September 1863, Hill Papers, NCDAH; Milner Diary, 6 September 1863, ADAH; Coleman Diary, 6 September 1863, UNC; Seaton, *Bugle*, 39; Heartsill, *Fourteen Hundred*, 146; Breckinridge to Anderson, 6:45 P.M., 6 September 1863, Hill Papers, LV; Jackman Journal, 6 September 1863, LC; John McGrath to "Friend Danl," 24 September 1863, McGrath Papers, LSU; Pasco Diary, 6 September 1863, CCNMP; Dillon Diary, 6 September 1863, TSLA; Johnson Diary, 6 September 1863, Johnson Papers, NARA; Watson Journal, 6 September 1863, CCNMP; Dugger Diary, 6 September 1863, *Watauga (N.C.) Democrat*, 21 May 1891; Richmond Diary, 6 September 1863, Polk Papers, US; *OR* 30(2):70–71.

CHAPTER 16

1. *OR* 30(3):322–23, 397–98, 412, 432.

2. *OR* 30(3):414, 986–87, 989; John J. McCook to James Garfield, 1:00 A.M., 7 September 1863, DC, Letters Received, NARA.

3. *OR* 30(3):414, 852, 989; *OR* 30(1):627–28.

4. *OR* 30(3):416–17, 419, 988.

5. *OR* 30(1):681–82, 688, 699, 701–4, 706; Hinman, *Sherman Brigade*, 410; *SOR* 62:413; *SOR* 65:390, 419, 423, 441, 445; Mallory Diary, 7 September 1863, HPL; Gillis Diary, 7 September 1863, OHS; Duncan Thompson to his parents, 8 September 1863, Thompson Letters, Timothy Brookes Collection, USAHEC; Clark, *Tigers*, 84; General Orders, No. 4, 8 September 1863, Emerson Opdycke to his wife, 7 September 1863, and Opdycke Diary, 7 September 1863, all in Opdycke Papers, OHS; Joseph Bruff to his wife, 9 September 1863, Bruff Family Letters, private collection; *SOR* 67:603, 611.

6. *OR* 30(3):414–17, 425.

7. *OR* 30(3):418–24, 989–90.

8. *OR* 30(1):727, 740, 755, 790, 821, 829, 831, 837, 843, 845, 848; McKee Diary, 7 September 1863, http://mckee-burns.pasttracker.com/mckee/cw_mckee/mckee_robert_t_cw_diary (15 June 2013); Mason Diary, 7 September 1863, SRNB; Connelly Diary, 7 September 1863, IHS; Hyde Diary, 7 September 1863, KYHS; Busbey Diary, 7 September 1863, SRNB; *SOR* 34:90; Marshall Diary, 7 September 1863, OHS; Harden, *90th Ohio*, 91; *SOR* 62:798, 803; Glisan Diary, 7 September 1863, CCNMP; Jonathan B. Holmes to "Anna," 7 September 1863, Holmes Letters, private collection; Hannaford,

Sixth Ohio, 443; Suiter Diary, 7 September 1863, ALPL; Walker Diary, 7 September 1863, Harrisburg Civil War Roundtable Collection, USAHEC; Willis Jones to his wife, 7 September 1863, Jones Papers, NC; Grose, *36th Indiana*, 173; Williams Diary, 7 September 1863, CCNMP; Palmer Journal, 7 September 1863, CCNMP; Benedict Diary, 7 September 1863, SRNB; Woodcock, *Southern Boy*, 186; Patton Diary, 7 September 1863, TSLA; Claggett Diary, 7 September 1863, CCNMP; *History, Seventy-Ninth Indiana*, 85; Tilford Diary, 7 September 1863, FHS; Huntzinger Diary, 7 September 1863, http://www.lafavre.us/huntzinger/hunt_3.htm (23 May 2016); Howe Diary, 7 September 1863, IHS; *SOR* 63:275; *SOR* 87:32; Barnes, Carnahan, and McCain, *Eighty-Sixth Indiana*, 158; Moore Diary, 7 September 1863, CCNMP; McCain, *Song*, 88; Decker Diary, 7 September 1863, WHS; Moses F. Yoder to his brother, 7 September 1863, Yoder Papers, LC; Claiborne J. Walton to his wife, 7 September 1863, Walton Letter, Lewis Leigh Collection, USAHEC; *OR* 30(3):411, 430.

9. *OR* 30(1):326, 384, 386, 393; *OR* 30(3):408–9; Beatty, *Citizen Soldier*, 329; Harris Diary, 7 September 1863, CCNMP; Hapeman Diary, 7 September 1863, ALPL; Calkins, *One Hundred and Fourth Illinois*, 113; George Marsh Jr. to his brother, 7 September 1863, Marsh Family Papers, ALPL; *SOR* 20:439; Johnston Diary, 7 September 1863, Johnston Collection, CHS; Haynie, *Nineteenth Illinois*, 215; *SOR* 21:358; Sheffield Diary, 7 September 1863, CCNMP; Bloom Diary, 7 September 1863, CCNMP; Shotts Diary, 7 September 1863, SRNB; Sturges Diary, 7 September 1863, Sturges Papers, *Civil War Times Illustrated* Collection, USAHEC; Shanks Diary, 7 September 1863, BGSU; Adams, "Diary," 649; Dilworth Journal, 7 September 1863, HC; Ward Diary, 7 September 1863, Ward Papers, DP; Ward Diary, 7 September 1863, IHS; Puntenny, *Thirty-Seventh Indiana*, 48; Weaver Diary, 7 September 1863, SRNB; John W. Baldwin to his wife, 5–12 September 1863, Baldwin Papers, OHS; Blackburn, *Letters*, 147; *SOR* 25:499, 508; Brown Diary, 7 September 1863, ALPL; Phillips, *Diary*, 25; King, *Three Years*, 112; Albert Woodcock to his wife, 7 September 1863, Woodcock Papers, NC; Runion Diary, 7 September 1863, http://civilwar.illinoisgenweb.org/scrapbk/runiondiary2.html (23 March 2013).

10. Christian Diary, 7 September 1863, CCNMP; *OR* 30(1):270, 398, 470; Jones Diary, 7 September 1863, SRNB; Memorandum, and Robert J. Bates to his parents, 9 September 1863, both in Bates Letters, WHS; Hinkley Diary, 7 September 1863, and Lucius D. Hinkley to his mother, 8 September 1863, both in Hinkley Papers, WHS; Webster Diary, 7 September 1863, Civil War Miscellaneous Collection, USAHEC; Wallace W. Darrah to his brother, 9 September 1863, Darrah Papers, NC; Frank M. Phelps to his friends, 9 September 1863, Phelps Letters, Lewis Leigh Collection, USAHEC; *SOR* 28:106, 155; *SOR* 86:118, 134; *Record, Ninety-Fourth Ohio*, 36; *SOR* 27:570; *SOR* 88:282; Johnston, *Soldier Boy*, 57; Clark Diary, 7 September 1863, Clark Papers, USAHEC; Galpin Diary, 7 September 1863, Galpin Family Papers, WHS; Hambright Report, Union Battle Reports, NARA; *SOR* 72:502, 521; *SOR* 87:138; *SOR* 21:646, 675; Williams, *Extracts*, 90; *OR* 30(3):410–11; Levering Account, 7 September 1863, CCNMP; Miller Journal, 7 September 1863, IHS; Floyd, *Seventy-Fifth Indiana*, 121; Morse, *Diaries*, 33; Tourgee, "Diary," 118; Tourgee, *Thousand*, 400; Parker Diary, 7 September 1863, HL; Taylor Diary, 7 September 1863, SRNB; *SOR* 67:121; Shera Diary, 7 September 1863, FHS; Alanson R. Ryman to Jane Ryman, 9 September 1863, Ryman Letters, IHS; *SOR* 29:821; Gates Diary, 7 September 1863, IHS; Hollingsworth Diary, 7 September 1863, IHS; *SOR* 27:637, 644; Ward Diary, 7 September 1863, Booth Papers, OHS; Owen Diary, 7 September 1863, AU; Steward Diary, 7 September 1863, clipping in *Chattanooga (Tenn.) Free Press*, 21 September 1938, CPL; Andrew, *Letters*, 75; Inskeep Diary, 7 September 1863, OHS; Frederick Marion to

his sister, 7 September 1863, Marion Letters, ALPL; Price Diary, 7 September 1863, Civil War Miscellaneous Collection, USAHEC; Small Diary, 7 September 1863, IHS; Bishop, *Story*, 94; Albertson, *Letters Home*, Letter 103; Donahower Account, 7 September 1863, Donahower Papers, MHS; Reed Diary, 7 September 1863, MHS; Bircher, *Drummer-Boy*, 72–73; Martling Diary, 7 September 1863, Martling Manuscript Collection, ISL; Davidson Diary, 7 September 1863, MCWM; Keegan, *Diaries*, 24–25; Bruce Diary, 7 September 1863, ISL; Ferdinand Van Derveer to his wife, 7 September 1863, Van Derveer Letters, SLRH.

11. *OR* 30(3):431–32; *OR* 30(1):895, 901, 909; Leonidas S. Stanton to Edward Ruger, 8 June 1867, Elijah S. Watts to Edward Ruger, 17 June 1867, and James P. Brownlow to Edward Ruger, 20 May 1867, all in Ruger Correspondence, Thomas Papers, NARA; Hempstead Diary, 7 September 1863, UMJ-B; *SOR* 41:722; Thomas Diary, 7 September 1863, Thomas Collection, UT; *SOR* 86:713; Merrill, *Diary*, 52; Persons Diary, 7 September 1863, WHS; Kendall Diary, 7 September 1863, HL; Mendenhall Diary, 7 September 1863, IHS; Baum Diary, 7 September 1863, IHS; Harris Diary, 7 September 1863, IHS; Lester Diary, 7 September 1863, ALPL; Nourse Diary, 7 September 1863, DU; Crofts, *Third Ohio Cavalry*, 112; Prickitt, *Company H*, 103; George Kryder to his wife, 7 September 1863, Kryder Papers, BGSU; Crane Diary, 7 September 1863, Thomas Papers, NARA; Feagles Diary, 7 September 1863, CCNMP; Crane Diary, 7 September 1863, CIHS; Thomson Diary, 7 September 1863, CCNMP.

12. *OR* 30(3):412–13, 988; Post Diary, 7 September 1863, Post Papers, KC; William McAdams to his wife, 7 September 1863, McAdams Letters, Lewis Leigh Collection, USAHEC; Mosman, *Rough Side*, 75; Mayfield Diary, 7 September 1863, IU; Lathrop, *Fifty-Ninth Illinois*, 216–17; *SOR* 24:393; Colyer Diary, 7 September 1863, ALPL; Patterson Diary, 7 September 1863, MHM; *SOR* 23:20, 208, 248, 371; Elbert J. Squire to his mother, 7 September 1863, Squire Letters, Regimental Papers, WRHS; Himoe Diary, 7 September 1863, NAHA; Rollin Olson to his wife and children, 5–7 September 1863, Olson Letters, WHS; James E. Love to "Molly," 6 August [7 September] 1863, Love Papers, MHM; Phillips Diary, 7 September 1863, Phillips Collection, HL; Pickering Diary, 7 September 1863, HL; Kiene, *Journal*, 172; Dean Diary, 7 September 1863, private collection; Jacob W. Bartmess to his wife, 7 September 1863, Bartmess Letters, IHS; Willoughby Diary, 7 September 1863, Willoughby Manuscript Collection, ISL; Robinson Diary, 7 September 1863, Regimental Papers, WRHS; Lyon Diary, 7 September 1863, OHS; Moon Diary, 7 September 1863, KSHS; Protsman Diary, 7 September 1863, WSU; E. T. Hooker to his daughter, 7 September 1863, private collection; Beck Diary, 7 September 1863, KSHS; Shideler Diary, 7 September 1863, CCNMP; *OR* 30(1):579, 583, 589; Smith, *Memoirs*, 57; Pirtle, "Leaves," CIHS; Pecoy Diary, 7 September 1863, CCNMP; Cummins Diary, 7 September 1863, Cummins Papers, ALPL; Bennett and Haigh, *Thirty-Sixth Illinois*, 450; L. W. Mann Diary, 7 September 1863, clipping from *Chattanooga (Tenn.) Times*, 25 April 1937, CPL; *SOR* 22:187, 585, 610; Cooley Diary, 7 September 1863, WHS; Ely Diary, 7 September 1863, CCNMP; Daniel E. Barnard to his sister, 9 September 1863, Howe Barnard Family Papers, NL; Merrill, *Soldier*, 2:436; Newlin, *Seventy-Third Illinois*, 212–13; *SOR* 48:304; Riley, *Diary*, 53; Simonds Diary, 7 September 1863, Simonds Papers, NIU; Lyman H. Needham to his brother and sister, 12 September 1863, Needham Papers, ALPL; Colburn/Gray Diary, 7 September 1863, private collection; Moody Diary, 7 September 1863, SRNB; Burns Diary, 7 September 1863, CCNMP; Tabler Diary, 7 September 1863, private collection; Crippin, "Diary," 280; Austin Diary, 7 September 1863, ALPL; Evans, *Inventory and Assessment, Dade County*, 143–58.

13. *OR* 30(3):425–30, 433; Marshall Diary, 7 September 1863, OHS; Dewees Diary,

7 September 1863, CCNMP; Hines Diary, 7 September 1863, Hines Manuscript Collection, ISL; Records Reminiscences, 7 September 1863, Records Manuscript Collection, ISL; Unidentified Diary, 7 September 1863, Meisner Collection, ISL; Kemper Diary, 7 September 1863, OHS; Griest Diary, 7 September 1863, CCNMP; Kemper Diary, 7 September 1863, OHS; Johnston Diary, 7 September 1863, FHS; Eighteenth Indiana Battery Chronology, 7 September 1863, Lilly Papers, LCA; McLain Diary, 7 September 1863, ISHS.

14. *OR* 30(3):430–31; Winans Diary, 7 September 1863, CCNMP; Hewes, *Tenth Michigan*, 50; Wilson, *Memoirs*, 193; Holmes, *Then and Now*, 5, 124; Thomas M. Burns to his father, 9 September 1863, Burns Letters, VT; Armstrong Diary, 7 September 1863, CCNMP; Kinnear, *Eighty-Sixth Illinois*, 22; Fahnestock Diary, 7 September 1863, ALPL; *OR* 30(1):864; *SOR* 25:681, 686; George Pepoon to his sister, 5 October 1863, Pepoon Letters, NIU; Hoch Journal, 7 September 1863, Illinois Historical Survey, UI; Nelson G. Huson to his parents, 11 September 1863, Huson Letters, HL; Partridge, *Ninety-Sixth Illinois*, 154–55; Sowers Diary, 7 September 1863, CCNMP; Royse, *115th Illinois*, 93; Royse Diary, 7 September 1863, Royse Manuscript Collection, ISL; Imboden, *Army of the Cumberland*, 9; *SOR* 26:407, 413; Robinson Diary, 7 September 1863, Robinson Papers, ALPL; Schwartz, *Diary*, 11; Boyd Diary, 6–7 September 1863, Boyd Family Papers, UCB; Beach, *Fortieth Ohio*, 39; Patton Diary, 7 September 1863, CCNMP; John M. Branum, *National Tribune*, 20 December 1900; Papers, DU; Batchelor Diary, 7 September 1863, ALPL; Linus A. Patrick to his father, 7 September 1863, Patrick Correspondence, BGSU; Members, *Battery M, First Illinois*, 76; Kennedy, "Army Life," SRNB; Goddard to Bingham, 7 September 1863, and Goddard to Carlton, 9:00 P.M., 6 September 1863, both in DC, Telegrams Sent, NARA; Keeler Diary, 7 September 1863, Keeler Papers, UM-B.

15. *OR* 30(3):412, 432; "Summaries of the News," 333–36, NARA.

16. *OR* 30(3):406–7, 409, 417; Bond to Van Duzer, 7 September 1863, Bond to Guthrie, 12:00 P.M., 7 September 1863, Thoms to R. S. Granger, 7 September 1863, Goddard to Dickson, 7 September 1863, Thoms to Brigadier General King, 7 September 1863, and Rosecrans to Halleck, midnight, 7 September 1863, all in DC, Telegrams Sent, NARA. At some point during the day, Lt. Col. Calvin Goddard telegraphed another staff officer in Nashville to forward a message to Goddard's wife, "All well so far," a sentiment probably not shared by his chief.

17. *OR* 30(4):616, 618, 623–24; *OR* 30(3):433–34; Maj. Frederick Sims to Maj. J. D. Whitford, Goldsboro, North Carolina, 7 September 1863, Sims Letter Book, HL.

18. Brent Diary, 7 September 1863, Brent to Beard, 7:00 A.M., 7 September 1863, Brent to Forrest, 7:30 A.M., 7 September 1863, and Brent to Buckner, 9:00 A.M., 7 September 1863, all in Bragg Papers, WRHS; *OR* 30(2):27.

19. Circular, 7 September 1863, Bragg Papers, WRHS; Circular, 7 September 1863, Buckner Papers, HL; Circular (Polk), 7 September 1863, Orders and Circulars, Army of Tennessee, NARA; *OR* 30(4):597–98, 621–23; Brent to Buckner (two messages), 7 September 1863, Brent to Polk (two messages), 7 September 1863, Brent to Mauldin, 7 September 1863, Brent to Rucker, 7 September 1863, Brent to Blanton, 7 September 1863, and Brent to Pegram, 7 September 1863, all in Bragg Papers, WRHS; Sloan Diary, 7 September 1863, TSLA; Leverich Diary, 7 September 1863, LSU.

20. *OR* 30(4):622; John Henry Smith Diary, 7 September 1863, CCNMP; Coleman Diary, 7 September 1863, UNC; Seaton, *Bugle*, 39; Heartsill, *Fourteen Hundred*, 146–47; Bush Diary, 7 September 1863, CCNMP; Jackman Journal, 7 September 1863, LC.

21. Thomas Jack to Hindman, 7 September 1863, and Thomas Jack to J. K. Jackson,

7 September 1863, both in Letters Sent, Polk's Command, NARA; *OR* 30(4):621; Rennolds Diary, 7 September 1863, CCNMP; Fielder Diary, 7 September 1863, TSLA; Oldham Diary, 7 September 1863, CCNMP; Moorman, "Moorman Memorandum," 79; Lindsley, *Annals*, 2:820; Richmond Diary, 7 September 1863, Polk Papers, US; *OR* 30(2):71. The notes penned by Lt. W. B. Richmond were shorn of many personal references by the editors of the *Official Records*. A complete transcript may be found in the Leonidas Polk Papers at the University of the South, Sewanee, Tennessee.

22. *OR* 30(4):621; Bragg to Cooper, 7 September 1863, Brent to Wayne, 7 September 1863, Brent to Garland, 7 September 1863, Falconer to Horbach, 7 September 1863, Brent to Commanding Officer, Chickamauga Station, 7 September 1863, Brent to Buckner, 9:00 P.M., 7 September 1863, and Brent to J. W. Davis, 7 September 1863, all in Bragg Papers, WRHS; Wayne to Brown, 13 September 1863, Cuyler Collection, UGA; Adamson, *Thirtieth Georgia*, 33; Flewellen to McMicken, 7 September 1863, Letters, Orders, and Circulars Sent, Medical Director, AT, NARA; Cumming, *Kate*, 137–38.

23. John Henry Smith Diary, 7 September 1863, CCNMP; *SOR* 13:644, 646; Milner Diary, 7 September 1863, ADAH; Armstrong Diary, 7 September 1863, ADAH; Williamson, *45th Mississippi*, 120; *SOR* 46:72; Coleman Diary, 7 September 1863, UNC; Seaton, *Bugle*, 39; *SOR* 80:74, 160, 181; Heartsill, *Fourteen Hundred*, 146–47; Sparkman Diary, 7 September 1863, BPL; *SOR* 79:420; Estes Diary, 7 September 1863, MC; *SOR* 14:281; Jackman Journal, 7 September 1863, LC; *SOR* 35:199, 203, 266, 273, 350, 354, 404, 408; Bush Diary, 7 September 1863, CCNMP; John McGrath to "Friend Danl," 24 September 1863, McGrath Papers, LSU; *SOR* 36:434; Pasco Diary, 7 September 1863, CCNMP; Lumsden Diary, 7 September 1863, ADAH; John Snow to his sister, 30 September 1863, Snow Papers, DU.

24. Fraser Diary, 7 September 1863, CCNMP; Rand Diary, 7 September 1863, MDAH; John A. James to his wife, 7 September 1863, UDC Collection, vol. 8, GDAH; Rennolds Diary, 7 September 1863, CCNMP; Magee Diary, 7 September 1863, DU; Brown Notebook, 7 September 1863, CCNMP; Richmond Diary, 7 September 1863, Polk Papers, US; *OR* 30(2):71; Otey, "Signal Corps," 130.

25. Daniel Diary, 7 September 1863, SRNB; *SOR* 14:366, 370, 438, 441, 491, 501, 539, 542; Grammer Diary, 7 September 1863, CCNMP; Freeman Diary, 7 September 1863, TSLA; Capers Diary, 7 September 1863, Capers Papers, CI; Adamson, *Thirtieth Georgia*, 33; Gentry Diary, 7 September 1863, CCNMP; General Orders, Nos. 13 and 14, 7 September 1863, Orders and Circulars, AT, NARA; Dillon Diary, 7 September 1863, TSLA; *SOR* 78:685; Owen, *Camp and Battle*, 269; *SOR* 13:917, 925, 929; Dugger Diary, 7 September 1863, *Watauga (N.C.) Democrat*, 21 May 1891; *SOR* 19:194; Johnson Diary, 7 September 1863, Johnson Papers, NARA; Holmes, *Diary*, 17; Watson Journal, 7 September 1863, CCNMP. Scarcity of information precludes determining either the order of march of Buckner's divisions or their exact locations during the night.

26. Sanders Diary, 7 September 1863, SRNB; Simpson Diary, 7 September 1863, TSLA; Farris, "Letters to Mary," 99; Jones, "Train Wreck," 15; *SOR* 78:474, 476; *SOR* 80:677, 684; *OR* 30(4):608, 619–20; *OR* 52(2):522; Leeper, *Rebels Valiant*, 185–86; *SOR* 14:193, 203, 340–41, 344; *SOR* 61:188; Lawton to Lee, 7 September 1863, Quartermaster General's Office, Letters and Telegrams Sent, NARA; Sims to Lee, 7 September 1863, and Sims to John D. Whitford, 7 September 1863 (two messages), both in Sims Letter Book, HL; Whitford to Sims, 7 September 1863, Railroad Bureau Telegrams, VM; Giles, *Rags and Hope*, 196; Lowrey Diary, 7 September 1863, HC; Campbell, *Lone Star Confederate*, 96; Ballard Diary, 7 September 1863, CCNMP; *SOR* 18:397, 406; Screven Diary, 7 September

1863, SCHS; Wyckoff, *2nd South Carolina*, 87; Wyckoff, *Third South Carolina*, 132–33; Belue Diary, 7 September 1863, WU; Hill Diary, 7 September 1863, Rietti Papers, MDAH; *SOR* 45:471; Montgomery Diary, 7 September 1863, GDAH; Moore, *Life*, 164. Originally scheduled to travel via Selma, Alabama, McNair's Brigade was redirected to go via the Mobile route. Nevertheless, it appears that at least two regiments, the Fourth and Twenty-Fifth Arkansas, took the route through Selma. *SOR* 14:340–41, 344, 346, 348, 350, 685, 692.

27. John M. Palmer to his wife, 8 September 1863, Palmer Papers II, ALPL; *OR* 30(1):710, 727, 740, 744, 751, 755, 790, 821, 837, 843, 848; *SOR* 34:70, 74, 106; Busbey Diary, 8 September 1863, SRNB; Hyde Diary, 8 September 1863, KYHS; Pate Diary, 8 September 1863, CCNMP; McKee Diary, 8 September 1863, http://mckee-burns.pasttracker.com/mckee/cw_mckee/mckee_robert_t_cw_diary_1 (15 June 2013); Connelly Diary, 8 September 1863, IHS; Harden, *90th Ohio*, 91; Hannaford, *Sixth Ohio*, 444; Glisan Diary, 8 September 1863, CCNMP; *SOR* 62:781, 786; Simmons, *84th Illinois*, 78; Suiter Diary, 8 September 1863, ALPL; Walker Diary, 8 September 1863, Harrisburg Civil War Roundtable Collection, USAHEC; Palmer Journal, 8 September 1863, CCNMP; Williams Diary, 8 September 1863, CCNMP; Grose, *36th Indiana*, 173; *OR* 30(3):462–63; 466; Van Cleve to Edward Ruger, 24 May 1867, Ruger Correspondence, Thomas Papers, NARA; Howe Diary, 8 September 1863, IHS; *History, Seventy-Ninth Indiana*, 85; Reep Manuscript, private collection; Benedict Diary, 8 September 1863, SRNB; Patton Diary, 8 September 1863, TSLA; Woodcock, *Southern Boy*, 186; Claggett Diary, 8 September 1863, CCNMP; Huntzinger Diary, 8 September 1863, http://www.lafavre.us/huntzinger/hunt_3.htm (23 May 2016); Tilford Diary, 8 September 1863, FHS; Wright, *Eighth Kentucky*, 178; Barnes, Carnahan, and McCain, *Eighty-Sixth Indiana*, 158; Moore Diary, 8 September 1863, CCNMP; McCain, *Song*, 88; Decker Diary, 8 September 1863, WHS; Horatio Van Cleve to his wife, 8 September 1863, Van Cleve Papers, MHS.

28. Woodruff, *Fifteen Years*, 280–81; William J. Carroll to his sister, 8 September 1863, Carroll Papers, UM-B; *OR* 30(1):688–89, 699, 702, 704; Hinman, *Sherman Brigade*, 410; Duncan Thompson to his parents, 8 September 1863, Thompson Letters, Timothy Brookes Collection, USAHEC; Clark, *Tigers*, 84; Opdycke Diary, 8 September 1863, Opdycke Papers, OHS; *OR* 30(3):424–25, 452–53, 455–58, 991–92.

29. *OR* 30(3):453–54, 462–63; *OR* (1):602, 710, 727, 751; *SOR* 34:106; Pate Diary, 8 September 1863, CCNMP; Williams Diary, 8 September 1863, CCNMP; Grose, *36th Indiana*, 173; Evans, *Inventory and Assessment, Dade County*, 187–90.

30. *OR* 30(1):326, 387, 393, 396; *OR* 30(3):446, 448–49; Beatty, *Citizen Soldier*, 329–30; Hapeman Diary, 8 September 1863, ALPL; Calkins, *One Hundred and Fourth Illinois*, 114; George Marsh Jr. to his brother, 1–8 September 1863, Marsh Family Papers, ALPL; Sheffield Diary, 8 September 1863, CCNMP; Bloom Diary, 8 September 1863, CCNMP; Hicks, "Personal Recollections," 527; Shanks Diary, 8 September 1863, BGSU; Adams, "Diary," 649; Dilworth Journal, 8 September 1863, HC; Canfield, *21st Ohio*, 105; Weaver Diary, 8 September 1863, SRNB; John W. Baldwin to his wife, 5–12 September 1863, Baldwin Papers, OHS; Blackburn, *Letters*, 147; *SOR* 65:673, 679; Nupp Diary, 7–8 September 1863, CCNMP; Millen Diary, 8 September 1863, SRNB; Gibson, *Seventy-Eighth Pennsylvania*, 84; *SOR* 62:350.

31. *OR* 30(3):411, 445–48; Jones Diary, 8 September 1863, SRNB; Hinkley Diary, 8 September 1863, and Lucius D. Hinkley to his mother, 8 September 1863, both in Hinkley Papers, WHS; Frank M. Phelps to his friends, 9 September 1863, Phelps Letters, Lewis Leigh Collection, USAHEC; Webster Diary, 8 September 1863, Civil War Miscellaneous Collection, USAHEC; Edmonds Diary, 8 September 1863, USAHEC; *Record, Ninety-*

Fourth Ohio, 36; *SOR* 88:283; Johnston, *Soldier Boy*, 57; Clark Diary, 8 September 1863, Clark Papers, USAHEC; *SOR* 72:516; Hambright Report, Union Battle Reports, NARA; Galpin Diary, 8 September 1863, Galpin Family Papers, WHS; Charles K. Bailer to his sister, 27 September 1863, Bailer Letters, Regimental Papers, WRHS; Morledge Diary, 8 September 1863, KMNMP; Levering Account, 8 September 1863, CCNMP; Williams, *Extracts*, 91; Owen Diary, 8 September 1863, AU; Ward Diary, 8 September 1863, Booth Papers, OHS; *SOR* 29:803, 806; Shera Diary, 8 September 1863, FHS; Miller Journal, 8 September 1863, IHS; *SOR* 30:98; Floyd, *Seventy-Fifth Indiana*, 121; Tourgee, "Diary," 118; Parker Diary, 8 September 1863, HL; Morse, *Diaries*, 33; Hollingsworth Diary, 8 September 1863, IHS; Benjamin Mabrey to Lou and Alis Mabrey, 8 September 1863, Mabrey Letters, IHS; Inskeep Diary, 8 September 1863, OHS; Price Diary, 8 September 1863, Civil War Miscellaneous Collection, USAHEC; Small Diary, 8 September 1863, IHS; Everett F. Abbott to his mother, 8 September 1863, Chamberlain Papers, IHS; Keegan, *Diaries*, 25; Martling Diary, 8 September 1863, Martling Manuscript Collection, ISL; Davidson Diary, 8 September 1863, NCWM; Solomon M. Deacon to his sister, 8 September 1863, Deacon Letter, CCNMP; Bruce Diary, 8 September 1863, ISL; Reed Diary, 8 September 1863, MHS; Bircher, *Drummer-Boy*, 73; Horatio Van Cleve to his wife, 8 September 1863, Van Cleve Papers, MHS.

32. Thomas Diary, 8 September 1863, Thomas Collection, UT; Merrill, *Diary*, 52–53; Persons Diary, 8 September 1863, WHS; Baum Diary, 8 September 1863, IHS; Kendall Diary, 8 September 1863, HL; Stanley, *Memoirs*, 140, 153–55; Lubetkin, *Before Custer*, 33, 280–81; *OR* 30(1):220; *OR* 30(3):468, 652–53; Belcher, *Stanley*, 155–56, 158–59, 161–67. Stanley's biographer, Dennis W. Belcher, while admitting Stanley's fondness for alcohol, dismisses that as a reason for Stanley's poor performance. He ascribes Stanley's problem purely to illness, arguing that Stanley had been sick since the beginning of September. Unfortunately, part of Belcher's argument depends on a 13 September message from Alexander McCook, misdated 3 September in the *Official Records*. *OR* 30(3):332.

33. Mayfield Diary, 8 September 1863, IU; Mosman, *Rough Side*, 75–76; Morris, *Eighty-First Indiana*, 56; Colyer Diary, 8 September 1863, ALPL; Pickering Diary, 8 September 1863, HL; Cope, *Fifteenth Ohio*, 303; Kiene, *Journal*, 172; Stahl Diary, 8 September 1863, BGSU; Phillips Diary, 8 September 1863, Phillips Collection, HL; Davidson, *Battery A*, 83; Robinson Diary, 8 September 1863, Regimental Papers, WRHS; Protsman Diary, 8 September 1863, WSU; Beck Diary, 8 September 1863, KSHS; Lyon Diary, 8 September 1863, OHS; *SOR* 62:541; Shideler Diary, 8 September 1863, CCNMP; Doll, *Sixth Indiana*, 68; *OR* 30(1):579, 583; Pirtle, "Leaves," CIHS; Cooley Diary, 8 September 1863, WHS; Cummins Diary, 8 September 1863, Cummins Papers, ALPL; Pecoy Diary, 8 September 1863, CCNMP; *SOR* 22:610, 627; Ely Diary, 8 September 1863, CCNMP; Simonds Diary, 8 September 1863, Simonds Papers, NIU; Riley, *Diary*, 53; Lyman H. Needham to his brother and sister, 12 September 1863, Needham Papers, ALPL; Burns Diary, 8 September 1863, CCNMP; Moody Diary, 8 September 1863, SRNB; Tabler Diary, 8 September 1863, private collection; Crippin, "Diary," 280; Austin Diary, 8 September 1863, ALPL; Luther Bradley to his wife, 8 September 1863, Bradley Papers, USAHEC; Merrill, *Soldier*, 2:437.

34. *OR* 30(3):468–70; *OR* 30(1):891, 901, 909; *SOR* 41:722; Leonidas S. Stanton to Edward Ruger, 8 June 1867, Elijah Watts to Edward Ruger, 17 June 1867, and O. O. Smith to Edward Ruger, 21 April 1867, all in Ruger Correspondence, Thomas Papers, NARA; Hempstead Diary, 8 September 1863, UM-B; Merrill, *Diary*, 52–53; Read Diary, 8 September 1863, KSHS; Persons Diary, 8 September 1863, WHS; Charles A. Pettibone, Receipt from Horace T. Persons, 8 September 1863, Persons Letters, WHS; Baum

Diary, 8 September 1863, IHS; Kendall Diary, 8 September 1863, HL; Harris Diary, 8 September 1863, IHS; Watts, "Chickamauga Campaign," Watts Papers, FHS; Prickitt, *Company H*, 103–4; Feagles Diary, 8 September 1863, CCNMP; Crane Diary, 8 September 1863, Thomas Papers, NARA; Crane Diary, 8 September 1863, CIHS; Thomson Diary, 8 September 1863, CCNMP; *Proceedings, 30th Reunion*, 16; Nourse Diary, 8 September 1863, DU.

35. *OR* 30(1):679, 760; *OR* 30(3):459–65, 470–71; Marshall Diary, 8 September 1863, OHS; Dewees Diary, 8 September 1863, CCNMP; Campbell Journal, 8 September 1863, CCNMP; Benefiel, *Souvenir, Seventeenth Indiana*, unpaginated; Banta Diary, 8 September 1863, CCNMP; Kemper Diary, 8 September 1863, OHS; Records Diary, 8 September 1863, and Records Reminiscences, both in Records Manuscript Collection, ISL; Griest Diary, 8 September 1863, CCNMP; McGee, *72nd Indiana*, 153.

36. *OR* 52(1):443; *OR* 30(3):467; Winans Diary, 8 September 1863, CCNMP; Hewes, *Tenth Michigan*, 50; Porter Diary, 8 September 1863, OHS; Holmes, *Then and Now*, 5, 124; Thomas M. Burns to his father, 9 September 1863, Burns Letters, VT; Thomas Green to Dear ______, 30 September 1863, Civil War Miscellaneous Collection, USAHEC; Alexander M. Ayers to his wife, 8 September 1863, Ayers Papers, EU; Harmon, *Life and Letters*, 97–98; Armstrong Diary, 8 September 1863, CCNMP; *SOR* 20:421; Brown, Murphy, and Putney, *Behind the Guns*, 53–54; Fahnestock Diary, 8 September 1863, ALPL; Kinnear, *Eighty-Sixth Illinois*, 23; Boyd Diary, 8 September 1863, and newspaper clippings, Boyd Family Papers, UCB; Partridge, *Ninety-Sixth Illinois*, 155; Sowers Diary, 8 September 1863, CCNMP; Schwartz, *Diary*, 11; Robinson Diary, 8 September 1863, Robinson Papers, ALPL; Patton Diary, 8 September 1863, CCNMP; McAdams, *One Hundred and Thirteenth Ohio*, 38–39; Members, *Battery M, First Illinois*, 76–77; Caleb Carlton to his wife, 8 September 1863, Carlton Papers, LC. Capt. Ephraim Wilson, one of Tillson's officers, described Stevenson at this time: "This town of Stevenson is a perfect sandhole and is uninviting in every respect. The stench from dead horses and mules lying around in the brush almost everywhere is enough to breed a pestilence. The town is small and dirty, and has a genuine rebel look about it that is woe-begone in every feature. The natives have all left—they attended to that just before the Yankees arrived—they might have stayed. But they did wisely by going and leaving behind them such a looking place as this. We simply make use of the name of the town instead of the town itself for a military Camp, and a sort of an intermediate or secondary base for the supplies necessary for the operations of the army." Wilson, *Memoirs*, 198–99.

37. *OR* 30(3):411, 442–43, 446, 458; Wilson, *Column South*, 86; Kirk, *Fifteenth Pennsylvania Cavalry*, 229; *OR* 30(1):453; *SOR* 25:499, 530; Phillips, *Diary*, 25; Brown Diary, 8 September 1863, ALPL. Nickajack Trace is described in Evans, *Inventory and Assessment, Dade County*, 85–90. The McKaig Trace described in the same work (177–80), however, is in Johnson's Crook, and is not the McKaig Trace identified by the Federals. The latter trail was just north of Trenton, and is shown in Col. William Palmer's sketch in *OR* 30(3):443.

38. *OR* 30(3):444, 452, 459–60, 990–91; G. P. Thruston to Philip Sheridan, 8:00 P.M., 8 September 1863, Sheridan Papers, LC; Richard L. Owen CSR, NARA; "Summaries of the News," 336–38, NARA; *OR* 30(1):602. The possibility exists that Owen was a Federal agent. His Compiled Service Record shows that he enlisted at Bardstown, Kentucky, in September 1862, was captured by Union forces at Auburn, Tennessee (his home), on 7 February 1863, was paroled and quickly processed through Nashville; Louisville; and Columbus, Ohio; to City Point, Virginia, for exchange on 1 April. Present with his

regiment, the Fourth [Eighth] Tennessee Cavalry, in May and June 1863, he thereafter disappears from the record, both Union and Confederate, except for the mention in Rosecrans's "Summaries of the News." Unlike Owen's first experience with the Federal prisoner of war system, there are no records of another incarceration of any kind, or indeed any record at all.

39. *OR* 30(3):451, 467–69. Two versions of Rosecrans's message to Halleck are printed in *OR* 30(3):442, 479, with insignificant differences in wording. As for Garfield's, and possibly Rosecrans's, misunderstanding of the geography east of Lookout Mountain, Pigeon Mountain, a spur of Lookout, intervened between Alpine and the southern end of Missionary Ridge, which lay in McLemore's Cove. Garfield made no mention of this salient fact in his orders to Stanley and McCook. Pigeon Mountain would play a much greater role in the days ahead.

40. Brent Diary, 8 September 1863, Bragg Papers, WRHS; Richmond Diary, 8 September 1863, Polk Papers, US; *OR* 30(2):71; Samuel Chester Reid Diary, 5 and 8 September 1863, Reid Family Papers, LC; Braxton Bragg to Marcus J. Wright, 7 March 1864, Wright Papers, UNC; Marriner, "Chickamauga," 8–9; Lumsden Diary, 8 September 1863, ADAH; John Snow to his sister, 30 September 1863, Snow Papers, DU; Hollingsworth, *Barefoot Confederate*, 12; *Macon (Ga.) Telegraph*, 11 September 1863, quoting *Atlanta Daily Intelligencer*, 10 September 1863; *Atlanta Daily Intelligencer*, 12 September 1863; Jackman Journal, 8 September 1863, LC; Sparkman Diary, 8 September 1863, BPL; Harder Reminiscences, TSLA; Johnson Diary, 8 September 1863, Johnson Papers, NARA; *SOR* 78:787; *SOR* 79:39, 352; Huntzinger Diary, 2 October 1863, http://www.lafavre.us/huntzinger/hunt_3.htm (23 May 2016).

41. Sloan Diary, 8 September 1863, TSLA; Leverich Diary, 8 September 1863, LSU; Louis DeLaigle to Samuel D. Stockman, 8 September 1863, Louis DeLaigle CSR, NARA; Watson Journal, 8 September 1863, CCNMP; *Memphis Daily Appeal*, 10 September 1863; Cumming, *Kate*, 138–40; Record of Events, Company B, Third Regiment, Engineer Troops, C.S.A., Muster Roll, 31 October 1863, NARA; Henry C. Wayne to Joseph Brown, 15 September 1863, Cuyler Collection, UGA.

42. Coleman Diary, 8 September 1863, UNC; *SOR* 46:72; Milner Diary, 8 September 1863, ADAH; Armstrong Diary, 8 September 1863, ADAH; John Henry Smith Diary, 8 September 1863, CCNMP; *SOR* 13:156, 573, 640–41; Heartsill, *Fourteen Hundred*, 147; Seaton, *Bugle*, 39; *SOR* 80:74, 160, 181; *SOR* 14:281; Evans, *Civil War Sites Assessment for Walker County*, 141–50; *SOR* 35:340, 404; Bush Diary, 8 September 1863, CCNMP; Ellis Diary, 8 September 1863, LSU; Pasco Diary, 8 September 1863, CCNMP; *OR* 30(2):71; Richmond Diary, 8 September 1863, Polk Papers, US; Anonymous Diary, 8 September 1863, Baker Papers, MDAH; *SOR* 45:95, 136, 192; *SOR* 46:180, 314; Hugh A. McLaurin to his father, 15 September 1863, McLaurin Papers, WHS; Rand Diary, 8 September 1863, MDAH; Fraser Diary, 8 September 1863, CCNMP; McAdory Memorandum, Twenty-Fifth Alabama File, ADAH; Manigault, *Carolinian*, 103–4; *SOR* 76:810; *SOR* 77:138; *SOR* 79:15, 24, 141, 197, 410; Rennolds Diary, 8 September 1863, CCNMP; James M. Brannock to his wife, 30 September 1863, Brannock Papers, VHS; David Godwin to "Miss B.," 30 September 1863, Godwin Letters, CCNMP; *SOR* 78:609, 743; Magee Diary, 8 September 1863, DU; Brown Notebook, 8 September 1863, CCNMP; Head, *Sixteenth Tennessee*, 117; Etter Diary, 8 September 1863, SRNB; Lindsley, *Annals*, 2:820; Jones Diary, 8 September 1863, CCNMP; Fielder Diary, 8 September 1863, TSLA; Moorman, "Moorman Memorandum," 79; U.S. Federal Census, 1860, Walker County, Georgia, NARA.

43. Freeman Diary, 8 September 1863, TSLA; Daniel Diary, 8 September 1863, SRNB;

SOR 14:548, 552; Grammer Diary, 8 September 1863, CCNMP; Swett, "Warren Light Artillery," http://www.perryvillebattlefield.org/html/ms-swett-charles-cs.html (24 July 2012); Capers Diary, 8 September 1863, Capers Papers, CI; Adamson, *Thirtieth Georgia*, 33; Owen, *Camp and Battle*, 269; William Alexander Brown Diary, 8 September 1863, CCNMP; *SOR* 13:917; Holmes, *Diary*, 17; *SOR* 19:194–95; Dugger/White Diary, 8 September 1863, *Watauga (N.C.) Democrat*, 21 May 1891; Anonymous Diary, 8 September 1863, MC; Andrew J. Neal to his father, 8 September 1863, Neal Letters, UDC Collection, vol. 4, GDAH; Dillon Diary, 8 September 1863, TSLA; *OR* 30(4):628.

44. *OR* 30(4):627–28; Dyer, *Diary*, 20; Davis Diary, 8 September 1863, TSLA; Corbitt Diary, 8 September 1863, EU.

45. Joseph Wheeler to Samuel Cooper, 17 May 1863, and Braxton Bragg endorsement, in James Hagan CSR, NARA; Knox Miller to "My dear Cellie," 15 September 1863, Miller Letters, UNC; *OR* 30(4):585, 611; Brent to Polk, and Brent to Mauldin, both 7 September 1863, in Bragg Papers, WRHS; *OR* 30(2):19, 522–23. For a detailed estimate of Wharton's and Martin's respective strengths, see Powell, *Failure*, 251–55.

46. Falconer to Buckner, 6:30 P.M., 8 September 1863, Brent to Polk, 8 September 1863, Brent to Hill, 11:30 P.M., 8 September 1863, Brent to Walker, 8 September 1863, Brent to Forrest, 11:30 P.M., 8 September 1863, and Brent to Wheeler, 11:30 P.M., 8 September 1863, all in Bragg Papers, WRHS; Brent to Hill, 11:30 P.M., 8 September 1863, Hill Papers, LV; Richmond Diary, 8–9 September 1863, Polk Papers, US; *OR* 30(2):71; *OR* 30(4):626–27.

47. Sims to Thomas Dodamead, 8 September 1863, Sims to John D. Whitford, 8 September 1863 (two messages), Sims to Henry T. Peake, 8 September 1863 (two messages), Sims to Thomas R. Sharp, 8 September 1863, Sims to Henry M. Drane, 8 September 1863 (two messages), Sims to George Yonge, 8 September 1863, Sims to Thomas Peters, 8 September 1863, and Sims to Mason Morfit, 8 September 1863, all in Sims Letter Book, HL; Henry M. Drane to Sims, 8 September 1863, Railroad Bureau Telegrams, VM; H. A. Troutman to John F. Divine, 8 September 1863, Confederate Citizens Files, NARA; Alexander R. Lawton to Lafayette McLaws, 8 September 1863, Quartermaster General's Office, Letters and Telegrams Sent, NARA.

48. Sanders Diary, 8 September 1863, SRNB; Simpson Diary, 8 September 1863, TSLA; Farris, "Letters to Mary," 99–100; *SOR* 14:340–41, 685; Reynolds, *Worthy*, 103; Henry S. Figures to his mother, 26 September 1863, Figures Letter, private collection; Laine and Penny, *Law's Alabama Brigade*, 139; Ballard Diary, 8 September 1863, CCNMP; Simpson, *Gaines' Mill*, 151–52; *SOR* 80:614; Joskins, "Sketch," HC; Campbell, *Lone Star Confederate*, 96; Lowrey Diary, 8 September 1863, HC; Joab Goodson to his niece, 28 September 1863, Goodson Letter, CCNMP; *SOR* 13:277, 744, 760; Vaughan Diary, 8 September 1863, Vaughan Papers, UNC; *SOR* 76:695, 754; *SOR* 77:65; Belue Diary, 8 September 1863, WU; Screven Diary, 8 September 1863, SCHS; Humphreys, "Sunflower Guards," Claiborne Papers, UNC; Cooper, *Confederate Soldier*, 25; Moore, *Life*, 164; *SOR* 45:280, 610; Hill Diary, 8 September 1863, Rietti Papers, MDAH; Mitchell Journal, 8 September 1863, CCNMP; Montgomery Diary, 8 September 1863, GDAH; Stillwell, *Letters*, 211; Brown Diary, 8 September 1863, CCNMP; *SOR* 82:586; *SOR* 83:157, 178, 355, 454, 536, 633, 796; *SOR* 84:106, 502; *New York Herald*, 8 September 1863.

CHAPTER 17

1. *OR* 30(3):481, 491–92; Bond to Crittenden, 2:30 A.M., 9 September 1863, and Bond to Merrill, 2:35 A.M., 9 September 1863, both in DC, Telegrams Sent, NARA; *OR* 30(1):780,

786, 807; Suiter Diary, 9 September 1863, ALPL; Claggett Diary, 9 September 1863, CCNMP; Evans, *Inventory and Assessment, Dade County*, 85–90, 187–90. For accounts of Rosecrans's headquarters routine, see Garfield, *Wild Life*, 233, 263; and Bickham, *Rosecrans' Campaign*, 28–29.

2. *OR* 30(3):460, 480, 482, 492, 496; *OR* 30(1):240–41; Van Duzer to Bond, 9 September 1863 and 1:00 P.M., 9 September 1863, both in DC, Letters Received, NARA; Plum, *Military Telegraph*, 2:66–67. For an excellent discussion of the means through which Wagner's message was communicated to Rosecrans, see Baker, "Command and Control Mechanisms," esp. 89–93. James Garfield's role, if any, in the decision to mount an immediate pursuit is unknown. His most astute biographer, Theodore C. Smith, commented, "That he was responsible for Rosecrans's adventurous decision it is too much to assume, but that he heartily sympathized with it and embodied his own aggressive spirit in his dispatches may be conjectured with some show of probability." Smith, *Garfield*, 1:319. Certainly Garfield opposed turning places into army objectives, writing to Secretary of the Treasury Salmon P. Chase on 5 May 1863, "I [have] been anxious to impress upon the General [Rosecrans] the truth that our true objective point of operations is the rebel army and not any particular position or territory." Garfield, *Wild Life*, 266.

3. *OR* 30(1):247; Carpenter Diary, 9 September 1863, SRNB; Bennett, *Ninth Michigan*, 33; Van Horne, *Army of the Cumberland*, 1:315–18; Van Horne, *Life of Thomas*, 103–6; Thomas B. Van Horne to Emerson Opdycke, 20 February 1884, Opdycke Papers, OHS. Van Horne's letter to Opdycke continued, "Had the General lived he would doubtless have given me a statement of these facts in writing. I thought the facts too important to be omitted and consequently have no other support than my own assertion as to their communication to me by him." Thomas biographers Francis McKinney, Benson Bobrick, and Christopher Einolf accept Van Horne's account as factual, while biographer Brian Wills does not mention Thomas's meeting with Rosecrans. Larry Daniel, in his history of the Army of the Cumberland, dismisses Van Horne's account out of hand. McKinney, *Education in Violence*, 224–25; Bobrick, *Master of War*, 175–76; Einolf, *Thomas*, 158–59; Wills, *Thomas*, 194–95, Daniel, *Days of Glory*, 299.

4. *OR* 30(3):349–50, 393–97, 426, 458–59, 495; David G. Blodgett and W. A. Naylor, *National Tribune*, 21 October 1886; A. B. Smith, *National Tribune*, 15 July 1882; P. S. Moore, *National Tribune*, 11 March 1886; Milton Barnes, *National Tribune*, 15 April 1886; Cy Crisman and Craig Jackson, *National Tribune*, 1 July 1886; C. J. Gardner, *National Tribune*, 5 August 1886; Joshua Dewees, *National Tribune*, 2 June 1887; Joshua Dewees, *National Tribune*, 11 April 1901. The various accounts differ slightly in detail, especially in regard to how the original boat was acquired, but in the main they are consistent with the account provided in the text.

5. *OR* 30(1):454, 603, 653, 689, 699, 727, 740, 751, 786, 802, 807, 821, 837, 843; Kelly, *Historic Sketch*, 10–11; Woodruff, *Fifteen Years*, 281; Mallory Diary, 9 September 1863, HPL; Gillis Diary, 9 September 1863, OHS; Opdycke Diary, 9 September 1863, Opdycke Papers, OHS; *SOR* 62:413; Williams Diary, 9 September 1863, CCNMP; Suiter Diary, 9 September 1863, ALPL; Glisan Diary, 9 September 1863, CCNMP; Hannaford, *Sixth Ohio*, 444–45; Connelly Diary, 9 September 1863, IHS; Woodcock, *Southern Boy*, 186–89; Patton Diary, 9 September 1863, TSLA; Claggett Diary, 9 September 1863, CCNMP; Reep Manuscript, private collection; Tilford Diary, 9 September 1863, FHS; Huntzinger Diary, 9 September 1863, http://www.lafavre.us/huntzinger/hunt_3.htm (23 May 2016); Howe Diary, 9 September 1863, IHS; Horatio Van Cleve to his wife, 9 September 1863, Van Cleve Papers, MHS; Barnes, Carnahan, and McCain, *Eighty-Sixth Indiana*, 160; Moore Diary,

9 September 1863, CCNMP; McCain, *Song*, 88; Decker Diary, 9 September 1863, WHS; Rerick, *Forty-Fourth Indiana*, 91; Atkins, *Chickamauga*, 6–7; *Ninety-Second Illinois*, 100–101.

6. Atkins, *Chickamauga*, 6–7; *Ninety-Second Illinois*, 100–101; *OR* 30(1):454, 628–29; *OR* 30(2):71; Campbell Journal, 9 September 1863, CCNMP; Itinerary, Eighteenth Indiana Battery, Lilly Papers, LCA. A story in the 12 August 1881 edition of the *Cincinnati Enquirer* by "Jayhawker [James H. Woodard]" claimed that Crittenden attempted to restrain Wood's impetuous push into Chattanooga, but that Wood contemptuously disregarded Crittenden's instructions. "Jayhawker" claimed to be an eyewitness to the events he described. Given the bad relationship then existing between Wood and Crittenden and the personalities of the two men, the story is plausible, but it is utterly undocumented otherwise. At some point after the original story reached print, Eli Lilly drafted a partial response to "Jayhawker," touting the primacy of the Ninety-Second Illinois's entry into the city, but his unfinished commentary was apparently never published. Eli Lilly to *Cincinnati Enquirer*, undated, Lilly Papers, LCA.

7. Atkins, *Chickamauga*, 7; *Ninety-Second Illinois*, 101; *OR* 30(1):454, 653, 699, 702, 704, 706; *OR* 30(3):487–88; Levering Account, CCNMP; John H. Bohn, *National Tribune*, 31 December 1885; Benjamin F. McMillan, *National Tribune*, 3 January 1901; Cy Crisman and Craig Jackson, *National Tribune*, 1 July 1886; Joshua Dewees, *National Tribune*, 2 June 1887; Dewees Diary, undated fragment, CCNMP; Hines Diary, 9 September 1863, Hines Manuscript Collection, ISL; Marshall Diary, 9 September 1863, OHS; Hight, *Fifty-Eighth Indiana*, 173–74; *SOR* 43:123; Woodruff, *Fifteen Years*, 281; S. L. Coulter, *National Tribune*, 12 November 1885; Mallory Diary, 9 September 1863, HPL; Gillis Diary, 9 September 1863, OHS; *SOR* 65:381, 419; Emerson Opdycke to his wife, 9 September 1863, and Opdycke Diary, 9 September 1863, both in Opdycke Papers, OHS; *SOR* 67:603; Joseph Bruff to his wife, 9 September 1863, Bruff Family Letters, private collection; *SOR* 34:146; *SOR* 62:413.

8. W. J. Carroll to his sister, 16 September 1863, Carroll Papers, UM-B; Hoobler, *Cities under the Gun*, 163; Hight, *Fifty-Eighth Indiana*, 173–74; Long, "War Time," *Chattanooga (Tenn.) Star*, 23 November 1907, clipping in CPL; Thomas Crutchfield Jr. to James R. Hood, 27 December 1863, Crutchfield Family Papers, TSLA; Cy Crisman and Craig Jackson, *National Tribune*, 1 July 1886; *OR* 30(3):481; U.S. Federal Census, 1850, Morgan County, Alabama, 1860, 1870, and 1880, Hamilton County, Tennessee (see also chap. 5, n. 30); McCallie, "Bragg Headquarters," *Chattanooga (Tenn.) Free Press*, 21 September 1938, clipping in CPL.

9. *OR* 30(1):603; *OR* 30(3):493–95.

10. Suiter Diary, 9 September 1863, ALPL; *OR* 30(1):780, 786, 798, 807; Walker Diary, 9 September 1863, Harrisburg Civil War Roundtable Collection, USAHEC; Palmer Journal, 9 September 1863, CCNMP; A. Brandley, *National Tribune*, 15 February 1894; William C. Margedant Account, Rosecrans Papers, UCLA; *OR* 30(3):498; Woodcock, *Southern Boy*, 186–89; Patton Diary, 9 September 1863, TSLA; Claggett Diary, 9 September 1863, CCNMP; *SOR* 34:440; Benedict Diary, 9 September 1863, SRNB; Hurd Diary, 9 September 1863, private collection; Reep Manuscript, private collection; Huntzinger Diary, 9 September 1863, http://www.lafavre.us/huntzinger/hunt_3.htm (23 May 2016); Tilford Diary, 9 September 1863, FHS; Howe Diary, 9 September 1863, IHS; *History, Seventy-Ninth Indiana*, 85–87.

11. *OR* 30(3):488, 495–96, 498, 500–501; Benefiel, *Souvenir, Seventeenth Indiana*, unpaginated; Kemper Diary, 9 September 1863, OHS; Henry Campbell Journal, 9 September 1863, CCNMP; *OR* 30(1):449, 767; Records Diary, 9 September 1863, and Records Reminiscences, both in Records Manuscript Collection, ISL; Griest Diary,

9 September 1863, CCNMP; Kitchell Diary, 9 September 1863, ALPL; McManus, *Morning*, 112; *Ninety-Second Illinois*, 101–2; Samuel Kessler to his uncle, 1 October 1863, Thomas J. Kessler Letters, NC; *SOR* 28:13; *SOR* 67:582; Johnston Diary, 9 September 1863, FHS; *SOR* 34:207; Potter Diary, 9 September 1863, Potter Papers, UM-B; McLain Diary, 9 September 1863, ISHS.

12. *OR* 30(3):488–89, 500.

13. Kirk, *Fifteenth Pennsylvania Cavalry*, 229–30; Wilson, *Column South*, 86; Weller Journal, 9 September 1863, *Civil War Times Illustrated* Collection, USAHEC; *SOR* 69:371–79, 405; *OR* 30(3):451, 483. The deserter statements referenced by McCook may be those described in "Summaries of the News," 336–38, NARA, as they were recorded on 8 September but forwarded to army headquarters a day later.

14. *OR* 30(3):489–90, 992–94; *OR* 30(1):497; Mosman, *Rough Side*, 76; William P. Carlin, *National Tribune*, 2 April 1885; Morris, *Eighty-First Indiana*, 56; Patterson Diary, 9 September 1863, ALPL; Colyer Diary, 9 September 1863, ALPL; *SOR* 21:449; Day, *One Hundred and First Ohio*, 144; I. P. Rule to his brother, 15 September 1863, Rule Letters, HPL; Himoe Diary, 9 September 1863, NAHA; *SOR* 88:6; *SOR* 22:61, 548; James E. Love to "Dearest Molly," 12 September 1863, Love Papers, MHM.

15. *OR* 30(1):887–88, 891, 895, 899, 901, 927; Elijah S. Watts to Edward Ruger, 17 June 1867, Leonidas S. Scranton to Edward Ruger, 8 June 1867, and Roswell M. Russell to Edward Ruger, 12 June 1867, all in Ruger Correspondence, Thomas Papers, NARA; Watts, "Chickamauga Campaign," Watts Papers, FHS; Mosman, *Rough Side*, 76; Hempstead Diary, 9 September 1863, UM-B; Thomas Diary, 9 September 1863, Thomas Collection, UT; Merrill, *Diary*, 53; Read Diary, 9 September 1863, KSHS; Persons Diary, 9 September 1863, WHS; John Smith CSR, NARA; Crane Diary, 9 September 1863, Thomas Papers, NARA; Crane Diary, 9 September 1863, CIHS; Crook, *Autobiography*, 103–4.

16. *OR* 30(1):887–88, 891, 895, 899, 903, 906–10, 912, 918, 927; Greenwood Diary, 9 September 1863, Knight Papers, UAK; Elijah S. Watts to Edward Ruger, 17 June 1867, O. O. Smith to Edward Ruger, 27 April 1867, and Roswell M. Russell to Edward Ruger, 12 June 1867, all in Ruger Correspondence, Thomas Papers, NARA; Watts, "Chickamauga Campaign," FHS; *Proceedings, 30th Reunion*, 16; Curry, *Four Years*, 109–10; Crofts, *Third Ohio Cavalry*, 112; Feagles Diary, 9 September 1863, CCNMP; Crane Diary, 9 September 1863, Thomas Papers, NARA; Crane Diary, 9 September 1863, CIHS; Thomson Diary, 9 September 1863, CCNMP; Second Cavalry Division Itinerary, CCNMP; Nourse Diary, 9 September 1863, DU; Hempstead Diary, 9 September 1863, UM-B; *SOR* 41:722; Thatcher, *Hundred Battles*, 141; Thomas Diary, 9 September 1863, UT; Carter, *First Tennessee Cavalry*, 86–87; Merrill, *Diary*, 53; Read Diary, 9 September 1863, KSHS; Persons Diary, 9 September 1863, WHS; *SOR* 86:654; Kendall Diary, 9 September 1863, HL; Mendenhall Diary, 9 September 1863, IHS; Baum Diary, 9 September 1863, IHS; Harris Diary, 9 September 1863, IHS; McCammon, *Loyal Mountain Troopers*, 64. A reporter for the *Cincinnati Commercial* considered Crook to be the hero of the action, but Lt. Col. Elijah S. Watts, a participant, believed the Confederates escaped because Crook was too slow in his flanking maneuver. *Cincinnati Commercial*, 22 September 1863; Watts, "Chickamauga Campaign," FHS.

17. *OR* 30(3):345–46 [misdated 4 September], 483, 489, 490–91; McCook to Garfield, 9 September 1863, Twentieth Army Corps, Letters Sent, NARA; *OR* 30(1):485–86, 497, 505–6, 510, 529; *OR* 30(4):127; Post Diary, 9 September 1863, Post Papers, KC; Mayfield Diary, 9 September 1863, IU; Mosman, *Rough Side*, 76; Rogers, "Diary," 11; James E. Love to "Dearest Molly," 12 September 1863, Love Papers, MHM; *Report of the Adjutant General*

of the State of Kansas, 121–22; Himoe Diary, 9 September 1863, NAHA; *SOR* 88:6; *SOR* 22:61, 548; *SOR* 33:541.

18. *OR* 30(3):489–91, 993–94.

19. *OR* 30(3):483–86; *OR* 30(1):247, 326; Hinkley Diary, 9 September 1863, Hinkley Papers, WHS; Edmonds Diary, 9 September 1863, USAHEC; Johnston, *Soldier Boy,* 57; Galpin Diary, 9 September 1863, Galpin Family Papers, WHS; Charles K. Bailer to his sister, 27 September 1863, Bailer Letters, Regimental Papers, WRHS; Levering Account, CCNMP; Miller Journal, 9 September 1863, IHS; Tourgee, "Diary," 118, 120; Parker Diary, 9 September 1863, HL; Hollingsworth Diary, 9 September 1863, IHS; Turchin, "Diary," 62–63; Williams, *Extracts,* 90–91; Ward Diary, 9 September 1863, Booth Papers, OHS; Owen Diary, 9 September 1863, AU; George Butler Turner to his mother, 9 September 1863, Turner Papers, OHS; Inskeep Diary, 9 September 1863, OHS; Price Diary, 9 September 1863, Civil War Miscellaneous Collection, USAHEC; Small Diary, 9 September 1863, IHS; Everett F. Abbott Letter Extracts, Chamberlain Papers, IHS; Keegan, *Diaries,* 25; Reed Diary, 9 September 1863, MHS; John Reed Beatty to "Dearest Laura," 9 September 1863, Beatty Papers, MHS; Bircher, *Drummer-Boy,* 73; Carpenter Diary, 9 September 1863, SRNB; Bennett, *Ninth Michigan,* 33; John Parkhurst to his sisters, 9 September 1863, Parkhurst Papers, UM-B.

20. *OR* 30(3):448; *OR* 30(1):326, 387, 393, 396, 1064; Sheffield Diary, 9 September 1863, CCNMP; Bloom Diary, 9 September 1863, CCNMP; Shotts Diary, 9 September 1863, SRNB; Haynie, *Nineteenth Illinois,* 215; Johnston Diary, 9 September 1863, Johnston Collection, CHS; Christian Diary, 9 September 1863, CCNMP; *SOR* 21:376; Sturges Diary, 9 September 1863, Sturges Papers, *Civil War Times Illustrated* Collection, USAHEC; Beatty, *Citizen Soldier,* 330; Harris Diary, 9 September 1863, CCNMP; Hapeman Diary, 9 September 1863, ALPL; Calkins, *One Hundred and Fourth Illinois,* 116; Shanks Diary, 9 September 1863, BGSU; Canfield, *21st Ohio,* 105; Dilworth Journal, 9 September 1863, HC; Adams, "Diary," 650; Weaver Diary, 9 September 1863, SRNB; John W. Baldwin to his wife, 5–12 September 1863, Baldwin Papers, OHS; *SOR* 65:673; Blackburn, *Letters,* 147–48; Nupp Diary, 9 September 1863, CCNMP; Millen Diary, 9 September 1863, SRNB; Gibson, *Seventy-Eighth Pennsylvania,* 84; Ward Diary, 9 September 1863, Ward Papers, DP; *SOR* 62:350; Evans, *Civil War Sites Assessment for Walker County,* 25–49.

21. Evans, *Civil War Sites Assessment for Walker County,* 29, 33, 37; *OR* 30(3):484–86; Sheffield Diary, 9 September 1863, CCNMP; Bloom Diary, 9 September 1863, CCNMP; Shotts Diary, 9 September 1863, SRNB; Haynie, *Nineteenth Illinois,* 215–16; Johnston Diary, 9 September 1863, Johnston Collection, CHS; Christian Diary, 9 September 1863, CCNMP; *SOR* 21:376.

22. *OR* 30(3):485–86; *OR* 30(1):270; Hinkley Diary, 9 September 1863, and Lucius D. Hinkley to his sister, 14 September 1863, both in Hinkley Papers, WHS; Frank M. Phelps to his friends, 9 September 1863, Phelps Letters, Lewis Leigh Collection, USAHEC; Webster Diary, 9 September 1863, Civil War Miscellaneous Collection, USAHEC; Robert J. Bates to his parents, 9 September 1863, Bates Letters, WHS; *Record, Ninety-Fourth Ohio,* 36; Edmonds Diary, 9 September 1863, USAHEC; Johnston, *Soldier Boy,* 57; Clark Diary, 9 September 1863, Clark Papers, USAHEC; Inskeep Diary, 9 September 1863, OHS; Price Diary, 9 September 1863, Civil War Miscellaneous Collection, USAHEC; Small Diary, 9 September 1863, IHS; Everett F. Abbott Letter Extracts, Chamberlain Papers, IHS; West, "Personal Recollections," 7; Martling Diary, 9 September 1863, Martling Manuscript Collection, ISL; Davidson Diary, 9 September 1863, NCWM; Keegan, *Diaries,* 25; Reed Diary, 9 September 1863, MHS; John Reed Beatty to "Dearest

Laura," 9 September 1863, Beatty Papers, MHS; Bircher, *Drummer-Boy*, 73; Gates Diary, 9 September 1863, IHS; Shera Diary, 9 September 1863, FHS; Miller Journal, 9 September 1863, IHS; Tourgee, "Diary," 118, 120; Parker Diary, 9 September 1863, HL; Hollingsworth Diary, 9 September 1863, IHS; Turchin, "Diary," 62–63; Williams, *Extracts*, 90–91; Ward Diary, 9 September 1863, Booth Papers, OHS; Josiah D. Cotton to his wife, 9 September 1863, Cotton Papers, LC.

23. Holmes, *Then and Now*, 5, 118–19, 124; Fahnestock Diary, 9 September 1863, ALPL; W. and J. F. Evans to their brother, 9 September 1863, Evans Letters, Civil War Miscellaneous Collection, USAHEC; Alexander M. Ayers to his wife, 10 September 1863, Ayers Papers, EU; Harmon, *Life and Letters*, 98; George Dillon to his wife, 9–10 September 1863, Dillon Letters, DPL; Armstrong Diary, 9 September 1863, CCNMP; Brown, Murphy, and Putney, *Behind the Guns*, 54; *SOR* 20:421; Boyd Diary, 9 September 1863, Boyd Family Papers, UCB; Partridge, *Ninety-Sixth Illinois*, 155–56; Royse Diary, 9 September 1863, Royse Manuscript Collection, ISL; Schwartz, *Diary*, 11; Robinson Diary, 9 September 1863, Robinson Papers, ALPL; Sowers Diary, 9 September 1863, CCNMP; Patton Diary, 9 September 1863, CCNMP; J. M. Branum, *National Tribune*, 20 December 1900; McAdams, *One Hundred and Thirteenth Ohio*, 39; Van Vleck, *Leader*, 166–67; Members, *Battery M, First Illinois*, 77; Winans Diary, 9 September 1863, CCNMP; Busbey Diary, 9 September 1863, SRNB; *OR* 30(1):744–45; Charles K. Bailer to his sister, 27 September 1863, Bailer Letters, Regimental Papers, WRHS; Albert G. Riley to "My Dearest Boy," 14 March 1864, Riley Letter, CCNMP; Lucius Brown to his sister, 10 September 1863, Brown Papers, EU; Barringer Diary, 9 September 1863, private collection; Augustus B. Carpenter to his parents, 16 September 1863, Carpenter Letters, YU; *OR* 30(3):499, 521; *OR* 52(1):443–44.

24. Calvin Goddard to his wife, 9 September 1863, Goddard to Commanding Officer, Bridgeport, 7:40 P.M., 9 September 1863, Bond to Innes, 9 September 1863, Drouillard to Purcell, 9 September 1863, and Rosecrans to Halleck, 9 September 1863, all in DC, Telegrams Sent, NARA; *OR* 30(3):479–80, 493–94; Henry Cist to his mother, 9 September 1863, Cist Family Papers, CIHS; McCullough Diary, 9 September 1863, ISL.

25. Richmond Diary, 9 September 1863, Polk Papers, US; *OR* 30(2):71, 522–23; Falconer to Polk, 5:30 A.M., 9 September 1863, Bragg Papers, WRHS; *OR* 30(4):626, 629.

26. Brent Diary, 9 September 1863, Bragg Papers, WRHS; Falconer to Mauldin, 7:00 A.M., 9 September 1863, Falconer to Polk, 7:30 A.M. 9 September 1863, Brent to Hill, 7:30 A.M., 9 September 1863, Brent to Wheeler, 8:00 A.M., 9 September 1863, Brent to Walker, 8:30 A.M., 9 September 1863, Brent to Buckner, 7:00 A.M., 9 September 1863, and Brent to Buckner, untimed (three messages), 9 September 1863, all in Bragg Papers, WRHS; Brent to Hill, 7:30 A.M., 9 September 1863, Hill Papers, LV; *OR* 30(4):629–30.

27. Davis Diary, 8–9 September 1863, TSLA; *OR* 30(3):495; Marriner, "Chickamauga," 8–9; Brent to Rucker, 7 September 1863, Brent to Buckner, 7 September 1863, Brent to Pegram, 7 September 1863, Brent to Polk, 9 September 1863, and Brent to Forrest, 3:00 P.M., 9 September 1863, all in Bragg Papers, WRHS; Milton Barnes, *National Tribune*, 15 April 1886; Long, "War Time," *Chattanooga (Tenn.) Star*, 23 November 1907, clipping in CPL; Richmond Diary, 9 September 1863, Polk Papers, US; *OR* 30(2):71.

28. Hill to Breckinridge, 9 September 1863, Hill Papers, NCDAH; *SOR* 35:282, 327, 404; Bush Diary, 9 September 1863, CCNMP; *SOR* 36:452; Pasco Diary, 9 September 1863, CCNMP; Ives, *Journal and Letters*, 42; Coleman Diary, 9 September 1863, UNC; Milner Diary, 9 September 1863, ADAH; Smith Diary, 9 September 1863, CCNMP; Armstrong Diary, 9 September 1863, ADAH; *SOR* 13:637, 641, 912; Heartsill, *Fourteen*

Hundred, 147; Adamson, *Thirtieth Georgia*, 33; Gentry Diary, 9 September 1863, CCNMP; *SOR* 14:370; Grammer Diary, 9 September 1863, CCNMP; Freeman Diary, 9 September 1863, TSLA; Daniel Diary, 9 September 1863, SRNB; Dillon Diary, 9 September 1863, TSLA; Bodenhamer Memoir, TSLA; Moore Diary, 9 September 1863, UDC Collection, vol. 6, GDAH; *SOR* 18:196; Owen, *Camp and Battle*, 269; Brown Diary, 9 September 1863, CCNMP; *SOR* 79:554; Holmes, *Diary*, 17; *SOR* 19:194; Dugger/White Diary, 9 September 1863, *Watauga (N.C.) Democrat*, 21 May 1891; Anonymous Diary [Fifty-Fourth Virginia Infantry regiment], 9 September 1863, MC.

29. Johnson Diary, 9 September 1863, Johnson Papers, NARA; *SOR* 78:787; *SOR* 79:39, 352, 420; Jackman Journal, 9 September 1863, LC; Watson Journal, 9 September 1863, CCNMP; Sparkman Diary, 9 September 1863, BPL; Estes Diary, 9 September 1863, MC.

30. *OR* 30(4):627; Dyer, *Diary*, 20; Brent to Wheeler, 11:30 P.M., 8 September 1863, and Brent to Wheeler, 8:00 A.M., 9 September 1863, both in Bragg Papers, WRHS; *SOR* 17:586; Corbitt Diary, 9 September 1863, EU; Davis Diary, 9 September 1863, TSLA; Eugene H. Smith to his mother, 19 October 1863, UDC Collection, GDAH; *SOR* 79:797; Bunting, *Civil War Letters*, 196; A. W. Hart CSR, NARA; *OR* 30(1):888–89; Foote, *Recollections*, 4–5; *OR* 30(2):523–24; Jordan and Pryor, *Campaigns of Forrest*, 305–6.

31. Foote, *Recollections*, 4–5; Richmond Diary, 9 September 1863, Polk Papers, US; *OR* 30(2):21–22, 71; General Orders, No. 178, 9 September 1863, Bragg Papers, WRHS, and Orders Received, First Kentucky Brigade, NARA; Brent to Polk, 9 September 1863, and Falconer to Polk, 9 September 1863, both in Bragg Papers, WRHS; *OR* 30(3):501; Brent Diary, 9 September 1863, Bragg Papers, WRHS; Fielder Diary, 9 September 1863, TSLA; Moorman, "Moorman Memorandum," 79–80; Oldham Diary, 9 September 1863, CCNMP; Rennolds Diary, 9 September 1863, CCNMP; Magee Diary, 9 September 1863, DU; Brown Notebook, 9 September 1863, CCNMP; Etter Diary, 9 September 1863, SRNB; Jones Diary, 9 September 1863, CCNMP; Joshua K. Callaway to his wife, 24 September 1863, Callaway Papers, UTX; Jack to Cheatham and Hindman, 9 September 1863, and Jack to Cheatham, 5:00 P.M., 9 September 1863, both in Letters Sent, Polk's Command, NARA; Jack to Mackall, 2:00 P.M., 9 September 1863, Dispatches, Polk's Corps, NARA; *SOR* 78:614; *SOR* 79:405, 407–8.

32. Sanders Diary, 9 September 1863, SRNB; Simpson Diary, 9 September 1863, TSLA; Farris, "Letters to Mary," 100; *SOR* 14:340–41, 685; Reynolds, *Worthy*, 103; Lawton to McLaws (two messages), 9 September 1863, Letters and Telegrams Sent, Quartermaster General's Office, NARA; *SOR* 76:695; Henry S. Figures to his mother, 26 September 1863, Figures Letter, private collection; Belue Diary, 9 September 1863, WU; Screven Diary, 9 September 1863, SCHS; Shields and Wyckoff, *Legacy*, 98; Moore, *Life*, 164; *SOR* 45:441; Hill Diary, 9 September 1863, Rietti Papers, MDAH; Mitchell Journal, 9 September 1863, CCNMP; Montgomery Diary, 9 September 1863, GDAH; Stillwell, *Letters*, 211; Sims to H. M. Drane, 9 September 1863, Sims to Campbell Wallace, 9 September 1863, and Sims to T. R. Sharp, 9 September 1863, all in Sims Letter Book, HL; Troutman to Capt. Eugene Carrington, Richmond, 9 September 1863, and Troutman to Maj. Mason Morfit, Petersburg, 9 September 1863, Confederate Citizens File, NARA.

33. Ballard Diary, 9 September 1863, CCNMP; Benjamin F. Abbott to Green Haygood, 26 September 1863, Confederate Miscellany, GDAH; Troutman to Maj. W. W. Peirce, Raleigh, undated, Troutman to Capt. C. W. Styron, Wilmington (two messages), 9 September 1863, Troutman to Hood, 9 September 1863, and Troutman to Peirce and Styron, 9 September 1863, all in Confederate Citizens File, NARA; Simpson, *Gaines' Mill*, 151–52; *SOR* 80:630; Joskins, "Sketch," HC; Campbell, *Lone Star Confederate*, 96;

Lowrey Diary, 9 September 1863, HC; Cooper to Benning, 18 September 1863, Shepherd to Cooper, 6 October 1863, Shepherd to Benning, 8 October 1863, Vance to Seddon, 15 October 1863, Seddon to Benning, 20 October 1863, Whitford to Vance, 31 October 1863, and Vance to Whitford, 10 November 1863, all in Benning Papers, UNC; Barrett, *Civil War in North Carolina*, 195–96; Houghton and Houghton, *Two Boys*, 137. For a detailed account of the "riot" at the *Standard* office, see the *Richmond Daily Dispatch* of 14 September 1863, which reprinted a lengthy article from the *Raleigh Daily Progress* of 11 September 1863.

34. Brent Diary, 9 September 1863, Bragg Papers, WRHS; Richmond Diary, 9 September 1863, Polk Papers, US; *OR* 30(2):72; *OR* 30(4):630. Martin's original dispatch to Bragg has not come to light. In an 1867 draft letter to Bragg, he described it as follows: "Thinking, as I then saw no effort to avail ourselves of the enemy's extraordinary dispersion of his army, that his object & position might be misapprehended I wrote directly to you a somewhat lengthy communication in regard to the isolated fragment of Thomas' Corps, then at Davis' Cross Roads in the Cove, between 9 and 11,000 strong, of all arms. This communication was dispatched to you at Lee & Gordon's Mills the day preceding the abortive movement." The 1867 draft letter can be found in the Will T. Martin Papers, UTX. Martin described the circumstances prompting the 1867 letter and published the draft in slightly modified form in 1883 in "A Defence of General Bragg's Conduct at Chickamauga," 201–6. It is possible that Major Johnson, identified by George Brent as the bearer of the critical information, carried Martin's message.

35. T. B. Mackall to Hindman, 10:00 P.M., 9 September 863, Hindman Papers, NARA; Falconer to Hindman, 11:45 P.M., 9 September 1863, Bragg Papers, WRHS; Brent Diary, 9 September 1863, Bragg Papers, WRHS; *OR* 30(2):298–99; Anderson Paper, NCDAH. William Polk's assertion that his father was the author of the plan can be found in Polk, "Chickamauga," 4; and in Polk, *Polk*, 2:237–38. In the latter account, Polk stated that his father was responding to a query from Bragg. In both accounts, Polk posits specific knowledge of Federal dispositions known in only the most general way by the Confederate high command through most of 9 September 1863. In contrast, Lt. William Richmond, a Polk aide and favorite, wrote in his diary that on that day information on Federal activity beyond Lookout Mountain was utterly lacking. Richmond Diary, 9 September 1863, Polk Papers, US. According to Richmond, Bragg and Polk shared lunch on 9 September. They certainly could have discussed offensive possibilities at that time in a general way, but the information upon which Bragg acted did not reach army headquarters until after nightfall. Unless Polk happened to be at Bragg's headquarters that night, a highly unlikely event given the relationship between the two men, there was little time for Polk to be consulted before Hindman was summoned at 10:00 P.M. to receive his orders. Had Polk been present at that time, it would have been superfluous for Major Falconer to write to Polk subsequently, "Orders have been given Maj. Genl. Hindman, detaching him from your corps. He is directed to move at once." Falconer to Polk, 9 September 1863, Bragg Papers, WRHS.

36. Falconer to Hindman, 11:45 P.M., 9 September 1863, copies in Bragg Papers, WRHS, Hill Papers, LV, Buckner Papers, HL, and *OR* 30(2):28, 298–99; Falconer to Hill, 11:45 P.M., 9 September 1863, copies in Bragg Papers, WRHS, Hill Papers, LV, Hill Papers, NCDAH, Buckner Papers, HL, and *OR* 30(2):28, 137–38; Anderson Paper, NCDAH; Falconer to Buckner, 9 September 1863, and Falconer to Polk, 9 September 1863, both in Bragg Papers, WRHS; *OR* 30(4):629; Field Return of T. C. Hindman's Division, 31 August 1863, NARA.

37. Foote, *Recollections*, 5.

» BIBLIOGRAPHY «

ARCHIVAL COLLECTIONS

Alabama

Alabama Department of Archives and History (Montgomery)

C. J. Armstrong Diary

Robert Lewis Bliss Letters

Newton N. Davis Letters

Bolling Hall Family Papers

William Riley Jones Civil War Letters

William C. Jordan Account of Chickamauga

Charles L. Lumsden Diary

Isaac W. McAdory Memorandum

Willis J. Milner Diary

Sydenham Moore Family Papers

Jeanette H. Parsons Letters

James R. Riggs Civil War Letters

James T. Searcy Letters

Thomas Warrick Papers

Sterling A. M. Wood Papers

Belser L. Wyman Letters

Auburn University

Thomas T. Bigbie Letters

Nathaniel P. Charlot Papers

Stouten Hubert Dent Collection

Hiram Talbert Holt Letters, Robert Partin Papers

Birmingham Public Library

John W. Sparkman Sr. Diary

California

Huntington Library (San Marino)

Simon B. Buckner Papers

James M. Forbes Collection

Nelson G. Huson Letters

Thomas J. Kendall Diary

William D. Kendall Papers
L. Newton Parker Diary
George Phillips Collection
John E. Pickering Diary
Frederick W. Sims Letter Book
University of California, Berkeley
Boyd Family Papers
University of California at Los Angeles
William S. Rosecrans Papers
Connecticut
Yale University
Augustus B. Carpenter Letters
District of Columbia
Library of Congress
Caleb H. Carlton Papers
Josiah Dexter Cotton Papers
John S. Jackman Journal
Horace Porter Papers
Samuel Chester Reid Family Papers
Philip Sheridan Papers
Louis T. Wigfall Papers
Samuel S. Yoder Papers
National Archives and Records Administration
Accounts of Secret Service Agents, Compiled 1861–1867 (RG 110)
Bushrod R. Johnson Papers (RG 109)
Compiled Service Records of Confederate General and Staff Officers, and Non-regimental Enlisted Men (RG 109)
Compiled Service Records of Confederate Soldiers Who Served in Military Organizations Raised Directly by the Confederate Government (RG 109)
Compiled Service Records of Confederate Soldiers Who Served in Organizations from the State of Alabama (RG 109)
Compiled Service Records of Confederate Soldiers Who Served in Organizations from the State of Arkansas (RG 109)
Compiled Service Records of Confederate Soldiers Who Served in Organizations from the State of Kentucky (RG 109)
Compiled Service Records of Confederate Soldiers Who Served in Organizations from the State of Tennessee (RG 109)
Compiled Service Records of Confederate Soldiers Who Served in Organizations from the State of Texas (RG 109)
Compiled Service Records of Volunteer Union Soldiers Who Served in Organizations from the State of Kentucky (RG 94)
Compiled Service Records for Union Army Volunteers (RG 94)
Confederate Citizens File (RG 109)
Department of the Cumberland, Letters Received, 1862–1865 (RG 393)
Department of the Cumberland, Letters Sent, November 1862–June 1865 (RG 393)
Department of the Cumberland, Telegrams Received (RG 393)

Department of the Cumberland, Telegrams Sent, October 1862–June 1865 (RG 393)
Dispatches, Orders, and Circulars, General Polk's Corps, Army of Tennessee, September 1863
Eighteenth United States Infantry, Unit Returns (RG 98)
Field Returns of Maj. Gen. T. C. Hindman's Division, 1862–1864 (RG 109)
General Thomas's Papers (RG 94)
XIV Corps Journal
William E. Crane Diary
Edward Ruger Correspondence
M. B. Walker, "A History of 1st Brigade. 3rd Div. 14th A.C. during the period in which Maj. Gen. Rosecrans Com'd Army of Cumberland"
Hardee's Corps, Special Orders, Circulars, and General Orders, 14 February 1863–14 March 1865 (RG 109)
Letters, 1st Kentucky Brigade, 1861–1863 (RG 109)
Letters Received by the Office of the Adjutant General, 1861–1870 (RG 94)
Letters Sent by General Polk's Command, 21 March 1862–7 October 1864 (RG 109)
Letters, Orders, and Circulars Sent and Received, Medical Director, Army of Tennessee, 1863–1865 (RG 109)
Letters Sent, Ordnance Office, Army of Tennessee (RG 109)
Letters and Telegrams Sent, Quartermaster General's Office, CSA (RG 109)
Letters and Telegrams Sent by Braxton Bragg, Army of Tennessee (RG 109)
Office of the Adjutant General, Union Battle Reports (RG 94)
Office of Quartermaster General, U.S. Military Railroads, Letters Sent, J. B. Anderson (RG 92)
Orders and Circulars, Army of Tennessee (RG 109)
Orders Received, Morning Reports and Returns, 1st Kentucky Brigade, January 1863–May 1864 (RG 109)
Papers of Lt. George Burroughs, Engineer on Rosecrans's Staff, 1863 (RG 393)
Returns from Regular Army Infantry Regiments, June 1825–December 1916 (RG 94)
Summaries of the News Reaching Headquarters of General W. S. Rosecrans (RG 393)
20th Army Corps, Letters Sent, October 1862–September 1863 (RG 393)
Thomas C. Hindman Papers (RG 109)
Union Provost Marshals' Files of Papers Relating to Individual Civilians (M345)

Florida

University of Florida (Gainesville)
James Patton Anderson Papers

Georgia

Atlanta Historical Society
James Dawson Letters
Chickamauga and Chattanooga National Military Park
William Kennett Armstrong Diary
George P. Ashmun Diary

John Jasper Ballard Diary
Henry Banta Diary
John J. Bloom Diary
Curtis A. Brasher Diary
Thaddeus Marion Brindley Letters
J. Thompson Brown Diary
William A. Brown Notebook
William Alexander Brown Diary
Edward Burns Diary
Squire Helm Bush Diary
DeWayne K. Calkins Letters
Henry Campbell Journal
William H. Christian Diary
David M. Claggett Diary
Solomon M. Deacon Letter
Joshua Dewees Diary
John Ely Diary
Josiah Feagles Diary
Joshua D. Foster Letters
James H. Fraser Diary
Martin Van Buren Gentry Diary
William Ross Glisan Diary
David George Godwin Letters
Joab Goodson Letter
George A. Grammer Diary
Alva Griest Diary
Luman G. Grist Letter
Albert Gsell Diary
G. W. Harris Diary
Frank M. Hayley Letter
James M. [L.] Hickerson Memoranda
John Calhoun Higdon Account
Christian Hinchberger Diary
James Harvey Houston Letters
Whit Isreal Letters
Itinerary, 2nd Cavalry Division
Robert A. Jarman Account
Russell J. Jones Diary
Ebenezer Lamb Diary
Leonard/Kleckner Letters
John Levering Account
Thomas M. Mitchell Journal
William S. Mitchell Letters
John Keith Moore Diary
Kingman Porter Moore Memoirs
John W. Nesbitt Letters
Franklin Nupp Diary

Van Buren Oldham Diary
Hannibal Paine Letters
Hulbert H. Palmer Journal
Samuel Pasco Diary
John W. Pate Diary
George M. Patton Diary
Chauncy H. Peck Letters
Oscar Pecoy Diary
Alfred M. Peterson Letter
Richard B. Pittman Letters
Axel H. Reed Diary
E. H. Rennolds Diary
Albert G. Riley Letter
Ezekiah B. Rorie Letter
Alex E. Spence Letter
Francis L. Wadsworth Letter
George Washington Sexton Diary
George S. Sheffield Diary
David L. Shideler Diary
Amandus Silsby Letters
Charles A. Smith Diary
John Henry Smith Diary
Edward Tyndall Sowers Diary
Thomas Stephenson Letter
Hiram Strong Letters
James Thomson Diary
Glenn Tucker Correspondence
Robert Watson Journal
Philip Welshimer Letters
Lyman S. Widney Letters
John Wilcox Letters
Maurice J. Williams Diary
Joel Winans Diary
Emory University (Atlanta)
Alexander Miller Ayers Papers
Lucius F. Brown Letters
W. B. Corbitt Diary
Honnoll Family Papers
Nimrod W. E. Long Papers
Isaac Roseberry Diary
Georgia Department of Archives and History
Civil War Miscellany
Julius L. Dowda Diary
James Longstreet Papers
William R. Montgomery Diary and Letters
United Daughters of the Confederacy Collection of Typescripts
Augustus P. Adamson Letter

- John A. James Letter
- Isaac V. Moore Diary
- Andrew Jackson Neal Letters
- Eugene H. Smith Letters

Georgia Historical Society (Savannah)
- Joseph Bryan Cumming Papers
- Claudius C. Wilson Papers

Kennesaw Mountain National Military Park
- John R. Morledge Diary
- Daniel O'Leary Letters
- W. G. Putney Diary
- Lyman S. Widney Diary

University of Georgia (Athens)
- Telamon Cuyler Collection

Illinois

Abraham Lincoln Presidential Library (Springfield)
- William Montgomery Austin Diary
- John Batchelor Diary
- David S. Blackburn Papers
- William H. Brown Diary
- Edward Colyer Diary
- George A. Cummins Papers
- George W. Dodd Papers
- Allen L. Fahnestock Diary
- James Fenton Diary [Reminiscence]
- Thomas J. Frazee Papers
- John Glenn Papers
- Douglas Hapeman Diary
- Edward Kitchell Diary
- A. W. Lester Diary
- Frederick Marion Letters
- Marsh Family Papers
- Lyman H. Needham Papers
- David Woodman Norton Letters
- John M. Palmer Papers II
- William E. Patterson Diary
- Edwin W. Payne Papers
- Gifford S. Robinson Papers
- Benjamin T. Smith Papers
- James P. Suiter Diary

Chicago Historical Society
- Day Elmore Letters
- Joseph Sturge Johnston Collection
- George Thomas Camp, G.A.R., Collection
- Henry T. Wulff Letter

Danville Public Library (Danville)
- George Dillon Letters

Knox College (Galesburg)
Phillip Sidney Post Papers
Newberry Library (Chicago)
Howe Barnard Family Papers
Edward W. Curtis Letters
John C. Fleming Letters
Northern Illinois University (DeKalb)
George Pepoon Letters
Merritt J. Simonds Papers
University of Illinois (Urbana-Champaign)
John Hoch Journal
Illinois Historical Survey
William E. Lodge Collection
Montraville Reeves Papers
James G. Watson Letters
Urbana Free Library (Urbana)
Oliver Perry Hunt Letters
Western Illinois University (Macomb)
Robert Everett Letter Excerpts
Christopher Wetsel Letters

Indiana

DePauw University (Greencastle)
William D. Ward Papers
Eli Lilly & Company Archives (Indianapolis)
Eli Lilly Papers
Indiana Historical Society (Indianapolis)
John M. Barnard Letters
Jacob W. Bartmess Letters
George W. Baum Diary
Bergun H. Brown Papers
Orville T. Chamberlain Papers
Jesse B. Connelly Diary
Jefferson C. Davis Papers
James G. Essington Papers
William Forder Letters
Arthur J. Gates Diary
Miriam Wilson Green Letters
Joseph C. Haddock Papers
James Henry Harris Diary
Thomas J. Harrison Letters
Jonathan E. Hollingsworth Diary
Daniel Wait Howe Diary
John C. Jessup Letters
Garrett Larew Diary
Uriah J. Loop Letters
Benjamin B. Mabrey Letters
John A. Mendenhall Diary

William Bluffton Miller Journal
Thomas Prickett Letters
Alanson R. Ryman Letters
Oliver Shelly Letters
Thomas M. Small Diary
Joseph Taylor Smith Letters
William R. Stookey Letters
John W. Switzer Letters
James S. Thomas Letters
Robert Tribbett Letters
William D. Ward Diary
Elias D. Work Letters
Indiana State Library (Indianapolis)
Chauncey Brooks Papers
Daniel E. Bruce Diary
Eli H. Clampitt Letters
Hiram Hines Manuscript Collection
William D. Hynes Letters
George H. Martling Manuscript Collection
Jacob S. McCullough Diary
John S. McGraw Letters
M. D. Meisner Collection (Unidentified Diary, 72nd Indiana Infantry)
William H. Records Manuscript Collection
I. H. C. Royse Manuscript Collection
Samuel Shepardson Letters
John T. Wilder Papers
Aurelius M. Willoughby Manuscript Collection
Indiana University (Bloomington)
Henry F. Dillman Diary
Leroy S. Mayfield Diary
Neeley Manuscripts (James Prosser Letters)
Ambrose Remley Letters
University of Notre Dame (South Bend)
Albert J. Baldwin Letters
David Power Conyngham Manuscript, "Soldiers of the Cross"
Johnston/Rhoads Family Correspondence
William T. Presley Letters
Vigo County Public Library (Terre Haute)
John H. Rippetoe Letters
Wabash College (Crawfordsville)
Henry Campbell Journal

Iowa

Iowa State Historical Society
John C. McLain Diary

Kansas

Kansas State Historical Society (Topeka)
Anderson Family Papers

Aaron N. Beck Diary
John A. Martin Letters
Franklin Darwin Moon Diary
John Andrews Read Diary

Kentucky

Filson Historical Society
Samuel H. Brodnax Memoirs
James J. Johnston Diary
J. Stoddard Johnston Military Papers
Alfred Pirtle Letters
James Shera Diary
John H. Tilford Diary
Elijah S. Watts Papers

Kentucky Historical Society
Jesse Hyde Diary

University of Kentucky
Winchester Byron Rudy Diary

Louisiana

Louisiana State University
E. John Ellis Diary
Charles E. Leverich Diary
John McGrath Papers

Tulane University (New Orleans)
George Brent Papers

Maryland

Maryland Historical Society
Osmun Latrobe Diary

National Library of Medicine (Bethesda)
Thomas Winston Papers

Michigan

Bentley Historical Library, University of Michigan (Ann Arbor)
Harold J. Bartlett Letters
William J. Carroll Papers
George W. Chase Letters
D. L. Haines Ms., "Record of Fourth Michigan Cavalry."
Henry Mortimer Hempstead Diary
Alonzo Merrill Keeler Papers
John C. Love Letters
John G. Parkhurst Papers
Henry Albert Potter Papers
Sligh Family Papers
Ezra Stearns Diary

William L. Clements Library, University of Michigan (Ann Arbor)
Henry H. Seys Letters
William A. and Julius S. Smith Papers

Western Michigan University (Kalamazoo)
Don DeYoung Collection

Minnesota
Minnesota Historical Society (St. Paul)
John Reed Beatty Papers
Judson W. Bishop Papers
Robert Burns Letters
Jeremiah C. Donahower Papers
Axel Reed Diary
Billings D. Sibley Papers
Moody Cook Tolman Papers
Horatio Van Cleve Papers
Norwegian-American Historical Association (Northfield)
Stephen O. Himoe Diary
Mississippi
Mississippi Department of Archives and History (Jackson)
T. Otis Baker Papers
Joseph Miller Rand Diary
John C. Rietti Papers
Oscar J. E. Stuart and Family Papers
Missouri
Missouri History Museum (St. Louis)
Braxton Bragg Papers
James E. Love Papers
Eleanor Waddle McCoy Papers
William E. Patterson Diary
Dexter P. Tiffany Collection
Nebraska
Nebraska State Historical Society (Lincoln)
John Holden McBride Correspondence
New York
New York Public Library
Ezra Carman Papers
North Carolina
Duke University (Durham)
William L. Broaddus Papers
Ellison Capers Papers
John Euclid Magee Diary
James Nourse Diary
John Snow Papers
Charles H. Sowle Papers
William H. T. Walker Papers
North Carolina Department of Archives and History (Raleigh)
James Patton Anderson Paper
D. H. Hill Papers
University of North Carolina (Chapel Hill)
James Patton Anderson Papers
Taylor Beatty Diary
Henry L. Benning Papers

J. F. H. Claiborne Papers
Daniel Coleman Diary
Espey Family Papers
John F. Leonard Papers
W. W. Mackall Papers
George Knox Miller Letters
Leroy Moncure Nutt Papers (Gustave Huwald Account)
Leonidas Polk Papers (Microfilm Edition)
John Henry Steinmeyer Memoir
Isaac Barton Ulmer Papers
Paul Turner Vaughan Papers
Henry Duplessis Wells Papers
Marcus J. Wright Papers

Ohio

University of Akron (Akron)
Charles M. Knight Family Papers (William Henry Greenwood Diary and Letters)
Bowling Green State University (Bowling Green)
John E. Cummins Letters (McCray Research Archive)
George Kryder Papers
Linus Anthony Patrick Correspondence
William Shanks Diary
William Stahl Diary
John Welk Diary
Loyal Wort Letters
21st Ohio Infantry Regiment Collection
Cincinnati Historical Society (Cincinnati)
Cist Family Papers
William E. Crane Diary
Frank Johnston Jones Papers
Alfred Pirtle Manuscript ("Leaves from My Journal")
Marietta College (Marietta)
William Rufus Putnam Collection
Miami University (Oxford)
Gilbert-Richards Papers
Ohio Historical Society (Columbus)
Sidney C. Baker Correspondence (George W. Botkin Diary and Letters)
John William Baldwin Papers
Alpheus S. Bloomfield Letters
Dr. John Booth Papers (A. T. Ward Diary)
Clark-Williams Family Letters
Robert Newell Elder Letters
A. L. Gierhart Papers
John A. Gillis Diary
Thomas C. Honnell Letters
John D. Inskeep Diary
William H. Kemper Diary

- Jabiel D. Lyon Diary
- John Wesley Marshall Diary
- James P. Mitchell Papers
- Emerson Opdycke Papers
- William M. Parkinson Papers
- Styles W. Porter Diary
- Nelson Purdum Papers
- John P. Sanderson Journal
- Isaac N. Schnorf Letter
- Frank Shearer Papers
- George Butler Turner Papers
- Oscar N. Wheeler Diary

Rutherford B. Hayes Presidential Library (Fremont)
- Charles Barney Dennis Memoir
- Silas S. Mallory Diary
- Andrew C. Parker Letters
- Isaac P. Rule Letters

Smith Library of Regional History (Oxford)
- Ferdinand Van Derveer Letters

Western Reserve Historical Society (Cleveland)
- Braxton Bragg Papers
- Albert G. Hart Papers
- George W. Hodges Papers
- William P. Palmer Collection
  - William B. Hazen Letter
- Regimental Papers
  - Charles K. Bailer Letters
  - William A. Robinson Diary
  - Elbert J. Squire Letters
  - C. Irvine Walker Letters
- Aquila Wiley Papers

Wright State University (Fairborn)
- Patterson Family Papers
- Oliver H. Protsman Diary

Pennsylvania

Historical Society of Pennsylvania (Philadelphia)
- Thomas S. McCahan Diary

National Civil War Museum (Harrisburg)
- Robert B. Davidson Diary

U.S. Army Heritage and Education Center (Carlisle)
- William H. Ball Letters
- Luther P. Bradley Papers
- Timothy Brookes Collection
  - Duncan Thompson Letters
- Civil War Miscellaneous Collection
  - George H. Alverson Letters
  - William D. Cole Letters

Rufus W. Daniel Diary
George Desforges Letters
Strader W. and Jesse Evans Letters
Thomas Green Letter
John H. Hoffman Letters
James A. Price Diary
Lewis Tripp Letters
Jackson E. Webster Diary
Civil War Times Illustrated Collection
Quintus S. Adams Letters
William H. Brown Diary
Abram M. Glazener Letters
John L. Rolison Diary
John Russell Letters
Eben P. Sturges Papers
Levi Wagner Reminiscences
Charles Weller Letters and Journals
William T. Clark Papers
James E. Edmonds Diary
Earl Hess Collection
George Sowers Letter
Claiborne J. Walton Letter
Harrisburg Civil War Roundtable Collection
John Meredith Diary
George Shuman Letters
Eli M. Tarbell Diary
John S. Walker Diary
George S. Lea Family Papers
Lewis Leigh Collection
William McAdams Letters
Frank M. Phelps Letters
Claiborne J. Walton Letter
Mungo P. Murray Letters
Michael Musick Collection
Hezekiah Rabb Letters
Wiley Sword Collection
Edgar N. Wilcox Diary

South Carolina

The Citadel
Ellison Capers Papers
South Carolina Historical Society (Charleston)
Reginald H. Screven Diary
Winthrop University (Rock Hill)
Thomas Belue Diary

Tennessee

Chattanooga Public Library (Chattanooga)

Clipping, Zella Armstrong, "Mrs. Davenport Remembers Campaign," *Chattanooga Times*, 12 July 1937.
Clipping, S. M. Cherry, "Church Leader Jots Notes on Battles Here," *Chattanooga Free Press*, 21 September 1938.
Clipping, S. J. A. Frazier, "Reminiscences of Chickamauga," *Chattanooga Lookout*, 20 May 1909.
Clipping, S. J. A. Frazier, "Reminiscences of a Soldier Who Fought at Chickamauga," *Chattanooga Times*, 23 October 1921.
Clipping, Marcus B. Long, "Chattanooga in War Time," *Chattanooga Star*, 23 November 1907.
Clipping, Thomas H. McCallie, "Bragg Headquarters Moved into City after Retreat," *Chattanooga Free Press*, 21 September 1938.
Clipping, Queenie Lee Rowles, "Some Stories of War Times," *Chattanooga Times*, 23 December 1909.
Clipping, Thomas L. Steward, "Bodies Found on Battlefield 90 Days after Chickamauga, Discloses Diary of Federal," *Chattanooga Free Press*, 21 September 1938.
Clipping, Robert Sparks Walker, "A Union Soldier's Diary [L. W. Mann]," *Chattanooga Times*, 25 April 1937.
"Part of the War Experience of a Little Girl (Louisa Emma Corbin) Told in Later Life to Her Daughter."

Stones River National Battlefield (Murfreesboro)
Charles Benedict Diary
William H. Busbey Diary
Jonah H. Carpenter Diary
James A. Colehour Account
Rufus W. Daniel Diary
Augustus F. Davis Letters
Isaiah Decker Letters
Risenar Etter Diary
John M. Ferree Diary
Reuben D. Jones Diary
Robert Kennedy, "Army Life and Experiences of Robert Kennedy, 1861–1865"
Jesse Leeper Diary
Samuel F. Mason Diary
William A. Millen Diary
Otis Moody Diary
Hiram Russell Letters
L. Jackson Sanders Diary
David Christopher Shotts Diary
Elbert J. Squire Letters
David Henry Talbot Diary
Lester Dewitt Taylor Diary
Perry Weaver Diary

Tennessee State Library and Archives (Nashville)
William Gibbs Allen Memoirs
David Shires Myers Bodenhamer Memoir

Bostick Family Collection
Crutchfield Family Papers
Thomas W. Davis Diary
George Washington Dillon Diary
Alfred T. Fielder Diary
John H. Freeman Diary
D. G. Godwin Letters
William Henry Harder Reminiscences
John W. Harris Letters
Milton P. Jarnagin Reminiscences
Isaac Madden [Miller] Letter
Joseph Branch O'Bryan Letters
Elijah M. Patton Diary
Samuel Robert Simpson Diary
William E. Sloan Diary
University of the South (Sewanee)
Leonidas Polk Papers
University of Tennessee, Chattanooga
John T. Wilder Papers
University of Tennessee, Knoxville
Julius E. Thomas Collection
Andrew G. Wickham Letter

Texas

Baylor University (Waco)
Nathaniel Alexander Morgan Letters
Hill College (Hillsboro)
Robert Sample Dilworth Journal
Joe Joskins, "A Sketch of Hood's Texas Brigade of the Virginia Army"
Robert James Lowrey Diary
William G. Young Letters
Navarro College (Corsicana)
Audley Anderson Letter
Wallace W. Darrah Papers
Willis Jones Papers
Thomas J. Kessler Letters
Robert James Lowrey Diary
Dempsey C. Neal Diary
Simon [Simeon] C. Wilkerson Letter
Albert Woodcock Papers
Texas Christian University
Love Family Letters
University of Texas (Austin)
Joshua K. Callaway Papers
Confederate States of America Records
Joseph W. Ward Letters
John Crittenden Letters
George A. Gordon Letters

John W. Hill Papers
Will T. Martin Papers

Virginia

Library of Virginia
D. H. Hill Papers
Museum of the Confederacy
Anonymous Diary, 54th Virginia Infantry
William Kenedy Estes Diary
Order and Letter Book, Hardee's Corps
Scout Book, Army of Tennessee
Samuel H. Stout Papers
Valentine Museum (Richmond)
Railroad Bureau Telegrams
Virginia Historical Society (Richmond)
James Madison Brannock Papers
Miller Family Papers
James Miller Wysor Letters
Virginia Military Institute (Lexington)
John R. Hurley Letters
Septimus Knight Account
Virginia Polytechnic Institute and State University (Blacksburg)
Thomas M. Burns Letters

West Virginia

West Virginia University Library (Morgantown)
Allen D. Frankenberry Diary

Wisconsin

Carroll University (Waukesha)
Clinton Family Papers
Wisconsin State Historical Society
Kelsey M. Adams Letters
Farlin Quigley Ball Letters (William H. Ball)
Robert J. Bates Letters
Eugene E. Comstock Papers
George A. Cooley Diary
Gasherie Decker Diary and Letters
Henry Drake Letters
Alfred Galpin Family Papers
Lucius Dwight Hinkley Papers
Franklin B. Howard Letters
Newton Jones Papers
Abraham V. Knapp Diary
Hugh A. McLaurin Letters
Rollin Olson Letters
Horace T. Persons Letters and Diary
Henry Clay Taylor Papers
Wisconsin Veterans Museum (Madison)
James M. Chatfield Letters

PRIVATE COLLECTIONS

Michael James Barringer Diary

Joseph Bruff Family Letters

L. Otis Colburn/Allen W. Gray Composite Diary

Kirkland N. Cowing Letter

Franklin F. Dean Diary

Henry S. Figures Letter

Charles Harker Letter

Jonathan B. Holmes Letters

E. T. Hooker Letter

Jason Hurd Diary

David F. Lawler Letter

J. A. Reep Manuscript ("Guttmachrala, or Four Years at the Front as a Private")

"Regimental Strengths at Chickamauga"

John Franklin Roberts Diary

Edward Leroy Tabler Diary

"Tri-monthly Return of Cavalry Corps of the Army of Tennessee, Trenton, Ga., 10 July 1863"

NEWSPAPERS

Atlanta Daily Intelligencer
Augusta (Ga.) Daily Constitutionalist
Augusta (Ga.) Chronicle
Charleston (S.C.) Mercury
Chattanooga (Tenn.) Daily Rebel
Chattanooga (Tenn.) Free Press
Chattanooga (Tenn.) Lookout
Chattanooga (Tenn.) Star
Chattanooga (Tenn.) Times
Cincinnati Daily Commercial
Cincinnati Enquirer
Dayton (Ohio) Weekly Journal
Indianapolis Journal
Macon (Ga.) Telegraph
Memphis Daily Appeal
Natchez (Miss.) Weekly Courier
National Tribune (Washington, D.C.)
New York Herald
New York Times
New York Tribune
Richmond Daily Dispatch
Richmond Examiner
Richmond Whig
Washington (D.C.) Evening Times
Watauga (N.C.) Democrat
Wisconsin State Journal (Madison)

PUBLISHED SOURCES

Abdill, George B. *Civil War Railroads*. Seattle: Superior, 1961.

Adams, Jacob. "Diary of Jacob Adams, Private Company F, 21st O.V.V.I." *Ohio Archaeological and Historical Quarterly* 38 (October 1929): 627–721.

Adamson, Augustus Pitt. *Brief History of the Thirtieth Georgia Regiment*. Griffin, Ga.: Mills, 1912.

Albertson, Joan W., comp. *Letters Home to Minnesota: 2nd Minnesota Volunteers*. Spokane, Wash.: P. D. Enterprises, 1992.

Allardice, Bruce S. *Confederate Colonels: A Biographical Register*. Columbia: University of Missouri Press, 2008.

———. *More Generals in Gray*. Baton Rouge: Louisiana State University Press, 1995.

Allen, W. G. "The Burning of Loudon Bridge." *Confederate Veteran* 24 (January 1918): 44.

———. *Reminiscences of William G. Allen*. Dayton, Tenn.: Rhea County Historical and Genealogical Society, 2000.

Alotta, Robert I. *Civil War Justice: Union Army Executions under Lincoln*. Shippensburg, Penn.: White Mane, 1989.

Andrew, A. Piatt, III. *Some Civil War Letters*. Gloucester, Mass.: Privately printed, 1925.

Andrews, J. Cutler. *The South Reports the Civil War*. Princeton, N.J.: Princeton University Press, 1970.

Arbuckle, J. W. *Cowan Pusher District and Tunnel*. Winchester, Tenn.: Herald-Chronicle, n.d.

Arbuckle, J. W., and Alan C. Shook. *The Mountain Goat*. Johnson City, Tenn.: Overmountain, 1992.

Armstrong, Zella. *The History of Hamilton County and Chattanooga, Tennessee*. 2 vols. 1940. Reprint, Johnson City, Tenn.: Overmountain, 1993.

Association of Survivors, Regular Brigade, Fourteenth Corps, Army of the Cumberland. *Proceedings of Reunions Held at Pittsburgh, Pa., Sept. 11–12, 1894, Crawfish Springs, Ga., Sept. 18–19, 1895, St. Paul, Minn., Sept. 1–2, 1896, Columbus, Ohio, Sept. 22–23, 1897*. Columbus, Ohio: John L. Trauger, 1898.

Aten, Henry J. *History of the Eighty-Fifth Regiment, Illinois Volunteer Infantry*. Hiawatha, Kans.: n.p., 1901.

Atkins, Smith D. *Chickamauga: Useless Disastrous Battle*. Mendota, Ill.: 1907.

Baird, John A., Jr. *Profile of a Hero: The Story of Absalom Baird, His Family, and the American Military Tradition*. Philadelphia: Dorrance, 1977.

Baldwin, Charles Candee. *Baldwin Genealogy, from 1500 to 1881*. Cleveland: Leader, 1881.

Baldwin, James J., III. *The Struck Eagle: A Biography of Brigadier General Micah Jenkins, and a History of the Fifth South Carolina Volunteers and the Palmetto Sharpshooters*. Shippensburg, Penn.: Burd Street, 1996.

Barnes, James A., James R. Carnahan, and Thomas H. B. McCain. *The Eighty-Sixth Regiment Indiana Volunteer Infantry: A Narrative of Its Services in the Civil War of 1861–1865*. Crawfordsville, Ind.: Journal Company, 1895.

Barrett, John G. *The Civil War in North Carolina*. Chapel Hill: University of North Carolina Press, 1963.

Batchelor, B. Frank, and George Q. Turner. *Batchelor-Turner Letters, 1861–1864*. Annotated by H. J. H. Rugeley. Austin, Tex.: Steck, 1961.

Baumgartner, Richard A. *Blue Lightning: Wilder's Mounted Infantry Brigade in the Battle of Chickamauga*. Huntington, W.Va.: Blue Acorn, 2007.

———, ed. *Yankee Tigers II: Civil War Field Correspondence from the Tiger Regiment of Ohio*. Huntington, W.Va.: Blue Acorn, 2004.

Beach, John N. *History of the Fortieth Ohio Volunteer Infantry*. London, Ohio: Shepherd & Craig, 1884.

Beatty, John. *The Citizen Soldier; or, Memoirs of a Volunteer*. Cincinnati: Wilstach, Baldwin, 1879.

Beers, Fannie A. *Memories: A Record of Personal Experience and Adventure during Four Years of War*. Philadelphia: J. B. Lippincott, 1889.

Belcher, Dennis W. *General David S. Stanley, USA: A Civil War Biography*. Jefferson, N.C.: McFarland, 2014.

Belknap, Charles E. *History of the Michigan Organizations at Chickamauga, Chattanooga, and Missionary Ridge, 1863*. Lansing, Mich.: Robert Smith, 1899.

Benefiel, William H. H. *Souvenir, the Seventeenth Indiana Regiment: A History from Its Organization to the End of the War*. Elwood, Ind.: Model, 1913.

Bennett, Charles W. *Historical Sketches of the Ninth Michigan Infantry*. Coldwater, Mich.: Daily Courier, 1913.

Bennett, L. G., and Wm. M. Haigh. *History of the Thirty-Sixth Regiment Illinois Volunteers, during the War of the Rebellion*. Aurora, Ill.: Knickerbocker & Hodder, 1876.

Bergeron, Arthur W., Jr. *Confederate Mobile*. Jackson: University of Mississippi Press, 1991.

———. *Guide to Louisiana Confederate Military Units, 1861–1865*. Baton Rouge: Louisiana State University Press, 1989.

Bevens, W. E. *Reminiscences of a Private: William E. Bevens of the First Arkansas Infantry, C.S.A.* Edited by Daniel E. Sutherland. Fayetteville: University of Arkansas Press, 1992.

Bianculli, Anthony J. *Trains and Technology: The American Railroad in the Nineteenth Century*. Vol. 1, *Locomotives*. Newark: University of Delaware Press, 2001.

Bickham, William D. *Rosecrans' Campaign with the Fourteenth Army Corps, or the Army of the Cumberland*. Cincinnati: Moore, Wilstach, Keys, 1863.

Bircher, William. *A Drummer-Boy's Diary, Comprising Four Years of Service with the Second Regiment Minnesota Veteran Volunteers, 1861 to 1865*. St. Paul, Minn.: St. Paul Book and Stationery, 1889.

Bishop, Judson W. *The Story of a Regiment: Being a Narrative of the Service of the Second Regiment Minnesota Veteran Volunteer Infantry, in the Civil War of 1861–1865*. St. Paul, Minn.: n.p., 1890.

Bishop, Lyle D., III. "The 58th Regiment of North Carolina Infantry: A History of Its Travels." *Watauga County (N.C.) Times . . . Past* 22/23 (June/September 1987): 2–28.

Black, Hugh. *Letters of Captain Hugh Black to His Family in Florida during the War between the States, 1862–1864*. Compiled by Elizabeth Coldwell Frano. Evansville, Ind.: Evansville Bindery, 1998.

Black, Robert C., III. *The Railroads of the Confederacy*. Chapel Hill: University of North Carolina Press, 1952.

Blackburn, J. K. P., L. B. Giles, and E. S. Dodd. *Terry Texas Ranger Trilogy*. Edited by Thomas W. Cutrer. Austin, Tex.: State House, 1996.

Blackburn, Theodore W. *Letters from the Front: A Union "Preacher" Regiment (74th Ohio) in the Civil War*. Dayton, Ohio: Morningside Bookshop, 1981.

Blanton, DeAnne, and Lauren M. Cook. *They Fought Like Demons: Women Soldiers in the American Civil War*. Baton Rouge: Louisiana State University Press, 2002.

Boatner, Mark M., III. *The Civil War Dictionary*. New York: McKay, 1959.

Bobrick, Benson. *Master of War: The Life of General George H. Thomas*. New York: Simon & Schuster, 2009.

Boon, John A. *The Civil War Letters of John A. Boon*. Lincoln, Neb.: Richard C. Ludden, 1994.

Boyd, Kenneth W. *The Historical Markers of North Georgia*. Atlanta: Cherokee, 1993.

Boynton, H. V. *Chattanooga and Chickamauga: Reprint of Gen. H. V. Boynton's Letters to the* Cincinnati Commercial Gazette, *August 1888*. Washington, D.C.: Gray & Clarkson, 1888.

———. "The Chickamauga Campaign." In *Campaigns in Kentucky and Tennessee Including the Battle of Chickamauga*, 321–72. Vol. 7 of *Papers of the Military Historical Society of Massachusetts*. 1908. Reprint, Wilmington, N.C.: Broadfoot, 1989.

Bradley, Michael R. *Tullahoma: The 1863 Campaign for the Control of Middle Tennessee*. Shippensburg, Penn.: Burd Street, 200.

Bragg, Braxton. "'We Sowed & We Have Reaped': A Postwar Letter from Braxton Bragg." Edited by Aaron M. Boom. *Journal of Southern History* 31 (February 1965): 75–79.

Bragg, C. L. *Distinction in Every Service: Brigadier General Marcellus A. Stovall, C.S.A.* Shippensburg, Penn.: White Mane, 2002.

Bragg, William Harris. *Joe Brown's Army: The Georgia State Line, 1862–1865*. Macon, Ga.: Mercer University Press, 1987.

Brennan, J. Fletcher, ed. *Biographical Cyclopaedia and Portrait Gallery of Distinguished Men, with an Historical Sketch, of the State of Ohio*. Vol. 1. Cincinnati: J. C. Yorston, 1880.

Brewer, Willis. *Alabama: Her History, Resources, War Record, and Public Men, from 1540 to 1872*. Montgomery, Ala.: Barrett & Brown, 1872.

Briant, C. C. *History of the Sixth Regiment Indiana Volunteer Infantry*. Indianapolis: Wm. B. Burford, 1891.

Bridges, Hal. *Lee's Maverick General: Daniel Harvey Hill*. New York: McGraw-Hill, 1961.

Brown, J. Willard. *The Signal Corps USA in the War of the Rebellion*. 1896. Reprint, New York: Arno, 1974.

Brown, Russell K. *To the Manner Born: The Life of General William H. T. Walker*. Athens: University of Georgia Press, 1994.

———. "Unlucky in Command, Unwise in Loyalty: General John K. Jackson." *Journal of America's Past* 36 (Winter 2011): 5–18.

Brown, Thaddeus C. S., Samuel J. Murphy, and William G. Putney. *Behind the Guns: The History of Battery I, 2nd Regiment, Illinois Light Artillery*. Edited by Clyde C. Walton. Carbondale: Southern Illinois University Press, 1965.

Brown, William H. "Soldier of the 92nd Illinois: Letters of William H. Brown and His Fiancee, Emma Jane Frazey." Edited by Vivian C. Hopkins. *Bulletin of the New York Public Library* 73 (February 1969): 114–36.

Brunsted, George H. "Letters from a Canadian Recruit in the Union Army." Edited by Doris Fleming. *Tennessee Historical Quarterly* 16 (1957): 159–66.

Buck, Irving A. *Cleburne and His Command*. 1908. Reprint, Dayton, Ohio: Morningside, 1982.

Bunch, Jack A. *Military Justice in the Confederate States Armies*. Shippensburg, Penn.: White Mane, 2000.

Bunting, Robert Franklin. *Our Trust Is in the God of Battles: The Civil War Letters of Robert Franklin Bunting, Chaplain, Terry's Texas Rangers, C.S.A.* Edited by Thomas W. Cutrer. Knoxville: University of Tennessee Press, 2006.

Butler, Jay Caldwell. *Letters Home*. Binghamton, N.Y.: Privately printed, 1930.

Calkins, William Wirt. *The History of the One Hundred and Fourth Regiment of Illinois Volunteer Infantry, War of the Great Rebellion, 1862–1865*. Chicago: Donohue & Henneberry, 1895.

Callaway, Joshua K. *The Civil War Letters of Joshua K. Callaway*. Edited by Judith Lee Hallock. Athens: University of Georgia Press, 1997.

Campbell, Robert. *Lone Star Confederate: A Gallant and Good Soldier of the 5th Texas Infantry*. Edited by George Skoch and Mark W. Perkins. College Station: Texas A&M University Press, 2003.

Canfield, Silas S. *History of the 21st Regiment Ohio Volunteer Infantry, in the War of the Rebellion*. Toledo, Ohio: Vrooman, Anderson & Bateman, 1893.

Carlin, William Passmore. *The Memoirs of Brigadier General William Passmore Carlin, U.S.A.* Edited by Robert I. Girardi and Nathaniel Cheairs Hughes Jr. Lincoln: University of Nebraska Press, 1999.

Carter, W. R. *History of the First Regiment of Tennessee Volunteer Cavalry in the Great War of the Rebellion*. Knoxville, Tenn.: Gaut-Ogden, 1902.

Chapin, James W. "With the Army of the Cumberland in the Chickamauga Campaign: The Diary of James W. Chapin, Thirty-Ninth Indiana Volunteers." Edited by Donald E. Reynolds and Max H. Kele. *Georgia Historical Quarterly* 59, no. 2: 223–42.

Chase, J. A. *History of the Fourteenth Ohio Regiment, O.V.V.I.* Toledo, Ohio: St. John, 1881.

Chattanooga Area Civil War Sites Assessment. Chattanooga, Tenn.: 1998.

Cisco, Walter Brian. *States Rights Gist: A South Carolina General of the Civil War*. Shippensburg, Penn.: White Mane, 1991.

Clark, Charles T. *Opdycke Tigers, 125th O.V.I.: A History of the Regiment and of the Campaigns and Battles of the Army of the Cumberland*. Columbus, Ohio: Spahr & Glenn, 1895.

Clay, A. [H.] B. "On the Right at Chickamauga." *Confederate Veteran* 19 (July 1911): 329–30.

Clifton, Rob. *Chattanooga Then and Now*. Chattanooga, Tenn.: Privately printed, 2006.

Coggins, Jack. *Arms and Equipment of the Civil War*. Garden City, N.Y.: Doubleday, 1962.

Collins, R. M. *Chapters from the Unwritten History of the War between the States*. Dayton, Ohio: Morningside, 1982.

Colton, Matthias Baldwin. *The Civil War Journal and Correspondence of Matthias Baldwin Colton*. Edited by Jessie Sellers Colton. Philadelphia: MacRae-Smith, 1931.

Commemorative Biographical Record of Prominent and Representative Men of Indianapolis and Vicinity. Chicago: J. H. Beers, 1908.

Cone, Stephen D. *A Concise History of Hamilton, Ohio*. 2 vols. Middletown, Ohio: George Mitchell, 1901.

Connelly, Thomas Lawrence. *Army of the Heartland: The Army of Tennessee, 1861–1862*. Baton Rouge: Louisiana State University Press, 1967.

———. *Autumn of Glory: The Army of Tennessee, 1862–1865*. Baton Rouge: Louisiana State University Press, 1971.

Connelly, Thomas Lawrence, and Archer Jones. *The Politics of Command: Factions and Ideas in Confederate Strategy*. Baton Rouge: Louisiana State University Press, 1973.

Conner, Robert C. *General Gordon Granger: The Savior of Chickamauga and the Man behind "Juneteenth."* Havertown, Penn.: Casemate, 2013.

Connolly, James A. *Three Years in the Army of the Cumberland: The Letters and Diary of Major James A. Connolly*. Edited by Paul M. Angle. Bloomington: Indiana University Press, 1959.

Cooney, Peter Paul. "The War Letters of Father Peter Paul Cooney of the Congregation of Holy Cross." *Records of the American Catholic Historical Society* 44 (1933): 151–69.

Cooper, Norman Lee. *A Confederate Soldier and His Descendants*. Bowie, Md.: Norm Cooper, 1982.

Cope, Alexis. *The Fifteenth Ohio Volunteers and Its Campaigns*. Columbus, Ohio: Cope, 1916.

Cornish, Dudley Taylor. *The Sable Arm: Negro Troops in the Union Army, 1861–1865*. 1956. Reprint, New York: Norton, 1966.

Cort, Charles Edwin. *"Dear Friends": The Civil War Letters and Diary of Charles Edwin Cort*. Edited by Helyn W. Tomlinson. Minneapolis: n. p., 1962.

Cowles, Calvin D., comp. *Atlas to Accompany the Official Records of the Union and Confederate Armies*. Washington, D.C.: Government Printing Office, 1891–95.

Cox, Charles Harding. "'Gone for a Soldier': The Civil War Letters of Charles Harding Cox, 1862–1863." Edited by Lorna Lutes Sylvester. *Indiana Magazine of History* 68, no. 1 (March 1972): 24–78.

Cox, Jacob D. "The Chickamauga Crisis." *Century Illustrated Monthly* 27 (1900): 326–39.

Cozzens, Peter. *The Darkest Days of the War: The Battles of Iuka & Corinth.* Chapel Hill: University of North Carolina Press, 1997.

———. "Forgotten Hero: Philip Sidney Post." *Illinois Historical Journal* 84 (Summer 1991): 75–100.

———. *No Better Place to Die: The Battle of Stones River.* Urbana: University of Illinois Press, 1990.

———. *This Terrible Sound: The Battle of Chickamauga.* Urbana: University of Illinois Press, 1992.

Crippin, Edward W. "The Diary of Edward W. Crippin, Private 27th Illinois Volunteers, War of the Rebellion, August 7, 1861, to September 19, 1863." Edited by Robert J. Kerner. *Transactions of the Illinois State Historical Society for the Year 1909.* Springfield, Ill.: State Journal, 1910.

Crofts, Thomas. *History of the Service of the Third Ohio Veteran Volunteer Cavalry in the War for the Preservation of the Union from 1861–1865.* Toledo, Ohio: Stoneman, 1910.

Crook, George. *General George Crook: His Autobiography.* Edited by Martin F. Schmitt. 1946. New ed. Norman: University of Oklahoma Press, 1960.

Cullens, Clarence E. "41st Mississippi: Adventures with the Guerilla in East Tennessee." *Sunny South,* 6 July 1895.

Cullum, George Washington. *Biographical Register of the Officers and Graduates of the U.S. Military Academy.* 3 vols. Boston: Houghton Mifflin, 1891.

Cumming, Kate. *Kate: The Journal of a Confederate Nurse.* Edited by Richard Barksdale Harwell. Baton Rouge: Louisiana State University Press, 1959.

Cummings, Charles M. "Otho French Strahl: 'Choicest Spirit to Embrace the South.'" *Tennessee Historical Quarterly* 24 (1965): 341–55.

———. *Yankee Quaker Confederate General: The Curious Career of Bushrod Rust Johnson.* Cranbury, N.J.: Fairleigh Dickinson University Press, 1971.

Cunningham, H. H. *Doctors in Gray: The Confederate Medical Service.* Baton Rouge: Louisiana State University Press, 1958.

Cunningham, O. Edward. *Shiloh and the Western Campaign of 1862.* Edited by Gary D. Joiner and Timothy B. Smith. New York: Savas Beatie, 2007.

Curry, W. L., comp. *Four Years in the Saddle: History of the First Regiment Ohio Volunteer Cavalry.* 1898. New ed. Jonesboro, Ga.: Freedom Hill, 1984.

Cutter, Orlando Phelps. *Our Battery; or, the Journal of Company B, 1st O.V.A.* Cleveland: Nevins, 1864.

Dana, Charles A. *Recollections of the Civil War.* New York: D. Appleton, 1898.

Daniel, Larry J. *Cannoneers in Gray: The Field Artillery of the Army of Tennessee, 1861–1865.* University: University of Alabama Press, 1984.

———. *Days of Glory: The Army of the Cumberland, 1861–1865.* Baton Rouge: Louisiana State University Press, 2004.

———. *Shiloh: The Battle That Changed the Civil War.* New York: Simon & Schuster, 1997.

———. *Soldiering in the Army of Tennessee: A Portrait of Life in a Confederate Army.* Chapel Hill: University of North Carolina Press, 1991.

Daniel, Larry J., and Lynn N. Bock. *Island No. 10: Struggle for the Mississippi Valley.* Tuscaloosa: University of Alabama Press, 1996.

Darst, Maury. "Robert Hodges, Jr.: Confederate Soldier." *East Texas Historical Journal* 9 (March 1971): 20–49.

Davidson, Henry M. *History of Battery A, First Regiment of Ohio Vol. Light Artillery*. Milwaukee: Daily Wisconsin Steam Printing, 1865.

Davis, Burke. *Our Incredible Civil War*. New York: Holt, Rinehart and Winston, 1960.

Davis, Jefferson. *The Papers of Jefferson Davis*. Vol. 9, *January–September, 1863*. Edited by Lynda L. Crist, Mary S. Dix, and Kenneth H. Williams. Baton Rouge: Louisiana State University Press, 1997.

Davis, Stephen. "A Georgia Firebrand: Major General W. H. T. Walker, C.S.A." *Confederate Historical Journal* 2 (Summer 1981): 1–15.

Davis, William C. *Breckinridge: Statesman, Soldier, Symbol*. Baton Rouge: Louisiana State University Press, 1974.

———. *Inventing Loreta Velasquez: Confederate Soldier Impersonator, Media Celebrity, and Con Artist*. Carbondale: Southern Illinois University Press, 2016.

———. *Jefferson Davis: The Man and His Hour, a Biography*. New York: HarperCollins, 1991.

Davis, William C., and Julie Hoffman, eds. *The Confederate General*. 6 vols. Harrisburg, Penn.: National Historical Society, 1991.

Dawson, Francis W. *Reminiscences of Confederate Service, 1861–1865*. Baton Rouge: Louisiana State University Press, 1980.

Day, L. W. *Story of the One Hundred and First Ohio Infantry*. Cleveland: W. M. Bayne, 1894.

Demoret, Alfred. *A Brief History of the Ninety-Third Regiment Ohio Volunteer Infantry: Recollections of a Private*. Ross, Ohio: Graphic Print, 1898.

DeVelling, C. T. *History of the Seventeenth Regiment* [Ohio]. Zanesville, Ohio: E. R. Sullivan, 1889.

Dillman, Henry F. *Pvt. Henry F. Dillman, Co. G, 31st Indiana Volunteer Infantry*. Edited by Henry E. Wahl. Bloomington, Ind.: Monroe County Historical Society, 1962.

Dodd, Ephraim Shelby. *Diary of Ephraim Shelby Dodd*. Austin, Tex.: E. L. Steck, 1914.

Dodson, W. C., ed. *Campaigns of Wheeler and His Cavalry, 1862–1865*. Atlanta: Hudgins, 1899.

Dodge, William Sumner. *History of the Old Second Division, Army of the Cumberland*. Chicago: Church & Goodman, 1864.

———. *A Waif of the War; or, the History of the Seventy-Fifth Illinois Infantry, Embracing the Entire Campaigns of the Army of the Cumberland*. Chicago: Church and Goodman, 1866.

Doll, William H. *History of the Sixth Regiment Indiana Volunteer Infantry in the Civil War*. Columbus, Ind.: Republican Job Print, 1903.

Drake, Edwin L., ed. *The Annals of the Army of Tennessee and Early Western History*. Vol. 1, *April–December, 1878*. 1878. Reprint, Jackson, Tenn.: Guild Bindery, n.d.

Duncan, Louis C. *The Medical Department of the United States Army in the Civil War*. 191[?]. Reprint, Gaithersburg, Md.: Olde Soldier, 1987.

Durham, Walter T. *Nashville: The Occupied City*. Nashville: Tennessee Historical Society, 1985.

———. *Reluctant Partners: Nashville and the Union*. Nashville: Tennessee Historical Society, 1987.

Dyer, Frederick H. *A Compendium of the War of the Rebellion*. 3 vols. 1908. Reprint, New York: Thomas Yoseloff, 1959.

Dyer, John P. *"Fightin' Joe" Wheeler*. University: Louisiana State University Press, 1941.

Dyer, William R. *The Civil War Diary of William R. Dyer, A Member of Forrest's Escort*. Edited by Wayne Bradshaw. Lexington, Ky.: Booksurge, 2009.

East, Ernest E. "Lincoln's Russian General." *Journal of the Illinois State Historical Society* 52 (1959): 106–22.

Eicher, John H., and David J. Eicher. *Civil War High Commands*. Stanford, Calif.: Stanford University Press, 2001.

Einolf, Christopher J. *George Thomas: Virginian for the Union*. Norman: University of Oklahoma Press, 2007.

Elliott, Sam Davis. *Isham G. Harris of Tennessee: Confederate Governor and United States Senator*. Baton Rouge: Louisiana State University Press, 2010.

———. *Soldier of Tennessee: General Alexander P. Stewart and the Civil War in the West*. Baton Rouge: Louisiana State University Press, 1999.

Eubank, Damon R. *In the Shadow of the Patriarch: The John J. Crittenden Family in War & Peace*. Macon, Ga.: Mercer University Press, 2009.

Evans, Raymond. *Civil War Sites Assessment for Walker County, Georgia*. Lafayette, Ga.: Walker County Commission, 2002.

———. *Inventory and Assessment of Civil War Period Cultural Resources in Dade County, Georgia*. Trenton, Ga.: Dade County Chamber of Commerce, 2001.

Fanebust, Wayne. *Major General Alexander M. McCook, USA: A Civil War Biography*. Jefferson, N.C.: McFarland, 2013.

Farris, John Kennerly. "Letters to Mary: The Civil War Diary of John Kennerly Farris." Edited by John Abernathy Smith. Winchester, Tenn.: Franklin County Historical Society, 1994.

Feis, William B. "'There Is a Bad Enemy in This City': Colonel William Truesdail's Army Police and the Occupation of Nashville, 1862–1863." *North & South*, March 2005, 34–45.

Fishel, Edwin C. "The Mythology of Civil War Intelligence." In *Battles Lost and Won: Essays from Civil War History*, edited by John T. Hubbell, 83–106. Westport, Conn.: Greenwood, 1975.

Fisher, Horace Cecil. *A Staff Officer's Story: The Personal Experiences of Colonel Horace Newton Fisher in the Civil War*. Boston: Thomas Todd, 1960.

Fitch, John. *Annals of the Army of the Cumberland*. Philadelphia: J. B. Lippincott, 1864.

Fitch, Michael H. *Echoes of the Civil War as I Hear Them*. New York: R. F. Fenno, 1905.

Floyd, David Bittle. *History of the Seventy-Fifth Regiment of Indiana Infantry Volunteers, Its Organization, Campaigns, and Battles (1862–65)*. Philadelphia: Lutheran Publication Society, 1893.

Foote, Henry S. *Recollections of the Chickamauga Campaign*. N.p., n.d.

Fox, William F. *New York at Gettysburg: Final Report of the Battlefield of Gettysburg*. 3 vols. Albany, N.Y.: J. B. Lyon, 1900.

Fradenburgh, J. N. *In Memoriam: Henry Harrison Cumings, Charlotte J. Cumings*. Oil City, Penn.: Derrick, 1913.

Freeman, Douglas Southall. *Lee's Lieutenants: A Study in Command*. 3 vols. New York: Charles Scribner's Sons, 1942–44.

———. *R. E. Lee: A Biography*. 4 vols. New York: Charles Scribner's Sons, 1935.

Fremantle, Arthur James Lyon. *The Fremantle Diary*. Edited by Walter Lord. Boston: Little, Brown, 1954.

French, Samuel G. *Two Wars: An Autobiography of Gen. Samuel G. French*. Nashville: Confederate Veteran, 1901.

Furey, J. Milton. *Historical and Biographical Work, or Past and Present of Clinton County*. Williamsport: Pennsylvania Grit, 1892.

Gancas, Ron. *The Gallant Seventy-Eighth: Stones River to Pickett's Mill.* Murrysville, Penn.: Mark V, 1994.

Garfield, James A. *The Wild Life of the Army: Civil War Letters of James A. Garfield.* Edited by Frederick D. Williams. East Lansing: Michigan State University Press, 1964.

Geary, James W. *We Need Men: The Union Draft in the Civil War.* DeKalb: Northern Illinois University Press, 1991.

"Gen. E. C. Walthall." *Confederate Veteran* 6 (July 1898): 305–7.

"Gen. William B. Bate." *Confederate Veteran* 2 (November 1894): 336–37.

Genco, James G. *To the Sound of Musketry and Tap of the Drum.* Rochester, Mich.: Ray Russell, 1983.

Gibson, Charles Dana, and E. Kay Gibson, comp. *Dictionary of Transports and Combatant Vessels Steam and Sail Employed by the Union Army, 1861–1868.* Camden, Me.: Ensign, 1995.

Gibson, Joseph Thompson. "Co. A, 78th Regiment Pa. Vols." *Presbyterian Messenger* 5 (1898): 37, 69–70, 101–2, 133–34, 164–66, 301–2.

———, ed. *History of the Seventy-Eighth Pennsylvania Volunteer Infantry.* Pittsburgh: Pittsburgh Printing, 1905.

Giles, Valerius Cincinnatus. *Rags and Hope, the Recollections of Val. C. Giles, Four Years with Hood's Brigade, Fourth Texas Infantry, 1861–1865.* Edited by Mary Lasswell. New York: Coward-McCann, 1961.

Goff, Richard D. *Confederate Supply.* Durham, N.C.: Duke University Press, 1969.

Goode, G. Brown. *Virginia Cousins: A Study of the Ancestry and Posterity of John Goode of Whitby.* Richmond: Randolph & English, 1887.

Govan, Gilbert E., and James W. Livingood. *The Chattanooga Country, 1540–1976.* 3rd ed. Knoxville: University of Tennessee Press, 1977.

Gow, June I. "Chiefs of Staff in the Army of Tennessee under Braxton Bragg." *Tennessee Historical Quarterly* 27 (1970): 341–60.

———. "Military Administration in the Confederate Army of Tennessee." *Journal of Southern History* 40 (May 1974): 183–98.

Grant, Ulysses S. *The Papers of Ulysses S. Grant.* Vol. 9, *July 7–December 31, 1863.* Edited by John Y. Simon. Carbondale: Southern Illinois University Press, 1982.

Grebner, Constantin. *"We Were the Ninth": A History of the Ninth Regiment, Ohio Volunteer Infantry, April 17, 1861 to June 7, 1864.* Translated and edited by Frederic Trautmann. Kent, Ohio: Kent State University Press, 1987.

Green, John Williams. *Johnny Green of the Orphan Brigade: The Journal of a Confederate Soldier.* Edited by Albert D. Kirwan. Lexington: University of Kentucky Press, 1956.

Greiner, H. C. *General Phil Sheridan: As I Knew Him, Playmate-Comrade-Friend.* Chicago: J. S. Hyland, 1908.

Griggs, Walter S., Jr. *General John Pegram, C.S.A.* Lynchburg, Va.: H. E. Howard, 1993.

Grose, William. *The Story of the Marches, Battles and Incidents of the 36th Regiment Indiana Volunteer Infantry.* New Castle, Ind.: Courier, 1891.

Hafendorfer, Kenneth A. *Perryville: Battle for Kentucky.* 2nd ed. Louisville, Ky.: KH, 1991.

Hallock, Judith Lee. *Braxton Bragg and Confederate Defeat.* Vol. 2. Tuscaloosa: University of Alabama Press, 1991.

Hannaford, E. *The Story of a Regiment: A History of the Campaigns, and Associations in the Field, of the Sixth Regiment Ohio Volunteer Infantry.* Cincinnati: n.p., 1868.

Harden, H. O. *History of the 90th Ohio Volunteer Infantry in the War of the Great Rebellion in the United States, 1861 to 1865.* Stoutsville, Ohio: Fairfield-Pickaway News, 1902.

Harmon, Oscar Fitzalan. *Life and Letters of Oscar Fitzalan Harmon, Colonel of the 125th Regiment Illinois Volunteers, Infantry*. Edited by Lucy Harmon McPherson. Trenton, N.J.: MacCrellish & Quigley, 1914.

Hartzell, John Calvin. *Ohio Volunteer: The Childhood & Civil War Memoirs of Captain John Calvin Hartzell OVI*. Edited by Charles I. Switzer. Athens: Ohio University Press, 2005.

Haughton, Andrew. *Training, Tactics and Leadership in the Confederate Army of Tennessee: Seeds of Failure*. London: Frank Cass, 2000.

Haverstock, Mary Sayre, Jeannette Mahoney Vance, and Brian L. Meggitt, eds. *Artists in Ohio, 1787–1900: A Biographical Dictionary*. Kent, Ohio: Kent State University Press, 2000.

Hay, Thomas Robson. "Braxton Bragg and the Southern Confederacy." *Georgia Historical Quarterly* 9 (December 1925): 267–316.

Haynie, J. Henry, ed. *The Nineteenth Illinois: A Memoir of a Regiment of Volunteer Infantry Famous in the Civil War of Fifty Years Ago for Its Drill, Bravery, and Distinguished Services*. Chicago: M. A. Donohue, 1912.

Hazen, William B. *A Narrative of Military Service*. 1885. Reprint, Huntington, W.Va.: Blue Acorn, 1993.

Hazzard, George. *Hazzard's History of Henry County, Indiana, 1822–1906*. 2 vols. New Castle, Ind.: George Hazzard, 1906.

Head, Thomas A. *Campaigns and Battles of the Sixteenth Regiment Tennessee Volunteers, in the War between the States*. Nashville: Cumberland Presbyterian, 1885.

Heartsill, W. W. *Fourteen Hundred and 91 Days in the Confederate Army*. Edited by Bell Irvin Wiley. Jackson, Tenn.: McCowat-Mercer, 1954.

Heg, Hans C. *The Civil War Letters of Colonel Hans Christian Heg*. Edited by Theodore C. Blegen. Northfield, Minn.: Norwegian-American Historical Association, 1936.

Heitman, Francis B. *Historical Register and Dictionary of the United States Army, from Its Organization, September 29, 1789, to March 2, 1903*. Washington, D.C.: Government Printing Office, 1903.

Herr, George W. *Nine Campaigns in Nine States*. San Francisco: Bancroft, 1890.

Hess, Earl J. *Braxton Bragg: The Most Hated Man of the Confederacy*. Chapel Hill: University of North Carolina Press, 2016.

———. *The Knoxville Campaign: Burnside and Longstreet in East Tennessee*. Knoxville: University of Tennessee Press, 2012.

Hewes, Fletcher Willis. *History of the Formation, Movements, Camps, Scouts and Battles of the Tenth Regiment Michigan Volunteer Infantry*. Detroit: John Slater, 1864.

Hewitt, Janet B., et al., eds. *Supplement to the Official Records of the Union and Confederate Armies*. 100 vols. Wilmington, N.C.: Broadfoot, 1994–2001.

Hewitt, Lawrence Lee. "Braxton Bragg and the Confederate Invasion of Kentucky in 1862." In *Confederate Generals in the Western Theater*, vol. 1, edited by Lawrence Lee Hewitt and Arthur W. Bergeron Jr., 70–86. Knoxville: University of Tennessee Press, 2010.

Hicks, Borden M. "Personal Recollections of the War of the Rebellion." In *Glimpses of the Nation's Struggle, Sixth Series, Papers Read before the Minnesota Commandery of the Military Order of the Loyal Legion of the United States, January, 1903–1908*, 519–44. Minneapolis: Aug. Davis, 1909.

High, Edwin W. *History of the Sixty-Eighth Regiment Indiana Volunteer Infantry, 1862–1865*. Metamora, Ind.: Regimental Association, 1902.

Hight, John J. *History of the Fifty-Eighth Regiment of Indiana Volunteer Infantry*. Princeton, Ind.: Clarion, 1895.

Hill, Daniel H. "Chickamauga: The Great Battle of the West." In *Battles and Leaders of the Civil War*, edited by Robert Underwood Johnson and Clarence Clough Buel, 3:638–62. New York: Century, 1884.

Hinman, Wilbur F. *The Story of the Sherman Brigade*. Alliance, Ohio: Daily Review, 1897.

Historical Sketch of the Chicago Board of Trade Battery. Chicago: Henneberry, 1902.

History of the Seventy-Ninth Regiment Indiana Volunteer Infantry in the Civil War of Eighteen Sixty-One. Indianapolis: Hollenbeck, 1899.

Hoffman, Mark. *"My Brave Mechanics": The First Michigan Engineers and Their Civil War*. Detroit: Wayne State University Press, 2007.

Hollingsworth, Dixon. *The Barefoot Confederate: A History of Company D, 47th Georgia Infantry Regiment, CSA*. Sylvania, Ga.: Partridge Pond, 1990.

Holm, D. D. *History of the Fifth Indiana Battery*. N.p., n.d.

Holmes, Henry McCall. *Diary of Henry McCall Holmes, Army of Tennessee, Assistant Surgeon Florida Troops*. State College, Miss.: n.p., 1968.

Holmes, J. T. *52d O.V.I. Then and Now*. Columbus, Ohio: Berlin, 1898.

Hoobler, James A. *Cities under the Gun: Images of Occupied Nashville and Chattanooga*. Nashville: Rutledge Hill, 1986.

Horton, Joshua H. *A History of the Eleventh Regiment, Ohio Volunteer Infantry*. Dayton, Ohio: W. J. Shuey, 1866.

Hough, Alfred Lacy. *Soldier in the West: The Civil War Letters of Alfred Lacey Hough*. Edited by Robert G. Athearn. Philadelphia: University of Pennsylvania Press, 1957.

Houghton, W. R., and M. B. Houghton. *Two Boys in the Civil War and After*. Montgomery, Ala.: Paragon, 1912.

Howe, Henry. *Historical Collections of Ohio*. 2 vols. Columbus, Ohio: Henry Howe & Son, 1889.

Hubbard, Gurdon S. *The Autobiography of Gurdon Saltonstall Hubbard*. Chicago: R. R. Donnelley, 1911.

Hudson, Patricia L. "The Old Anderson Road: Lifeline to Chattanooga." *Tennessee Historical Quarterly* 42 (Summer 1983): 165–78.

Hughes, Nathaniel Cheairs, Jr. *General William J. Hardee: Old Reliable*. Baton Rouge: Louisiana State University Press, 1965.

———. *The Pride of the Confederate Artillery: The Washington Artillery in the Army of Tennessee*. Baton Rouge: Louisiana State University Press, 1997.

———. *Yale's Confederates: A Biographical Dictionary*. Knoxville: University of Tennessee Press, 2008.

Hughes, Nathaniel Cheairs, Jr., and Roy P. Stonesifer Jr. *The Life and Wars of Gideon J. Pillow*. Chapel Hill: University of North Carolina Press, 1993.

Hughes, Nathaniel Cheairs, Jr., and Gordon D. Whitney. *Jefferson Davis in Blue: The Life of Sherman's Relentless Warrior*. Baton Rouge: Louisiana State University Press, 2002.

Hunt, Roger D. *Colonels in Blue: Michigan, Ohio and West Virginia*. Jefferson, N.C.: McFarland, 2011.

Hunt, Roger D., and Jack R. Brown. *Brevet Brigadier Generals in Blue*. Gaithersburg, Md.: Olde Soldier, 1990.

Hunter, Alf. G. *History of the Eighty-Second Indiana Volunteer Infantry*. Indianapolis: Wm. B. Burford, 1893.

Hurst, Jack. *Nathan Bedford Forrest: A Biography*. New York: Knopf, 1993.

Imboden, Cyrus M. *With the Army of the Cumberland*. Blandinsville, Ill.: Helen Fleming Rolofson, 1969.

Indiana at Chickamauga, 1863–1900: Report of Indiana Commissioners Chickamauga National Military Park. Indianapolis: Wm. B. Burford, 1901.

Ives, Washington. *Civil War Journal and Letters of Serg. Washington Ives, 4th Florida C.S.A.* Edited by Jim R. Cabaniss. Tallahassee, Fla.: J. R. Cabaniss, 1987.

Jackson, Benjamin Franklin. *So Mourns the Dove: Letters of a Confederate Infantryman and His Family*. Edited by Alto Loftin Jackson. New York: Exposition, 1965.

James, Alfred P. "General James Scott Negley." *Western Pennsylvania Historical Magazine* 14 (April 1931): 69–91.

Jamison, Robert D. *Letters and Recollections of a Confederate Soldier, 1860–1865*. Compiled by Henry Downs Jamison Jr. and Marguerite Jamison McTigue. Nashville: H. D. Jamison, 1964.

Johansson, M. Jane. "Daniel Weisiger Adams: Defender of the Confederacy's Heartland." In *Confederate Generals in the Western Theater*, edited by Lawrence Lee Hewitt and Arthur W. Bergeron Jr., 3:86–119. Knoxville: University of Tennessee Press, 2011.

Johnson, Andrew. *The Papers of Andrew Johnson*. Edited by Ralph W. Haskins, LeRoy P. Graf, and Paul Bergeron. 16 vols. Knoxville: University of Tennessee Press, 1967–2000.

Johnson, Mark W. *That Body of Brave Men: The U.S. Regular Infantry and the Civil War in the West*. Cambridge, Mass.: DaCapo, 2003.

Johnson, R. W. *A Soldier's Reminiscences in Peace and War*. Philadelphia: J. B. Lippincott, 1886.

Johnson, Timothy D. "Benjamin Franklin Cheatham: The Early Years." *Tennessee Historical Quarterly* 42 (Fall 1983): 266–80.

Johnston, Adam S. *The Soldier Boy's Diary Book; or, Memorandums of the Alphabetical First Lessons of Military Tactics*. Pittsburgh: n.p., 1866.

Johnston, Joseph E. *Narrative of Military Operations*. New York: D. Appleton, 1874.

Johnston, William Preston. *The Life of Gen. Albert Sidney Johnston*. New York: D. Appleton, 1879.

Jones, Eugene W., Jr. *Enlisted for the War: The Struggles of the 24th Regiment, South Carolina Volunteers, Infantry, 1861–1865*. Hightstown, N.J.: Longstreet House, 1997.

Jones, Frank J. "Personal Recollections and Experience of a Soldier during the War of the Rebellion." In *Sketches of War History, 1861–1865, Papers Prepared for the Commandery of the State of Ohio, Military Order of the Loyal Legion of the United States*, 6:111–31. Cincinnati: Monfort, 1908.

Jones, John Beauchamp. *A Rebel War Clerk's Diary at the Confederate States Capital*. 2 vols. Philadelphia: J. B. Lippincott, 1866.

Jones, R. Steven. *The Right Hand of Command: Use & Disuse of Personal Staffs in the Civil War*. Mechanicsburg, Penn.: Stackpole, 2000.

Jones, Shirley Farris. "A Train Wreck in Georgia: From the War between the States Diary of Dr. John Kennerly Farris." *UDC Magazine*, May 1994, 15–17.

Jordan, Holman D. "The Military Career of Henry D. Clayton." *Alabama Review* 13 (April 1960): 127–34.

Jordan, Thomas, and J. P. Pryor. *The Campaigns of Lieut.-Gen. N. B. Forrest, and of Forrest's Cavalry*. 1868. Reprint, Dayton, Ohio: Morningside, 1977.

Jordan, Weymouth T., Jr., comp. *North Carolina Troops, 1861–1865: A Roster*. Vol. 5. Raleigh, N.C.: Archives and History, 1973.

Jordan, William C. *Some Events and Incidents during the Civil War*. Montgomery, Ala.: Paragon, 1909.

Joslyn, Mauriel Phillips, ed. *A Meteor Shining Brightly: Essays on Maj. Gen. Patrick R. Cleburne*. Milledgeville, Ga.: Terrell House, 1997.

Kean, Robert Garlick Hill. *Inside the Confederate Government: The Diary of Robert Garlick Hill Kean*. Edited by Edward Younger. New York: Oxford University Press, 1957.

Keegan, Peter. *The Diaries of Peter Keegan*. Edited by Dwight Reynolds. Indianapolis: Privately printed, 1938.

Keil, F. W. *Thirty-Fifth Ohio: A Narrative of Service from August, 1861 to 1864*. Fort Wayne, Ohio: Archer, Housh, 1894.

Kelly, Dennis. "Back in the Saddle: The War Record of William Bate." *Civil War Times Illustrated* 27 (December 1988): 27–33.

Kelly, Welden. *A Historic Sketch Lest We Forget Company "E" 26th Ohio Infantry in the War for the Union, 1861–65*. Osborn, Mo.: 1909.

Kempfer, Lester L. *The Salem Light Guard: Company G, 36th Regiment Ohio Volunteer Infantry, Marietta, Ohio, 1861–5*. Chicago: Adams, 1973.

Kerwood, A. L. *Annals of the Fifty-Seventh Regiment Indiana Volunteers*. Dayton, Ohio: W. J. Shuey, 1868.

Kiene, Francis A. *A Civil War Diary: The Journal of Francis A. Kiene, 1861–1864. A Family History*. Edited By Ralph E. Kiene Jr. Kansas City, Mo.: Yearbook House, 1974.

Kimberly, Robert L., and Ephraim S. Holloway. *The Forty-First Ohio Veteran Volunteer Infantry in the War of the Rebellion, 1861–1865*. Cleveland: W. R. Smellie, 1897.

King, Cameron Haight, comp. *The King Family of Suffield, Connecticut: Its English Ancestry, A.D. 1389–1662, and American Descendants, A.D. 1662–1908*. San Francisco: Walter N. Brunt, 1908.

King, John M. *Three Years with the 92d Illinois: The Civil War Diary of John M. King*. Edited by Claire E. Swedberg. Mechanicsburg, Penn.: Stackpole, 1999.

Kinnear, J. R. *History of the Eighty-Sixth Regiment Illinois Volunteer Infantry*. Chicago: Tribune, 1866.

Kirk, Charles H., ed. *History of the Fifteenth Pennsylvania Volunteer Cavalry*. Philadelphia: n.p., 1906.

Kirkpatrick, George Morgan. *The Experiences of a Private Soldier in the Civil War*. 1924. Reprint, Indianapolis: Hoosier Bookshop, 1973.

Kirwan, Albert D. *John J. Crittenden: The Struggle for the Union*. Lexington: University of Kentucky Press, 1962.

Kundahl, George G. *Confederate Engineer: Training and Campaigning with John Morris Wampler*. Knoxville: University of Tennessee Press, 2000.

Laine, J. Gary, and Morris M. Penny. *Law's Alabama Brigade in the War between the Union and the Confederacy*. Shippensburg, Penn.: White Mane, 1996.

Lamers, William M. *The Edge of Glory: A Biography of General William S. Rosecrans, U.S.A.* New York: Harcourt, Brace & World, 1961.

Lathrop, D. *The History of the Fifty-Ninth Regiment Illinois Volunteers*. Indianapolis: Hall & Hutchinson, 1865.

Le Duc, William G. *Recollections of a Civil War Quartermaster: The Autobiography of William G. Le Duc*. St. Paul, Minn.: North Central, 1963.

Lee, Dan. *Kentuckian in Blue: A Biography of Major General Lovell Harrison Rousseau*. Jefferson, N.C.: McFarland, 2010.

———. *Thomas J. Wood: A Biography of the Union General in the Civil War*. Jefferson, N.C.: McFarland, 2012.

Leeper, Wesley Thurman. *Rebels Valiant: Second Arkansas Mounted Rifles (Dismounted)*. Little Rock, Ark.: Pioneer, 1964.

Leonard, Elizabeth D. *All the Daring of the Soldier: Women of the Civil War Armies*. New York: W. W. Norton, 1999.

Lewis, R. "Reminiscences about Chattanooga." *Confederate Veteran* 1 (August 1893): 243.

Liddell, St. John Richardson. *Liddell's Record*. Edited by Nathaniel C. Hughes. Dayton, Ohio: Morningside House, 1985.

Lindsley, John Berrien, ed. *The Military Annals of Tennessee, Confederate*. 2 vols.1886. Reprint, Wilmington, N.C.: Broadfoot, 1995.

Livingood, James W. "The *Chattanooga Rebel*." East Tennessee Historical Society Publications 39 (1967): 42–55.

Longacre, Edward G. *A Soldier to the Last: Maj. Gen. Joseph Wheeler in Blue and Gray*. Washington, D.C.: Potomac, 2007.

Longstreet, James. *From Manassas to Appomattox: Memoirs of the Civil War in America*. 1896. Reprint, Bloomington: Indiana University Press, 1960.

Losson, Christopher. *Tennessee's Forgotten Warriors: Frank Cheatham and His Confederate Division*. Knoxville: University of Tennessee Press, 1989.

Lubetkin, M. John, ed. *Before Custer: Surveying the Yellowstone, 1872*. Norman, Okla.: Arthur H. Clark, 2015.

Lyle, W. W. *Lights and Shadows of Army Life*. Cincinnati: R. W. Carroll, 1865.

Lyman, George H. "Some Aspects of the Medical Service in the Armies of the United States during the War of the Rebellion." In *Civil and Mexican Wars, 1861, 1846*, 175–228. Vol. 13 of *Papers of the Military Historical Society of Massachusetts*, 1913. Reprint, Wilmington, N.C.: Broadfoot, 1990.

Lyman, Theodore. *Meade's Headquarters, 1863–1865: Letters of Colonel Theodore Lyman from the Wilderness to Appomattox*. Edited by George R. Agassiz. Boston: Atlantic Monthly Press, 1922.

Lytle, William Haines. *For Honor, Glory & Union: The Mexican & Civil War Letters of Brig. Gen. William Haines Lytle*. Edited by Ruth C. Carter. Lexington: University Press of Kentucky, 1999.

Magid, Paul. *George Crook: From the Redwoods to Appomattox*. Norman: University of Oklahoma Press, 2011.

Manigault, Arthur Middleton. *A Carolinian Goes to War: The Civil War Narrative of Arthur Middleton Manigault*. Edited by R. Lockwood Tower. Columbia: University of South Carolina Press, 1983.

Marcoot, Maurice. *Five Years in the Sunny South*. N.p., n.d.

Marriner, W. M. "Chickamauga: The Opening." *Southern Bivouac* 3 (September 1884): 8–11.

Marsh, Bryan. "The Confederate Letters of Bryan Marsh." *Chronicles of Smith County, Texas* 14 (Winter 1975): 9–30, 43–55.

Marshall, Emogene Niver. *To the Memory of My Brother, Edwin W. Niver*. Sandusky, Ohio: Krewson's, 1932.

Martin, Samuel J. *General Braxton Bragg, C.S.A.* Jefferson, N.C.: McFarland, 2011.

Martin, W. L. [T.]. "A Defence of General Bragg's Conduct at Chickamauga." *Southern Historical Society Papers* 11 (April–May 1883): 201–6.

Marvel, William. *Burnside*. Chapel Hill: University of North Carolina Press, 1991.

Massey, John. *Reminiscences*. Nashville: M. E. Church, South, 1916.
Mattes, Merrill J. *Indians, Infants and Infantry: Andrew and Elizabeth Burt on the Frontier*. 1960. Reprint, Lincoln: University of Nebraska Press, 1988.
Mauzy, James H. *Historical Sketch of the Sixty-Eighth Regiment Indiana Volunteers*. Rushville, Ind.: Republican, 1887.
McAdams, F. M. *Every-day Soldier Life, or a History of the One Hundred and Thirteenth Ohio Volunteer Infantry*. Columbus, Ohio: Chas. M. Cott, 1884.
McCain, Thomas Hart Benton. *In Song and Sorrow: The Daily Journal of Thomas Hart Benton McCain, 86th Indiana Volunteer Infantry*. Edited by Richard K. Rue and Geraldine M. Rue. Carmel, Ind.: Guild, 1998.
McCallie, Samuel Washington. *Report on the Fossil Iron Ores of Georgia: Geological Survey of Georgia Bulletin No. 17, 1908*. Atlanta: Geological Survey of Georgia, 1908.
McCammon, Charles S. *Loyal Mountain Troopers: The Second and Third Tennessee Volunteer Cavalry in the Civil War*. Maryville, Tenn.: Blount County Genealogical and Historical Society, 1992.
McClellan, George B. *The Civil War Papers of George B. McClellan: Selected Correspondence, 1860–1865*. Edited by Stephen W. Sears. New York: Ticknor & Fields, 1989.
McDonough, James Lee. *Shiloh: In Hell before Night*. Knoxville: University of Tennessee Press, 1977.
———. *Stones River: Bloody Winter in Tennessee*. Knoxville: University of Tennessee Press, 1980.
———. *War in Kentucky: From Shiloh to Perryville*. Knoxville: University of Tennessee Press, 1994.
McGee, B. F. *History of the 72nd Indiana Volunteer Infantry of the Mounted Lightning Brigade*. Lafayette, Ind.: S. Vater, 1882.
McKinney, Francis F. *Education in Violence: The Life of George H. Thomas and the History of the Army of the Cumberland*. Detroit: Wayne State University Press, 1961.
McLaws, Lafayette. "After Chickamauga." *Addresses Delivered before the Confederate Veterans' Association, Savannah, Georgia*. Savannah, Ga.: 1898.
McManus, Otho J. *Morning to Midnight in the Saddle: Civil War Letters of a Soldier in Wilder's Lightning Brigade*. Edited by Christopher D. McManus, Thomas H. Inglis, and Otho James Hicks. XLIBRIS, 2012.
McMurtry, R. Gerald. *Ben Hardin Helm: "Rebel" Brother-in-Law of Abraham Lincoln—with a Biographical Sketch of His Wife and an Account of the Todd Family of Kentucky*. Chicago: Civil War Round Table, 1943.
McNeil, Samuel A. *Personal Recollections of Service in the Army of the Cumberland and Sherman's Army, from August 17, 1861 to July 20, 1865*. Richwood, Ohio: S. A. McNeil, 1910.
McWhiney, Grady. *Braxton Bragg and Confederate Defeat*. Vol. 1, *Field Command*. New York: Columbia University Press, 1969.
Members of the Battery. *History of the Organization, Marches, Campings, General Services and Final Muster Out of Battery M, First Regiment Illinois Light Artillery*. Princeton, Ill.: Mercer & Dean, 1892.
Memoir of Gen. A. C. Ducat. Chicago: Rand, McNally, 1897.
Memorial of Lieutenant Howard M. Burnham, United States Army, Who Fell in the Battle of Chicamauga, Tenn., September 19th, 1863. Springfield, Mass.: Samuel Bowles, 1864.
Merrill, Catherine. *The Soldier of Indiana in the War for the Union*. 2 vols. Indianapolis: Merrill, 1869.
Merrill, Robert Sidney. *Diary*. Cedarburg, Wisc.: MGS, 1995.

Miller, Francis Trevelyan, ed. *The Photographic History of the Civil War*. 10 vols. New York: Review of Reviews, 1911.

Miller, Robert J. *Both Prayed to the Same God: Religion and Faith in the American Civil War*. Lanham, Md.: Lexington, 2007.

Moore, David G. *William S. Rosecrans and the Union Victory: A Civil War Biography*. Jefferson, N.C.: McFarland, 2014.

Moore, Robert A. *A Life for the Confederacy*. Edited by James W. Silver. Jackson, Tenn.: McCowat-Mercer, 1959.

Moorman, Hiram Clark. "The Moorman Memorandum." *Confederate Chronicles of Tennessee* 3 (1989): 52–142.

Morgan, O. H., and E. R. Murphy. *History of the 7th Independent Battery Indiana Light Artillery*. Bedford, Ind.: Press of the Democrat, 1898.

Morris, George W. *History of the Eighty-First Regiment of Indiana Volunteer Infantry in the Great War of the Rebellion, 1861 to 1865*. Louisville, Ky.: Franklin, 1901.

Morris, Roy, Jr. "Eastern Ohio Quaker in Gray: Bushrod Johnson's Strange Career." *Blue and Gray* 2 (February–March 1985): 52–57.

———. *Sheridan: The Life and Wars of General Phil Sheridan*. New York: Crown, 1992.

Morse, Bliss. *Civil War Diaries of Bliss Morse*. Edited by Loren J. Morse. Pittsburg, Kans.: Pittcraft, 1964.

Morton, John Watson. *The Artillery of Nathan Bedford Forrest's Cavalry*. Nashville: M. E. Church, South, 1909.

Mosman, Chesley A. *The Rough Side of War: The Civil War Journal of Chesley A. Mosman, 1st Lieutenant, Company D 59th Illinois Volunteer Infantry Regiment*. Edited by Arnold Gates. Garden City, N.Y.: Basin, 1987.

Mulhane, L. W. *Memorial of Major-General William Stark Rosecrans*. Columbus, Ohio: Columbian, 1898.

Murdock, Eugene Converse. *Patriotism Limited, 1862–1865: The Civil War Draft and the Bounty System*. Kent, Ohio: Kent State University Press, 1967.

Nance, C. Roger, and Beverly E. Bastian. "Report on Old Bellefonte: An Historical Site in Northern Alabama." Chattanooga: Tennessee Valley Authority, 1974.

Nash, Charles Edward. *Biographical Sketches of Gen. Pat Cleburne and Gen. T. C. Hindman*. 1898. Reprint, Dayton, Ohio: Morningside, 1977.

Neal, Diane, and Thomas W. Kremm. *Lion of the South: General Thomas C. Hindman*. Macon, Ga.: Mercer University Press, 1993.

Nelson, William Cowper. *The Hour of Our Nation's Agony: The Civil War Letters of Lt. William Cowper Nelson of Mississippi*. Edited by Jennifer W. Ford. Knoxville: University of Tennessee Press, 2007.

Newell, Clayton R. *Lee vs. McClellan: The First Campaign*. Washington, D.C.: Regnery, 1996.

Newlin, William Henry. *A History of the Seventy-Third Regiment of Illinois Infantry Volunteers*. Springfield, Ill., 1890.

Ninety-Second Illinois Volunteers. Freeport, Ill.: Journal Steam Publishing, 1875.

Noe, Kenneth W. *Perryville: This Grand Havoc of Battle*. Lexington: University Press of Kentucky, 2001.

Norman, Matthew W. *Colonel Burton's Spiller & Burr Revolver: An Untimely Venture in Confederate Small-Arms Manufacturing*. Macon, Ga.: Mercer University Press, 1996.

Obreiter, John. *The Seventy-Seventh Pennsylvania at Shiloh: History of the Regiment*. Harrisburg, Penn.: Harrisburg Publishing, 1905.

Official Roster of the Soldiers of the State of Ohio in the War of the Rebellion, 1861–1866. 12 vols. Akron, Ohio: Werner, 1886–95.

Oliphant, William J. *Only a Private: A Texan Remembers the Civil War. The Memoirs of William J. Oliphant.* Edited by James M. McCaffrey. Houston: Halcyon, 2004.

Olmsted, Frederick Law. *Defending the Union: The Civil War and the U.S. Sanitary Commission, 1861–1863.* Vol. 4 of *The Papers of Frederick Law Olmsted.* Edited by Jane Turner Censer. Baltimore: Johns Hopkins University Press, 1986.

Otey, W. N. Mercer. "Operations of the Signal Corps." *Confederate Veteran* 8 (1900): 129–30.

Otto, John. *History of the 11th Indiana Battery, Connected with an Outline History of the Army of the Cumberland during the War of the Rebellion, 1861–1865.* Auburn, Ind.: W. D. Page, 1891.

Otto, John Henry. *Memoirs of a Dutch Mudsill: The "War Memories" of John Henry Otto, Captain, Company D, 21st Regiment Wisconsin Volunteer Infantry.* Edited by David Gould and James B. Kennedy. Kent, Ohio: Kent State University Press, 2004.

Owen, Thomas McAdory. *History of Alabama and Dictionary of Alabama Biography.* 4 vols. Chicago: Clarke, 1921.

Owen, Urban G. "Letters of a Confederate Surgeon in the Army of Tennessee to His Wife." Edited by Enoch L. Mitchell. *Tennessee Historical Quarterly* 4 (1945): 341–53; and 5 (1946): 60–81, 142–81.

Owen, William Miller. *In Camp and Battle with the Washington Artillery.* Boston: Ticknor, 1885.

Palmer, George Thomas. *A Conscientious Turncoat: The Story of John M. Palmer, 1817–1900.* New Haven, Conn.: Yale University Press, 1941.

Palmer, John M. *Personal Recollections of John M. Palmer: The Story of an Earnest Life.* Cincinnati: Robert Clarke, 1901.

Palmer, William Jackson. *Letters, 1853–1868, Gen'l Wm. J. Palmer.* Compiled by Isaac H. Clothier. Philadelphia: Ketterlinus, 1906.

Pape-Findley, Nancy. *The Invincibles: The Story of the Fourth Ohio Veteran Volunteer Cavalry, 1861–1865.* Tecumseh, Mich.: Blood Road, 2002.

Parks, Joseph H. *General Edmund Kirby Smith, C.S.A.* Baton Rouge: Louisiana State University Press, 1954.

———. *General Leonidas Polk, C.S.A.* Baton Rouge: Louisiana State University Press, 1962.

Partridge, Charles A., ed. *History of the Ninety-Sixth Regiment Illinois Volunteer Infantry.* Chicago: Brown, Pettibone, 1887.

Paul, Franc M. "The Chattanooga Rebel." In *Tennessee Old and New: 1796–1946,* 2:273–79. Kingsport, Tenn.: Kingsport Press, 1946.

Perry, Henry Fales. *History of the Thirty-Eighth Regiment Indiana Volunteer Infantry.* Palo Alto, Calif.: F. A. Stuart, 1906.

Peskin, Allan. *Garfield.* Kent, Ohio: Kent State University Press, 1978.

Phillips, Alfred R. *Fighting with Turchin.* Privately printed, n.d.

Phillips, James M. *Civil War Diary & Letters of James Martin Phillips, Company G, 92nd Illinois Volunteers.* Compiled by Harriet Phillips Bone. St. Louis: Genealogical Research, 1984.

Pickerill, W. N. *History of the Third Indiana Cavalry.* Indianapolis: Aetna, 1906.

Piston, William Garrett. *Lee's Tarnished Lieutenant: James Longstreet and His Place in Southern History.* Athens: University of Georgia Press, 1987.

Plum, William R. *The Military Telegraph during the Civil War in the United States*. 2 vols. 1882. Reprint, New York: Arno, 1974.

Polk, J. M. *The North and South American Review*. Austin, Tex.: Von Boeckmann-Jones, 1914.

Polk, W. N. [M.]. "The Battle of Chickamauga: Letter from Captain W. N. [M.] Polk." *Southern Historical Society Papers* 10 (1882): 2–25, 236–38.

———. *Leonidas Polk: Bishop and General*. 2 vols. New York: Longmans, Green, 1915.

Poole, John Randolph. *Cracker Cavaliers: The 2nd Georgia Cavalry under Wheeler and Forrest*. Macon, Ga.: Mercer University Press, 2000.

Portrait and Biographical Record of Hancock, McDonough and Henderson Counties, Illinois. Chicago: Lake City, 1894.

Portrait and Biographical Record of Marion and Hardin Counties, Ohio. Chicago: Chapman, 1895.

Powell, David A. *Failure in the Saddle: Nathan Bedford Forrest, Joseph Wheeler, and the Confederate Cavalry in the Chickamauga Campaign*. New York: Savas Beatie, 2010.

Powell, William H., ed. *Officers of the Army and Navy (Volunteer) Who Served in the Civil War*. Philadelphia: L. R. Hamersly, 1893.

Powell, William H., and Edward Shippen, eds. *Officers of the Army and Navy (Regular) Who Served in the Civil War*. Philadelphia: L. R. Hamersly, 1892.

Prickitt, Daniel J. *Daniel J. Prickitt, Sergeant, Company H, Third Ohio Cavalry, 1861–1865*. Edited by E. D. Stoltz. Archibold, Ohio: Edwin D. Stoltz, 1988.

Prince, Richard E. *Nashville, Chattanooga & St. Louis Railway: History and Steam Locomotives*. 1967. Reprint, Bloomington: Indiana University Press, 2001.

Proceedings of the Thirtieth Annual Reunion, 1st O.V.V.C. Columbus, Ohio: n.p., 1909.

Puntenny, George H. *History of the Thirty-Seventh Regiment of Indiana Infantry, Volunteers: Its Organization, Campaigns, and Battles, Sept. '61–Oct. '64*. Rushville, Ind.: Jacksonian Book and Job, 1896.

Purdue, Howell, and Elizabeth Purdue. *Pat Cleburne, Confederate General*. 2nd ed. Tuscaloosa, Ala.: Portals, 1977.

Quiner, E. B. *The Military History of Wisconsin: A Record of the Civil and Military Patriotism of the State, in the War for the Union*. Chicago: Clarke, 1866.

Quinlin, Bradley, and Joshua Haugh. *Duty Well Performed: The Twenty-First Ohio Volunteer Infantry in the Civil War*. Milford, Ohio: Little Miami, 2011.

Quintard, Charles Todd. *Doctor Quintard, Chaplain C.S.A. and Second Bishop of Tennessee*. Edited by Sam Davis Elliott. Baton Rouge: Louisiana State University Press, 2003.

Raab, James W. *J. Patton Anderson, Confederate General: A Biography*. Jefferson, N.C.: McFarland, 2004.

Rabb, John Wesley. "'We Are Stern and Resolved': The Civil War Letters of John Wesley Rabb, Terry's Texas Rangers." Edited by Thomas W. Cutrer. *Southwestern Historical Quarterly* 91 (1987): 185–226.

Radley, Kenneth. *Rebel Watchdog: The Confederate States Army Provost Guard*. Baton Rouge: Louisiana State University Press, 1989.

Ramage, James A. *Rebel Raider: The Life of General John Hunt Morgan*. Lexington: University Press of Kentucky, 1986.

Record of the Ninety-Fourth Regiment Ohio Volunteer Infantry, in the War of the Rebellion. Cincinnati: Ohio Valley Press, n.d.

Report of the Adjutant General of the State of Kansas, 1861–65. Vol. 1. Topeka: J. K. Hudson, 1896.

Reid, Whitelaw. *Ohio in the War: Her Statesmen, Her Generals, and Soldiers*. 2 vols. Cincinnati: Moore, Wilstach & Baldwin, 1868.

Reinhart, Joseph R., ed. *August Willich's Gallant Dutchmen: Civil War Letters from the 32nd Indiana Infantry*. Kent, Ohio: Kent State University Press, 2006.

Rerick, John H. *The Forty-Fourth Indiana Volunteer Infantry: History of Its Services in the War of the Rebellion and a Personal Record of Its Members*. Lagrange, Ind.: Rerick, 1880.

Reynolds, Daniel Harris. *Worthy of the Cause for Which They Fight: The Civil War Diary of Brigadier General Daniel Harris Reynolds, 1861–1865*. Edited by Robert Patrick Bender. Fayetteville: University of Arkansas Press, 2011.

Rice, Ralsa C. *Yankee Tigers: Through the Civil War with the 125th Ohio*. Edited by Richard A. Baumgartner and Larry M. Strayer. Huntington, W.Va.: Blue Acorn, 1992.

Richards, Henry. *Letters of Captain Henry Richards of the Ninety-Third Ohio Infantry*. Cincinnati: Wrightson, 1883.

Ridley, Bromfield L. *Battles and Sketches of the Army of Tennessee*. 1906. Reprint, Dayton, Ohio: Morningside, 1978.

Riley, James Wesley. *Civil War Diary of James Wesley Riley*. N.p.: C. W. Denslinger, 1960.

Robertson, John, comp. *Michigan in the War*. Lansing, Mich.: W. S. George, 1882.

Robertson, William G. "Bull of the Woods? James Longstreet at Chickamauga." In *The Chickamauga Campaign*, edited by Steven E. Woodworth, 116–39. Carbondale: Southern Illinois University Press, 2010.

———. "Rails to the River of Death: Railroads in the Chickamauga Campaign." *Civil War: The Magazine of the Civil War Society* 9 (1991): 50–55, 70–71.

Robins, Glenn. *The Bishop of the Old South: The Ministry and Civil War Legacy of Leonidas Polk*. Macon, Ga.: Mercer University Press, 2006.

Rogers, Lucien Payne. "Excerpts from the Civil War Diary of Lucien Payne Rogers." Edited by P. Burwell Rogers. *Bucknell University Studies* 4 (March 1954): 1–28.

Rose, Joseph A. *Grant under Fire: An Expose of Generalship & Character in the American Civil War*. New York: Alderhanna, 2015.

Rosecrans, William S. "The Mistakes of Grant." *North American Review* (December 1885): 580–99.

Rowland, Dunbar, ed. *Encyclopedia of Mississippi History*. 2 vols. Madison, Wisc.: Selwyn A. Brant, 1907.

Royse, Isaac Henry Clay. *History of the 115th Regiment Illinois Volunteer Infantry*. Terre Haute, Ind.: 1900.

Russell, William Howard. *My Diary North and South*. Boston: Burnham, 1863.

Salling, Stuart. *Louisianians in the Western Confederacy: The Adams-Gibson Brigade in the Civil War*. Jefferson, N.C.: McFarland, 2010.

Scharf, John Thomas. *History of Saint Louis City and County*. 2 vols. Philadelphia: Louis H. Everts, 1883.

Schlinger, Peter J. *Kentucky's Last Cavalier: General William Preston, 1816–1887*. Lexington: Kentucky Historical Society, 2004.

Schroeder-Lein, Glenna R. *Confederate Hospitals on the Move: Samuel H. Stout and the Army of Tennessee*. Columbia: University of South Carolina Press, 1994.

Schult, Dain L. *Nashville, Chattanooga & St. Louis: A History of the "Dixie Line."* Lynchburg, Va.: TLC, 2002.

Schwartz, Ezekiel Koehler. *Civil War Diary of Ezekiel Koehler Schwartz, March 1863 to June 1865, and History of E. K. Schwartz Family*. Shelbyville, Ill.: Shelby County Historical and Genealogical Society, 1989.

Scott, William Forse. *Philander P. Lane: Colonel of Volunteers in the Civil War*. Privately printed, 1920.

Scribner, Benjamin Franklin. *How Soldiers Were Made; or the War as I Saw it under Buell, Rosecrans, Thomas, Grant, and Sherman*. New Albany, Ind.: 1887.

Seaton, Benjamin M. *The Bugle Softly Blows: The Confederate Diary of Benjamin M. Seaton.* Edited by Harold B. Simpson. Waco, Tex.: Texian, 1965.

Seitz, Don C. *Braxton Bragg: General of the Confederacy*. Columbia, S.C.: State, 1924.

Shanks, William F. G. *Personal Recollections of Distinguished Generals.* New York: Harper & Brothers, 1866.

Shaw, James Birney. *History of the Tenth Regiment Indiana Volunteer Infantry*. Lafayette, Ind.: n.p., 1912.

Sheridan, P. H. *Personal Memoirs of P. H. Sheridan.* Vol. 1. New York: Charles L. Webster, 1888.

Sherman, Francis T. *Quest for a Star: The Civil War Letters and Diaries of Colonel Francis T. Sherman of the 88th Illinois.* Edited by C. Knight Aldrich. Knoxville: University of Tennessee Press, 1999.

Shields, Aliene, and Mac Wyckoff. *The Legacy of a Common Civil War Soldier, Private Thomas Marion Shields: A Collection of 34 Letters, 1861–1865*. North Charleston, S.C.: CreateSpace, 2010.

Shiman, Philip D. "Engineering and Command: The Case of William S. Rosecrans." In *The Art of Command in the Civil War*, edited by Steven E. Woodworth, 84–117. Lincoln: University of Nebraska Press, 1998.

Shook, Robert Donnell. "Timely Information to General Bragg." *Confederate Veteran* 18 (July 1910): 319.

Shultz, John A. *One Year at War: The Diary of Private John A. Shultz, August 1, 1863–August 1, 1864*. Edited by Hobart L. Morris Jr. New York: Vantage, 1968.

Silverstone, Paul H. *Warships of the Civil War Navies.* Annapolis, Md.: Naval Institute, 1989.

Simmons, L. A. *The History of the 84th Reg't Ill. Vols.* Macomb, Ill.: Hampton Brothers, 1866.

Simpson, Harold B. *Gaines' Mill to Appomattox: Waco & McLennan County in Hood's Texas Brigade.* Waco, Tex.: Texian, 1963.

Sipes, William B. *The Seventh Pennsylvania Veteran Volunteer Cavalry: Its Record, Reminiscences and Roster*. Pottsville, Penn.: Miners' Journal, 1906.

Skellie, Ron. *Lest We Forget: The Immortal Seventh Mississippi.* Acworth, Ga.: Privately printed, 2012.

Skinner, George W., comp. *Pennsylvania at Chickamauga and Chattanooga: Ceremonies at the Dedication of the Monuments Erected by the Commonwealth of Pennsylvania to Mark the Positions of the Pennsylvania Commands Engaged in the Battles, 1897*. Harrisburg, Penn.: W. S. Ray, 1901.

Smith, Benjamin Taylor. *Memoirs of a Soldier*. Edited by Martin P. Mullen. Bloomington, Ind.: 1st Books Library, 2001.

———. *Private Smith's Journal: Recollections of the Late War*. Edited by Clyde C. Walton. Chicago: R. R. Donnelley, 1963.

Smith, J. K. B. Untitled. *Confederate Veteran* 1 (June 1893): 164.

Smith, John Thomas. *A History of the Thirty-First Regiment of Indiana Volunteer Infantry in the War of the Rebellion*. Cincinnati: Western Methodist Book Concern, 1900.

Smith, Lanny Kelton. *The Stones River Campaign, 26 December 1862–5 January 1863, Army of Tennessee*. Privately printed, 2010.

———. *The Stones River Campaign, 26 December 1862–5 January 1863, the Union Army*. Privately printed, 2008.

Smith, Lyn Terese Miller. *Write as Soon as You Git This*. Bloomington, Ind.: Authorhouse, 2006.

Smith, Marion O. *Civil War Tour for Cavers: Sewanee to Chattanooga*. Louisville, Tenn.: Byron's Graphic Arts, 1998.

———. *Confederate Niter District Eight: Middle Tennessee & Northwest Georgia*. Cookeville, Tenn.: Tennessee Cave Survey, 2011.

———. "General Rosecrans' Visit to Long Island Saltpeter Cave." *Georgia Underground* 10 (March/April 1973): 37–46.

Smith, Samuel Thomas. *The Life and Letters of Pvt. Samuel Thomas Smith, Fifteenth Indiana Regiment Volunteers Civil War*. Edited by Rev. Harry Virgil Smith. Bloomington, Ind.: Monroe County Historical Society, 1976.

Smith, Theodore Clarke. *The Life and Letters of James Abram Garfield*. 2 vols. New Haven, Conn.: Yale University Press, 1925.

Society of the Army of the Cumberland: Twenty-Third Reunion, Chickamauga, Georgia, 1892. Cincinnati: Robert Clarke, 1892.

Society of the Army of the Cumberland: Twenty-Fourth Reunion, Cleveland, Ohio, 1893. Cincinnati: Robert Clarke, 1894.

Society of the Seventy-Fourth Illinois Volunteer Infantry. *Reunion Proceedings of the Regiment*. Rockford, Ill.: W. P. Lamb, 1903.

Spencer, John W. *From Corsicana to Appomattox*. Corsicana, Tex.: Texas Press, 1984.

Stanley, David S. *Personal Memoirs of Major-General D. S. Stanley, U.S.A.* Cambridge, Mass.: Harvard University Press, 1917.

Starkweather, John C. *Statement of Military Services of Brigadier General John C. Starkweather, of Wisconsin, since the 4th of March, 1861*. Milwaukee, Wisc.: Daily Sentinel, 1864.

Steenburn, Donald H. *The Man Called Gurley*. Meridianville, Ala.: Elk River, 1999.

Steiner, Paul E. *Medical-Military Portraits of Union and Confederate Generals*. Philadelphia: Whitmore, 1968.

Stevenson, William Robert. "Robert Alexander Smith: A Southern Son." *Alabama Historical Quarterly* 20 (1958): 35–60.

Stewart, Charles D. "A Bachelor General." *Wisconsin Magazine of History* 17 (1933): 131–54.

Stewart, Nixon B. *Dan McCook's Regiment, 52nd O.V.I.* Alliance, Ohio: Review Print, 1900.

Stickles, Arndt M. *Simon Bolivar Buckner: Borderland Knight*. Chapel Hill: University of North Carolina Press, 1940.

Stilwell, William Ross. *The Stilwell Letters: A Georgian in Longstreet's Corps, Army of Northern Virginia*. Edited by Ronald H. Moseley. Macon, Ga.: Mercer University Press, 2002.

Stout, Samuel H. "Outline of the Organization of the Medical Department of the Confederate Army and Department of Tennessee." Edited by Sam L. Clark and H. D. Riley Jr. *Tennessee Historical Quarterly* 14 (1957): 55–82.

Stroud, David V. *Ector's Texas Brigade and the Army of Tennessee, 1862–1865*. Longview, Tex.: Ranger, 2004.

Sword, Wiley. *Shiloh: Bloody April*. New York: William Morrow, 1974.

Sykes, E. T. *Walthall's Brigade: A Cursory Sketch, with Personal Experiences of Walthall's Brigade, Army of Tennessee, C.S A., 1862–1865*, 477–623. In *Mississippi Historical Society Publications*, Centenary Series, 1916.

Symonds, Craig L. *Joseph E. Johnston: A Civil War Biography*. New York: W. W. Norton, 1992.

———. *Stonewall of the West: Patrick Cleburne & the Civil War*. Lawrence: University Press of Kansas, 1997.

Taylor, Lenette S. *"The Supply for Tomorrow Must Not Fail": The Civil War of Captain Simon Perkins Jr., a Union Quartermaster*. Kent, Ohio: Kent State University Press, 2004.

Taylor, Richard. *Destruction and Reconstruction: Personal Experiences of the Late War*. New York: D. Appleton, 1879.

Tennesseans in the Civil War: A Military History of Confederate and Union Units with Available Rosters of Personnel. Part 1. Nashville: Civil War Centennial Commission, 1964.

Tennessee Historical Commission. *Tennessee Historical Markers*. 8th ed. Nashville: Tennessee Historical Commission, 1996.

Tennessee Historical Society. *Tennessee Old and New: 1796–1946*. 2 vols. Kingsport, Tenn.: Kingsport Press, 1946.

Thatcher, Marshall P. *A Hundred Battles in the West: St. Louis to Atlanta, 1861–65*. Detroit: Privately printed, 1884.

Thomas, Benjamin P., and Harold M. Hyman. *Stanton: The Life and Times of Lincoln's Secretary of War*. New York: Alfred A. Knopf, 1962.

Thornton, Leland W. *When Gallantry Was Commonplace: The History of the Michigan Eleventh Volunteer Infantry, 1861–1864*. New York: Peter Lang, 1991.

Tourgee, Albion W. "A Civil War Diary of Albion W. Tourgee." Edited by Dean H. Keller. *Ohio History* 74 (Spring 1965): 99–131.

———. *The Story of a Thousand*. Buffalo: S. McGerald, 1896.

Turchin, John B. *Chickamauga*. Chicago: Fergus, 1888.

Turchin, Nadine. "'A Monotony Full of Sadness': The Diary of Nadine Turchin, May 1863–April 1864." Edited by Mary Ellen McElligott. *Journal of the Illinois State Historical Society* 70 (February 1977): 27–89.

Turner, Jim. "Jim Turner, Co. G, 6th Texas Infantry, C.S.A., from 1861–1865." *Texana* 12 (1974): 149–78.

Tuttle, John W. *The Union, the Civil War, and John W. Tuttle: A Kentucky Captain's Account*. Edited by Hambleton Tapp and James C. Klotter. Frankfort: Kentucky Historical Society, 1980.

Ulmer, Herman, Jr. *The Correspondence of Will and Ju Stockton, 1845–1869*. Jacksonville, Fla.: 1986.

Urquhart, David. "Bragg's Advance and Retreat." In *Battles and Leaders of the Civil War*, edited by Robert Underwood Johnson and Clarence Clough Buel, 3:600–609. New York: Century, 1884.

U.S. Congress. *Report of the Joint Committee on the Conduct of the War, at the Second Session Thirty-Eighth Congress*. 3 vols. Washington, D.C.: Government Printing Office, 1865.

U.S. Congress. House of Representatives Document No. 514. *Atlas of Chickamauga, Chattanooga, and Vicinity*. 56th Cong., 2nd sess., 1901. Washington, D.C.: Government Printing Office, 1901.

U.S. Surgeon-General's Office. *The Medical and Surgical History of the War of the Rebellion*. 3 vols. Washington, D.C.: Government Printing Office, 1870–88.

U.S. War Department. *The War of the Rebellion: A Compilation of the Official Records of the Union and Confederate Armies*. 128 vols. Washington, D.C.: Government Printing Office, 1880–1901.

Vale, Joseph G. *Minty and the Cavalry: A History of Cavalry Campaigns in the Western Armies*. Harrisburg, Penn.: Edwin K. Meyers, 1886.

Vance, Wilson. *God's War*. New York: F. Tennyson Neely, 1899.

Vandiver, Frank E. *Ploughshares into Swords: Josiah Gorgas and Confederate Ordnance*. Austin: University of Texas Press, 1952.

Van Horne, Thomas B. *History of the Army of the Cumberland*. Cincinnati: Robert Clarke, 1875.

———. *The Life of Major-General George H. Thomas*. New York: Charles Scribner's Sons, 1882.

Van Vleck, Carter. *Emerging Leader: The Letters of Carter Van Vleck*. Edited by Teresa K. Lehr and Philip L. Gerber. Bloomington, Ind.: iUniverse, 2012.

Varney, Frank P. *General Grant and the Rewriting of History*. El Dorado Hills, Calif.: Savas Beatie, 2013.

Velazquez, Loreta Janeta. *The Woman in Battle: A Narrative of the Exploits, Adventures and Travels of Madame Loreta Janeta Velazquez, Otherwise Known as Lieutenant Harry T. Buford, Confederate States Army*. Richmond: Dustin, Gilman, 1876.

Villard, Henry. *Memoirs of Henry Villard, Journalist and Financier, 1835–1900*. Vol. 2. Boston: Houghton, Mifflin, 1904.

Wall, Joseph Frazier. *Henry Watterson: Reconstructed Rebel*. New York: Oxford University Press, 1956.

Warner, Ezra J. *Generals in Blue: Lives of the Union Commanders*. Baton Rouge: Louisiana State University Press, 1964.

———. *Generals in Gray: Lives of the Confederate Commanders*. Baton Rouge: Louisiana State University Press, 1959.

Warner, Seth. "George Earl Maney: Soldier, Railroader, and Diplomat." *Tennessee Historical Quarterly* 65 (2006): 130–47.

Warren, Israel P. *The Stanley Families of America*. Portland, Me.: B. Thurston, 1887.

Watson, William. *Life in the Confederate Army*. New York: Scribner and Welford, 1888.

Watterson, Henry. *"Marse Henry": An Autobiography*. 2 vols. New York: George H. Doran, 1919.

Weber, Thomas. *The Northern Railroads in the Civil War, 1861–1865*. 1952. Reprint, Westport, Conn.: Greenwood, 1970.

Weigley, Russell F. *Quartermaster General of the Union Army: A Biography of M. C. Meigs*. New York: Columbia University Press, 1959.

Welcher, Frank J. *The Union Army, 1861–1865: Organization and Operations*. 2 vols. Bloomington: Indiana University Press, 1989–93.

Weller, Jac. "Nathan Bedford Forrest: An Analysis of Untutored Military Genius." *Tennessee Historical Quarterly* 18 (September 1959): 213–51.

Wellman, Manly Wade. *The County of Warren, North Carolina, 1586–1917*. Chapel Hill: University of North Carolina Press, 1959.

Wells, Ebenezer Tracy. "The Campaign and Battle of Chickamauga." *United Service* 16 (1896): 205–33.

Welsh, Jack D. *Medical Histories of Confederate Generals*. Kent, Ohio: Kent State University Press, 1995.

———. *Medical Histories of Union Generals*. Kent, Ohio: Kent State University Press, 1996.

Wert, Jeffry D. *General James Longstreet: The Confederacy's Most Controversial Soldier, a Biography*. New York: Simon & Schuster, 1993.

West, Granville C. "Personal Recollections of the Chickamauga Campaign." In *War Papers*, no. 95. Military Order of the Loyal Legion of the United States, Commandery of the District of Columbia, 1913.

Whalen, Charles, and Barbara Whalen. *The Fighting McCooks*. Bethesda, Md.: Westmoreland, 2006.

White, John H., Jr. *The American Railroad Passenger Car*. Baltimore: Johns Hopkins University Press, 1978.

Wilder, John T. "Preliminary Movements of the Army of the Cumberland before the Battle of Chickamauga." In *Sketches of War History*, 7:261–72. 1908. Reprint, Wilmington, N.C.: Broadfoot, 1993.

Williams, Edward P. *Extracts from Letters to A. B. T. from Edward P. Williams during His Service in the Civil War, 1862–1864*. New York: Privately printed, 1903.

Williams, Samuel C. *General John T. Wilder: Commander of the Lightning Brigade*. Bloomington: Indiana University Press, 1936.

Williams, T. Harry. *Lincoln and His Generals*. New York: Alfred A. Knopf, 1952.

Williamson, David. *The Third Battalion Mississippi Infantry and the 45th Mississippi Regiment: A Civil War History*. Jefferson, N.C.: McFarland, 2004.

Wills, Brian Steel. *A Battle from the Start: The Life of Nathan Bedford Forrest*. New York: HarperCollins, 1992.

———. *George Henry Thomas: As True as Steel*. Lawrence: University Press of Kansas, 2012.

Wilson, Ephraim A. *Memoirs of the War*. Cleveland: W. M. Bayne, 1893.

Wilson, James Harrison. *The Life of Charles A. Dana*. New York: Harper, 1907.

Wilson, Suzanne Colton, comp., *Column South: With the Fifteenth Pennsylvania Cavalry from Antietam to the Capture of Jefferson Davis*. Flagstaff, Ariz.: J. F. Colton, 1960.

Wingfield, Marshall. *General A. P. Stewart: His Life and Letters*. Memphis: West Tennessee Historical Society, 1954.

Woodall, Eliza B. *The Stevenson Story*. Stevenson, Ala.: Stevenson Depot Museum, 1982.

Woodcock, Marcus. *A Southern Boy in Blue: The Memoirs of Marcus Woodcock, 9th Kentucky Infantry (U.S.A.)*. Edited by Kenneth W. Noe. Knoxville: University of Tennessee Press, 1996.

Woodruff, George H. *Fifteen Years Ago; or, The Patriotism of Will County*. Joliet, Ill.: Joliet Republican, 1876.

Woodworth, Steven E. "Braxton Bragg and the Tullahoma Campaign." In *The Art of Command in the Civil War*, edited by Steven E. Woodworth, 157–82. Lincoln: University of Nebraska Press, 1998.

———. *Jefferson Davis and His Generals: The Failure of Confederate Command in the West*. Lawrence: University of Kansas Press, 1990.

Worsham, W. J. *The Old Nineteenth Tennessee Regiment, C.S.A.* Knoxville, Tenn.: Paragon, 1902.

Wright, Marcus J. *Diary of Brigadier-General Marcus J. Wright, C.S.A., April 23, 1861–February 26, 1863*. Electronic ed. Chapel Hill: University of North Carolina, 1998.

Wright, T. J. *History of the Eighth Regiment Kentucky Vol. Inf., during Its Three Years Campaigns*. St. Joseph, Mo.: St. Joseph Steam Printing, 1880.

Wyckoff, Mac. *A History of the 2nd South Carolina Infantry: 1861–65*. Fredericksburg, Va.: Sergeant Kirkland's Museum, 1994.

———. *A History of the Third South Carolina Infantry: 1861–1865*. Fredericksburg, Va.: Sergeant Kirkland's Museum, 1995.

Wyeth, John Allan. *Life of General Nathan Bedford Forrest*. 1899. Reprint, Dayton, Ohio: Morningside, 1975.

———. *With Sabre and Scalpel: The Autobiography of a Soldier and Surgeon*. New York: Harper, 1914.

THESES AND DISSERTATIONS

Baker, Philip J., Jr. "Command and Control Mechanisms in the Chickamauga Campaign: The Union Experience." MMAS thesis, U.S. Army Command and General Staff College, 1989.

Barclay, Keith A. "Major General James Scott Negley and His Division at Chickamauga: A Historical Analysis." MMAS thesis, U.S. Army Command and General Staff College, 2001.

Brewer, Richard J. "The Tullahoma Campaign: Operational Insights." MMAS thesis, U.S. Army Command and General Staff College, 1991.

Dalessandro, Robert J. "Morale in the Army of the Cumberland during the Tullahoma and Chickamauga Campaigns." MMAS thesis, U.S. Army Command and General Staff College, 1995.

Davis, Michael John. "The Role of Ordnance Logistics in the Chickamauga Campaign." MMAS thesis, U.S. Army Command and General Staff College, 1995.

Gow, June I. "Military Administration in the Confederacy: The Army of Tennessee, 1862–1864." PhD diss., University of British Columbia, 1970.

Johnson, Robert Lewis. "Confederate Staff Work at Chickamauga: An Analysis of the Staff of the Army of Tennessee." MMAS thesis, U.S. Army Command and General Staff College, 1992.

Kapaun, David M., Jr. "Major General Joseph J. Reynolds and His Division at Chickamauga: A Historical Analysis." MMAS thesis, U.S. Army Command and General Staff College, 1999.

Lott, Robert P., Jr. "Van Cleve at Chickamauga: The Study of a Division's Performance in Battle." MMAS thesis, U.S. Army Command and General Staff College, 1996.

Mammay, Michael J. "Union Artillery at the Battle of Chickamauga." MMAS thesis, U.S. Army Command and General Staff College, 2001.

Manville, Craig Julian. "The Limits of Obedience: Brigadier General Thomas J. Wood's Performance during the Battle of Chickamauga." MMAS thesis, U.S. Army Command and General Staff College, 2005.

McCaffrey, James M. "Only a Private: The Civil War Memoirs of William J. Oliphant, Company G, 6th Texas Infantry Regiment." MA thesis, University of Houston, 1987.

Morris, Andrew N. "Forgotten Decisiveness: The Middle Tennessee Campaign of 1863." PhD diss., University of Kansas, 1996.

Richardson, Robert D. "Rosecrans' Staff at Chickamauga: The Significance of Major General William S. Rosecrans' Staff on the Outcome of the Chickamauga Campaign." MMAS thesis, U.S. Army Command and General Staff College, 1989.

Rubenstein, David A. "A Study of the Medical Support to the Union and Confederate

Armies during the Battle of Chickamauga: Lessons and Implications for Today's US Army Medical Department Leaders." MMAS thesis, U.S. Army Command and General Staff College, 1990.
Sones, Bruce V. "Brigadier General Jefferson C. Davis: Civil War General." MMAS thesis, U.S. Army Command and General Staff College, 2002.

» INDEX «